DATE DUE			
			PRINTED IN U.S.A.

Literature Criticism from 1400 to 1800

Guide to Gale Literary Criticism Series

When you need to review criticism of literary works, these are the Gale series to use:

If the author's death date is:

You should turn to:

After Dec. 31, 1959
(or author is still living)

CONTEMPORARY LITERARY CRITICISM

for example: Jorge Luis Borges, Anthony Burgess,
William Faulkner, Mary Gordon,
Ernest Hemingway, Iris Murdoch

1900 through 1959

TWENTIETH-CENTURY LITERARY CRITICISM

for example: Willa Cather, F. Scott Fitzgerald,
Henry James, Mark Twain, Virginia Woolf

1800 through 1899

NINETEENTH-CENTURY LITERATURE CRITICISM

for example: Fedor Dostoevski, Nathaniel Hawthorne,
George Sand, William Wordsworth

1400 through 1799

LITERATURE CRITICISM FROM 1400 TO 1800
(excluding Shakespeare)

for example: Anne Bradstreet, Daniel Defoe,
Alexander Pope, François Rabelais,
Jonathan Swift, Phillis Wheatley

SHAKESPEAREAN CRITICISM

Shakespeare's plays and poetry

Antiquity through 1399

CLASSICAL AND MEDIEVAL LITERATURE CRITICISM

for example: Dante, Homer, Plato, Sophocles, Vergil,
the Beowulf Poet

Gale also publishes related criticism series:

CHILDREN'S LITERATURE REVIEW

This series covers authors of all eras who write for the preschool
through high school audience.

SHORT STORY CRITICISM

This series covers the major short fiction writers of all nationalities
and periods of literary history.

ISSN 0740-2880

Volume 10

Literature Criticism from 1400 to 1800

Excerpts from Criticism of the Works
of Fifteenth-, Sixteenth-, Seventeenth-, and
Eighteenth-Century Novelists, Poets, Playwrights,
Philosophers, and Other Creative Writers, from
the First Published Critical Appraisals
to Current Evaluations

James E. Person, Jr.
Editor

James P. Draper
Associate Editor

 **Gale Research Inc.** · DETROIT · LONDON

STAFF

James E. Person, Jr., *Editor*
James P. Draper, *Associate Editor*

oomis, Shannon J. Young, *Assistant Editors*

Gough, *Permissions and Production Manager*

beth A. Purdy, *Production Supervisor*
Cathy Beranek, Christine A. Galbraith, David G. Oblender, Suzanne Powers,
Linda M. Ross, Kristine Tipton, Lee Ann Welsh, *Editorial Assistants*

Linda M. Pugliese, *Manuscript Coordinator*
Maureen A. Puhl, *Senior Manuscript Assistant*
Donna Craft, Jennifer E. Gale, *Manuscript Assistants*

Victoria B. Cariappa, *Research Supervisor*
Maureen R. Richards, *Research Coordinator*
Mary D. Wise, *Senior Research Assistant*
Joyce E. Doyle, Rogene M. Fisher, Kevin B. Hillstrom, Karen D. Kaus,
Eric Priehs, Filomena Sgambati, Laura B. Standley, *Research Assistants*

Janice M. Mach, *Text Permissions Supervisor*
Kathy Grell, Mabel E. Gurney, *Text Permissions Coordinators*
Josephine M. Keene, *Senior Permissions Assistant*
H. Diane Cooper, Kimberly F. Smilay, *Permissions Assistants*
Melissa A. Brantley, Denise M. Singleton, Sharon D. Valentine, Lisa M. Wimmer, *Permissions Clerks*

Patricia A. Seefelt, *Picture Permissions Supervisor*
Margaret A. Chamberlain, *Picture Permissions Coordinator*
Pamela A. Hayes, Lillian Quickley, *Permissions Clerks*

Mary Beth Trimper, *Production Manager*
Arthur Chartow, *Art Director*
Linda A. Davis, *Production Assistant*

Laura Bryant, *Production Supervisor*
Louise Gagné, *Internal Production Associate*

The paper used in this publication meets the minimum requirements
of American National Standard for Information Sciences—Permanence
Paper for Printed Library Materials, ANSI Z39.48-1984. ∞™

Library of Congress Catalog Card Number 84-643570
ISBN 0-8103-6109-4
ISSN 0740-2880

Printed in the United States of America.

Published simultaneously in the United Kingdom
by Gale Research International Limited
(An affiliated company of Gale Research Inc.)

Contents

Preface   vii

Authors to Appear in Future Volumes   xi

Acknowledgments   489

Preface

"If I have seen farther," wrote Sir Isaac Newton, echoing Fulbert of Chartres and commenting on his own indebtedness to the sages who preceded him, "it is by standing on the shoulders of giants"; this is a statement as applicable to ourselves today as it was to Newton and his world. Many of the political and intellectual foundations of the modern world can be found in the art and thought of the fifteenth through eighteenth centuries. During this time the modern nation-state was born, the sciences grew tremendously, and many of the political, social, economic, and moral philosophies that are influential today were formulated. The literature of these centuries reflects this turbulent time of radical change: the period saw the rise of drama equal in critical stature to that of classical Greece, the birth of the novel and personal essay forms, the emergence of newspapers and periodicals, and significant achievements in poetry and philosophy. Much of modern literature reflects the influence of these centuries' developments. Thus the literature of this period provides insight into the universal nature of human experience, as well as into the life and thought of the past.

Literary criticism can also give us insight into the human condition, as well as into the specific moral and intellectual atmosphere of an era, for the criteria by which a work of art is judged reflect contemporary philosophical and social attitudes. Literary criticism takes many forms: the traditional essay, the book or play review, even the parodic poem. Criticism can also be of several kinds, including descriptive, interpretive, textual, appreciative, and generic, among others. Collectively, the range of critical response helps us understand a work of art, an author, an era.

Scope of the Series

Literature Criticism from 1400 to 1800 (LC) is designed to serve as an introduction to the authors of the fifteenth through eighteenth centuries and to the most significant commentators on these authors. The works of the great poets, dramatists, novelists, essayists, and philosophers of those years are considered classics in every secondary school and college or university curriculum. Because criticism of this literature spans a period of up to six hundred years, an overwhelming amount of critical material confronts the student. To help students locate and select criticism of the works of authors who died between 1400 and 1800, *LC* presents significant passages from the most noteworthy published criticism of authors of these centuries. Each volume of *LC* is carefully compiled to represent the critical heritage of the most important writers from a variety of nationalities. In addition to major authors, *LC* also presents criticism of lesser-known writers whose significant contributions to literary history are reflected in continuing critical assessments of their works.

The need for *LC* among students and teachers of literature of the fifteenth through eighteenth centuries was suggested by the proven usefulness of Gale's *Contemporary Literary Criticism (CLC), Twentieth-Century Literary Criticism (TCLC),* and *Nineteenth-Century Literature Criticism (NCLC),* which excerpt criticism of works by nineteenth- and twentieth-century authors. Because of the different time periods covered, there is no duplication of authors or critical material among any of Gale's literary criticism series. For further information about these series, readers should consult the Guide to Gale Literary Criticism Series preceding the title page of this volume. Here, the reader will note that there is a separate Gale reference series devoted to Shakespearean studies. For though belonging properly to the literary period covered in *LC,* William Shakespeare has inspired such a tremendous and ever-growing corpus of secondary material that the editors have deemed it best to give his works the extensive critical coverage best served by a separate series, *Shakespearean Criticism.*

Each author entry in *LC* provides an overview of major criticism of an author. Therefore, the editors include approximately ten authors in each 550-page volume (compared with approximately forty authors in a *CLC* volume of similar size) so that more attention may be given each author. Each author entry presents a historical survey of the critical response to an author's work: early criticism is offered to indicate initial responses, later selections document any rise or decline in the author's literary reputation and describe the effects of social or historical forces on the work of an author, and retrospective analyses provide students with a modern view. The length of an author entry is intended to present the author's critical reception in English or foreign criticism in translation. Articles and books that have not been translated into English are therefore excluded. Every attempt has been made to identify and include excerpts from the seminal essays on each author's work and to include recent critical commentary providing modern perspectives on the writer. An author may appear more than once in the series because of the great quantity of critical material available, or because of a resurgence of criticism generated by such events as an author's anniversary celebration, the republication of an author's works, or the publication of a newly translated work.

Organization of the Book

An author entry consists of the following elements: author heading, biographical and critical introduction, list of principal works, excerpts of criticism (each followed by a bibliographical citation), and a bibliography of further reading. Also, most author entries reproduce author portraits and other illustrations pertinent to the author's life and career.

- The *author heading* consists of the author's full name, followed by birth and death dates. The portion of the name not parenthesized denotes the form under which the author most commonly wrote. If an author wrote consistently under a pseudonym, the pseudonym will be used in the author heading, with the real name given in parentheses on the first line of the biographical and critical introduction. Also located at the beginning of the introduction to the author entry are any name variations under which an author wrote, including transliterated forms for authors whose native languages use nonroman alphabets. Uncertain birth or death dates are indicated by question marks.

- The *biographical and critical introduction* contains background information designed to introduce the reader to an author and to the critical discussion surrounding his or her work. Parenthetical material following many of the introductions provides references to biographical and critical reference series published by Gale in which additional material on the author may be found, including *Children's Literature Review, Dictionary of Literary Biography, Something about the Author,* and *Yesterday's Authors of Books for Children.*

- Most *LC* entries include *portraits* of the author. Many entries also contain illustrations of materials pertinent to an author's career, including selected author holographs, title pages, letters, or representations of important people, places, and events in an author's life.

- The *list of principal works* is chronological by date of first book publication and identifies the genre of each work. In the case of foreign authors whose works have been translated into English, the title and date of the first English-language edition are given in brackets following the foreign-language listing. Unless otherwise indicated, dramas are dated by first performance, not first publication.

- *Criticism* is arranged chronologically in each author entry to provide a useful perspective on changes in critical evaluation over the years. All titles by the author featured in the critical entry are printed in boldface type to enable the user to ascertain without difficulty the works being discussed. Also for purposes of easier identification, the critic's name and the composition or publication date of the critical work are given at the beginning of each excerpt. Unsigned criticism is preceded by the title of the source in which it appeared. When an anonymous essay has been attributed to a critic, the critic's name appears in brackets at the beginning of the excerpt and in the bibliographical citation. Publication information (such as publisher names and book prices) and parenthetical numerical references (such as footnotes or page and line references to specific editions of works) have been deleted at the editor's discretion to provide smoother reading of the text.

- Critical essays are prefaced by *explanatory notes* as an additional aid to students using *LC*. The explanatory notes may provide several types of useful information, including: the reputation of a critic, the importance of a work of criticism, the specific type of criticism (biographical, psychoanalytic, structuralist, etc.), the intent of the criticism, and the growth of critical controversy or changes in critical trends regarding an author's work. In some cases, these notes cross-reference the work of critics who agree or disagree with each other. Dates in parentheses within the explanatory notes refer to a book publication date when they follow a book title and to the date of an essay excerpted and reprinted elsewhere in the author entry when they follow a critic's name.

- A complete *bibliographical citation* designed to facilitate location of the original essay or book by the reader follows each piece of criticism.

- The *additional bibliography* appearing at the end of each author entry suggests further reading on the author. In a few rare cases it includes essays for which the editors could not obtain reprint rights.

An appendix lists the sources from which material in each volume has been reprinted. It does not, however, list every book and periodical consulted in the preparation of the volume.

Cumulative Indexes

Each volume of *LC* includes a cumulative index to authors listing all the authors that have appeared in *Contemporary Literary Criticism, Twentieth-Century Literary Criticism, Nineteenth-Century Literature Criticism, Literature Criticism from 1400 to 1800,* and *Classical and Medieval Literature Criticism,* along with cross-references to the Gale series *Short Story Criticism, Children's Literature Review, Authors in the News, Contemporary Authors, Contemporary Authors Autobiography Series, Contemporary Authors Bibliographical Series, Dictionary of Literary Biography, Concise Dictionary of Literary Biography, Something about the Author, Something about the Author Autobiography Series,* and *Yesterday's Authors of Books for Children.* Readers will welcome this cumulative author index as a useful tool for locating an author within the various series. The index, which includes authors' birth and death dates, is particularly valuable for those authors who are identified with a certain period but whose death dates cause them to be placed in another, or for those authors whose careers span two periods. For example, F. Scott Fitzgerald is found in *TCLC,* yet a writer often associated with him, Ernest Hemingway, is found in *CLC.*

Each volume of *LC* also includes a cumulative nationality index, in which authors' names are arranged alphabetically under their respective nationalities and followed by the numbers of the volumes in which they appear. In addition, each volume of *LC* includes a cumulative index to titles, an alphabetical listing of the literary works discussed in the series since its inception. Each title listing includes the corresponding volume and page numbers where criticism may be located. Foreign-language titles that have been translated are followed by the titles of the translations—for example, *El ingenioso hidalgo Don Quixote de la Mancha (Don Quixote).* Page numbers following these translated titles refer to all pages on which any form of the titles, either foreign-language or translated, appear. Titles of novels, dramas, nonfiction books, and poetry, short story, or essay collections are printed in italics, while all individual poems, short stories, and essays are printed in roman type within quotation marks. In cases where the same title is used by different authors, the author's surname is given in parentheses after the title, e.g., *Poems* (Bradstreet) and *Poems* (Killigrew).

Acknowledgments

No work of this scope can be accomplished without the cooperation of many people. The editors especially wish to thank the copyright holders of the excerpts included in this volume, the permissions managers of many book and magazine publishing companies for assisting us in locating copyright holders, and Anthony Bogucki for assistance with copyright research. We are also grateful to the staffs of the Detroit Public Library, the Library of Congress, University of Detroit Library, University of Michigan Library, and Wayne State University Library for making their resources available to us.

Suggestions Are Welcome

Readers who wish to suggest authors to appear in future volumes, or who have other suggestions, are cordially invited to write the editor.

Authors to Appear in Future Volumes

Abravenel, Isaac 1437-1508
Abravenel, Judah 1460-1535
Addison, Joseph 1672-1719
Agricola, Johannes 1494?-1566
Akenside, Mark 1721-1770
Alabaster, William 1567-1640
Alarcón y Mendoza, Juan Rúiz
  1581-1634
Alberti, Leon Battista 1404-1472
Alembert, Jean Le Rond d' 1717-1783
Amory, Thomas 1691?-1788
Anton Ulrich, Duke of Brunswick
  1633-1714
Aretino, Pietro 1492-1556
Ascham, Roger 1515-1568
Aubigne, Théodore Agrippa d'
  1552-1630
Aubrey, John 1620-1697
Bâbur 1483-1530
Bacon, Sir Francis 1561-1626
Bale, John 1495-1563
Barber, Mary 1690-1757
Baretti, Giuseppi 1719-1789
Barker, Jane 1652-1727?
Bartas, Guillaume de Salluste du
  1544-1590
Baxter, Richard 1615-1691
Bayle, Pierre 1647-1706
Beaumarchais, Pierre-Augustin Caron
  de 1732-1799
Beaumont, Francis 1584-1616
Belleau, Rémy 1528-1577
Berkeley, George 1685-1753
Bessarion, Johannes 1403-1472
Bijns, Anna 1493-1575
Bisticci, Vespasiano da 1421-1498
Blackmore, Sir Richard 1650-1729
Boccalini, Traiano 1556-1613
Bodin, Jean 1530-1596
Bolingbroke, Henry St. John
  1678-1751
Boyle, Roger 1621-1679
Bradford, William 1590-1657
Brant, Sebastian 1457-1521
Bredero, Gerbrand Adriaanszoon
  1585-1618
Breitinger, Johann Jakob 1701-1776
Breton, Nicholas 1545-1626
Broome, William 1689-1745
Brown, Thomas 1663-1704
Browne, Sir Thomas 1605-1682
Bruni, Leonardo 1370-1444
Bruno, Giordano 1548-1600
Buffon, George-Louis Leclerc, Comte
  de 1707-1788
Burgoyne, John 1722-1792

Burnet, Gilbert 1643-1715
Burton, Robert 1577-1640
Butler, Samuel 1612-1680
Byrd, William, II 1674-1744
Byrom, John 1692-1763
Calderón de la Barca, Pedro 1600-1681
Camden, William 1551-1623
Campion, Thomas 1567-1620
Carew, Richard 1555-1620
Carew, Thomas 1594-1640
Carver, Jonathan 1710-1780
Casanova di Seingalt, Giacomo
  Girolamo 1725-1798
Castiglione, Baldassare 1478-1529
Castillejo, Cristobalde 1492-1550
Cavendish, William 1592-1676
Caxton, William 1421?-1491
Centlivre, Susanna 1667?-1723
Chapman, George 1560-1634
Chartier, Alain 1390-1440
Chaucer, Geoffrey 1340?-1400
Cibber, Colley 1671-1757
Cleveland, John 1613-1658
Collyer, Mary 1716?-1763?
Colonna, Vittoria 1490-1547
Commynes, Philippe de 1445-1511
Condillac, Etienne Bonnot, Abbé de
  1714?-1780
Cook, James 1728-1779
Corneille, Pierre 1606-1684
Cortés, Hernán 1485-1547
Cotton, John 1584-1652
Courtilz de Sandras, Gatiende
  1644-1712
Cowley, Abraham 1618-1667
Cranmer, Thomas 1489-1556
Crashaw, Richard 1612-1649
Crébillon, Prosper Jolyot de 1674-1762
Cruden, Alexander 1701-1770
Curll, Edmund 1675-1747
Dampier, William 1653-1715
Daniel, Samuel 1562-1619
Davenant, Sir William 1606-1668
Davidson, John 1549?-1603
Da Vinci, Leonardo 1452-1519
Day, John 1574-1640
Dekker, Thomas 1572-1632
Delany, Mary Pendarves 1700-1788
Denham, Sir John 1615-1669
Dennis, John 1657-1734
Deloney, Thomas 1543?-1600?
Descartes, René 1596-1650
Desfontaines, Pierre François Guyot,
  Abbé 1685-1745
Diaz del Castillo, Bernal 1492?-1584
Diderot, Denis 1713-1784
Drummond, William 1585-1649

Du Guillet, Pernette 1520?-1545
Dunbar, William 1460?-1520?
Elyot, Thomas 1490-1546
Emin, Fedor ?-1770
Erasmus, Desiderius 1466-1536
Etherege, Sir George 1635-1691
Eusden, Laurence 1688-1730
Evelyn, John 1620-1706
Fabyan, Robert ?-1513
Fairfax, Thomas 1621-1671
Fanshawe, Lady Anne 1625-1680
Fanshawe, Sir Richard 1608-1666
Farquhar, George 1678-1707
Fénelon, François 1651-1715
Fergusson, Robert 1750-1774
Ficino, Marsilio 1433-1499
Fletcher, John 1579-1625
Florian, Jean Pierre Claris de
  1755-1794
Florio, John 1553?-1625
Fontaine, Charles 1514-1565
Fontenelle, Bernard Le Bovier de
  1657-1757
Fonvizin, Denis Ivanovich 1745-1792
Ford, John 1586-1640
Foxe, John 1517-1587
Franklin, Benjamin 1706-1790
Froissart, Jean 1337-1404?
Fuller, Thomas 1608-1661
Galilei, Galileo 1564-1642
Garrick, David 1717-1779
Gascoigne, George 1530?-1577
Gay, John 1685-1732
Gibbon, Edward 1737-1794
Gildon, Charles 1665-1724
Glanvill, Joseph 1636-1680
Góngora y Argote, Luis de 1561-1627
Gosson, Stephen 1554-1624
Gottsched, Johann Christoph
  1700-1766
Gower, John 1330?-1408
Gracian y Morales, Baltasar 1601-1658
Graham, Dougal 1724-1779
Greene, Robert 1558?-1592
Griffith, Elizabeth 1727?-1793
Guarini, Giambattista 1538-1612
Hakluyt, Richard 1553-1616
Hall, Edward 1498-1547
Harrington, James 1611-1677
Hartley, David 1705-1757
Helvetius, Claude Arien 1715-1771
Henslowe, Philip ?-1616
Herbert, George 1593-1633
Herrick, Robert 1591-1674
Heywood, Thomas 1574-1641
Hobbes, Thomas 1588-1679
Hogarth, William 1697-1764

Holbach, Paul Heinrich Dietrich 1723-1789
Holinshed, Raphael ?-1582?
Hooker, Richard 1544-1600
Hooker, Thomas 1586-1647
Howard, Henry, Earl of Surrey 1517-1547
Hung Sheng 1646-1704
Hutcheson, Francis 1694-1746
Ibn Khaldun, Abd al-Rahman ibn Muhammad 1332-1406
Iriarte, Tomas de 1750-1791
Isla y Rojo, José Francisco de 1703-1781
Ivan IV 1533-1584
James I, King of Scotland 1394-1437
Johnson, Samuel 1709-1784
King, William 1662-1712
Knox, John 1514?-1572
Kyd, Thomas 1558-1594
La Bruyére, Jean de 1645-1696
La Fontaine, Jean de 1621-1695
Langland, William 1330?-1400
La Rochefoucauld, Francois de 1613-1680
Law, William 1686-1761
L'Estrange, Sir Roger 1616-1704
Let-we Thon-dara 1752-1783
Lipsius, Justus 1547-1606
Littleton, Sir Thomas 1422-1481
Lo Kuan-chung c.1400
Lodge, Thomas 1558-1625
Lope de Vega 1562-1635
Lopez de Ayala, Pero 1332-1407?
Lovelace, Richard 1618-1657
Loyola, Ignacio de 1491-1556
Lydgate, John 1370?-1452
Lyly, John 1554-1606
MacDomhnaill, Sean Clarach 1691-1754
Macpherson, James 1736-1796
Maitland, Sir Richard 1496-1586
Malory, Sir Thomas ?-1471
Mandeville, Bernard de 1670-1733
Marlowe, Christopher 1564-1593
Marston, John 1576-1634
Massinger, Philip 1583-1640
Mather, Cotton 1663-1728
Mather, Increase 1639-1723
Mendelssohn, Moses 1729-1786
Metastasio, Pietro 1698-1782
Michelangelo Buonarrotti 1475-1564
Middleton, Thomas 1580-1627
Montfort, Hugo von 1357-1423

Morton, Thomas 1575-1647
Muret, Marc-Antoine de 1526-1585
Nashe, Thomas 1567-1601
Nawa i 1441-1501
Newton, Sir Isaac 1642-1727
North, Sir Thomas 1535?-1601?
Norton, Thomas 1532-1584
Oldham, John 1653-1683
Otway, Thomas 1652-1685
Pade-tha-ya-za 1684-1754
Painter, William 1540?-1594
Paracelsus 1493-1541
Parr, Catharine 1512-1548
Pascal, Blaise 1623-1662
Pasek, Jan Chryzostom 1636-1701
Peele, George 1556-1596
Pembroke, Mary Sidney, Countess of 1561-1621
Penn, William 1644-1718
Pepys, Samuel 1633-1703
Pico della Mirandola, Giovanni 1463-1494
Poliziano, Angelo 1454-1494
Quarles, Francis 1592-1644
Quevedo y Villegas, Francisco Gomez de 1580-1645
Racine, Jean 1639-1699
Raleigh, Sir Walter 1552-1618
Reuter, Christian 1665-1712
Revius, Jacobus 1586-1658
Reynolds, Sir Joshua 1723-1792
Rochester, John Wilmot, Earl of 1648-1680
Rojas Zorilla, Francisco de 1607-1648
Rousseau, Jean-Jacques 1712-1788
Rowe, Elizabeth 1674-1737
Rutherford, Samuel 1600?-1661
Sackville, Thomas 1536-1608
Saint-Simon, Louis de Rouvroy 1675-1755
Santeuil, Jean Baptiste de 1630-1697
Savage, Richard 1696-1742
Savonarola, Girolamo 1452-1498
Scarron, Paul 1610-1660
Scott, Sarah 1723-1795
Selden, John 1584-1654
Sévigné, Madame de 1626-1696
Sewall, Samuel 1652-1730
Shadwell, Thomas 1642-1692
Shaftesbury, Anthony Ashley Cooper, Earl of 1671-1713
Shenstone, William 1714-1763
Shirley, James 1596-1666
Sidney, Sir Philip 1554-1586

Skelton, John 1464?-1529
Smith, Adam 1723-1790
Sorsky, Nil 1433-1508
Spee, Friedrich von 1591-1635
Sprat, Thomas 1635-1713
Stanhope, Philip 1694-1773
Steele, Sir Richard 1672-1729
Suckling, Sir John 1609-1642
Swedenborg, Emanuel 1688-1772
Takeda Izumo 1690-1756
Tasso, Bernardo 1494-1569
Taylor, Edward 1645-1729
Taylor, Jeremy 1613-1667
Temple, Sir William 1629-1699
Tencin, Madame de 1682-1749
Teresa de Jesús 1515-1582
Testi, Fulvio 1593-1646
Thomas à Kempis 1380?-1471
Thomson, James 1700-1748
Tourneur, Cyril 1570-1626
Traherne, Thomas 1637-1674
Trai, Nguyen 1380-1442
Tristan 1601-1655
Tyndale, William 1494?-1536
Urquhart, Sir Thomas 1611-1660
Ussher, James 1581-1656
Vasari, Giorgio 1511-1574
Vaughan, Henry 1621-1695
Vaughan, Thomas 1622-1666
Vico, Giambattista 1668-1744
Villiers, George 1628-1687
Villon, François 1431-1463
Voltaire 1694-1778
Waller, Edmund 1606-1687
Walton, Izaak 1593-1683
Warburton, William 1698-1779
Warner, William 1558-1609
Warton, Thomas 1728-1790
Webster, John 1580-1638
Weise, Christian 1642-1708
Wesley, Charles 1701?-1788
Wesley, John 1703-1791
Whetstone, George 1544?-1587?
White, Gilbert 1720-1793
Wigglesworth, Michael 1631-1705
Williams, Roger 1603-1683
Winckelman, Johann Joachim 1717-1768
Winthrop, John 1588-1649
Wyatt, Sir Thomas 1503-1542
Yuan Mei 1716-1797
Zólkiewski, Stanislaw 1547-1620
Zrinyi, Miklos 1620-1664

Readers are cordially invited to suggest additional authors to the editors.

John Donne

1572-1631

English poet, epigrammist, and sermonist.

Renowned by some scholars as the greatest Anglican divine of his day, Donne is also considered one of the most accomplished, if controversial, poets of the seventeenth century. He was at the head of the metaphysical school of English poetry, whose number also included Richard Crashaw, Abraham Cowley, George Herbert, and Thomas Vaughan, among others. The Metaphysicals' poetry is characterized by complex, witty conceits, sudden (even jarring) paradoxes and contrasts, imagery that combines the ornate with the mundane, and contemplations melding the natural world with the divine. To modern readers, Donne is perhaps best known for his short prose devotion beginning "No man is an island, entire of itself," and ending "Therefore never send to know for whom the bell tolls; it tolls for thee." His life and work are perceived as forming a study in contrasts, reflecting both the sensual rake who celebrated the joys of the young, nude body in lovemaking as well as the severe Christian humanist who calmly contemplated physical suffering, the end of earthly endeavor, and the subservient relationship of humanity to God.

Donne was born into a Roman Catholic family in 1572 in London. His father was a prosperous merchant who died when John was a small boy; and his mother, Elizabeth Heywood, was a relative of the Catholic martyr Sir Thomas More. The family suffered much for their faith under the Tudors; two Jesuit uncles of Donne died in exile, and his younger brother, Henry, died of an illness in jail in 1593, having been imprisoned for sheltering a Roman priest. In 1584 Donne went up to Oxford, but because of his Catholic background he was unable to take the oath of supremacy (recognizing the reigning British monarch, not the pope, as head of the Anglo-Catholic church) required for taking a degree and left after about three years. He began legal studies in 1591 at the Inns of Court in London, and it was there that the duality of his temperament and interests was first made strongly evident. For there Donne became known as both something of a free-spending libertine and a serious scholar of law and the religious questions of the day. Sir Richard Baker, writing in *A Chronicle of the Kings of England* (1643), described young Donne as "not dissolute, but very neat, a great visitor of Ladies, a great frequenter of Playes, a great writer of conceited Verses," while Donne's first biographer, Izaak Walton, described his subject as a man who would rise well before dawn and not leave his studies until late morning. Donne spent much of that time studying the Roman and Anglican churches from a comparative viewpoint, seeking to decide upon which church to embrace. During his years at the Inns of Court (1591-96), he wrote his *Elegies* and *Satyres*, which reflect variously his wit, dandyism, and gravity. Upon completing his studies, Donne accompanied the earl of Essex on two naval expeditions against the Spanish, writing, upon returning from the second, such accomplished poems as "The Storm" and "The Calm" as well as the horrifying "The Burnt Ship." Back in England, Donne embarked upon a promising occupation, serving as secre-

John Donne

tary to Sir Thomas Egerton, whom he had met aboard ship while serving with Essex. His hopes for success and advancement vanished, though, after he secretly married Egerton's niece, Ann More. Learning of the marriage shortly afterward, her enraged father arranged that Donne be jailed and released from his brother-in-law's service. Sometime afterward, Donne sadly wrote a brief epigram describing his lot: "John Donne/Ann Donne/Undone."

Released from prison in 1602, Donne had little money and even less chance of again obtaining gainful employment such as he had recently lost. He spent the next 13 years undergoing long stretches of grinding poverty broken by brief periods of modest gain, desperately seeking patronage to support his rapidly growing family. (Ann Donne bore 12 children before her death in 1617.) At first he lived on charity, and then he came under the patronage of three influential peers: Sir Thomas Morton; Lucy, countess of Bedford; and, finally, Sir Robert Drury. Having embraced the Church of England, Donne was enlisted by Morton to aid him in writing anti-Roman Catholic broadsides. *Pseudo-Martyr* (1610), Donne's first published work, was thus written to persuade English Catholics to foreswear their allegiance to Rome and instead take the

1

oath of allegiance to the British crown. This work, which brought the author to the attention of James I, was followed by the anti-Jesuit polemic *Ignatius His Conclave*, published in 1611, and a treatise arguing for the lawfulness of suicide, *Biathanatos*, which Donne witheld from publication. He also wrote two of his longest (and, in later years, critically controversial) poems, *An Anatomie of the World* and *Of the Progres of the Soule*. These works, also known as the *Anniversaries*, were composed for the sorrowing Drury on the first two anniversaries of his 15-year-old daughter's death. Drury took Donne with him to France on a long diplomatic mission from 1611 to 1612, during which time Donne wrote one of his most praised and critically discussed love poems, "A Valediction: forbidding mourning," at being parted reluctantly from his wife. Upon his return to England, Donne sought to secure a diplomatic post with the help of Robert Carr, Viscount Rochester, a court favorite of James—who himself had other plans for Donne.

Believing that Donne could be of greatest service to the Crown in a much different capacity, the king soon began to pressure Donne to take clerical orders. After some resistance, Donne acquiesced to James's wishes and was ordained in early 1615. After his ordination Donne wrote little poetry, instead devoting his time to writing sermons and devotions and attending to other priestly duties. By all accounts, Donne took his new vocation seriously and performed his ecclesiastical duties quite well, acquiring a great reputation as an impressive deliverer of insightful sermons. During the years immediately following his ordination, he held several important posts, culminating in his appointment—again at James's insistence—as Dean of St. Paul's in 1621. Two years later he suffered an attack of spotted fever, during which he apparently believed himself dying and wrote his renowned *Devotions upon Emergent Occassions*, a collection of somber meditations which includes the prose work "No man is an island." At this time he also wrote two poems of hopeful resignation, "Hymn to God the Father" and "Hymn to God my God, in my sicknesse." Donne's last (and most famous) sermon, *Deaths Duell*, was preached before Charles I during Lent, 1631. Walton stated that Donne, by then clearly a dying man, appeared so gaunt before the congregation and spoke in such a weakened voice that many of his hearers believed they had witnessed a man who *"preach't his own Funeral Sermon."* Walton also recorded that shortly after delivering this final sermon, Donne commissioned a portrait rendered of himself dressed in his burial shroud. Lying thus enshrouded upon his sickbed, Donne meditated upon the completed likeness during the few remaining weeks of his life. After his death, his body was interred in St. Paul's beneath a monument modeled on the deathbed portrait. (This statue was the only such monument to survive the fire that swept St. Paul's in 1666, and it may still be viewed today.)

Commentators note that Donne excelled in both poetry and prose. There was no definitive edition of Donne's poetry until H. J. C. Grierson's edition appeared in 1912. While settling questions of spelling, authenticity, and misattribution, Grierson's *Poems of John Donne* also divided the poems into the categories by which they are discussed today: among them *Songs and Sonets, Elegies,* and *Holy Sonnets*. Having studied the poems, N. J. C. Andreasen described Donne as a "conservative revolutionary," dem-

onstrating that as a poet he worked firmly within a Christian and traditional framework throughout his career—though he was a poetic innovator, nonetheless. Those poems deemed his best, the *Songs and Sonets*—notably "The Canonization," "The Ecstasie," "A Valediction: forbidding mourning," and "The Flea" —abound in the unexpected metaphors, original imagery, startling paradoxes, and avoidance of poetic diction for which the Metaphysicals are known, all voiced in a tone of immediacy and passion in which thought and feeling are intimately melded. In "The Flea," for example, the speaker seeks to coax a desirable woman to his bed, telling her that the flea she just caught has sucked her blood as well as his; their blood has already been mixed within the flea, foreshadowing (he hopes and hints) a more complete and enjoyable intercourse to come. Donne's *Elegies* are praised for similar qualities, as are the *Anniversaries*, "A Valediction: forbidding mourning," and "Goodfriday 1613: Riding Westward," with this last-named poem being considered one of the poet's most richly symbolic meditations upon mortality. Also considered intriguing in its use of imagery is the late "Hymn to God my God, in my sicknesse," in which Donne likens his prone, sick body to a map which doctors, like explorers, have been recently and intimately scrutinizing.

Donne's sermons and devotions are considered eloquent witnesses to a mind attuned to Christian orthodoxy, the style demanded of seventeenth-century religious writing, and the imagery and concerns congenial to the common man of the day. Sometimes the imagery evoked is shocking to twentieth-century readers unaccustomed to the strict doctrines and pulpit style of Jacobean Anglicanism. *Deaths Duell*, with its relentless return to the theme of life as a deceptive prelude to death, is sometimes considered especially so. As with the poetry, though, cultural allowances must be made to enable readers to discern Donne's skill—in this case, in introducing, developing, illustrating, and concluding his exposition in *Deaths Duell* and the other religious writings. As a seventeenth-century divine, Donne has been judged a worthy successor to the accomplished Lancelot Andrewes, with some calling him Andrewes's superior.

The critical history of Donne's works is a checkered one. The first collection of Donne's poetry was not published until two years after the author's death, the poems having previously circulated in manuscript only. Entitled *Poems*, this collection was prefaced with elegies by Walton, Thomas Carew, and other contemporaries of Donne. These writers represented one side of early criticism of Donne's poetry—those who honored Donne as a master—with Carew eloquently lamenting the passing of "*a King, that rul'd as hee thought fit/the universall Monarchy of wit*," and Walton later writing his insightful—if perhaps overly reverent—life of Donne as a preface to the latter's *LXXX Sermons* (1640). Another early view was first voiced by Ben Jonson in his famous recorded conversations with William Drummond of Hawthornden. While giving much praise to Donne's poetry, Jonson also faulted it for its profanity and innovative meter (for which latter quality Donne "deserved hanging"). He also criticized the first *Anniversarie* as obsequious, relating to Drummond his having bluntly told Donne to his face that the poem was so full of extravagant flattery as to more appropriately serve as an ode of praise to the Virgin Mary than to a fifteen-year-old girl he had never even known. Jonson's criticisms, expressed to Drummond in 1618 or 1619, were adopted and developed by critics of Donne's poetry for nearly the next two centuries. In his "The Original and Progress of Poetry" (1693), John Dryden used the term "metaphysical" for the first time to describe Donne's poetry, characterizing Donne as more a wit than a poet. Other critics seized upon this criticism over the next decades, with Samuel Johnson eventually writing a crushing critique of Donne's poetry in his "Life of Cowley" (1779), an attack on the metaphysical school in general and Donne, Abraham Cowley, and John Cleveland in particular. In this famous essay, Johnson used the term "metaphysical" as a term of abuse to describe poets whose aim, he believed, was to show off their own cleverness and learning and to construct paradoxes so outlandish and inadvertantly pretentious as to be ludicrous, indecent, or both. Predominantly negative criticisms of Donne's poetry continued into the early nineteenth century, with William Hazlitt, writing in 1819, being one of the last major critics to affirm Johnson's condemnation of Donne's work.

The early nineteenth century saw growing critical and popular interest in and acceptance of Donne's poetry. Samuel Taylor Coleridge, Robert Browning, and Thomas De Quincey were especially instrumental in focusing a favorable light on the works: Coleridge praised the power and vivacity of the poems; Browning wrote what G. K. Chesterton later described as "poetry which utters the primeval and indivisible emotions" in a manner reminiscent of Donne—whom Browning acknowledged publicly as a major influence; and De Quincey turned aside Johnson's arguments, hailing Donne's skill as a rhetorician. Donne's complete works were published in 1839, and thus the sermons and devotions began to be discussed, while several editions of the poems appeared throughout the century. Edmund Gosse's *Life and Letters of Dr. John Donne, Dean of St. Paul's* (1899), the first biography of Donne since Walton's "Life" of 1640, prepared the way for Grierson's definitive edition of the poems, published a few years later. Major literary figures—including Arthur Symons, Leslie Stephen, Lytton Strachey, Walter de la Mare, and Rupert Brooke—reviewed these works at length, bolstering a ground swell of popular and critical interest in Donne's accomplishment. This came too a flood in the early 1920s and continues to the present day. In 1921, T. S. Eliot wrote a major article, "The Metaphysical Poets," in which he focused attention on Donne and the Metaphysicals as poets of signal stature who had been to their age what the twentieth-century Modernists were to theirs. Like the Modernists, who were constructing complex, distanced poetry to reflect the spiritual vacuum at the center of modern life, Eliot argued, the Metaphysicals had written complex, emotionally charged celebrations of the joys, sorrows, and dilemmas of their own age, an age of both fleshliness and faith. Other essayists, following Eliot's lead or working independently, wrote about Donne's poetry in a similar vein, with some—notably Hugh I'Anson Fausset—proclaiming Donne a Zarathustra-like figure who had thrown off all Christian morality in celebration of *ethos* unfettered and *eros* unbound. Not all criticism of Donne's work was favorable at this time, however. C. S. Lewis, for example, a literary traditionalist and longtime nemesis of Eliot, found the love poetry vastly overrated, while several other commentators faulted the meter, structure, and subject matter of selected poems. Otherwise, Donne was perceived in modern eyes as an Elizabethan playboy-poet unfairly transformed by hard circumstances into a stiff, morbid, Jacobean divine.

In succeeding decades, this estimation was altered as closer study of Donne's devotions and sermons, along with fresh examinations of the record of his life, compelled scholars to view their subject as far more complex than originally perceived. From mid-century to the present day, Donne's canon has been scrutinized according to the methods of various critical schools, with representatives of the New Critics, the deconstructionists, and others offering diverse interpretations of the works. Critics of the stature of Lionel Trilling, I. A. Richards, and Cleanth Brooks have commented on Donne's poetry. In addition, twentieth-century writers have used phrases from Donne's poetry to adorn their own works in the form of epigrams and titles. A phrase from Donne's best-known religious devotion was adopted by Ernest Hemingway as the title of his novel of the Spanish Civil War, *For Whom the Bell Tolls* (1940). (Hemingway later told one correspondent that Donne's works were rife with such lines for use by authors searching for titles for their works.) And as the title of one of his better-known essays on the Christian life, Lewis used the last four words of one poem's opening line, "What if this Present were the world's last night?"—and used the entire line as his essay theme.

Once considered the story of an abrupt transformation from worldly audacity to Christian conformity, Donne's life and career are today seen in terms of an artistically sensitive man's spiritual growth in a lifelong search for meaning and wholeness. That there was a break between the younger Donne who wrote the gay *Songs and Sonets*, the Donne of middle years who wrote to please his patrons and gain favor with influential readers, and the older Donne so much concerned with the meaning of sanctification is undeniable. But there is evidence that Donne was deeply interested in spiritual truths throughout his life, and it is certain that he did not abandon poetry altogether after taking orders. Further, it has been emphasized that the modern reader of Donne's poems and the interpreter of his life must take into account the cultural mores and atmosphere of Donne's age: a time when the fleshly and the solemnly spiritual were comfortably married in English life: a time of plagues in which a widespread sense of life's brevity and fleeting beauty was acknowledged: a time of schism and doubt as people in a once-Roman Catholic nation searched for certainty in a land now under the control of a state church and a spiritual leader of questionable spiritual authority. As a poet, Donne served as the inspiration to an entire school of poets—"the school of Donne" —who collectively wrote some of the most accomplished religious poetry in English history. He is seen as the forerunner of many modern poets, notably those Modernist innovators of the first half of the twentieth century. Frank Kermode has praised Donne as "at least as original and idiosyncratic" as his near-contemporaries Edmund Spenser and William Shakespeare. Perhaps Carew, writing three centuries earlier, wrote the most succinct and eloquent summary of Donne's accomplishment, concluding his elegy: "*Here lie two Flamens, and both those, the best,/ Apollo's first, at last, the true Gods Priest.*"

PRINCIPAL WORKS

Pseudo-Martyr (essay) 1610

Ignatius His Conclave; or His Inthronisation in a Late Election in Hell: wherein many things are mingled by way of satyr; concerning the disposition of Jesuits, the creation of a new hell, the establishing of a church in the moone (essay) 1611

*The First Anniversarie. An Anatomie of the World. Wherein By Occasion Of the untimely death of Mistris Elizabeth Drury, the frailtie and decay of this whole World is represented (poetry) 1611

*The Second Anniversarie. Of the Progres of the Soule. Wherein, By Occasion Of the Religious death of Mistris Elizabeth Drury, the incommodities of the Soule in this life, and her exaltation in the next, are Contemplated (poetry) 1612

Devotions upon Emergent Occasions, and Severall steps in my sickness (devotions) 1624

Deaths Duell (sermon) 1632

Juvenilia; or, Certaine paradoxes, and problems (prose) 1633

†Poems (poetry) 1633

LXXX Sermons (sermons) 1640

ΒΙΑΘΑΝΑΤΟΣ. A declaration of that paradoxe, or thesis, that self-homicide is not so naturally sinne, that it may never be otherwise. Wherein the nature, and the extent of all those lawes, which seeme to be violated by this act, are diligently surveyed (essay) 1646

‡Essayes in Divinity (essays) 1652

Works. 6 vols. (poetry, essays, sermons, devotions, epistles, and prose) 1839

Selected Passages from the Sermons (sermons) 1919

The Showing forth of Christ: Sermons of John Donne (sermons) 1964

*These works were published together as *The Anniversaries* in 1963.

†In later centuries, this first edition of Donne's poetry was succeeded by other, more authoritative editions, notably those issued in 1895 and 1912. H. J. C. Grierson's 1912 edition is considered definitive and contains *Songs and Sonets, Epigrams, Elegies, Heroicall Epistle, Epithalamions, Satyres, Letters to Severall Personages, An Anatomie of the World, Of the Progresse of the Soule, Epicedes and Obsequies upon the Deaths of Sundry Personages, Epitaphs, Infinitati Sacrum, Divine Poems, Holy Sonnets*, Donne's Latin poems and translations, and poems of questionable authorship attributed to Donne in early editions.

‡This work was published with a 1652 printing of *Juvenilia; or, Certaine paradoxes, and problems.*

BEN JONSON (poem date 1610)

[*The first (though unofficial) poet laureate of England, Jonson was among the most prominent writers of the Elizabethan Age. He is especially esteemed for such satirical plays as* Every Man in His Humor *(1598),* Volpone *(1605-06), and* The Alchemist *(1610). Jonson distinguished himself, as well, as a writer of court masques and in several varieties of verse, displaying an unrivaled classical learning. In the following epigram written in 1610, he offers high praise to Donne.*]

DONNE, the delight of Phoebus and each Muse,

Who, to thy one, all other brains refuse;
Whose every work, of thy most early wit,
Came forth example, and remains so yet:
Longer a knowing than most wits do live,
And which no affection praise enough can give!
To it, thy language, letters, arts, best life,
Which might with half mankind maintain a strife;
All which I meant to praise, and yet I would;
But leave, because I cannot as I should!

> *Ben Jonson, "To John Donne," in his* The Works of Ben Jonson, Vol. III, *edited by Francis Cunningham, John Camden Hotten, 1875, p. 229.*

BEN JONSON (conversation date 1618-19)

[*In the following excerpt from a series of conversations held in December 1618 or January 1619 with William Drummond of Hawthornden, Jonson expresses mixed thoughts on Donne's poetic skill. Some of Jonson's remarks reprinted below are among the most famous recorded assessments of Donne's poetry.*]

Certain informations and maners of Ben Johnsons to W. Drumond.

That Dones *Anniversarie* ["An Anatomie of the World"] was profane and full of Blasphemies: that he told Mr. Donne, if it had been written of the Virgin Marie it had been something; to which he answered, that he described the Idea of a Woman, and not as she was.

That Done, for not keeping of accent, deserved hanging. (p. 5)

He esteemeth John Done the first poet in the World, in some things: his verses of the Lost Chaine ["**Elegie XI: The Bracelet**"] he heth by heart; and that passage of the "**Calme,**" That dust and feathers doe not stirr, all was so quiet. Affirmeth Done to have written all his best pieces ere he was 25 years old. (p. 11)

That Done said to him he wrott that Epitaph on Prince Henry ["**Elegie upon the untimely death of the incomparable Prince Henry**"] Look to me, Fath, to match Sir Ed: Herbert in obscurenesse. (p. 12)

The conceit of Dones Transformation or Μετεμψυχωσιζ ["**The Progresse of the Soule**"] was, that he sought the soule of that Aple which Eva pulled, and thereafter made it the soule of a bitch, then of a shee wolf, and so of a woman: his generall purpose was to have brought in all the bodies of the Hereticks from the soule of Cain, and at last left it in the bodie of Calvin: Of this he never wrotte but one sheet, and now, since he was made Doctor, repenteth highlie, and seeketh to destroy all his poems. (pp. 12-13)

That Done himself, for not being understood, would perish. (p. 18)

> *Ben Jonson, in his* Ben Jonson's Conversations with William Drummond of Hawthornden, *edited by R. F. Patterson, 1923. Reprint by Haskell House Publishers Ltd., 1974, 60 p.*

THOMAS CAREW (poem date 1633)

[*Carew was one of the Cavalier poets, whose number also included Robert Herrick, Sir John Suckling, and Edmund Waller, among others. Influenced primarily by Ben Jonson and Donne, he is best known for his early love poetry, notably "The Rapture." In the following poem, he offers high praise to Donne's accomplishment, concluding with lines that are among the most famous ever written on Donne's poetic stature.*]

Can we not force from widdowed Poetry,
Now thou art Dead (Great DONNE) one Elegie
To crowne thy Hearse? Why yet dare we not trust
Though with unkneaded dowe-bak't prose thy dust,
Such as the uncisor'd Churchman from the flower
Of fading Rhetorique, short liv'd as his houre,
Dry as the sand that measures it, should lay
Upon thy Ashes, on the funerall day?
Have we no voice, no tune? Did'st thou dispense
Through all our language, both the words and sense?
'Tis a sad truth; The Pulpit may her plaine,
And sober Christian precepts still retaine,
Doctrines it may, and wholesome Uses frame,
Grave Homilies, and Lectures, But the flame
Of thy brave Soule, that shot such heat and light,
As burnt our earth, and made our darknesse bright,
Committed holy Rapes upon our Will,
Did through the eye the melting heart distill;
And the deepe knowledge of darke truths so teach,
As sense might judge, what phansie could not reach;
Must be desir'd for ever. So the fire,
That fills with spirit and heat the Delphique quire,
Which kindled first by thy Promethean breath,
Glow'd here a while, lies quench't now in thy death;
The Muses garden with Pedantique weedes
O'rspred, was purg'd by thee; The lazie feeds
Of servile imitations throwne away;
And fresh invention planted, Thou didst pay
The debts of our penurious bankrupt age;
Licentious thefts, that make poëtique rage
A Mimique fury, when our soules must bee
Possest, or with Anacreons Extasie,
Or Pindars, not their owne; The subtle cheat
Of slie Exchanges, and the jugling feat
Of two-edg'd words, or whatsoever wrong
By ours was done the Greeke, or Latine tongue,
Thou hast redeem'd, and open'd Us a Mine
Of rich and pregnant phansie, drawne a line
Of masculine expression, which had good
Old Orpheus seene, Or all the ancient Brood
Our superstitious fooles admire, and hold
Their lead more precious, then thy burnish't Gold,
Thou hadst beene their Exchequer, and no more
They each in others dust, had rak'd for Ore.
Thou shalt yield no precedence, but of time,
And the blinde fate of language, whose tun'd chime
More charmes the outward sense; Yet though maist claime
From so great disadvantage greater fame,
Since to the awe of thy imperious wit
Our stubborne language bends, made only fit
With her tough-thich-rib'd hoopes to gird about
Thy Giant phansie, which had prov'd too stout
For their soft melting Phrases. As in time
They had the start, so did they cull the prime
Buds of invention many a hundred yeare,
And left the rifled fields, besides the feare
To touch their Harvest, yet from those bare lands
Of what is purely thine, thy only hands
(And that thy smallest worke) have gleaned more
Then all those times, and tongues could reape before;
But thou art gone, and thy strict lawes will be
Too hard for Libertines in Poetrie.

They will repeale the goodly exil'd traine
Of gods and goddesses, which in thy just raigne
Were banish'd nobler Poems, now, with these
The silenc'd tales o' th' Metamorphoses
Shall stuffe their lines, and swell the windy Page,
Till Verse refin'd by thee, in this last Age,
Turne ballad rime, Or those old Idolls bee
Ador'd againe, with new apostasie;
Oh, pardon mee, that breake with untun'd verse
The reverend silence that attends thy herse,
Whose awfull solemne murmures were to thee
More then these faint lines, A loud Elegie,
That did proclaime in a dumbe eloquence
The death of all the Arts, whose influence
Growne feeble, in these panting numbers lies
Gasping short winded Accents, and so dies:
So doth the swiftly turning wheele not stand
In th' instant we withdraw the moving hand,
But some small time maintaine a faint weake course
By vertue of the first impulsive force:
And so whil'st I cast on thy funerall pile
Thy crowne of Bayes, Oh, let it crack a while,
And spit disdaine, till the devouring flashes
Suck all the moysture up, then turne to ashes.
I will not draw the envy to engrosse
All thy perfections, or weepe all our losse;
Those are too numerous for an Elegie,
And this too great, to be express'd by mee.
Though every pen should share a distinct part,
Yet art thou Theme enough to tyre all Art;
Let others carve the rest, it shall suffice
I on thy Tombe this Epitaph incise.

*Here lies a King, that rul'd as hee thought fit
The universall Monarchy of wit;
Here lie two Flamens, and both those, the best,
Apollo's first, at last, the true Gods Priest.* (pp. 385-88)

Thomas Carew, "An Elegie upon the Death of the Deane of Pauls, Dr. John Donne," in Poems by J. D., John Marriot, 1633, pp. 385-88.

IZAAK WALTON (essay date 1640)

[*Walton was the author of the celebrated work* The Compleat Angler *(1653) and the equally esteemed* Lives *of such contemporaries as Donne (1640), Richard Hooker (1665), and George Herbert (1670). In the following excerpt from "The Life of Dr. Donne," a short biography originally published as an introduction to Donne's* LXXX Sermons *(1640), Walton tells of the peculiar circumstances surrounding the poem "A Valediction, forbidding mourning." In the second part of the excerpt, he describes an event which occured near the very end of Donne's life: the delivery of the sermon* Deaths Duell.]

At this time of Mr. *Donne's*, and his wives living in Sir *Roberts* house, the Lord *Hay* was by King *James* sent upon a glorious Embassie to the then *French* King *Henry* the fourth, and, Sir *Robert* put on a suddain resolution to accompany him to the *French* Court, and, to be present at his audience there. And, Sir *Robert* put on as suddain a resolution, to solicit Mr. *Donne* to be his Companion in that Journey: And this desire was suddainly made known to his wife, who was then with Child, and otherways under so dangerous a habit of body, as to her health, that she profest an unwillingness to allow him any absence from her; saying, *her divining soul boded her some ill in his absence*; and therefore, desired him not to leave her. This made Mr. *Donne* lay aside all thoughts of the Journey, and really to resolve against it. But Sir *Robert* became restless in his perswasions for it; and Mr. *Donne* was so generous, as to think he had sold his liberty when he received so many Charitable kindnesses from him: and, told his wife so; who did therefore with an unwilling-willingness give a faint Consent to the Journey, which was proposed to be but for two months: for about that time they determin'd their return.—Within a few days after this resolve, the *Embassador*, Sir *Robert*, and Mr. *Donne* left *London*; and were the twelfth day got all safe to *Paris*.—two days after their arrival there, Mr. *Donne* was left alone, in that room in which Sir *Robert*, and he, and some other friends had din'd together. To this place Sir *Robert* return'd within half an hour; and, as he left, so he found Mr. *Donne* alone; but, in such an Extasie, and so alter'd as to his looks, as amaz'd Sir *Robert* to behold him: insomuch that he earnestly desired Mr. *Donne* to declare what had befaln him in the short time of his absence? to which, Mr. *Donne* was not able to make a present answer: but, after a long and perplext pause, did at last say, *I have seen a dreadful Vision since I saw you: I have seen my dear wife pass twice by me through this room, with her hair hanging about her shoulders, and a dead child in her arms: this, I have seen since I saw you.* To which, Sir *Robert* reply'd; *Sure Sir, you have slept since I saw you; and, this is the result of some melancholy dream, which I desire you to forget, for you are now awake.* To which Mr. *Donne's* reply was: *I cannot be surer that I now live, then that I have not slept since I saw you: and am, as sure, that at her second appearing, she stopt, and look'd me in the face, and vanisht.*——Rest and sleep, had not alter'd Mr. *Donne's* opinion the next day: for, he then affirm'd this Vision with a more deliberate, and, so confirm'd a confidence, that he inclin'd Sir *Robert* to a faint belief that the Vision was true.——It is truly said, *that desire, and doubt, have no rest*: and it prov'd so with Sir *Robert*, for he immediately sent a servant to *Drewry* house with a charge to hasten back, and bring him word, whether Mrs. *Donne* were alive? and if alive, in what condition she was, as to her health?—The twelfth day the Messenger returned with this account—That he found and left Mrs. *Donne* very sad, and sick in her bed: and, that after a long and dangerous labor she had deliver'd of a dead child. And, upon examination, the abortion prov'd to be the same day, and about the very hour that Mr. *Donne* affirm'd he saw her pass by him in his Chamber.

This is a relation that will beget some wonder: and, it well may; for most of our world are at present possest with an opinion that *Visions* and *Miracles* are ceas'd. (pp. 39-41)

I forbear the Readers farther trouble, as to the relation, and what concerns it; and will conclude mine, with commending to his view . . . **["A Valediction: forbidding mourning,"]** Verses given by Mr. *Donne* to his wife at the time that he then parted from her. And I beg to leave to tell, that I have heard some Criticks, learned, both in Languages and Poetry, say, that none of the Greek or Latine Poets did ever equal them.

• • • • •

Before that month [January 1630] ended, he was appointed to preach upon his old constant day, the first *Friday* in *Lent*; he had notice of it, and had in his sickness so prepared for that imployment, that as he had long thirsted for it: so he resolved his weakness should not hinder his journey; he came therefore to *London*, some few days before

his appointed day of preaching. . . . And, when to the amazement of some beholders he appeared in the Pulpit, many of them thought he presented himself not to preach mortification by a living voice: but, mortality by a decayed body and a dying face. And doubtless, many did secretly ask that question in *Ezekiel*; *Do these bones live? or, can that soul organize that tongue, to speak so long time as the sand in that glass will move towards its centre, and measure out an hour of this dying mans unspent life?* Doubtless it cannot; and yet, after some faint pauses in his zealous prayer, his strong desires enabled his weak body to discharge his memory of his preconceived meditations, which were of dying: the Text being, *To God the Lord belong the issues from death.* Many that then saw his tears, and heard his faint and hollow voice, professing they thought the Text prophetically chosen, and that Dr. *Donne had preach't his own Funeral Sermon.*

Being full of joy that God had enabled him to perform this desired duty, he hastened to his house; out of which he never moved, till like St. *Stephen*, he was carried by devout men to his Grave. (pp. 74-5)

Izaak Walton, "Life of Dr. John Donne," in his The Lives of John Donne, Sir Henry Wotton, Richard Hooker, George Herbert and Robert Sanderson, Oxford University Press, London, 1927, pp. 20-89.

JOHN DRYDEN (essay date 1693)

[*Regarded by many scholars as the father of modern English poetry and criticism, Dryden dominated literary life in England during the last four decades of the seventeenth century. He deliberately and comprehensively refined the language of Elizabethan England in all his works, developing an expressive, universal diction which has had immense impact on the development of speech and writing in Great Britain and North America. Although recognized as a prolific and accomplished Restoration dramatist, Dryden also wrote a number of satirical poems and critical writings, some of which are acknowledged as his greatest literary achievements. In the former, most notably* Absalom and Achitophel *(1681),* Religio Laici *(1682), and* The Hind and the Panther *(1687), he displayed an irrepressible wit and forceful line of argument which later satirists adopted as their model. In the latter, particularly* Of Dramatic Poesy *(1668), Dryden originated the extended form of objective, practical analysis that has come to characterize most modern criticism. In the following excerpt from his "A Discourse on the Original and Progress of Satire" (1693), an essay dedicated to Charles, Earl of Dorset and Middlesex, Dryden first compares the poetry of Dorset and Donne—to Donne's disadvantage. He then faults Donne's skill as a Horatian satirist, finding him more a wit than a poet. This judgment of Donne as a clever craftsman, not a poetic artist, marked the beginning of a theme which recurred in negative criticisms of Donne's work for over a century.*]

There is not an English writer this day living, who is not perfectly convinced that your Lordship excels all others in all the several parts of poetry which you have undertaken to adorn. (p. 18)

Donne alone, of all our countrymen, had your talent; but was not happy enough to arrive at your versification; and were he translated into numbers, and English, he would yet be wanting in the dignity of expression. That which is the prime virtue, and chief ornament, of Virgil, which distinguishes him from the rest of writers, is so conspicuous in your verses, that it casts a shadow on all your contemporaries; we cannot be seen, or but obscurely, while you are present. You equal Donne in the variety, multiplicity, and choice of thoughts; you excel him in the manner and the words. I read you both with the same admiration, but not with the same delight. He affects the metaphysics, not only in his satires, but in his amorous verses, where nature only should reign; and perplexes the minds of the fair sex with nice speculations of philosophy, when he should engage their hearts, and entertain them with the softnesses of love.

• • • • •

'Tis but necessary, that after so much has been said of Satire some definition of it should be given. Heinsius, in his dissertations on Horace, makes it for me, in these words: 'Satire is a kind of poetry, without a series of action, invented for the purging of our minds; in which human vices, ignorance, and errors, and all things besides, which are produced from them in every man, are severely reprehended; partly dramatically, partly simply, and sometimes in both kinds of speaking; but, for the most part, figuratively, and occultly; consisting in a low familiar way, chiefly in a sharp and pungent manner of speech; but partly, also, in a facetious and civil way of jesting; by which either hatred, or laughter, or indignation, is moved.'— Where I cannot but observe, that this obscure and perplexed definition, or rather description, of satire, is wholly accommodated to the Horatian way; and excluding the works of Juvenal and Persius, as foreign from that kind of poem. The clause in the beginning of it *without a series of action* distinguishes satire properly from stage-plays, which are all of one action, and one continued series of action. The end or scope of satire is to purge the passions; so far it is common to the satires of Juvenal and Persius. The rest which follows is also generally belonging to all three; till he comes upon us, with the excluding clause *consisting in a low familiar way of speech*, which is the proper character of Horace; and from which the other two, for their honour be it spoken, are far distant. But how come lowness of style, and the familiarity of words, to be so much the propriety of satire, that without them a poet can be no more a satirist, than without risibility he can be a man? Is the fault of Horace to be made the virtue and standing rule of this poem? Is the *grande sophos* of Persius, and the sublimity of Juvenal, to be circumscribed with the meanness of words and vulgarity of expression? If Horace refused the pains of numbers, and the loftiness of figures, are they bound to follow so ill a precedent? Let him walk afoot, with his pad in his hand, for his own pleasure; but let not them be accounted no poets, who choose to mount, and show their horsemanship.... Would not Donne's **Satires**, which abound with so much wit, appear more charming, if he had taken care of his words, and of his numbers? But he followed Horace so very close, that of necessity he must fall with him; and I may safely say it of this present age, that if we are not so great wits as Donne, yet certainly we are better poets. (pp. 100-02)

> *John Dryden, "A Discourse concerning the Original and Progress of Satire," in his* Essays of John Dryden, Vol. II, *edited by W. P. Ker, Oxford at the Clarendon Press, 1900. pp. 15-114.*

LEWIS THEOBALD   (essay date 1734)

[*Theobald was an English editor and translator who is remembered primarily as the compiler of an eighteenth-century edition of Shakespeare's plays and as the hero of Alexander Pope's* The Dunciad *(1728). In the following excerpt, he scorns Donne and the poets of his era for their pretentious obscurity.*]

Besides, *Wit* lying mostly in the Assemblage of *Ideas*, and in the putting Those together with Quickness and Variety, wherein can be found any Resemblance, or Congruity, to make up pleasant Pictures, and agreeable Visions in the Fancy; the Writer, who aims at Wit, must of course range far and wide for Materials. Now, the Age, in which *Shakespeare* liv'd, having, above all others, a wonderful Affection to appear Learned, They declined vulgar Images, such as are immediately fetch'd from Nature, and rang'd thro' the Circle of the Sciences to fetch their Ideas from thence. But as the Resemblances of such Ideas to the Subject must necessarily lie very much out of the common Way, and every piece of Wit appear a Riddle to the Vulgar; This, that should have taught them the forced, quaint, unnatural Tract they were in, (and induce them to follow a more natural One,) was the very Thing that kept them attach'd to it. The ostentatious Affectation of abstruse Learning, peculiar to that Time, the Love that Men naturally have to every Thing that looks like Mystery, fixed them down to this Habit of Obscurity. Thus became the Poetry of Donne (tho' the wittiest Man of that Age,) nothing but a continued Heap of Riddles. (p. xlvi)

> *Lewis Theobald, in an excerpt in his* Preface to The Works of Shakespeare, *(1734),* William Andrews Clark Memorial Library, University of California, 1949, p. xlvi.

DAVID HUME   (essay date 1754)

[*Hume is considered an outstanding figure in world philosophy. He was a major promoter of what he called a "mitigated" form of philosophical skepticism—the doctrine that true knowledge is uncertain—and a profound explorer of the human mind. Also a prolific historian, he wrote an important multivolume history of England. In the following excerpt from the first volume of that work,* The History of Great Britain, Vol. I: Containing the Reigns of James I. and Charles I. *(1754), he briefly denigrates Donne's satires as the degenerate products of a decadent literary age.*]

Tho' the age [of James I] was by no means destitute of eminent writers, a very bad taste in general prevailed during that period; and the monarch himself was not a little infected with it.

On the first origin of letters among the Greeks, the genius of poets and orators, as might naturally be expected, was distinguished by an amiable simplicity, which, whatever rudeness might sometimes attend it, is so fitted to express the genuine movements of nature and passion, that the compositions, possessed of it, must for ever appear valuable to the discerning part of mankind. The glaring figures of discourse, the pointed antithesis, the unnatural conceit, the jingle of words; such false ornaments are not employed by early writers; not because they were rejected, but because they scarce ever occurred to them. An easy, unforced strain of sentiment runs thro' their compositions; tho' at the same time we may observe, that, amid the most elegant simplicity of thought and expression, one is some-times surprised to meet with a poor conceit, which had presented itself unsought for, and which the author had not acquired critical observation enough to condemn. A bad taste seizes with avidity these frivolous beauties, and even perhaps a good taste, 'ere furfeited by them: They multiply every day more and more, in the fashionable compositions: Nature and good sense are neglected: Lab-oured ornaments, studied and admired: And a total degen-eracy of style and language prepares the way for barbarism and ignorance. Hence the Asiatic manner was found to de-part so much from the simple purity of Athens: Hence that tinsel eloquence, which is observable in many of the Roman writers, from which Cicero himself is not wholly exempted, and which so much prevails in Ovid, Seneca, Lucan, Martial, and the Plinys. (pp. 245-46)

A like character may be extended to the first English writ-ers; such as flourished during the reign of Elizabeth and James, and was even till long afterwards. Learning, on its revival, in this island, was attired in the same unnatural garb, which it wore at the time of its decay among the Greeks and Romans. And, what may be regarded as a mis-fortune, the English writers were possessed of great genius before they were endued with any degree of taste, and by that means gave a kind of sanction to those forced turns and sentiments, which they so much affected. Their dis-torted conceptions are attended with such vigor of mind, that we admire the imagination, which produced them; as much as we blame the want of judgment, which gave them admittance. (p. 247)

In Donne's satyres, when carefully inspected, there appear some flashes of wit and ingenuity; but these totally suffo-cated and buried by the harshest and most uncouth ex-pression, which is any where to be met with. (p. 249)

> *David Hume, "James I: Chapter VI," in his* The History of Great Britain: The Reigns of James I and Charles I, *edited by Duncan Forbes, Penguin Books, 1970, pp. 219-54.*

THE MONTHLY REVIEW   (essay date 1756)

[*The* Monthly Review *(1749-1844) was the first English se-rial devoted to reviewing the full spectrum of current publi-cations for the general reading public. The prestige and lon-gevity of this periodical is attributed largely to founding editor Ralph Griffiths's ambition in assembling an illustri-ous and learned staff of reviewers—including Oliver Gold-smith and Owen Ruffhead—and skill as a businessman. De-spite the magazine's pro-Whig and anti-Church bias, Griffiths for the most part made it into an impartial forum over which he retained control by assigning books to review-ers most likely to give them a fair consideration and by pub-lishing these reviews anonymously, thus discouraging liter-ary feuds that might undermine the objectivity he desired for his publication. In the following excerpt from a review of Jo-seph Warton's anonymously published* Essay on the Genius and Writings Pope *(1756), the critic "Dr. G." takes Warton to task for overrating Donne's importance. In later editions of his book, Warton altered his assessment of English poets, dropping Donne much further down than originally ranked (see excerpt dated 1782).*]

Of all eminent men, none have been so much the butt of censure, and the subject of praise, as the poets; and among these, none, perhaps, ever suffered more from either, than

POPE; with this felicity, however, that if he has had a Zoilus in Gildon, he has had an Aristarchus in Spence, and in the Author [Joseph Warton] of the present Essay.

But though we think very highly of the critical and literary abilities of our unknown Essayist, and have perused his work with no less profit than pleasure, yet can we not im-plicitly subscribe to all his decisions, and illustrations. As he has ventured, in some things, to differ from the re-ceived opinion, so shall we be the less scrupulous in dis-senting from him. (p. 528)

'Our English Poets ([says] our Author) may, I think, 'be disposed in four different classes and degrees. In the first class he would place Spencer, Shakespear, and Milton; and then, at proper intervals, Otway and Lee.

In the second class he places such as possessed the *true po-etical genius,* 'in a more moderate degree,' but had noble talents for *ethical poetry.* At the head of these is Dryden. (pp. 533-34)

In the second class after Dryden, the Critic places Donne, as possessing the *true poetical genius, with noble talents for moral poesy.* And yet, but two pages before, he character-izes this author, as a man of wit, and a man of sense, but asks what traces he had left of pure poetry? We readily agree that he has left none; for as an elegant genius of the north [Drummond of Hawthornden] has expressed it, we shall never be induced to regard that as poetry, which Ho-mer and Virgil, if alive, would not have understood. Did any man with a poetical ear, ever yet read ten lines of Donne without disgust? or are there ten lines of poetry in all his works? No. How then comes this Adjuster of liter-ary rank to post him before Denham, Waller, Cowley, &c. In truth, Daniel, Drayton, Randolph, or almost any other of his contemporary poets, the translator of Du Bartas not excepted, deserve the place better than he. (p. 535)

> *Dr. G., "An Essay on the Writings and Genius of Pope," in* The Monthly Review, *London, Vol. XIV, April, 1756, pp. 528-54.*

SAMUEL JOHNSON   (essay date 1779)

[*Johnson is one of the outstanding figures in English litera-ture and a leader in the history of textual and easthetic criti-cism. Popularly known in his own day as the "Great Cham of Literature," Johnson was a prolific lexicographer, essay-ist, poet, and critic whose lucid and extensively illustrated* Dictionary of the English Language *(1755) and* Prefaces, Biographical and Critical, to the Works of the English Po-ets *(10 vols., 1779-81; reissued in 1783 as* The Lives of the Most Eminent English Poets*) were new departures in lexi-cography and biographical criticism, respectively. As a liter-ary critic he was neither a rigid theorist nor a strict follower of neoclassical rules, tending instead to rely on common sense and empirical knowledge. Basically skeptical in all matters but religion and always ready to shift his argu-ment's ground if necessary, he had in his criticism one crite-rion in mind: the power of a work to please and instruct. At his best a direct and pungent prosodist, Johnson could be a perceptive and acute judge of both the defects and merits of a work, but because of his forceful style his listings of defects are often more memorable than his extensive general praise. In the following excerpt from an essay originally published in the first edition of his* Lives, *Johnson uses the word "metaphysical" as a term of abuse, describing and denigrat-*

ing the metaphysical poets while displaying examples from Donne's poetry to illustrate his argument.]

Wit, like all other things subject by their nature to the choice of man, has its changes and fashions, and at different times takes different forms. About the beginning of the seventeenth century appeared a race of writers that may be termed the metaphysical poets; of whom, in a criticism on the works of Cowley, it is not improper to give some account.

The metaphysical poets were men of learning, and to show their learning was their whole endeavour; but, unluckily resolving to shew it in rhyme,instead of writing poetry, they only wrote verses, and very often such verses as stood the trial of the finger better than of the ear; for the modulation was so imperfect, that they were only found to be verses by counting the syllables.

If the father of criticism has rightly denominated poetry *an imitative art,* these writers will, without great wrong, . . . lose their right to the name of poets; for they cannot be said to have imitated any thing; they neither copied nature nor life; neither painted the forms of matter, nor represented the operations of intellect.

Those, however, who deny them to be poets, allow them to be wits. Dryden confesses of himself and his contemporaries, that they fall below Donne in wit, but maintains that they surpass him in poetry. (pp. 12-13)

Critical remarks are not easily understood without examples; and I have therefore collected instances of the modes of writing by which this species of poets, for poets they were called by themselves and their admirers, was eminently distinguished.

As the authors of this race were perhaps more desirous of being admired than understood, they sometimes drew their conceits from recesses of learning not very much frequented by common readers of poetry. (p. 16)

Thus *Donne* shews his medicinal knowledge in some encomiastick verses ['**To the Countes of Bedford. "Madame, reason is"'**]:

> In every thing there naturally grows
> A Balsamum to keep it fresh and new,
> If 'twere not injur'd by extrinsique blows;
> Your youth and beauty are this balm in you.
> But you, of learning and religion,
> And virtue and such ingredients, have made
> A mithridate, whose operation
> Keeps off, or cures what can be done or said.

Though the following lines of Donne [from '**To the Countesse of Bedford, "This twilight of"'**], on the last night of the year, have something in them too scholastick, they are not inelegant:

> This twilight of two years, not past nor next,
> Some emblem is of me, or I of this,
> Who, meteor-like, of stuff and form perplext,
> Whose what and where, in disputation is,
> If I should call me any thing, should miss.
>
> I sum the years and me, and find me not
> Debtor to th' old, nor creditor to th' new,
> That cannot say, my thanks I have forgot,
> Nor trust I this with hopes; and yet scarce true

This bravery is, since these times shew'd me you. . . .

Yet more abstruse and profound is *Donne's* reflection upon Man as a Microcosm [in '**To Mr. R. W. "If as mine is"'**]:

> If men be worlds, there is in every one
> Something to answer in some proportion
> All the world's riches: and in good men, this
> Virtue our form's form, and our soul's soul is.
>
> (p. 17)

The tears of lovers are always of great poetical account; but Donne has extended them into worlds. If the lines [which follow, from '**A Valediction: of weeping**'] are not easily understood, they may be read again.

> On a round ball
> A workman, that hath copies by, can lay
> An Europe, Afric, and an Asia,
> And quickly make that, which was nothing, all.
>
> So doth each tear,
> Which thee doth wear,
> A globe, yea world, by that impression grow,
> Till thy tears mixt with mine do overflow
> This world, by waters sent from thee my heaven
> dissolved so.

On reading the following lines [from '**An Epithalamion, Or mariage Song on the Lady Elizabeth, and Count Palatine being married on St. Valentine's day**'], the reader may perhaps cry out—*Confusion worse confounded.*

> Here lies a she sun, and a he moon there,
> She gives the best light to his sphere,
> Or each is both, and all, and so
> They unto one another nothing owe.
>
> (pp. 19-20)

Who but Donne would have thought that a good man is a telescope?

> Though God be our true glass, through which we see
> All, since the being of all things is he,
> Yet are the trunks, which do to us derive
> Things, in proportion fit, by perspective
> Deeds of good men; for by their living here,
> Virtues, indeed remote, seem to be near.
>
> (p. 20)

That prayer and labour should co-operate, are thus taught by Donne:

> In none but us, are such mixt engines found,
> As hands of double office: for the ground
> We till with them; and them to heaven we raise;
> Who prayerless labours, or without this, prays,
> Doth but one half, that's none.

By the same author, a common topick, the danger of procrastination, is thus illustrated:

> —That which I should have begun
> In my youth's morning, now late must be done;
> And I, as giddy travellers must do,
> Which stray or sleep all day, and having lost
> Light and strength, dark and tir'd, must then ride post.

All that Man has to do is to live and die; the sum of humanity is comprehended by Donne in the following lines:

> Think in how poor a prison thou didst lie;

After, enabled but to suck and cry.
Think, when 'twas grown to most, 'twas a poor inn,
A province pack'd up in two yards of skin,
And that usurp'd, or threaten'd with a rage
Of sicknesses, or their true mother, age.
But think that death hath now enfranchis'd thee;
Thou hast thy expansion now, and liberty;
Think, that a rusty piece discharg'd is flown
In pieces, and the bullet is his own,
And freely flies: this to thy soul allow,
Think thy shell broke, think thy soul hatch'd but now.

They were sometimes [as in **'Twicknam garden'**] indelicate and disgusting. (pp, 24-5)

Hither with crystal vials, lovers, come,
And take my tears, which are Love's wine,
And try your mistress' tears at home;
For all are false, that taste not just like mine.

This [from **'Elegie VIII. The Comparison'**] is yet more indelicate:

As the sweet sweat of roses in a still,
As that which from chaf'd musk-cat's pores doth trill,
As the almighty balm of th' early East;
Such are the sweat-drops of my mistress' breast.
And on her neck her skin such lustre sets,
They seem no sweat-drops, but pearl coronets:
Rank sweaty froth thy mistress' brow defiles.

(p. 26)

To the following comparison [in **'A Valediction: forbidding mourning'**] of a man that travels, and his wife that stays at home, with a pair of compasses, it may be doubted whether absurdity or ingenuity has the better claim:

Our two souls therefore, which are one,
Though I must go, endure not yet
A breach, but an expansion,
Like gold to airy thinness beat.

If they be two, they are two so
As stiff twin-compasses are two;
Thy soul the fixt foot, makes no show
To move, but doth, if th' other do.

And though it in the centre sit,
Yet when the other far doth roam,
It leans, and hearkens after it,
And grows erect, as that comes home.

Such wilt thou be to me, who must
Like th' other foot, obliquely run.
Thy firmness makes my circle just,
And makes me end, where I begun.

In all these examples it is apparent, that whatever is improper or vicious, is produced by a voluntary deviation from nature in pursuit of something new and strange; and that [Donne and the metaphysical] writers fail to give delight, by their desire of exciting admiration. (p. 28)

Samuel Johnson, "Cowley," in his Lives of the English Poets, *Vol. I, 1906. Reprint by Oxford University Press, 1955-56, pp. 1-53.*

JOSEPH WARTON (essay date 1782)

[*Warton was an eighteenth-century English poet and critic. He is noted for poetry criticism in which he stressed that "the fashion of moralizing in verse had been carried too far"*

by mid-century and that the faculties of the true poet were "invention and imagination." In the following excerpt from the fourth (1782) edition of his Essay on the Genius and Writings of Pope, *Warton sides with John Dryden (see excerpt dated 1693) in judging Donne more a wit than a poet. In the first (1756) edition of this work, Warton had placed Donne in the second rank of English poets—overrating him, according to an anonymous reviewer of the day (see excerpt dated 1756). By the time he came to compose the fourth edition, Warton had consigned Donne to the third rank.*]

We do not, it should seem, sufficiently attend to the difference there is, betwixt a MAN OF WIT, a MAN OF SENSE, and a TRUE POET. Donne and Swift were undoubtedly men of wit, and men of sense: but what traces have they left of PURE POETRY? It is remarkable, that Dryden says of Donne; He was the greatest wit, tho' not the greatest poet of this nation [see excerpt dated 1693].

Our English poets may, I think, be disposed in four different classes and degrees. In the first class, I would place, our only three sublime and pathetic poets; SPENSER, SHAKESPEARE, MILTON. In the second class should be ranked, such as possessed the true poetical genius, in a more moderate degree, but who had noble talents for moral, ethical, and panegyrical poesy. At the head of these are DRYDEN, PRIOR, ADDISON, COWLEY, WALLER, GARTH, FENTON, GAY, DENHAM, PARNELL. In the third class may be placed, men of wit, of elegant taste, and lively fancy in describing familiar life, tho' not the higher scenes of poetry. Here may be numbered, BUTLER, SWIFT, ROCHESTER, DONNE, DORSET, OLDHAM. In the fourth class, the mere versifiers, however smooth and mellifluous some of them may be thought, should be disposed. Such as PITT, SANDYS, FAIRFAX, BROOME, BUCKINGHAM, LANSDOWN. (pp. xi-xiii)

• • • • •

Two noblemen of taste and learning, the Duke of Shrewsbury and the Earl of Oxford, desired POPE to melt down and cast anew the weighty bullion of Dr. Donne's satires; who had degraded and deformed a vast fund of sterling wit and strong sense, by the most harsh and uncouth diction. POPE succeeded in giving harmony to a writer, more rough and rugged than even any of his age; and who profited to little by the example *Spenser* had set, of a most musical and mellifluous versification; far beyond the versification of *Fairfax*, who is so frequently mentioned as the greatest improver of the harmony of our language. The satires of *Hall*, written in very smooth and pleasing numbers, preceded those of *Donne* many years; for his *Virgidemiarum* were published, in six books, in the year 1597; in which he calls himself the very first English satirist. This, however, was not true in fact; for Sir Thomas Wyatt, of Allington Castle in Kent, the friend and favourite of *Henry VIII.* and, as was suggested, of *Ann Boleyn*, was our first writer of satire worth notice. But it was not in his numbers only that Donne was reprehensible. He abounds in false thoughts, in far-sought sentiments, in forced unnatural conceits. He was the corrupter of *Cowley*. *Dryden* was the first who called him a *metaphysical* poet. He had a considerable share of learning; and, though he entered late into orders, yet was esteemed a good divine. (pp. 353-54)

Joseph Warton, in excerpts in his An Essay on the Genius and Writings of Pope, *Vols. I & II, fourth edition, 1782. Reprint by Gregg International Publishers Ltd., 1969, pp.iii-xiii; 353-54.*

VICESIMUS KNOX (essay date 1782)

[*An English educator, clergyman, and essayist, Knox is best known for his* Essays, Moral and Literary *(1777). In the following excerpt from the 1782 edition of this work, he expresses a low opinion of Donne's satires and poetic legacy.*]

The English [satirists] seem to have copied the manner of Juvenal rather than of Horace. Our national spirit is indeed of the manly and rougher kind, and feels something congenial with itself in the vehemence of the indignant Juvenal.

The Roman is remarkably harmonious. But Donne, his imitator, seems to have thought roughness of verse, as well as of sentiment, a real grace. It is scarcely possible, that a writer who did not studiously avoid a smooth versification, could have written so many lines without stumbling on a good one. Pope has revived his fame by attuning his harsh numbers; a work whose very excellence makes us regret that a genius so fertile as was the bard's of Twickenham, should have wasted its vigour in paraphrases and translations. (pp. 167-68)

[As for Cowley:] Was it a compliance with the taste of the age, that induced him to affect deformity? unfortunate compliance with a deplorable taste! He as well as they whom he imitated, Donne and Jonson, were unquestionably possessed of great learning and ingenuity; but they all neglected the graces of composition, and will therefore soon be numbered among those once celebrated writers, whose utility now consists in filling a vacancy on the upper shelf of some dusty and deserted library. (p. 440)

> *Vicesimus Knox, in excerpts in his* Essays: Moral and Literary, *Vol. 3, n.p., 1782, pp. 167-68, 440.*

ANDREW KIPPIS (essay date 1793)

[*Kippis was an English divine, editor, biographer, and critic. He is remembered chiefly as coauthor and editor of* Biographia Britannica *(1778-93). In the following excerpt from that work, he defends Donne's poetry but offers a generally unfavorable view of Donne's prose.*]

The name of Dr. Donne is now more generally known as a poet than in any other capacity, though none of his poetical works are read at present, excepting his Satires, which [have been] modernized by Mr. Pope. . . . His versification is allowed to be intolerably harsh and unmusical; but different accounts have been given of his genius as a poet. [In his *The Life of the Most Reverend Dr. John Tillotson* (1752)] Dr. Birch observes, that his poetical works shew a prodigious fund of genius, under the disguise of an affected and obscure stile, and a most inharmonious versification. A far superior arbiter in subjects of taste (Dr. Warton) has asserted, that Dr. Donne possessed the true poetical genius, with noble talents for moral poesy [see excerpt dated 1782]. The same writer having before characterized him as a man of wit, and a man of sense, but asked what traces he had left of pure poetry, hath been thought by a periodical critic to be guilty of an inconsistency [see excerpt dated 1756]. This, however, we do not perceive to be the case; for Dr. Donne might have noble talents for moral poesy, and yet they might be perverted from being properly displayed, by his want of taste and neglect of harmony. The critic referred to farther says, "Did any man, with a poetical ear, ever yet read ten lines of Donne without disgust? or are there ten lines of poetry in all his works? No." We as confidently answer, "Yes;" and, for the truth of our answer, we shall only appeal to the four stanzas [that conclude "**A Valediction: forbidding mourning**"], where there are sixteen lines which, notwithstanding their quaintness, may be read without disgust, and *have in them a true spirit of poetry.* (pp. 336-37)

Of Dr. Donne's prose works little remembrance now remains. Dr. Birch remarks, that all his wit and learning cannot secure his sermons from universal neglect. The most valuable of his prose-writings is his **Pseudo Martyr,** which contains an unanswerable confutation of the Papal Supremacy. Granger [in volume I of his *A Biographical History of England* (1769)] is of the same opinion.

There is one of Dr. Donne's productions, which had long slept in Oblivion, that has lately been brought into notice. We mean his **BIATHANATOS: or a declaration of that Paradox or Thesis, that Self-Homicide is not so naturally a Sin, that it may not be otherwise.** Mr. Moore, in his elaborate work on Suicide [*A Full Inquiry into the subject of suicide* (1790)], a work in which every thing relative to the subject is critically and amply considered, hath entered into an examination of Dr. Donne's positions, and shewn *that they will not stand the test of a strict enquiry.* (p. 337)

> *Andrew Kippis, "Donne," in* Biographia Britannica, *Vol. V, edited by Andrew Kippis, second edition, 1793. Reprint by George Olms Verlag, 1974, pp. 331-37.*

ROBERT SOUTHEY (essay date 1807)

[*A late-eighteenth- and early-nineteenth-century English man of letters, Southey was a key member of the so-called Lake School of poetry, a group that included the celebrated authors William Wordsworth and Samuel Taylor Coleridge. Southey's poetry consists mainly of short verse, ballads, and epics, many of which are notable for their novel versification and meter. His prose writings—which are generally more highly praised than his poetry—include ambitious histories, biographies, and conservative social commentaries. Today Southey is primarily remembered as a conservative theorist and as the biographer of such figures as Horatio Nelson and John Wesley. In the following excerpt from a historical overview of English poetry, he notices Donne as a man of true intellect but with no real talent for poetry.*]

From the time of Shakspeare to that of Milton, our taste was rather retrograde than progressive. The metaphysical poetry, as it has not very happily been termed, gained ground, and seduced many men whose quick and shaping fancy might else have produced works worthy of immortality. Donne could never have become a Poet, unless Apollo, taking his ears under his divine care, would have wrought as miraculous a change in their internal structure, as of old he wrought in the external of those of Midas. The power of versifying is a distinct talent, and a metrical ear has little more connexion with intellect than a musical one. Of this, Donne is a sufficient example. (pp. xxiv-xxv)

> *Robert Southey, in a preface to his* Specimens of the Later English Poets, *Vol. I, Longman, Hurst, Rees and Orme, 1807, pp. iii-xxxii.*

SAMUEL TAYLOR COLERIDGE (essay date 1811)

[*Coleridge was at the intellectual center of the English Romantic movement and is considered one of the greatest literary critics in the English language. He was also the first prominent spokesman for German idealistic metaphysics in England and one of the original proponents of modern psychological criticism, specifically in his conception of the organic nature of literary form. Coleridge theorized that works of literature derive from and are determined by inspiration rather than by external rules. Though most scholars agree on Coleridge's importance in world literature, they also realize that much of his aesthetic philosophy and literary criticism was borrowed, and at times directly translated, from such German thinkers as Friedrich von Schelling, A. W. Schlegel, Immanuel Kant, and Johann Wolfgang von Goethe. What makes Coleridge such an imposing figure in English literary criticism is the fact that he introduced their concepts to the English-speaking world and combined them with elements of neoclassicism and English empiricism. He differs drastically from most preceding English writers in his attempt to develop a consistent philosophy of thought, language, and knowledge from which to derive critical principles and a theory of literature. Though in his own work he failed to realize this goal, Coleridge has consistently been praised for the sincerity of his efforts. For modern critics, his most important achievement remains his attempt to fuse such variant ideas as fancy and imagination, talent and genius, mechanical and organic form, taste and judgment, symbol and allegory, even though they concur that his efforts to create a "graceful and intelligent whole" were self-defeating and poor criteria for the actual study of literature. Nevertheless, Coleridge is counted among the most important critics in the history of world literature. During the spring of 1811, he wrote his impressions of Donne's poetry in the margins of a famous friend's copy of Donne's collected poems, concluding: "I shall die soon, my dear Charles Lamb, and then you will not be vexed that I had bescribbled your book." In the following excerpt from this marginalia, Coleridge offers diverse judgments of Donne's work.*]

To read Dryden, Pope, &c., you need only count syllables; but to read Donne you must measure *time*, and discover the time of each word by the sense of passion. (p. 133)

Doubtless, all the copies I have ever seen of Donne's poems are grievously misprinted. Wonderful that they are not more so, considering that not one in a thousand of his readers has any notion how his lines are to be read—to the many, five out of six appear anti-metrical. How greatly this aided the compositor's negligence or ignorance, and prevented the corrector's remedy, any man may ascertain by examining the earliest editions of blank verse plays, Massinger, Beaumont and Fletcher, &c. Now, Donne's rhythm was as inexplicable to the many as blank verse, spite of his rhymes —*ergo*, as blank verse, misprinted. I am convinced that where no mode of rational declamation by pause, hurrying of voice, or apt and sometimes double emphasis, can at once make the verse metrical and bring out the sense of passion more prominently, that there we are entitled to alter the text, when it can be done by simple omission or addition of *that*, *which*, *and*, and such "small deer"; or by mere new placing of the same words—I would venture nothing beyond.

"The Triple Fool", v. 15.

   And by delighting many, frees again
   Grief which Verse did restrain.

A good instance how Donne read his own verses. We should write, "The Grief, verse did restrain;" but Donne

roughly emphasized the two main words, Grief and Verse, and, therefore, made each the first syllable of a trochee or dactyl:—

   Grïef, whïch / vĕrse dĭd rĕ / strāin.

"Song"

   Aňd wē joĭn to't ōur strĕngth,
   Aňd wē teăch ĭt ařt aňd leňgth.

The anapest judiciously used, in the eagerness and haste to confirm and aggravate. This beautiful and perfect poem proves, by its title "Song," that *all* Donne's poems are equally *metrical* (misprints allowed for) though smoothness (*i.e.*, the metre necessitating the proper reading) be deemed appropriate to *songs;* but in poems where the writer *thinks*, and expects the reader to do so, the sense must be understood in order to ascertain the metre.

"Satire III"

If you would teach a scholar in the highest form how to *read*, take Donne, and of Donne this satire. When he has learnt to read Donne, with all the force and meaning which are involved in the words, then send him to Milton, and he will stalk on like a master, *enjoying* his walk.

On Donne's Poem **"The Flea"**

   Be proud as Spaniards. Leap for pride, ye Fleas!
   In Nature's *minim* realm ye're now grandees.
   Skip-jacks no more, nor civiller skip-johns;
   Thrice-honored Fleas! I greet you all as *Dons*.
   In Phoebus's archives registered are ye,
   And this your patent of nobility.

"The Good Morrow"

   What ever dies is not mixt equally;
   If our two loves be one, both thou and I
   Love just alike in all; none of these loves can die.

Too good for mere wit. It contains a deep practical truth, this triplet.

"Woman's Constancy"

After all, there is but one Donne! and now tell me yet, wherein, in *his own kind*, he differs from the similar power in Shakespeare? Shakespeare was all men, potentially, except Milton; and they differ from him by negation, or privation, or both. This power of dissolving orient pearls, worth a kingdom, in a health to a whore!—this absolute right of dominion over all thoughts, that dukes are bid to clean his shoes, and are yet honored by it! But, I say, in this lordliness of opulence, in which *the* positive of Donne agrees with *a* positive of Shakespeare, what is it that makes them *homoi*ousian, indeed: yet not homoousian? (pp. 133-35)

["The Sun Rising"]

Fine, vigorous exultation, both soul and body in full puissance.

"The Indifferent"

   I can love both fair and brown;
   Her whom abundance melts, and her whom want betrays;
   Her who loves loneness best, and her who sports and
      plays;
   Her whom the country formed, and whom the town;
   Her who believes, and her who tries,
   Her who still weeps with spungy eyes,
   And her who is dry cork and never cries;
   I can love her, and her, and you, and you;
   I can love any, so she be not true.

How legitimate a child was not Cowley of Donne; but Cowley had a soul-*mother* as well as a soul-*father*, and who was she? What was that? Perhaps, sickly court-loyalty, conscientious per accident—a discursive intellect, *naturally* less vigorous and daring, and then *cowed* by king-worship. The populousness, the activity, is as great in C. as in D.; but the *vigor*, the insufficiency to the poet of active fancy without a substrate of profound, tho' mislocate thinking,—the willworship, in squandering golden hecatombs on a fetisch, on the first stick or straw met with at rising—this pride of doing what he likes with his own, fearless of an immense surplus to pay all lawful debts to self-subsisting themes, that rule, while they cannot create, the moral will—this is Donne! He was an orthodox Christian only because he could have been an infidel *more* easily; and, therefore willed to be a Christian: and he was a Protestant, because it enabled him to lash about to the right and the left, and without a *motive*, to say better things for the Papists than they could say for themselves. It was the impulse of a purse-proud opulence of innate power! In the sluggish pond the waves roll this or that way; for such is the wind's direction: but in the brisk spring or lake, boiling at bottom, wind this way, that way, all ways, most irregular in the calm, yet inexplicable by the most violent *ab extra* tempest.

"Canonization"

One of my favourite poems. As late as ten years ago, I used to seek and find out grand lines and fine stanzas; but my delight has been far greater since it has consisted more in tracing the leading thought thro'out the whole. The former is too much like coveting your neighbour's goods; in the latter you merge yourself in the author, you *become He.*

"A Fever"

Yet I had rather owner be
Of thee one hour, than all else ever.

Just and affecting, as *dramatic; i.e.*, the outburst of a transient feeling, itself the symbol of a deeper feeling, that would have made *one* hour, *known* to be *only* one hour (or even one year), a perfect hell! All the preceding verses are detestable. Shakespeare has nothing of this. He is never *positively* bad, even in his Sonnets. He may be sometimes worthless (N.B., I don't say he *is*), but nowhere is he *unworthy.*

"A Valediction forbidding Mourning"

An admirable peom which none but Donne could have written. Nothing was ever more admirably made out than the figure of the Compass. (pp. 136-38)

"The Extacy"

I should never find fault with metaphysical poems, were they all like this, or but half as excellent.

"The Primrose"

I am tired of expressing my admiration; else I could not have passed by **"The Will"**, **"The Blossom"**, and **"The Primrose"**, with **"The Relique"**. (p. 138)

Samuel Taylor Coleridge, "Donne," in his Coleridge's Miscellaneous Criticism, *edited by Thom-* *as Middleton Raysor, 1936. Reprint by The Folcroft Press, Inc., 1969, pp. 131-45.*

NATHAN DRAKE (essay date 1817)

[*Drake was an English physician and literary essayist. In the following excerpt, he joins with critics of the previous century in scorning Donne's poetry.*]

The greater part of the poetry of this prelate [John Donne], though not published, was written, according to Ben Jonson, before he was twenty-five years of age; and as he was born in London in 1573, he must consequently be ranked as a bard of the sixteenth century. His poems consist of elegies, satires, letters, epigrams, divine poems, and miscellaneous pieces, and procured for him, among his contemporaries, through private circulation and with the public when printed, during the greater part of the seventeenth century, an extraordinary share of reputation. A more refined age, however, and a more chastised taste, have very justly consigned his poetical labours to the shelf of the philologer. A total want of harmony in versification, and a total want of simplicity both in thought and expression, are the vital defects of Donne. Wit he has in abundance, and even erudition, but they are miserably misplaced; and even his amatory pieces exhibit little else than cold conceits and metaphysical subtleties. He may be considered as one of the principal establishers of a school of poetry founded on the worst Italian model, commencing towards the close of Elizabeth's reign, continued to the decease of Charles the Second, and including among its most brilliant cultivators the once popular names of Crashaw, Cleveland, Cowley, and Sprat. (p. 615)

Nathan Drake, "View of Miscellaneous Poetry during the Same Period," in his Shakspeare and His Times, *Vol. I, T. Cadell and W. Davies, 1817, pp. 594-735.*

WILLIAM HAZLITT (essay date 1819)

[*Hazlitt was one of the most important literary critics of the Romantic age. He was a deft stylist, a master of the prose essay, and a leader of what was later termed "impressionist criticism"—a form of personal analysis directly opposed to the universal standards of critical judgment accepted by many eighteenth-century critics. Hazlitt, like Samuel Taylor Coleridge before him, played a substantial role in reinterpreting Shakespeare's characters during the nineteenth century, and he contributed significantly to the revival of interest in a number of Elizabethan dramatists, including John Webster and Thomas Heywood. Although he has often been considered a follower of Coleridge, he is closer in spirit and critical methodology to Charles Lamb. Like Lamb, Hazlitt utilized the critical techniques of evocation, metaphor, and personal reference—three innovations that greatly altered the development of literary criticism in the nineteenth and twentieth centuries. Hazlitt did not see the goal of criticism as rendering ultimate judgments of literary works; instead, the critic should serve as a guide to help determine the reader's response to literature. As a journalist who lived by his pen, Hazlitt was acutely aware of the abstract nature of literature as well as the limitations of his audience in understanding questions of aesthetics and style. For this reason he purposely made his criticism palatable by using illustrations, digressions, and repetitions. In the following excerpt from* Lectures on the English Comic Writers *1819), Hazlitt lambasts Donne's poetry.*]

Donne, who was considerably before Cowley, is without his fancy, but was more recondite in his logic, and rigid in his descriptions. He is hence led, particularly in his satires, to tell disagreeable truths in as disagreeable a way as possible, or to convey a pleasing and affecting thought (of which there are many to be found in his other writings) by the harshest means, and with the most painful effort. His Muse suffers continual pangs and throes. His thoughts are delivered by the Caesarean operation. The sentiments, profound and tender as they often are, are stifled in the expression; and 'heaved pantingly forth,' are 'buried quick again' under the ruins and rubbish of analytical distinctions. It is like poetry waking from a trance: with an eye bent idly on the outward world, and half-forgotten feelings crowding about the heart; with vivid impressions, dim notions, and disjointed words. The following may serve as instances of beautiful or passioned reflections losing themselves in obscure and difficult applications. He has some lines to a Blossom, which begin thus:

> Little think'st thou, poor flow'r,
> Whom I have watched six or seven days,
> And seen thy birth, and seen what every hour
> Gave to thy growth, thee to this height to raise,
> And now dost laugh and triumph on this bough.
> Little think'st thou
> That it will freeze anon, and that I shall
> To-morrow find thee fall'n, or not at all.

This simple and delicate description is only introduced as a foundation for an elaborate metaphysical conceit as a parallel to it, in the next stanza.

> Little think'st thou (poor heart
> That labour'st yet to nestle thee,
> And think'st by hovering here to get a part
> In a forbidden or forbidding tree,
> And hop'st her stiffness by long siege to bow:)
> Little think'st thou,
> That thou to-morrow, ere the sun doth wake,
> Must with this sun and me a journey take.

This is but a lame and impotent conclusion from so delightful a beginning.—He thus notices the circumstance of his wearing his late wife's hair about his arm, in a little poem which is called the Funeral:

> Whoever comes to shroud me, do not harm
> Nor question much
> That subtle wreath of hair, about mine arm;
> The mystery, the sign you must not touch.

The scholastic reason he gives quite dissolves the charm of tender and touching grace in the sentiment itself—

> For 'tis my outward soul,
> Viceroy to that, which unto heaven being gone,
> Will leave this to control,
> And keep these limbs, her provinces, from dissolution.

Again, the following lines, the title of which is Love's Deity, are highly characteristic of this author's manner, in which the thoughts are inlaid in a costly but imperfect mosaic-work.

> *I long to talk with some old lover's ghost,*
> *Who died before the God of Love was born:*
> I cannot think that he, who then lov'd most,
> Sunk so low, as to love one which did scorn.
> But since this God produc'd a destiny,
> And that vice-nature, custom, lets it be;
> I must love her that loves not me.

The stanza in the Epithalamion on a Count Palatine of the Rhine, has been often quoted against him, and is an almost irresistible illustration of the extravagances to which this kind of writing which turns upon a pivot of words and possible allusions, is liable. His love-verses and epistles to his friends give the most favourable idea of Donne. His satires are too clerical. He shews, if I may so speak, too much disgust, and, at the same time, too much contempt for vice. His dogmatical invectives hardly redeem the nauseousness of his descriptions, and compromise the imagination of his readers more than they assist their reason. The satirist does not write with the same authority as the divine, and should use his poetical privileges more sparingly. 'To the pure all things are pure,' is a maxim which a man like Dr. Donne may be justified in applying to himself; but he might have recollected that it could not be construed to extend to the generality of his readers, *without benefit of clergy.* (pp. 51-3)

William Hazlitt, "On Cowley, Butler, Suckling, Etherege, Etc.,"in his Lectures on the English Comic Writers with Miscellaneous Essays, *E. P. Dutton & Co., 1910, pp. 49-69.*

THOMAS DE QUINCEY (essay date 1828)

[*An English critic and essayist, De Quincey used his own life as the subject of his best-known work,* Confessions of an English Opium Eater *(1822), in which he chronicled his addiction to opium. De Quincey contributed reviews to a number of London journals and earned a reputation as an insightful, if occasionally long-winded, literary critic. At the time of his death, his critical expertise was underestimated, though his talent as a prose writer had long been acknowledged. In the twentieth century, some critics still disdain the digressive qualities of De Quincey's writing, yet others find that his essays display an acute psychological awareness. In the following excerpt from an essay originally published in 1828 in* Blackwood's Edinburgh Magazine, *De Quincey praises Donne's skill as a rhetorician, defending the poet against Samuel Johnson's strictures (see excerpt dated 1779).*]

Omitting Sir Philip Sidney, and omitting his friend, Fulke Greville, Lord Brooke (in whose prose there are some bursts of pathetic eloquence, as there is of rhetoric in his verse, though too often harsh and cloudy), the first very eminent rhetorician in the English Literature is Donne. Dr. Johnson inconsiderately classes him in company with Cowley, &c., under the title of *Metaphysical* Poets [see excerpt dated 1779]: metaphysical they were not; *Rhetorical* would have been a more accurate designation. In saying *that*, however, we must remind our readers that we revert to the original use of the word *Rhetoric*, as laying the principal stress upon the management of the thoughts, and only a secondary one upon the ornaments of style. Few writers have shown a more extraordinary compass of powers than Donne; for he combined—what no other man has ever done—the last sublimation of dialectical subtlety and address with the most impassioned majesty. Massy diamonds compose the very substance of his poem on the Metempsychosis [**"The Progresse of the Soule"**], thoughts and descriptions which have the fervent and gloomy sublimity of Ezekiel or Æschylus, whilst a diamond dust of rhetorical brilliancies is strewed over the whole of his occasional verses and his prose. No criticism was ever more unhappy than that of Dr. Johnson's which denounces all this artificial display as so much perversion of taste. There cannot be a falser thought than this; for upon that principle a whole class of compositions might be vicious by conforming to its own ideal. The artifice and machinery of rhetoric furnishes in its degree as legitimate a basis for intellectual pleasure as any other; that the pleasure is of an inferior order, can no more attaint the idea or model of the composition than it can impeach the excellence of an epigram that it is not a tragedy. Every species of composition is to be tried by its own laws; and, if Dr. Johnson had urged explicitly (what was evidently moving in his thoughts) that a metrical structure, by holding forth the promise of poetry, defrauds the mind of its just expectations, he would have said what is notoriously false. Metre is open to any form of composition, provided it will aid the expression of the thoughts; and the only sound objection to it is that it has *not* done so. Weak criticism, indeed, is that which condemns a copy of verses under the ideal of poetry, when the mere substitution of another name and classification suffices to evade the sentence, and to reinstate the composition in its rights as rhetoric. It may be very true that the age of Donne gave too much encouragement to his particular vein of composition. That, however, argues no depravity of taste, but a taste erring only in being too limited and exclusive. (pp. 100-02)

Thomas De Quincey, "Rhetoric," in his The Collected Writings of Thomas De Quincey: Literary Theory and Criticism, Vol. X, *revised edition, Adam and Charles Black, 1890, pp. 81-133.*

LEIGH HUNT   (essay date 1841)

[*An English poet and essayist, Hunt is remembered as a literary critic who encouraged and influenced several Romantic poets, especially John Keats and Percy Bysshe Shelley. Hunt produced volumes of poetry and critical essays and, with his brother John, established the* Examiner, *a weekly liberal newspaper. In his criticism, Hunt articulated the principles of Romanticism, emphasizing imaginative freedom and the expression of a personal emotional or spiritual state. Although his critical works were overshadowed by those of more prominent Romantic critics, such as his friends Samuel Taylor Coleridge, William Hazlitt, and Charles Lamb, his essays are considered insightful and generous to the fledgling writers he supported. In the following excerpt from an essay originally published in 1841, he briefly describes Donne's skill as a writer of epithalamia, or marriage poems, comparing Donne's achievement with that of Edmund Spenser.*]

The celebrated Epithalamium of Spencer, perhaps the best altogether in the language, is gorgeous, voluptuous, full of the most refined sensual elegance, and consecrated moreover by the stars; yet like those of Tasso, is somehow too stately, and scholar-like—too loftily serious, even in its gaieties. One fancies that a kind of celestial schoolmaster is going to be married. And yet never was mythology so daintily managed. (p. 497)

Next to Spenser's poem, our best Epithalamiums, and the only ones, we fear, worth much remembrance, are those of a great wit and intellect, who is supposed, by some, to be nothing but a bundle of conceits—Dr. Donne. In occasional passages, they are even superior in depth and feeling, though the very audacity of their truthfulness (honest in that depth) hinders them from being quotable to the "general ear." One of them is upon the marriage of poor wretched Car, Earl of Somerset, with Lady

Essex—singular personages for the feeling and thoughtful Donne to panegyrize. The faith expressed in their love, however, by this good and great child-like man, however startling to us when we know under what circumstances they were married, was, no doubt, as far as regards himself, good and true. Let us hope, therefore, there were more circumstances than we are aware of, to extenuate, if possible, their crimes. One thing there certainly was—they were victims of their own beauty. (pp. 497-98)

Leigh Hunt, "Epithalamiums. Wedding Days. 'Vivia Perpetua','" in his Literary Criticism, *edited by Lawrence Huston Houtchens and Carolyn Washburn Houtchens, Columbia University Press, 1956, pp. 494-508.*

GEORGE MacDONALD   (essay date 1868)

[*A Scottish man of letters, MacDonald was a key figure in shaping the fantastic and mythopoeic literature of the nineteenth and twentieth centuries. Such novels as* Phantastes *(1858) and* The Princess and the Goblin *(1872) are considered classics of fantasy literature. These works have influenced C. S. Lewis, Charles Williams, J. R. R. Tolkien, and others interested in divine truth, adventure, and escape from mortal limitations. During his long, prolific career, MacDonald also wrote in other genres and on other themes, achieving particular success with his novels of British country life. These are little read today. In the following excerpt from his survey study* England's Antiphon *(1868), he provides a balanced general summary of Donne's poetic skill and an illustrative sampling of Donne's poetry.*]

[Mr. Donne] is represented by Dr. Johnson as one of the chief examples of that school of poets called by himself the *metaphysical*, an epithet which, as a definition, is almost false [see excerpt dated 1779]. True it is that Donne and his followers were always ready to deal with metaphysical subjects, but it was from their mode, and not their subjects, that Dr. Johnson classed them. What this mode was we shall see presently, for I shall be justified in setting forth its strangeness, even absurdity, by the fact that Dr. Donne was the dear friend of George Herbert, and had much to do with the formation of his poetic habits. Just twenty years older than Herbert, and the valued and intimate friend of his mother, Donne was in precisely that relation of age and circumstance to influence the other in the highest degree.

The central thought of Dr. Donne is nearly sure to be just: the subordinate thoughts by means of which he unfolds it are often grotesque, and so wildly associated as to remind one of the lawlessness of a dream, wherein mere suggestion without choice or fitness rules the sequence. As some . . . [writers] would play with words, Dr. Donne would sport with ideas, and with the visual images or embodiments of them. Certainly in his case much knowledge reveals itself in the association of his ideas, and great facility in the management and utterance of them. True likewise, he says nothing unrelated to the main idea of the poem; but not the less certainly does the whole resemble the speech of a child of active imagination, to whom judgment as to the character of his suggestions is impossible, his taste being equally gratified with a lovely image and a brilliant absurdity: a butterfly and a shining potsherd are to him similarly desirable. Whatever wild thing starts from the thicket of thought, all is worthy game to the hunting intellect of Dr. Donne, and is followed without question of tone, keeping, or harmony. In his play with words, Sir Philip Sidney kept good heed that even that should serve the end in view; in his play with ideas, Dr. John Donne, so far from serving the end, sometimes obscures it almost hopelessly: the hart escapes while he follows the squirrels and weasels and bats. It is not surprising that, their author being so inartistic with regard to their object, his verses themselves should be harsh and unmusical beyond the worst that one would imagine fit to be called verse. He enjoys the unenviable distinction of having no rival in ruggedness of metric movement and associated sounds. This is clearly the result of indifference; an indifference, however, which grows very strange to us when we find that he *can* write a lovely verse and even an exquisite stanza.

Greatly for its own sake, partly for the sake of illustration, I quote a poem containing at once his best and his worst, the result being such an incongruity that we wonder whether it might not be called his best, *and* his worst, because we cannot determine which. He calls it **"Hymn to God, my God, in my Sickness."** The first stanza is worthy of George Herbert in his best mood.

> Since I am coming to that holy room,
> Where with the choir of saints for evermore
> I shall be made thy music, as I come
> I tune the instrument here at the door,
> And what I must do then, think here before.

To recognize its beauty, leaving aside the depth and truth of the phrase, "Where I shall be made thy music," we must recall the custom of those days to send out for "a noise of musicians." Hence he imagines that he has been summoned as one of a band already gone in to play before the king of "The High Countries:" he is now at the door, where he is listening to catch the tone, that he may have his instrument tuned and ready before he enters. But with what a jar the next stanza breaks on heart, mind, and ear!

> Whilst my physicians by their love are grown
> Cosmographers, and I their map, who lie
> Flat on this bed, that by them may be shown
> That this is my south-west discovery,
> *Per fretum febris*—by these straits to die;—

Here, in the midst of comparing himself to a map, and his physicians to cosmographers consulting the map, he changes without warning into a navigator whom they are trying to follow upon the map as he passes through certain straits—namely, those of the fever—towards his south-west discovery, Death. Grotesque as this is, the absurdity deepens in the end of the next stanza by a return to the former idea. He is alternately a map and a man sailing on the map of himself. But the first half of the stanza is lovely: my reader must remember that the region of the West was at that time the Land of Promise to England.

> I joy that in these straits I see my West;
> For though those currents yield return to none,
> What shall my West hurt me? As west and east
> In all flat maps (and I am one) are one,
> So death doth touch the resurrection.

It is hardly worth while, except for the strangeness of the phenomenon, to spend any time in elucidating this. Once more a map, he is that of the two hemispheres, in which the east of the one touches the west of the other. Could

anything be much more unmusical than the line, "In all flat maps (and I am one) are one"? But the next stanza is worse.

> Is the Pacific sea my home? Or are
> The eastern riches? Is Jerusalem?
> Anvan, and Magellan, and Gibraltar?
> All straits, and none but straits are ways to them,
> Whether where Japhet dwelt, or Cham, or Sem.

The meaning of the stanza is this: there is no earthly home: all these places are only straits that lead home, just as they themselves cannot be reached but through straits.

Let my reader now forget all but the first stanza, and take it along with the following, the last two:

> We think that Paradise and Calvary,
> Christ's cross and Adam's tree, stood in one place:
> Look, Lord, and find both Adams met in me;
> As the first Adam's sweat surrounds my face,
> May the last Adam's blood my soul embrace.
>
> So, in his purple wrapped, receive me, Lord;
> By these his thorns give me his other crown;
> And as to others' souls I preached thy word,
> Be this my text, my sermon to mine own:
> *Therefore, that he may raise, the Lord throws down.*

Surely these are very fine, especially the middle verse of the former and the first verse of the latter stanza. The three stanzas together make us lovingly regret that Dr. Donne should have ridden his Pegasus over quarry and housetop, instead of teaching him his paces. (pp. 114-18)

["**A Hymn to God the Father**"] is artistic throughout. Perhaps the fact, of which we are informed by Izaak Walton, "that he caused it to be set to a grave and solemn tune, and to be often sung to the organ by the choristers of St. Paul's church in his own hearing, especially at the evening service," may have something to do with its degree of perfection. There is no sign of his usual haste about it. It is even elaborately rhymed after Norman fashion, the rhymes in each stanza being consonant with the rhymes in every stanza.

In those days even a pun might be a serious thing: witness the play in the last stanza on the words *son* and *sun*—not a mere pun, for the Son of the Father is the Sun of Righteousness: he is Life *and* Light.

What the Doctor himself says concerning the hymn, appears to me not only interesting but of practical value. He "did occasionally say to a friend, 'The words of this hymn have restored to me the same thoughts of joy that possessed my soul in my sickness, when I composed it.'" What a help it would be to many, if in their more gloomy times they would but recall the visions of truth they had, and were assured of, in better moments! (pp. 119-20)

["**A Hymn to Christ**"] is a somewhat strange hymn, which yet possesses, rightly understood, a real grandeur.... (p. 120)

To do justice to this poem, the reader must take some trouble to enter into the poet's mood. (p. 121)

In a poem called **"The Cross,"** full of fantastic conceits, we find the following remarkable lines, embodying the profoundest truth.

As perchance carvers do not faces make,
But that away, which hid them there, do take:
Let crosses so take what hid Christ in thee,
And be his image, or not his, but he.

One more, and we shall take our leave of Dr. Donne. It is
called a fragment; but it seems to me complete. It will
serve as a specimen of his best and at the same time of his
most characteristic mode of presenting fine thoughts grotesquely attired.

"Resurrection"

Sleep, sleep, old sun; thou canst not have re-past
As yet the wound thou took'st on Friday last.
Sleep then, and rest: the world may bear thy stay;
A better sun rose before thee to-day;
Who, not content to enlighten all that dwell
On the earth's face as thou, enlightened hell,
And made the dark fires languish in that vale,
As at thy presence here our fires grow pale;
Whose body, having walked on earth and now
Hastening to heaven, would, that he might allow
Himself unto all stations and fill all,
For these three days become a mineral.
He was all gold when he lay down, but rose
All tincture; and doth not alone dispose
Leaden and iron wills to good, but is
Of power to make even sinful flesh like his.
Had one of those, whose credulous piety
Thought that a soul one might discern and see
Go from a body, at this sepulchre been,
And issuing from the sheet this body seen,
He would have justly thought this body a soul,
If not of any man, yet of the whole.

What a strange mode of saying that he is our head, the
captain of our salvation, the perfect humanity in which
our life is hid! Yet it has its dignity. When one has got
over the oddity of these last six lines, the figure contained
in them shows itself almost grand.

As an individual specimen of the grotesque form holding
a fine sense, regard for a moment the words,

He was all gold when he lay down, but rose
All tincture;

which means, that, entirely good when he died, he was
something yet greater when he rose, for he had gained the
power of making others good: the *tincture* intended here
was a substance whose touch would turn the basest metal
into gold. (pp. 122-24)

> *George MacDonald, "Dr. Donne," in his* En-
> gland's Antiphon, *Macmillan & Co., 1868, pp.
> 113-24.*

ALGERNON CHARLES SWINBURNE (essay date 1889)

[*Swinburne was an English poet, dramatist, and critic.
Though renowned during his lifetime for his lyric poetry, he
is remembered today for his rejection of Victorian mores.
His explicitly sensual themes shocked many of his contemporaries: while they demanded that poetry reflect and uphold current moral standards, Swinburne's only goal, implicit in his poetry and explicit in his critical writings, was
to express beauty. In the following excerpt from his with
Study of Ben Johnson (1889), he favorably compares
Donne's poetry with that of Thomas Gray.*]

[It] would be difficult for any competent and careful student to maintain that chance is not the ruler of the world
of letters. Gray's odes are still, I suppose, familiar to thousands who know nothing of Donne's **Anniversaries**; and
Bacon's Essays are conventionally if not actually familiar
to thousands who know nothing of Ben Jonson's *Discoveries.* And yet it is certain that in fervour of inspiration, in
depth and force and glow of thought and emotion and expression, Donne's verses are as far above Gray's as Jonson's notes or observations on men and morals, on principles and on facts, are superior to Bacon's in truth of
insight, in breadth of view, in vigour of reflection and in
concision of eloquence. (p. 129)

> *Algernon Charles Swinburne, "Discoveries," in his*
> A Study of Ben Jonson, *1889. Reprint by Haskell
> House Publishers Ltd., 1968, pp.127-81.*

CHARLES ELIOT NORTON (essay date 1895)

[*Norton was a nineteenth-century American essayist, critic,
educator, translator, and editor. He was founding editor of
the liberal weekly the* Nation, *a coeditor of the* North American Review, *and a regular contributor to the* Atlantic
Monthly. *He also translated Dante's* Divina commedia *and
edited collections of Thomas Carlyle's letters and Donne's
poetry. In the following excerpt, Norton outlines some of the
historical forces that shaped Donne's poetry and surveys
some earlier criticism of his work.*]

No name of a contemporary occurs more frequently than
that of Donne in Drummond of Hawthornden's *Notes of
Ben Jonson's Conversations,* on the occasion of Jonson's
famous visit to him in 1618. He reports Jonson as declaring that "He esteemeth John Donne the first poet in the
world in some things," but also as asserting that "Donne
for not being understood would perish," and that "for not
keeping of accent he deserved hanging" [see excerpt dated
1618-19]. Jonson, when his judgment was not warped by
jealousy or dislike, was a sound critic, and there is truth
in each of these sayings about Donne. In some things
Donne was indeed the first poet of his time, Shakespeare
alone excepted, and yet this place is not generally accorded to him, because, if he do not wholly perish, he
does suffer neglect for not being understood, and is hard
to read for not keeping of accent. More than this, few poets are so unequal as Donne; few, capable of such high
reaches as he, sink lower than he at times descends. His
verse must be sifted with a coarse sieve; much of it will
run through the meshes, but when all that is worthless or
worse has been sifted out, there remains a residue of the
pure grain of poetry, of poetry rich in imagination, fancy,
wit, passion, and reflection, and in strong and often not
unmusical verse. (pp. xvii-xviii)

His better poetry is the revelation of a curiously interesting and complex nature, of a soul with rare capacity of intense feeling, of an intelligence at once deep and subtle,
and of a varied experience of life.

His nature was essentially a product of the Elizabethan
age. The growth and consciousness of national power and
the jealous pride of national independence in England,
during the last half of the sixteenth century, had quickened the imagination of her people. The vast discoveries
of the world combined with the new learning to animate
the intelligence alike of men of affairs and of men of

thought with fresh and stimulating inspiration. The tremendous debate of the Reformation, with the social and material changes to which it led, called forth constant discussion of the deepest problems, not as mere abstract subjects of controversy, but as bearing directly on the lives and fortunes of the disputants. The debate was at fire heat with passion. The conditions of the world, moreover, afforded unwonted variety of opportunity for the display of strong individualities, yet society was gaining the settled order and the established form requisite for the higher development of intellectual life. The language itself had just reached that stage in its evolution which made it responsive to the new demands of widening thought and more varied emotion, and, in answering them, it was shaping itself into the most serviceable instrument of expression which man has ever had at his command.

Another influence also was deeply affecting the intellectual life of England, that of the spirit of the Italian Renaissance. Donne was a child of this spirit. He shared in its exaltations and debasements, in its confusion of the sensual and the supersensual, in its love of physical and its adoration of spiritual beauty, in its poetic fervor, its ardor for experience and for learning, its rapid changes of mood, its subjection to the things of the flesh, its ascetic aspiration for the things of the spirit. (pp. xxi-xxii)

The moods and conditions of this period are displayed in Donne's poetry in such degree as to make it a sort of epitome and school of them all. Putting Shakespeare out of the question, as forming a class by himself, there is no poet of the time who surpasses Donne in the occasional power of his imagination, in easy flight of fancy, in sincerity of passionate utterance, in sweetness and purity of sentiment, in depth and substance of reflection, in terse expression of thought. But, on the other hand, his poems equally reflect the poetic age in its gross sensuality and coarse obscenity; in studied obscurity, fantasticality of conceit, exaggeration of affected feeling, harshness of diction, and cumbrousness of construction. The mingling of good and bad is often intricate. The sensualism of the verses of his youth is now and then lifted by a stroke of the wing of imagination out of the lower into the higher regions of life. The dreariness of a long stretch of labored and intricate conceits is not seldom lighted up by a flash of wit, or the illumination of an original and impressive thought. The extravagance of eulogy is here and there stoned for by a passage full of natural feeling, expressed with penetrating simplicity.

Much of his poetry seems to have been rapidly composed, and never subjected to considerate revision. To this no doubt are due something of its obscurity, as well as those grave faults of art in his verse which show not so much a defect of poetic capacity, as carelessness, and indifference to perfection of rhythmical form. "Donne," says Mr. Lowell in his *Shakespeare Once More*, "is full of salient verses that would take the rudest March winds of criticism with their beauty, of thoughts that first tease us like charades, and then delight us with the felicity of their solution; but these have not saved him. He is exiled to the limbo of the formless and the fragmentary." And yet, one may add, if he be adjudged to this limbo, he is one "of the people of great worth who are suspended there."

In another essay Mr. Lowell, citing Drayton's fine words about Marlowe, says: "As a poet Donne had in him' those

brave translunary things that our first poets had.' To open vistas for the imagination through the blind wall of the senses, as he could sometimes do, is the supreme function of peotry."

The result of all his poetic faults has not been, as Jonson prophesied, that Donne has perished, but that his merits have been largely overlooked, or falsely measured. (pp. xxii-xxiv)

Southey, with a somewhat characteristic want of taste and appreciation of poetic excellence, goes so far as to say, "Nothing, indeed, could have made Donne a poet, unless as great a change had been worked in the structure of his ears as what wrought in elongating those of Midas" [see excerpt dated 1807].

Surely it could only be the ears of Midas himself that would not find music and poetry in,—

> Little think'st thou, poor flower,
> Whom I have watched six or seven days,
> And seen thy birth, and seen what every hour
> Gave to thy growth thee to this height to raise,
> And now dost laugh and triumph on this bough,
> Little think'st thou
> That it will freeze anon, and that I shall
> To-morrow find thee fallen, or not at all.

And in **"The Relic"** there is a metrical felicity which corresponds with the intimate poetic sentiment and gives perfect expression to it:

> When my grave is broke up again
> Some second guest to entertain,
> And he that digs it spies
> A bracelet of bright hair about the bone,
> Will he not let us alone,
> And think that there a loving couple lies,
> Who thought that this device might be some way
> To make their souls at the last busy day,
> Meet at this grave and make a little stay?

I have omitted two verses of this stanza in which Donne's fondness for quips and his lack of refinement are characteristically displayed, but the number of single stanzas fine as this which might be chosen from his earlier poems is very large, and it is surprising that any lover of poetry should fail to take delight in the audacious, picturesque fancy of such a poem as **"The Sun-rising,"** the brilliant wit of **"The Will,"** the depth of sentiment in **"Love's Growth," "The Ecstacy," "The Anniversary,"** and **"The Shadow,"** the subtle delicacy of **"The Undertaking,"** and the exquisite imagery and true feeling of **"A Valediction forbidding Mourning,"** in all of which, as well as in many others, there is no defect of measure to interfere with the poetic charm.

I do not impugn Ben Jonson's opinion that Donne deserved hanging for not keeping of accent. His sins in this respect are, indeed, unpardonable and unaccountable. He puts accent where he likes, forcing it from one syllable to another as if it had no settled place of its own . . . Accent seems as indifferent to him as spelling, and he writes cómplaint, éxtreme, úsurpers, tortúre, pícture, ánswér, papér, giánt, prisón, kingdóm, presénce, and more than fifty other words, with similar disregard of English usage. I say English usage, for it is obvious that in many of these words Donne was following the French accentuation.

POEMS,

By J. D.

WITH

ELEGIES

ON THE AUTHORS

DEATH.

LONDON.

Printed by *M. F.* for IOHN MARRIOT,
and are to be fold at his fhop in St *Dunftans*
Church-yard in *Fleet-ftreet.* 1633.

Title page of the first collection of Donne's *poetry.*

Even when the accent is correct his lines are often harsh, and he employs slurs and elisions to a degree that makes his verse difficult to a reader whose eyes and ears are not accustomed to the freedom in this respect which the poets of Donne's time allowed themselves, and who thus lies open to the charge which Holophernes brings against Sir Nathaniel's reading of Biron's sonnet: "You find not the apostrophes and so miss the accent." (pp. xxviii-xxx)

In Donne's longer poems there are few passages of many continuous verses of sustained excellence, but single verses or couplets are frequent which express a striking thought or a profound reflection with epigrammatic terseness. Some few of them have become familiar quotations, as, for example:

Her pure and eloquent blood
Spoke in her cheeks and so divinely wrought
That one might almost say her body thought;

and,

No Spring nor Summer's beauty hath such grace
As I have seen in one Autumnal face;

and again,

In laborers' ballads oft more piety
God finds than in Te Deums' melody.
(p. xxxi)

But it is, perhaps, doing the poet wrong thus to choose out these verses. For, as Donne himself said, "Sentences in au-

thors, like hairs in horsetails, concur in one root of beauty and strength; but being plucked out one by one, serve only for springes and snares." Donne's better poems deserve to be read not only complete, but over and over again. They allure and hold the lover of poetry with an abiding charm. They have secure place in the small volume of immortal verse. (p. xxxii)

Charles Eliot Norton, in an introduction to The Poems of Donne, Vol. I, *edited by Charles Eliot Norton, revised edition, The Grolier Club, 1895, pp. xvii-xxxii.*

EDMUND GOSSE (essay date 1899)

[*Gosse's importance as a critic is due primarily to his introduction of Henrik Ibsen's "new drama" to an English audience. He was among the chief English translators and critics of Scandinavian literature and was decorated by the Norwegian, Swedish, and Danish governments for his efforts. Among his other works are studies of Donne, Thomas Gray, Sir Thomas Browne, and a number of late-nineteenth-century French authors. Although Gosse's works are varied and voluminous, he was largely a popularizer, with the consequence that his commentary lacks depth and is not considered in the first rank of modern critical thought. However, his broad interests and knowledge of foreign literatures give his works much more than a documentary value. His* The Life and Letters of John Donne, Dean of St. Paul's, *(1899), from which the following excerpt is taken, was the first biography of Donne since Walton's "Life" (1640). Here, Gosse discusses* The Progresse of the Soule.]

It is very satisfactory to the biographer of the mind of Donne that [one lengthy] poem, which he began by naming "Metempsychosis," and which is now known as **"The Progress of the Soul"**, happens to be exactly dated, since it is a highly characteristic example of his style, and displays it at its climacteric. As we now posses it, the brief prose preface is headed with the words "Infinitati Sacrum, 16 Augusti 1601."

The preface is a curious tirade, not lacking in a certain unexpected lucidity and modernness of style, but of the most fantastic and even giddy import. Donne announces that he is going to paint his own picture at the head of his poem, "if any colours can deliver a mind so plain and flat and throughlight [translucent] as mine." Here sarcasm stalks unabashed, for Queen Elizabeth possessed no subject whose mind was less translucent, flat or plain, than that of Donne. He presents himself as still above all things a satirist, but he is tired of damning others, especially authors. He has therefore determined to contribute to contemporary literature, as we should say, an independent work of his own, thus to give other men a chance of censuring him. But he will borrow nothing, either from the classics or from the poets of his own day; the only person to whom he will be indebted shall be an unnamed scholar, who from some obscure Rabbinical or Spanish source has digged out the treasure of the odd subject he chooses. That is to say, some one has pointed out to Donne that if he wants to write a startling poem, illustrative of his peculiarities of soul and style, here is a theme made to his hand.

The theme is an adaptation of the Pythagorean theory of metempsychosis, which has been too narrowly bound down to a circulation through men and animals; the vegetable world is no less open to its incursions; a soul may fly from a whale to a cauliflower, and from a bean to a mammoth. What resided in an emperor yesterday, may animate a post-horse to-day, and flit into a "macaroon" (or fop) to-morrow. And Donne flings himself forth upon the glittering and elastic strands of his fancy. The soul may forget that it once lived in a melon, yet dimly recall the lascivious banquet at which it was served. It may remember not the time when it was a spider, yet recollect the vivid moment when a secret hand dropped it as poison into a cup of wine. The poet, therefore, will recount the adventures of the memory of a soul from Paradise until the present year of grace, sparing us all but its spasms of passion, its moments of intensest experience.

The scheme of this poem offers not a little attraction, and might have been treated with brilliant success in prose by some such follower of Rabelais as Bonaventure des Périers, who would have brought to the task of its composition a bitter scepticism and a pedantic erudition, wrapping up caustic and detestable insinuations in a cloak of wilful obscurity. It seems as though, for a moment, Donne had intended to adopt this line, and we cannot doubt that Ben Jonson, with whom he took counsel, commended this conception of the task. **"The Progress of the Soul"**, as it now stands, is not an easy poem to read, and our critics have found it simple to accept, as appropriate to its text, the words of Ben Jonson to Drummond of Hawthornden: "The conceit of Donne's Transformation . . . was, that he sought the soul of that apple which Eve pulled, and thereafter made it the soul of a bitch, then of a she-wolf, and so of a woman: his general purpose was to have brought in all the bodies of the Heretics from the soul of Cain, and at last left it in the body of Calvin. Of this he never wrote but one sheet, and now, since he was made Doctor, repenteth highly, and seeketh to destroy all his poems" [see excerpt dated 1618-19].

This is an invaluable piece of information, but it does not absolve us from a study of the poem itself. The poet begins, in the approved epic manner, by announcing to us his subject—

> I sing the progress of a deathless soul,
> Whom Fate,—which God made, but does not control,—
> Placed in most shapes.

He will make the adventures of this hunted soul his theme,

> And the great world to's agèd evening
> From infant morn, through manly noon, I draw:
> What the gold Chaldee, or silver Persian saw,
> Greek brass, or Roman iron, is in this one.

He then addresses the sun, as he did long afterwards in his great sonnet to Lord Doncaster, celebrating the fecundity of its "hot masculine flame," its "male force," which first drew out the island spices in the far, dim chambers of the East. He bids the wheeling luminary concede that the fragile Soul of whom the poet sings has seen as many realms as he in his loose-reined career, and shall long survive his frail flight. Noah, under the name of "holy Janus," is then introduced, with a humorous description of the varieties of life provisionally cooped up together, and we are reminded that this Soul has moved and informed more different shapes than inhabited the Ark. After an appeal, suddenly serious, to the Destiny of God to guide the poet in his task of chronicling the strange divagations of the Soul,

these stanzas occur. As the text at present exists, copied in all probability by careless hands from one rude draft, it is evident that they are corrupt in themselves, and are embedded without proper fusion in the general mass of the poem. But they possess great autobiographical value, and the body of their obscurity flashes with embedded jewels of poetry—

> To my six lusters almost now outwore,
> Except thy book owe me so many more,
> Except my legend be free from the lets
> Of steep ambition, sleepy poverty,
> Spirit-quenching sickness, dull captivity,
> Distracting business, and from beauty's nets,
> And all that calls from this, and to others whets,
> O let me not launch out, but let me save
> Th' expense of brain and spirit, that my grave
> His right and due, a whole unwasted man, may have.

The meaning of this seems to me, that, being nearly thirty years of age, Donne is not inclined, unless the book of destiny promises him at least thirty more, with a fair prospect of health and wealth and bodily comfort, to adventure in arduous, intellectual enterprise. If he is going to continue the distracting life he has endured hitherto, without respite from illness and business, the ennuis of love and the frets of ambition, the game is positively not worth the candle; he will retire from the intolerable struggle, and will go down quietly to his grave, when his time comes, "a whole, unwasted man." This is what he fancies he would prefer—a quiet life, without events, where there should be no "expense of brain or spirit," and rest should come early to him—

> But if my days be long, and good enough,
> In vain this sea shall énlarge or enrough
> Itself, *for I will through the wave and foam;*
> *And shall in sad lone ways, a lively sprite,*
> *Make my dark heavy poem light,* and light.
> For, though through many straits and lands I roam,
> *I launch at Paradise, and I sail towards home;*
> The course I there began shall here be stay'd,
> Sails hoisted there, struck here, and anchors laid
> In Thames, which were at Tigris and Euphrates weigh'd.

It will be remembered that Ben Jonson reported that the Soul was at last to be left in the body of Calvin. This seems to be either a misunderstanding on Jonson's part or else to indicate a change of Donne's intention, for it now becomes certain that the Soul was to be represented as finding its final habitation in Queen Elizabeth—

> For the great Soul which here amongst us now
> Doth dwell, and moves that hand, and tongue, and brow,
> Which, as the Moon the sea, moves us,

can be none other than she of whom Shakespeare a few months later was to say—

> The mortal Moon hath her eclipse endured,

and, if so, Donne's language is explicit. The story of the Queen, perhaps as the great tyrannical persecutor of the Catholics, was to wind up his satire—

> For 'tis the crown and last strain of my song—
> This Soul, to whom Luther and Mahomet were
> Prisons of flesh; this Soul, which oft did tear
> And mend the wracks of th' Empire and late Rome,
> And lived when every great change did come,
> Had first in Paradise a low, but fatal room.

We are then informed what room that was. It hung in Paradise, at the flushed end of one of the boughs of that "forbidden learnèd tree" whence came all our woe. It was born in the flesh of the fruit of the knowledge of good and evil—

> Prince of the orchard, fair as dawning morn,
> Fenced with the law, and ripe as soon as born,
> That apple grew, which this Soul did enlive.

When the Serpent offered it to Eve, the Soul went with the apple, and

> Man all at once was there by Woman slain,

yet it was not delivered for a moment into Eve's custody for—

> Just in that instant when the Serpent's grip
> Broke the slight veins and tender conduit-pipe,
> Thro' which this Soul from the tree's root did draw
> Life and growth to this apple, fled away
> This loose Soul,

and, fluttering to the ground, sank through a boggy piece of ground into the roots of a Mandrake. Donne had a great partiality for mandrakes, in the half-human roots of which the superstition of the age saw aphrodisiac and lethal powers. . . . Here the Soul in her progress now resides, and a most vivid and grotesque picture is given of the malign human vegetable. But Eve disturbs the Soul in this "lone, unhaunted place," for, sin having come into the world, her child is vexed with fever, and she seeks in waste places for a herb to restore it to health. In her search she is led to the mandrake and the poppy,

> And tore up both, and so cool'd her child's blood.

Donne reflects that these plants were the first to die because of their virtues; had they been base weeds they might have lived long.

> Thinner than burnt air flies this soul,

and, seeking for a fresh habitation, insinuates herself

> Into a small blue shell, the which a poor
> Warm bird o'erspread, and sat still evermore,
> Till her enclos'd child kick'd, and peck'd itself a door.

The Soul occupies as its new inn a grim little freshly-hatched sparrow, which is thus described, in Donne's most vigorously realistics manner—

> Out crept a sparrow . . .
> On whose raw arms stiff feathers now begin,
> As children's teeth thro' gums, to break with pain;
> His flesh is jelly yet, and his bones threads;
> All a new downy mantle overspreads;
> A mouth he opes, which would as much contain
> As his late house, and the first hour speaks plain,
>
> And chirps aloud for meat. Meat fit for men
> His father steals for him, and so feeds then
> One that, within a month, will beat him from his hen.

The little cock-sparrow has a brilliant existence, but might have sheltered the Soul longer if it had garnered its forces better; it is a spendthrift of its vital energy, and dies of exhaustion. The Soul flits down into a brook, and hides in one ovum of a fish's roe. It is next swallowed by a swan, and the Soul has two prisons,

> Till, melted by the Swan's digestive fire,
> She left her house, the Fish, and vapour'd forth.

She enters another fish, is pursued by a pike, and swallowed by an oyster-catcher. (pp. 131-37)

A sudden stiff land-wind drives the oyster-catcher out to sea, and the Soul enters the embryo of a whale. Donne outdoes himself in the preposterous description of this monster, which seems to be copied from a print in some fabulous book of voyages. . . . This whale is long the tyrant of the ocean, but at length two little fishes, a thresher and a swordfish, combine to attack and slay him. The Soul, indignant that even so enormous a mansion can be battered down about her ears, flies to shore again, and for her next home

> Got the strait cloister of a wretched mouse.

The mouse climbs up the proboscis of an elephant, and gnaws its brain, but is killed by the death-fall of the huge beast; the Soul flies forth and takes refuge in a wolf, and then in a whelp, and then in an ape, which intrudes itself on Siphatecia, Adam's fifth daughter, sister and wife to Cain. Here, at last, the Soul finds a human habitation; but we have not yet advanced out of sight of the Garden of Eden, and at this rate of progress it would have taken millions of verses to bring us safey down to Queen Elizabeth. The poet evidently felt the inherent weakness of his scheme, and here abandoned it, drawing the threads loosely together in a final stanza when he says that his "sullen" poem is written to please himself and not other people, and declares that there is no such thing as positive good or positive evil, but all is a question of relative values, and to be judged by the average of public opinion.

"The Progress of the Soul" may help us to understand why, with gifts of intellectual appreciation and keen refinement perhaps unsurpassed even in that consummate age, Donne never contrived to reach the first rank among men of letters. The puerility of the central idea is extraordinary; the Soul flits from body to body, without growth, without change, as a parasite leaps from one harbouring object to another. In this notion of the undeveloping restlessness of the Soul, if there is any thought at all, it is the bare satiric one, too cheap to be so magnificently extended and embroidered. It is probable that Donne's intention was to irradiate the dark places of ignorance and brutality as his narrative descended the ages, but, as we have seen, he could not induce the hare to start. He had little dramatic and positively no epic talent; and this is implicitly admitted even by De Quincey, who is the solitary uncompromising admirer of **"The Progress of the Soul"** whom three centuries have produced, [see excerpt dated 1828].

But when all this is conceded, the poem remains one of the most extraordinary in a majestic age. De Quincey, to quote him at the height of his argument, declares that "massy diamonds compose the very substance of his poem on the Metempsychosis, thoughts and descriptions which have the fervent and gloomy sublimity of Ezekiel or Æschylus." If a sober criticism may hesitate to admit the "massy diamonds," there is yet no question that diamond dust is sprinkled broadcast over the stanzas of this grotesque poem. The effort after a complete novelty of style is apparent, and the result of this is occasionally, although not invariably, happy. What we notice in it first is resistance to the accepted Spenserian glow and amenity. The author is absolutely in revolt against the tendency and mode of Spenser. He is not less opposed to a dry and even manner of writing intellectual poetry, which was a revival, in measure, of what Spenser had cast forth, and which had been exemplified in the graceful and highly popular miscellanies of Samuel Daniel, first collected in this very year 1601; in the *Nosce Teipsum* of Sir John Davys, in 1599; and in the historical verse of Drayton (1597 and onwards). My own conviction is that it was the even flow of versification of these academic writers which, more than anything else, goaded Donne to the cultivation of that violently varied tonality in verse of which **"The Progress of the Soul"** gives innumerable examples. (pp. 137-39)

If we look around for any contemporary poetry which shall in measure remind us of Donne, we are confined to one or two works of pure eccentricity, such as Chapman's *Amorous Zodiac,* published in 1595, and Cyril Tourneur's *Transform'd Metamorphosis* of 1600. In the former unseemly and ingenious rhapsody there is a certain resemblance to **"The Progress of the Soul"** in its superficial aspect, while the verse of Tourneur may be said to suit Donne's ear better than that of any other contemporay. But Donne affects neither the turbidity of Chapman nor the Alexandrian allusiveness of Cyril Tourneur, while his language, although frequently hard and abrupt, is genuine and lucid English, and not darkened by a thick flight of detestable and useless neologisms. Our quotations will suffice to show with what brilliant intrepidity he will dart in a moment into the very central shrine of imaginative expression. Here, as in his lyrics, the general aspect of the work is, as he said himself, "sullen," with the leaden colours of the thunderstorm, but ever and again the lightning plays amongst it in lambent and intolerable radiance.

From the biographical standpoint, **"The Progress of the Soul"** offers us a few details of importance. The entire tone and character of it are un-Christian; it is penetrated by the mocking, sensuous scepticism of the Renaissance. The author is akin to Marlowe's Faustus, without veneration, without fear, pursued by an absolutely unflinching curiosity into unfamiliar fields of physical inquiry. No one can read this poem of August 1601 and believe that Donne's memory was not, in later years, amiably deceived when he told Izaak Walton that he continued through these years to "proceed with humility and diffidence in disquisition and search" after religious truth. It is quite certain, from all the evidence we posses—if we regard it honestly—that Donne's conscience was not yet touched. (pp. 139-40)

Edmund Gosse, "The Progress of the Soul," in The Life and Letters of John Donne, Vol. I *edited by Edmund Gosse, revised edition, 1899. Reprint by Peter Smith, 1959, pp. 129-41.*

LESLIE STEPHEN   (essay date 1902)

[*Many scholars consider Stephen the most important literary critic of the Victorian age after Matthew Arnold. He has been praised for his moral insight and judgment, as well as for his intellectual vigor. The key to Stephen's moral criticism is his theory that all literature is nothing more than an imaginative rendering, in concrete terms, of a writer's philosophy or beliefs. It is the role of criticism, he contends, to translate into intellectual terms what the writer has told the reader through character, symbol, and event. More often than not, Stephen's analysis passes into biographical judgment of the writer rather than the work. As he once observed. "The whole art of criticism consists in learning to know the human being who is partially revealed to us in his spoken or his written words." Nonetheless, Stephen's emphasis on the writer's philosophy, rather than the formal aspects of literature, has led Desmond MacCarthy to call him "the least aesthetic of noteworthy critics." In the following excerpt, Stephen discusses the rhetorical characteristics of Donne's sermons.*]

Donne's sermons, whatever else they may be, are astonishing intellectual feats. In spite of ill-health and many distractions, he published, as Dr. Jessopp counts, one hundred and eighty sermons; each itself rather a short treatise than a brief flight of rhetoric; first elaborated, then spoken, and then elaborately rewritten. As mere exhibitions of learning they are remarkable, and the more so, because Donne does not seem to be turning out a commonplace book, or going out of his way to display learning. He has a mind so full of learning that references crowd in spontaneously. He makes, it may be noticed, few allusions to the classics, but he is thoroughly at home with all the fathers and ecclesiastical history; Augustine is at his fingers' ends, and St. Bernard is a special favourite. Then he applies Aquinas and the schoolmen; or shows his profound familiarity with the whole Catholic theology of his time; or calls in the Protestant champions, Luther, and Melanchthon, and Calvin; or is attracted by some great writer of the day, now forgotten, such as Collius, who had investigated with untiring industry the posthumous fate of Pagan souls. Evidently his hydroptic thirst has stored his mind with masses of anecdote, argument, and reflection, over which he can range at will whenever he needs an apt illustration. Then, as he quaintly remarks, the pastor must not only distribute 'manna'—fruits known to all—but 'quails,' 'meat of a stronger digestion'—that is, be at home in whole systems of dogmatic and casuistical theology. The congregation is in the mental attitude of students in a professor's lecture-room. The preacher claims the authority of an expert, and speaks as the exponent of the judgments of countless learned doctors. The doctors did not all agree, it is true; but the mere weight of so many great names warns the ignorant that he is not to presume an opinion of his own.

This attitude of mind, the impression that the preacher is condescending from the vantage-ground of mysterious learning, has become as strange as Donne's political attitude. The King for him is scarcely short of an earthly god. We wonder whether he was perfectly sincere. In one of his most elaborate performances Donne applies a text from Proverbs, saying, that the King shall be the friend of him 'that loveth pureness of heart.' In a glowing peroration this is applied to James. Donne, of course, includes purity of doctrine, to which James might make a claim; but nobody knew better than Donne what was the moral purity of the favourites who had been rewarded by James's friendship. Neither he nor his congregation, we must presume, looked too closely; but Donne, if he turned over a certain satire which lay in his desk, might have remembered that such a panegyric might be turned into the bitterest irony.

But, putting this aside, we must admit another point. Donne's learning is, after all, subsidiary to a marvellous intellectual activity. In his poems the dialectical subtlety seems to fetter him. The fancy is condensed as well as constrained. He seems to labour till he can squeeze the imaginative impulse into a logical formula at the price of crabbed obscurity. But in the prose the two faculties play freely into each other's hands. There is a crowd and rush of thoughts and illustrations. His subtle intellect evolves endless distinctions and startling paradoxes and quaint analogies so abundantly, that he might apparently have preached for a week as easily as for an hour. He takes up one fancy after another, and revels in various applications till the display becomes astonishing. His most famous predecessor, Andrewes, was perhaps equally learned and logically subtle; but—so far as I have been able to get, not, I confess, very far—his desire to be logically convincing overweights him and keeps him to the earth. Jeremy Taylor, Donne's greatest successor, can yield frankly to his imagination, and takes daring flights into the region of pure poetry. Donne represents the fusion of the two faculties. He conscientiously begins his sermons by laying down his logical framework. Any text on his method may serve, as he says of one, for introducing a lecture upon grammar logic, ethic, rhetoric, or philosophy; though, of course, every clause, or even single word, may have to be strangely tortured and sublimated in the process. The style, again, is essentially logical, perfectly clear, and thoroughly articulate even in the longest sentences, now that he has not to force his words into metrical fetters. It is thoroughly alive; never flagging, relaxed, or clumsy, however elaborate. He is specially master of one device. He reaches a climax, as you suppose, and that only leads to another more surprising, and so to a third, which eclipses its predecessors. Or sometimes a sentence contains an accumulation of apparent synonyms, intended to make the idea flash new sparkles from different facets. Donne, at least, never goes to sleep, and the alertness and versatility indicated is constantly surprising.

This, of course, involves the string of quibbles and conceits which would strike a modern congregation sometimes as puerile and sometimes as profane. He can take suggestions from all manner of topics. He can at times appeal to mathematical analogies. He has been amused by the remark that you have only to join the ends of a flat map to make east coincide with west, and more than once uses it for edification. The natural history of those days, whose animals seem to come partly out of folk-lore and partly from *Æsop's Fables*, offers delightful suggestions. One of his most singular passages relates to the well-known fact (used also in his **Progress of the Soul**) that the mouse is a deadly enemy of the elephant. It creeps up the elephant's trunk and 'gnaws the life-cords.' This is applied to the relations between man and the Being who made him out of nothing, 'which is infinitely less than a mathematical point.' Can man dare to be at enmity with his Creator, 'who is not only a multiplied elephant, millions of elephants multiplied into one, but a multiplied world, a multiplied all, all that can be conceived by us, infinite many times over?' Do modern preachers regret, I wonder, that they are not allowed such extravagances, which at least would be fatal to slumbers, or rejoice that such efforts are not expected of them? Anyway, with so wide a field, Donne had ample opportunities for startling his hearers and stimulating their attention. Whatever the eccentricities, each sermon plays round some definite central thought, and has a certain unity through the endless ramifications of exuberant illustration. Such performances

might be amazing feats of intellectual juggling; but could they produce 'raptures' and 'tears'? I can manage to believe it, though I must confess that I have to take it rather on trust. It wants an effort to suppose that the sense of man's littleness in the Universe could be really driven home by comparing the Creator to a 'multiplied elephant.' If a man were not shocked by the incongruity, he might recognise a true sentiment, which, uttered in a different dialect, may still impress us all at times. But, then, if we strip off the subtleties, we are apt to come upon a commonplace, and at last must confess that a good many of Donne's refinements suggest rather a yawn than a rapture. If, however, we deliberately make the effort, get back as well as we can to the seventeenth century, and try to get up a rapture, we can perhaps understand, though it is difficult quite to sympathise. There are passages enough in which Donne reveals his heart, and the veil of subtlety becomes transparent. Using a comparison generally attributed to Newton, he speaks of the worthlessness of mere human wisdom, and says that men who have followed by this light 'all the ways both of wisdom and of craft, have got no further than to have walked by the side of a tempestuous sea, and to have gathered pebbles and speckled cockle-shells.' There, happily, his faculty for analogies stops, within legitimate bounds, and the phrase illustrates the vein in which we can really imagine Donne to have moved tears as well as wonder. Showing here and there throughout the subtlety and the learning and the controversy, we have glimpses of the ghastly figure which preached his own funeral sermon. Donne, indeed, represents that strangely materialist view of death, the dwelling upon corruption and the physically repulsive, characteristic of the time. Inevitably it leads him into queer speculations, as, for example, into the problem how the body is to be put together after it has been assimilated by a fish or a cannibal, and therefore become the common property of two souls. But beneath all this is the strong sentiment which might now be congenial to pessimism. Donne was a saint in the eyes of his hearers, and a saint of the ascetic type. His conscience is still haunted by remorse, tempted to self-torture and disillusionment with the world. The sensual appetites have been conquered, but at the price of constantly fixing his eyes upon the hideous side of things; he thinks of the treachery and the villainy which underlies the decorous outside of the world, and checks the worship of beauty by thoughts of what will happen to beauty in the grave. There, again, Hamlet in the churchyard gave pithy utterance to a theme which Donne extends into elaborate subtleties, and considers a 'little too curiously.' If he has in some sense found peace and consolation, he has to be always mortifying the flesh and scourging himself to keep down the old man. He meditates upon hell and the gloomy aspect of the world, which preoccupies him and leads to his most effective passages. To give specimens would be difficult, if only on account of the excessive luxuriance of his rhetoric. A singularly fine passage is the peroration to a sermon upon the text, 'He that believeth not shall be damned,' where the real torment of hell is described as the hopeless separation of the soul from God. That, perhaps, of which a slight indication can be most easily given is an appeal to the atheist. He challenges the 'poor, intricated, perplexed, labyrinthical soul' to stand by its creed. If I asked, he says, whether there be a God when you are at church or in the world or at a theatre, you might consider that religion was an invention of priests or poets or rulers. But, he proceeds, 'I respite thee not till the day of judgment, when thou wilt call upon the hills to cover thee; nor till the day of thine own death, when thou shalt have evidence enough of thy Maker by feeling hell. 'I respite thee but a few hours, but six hours, but till midnight. Wake then, and then, dark and alone, hear God ask thee then, and remembered that I asked thee now. Is there a God? And if thou darest, say No!'

This passage must be enough to illustrate the vigour with which Donne can often throw aside his 'mouse and elephant,' and his elaborate refinements on grammatical and logical niceties, and glow with genuine fire, though frequently we have to exclude so much uncongenial matter that our appreciation ceases to be spontaneous. And there is perhaps the final interest of Donne. In one way he has partly become obsolete because he belonged so completely to the dying epoch. The scholasticism in which his mind was steeped was to become hateful and then contemptible to the rising philosophy; the literature which he had assimilated went to the dust-heaps; preachers condescended to drop their doctorial robes; downright common-sense came in with Tillotson and South in the next generation; and not only the learning but the congenial habit of thought became unintelligible. Donne's poetical creed went the same way, and if Pope and Parnell perceived that there was some genuine ore in his verses and tried to beat it into the coinage of their own day, they only spoilt it in trying to polish it. But on the other side, Donne's depth of feeling, whether tortured into short lyrics or expanding into voluble rhetoric, has a charm which perhaps gains a new charm from modern sentimentalists. His morbid or 'neurotic' constitution has a real affinity for latter-day pessimists. If they talk philosophy where he had to be content with scholastic theology, the substance is pretty much the same. He has the characteristic love for getting pungency at any price; for dwelling upon the horrible till we cannot say whether it attracts or repels him; and can love the 'intense' and super-sublimated as much as if he were skilled in all the latest aesthetic canons. People sometimes talk as if pessimism were a new invention. It is merely a new way of saying the old things. The good old hearty belief in the devil had certainly one advantage: it enabled a gloomy person to cover his misanthropical sentiments by an edifying mask. The conviction that man's nature is corrupt, and that the great majority will be damned, enabled you to discharge your melancholy and yet ostensibly to believe that everything was for the best. Now that the devil has gone out of fashion, the pessimist cannot find even a verbal excuse for his mismanagements of 'Nature,' and has to appear in his true character. It is, in fact, the affinity of Donne to such teaching which suggests a certain ambiguity in the eulogies bestowed upon his religion. His view may be right or wrong; but it implies something very unlike the amiable and optimistic view of the universe which seems to be generally taken as religious by modern preachers. (pp. 71-82)

> *Leslie Stephen, "John Donne," in his* Studies of a Biographer, *Vol. III, second series,* Duckworth & Co., *1902, pp. 36-82.*

LYTTON STRACHEY (essay date 1913)

[*Strachey was a twentieth-century English literary critic and biographer whose iconoclastic reexamination of historical figures revolutionized the course of modern biography. He conceived a type of biography that integrated established facts, speculative psychological interpretations, and imaginative recreations of his subjects' thoughts and actions, resulting in lively, perceptive, and above all "human" biographical portraits. In his major biographies,* Eminent Victorians *(1918),* Queen Victoria *(1912 and* Elizabeth and Essex: A Tragic History *(1928), Strachey helped disclose his subjects' previously overlooked complexities of personality. Like his biographies, Strachey's literary criticism is considered extremely incisive. In the following excerpt from a 1913* Spectator *review of H. J. C. Grierson's recently published edition of Donne's poems, Strachey praises Donne as both a poet and a poetic influence.*]

Donne's work is peculiarly interesting, not only on account of its high intrinsic merits, but owing to the extraordinary strength and the no less extraordinary diversity of its influence upon subsequent writers. It is a curious paradox that a poet whose traces are to be found all over English literature should still be almost unknown to the majority of English readers. It would be difficult, for instance, to name two works more remote from each other in style, in subject, in feeling, in general conception, than Butler's *Hudibras* and Crashaw's *Hymn to Saint Teresa*; yet both the ingenious ribaldry of the one and the mystical frenzies of the other are the direct offspring of Donne's poetry. More important, because more far-reaching, was his influence on Dryden. Dryden, we know, was in his youth an enthusiastic disciple of Donne, and his early work shows the signs of his admiration plainly enough. There is nothing surprising in this. Apart from Chaucer, Donne was the first English writer to grasp to the full the importance of the realistic and intellectual elements in poetry. It was he who, by leading a revolt against the sugared and sensuous style of Spenser, opened the way to that great movement in our literature which culminated in the *Satires* of Pope. And it was through Dryden that the way lay. Dryden's eminently rationalistic and mundane mind recognized in Donne the master who could teach him how to use verse both as an instrument of argumentative exposition and as a brilliant mirror of actual life. Having learnt this, he went a step further, discarded what was *baroque* and unessential in Donne's manner, and introduced once for all the modern spirit into poetry. Thus, in a sense, he superseded Donne, but the magnificent original conception of the great Elizabethan lies at the root of Dryden's finest work, and of that of his numerous spiritual progeny. Just as *Endymion* is implicit in the *Faerie Queen*, so is *English Bards and Scotch Reviewers* implicit in the *Satires* of Donne.

But though the main importance of Donne's influence lay in this direction, the actual characteristics of his poetry itself are curiously complex, and the essential nature of his work differs entirely from that of any of his successors. The intellectuality of Dryden and Pope, the mysticism of Crashaw and Vaughan, the gallantry of Cowley, the bitter wit of Butler, all these elements are to be found in him, not side by side, but completely interfused and compounded together into a strange and unique whole. It is here that the peculiar interest of his poetry lies—in the amazing many-sidedness of the personality which it reveals. It shows us a man who was at once religious, sensual, erudite, passionate, and argumentative. 'He combined,' says De Quincey, 'what no other man has ever done—the last sublimation of dialectical subtlety and address with the most impassioned majesty' [see excerpt dated 1828]. His love poems are probably the most extraordinary in the world. Loaded with complicated reasonings, learned allusions to obscure writers, abstruse references to philosophical systems, it seems almost impossible that they should be anything but frigid and absurd. And, of course, many critics—with Dr Johnson at the head of them—have failed to see more in Donne's poetry than a preposterous collection of 'conceits'. Dryden himself, with the blindness of a reformer, wrote of Donne that 'he affects the metaphysics, not only in his satires, but in his amorous verses, where nature only should reign; and perplexes the minds of the fair sex with nice speculations of philosophy when he should engage their hearts, and entertain them with the softnesses of love' [see except dated 1693]. The criticism seems perfectly just until we turn to the poems themselves, and find that Donne really has achieved the impossible. The ardours of his passionate soul transfuse his antiquated mannerisms, his contorted and remote conceptions, and fill them with an intensely human significance. He has the art of endowing the strangest speculations with a personal thrill:

> I long to talk with some old lover's ghost,
> Who died before the god of Love was born.

He can make a far-fetched, complicated simile the occasion for a lyric outburst of astonishing beauty:

> O more than moon!
> Draw not up tears to drown me in thy sphere,
> Weep me not dead in thine arms. . . .

Or he can turn an epigram into an intimate confession of adoration:

> I must confess, it could not choose but be
> Profane, to think thee anything but thee.

Nor is it only in his love poems that the remarkable qualities of Donne's poignant and powerful nature are apparent. In his elegies, his satires, and his devotional verses the same bizarre and highly-strung individuality makes itself felt. Perhaps the most characteristic of all his works are the two *Anniversaries* written to commemorate the early death at the age of fifteen of Elizabeth Drury, the daughter of one of Donne's patrons. In these strange poems his genius seems to pour itself forth without restraint in a sort of intoxication. No one has a right to consider himself a true worshipper of Donne unless he can admire wholeheartedly these extraordinary productions. Whether Professor Grierson comes within the category is a little doubtful. He seems to apologize for the tremendous and elaborate structure of hyperboles which Donne has erected over the grave of this young girl. But here apologies are out of place; one must either reject wholly or accept wholly; Donne is either revolting or magnificent. Probably it is the very intensity of his seriousness that tends to mislead some of his modern readers. To him God and Heaven were blazing and palpitating realities, and the human soul was a miracle about which no exaggeration of statement was possible. He saw in Elizabeth Drury, not only the type, but the actual presence, of all that is most marvellous in the spirit of man.

> One, whose clear body was so pure and thin,
> Because it need disguise no thought within:
> 'Twas but a through-light scraf, her mind t' inroll;
> Or exhalation-out from her Soul.

And he meant not less, but more, than what he wrote of her:

> She to whose person Paradise adhered
> As courts to Princes, she whose eyes ensphered
> Starlight enough to have made the South control
> (Had she been there) the star-full Northern Pole,
> She, she is gone; she is gone; when thou knowest this,
> What fragment rubbidge this world is
> Thou knowest, and that it is not worth a thought.

In such lines as these one recognize the same spirit which led Donne, on his death-bed, to wrap himself in his shroud to have his portrait painted. For that strange nature rhetorical eccentricity seems to have been the sincerest expression of mystical ravishment, just as dialectical quibbling was the natural language of his most passionate love. (pp. 90-3)

> *Lytton Strachey, "The Poetry of John Donne," in his* Spectatorial Essays, *Harcourt Brace Jovanovich, 1965, pp.88-93.*

WALTER DE LA MARE   (essay date 1913)

[An English man of letters, de la Mare is considered one of the chief exemplars of the romantic imagination in twentieth-century literature. His poems, short stories, and novels together form a sustained treatment of romantic concerns: dreams, rare states of mind and emotion, fantasy worlds of childhood, and the pursuit of the transcendent. In the following excerpt from a review of H. J. C. Grierson's edition of Donne's poetry, de la Mare praises Donne as a poet whose work is best apprehended by a select and mature readership.]

[Beauty] depends for its being less on that which reveals it than on him who perceives it. The best things—if in a sense it is true that the best is not only highest good but what is rarest—can, therefore, never be really popular. And so, as Ben Jonson wrote to Lucy, Countess of Bedford, in one of his 'Epigrams', published in 1616, and prefixed to the 1650 edition of the works of John Donne: 'Rare poems ask rare friends.' Even regarding the *Satires*, Jonson argued that since the majority of mankind is the subject of them, few can appreciate them without offence; and those few must be of the best. And, turning from Donne's 'Egeria' to the poet himself, he scornfully dismisses 'those that for claps 'doe write':

> A man should seek great glory, and not broad.

That will always, as things go, be Donne's fate as a poet— great glory, but not broad. He captures an ardent, almost impassioned, few; but has little share in the admiration of the many. He is too bare and direct, and he is too obscure and abstruse. He is at the same time too little and too much a poet. Jonson, indeed, though he enthusiastically acknowledged him as 'the first poet in the world for some things,' also remarked in convivial confidence to Drummond, that 'Done himself, for 'not being understood, would perish, [see excerpt dated 1618-19]. It is undeniable that the full appreciation of his work, even by his devotees, needs not only all the research, scholarship, acute analysis, and sustained and penetrating diligence and thought that Professor Grierson has given to this new and surely definitive edition: it needs also some temperamental affinity, a certain openness of mind, and freedom from prjudice. To some extent, too, even in regard to the work of Donne's headlong, hedonistic youth, such appreciation is a question of age. Life, fortunately, does not empty her whole cornucopia of delights on man's devoted head in one generous gesture. She refuses to let him ever irretrievably 'come of age.' She reserves joys for maturity, joys for antiquity. And Donne is among those intended for life's meridian—when we look before and after and are compelled to realise that thenceforth, though our wisdom may ripen, it will ripen at the expense of the tree. (pp. 372-73)

The finest achievement of most lyrical poets—Keats, Coleridge, Herrick, Blake, Shelley—seems to be something apart and aloof from their mere workaday selves. It is the outcome of rare, heightened moments, of an elusive and, to a certain degree, alien impulse. We speak of inspiration and so imply an instrument attuned. We speak of art and so imply a direct choice and rejection. And such poetry, alike for writer and reader, is the fruit of a golden pause in life, when time's chariot-wheels are at rest, and the heart no longer tolls *memento mori*, or whisper a feverish *carpe diem,* but beats for a while to an immortal rhythm. Existence is simplified in this intensified and isolated moment. Life is no longer a riddle but a dream.

Donne's poetry is different. He is the poet not of escape from, but into, the depths and mysteries of personality. It is his personality that enslaves us. 'By our first strange and fatal interview,' we are once and for all made captive. He can be almost as intolerably coarse as Swift, as ecstatic as Shelley, as imaginative as Sir Thomas Browne, as nimble and insolent as Mercutio, as thought-ridden as Hamlet, as solemn as the *Dies Irae*, as paradoxical as a latter-day moralist. He may overwhelm a lyric with learning, juggle with the erudite ideas of 'wrangling schooles,' be affectedly and fantastically intellectual, tediously labyrinthine. 'Subtile to plague him'self' he was; but however straitened the view we catch of him, he is always in some indefinable and virtual fashion the man—John Donne. And it is from out of the midst of his obscurity, in the hugger-mugger, as it were, of his alembics and retorts, that we are suddenly dazzled and enthralled by a sheer incandescence of thought and feeling—the attar of his poetry. Donne 'perplexes the mind of the fair sex,' said Dr. Johnson. None the less, except it be Browning, far more of a sentimetalist, in spite of his philosophical gallantry, than Donne, to no other poet do women—apart from the 'fair sex'—owe a rarer debt for his insight, exquisite tenderness, and masculine understanding. No man ever 'deeper digg'd loves Myne' than Donne, nor retrieved from it a stranger treasure. Who that has really read him does not know 'by heart' **The undertaking,** 'Sweetest love, I do not goe,' 'The Funerall,' 'The Exstasie,' 'A Nocturnall,' 'A Valediction: of weeping,' the *Anniversaries,* the best of the *Elegies;* the wonderful onset of **'Aire and Angels,'** of **'Loves Deitie,' 'The Legacie,' 'A Feaver,'** of **'The good-morrow'?**

Throughout his life the same bare, emotional directness is apparent, from 'The Canonization'—'For Godsake hold your tongue, and let me love,'—to the *Holy Sonnets.* . . . (pp. 375-76)

Reading him, we do not throw off the world; we are not, as by a miracle, made innocent and happy. 'Witty depravity,' the sharpest actuality, extremes of exultation and despair, passion and disillusionment, love, death, the grave, corruption—all this is the material of his verse—a verse that breaks into beauty and music the moment feeling and thought are clear and free. Everything that we have—mind, body, soul—he invites to his intimacy.

> A naked thinking heart, that makes no show,

is his demand; a reader 'mad with much heart,' rather than 'ideott with none'; but he exercises also all our mature, modern complexity, for 'man is a lumpe, where all beats 'kneaded bee.' 'Made one anothers hermitage,' we share with him a tense, vigilant, silence in some withdrawn chamber of our minds.

> as men who through a Cipres see
> The rising sun.

'Forget this rotten world!' he cries; what 'fragmentary 'rubbidge' it all is!

> And unto thee
> Let thine own times as an old story be.

The house of life, darkened, haunted, is above and around us. Brightest lover and friend, like clear-illumined ghosts, offer their wordless company. Passionately realised, or dimmed in ecstatic brooding, long they have been away,

> long, long, yet none
> Offers to tell us who it is that's gone.

For us in this solitude with him, at any moment a further door may quietly open, and Death, like a groom, will bring a 'taper to the outward room.' 'The last busie day done, we shall 'ebbe out with them, who homeward goe': and then, 'good morrow to our waking soules.' Only the best of life is in most poets; all man's inward life is in Donne—from his reckless, squandered youth, the youth of the long sensual face, with its high, sloping forehead, wide, dreaming, searching, interrogative eyes, to the shroud-swathed, 'ruinous Anatomie' of the Droeshout engraving. And his poetry has conferred upon him, so far as this world is concerned, life's only real immortality. (pp. 376-77)

Walter de la Mare, "An Elizabethan Poet and Modern Poetry," in The Edinburgh Review *Vol. CCXVII, No. CDXLIV, April, 1913, pp. 372-86.*

RUPERT BROOKE   (essay date 1913)

[*One of the Georgian movements's primary organizers and contributors, Brooke is best known today for his war poetry and for his mystique as the embodiment of idealized youth. He is remembered especially for his sonnet "The Soldier," which celebrates a life gladly given in battle in service to England. In the following excerpt from his review of H. J. C. Grierson's edition of Donne's poetry he offers high praise to Donne's poetic accomplishment.*]

Donne was labelled, by Johnson, a "metaphysical" post [see excerpt dated 1779], and the term has been repeated ever since, to the great confusion of critics. Mr. Grierson attempts to believe that it means erudite, and that erudition is one of the remarkable and eponymous characteristics of Donne's poetry. It rested on erudition, no doubt, as Mr. Grierson has valuably shown; but it was not so especially erudite—not so erudite as the writings of Ben Jonson, a far less "metaphysical" poet. But the continual use of this phrase may have aimed vaguely at a most important feature there is in Donne's poetry. He is the most *intellectual* poet in English; and his intellectualism had, even, sometimes, a tendency to the abstract. But to be an intellectual poet does not mean that one writes about intellectual things. The pageant of the outer world of matter and the mind-region world of the passions came to Donne through the brain. The whole composition of the man was made up of brain, soul, and heart in a different proportion from the ordinary prescription. This does not mean that he felt less keenly than others; but when passion shook him, and his being ached for utterance, to relieve the stress, expression came through the intellect. Under the storm of emotion, it is common to seek for relief by twisting some strong stuff. Donne, as Coleridge said, turns intellectual pokers into love-knots. An ordinary poet, whose feelings find far stronger expression than a common man's, but an expression according to the same prescription, praises his mistress with some common idea, intensely felt:

> Oh, thou art fairer than the evening air,
> Clad in the beauty of a thousand stars!

Donne, equally moved and equally sincere, would compare her to a perfectly equilateral triangle, or to the solar system. His intellect must find satisfaction. If a normal poet—it is not very probable—in thinking of his mistress being ill with a fever, had had suggested to him the simile of these fevers soon passing and dying away in her, just as shooting stars consume and vanish in the vastness and purity of the sky, he would have tried to bring the force of his thought home by sharpening and beautifying the imagined vision. He might have approached it on the lines of:

> Through the serene wide dark of you
> They trail their transient gold, and die.

Donne feels only the idea. He does not try to visualise it. He never visualises, or suggests that he has any pleasure in looking at things. His poems might all have been written by a blind man in a world of blind men. In **"The Feaver"** he gives you the thought thus:

> These burning fits but meteors be,
> Whose matter in thee is soon spent.
> Thy beauty, and all parts, which are thee,
> Are unchangeable firmament.

The mediation of the senses is spurned. Brain does all.

And as Donne saw everything through his intellect, it follows, in some degree, that he could see everything humorously. He could see it the other way, too. But humour was always at his command. It was part of his realism; especially in the bulk of his work, his poems dealing with love. There is no true lover but has sometimes laughed at his mistress, and often at himself. But you would not guess that from the love-songs of many poets. Their poems run the risk of looking a little flat. They are unreal to the side of Donne. For while his passion enabled him to see the face of love, his humour allowed him to look at it from the other side. So we behold his affairs in the round.

But it must not appear that his humour, or his wit, and his passion, alternated. The other two are his passion's handmaids. It should not be forgotten that Donne was one of the first great English satirists, and the most typical and prominent figure of a satirical age. Satire comes with the

Bible of truth in one hand and the sword of laughter in the other. Donne was true to the reality of his own heart. Sometimes you hear the confident laughter of lovers who have found their love:

> I wonder, by my troth, what thou and I
> Did, till we loved? were we not weaned till then?
> But sucked on country pleasures, childishly?
> Or snorted we in the Seven Sleepers' den?

and there is the bitterer mirth of the famous—

> For God's sake, hold your tongue, and let me love.

He could combine either the light or the grave aspects of love with this lack of solemnity that does but heighten the sharpness of the seriousness. His colloquialism helped him. It has been the repeated endeavour of half the great English poets to bring the language of poetry, and the accent and rhythm of poetry, nearer to those of the intensest moments of common speech. To attempt this was especially the mark of many of the greatest of the Elizabethans. Shakespeare's "Prithee, undo this button!" finds its lyrical counterpart in several of Donne's poems. Yet he did not confine his effects to laughter and slang. He could curiously wed fantastic imagination with the most grave and lofty music of poetry; as in the great poem where he compares his wife to the stationary leg of a compass, himself to the voyaging one. . . . For indeed, while the quality of his imagination was unique and astonishing, he expressed it most normally as a great poet, with all the significance and beauty that English metre and poetry can give:

> O more than moon,
> Draw not up seas to drown me in thy sphere!

and—

> Thou art not soft, and clear, and straight, and fair,
> As down, as stars, cedars, and lilies are;
> But thy right hand, and cheek, and eye, only
> Are like thy other hand, and cheek, and eye—

contain as much inexplicable loveliness and strangeness as any of the writings of the Romantics. The mere technique of his poetry has been imitated and followed by many of all the poets who followed him and loved him, from Dryden to Swinburne. It is a good thing that he is slowly spreading from that select band of readers to a wider public. . . . It is fitting he should be read in an age when poetry is beginning to go back from nature, romance, the great world, and the other fine hunting-places of the Romantics, by devious ways and long *ambages*, to that wider home which Donne knew better than any of the great English poets, the human heart. "The heart's a wonder." (pp. 186-88)

Rupert Brooke, "John Donne," in Poetry & Drama, *Vol. 1, No. 2, June, 1913, pp 185-88.*

ALDOUS HUXLEY (essay date 1920)

[*Known primarily for his dystopian novel* Brave New World *(1932). Huxley was an English writer who is considered a novelist of ideas. The grandson of noted Darwinist T. H. Huxley and the brother of scientist Julian Huxley, he was interested in many fields of knowledge, and daring conceptions of science, philosophy, and religion are woven through-*

*out hs fiction. In the following excerpt from an essay origi-
nally published in the* Chapbook *in 1920, he praises Donne
as a poet of accomplishment unmatched by modern poets.*]

It will not be unprofitable to compare the literary situation in this early twentieth century of ours with the literary situation of the early seventeenth century. In both epochs we see a reaction against a rich and somewhat
formalized poetical tradition expressing itself in a determination to extend the range of subject-matter, to get back
to real life, and to use more natural forms of expression.
The difference between the two epochs lies in the fact that
the twentieth-century revolution has been the product of
a number of minor poets, none of them quite powerful
enough to achieve what he theoretically meant to do,
while the seventeenth-century revolution was the work of
a single poet of genius, John Donne. Donne substituted
for the rich formalism of non-dramatic Elizabethan poetry
a completely realized new style, the style of the so-called
metaphysical poetry of the seventeenth century. He was a
Poet-philosopher-man-of-action whose passionate curiosity about facts enabled him to make poetry out of the most
unlikely aspects of material life, and whose passionate apprehension of ideas enabled him to extend the bounds of
poetry beyond the frontiers of common life and its emotions into the void of intellectual abstraction. He put the
whole life and the whole mind of his age into poetry. (pp.
40-1)

We to-day are metaphysicals without our Donne. Theoretically we are free to make poetry of everything in the universe; in practice we are kept within the old limits, for the
simple reason that no great man has appeared to show us
how we can use our freedom. A certain amount of the life
of the twentieth century is to be found in our poetry, but
precious little of its mind. We have no poet to-day like
that strange old Dean of St. Paul's three hundred years
ago—no poet who can skip from the heights of scholastic
philosophy to the heights of carnal passion, from the contemplation of divinity to the contemplation of a flea, from
the rapt examination of self to a enumeration of the most
remote external facts of science, and make all, by his
strangely passionate apprehension, into an intensely lyrical
poetry. (pp. 40-1)

> *Aldous Huxley, "Subject-Matter of Poetry," in his*
> On the Margin: Notes and Essays, *George H. Do-
> ran Company, 1923, pp. 32-42.*

T. S. ELIOT (essay date 1923)

[*Perhaps the most influential poet and critic to write in the
English language during the first half of the twentieth century, Eliot is closely identified with many of the qualities de-
noted by the term Modernism: experimentation, formal
complexity, artistic and intellectual eclecticism, and a classicist's view of the artist working at an emotional distance
from his creation. He introduced a number of terms and
concepts that strongly affected critical thought in his lifetime, among them the idea that poets must be conscious of
the living tradition of literature in order for their work to
have artistic and spiritual validity. In general, Eliot upheld
values of traditionalism and discipline, and in 1928 he an-
nexed Christian theology to his overall conservative world
view. Of his criticism, he stated: "It is a by-product of my
private poetry-workshop: or a prolongation of the thinking
that went into the formation of my verse." Eliot was one of
the key revivifiers of modern critical interest in metaphysical*

*poetry, thanks largely to his seminal essay "The Metaphysi-
cal Poets," originally published in 1921 and later reprinted
in his* Selected Essays *(1932). In the following excerpt from
a review of* Love Poems of John Donne, *he expands upon
the argument stated in the earlier essay, holding that Donne
reflected the preoccupations and intellectual tone of his day
in a manner foreshadowing the work of the twentieth-
century Modernists.*]

One of the characteristics of Donne which wins him, I fancy, his interest for the present age, is his fidelity to emotion as he finds it; his recognition of the complexity of
feeling and its rapid alterations and antitheses. A change
of feeling, with Donne, is rather the regrouping of the
same elements under a mood which was previously subordinate: it is not the substitution of one mood for a wholly
different one.

Impossible to isolate his ecstasy, his sensuality, and his
cynicism.

With sincerity in the practical sense, poetry has little to
do; the poet is responsible to a much more difficult consciousness and honesty. And it is because he has this honesty, because he is so often expressing his genuine whole
of tangled feelings, that Donne is, like the early Italians,
like Heine, like Baudelaire, a poet of the world's literature.

There are two ways in which we may find a poet to be
modern: he may have made a statement which is true everywhere and for all time (so far as "everywhere" and "for
all time" have meaning), or there may be an accidental relationship between his mind and our own. The latter is
fashion; we are all susceptible to fashion in literature as in
everything else, and we all require some indulgence for it.
The age of Donne, and the age of Marvell, are sympathetic to us, and it demands a considerable effort of dissociation to decide to what degree we are deflected toward him by
local or temporary bias.

The age objects to the heroic and sublime, and it objects
to the simplification and separation of the mental faculties. The objections are largely well grounded, and react
against the nineteenth century; they are partly—how far I
do not inquire—a product of the popularization of the
study of mental phenomena. Ethics having been eclipsed
by psychology, we accept the belief that any state of mind
is extremely complex, and chiefly composed of odds and
ends in constant flux manipulated by desire and fear.
When, therefore, we find a poet who neither suppresses
nor falsifies, and who expresses complicated states of
mind, we give him welcome. And when we find his poetry
containing everywhere potential or actual *wit,* our thirst
has been relieved.

Neither the fantastic (Clevelandism is becoming popular)
nor the cynical nor the sensual occupies an excessive importance with Donne; the elements in his mind had an order and congruity. The range of his feeling was great, but
no more remarkable than its unity. He was altogether
present in every thought and in every feeling. It is the
same kind of unity as pervades the work of Chapman, for
whom thought is an intense feeling which is one with every other feeling. Compared with these men, almost every
nineteenth-century English poet is in some way limited or
deformed.

Our appreciation of Donne must be an appreciation of
what we lack, as well as of what we have in common with

him. What is true of his mind is true, in different terms, of his language and versification. A style, a rhythm, to be significant, must embody a significant mind, must be produced by the necessity of a new form for a new content.... The dogmatic slumbers of the last hundred years are broken, and the chaos must be faced: we cannot return to sleep and call it order, and we cannot have any order but our own, but from Donne and his contemporaries we can draw instruction and encouragement. (p. 332)

T. S. Eliot, "John Donne," in The Nation and the Athenaeum *Vol. XXXIII, No. 10, June 9, 1923, pp. 331-32.*

HUGH I'ANSON FAUSSET   (essay date 1924)

[*Fausset was an English man of letters known primarily as a biographer and literary essayist. He wrote critical biographies of John Keats (1922), Lord Tennyson (1923), and Leo Tolstoy (1927), among others. In the following excerpt from his* John Donne, *Fausset celebrates Donne as a near-pagan liberator of human thought and religious beliefs.*]

Our modern world, with the emphasis which it lays upon the rights of individual judgment and the duties of human discretion, may be dated from the Reformation, if only because from that moment men began to rèsent the conception of an arbitrary God, Who had made man in His own image, and to strive, however darkly, to make God in theirs, to realize the divinity in themselves rather than fall prostrate before the divinity of Life or yield blindly to its errant passions; in short, to be rational as well as vital, and, by the union of the social and scientific ideas, of instinct and intelligence, to transcend the violence of the beast and verify the revelation of the seer.

The Reformation is the religious expression of the Renaissance: the one announces the liberation of life, of generous, abounding, and increasingly self-conscious instinct; the other the first step in the distinctive emancipation of mind.

And as with ages, so with individuals. The two are related and even analogous, but while the microcosm reflects the macrocosm, it also forestalls its processes by speedier and more concentrated development. While therefore the vital man is of his time, he is also behind it and before it. He is a 'little world made cunningly' to demonstrate in his short span of years both the depths out of which man has emerged and the heights to which he may yet attain.

Such men are rebels against the conventions of their times because they are driven to explore the realities of all times. It is not only for their greater sincerity that they are most worthy of study, but also for their wider reach. They renew the past in their lives and image the future. Exulting in the primitive impulses of nature, they doff the garment of contemporary civilization, and by ways of bitter experience re-fashion it to clothe their nakedness. And since life's verities are most luminous when its form is no longer congealed by convention and its elements are for the moment resolved, the rebel whom passion animates and who is also self-conscious enough to record and analyse the phases of his experience is a history in miniature. His errors and distractions, even his failure, are more

charged with significance for posterity than all the maxims of complacent conformity.

Such a man was John Donne, a genius physically and intellectually 'possessed,' one who ranged almost every scale of experience, and upon each struck some note, harsh, cunning, arrogant or poignant, which lingers down the roof of time; a poet who was at times near a monster, full-blooded, cynical and gross, a thinker, curious, ingenious and mathematical, a seer brooding morbidly over the dark flux of things, a saint aspiring to the celestial harmony.

This catholicity of faculty of experience is rare. History shows us few men who serve the flesh with the same ardour with which they seek the ideal. The sensualist is seldom the thinker, or the poet the priest, or the Pagan the Christian. Donne was all of these; his carnality blossomed into spirituality as a flower that springs from the dung.

And not only is his personal history a parable of 'Everyman,' and, as such, applicable to any age, but he also represents, more fully than any of his contemporaries, the three aspects of life which met in confused association in the England of the seventeenth century, those of Mediævalism, the Renaissance, and the Reformation. Sensual, scientific, egotistic, he is alike Pagan, Scholar, Courtier, and Puritan, a child of the old darkness and the new dawn. He has shed the stupor of mediævalism and most of its superstition, but not its innate savagery, nor its fear of the unknown. That sudden intoxication with life, which led the men of the Renaissance to enthrone anew in a burst of artistic adoration the body in its beauty and its pride, is his also, but with him the intoxication is not æsthetic but realistic; and so, in common with the ascetic whom the Renaissance renounced, he discovers the ugliness of the body by observing with critical detachment the gross impulses by which it is mastered. His passion for life, in brief, is not ecstatic enough to subdue his mediæval fear of death or console with a renaissance sense of beauty. And lastly the Puritan in him, the awaking rationality which he shared with his own age and country, led him to associate the fact of death with the idea of sin, and the state of virtue with the hope of immortality.

Thus, to simplify the elements which his personality expressed, we see in him a Pagan, stricken with that longing for spiritual consciousness which is the Christian's eventual compensation for ceasing to enjoy uncritically a state of Nature. And his peculiar value to us, as an expression of life, lies in the fact that he never compromised.

He never confused the spiritual and the sensual either through false fear or false reverence. He is never sentimental, because he experienced and expressed the physical with complete candour, and so was never tempted to linger over it in secretive cunning, sanctifying the sensuous with fine phrases, or smudging the spiritual with vague emotions. He knew that there can be no escape from the physical to the spiritual. Each is the condition of the other, and the transmutation must be complete and unqualified like some sudden fusion of elements.

And so the physical, intellectual and spiritual elements in him preserve for most of his life a singular detachment from each other. They do not mix, but each in turn dominates his personality. (pp. 18-22)

As a lover he is in turn the sensualist and the cynic, passion's slave and passion's critic, the Platonist and the devoted husband.

In religion he escapes from Catholicism to agnosticism, becomes the paid casuist and the learned theologian: embraces at last, at the bidding of circumstance, the ministry of the English Church, and in the anguish of his spirit converts a professional into a spiritual vocation, which for pure intensity of expression has never been surpassed. (p. 23)

With him we learn that religion is real. He, like all of us, was limited by his age: keen as his intellect was, he lacked the knowledge which renders many of the dogmas that he ultimately accepted utterly void of reality to-day. (But far beyond the limits of his time, he related poetry to religion, and religion to truth.) He teaches us, not how to worship God, but how to relate ourselves to God, and he shows that spiritual satisfaction, however exquisite, is unworthy of the name if it be achieved at the sacrifice of intellectual honesty; that religious experience is the prize of perpetual conflict, of that battle between life and death which is the agony and exultation of the creature in us striving after the divine. (p. 24)

'Poor intricated soul!' he once said of '**The Atheist**,' 'Riddling, perplexed, labyrinthicall soul!' and essentially it was of himself that he spoke. His theology, his doctrine may have been unexceptionable on grounds of orthodoxy, but his Christianity was no more than the veneer of the savage. He did not so much evolve a religion as represent a complex, and because that complex is typical of Puritanism in its origin, and, as such, of a stage in the spiritual development of man, repeated from generation to generation in the individual, his life has more than a personal significance.

It should make a particular appeal to an age such as ours, which is even more puzzled how to bring the head into harmony with life than the heart. We, in a very different way, are in danger of losing touch with any unifying idea external to ourselves, of being prisoned within the relativity of our own conceptions, and so of becoming dwarfed and mechanical for want of that apprehension of creative purpose in the universe which invites to self-forgetfulness, and which it is art's and religion's aim to supply.

To the Puritan of the seventeenth century a gulf suddenly yawned between nature and man. The old joy of the senses, the old care-free innocence of instinct was tarnished, because man had begun to be self-conscious and to exploit the material of life to his own hurt and to the disturbing of Nature's economy. He had discovered how consciously to abuse and criticize the physical impulses which before he had almost unthinkingly accepted.

And from such criticism sprang self-disgust and cynicism—or, as religion names it, a sense of sin—the first symptoms of man's superiority to the flesh, of his human and rational prerogative.

But if intellectual man was born out of natural man, he was still the slave to the physical which he criticized. It was that which made his criticism so agonized. He was drowning, even while he cursed the ocean that engulfed him. (pp. 313-14)

It was Donne's great and tragic destiny to experience the worst agonies of that inconclusive battle, and to bequeath to literature the tale of it. With a kindred fierceness he loved life and hated it, accepted and denied it. He was as sensual in his later asceticism as in his earlier indulgence, at once too Pagan to be a Christian and too Christian to be a Pagan. The corollary of his lust for life was his dread of death; for death meant surely an end to sensation, against which his goaded instinct rose in horrified rebellion which no philosophy might quell. (p. 315)

He could not create beauty out of life, he could not even see the beauty in which the limbs of life were veiled, which flowed through and over the bleak anatomy of fact, consecrating the perishable dust and redeeming it of squalor and grossness—because he lacked harmony in himself; and for the same reason he could only aggravate the horrors of death by endowing it with his own animality.

Too mature for that Classic Grace which even in its wantonness preserved an innocence of body and of mind, a divine naturalness, he was yet too primitive for Romantic vision. He represents as it were only the tangled roots of the Gothic, that turbulent obscurity out of which were born, in purer souls than his, not only grinning gargoyles but a miracle of tapering spires. (pp. 316-17)

It is the rich physical nature of Donne that makes him so passionately expressive, even in his defeat; and in his rare moments of imaginative victory, of conflict culminating in unity only to relapse again into discord, 'through the ragged apparel of the afflictions of this life; through the scars and wounds and paleness, and morphews of sin, and corruption, we can look upon the soul itself.' (p. 317)

In the stress of such a nature the problem of human life is starkly presented. Like some distracted microcosm, Donne reflects and condenses, the long labour of the man to outgrow the beast and approach the divine. And he shows that religion for an honest man is something other than an escape: that it is an adventure which demands in the region of the ideal as much moral courage and tenacity, and reveals the same flaws of character, as do the yards in a pelting gale for the sailor rounding the Horn. (p. 318)

Hugh I'Anson Fausset, in his John Donne: A Study in Discord, *1924. Reprint by Russell & Russell, 1967, 318 p.*

[JOHN MIDDLETON MURRY] (essay date 1926)

[*Murry is recognized as one of the most significant English critics and editors of the twentieth century. Anticipating later scholarly opinion, he championed—through his positions as founding editor of the* Adelphi *and as a regular contributor to the* Times Literary Supplement, *among other periodicals—the writings of Marcel Proust, James Joyce, Paul Valery, D. H. Lawrence, and Thomas Hardy. His early exposition on literary appreciation,* The Problem of Style *(1922), is considered an informed guidebook for both critics and general readers to employ when considering not only the style of a literary work, but also its theme and viewpoint. In it Murry espouses the theoretical premise underlying all his criticism, that in order to evaluate fully a writer's achievement, the critic must search for the crucial passages that effectively "crystallize" the writer's innermost impressions and convictions. In the following excerpt, Murry offers an essentially negative assessment of* Devotions upon Emergent Occasions.]

The vogue of Donne in recent years has been, like most other sudden elections into popularity, a little undiscriminating. The author of some great and dazzling, and many smaller and fascinating, poems was precipitately discovered to be a master of prose. People not generally given to reading sermons read Donne's. The unfamiliarity went to their heads. Donne's sermons [collected in **Devotions upon Emergent Occasions**] are not at all like the sermons we hear (or hear of) nowadays, but it does not necessarily follow that they are unlike the sermons Donne's contemporaries used to hear. In fact they are not; nor are they better than other sermons of the spacious days. To the finest of Elizabethan and Jacobean sermons they are conspicuously inferior—both as divinity and as prose. . . .

Donne has been regarded as though he were the one intelligent man in the Church of his day. In fact there were others; and the only reason why they have been comparatively forgotten is that the ardours of high theological thinking have become unpopular. But that unpopularity, we believe, is only temporary; for theological thinking of the highest order is a different kind of thinking from any to which the modern mind is accustomed, and we may venture the assertion that it is a kind of thinking of which the modern mind stands in need. The effort of centuries to make spiritual realities amenable to the logic of discourse will, sooner or later, be recognized and drawn upon by minds which are beginning to suspect the necessity of a like effort to-day.

Donne's sermons and devotions have to be considered in their place as part of the religious thought and writing of his day. Compare them, say, with the sermons and devotions of his great contemporary, Bishop Andrewes. Andrewes is not less striking but he is far less eccentric than Donne. In Donne's illness the physicians of the day put pigeons to his feet to draw the vapours from his heart; in the Dean's meditations the pigeon is likened to the dove hovering above his head. He breaks out into spots; the spots are a symbol of the stars in heaven. Such eccentricities—to call them no worse—would have been impossible for Bishop Andrewes. Nor shall we say that it was because Andrewes had better taste, though that would be the effect of the comparison on a critic who had no interest in their subjects; it was because Andrewes had an ever-present sense of the Divine reality. He knew immediately, what Donne seems never to have known, when the self-satisfied intellect was getting the upper hand. He used his intellect, and used it magnificently; but he kept it always harmoniously subordinate to his religious perception. The light in Andrewes's writing is steady; divine illumination and intellectual clarity appear as one. Far otherwise with Donne. At moments one might fairly accuse him of using the categories of high theology simply for the purpose either of self-indulgent introspection or to astonish his fashionable audience, or for both purposes at once. And in the process inevitably the categories themselves become all but meaningless; for theological thinking that is suffered to proliferate, in divorce from the immediate religious perception which is its source, must become merely a debased variety of philosophy. And much of Donne's religious writing deserves no better name.

There are flashes, of course, both of profound psychological intuition and of intuition into the religious mystery; and sometimes his figures are as fine as they are curious, as in this from his meditation on the tolling of the passing-bell:—

> The church is Catholic, universal, so are all her actions; all that she does belongs to all. When she baptizes a child, that action concerns me; for that child is thereby connected to that body which is my head too, and ingrafted into that body whereof I am a member. And when she buries a man, that action concerns me; all mankind is of one author, and is one volume; when one man dies one chapter is not torn out of the book, but translated into a better language; and every chapter must be so translated. God employs several translators; some pieces are translated by age, some by sickness, some by war, some by justice; but God's hand is in every translation, and his hand shall bind up all our scattered leaves again for that library where every book shall lie open to one another.

But for all that, catholicity is the virtue in which Donne as a religious writer (perhaps also as a poet) is certainly wanting. He has a queer and surprising but not a great mind. The luminous simplicity that is born of the complete congruity of thought and emotion is much rarer in his religious writing than in his poetry, but it is rare even in his poetry. What failed him in his first profession was bound to fail him more obviously in his second, unless a profound conversion had intervened. Religious conviction is a reality, and men are not converted to it by Royal, but by Divine solicitation.

> *[John Middleton Murry], "Donne's Devotions," in The Times Literary Supplement No. 1260, March 11, 1926, p.178.*

PIERRE LEGOUIS (essay date 1928)

> [*Legouis is a French educator who has written several studies on the works of Andrew Marvell and Donne. In the following excerpt from a work originally published in 1928, he examines the imagery and dramatic elements in several of the* Songs and Sonets.]

That Donne possessed dramatic power has generally been acknowledged. Indeed one of the generation which came to manhood in the last decade of the XVIth century might be credited with some measure of the instinct at work in Shakespeare and so many lesser playwrights, even before he had given evidence of it. In his fervid youth Donne was "a great Frequenter of Plays" though the theatres probably found in him a hard patron to please; and even in his sermons he will not boggle at comparisons drawn from play-acting. (pp. 47-8)

The four pieces which go by the common title of **"Valediction"** are dramas of the simplest kind. In one of them at least, possibly in others, the mistress from whom the poet-lover parts is weeping. But the interest centres on the symbol which provides three of the pieces with their subtitles: **"of my name, in the window"**,—**"of the booke"**,—**"of weeping"**;—and though Donne called the fourth **"A Valediction: forbidding mourning"**, the reader will be sure to remember it as the piece in which the parted lovers are compared to "stiffe twin compasses".—The song **"Sweetest love, I do not goe"** is to all intents and purposes a valediction, though Donne did not choose to entitle it so, perhaps because there was no symbol in it to emphasize its difference in sameness; but it is all the more touching for the directness of its appeal, since attention is not with-drawn from the characters and the scene to a mere term of comparison.—"**Breake of day**" also is a valediction, more precisely a descendant of the medieval *aube* as Professor Grierson points out. Here, for once in the *Songs and Sonets,* the woman speaks, and so well that this piece alone would suffice to prove Donne's ability to express the feelings of others, and allow us to surmise that even when the speaker is a man he need not be the poet's own self. "**Breake of day**" stands not unworthy of comparison with the parting scene in *Romeo and Juliet.* True we hear in it no lark's song, which the lovers would persuade themselves to be the nightingale's; no "jocund day—Stands tiptoe on the misty mountain tops". The language is as naked as can be, but its very nakedness speaks passion:

> 'Tis true, 'tis day; what though it be?
> O wilt thou therefore rise from me?
> Why sould we rise, because 'tis light?
> Did we lie downe, because 'twas night?
> Love which in spight of darknesse brought us hether,
> Should in despight of light keepe us together.
>
> (pp. 51-2)

In "**The Sunne Rising**" we find the same situation and a similar feeling; but here the lover addresses the sun, and his railings sound more rhetorical than dramatic. Yet the scenery, sketched in a few skilful strokes, redeems the piece from the fault of ranting in cold blood: the sunrays peer through windows and drawn curtains into the bed, a property only alluded to in "**Breake of day**" but here brazenly mentioned in the concluding lines of the last two stanzas, so as to leave us in no doubt of its paramount importance:

> Aske for those Kings whom thou saw'st yesterday,
> And thou shalt heare, All here in one bed lay.
> Shine here to us, and thou art every where;
> This bed thy center is, these walls, thy spheare.

"**The good-morrow**" seems related to the foregoing group of poems, but the connexion is merely metaphorical. The lovers are not parting, neither does the sun remind them it were time to part. Their souls, not their bodies, have just awakened. Their happiness is for the nonce unalloyed; they wonder how they lived before they loved. Therefore the dramatic element appears less vividly than in those pieces where there is fear, or at least a sense that joy is ephemeral. Yet "**The good-morrow**" is no madrigal indited in the closet to a distant mistress; it is the report of an impassioned dialogue in that "little room" where the lovers have met and which has become to them "an every where". The woman remains silent, or rather her words are not given; but her presence is felt: "*her* face in *his* eye, *his* in *hers* appeares".—Let no one misunderstand me: this piece *was* written by Donne in his closet, and with much care; it was revised by him ... at leisure: what I mean is that it succeeds in creating a voluptuous atmosphere and calling up in it two flesh-and-blood human beings who act in relation to each other. The impression of passionate reality made upon the reader results partly from the poet's artfully concealed art, an art which is nothing if not dramatic.

However, against the applying of this epithet to "**The good-morrow**", as indeed to almost every one of the pieces we have considered so far, it might be objected that they lack progression; the situation and even the feelings are at the end what they were at the beginning. But there remain for study a few of the *Songs and Sonets* in which Donne's technique shows itself more complex: the initial situation evolves more or less, there are episodes and vicissitudes, or at least development.

The song "**Sweetest Love, I do not goe . . .**" differs, as we have noted, from the "**Valedictions**" in that it appeals to the heart, not through the medium of a symbol, but directly. It also gives more importance to the woman's part. The poet really speaks to her, not above her head, and he alters his tone according to the effect produced upon her by what he has just said. In the first stanza he tries to make her smile; but we see that he fails, since the second stanza more seriously attempts to comfort her by promising a speedy return. Yet this also proves unavailing, and he, feeling helpless at the sight of her redoubling grief, gives vent in the third stanza to his own despondency. Man, he generalizes, "cannot add another houre" to his good fortune, "nor a lost houre recall"; but we know how to assist misery when it comes and "teach it art and length,—It selfe o'r us to'advance". Such sombre wisdom rather justifies the woman's grief as being consonant to human nature. So in the fourth stanza he returns to their own sad plight and entreats her to spare him; her grief is his death. . . . Besides, adds the first half of the fifth stanza, foreseeing of evil will bring it to pass. Pity, with a touch of superstition in it, succeeds where wit, sense, philosophy, have been of no avail. And now she listens, outwardly quieter, to his renewed invitation to make light of his absence, and to his assurance that no separation ever takes place between those "who one another keepe—Alive". Thus interpreted dramatically, this beautiful piece achieves a unity which was not apparent when one considered it as a lyric of the ordinary type. The reader must fill the logical gaps with kisses and embraces, sighs and sobs, weeping and the wiping away of tears, and gazings into the woman's eyes to read her thoughts; he must also realize the failure of the lover's first efforts in order to understand the crescendo of pathos, and the relative success that ensues so as to appreciate the more subdued and pacified tone of the conclusion.

"**The Canonization**" stands alone among the *Songs and Sonets* because the person addressed in it is a male friend, but love is still the theme. The character who is speaking rejects the wordly-wise advice offered to him and vindicates his own abandonment to passion. . . . "**The Canonization**" appears almost incoherent at the first reading, so much does the tone (not the theme) change in the course of its five stanzas. Of these the title fits only the last two: the first three have nothing to do with the admitting of the lovers to the calendar of saints. To discover the essential unity of the piece one must analyse it in a detailed manner.

The famous opening line:

> For Godsake hold your tongue, and let me love,

shows us Donne at his best in the brusque familiar style. In the rest of the stanza he makes fun of himself:

> Or chide my palsie, or my gout,
> My five gray haires, or ruin'd fortune flout,

and then of his friend:

> Observe his honour, or his grace,
> Or the Kings reall, or his stamped face
> Contemplate, what you will, approve,

but shows all the strength of his passion in the appeal: do anything

> So you will let me love.

The satirical note reappears in the second stanza, where it sounds still more clearly. The first line states the simple thought in simple terms:

> Alas, alas, who's injur'd by my love?

The next lines are a rhetorical amplification of that thought. The poet here parodies the hyperbolical metaphors of the Petrarchists, used elsewhere by himself more seriously:

> What merchants ships have my sighs drown'd?
> Who saies my teares have overflow'd his ground?
> When did my colds a forward spring remove?
> When did the heats which my veines fill
> Adde one more to the plaguie Bill?

In the last three lines satire becomes more stinging; it still hits the love-poets who have exaggerated the influence of their heart-beats upon the world at large, but it also exposes the selfishness of the professional man:

> Soldiers finde warres, and Lawyers finde out still
> Litigious men, which quarrels move,
> Though she and I do love.

Among the accusations from which the lover pretends to be particularly anxious to clear himself, he places last, as the most heinous, that of having stopped all wars and lawsuits, which would have brought upon him the just anger of two dangerous and vindictive kinds of men.

After this ironical outburst the lover pauses awhile to catch his breath, and the friend tries to get a word in. He upbraids the passionate couple with lack of sense: they are night-moths dazzled by a light. This speech, which takes place, if we may coin the word, in the inter-stanza, turns the lover's ardour from satire to self-glorification. So far he has told others to mind their own business and proved the harmlessness of his own all-engrossing pursuit; that strain recurs in the third stanza:

> Call her one, mee another flye,
> We are Tapers too, and at our owne cost die,

which means: nobody suffers a loss by our death. But the main idea now is that of justification by love:

> Call us what you will, wee are made such by love,

—nay, more, than justification, ennoblement:

> And wee in us finde the Eagle and the Dove.

Probably the metaphor of the birds was suggested by that of the insects, and corrects it; in the erotic-mystical language of the time "eagle" stands for "strength" and "dove" for "tenderness and purity"; let us remember Crashaw's rapturous appeal to Saint Theresa:

> By all the eagle in thee, all the dove.

But the metaphor of the Phoenix, which comes up in the next line and proceeds from that of the self-burning night-moth, makes it likely that the eagle and the dove also arise from fire.... [with] the Phenix Donne openly reverts to the type of traditional hyperbole he has just ridiculed, but he wears the hackneyed symbol with a difference:

> The Phoenix ridle hath more wit
> By us, we two being one, are it.

The fabulous bird, being unique of its kind, united in himself both sexes; the two lovers, having combined into one "neutrall" (not a very happy substitute for "hermaphrodite") thing, have also acquired that other property of the phenix: they "dye and rise the same" as before.

Here the friend once more gets a chance and must be understood prosaically to object that, unless the poet means the metaphorical deaths and resurrections of parting and meeting again, he is straying very far from the truth: their love may well destroy the lovers, but not call them back to this nether world, not even provide them with a living while they are in it. The fourth stanza admits the hard fact, but answers defiantly:

> Wee can dye by it, if not live by love.

It then proceeds to improve upon a hint given in the last line of the third stanza: the love of the pair is a mystery; therefore they will have a "legend", *i.e.* their marvellous but true story will be written for the edification of the faithful in after ages; their fame will rest safely, if not in a "Chronicle", at least in "hymns": This last word, with its religious import, leads up naturally to the announcement that the poet and his mistress will be *Canoniz'd for love* on which the fourth stanza ends. The friend this time probably opens his mouth to remonstrate against pride amounting to blasphemy, if the is a Roman catholic, or idolatry if he is a protestant; but no word of his can be even overheard, for the fourth stanza runs into the fifth, without a period. The new-made saints are already "invoked" by lovers who come after them; their intercession is prayed for in the most approved papistical style; the repetition of the words "You whom", "You do whom . . .; who . . ." suggests a litany. Here Donne the lover turns to good account the learning of Donne the schoolman, and, in the impassioned subtleties of that imaginary address, the reader may well forget the friend who was the occasion of the piece. Yet without him, and unless we fill in his interruptions, we do not thoroughly realize why the lover-poet gradually warms himself up and passes from jesting impatience to an almost ecstatic vision.

These last words naturally call to our minds the title of another among the **Songs and Sonets,** which recent critics generally agree in praising as the finest and most characteristic of all, but of which they give divergent interpretations, none of then, I think, adequate. **"The Extasie"** resembles **"The Canonization"** in its use of scholastic notions for lyric-dramatic effect; it differs from the piece we have just analysed because it is partly narrative and the dumb character, here a woman, takes no such active share in the dramatic part as the male friend did. On the other hand the scenery is described in **"The Extasie"** at greater length than in any other of Donne's lyrics (except **"The Primrose"**, which is not dramatic), but the description assumes, so to speak, the form of a stage-direction, instead of occuring in the speeches themselves, after the more artistic manner of **"The Apparition"** and **"The Sunne Rising"**:

> Where, like a pillow on a bed,
> A Pregnant banke swel'd up, to rest
> The violets reclining head,
> Sat we two, one anothers best.

Donne is no poet of nature; his proper study is man; even when he for once lays the scene of his action outdoors, his metaphors take us back to the boudoir or the rake's den. The epithet "pregnant", though not voluptuous, is also sexual, and the drooping violets suggest languor. The feelings of the lovers are in keeping with the place; indeed, rather than feelings I should say sensations:

> Our hands were firmely cimented
> With a fast balme, which thence did spring.

In like words but with bitter irony Othello praises Desdemona's hand, "moist . . ., hot, hot, and moist", which "argues fruitfulness and liberal heart", but warns her against the "young and sweating devil" there. — Donne goes on:

> Our eyes-beames twisted, and did thred
> Our eyes, upon one double string.

Generally sight, of all the senses, expresses love most spiritually; but here looking into each other's eyes becomes as material a link as joining hands. The metaphor of the string threading the two balls would reach the acme of bad taste if it did not fitly convey the physical intensity of the situation.—The next stanza, ostensibly telling us what has not yet taken place between the lovers, hints it were time it took place, and so puts the problem which is the *raison d'être* of the whole piece:

> So to'entergraft our hands, as yet
> Was all the meanes to make us one,
> And pictures in our eyes to get
> Was all our propagation.

But the poet would defeat his own purpose if he opened it too clearly and too soon. He has said enough of the bodies for the nonce, and now passes to the souls whose meeting he depicts in the loftiest language; he insists upon the perfect stillness of the lovers in order to emphasize their Platonic purity:

> As 'twixt two equal! Armies, Fate
> Suspends uncertaine victorie,
> Our soules, (which to advance their state,
> Were gone out, hung 'twixt her, and mee.
> And whil'st our soules negociate there,
> Wee like sepulchrall statues lay;
> All day, the same our postures were,
> And wee said nothing, all the day.

Even words are too gross, it seems, for such ethereal passion; but the cynical reader remembers the balm cementing the hands, and smiles. Donne, however, preserves a most serious countenance, and introduced an hypothetical listener who bears witness to the ennobling quality of the scene:

> If any, so by love refin'd,
> That he soules language understood,
> And by good love were growen all minde,
> Within convenient distance stood,
> He (though he knew not which soule spake,
> Because both meant, both spake the same)
> Might thence a new concoction take,
> And part farre purer then he came.

So ends the narrative prelude to the speech which contains the gist of the matter. Let us note the use of the preterite to report the circumstances in which the incident happened. It is undramatic; so is the introduction of a third party whom the poet does not even invest with more than a virtual existence. And the reader is puzzled, because the poet has not frankly taken him into his confidence though he has thrown out hints of an unscrupulous and selfish scheme veiled behind transcendental pretence.

As soon as the speech begins, one thing at least becomes clear: the supposed impossibility for the listener to tell whose voice he heard and the ensuing use of "we" instead of "I" are mere flattery and wile on the lover's part. The woman will feel pleased, her vanity will be tickled when she thinks she is considered able to utter such high-flown conceits; she will not notice the moment when it is no longer safe for her to agree to the man's metaphysics, which she interprets with a weaker head and more fervid heart.

The first half of the speech exalts Platonic love and explains its workings:

> This Extasie doth unperplex
> (We said) and tell us what we love,
> Wee see by this, it was not sexe,
> Wee see, we saw not what did move:

As Professor Grierson points out, that theory of the new insight acquired in ecstasy comes, directly or indirectly, from Plotinus; and so does that of the contact and union of souls in the next lines:

> But as all severall soules containe
> Mixture of things, they know not what,
> Love, these mixt soules, doth mixe againe,
> And makes both one, each this and that.

The poet, however, stops borrowing to insert one of his curiously matter-of-fact comparisons, at once familiar and unexpected:

> A single violet transplant,
> The strength, the colour, and the size,
> (All which before was poore, and scant,)
> Redoubles still, and multiplies.

After "transplant" the reader must supply: "to a richer soil"; the remark sounds like a sensible gardener's, not and idle dilettante's. Indeed it does not interrupt the logical process, being neither emotional nor picturesque, the poet is reasoning by anology, as Bacon himself so often does: a violet improves by transplanting, so will a soul:

> When love, with one another so
> Interinanimates two soules,
> That abler soule, which thence doth flow,
> Defects of loneliness controules.
> Wee then, who are this new soule, know,
> Of what we are compos'd and made, . . .

These last two lines take us back to the new insight, for which the preceding ones have sufficiently accounted: they are the logical conclusion of that half of the speech: the demonstration of the superior quality of Platonic love seems now complete. But the poet goes on with it, and rather impairs it from the philosopher's point of view:

> For, th'Atomies of which we grow,
> Are soules, whom no change can invade.

Grammar will hardly admit of any other antecedent to "whom" than "soules". If so, one might well ask how the "mixture of things" scornfully mentioned in 1.34, has now become an "atomy", something perfectly simple and pure. But Donne may well risk this sophism; he knows the woman has been out of her intellectual depth for some time, and wants anyhow to impress her with the notion that they are now secure from change, whatever they do.

Now the lover boldly comes to the point and says what he has been thinking of all the time:

> But O alas, so long, so farre
> Our bodies why doe wee forbeare?

And without allowing the woman time to consider this startling proposition by the light of her own moral sense, he hastens to ply her with arguments for consenting. He appeals now to her reason, somewhat stunned by this time:

> They are ours, though they are not wee, wee are
> The intelligences, they the spheare,

(remember that in line 20 the bodies were "wee", now to her feeling, namely gratitude:

> We owe them thankes, because they thus,
> Did us, to us, at first convay,
> Yeelded their forces, sense, to us,
> Nor are drosse to us, but allay.

But reason is better; the woman will mistrust it less readily, and the compliment paid to her as one above her sex in intellect will go a long way towards removing her last scruples; besides, the lover's reputation as a casuist requires that he should at least seem to reconcile the two sharply opposed definitions of love that he has just been and is now giving. Scientific comparisons will be helpful, first an astrological one:

> On man heavens influence workes not so,
> But that it first imprints the ayre,
> Soe soule into the soule may flow,
> Through it to body first repaire;

secondly a physiological one:

> As our blood labours to beget
> Spirits, as like soules as it can,
> Because such fingers need to knit
> That subtile knot, which makes us man:
> So must pure lovers soules descend
> T'affections, and to faculties,
> Which sense may reach and apprehend,
> Else a great Prince is prison lies.

In the last line the appeal to reason again passes into an appeal to feeling, no longer gratitude but pity, that most insidious enemy to virtue in woman as in man. The magnificent language takes us very far above the seducer's scheme, and alone explains Coleridge's selection of **"The Extasie"** for special praise: "I should never find fault with metaphysical poems if they were all like this or but half as excellent" [see excerpt dated 1811]. But immediately after this flight we fall back to earth:

> To'our bodies turne wee then, that so
> Weake men on love reveal'd may looke;
> Loves mysteries in soules doe grow,
> But yet the body is his booke.
> And if some lover, such as wee,
> Have heard this dialogue of one,
> Let him still marke us, he shall see
> Small change, when we'are to bodies gone.

Probably Coleridge read a spiritual meaning into these last two stanzas; we may regret he did not write it down for us, since the plain and literal meaning sounds queer and unpleasant enough. The hypothetical listener of the prelude reappears and turns spectator at a time when the lovers as well as we could well wish him away. And is the woman so dazed that she should fail to suspect triumphant cynicism in that conclusion? Logical symmetry, however, receives this satisfaction that the final line of the second part of the speech repeats, with some variation, the last line of the first part: "no change" becomes "small change", the difference between the two terms representing what the man has won and the woman lost.

Donne, his latest biographer affirms, maintained his search for truth with a persistent honesty of purpose. If by truth is meant *adequatio spiritus et rei*, as the poet himself would have said, or objective truth, as the new schoolmen now say, I feel bound to disagree. Such truth in **"The Extasie"** at best occupies a very subordinate position. Donne does not set to solve once for all the difficult problem of the relations between soul and body in love. He considers the particular case of a couple who have been playing at Platonic love, sincerely enough on the woman's part, and imagines how they would pass from it to carnal enjoyment; whether he thinks this *in abstracto* a natural consummation or a sad falling off matters little; the chief interest of the piece is psychological, and character being represented here in action, dramatic. The heroine remains indeed for the reader to shape, but the hero stands before us, self-revealed in his hypocritical game. If truth exists here, it is the truth that we find in the speeches of Molière's Don Juan, who can call on Heaven when convenient and cloak his wicked designs in religious cant, the truth of the playwright who holds up the mirror to human nature.

In the scholastic Don Juan of **"The Extasie"**, has Donne portrayed himself? Is this piece the record of one youthful adventure of his? The answer to this question, even if it were safe to answer it, lies beyond the scope of this essay. At any rate the supposition contains no internal improbability, since Donne was sensual, yet dabbled in platonics; he certainly resembled his hero closely, while Molière had very little of the Spanish libertine, least of all his hypocrisy. This amounts to saying that Donne's dramatic power mostly worked upon his personal experience, however freely he may have dealt with the setting and circumstances of each incident. **"The Extasie"** is the strongest of the *Songs and Sonets,* not because it reveals his final creed about love, but because it pictures the type of lover he knew most intimately, from the inside, and no other poet ever knew and sympathized with so well as he. (pp. 53-7)

Pierre Legouis, in his Donne the Craftsman: An Essay upon the Structure of the "Songs and Sonets," *Russell & Russell, Inc., 1962, 98 p.*

H. J. C. GRIERSON (essay date 1929)

[*Grierson was a Scottish educator and scholar who was considered in his time a leading authority on John Milton, Sir Walter Scott, and Donne. It was he who compiled what is today considered the most complete and authoritative collection of Donne's poetry,* The Poems of John Donne *(1912), a well-researched, well-annotated collection which settled critical controversies about definitive versions of poems and of poems falsely attributed to Donne. Grierson's edition was critically applauded by such poets as Walter de la Mare and Rupert Brooke (see excerpts dated 1913 and 1913). In the following excerpt from his 1929 introduction to a later edition of the collection, Grierson surveys Donne's career.]*

Sensual Donne has been called, but it is not quite the right word. Hot-blooded and passionate he was, with a passion in which body and soul are sometimes inextricably blended, again in open conflict, and again conceived in abstract separation from one another, but sensual in a more general and deliberate way, without the appeal of passion, he is not. His poetry has nothing to say of the pleasures of eating and drinking, like that of his friend Ben Jonson, and the impression one gathers from poems, records, and letters is of one indifferent or even ascetic in regard to such pleasures. Even the most audacious of the *Elegies*, compared with similar exercises by Carew and others, are agitated and aerated by a passionate play of wit that makes a difference, the absence of which, the more frigidly sensuous tone, marks clearly as *not* by Donne many poems that have been attributed to him. It is noteworthy too how little stress Donne lays on beauty in his love-poems, the aesthetic element in passion. The feeling for pure beauty was somewhat defective in his composition. The want of it is the most definite limitation to the high quality of his poetry.

Not sensual nor sensuous but passionate is the note of the young Donne and his verse, an intense susceptibility to the fascination of sex, a fascination that at once allures and repels, enthralls and awakens a spirit of scornful rebellion. He ranges through the whole gamut of passion from its earthliest to its most abstractly detached moods. For there are different strata in the love poems thrown down together in such confused order by the first editors. At the one extreme are poems of seduction and illicit love with its accompaniment of passion and scorn. Such are most of the *Elegies*, and in the *Songs and Sonets* a concentrated outburst as 'The Apparition,' or so finely woven a web of thought as 'The Extasie,' though the latter, as the poet warms to his theme, as the wheels of his chariot grow hot with driving, becomes a vindication of the interconnexion and interdependence of soul and body, which was to be a cardinal principle of Donne's religious thought at a later period. One may, if one pleases, descry through these poems a liaison with a married woman, an intrigue with an unmarried girl in 'The Perfume,' or one may read them as witty and paradoxical elaborations of general theses suggested by Donne's naturalistic revolt against the insincerities of Petrarchian sonnetteers,—the fickleness of women, his own delight in change, the folly of confining love by rules and relationships, sophisticated justifications of seduction, scorn of women's affected constancy, and of the physical basis of love which no refinements and hyperboles of love-poets can disguise. Some breathe, even if the main theme be the same, a purer and more simply passionate note, the twelfth *Elegy* ['**His parting from her**'] which seems to tell of a wife passionately loved in secret though over them hung the

> husband's threatening eyes
> That flam'd with the oily sweat of jealousy,

and a large body of the songs as '**I wonder by my troth**', '**For God's sake hold your tongue and let me love**', '**If yet I have not all thy love**', '**Oh do not die**', '**Twice or thrice**

had I loved thee', 'All kings and all their favourites', 'I'll tell thee now, dear love, what thou shalt do', 'Whoever comes to shroud me do not harm', 'Take heed of loving me', 'So, so break off this last lamenting kiss'. Some of these may, though I rather doubt it, belong to a later period when Donne was the lover and wooer of Ann More. To a later period certainly belongs a small group of songs, and perhaps the sixteenth *Elegy,* ['**On his Mistris**']. The songs are 'Sweetest love, I do not go', 'As virtuous men pass mildly away', and 'A Valediction: of weeping.' These were written after his marriage when business of one kind or another called Donne away from his home. They are a beautifully patterned expression of the depth and sweetness of the affection which united the sorely tried couple and contrast strangely with some of the poems with which they stand cheek by jowl.

There remains a group of songs that present somewhat of a problem. They show us Donne in the, rather unusual for him, traditional attitude of the Petrarchian wooer of a fair but obdurate Laura, a lady whom he reproaches, not for fickleness or sensuality or a halfhearted reluctance to yield to love, but for a too impeccable coldness:

> O perverse sex where none is true but shee,
> Who's therefore true because her truth kills mee.

These poems are '**Twicknam Garden,**' the sombre and powerful '**Nocturnall upon St. Lucies Day,**' '**The Blossome,**' '**The Primrose,**' '**The Relique,**' and '**The Dampe**'. None of the *Elegies* is in this key. In them the tone is set, not by Petrarch, but by Ovid.

It would be easier, probably, to accept the explanation which I have already ventured to propound if one might eliminate '**The Blossome,**' '**The Primrose,**' and '**The Dampe,**' for in these there is a strain of the more familiar Donne, sardonic and sensual. Apart from these, and perhaps including them, I am disposed to argue that the change of tone in this group of poems represents a difference in the social status of the persons addressed, that he is here, like other poets, adopting the Petrarchian convention to pay compliments to the noble ladies of his acquaintance. The class of women to whom, or on whom, he had composed the *Elegies* and *Songs and Sonets* of a similar kind had been that common object of young lawyers' and courtiers' freer advances and more audacious wit, the wives and daughters of citizens, women of Donne's own rank and station. In the group under consideration, as in the '**Letter to the Countesse of Huntingdon,**' the persons addressed, actual or ideal, more probably the first, are of a higher rank. It may be an accident that the titles of three of them, '**Twicknam Garden,**' '**A Nocturnall upon St. Lucies Day,**' and '**The Primrose**' suggest a connexion with the Countess of Bedford and Mrs. Magdalen Herbert. . . . I have a lurking suspicion that '**Twicknam Garden**', and '**St. Lucies Day,**' were exquisite and passionate compliments to his great lady-patron, Lucy, Countess of Bedford, who occupied Twickenham Park from 1608 to 1617. Nor need even the devout Mrs. Herbert, of whose earlier years we know little, have felt indignant on the receipt of such an impassioned compliment as '**The Relique**':

> These miracles we did; but now alas,
> All measure and all language I should pass,
> Should I tell what a miracle she was.

It is more difficult to imagine her the person addressed in **'The Primrose'** and **'The Dampe.'** If a reference to her is ruled out, on the strength of what we know of her from Walton and on general considerations, then these poems may be the product of the years in which Donne began, as a member of Sir Thomas Egerton's household, to move in a more exalted sphere than that which the young law-student had frequented in his more unregenerate days. They are the compliments he paid to ladies like the Countess of Huntingdon and others, charming because passionate compliments with just a touch of more daring suggestion which quite possibly these not too prudish young ladies would not resent. They heard in the theatre and at Court abundance of such frank speech as a later age would not have tolerated. It is after all convention that regulates both the length of a lady's skirt and the kind of compliments one may pay her. Lady Bedford would have been more scandalized at the thought of going through the street in the attire of a Highland regiment than at some freedom of language in a kind of poetry which everyone understood to be purely conventional.

The conflict of moods which the first group of these poems betrays, the war of sense and spirit, the awareness of body and soul as complementary and yet antagonistic, becomes more intelligible against such a background as I have suggested, the revolt against a too strong superimposed bias. Donne's nature had revolted, asserted its claim to life and experience. But experience is bitter as well as sweet—sweet in the mouth but bitter in the belly. Inde-

Autograph copy of "The Damp."

pendence humiliates as well as exalts. The emancipated instincts realize their limitations. The spiritual and ascetic impulses reassert their claim when passion has spent itself. Strife and bitterness succeed, finding vent in scornful satire and an exaggeration of sensuality or an equally extravagant and abstract idealism, till the tumult subsides, feeling gathers strength again, and body and soul are merged in the passion of the moment. 'The imagination of a boy is healthy and the mature imagination of a man is healthy; but there is a space of life between in which the soul is in a ferment, the character is undecided, the way of life uncertain, the ambition thick-sighted: thence proceeds mawkishness and all the thousand bitters which these men I speak of necessarily taste of in going over these pages.' So says Keats in the preface to *Endymion*. There were factors and elements in the ferment of Donne's soul which Keats did not know till he was a dying man; and the instinct for beauty was too uncertain in the older poet, too arrogantly controlled by a restless intellect, for him ever to attain to the peace of great imaginative work, though he perhaps comes nearest to it in the beautiful prose of some of the passages in his sermons.

But Donne was no ordinary young man carried by a swing of the pendulum from a too strict education to a life of debauchery and then again to repentance. The movement which these poems reflect in its excesses was one of thought as well as feeling, and the thought remained a central one in all his later development, even if he never succeeded in working it out to a balanced and harmonious conception of life. The dualism of body and soul he refused to accept as the absolute one to which medieval thought, influenced by Neo-Platonism, had tended. The body is not simply evil, the spirit good, sense a corrupter and misleader, the soul pure and heavenward aspiring. Man is body and soul, and neither can be complete without the other. To separate them absolutely is heresy alike in love and in religion:

> Love's not so pure and abstract as they use
> To say which have no mistress but the Muse;
> But as all else being elemented too,
> Love sometimes would contemplate, sometimes do.

The same thought in its religious bearing was to recur in many of his poems and letters and sermons:

> A resurrection is a second rising to that state from which anything is formerly fallen. Now though by death the soul do not fall into any such state as that it can complain (for what can that lack which God fills?), yet by death the soul falls from that for which it was infused and poured into man at first, that is to be the form of that body, the king of that kingdom; and therefore when in the general resurrection the soul returns to that state for which it was created and to which it hath an affection even in the fulness of the joys of Heaven; then when the soul returns to her office, to make up the man, because the whole man hath, therefore the soul hath a resurrection.

Just so Blake pictures the passionate reunion of soul and body.

But Donne was not yet a preacher penitent for his early excesses. The experience through which he passed in these early years is really a typical though salient instance of the movement of thought and feeling which we call the Renaissance. It is the movement, thrown into sharp relief by the peculiar character of Donne's upbringing, from conceptions of life and morality which made the joys of another world the goal of life and the measure of man's conduct to conceptions in which this world and man's sensible nature are at least constituent elements in the good for which he strives.

Love and poetry were quite certainly not the sole concern of the years between 1592 and 1596 when Donne was a student of law at Lincoln's Inn, 'giggling and making giggle' with Davies and Hoskins and others, like himself,

> Of study and play made strange hermaphrodites.

'In the most unsettled days of his youth', says Walton, 'his bed was not able to detain him beyond the hour of four in the morning; and it was no common business that drew him out of his chamber till past ten; all which time was employed in study, although he took great liberty after it.' For these are the years in which Donne wrote the first three *Satyres*. Several things in them show his familiarity with the London of 1594-6. Bank's performing horse and the performing elephant, the ape that would come over the chain for a mention of the Queen (as later of King James) but sit still . . . for the Pope and the King of Spain, figure alike in Donne's *Satyres* and the *Epigrams* which Davies composed in 1594. Donne's second *Satyre* ['**Satyre II**'] and Davies's 'Gulling Sonnets' were directed against the same person, a lawyer who had turned poet and published in 1594 *Zepheria*, a series of sonnets full of legal terms and long, harsh words, though Donne covertly extends the satire to include the mean lawyer who makes money by denouncing Catholics. And the picture these *Satyres* present is just such as Walton indicates. 'Away, thou fondling, motley humourist,' he cries to a young gallant, like himself 'a visiter of ladies', but not able to share his graver studies, who has broken in upon him before the hour of ten in the morning:

> Leave me and in this standing wooden chest
> Consorted with these few books let me lie
> In prison and here be coffin'd when I die.
> Here are God's conduits, grave divines; and here
> Nature's Secretary, the philosopher,
> And jolly statesman which teach how to tie
> The sinews of a city's mystic body;
> Here gathering chroniclers, and by them stand
> Giddy fantastic poets of each land.

The poets we know from a later letter to Buckingham included Spanish poets, and doubtless also Latin, Italian, French and English. Among the chroniclers were Holinshed and Stowe, but also more serious historians as Surius and Sleidan. Nature's Secretary is, of course, Aristotle. Among the divines would be Thomas Aquinas and some of the older theologians, but the majority would be modern controversialists—Spanish, French, Italian and German; and the latest volumes on Donne's shelf in 1594-5 would be the *Disputationes de Controversiis Christianae Religionis* of Cardinal Bellarmine, issued in 1593, for he later showed 'the then Dean of Gloucester . . . all the Cardinal's works with many weighty observations under his own hand' (Walton). The trend of his thought on religious controversies, the line of escape by which he made his way to conformity, is indicated in the third of the *Satyres* ['**Satyre III**']. (pp. xxv-xxvi)

Donnes's poems abound in thinly veiled allusions to the unhappy lot of his co-religionists. His position was difficult, the way of escape which he found is interesting, though easy to misrepresent by a critic who has no sympathy with or understanding of the complexities of the human heart. It is very clearly indicated in the *Satyre* in question. He had studied the religious controversies of the day. . . . He sees that the religion of most men is largely a matter of accident, the country they were born in, the religion of their godfathers, or of capricious choice. A taste for antiquity draws some men to Rome; a distaste for ceremonies and the fringes of worship drives others to Geveva. It is a toss up between a 'church in the lake' and a 'church upon seven hills'. Yet surely of all things religion should be the subject of careful consideration and deliberate choice, to the making of which tradition and reason should both contribute. But for Donne as for a later poet:

> There lives more faith in honest doubt
> Believe me than in half the creeds.
> believe me this
> He's not of none nor worst, that seeks the best.
> To adore or scorn an image, or protest,
> May all be bad; doubt wisely; in strange way
> To stand inquiring right is not to stray;
> To sleep or run wrong is. On a huge hill
> Cragged and steep truth stands, and he that will
> Reach her about must and about must go
> And what the hill's suddenness resists win so.

It was along this line of intellectual inquiry that Donne detached himself from Catholicism rather than by any change of heart. The position he reached is clearly stated in a later letter to his friend Goodyere: 'You know I never fettered nor imprisoned the word religion; not straitening it Friarly *ad religiones factitias* (as the Romans well call their orders of religion) nor immuring it in a Rome or a Wittenberg or a Geneva. They are all virtual beams of one sun, and wheresoever they find clay hearts they harden them into dust and they entender and mollify waxen.' But the natural inference from such a premise is that one may, and so ought, to conform to the Church of one's King and country. There, had Donne found a secular career, he would probably have left it; but King James and circumstances made him rather, one suspects, against his will a controversialist. (pp. xxvii-xxviii)

For Donne the consequences were disastrous. He never again until, after long internal strife and the disappointment of other hopes he entered the ministry, found honourable employment which could give him real independence. The years that followed were years of wearing poverty and humiliating dependence. (p. xxxiii)

The record of these years in writings, private and intended for publication, form a mirror reflecting vividly the complexity of his character, his many-sided erudition, his vigorous and subtle mind. 'Jack Donne' was not dead and buried in Benedick the married man or the melancholy suitor and dependent. The audacious wit of the early poems still found an outlet in his intercourse with the gallants and courtiers of his acquaintance, the Roes, Thomas and John, cousins, of whom the one after a wild career died in Jonson's arms of the plague, the other became the great ambassador to the Mogul and the friend of the Queen of Bohemia, Henry Goodyere to whom Donne gave so much unavailing good advice, Thomas Coryat; John Hoskins, the young men who contributed to Overbury's *Characters*, and others. Numerous *jeux d'esprit*, clever but marred by the bad taste of the time, survive in manuscript or in badly printed texts. The fourteenth *Elegy* ['**A Tale of a Citizen and His Wife**'], if it be Donne's (and there is no sufficient evidence to reject if) cannot have been written earlier than 1609, a year in which he was also composing 'divine poems'. Some of the Paradoxes and Problems, of which not all have found their way into print, Seem to belong to this period. He had hardly finished the serious and heavy *Pseudo-Martyr* in 1610 when he assailed the Jesuits, for, whatever his sympathies with old English Catholics, he always hated the Society, in *Ignatius, his Conclave*, in Latin and English, a wildly paradoxical pamphlet full of the clever but execrable wit which polluted politico-religious controversy in those good Christian days. One will never comprehend or even state aright the problem of Donne's character if one fails to recognize that these 'evaporations of wit', as he calls them, seemed to him quite compatible with more serious pursuits controversial and devout.

The record of these more serious pursuits in this interval of fourteen years is the *Pseudo-Martyr;* the *Biathanatos*; poems in the form of verse-letters to friends and to noble ladies and other patrons; as well as prose-letters to the same persons. The first is not a work of interest to the student of Donne's character. His controversial prose has not the poetic quality of his sermons. The close, acute controversial methods of the day did not encourage eloquence. The *Biathanatos*, written in the same crabbed style, has a much greater interest. It was not published till 1644, long after the author's death, but it was sent in MS. from time to time to his friends with the prayer that it should not be published: 'Preserve it for me if I live, and if I die ... publish it not, but yet burn it not'. The treatise is not a defence of suicide as a modern might write such a defence, a grave consideration of the right of a man to commit suicide to escape from inevitable suffering provided his doing so did not entail loss or suffering upon others. Donne was a Christian and could never have raised such a question, for on no duty had the Church since the days of St. Augustine and earlier spoken more clearly, and there is no moral question the answer to which depends so obviously on the belief or disbelief in another world, on a religious sanction for morality. Donne, indeed, raises the question as though that were what he was going to discuss. He wrote the work probably, as Goethe sometimes did, to work off a mood with which he was beset; but the answer which he gives in the end is not one which in itself could dispel the mood in which the question has originated. What that mood was he states very clearly: 'Beza, a man as eminent and illustrious in the full glory and noon of learning, as others were in the dawning and morning, when any the least sparkle was notorious, confesseth of himself that only for the anguish of a scurf which overran his head he had once drowned himself from the miller's bridge in Paris, if his uncle had not by chance come that way. I have often such a sickly inclination; and whether it be because I had my first breeding and conversation with men of a suppressed and afflicted religion, accustomed to the despite of death and hungry of an imagined martyrdom; or that the common enemy find that door worst locked against him in me, or that there be a perplexity and flexibility in the doctrine itself; or because my conscience assures me that no rebellious grudging at God's gift, nor other sinful concurrence accompanies these thoughts in me, or that a brave scorn or that a faint cowardliness beget it, whensoever any affliction assails me methinks I

have the keys of my prison in mine own hand, and no remedy presents itself so soon to my heart as mine own sword. Often meditation of this hath won me to a charitable interpretation of their action who die so; and provoked me a little to watch and exagitate their reasons which pronounce so peremptory judgements upon them.' So speaks the man of the Renaissance in Donne, but the answer is worked out on the lines of a fine question in Christian casuistry, and it is difficult to see what consolation for such a mood is to be extracted from what in the end Donne concludes, namely, that there may be, and have been, cases in which a man may legitimately lay down his life by his own action to serve God and his fellow-men, as Samson did, and the death of Christ on the cross was itself a voluntary surrender of His life, 'for we say the same that this may be done only when the honour of God may be promoted that way and no other'. (pp. xxxiii-xxxvi)

Only a few of the verse-letters are actually dated, but it is not difficult to group them with sufficient approximation to their chronological sequence. ... The letter which [begins] '**Sir, more than kisses**' was written before April 1598; and the letter '**Here's no more news**' belongs to the same year or to 1599, when in '**Went you to conquer**' Donne writes to Wotton, now campaigning with Essex in Ireland. These letters and one or two perhaps of the shorter notes to the Woodwards (e.g. '**If, as mine is, thy life a slumber be**') belong to the interval between the Islands Voyage and the date of Donne's marriage. They have a note of the *insouciance* of the young man who wrote the earlier songs and elegies. The rest of those addressed to personal friends, as Sir Henry Goodyere, Rowland Woodward, Henry Wotton departing as an ambassador to Venice, are subsequent to that date and are saturated with the melancholy and almost listless resignation of the prose-letters of these years, the years spent at Pyrford, Mitcham, and London, before in 1608 or 1609 the hopes of a turn of fortune and the favours of the Countess of Bedford brightened Donne's mercurial spirits.

The letters to the Duchess and other noble ladies form a group by themselves. They lack the intimate self-revealing note of those to Goodyere and Wotton and Woodward. They abound in extravagances of metaphysical compliment. Even more than the early extravagances of perverse wit one might regard the excesses of flattery in these letters and the worse funeral elegies as 'an expense of spirit in a waste of shame', but what was a poor man to do who had no profession and to whom a child was born every year? It is difficult to exempt from this censure even the much-lauded *Anniversaries*, at least in their entirety. There are two interwoven strands in these strange poems, a eulogy of the young Elizabeth Drury, which passes all limits of decent or convincing hyperbole, even the hyperbole of extravagant grief, and a *de contemptu mundi* passing in the *Second Anniversarie* into a contemplation of the glories of heaven the soul's true home, which is the finest thing in the poem and is developed with the close-packed eloquence, the passionate feeling quickening the subtle thought and manifold erudition, the shining felicity of phrase, the impressive rhetoric of the great passages in the sermons. It is one of the strangest poems in the language in its combination of what is execrable with what is magnificent, of the ingenuities of a too subtle and erudite wit irradiated by a passionate imaginative apprehension of the spiritual and transcendent, of frigidities and harshness of imagery and phrasing with felicitous and incandescent phrases and varied harmonies.

These manifold contradictions encounter us at every turn in the study of Donne's life and character and work. No one can trace what Dr. Jessop called his 'steps to the altar', as Sir Edmund Gosse's biography has illuminated them, with entire equanimity or without a sense of the strange complexity of the human mind which makes compatible with one another sincere religious feeling and essential moral soundness and the strangest acquiescences and aberrations of moral judgement and taste. Donne was a sincerely religious man before he became a divine. The whole spirit of his work risks being misapprehended if one think of him as fundamentally insincere, or fail to recognize that neither the extravaganes of his youth, the ambitious compliances of his later years, nor the sceptical sense he reveals of the contradictions inherent in theology and science—of which no man of his day was more acutely aware—ever effaced the impression of his early religious upbringing or corrupted the fundamental honesty and loyalty of his nature. As a son, as a husband, as a friend, Donne's character whenever it reveals itself is unexceptionable. Nothing could be finer than the tone and spirit of some of the most intimate of his letters to Goodyere, and no man had a larger cortege of loyal and devoted friends, from Goodyere and Wotton and the Brookes and the Woodwards of his youth to Sir Robert Ker and the Earl of Carlisle and Bishop King and Izaak Walton in his older age. Yet on the other hand there are elements in Donne's writings, not the early poems alone, but in his later writings (even in his sermons), and there are incidents in his life, not his early life alone, of which our knowledge is largely conjectural, but in his progress towards the altar, and even in his clerical career, which are morally and aesthetically jarring and repellent. It will not do to cut Donne's life across, as some of his clerical critics would do, and turning away pained eyes from his early extravagances portray with unction his later life as a glorious example of the great penitent. To some of us the early excesses in wit and indecency of his poems are more easily condoned than some of the compliances of his later life—his fulsome flattery of noble ladies, his protestations of devotion to the service of Jame's abominable favourites, Somerset and Buckingham, his pluralities and eager touting for preferment. (pp. xxxvii-xxxix)

The chief works of these last years were his numerous sermons, his strange *Essays on Divinity* (published in 1652), the *Devotions upon Emergent Occasions, and Severall steps in my Sicknes* and the best of his *Divine Poems.* The latter do not all belong to this period. A fair number date from the distressful years which followed his marriage, the years when, if in trouble, Donne's thoughts turned towards the Church, but, when the warm sun of favour reappeared reawakening ambition, his interests grew more secular. The sonnets called *La Corona,* because of the way they are linked together, were sent to Mrs. Herbert and to the Earl of Dorset in 1608 or 1609, in which year the **'Litanie'** was also composed. **'On the Annuntiation and Passion'** was written on the last day of 1608, as that was counted, i.e. March 25, 1609. **'The Crosse'** and the fragment on the **'Resurrection'** date from about the same time. **'Goodfriday'** is dated 1613, two years before his ordination and shortly after he had completed the very pagan and sensuous **'Epithalamion'** on the marriage of the Princess Elizabeth. But

the finest of these poems are the expression of his heart under the influence of the death of his wife in 1617 and the sicknesses that preceded his own death. In these and in his sermons Donne's work recaptures the peculiar charm of his early love verses at their best, the unique blend of passionate feeling and rapid subtle thinking, the strange sense that his verse gives of a certain conflict between the passionate thought and the varied and often elaborate pattern into which he moulds its expression, resulting in a strange blend of harshness and constraint with reverberating and penetrating harmony. No poems give more than the *Holy Sonnets* and the three hymns composed in 1619 and 1623, **'In what torn ship'**, **'Since I am coming'**, and **'Wilt thou forgive'**, the sense of conflict of soul, of faith and hope snatched and held desperately, of harmony evoked from harsh combinations as of one who tears his

> Pleasures with rough strife
> Thorough the iron gates of life.

The note of these poems is that of the greatest of the sermons. The same spirit is at work in both, the same restless and subtle wit, the same poetic fancy, but in the latter the wit is more subdued, the fancy more sustained by the dominant mood of religious solemnity. As they stand, each sermon is a careful work of art. The sermon as delivered was not the sermon as we have it. The printed sermon is the spoken sermon set down subsequently by the preacher, corrected, polished, expanded at times from one sermon into two. 'At the Haghe, December 16, 1619. I preached upon this text. Since in my sickness at Abrey Hatch in Essex, 1630, revising my short notes of that sermon I digested them into two.'

Donne is the only English poet of the first rank who is also a great orator, it may be as some have claimed a greater orator than poet; but in fact his poetry and his oratory have much in common, for poetry as an art may be said to move between the poles of song or music on the one hand and of eloquence on the other, pure song in which the melody itself is the chief communicant of the feeling, as in Shelley's poetry:

> My soul is an enchanted boat
> Which like a sleeping swan doth float
> Upon the silver waves of thy sweet singing;
> And thine doth like an angel sit
> Beside the helm conducting it,
> Whilst all the winds with melody are ringing.

That is one extreme, the other is the ordered, polished eloquence to which serious English poetry moved under the influence of Milton whose successors were Dryden, Pope, Gray, and others of lesser rank, and to which it returned in Tennyson after the explosive and technically somewhat uncertain romantic revival, in the main a lyrical revival. But the poetry of Donne and his most notable followers is neither the one nor the other. It is a poetry of talk vigorous and direct, but poetry because it is 'musicè composita'. His abrupt openings, his vigorous, unconventional, unpolished yet felicitous phrasing, his wit, his imagery homely and erudite—all suggest one who is talking, arguing, expostulating, playing with his thoughts, but neither polishing his eloquence nor surrendering himself to the pure delight of song. But his talk is poetry because it is musically drawn out from line to line in surprisingly varied and elaborate stanzas or paragraphs. And his oratory is of the same kind, not the oratory of the great French preachers or of Burke, carrying one on from point to point in the development of an elaborate, coherent, carefully jointed argument. That was not the method of the preacher in the seventeenth century, of Andrews or of Donne. A sermon of Donne's is the exposition, word by word, of a text, not what we should call to-day a scientific exposition trying to discover by every availabe means philological, philosophical, historical, what the words meant for the writer who used them and when he used them, but an exposition erudite, that is based on the tradition of the Fathers and the Schoolmen, fanciful, practical, applying the word to the conscience and faith of his hearers; and the style is that of one holding with his audience a heart-to-heart talk.

An artistic consequence of the method is that the greater flights are not gradually led up to by a *crescendo*, not elaborate perorations as in Burke's speeches. They spring from the thought of the moment, the word or doctrine immediately under consideration, and sometimes there are no such moments. Donne is not a showy preacher on the quest for opportunities to introduce purple passages. Some of the best of his sermons, as that preached before Princess Elizabeth at Heidelberg, move on a steady level of grave and sober reflection, just thoughts, happy fancies, weighty sentences, but no bursts of eloquence. It is when the course of his reflective exposition brings him to some moving theme, the occasional mercies of God death and the resurrection prayer, sin, the Last Judgement, that the preacher rises to moving imagery and pealing harmonies, and even here it is the eloquence of one who talks rather than declaims, talks to himself as well as to his audience. A sermon will open in the same abrupt way as a poem. A good example is the fine exordium to the sermon preached at the Cross on the 15th of September, 1622, and printed in the same year. The text is: 'They fought from Heaven; the stars in their courses fought against Sisera,' and the preacher opens thus: 'All the words of God are always sweet in themselves, says David; but sweeter in the mouth, and in the pen of some of the prophets, and some of the Apostles than of others, as they differed in their natural gifts, or in their education: but sweetest of all, where the Holy Ghost hath been pleased to set the words of God to music, and to convey it in a song; and this text is of that kind.' And so for a paragraph of two or three pages (in the first quarto) he sustains the effect of varying cadences and the blowing of silver trumpets before he settles down to the 'division' of his text. Such preaching is more akin both to talk and to poetry than it is to declamation, even the declamation of Burke. From one point of view a sermon by Donne has the appearance of a closely knotted rope, point succeeding point in a continuous, conversational exposition; from another, of a sustained poetical rhapsody, rising and falling with the inspiration of the moment, always earnest, passionate, pleading, but ever and again pealing out in notes of warning or with the music of the spheres. Neither the argument nor the appeal to the feelings have all the power they once possessed. Statements are made as indisputable which seem to us far from being so; that called right which our conscience would arraign. But the fancy is still vivid; the feeling still warm; the music of the periods undulled. (pp. xli-xlv)

[Donne was] one of the strangest and greatest ornaments of the Church of England and of English poetry and prose.

Great and strange—Donne is not one of the lesser yet interesting figures whose merits and limitations it is equally easy to appreciate. His is the more difficult case of one whose great virtues and great faults are equally undeniable and inextricably blended. In his life and in his poetry they are always present to repel and to fascinate ; and one or other has to gain the upper hand. You must feel the fascination of Donne as man and poet with all his faults, or leave him alone. There was nothing in his poetry that appealed to the taste to which Tennyson ministered, though Browning felt his fascination to the full. No verse of his found its way into the *Golden Treasury* for 'Absence, hear thou my protestation' is not by Donne, nor has it the essential quality of Donne's poetry in thought or style or prosody. It is a relic of the poetry inspired by Sidney. The present Poet Laureate and Sir William Watson feel nothing but distaste for the frequent ugliness of his imagery and wit, his prosody 'which is not Milton's but the forerunner of Dryden's', the evil strain in his psychology, the 'pestilential' character of his theological and pseudo-scientific erudition. To Donne has fallen the unhappy lot, says Sir William Watson, of being read only by scholars. But this is not quite true. No English poet of the past has exercised a stronger influence upon the poetry of the younger poets of to-day, for their experiments too have a root in the consciousness that the ugly and the beautiful are stangely blended in passionate experience, their prosody is a result of an effort to keep metre in touch, not alone with music, but with human speech, phrases and cadences such as men do use, and their poetry seeks to charge itself, not with experience only, but with the metaphysic which strives to transcend and to interpret experience. (pp. xlvi-xlvii)

H. J. C. Grierson, in an introduction to The Poems of John Donne, *edited by H. J. C. Grierson, Oxford University Press, London, 1929, pp. xiii-xlvii.*

VIRGINIA WOOLF (essay date 1931)

[*An English novelist, essayist, and short story writer. Woolf is considered one of the most prominent literary figures of twentieth-century English literature. Like her contemporary James Joyce, with whom she is often compared. Woolf is remembered as one of the most innovative of the stream-of-consciousness novelists. Concerned primarily with depicting the life of the mind, she revolted against traditional narrative techniques and developed her own highly individualized style. Woolf's works, noted for their subjective explorations of character's inner lives and for their delicate poetic quality have had a lasting effect on the art of the novel. A discerning and influential critic and essayist as well as a novelist. Woolf began writing reviews for the* Times Literary Supplement *at an early age. Her critical essays, termed "creative, appreciative, and subjective" by Barbara Currier Bell and Carol Ohmann, cover almost the entire range of English literature and contain some of her finest prose. Along with Lytton Strachey, Roger Fry, Clive Bell, and others. Woolf and her husband Leonard formed the literary coterie known as the "Bloomsbury Group." In the following excerpt from an essay written in 1931 and published the following year in* The Common Reader, second series, *Woolf celebrates the tercentenary of the death of Donne by "trying to analyze the meaning that his voice has for us as it strikes upon the ear after this long flight across the story seas that separate us from the age of Elizabeth."*]

When we think how many millions of words have been written and printed in England in the past three hundred years, and how the vast majority have died out without leaving any trace, it is tempting to wonder what quality the words of Donne possess that we should still hear them distinctly today. Far be it from us to suggest even in this year of celebration and pardonable adulation (1931) that the poems of Donne are popular reading or that the typist if we look over her shoulder in the Tube, is to be discovered reading Donne as she returns from her office. But he is read; he is audible—to that fact new editions and frequent articles testify, and it is worth perhaps trying to analyse the meaning that his voice has for us as it strikes upon the ear after this long flight across the stormy seas that separate us from the age of Elizabeth.

But the first quality that attracts us is not his meaning, charged with meaning as his poetry is, but something much more unmixed and immediate; it is the explosion with which he bursts into speech. All preface, all parleying have been consumed; he leaps into poetry the shortest way. One phrase consumes all preparation:

> I long to talke with some old lover's ghost, or

> He is starke mad, whoever sayes,
> That he hath beene in love an houre.

At once we are arrested. Stand still, he commands.

> Stand still, and I will read to thee
> A Lecture, Love, in love's philosophy.

And stand still we must. With the first words a shock passes through us; perceptions, previously numb and torpid, quiver into being; the nerves of sight and hearing are quickened; the 'bracelet of bright hair' burns in our eyes. But, more remarkably, we do not merely become aware of beautiful remembered lines; we feel ourselves compelled to a particular attitude of mind. Elements that were dispersed in the usual stream of life become, under the stroke of Donne's passion, one and entire. The world, a moment before, cheerful, humdrum, bursting with character and variety, is consumed. We are in Donne's world now. All other views are sharply cut off.

In this power of suddenly surprising and subjugating the reader, Donne excels most poets. It is his characteristic quality; it is thus that he lays hold upon us, summing up his essence in a word or two. But it is an essence that, as it works in us, separates into strange contraries at odds with one another. Soon we begin to ask ourselves of what this essence is composed, what elements have met together to cut so deep and complex an impression. Some obvious clues lie strewn on the surface of the poems. When we read the **Satyres,** for example, we need no external proof to tell us that these are the work of a boy. He has all the ruthlessness and definiteness of youth, its hatred of the follies of middle age and of convention. Bores, liars, courtiers—detestable humbugs and hypocrites as they are, why not sum them up and sweep them off the face of the earth with a few strokes of the pen? And so these foolish figures are drubbed with an ardour that proves how much hope and faith and delight in life inspire the savagery of youthful scorn. But, as we read on, we begin to suspect that the boy with the complex and curious face of the early portrait—bold yet subtle, sensual yer nerve drawn—possessed qualities that made him singular among the young. It is

not simply that the huddle and pressure of youth which outthinks its words had urged him on too fast for grace or clarity. It may be that there is in this clipping and curtailing, this abrupt heaping of thought on thought, some deeper dissatisfaction than that of youth with age, of honesty with corruption. He is in rebellion, not merely against his elders, but against something antipathetic to him in the temper of his time. His verse has the deliberate bareness of those who refuse to avail themselves of the current usage. It has the extravagance of those who do not feel the pressure of opinion, so that sometimes judgment fails them, and they heap up strangeness for strangeness' sake. He is one of those nonconformists, like Browning and Meredith, who cannot resist glorifying their nonconformity by a dash of wilful and gratuitous eccentricity. But to discover what Donne disliked in his own age, let us imagine some of the more obvious influences that must have told upon him when he wrote his early poems—let us ask what books he read. And by Donne's own testimony we find that his chosen books were the works of 'grave Divines'; of philosophers; of 'jolly Statesmen, which teach how to tie The sinewes of a cities mistique bodie'; and chroniclers. Clearly he liked facts and arguments. If there are also poets among his books, the epithets he applies to them, 'Giddie fantastique', seem to disparage the art, or at least to show that Donne knew perfectly well what qualities were antipathetic to him in poetry. And yet he was living in the very spring of English poetry. Some of Spenser might have been on his shelves; and Sidney's *Arcadia;* and the *Paradise of Dainty Devices,* and Lylys's *Euphues.* He had the chance, and apparently took it— 'I tell him of new playes'—of going to the theatre; of seeing the plays of Marlowe and Shakespeare acted. When he went abroad in London, he must have met all the writers of that time—Spenser and Sidney and Shakespeare and Jonson; he must have heard at this tavern or at that talk of new plays, of new fashions in verse, heated and learned discussion of the possibilities of he English language and the future of English poetry. And yet, if we turn to his biography, we find that he neither consorted with his contemporaries nor read what they wrote. He was one of those original beings who cannot draw profit, but are rather disturbed and distracted by what is being done round them at the moment. If we turn again to **Satyres,** it is easy to see why this should be so. Here is a bold and active mind that loves to deal with actual things, which struggles to express each shock exactly as it impinges upon his tight-stretched senses. A bore stops him in the street. He sees him exactly, vividly. . . . Then he likes to give the actual words that people say:

> He, like to a high stretcht lute string squeakt, O Sir,
> 'Tis sweet to talke of Kings. At Westminster,
> Said I, The man that keepes the Abbey tombes,
> And for his price doth with who ever comes,
> Of all our Harries, and our Edwards talke,
> From King to King and all their kin can walke:
> Your eares shall heare nought, but Kings; your eyes meet
> Kings only; The way to it, is Kingstreet.

His strength and his weakness are both to be found here. He selects one detail and stares at it until he has reduced it to the few words that express its oddity:

> And like a bunch of ragged carrets stand
> The short swolne fingers of thy gouty hand,

but he cannot see in the round, as a whole. He cannot stand apart and survey the large outline so that the description is always of some momentary intensity, seldom of the broader aspect of things. Naturally, then, he found it difficult to use the drama with its conflict of other characters; he must always speak from his own centre in soliloquy, in satire, in self-analysis. Spenser, Sidney, and Marlowe provided no helpful models for a man who looked out from this angle of vision. The typical Elizabethan with his love of eloquence, with his longing for brave new words, tended to enlarge and generalize. He loved wide landscapes, heroic virtues, and figures seen sublimely in outline or in heroic conflict. Even the prose-writers have the same habit of aggrandisement. When Dekker sets out to tell us how Queen Elizabeth died in the spring, he cannot describe her death in particular or that spring in particular; he must dilate upon all deaths and all springs.... (pp. 32-5)

Donne's genius was precisely the opposite of this. He diminished; he particularized. Not only did he see each spot and wrinkle which defaced the fair outline; but he noted with the utmost curiosity his own reaction to such contrasts and was eager to lay side by side the two conflicting views and to let them make their own dissonance. It is desire for nakedness in an age that was florid, this determination to record not the likenesses which go to compose a rounded and seemly whole, but the inconsistencies that break up semblances, the power to make us feel the different emotions of love and hate and laughter at the same time, that separate Donne from his contemporaries. And if the usual traffic of the day—to be buttonholed by a bore, to be snared by a lawyer, to be snubbed by a courtier—made so sharp an impression on Donne, the effect of falling in love was bound to be incomparably greater. Falling in love meant, to Donne, a thousand things; it meant being tormented and disgusted, disillusioned and enraptured but it also meant speaking the truth. The love poems, the elegies, and the letters thus reveal a figure of a very different calibre from the typical figure of Elizabethan love poetry. That great ideal, built up by a score of eloquent pens, still burns bright in our eyes. Her body was of alabaster, her legs of ivory; her hair was golden wire and her teeth pearls from the Orient. Music was in her voice and stateliness in her walk. She could love and sport and be faithless and yielding and cruel and true; but her emotions were simple, as befitted her person. Donne's poems reveal a lady of a very different cast. She was brown but she was also fair; she was solitary but also sociable; she was rustic yet also fond of city life; she was sceptical yet devout, emotional but reserved—in short she was a various and complex as Donne himself. As for choosing one type of human perfection and restricting himself to love her and her only, how could Donne, or any man who allowed his senses full play and honestly recorded his own moods, so limit his nature and tell such lies to placate the conventional and the decorous? Was not 'love's sweetest part, Variety'? 'Of music, joy, life and eternity Change is the nursery', he sang. The timid fashion of the age might limit a love to one woman. For his part he envied and admired the ancients, 'who held plurality of loves no crime':

But since this title honour hath been us'd,
Our weak credulity hath been abus'd.

We have fallen from our high estate; the golden laws of nature are repealed.

So through the glass of Donne's poetry, now darkly clouded, now brilliantly clear, we see pass in procession the many women whom he loved and hated—the common Julia whom he despised; the simpleton, to whom he taught the art to love; she who was married to an invalid husband, 'cag'd in a basket chair'; she who could only be loved dangerously by strategy; she who dreamt of him and saw him murdered as he crossed the Alps; she whom he had to dissuade from the risk of loving him; and lastly, the autumnal, the aristocratic lady for whom he felt more of reverence than of love—so they pass, common and rare, simple and sophisticated, young and old, noble and plebeian, and each casts a different spell and brings out a different lover, although the man is the same man, and the women, perhaps, are also phases of womanhood rather than separate and distinct women. In later years the Dean of St. Paul's would willingly have edited some of these poems and suppressed one of these lovers—the poet presumably of '**Going to Bed**' and '**Love's Warr**'. But the Dean would have been wrong. It is the union of so many different desires that gives Donne's love poetry not only its vitality but also a quality that is seldom found with such strength in the conventional and orthodox lover—its spirituality. If we do not love with the body, can we love with the mind? If we do not love variously, freely, admitting the lure first of this quality and then of that, can we at length choose out the one quality that is essential and adhere to it and so make peace among the warring elements and pass into a state of being which transcends the 'Hee and Shee'? Even while he was at his most fickle and gave fullest scope to his youthful lusts, Donne could predict the season of maturity when he would love differently, with pain and difficulty, one and one only. Even while he scorned and railed and abused, he divined another relationship which transcended change and parting and might, even in the bodies' absence, lead to unity and communion.... Such hints and premonitions of a further and finer state urged him on and condemn him to perpetual unrest and dissatisfaction with the present. He is tantalized by the sense that there is a miracle beyond any of these transient delights and disgusts. Lovers can, if only for a short space, reach a state of unity beyond time, beyond sex, beyond the body. And at last, for one moment, they reach it. In the '**Extasie**' they lie together on a bank,

All day, the same our postures were,
And wee said nothing, all the day....

This Extasie doth unperplex
(We said) and tell us what we love,
Wee see by this, it was not sexe,
Wee see, we saw not what did move....

Wee then, who are this new soule, know,
Of what we are compos'd, and made,
For, th'Atomies of which we grow,
Are soules, whom no change can invade.
But O alas, so long, so farre
Our bodies why doe wee forbeare?...

But O alas, he breaks off, and the words remind us that however much we may wish to keep Donne in one posture—for it is in these Extasies that lines of pure poetry suddenly flow as if liquefied by a great heat—so to remain in one posture was against his nature. Perhaps it is against the nature of things also. Donne snatches the intensity because he is aware of the change that must alter, of the discord that must interrupt.

Circumstances, at any rate, put it beyond his power to maintain that ecstasy for long. He had married secretly; he was a father; he was, as we are soon reminded, a vey poor yet a very ambitious man, living in a damp little house at Mitcham with a family of small children. The children were frequently ill. They cried, and their cries, cutting through the thin walls of the jerry-built house, disturbed him at his work. He sought sanctuary naturally enough elsewhere, and naturally had to pay rent for that relief. Great ladies—Lady Bedford, Lady Huntingdon, Mrs. Herbert—with well-spread tables and fair gardens, must be conciliated; rich men with the gift of rooms in their possession must be placated. Thus, after Donne the harsh satirist, and Donne the imperious lover, comes the servile and obsequious figure of Donne the devout servant of the great, the extravagant eulogist of little girls. And our relationship with him suddenly changes. In the satires and the love poems there was a quality—some psychological intensity and complexity—that brings him closer than his contemporaries, who often seem to be caught up in a different world from ours and to exist immune from our perplexities and swept by passions which we admire but cannot feel. Easy as it is to exaggerate affinities, still we may claim to be akin to Donne in our readiness to admit contrasts, in our desire for openness, in that psychological intricacy which the novelists have taught us with their slow, subtle, and analytic prose. But now, as we follow Donne in his progress, he leaves us in the lurch. He becomes more remote, inaccessible, and obsolete than any of the Elizabethans. It is as if the spirit of the age, which he had scorned and flouted, suddenly asserted itself and made this rebel its slave. And as we lose sight of the outspoken young man who hated society, and of the passionate lover, seeking some mysterious unity with his love and finding it miraculously, now here, now there, it is natural to abuse the system of patrons and patronage that thus seduced the most incorruptible of men. Yet it may be that we are too hasty. Every writer has an audience in view, and it may well be doubted if the Bedfords and the Drurys and the Herberts were worse influences than the libraries and the newspaper proprietors who fill the office of patron nowadays.

The comparison, it is true, presents great difficulties. The noble ladies who brought so strange an element into Donne's poetry, live only in the reflection, or in the distortion, that we find in the poems themselves. The age of memoirs and letter-writing was still to come. If they wrote themselves, and it is said that both Lady Pembroke and Lady Bedford were poets of merit, they did not dare to put their names to what they wrote, and it has vanished. But a diary here and there survives from which we may see the patroness more closely and less romantically. Lady Ann Clifford, for example, the daughter of a Clifford and a Russell, though active and practical and little educated—she was not allowed 'to learn any language because her father would not permit it'—felt, we can gather from the bald statements of her diary, a duty towards literature and to the makers of it as her mother, the patroness of the poet Daniel, had done before her. . . . It was she who paid for the first monument to Spenser in Westminster Abbey, and if, when she raised a tomb to her old tutor, she dwelt largely upon her own virtues and titles, she still acknowledged that even so great a lady as herself owed gratitude to the makers of books. Words from great writers nailed to the walls of the room in which she sat, eternally trans-

acting business, surrounded her as she worked, as they surrounded Montaigne in his tower in Burgundy.

Thus we may infer that Donne's relation to the Countess of Bedford was very different from any that could exist between a poet and a countess at the present time. There was something distant and ceremonious about it. To him she was 'as a vertuous Prince farre off'. The greatness of her office inspired reverence apart from her personality, just as the rewards within her gift inspired humility. He was her Laureate, and his songs in her praise were rewarded by invitations to stay with her at Twickenham and by those friendly meetings with men in power which were so effective in furthering the career of an ambitious man—and Donne was highly ambitious, not indeed for the fame of a poet, but for the power of a statesman. Thus when we read that Lady Bedford was 'God's Masterpiece', that she excelled all women in all ages, we realise that John Donne is not writing to Lucy Bedford; Poetry is saluting Rank. And this distance served to inspire reason rather than passion. Lady Bedford must have been a very clever woman, well versed in the finer shades of theology, to derive an instant or an intoxicating pleasure from the praises of her servant. Indeed, the extreme subtlety and erudition of Donne's poems to his patrons seems to show that one effect of writing for such an audience is to exaggerate the poet's ingenuity. What is not poetry but something tortured and difficult will prove to the patron that the poet is exerting his skill on her behalf. Then again, a learned poem can be handed round among statesmen and men of affairs to prove that the poet is no mere versifier, but capable of office and responsibility. But a change of inspiration that has killed many poets—witness Tennyson and the *Idylls of the King*—only stimulated another side of Donne's many-sided nature and many-faceted brain. As we read the long poems written ostensibly in praise of Lady Bedford, or in celebration of Elizabeth Drury (*An Anatomie of the World* and the *Progresse of the Soul),* we are made to reflect how much remains for a poet to write about when the season of love is over. When May and June are passed, most poets cease to write or sing the songs of their youth out of tune. But Donne survived the perils of middle age by virtue of the acuteness and ardour of his intellect. When 'the satyrique fires which urg'd me to have writt in skorne of all' were quenched, when 'My muse (for I had one), because I'm cold, Divorced herself', there still remained the power to turn upon the nature of things and dissect that. Even in the passionate days of youth Donne had been a thinking poet. He had dissected and analysed his own love. To turn from that to the anatomy of the world, from the personal to the impersonal, was the natural development of a complex nature. And the new angle to which his mind now pointed under the influence of middle age and traffic with the world, released powers that were held in check when they were directed against some particular courtier or some particular woman. Now his imagination, as if freed from impediment, goes rocketing up in flights of extravagant exaggeration. True, the rocket bursts; it scatters in a shower of minute, separate particles— curious speculations, wire-drawn comparisons, obsolete erudition; but, winged by the double pressure of mind and heart, of reason and imagination, it soars far and fast into a finer air. (pp. 36-42)

[These poems] need to be read currently rather to grasp the energy and power of the whole than to admire those separate lines which Donne suddenly strikes to illumine the stages of our long climb.

Thus, finally, we reach the last section of the book, the **Holy Sonnets** and **Divine Poems**. Again the poetry changes with the change of circumstances and of years. The patron has gone with the need of patronage. Lady Bedford has been replaced by a Prince still more virtuous and still more remote. To Him the prosperous, the important, the famous Dean of St. Paul's now turns. But how different is the divine poetry of this great dignitary from the divine poetry of the Herberts and the Vaughans! The memory of his sins returns to him as he writes. He has been burnt with 'lust and envy'; he has followed profane loves; he has been scornful and fickle and passionate and servile and ambitious. He has attained his end; but he is weaker and worse than the horse or the bull. Now too he is lonely. 'Since she whom I lov'd' is dead 'My good is dead.' Now at last his mind is 'wholly sett on heavenly things'. And yet how could Donne—that 'little world made cunningly of elements—be wholly set on any one thing. . . . It was impossible for the poet who had noted so curiously the flow and change of human life, and its contrasts, who was at once so inquisitive of knowledge and so sceptical, . . . who had owned allegiance to so many great Princess, the body, the King, the Church of England, to reach that state of wholeness and certainty which poets of purer life were able to maintain. His devotions themselves were feverish and fitful. 'My devout fitts come and goe away like a fantastique Ague.' They are full of contraries and agonies. Just as his love poetry at its most sensual will suddenly reveal the desire for a transcendent unity 'beyond the Hee and Shee', and his most reverential letters to great ladies will suddenly become love poems addressed by an amorous man to a woman of flesh and blood, so these last divine poems are poems of climbing and falling, of incongruous clamours and solemnities, as if the church door opened on the uproar of the street. That perhaps is why they still excite interest and disgust, contempt and admiration. For the Dean still retained the incorrigible curiosity of his youth. The temptation to speak the truth in defiance of the world even when he had taken all that the world had to give, still worked in him. An obstinate interest in the nature of his own sensations still troubled his age and broke its repose as it had troubled his youth and made him the most vigorous of satirists and the most passionate of lovers. There was no rest, no end, no solution even at the height of fame and on the edge of the grave for a nature plaited together of such diverse strands. The famous preparations that he made, lying in his shroud, being carved for his tomb, when he felt death approach are poles asunder from the falling asleep of the tired and content. He must still cut a figure and still stand erect—a warning perhaps, a portent certainly, but always consciously and conspicuously himself. That, finally, is one of the reasons why we still seek out Donne; why after three hundred years and more we still hear the sound of his voice speaking across the ages so distinctly. It may be true that when from curiosity we come to cut up and 'survey each part', we are like the doctors and 'know not why— we cannot see how so many different qualities meet together in one man. But we have only to read him, to submit to the sound of that passionate and penetrating voice, and his figure rises again across the waste of the years more erect, more imperious, more inscrutable than any of his time. (pp. 43-5)

Virginia Woolf, "Donne after Three Centuries," in her Collected Essays, *Vol. I, Harcourt Brace Jovanovich, 1967, pp. 32-45.*

THOMAS STEARNS ELIOT (essay date 1931)

[*In the following excerpt from an essay contributed to* A Garland for John Donne *(1931), a tercentenary collection of appreciative essays by various hands. Eliot modifies somewhat his earlier enthusiasm for Donne (see excerpt dated 1923 and the Additional Bibliography), praising his accomplishment as more a significant influence on poetry than a major literary artist.*]

Donne's poetry is a concern of the present and the recent past, rather than of the future. (p. 5)

The progress of the reputation of Donne in the last twenty years or so is a curious chapter in the history of reputations. First he was supposed to be "mediaeval"; and our notions of "mediaeval" have themselves undergone change. This adjective was forcibly propelled at Donne by Miss Ramsay. Fortunately, however, Miss Ramsay has provided in the body of her book a mass of information which enables us to question the conclusions set out in her foreword. That Donne was well read in scholastic philosophy is undoubted; but there is no reason to suppose that he was any better read than Hooker, or that he was so deeply influenced by mediaeval thought as Hooker. Donne had also read or consulted all the principal theological writers up to date; he had also read the Protestant authorities and had read pretty widely in still more heretical authors; it is pertinent to remember that his great grandmother was a sister of Sir Thomas More, who translated Pico della Mirandola. (p. 7)

In his whole temper, indeed, Donne is the antithesis of the scholastic, of the mystic and of the philosophical system maker. The encyclopaedic ambitions of the schoolmen were directed always towards unification: a *summa* was the end to be attained, and every branch of knowledge and practice was to have its relation to the whole. In Donne, there is a manifest fissure between thought and sensibility, a chasm which in his poetry he bridged in his own way, which was not the way of mediaeval poetry. His learning is just information suffused with emotion, or combined with emotion not essentially relevant to it. In the poetry of Dante, and even of Guido Cavalcanti, there is always the assumption of an ideal unity in experience, the faith in an ultimate rationalisation and harmonisation of experience, the subsumption of the lower under the higher, an ordering of the world more or less Aristotelian. But perhaps one reason why Donne has appealed so powerfully to the recent time is that there is in his poetry hardly any attempt at organisation; rather a puzzled and humorous shuffling of the pieces; and we are inclined to read our own more conscious awareness of the apparent irrelevance and unrelatedness of things into the mind of Donne.

But to suggest that Donne was not a believer, in the sense in which it was a category of mediaeval thought that there was a unity in existence, a relation of real to ideal, which was not beyond the mind of man to trace in its outlines, is not to imply that he was, in the modern sense, a sceptic. To say that his cast of mind was such as made it impossible for him to be a constructive philosopher or a mystic is not to say that he knew *doubt* as the modern world has known it. The metaphysician and the mystic work differently and with different tools; but alike for metaphysics and for mysticism a unification is required which was alien to Donne. On the other hand, it was still possible for Donne to be, and I am sure that he was, genuinely *devout.* But he was a sincere churchman not because he had passed through the doubt which his type of mind finds congenial (I say his *type* of mind), but because in theology he had not yet arrived there. In short, his kind of religious belief differs both from that of the thirteenth century and that of the nineteenth and twentieth; it was sincere, but represents a period of transition.

The question of the nature of Donne's religious faith determines our solution of the "problem" of his conversion. Nobody now, I suppose, divides Donne's life into two periods, one dissolute and irreligious, the other a revulsion to intense and austere piety, a division so complete as to suggest an alternation of personality. We agree that it is one and the same man in both early and later life. But some of the best informed critics and scholars are still inclined to take for granted a period of debauchery and to emphasize it. Thus a very competent scholar, Mr. John Sparrow (writing in *Theology,* March, 1931) says: "We need only look at one of his earliest poems to see that even in his most dissolute days religion was to Donne something more than a merely intellectual interest." Well, I suppose that this sentence needed saying; and yet I do not think that we have sufficient evidence that Donne was so *very* dissipated; we are in danger of making an attractive romance about him. The able pamphlet of M. Legouis [see excerpt dated 1928] convinces me that we can easily exaggerate the mystical element in such a poem as "**The Ecstacy**"; but I suspect that we can easily exaggerate the erotic element as well. No one now is likely to follow Sir Edmund Gosse in reading Donne's *Elegies* as exact autobiography. My intention here is not to whitewash the evidence of a dissipated or immoral youth; but merely to affirm that we have no satisfactory evidence, and that it is a point of the very slightest interest anyhow. The courtly cynicism was a poetic convention of the time; Donne's sometimes scoffing attitude towards the fickleness of women may be hardly more than immature bravado; it comes to me with none of the terrible sincerity of Swift's vituperation of the human race. Nor can I take very seriously Donne's later remorse or repentance. It is pleasant in youth to think that one is a gay dog, and it is pleasant in age to think that one *was* a gay dog; because as we grow old we all like to think that we have changed, developed and improved; people shrink from acknowledging that they are exactly the same at fifty as they were at twenty-five— sometimes, indeed, men alter in order to congratulate themselves that they have altered, and not out of inner necessity. If Donne in youth was a rake, then I suspect that he a was conventional rake; If Donne in age was devout, then I suspect that he was conventionally devout. An observation which, even if true, is not necessarily destructive.

The kind of religious faith expressed in Donne's religious writings is wholly consistent with the employment in his poetry of the many scraps of various philosophies which appear there. His attitude towards philosophic notions in his poetry may be put by saying that he was more interested in *ideas* themselves as objects than in the *truth* of ideas. In an odd way, he almost anticipates the philosopher of

the coming age, Descartes.... Donne was, I insist, no sceptic: it is only that he is interested in and amused by ideas in themselves, and interested in the way in which he *feels* an idea; almost as if it were something that he could touch and stroke. To turn the attention to the mind in this way is a kind of creation, because the objects alter by being observed so curiously. To contemplate an idea, because it is present for the moment in my own mind, to observe my emotion colour it, and to observe it colour my emotions, to play with it, instead of using it as a plain and simple meaning, brings often odd or beautiful objects to light, as a deep sea diver inspects the darting and crawling life of the depths; though it may lend itself, this petting and teasing of one's mental objects, to extremities of torturing of language. With Donne it is not, as it is with the Elizabethans in their worst excesses, the word, the vocabulary that is tormented—it is the thought itself. In the poem

> I wonder by my troth, what thou, and I ...

the *idea* is thoroughly teased and touseled. The choice and arrangement of words is simple and direct and felicitous. There is a startling directness (as often at the beginning of Donne's poems) about the idea, which must have occurred to many lovers, of the abrupt break and alteration of the new life. These *trouvailles* themselves are enough to set Donne apart from some of his imitators: Cowley never found anything so good. But the usual course for Donne is not to pursue the meaning of the idea, but to arrest it, to play catlike with it, to develop it dialectically, to extract every minim of the emotion suspended in it. (pp. 8-13)

As long as we thought of Donne as a mediaeval, as a mystic, as a philosopher, as a rake turned devout, or a convert, we did not see his poetry as it is. Donne is not even an absolutely first-rate devotional poet: fine as some of his religious verse is, *Crashaw, Herbert and Vaughan each in his limited scope surpasses Donne*; and yet Donne is absolutely a greater poet, a greater master of language, than any of them.

And detaching Donne from his relation to a particular generation, our own, a relation which may never be repeated at any subsequent time, this I think we can say at least. Donne will remain permanently in a higher place than he has occupied before. For he was a great reformer of the English language, of English verse. We may continue always to find him more of a poet, of deeper knowledge and more intense and moving expression, than Dryden; but here we can compare him favourably to Dryden in the very matter in which Dryden deserves our warmest gratitude and admiration. The verse of Dryden was once thought artificial, pedestrian and prosaic; just as in a previous century the verse of Donne was thought to be artificial, pedestrian and prosaic, as well as uncouth. But in truth Dryden and Donne are both highly natural; and the merit of both is to have established a natural conversational diction instead of a conventional one. Each effected a revolution of the kind which has to occur from time to time, which will have to occur again in nearly measurable time, if the English language is to retain its vigour. (pp. 13-14)

It is hardly too much to say that Donne enlarged the possibilities of lyric verse as no other English poet has done. M. Legouis has pointed out very pertinently how largely his lyrics are dramatic, in monologue and dialogue. The possibilities of this kind of verse, however, were not considerably developed by any of Donne's immediate successors; and however closely they depended upon him for their language, and however they excelled him in various departments of devotional verse, none could follow so delicately the movements of the human mind or the comedy and tragedy of human behaviour and feeling. The path of exploration started by Donne ended in the blind alley of the Pindaric ode of Cowley, and the lyric ran on into tender sentiment, *vers de société* and satire. We must accordingly dissociate Donne from the "school of Donne"; so far as these followers enjoy any particular vogue in our time, it is a popularity reflected from that of Donne, or partly one arising from a new interest in devotional verse. From one point of view, George Herbert is far more to the taste of an admirer of Christina Rossetti than necessarily to the taste of an admirer of Donne. For the technique of verse, and for its adaptibility to purposes, Donne has closer affinity to Browning, to Laforgue and to Corbière. The place of Browning in this group is obscured by several accidents: by the fact that he is often tediously longwinded, that he is far less a wit and ironist, and perhaps more than anything by the fact that his knowledge of the particular human heart is adulterated by an optimism which has proved offensive to our time, though a later age may succeed in ignoring it. Browning, moreover, is perhaps *too* objective, without having that large and intricate pattern which objectivity requires: Donne, Corbière, Laforgue begin with their own feelings, and their limitation is that they do not always get much outside or beyond; Shakespeare, one feels, arrives at an objective world by a process from himself, whoever he was, as the centre and starting point; but too often, one thinks with Browning, here is a world with no particular interesting man inside it, no consistent point of view. But the verse method, in all these four men, is similar: either dramatic monologue or dramatic dialogue; and with Donne and the French poets, the pattern is given by what goes on within the mind, rather than by the exterior events which provoke the mental activity and play of thought and feeling.

But Donne effected not only a development, but a reform, of the language, just as Dryden, in his turn, reformed the language from the excesses of the minor followers of Donne. The minor Elizabethan dramatists sometimes tormented the language; where the content is often quite simple, the expression is perverse. In the verse of Donne the thought is sometimes overingenious and perverse, but the language is always pure and simple. . . . Donne introduced the natural or conversational style, which the Elizabethans at their best had excelled in producing in a highly sophisticated metric of blank verse, into the lyric; he first made it possible to think in lyric verse, and in a variety of rhythms and stanza schemes which forms an inexhaustible subject of study; and at the same time retained a quality of song and the suggestion of the instrumental accompaniment of the earlier lyric. No poet has excelled him in this peculiar combination of qualities. (pp. 14-17)

Such, I believe, are some of the conclusions of praise which another generation, not enjoying that fulness of satisfaction in Donne that we have felt, will be able to confer upon him. The fascination of the "personality" of an author is an undependable and fluctuating influence upon posterity; the affinity which we find or invent for ourselves and various authors of various periods is uncertain, variable but partly relevant to their greatness. Yet certainly that of Donne is as definite, and as impressive, as that of Montaigne; and we are not wholly fanciful in believing that he has, in the old sense of the word, "prevented" us. The last stage in the discovery and rehabilitation of Donne—if that can be called a rehabilitation which is really an habilitation—is the current applause of his works of divinity. I feel, myself (it is perhaps to-day an heretical sensation), that the essential originality of Donne is rather in the **Songs and Sonets**, in the **Elegies**, and in the **Satires**, than in the **Sermons**. We find in the gorgeous prose of the last something more than what is there, for we find now and then what is not to be expected, the knowledge of the weaknesses of the human soul, the frankness of admission as of Montaigne, which is not in the view of the greater Jacobean and Caroline divines. But actually (I for one have always been convinced) in the history of English Theology it is not Donne, but Cranmer and Latimer and Andrewes, who are the great prose masters; and for the theologian even the high-sounding Bramhall and the depressive Thorndike are more important names than Donne's. His sermons will disappear as suddenly as they have appeared. For one age or another his personality may be no more interesting than has been, for the last seventy-five years or so (I am not at the moment careful to answer in respect of that reputation), the personality of Byron. But at any time Donne ought always to be recognized as one of the few great reformers and preservers of the English tongue. (pp. 18-19)

Engraved title page of the first collection of Donne's sermons.

Thomas Stearns Eliot, "Donne in Our Time," in A Garland for John Donne: 1631-1931, *edited by Theodore Spencer, 1931. Reprint by Peter Smith, 1958, pp. 1-19.*

F. R. LEAVIS (essay date 1935)

[*An influential English educator and critic. Leavis articulated his views in his lectures, in his many critical works, and in* Scrutiny, *a quarterly he cofounded and edited from 1932 to 1953. His critical methodology combined close textual analysis, predominantly moral and social concerns, and emphasis on the development of "the individual sensibility." Leavis believed that the writer, who represents "the most conscious point of the race" in his or her lifetime, should strive to eliminate "ego-centered distortion and all impure motives" and thereby promote "sincerity," or the realization of the individual's proper place in human society. Literature that accomplishes this he deemed "mature." Although Leavis's advocacy of a cultural elite, the vagueness of his moral assumptions, and his refusal to develop a systematic philosophy have alienated many scholars from his work, his writings remain an important, if controversial, force in literary criticism. In the following excerpt from an essay originally published in 1935 in* Scrutiny, *Leavis uses the occasion of his reviewing the* Oxford Book of Seventeenth Century Verse *to discourse upon what he considers Donne's high achievement in poetry.*]

Few who handle the new *Oxford Book [of Seventeenth Century Verse]* will think of reading it straight through, and fewer will actually read through it, but to persist only moderately in the undertaking is to assure oneself that one valuation at least, and that a key one, among current acceptances needs no downward revision. After ninety pages of (with some minor representation) Fulk Greville, Chapman and Drayton, respectable figures who, if one works through their allotments, serve at any rate to set up a critically useful background, we come to this:

> I wonder by my troth, what thou, and I
> Did, till we lov'd? were we not wean'd till then?
> But suck'd on country pleasures, childishly?
> Or snorted we in the seven sleepers den?
> 'Twas so; But this, all pleasures fancies bee.
> If ever any beauty I did see,
> Which I desir'd, and got, 'twas but a dreame of thee.

At this we cease reading as students, or as connoisseurs of anthology-pieces, and read on as we read the living. The extraordinary force of originality that made Donne so potent an influence in the seventeenth century makes him now at once for us, without his being the less felt as of his period, contemporary—obviously a living poet in the most important sense. And it is not any eccentricity or defiant audacity that makes the effect here so immediate, but rather an irresistible rightness.

With all that has been written of late about Donne it is still, perhaps, not altogether easy to realize how powerful an originality is represented by the stanza quoted above. In an age when music is for all classes an important part of daily life, when poets are, along with so large a proportion of their fellow-countrymen, musicians and write their lyrics to be sung, Donne uses in complete dissociation from music a stanza-form that proclaims the union of poetry and music. The dissociation is positive; utterance, movement and intonation are those of the talking voice. And consider the way in which the stress is got on 'Did,' and the intonation controlled, here:

> I wonder by my troth, what thou, and I
> Did, till we lov'd?

This is the spirit in which Donne uses the stanza-form—for he does indeed strictly use it: the exigencies of the pattern become means to the inevitable naturalness; they play an essential part in the consummate control of intonation, gesture, movement and larger rhythm. But that Donne is a great artist is now commonly recognized, and we are not likely to hear much more of his harsh and rugged verse and his faults of phrasing and harmony (though no doubt these could still be found). The commonplaces now regard the magnificent handling of the stanza, the building-up of varied cumulative effects within it, exemplified by (say) *The Anniversarie* and 'A nocturnall upon S. Lucies day'.

There remains, perhaps, something to be said about such mastery of tone as is exhibited in (to take the example at which the book happens to be open) 'Aire and Angells'—the passage from the gravely gallant and conventional exaltation of the opening to the blandly insolent matter-of-factness of the close. Indeed, the subtleties of Donne's use of the speaking voice and the spoken language are inexhaustible—or might, by a reasonable hyperbole, be called so, if we were not reminded of Shakespeare. For of Shakespeare we are, in fact, notably reminded. Whether or not Donne did actually get anything from dramatic verse can only be a matter of idle speculation, but his own verse—the technique, the spirit in which the sinew and living nerve of English are used—suggests an appropriate development of impressions that his ear might have recorded in the theatre.

And there is, of course, about Donne's characteristic poetry—in the presentment of situations, the liveliness of enactment—something fairly to be called dramatic. 'Satyre iii', which one is glad to find in this *Oxford Book,* very obviously justifies the adjective (though not, perhaps, more obviously than many of the poems in stanzas), and the handling in it of the decasyllabic line reminds us peculiarly of dramatic blank verse. Consider, for instance, the way in which Donne here, playing his sense-movement across the rimes, controls his tone and gets his key stresses, coming finally down with retarded emphasis on 'damn'd':

> Are not heavens joyes as valiant to asswage
> Lusts, as earths honour was to them? Alas,
> As wee do them in meanes, shall they surpasse
> Us in the end, and shall thy fathers spirit
> Meete blinde Philosophers in heaven, whose merit
> Of strict life may be imputed faith, and heare
> Thee, whom he taught so easie wayes and neare
> To follow, damn'd?

This art has evident affinities with Shakespeare's; nevertheless Donne is writing something original and quite different from blank verse. For all their apparent casualness, the rimes, it should be plain, are strictly *used*; the couplet-structure; though not in Pope's way, is functional. If, for instance, 'asswage' had not been a rime-word, there would not have been quite that lagging diliberation of stress upon 'lusts'; just as, in the following, the riming upon the first syllable of 'blindnesse' secures a natural speaking stress and intonation and an economy that is the privilege of speech (the effect is: 'this state of blindness—for that's what it amounts to . . .'):

> Careless Phrygius doth abhorre

All, because all cannot be good, as one
Knowing some women whores, dares marry none.
Gracchus loves all as one, and thinkes that so
As women do in divers countries goe
In divers habits, yet are still one kinde,
So doth, so is Religion; and this
blindnesse too much light breeds . . .

Even so short a passage as this suggests the mimetic flexibility for which the whole piece is remarkable. The poised logical deliberation of the first three lines, suggesting the voice of invincibly rational caution, sets off the rakish levity, the bland Restoration insolence, that follows ('So doth, so is . . .'—it is an extraordinarily different logic).

But enough illustration (out of an embarrassment of choice) has been given to bring home how dramatic Donne's use of his medium can be; how subtly, in a consummately managed verse, he can exploit the strength of spoken English. But it is not enough to leave the stress there; a Donne whose art was fully represented by **'Satyre iii'** could not have been as important or pervasive an influence in the century as actually he was. He also wrote this:

Sweetest love, I do not goe,
For wearinesse of thee,
Nor in hope the world can show
A fitter Love for mee;
But since that I
Must dye at last, 'tis best,
To use my selfe in jest
Thus by fain'd deaths to dye.

This is not Campion, yet it is a song. And Donne's songs are, though a continuity of intermediate modes, in touch at the other end of the scale with the mode of **'Satyre iii.'** (pp. 10-15)

> *F. R. Leavis, "The Line of Wit," in his* Revaluation: Tradition & Development in English Poetry, *1936. Reprint by George W. Stewart, Publisher, Inc., 1947, pp. 10-41.*

C. S. LEWIS (essay date 1938)

[*Lewis is considered one of the foremost mythopoeic authors of the twentieth century. Indebted principally to George MacDonald, G. K. Chesterton, Charles Williams, and the writers of ancient Norse myths, he is regarded as a formidable logician and Christian polemicist, a perceptive literary critic, and an accomplished writer of fantasy literature. Also a noted academic and scholar. Lewis was an acknowledged authority on medieval and Renaissance literature, holding posts at Oxford and Cambridge. A traditionalist in his approach to life and art, he opposed the modern critical movement toward biographical and psychological interpretation, preferring to practice and propound a theory of criticism that stresses the author's intent rather than the reader's presuppositions and prejudices. In the following excerpt, he describes and negatively appraises Donne's love poetry.*]

It is not impossible to see why Donne's poetry should be overrated in the twentieth and underrated in the eighteenth century; and in so far as we detect these temporary disturbing factors and explain the varying appearances of the object by the varying positions of the observers, we shall come appreciably nearer to a glimpse of Donne *simpliciter*. I shall concern myself in what follows chiefly with his love poetry.

In style this poetry is primarily a development of one of the two styles which we find in the work of Donne's immediate predecessors. One of these is the mellifluous, luxurious, 'builded rhyme,' as in Spenser's *Amoretti*: the other is the abrupt, familiar, and consciously 'manly' style in which nearly all Wyatt's lyrics are written. . . . Wyatt remains, if not the finest, yet much the purest example of the plainer manner, and in reading his songs, with their conversational openings, their surly (not to say sulky) defiances, and their lack of obviously poetic ornament, I find myself again and again reminded of Donne. But of course he is a Donne with most of the genius left out. Indeed, the first and most obvious achievement of the younger poet is to have raised this kind of thing to a much higher power; to have kept the vividness of conversation where Wyatt too often had only the flatness; to sting like a lash where Wyatt merely grumbled. The difference in degree between the two poets thus obscures the similarity in kind. Donne has so far surpassed not only Wyatt but all the Elizabethans in what may be called their Wyatt moments, and has so generally abstained from attempting to rival them in their other vein, that we hardly think of him as continuing one side of their complex tradition; he appears rather as the innovator who substituted a realistic for a decorated kind of love poetry. (pp. 64-5)

But of course when we have identified the Wyatt element in Donne, we have still a very imperfect notion of his manner. We have described **'Busie old foole'** and **'I wonder by my troth'** and **'For Godsake hold your tongue, and let me love'**; but we have left out the cleaving remora, the triple soul, the stiff twin compasses, and a hundred other things that were not in Wyatt. There were indeed a great many things not in Wyatt, and his manly plainness can easily be over-praised—'pauper videri Cinna vult et est pauper'. If Donne had not reinforced the style with new attractions it would soon have died of very simplicity. An account of these reinforcements will give us a rough notion of the unhappily named 'metaphysical' manner.

The first of them is the multiplication of conceits—not conceits of any special 'metaphysical' type but conceits such as we find in all the Elizabethans. When Donne speaks of the morning coming from his mistress's eyes, or tells how they wake him like the light of a taper, these fanciful hyperboles are not, in themselves, a novelty. But, side by side with these, we find, as his second characteristic, what may be called the difficult conceit. This is clearly a class which no two readers will fill up in quite the same way. An example of what I mean comes at the end of **'The Sunne Rising'** where the sun is congratulated on the fact that the two lovers have shortened his task for him. Even the quickest reader will be checked, if only for an infinitesimal time, before he sees how and why the lovers have done this, and will experience a kind of astonished relief at the unexpected answer. The pleasure of the thing, which can be paralleled in other artistic devices, perhaps in rhyme itself, would seem to depend on recurrent tension and relaxation. In the third place, we have Donne's characteristic choice of imagery. The Petrarchans (I will call them so for convenience) had relied for their images mainly on mythology and on natural objects. Donne uses both of these sparingly—though his sea that 'Leaves embroider'd works upon the sand' is as fine an image from nature as I know—and taps new sources such as law, science, philosophy, and the commonplaces of urban life. It is this that has given the Metaphysicals their name and been much misunderstood. When Johnson said that they were resolved to show their learning he said truth in fact [see excerpt dated 1779] for there is an element of pedantry, of dandyism, an *odi profanos* air, about Donne—the old printer's address not to the *readers* but to the *understanders* is illuminating. But Johnson was none the less misleading. He encouraged the idea that the abstruse nature of some of Donne's similes was poetically relevant for good or ill. In fact, of course, when we have once found out what Donne is talking about—that is, when Sir Herbert Grierson has told us—the learning of the poet becomes unimportant. The image will stand or fall like any other by its intrinsic merit—its power of conveying a meaning 'more luminously and with a sensation of delight'. The matter is worth mentioning only because Donne's reputation in this respect repels some humble readers and attracts some prigs. What is important for criticism is his avoidance of the obviously poetical image; whether the intractable which he is determined to poetize is fetched from Thomas Aquinas or from the London underworld, the method is essentially the same. Indeed it would be easy to exaggerate the amount of learned imagery in his poems and even the amount of his learning. He knows much, but he seems to know even more because his knowledge so seldom overlaps with our own; and some scraps of his learning, such as that of angelic consciousness or of the three souls in man, come rather too often—like the soldiers in a stage army, and with the same result. This choice of imagery is closely connected with the surprising and ingenious nature of the connexions which Donne makes between the image and the matter in hand, thus getting a double surprise. No one, in the first place, expects lovers to be compared to compasses; and no one, even granted the comparison, would guess in what respect they are going to be compared.

But all these characteristics, in their mere enumeration, are what Donne would have called a 'ruinous anatomie'. They might all be used—indeed they all are used by Herbert—to produce a result very unlike Donne's. What gives their peculiar character to most of the *Songs and Sonets* is that they are dramatic in the sense of being addresses to an imagined hearer in the heat of an imagined conversation, and usually addresses of a violently argumentative character. The majority of lyrics, even where nominally addressed to a god, a woman, or a friend, are meditations or introspective narratives. Thus Herbert's 'Throw away thy rod' is formally an apostrophe; in fact, it is a picture of Herbert's own state of mind. But the majority of the *Songs and Sonets,* including some that are addressed to abstractions like Love, present the poet's state of mind only indirectly and are ostensibly concerned with badgering, wheedling, convincing, or upbraiding an imagined hearer. No poet, not even Browning, buttonholes us or, as we say, 'goes for' us like Donne. There are, of course, exceptions. **'Goe and catche a falling starre,'** though it is in the form of an address, has not this effect; and **'Twicknam Garden'** or the **'Nocturnall'** are in fact, as well as in pretension, soliloquies. These exceptions include some of Donne's best work; and indeed, one of the errors of contemporary criticism, to my mind, is an insufficient distinction between Donne's best and Donne's most characteristic. But I do not at present wish to emphasize this. For the moment it is enough to notice that the majority of his love lyrics, and of the *Elegies*, are of the type I have described. And since

they are, nearly always, in the form of arguments, since they attempt to extort something from us, they are poetry of an extremely exacting kind. This exacting quality, this urgency and pressure of the poet upon the reader in every line, seems to me to be the root both of Donne's weakness and his strength. When the thing fails it exercises the same dreadful fascination that we feel in the grip of the worst kind of bore—the hot-eyed, unescapable kind. When it succeeds it produces a rare intensity in our enjoyment—which is what a modern critic meant (I fancy) when he claimed that Donne made all other poetry sound less 'serious'. The point is worth investigation.

For, of course, in one sense these poems are not serious at all. Poem after poem consists of extravagant conceits woven into the preposterous semblance of an argument. The preposterousness is the point. Donne intends to take your breath away by the combined subtlety and impudence of the steps that lead to his conclusion. Any attempt to overlook Donne's 'wit' in this sense, or to pretend that his rare excursions into the direct expression of passion are typical, is false criticism. The paradox, the surprise, are essential; if you are not enjoying these you are not enjoying what Donne intended. Thus **'Womans Constancy'** is of no interest as a document of Donne's 'cynicism'— any fool can be promiscuously unchaste and any fool can say so. The merit of the poem consists in the skill with which it leads us to expect a certain conclusion and then gives us precisely the opposite conclusion, and that, too with an appearance of reasonableness. Thus, again, the art of **'The Will'** consists in keeping us guessing through each stanza what universal in the concluding triplet will bind together the odd particulars in the preceding six lines. The test case is **'The Flea'**. If you think this very different from Donne's other poems you may be sure that you have no taste for the real Donne. But for the accident that modern cleanliness by rendering this insect disgusting has also rendered it comic, the conceit is exactly on the same level as that of the tears in **'A Valediction: of weeping'**.

And yet the modern critic was right. The effect of all these poems is somehow serious. 'Serious' indeed is the only word. Seldom profound in thought, not always passionate in feeling, they are none the less the very opposite of gay. It is as though Donne performed in deepest depression those gymnastics which are usually a sign of intellectual high spirits. He himself speaks of his *concupiscence* of wit.' The hot, dark word is well chosen. We are all familiar—at least if we have lived in Ireland—with the type of mind which combines furious anger with a revelling delight in eloquence, nay grows more rhetorical as anger increases. In the same way, wit and the delight in wit are, for Donne, not only compatible with, but actually provoked by, the most uneasy passions—by contempt and self-contempt and unconvinced sensuality. His wit is not so much the play as the irritability of intellect. But none the less, like the angry Irishman's *clausulae,* it is still enjoyed and still intends to produce admiration; and if we do not hold our breaths as we read, wondering in the middle of each complication how he will resolve it, and exclaiming at the end 'How ever did you think of *that*? (Carew speaks of his 'fresh invention' [see excerpt dated 1633]), we are not enjoying Donne.

Now this kind of thing can produce a very strong and a very peculiar pleasure. Our age has nothing to repent of in having learned to relish it. If the Augustans, in their love for the obviously poetical and harmonious, were blind to its merits, so much the worse for them. At the same time it is desirable not to overlook the special congeniality of such poetry to the twentieth century, and to beware of giving to this highly specialized and, in truth, very limited kind of excellence, a place in our scheme of literary values which it does not deserve. Donne's rejection of the obviously poetical image was a good method—for Donne; but if we think that there is some intrinsic superiority in this method, so that all poetry about pylons and *non obstantes* must needs be of a higher order than poetry about lawns and lips and breasts and orient skies, we are deceived—deceived by the fact that we, like Donne, happen to live at the end of a great period of rich and nobly obvious poetry. It is natural to want your savoury after your sweets; but you must not base a philosophy of cookery on that momentary preference. Again, Donne's obscurity and occasional abstruseness have sometimes (not always) produced magnificent results, and we do well to praise them. But, as I have hinted, an element of dandyism was present in Donne himself—he 'would have no such readers as he could teach'—and we must be very cautious here lest shallow call to shallow. There is a great deal of dandyism (largely of Franco-American importation) in the modern literary world. And finally, what shall we say of Donne's 'seriousness', of that persistency, that nimiety, that astringent quality (as Boehme would have said) which makes him, if not the saddest, at least the most uncomfortable, of our poets? Here, surely, we find the clearest and most disturbing congeniality of all. It would be foolish not to recognize the growth in our criticism of something that I can only describe as literary Manichaeism—a dislike of peace and pleasure and heartsease simply as such. To be bilious is, in some circles, almost the first qualification for a place in the Temple of Fame. We distrust the pleasures of imagination, however hotly and unmerrily we preach the pleasures of the body. This seriousness must not be confused with profundity. We do not like poetry that essays to be wise, and Chaucer would think we had rejected 'doctryne' and 'solas' about equally. We want, in fact, just what Donne can give us—something stern and tough, though not necessarily virtuous, something that does not conciliate. Born under Saturn, we do well to confess the liking complexionally forced upon us; but not to attempt that wisdom which dominates the stars is pusillanimous, and to set up our limitation as a norm—to believe, against all experience, in a Saturnocentric universe—is folly.

The sentiment of Donne's love poems is easier to describe than their manner, and its charm for modern readers easier to explain. No one will deny that the twentieth century, so far, has shown an extraordinary interest in the sexual appetite and has been generally marked by a reaction from the romantic idealization of that appetite. We have agreed with the romantics in regarding sexual love as a subject of overwhelming importance, but hardly in anything else. On the purely literary side we are wearied with the floods of uxorious bathos which the romantic conception undoubtedly liberated. As psychologists we are interested in the new discovery of the secreter and less reputable operations of the instinct. As practical philosophers we are living in an age of sexual experiment. The whole subject offers us an admirable field for the kind of seriousness I have just described. It seems odd, at first sight, that a sixteenth-century poet should give us so exactly what we want; but it can be explained.

The great central movement of love poetry, and of fiction about love, in Donne's time is that represented by Shakespeare and Spenser. This movement consisted in the final transmutation of the medieval courtly love or romance of adultery into an equally romantic love that looked to marriage as its natural conclusion. The process, of course, had begun far earlier—as early, indeed, as the *Kingis Quhair*—but its triumph belongs to the sixteenth century. It is most powerfully expressed by Spenser, but more clearly and philosophically by Chapman in that underestimated poem, his *Hero and Leander*. These poets were engaged, as Professor Vinaver would say, in reconciling Carbonek and Camelot, virtue and courtesy, divine and human love; and incidentally in laying down the lines which love poetry was to follow till the nineteenth century. We who live at the end of the dispensation which they inaugurated and in reaction against it are not well placed for evaluating their work. Precisely what is revolutionary and creative in it seems to us platitudinous, orthodox, and stale. If there were a poet, and a strong poet, alive in their time who was failing to move with them, he would inevitably appear to us more 'modern' than they.

But was Donne such a poet? A great critic has assigned him an almost opposite role, and it behoves us to proceed with caution. It may be admitted at once that Donne's work is not, in this respect, all of a piece; no poet fits perfectly into such a scheme as I have outlined—it can be true only by round and by large. There are poems in which Donne attempts to sing a love perfectly in harmony with the moral law, but they are not very numerous and I do not think they are usually his best pieces. Donne never for long gets rid of a medieval sense of the sinfulness of sexuality; indeed, just because the old conventional division between Carbonek and Camelot is breaking up, he feels this more continuously and restively than any poet of the Middle Ages. (pp. 73-4)

I trace in his poetry three levels of sentiment. On the lowest level (lowest, that is, in order of complexity), we have the celebration of simple appetite, as in **'Elegy XIX.'** If I call this a pornographic poem, I must be understood to use that ugly word as a descriptive, not a dyslogistic, term. I mean by it hat this poem, in my opinion, is intended to arouse the appetite it describes, to affect not only the imagination but the nervous system of the reader. And I may as well say at once—but who would willingly claim to be a judge in such matters—that it seems to me to be very nearly perfect in its kind. Nor would I call it an immoral poem. Under what conditions the reading of it could be an innocent act is a real moral question; but the poem itself contains nothing intrinsically evil.

On the highest, or what Donne supposed to be the highest, level we have the poems of ostentatiously virtuous love, **'The Undertaking,' 'A Valediction: forbidding mourning', and 'The Extasie'**. It is here that the contrast between Donne and his happier contemporaries is most marked. He is trying to follow them into the new age, to be at once passionate and innocent; and if any reader will make the experiment of imagining Beatrice or Juliet or Perdita, or again, Amoret or Britomart, or even Philoclea or Pamela, as the auditress throughout these poems, he will quickly feel that something is wrong. You may deny, as perhaps some do, that the romantic conception of 'pure' passion has any meaning; but certainly, if there is such a thing, it is not like this. It does not prove itself pure by talking about purity. It does not keep on drawing distinctions between spirit and flesh to the detriment of the latter and then explaining why the flesh is, after all, to be used. This is what Donne does, and the result is singularly unpleasant. The more he labours the deeper 'Dun is in the mire,' and it is quite arguable that **'The Extasie'** is a much nastier poem than the nineteenth **'Elegy'**. What any sensible woman would make of such a wooing it is difficult to imagine—or would be difficult if we forgot the amazing protective faculty which each sex possesses of not listening to the other.

Between these two extremes falls the great body of Donne's love poetry. In certain obvious, but superficial, respects, it continues the medieval tradition. Love is still a god and lovers his 'clergie'; oaths may be made in 'reverentiall feare' of his 'wrath'; and the man who resists him is 'rebell and atheist'. Donne can even doubt, like Soredamors, whether those who admit Love after a struggle have not forfeited his grace by their resistance, like

> Small townes which stand stiffe, til great shot
> Enforce them.

He can personify the attributes of his mistress, the 'enormous gyant' her Disdain and the 'enchantress *Honor'*, quite in the manner of *The Romance of the Rose*. He writes *Albas* for both sexes, and in the **Holy Sonnets** repents of his love poetry, writing his palinode, in true medieval fashion. A reader may wonder, at first, why the total effect is so foreign to the Middle Ages: but Donne himself has explained this when he says, speaking of the god of Love,

> If he wroung from mee a teare, I brin'd it so
> With scorne or shame, that him it nourish'd not.

This admirable couplet not only tells us, in brief, what Donne has effected but shows us that he knew what he was doing. It does not, of course, cover every single poem. A few pieces admittedly express delighted love and they are among Donne's most popular works; such are **'The Good-morrow'** and **'The Anniversarie'**—poems that again remind us of the difference between his best and his typical. But the majority of the poems ring the changes on five themes, all of them grim ones—on the sorrow of parting (including death), the miseries of secrecy, the falseness of the mistress, the fickleness of Donne, and finally on contempt for love itself. The poems of parting stand next to the poems of happy love in general popularity and are often extremely affecting. We may hear little of the delights of Donne's loves, and dislike what we hear of their 'purity'; the pains ring true. The song **'Sweetest love, I do not goe'** is remarkable for its broken, but haunting, melody, and nowhere else has Donne fused argument, conceit, and classical imitation into a more perfect unity. **'The Feaver'** is equally remarkable, and that for a merit very rare in Donne—its inevitability. It is a single jet of music and feeling, a straight flight without appearance of effort. The remaining four of our five themes are all various articulations of the 'scorne or shame' with which Donne 'brines' his reluctantly extorted tributes to the god of Love; monuments, unparalleled outside Catullus, to the close kinship between certain kinds of love and certain kinds of hate. The faithlessness of women is sometimes treated, in a sense, playfully; but there is always something— the clever surprise in **'Womans Constancy'** or the grotesque in **'Goe and catche a falling starre'**—which stops these poems short of a true anacreontic gaiety. The theme of faithlessness rouses Donne to a more characteristic, and also a better, poetry in such a hymn of hate as **'The Apparition,'** or in the sad mingling of fear, contempt, and self-contempt in **'A Lecture upon the Shadow'**. The pains of secrecy give opportunity for equally fierce and turbulent writing. I may be deceived when I find in the sixteenth **'Elegy'**, along with many other nauseas and indignations, a sickened male contempt for the whole female world of nurses and 'midnight startings' and hysterics; but **'The Curse'** is unambiguous. The ending here is particularly delicious just because the main theme—an attack on *Falosie* or the 'lozengiers'—is so medieval and so associated with the 'honour of love'. Of the poet's own fickleness one might expect, at last, a merry treatment; and perhaps in **'The Indifferent'** we get it. But I am not sure. Even this seems to have a sting in it. And of **'Loves Usury'** what shall I say? The struggle between lust and reason, the struggle between love and reason, these we know; but Donne is perhaps the first poet who has ever painted lust holding love at arm's length, in the hope 'that there's no need to trouble himself with any such thoughts yet'—and all this only as an introduction to the crowning paradox that in old age even a reciprocated love must be endured. The poem is, in its way, a masterpiece, and a powerful indirect expression of Donne's habitual 'shame and scorne'. For, in the long run, it must be admitted that 'the love of hatred and the hate of love' is the main, though not the only, theme of the **Songs and Sonets**. A man is a fool for loving and a double fool for saying so in 'whinning poetry'; the only excuse is that the sheer difficulty of drawing one's pains through rhyme's vexation 'allays' them. A woman's love at best will be only the 'spheare' of a man's— inferior to it as the heavenly spheres are to their intelligences or air to angels. Love is a spider that can transubstantiate all sweets into bitter: a devil who differs from his fellow devils at court by taking the soul and giving nothing in exchange. The mystery which the Petrarchans or their medieval predecessors made of it is 'imposture all', like the claims of alchemists. It is a very simple matter (*foeda et brevis voluptas*), and all it comes to in the end is

> that my man
> Can be as happy as I can.

Unsuccessful love is a plague and tyranny; but there is a plague even worse—Love might try

> A deeper plague, to make her love mee too!

Love enjoyed is like gingerbread with the gilt off. What pleased the whole man now pleases one sense only—

> And that so lamely, as it leaves behind
> A kinde of sorrowing dulnesse to the minde.

The doctors say it shortens life.

It may be urged that this is an unfair selection of quotations, or even that I have arrived at my picture of Donne by leaving out all his best poems, for one reason or another, as 'exceptions', and then describing what remains. There is one sense in which I admit this. Any account of Donne which concentrates on his love poetry must be unfair to the poet, for it leaves out much of his best work. By hypothesis, it must neglect the dazzling sublimity of his best religious poems, the grotesque charm of *The Progresse of the Soule,* and those scattered, but exquisite, patches of poetry that appear from time to time amidst the insanity of *The First and Second Anniversaries.* Even in the *Epistles* [*Letters to Severall Personages*] there are good passages. But as far as concerns his love poetry, I believe I am just. I have no wish to rule out the exceptions, provided that they are admitted to be exceptions. I am attempting to describe the prevailing tone of his work, and in my description no judgement is yet implied.

To judgement let us now proceed. Here is a collection of verse describing with unusual and disturbing energy the torments of a mind which has been baffled in its relation to sexual love by certain temporary and highly special conditions. What is its value? To admit the 'unusual and disturbing energy' is, of course, to admit that Donne is a poet; he has, in the modern phrase, 'put his stuff across'. Those who believe that criticism can separate inquiry into the success of communication from that into the value of the thing communicated will demand that we should now proceed to evaluate the 'stuff'; and if we do so, it would not be hard to point out how transitory and limited and, as it were, accidental the appeal of such 'stuff' must be. But something of the real problem escapes under this treatment. It would not be impossible to imagine a poet dealing with this same stuff, marginal and precarious as it is, in a way that would permanently engage our attention. Donne's real limitation is not that he writes *about,* but that he writes *in,* a chaos of violent and transitory passions. He is perpetually excited and therefore perpetually cut off from the deeper and more permanent springs of his own excitement. But how is this to be seperated from his technique—the nagging, nudging, quibbling stridency of his manner? If a man writes thus, what can be communicate but excitement? Or again, if he finds nothing but excitement to communicate, how else should he write? It is impossible here to distinguish cause from effect. Our concern, in the long run, must be with the actual poetry (the 'stuff' *thus* communicated, this communication of *such* 'stuff') and with the question how far that total phenomenon is calculated to interest human imagination. And to this question I can see only one answer: that its interest, save for a mind specially predisposed in its favour, must be short-lived and superficial, though intense. Paradoxical as it may seem, Donne's poetry is too simple to satisfy. Its complexity is all on the surface—an intellectual and fully conscious complexity that we soon come to the end of. Beneath this we find nothing but a limited series of 'passions'— explicit, mutually exclusive passions which can be instantly and adequately labelled as such—things which can be readily talked about, and indeed, must be talked about because, in silence, they begin to lose their hard outlines and overlap, to betray themselves as partly fictitious. That is why Donne is always arguing. There are puzzles in his work, but we can solve them all if we are clever enough; there is none of the depth and ambiguity of real experience in him, such as underlies the apparent simplicity of *How sleep the brave* or *Songs of Innocence,* or even Αιαι Λειψυδριον. The same is true, for the most part, of the specifically 'metaphysical comparisons. One idea has been put into each and nothing more can come out of it. Hence they tend to die on our hands, where some seemingly banal comparison of a woman to a flower or God's anger to flame can touch us at innumerable levels and renew its virginity at every reading. Of all literary virtues 'originality', in the vulgar sense, has, for this reason, the

shortest life. When we have once mastered a poem by Donne there is nothing more to do with it. To use his own simile, he deals in earthquakes, not in that 'trepidation of the spheres' which is so much less violent but 'greater far'.

Some, of course, will contend that his love poems should interest me permanently because of their 'truth'. They will say that he has shown me passion with the mask off, and catch at my word 'uncomfortable' to prove that I am running away from him because he tells me more truth than I can bear. But this is the mere frenzy of anti-romanticism. Of course, Donne is true in the sense that passions such as he presents do occur in human experience. So do a great many other things. He makes his own selection, like Dickens, or Gower, or Herrick, and his world is neither more nor less 'real' than theirs; while it is obviously less real than the world of Homer, or Virgil, or Tolstoy. In one way, indeed, Donne's love poetry is less true than that of the Petrarchans, in so far as it largely omits the very thing that all the pother is about. Donne shows us a variety of sorrows, scorns, angers, disgusts, and the like which arise out of love. But if any one asked 'What is all this *about*? What is the attraction which makes these partings so sorrowful? What is the peculiarity about this physical pleasure which he speaks of so contemptuously, and how has it got tangled up with such a storm of emotions?', I do not know how we could reply except by pointing to some ordinary love poetry. The feeblest sonnet, almost, of the other school would give us an answer with coral lips and Cupid's golden wings and the opening rose, with perfumes and instruments of music, with some attempt, however trite, to paint that iridescence which explains why people write poems about love at all. In this sense Donne's love poetry is parasitic. I do not use this word as a term of reproach; there are so many good poets, by now, in the world that one particular poet is entitled to take for granted the depth of a passion and deal with its froth. But as a purely descriptive term, 'parasitic' seems to me true. Donne's love poems could not exist unless love poems of a more genial character existed first. He shows us amazing shadows cast by love upon the intellect, the passions, and the appetite; to learn of the substance which casts them we must go to other poets, more balanced, more magnanimous, and more humane. There are, I well remember, poems (some two or three) in which Donne himself presents the substance; and the fact that he does so without much luxury of language and symbol endears them to our temporarily austere taste. But in the main, his love poetry is *Hamlet* without the prince. (pp. 75-82)

C. S. Lewis, "Donne and Love Poetry in the Seventeenth Century," in Seventeenth Century Studies Presented to Sir Herbert Grierson, *1938. Reprint by Octagon Books, Inc., 1967, pp. 64-84.*

JOAN BENNETT (essay date 1938)

[*Bennett was an English educator who wrote studies on the works of Virginia Woolf (1945) and George Eliot (1948). She is also the author of* Four Metaphysical Poets: Donne, Herbert, Vaughan, Crashaw *(1934; see Additional Bibliography). In the following excerpt from an essay she contributed to the festschrift* Seventeenth Century Studies Presented to Sir Herbert Grierson *(1938). Bennett offers a point-by-point rebuttal of C. S. Lewis's negative assessment of Donne's love poetry (see excerpt dated 1938).*]

In that brilliant and learned book *The Allegory of Love* Mr. Lewis writes, 'cynicism and idealism about women are twin fruits on the same branch—are the positive and negative poles of a single thing'. Few poets provide a better illustration of this than John Donne. These **Songs and Sonets** and **Elegies** which, Mr. Lewis would have us believe, never explain 'why people write poems about love at all' [see excerpt dated 1938] are the work of one who has tasted every fruit in love's orchard, from that which pleased only while he ate it—

> And when hee hath the kernell eate
> Who doth not fling away the shell?—

to that which raised a thirst for even fuller spiritual satisfaction, so that he wrote:

> Here the admyring her my mind did whett
> To seeke thee God.

How is it then that distinguished critics wonder what it is all about; that Dryden declares 'Donne perplexes the minds of the fair sex with nice speculations of philosophy, when he should engage their hearts and entertain them with the softness of love'; and that Mr. Lewis wonders 'what any sensible woman can make of such love-making'? A part of the trouble is, I believe, that they are accustomed to, or that they prefer, another kind of love poetry, in which the poet endeavours to paint the charms of his mistress. (p. 85)

Donne tells us very little about that beauty of 'colour and skin' which he describes in **'The Undertaking'** as 'but their oldest clothes'. He writes almost exclusively about the emotion, and not about its cause; he describes and analyses the experience of being in love, if I may use that word for the moment to cover his many kinds of experience which range from the mere sensual delight presupposed in **'Elegy XIX'** to the 'marriage of true minds' celebrated in **'The Good-morrow,'** or in **'The Valediction: forbidding mourning.'** In **'Elegy XIX,'** for instance, Donne is writing of the same kind of experience as that of which Carew writes in 'The Rapture.' But Carew expends his poetic gifts in description of the exquisite body of the woman, so that the reader can vicariously share his joys. Donne, on the other hand, gives two lines to description, and even so they are not really about what he sees; he is content to suggest by analogy the delight of the eye when the woman undresses:

> Your gown off, such beauteous state reveals,
> As when from flowry meads th' hills shadow steales.

The poem is not about her exquisite body, but about what he feels like when he stands there waiting for her to undress. Now it may be that 'any sensible woman' would rather be told of

> Thy bared snow and thy unbraided gold,

but I am not sure. She can see that in her looking-glass, or she may believe she sees these things reflected in the work of some painter, for the painter's art can show such things better than any words. It may interest her more to know what it feels like to be a man in love. In any case, it is of that that Donne chooses to write. He is not incapable of describing physical charms. . . . But the fact remains that such touches of description are very rare in Donne's poetry. His interest lay elsewhere, namely in dramatizing, and

analysing, and illustrating by a wealth of analogy the state, or rather states, of being in love.

But what does he mean by love? We have the whole mass of Donne's poems before us, thrown together higgledy-piggledy with no external evidence as to when or to whom any one of them was written. And in some of them love is 'imposture all', or 'a winter-seeming summers night'; in others physical union is all in all so that two lovers in bed are a whole world; and elsewhere we are told that

> Difference of sex no more wee knew
> Than our Guardian Angells doe.

And elsewhere again:

> Our bodies why doe wee forbeare?
> They are ours, though they are not wee, Wee are
> The intelligences, they the spheare.
> We owe them thankes because they thus
> Did us, to us, at first convay,
> Yeelded their forces, sense, to us,
> Nor are drosse to us, but allay.

The temptation to assign each poem to a particular period and to associate each with a particular woman is very strong. It has been yielded to again and again, not only in Sir Edmund Gosse's biography, but much more recently. Yet it must be resisted for two reasons: first because we have no evidence as to when any one of the **Songs and Sonets** was written, and secondly because we cannot know how far the experience of which any one of them treats was real or imaginary. Mr. Lewis is very well aware of these things. But it is no less misleading to go to the other extreme and read them as though they were all written at one time, or all with equal seriousness and sincerity. We have some important facts to guide us. Between the years 1597 and 1601 Donne fell in love with Anne More. He married her in 1601, as Walton puts it, 'without the allowance of those friends whose approbation always was, and ever will be necessary, to make even a virtuous love become lawful'. He had nine children by her, and watched over them with her when they were sick, and suffered with her when some of them died. (pp. 86-8)

In 1614, thirteen years after his marriage, we have further evidence of the constancy and of the quality of Donne's love for his wife. In a letter to Sir Robert More, on 10 August of that year, he again explains why he cannot and will not leave Anne in solitude:

> When I begin to apprehend that, even to myself, who can relieve myself upon books, solitariness was a little burdensome, I believe it would be much more to say to my wife if she were left alone. So much company therefore, as I am, she shall not want; and we had not one another at so cheap a rate as that we should ever be weary of one another.

Such words need no comment. But if any more evidence is required as to the nature and endurance of Donne's love for his wife, we have **'Holy Sonnet XVII,'** written after her death in 1617:

> Since she whom I lov'd hath payd her last debt
> To Nature, and to hers, and my good is dead,
> And her Soule early into heaven ravished,
> Wholly on heavenly things my mind is sett.
> Here the admyring her my mind did whett
> To seeke thee God; so streames do shew their head.

Without claiming any knowledge as to the dates of particular poems, we are bound to recognize that seventeen years of married love will have taught Donne something he did not know when he wrote, for instance, 'Elegy VII.' And we do, in fact, find that the poems express views of love which could scarcely all have been held at the same time.

Mr. Lewis, of course, recognizes that Donne's love poetry is 'not all of piece'. 'There are poems', he admits, 'in which Donne attempts to sing of a love perfectly in harmony with the moral law, but they are not very numerous and I do not think they are usually among his best pieces'. That judgements seems to me very odd, but it is impossible to discuss it without first deciding of what 'moral law' we are thinking. The moral law governing sexual relations has been very differently conceived of in different periods of the world's history. . . . Mr. Lewis believes that Donne never for long freed himself from [the] 'medieval sense of the sinfulness of sexuality'. Born a Roman Catholic, and deeply read in the Fathers of the Church, he must of course have considered it. But does his poetry support [the] belief that he continued to accept it? The value of Donne's love poetry largely depends upon the answer. 'The great central movement of love poetry in Donne's time', Mr. Lewis reminds us, was at variance with the medieval view. It was now believed that marriage sanctified sexual love; and for Spenser, once the marriage ceremony is over, the sexual act is its proper consummation and the chaste moon bears witness to it in the 'Epithalamion':

> Who is the same, which at any window peepes?
> Or whose is that faire face that shines so bright?
> Is it not Cinthia, she that never sleepes,
> But walkes about high heaven al the night?
> O fayrest goddesse, do thou not envy
> My love with me to spy:
> For thou likewise didst love, though now unthought,
> And for a fleece of wooll, which privily
> The Latmian shepherd once unto thee brought,
> His pleasure with the wrought.
> Therefore to us be favorable now;
> And sith of womens labours thou hast charge,
> And generation goodly dost enlarge,
> Encline thy will t'effect our wishful vow,
> And the chaste wombe informe with timely seed,
> That may our comfort breed:
> Till which we cease our hopeful hap to sing,
> Ne let the woods us answere, nor our Eccho ring . . .

Where does Donne stand in relation either to this belief that marriage, and marriage alone, sanctifies the sexual act, or to the medieval view that it is alike sinful within or without the marriage bond? If I read the poetry aright, he accepts neither view, or rather he totally rejects the second and does not consider the first. The purity or otherwise of the act depends for him on the quality of the relation between the lovers. We have in 'The Sunne Rising' a celebration of the same event as in the stanza quoted from 'Epithalamion'; but the difference in treatment is noteworthy. Donne is joyously impudent to the sun, whereas Spenser is ceremoniously respectful to the moon, and (which is the point here relevant), in Donne's poem we neither know nor care whether the marriage ceremony has taken place. For Donne, if delight in one another is mutual, physical union is its proper consummation; but, if the lovers are not 'inter-assuréd of the mind', then 'the sport' is 'but a winter-seeming summers night', and

> at their best
> Sweetnesse and wit they are but *mummy* possest.

There are a number of poems in which Donne is writing about love which has not reached physical consummation, but there is only one, 'The Undertaking,' in which he writes as though this state of affairs were satisfactory. Elsewhere he makes it plain that he has merely acquiesced, not without protest, in the human laws that forbade what he holds to be the natural expression of human loves. This reluctant obedience to the rules is most clearly stated in 'The Relique,' where he explains precisely how he and the woman behaved, and makes known in a parenthesis what he thinks of the law that inhibited them:

> Comming and going, wee
> Perchance might kisse, but not between those meales
> Our hands ne'er toucht the seales,
> Which nature, injur'd by late law, sets free.

Donne's poetry is not about the difference between marriage and adultery, but about the difference between love and lust. He does not establish the contrast between them in any one poem, but we arrive at his views by submitting ourselves to the cumulative evidence of all his poetry and, in so far as they are relevant, of his prose and of his life as well. The most important part of this evidence is the violent contrast between his cynical poems and those in which he celebrates

> our waking souls
> Which watch not one another out of feare.

In order to establish that contrast I must, unfortunately, refer to the vexed question of Donne's rhythm. Mr. Lewis assures us that 'most modern readers do not know how to scan'. However that may be, unless they can hear the difference between quick and slow movements, or between smooth and staccato, and unless they can submit to the rhythm sufficiently to throw the emphasis precisely where Donne has arranged for it to fall, they cannot understand his poetry. (pp. 88-9)

The greatness of Donne's love poetry is largely due to the fact that his experience of the passion ranged from its lowest depths to its highest reaches. No one, not even Shakespeare, knew better than he that

> The expense of spirit in a waste of shame
> Is lust in action; and till action, lust
> Is perjured, murderous, bloody, full of blame,
> Savage, extreme, rude, cruel, not to trust;
> Enjoy'd no sooner but despised straight;
> Past reason hunted; and no sooner had,
> Past reason hated.

Many of the *Songs and Sonets* and the *Elegies* dramatize the experience which Shakespeare here describes. But Donne came to know also the 'marriage of true minds', and many of his poems are about that experience. Nor does he repent of this love poetry in the *Holy Sonnets*; on the contrary, he expressly states that love for his wife led directly to the love of God. He does not even overlook his grosser experiences, but is prepared to use 'prophane love' to illustrate his faith in Christ's pity:

> No, no, but as in my idolatrie
> I said to all my profane mistresses
> Beauty, of pitty, foulnesse only is
> A signe of rigour: so I say to thee,
> To wicked spirits are horrid shapes assign'd
> This beauteous forme assures a piteous minde.

There is no note of shame here, neither wallowing self-abasement nor a hiding or forgetting of the past. He is simply using, characteristically, just what is relevant for his present purpose. Physical beauty, which his poetry so seldom describes, he nevertheless accepts as a type of the soul's beauty:

> For though mind be the heaven where love doth sit
> Beauty a convenient type may be to figure it.

Donne never despised the flesh. Even in a Lenten sermon he asks his hearers 'what Christian is denied a care of his health and a good habitude of body, or the use of those things which may give a cheerfulness to his heart and a cheerfulness to his countenance', and in his **'Litany'** he prays

> From thinking us all soule, neglecting thus
> Our mutuall duties, Lord deliver us.

Mr. Lewis's objections to **'The Extasie'** depend upon Donne's treatment of the relation between soul and body, and it is therefore important to discover what in fact Donne thought about this. 'Love does not', writes Mr. Lewis, 'prove itself pure by talking about purity. It does not keep on drawing distinctions between spirit and flesh to the detriment of the latter and then explaining that the flesh is after all to be used.' I must admit that I find this rather perplexing. Perhaps nothing can be proved by talking about it, neither the purity of love nor the purity of Donne's poetry. But language is the poet's only means of communication, and if Chapman is allowed to express his conception of the immorality of premarital relations by talking about it, why may not Donne, by the same means, express his belief that

> As our blood labours to beget
> Spirits as like soules as it can,
> Because such fingers need to knit
> That subtile knot that makes us man:
> So must pure lovers soules descend
> T'affections, and to faculties,
> Which sense may reach and apprehend,
> Else a great Prince in prison lies.

On what grounds does Mr. Lewis object to Donne's 'drawing distinctions between spirit and flesh to the detriment of the latter'? What else could he do? Could a man of his time and of his religion have thought of the flesh either as equal to or as indistinguishable from the spirit? Donne, like any man of his time, and, I suppose, any Christian of any time, thinks of the body as inferior to the soul, although it can be the 'temple of the Holy Ghost'. He is not singular in supposing that, in this life, the soul can and must express itself through the body. Milton goes so far as to assert that even the Angels need some equivalent for this means of expression:

> Whatever pure thou in body enjoy'st
> (And pure thou wert created,) we enjoy
> In eminence; and obstacle find none
> Of membrane, joint, or limb, exclusive bars;
> Easier than air with air, if Spirits embrace,
> Total they mix, union of pure with pure
> Desiring, nor restrain'd conveyance need,
> As flesh to mix with flesh, or soul with soul.

Donne, in **'The Extasie,'** is attempting (by his usual means of employing a series of analogies) to explain that the union of spirit with spirit expresses itself in the flesh, just as the soul lives in the body and, in this world, cannot exist without it. . . . The point Donne wishes to make in **'The Extasie,'** as in so many of his serious love poems, is that a man and a woman united by love may approach perfection more nearly than either could do alone:

> A single violet transplant
> The strength, the colour, and the size,
> (All which before was poore, and scant,)
> Redoubles still, and multiplies.
> When love, with one another so
> Interinanimates two soules,
> That abler soule, which thence doth flow,
> Defects of lonelinesse controules.

I have tried to show that Donne was very far from retaining 'the medieval view of the sinfulness of sex'; but Mr. Lewis has yet another accusation to bring, equally incompatible with my own belief that Donne is one of the greatest love poets in the English language. Contempt for women seems to him to permeate the poetry. Once again I shall be forced to assume that readers are more sensitive to rhythm than Mr. Lewis supposes, for I am going to quarrel with Mr. Lewis's interpretation of **'Elegy XVI'** largely by appealing to the readers's ear. He admits that he 'may be deceived' when he finds here 'a sickened male contempt for the whole female world of nurses and "midnight starting"'. Most certainly he is deceived, and the varied rhythms of that poem are an important index of the extent of that deception. One of the most remarkable things about the poem is the contrast between the solemn, tender music of the verse whenever Donne addresses the woman, and the boisterous staccato in which he describes the foreign lands to whose dangers she will be exposed if she insists upon following him abroad. I must beg leave to quote the poem at sufficient length to illustrate the nature and extent of this difference.

> By our first strange and fatall interview,
> By all desires which thereof did ensue,
> By our long starving hopes, by that remorse
> Which my words masculine perswasive force
> Begot in thee, and by the memory
> Of hurts, which spies and rivals threatned me,
> I calmly beg: But by thy fathers wrath,
> By all paines, which want and divorcement hath
>
> I conjure thee, and all the oathes which I
> And thou have sworne to seale joynt constancy,
> Here I unsweare, and overswear them thus,
> Thou shalt not love by wayes so dangerous.
> Temper, O faire love, loves impetuous rage,
> Be my true Mistris still, not my faign'd Page.

It is tempting to quote even more of this melodious pleading, but this is enough to illustrate the liturgical music of his address to this beloved of whom Mr. Lewis can think Donne is contemptuous. When, in the same poem, he wants to express contempt, his music is very different:

> Men of France, changeable Camelions,
> Spittles of diseases, shops of fashions,
> Loves fuellers, and the rightest company
> Of Players, which upon the worlds stage be,
> Will quickly know thee, and no lesse, alas!
> Th'indifferent Italian, as we passe
> His warme land, well content to thinke thee Page,
> Will hunt thee with such lust, and hideous rage,
> As *Lots* faire guests were vext.

And now, in case the point is not yet proven, let us hear how he speaks of her 'midnight startings', and how the rhythm changes once again as she comes back into the picture:

> When I am gone, dreame me some hapinesse,
> Nor let thy lookes our long hid love confesse,
> Nor praise, nor dispraise me, nor blesse, nor curse
> Openly loves force, nor in bed fright thy Nurse
> With midnight startings, crying out oh, oh
> Nurse, O my love is slaine, I saw him goe
> O'r the white Alpes alone; I saw him I,
> Assail'd, fight, taken, stabb'd, bleed, fall, and die.
> Augure me better chance, except dread *Jove*
> Thinke it enough for me to'have had thy love.

I said I would argue my case 'almost' solely on the grounds of rhythm, but in case Mr. Lewis is right in thinking modern readers are for the most part impervious to the music of verse, they will, I trust, be convinced that the mere prose sense of the last line is incompatible with contempt for the woman.

No one will deny that at one period of his life Donne wrote of women with contempt. At this time he despised them equally for yielding to his lust or for denying themselves to him. . . . But the measure of his contempt for easy virtue, coyness, and faithlessness is the measure of his admiration when he finds a woman to whom he can say

> So thy love may be my love's sphere.

But to Mr. Lewis that, too, sounds contemptuous; and as **'Aire and Angels'** has been variously understood, it is worth while to pause and examine the sentence in its context. The poem is an account of Donne's search for, and final discovery of, the true object of love. It begins with much the same idea as he express in the first stanza of **'The Good-morrow'**:

> If ever any beauty I did see,
> Which I desired, and got, 'twas but a dream of thee.

In **'Aire and Angels'**:

> Twice or thrice had I loved thee,
> Before I knew thy face or name;
> So in a voice, so in a shapelesse flame,
> *Angells* affect us oft, and worship'd bee;
> Still when, to where thou wert, I came
> Some lovely glorious nothing I did see.

And here, as so often elsewhere in the **Songs and Sonets**, Donne asserts his belief that 'pure lovers soules' must 'descend t'affections, and to faculties':

> But since my soule, whose child love is,
> Takes limmes of flesh, and else could nothing doe,
> More subtile than the parent is,
> Love must not be, but take a body too.

And at first he imagines that the physical beauty of the loved woman is the object of his search:

> And therefore what thou wert, and who,
> I bid love aske, and now
> That it assume thy body, I allow,
> And fix it selfe in thy lip, eye, and brow.

So far the progress is one to which we are accustomed, both in the literature of love and in experience; from a general reaching out after beauty to a particular worship of one person who sums up and overreaches all that had seemed fair in others. So Romeo catches sight of Juliet and forgets Rosalind:

> Did my heart love till now? forswear it, sight!
> For I ne'er saw true beauty till this night.

But Donne is not satisfied. There is no rest for his love in the bewildering beauty of his mistress:

> Whilst thus to ballast love, I thought,
> And so more steddily to have gone,
> With wares that would sinke admiration,
> I saw, I had loves pinnace overfraught,
> Ev'ry thy haire for love to worke upon
> Is much too much, some fitter must be sought;
> For, nor in nothing, nor in things
> Extreme, and scatt'ring bright, can love inhere.

The search is not yet over. But it is to end in a discovery surely more pleasing to any woman in love than would be the mere worship of her beauty. Beauty is transient, but love can last if it be for something which, though expressed in the body, is yet not the body:

> Then as an Angell, face and wings
> Of aire, not pure as it, yet pure doth weare,
> So thy love may be my loves spheare.

The doctrine of St. Thomas Aquinas, about the Angels assuming a body of air provided Donne with the analogy he wanted. . . . [The] point of the image for Donne is that the air-body of the Angels is neither nothing, nor too much, but just sufficient to confine a spirit on earth. So the woman's love for him is a resting-place for his spirit. It is of course, the final couplet of the poem that has led to misunderstanding. Dr. Leavis, in *Revaluations,* speaks of 'the blandly insolent matter-of-factness of the close' of **'Aire and Angels'** [see excerpt dated 1935]; and, isolated from its context, that is how it sounds:

> Just such disparitie
> As is twixt Aire and Angells puritie,
> 'Twixt womens love, and mens will ever bee.

There are two possible ways of reading this. The way which I am combating supposes that Donne, reversing the sentiment of the rest of the poem throws out a contemptuous generalization about the impurity of woman's love in comparison with man's. My own view is that Donne, satisfied with the logical aptness of his image, is, characteristically, indifferent to the associations of the word 'purity', whose meaning is, to his mind, made sufficiently clear by the context. The air-body is only less pure than the angel in so far as it can exist on earth and so enable a spirit to appear to men. A woman's love is only less pure than a man's in so far as it is focused upon a single object and does not continually reach out towards 'some lovely glorious nothing'. I would support this view by referring the reader to other instances in which Donne shows a similar indifference to the irrelevant associations his words may suggest. The use of the word 'pure' in **'Loves Growth'** is similarly circumscribed by its context:

> I scarce believe my love to be so pure
> As I had thought it was,
> Because it doth endure
> Vicissitude, and season as the grasse.

The sense in which it is not so pure is explained in the next stanza:

> Love's not so pure, and abstract, as they use
> To say, which have no Mistresse but their Muse,
> But as all else, being elemented too,
> Love sometimes would contemplate, sometimes do.

Donne is not saying that love is unclean, or less clean than he had supposed; we have already seen that he does not think of the flesh as impure in that sense, but that, like everything else on earth, it is composed of diverse elements. He is arguing that the quickening of love in the springtime is not an increase, since his love was complete before,

> And yet no greater, but more eminent
> Love by the spring is growne;
> As, in the firmament,
> Starres by the sunne are not inlarg'd, but showne;

and, to make his meaning clear, Donne adds three more images or illustrations:

> Gentle love deeds, as blossomes on a bough,
> From loves awakened root do bud out now.
> If, as in water stir'd more circles bee
> Produc'd by one, love such additions take,
> Those like so many spheares, but one heaven make,
> For, they are all concentrique unto thee.

And finally, the 'blandly matter-of-fact' image:

> As princes doe in times of action get
> New taxes, but remit them not in peace.

Here, however, the last line of the poem,

> No winter shall abate this spring's increase,

prevents the reader from supposing that the prosaic image implies a reversal of the emotional tone of the poem. The point relevant to my argument about **'Aire and Angels'** is that Donne always trusts the reader to ignore irrelevant associations. The political image here is logically apt, and that is a sufficient reason for him to use it. (pp. 93-101)

I hope I may have persuaded some readers that Donne did not think sex sinful, and that contempt for women is not a general characteristic of his love poetry. But Mr. Lewis brings yet one more accusation against him: 'He is perpetually excited and therefore perpetually cut off from the deeper and more permanent springs of his own excitement.' Now one way of answering this would be to say that love is an exciting experience, and that great love poetry is therefore bound to communicate excitement. But with this I am not quite content. Love is exciting, but it is also restful. Unreciprocated love is a torment of the spirit, but reciprocated love is peace and happiness. In the astonishment and uncertainty of the early stages of love there is excitement and there is also fear, but there comes a time when there is confidence and a sense of profound security. Donne is a great love poet because his poetry records and communicates these diverse experiences. He would be less great if it were true that he is 'perpetually excited'. The truth is that, just as his early contempt for women is the measure of his later reverence for one woman, so his vivid experience of the torment of insecure love has made him the more keenly relish the peace of a love

> inter-assured of the mind.

In **'The Canonization'** he tells us that future lovers will address him and his mistress as

> You to whom love was peace, that now is rage.

And in **'The Dissolution'** we read of a love so secure that the 'elements' of love, 'fire of Passion, sighs of ayre, water of teares and earthly sad despaire' were 'ne'ere worne out by loves securitie'. There are two alternative readings of this line; it may be 'ne'ere worne out' (never) or 'neere worne out' (nearly). The former seems to me the more probable reading, since Donne is arguing that he is now overburdened with elements, which he is more likely to be if they had not been spent. Moreover, in 'loves securitie', 'fire of Passion, sighs of ayre, water of teares and earthly sad despaire' are not 'worne out' (such love does not call for the expense of spirit); 'never' fits the sense better than 'nearly', but, for my present argument, it is not of vital importance which reading we choose, the significant word is 'securitie'. Nor does Donne merely tell us of the fearlessness, safety, peace, and security that love may give; the serenity of which he speaks is reflected in the movement of his verse, the quiet speaking voice is heard in the rhythm of **'The Good-morrow**, and in **'A Valediction: forbidding mourning'**, and quiet pleading in the last stanza of **'A Valediction: of weeping'**:

> O more then Moone,
> Draw not up seas to drowne me in thy spheare,
> Weepe me not dead, in thine armes but forbeare
> To teach the sea, what it may do too soone;
> Let not the winde
> Example finde,
> To doe me more harme, than it purposeth;
> Since thou and I sigh one another's breath,
> Who e'r sighs most, is cruellest, and hasts the others death;

and in that gracious lyric, **'Sweetest love I do not goe'**. (pp. 102-03)

> *Joan Bennett, "The Love Poetry of John Donne: A Reply to Mr. C. S. Lewis," in* Seventeenth Century Studies Presented to Sir Herbert Grierson, *1938. Reprint by Octagon Books, Inc., 1967, pp. 85-104.*

CLEANTH BROOKS (essay date 1942)

[Brooks is the most prominent exponent of the New Criticism movement. Although he and the other New Critics did not subscribe to a single set of principles, all believed that a work of literature had to be examined as an object in itself through a process of close analysis of symbol, image, and metaphor. For the New Critics, a literary work was not a manifestation of ethics, sociology, or psychology, nor could it be evaluated in the general terms of any nonliterary discipline. For Brooks, metaphor was the primary element of literary art, and the effect of that metaphor of primary importance. Brook's most characteristic essays are detailed studies of metaphoric structure, particularly in poetry. According to René Wellek, "Brooks analyzes poems as structures of opposites, tensions, paradoxes, and ironies with unparalleled skill." For Brooks, irony is the most important of these elements and, as Wellek notes, "indicates the recognition of incongruities, the ambiguity, the reconciliation of opposites which Brooks finds in all good, that is, complex poetry." In the following excerpt, Brooks reads "The Canonization" as a poem laden with daring paradoxical conceits.]

Few of us are prepared to accept the statement that the language of poetry is the language of paradox. Paradox is the language of sophistry, hard, bright, witty; it is hardly the language of the soul. We are willing to allow that paradox is a permissible weapon which a Chesterton may on occasion exploit. We may permit it in epigram, a special subvariety of poetry; and in satire, which though useful, we are hardly willing to allow to be poetry at all. Our prejudices force us to regard paradox as intellectual rather than emotional, clever rather than profound, rational rather than divinely irrational.

Yet there is a sense in which paradox is the language appropriate and inevitable to poetry. It is the scientist whose truth requires a language purged of every trace of paradox; apparently the truth which the poet utters can be approached only in terms of paradox. (p. 37)

Seeing this, we should not be surprised to find poets who consciously employ it to gain a compression and precision otherwise unobtainable. Such a method, like any other, carries with it its own perils. But the dangers are not overpowering; the poem is not predetermined to a shallow and glittering sophistry. The method is an extension of the normal language of poetry, not a perversion of it.

I should like to refer you to a concrete case. Donne's **"Canonization"** ought to provide a sufficiently extreme instance. (p. 46)

The basic metaphor which underlies the poems (and which is reflected in the title) involves a sort of paradox. For the poet daringly treats profane love as if it were divine love. The canonization is not that of a pair of holy anchorites who have renounced the world and the flesh. The hermitage of each is the other's body; but they do renounce the world, and so their title to sainthood is cunningly argued. The poem then is a parody of Christian sainthood; but it is an intensely serious parody of a sort that modern man, habituated as he is to an easy yes or no, can hardly understand. He refuses to accept the paradox as a serious rhetorical device; and since he is able to accept it only as a cheap trick, he is forced into this dilemma. Either: Donne does not take love seriously; here he is merely sharpening his wit as a sort of mechanical exercise. Or: Donne does not take sainthood seriously; here he is merely undulging in a cynical and bawdy parody.

Neither account is true; a reading of the poem will show that Donne takes both love and religion seriously; it will show, further, that the paradox is here his inevitable instrument. But to see this plainly will require a closer reading than most of us give to poetry.

The poem opens dramatically on a note of exasperation. The "you" whom the speaker addresses is not identified. We can imagine that it is a person, perhaps a friend, who is objecting to the speaker's love affair. At any rate, the person represents the practical world which regards love as a silly affectation. To use the metaphor on which the poem is built, the friend represents the secular world which the lovers have renounced.

Donne begins to suggest this metaphor in the first stanza by the contemptuous alternatives which he suggests to the friend

> . . . chide my palsy, or my gout,
> My five gray haires, or ruin'd fortune flout . . .

The implications are: (1) All right, consider my love as an infirmity, as a disease, if you will, but confine yourself to my other infirmities, my palsy, my approaching old age, my ruined fortune. You stand a better chance of curing those; in chiding me for this one, you are simply wasting your time as well as mine. (2)Why don't you pay attention to your own welfare —go on and get wealth and honor for yourself. What should you care if I do give these up in pursuing my love?

The two main categories of secular success are neatly, and contemptuously epitomized in the line

> Or the Kings reall, or his stamped face.

Cultivate the court and gaze at the king's face there, or, if you prefer, get into business and look at his face stamped on coins. But let me alone.

This conflict between the "real" world and the lover absorbed in the world of love runs through the poem; it dominates the second stanza in which the torments of love, so vivid to the lover, affect the real world not at all—

> What merchants ships have my sighs drown'd?

It is touched on in the fourth stanza in the contrast between the word "Chronicle" which suggests secular history with its pomp and magnificence, the history of kings and princes, and the word "sonnets" with its suggestions of trivial and precious intricacy. The conflict appears again in the last stanza, only to be resolved when the unworldly lovers, love's saints who have given up the world, paradoxically achieve a more intense world. But here the paradox is still contained in, and supported by, the dominant metaphor: so does the holy anchorite win a better world by giving up this one.

But before going on to discuss this development of the theme, it is important to see what else the second stanza does. For it is in this second stanza and the third, that the poet shifts the tone of the poem, modulating from the note of irritation with which the poem opens into the quite different tone with which it closes.

Donne accomplishes the modulation of tone by what may be called an analysis of love-metaphor. Here, as in many of his poems, he shows that he is thoroughly self-conscious about what he is doing. This second stanza he fills with the conventionalized figures of the Petrarchan tradition: the wind of lover's sighs, the floods of lovers' tears, etc—extravagant figures with which the contemptuous secular friend might be expected to tease the lover. The implication is that the poet himself recognizes the absurdity of the Petrarchan love metaphors. But what of it? The very absurdity of the jargon which lovers are expected to talk makes for his argument: their love, however absurd it may appear to the world, does no harm to the world. The practical friend need have no fears: there will still be wars to fight and lawsuits to argue.

The opening of the third stanza suggests that this vein of irony is to be maintained. The poet points out to his friend the infinite fund of such absurdities which can be applied to lovers:

Call her one, mee another flye,
We'are Tapers too, and at our owne cost die . . .

For that matter, the lovers can conjure up for themselves plenty of such fantastics comparisons: *they* know what the world thinks of them. But these figures of the third stanza are no longer the threadbare Petrarchan conventionalities; they have sharpness and bite. The last one, the likening of the lovers to the phoenix, is fully serious, and with it, the tone has shifted from ironic banter into a defiant but controlled tenderness.

The effect of this implied awareness of the lovers' apparent madness is to cleanse and revivify metaphor; to indicate the sense in which the poet accepts it, and thus to prepare us for accepting seriously the fine and seriously intended metaphors which dominate the last two stanzas of the poem.

The opening line of the fourth stanza,
Wee can dye by it, if not live by love,

achieves an effect of tenderness and deliberate resolution. The lovers are ready to die to the world; they are committed; they are not callow but confident. (The basic metaphor of the saint, one notices, is being carried on; the lovers in their renunciation of the world, have something of the confident resolution of the saint. By the bye, the word "legend"—

. . . if unfit for tombes and hearse
Our legend bee—

in Donne's time meant "the life of a saint.") The lovers are willing to forego the ponderous and stately chronicle and to accept the trifling and insubstantial "sonnet" instead; but then if the urn be well-wrought it provides a finer memorial for one's ashes than does the pompous and grotesque monument. With the finely contemptuous, yet quiet phrase, "half-acre tombes," the world which the lovers reject expands into something gross and vulgar. But the figure works further; the pretty sonnets will not merely hold their ashes as a decent earthly memorial. Their legend, their story, will gain them canonization; and approved as love's saints, other lovers will invoke them.

In this last stanza, the theme receives a final complication. The lovers in rejecting life actually win to the most intense life. This paradox has been hinted at earlier in the phoenix metaphor. Here it receives a powerful dramatization. The lovers in becoming hermits, find that they have not lost the world, but have gained the world in each other, now a more intense, more meaningful world. Donne is not content to treat the lovers' discovery as something which comes to them passively, but rather as something which they actively achieve. They are like the saint, God's athlete:

Who did the whole worlds soule *contract,* and *drove*
Into the glasses of your eyes. . . .

The image is that of a violent squeezing as of a powerful hand. And what do the lovers "drive" into each other's eyes? The "Countries, Townes," and "Courts," which they renounced in the first stanza of the poem. The unworldly lovers thus become the most "wordly" of all.

The tone with which the poem closes is one of triumphant achievements, but the tone is a development contributed

to by various earlier elements. One of the more important elements which works toward our acceptance of the final paradox is the figure of the phoenix, which will bear a little further analysis.

The comparison of the lovers to the phoenix is very skilfully related to the two earlier comparisons, that in which the lovers are like burning tapers, and that in which they are like the eagle and the dove. The phoenix comparison gathers up both: the phoenix is a bird, and like the tapers, it burns. We have a selected series of items: the phoenix figure seems to come in a natural stream of association. "Call us what you will," the lover says, and rattles off in his desperation the first comparisons that occur to him. The comparison to the phoenix seems thus merely another outlandish one, the most outrageous of all. But it is this most fantastic one, stumbled over apparently in his haste, that the poet goes on to develop. It really describes the lovers best and justifies their renunciation. For the phoenix is not two but one, "we two being one, are it"; and it burns, not like the taper at its own cost, but to live again. Its death is life: "Wee dye and rise the same. . . ." The poet literally justifies the fantastic assertion. In the sixteenth and seventeenth centuries to "die" means to experience the consummation of the act of love. The lovers after the act are the same. Their love is not exhausted in mere lust. This is their title to canonization. Their love is like the phoenix.

I hope that I do not seem to juggle the meaning of *die.* The meaning that I have cited can be abundantly justified in the literature of the period; Shakespeare uses "die" in this sense; so does Dryden. Moreover, I do not think that I give it undue emphasis. The word is in a crucial position. On it is pivoted the transition to the next stanza,

Wee can dye by it, if not live by love,
And if unfit for tombes. . . .

Most important of all, the sexual submeaning of "die" does not contradict the other meanings: the poet is saying: "Our death is really a more intense life"; "We can afford to trade life (the world) for death (love), for that death is the consummation of life"; "After all, one does not expect to live *by* love, one expects, and wants, to die *by* it." But in the total passage he is also saying "Because our love is not mundane, we can give up the world"; "because our love is not merely lust, we can give up the other lusts, the lust for wealth and power"; "because," and this is said with a little vein of irony as by one who knows the world too well, "because our love can outlast its consummation, we are a minor miracle; we are love's saints." This passage with its ironical tenderness and its realism feeds and supports the brilliant paradox with which the poem closes.

There is one more factor in developing and sustaining the final effect. The poem is an instance of the doctrine which it asserts; it is both the assertion and the realization of the assertion. The poet has actually before our eyes built within the song the "pretty room" with which he says the lovers can be content. The poem itself is the well-wrought urn which can hold the lovers' ashes and which will not suffer in comparison with the prince's "half-acre tomb."

And how necessary are the paradoxes? Donne might have said directly, "Love in a cottage is enough." **"The Canonization"** contains this admirable thesis, but it contains a great deal more. He might have been as forthright as a later lyricist who wrote, "We'll build a sweet little nest, / Somewhere out in the West, / And let the rest of the world go by." He might even have imitated that more metaphysical lyric, which maintains, "You're the cream in my coffee." **"The Canonization"** touches on all these observations, but it goes beyond them, not merely in dignity, but in precision.

I submit that the only way by which the poet could say what **"The Canonization"** says is by paradox. More direct methods may be tempting but all of them enfeeble and distort what is to be said. This statement may seem the less surprising when we reflect on how many of the important things which the poet has to say have to be said by means of paradox:—most of the language of lovers is such; **"The Canonization"** is a good example; most of the language of religion: "He who would save his life, must lose it"; "The last shall be first." (pp. 48-56)

> *Cleanth Brooks, "The Language of Paradox," in* The Language of Poetry by *by Philip Wheelwright and others, edited by Allen Tate, Princeton University Press, 1942, pp. 37-61.*

KATHLEEN RAINE (essay date 1945)

[*Raine is an English poet, essayist, autobiographer, and translator. As a literary essayist, she is best known for her numerous works on the poetry of William Blake. In the following excerpt, Raine examines Donnes' poetry as reflective of a sensitive life lived at the intersection of the medieval age of faith and spirituality and the modern age of doubt and materialism.*]

It is now for an entire literary generation that the methaphysical poets have seemed to have the clue to our own situation. It is not difficult to see why. For we, probably the most unhappy, and certainly the most torn by conflict, of all the generations since the seventeenth century, have to make a choice, as they had, between the desirable but doomed, and the less desirable but inevitable. To make a choice, or to find a solution. Whether one sees in Baroque art a resolved or an unresolved conflict, a consideration of what that conflict essentially was, cannot fail to compel our respect for the intellectual courage, not to say heroism, of the poet John Donne, who among other great figures of the Baroque period felt its full impact, and held in equipoise, even if only for a moment, those forces of change that in a few years transformed the medieval into the modern world. (p. 371)

Those who saw the turn of the sixteenth century, saw the passing of the Renaissance into the first dawning of the centuries of the Common Man, in the beginnings of Puritanism; they saw the last, superb expression of the ancient faith in Spanish Baroque art, and the Spanish Baroque saints; the highest point ever attained in Christian mysticism, in the period of Saint Teresa of Avila and Saint John of the Cross (both also poets) came late in the sixteenth century. Saint Teresa died in 1582, St. John in 1591. But Copernicus had already set the round earth in motion, and the little world of his new astronomy was already a diminished part in an expanding universe, and Europe itself a diminishing part of a world in which America was already appearing on the western horizon. The medieval world and the modern, the setting and the

rising stars, were in the sky together, for those who would to compare the values that had shaped the human world of the past, with those that were to shape its future.

As the rift between the spiritual and the material values widened, the Great picked sides. England was then the great protagonist of the modern, Spain of the ancient, order. And in this polarity, English thought and poetry were strong influenced by Spanish for the first and last time in history. The metaphysical poets are the fruits of this close contact with Spain, and that at a time when both countries were in their golden age. (p. 372)

What was great in the Baroque poets was that they did not underrate either kind of truth. They tried to hold the two hemispheres (the very word is characteristic of Baroque poetry) together, and if even partially they succeeded, their achievement was a tremendous one. Then, as now, the price of seeing too clearly both systems of value, was conflict and unhappiness. But then, as now, neither the revolutionary nor the reactionary, both of whom see things more simply, was wholly civilized.

The greatness of Baroque art, therefore, may be seen to be not in its destructive element, but in its attempt to reconcile those kinds of knowledge that at certain times seem impossible to reconcile, except in art.

Professor Edouardo Sarmiento, writing of Spanish Baroque art, point out how, the counter-reformation notwithstanding, even in Catholic Spain, this sense of strain reveals a latent doubt, disbelief, and loss of faith. 'If we may believe', he writes, 'the involuntary evidence of the art-style of an age for the state of its soul, then we cannot doubt that some such diagnosis of the Spanish counter-reform is true. The Baroque bears the stigmata of disbelief, anxiety and decadence, as certainly as the Gothic bears marks of faith, joy, and vigour.'

The strain characteristic of Baroque art is typically expressed in the use of perspective. In Baroque painting, the human figure is by this means seen to stand not firmly anchored to the earth, but is represented in often tormented and sensational attitudes rising towards heaven, or some other infinite point introduced into the composition by this exaggeration of perspective. (p. 374)

This may seem to be a digression from the subject—the metaphysical poetry of John Donne. But it is not so. For in poetry, a comparable attempt to bring together into focus the finite and the infinite, is the typical metaphysical figure, common to English and Spanish baroque poets, the conceit. Like the Baroque façade, this is not, as it might appear, a merely decorative device, but an attempt, in poetry, to harness together the tremendous forces of the temporal and the eternal, felt, as they were at the time, to be pulling apart. Here is a piece of John Donne from the poem *'Goodfriday 1613—Riding Westward'*, in which the space—the literal physical poles of the earth—are straining against the Christian image.

> Let mans Soule be a Spheare, and then, in this,
> The intelligence that moves, devotion is,
> And as the other Spheares, by being growne
> Subject to forraigne motions, lose their owne,
> And being by others hurried every day,
> Scarce in a yeare their naturall forme obey:
> Pleasure or businesse, so, our Soules admit
> For their first mover, and are whirld by it.
> Hence is't, that I am carryed towards the West
> This day, when my Soules forme bends towards the East.

> There I should see a Sunne, by rising set,
> And by that setting endlesse day beget;
> But that Christ on this Crosse, did rise and fall,
> Sinne had eternally benighted all.

In this poem, Donne achieves something, in poetic terms very like the *Transparente* of Spanish Baroque architecture. The static image of Christ, the earth's fixed centre, is harnessed to the whirling image of the Copernican movement of the revolving earth, the moving spheres.

> Could I behold those hands which span the Poles,
> And tune all spheares at once, pierc'd with those holes?
> Could I behold that endlesse height which is
> Zenith to us, and our Antipodes,
> Humbled below us? or that blood which is
> The seat of all our Soules, if not of his,
> Made durt of dust, or that flesh which was worne
> By God, for his apparell, rag'd, and torne?

The tension is immense. But the poem holds as it intends to hold, the two orders of reality together, not scientifically, or theologically, but as poetry—the only force perhaps that can harness together truths of different orders.

That is an extreme example of the constant characteristic of the conceit, which is to bring together, using as a focal point some light similarity between them, sharply contrasting images, belonging, often, to different orders of reality (as in the passage just quoted). Other figures are commonly used to accomplish the same end. Of metaphysical poems it is less the figures used than the purpose they serve that is characteristic.

In this other quoted passage from **'The Relique'**, it is not science and the image of Christ that pull apart and are held by the conceit, but that other basic conflict that tormented the Baroque period, the paradox of life and death, sex and corruption.

> When my grave is broke up againe
> Some second ghest to entertaine,
> (For graves have learn'd that woman-head
> To be to more than one a Bed)
> And he that digs it, spies
> A bracelet of bright haire about the bone,
>
> Will he not let'us alone,
> And thinks that there a loving couple lies,
> Who thought that this device might be some way
> To make their soules, at the last busie day,
> Meet at this grave, and make a little stay?

There are other subsidiary antitheses; there is the juxtaposition of the old half-legendary medievalism, Adam and Eve in the Garden of Eden, Noah and the flood and the rest—with the new Copernican pattern of the world (pp. 375-77)

Or again, the microcosm and the macrocosm are harnessed together in an image that recurs often in Donne, of life as land, death as sea:

> Man is the world, and death the ocean
> To which God gives the lower parts of men.
> This sea invirons all land though as yet
> God hath set marks and bounds twixt us and it,
> Yet doth it rore and gnaw, and still pretend,
> And breakes our banks whenere it takes a friend,
> Then our land waters (tears of passion) vent,
> Our waters, then above the firmament
> (Tears which our Soul doth for her sins let fall)
> Take all a brakish taste, and funerall.

'My America, my newfound land,' Donne called his mistress. One meets everywhere images of latitude and longitude, lengthening and shortening shadows: the new Copernican framework of the universe. Superimposed on the human measure of the Christian myth with eternity and infinity, God-in-man, at the centre, is a new order in which eternity and infinity are being banished to the circumference of an expanding universe, no longer infinitely present, but infinitely remote. (p. 377)

Want of beauty is a charge that has been made against Donne's poetry; and in a certain sense with justice. For the worlds of beauty and of reality, too, were pulling apart at the turn of the century. Shakespeare wrote in a language at once near the real speech of men, and equally capable of speaking for that inner voice of the soul (heard all too often in the nineteenth century), for the two were not very different in an age when soldiers like Sydney and Essex, and seamen like Sir Walter Raleigh found it natural to be poets. But at the turn of the century, Shakespeare himself wrote:

> Truth may see, but cannot be,
> Beauty brag, but 'tis not she,
> Truth and beauty buried be.

Donne spoke a language stripped of magic, bare, in that sense, of beauty. Milton inherited the beauty, but no longer wrote poetry in a language that men spoke. One might see in this division, too, another symptom of the repression of the soul. (p. 379)

Each poem that he wrotes is like a finely poised needle, suspended between the great magnets of science and religion, action and learning, the pleasures of love, the call to martyrdom; the infirm glory of the greatest court on earth; and the annihilation of all in death. The needle, for Donne, comes to rest only when it points to the one true North—that of love. And for Donne, as for Dante, it was through woman's love that his way lay towards the divine love that was his final point of rest.

In two of his longer works, we can see Donne's speculative mind at work in a way essentially modern, on changes of the medieval pattern of thought. **'The Progresse of the Soule,'** written in 1601, and one of Donne's finest poems, combines the Garden of Eden myth with a fine intuitive forecasting of modern biological theory. The transmigration of a 'soul', beginning its life in an apple on the tree of Eden, and ending just as it reached the human level (rather in mid-air, as Donne did not finish the poem as he had originally planned it) are traced from plant to bird, to fish, whale, elephant, dog, ape, and finally to man. Donne having no theory of science to prove cannot be blamed if the order is a little out at one or two places. But that the 'progresse' in the poem is so close to the picture that Darwin later established, is a measure of the natural scientific bent of Donne's mind. And all this is combined in a series of Duerer-like pictures of plant and animal life, suggesting the herbals and bestiaries of the middle ages, in which walks Eve herself, as true to life as detail can make her; her mythical figure pulls up a real mandrake plant to give, as medicine, to a real baby. Like Duerer, Donne makes the myth credible by the realism of the detail.

Nine years later; in 1610, Donne wrote *Ignatius his Conclave.* This satire is amusing reading even now; Donne describes his 'vision', in which 'I had liberty to wander through all places and to survey and reckon all the roomes, and all the volumes of the heavens, and to comprehend the situation, the dimensions, the nature, the people, and the policy, both of the swimming Islands, the *Planets* and of all those which are fixed in the firmament. Of which, I thinke it an honester part as yet to be silent, than to do *Galileo* wrong by speaking of it, who of late hath summoned the other worlds, the Stars to come nearer to him. and give him an account of themselves. Or to *Keppler*, who as himselfe testifies of himselfe, ever since Tycho Braches death hath received it into his care, that no new thing should be done in heaven without his knowledge.' 'In the twinkling of an eye', writes Donne, 'I saw all the roomes in Hell open to my sight. And by the benefit of certaine spectacles, I know not of what making, but I thinke, of the same, by which *Gregory*, the great, and *Beda* did discerne so distinctly the soules of their friends, when they were discharged from their bodies, and sometimes the soules of such men as they knew not by sight, and of some that never were in the world, and yet they could distinguish them flying into Heaven, or conversing with living men, I saw all the channels in the bowels of the Earth; and all the inhabitants of all nations, and of all ages were suddenly made familiar to me. I think truely, *Robert Aquinas* when he tooke *Christs* long Oration, as he hung upon the Crosse, did use some such instrument as this, but applied to the eare; And so I thinke did he, which dedicated to *Adrian 6*, the Sermon which *Christ* made in prayse of his father *Joseph*; for else how did they heare that, which none but they ever heard?' To proceed, Donne describes how (in Hell that is) 'I saw a secret place, where there were not many, beside Lucifer himselfe; to which, onely they had title, which had so attempted any innovation in this life, that they gave an affront to all antiquitie, and induced doubts, and anxieties, and scruples, and after, a libertie of beleeving waht they would; at length established opinions, directly contrary to all established before.'

Here we recognize, in comic dress, the same Baroque conflict of ideas, of new and uncontrollable ideas that are far-reaching enough quite to overturn the foundations of the world. There is very little comic Baroque art, but **Ignatius his Conclave** may be claimed as a rare example of this category.

In this imaginary 'hell' the Jesuits take a high place as the arch equivocators. Here Donne 'saw' St. Ignatious (like Jouvet, in monk's habit) standing very close to Lucifer himself, advising him on the cases of those pretenders who sought admission to Hell's most exalted rank, as distorters of the universe.

The pretenders and their claims are interesting. Copernicus puts his case: 'Shall these gates be open to such as have innovated in small matters? and shall they be shut against me, who have turned the whole frame of the world, and am thereby almost a new "Creator"?'. Ignatius opposes his claim. 'Who cares', Ignatius asks, 'whether the earth travell, or stand still? Hath your raising up of the earth into heaven, brought men to that confidence, that they build new towers or threaten God againe? Or do they out of this motion of the earth conclude, that there is no hell, or deny the punishment of sin? Do not men beleeve? do they not live just, as they did before?' Also 'those opinions of yours may very well be true'—and that in itself must exclude Copernicus from the highest honours of Hell. In the light of subsequent history, one is inclined to

think that Donne's Ignatius was premature in his conclusion that men went on living 'just as they did before' after Copernicus.

Paracelsus was excluded likewise, because such as his discoveries were, they were of minor importance. Machiavelli had a better case: 'although the entrance into his place may be decreed to none but the Innovators, and onely such of them as have dealt in *Christian* businesse; and of them also, to those only which have had the fortune to doe much harme, I cannot see but that next to the Jesuites, I must bee invited to enter, since I did not onely teach those wayes by which, through *perfidiousness* and *dissembling of Religion,* a man might possesse, and usurpe upon the liberty of free *Commonwealths*; but also did arme and furnish the people with my intructions, how when they were under this oppression, they might safeliest conspire, and remove a *tyrant* or revenge themselves of their *Prince*, and redeeme their former losses; so that from both sides, both from *Prince* and *People*, I brought an abundant harvest, and a noble increase to this kingdome. By this time I perceived *Lucifer* to bee much moved with this Oration, and to incline much towards *Machiavel*. For he did acknowledge him to bee a kind of *Patriarke*, of those whom they call *Laymen*. And he had long observed, that the *Clergie* of *Rome* tumbled downe to *Hell* daily, easily, voluntarily, and by troupes, because they were accustomed to sinne against their conscience, and knowledge; but that the *Layitie* sinning out of a slouthfulnesse, and negligence of finding the truth, did rather offend by ignorance, and omission. And therefore he thought himselfe bound to reward *Machiavel,* which had awakened this drowsie and implicite *Layitie* to greater, and more bloody undertakings.'

'Vision' or not, what Donne wrote had this much truth in it. These were ideas whose conflict was on an earthly plan 'inducing doubts, and anxieties, and scruples, and after, a liberty of believing what they would'. (pp. 381-84)

Donne's middle period—the years of poverty and worry that drove him to the necessity of a servility to possible patrons that became him vey ill; in a series of always frustrated attempts to get back into a career of some sort—produced no poems as fine in their kind as the early **Songs and Sonnets**, or later **Holy Sonnets** and religious verse. But those he wrote at that time are revealing, bringing to light as they do the measure of the spiritual maladjustment of Donne to his world, and that world to itself; and the growing seriouness with which the poet now sought to find a solution for a problem whose implications he increasingly realized. The clue is to be found in **'The Anatomie of the World'** and the **'First and Second Anniversaries.** These ambitious poems, full of fine passages, have something deeply wrong about them, and are embarrasing reading even now. This is not so much because they were written to some extent (possibly, or partly) with an eye to getting a patron (which they did), but because they open a religious void that it is saddening to contemplate.

These Rilke-like poems were written, like the Duino Elegies, on the occasion of the untimely death of a young girl—a girl whom the poet had never seen—Miss Elizabeth Drury, only daughter of that Sir Robert Drury who was to be Donne's patron for a number of years. And if ever poems rang false, these do. 'If it had been written of the Virgin Mary it had been something,' Ben Jonson said of the '**Anatomie of the World**'—and he has put his finger on the very point of the weakness. They were not written of the Virgin Mary. They were, however (as Donne said), written 'of the idea of a woman, not as she was'. They were, in fact, a lamentable, trumped-up attempt to put a personal image and personal 'idea of a woman' in the place of the old and universal Christian pantheon—even of the Mother of God herself—who were gone from the empty niches of the reformed churches of England. This pompous, inflated, home-made improvisation tagged on to the corpse of Miss Elizabeth Drury reveals jut how far adulation falls short of canonization. The root of medieval faith had been severed. Not one of the elegies that Donne wrote in succeeding years, attributing to the nobility and to princes virtues that they may have possessed, or may not, ever could bridge that gulf between the scepticism of the reform and the lost medieval faith. They remain mere epitaphs: these poems, and all Donne's poetry of the grave and the dead, is like a dark after-image of the light of faith and bears to the medieval faith the skull-like resemblance that the negative photograph bears to the positive.

Donne did indeed, like an apostle not of faith but of mortality, put something in those empty niches, in those churches deserted by their saints. But not the carved angels, not the shrines of gothic saints. He hung those empty walls with emblems of mortality, urns, marmoreals, symbols of death and physical corruption; the pomp of the grave, not the symbols of life. These silent testimonies of doubt have, in the English churches, replaced the saints in their shrines. Donne was, of that tradition, one of the orginators, who left imprinted on the English Church its characteristic grand, but essential, though reluctant, scepticism. (pp. 386-87)

And yet there is greatness in the scepticism of the reform—for it is a relative, not an absolute scepticism that we find in the English Baroque; a scepticism that would fain believe, not one that belittles, with the diabolical 'spirit that denies'. One that does still, in fact, hold to the desirability of faith, and therewith, some faith also. (p. 388)

Two years after Donne's ordination, and four before his appointment as Dean of St. Paul's, Anne Donne died in giving birth to their twelfth child. If one sees the events of a life as stages of a pilgrimage, it is difficult not to see in Anne Donne's death as the departure of one of those legendary guides—like Dante's Virgil, or Beatrice, who stayed with the poet only until her work was accomplished, for now Donne had entered the last stage of his strange development. Henceforth his inner life was to be lived in relation only to God.

Look at the beginning of Donne's life—those love-poems, so subtly introspective, yet so worldly, so far from serious; at the portrait of Jack Donne at eighteen, the young man with the earrings, at the end of his three years at Cambridge; and look at the end—the eloquent divine, who, in the words of one critic, now 'put a trumpet to his lips'; who himself chose that posterity should remember him in the aspect of his death, the features burned out, the winding sheet tied about his face. How did the one change into the other? It happened imperceptibly, naturally. It is the same man. That unmistakable personal idiom, the rapid ardent sentences, the very imagery of the early love poems are found in the **Holy Sonnets**. The very imagery of erotic

love is retained, and amplified into a symbolic language to speak of God, and to God.

> Take mee to you, imprison me, for I
> Except you enthrall mee, never shall be free,
> Norever chast, except you ravish mee.

The first and the last poems that he wrote, use almost precisely the same images.

Donne indeed put a trumpet to his lips in those later years, when he preached at Paul's Cross, to the people, and before two kings—James I, and later King Charles—at Whitehall; when he summoned up the angels in Baroque imagery of unsurpassed grandeur—

> At the round earth's imagin'd corners, blow
> Your trumpets, Angells, and arise, arise
> From death, you numberlesse infinities
> Of soules, and to your scattred bodies goe,
> All whom flood did, and fire shall o'erthrow,
> All whom warre, dearth, age, agues, tyrannies,
> Despaire, law, chance, hath slaine, and you whose eyes,
> Shall behold God, and never tast deaths woe.

But a trumpet does not necessarily mean a release from doubts. With Donne, the light and shade was deeper, that was all, as his life declined from evening into night. In his youth, that we cannot know all seemed reason to doubt God; in his maturity, a reason for trusting Him. But as the noon of love darkened into the shadow of death, the witty scepticism of youth darkened into the agonizing doubts of age. It is still a poetry of doubt, of decline from faith, struggling to find certainty at the brink of the grave, that no other times of life, neither the love nor the learning of his prime, had yielded the poet. For all Donne's doubts gradually focused on one point—Death. As in loving women he was introspective, analysing his love, so in his sickness he analysed himself as thoroughly as Freud could ever have searched the submerged regions of instinct and the unconscious. If only he could have found the soul, and brought it out like an undiscovered organ! But deep as he might search, it was not to be found. The **Devotions on Sundrie Occasions** are in their way as searchingly introspective as the *Ascent of Mount Carmel*. But they are the voice of the body, the unconscious, the dark chaos of man, not his incandescence, as is St. John's great introspective analysis.

To pass over the twenty years of his preaching and ministry, we reach the story of Donne's death. In the winter of 1630, Donne was a dying man. He was too ill to preach at Christmas, but at the beginning of Lent, knowing that it was for the last time, he rose from his bed to preach perhaps his greatest sermon of all— **Death's Duell, or A Consolation to the Soul against the Dying Life, and Living Death of the Body**. This sermon was 'Delivered at Whitehall, before the King's Majesty' on 25 February, 1630, 'Being his last Sermon and called by His Majesties' Household, the Doctor's owne Funerall Sermon'. He took as his text the terrible sentence 'And unto God the Lord, belong the issues of death'. Here at its most sublime is that 'metaphysical shudder'. the horror of mortality. (pp. 390-92)

But in the very toils of this death, Donne was to portray, as it has never before or since been portrayed in England in poetry, or in any other art, the scene of the Crucifixion, in a baroque magnificence comparable only to the painting of El Greco:

DEATHS
DVELL,
O R,
A Confolation to the Soule, againft
the dying Life, and liuing
Death of the Body.

Deliuered in a Sermon at White Hall, before the
KINGS MAIESTY, in the beginning
of Lent, 1630.

By that late learned and Reuerend Diuine,
IOHN DONNE, Dr. in Diuinity,
& Deane of S.Pauls, London.

Being his laft Sermon, and called by his Maiefties houfhold
THE DOCTORS OWNE FVNERALL SERMON:

LONDON,
Printed by THOMAS HARPER, for Richard Redmer
and Beniamin Fisher, and are to be fold at the figne
of the Talbot in Alderf-gate ftreet.
M. DC. XXXII.

Title page of the work described by Donne's contemporaries as "the Doctor's own funeral sermon."

There now hangs that sacred Body upon the Crosse, re-baptized in his owne teares and sweat, and embalmed in his owne blood alive. There are those bowells of compassion, which are so conspicuous, so manifested, as that you may see them through his wounds. There those glorious eyes grew faint in their light: so as the Sun ashamed to survive them, departed with his light too. And then that Sonne of God, who was never from us, and yet had now come a new way unto us in assuming our nature, delivers that soule (which was never out of his Father's hand) by a new way, a voluntary emission of it into his Father's hands; For though to his God our Lord, belong'd these issues of death, so that considered in his owne contract, he must necessarily die, yet at no breach or battery, which they had made upon his sacred Body, issued his soule, but emisit, hee gave up the Ghost, and as God breathed a soule into the first Adam, so this second Adam breathed his soule into God, into the hands of God. There wee leave you in that blessed dependancy, to hang upon him that hangs upon the Crosse, there bath in his teares, there suck at his woundes, and lie downe in peace in his grave, till hee vouchsafe you a resurrection, and an ascension into that Kingdome, which hee hath purchas'd for you, with the inestimable price of his incorruptible blood.

Here indeed we have doubt at its most heroic, redeemed by its own intensity, and achieving the stature of faith. For greater than a complacent belief in something trivial, is the doubt of something great. For to doubt is in itself to assert and establish the values doubted. So Baroque art takes its stature from medieval faith. Never again, perhaps, will a decline of faith produce anything comparable, for never again will the world have so much to lose, as the medieval Christian faith. Compared with the struggle with which then were relinquished the values of a passing age, it is frightening to see, in our period, with what ease, what lack of spiritual struggle, values are discarded. For the gulf that opens for us (in *Mein Kampf*, the Communist Manifesto, and our own and the American materialist Utopias) is as much deeper than Donne's relative doubt as medieval Christianity was higher than the liberal humanism that succeeded it, and is now in its turn the vanishing faith.

The image of Christ crucified is, of all the Christian images, the one that in itself contains the full paradox of human doubt and human faith, the focal point of temporal and eternal, at which the eternal is at once most essentially challenged, and most essentially triumphant. For Donne, the pull was not only away from faith, but also, with equal, and perhaps finally with greater strength, towards it. At the end of his life only two magnets retained any power over him—the image of the grave and the image of God.

In the seven weeks that lay between the preaching of **Death's Duell** and death itself, Donne prepared for his promised end, still seeking God with a courage equal to that of any saint who ever battled his way out of this world. (pp. 392-93)

To these last weeks also belong two of the greatest of his lyrical poems—the **'Hymne to God my God, in my sicknesse'**, and **'A Hymne to God the Father'**.

In the first Donne, for a moment echoing the faith of Saint John of the Cross who wrote of the soul:

> Oh night more lovely than the day
> Oh night that joined the beloved with her lover,
> *and changed her into her love,*

writes like a mystic 'Since I am coming to that Holy roome Where, with thy Quire of Saints for evermore *I shall be made thy Musique'*.

He takes his last backward look on the world. How long ago it was that he had written of his mistress' body,

> without sharp north, without declining west.

How long ago those voyages with Essex, long dead, to Cadiz and the Azores! Now these images of life are seen down the lengthening perspective of death:

> Whilst my Physitians by their love are growne
> Cosmographers, and I their Mapp, who lie
> Flat on his bed, that by them may be showne
> That this is my South-west discoverie
> Per fretum febris, by these streights to die,
>
> I joy, that in these straits, I see my West;
> For, though theire currants yeeld returne to none,
> What shall my West hurt me? As West and East
> In all flatt Maps (and I am one) are one,
> So death doth touch the Resurrection.

And for the last time for centuries to come, the natural and the spiritual orders are brought together in a Baroque image of unsurpassed power; for one last time the poles of the natural world, of the human measure and of supernatural truth, were one:

> We thinke that Paradise and Calvarie,
> Christs Crosse, and Adams tree, stood in one place;
> Looke Lord, and finde both Adams met in me;
> As the first Adams sweat surrounds my face,
> May the last Adams blood my soule embrace.

But to his very death, doubt and faith struggled for the soul of John Donne. His last written words were these:

> I have a sinne of feare, that when I have spunne
> My last thred, I shall perish on the shore;
> Sweare by thy selfe, that at my death thy sonne
> Shall shine as he shines now, and heretofore;
> And, having done that, Thou haste done,
> I feare no more.

It has remained for a painter of our own tormented age, Stanley Spenser, to paint the scene that the monument he himself designed has for so long obscured, of 'John Donne arriving at the Gates of Heaven'. For though much had perished in doubt, enough faith finally remained to bring within their reach that heroic soul who welded together in his poetry the hemispheres of broken truth. (pp. 394-95)

> Kathleen Raine, "John Donne and the Baroque Doubt," in Horizon, London, Vol. XI, No. 66, June, 1945, pp. 371-95.

J. B. LEISHMAN   (essay date 1951)

[*An English educator and translator, Leishman was the author of* The Metaphysical Poets *(1934) and* Themes and Variations in Shakespeare's Sonnets *(1961). In the following excerpt, he illuminates the influence of Ovid upon Donne's* Elegies.]

In nearly all Donne's poetry what one may call sheer wit plays a very great part, and this element of sheer wit, is, I think, more immediately apparent in the couplet poems than in the ***Songs and Sonets,*** where it has often been mistaken for the expression of actual convictions, attitudes and experiences. (p. 50)

Only part of Donne's poetry is wholly of this kind, but a great deal of it is partly of this kind—a fact we must remember when we feel tempted to interpret it autobiographically. We must always be prepared to make very large allowance for the element of sheer wit. (P. 52)

What is most peculiar and characteristic in Donne's genius and method, the great part played in his poetry by sheer wit, emerges, perhaps, most clearly and rapidly from a careful study of the Elegies. *They may be divided into three main groups: (1) witty discourses on a broomstick, where the subject is a mere occasion for displaying wit; (2) apparently serious defences of outrageous propositions; (3) dramatic situations, real or imaginary, in which also considerable elements of sheer wit or sheer paradox may be incidentally* present.

Let us begin with the third group, which I have called the dramatic elegies, but before doing so let us glance briefly at a book which had, I think, no inconsiderable influence on the tone and on the situations of several of them, Ovid's *Amores*. Ovid's *Elegies* the Elizabethans called them, and that was the title of the not always very accu-

rate or felicitous translation by the youthful Marlowe, which, together with the *Epigrams* of Sir John Davies, appeared in an undated volume which claimed to have been printed at Middleburgh, and which must certainly have been printed before 1599. The original meaning of *elegia* or *elegeia* was a funeral elegy written in elegiacs (*elegi*), that is to say, in couplets consisting of an hexameter followed by a pentameter, but Ovid and other Roman poets used the word to describe a love-poem written in that metre.... Donne's predecessors had exploited classical mythology and classical legend and had drawn largely on the Ovid of the *Metamorphoses*; Donne, who despised such mere ornaments and childish fancies, proceeded to do something much more daring and original, something, too, which was the almost complete antithesis of that Petrarchan adoration and Platonic idealism of which, together with classical mythology and classical allusions, he and many of his contemporaries had had more than enough: he proceeded *to reproduce something of the tone, the situations and the cynical wit of Ovid's Amores.* There are, it is true, great differences in style: the smooth progression, the details seldom in themselves extravagant, the crackling fire of epigram which distinguish Ovid's Amores are very different from the drama, the extravagance, the vivid realism, the subtle analogies and syllogistic arguments of Donne. What Donne has caught are the impudence and insolence and the assumptions about the true nature and end of love and the proper attitude to husbands. One of the most consistently witty and epigrammatic of all Ovid's elegies is the nineteenth of the Second Book, where he contemptuously tells Corinna's complacent husband to guard her for her lover's sake if not for his own, since things too easily obtained lose their attraction. 'If you yourself, you fool,' he begins, 'feel no need to guard your wife, at least guard her for my sake so that I may desire her more passionately. What is lawful gives no pleasure, what is not excites us all the more keenly'. (pp. 52-4)

The Ovid of the *Metamorphoses*, the mythological Ovid, had already been exploited *and mauseam;* Donne seems to have been the first to perceive what novel, surprising and shocking effects might be produced by exploiting the more realistic and naturalistic Ovid of the *Amores*. To transfer some of Ovid's characteristic situations and assumptions to Elizabethan London, and to express them as though they were a matter of course, was in itself a daring piece of originality. We must, of course, resist the temptation to regard such poems as autobiographical, or to infer from them anything about Donne's own conduct, morals and opinions. The fact that in several of them there appears the triangular situation of poet, mistress and husband, led Gosse to infer that round about 1596 Donne was having an intrigue with some married woman; it is, though, much more probable that he was simply dramatizing the situation he found in Ovid's *Amores*. We should remember, too, a remark of the later and graver Donne about the poetry he had written in youth; 'I did best', he said, 'when I had least truth for my subjects'.

Proceeding now to our study of what I have called the dramatic elegies, let us begin with the First Elegy, entitled **"Jealosie"**.... The situation, as I have said, comes Ovid's *Amores*, but, here as elsewhere, there is much more drama and play of mind than in Ovid.

> Wee must not, as wee us'd, flout openly,
> In scoffing ridles, his deformitie;
> Nor at his boord together being satt,
> With words, nor touch, scarce lookes adulterate.

These lines were almost certainly suggested by a much longer passage in the fourth elegy of Ovid's First Book, but how different is Donne's rapidity and vivid concentration from the leisurely elaboration of Ovid, who is, as it were, rather coolly, methodically and exhaustively working out a prescribed theme than, like Donne, setting down images and impressions which seem to have occurred to him for the first time in the heat of composition.

Ovid, one may say in general, is continually describing, and making witty and epigrammatic remarks about, situations which are static or given, is, as it were, contemplating them from the outside, in detachment; Donne, at any rate in the elegies we are now considering, is much more dramatic, continually throwing himself, as it were, into a part, continually imagining new aspects of the triangular situation, and speaking, thinking, and feeling vividly and rapidly as in a play. While Ovid merely describes situations, Donne enacts them: the nature and details of the situation emerge, as it were, incidentally, from an overheard discourse or tirade. Such elegies are essentially dramatic monologues—monologues, that is to say, whose tone is modified by, adapted to, the particular kind of person Donne imagines himself to be addressing. (pp. 56-9)

In the Fourth Elegy, entitled **'The Perfume'**, the mistress is a young unmarried woman, a mere girl. One can still feel Ovid in the background, and the desire to surprise, to shock, by the pretended acceptance of an immoral and cynical code which, I think we may be pretty sure, was never Donne's own; but, although there is more detail than in **'Jealosie'**, it is entirely unimitative, entirely English, and most brilliantly, vividly and concentratedly imagined. Indeed, the description of the mother's careful examination of her daughter is, in its elaborately but at the same time concentratedly imagined detail, reminiscent of some of the best things in Jonson's comedies.... [The] first forty-two lines [form] the most brilliant and characteristic passage, I think, in all Donne's dramatic elegies.... (p. 60)

The Fifteenth Elegy, **'The Expostulation'**, though still essentially dramatic, is, as it were, more internally and less externally so, less descriptive, more continuously argumentative, than the elegies we have been considering. He first accuses his mistress of inconstancy, then suddenly rebukes himself, curses the person in whom she innocently confided and who made them jealous and mistrustful of one another, and insists that everything between them is just as it was before. In the concluding lines which, like **'His parting from her'**, are tender as well as witty, and, though full of intellectual activity, never abstract, there is an almost certain reminiscence of a passage at the beginning of the second elegy of Ovid's Third Book, where he describes himself at the circus with Corinna, she watching the races, he watching her, though Donne substitutes the playhouse for the circus. (P. 64)

[We now] come to the famous Sixteenth, **'On his Mistris'**, dissuading her from her wish to accompany him on a foreign journey disguised as a page, which in one manuscript alone, the Bridgewater, has the title **'His wife would have gone as his page'**. For various reasons I agree with Grierson that this poem was almost certainly not addressed by Donne to his wife. In the first place, so far as we know, the first time that Donne travelled abroad after his marriage was when he went to Paris with Sir Robert Drury in

1611. Before leaving her, he gave his wife, as Walton tells us, the **'Valediction: forbidding mourning'** [see excerpt dated 1640], and it seems to me almost certain that it was knowledge of the circumstances under which this poem had been written which led the writer of the Bridgewater MS. to assume, rather superficially, that the Sixteenth Elegy had been written at the same time. In the second place, it is perfectly clear from internal evidence that the real or imaginary addressee of this elegy was neither in reality nor in imagination Donne's wife: he calls her his 'Mistris', and she is still a mere girl and has a nurse. Some might object that the writer of the Bridgewater MS. meant no more than that the elegy had been addressed by Donne to his *future* wife, that is to say, to Ann More, on some occasion before their marriage, but the fact that at l.7 all the manuscripts except one, and that a late one, read 'by thy parents wrath', suggests that the reading of the printed texts 'by thy fathers wrath', was introduced later by someone who believed, like the writer of the Bridgewater MS., that the poem had been addressed, either before or after marriage, to Donne's wife, and who knew that, as a matter of fact, not both her parents but only her father was alive at the time of their first acquaintance. It is, of course, possible that at some time before their marriage Donne had imagined a situation in which Ann, who was only seventeen when he married her in 1601, had wished to accompany him on a foreign journey disguised as a page; but is it really more necessary to posit a real existence for the young girl of this elegy than for the young daughter of the 'hydroptique father' and 'immortall mother', guarded by

The grim eight-foot-high iron-bound serving-man

in **'The Perfume'**? I ask the question, because it seems to be so generally assumed that whenever Donne is writing tenderly rather than merely wittily, cynically and impudently, whenever he is expressing himself, as one might say, Shakespeareanly rather than Ovidianly, he must have been writing out of actual experience, not just out of his imagination. Even Grierson groups together the present elegy, **'His parting from her'**, **'The Expostulation'**, and **'His Picture'**, which we have still to consider, as bearing what he calls 'the imprint of some actual experience'. But why, as I have asked before, should not Donne, if only for the sake of variety, have now and then dramatized other moods of his very diverse and volatile self besides that of mere outrageousness? Whether, though, the experience behind this elegy was real or imaginary, it is a superb piece of drama. (pp. 67-8)

The last elegy I would classify as primarily dramatic is the Fifth, **'His Picture'**, which some may like to think of as having been written before his departure with the Cadiz expedition in June 1596.... From this elegy we can infer absolutely nothing about the woman to whom it is addressed, whether she was married or single, whether, even, she was real or imaginary. She may well have been composite. Even if Donne had not happened to have one, or a particular one, in mind, or, perhaps I should rather say, in heart, at the time, to write a farewell to his mistress would have been dramatically appropriate to the situation of one departing on a military expedition, and Donne, like Shakespeare's Richard II, was a born self-dramatizer.

When Ben Jonson told Donne that the two *Anniversaries* he had written in 1611 and 1612 to commemorate the daughter of his patron Sir Robert Drury, who had died at the age of fifteen, 'were profane and full of blasphemies', and that 'if it had been written of the Virgin Marie it had been something', Donne replied that 'he described the Idea of a woman, and not as she was' [see excerpt dated 1618-19]. So, too, in these dramatic elegies Donne, it seems to me, is playing with, dramatizing, various ideas of women, various ideas of himself, in various imaginary situations, and not describing either them or himself 'as they were'. To conclude with a brief review of the elegies we have been considering, in **'Jealosie'** we have cynical . . . in and in **'His parting from her'** a tender address to a married woman; in **'The Perfume'** we have a high-spirited but rather cynical, and in **'On his Mistris'** a tender and impassioned, address to a young girl; in **'The Expostulation'** a misunderstanding is cleared up and renewed affection protested to a woman whom what we may call the hero presumably regards with honourable intentions, while in **'His Picture'** the hero takes a witty but not untender farewell of some indeterminate mistress before departing on an expedition. Much in these elegies is witty and outrageous and cynical and satirical and realistic, and much is tender and impassioned, but, if one wanted to describe their author in one appropriate word, one would have to call him, I think, an essentially *dramatic* poet. About the last thing one would think of calling him, if one knew him from these poems alone, would be a 'metaphysical' poet. That, indeed, is the question we must always keep before us: *what are the really essential characteristics of Donne's poetry, and how much of it may appropriately be called metaphysical?* The affixing of the label 'metaphysical' to Donne has, I fear, saved far too many people the trouble and deprived them of the fascination of trying to discover what his poetry is really like.

Let us now turn to those *elegies which are primarily 'witty' rather than dramatic. In three of them the wit may perhaps best be described as Ovidian, while in the rest it is of a more scholastic kind than we have yet encountered. Although in several of them some kind of situation is indeed implied, I have classified them as 'witty' rather than 'dramatic', because what we are primarily aware of is not, as in the elegies we have been considering, the situation, the characters (real or imaginary) and their emotions and attitudes, but simply the writer's wit, his ingenious comparisons, analogies and arguments, his power, as it were, to keep going for so long on subjects one might have supposed very rapidly exhaustible. His attitude to his subject is much more external than in the dramatic elegies—is often, indeed, almost indifferent. The subject does not matter—the important thing is what Donne can find to say about it.*

Let us first consider the three Ovidian elegies. The Twentieth, **'Loves Warre'**, . . . has affinities with at least three of Ovid's *Amores*: with the ninth of the First Book, . . . in which Ovid very wittily and antithetically insists on the similarity between the qualities of a good lover and a good soldier, such as capacity to endure night watches, to sleep on the ground, not to fear the face of an enemy, to besiege and take by storm, to surprise the enemy while he is asleep, to elude watchmen and sentries: although it is true that Donne, unlike Ovid, is concerned not with the similarities but with the differences. Then there is that impudent elegy which I have already referred to, the tenth of the Second Book, with that passage beginning:

Felix quem Veneris certamina mutua rumpunt,

which almost seems to parody what Virgil and Horace had written in praise of the simple life; and the twelfth elegy of the Second Book in which Ovid celebrates his bloodless victory over Corinna, declaring that by his own generalship alone he has overcome countless enemies without shedding a drop of blood and without causing a new war:

Haec est praecipuo victoria digna triumpho,
In qua, quaecumque est, sanguine praeda caret.

The victory which above all deserves a triumph is that in which the prize, whatever it be, is got without bloodshed.

Me quoque, qui multos, sed me sine caede, Cupido
Iussit militiae signa mouere suae.

Me too, after so many others, Cupid commanded to raise his standard, but without shedding blood.

Donne has not imitated any of the verbal detail of these elegies, but some of his epigrammatic lines are quite in Ovid's manner:

Other men war that they their rest may gayne;
But wee will rest that wee may fight agayne.
Those warrs the ignorant, these th'experienc'd love,
There wee are alwayes under, here above.

One is not aware, as one is in the dramatic elegies, as one is even in **'His Picture'**, which is almost a limiting case—*one is not even momentarily aware of a person whom Donne is addressing and whose real or imaginary personality is to some extent dictating and qualifying what he says: one is aware only of Donne himself, wittily developing a paradox.* He might just as well have addressed the elegy to a friend, have substituted the third person for the second, and have begun:

Till I have-peace with *her,* warr other men.

In the *Eighteenth Elegy,* **'Loves Progress'**, which begins:

Who ever loves, if he do not propose
The right true end of love, he's one that goes
To sea for nothing but to make him sick

he describes the progress from the face, or better, he contends, from the feet, to the 'centrique part.' The impudence is Ovidian, but the ingenious comparisons Donne uses in order to describe the lover's progress in terms of a voyage could never possibly have occurred to Ovid or to any classical poet:

The brow becalms us when 'tis smooth and plain,
And when 'tis wrinckled, shipwracks us again.
Smooth, 'tis a Paradice, where we would have
Immortal stay, and wrinkled 'tis our grave.
The Nose (like to the first Meridian) runs
Not 'twixt an East and West, but 'twixt two suns;
It leaves a Cheek, a rosie Hemisphere
On either side, and then directs us where
Upon the Islands fortunate we fall,
(Not faynte *Canaries,* but *Ambrosiall*)
Her swelling lips; To which when wee are come,
We anchor there, and think our selves at home,
For they seem all: there Syrens songs, and there
Wise Delphick Oracles do fill the ear.

The Nineteenth Elegy, **'Going to Bed'**, may perhaps have been suggested by the fifth in Ovid's First Book, where he describes how Corinna came to him one hot noon while he was resting on his couch, but it was not altogether without some kind of English precedent in Nashe's *Choice of Valentines*, a poem which never got into print, and for which Nashe and the noble patron for whom he wrote it were severely reproved by Hall and other satirists. (pp. 70-4)

> J. B. Leishman, in his The Monarch of Wit: An Analytical and Comparative Study of the Poetry of John Donne, *Hutchinson's University Library, 1951, 278 p.*

ALLEN TATE (essay date 1953)

[*Tate's criticism is closely associated with two critical movements, Agrarianism and New Criticism. The Agrarians were concerned with political and social issues as well as literature, and they were dedicated to preserving the Southern way of life and traditional Southern values. In particular, they attacked Northern industrialism as they sought to preserve the Southern farming economy. The New Critics, a group that included Cleanth Brooks and Robert Penn Warren, among others, comprised one of the most influential critical movements of the mid-twentieth century. Although the New Critics did not subscribe to a single set of principles, all believed that a work of literature had to be examined as an object in itself through close analysis of symbol, image, and metaphor. For the New Critics, a literary work was not a manifestation of ethics, sociology, or psychology, nor could be evaluated in the general terms of any nonliterary discipline. However, Tate adhered to a different vision of literature's purpose than did the other New Critics. A conservative thinker and convert to Catholicism, Tate attacked the tradition of Western philosophy which he felt has alienated persons from themselves, from each, other, and from nature by divorcing intellectual from natural functions in human life. For Tate, literature is the principal form of knowledge and revelation, one that restores human beings to a proper relationship with nature and the spiritual realm. Although this vision informs much of his work, Tate is like T. S. Eliot in that an appreciation of his criticism is not wholly dependent upon an acceptance of his spiritual convictions. His most important critical essays are on modern poetry, and on Southern traditions and the legacy of the Civil War. The following essay was originally published in 1953, first in the Sewanee Review, then in Tate's essay collection* The Forlorn Demon: Didactic and Critical Essays. *Tate later explained his purpose in writing the essay: "A few years before 1952 Professor Douglas Bush had read an article at a meeting of the Modern Language Association, in which he said that most of the New Critics were ignorant, and that I in paticular seemed to know nothing about Elizabethan literature except the habit of the poets of punning on the verb to die (to die=to complete the act of love). I had said somewhere that this pun was concealed in the first two stanzas of Donne's "A Valediction: Forbidding Mourning"; Professor Bush said it wasn't there. I wrote "The Point of Dying" to prove that it was, and I think I proved it."*]

As virtuous men passe mildly away
And whisper to their souls, to goe,
Whilst some of their sad friends do say,
The breath goes now, and some say no:
So let us melt and make no noise,
No teare-floods nor sigh tempests move;
'Twere prophanation of our joyes
To tell the layetie our love.

I believe that none of Donne's commentators has tried to follow up the implications of the analogy: the moment of death is like the secret communion of lovers. The first thing that we see is that lovers die *out of* something *into* something else. They die in order to live. This is the particular *virtue*, the Christian entelechy or final cause of mankind, and the actualization of what it is to be human.

The logical argument of **"A Valediction: Forbidding Mourning"** is a Christian commonplace. Through the higher love lovers achieve a unity of being which physical love, the analogue of the divine, not only preserves but both intensifies and enlarges. The implicit symbol of this union is the Aristotelian circle of archetypal motion. Union is imagined first as a mathematical point where physical and spiritual union are the same; then as an expanding circle of which the point is the center. The analogy is complete when the two legs of the draftman's compasses become congruent in the lover's embrace, so that the legs from a vertical line standing on the "same" point. Thus Donne "reduces" a Platonic abstraction to actual form by contracting the circumference, "absence," to the point, "reunion," on the human scale, of the lovers.

Logically the mathematical point precedes the circle of which it is the center; literally it also has priority, since the lover begins his journey from the point. But the poem as action, as trope, asserts the priority of the circle, for without it nothing in the poem would move: the lovers in order to be united, or reunited, have got first to be "separated," the woman at the center, the man at the enlarging circumference, even though the separation is further and larger union. The visual image of the expanding circle is the malleable gold, which by becoming materially thinner under the hammer expands indefinitely, but not into infinity; for this joint soul of the lovers is a "formulable essence" which abhors infinity. The material gold disappears as it becomes absolutely thin, and is replaced by pure, anagogical "light"—another Christian commonplace that needs no explanation. Donne fills his circle with a physical substance that can be touched and seen; but it is the particular substance which archetypically reflects the light of heaven. Yet all this light which is contained by the circle is only an expanded point; that is to say, whether we see the lovers as occupying the contracted circle in the figure of the compasses, or the expanded point of the gold, they always occupy the same "space," and are never separated. Space is here the "letter" of a nondimensional anagoge; and likewise the circle widening towards infinity. Thus spatial essences are the analogical rhetoric of a suprarational intuition.

But **"A Valediction: Forbidding Mourning"** is a poem, not a philosophical discourse. And since a poem is a movement of a certain kind in which its logical definition is only a participant, we have got to try to see this poem, like any other, as an action more or less complete. For an action, even of the simplest outline, in life or in art, is not what we can say about it; it rather is what prompts us to speak. The Christian commonplaces that I have pointed out are not Donne's poem; they are, as letter and allegory, material factors that it is the business of the poet to bring to full actualization in rhetoric; and here, as always, the rhetoric, the full linguistic body of the poem which ultimately resists our analysis, is the action, the trope, the "turning" from one thing to another: from darkness to light, from ignorance to knowledge, from sight to insight. This tropological motion is the final cause ... of the poem, that towards which it moves, on account of which its logical definition, its formulable essence, exists. And it is the business of criticism to examine this motion, not the formulable essence as such.

Donne's two opening stanzas announce the theme of indissoluble spiritual union in an analogy to what seems at first glance its opposite: dissolution of soul from body. First we have dying men (not one man, not trope but allegory) who "whisper to their souls, to,goe"; then, in the second stanza, lovers who "melt *and* (my italics) make no noise." The moment of death is a *separation* which virtuous men welcome, and the lovers are about to *separate* in quiet joy ("no teare-floods nor sigh-tempests move"). For the lovers too are "virtuous"—infused with a certain power or potency to be realized. They have no more to fear from separation from each other than dying men from death, or separation from life. If the lovers foresee no loss, they may expect a gain similar to that of the dying men.

At this point we may pass to another phase of the analogy. Here the difficult word is "melt." I cannot find in the history of the word, even as a secondary meaning, the idea of human separation. The meanings range from change of physical identity to feelings of tenderness. Tenderness is no doubt felt by the lovers at parting, and by the sad friends at the deathbed. But it is difficult to imagine these virtuous men feeling tender towards themselves, or sorry that they are dying. They might feel some "tenderness" for or yearning towards something beyond life, i.e., union with God, the realization of their virtue. Here the analogy holds for both lovers and dying men, but here also melting as tenderness becomes very remote; and we must fall back upon change of physical identity as the analogue to change of spiritual identity. The figure has got to work in the first place this side of a remote "higher" meaning, a univocal abstraction not caught in the burning bush of rhetorical analogy. Donne is one of the last Catholic allergorists; to him aiming high is meaningless unless the aim is sighted from a point below. Thus the sense in which both dying men and lovers may be said to melt is restricted to loss of physical substance, of physical identity. The verb "to goe" applies then to both lovers and dying men; both go out of the body, yet through the body, to unite with the object of love. "To goe" thus means to join, to unite with; to "melt" must be equated with "to goe"; it means going into something other than itself. Melting and going are species of dying, but the underlying universal is affirmed, implicitly, not overtly. If lovers die in this analogical sense, they lose their identity in each other, and the physical separation is the letter of the great anagoge, spiritual union. The lover dies out of himself into the beloved in order to gain spiritual union; and spiritual union having been gained, the bodies are no longer there; they are absent, separated. The lover leaves not only the body of the beloved, but his own; and the movement of action, the trope, provides for both journeys. For "mourning" is forbidden for two reasons. They must not mourn because "Donne" is going off to the continent; they must not mourn, since through the letter of sexual union they pass tropologically from body to spirit, where body is left behind for another kind of journey.

The structure of the poem, *at the level of trope,* turns on the pun *to die:* orgasmic ectasy as the literal analogue to spiritual ecstasy; physical union as the analogue to spritual. Between these extremes of inert analogy we find the moral, or tropological, movement of the poem, the central action— the passage in actualized experience from the lower to the higher. But without this egregious pun, the whole range of the pun, at that: its witty, anecdotal, even obscene implications: without it the poem would not move; for the pun is its mover, its propeller, its efficient cause.

A grammatical peculiarity of stanza two will offer indirect support for this argument. I refer to "and" between "melt *and* make no noise." I have I believe disposed of "let us be tender" as a plausible meaning of "melt." But if that were the right meaning, the conjunction should be "but," not "and." As Donne wrote the passage (we are entitled to read only what he wrote), it evidently means: Let us pass through the body, let us "die" in both senses, *and* the loss of physical self will prevent the noisy grief of "sublunary lovers" at parting and the noisy love making of physical union. Thus if "melt" were not an extension of the pun, Donne would probably have written "but make no noise" —a prudential injunction to protect the neighbors from scandal.

Two other features of the analogy seem to me to reinforce this reading. Why are the sad friends at the deathbed incapable of detecting the exact moment of death? Affection and anxiety account for it in life. This is obviously the first and literal meaning. But here it must be considered along with the lovers' reluctance to tell their love to the "laity." For the logic of the poem contains a third Christian commonplace: death-in-life of this world, life-in-death of the next. The sad friends are a similar laity and the laity is the world, where men do not know the difference between appearance and reality, between death and life. But men at the moment of death, lovers at the moment of spiritual union (through and beyond the body), have a sacerdotal secret, access to a sacramental rite, beyond the understanding of the "laity" who have not had these ultimate experiences. The dying of the lovers into life and the dying of death into life are reciprocally analogous. Donne is not saying that death is *like* love, or that love is *like* death; there is the identity, death-love, a third something, a reality that can be found only through analogy since it has no name. This reality, whether of "dying" lovers or of "dying" men, is the ultimate experience. The reciprocal conversion of the one into the other is the moral motion of the poem, its peripety, the "action" which eventually issues in the great top-level significance that Dante understood as the anagoge. This is nothing less, as it is surely nothing more, than the entire poem, an actual linguistic object that is at once all that our discourse can make of it and nothing that at any moment of discourse we are able to make of it. (pp. 247-52)

Allen Tate, "The Point of Dying: Donne's 'Virtuous Men'," in his Essays of Four Decades, *The Swallow Press Inc., 1968, pp. 247-52.*

WILLIAM EMPSON (essay date 1953)

[*Empson was an English critic, poet, and editor. He is best known for* Seven Types of Ambiguity *(1930), a seminal contribution to the formalist school of New Criticism. Much of Empson's work reflects the influence of I. A. Richards and the atmosphere of Cambridge University in the late 1920s: scientific thought and theory strongly influenced the arts; literature emphasized complex, rational techniques and themes; and critical approaches were likewise based on the belief that literature could be analyzed using formal, objective criteria derived from the scientific method. Empson's criticism is thus characterized by close textual analysis which focuses on the ambiguities of poetic diction, and his poetry is noted for its precision of style and form. Empson's poems often present an argument and follow it through its various complexities. This tendency to "argufy" has led many critics to link Empson with the seventeeth-century metaphysical poets. Empson's critical theory is based on the assumption that all great poetry is ambiguous and that this ambiguity can often be traced to the multiple meanings of words. He therefore analyzed texts by enumerating and discussing these various meanings and examining how they fit together to communicate ideas and emotions. His method of "puzzling" a text has been widely attacked as well as praised. While Empson is almost unanimously respected for his intelligence and ingenuity, he has been faulted for the limitations of his approach. In the following excerpt from a later edition of* Seven Types of Ambiguity—*in which "ambiguity" is defined as "any verbal nuance, however slight, which gives room for alternative reactions to the same piece of literature"*—*Empson closely explicates three of Donne's poems as examples of the "fourth type" of ambiguity. This he identifies as the case in which alternative meanings combine to make clear a complicated state of mind in the author.*]

'A Valediction, of weeping' weeps for two reasons, which may not at first sight seem very different; because their love when they are together, which they must lose, is so valuable, and because they are 'nothing' when they are apart. There is none of the Platonic pretence Donne keeps up elsewhere, that their love is independent of being together; he can find no satisfaction in his hopelessness but to make as much of the actual situation of parting as possible; and the language of the poem is shot through with a suspicion which for once he is too delicate or too preoccupied to state unambiguously, that when he is gone she will be unfaithful to him. Those critics who say the poem is sincere, by the way, and therefore must have been written to poor Anne, know not what they do.

> Let me powre forth
> My teares before thy face, whil'st I stay here,
> For thy face coins them, and thy stampe they beare,
> And by this Mintage they are something worth,
> For thus they be
> Pregnant of thee,
> Fruits of much grief they are, emblemes of more,
> When a tear falls, that thou falst which it bore,
> So thou and I are nothing then, when on a divers shore.

'Allow me this foolishness; let me cry thoroughly while I can yet see your face, because my tears will be worth nothing, may, in fact, not flow at all, when once I have lost sight of you.' 'Let me plunge, at this dramatic moment, into my despair, so that by its completeness I may be freed from it, and my tears may be coined into something more valuable.'

The metaphor of coining is suitable at first sight only 'because your worth and your beauty are both royal,' but other deductions from it can be made. In that his *tears* will not reflect her *face* unless he *stays here*, it may imply 'because it is only when I am seeing your beauty that it matters so much to me; I only shed valuable tears about you when I am at your side.' There is a shift of the metaphor in this, brought out by line 3, from the *tears* as molten metal which must be *stamped* with her value to the *tears* themselves as the completed *coin*; 'because,' then, 'you are so fruitful of unhappiness'; and in either case, far in the background, in so far as she is not really such a queenly figure, 'because you are public, mercenary, and illegal.'

In each of the three verses of the poem the two short middle lines are separated only by commas from the lines before and after them; Professor Grierson on the two occasions that he has corrected this has accurately chosen the more important meaning, and unnecessarily cut off the less. In this verse, *for thus they be* may be a note to give the reasons why the tears are *something worth*, or may be parallel to *for thy face coins them*, so that it leads on to the rest of the stanza. Going backwards, 'Let me pour out at once the tears I shall have to shed sooner or later, because if I do it now they will reflect your face and become valuable because they contain you'; going forwards, 'Let me pour forth my tears before your face, because they are epitomes of you in this way, that they are born in sorrow, and are signs that there is more sorrow to come after.' *Pregnant* because they are like her, in that they *fall* and are *emblems of grief*, and give true information about her (as in 'a pregnant sentence'), because they are round and large like a pregnancy, because they hold a reflection of her inside them, and because, if they are wept in her presence, they will carry her more completely with them, and so do him more good. It is this last obscure sense, that he is getting rid of her, or satisfying her, or getting his feeling for her into a more manageable form, by a storm of emotion in her presence, that gives energy to the metaphor of *pregnancy*, and logic to the second alternative—the idea that she normally causes sorrow.

Corresponding to these alternative meanings of *for thus, that thou* means 'the fact that you' and 'that particular case of you.' 'The tears are emblems of more grief by foreshowing, when they fall, that you will fall who were the cause of them' (if *which* refers to a person it should be the subject of *bore*), or, beginning a new sentence at *when*, 'when a tear falls, that reflection of you which it carries in it falls too' (*(which* now refers to a thing and so can be the object).

And corresponding to these again, there is a slight variation in the meaning of *so*, according as the last line stands alone or follows on from the one before. 'These tears by falling show that you will fall who were the cause of them. And therefore, because you will fall when we are separated, when we are separated we shall both become nothing,' or 'When the reflection of you is detached from my eye and put on a separate tear it falls; in the same way we shall ourselves fall and be nothing when we are separated by water.'

All these versions imply that their love was bound to lead to unhappiness; the word *fall* expects unfaithfulness, as well as negation, from her absence; *then* means both 'when you fall' and 'when we are separated,' as if they were much the same thing; and *nothing* (never name her, child, if she be nought, advised Mrs. Quickly) says the same of himself also, when a channel divides them deeper, but no less salt, than their pool of tears.

> On a round ball,
> A workeman that hath copies by, can lay
> An Europe, Afrique, and an Asia,
> And quickly make that, which was nothing, *All*,
> So doth each teare
> Which thee doth weare,
> A globe, yea world by that impression grow
> Till my tears mixed with thine do overflow
> This world, by waters sent from thee, my heaven dissolved
> so.

The first four lines are defining the new theme, and their grammar is straightforward. Then the *teare* may be active or passive, like the *workeman* or like the *ball*, on the face of it, it is like the *ball*, but *so doth* may treat it as like the *workeman*. For *doth* may be a separate verb as well as an auxiliary of *grow*; while, in any case, *grow* may either mean 'turn into' or 'grow larger.' The *globe* and the *world* may be either the *teare* or *thee*. The other meanings of *impression* would be possible here. Either, then, 'In the same way each tear that wears you, who are a whole world yourself or at least the copy of one, grows into a world, or 'And so does every tear that wears you; each tear, that is, grows, so as to include everything, or to produce a great deal more water'; it is only this second, vaguer meaning which gives a precise meaning to *till*, and suggests, instead of a mere heap of world-tears, such a flood as descended upon the wickedness of the antediluvians.

Which thee doth weare suggests by the order of the words a more normal meaning, that her *tears* are jewels and she is *wearing* them; this is inverted by the grammar, so as to leave an impression that she is uniquely and unnaturally under the control of her tears, or even has no existence independent of them.

The last line but one may stand alone, with *overflow* meaning simply 'flow excessively,' or 'flow into each other,' so as to spoil each other's shape, and then the last line, by itself, means, 'In the same way, the necessities of this, the real, world have dissolved my precarious heaven by means of, or into, tears.' Or making *world* the object of *overflow*, it may mean, according as *this world* is the real world or the *tear*, either 'we produce more and more tears till we drown the world altogether, and can no longer see things like ordinary people,' or 'my tear reflects you and so is a world till one of your tears falls on it, spoils its shape and leaves only a splash'; it is she who has made the *world* which is his *heaven,* and she who destroys it. The rest of the line then says, 'in the same way my happiness in our love has been dissolved, by this meeting with your tears,' making *heaven* the subject of the intransitive verb *dissolved*. But *my heaven* may be in apposition to *thee*; *dissolved* may be a participle; and *so* may be not 'in the same way' but 'so completely, so terribly'; it is not merely his memory and idea and understanding of her, it is the actual woman herself, as she was when they were happy together, who is *dissolving* under his eyes into the *tears* of this separation; *dissolved,* it has already happened. The waters are falling that were above the firmament; the heaven and crystalline spheres, which were she, are broken; she is no longer the person he made her, and will soon be made into a different person by another lover. These broken pieces of grammar which may be fitted together in so many ways are lost phrases jerked out whilst sobbing, and in the reading, 'so my heaven dissolved this world,' which though far in the background is developed in the following stanza, there is a final echo of unexplained reproach.

> O more than Moone,
> Draw not up seas to drowne me in thy spheare,
> Weep me not dead, in thine armes, but forbeare
> To teach the sea, what it may doe too soone,
> Let not the winde
> Example finde,
> To do me more harm, then it purposeth,
> Since thou and I sigh one another's breath,
> Whoe'er sighs most, is cruellest, and hasts the other's
>   death.

She is *Moone,* with a unifying reference to the first line of the poem, because she draws up the tides of weeping both from him and from herself, a power not necessarily to her credit, but at any rate deserving adoration; the moon, too, is female inconstant, chaste because though bright cold, and has *armes* in which the new moon holds the old one. Some of the lyrical release in the line may be explained as because it is deifying her, and remembering the Sidney tradition, even now after so many faults in her have been implied, and are still being implied. She is *more than Moone* because she is more valuable to him than anything in the real world to which he is being recalled; because she has just been called either the earth or the heavens and they are larger than the moon; as controlling tides more important or more dangerous than those of the sea; as making the world more hushed and glamorous than does moonlight; as being more inconstant, or as being more constant, than the moon; as being able to draw tides right up to her own sphere; as shining by her own light; and as being more powerful because closer.

In thy spheare may be taken with *me*, 'don't drown me, whether with my tears or your own, now that I am still fairly happy and up in your sphere beside you; don't trouble to draw up the seas so high, or be so cruel as to draw up the seas so high, that they drown me now, since tomorrow they will drown me easily, when I am thrown down into the world'; may be taken alone, as 'your sphere of influence,' your sort of drowning, 'don't *you* go drowning me; I have the whole sea to drown me when I take ship to-morrow'; or may be taken with *Moone,* 'you, far in your sphere, high and safe from sorrow in your permanence and your power to change, do not drown a poor mortal who is not in your sphere, to whom these things matter more deeply.'

The machinery of interpretation is becoming too cumbrous here, in that I cannot see how these meanings come to convey tenderness rather than the passion of grief which has preceded them, how they come to mark a particular change of tone, a return towards control over the situation, which makes them seem more vividly words actually spoken. It is a question of the proportions in which these meanings are accepted, and their interactions; it is not surprising that the effect should be what it is, but I do not know that it could have been foreseen. Perhaps it is enough to say that the request, in its fantastic way, is more practical, and draws its point from the immediate situation.

Weep me not dead means: 'do not make me cry myself to death; do not kill me with the sight of your tears; do not cry for me as for a man already dead, when, in fact, I am in your arms,' and, with a different sort of feeling, 'do not exert your power over the sea so as to make it drown me by sympathetic magic'; there is a conscious neatness in the ingenuity of the phrasing, perhaps because the same idea is being repeated, which brings out the change of tone in this verse. *What it may doe too soone*, since the middle lines may as usual go forwards or backwards, may be said of the *sea* or of the *winde*; if of the *winde* the earlier syntax may be 'forbeare in order to teach the sea to be calm'; this gives point to the crude logic, which has in any case a sort of lyrical ease, of 'do not weep, but forbeare to weep.' The *sea* is going to separate them; it *may* be going to drown him; and so it *may* drown him, for all he cares, when he has lost her. The *winde purposeth* to blow him from her, and if she doesn't stop sighing she will *teach* it to do *more harm,* and upset the boat. One may notice the contrast between the danger and discomfort of this prospect, also the playfulness or brutality of the request, and the cooing assured seductive murmur or the sound *doe too soone*; by this time he is trying to soothe her.

I always think of this poem as written before Donne's first voyage with Essex, which he said he undertook to escape from 'the queasy pain of loving and being loved'; the fancy is trivial but brings out the change of tone in the last two lines. In itself the notion is a beautiful one, 'our sympathy is so perfect that any expression of sorrow will give more pain to the other party than relief to its owner, so we ought to be trying to cheer each other up,' but to say this is to abandon the honest luxuriance of sorrow with which they have been enlivening their parting, to try to forget feeling in a bright, argumentative, hearty quaintness (the good characters in Dickens make the orphan girl smile through her tears in this way); the language itself has become flattened and explanatory: so that he almost seems to be feeling for his hat. But perhaps I am libelling this masterpiece; all one can say is that its passion exhausts itself; it achieves at the end the sense of reality he was looking for, and some calm of mind.

This poem is ambiguous because his feelings were painfully' mixed, and because he felt that at such a time it would be ungenerous to spread them out clearly in his mind; to express sorrow at the obvious fact of parting gave an adequate to relief to his disturbance, and the variety of irrelevant, incompatible ways of feeling about the affair that were lying about in his mind were able so to modify, enrich, leave their mark upon this plain lyrical relief as to make it something more memorable.

I hope I have now made clear what the fourth type is like when it really gets under way; I shall add some much slighter cases which seemed illuminating.

> What if this present were the world's last night?
> Mark in my heart, O Soule, where thou dost dwell,
> The picture of Christ crucified, and tell
> Whether that countenance can thee affright,
> Teares in his eyes quench the amasing light,
> Blood fills his frownes, which from his pierc'd head fell.
> And can that tongue adjudge thee unto hell,
> Which prayed forgivenesse for his foes fierce spight?
> No, no; but as in my idolatrie
> I said to all my profane mistresses,
> Beauty, of pitty, foulness onely is
> A sign of rigour; so I say to thee,
> To wicked spirits are horrid shapes assign'd
> This beauteous form assures a piteous mind.

In one's first reading of the first line [of **"What if this present were the world's last night?"**], the dramatic idea is of Donne pausing in the very act of sin, stricken and swaddled by a black unexpected terror: suppose the end of the world came *now*? The preacher proceeds to comfort us after this shock has secured our attention. But looking back, and taking for granted the end's general impression of security, the first line no longer conflicts with it. 'Why, this *may* be the last night, but God is loving. What if it were?' In the first notion one must collect one's mind to answer the Lord suddenly, and Donne, in fact, shuffles up an old sophistry from Plato, belonging to the lyrical tradition he rather despised, and here even more absurdly flat-

tering to the person addressed and doubtful as to its general truth than on the previous occassions he has found it handy. Is a man in the last stages of torture so beautiful, even if blood hides his frowns? Never mind about that, he is pleased, we have carried it off all right; the great thing on these occasions is to have a ready tongue.

A similar doubt as to emphasis runs through the **'Apparition'** and almost leaves one in doubt between two moods; an amused pert and fanciful contempt, written up with more elaboration than it deserves, so as to give him an air of being detached from her and interested in literature; and the scream of agony and hatred by which this is blown aside.

> *Then* thy sicke taper will begin to *winke*

is a bumping line full of guttering and oddity, but brisk with a sense of power over her. This has reached a certain intensity by the time we get to

> thinke
> Thou call'st for more,
> And *in false sleepe* will from thee *shrinke.*

with the stresses in the line almost equal; Crashaw uses a similar rhythm to convey a chanting and mystical certainty,

> And in her *first ranks* make thee *room.*

Donne's version conveys: 'I am speaking quite seriously, with conviction, but with personal indifference, to this toad.'

> And *then* poore *Asp*en *wretch, neglected* thou
> All in a cold quicksilver sweat wilt lye
> A veryer ghost than I.

The stress is on *neglected*; 'you would be glad to get me back now if you could.' But

> since my love is spent
> I had *rather* thou shouldst *pain* fully re*pent*
> Than by my threatenings rest still innocent.

What a placid epigrammatical way of stopping, we are to think, and how trivial the affair is made by this final admission that she is innocent! he would not say that if he cared for her any more.

But, after all, the first line calls her a *murderess*, and the way most people read the poem makes the poet more seriously involved;

> Then *thy* sicke taper will begin to winke

('As does mine now; you have left me ill and exhausted,' and the last part of the line gabbles with fury.)

> And in false sleepe will from *thee* shrinke

('As you, if I can credit it, as you have shrunk from *me*; with a disgust which I shall yet turn to terror.')

> And *then* poore Aspen wretch, neglected *thou*

(It is almost a childish cry; 'I find it *intolerable* to be so neglected.')

> A veryer ghost than *I*

('Than I am now,' not 'than I shall be then'); that his *love* is *spent* has become pathetically unbelievable;

> I had rather *thou* shouldst painfully repent

('As I am repenting, in agony'); and *innocent* has become a scream of jealous hatred at her hypocrisy, of an impotent desire to give any pain he can find.

The meaning of an English sentence is largely decided by the accent, and yet one learns in conversation to put the accent in several places at once; it may be possible to read the poem so as to combine these two ways of underlining it. But these last two cases are curious in that the alternative versions seem particularly hard to unite into a single vocal effect. You may be intended, while reading a line one way, to be conscious that it could be read in another; so that if it is to be read aloud it must be read twice; or you may be intended to read it in some way different from the colloquial speech-movement so as to imply both ways at once. Different styles of reading poetry aloud use these methods in different proportions, but perhaps these two examples from Donne respectively demand the two methods in isolation. (pp. 139-48)

> *William Empson, "Chapter IV," in his* Seven Types of Ambiguity, *third edition, 1953. Reprint by New Directions, 1966, pp. 133-54.*

LOUIS L. MARTZ (essay date 1954)

[Martz is an American literary scholar who has written extensively on seventeenth- and eighteenth-century English literature. He has also edited many works by and about the authors of that time period, including Milton: A Collection of Critical Essays *(1966), and serves as editorial chairman of the "Yale Edition of the Works of Thomas More." In the following excerpt from* The Poetry of Meditation: A Study in English Religious Literature of the Seventeenth Century, *he examines* Of the Progresse of the Soule, *seeking to demostrate that "despite some flaws, [it] is as a whole one of the great religious poems of the seventeenth century."]*

Everything that we know of Donne indicates that, during the years from his marriage in 1601 down through the time of his ordination in 1615, he was engaging in the most fervent and painful self-analysis, directed toward the problem of his vocation. The crisis and culmination of these efforts, I believe, is represented in the two *Anniversaries*, both of which, surprisingly enough, may have been written in the year 1611. (pp. 218-19)

It was a period when his weighing of the sacred and profane tendencies within himself must have reached a climax of intensity; and this, I believe, is why the two poems represent Donne's most elaborate examples of the art of sacred parody and his most extensive efforts in the art of poetical meditation.

Yet the *Anniversaries* are not usually treated as whole poems. For one thing, the biographical facts underlying these poems lead readers to approach them with suspicion, since they were written in memory of the daughter of Donne's generous patron, Sir Robert Drury—a girl who died in her fifteenth year, and whom Donne admits he never saw. As a result, the elaborate eulogies of Elizabeth Drury are frequently dismissed as venal and insincere, while interest in the poems centers on those passages which reflect Donne's awareness of the "new philosophy," on explicitly religious portions, or on any portions which provide illustrative quotations for special studies of Donne and his period.

Such fragmentary appreciation of the poems has, I think, hampered an understanding of their full significance. For each poem is carefully designed as a whole, and the full meaning of each grows out of a deliberately articulated structure. Furthermore, a close reading of each poem shows that the two *Anniversaries* are significantly different in structure and in the handling of Petrarchan imagery, and are consequently different in value. The *First Anniversary,* despite its careful structure, is, it must be admitted, successful only in brilliant patches; but I think it can be shown that the *Second Anniversary*, despite some flaws, is as a whole one of the great religious poems of the seventeenth century. (pp. 220-21)

The full title of Donne's *Second Anniversary* itself suggests the possibilities of a unity not achieved in the earlier poem: *Of the Progresse of the Soule. Wherein, By occasion of the Religious death of Mistris Elizabeth Drury, the incommodities of the Soule in this life, and her exaltation in the next, are contemplated.* Here, clearly, is an "occasion" to use Mistress Drury as a symbol naturally integrated with the traditional matter of religious meditation: a "Religious death" (not the "untimely death" of the *Anatomie*'s title) is the ultimate aim in this life for all the devout. The poem's structure indicates that Donne is indeed moving throughtout with the imaginative ease that marks the management of a truly unified conception.

The *Progresse* consists of an Introduction, only half as long as the Introduction to the preceding poem; a Conclusion, less than half as long; and seven sections which constitute the body of the work. These proportions, in a poem over fifty lines longer, indicate an important shift in emphasis. The Introduction and Conclusion to the *Anatomie*, with their emphasis on hyperbolic praise of the dead girl, make up a quarter of that poem; whereas these portions make up only about an eighth of the *Progresse*. Each section of the *Progresse* is subdivided in a manner reminiscent of the *Anatomie*. The first section contains (1) a Meditation on contempt of the world and one's self; (2) a Eulogy of the girl as the pattern of Virtue; (3) a Moral, introduced by lines which recall the refrain of the preceding poem:

> Shee, shee is gone; she is gone; when thou knowest this,
> What fragmentary rubbidge this world is
> Thou knowest, and that it is not worth a thought;
> He honors it too much that thinkes it nought.

But, as the following outline shows, the "refrain" does not appear hereafter, and of the remaining sections, only the second concludes with a distinct Moral; in the rest the moral is absorbed into the Eulogy. (p. 236)

This gradual modification of the strict mold which marked the sections of the *Anatomie* suggests a creative freedom that absorbs and transcends formal divisions. The first striking indication that this is true is found in the ease of the reader's movement from part to part. We are freed from the heavy pauses that marked the close of each section in the *Anatomie*: omission of the refrain and, above all, omission of the flat, prosy Morals, makes possible an easy transition from section to section; the only heavy pause occurs at the close of the long Moral in Section II. We are always aware that a new sequence is beginning: it is essential that we feel the form of the poem beneath us. But each new sequence, with the above exception, follows inevitably from the close of the preceding one, as at the close of the first section, where the words of the very brief Moral, "thought" and "thinkes," lead directly to the dominant command of the second Meditation: "Thinke then, my soule, that death is but a Groome . . . Thinke thee laid on thy death-bed . . . Thinke . . . Thinke . . ."; the traditional self-address of religious meditation.

The transition within each section from Meditation to Eulogy is even more fluent; we do not find here the sharp division of meaning which marked these two elements in the *Anatomie*. In the previous poem every Meditation was strictly a scourging of the world and of man, every Eulogy the picture of a lost hope. But in the *Progresse* every Meditation, together with this scourging, includes the hope of salvation which is imaged in the Eulogy, and in every Meditation except the first, this hope, this upward look, is stressed in the latter part of the Meditation, with the result that the reader is carried easily into the realm where the symbol of perfect virtue now lives.

In Sections III and V the distinction between Meditation and Eulogy is even further modified, for the Meditation itself falls into two contrasting parts. In Section III we have first a meditation on the loathsomeness of the body, which "could, beyond escape or helpe," infect the soul with Original Sin. But Donne does not dwell long on this; he lifts his eyes from these "ordures" to meditate, in a passage twice as long, his soul's flight to heaven after death—a flight that leads directly to the Eulogy. Likewise, in Section V, after meditating the corrupt company kept on earth Donne lifts his eyes to meditate the soul's "conversation" with the inhabitants of Heaven—a theme which leads naturally into the Eulogy of Heaven's new inhabitant.

Fundamentally, the union of Meditation with Eulogy is due to a difference in Donne's treatment of the Eulogies in this poem. Here he has avoided a clash between eulogy and religious meditation by giving up, except in the brief Introduction and first Eulogy, the Petrarchan hyperbole which in parts of the *Anatomie* attributed the decay of the world to the girl's death. This hyperbole, together with the single reminder of the refrain, appears to be brought in at the beginning of the *Progresse* to link this poem with its predecessor, in line with Donne's original plan of writing a poem in the girl's memory every year for an indefinite period. The labored Introduction to the *Progresse* is certainly a blemish on the poem; yet it may be said that the reminiscences of the *Anatomie* are functional: they suggest that the negative "anatomizing" of the other poem may be taken as a preparation for the positive spiritual progress to be imaged in the second poem. At any rate, Donne does not use this hyperbole in the six later Eulogies, nor in the brief Conclusion, of the second poem. Instead, he consistently attempts to transmute the girl into a symbol of virtue that may fitly represent the Image and Likeness of God in man, recognition of which is, according to St. Bernard, the chief end and aim of religious meditation.

Thus Juan de Ávila's *Audi Filia* begins its section on self-knowledge with a chapter summarizing the command to

"know thyself" which St. Bernard found in the famous verse of his beloved *Canticle:* "Si ignoras te, O pulchra inter mulieres, egredere,et abi post gregas sodalium tuorum. . . ." If the soul, the intended Bride, does not know herself—that is, does not know whence she comes, where she is, and whither she is going—she will live forever in the "Land of Unlikeness," that land of sin and disorder in which man forgets that he was made in God's Image and Likeness, and thus lives in a state of exile where the Image is defaced and the Likeness lost. . . . Take care, says St. Bernard, "now thou art sunk into the slime of the abyss, not to forget that thou art the image of God, and blush to have covered it over with an alien likeness. Remember thy nobility and take shame of such a defection. Forget not thy beauty, to be the more confounded at thy hideous aspect."

In accordance with the twofold aim of meditation implied in the last sentence, Donne's *Second Anniversary* presents seven Meditations which may be called, for the most part, a description of the "defaced image," the Land of Unlikeness; while the seven Eulogies, for the most part, create a symbol of the original Image and Likeness, the lost beauty and nobility that must not be forgotten. That is not to say that Donne gives up Petrarchan imagery; not at all—but this imagery is now attuned to the religious aims of the poem. The Eulogies are sometimes too ingenious; yet the excessive ingenuity remains a minor flaw: it does not destroy the poem's unity. . . . [Throughout] the *Progresse* Meditation and Eulogy combine to present its central theme: the true end of man.

Let us look now at the whole movement of the poem; we can then see that this central theme is clearly introduced at the beginning of the first Meditation, carried to a climax in the fourth and fifth sections, and resolved in the Eulogy of Section VI. There is no flagging of power in this poem: it is a true progress. After the labored Introduction, Donne strikes at once into the heart of his theme:

> These Hymnes, thy issue, may encrease so long,
> As till Gods great *Venite* change the song. (end of Intro.)
> Thirst for that time, O my insatiate soule,
> And serve thy thirst, with Gods safe-sealing Bowle.
> Be thirstie still, and drinke still till thou goe
> To th' only Health, to be Hydroptique so.

The "Bowle" is the Eucharist, a "seale of Grace," as Donne calls it in his sermons. One thinks of the "Anima sitiens Deum" it St. Bernard—the Soul, the Bride, which thirsts for God, desiring a union of will between herself and God, that union which at last results in Perfect Likeness after death. This imagery is then supported in Section II by the line, "And trust th' immaculate blood to wash thy score"; as well as by the lines of Section III where Donne refers to death as the soul's "third birth," with the very significant parenthesis, "Creation gave her one, a second, grace." One needs to recall that at the close of the *Anatomie* Donne has said that he

> Will yearely celebrate thy second birth,
> That is, thy death; for though the soule of man
> Be got when man is made, 'tis borne but than
> When man doth die.

The omission of Grace may be said to indicate the fundamental flaw of the *First Anniversary:* it lacks the firm religious center of the *Progresse.*

This promise of salvation is the positive aspect of the soul's progress; but, as Gilson says in his *The Mystical Theology of Saint Bernard* (1940)], "By this thirst for God we must further understand an absolute contempt for all that is not God." This complementary negative aspect is consequently introduced immediately after the above lines on the Eucharist:

> Forget this rotten world; And unto thee
> Let thine owne times as an old storie bee.
> Be not concern'd: studie not why, nor when;
> Doe not so much as not beleeve a man.

Donne is taking as his prime example of vanity that curiosity which forms the first downward step in St. Bernard's Twelve Degrees of Pride—curiosity, which occurs, St. Bernard tells us, "when a man allows his sight and other senses to stray after things which do not concern him."

> So since it [the soul] takes no heed to itself it is sent out of doors to feed the kids. And as these are the types of sin, I may quite correctly give the title of 'kids' to the eyes and the ears, since as death comes into the world through sin, so does sin enter the mind through these apertures. The curious man, therefore, busies himself with feeding them, though he takes no trouble to ascertain the state in which he has left himself. Yet if, O man, you look carefully into yourself, it is indeed a wonder that you can ever look at anything else.

This theme of curiosity remains dormant until Section III of the poem, where it emerges gradually from Donne's magnificent view of his own soul's flight to Heaven after death. It is important to note that this is not, strictly speaking, "the flight of Elizabeth Drury's soul to Heaven," as most commentators describe it. It is Donne's own soul which here is made a symbol of release, not only from physical bondage, but also from that mental bondage which is the deepest agony of the greatest souls:

> she stayes not in the ayre,
> To looke what Meteors there themselves prepare;
> She carries no desire to know, nor sense,
> Whether th' ayres middle region be intense;
> For th' Element of fire, she doth not know,
> Whether she past by such a place or no;
> She baits not at the Moone, nor cares to trie
> Whether in that new world, men live, and die.
> *Venus* retards her not, to 'enquire, how shee
> Can, (being one starre) *Hesper,* and *Vesper* bee.

In the last two lines Donne is renouncing one of his own witty *Paradoxes and Problems;* in the earlier part he renouncing the astronomical curiosity which had drawn his scorn in the greatest passage of the *Anatomie.* Here, however, as Coffin has well shown there is a much stronger emphasis on problems such as "fire" and the moon which were being debated in Donne's own day [see Additional Bibliography]. From all such vain controversies the soul is now freed and

> ere she can consider how she went,
> At once is at, and through the Firmament.

It is not until Section IV that this theme reaches its full, explicit development. Turning here from the heavens, Donne scourges the search for physical understanding of earth and its creatures; yet, as before, the very flagellation suggests an almost indomitable curiosity, and shows a mind that has ranged through all the reaches of human learning:

> Wee see in Authors, too stiffe to recant,
> A hundred controversies of an Ant;
> And yet one watches, starves, freeses, and sweats,
> To know but Catechismes and Alphabets
> Of unconcerning things, matters of fact—

matters which do not concern the true end of man, as implied in the following lines:

> When wilt thou shake off this Pedantery,
> Of being taught by sense, and Fantasie?
> Thou look'st through spectacles; small things seeme great
> Below; But up unto the watch-towre get,
> And see all things despoyl'd of fallacies:
> Thou shalt not peepe through lattices of eyes,
> Nor heare through Labyrinths of eares, nor learne
> By circuit, or collections to discerne.
> In heaven thou straight know'st all, concerning it,
> And what concernes it not, shalt straight forget.

All worldly philosophy is vain, for essential truth, says Donne, cannot be learned through sense-impressions of external things, nor through that "Fantasie" which transmits sense-impressions to the intellect. Such philosophy is the way of pride; true knowledge comes only through humility, as Donne, echoing St. Bernard, declares in a significant passage of his *Essayes:*

> It is then humility to study God, and a strange miraculous one; for it is an ascending humility, which the Divel, which emulates even Gods excellency in his goodnesse, and labours to be as ill, as he is good, hath corrupted in us by a pride, as much against reason; for he hath fill'd us with a descending pride, to forsake God, for the study and love of things worse then our selves.

True knowledge lies within and leads to virtue, the fourth Eulogy explains:

> Shee who all libraries had throughly read
> At home in her owne thoughts, and practised
> So much good as would make as many more:
> Shee whose example they must all implore,
> Who would or doe, or thinke well . . .
> She who in th' art of knowing Heaven, was growne
> Here upon earth, to such perfection,
> That she hath, ever since to Heaven she came,
> (In a far fairer print,) but read the same. . . .

Religious virtue creates, or rather *is,* the restored Likeness which, according to St. Bernard, makes possible some knowledge of God; with St. Bernard, as Gilson says, "the resemblance of subject and object is the indispensable condition of any knowledge of the one by the other." This is made plain in the sixth Eulogy, which provides the resolution of the whole poem by obliterating all traces of Petrarchan compliment and giving explicitly in the terms of St. Bernard a definition of the soul's perfection on earth. The sixth Meditation leads the way into this Eulogy by an abstract definition of "essential joy":

> Double on heaven thy thoughts on earth emploid;
> All will not serve; Only who have enjoy'd
> The sight of God, in fulnesse, can thinke it;
> For it is both the object, and the wit.
> This is essentiall joy, where neither hee
> Can suffer diminution, nor wee.

God is both the object of knowledge and the means of knowing; though this full knowledge and joy can never be achieved on earth, we can, the Eulogy explains, come closest to it by striving to restore the Divine Likeness, as did she,

> Who kept by diligent devotion,
> Gods Image, in such reparation,
> Within her heart, that what decay was growne,
> Was her first Parents fault, and not her owne:
> Who being solicited to any act,
> Still heard God pleading his safe precontract;
> Who by a faithfull confidence, was here
> Betroth'd to God, and now is married there . . .
> Who being here fil'd with grace, yet strove to bee,
> Both where more grace, and more capacitie
> At once is given. . . .

Compare the words of St. Bernard, speaking of that conformity between the soul's will and God's which leads to mystic ecstasy:

> It is that conformity which makes, as it were, a marriage between the soul and the Word, when, being already like unto Him by its nature, it endeavours to show itself like unto Him by its will, and loves Him as it is loved by Him. And if this love is perfected, the soul is wedded to the Word. What can be more full of happiness and joy than this conformity? what more to be desired than this love? which makes thee, O soul, no longer content with human guidance, to draw near with confidence thyself to the Word, to attach thyself with constancy to Him, to address Him with confidence, and consult Him upon all subjects, to become as receptive in thy intelligence, as fearless in thy desires. This is the contract of a marriage truly spiritual and sacred. And to say this is to say too little; it is more than a contract, it is a communion, an identification with the Beloved, in which the perfect correspondence of will makes of two, one spirit.

The "faithfull confidence" of Donne's poem is akin to the "confidence" (*fiducia*) of St. Bernard, an attribute of the soul which has passed beyond fear of divine punishment and stands on the threshold of mystic ecstasy. This recognition of the end of man on earth and in Heaven is the fulfillment of the poem; the brief remainder is summary and epilogue.

In such a poem of religious devotion the sevenfold division of sections assumes a significance beyond that of the fivefold division of the *Anatomie*. Seven is the favorite number for dividing religious meditations: into those *semaines* and *septaines* that were characteristic of the "New Devotion" in the Low Countries; or into the contrasting meditations for each day of the week that formed the basis of popular daily exercises throughout Europe. . . . But the sevenfold division of this poem suggests more than a relation to the practice of methodical meditation. As Donne says in his *Essayes*, "Seven is ever used to express infinite." It is the mystic's traditional division of the soul's progress toward ecstasy and union with the Divine. St. Augustine thus divides the progress of the soul into seven stages, and anyone familiar with mystical writings will realize how often the division has been used by later mystics, as in St. Teresa's *Interior Castle*. Thus Donne's *Progresse* uses both mystical structure and mystical imagery to express a goal: the Infinite, the One.

This does not mean that Donne's *Progresse* is, properly speaking, a mystical poem, even though he uses in his title the mystical term "contemplate," and in the poem cries, "Returne not, my Soule, from this extasie". The next line

after this—"And meditation of what thou shalt bee" —indicates that the ecstasy is metaphorical only. "Meditation" is always discursive, always works through the understanding; it is only the preparation for ascent to the truly mystical state now generally understood in the term "contemplation," which St. Bernard defines as "the soul's true unerring intuition," "the unhesitating apprehension of truth." Donne's use of the word "contemplate" in the title of his *Progresse* may indicate a higher spiritual aim than the "represent" of the *Anatomie's* title, but his *Progresse* remains a spiritual exercise of the purgative, ascetic life. It represents an attempt to achieve the state of conversion best described by Donne himself in a prayer at the close of his *Essayes in Divinity:*

> Begin in us here in this life an angelicall purity, an angelicall chastity, an angelicall integrity to thy service, an Angelicall acknowledgment that we alwaies stand in thy presence, and should direct al our actions to thy glory. Rebuke us not, O Lord, in thine anger, that we have not done so till now; but enable us now to begin that great work; and imprint in us an assurance that thou receivest us now graciously, as reconciled, though enemies; and fatherly, as children, though prodigals; and powerfully, as the God of our salvation, though our own consciences testifie against us. (pp. 237-48)

> *Louis L. Martz, "John Donne in Meditation: The 'Anniversaries'," in his* The Poetry of Meditation: A Study in English Religious Literature of the Seventeenth Century, *Yale University Press, 1954, pp. 211-48.*

E. M. W. TILLYARD   (essay date 1956)

[*Tillyard was an English scholar of Renaissance literature whose studies of John Milton, William Shakespeare, and the epic form are widely respected. In the following excerpt, he examines two of Donne's poems, comparing one to poems by Oliver Goldsmith and Samuel Taylor Coleridge and finding both expressive of one extraordinary man's self-expression.*]

In his poetry [Donne] shows little trace of that sense of public or social obligation which, largely inherited from Greece and Rome in the sixteenth century, was destined to reach its height a century and a half later. The briefest glance at *King Henry IV* and *Hamlet* together will show that it was possible to combine the public and the introspective sides in an eminent degree. And in a less eminent degree, the same combination is found in the *Alchemist* and *Sejanus*. Donne was weak in the values that rule *Sejanus* and *Henry IV*. But, since he is so very strong on the side of mental processes, and since there are other poets than Donne to satisfy where he is weak, we should do ill to complain. And instead of complaining I will go on to talk of a poem that illustrates with peculiar felicity Donne's habit of showing his self-centred interest in the workings of his own mind, the '**Blossom**'. And I choose to talk of it not only to illustrate Donne's introspection, what Allen Tate calls his habit of pitting his ideas against one another like characters in a play, but also to present the kind of excellence in Donne most likely to survive a long bout of special popularity that cannot in the nature of things suffer no decline. Donne wrote no comprehensive long poem; and no single poem of his can contain all the poetic parts he commands. The '**Blossom**' is not a religious poem like the sonnet to his dead wife, nor does it ap-

proach the fierce absorption of passions into a single monotony that makes the **'Nocturnal upon St. Lucy's Day'** so
notable. But it displays an unusual variety and it reveals
the divisions of Donne's personality in the most obvious
form I can imagine that at some future date the **'Blossom'**
will continue to charm while the **'Nocturnal'** will be treated with a mixture of astonishment and dislike.

The dramatic situation presented in the **'Blossom'** is the
following. Donne is in the country and next day, very early, he will set out for London. There, in London, he knows
there is an accommodating lady, ready to return affection,
physical and mental. But his perverse heart is not interested and has chosen to pay its attention, in foolish delusion
that it may succeed, to a woman in this country neigh-
bourhood whom it has no business to court and who repels his advances. And she is not even particularly desirable. She is cold mentally and physically; and though,
Donne conjectures, she might develop on the purely sensual side she will never turn out sincerely affectionate.
And Donne's conclusion is: 'What a fool I am! But there
it is; that's what I'm like. That's the sort of silly trick the
human mind insists on playing.' To express the mind divided within itself Donne adopts the antique method of
the disputation; only here it is not two persons or allego-
rised 'qualities that dispute but the portions of a single
brain. It is the method employed by Marvell in his *'Dialogue between the Soul and Body'* and by Yeats in his *'Dialogue of Self and Soul'* Donne does not dramatise as completely as Yeats; he does not label the speakers and
confine his poem to their words. He introduces in his own
words the speech that his heart makes. And now for the
way the poem evolves.

Donne begins by addressing his heart through two stanzas,
the first presenting an analogy with the case his heart is in,
an analogy with a blossom, and the second being a direct
address to that heart. It is a surprising beginning because
it is smoothly lyrical and it is beautiful much in the way
the conventional Elizabethan lyric is beautiful. Donne
says, as it were: I know by this time you expect me to begin violently and in a way no ordinary writer of lyrics habitually does, something like 'For God's sake, hold your
tongue and let me love' or 'He is stark mad whoever
says . . .' but this time I am giving another surprise, disap-
pointing what you have come to expect of me; I am being
lyrical and incantatory. Further, I enjoy showing you that
I am able to do this kind of old-fashioned stuff if I please;
possibly better than any of you.

> Little think'st thou, poor flower,
> Whom I have watch'd six or seven days,
> And seen thy birth and seen what every hour
> Gave to thy growth, thee to this height to raise,
> And now dost laugh and triumph on this bough,
> Little think'st thou
> That it will freeze anon, and that I shall
> Tomorrow find thee fallen or not at all.

> Little think'st thou, poor heart,
> That labour'st yet to nestle thee
> And think'st by hovering here to get a part
> In a forbidden or forbidding tree,
> And hop'st her stiffness by long siege to bow,
> Little think'st thou
> That thou tomorrow, ere that sun doth wake,
> Must with this sun and me a journey take.

Notice also how in these stanzas Donne not only sweetens
his rhythms but in the second stanza dwells on his images
less insistently than usual. The lady is first a tree in which
his heart tries birdlike to build a nest, she quickly becomes
the conventional image of the fortress besieged by the lover, and finally the regal sun with the hint that the lover's
efforts do no damage to the calm and length of her slumbers. Donne deliberately tones down his own metaphorical
habits and approximates them to the conventional. But in
being thus conventional he is also being satirical towards
his heart; he as it were mimics the Petrarchian sentiments
of hopeless adoration which his heart has been silly
enough to experience.

He goes on to say: of course my heart will have its retort
to this—

> But thou, which lov'st to be
> Subtle to plague thyself, wilt say—

and the heart's retort is that it prefers to stay near the lady
while the body goes to London; with the implication that
love is a purely spiritual business, a superior Platonic affair that can dispense with the physical presences. But
note that Donne's heart does not use the lyrical vein that
Donne had assumed in addressing it. No, it uses the
speech-rhythms normal to Donne's argumentation and it
drops all metaphors.

> Alas, if *you* must go, what's that to *me*?
> Here lies my business, and here I will stay:
> You go to friends, whose love and means present
> Various content
> To your eyes, ears, and tongue, and every part.
> If then your body go what need you a heart?

Is it over-ingenious to guess that, as Donne's speech to his
heart in the opening stanzas mimics ironically the Petrarchian sentiments that heart is foolish enough to feel, the
heart counter-attacks by putting *its* case in the unaureate
idiom that Donne habitually affects?

Then, in the two final stanzas, Donne has the last word:
a contemptuous snort that his heart is quite self-deceived
about the ways of women and a piece of advice. *They*
have no use for the refinements of disembodied or Platonic love. The woman you're pursuing, says Donne, won't
know *my* heart from another's in separation from my
body; indeed she won't recognise you for a heart at all, because not having one she has no idea what a heart is like.
Any further possibilities in her lie elsewhere. So my advice
is: wait a bit here, if you will; then join me in London,
where all the rest of me will have had a holiday from female society and will be in fine condition. If you are wise,
you will imitate this rest of me to your great advantage.
And when we've made it up, there is someone waiting to
welcome my reunited self.

> Well then, stay here; but know,
> When thou hast stay'd and done thy most,
> A naked thinking heart, that makes no show,
> Is to a woman but a kind of ghost.
> How shall she know *my* heart, or, having none,
> Know *thee* for one?
> Practice may make her know some other part,
> But, take my word, she doth not know a heart.

> Meet me in London, then,
> Twenty days hence, and thou shalt see

Me fresher and more fat by being with men
Than if I had stay'd still with her and thee.
For God's sake, if you can, be you so too:
I would give you
There to another friend, whom we shall find
As glad to have my body as my mind.

There is a delightful variety in the poem. The first stanzas, however self-consciously planned, convey the element of trance and the refusal to face the facts that the experience of being in love engenders. The total poem also conveys the truth that people very much in love and embarrassed by it can, notwithstanding, exercise their other faculties normally. (It was not Parnell's grand-scale love-affair that ruined him as a politician; indeed it may have stimulated other sides of him to special activity: the ruin came from what other people thought of it, when it became public). The whole tone is cynical, but no complete cynic could have achieved the lyrical beauty of the opening.

There are special reasons too why the **'Blossom'** should be widely liked. Though the evident work of Donne at his best and of no one else, it is less extreme in manifesting its author's favourite literary habits than most of his great lyrics. Donne could be heavy-handed and inflict his personality on you. But here he manipulates his matter deftly and elegantly; without applying undue pressure. There is even a touch of social consideration. He seems to mitigate his personal obsessions for the reader's benefit. His cleverness, though not free from exhibitionism, does not seek merely to dazzle or stun but is accommodated to the ordinary reader. Best of all he apologises for his divided mind by referring to it explicitly:

> But thou which lov'st to be
> Subtle to plague thyself . . .

It is only a minority of men who are bored with the normal range of the mind and need the torture of feeling, the ramifications of self-questioning, or the exploration of the fringes of consciousness bordering on the insane to awaken their interest. Most people think that life offers enough interest through the plagues it brings along in its ordinary course to make the subtlety to plague yourself superfluous. In those two lines Donne pays tribute to this majority feeling, reprimanding his heart for being so foolish. Finally, the **'Blossom'** goes back on itself only once (when Donne decides that his heart doesn't after all have to leave the country but can stay there) and genuinely leads up to a conclusion. There is what can be called a normal distribution of energy between journey and arrival, between means and end.

But, though there are reasons why the **'Blossom'** should be unusually acceptable to the reader not specially prejudiced in favour of Donne's personal and rhetorical peculiarities, its first claim to excellence is in the distinction and subtlety of mind it presents to our inspection. Although Donne may make allowance for his readers and in so doing show some social consideration, he is still far from the sense of public, not to say political, obligation that you find in the odes of Horace and even in some of the later Yeats.

To make still clearer these qualities which in spite of various mitigations appear in the **'Blossom'**, self-questioning and absence of social sense, I turn to a poem more extreme, more typical, and one of his greatest, **'A Nocturnal upon St. Lucy's Day'**. It is a difficult poem and has called forth much comment. There is, for instance, an exposition of it by W. A. Murray in an article called 'Donne and Paracelsus' [published in the *Review of English Studies* in 1949]. It seems that some of the terms Donne uses cannot be understood fully except in the light of Paracelsus's scientific theories. On the we do other hand the general trend of the poem is plain, and we do not need any Paracelsan knowledge to understand the drift of such a line as

> The general balm th' hydroptic earth hath drunk.

General balm has a technical meaning in Paracelsus, which Donne meant to include, but for poetical appreciation we can satisfy ourselves pretty well when we interpret it as a life-giving property generally and take the line to mean that this property has withdrawn into the earth to the utmost extent. Further, no one is likely to quarrel with W. A. Murray's description of the poem's theme as being 'the annihilation of spirit, the death-in-life which follows supreme loss'. The poem is typically true to Donne's peculiar cast of mind because his feeling increases as the thought becomes more complicated. In the culminating fourth stanza, when Donne describes the supreme nothingness to which the death of his beloved has reduced him (supreme compared with the lesser nothingnesses he had before experienced), the rhythm throbs more and more with emotion as he runs through the different hierarchies of creation, all of them, even the humblest, positive in some way, as he is not, to justify the colossal fantasy of his being the elixir or quintessence of the primal nothingness our of which God created the universe:

> But I am by her death (which word wrongs her)
> Of the first nothing the elixir grown.
> Were I a man, that I were one
> I needs must know; I should prefer,
> If I were any beast,
> Some ends, some means; yea stones detest
> And love: all some properties invest.
> If I an ordinary nothing were,
> As shadow, a light and body must be there.
> But I am none.

Note how Donne goes back on himself in the first line: she is dead, but of course she is not dead, being in heaven. He has leisure to be paradoxical even in the height of passion. But the paradox does not compromise the passion, which we should never dream of doubting to be authentic. On the contrary it has its emotional effect, which is to join with the other extravangances to impress on us the extraordinary cast of Donne's mind. And we watch that mind as if it were some unusual natural portent, a flood, a great wind, an eruption.

I ask you now to consider these two poems of Donne, and specially the **'Nocturnal'**, along with two poems by other men. The first is Goldsmith's *Traveller*. This is a poem based on living experience, for Goldsmith spent some two years drifting round western Europe on foot, the best possible way of learning the intimacies of a country. But, far from rendering any personal experience, he yields to the excessive social bent of his time and effaces every indication of giving an authentic, first-hand, personal account. . . . If Donne is uncompromisingly personal, Goldsmith goes right to the other extreme and errs in abandoning every advantage in vividness that the exploitation of the personal offered him.

My other comparison leads to more fundamental matters. Donne's **'Nocturnal'** described sensations of loneliness and annihilation; and now put it alongside another poem in its way equally fantastic and dealing with the same sensations, Coleridge's *Ancient Mariner*. The mariner, becalmed and among the dead, is, humanly, utterly alone:

> Alone, alone, all, all alone,
> Alone on a wide wide sea!
> And never a saint took pity on
> My soul in agony.

Further, when he has slept and the curse begins to relax its hold, he is less than a man, a species of nothing:

> I moved, and could not feel my limbs:
> I was so light—almost
> I thought that I had died in sleep,
> And was a blessèd ghost.

What then is the final effect on the mind of the two accounts of spiritual annihilation? (pp. 12-24)

Coleridge expresses the cosmic terror, potential or realised, of all men: Donne expresses the peculiar feeling of annihilation of a very extraordinary man. I do not think it accidental that the *Ancient Mariner* begins and ends in social life, and (at the end) in a social life that includes the animals.

> O Wedding-Guest! this soul hath been
> Alone on a wide wide sea:
> So lonely 'twas, that God himself
> Scarce seemed there to be.
>
> O sweeter than the marriage-feast,
> 'Tis sweeter far to me,
> To walk together to the kirk
> With a goodly company!—
>
>   *   *   *
>
> He prayeth best, who loveth best
> All things both great and small;
> For the dear God who loveth us,
> He made and loveth all.

The ultimate effect of a work of art depends only to a small degree on superficial complexities; and some of the immemorial simplicities of the fairy-tale stir our natures more fundamentally than the bright and rattling ingenuities of a good adventure story. Or one can point to the different areas of the mind which have interested the two modern psychologists who show the same kind of temperamental opposition as Plato and Aristotle among the Greeks, Jung and Freud. Jung did not deny the truth of much Freudian theorising about the mind but he thought it defective in leaving out those areas of the unconscious that mattered most: the primitive areas of instinctive wisdom accumulated through the ages by the collective efforts of the race. I do not either believe or disbelieve in the Jungian theory of the collective unconscious but I am clear in my own mind that in talking of it Jung points to certain basic mental possessions to which Freud and his kin are not very sensitive, and, further, that the poetry which appeals to those mental possessions has a special and at the same time wide-embracing power. I also think that the *Ancient Mariner* has that power, whereas the **'Nocturnal upon St. Lucy's Day'** has not. Since the power is wide-embracing, since it exists, even if usually dormant and unknown, in the minds of all men it implies a social

sense: something I found missing in Donne's poem. In its restricted way Donne's **'Nocturnal'** is superb. But Coleridge in the *Ancient Mariner*, while being eminently himself, speaks for the whole of normal humanity and, so doing, creates a work of art of a different, and of a larger, dimension. (pp. 25-6)

E. M. W. Tillyard, "Personal and Public," in his
The Metaphysicals and Milton, Chatto &
Windus, 1956, pp. 12-28.

FRANK KERMODE (essay date 1957)

[*Kermode is an English critic whose career combines modern critical methods with expert traditional scholarship, particularly in his work on Shakespeare. In his critical discussions of modern literature. Kermode has embraced many of the conceptions of structuralism and phenomenology. He characterizes all human knowledge as poetic, or fictive: constructed by humans and affected by the perceptual and emotional limitations of human consciousness. Because perceptions of life and the world change, so does human knowledge and the meaning attached to things and events. Thus, there is no single fixed reality over time. Similarly, for Kermode, a work of art has no single fixed meaning, but a multiplicity of possible interpretations; in fact, the best of modern writing is constructed so that it invites a variety of interpretations, all of which depend upon the sensibility of the reader. Kermode believes his critical writings exist to stimulate thought, to offer possible interpretations, but not to fix a single meaning to a work of art. True or "classic" literature, to Kermode, is thus a constantly reinterpreted living text, "complex and indeterminate enough to allow us our necessary pluralities." In the following excerpt from an essay originally published as a monograph for the British Council in 1957, he surveys Donne's career as a writer.*]

To have read Donne was once evidence of man's curious taste; now (though the vogue may be fading) it is a minimum requirement of civilized literary talk. We have seen the history of English poetry rewritten by critics convinced of his cardinal importance. This change was partly the effect of the reception into England of French Symbolist thought, and its assimilation to the native doctrines of Blake, Coleridge and Pater. Poets and critics were struck by the way Donne exhibits the play of an agile mind within the sensuous body of poetry, so that even his most passionate poems work by wit, abounding in argument and analogy; the poetry and the argument cannot be abstracted from each other. (p. 116)

Wit is a quality allowed Donne by all critics, of all parties. In his own time people admired his 'strong lines', and perhaps the best way of giving a general account of his wit is to try to explain what this expression meant. Donne is notoriously an obscure poet—in fact his obscurity is often overestimated, but he is never easy—and this is often because his manner is tortuous and, in his own word, 'harsh'. . . . Donne was not writing for the many. He expected his readers to enjoy difficulty, not only in the scholastic ingenuity of his arguments, but in the combination of complicated verseforms and apparently spontaneous thought—thought that doubled back, corrected itself, broke off in passionate interjections. This kind of writing belongs to a rhetorical tradition ignored by much Elizabethan poetry, which argued that language could directly represent the immediate play of mind—style as the instantaneous expression of thinking. And this is why Donne—if

I may translate from Mario Praz what I take to be the best thing ever said about Donne's style—will always appeal to readers 'whom the *rhythm of thought* itself attracts by virtue of its own peculiar convolutions'. (pp. 119-20)

As strong lines directly record mental activity, they contain concepts, or, in the contemporary form of the word, 'conceits'. The meaning we now attach to this word is a specialization directly due to the vogue for strong lines. The value of such lines obviously depends on the value (and that is almost the same thing as the *strangeness*) of the concepts they express, and these were usually metaphors. A high valuation was placed on metaphor, on the power of making what Dr. Johnson, who understood without approving, called the *discordia concors*. The world was regarded as a vast divine system of metaphors, and the mind was at its fullest stretch when observing them. Peculiar ability in this respect was called *acutezza* by the Italians and, by the English, Wit. But although the movement was European in scope, it is unnecessary to suppose that Donne owed much to its Spanish and Italian exponents; they were known in England, but they conspicuously lack Donne's colloquial convolution, and his argumentativeness.... We cannot think of Donne without thinking of relentless argument. He depends heavily upon dialectical sleight-of-hand, arriving at the point of wit by subtle syllogistic misdirections, inviting admiration by slight but significant perversities of analogue, which re-route every argument to parodox. Still, in view of the lack of contemporary English criticism on these points, it is wise to learn what we can from Continental critics of witty poetry, and the most important lesson, brilliantly suggested by S. L. Bethell, is that they regarded the conceit of *argument*—making a new and striking point by a syllogism concealing a logical error—as the highest and rarest kind of conceit. This is Donne's commonest device. Of course we are aware that we are being cleverly teased, but many of the love-poems, like '**The Extasie**' or '**The Flea**', depend on our wonder outlasting our critical attitude to argument. ... [In each of these last-named poems] the argument, a tissue of fallacies, sounds solemnly convincing and consecutive, so that it is surprising to find it ending with an immodest proposal. The highest powers of the mind are put to base use, but enchantingly demonstrated in the process.

Part of Donne's originality lies precisely in the use of such methods for amorous poetry. Properly they belong to the sphere of religion (of course there is always much commerce between the two). This human wit suggests the large design of God's wit in the creation. It is immemorially associated with biblical exegesis and preaching, sanctioned and practised by Ambrose and Augustine, and blended in the patristic tradition with the harshness of Tertullian, as well as with the enormous eloquence of Chrysostom. The Europe of Donne's time had enthusiastically taken up witty preaching.... Donne's youthful examination of 'the whole body of divinity controverted between the Churches of England and Rome' provided him not only with a religion but with a style. Some aspects of his Jesuit training would help him in the business of analogy; but primarily the conceit of his secular poetry is derived from his later religious studies. It is, in fact, a new, paradoxical use, for amorous purposes, of the *concetto predicabile*, the preacher's conceit. As usual, we see him all of a piece, yet all paradox; Donne the poet, with all his 'naturalist' passion, knowingness, obscenity indeed, is *anima naturaliter*

theologica. What made him a poet also made him an Anglican: the revaluation of a tradition.

It is for this reason that the old emphasis on the 'medieval' quality of Donne's thought, though in need of qualification, is more to the point than the more recent stress on his modernity. A great deal has been made of his interest in the 'new philosophy', and the disturbance supposed to have been caused him by such astronomical discoveries as the elliptical movement of planets, the impossibility of a sphere of fire, the corruptibility of the heavens, the movement of the earth, and so on. Certainly, as we know from *Ignatius* and elsewhere, Donne was aware of such developments, aware that it was no longer humanly satisfactory to look at the heavens through the spectacles of Ptolemy. But it is the greatest possible misunderstanding of Donne to suppose that he took this as any more than another proof, where none was needed, of the imperfection of human intellect. Mutability reached higher towards heaven than one had thought; but this only shows how unreliable human knowledge must always be.... There is always an antithesis, in Donne, between natural and divine knowledge, the first shadowy and inexact, the second clear and sure. New philosophy belongs to the first class. What we really know is what is revealed; later we shall know in full:

> Up into the watch-towre get,
> And see all things desployl'd of fallacies:
> Thou shalt not peepe through lattices of eyes,
> Nor heare through Labyrinths of eares, nor learne
> By circuit, or collections to discerne.
> In heaven thou straight know'st all, concerning it,
> And what concerns is not, shalt straight forget.

A mind habituated to such discriminations between the light of nature and 'light from above, from the fountain of light', as Milton calls it, may, in some spheres of knowledge, earn the epithet 'sceptical'. Donne deserted a Church which, as he and Hooker agreed, had mistaken mere custom for law. Liberated from the tyranny of custom, he turns, in his erotic poetry, a professionally disenchanted eye on conventional human behaviour. We may speak confidently of a 'libertine' or 'naturalist' Donne only if we use the terms as applying to literature and thought rather than to life; but it remains true that the **Songs and Sonets** are often (though without his shocking coolness) akin to the franker pronouncements of Montaigne. Consider, for example, his essay '**Upon some verses of Virgil**', where he professes his contempt for 'artised' love: he prefers the thing itself, and in accordance with his preference argues that amorous poetry also should be 'natural', colloquial, 'not so much innovating as filling language with more forcible and divers services, wrestling, straining, and enfolding it ... teaching it unwonted motions'.... Donne openly despises the ritual and indirection of Platonic love; he will follow Nature and pluck his rose (or roses; for Love's sweetest part is variety). The enemies of nature are such fictions as Honour; in the good old times, before Custom dominated humanity, things were very different: see '**Loves Deity**' and '**Elegy XVII**'.... This is the sense in which Donne often celebrates the passion of love—as immediate and natural, but constricted by social absurdities:

> Love's not so pure and abstract, as they use
> To say, which have no Mistresse but their Muse.

But of course we must allow for an element of formal paradox. Donne found this very congenial—it is in a way a theological, a liturgical device—and his *Juvenilia* contain such joke paradoxes as a defence of woman's inconstancy, an argument that it is possible to find some virtue in women, and so on, worked out with the same half-serious, half-ribald ingenuity that we find in some of the *Songs and Sonets.* . . . To take these poems too seriously, as moral or autobiographical pronouncements, is to spoil them; though some are clearly more serious than others.

This may suggest the possibility of dividing the secular poems into groups other than their obvious *genres*; but is a highly conjectural undertaking. There is a similar difficulty about their chronology; attempts to determine this depend on hypothetical links with events (and women) in Donne's life. We can say the Satires were written in the 'nineties; we can place many verse-letters over a twenty-year period; epithalamia and obsequies are datable; one or two references in the love-poems hint at dates. But in these last the evidence is scanty. . . . All we may be sure of is that Donne, with varying intensity, passion, and intellectual conviction, exercised his wit on the theme of sexual love, and that he was inclined to do this in a 'naturalist' way. We need not concern ourselves with dates, or with the identities of mistresses celebrated, cursed or mourned

The *Songs and Sonets* were read only in manuscript in Donne's lifetime, and so by a small and sophisticated circle. They certainly exhibit what Donne, in the little squib called *The Courtier's Library*, calls 'itchy outbreaks of farfetched wit'; and the wit is of the kind that depends both upon a harsh strangeness of expression and upon great acuity of illustration and argument. We are asked to *admire*, and that is why the poet creates difficulties for himself, choosing arbitrary and complex stanza forms, of which the main point often seems to be that they put tremendous obstacles in his way. Without underestimating the variety of tone in these poems, one may say they all offer this kind of pleasure—delight in a dazzling conjuring trick. Even the smoothest, simplest song, like **'Sweetest love, I do not goe'**, is full of *mind*. Donne would have despised Dryden's distinction between poets and wits. True, some of these poems deserve the censure that when we have once understood them they are exhausted: **'The Indifferent'**, **'The Triple Fool'**, and a dozen others fall into this class. Others, like **'The Flea'** and **'A Valediction: of my name, in the window'**, are admired primarily as incredibly perverse and subtle feats of wit; yet others, like **'The Apparition'**, as examples of how Donne could clothe a passion, in this case hatred, in a clever colloquial fury. This is the inimitable Donne: sometimes, as in **'The Broken Heart'**, we might be reading Cowley's sexless exercises.

One should here dwell at rather more length on one or two poems. I almost chose **'The Dampe'**, a fine example of Donne's dialectical wit (the main argument is attended by a ghost-argument, supported by slang double-meanings); and **'Farewell to Love'**, which would have pleased Montaigne by its grave obscenity; and, for its wide-ranging metaphor and brilliant farfetched conclusion, **'Loves Alchymie'**. **'Lovers Infinitenesse'** has the characteristic swerving argument, its stanzas beginning 'If . . . Or . . . Yet . . .' —compare **'The Feaver'**, with its 'But yet . . . Or if . . . And yet . . . Yet . . .' For his best use of 'the nice speculations of philosophy', **'Aire and Angells'** and **'The Extasie'** commend themselves. . . . But **'The Curse'** is both characteris-

tic and neglected, and **'A Nocturnall upon S. Lucies Day'** is Donne's finest poem. . . . (pp. 120-29)

Of Donne's twenty Elegies I have room to say little. They are love-poems in loose iambic pentameter couplets, owing a general debt, for tone and situation, to the *Amores* of Ovid; the Roman poet loses no wit, but acquires harshness, masculinity. These poems are full of sexual energy, whether it comes out in frank libertinism, or in the wit of some more serious attachment. **'The Anagram'** (ii) is an example of the wit that proved all too imitable, all too ready to degenerate into fooling—it is a series of paradoxes on somebody's foul mistress, a theme current at the time. Elegy viii [**'The Comparison'**] is a similar poem, comparing one's own and another's mistress, with plenty of unpleasant detail. But the Elegies have a considerable variety of tone, ranging from the set pieces on **'Change'** and **'Variety'** (iii and xvii) which are paralleled by several of the *Songs and Sonets*, to the passionate xvi [**'On his Mistres'**] and the sombre xii [**'His parting from her'**] on the theme of parting. . . . The Elegies have always had a reputation for indecency, and they certainly exploit the sexual puns so much enjoyed by Elizabethan readers. Among the poems excluded from the first edition is the magnificently erotic Elegy xix, **'Going to Bed'**: too curious a consideration of some of the metaphors in this poem (such as the passage about 'imputed grace') has led critics to charge it with blasphemy, a risk Donne often runs by the very nature of his method. Montaigne might have complained that Donne here substitutes a new mythology and metaphysics of love for those he had abandoned, new presbyter for old priest. But it is impossible not to admire the translation of sexual into mental activity. Elegy xix was later regarded as the poet's own epithalamion, a fancy as harmless as it is improbable, except that it has perhaps resulted in the acceptance of a very inferior reading in line 46. One beautiful and exceptional peom is Elegy ix, **'The Autumnall'** to Lady Danvers; but even this would not, I think, quite escape Sir Herbert Grierson's criticism, that Donne (especially in the Elegies) shows 'a radical want of delicacy'; for it has the wit and fantastic range of reference that mark the erotic Elegies.

The Satires belong to the same phase of Donne's talent as the work I have been discussing. They are, as Elizabethan satire was supposed to be, rough and harsh, written in that low style that Donne so often used, though here it is conventional. . . . [We] may say that they have the usual energy, a richness of contemporary observation rather splenetic, of course, in character. Pope thought them worth much trouble, but it is doubtful if, except for iii, they play much part in anybody's thinking about Donne. The same may be said of the epicedes and obsequies, funeral poems which in this period were often, when they were not pastoral elegies, poems of fantastically tormented wit. So Donne proves, in the elegy on Prince Henry, that 'wee May safelyer say, that we are dead, then hee'. The form suited him only too well. The same cannot be said of the epithalamion; Spenser is the poet to thrive here. Yet there are fine things in Donne's poem for the marriage of the Princess Elizabeth in 1613:

> Up, up, faire Bride, and call,
> Thy starres, from out their severall boxes, take
> Thy Rubies, Pearles, and Diamonds forth, and make
> Thy selfe a constellation, of them All,
> And by their blazing signifie,
> That a Great Princesse falls, but doth not die.

Donne could not speak without wit; it is this naturalness that often redeems him.

Of the occasional verse included under the title **Letters to Severall Personages** a word must suffice. There is a mistaken view that they are negligible because they occasionally flatter. They were written over many years, and not for all profit: notice the little-known verses to Goodyere which have the strong Jonsonian ring; the charming **'Mad paper, stay'** to Lady Herbert before her re-marriage. The best, probably, are to the Countess of Bedford, dependant though Donne may have been; and the poem beginning **'You have refin'd mee'** is a great poem, certainly no more 'blasphemous' in its compliment than **'Elegy xix'** in its persuasions.

This matter of blasphemous allusion comes to a head in the two **Anniversaries**, written for Sir Robert Drury on the death of his daughter Elizabeth, and published in 1611 and 1612. These are amazingly elaborate laments for a girl Donne had never seen. The first he called **'An Anatomy of the World'**, announcing in his full title that the death of Elizabeth Drury is the *occasion* for observations on the frailty and decay of the whole world, and representing the dead girl as Astraea, as the world's soul, as the preservative balm, and so on, her departure has left it lifeless, and he dissects it. The second, describing 'the Progresse of the Soule' after death, is similar: 'By occasion of the Religious death of Mistris Elizabeth Drury, the incommodities of the soule in this life, and her exaltation in the next, are contemplated.' From Jonson forward, critics have complained of the faulty taste of such hyperbolical praise of a young girl, and Donne defended himself more than once, though without much vigour; he would have little patience with this kind of misunderstanding. All we may say here is that these poems—now known to be planned in a highly original way as a series of formal religious meditations—are essential to the understanding of Donne; they come near to giving us a map of *the dark side of his wit.* (pp. 132-35)

The **Anniversaries** lead us into a consideration of Donne's religious life. But we shall find that the poet and the religious were the same man.

Donne's acceptance of the established Church is the most important single event of his life, because it involved all the powers of his mind and personality. His youthful sympathies must have been with the persecuted Romanists, and his Satires contain bitter allusions to 'pursuivants', tormentors of Jesuits; the odious Topcliffe is mentioned by name in some manuscripts. But he was familiar with the fanaticism as well as with the learning of Jesuits; and later he decided that the first of these was the hardest affliction of Christendom, though the second was to serve him well. No one can say exactly when he left one Church for the other; it was a gradual process. . . . Of the two communions—sister teats of his graces' he called them, 'yet both diseased and infected, but not both alike'—he was to choose the one truer to the Catholic tradition as he understood it. Like his learned contemporary Casaubon, he found this to be the Church of England— episcopal and sacramental, but divested of the Romanist accretions. (pp. 135-37)

Donne, then, accepted the Church of England because it was truly Catholic. He rejoiced to discover a Reformed Church which cultivated the Fathers and was slow to come 'to a final resolution' in 'particulars'. He wanted tradition but without its errors: Aquinas, but not the scholastic nonsense; the Fathers, but not their mistakes. The Catholic heritage was enormously more important to him than any 'new' knowledge, theological or physical, and he has little distinction as a speculative theologian, though his age is one of dogmatic controversy. He detested, for instance, the Calvinist teaching on Predestination, which had the intellectual presumption to dishonour God by suggesting that He could 'make us to damn us'; when it was necessary to pronounce on the matter he fell back on Aquinas ('God has appointed all future things to be, but so as they are, that is necessary things necessarily and contingent things contingently') but he disliked the whole argument: '*Resistibility*, and *Irresistibility*, of grace, which is every Artificers wearing now, was a stuff that our Fathers wore not, a language that pure antiquity spake not.' 'The best men', he says, 'are but Problematicall, only the Holy Ghost is Dogmaticall.' Though by no means a complete Sceptic, he knew the limits of reason, and often defined its relation to faith (in **Essayes in Divinity**, **Biathanatos**, a verse-letter to the Countess of Bedford, the Christmas sermon for 1621). His position is not dissimilar from Hooker's (e.g. *Laws* I.8). The limitations of human learning he sets forth in the famous Valediction Sermon of 1619, and the contrast between natural and heavenly knowledge . . . is developed in a splendid passage of the 1622 Easter sermon: 'God shall create us all Doctors in a minute.' Obviously the fierce certainties of some contemporaries were not for Donne. 'It is the text that saves us', he says. 'The interlineary glosses, and the marginal notes, and the *variae lectiones*, controversies and perplexities, undo us.' He was content with his Church's restoration of a good, lost tradition, just as, in his capacity as poet, he had used a traditional but neglected style that had its roots in the same great body of learning, the teaching of the Fathers.

No one, then, will read Donne for theological novelties; even in the **Essayes**, which are full of curious applications, Donne's regard for authority puts him at the opposite pole from the radically speculative Milton. And whatever may be offered by the vast array of sermons, it is not that kind of excitement.

It is not easy to give a general account of the sermons. They were preached on all manner of occasions, over fifteen years, and they take their colour from the audience, and from Donne's mood, as well as from the text and from the ecclesiastical occasion. Some were for a great audience, some for a small; some for lawyers, some for the Court; some for Lent and some for Easter; some were preached when the preacher had private reason for joy, some when he was miserable. The tone varies widely. There is truth in the often-repeated charge that Donne was preoccupied with sin and death; he confesses his melancholy temperament (calling it 'a disease of the times') and constantly quotes St. Paul's *cupio dissolvi* (Phil. i. 23), 'having a desire to depart and be with Christ'. 'If there were any other way to be saved and to get to Heaven,' he says, 'then by being born into this life, I would not wish to have come into this world.' There are terrible sermons on death, full of the poetry of charnel-house and worm. There are lamentations for the sins of youth: 'I preach the sense of Gods indignation upon mine own soul.' There are even rather grim sermons on apparently joyous occasions;

a wedding sermon for personal friends is a forbidding, though orthodox, account of the Church's teaching on marriage, with many gloomy strictures on women. But one can overdo this aspect of the sermons. Death and Sin are fully presented; but perhaps not inordinately. And, to balance them, there is a massive insistence on the theme of Resurrection, and far more humanity than one is led to expect— see, for example, the moving passages on the death of Augustine's son, and that of his own daughter, in the superb Easter sermon for 1627.... (pp. 138-40)

As a preacher Donne is guilty, by modern, standards, of pedantry. His style is artificial; he would have been angry to have been told otherwise. The pedantry was partly a matter of fashion, but also a token of his confidence in a truly Catholic tradition. The sermons are inconceivable without it, so is Donne himself. And if he makes our flesh creep, that was still part of his duty; if he almost ignores the ecstatic religion that flourished in his day, that was a defect of his central merit. If we want Donne as a modern poet we may find it tiresome that he was capable of so much archaic quibbling, so much jargon and flattery. But, while it is perfectly proper to read the **Songs and Sonets** and ignore the sermons, it is improper to construct an image of Donne without looking at them; and many such caricatures still circulate.

It was Donne's habit, in later life, to speak slightingly of his poetry; and although he considered, for a brief moment before his ordination, the possibility of publishing his poems, it seems he did not even possess copies of them. There are signs that it was regarded as slightly improper, after his ordination, for 'a man of his years and place' to be versifying, and indeed Donne wrote little verse as a priest.... In fact it now appears that the bulk of the divine poems belongs to 1607-15. These years produced the **Corona** sequence, most of the **Holy Sonnets**, the **'Litanie'**, **'Upon the Annunciation and Passion'**, **'Goodfriday, 1613'**, and probably **'The Crosse'**. The poem addressed to Tilman, the **'Lamentations of Jeremy'**, the lines on Sidney's 'Psalms', the three great Hymns, three Sonnets, and **'An hymne to the Saints, and to Marquesse Hamylton'**, which Donne wrote reluctantly in 1625, make up the extant poetical work of the priest. Most of the religious poetry, therefore, belongs to the period of many of the verse-letters, and the **Anniversaries**.

It is verse of remarkable originality. **'Satyre iii'** shows that even in his youth Donne considered the language of passionate exploration and rebuke appropriate to religious themes; and even when he is working in strict forms like the sonnet, and on devotional topics, we recognize at once that turbulent diction which spontaneously records the pressure of fervent and excited thought. But though he rejected some of the formalities in his secular poetry, Donne was habituated in matters of devotion to certain schematic disciplines. He had been taught to pray; and when his poems are prayers they are formed by this early training. When he undertook 'a serious meditation of God', he tended to do so by employing these meditative techniques.

Here a learned man committed to the reformed religion occupies himself with Papist devotion; but we should not exaggerate the paradox. Donne's Church did not reject what it found good in the tradition; many devotional practices were retained, and some were revived. Donne's **Corona** sonnets are an ingenious adaptation of an old Do-

minican system of meditation, based on an obsolete type of rosary called the *corona*. A Puritan might condemn this, but to Donne it was, theologically, an indifferent matter, and good in that it concentrated the devotional powers of a man easily distracted from prayer. More remarkable, perhaps, is the fact that some of the Holy Sonnets, and the **Anniversaries**, are indebted to meditative techniques defined and propagated by Ignatius Loyola and the Jesuits; yet these were so widely disseminated, and apparently so fruitful, that it was by no means exceptional for enemies of the Order to adopt them.

The **Corona**, with its linked sonnets and carefully balanced ingenuity, may strike us as 'mixt wit'; the Ignatian method is more interesting. The purpose of the technique is to concentrate all the powers of the soul, including the sensual, in the act of *prayer*.... [The] poem is another of Donne's exercises in the paradoxes of his religion, and the Trinity is one of the greatest of them. The epithet is obliquely justified by the intensity of the rhythmical conflicts throughout; in the opposition between the heavy 'Batter' and the weak, cadential 'knocke, breathe, shine and seek to mend'; in the divine absurdity of Heaven troubling to take the sinner by storm, laying him low that he may stand; finally by the imagery of rape. Love is figured as lust because it is to be rough and irresistible; God is a monster of mercy (but the Scripture compares him to a thief). The powerful paradoxes of the last couplet suggest an infinite series of such: God as infant, God as malefactor, Justice as mercy, Death as Life, and so forth. We respond crudely to this kind of challenge, and such a reading as this is clumsy and over-explicit. Similarly we are inclined to think of a poem that celebrates the coincidence of Lady Day and Good Friday as a toy; but for Donne it was a motive to reverence, a piece of calendar wit that challenged a Christian poet to prayer. We are usually content to be cleverer about the love of women than the love of God; therefore the **Songs and Sonets** keep better. But Donne was clever about both, and sometimes in much the same, way; our awkwardness here leads us to charge Elegy xix [**'Going to Bed'**] with blasphemy, and **'Show me, dear Christ'** with indelicacy. Donne himself was not blind to some of the dangers of his method: in the **'Litanie'** he writes, 'When wee are mov'd to seeme religious Only to vent wit, Lord deliver us'.

The finest of the other pre-ordination poems is **'Goodfriday, 1613'**. Here too Donne starts from a paradox; on this day of all days he is turned away from the East. This plunges him into that paradoxical series where he moves with such assurance; and his wit binds up the paradoxes, with just the neatness and passion of the love-poems, in a fine conclusion.... (pp. 144-48)

Of the poems written after ordination, only the sonnets of the Westmoreland MS. and the three Hymns are of the best of Donne. The little group of sonnets includes the moving poem about the death of his wife, and **'Show me, dear Christ'**. The Hymns are justly admired. **'A Hymn to Christ, at the Authors last going into Germany'** records a moment of intense personal feeling, and is a companion to the beautiful Valediction Sermon of 1619. The other two belong to the period of Donne's serious illness in 1623, when he also wrote, **Devotions**. 'Thou art a meta-physical God,' he says in that work, 'full of comparisons.' And although these poems abjure harshness in favour of the solemnity proper to hymns, they nevertheless live by their wit. **'A Hymn to God, my God, in my sicknesse'** is founded on a favourite conceit; the poet is a map over which the physicians pore.... The **'Hymn to God the Father'** contains the famous play on the poet's name (but so does the inscription on the portrait of the author in his shroud, prefixed to **'Deaths Duell'**); what in our time would be only a puerile joke is thrice repeated in this solemn masterpiece.

Donne's wit, of course, depends on the assumption that a joke can be a serious matter. Wit, as he understood it, was born of the preaching of the Word, whether employed in profane or in religious expression. 'His fancy', as Walton says, 'was unimitably high, equalled only by his great wit.... He was by nature highly passionate '[see excerpt date 1640]. It will never be regretted that the twentieth century, from whatever motive, restored him to his place among the English poets, and wit to its place in poetry. (p. 148)

> Frank Kermode, "John Donne," in his Shakespeare, Spenser, Donne: Renaissance Essays, *Routledge & Kegan Paul, 1971, pp. 116-48.*

I. A. RICHARDS   (lecture date 1957-58)

[*An English literary scholar, Richards is considered a forerunner of New Criticism, a critical movement that emphasizes the close reading and explication of a text over study informed by the apparent biographical, historical, or moral vision of the artist. Richard's studies often stress the nature of symbolic language. In the following excerpt from a talk originally broadcast on a Boston television program during the 1957-58 season. Richards provides a close reading of "The Exstasie."*]

I am taking a poem now which has been understood in very different ways and praised and blamed for surprisingly different reasons. It is John Donne's **"The Exstasie"**, first printed in 1633, probably written in 1611. (p. 85)

> Where, like a pillow on a bed,
> A Pregnant banke swel'd up, to rest
> The violets reclining head,
> Sat we two, one anothers best;

To a newcomer to the poem the first puzzling thing is the scenery, isn't it? This mixture of bedroom and out of doors. And many people feel a discomfort over this *violet* and it *reclining head*. How small a bank would do that?

However, violets are mentioned again: the lovers are in some way like violets and they are to rest their own reclining heads through most of the rest of the poem.

The fourth line is the one to ponder. Note that at this stage they are sitting

> Sat we two, one another's best;

Not only: each the one the other likes best, but: each the one who is best for the other. The poem is going to be about what this being *best* is, and in the deepest possible sense of *best*.

> Our hands were firmly cimented
> With a fast balme, which thence did spring,
> Our eye-beames twisted, and did thred
> Our eyes, upon one double string;

They are hand in hand. *cimented*: secured together, *fast balme*: balm of Gilead, warmth and comfort; a place of shelter and protection in the Alps is often a *balme*.

It's the next two lines which make people blink. These eyes which are gazing into one another so are close together here: so close that each pair of eyes sees and is seen as only one eye . . . over near . . . almost unseen and unseeing. Notice how the strain is conveyed. You can verify if you like—with a mirror.

> So to'entergraft our hands, as yet
> Was all our meanes to make us one,
> And pictures on our eyes to get
> Was all our propagation

Pictures on our eyes to get: The lovers separating their faces a little become able to see now—each on the gleaming surface of the other's eyes (or within the pupil's inkwell) miniature images of their own heads. It's not just "We can see reflections of one another" but "Within one another's eyes images of ourselves seem already to be living". (pp. 85-6)

To go back to Donne: *as yet* is fair warning—isn't it?—that far deeper *meanes to make us one* are to follow.

> As 'twixt two equal Armies, Fate
> Suspends uncertaine victorie,
> Our soules, (which to advance their state,
> Were gone out,) hung 'twixt her, and mee.

What is this sudden and surprising military metaphor doing here? We are suddenly swept off into the atmosphere of high politics or of *The Iliad*: Achilles chasing Hector round Troy and Zeus hanging up his golden balance.

Gone out: to battle, that is; "gone out" has been a way of saying 'fought a duel'.

To advance their state: in a spirit of self-aggrandisement, each the would-be out-doer, conquerer, subjugator, of the other. But they are *two egual Armies*. It won't do. There can be no military outcome. Nor can it be a sort of cold-war situation. They are *one another best*—as they are now coming to know.

> And whil'st our soules negotiate there,
> Wee like sepulchrall statues lay;
> All day, the same our postures were,
> And wee said nothing, all the day

What a change from the eye to eye posture of stanza 2. Here, in this grim tombstone image, they lie like effigies of the dead: *sepulchrall statues*. Why? Is it because that *victorie* business had threatened a sort of death to their love? Or is it rather a reminder that the going forth of the soul in ecstasy leaves the body as though it were dead?

> If any, so by love refin'd
> That he soules language understood,
> And by good love were grown all minde,
> Within convenient distance stood,

> He (though he knew not which soule spake,
> Because both meant, both spake the same)
> Might thence a new concoction take,
> And part farre purer then he came.

Poems do often, and rightly, stop off to tell the reader what they are doing. Here for 2 verses **"The Exstasie"** does this.

So by love refin'd: this poem is, I take it, a description of how this refining, this purifying is done. The root meaning of *fine,* here, is 'end, aim': made again as it should be. Refining is especially the process of separating metal from ore and the poem is going to talk of dross and alloy later.

Soules language: as distinguished from what tongues can say. They *said nothing, all the day.* But the souls in their negotiation talk on and on. What they agree upon is reported in the rest of the poem which is simply this report. *And by good love were grown all minde:* the report is going to explain, very exactly, that *grown all minde* doesn't mean the exclusion or disregard of the body but its development to become one with mind.

Concoction: a sort of ripening or remaking by heat, as in cooking; *farre purer:* the poem is going to explain what it means by that. Perhaps, though, an excerpt from the Book of Wisdom may be helpful:

> For wisdom, which is the worker of all things, taught me; for in her is an understanding spirit, holy, one only, manifold, subtil, lively, clear, having all power, overseeing all things, and going through all understanding, pure and most subtil spirits. For wisdom is more moving than any motion: she passeth and goeth through all things by reason of her pureness.

In what follows through the rest of the poem these two souls become one joint and abler soul—*both meant, both spake the same:* the outcome in any qualified hearer (reader) is a *new concoction* in him, the new truth that "the worker of all things" has enabled them, *who are this new soule,* to learn.

Here is the account of ecstasy which Grierson quotes from Plotinus:

> Even the word, 'vision', does not seem appropriate here. It is rather an ecstasy, a simplification, an abandonment of self, a desire of contact, a perfect quietude, in short, a wish to merge oneself in that which one contemplates in the Sanctuary.

> This Exstasie doth unperplex
> (We said) and tell us what we love,
> Wee see by this, it was not sexe,
> Wee see, we saw not what did move;

Doth unperplex: what has been perplexed, tangled, ravelled becomes simpler.

And tell us what we love: the greatest of all our quests is to learn what it is we love.

It was not sexe: according to the Oxford Dictionary this is the first appearance of the word *sex*—in this its distinctively modern use. It looks as if Donne introduced this meaning for it. What a career it has had!

Wee see, we saw not what did move: both (1) We see now, and did not see before, what did move; and (2) We see that we did not see then, what did move. Now *what did move?* What does this mean? — especially if we take it together with *what we love?*

Let me show you a passage from Plato's *Republic* and one from Aristotle's *Metaphysics* which, I think, can help a lot.

> Socrates: Isn't it clear that there are plenty of people who are ready enough to *seem* just, or to have what

seems beautiful, without its being at all so in fact; but when it comes to the good, everyone wants the thing itself and what only *seems* good isn't good. enough for anyone.

> Adeimantus: That's so.

> Socrates: This, then, is what every soul is looking for, and for this every soul does all that it does, feeling in some way what it is, but troubled and uncertain and unable to see clearly enough.

It is the Idea of the Good that is really, in and behind all we do, what everyone, all the time, is seeking.

And here is what Aristotle did with this hint:

> There is a mover which moves without being moved, being eternal . . . And the object of thought and the object of desire move in this way; they move without being moved.

Since the Ecstasy can *tell us what we love* it thereby makes us *see . . . what did move.*

> But as all severall soules containe
> Mixture of things, they know not what,
> Love, these mixt soules, doth mixe againe,
> And makes both one, each this and that.

Several soules: separate souls.

They know not what they have in them: When they become one soul they do know just that.

Each this and that: each is both. 'Each is both': here is Coomaraswamy on the Indian concept of love:

> In India . . . sexual love has a deep and spiritual significance. There is nothing with which we can better compare the 'mystic union' of the finite with its infinite ambient . . . than the selfoblivion of earthly lovers locked in each other's arms, where 'each is both'.

> A single violet transplant,
> The strength, the colour, and the size,
> (All which before was poore, and scant,)
> Redoubles still, and multiplies.

Helen Gardner comments: "I believe Donne is referring to the fact that transplantation will produce double from single flowers" and gives contemporary references.

> When love, with one another so
> Interinanimates two soules,
> That abler soule, which thence doth flow,
> Defects of lonelinesse controules.

Interinanimates: like two logs each of which makes the other flame the better.

Defects of lonelinesse: the chief of which is ignorance, ignorance of what we are.

When *that abler soule* comes into being

> Wee then, who are this new soule, know,
> Of what we are compos'd, and made,
> For, th'Atomies of which we grow,
> Are soules, whom no change can invade.

Now comes a turning point of the poem and the place from which the greatest differences of opinion as to what the poem is doing chiefly start out. We should remember that the two are still using *soules language* together.

> But O alas, so long, so farre
> Our bodies why doe wee forbeare?
> They'are ours, though they'are not wee, Wee are
> Th'intelligences, they the spheare.

Forbeare: some want to take this in the sense 'endure, put up with'. Push that far enough and you would get "Why don't we commit suicide?" Others take *forbeare* as 'control, refrain, desist and abstain, keep from using and enjoying'. You have to choose here according to how you understand the rest.

Th'intelligences ... the spheare: This is Ptolemaic astronomy: each of the nine concentric spheres has its angelic intelligence which governs it. Here the two souls who have become this abler soul have a joint sphere: their bodies.

> We owe them thankes, because they thus,
> Did us, to us, at first convay,
> Yeelded their forces, sense, to us,
> Nor are drosse to us, but allay.

Did us, to us, at first convay: For example, it was their bodies which first enabled them to see and talk to one another.

Yeelded their forces, sense, to us: their forces, that is to say their sensory powers, appetites etc. And they are not *drosse*—worthless remainder to be thrown away—but *alloy*—like the nickel, etc. which can make steel so much stronger, sharper etc. than iron.

> On man heavens influence workes not so,
> But that it first imprints the ayre.
> Soe soule into the soule may flow,
> Though it to body first repaire.

Medieval physics. They did not think that planets and stars could influence people except through doing something to the air. Action at a distance did not seem reasonable.

> As our blood labours to beget
> Spirits, as like soules as it can,
> Because such fingers need to knit
> That subtile knot, which makes us man:

Medieval physiology: The animal spirits produced by the blood were thought necessary to tie soul and body together. But, beyond this, and well within the probable influences from Plato impinging upon Donne (via whatever Leone Ebreo or other channels) is what may reasonably be regarded as the central thought of the theory of Government taught in *The Republic*: the role of Spirit in the governance of the individual, and equally, of the executive and police in the ruling of the state. This may most simply and directly be conveyed by a diagram. It is NOT Plato's but a recent derivative:

The head: Seat of the Government: the Guardians, Organ of knowledge, the *psyche,* the Guardians.

The thorax: Seat of Spirit, organ of courage and control, breathing and heart, the Guards.

The abdomen Source of energies, nutriment, desires, the productive component: the workers.

The Poem may be telling us that, correspondent to the physiological Spirits needed *to knit*

> That subtile knot, which makes us man:

there are, as Socrates so elaborately insists in *The Republic,* an order of agencies needed to intermediate BETWEEN the Guardians and the energy suppliers, the Workers, and equally between the soul and the senses. These intermediaries (the affections, feelings, and attitudes: 'the sentiments' we might call them: tenderness, pity, regard . . . and the faculties, the volitional system: resolution, courage, the impulse to help, to sustain . . .) are what the next, the key stanza, is about.

> So must pure lovers soules descend
> T'affections, and to faculties,
> Which sense may reach and apprehend
> Else a great Prince in prison lies.

Not altogether surprisingly it is these climactic lines which, textually as well as semiotically, have been less uniformly interpreted than any others. Donne's latest editor, Helen Gardner, has felt a difficulty so strongly that "against the consensus of 1633 and all manuscripts" she has "amended 'Which' to 'that' . . . assuming that 'Which' was substituted under the mistaken notion that 'That' was the relative and not the conjunction". She adds "If we read 'That' (in order that) the action of the souls parallels the action of the blood". But this can equally be secured if we retain 'Which' provided we give the poem credit for knowing and using here its *Republic*. The doubts Gardner mentions "over the genuineness of the poem's 'Platonism'" may have been the doubters' rather than the poem's fault. She reports—out of her unequalled acquaintance with and deep study of what has been written hitherto on **"The Exstasie"**—some questioning by the most qualified—typically, and most notably, by Grierson, himself—as to its complete success. My own feeling is that the poem, as Dame Helen suggests, set itself initially as its problem the exploration of ecstasy. I find that it succeeded, but by asking of its readers an understanding of Plato's prime theme in the *Republic* that they have not, all of them, been able to bring. In the *Republic* just as the philosopher kings, Lovers of Knowledge whose virtue is Wisdom, require their executives, Lovers of Honor whose virtue is Courage, in order to rule over the rest of the citizens, Lovers of Pleasure (or profit) whose virtue should be Sophrosyne, so in the man who is the small letter analogue to the great letters of the State, Knowledge and the senses (and their desires) are too far apart. They need recourse, both of them, to the intermediaries

> T'affections, and to faculties,
> Which sense may reach and apprehend,
> Else a great Prince in prison lies.

The grammatical possibilities are extraordinarily flexible here:

Which sense may reach and apprehend: Which way do you take that? Is it the affections and faculties which reach and apprehend sense—as a policeman can apprehend a disturber of the peace? Or is it sense which manages to understand and take in what the affections and the faculties would teach it? It makes curiously little difference provided we realize that only through this *descent* of the soul to *affections* and to *faculties* can this *great Prince* be free'd from prison.

And what is this great Prince? Some say it is Love; some say it is the Soul; some that it is Sense; and some that it is none of these separately but the whole Man which includes Soul, the affections and faculties AND sense. We should remember that it is the business of a Prince to rule.

Whatever it is, there is a conclusive sort of ring in *Else a great Prince in prison lies* which seems to warn us that here is the point, the end, the summit of the poem.

In the last two stanzas the lovers' souls returning from their ecstasy proceed exactly thus to *descend,* to put into effect their rule, via the sentiments, over the senses, and their appetites.

> To'our bodies turne wee then, that so
> Weake men on love reveal'd may looke;
> Loves mysteries in soules doe grow,
> But yet the body is his booke.

The poem continues to divide its readers into groups with extremely different positions for living.

To our bodies turne wee then: we have to choose a meaning for *To our bodies* which will join up with

> But O alas, so long, so farre
> Our bodies why doe wee forbeare?

And again in

> And if some lover, such as wee,
> Have heard this dialogue of one,
> Let him still marke us, he shall see
> Small change, when we'are to bodies gone.

for *to bodies gone.*

There are those . . . who put a very simple meaning into these phrases: physical intercourse. And of these, some profess to be shocked, as others are gleefully excited at what they take to be a startling exhibitionism. We have to remember, however, that this *lover, such as wee,* who has, throughout *this dialogue of one soules language understood,* as before he had to listen to what the lovers, who *said nothing, all the day,* did not utter, so now he is invited to *marke* what is invisible. The more closely we read the poem, I believe, the less we will be tempted to any simple meaning. We, like this witness, *shall see Small change.* Out of their ecstasy, as within it, order will rule. Their Spirits will continue *to knit*

> That subtile knot, which makes us man. (pp. 87-94)

> *I. A. Richards, "'The Exstasie'," in his* Poetries:
> Their Media and Ends, *edited by Trevor Eaton,
> Mouton, 1974, pp. 85-94.*

A. ALVAREZ   (essay date 1961)

[*Alvarez is an English poet, novelist, and critic. "Apparent in [his] fiction as well as in his criticism and his poetry," Sibyl L. Severance has written. "is Alvarez's belief that the artist must face 'the full range' of experience' with his full intelligence.' In his insistence upon seeing the whole individual, Alvarez stands as a modern Metaphysical, himself a follower of 'the school of Donne,'" In the following excerpt from his study* The School of Donne, *Alvarez appropriates and sharpens the thematic focus of one of T. S. Eliot's assessments of Donne (see excerpt dated 1923), outlining the nature of his poetic realism.*]

Donne was not only one of the most supremely intelligent poets in the language, he was also the first Englishman to write verse in a way that reflected the whole complex activity of intelligence. A number of Elizabethan poets embodied the philosophical truths of their period in verse of considerable elegance and power. But Donne created a poetic language of thought, a mode of expression which so took for granted the intellectual tone and preoccupations of his time that it made of them, as it were, the stage on which the intimate give-and-take of personal poetry was played. He was, in short, the first intellectual realist in poetry.

Eliot first made much the same point as early as 1923 in an article that has, to my knowledge, never been reprinted [see excerpt dated 1923]. . . . The difference between the time at which Eliot wrote this and our own lies in the way in which psychology can now be taken more or less for granted. The complexity and contradictoriness of the emotions are no longer fighting subjects. Instead, the contemporary problem is to write with an intelligence that recognizes this complexity and controls it in all its baffling fragmentariness.

Eliot's insights into Donne's originality were largely sidetracked by later critics in their search for a technique to produce certain effects. Hence the inordinate concentration on the 'outlandish conceit', as though the whole of Metaphysical poetry were reducible to a single, rather ostentatious trick of style. I simply want to replace the stress on the element of realism in Donne, the skill by which he created a poetic language in which technique was at the service of a fullness of the intelligence.

Nowadays 'realism' usually means a certain wilful harping on the facts of life, an insistence on the short, frank word and the daringly, or drearily, sordid detail. There is, of course, an element of this kind of frankness in Donne's poetry, but, as often as not, it enters when he is most classical: in, say, 'Elegie XIX. Going to Bed', where he is being a kind of new English Ovid. The realism I am referring to is, however something more diffused and its effect is distinctly not of grinding the reader's nose into the dirt. On the contrary, the final impression is one of a peculiarly heightened dignity.

This sense of personal dignity is at the centre of Donne's work. At the simplest level, it is his perennial theme:

> She'is all States, and all Princes, I,
> Nothing else is. is an extreme but typical way of putting it.
> This dignity measures his distance from the more
> conventional Elizabethans . . . [and] it is at the root of his
> 'masculine', 'strong' style. More important, it makes for
> the cohesion of his work, that unity and strength which
> give his collected poems an importance difficult to pin
> down in any single one of them. He is, after all, one of the
> few major poets before this century whose achievement is
> not summed up in any one really extended work.

Yet despite this unity there is considerable variation in his style. The *Elegies*, for example, seem definably younger work than the best *Songs and Sonets*. This is due to something more than their occasional self-consciousness, which was the young Donne's fatal Cleopatra. It is a question of technique. The key to Donne's mature style is his use of logic: the more subtle and complex the emotion, the greater the logical pressure. The mature Donne organizes his poems in such a way that each shift of feeling seems to be substantiated logically. In the *Elegies*, however, the emotions are simpler and are sustained in their singleness. He adopts a stance and then develops it dramatically, not logically. So instead of a piece of elaborate human dialectics, he leaves you with a situation presented in the vivid colouring of a more or less single strong feeling.

Even the best of the *Elegies*, in fact, are more uncomplicatedly assertive than most of Donne's other work of the same standard. **'Elegie IV. The Perfume'**, for instance, is perhaps the most inventive of all Donne's poems, but its wit is more ornamental than profound: it has gone into the puns, into the dramatic detail, into maintaining the overriding masculine independence. It is, in short, less analytic than energetic. The only deepening of tone comes at the moment when his masculinity itself is threatened:

> Onely, thou bitter sweet, whom I had laid
> Next mee, mee traiterously hast betraid...

It may seem odd that the perfume should inspire a couple of lines which are as moving and as moved as anything Donne ever wrote on the theme of the inconstant mistress. But the reason comes a few lines later:

> By thee, the greatest staine to mans estate
> Falls on us, to be call'd effeminate...

The perfume, in fact, has undermined the whole basis of this and most of the other *Elegies*: the almost belligerent masculinity of the young Donne who was 'a great visitor of ladies'. The difference between the *Elegies* and Donne's maturest technique [exemplified by 'A nocturnall upon S. Lucres day, Being the shortest day'] is large and clear.... This is the only one of Donne's poems which might validly be called 'modern'. As in *The Waste Land*, the poet is on the rack to define a complex negative state which he apparently cannot fully understand and, what is even more pertinent to Donne's difficulty, which he cannot properly dramatize. The theme is a depression so deep as to verge on annihilation (he wrote, after all, a defence of suicide). And its root, I think, is inaction, or the impossibility of action, as he described it in the famous letter to Goodyer:

> Therefore I would fain do something; but that I cannot
> tell what is no wonder. For to chuse, is to do: but to be
> no part of any body, is to be nothing.

He tries to force some kind of clearing through this swaddling depression by bringing to bear upon it an extraordinarily tense logic and a great concentration of learning. Each stanza moves forward to its own temporary resolution; the twisted, pausing, in-turning movement clears to make way for a direct but invariably negative statement:

"The worlds whole sap is sunke"

"Compar'd with mee, who am their Epitaph"

"For I am every dead thing"

"...things which are not"

"...made us carcasses"

"But I am None"...

Unlike most of his other lyrics, the logic of the **'Nocturnall'** does not exorcise his troubles. Despite all the dialectic and the learning, despite the invocation of the outside lovers and even, in the third stanza, the invocation of his own more dramatic love poems, he is left with the blank fact of his isolation. Yet although whatever pressure he brings to bear on the situation produces no clear answer, it does help him to achieve some kind of balance. The last lines of the poem—"since this/Both the yeares, and the dayes deep midnight is"—may simply be a restatement of the first—"Tis the yeares midnight, and it is the dayes, *Lucies*"—but they are a restatement with a difference: the difficult, questioning movement of the start has been resolved into a clearer, more measured statement. He finishes, that is, by *accepting* the depression, instead of trying, with all the intellectual ingenuity at his command, to wriggle through it. So the poem ends with his facing the adult necessity of living with grief and depression, instead of giving in to them. Donne's logic and learning, in short, were the prime forces in his emotional maturity *as a poet*.

It is the absence of this quality, incidentally, which marks off Shakespeare's formal verse from Donne's.... Like the **'Nocturnall'**, 'Sonnet XCIV' is also, in its way, a rather modern poem: its mode is complex, negative and founded perhaps on the same sexual anger and frustration that produced Othello's "O thou weed/Who art so lovely fair and smell's so sweet/ That the sense aches at thee, would thou hadst ne'er been born!" But unlike Donne's, Shakespeare's compression is all in the imagery rather than the argument. Where Donne often begins with a straightforward situation (those famous, or infamous, dramatic openings) and then produces infinitely complicated arguments to justify it, Shakespeare begins with the abstractions and then gives them body. (pp. 12-21)

However far, of course, Donne seems from the usual Elizabethan rhetoric, he did produce a rhetoric of his own. He produced it for his rare public performances—the two *Anniversaries*, for example—and it was the rhetoric of the intellectual, abstract and analytic. Hence, Ben Jonson's irritated declaration "That Dones *Anniversarie* was profane and full of Blasphemies. That he told Mr. Done, if it had been written of ye Virgin Marie it had been something to which he answered that he described the Idea of a Woman and not as she was." In the *First Anniversarie* Donne dissects 'the idea of a woman' in order to produce *An Anatomie of the World*, a theological and political analysis of the state of corruption; that is, he was using the occasion to be deliberately less Donne the poet than Donne the learned wit, author of *Pseudo-Martyr*. The *Second Anniversarie The Progresse of the Soule*, is less abstract, more dramatic and, seemingly, more deeply felt. It is possible, indeed, that its roots were much more personal than those of the *First Anniversarie*. Donne apparently wrote it well before the date it was due, while he was staying with Sir Robert Drury in Amiens. He had gone abroad unwillingly, full of anxiety for his wife whom he left ill and pregnant. It was at Amiens that he had the terrible dream in which his wife appeared to him with a dead child in her arms. It may be, then, that 'the idea of a woman' was, in this instance, his wife, not Elizabeth Drury. Be that as it may, the dramatic meditation on death and the after-life is closer to the style of Donne the preacher or Donne the author of the *Devotions* than to that of the more analytic theologian of the *First Anniversarie*. In both poems, his public personality is

PSEVDO-
MARTYR·

Wherein

OVT OF CERTAINE

Propofitions and Gradations, This

Conclufion is euicted.

THAT THOSE WHICH ARE

of the Romane Religion in this Kingdome,

may and ought to take the Oath of

Allegeance.

D E V T. 32. 15.

But he that fhould haue beene vpright, when he waxed fatte, fpurned with his heele: Thou art fat, thou art groffe, thou art laden with fatneffe.

I O B. 11. 5.

But oh that God would fpeake and open his lips againft thee, that he might fhew thee the fecrets of wifedome, how thou haft deferued double according to right.

2. C H R O. 28. 22.

In the time of his tribulation, did he yet trefpaffe more againft the Lord, for he facrificed vnto the gods of Damafcus, which plagued him.

L O N D O N

Printed by *W. Stansby* for *Walter Burre.*

1 6 1 0.

Title page of Donne's first published work.

foremost. Their rhetoric is formally and formidably that of the intellectual, the debater.

Yet fundamentally it is the same rhetoric which, on less public occasions, is used to heighten a personal strength and richness. Philosophy, science, logic, divinity, poetry itself are all means of enhancing the dignity of the individual. His realism lies in the richness of the resources he brings to bear upon more or less conventional subjects and his ability to falsify the full range of his response. Donne's achievement was to take a poetry over which the academic theorists were fiercely haggling, and break down the constrictions of mere aesthetic criteria; to take a dialectical form which had become rigid in centuries of scholastic wrangling, and break down its narrow casuistry; to take the sciences in all the imaginative strength of the new discoveries, and bring them all together as protagonists in the inward drama of his own powerful experience. He substantiated less a poetic technique than a form of intelligence which the most talented men of the following generation could use without, at any point, belying their natural gifts outside the realm of poetry. As a result, the style of Donne lasted until, under the imperative stresses of the Civil War, the whole mode of intelligence changed. We are now far enough removed from the tensions that split the seventeenth century to be able to judge Donne's monarchy of wit not as a trick or a fashion but as one of the greatest achievements of the poetic intelligence. (pp. 21-3)

A. Alvarez, in his The School of Donne, *1961. Reprint by Pantheon Books, 1962, 211 p.*

EDMUND FULLER   (essay date 1964)

[*Fuller is an American novelist and essayist who has written on a wide variety of literary and historical themes from a traditionalist and Christian perspective. He is the editor of an edition of Shakespeare's plays (1966-68), a selection of Samuel Johnson's "Lives" of the English poets (1965), and the essay collection* Myth, Allegory, and Gospel: An Interpretation of J. R. R. Tolkien, C. S. Lewis, G. K. Chesterton, and Charles Williams *(1974). He is also the author of* George Bernard Shaw: Critic of Western Morale *1950, among many other works. In the following excerpt from his introduction to a selection of Donne's sermons, Fuller illustrates Donne's exposition and his latitudinarian orthodoxy, emphasizing the timeliness of the sermons to the twentieth-century Christian.*]

In the 1930's, Ernest Hemingway popularized the passage beginning "No man is an island..." from which he took the title of *For Whom the Bell Tolls.* In 1959, the novelist William Styron derived a title, *Set This House on Fire,* from a great passage in a less consistently distinguished sermon preached before the Earl of Carlisle in 1622. These are small matters in themselves, but they are indications that much in Donne's thought and expression speaks with extraordinary directness and aptness to our own condition today. We find such indications throughout the sermons. There are analogies between his age and ours: both are animated and disturbed by breakthroughs of scientific knowledge and revolutions of thought. Donne's mind and spirit also often show a psychic harmony with twentieth-century man.

It is in the sermons that his finest prose is found. (pp. ix-x)

Donne has many cogent things to say—and to say marvelously well—to modern readers of apologetical, devotional, and homiletic writing. (p. x)

As Marjorie Hope Nicolson has observed..., Donne was an Elizabethan who became a modern, in the sense of his response to the great breakthroughs of scientific knowledge and the expanding world sense of his age. For this was the time, too, of Kepler and Galileo, following on the heels of Copernicus, of the opening of the Western hemisphere and the first circumnavigations of the world.

Donne's response to all these stimuli was very marked in his poems, especially in the famous passage from *The First Anniversary* in *An Anatomy of the World,* one of his funeral elegies (1610).

> And new Philosophy [science] calls all in doubt,
> The Element of fire is quite put out;
> The Sun is lost, and th' earth, and no man's wit
> Can well direct him where to look for it.
> And freely men confess that this world's spent,
> When in the Planets, and the Firmament
> They seek so many new; then see that this
> Is crumbled out again to his Atomies.
> 'Tis all in pieces, all coherence gone;
> All just supply, and all Relation.

The theological implications of such matters were touchy issues, for there was deep suspicion of heresy in the new cosmology. Donne did not explore scientific subjects widely in the sermons, thus it is all the more notable that we find, at the beginning of the first sermon in this volume, on Genesis 1:26, his use of the new astronomy as a source of images in discussing Creation. There he reflects awareness both of science and the great explorations, as he speaks of

> That Earth, which in some thousands of years men could not look over, nor discern what form it had ... that earth, which no man in his person is ever said to have compassed till our age ... all that earth, and then that heaven, which spreads so far as that subtle men have, with some appearance of probability, imagined that in that heaven, in those manifold spheres of the planets and the stars, there are many earths, many worlds, as big as this which we inhabit....

And in the sermon on Proverbs 8:17, he speaks of "the merit and passion of Christ Jesus, sufficient to save millions of worlds...."

So we encounter, here, numerous reflections of an age of new horizons—reflections which echo forcefully in our own age, as in the first sermon:

> ...remember that a frame may be thrown down in much less time than it was set up. A child, an ape, can give fire to a cannon: and a vapor can shake the earth: and these fires, and these vapors can throw down cities in a minute.

We can append to this, for pondering today, words from his sermon on the conversion of Paul (Acts 9:4):

> [God] can choose his way, he can call in nation against nation, he can cast a damp upon any nation, and make them afraid of one another, he can do an execution upon them by themselves.... (pp. xiii-xiv)

Whether from Old or New Testament, Christ is the center of all. Between the two Testaments he makes the nice distinction:

> ...that which was but a matter of prophecy to them (in the Old Testament they knew not when it should be done) to us in the New is matter of history, and we know when it was done. (Sermon on St. John 14:20)

Something of Donne's characteristic thought on all the great doctrines of Catholic Christianity is represented. He preaches on the Trinity, on Creation, the Incarnation and general Christology, on the doctrine of Man, on the Sacraments, on prayer, repentance, redemption, conversion, on birth, death and marriage, and the necessity for Christian life and worship to be fulfilled within the fold of the Church.

We must not let the controversies of his age confuse us about Donne's preaching within the great, historic Catholic continuity of theology. The Church of England was in conflict with Rome on the one hand and with nonconformist Puritanism on the other. Donne was clearly closer to Rome than to Puritanism; he was more anti-Jesuit than anti-Roman Catholic. In one of his letters he says:

> You know I never fettered nor imprisoned the word Religion; not straightening it Frierly ... nor immuring it in a *Rome*, or a *Wittemberg*, or a *Geneva*; they are all virtual beams of one Sun ... Religion is Christianity.

In his age, the controversies were inescapable, yet we find him looking beyond them in a spirit which is relevant to today's concern with Christian unity.

> If we would but make Christ Jesus and his peace the life and soul of all our actions and all our purposes; if we

would mingle that sweetness and suppleness which he loves and which he is, in all our undertakings; if in all controversies, book controversies and sword controversies, we would fit them to him and see how near they would meet in him, that is how near we might come to be friends and yet both sides be good Christian....
(Sermon on St. Matt. 21:44) (pp. xiv-xv)

Though he is far from Puritan theology, there is still a dark, occasionally even morbid, tone to much of his preaching, which reflects aspects of his temperament as well as the dramatic contrasting of lights and darks so typical of his age. Death and disease and pain and danger hovered close to men in Donne's time; 1625 saw one of the great plagues that assailed London. I need not cite only the somber notes; rather I would emphasize his celebrations of joy and of the happiness of religious fellowship. In the sermon on Proverbs 8:17 he says:

> And let no man be afraid to seek or find him [God] for fear of the loss of good company; religion is no sullen thing, it is not a melancholy, there is not so sociable a thing as the love of Christ Jesus.

Donne's preaching is not only great exposition, but reveals a great prose master, whose prose in turn reveals the poet. It is the prose of a Latinist, like Milton's after him. He is able to construct huge, balanced, perfectly controlled, architectonic sentences, clause built upon clause, image upon image, parallel upon parallel, to soaring climaxes. These qualties are seen abudantly in all these sermons, yet perhaps nowhere more notably than in his tenderly compassionate discussion of God's love for us in the sermon on Proverbs 8:17.

His imagery and all his rhetorical resources are displayed in his marriage sermon, on Hosea 2:19. After a discourse on earthy marriage, he develops the metaphor of the marriage of the soul of man to Christ, and culminates it in a rolling surge of language as he depicts the joy and glory of the soul's ultimate union with God in Heaven, at the time of the Last Things, in part freely adapted from burning images in the 6th chapter of the Revelation of St. John the Divine:

> I shall see the sun black as sackcloth of hair, and the moon become as blood, and the stars fall as a fig tree casts her untimely figs, and the heavens rolled up together as a scroll. I shall see a divorce between princes and their prerogatives, between nature and all her elements, between the spheres and all their intelligences between matter itself and all her forms, and my marriage shall be forever.

> I shall see an end of faith, nothing to be believed that I do not know; and an end of hope, nothing to be wished that I do not enjoy, but no end of that love in which I am married to the Lamb forever.

For all the savoring of such noble periods, for all the wish that we might have heard the music of the voice that uttered them, these delights of style are no more the prime purpose of this book than they were of Donne when he composed the sermons. It is a fine thing and "a good art to deliver deep points in a holy plainness, and plain points in a holy delightfulness" (Sermon on Job 16:17-19). Yet we must not suppose him to have preached chiefly for the display of skill, or chiefly to give aesthetic satisfaction to the hearers who thronged to him. This is no liberal, permissive, comfortable soothing, but rather a firm, sometimes stern, preaching on the demands of the Faith and the obligations that go with professing it.

In one of his discourses on the right preparation for receiving the Sacrament (in the lovely Christmas sermon, gravely joyous, on St. Luke 2:29, 30) Donne says of prayers and sermons:

> He that brings any collateral respect to prayers loses the benefit of the prayers of the congregation; and he that brings that to a sermon loses the blessings of God's ordinance in that sermon; he hears but the logic, or the rhetoric, or the ethic, or the poetry of the sermon, but the sermon of the sermon he hears not.

We should approach the [pages of *The Showing forth of Christ: Sermons of John Donne*] with this counsel in mind. It is for the sermons of the sermons that we owe must to Donne. (pp. xvii-xviii)

> *Edmund Fuller, in an introduction to* The Showing Forth of Christ: Sermons of John Donne, *edited by Edmund Fuller, Harper & Row, Publishers, 1964, pp. ix-xviii.*

N. J. C. ANDREASEN   (essay date 1967)

[*In the following excerpt, Andreasen argues for recognition of Donne as a "conservative revolutionary": a poet whose innovations and iconoclasm are actually rooted firmly in a traditional Christian ethic.*]

Literature is not written in a vacuum. When we are faced with difficulties in a poem or a group of poems, we can sometimes resolve them by observing the aesthetic assumptions and literary or intellectual traditions with which the poet is working. Customarily we do not, of course, think of Donne as a traditional poet. More than enough has been said in the past about his innovations in imagery. Few precedents exist for his stanza forms and rhyme schemes. And many poems seem to protest against old-fashioned beliefs about the purpose of love. But we still cannot lift Donne out of his Renaissance context. If he avoided the mythological allusions so popular among his contemporaries, he nevertheless forged his imagery from Renaissance materials, the less obviously "poetic" ones of contemporary alchemy, medicine, or astronomy. If he wrote "strong lines" and unusual stanzas, he still stuck to conventional genres—elegies, satires, sonnets and songs. And some critics have suggested that he mocked the Petrarchan tradition by drawing instead on the Ovidian tradition. *No one can invent everything anew.* Beneath Donne's surface innovations a firm bedrock of tradition—aesthetic, literary, and intellectual—necessarily remains. And the nature and structure of that bedrock helped dictate the form which Donne's poetry took, for it was the foundation upon which he built. (pp. 13-14)

When Donne wrote his love lyrics, a didactic aesthetic was overwhelmingly pervasive among his English contemporaries. Though they may disagree about which literary works are valuable and how literature should teach, men so diverse as Gosson and Lodge and Sidney are all agreed that it should provide moral instruction. Borrowing from the Horatian dictum that literature should be *dulcis et utilis*, Sidney, for example, asserts that it should delight and teach; that it should provide delight alone never seems to have entered his mind, and his discussion of

these dual objectives of the poet indicates that sweetness is for him but a means to the more important end of didacticism. Of the poets he says: "... these indeede doo meerely make to imitate, and imitate both to delight and teach, and delight to moue men to take that goodness in hande, which without delight they would flye as from a stranger; and teach, to make them know that goodness whereunto they are mooued...." Sidney even makes such high claims for poetry that in his view the poet surpasses the philosopher and the historian in ability to inspire moral improvement.

If we postulate that Donne shared this didactic aesthetic, then the problem of his wit can be partially resolved, for it must be functional rather than frivolous. His yoking of incongruities is not meant merely to trick or amuse, but to serve some useful purpose. Although he is certainly playing a word-and-idea game on the surface, he is also fulfilling his later plea in **"A Litanie:"**

> That wit, borne apt high good to doe,
> By dwelling lazily
> On Natures nothing, be not nothing too. . . .

And if at the time he wrote his love poetry he shared the beliefs of his era, implicit in this plea, then he not only wrote "apt high good to doe" but he also believed that art should not merely hold a mirror up to "Natures nothing." For according to Sidney, poetry teaches by dramatizing positive and negative moral *exempla,* and the poet is superior to the historian because he can improve upon reality by creating "feigned examples" which reflect a Reality above nature. And since Donne shared the Augustinian-Platonic metaphysic upon which Sidney's aesthetic is based, he probably shared the aesthetic as well. (pp. 14-16)

As we read through the *Elegies* and *Songs and Sonets,* trying to sense what kind of love relationship each poem dramatizes, we find most of them falling rather naturally into three groups. Donne is, of course, a poet of splendid variety, and we could if we wished define as many groups as there are poems, so individualized are the speakers and their situations. But though such a refusal to classify would pay tribute to the complexity of Donne's achievement, it would hardly be useful; and it is nearly as accurate to oversimplify a bit in order to generalize, for a sizable number of Donne's poems can with some fairness be seen as subtypes within three general categories, each of which concentrates on a particular kind of love and draws to some extent on a particular literary tradition. One group, those poems which treat love cynically or see it as limited to sexual attraction, follows the Ovidian tradition. Although Donne is sometimes said to be anti-Petrarchan, mostly because of the anti-idealism which characterizes his Ovidian poems, there is another group of poems (sometimes called the "courtly compliments") which draw on Petrarchanism and portray a more impassioned and romantic love. And finally there is a group which reflects the doctrines of Christian Platonism, although in this case the tradition upon which Donne draws is perhaps more philosophical than literary. But whenever he writes, Donne assumes an audience which accepts Christian teachings about love, and consequently its ethic indirectly informs nearly all his love poems, even the pagan Ovidian ones, and gives them unifying and governing principle.

J. B. Leishman has, in *The Monarch of Wit,* written a fine and suggestive treatment of Donne's Ovidian poetry [see excerpt dated 1951]. There he stresses Donne's indebtness to Ovid and makes some points that one wishes had been made sooner and more often: he argues that much of Donne's poetry is literary in inspiration rather than personal and that much of it is meant to be both fun and funny. He finds the wit which pervades the *Elegies* and the Ovidian poems within *Songs and Sonets* to be preposterous, impudent, ingenius, mockingly illogical and paradoxical, and intentionally shocking and outrageous. But because he does not read them within the context of the Renaissance Ovid, he also finds them totally playful. What one misses in Leishman's study is Ovid the moralist, the Ovid which Donne knew and used. (pp. 16-17)

Ovid's *Amores, Ars Amatoria,* and *Remedia Amoris* (the works which exercised the greatest influence on Donne) were often read in the Renaissance as didactic works, using techniques of comic irony and satire, and not as prurient lessons on the art of lust. Although an occasional Gosson might protest, Ovid was thought by most humanist to be presenting dramatic portraits of deviations from a moral ideal. And Donne seems to have written his Ovidian poems in a similar spirit. In those poems which seem to advocate a cheerful devotion to illicit lust, Donne is probably writing tongue in cheek and creating *personae* who are to be seen as deviations from a moral ideal, just as he does more obviously in his five formal verse satires, which were written about the same time. But in the *Elegies* and *Songs and Sonets* he follows Ovid rather than Horace and Juvenal, and he wields his irony more subtly. Admiration for the satiric qualities in this early poetry is probably behind the somewhat strange remark of Ben Johnson (no mean satirist himself) that he "esteemeth John Done the first poet in the World in some things..." and "affirmeth Done to have written all his best pieces err he was 25 years old" [see excerpt dated 1618-19]. If we ignore the moral satire behind the surface levity, we miss much of the humor which Donne's contemporaries probably enjoyed in these poems.

Nor is there any inconsistency between Donne's "Ovidian or naturalistic" poetry and his "Petranchan or idealistic" poetry. In some of his poems, in fact, Donne seems to be using elements from both the Petrarchan tradition and the Ovidian tradition within the same poem.... Petrarchan love was usually regarded in the Renaissance as profane and sinful, since the lover's emotions were excessively irrational and passionate. And Donne's Petrarchan poems usually reflect this moral judgement of his contemporaries. Neo-Petrarchan rather than anti-Petrarchan, Donne experiments with conventions in a number jof ways, but always retains their essential spirit. Petrarchanism offered to the Renaissance poet a convenient vehicle for treating profane love; its set themes—the beloved's scorn, the lover's frustration, floods of tears and tempests of sighs—are used and reused by Donne's fellow poets and refreshed by Donne himself. And when we encounter these standard images in Donne's poetry, we can speculate that he may be drawing on literature rather than life, that he could be transforming literary conventions rather than revealing persooal experience, that he is perhaps writing a poem rather than addressing the Countess of Bedford.

Donne's Ovidian and Petrarchan poems are dramatic monologues spoken by lovers who are in a sense meant to be seen as negative moral *exempla*. Since the Ovidian lovers err by placing excessive emphasis on physical love and the Petrarchan lovers by as misguided and excessive idealism, these two groups of poems complement one another. And they are further complemented by a third group, those poems which are at least partially inspired by Christian Platonism. The lovers who deliver these monologues are positive examples, men who experience a love which is joyous, satisfying, and righteous. Their love is the true ideal, from which the cynical Ovidian and the masochistic Petrarchan deviate.

Insofar as Donne has a "philosophy of love," it is to be found in this third group of poems. But for all his interest in intellectual matters, Donne is a great poet and psychologist rather than a great philosopher; and to say that the beliefs affirmed in these poems are essentially derivative hardly detracts from his originality. Donne did not need to invent a new philosophy of love, for he had an ample system of doctrines ready at hand in the Bible, the Church Fathers, and the works produced by the Florentine and French Academies. As Sidney says, however, the poet surpasses the philosopher in that the poet present both precepts and example, both doctrine and experience. And this is why Donne shines. Although he does not invent dogma, he so vivifies the old clichés about the nature of righteous human love, so brilliantly dramatizes the joy which it produces, so uncompromisingly refuses to soften or semtimentalize, that these poems emerge as his finest, strongest, and most admired.

When we thus look at Donne's poetry in the light of the traditions that it borrows from, the man who created it emerges as somewhat more conservative than he is sometimes considered to be. Of course he is also restless, skeptical, rebellious, and mercurial, but **"Satyre III"** reminds us that even the very young Donne saw his Prutean intellectual metamorphoses as a way of climbing a cragged and steep hill toward a Truth he knew was at the top. Like Dante's souls in purgatory (with whom he was no doubt identifying himself as he wrote those lines), that faith gives a continuity to his transformation and development. And if we see the man who wrote the love poems as a poet whose wit is functional rather than simply decorative and whose ethic is intrinsically Christian rather than pagan, we can resolve some of the paradoxes and problems which pervade his work. (pp. 18-20)

Donne's total system assumes that love can be as good as it is powerful; when it conforms to the moral order of the universe, love can produce intense joy and satisfaction, whether it is directed toward another human being or toward God, although divine love, because it is divine, gives man an intenser joy than human love. But if love is a good thing, it can also be abused; and when it is abused, it produces sorrow and bondage to sin rather than joy and liberation. The Ovidian and Petrarchan poems dramatize lovers who abuse love; behind the comic satire or the pathos of these poems is the belief that human affection can and should be used for better purposes, a belief pointed up by the religious images through which this negative love is often expressed. The poems of profane love reverberate more authentically when they are heard within the framework of the Christian Philosophy of love, when they are heard as a dull and distorted echo of the love expressed in the Platonic poems or *The Holy Sonnets.*

In his Ovidian and Petrarchan poems, Donne dramatizes a sinful and profane love which is dominated by change and rooted in self. The lovers in these poems place themselves upon love's wheel of fortune, for they focus their affections on objects which are not lasting and seek to gratify their desires through pleasure which are transient by nature. This improper love, whether lust or idolatry, brings misery upon lovers sooner or later, for it involves an excessively great commitment to the mortal and mutable. Things of the earth, so fickle and fragile, will not support the burden of devotion which profane lovers give them. Thus the lustful or idolatrous lover, having mistaken a lesser good for the greatest good, eventually faces disillusionment and despair.

What Donne sees in the things of the world, however, is not their inherent evilness. He sees, rather, the danger that men may overestimate their goodness and convert a potential source of happiness into a source of sin and misery. He sees, in short, that worldly goods may either lead men toward God or alienate them from God, depending on the way in which they are used. In his Ovidian and Petrarchan poems, he reveals the negative use of the things of the world: the lovers, overly committed to goods which are transient by nature, bring misery themselves because the joys of transient goods are transient joys; the lovers sin by making the things of the world an end rather than a means, and they punish themselves by choosing to love something which cannot fulfill their inordinate love. In his affirmative poems of human love Donne reveals the positive use of the things of the world. He dramatizes a state of grace in love, a love which thrives in the world and yet leads the lovers toward God, a love which surmounts the threats of worldly mutability. And whereas the sinful love which is tied to worldly goods is circumscribed and produces bondage, the state of grace in love is unlimited and liberating. Donne's sense of total system, which presupposes that love is a good which can be turned to evil through abuse or misuse, is behind his implicit condemnation of profane love in the Ovidian and Petrarchan poems. Love, these poems suggest, should produce something better than misery and disillusionment. His affirmative poems answer the negative poems by revealing how and why love can produce something better. Their dramatization of a secure and joyful love is perhaps Donne's most final and devastating exposé of profane love. (pp. 238-40)

> *N. J. C. Andreasen, in her* John Donne: Conservative Revolutionary, *Princeton University Press, 1967, 249 p.*

LIONEL TRILLING   (essay date 1967)

[*An American critic and literary historian, Trilling was also an essayist, editor, novelist, and short story writer. He judged the value of a text by its contribution to culture and, in turn, regarded culture as indispensible for human survival. Trilling focused in particular on the conflict between the individual and culture, maintaining that art had the power to "liberate the individual from the tyranny of his culture in the enviromental sense and to permit him to stand beyond it in an autonomy of perception and judgement." In the following excerpt from an essay originally published in 1967, he discusses the poetics, controversial imagery, and background of "A Valediction: forbidding mourning."*]

In reading **"A Valediction: Forbidding Mourning"** it is the voice of the poem that first engages our attention. The opening line is audacious in its avoidance of the metre that is to be established in the following lines of the stanza and maintained through the rest of the poem, although not in a strict or mechanical way; no matter how we read it, we cannot scan that opening line, and its bold freedom leads us to feel that it is saying something "actual" rather than "poetic." The succeeding lines, although controlled by metre, sustain this feeling; they sound in the ear as the utterance of a present speaker. It is in the ambience of the speaker's voice that the metaphysical elements of the poem are presented to us. The comparison between the significance of earthquakes and the "trepidation of the spheres" and the brief simile of the beaten gold, the elaborated simile of the pair of compasses, are the less likely to seem merely ingenious, or studied, or out of the way, because they are suffused with the tones of the voice that proposes them, its directness and masculine vigor, its gravity and its serious humor.

Dr. Johnson took particular notice of the compass simile, introducing his quotation of the three stanzas in which it is developed with this sentences: "To the following comparison of a man that travels and his wife that stays at home, with a pair of compasses, it may be doubted whether absurdity or ingenuity has a better claim" [see excerpt dated 1779]. For Johnson the absurdity lay in the fact that compasses seemed to him to be incongrous with the emotional circumstances they were meant to represent. A pair of compasses suggests what is mechanical and unfeeling: it is metallic and stiff, and an instrument of precision employed in, and emblematic of, the sternly rational and abstract discipline of geometry; it therefore stands at the furthest remove from the emotion of love. The simile of the compasses substantiated Johnson's opinion that metaphysical poetry cannot express emotion and is "void of fondness."

Although we will perceive as readily as Dr Johnson that there is some measure of unlikehood in the comparison, this will not prevent our having pleasure in it. On the contrary, we will tend to be pleased exactly because we are taken aback. For us, the figure's suggestion of cold rationally and abstractness is modified by the humor with which it is developed, a humor which does not in the least diminish the direct sincerity of the utterance. Isaac Walton, in his brief life of his friend, tells us that Donne composed the poem in 1611 while he was on a diplomatic mission to France and that it was addressed to his wife Anne [see excerpt dated 1640]. The marriage was a famous one in its day, both because of the tempestuous courtship that preceded it and the unbroken tender devotion of the husband and wife. Walton mentions the circumstance in which the poem was written and the person to whom it was addressed out of his sense that the poem, for all the ingenuity of its "conceits," is a direct, personal, and fully felt comunication, wholly appropriate to its occassion. With this judgement the modern reader would find it hard to disagree. (pp. 192-93)

> *Lionel Trilling, "John Donne: A Valediction, Forbidding Mourning," in his* Prefaces to The Experience of Literature, *Harcourt Brace Jovanovich, 1979, pp. 188-93.*

JOSEPH H. SUMMERS   (essay date 1970)

[*Summers is an American educator and literary essayist. In the following excerpt, he compares the poetry of Donne and Ben Jonson.*]

The most important distinctions between the poetry of Donne and the poetry of Jonson approximate the differences which John Buxton has recently described in his *Elizabethan Taste* (1963) between the kinds of poetry circulated in manuscripts among literary coteries in the 1590's and the kinds intended for publication: poetry imitating private voices in contrast to poetry imitating public voices, poetry written by conscious amateurs in contrast to poetry written by professionals. Donne was the man who wrote, shortly after the publication of his *Second Anniversary* in 1612, 'Of my *Anniversaries,* the fault that I acknowledge in my self, is to have descended to print any thing in verse, which though it have excuse even in our times, by men who professe, and practise much gravitie; yet I confesse I wonder how I declined to it, and do not pardon myself . . .'; and Jonson was the man who shocked and amused his contemporaries by disclosing his literary seriousness and ambition when, four years after Donne's remark, he published some of his plays and poems as his *Works.*

From the major contrast implied, one can easily move to the popular contrast between 'colloquial' and 'formal' styles. But that formulation can be misleading. It may seem to postulate a single, completely unselfconscious, 'natural' (and therefore for some readers 'good') style, so close to an abstraction called 'reality' as to be its inevitable voice, and another, 'artful,' 'artificial,' 'rhetorical,' completely removed from any spoken language—and therefore 'bad.' I doubt that things have ever been that simple; at any rate, such a distinction is too crude for an age as rhetorically aware as the late sixteenth and early seventeenth centuries. It is possible to hold theoretically that 'real,' 'essential' man is man utterly alone, with no thought of others or of an audience, but it is hardly possible to talk sensibly about such a notion. Once we admit the use of language, that incorrigibly social medium, we are involved, willy-nilly, with matters of audiences, stances, purposes, and all the rest. *Every* use of language is more or less 'artful' or 'formal' as its user is more or less conscious of what he is doing and successful in doing it; and every use of language has also some relation (although sometimes a sadly remote one) to language as it has been either spoken or sung. 'Formal' and 'colloquial' alone strike me as too vague to be very useful: 'colloquial' for whom? what kind of speakers in what mood? speaking directly to whom? overheard by whom? for what purposes? And what kind of 'formality'? inviting what sorts of recognitions or participations from what readers or hearers? I do not mean to imply that these are easy questions or that I have the answers to them. (What *can* one determine about the 'audience' and 'purposes' of a persuasion to love, written both in a middle style and in the form of a strict Italian sonnet, addressed to a real lady but published by the poet?) But they are questions which we might keep in mind when we read Donne and Jonson and the rest. And it may be helpful also to question some of our perhaps unconscious assumptions about colloquialism and linguistic 'realism' in general. Is the heightened speech of a passionate persuasion to love more 'colloquial' than the fairly neutral conversation of old lovers—or of a husband and wife? Is speech addressed to one hearer necessarily more 'realistic' than speech addressed to several hearers? Is language expressing anger or impatience intrinsically more 'authentic' than meditative language—or even social chatter? Is harshness always more 'real' or even 'colloquial' than euphony? (pp. 15-17)

There are advantages in beginning with the epigrams and *Paradoxes and Problems*, particularly since that seems to be about where Donne and Jonson began. Donne's few epigrams are off-hand squibs, most of them only two-lines long and many of them very funny; such as *'Antiquary'*:

> If in his study Hammon hath such care
> To 'hang all old strange things, let his wife beware.

Or, **'A Selfe Accuser'**:

> Your mistress, that you follow whores, still taxeth you:
> 'Tis strange she should confess it, though' it be true.

In his recent edition, W. Milgate attributes to Donne **'Manliness'**:

> Thou call'st me effeminate, for I love women's joys;
> I call not thee manly, though thou follow boys.

Jonson, by contrast, called his 'Epigrams' the 'ripest of my studies,' and published one-hundred-three; he included complimentary and elegiac as well as satiric epigrams and even expanded the term to include a scabrous mock-heroic of almost two-hundred lines, 'The Famous Voyage.' Jonson was usually serious about imitating (and attempting to surpass) Martial. In most of his epigrams he seems to have wanted a density, a deliberate and weighty judgement, a public and permanent status close to that of an actual inscription, even when they, too, contained only a single couplet:

> "To Alchemists"
>
> If all you boast of your great art be true;
> Sure, willing poverty lives most in you.

More characteristic (and more impressive) are epigrams of eight or ten lines, such as 'On some-thing, that walks some-where':

> At court I met it, in clothes brave enough,
> To be a courtier; and looks grave enough,
> To seem a statesman: as I near it came,
> It made me a great face, I asked the name.
> 'A lord,' it cried, 'buried in flesh, and blood,
> And such from whom let no man hope least good,
> For I will do none: and as little ill,
> For I will dare none.' Good Lord, walk dead still.

What we are invited to admire here is less the cleverness of the observer than the justice and precision of his observation. The symmetries of the poem ('brave enough' and 'grave enough,' 'To be' and 'to seem,' 'good' and 'ill,' 'do' and 'dare'), carefully climaxed by the implied contrast between walking dead and being alive, help convince us that private judgement has, in fact, correctly observed public reality. Jonson often gains something of that effect, even in his most personal and moving epitaphs. He seems to have begun, if not as an aged eagle, at least with the tone of a sober and fully mature citizen. One could almost deduce his admiration for Francis Bacon and Selden.

The witty, mercurial, 'interesting' young man who speaks Donne's epigrams is, I think, more clearly defined in *Paradoxes and Problems*, those prose juvenilia to which Donne devoted a good deal more care. He is, literally and quite intentionally, dazzling. He knows all the old arguments and can stand them on their heads. He is a master of wild analogy, semi-arcane lore, and false logic. He cannot only play the usual young man's game of hooting at generally accepted conventions and the gray-beards (by, for example, defending women's inconstancy or their duty to paint), but he can have even more sport in hoisting other such young men with their own petards: what fun to *defend* as paradoxes the notions that virginity is a virtue or that 'it is possible to find some virtue in some women'! And he is wonderfully inventive in thinking up multiple solutions for 'problems' such as **'Why Hath the Common Opinion Afforded Women Souls?'** and **'Why doth the Pox so much Affect to Undermine the Nose?'** The *Paradoxes and Problems* are virtuoso performances. Our chief pleasure is in the agility of the intellectual footwork, the fertility of the invention, the gaiety of all that energy. The usual pose is sceptical, satirical, endlessly knowing; but if the young speaker has any settled or serious convictions it is all to his present purpose that they should not show. The last thing he wishes is to give a sense of mature, public, and permanent judgement. Donne's young speaker could not possibly be imagined as the author of any of Jonson's epigrams— only, perhaps, as the subject of one. Although both poets went on to different and more ambitious kinds of poetry, I think one can continue to catch glimpses in the poems of these early speakers' stances and assumptions and values. (pp. 18-20)

Jonson seems to have believed that a poet should know and be able to imitate the best contemporary poets and styles. Furthermore, as the most thoroughgoing classicist England had yet produced, he believed that 'the true artificer' should be mastercraftsman enough to provide a demonstration of Milton's ideal of the well-educated man, by performing 'justly, skilfully, and magnanimously all the [*poetic*] offices, both private and public, of peace and war.' For Jonson such a demonstration included the composition of the epigrams, the verse-letters, the odes, the songs, the epithalamiums, the tragedies, the comedies, and those masques which combined entertainment and compliment, mythical fictions and social realities, as well as most of the beautiful arts. It seems inevitable that Jonson should have translated Horace's *Art of Poetry*. It is hard to imagine Donne's doing so. (p. 22)

If Jonson held in theory that a poet should be able to write exhaustively about almost everything, Donne came near to fulfilling such an ideal in practice on the one subject of the psychology of love. In his *Love Elegies* and *Songs and Sonnets,* the individual speaker sometimes loves all women and sometimes he curses or despairs of all or announces that he is through with love. Sometimes he says that he can love any woman, or any woman so long as she is true, or any woman so long as she is untrue. Sometimes he cares only for the woman's body and the physical act of love; on at least one occasion he claims to love only one woman's virtuous soul. In some of the best poems, he insists that love is properly fulfilled only when it embraces both body and soul. But before we conclude that these poems are direct reflections of one unusually varied sexual autobiography, we should notice that two of the poems are written in the voice of a woman, one of them arguing wittily for absolute female promiscuity ('Good is not good, unless / A thousand it possess'). In addition to their varied attitudes and speakers, the poems explore various forms of address (often, as Helen Gardner has suggested, owing something to Ovid, the classical epigrams, Petrarch, or the English drama): a lover advises other lovers on how best

to begin an affair; he satirizes the foulness of another lover's mistress; he celebrates his new day of love as the beginning of a new life; he celebrates a full year of love; he imagines the future canonization of himself and his mistress as saints of a new religion of love; he laments the death of his loved one; he imagines his own burial; he makes his will. And he frequently explores the technically metaphysical (Neoplatonic or scholastic) subtleties concerning the nature and number of the new being which results from the perfect union of lovers. There are, however, some limitations. Helen Gardner has remarked [in her introduction to *The "Elegies"*] that Donne 'never speaks in the tone of a man overhelmed by what he feels to be wholly undeserved good fortune.' I should think, too, that we value the note of simple tenderness in **'Sweetest love, I do not go'** partly because it is so rare in Donne. And **'The Flea'** is memorable, among other reasons, because it is one of the few occasions in which Donne used (and, I think, parodied) the traditional persuasion to love. It is almost as if Donne wished to explore all the possibilities of personal love poetry except the sort that had been most popular in the vernacular: the poem which declares initial passion or devotion and attempts to persuade the lady to respond. In nearly all of Donne's best love poems (and a number of them are surely among the best poems in the language), the speaker is either passionately engaged or outrageously witty and playful or both.

The contrast with Jonson is precise. Jonson began *The Forest* with 'Why I write not of Love':

> Some act of Love's bound to rehearse,
> I thought to bind him, in my verse:
> Which when he felt, 'Away' (quoth he)
> 'Can Poets hope to fetter me?
> It is enough, they once did get
> Mars, and my Mother, in their net:
> I wear not these my wings in vain.'
> With which he fled me: and again,
> Into my ri'mes could ne'er be got
> By any art. Then wonder not,
> That since, my numbers are so cold,
> When Love is fled, and I grow old.

The personal love poem, addressed by a recognizably individual speaker to a specific mistress (fictional or otherwise), is the realm of the amateur in more than etymology, and Jonson seems almost embarrassed by it. When he infrequently attempts such poems, he often presents himself as a ruefully comic figure. (pp. 24-7)

No one would claim that Jonson's four 'devotional' poems are at all commensurate literarily with Donne's *Divine Poems.* To judge from his poetry, Jonson was not much concerned with theology, and he did not devote much of his life to religious meditation, There is nothing in Jonson to match the intensity of **'Batter my heart, three-personed God,'** the drama of **'At the round earth's imagined corners,'** the imaginative intricacy of **'Good-friday, 1613. Riding Westward.'** But although the best of Donne's *Divine Poems* are incomparable, their very qualities sometimes made for problems. Sometimes, Donne had difficulty in constructing sestets which satisfactorily fulfilled the promise (or resolved the questions) of the usually brilliant octaves of his *Holy Sonnets.* And although it usually does not matter much if in reading a poem addressed to a mistress a reader becomes much more interested in the verbal play or a metaphor than in the subject or even in the speaker's attitude toward the subject, such distraction can sometimes be almost fatal to a poem addressed to God. In reading Donne's poems we are uncomfortably reminded at times of possible limits to the amount of individual, brilliant gymnastics which a benighted and repentant sinner can credibly display. Jonson's nearly 'anonymous' 'Hymm to God the Father' (*The Underwood*, I) manages the tone of humility more easily and convincingly than Donne usually does:

> Hear me, O God!
> A broken heart
> Is my best part:
> Use still thy rod,
> That I may prove
> Therein, thy Love.

And that single poem concludes with a sense of religious assurance which Donne hardly matched in his poetry except in his **'Hymn to God my God, in my sickness.'**

But despite Jonson's differing sorts of successes, there can be little doubt of Donne's greater achievement as a love poet and as a sacred poet. It is within the public and semi-public poems, the verse letters (composed with varying degrees of formality, depending on the closeness of the friendships and the degrees of social distance), the 'epicides' and epithalamiums, the poems celebrating men or events, that Jonson's commitment to public voices and social judgements gives him a distinct advantage. In his verse letters (sometimes in the form of a sonnet) to close friends, Donne often exaggerated, with the greatest self-consciousness, his penchant for creating a harsh, idiosyncratic voice:

> I sing not, Siren-like, to tempt; for I
> Am harsh; . . . (**'To Mr. S. B.: "O thou which to
> search out the secret parts"'**)

> Now if this song be too 'harsh for rime, yet as
> The Painter's bad god made a good devill,
> 'Twill be good prose, although the verse be evill,
> If thou forget the rime as thou dost pass.
>   (**'To Mr. T. W.: "All hail
>   sweet Poet"'**)

This can be good fun—although some readers have difficulty in remaining amused long enough to puzzle out the meter. (Jonson's remark that Donne deserved hanging for not keeping of accent [see conversation dated 1618-19] was a precise one: Donne did usually 'keep' the proper number of syllables; but by a large amount of elision and the free substitution of feet, he sometimes reduced the expected iambic pattern of accents to an almost incredible fiction. Jonson's remark conveys a conscientious citizen's outrage that a rascal has successfully cheated without actually breaking the laws.) In those set pieces Jonson admired, **'The Storm'** and **'The Calm,'** Donne is masterly; his letter to Sir Henry Goodyere is fine; and he is always near his best in the poems he addressed to Sir Henry Wotton. But in the letters to his Countesses (of Huntingdon, Bedford, and Salisbury), he is often at his worst. Those poems tend to overly-finespun ingenuities, slack quibblings, tedious lore. The limitless eulogy and the speaker's posture of rapt adoration are frequently distasteful. (If we feel this strongly, it may be because Donne's own better poems have taught us the ironic and self-limiting uses of such hyperbolic eulogy.) And, there are sometimes, too, grotesque lapses within Donne's more public attempts at eulogy or celebration. One is not at all surprised that Donne's 'Obsequies to the Lord Harrington' failed to please the Countess of Bedford, the dead man's sister. And it is difficult to imagine that the newlyweds of the **'Epithalamion Made at Lincoln's Inn'** were any more pleased than the Countess when Death melodramatically entered the church during their wedding:

> Thy two-leaved gate's fair Temple unfold,
> And these two in thy sacred bosom hold,
> Till, mystically joined, but one they be;
> Then may thy lean and hunger-starved womb
> Long time expect their bodies and their tomb,
> Long after their own parents fatten thee.

Even stranger is that poem's climatic description of the bride's awaiting the bridegroom's approach, lying 'Like an appointed lamb, when tenderly / The priest comes on his knees t' embowel her.'

Just when one is about to conclude that Donne could not create and sustain a proper tone for a fully public poem, one remembers the Ecolgue and Epithalamion for the scandalous marriage of Robert Carr, Earl of Somerset, and Frances Howard, Countess of Essex, a long and ambitious poem which is consistently interesting and entertaining and which, so far as I can judge, contains not a single lapse, social or literary. Perhaps Donne carefully sought for and attained an adequate public tone because the political, social, and moral issues of that marriage were so delicate. (The poem may provide evidence in support of Donne's later remark, that in poetry 'I did best when I had least truth for my subjects.') At any rate, Donne's poem surpasses, in both literary achievement and tact Jonson's verse-letter to Somerset upon the same occasion.

Yet Donne's Eclogue and Epithalamion are not central to his work as most of Jonson's public poems are to his. It is within those poems that one can see, firmly related, Jonson's chief moral and poetic concerns. (pp. 29-33)

Jonson attempted one of the most difficult things a poet can conceive in any age: to present an ideal of the mean, of rational control and fulfilled public function, so that it seizes the imagination of the reader and stirs his emotions. The clarity, the learning, and the labour were necessary for the successful communication of such an ideal; they also reflected it. Moreover, some glimpses we get of Jonson's temperament and actions (irascible, sometimes violent or drunken, dictatorial, professionally jealous, occasionally crude in personal relations, saturnine, enjoying the exposure of the sordid) suggest that he may have embraced both his ideal and the means to attain it less because they were easily congenial than because they were necessary for his survival. Jonson may have been more temperamentally inclined to a despairing pessimism than Donne. He seems to have found in his combination of a roughly neo-stoic ethic and a neo-classic aesthetic a major sustaining force analogous to what Donne discovered within the Church.

For a summary view of the differences involved in Donne's and Jonson's approach to the public poem, one might compare Donne's two *Anniversaries* on the death of Elizabeth Drury with Jonson's 'To the Immortal Memory, and Friendship of that Noble Pair, Sir Lucius Cary, and Sir H. Morison. I think that the word 'marvellous' may be the correct one for Donne's *Anniversaries*. Commissioned to honour the memory of a young girl he had not known,

Donne turned her into a symbol of all the lost perfection of the world and the poems into extraordinarily witty descants on two traditional themes: the anatomy of a corrupt world and the progress of the souls of the blessed from this world to the next. I differ from Professor Louis Martz in preferring the **First Anniversary** to the **Second** [see excerpt dated 1954]. I would agree that the **Second** is more nearly unified and probably more serious than the **First,** but I am not convinced that an anatomy requires a high degree of unity nor that the quality of religious meditation in the **Second** is greatly impressive. And surely the **First Anniversary** is much the wittier of the two. I find myself joining the responses of the man who wrote the prefatory puffing poem for **'An Anatomy of the World'** (probably Joseph Hall) both in his exclamation and in his formulation of the poem's fundamental paradox:

> Well died the World, that we might live to see
> This world of wit, in his Anatomy: . . . (II. 1-2)

> Yet how can I consent the world is dead
> While this Muse lives? which in his spirit's stead
> Seems to inform a World; and bids it be
> In spite of loss or frail mortality? (II. 7-10)

It would be difficult to discover elsewhere such spirited and inventive verse rushing so headlong to describe death, dissolution, and total decay:

> There is no health; Physicians say that we,
> At best, enjoy but a neutrality.
> And can there be worse sickness, than to know
> That we are never well, nor can be so?
> We are born ruinous: poor mothers cry,
> That children come not right nor orderly;
> Except they headlong come and fall upon
> An ominous precipitation.
> How witty's ruin: how importunate
> Upon mankind! It laboured to frustrate
> Even God's purpose; and made woman, sent
> For man's relief, cause of his languishment.
> They were to good ends, and they are so still,
> But accessory, and principal in ill;
> For that first marriage was our funeral:
> One woman at one blow, then killed us all,
> And singly, one by one, they kill us now.
> We doe delightfully our selves allow
> To that consumption; and profusely blind,
> We kill our selves to propagate our kind. (II. 91-110)

It is, I think, beside the point for us to spend much time wondering how suitable such a passage is for an elegy on a young girl or what the elder Drury's might have thought of it. And it is probably a mistake to object to the extravagance of the eulogy. Jonson thought that the poem was 'profane and full of Blasphemies' and told Donne 'if it had been written of the Virgin Marie it had been something,' but Donne answered that he did not describe a woman but the *Idea* of one [see excerpt dated 1618-19]. Granted that ideal perfection is what we have lost (always), we can rejoice in the wit and ingenuity with which the poem explores both the nature of perfection and the extremity of our own corruption. (pp. 34-7)

Jonson's Pindaric ode on Cary and Morison is another matter. It seems to me one of the best and most 'serious' poems of the age. (p. 37)

Considering these last poems and also some of Donne's finest **Songs and Sonnets** and **Divine Poems,** one is tempted to characterize the poetry of Donne and Jonson in terms of a whole series of seemingly opposed ideals and practices. Besides the private and the public, the amateur and the professional, the individual and the general, one thinks of extravagance and sobriety, excess and measure, spontaneity and deliberation, immediacy and distance, daring and propriety, roughness and elegance, tension and balance, agility and weight. And one can go on to expression and function, ecstacy and ethics, experience and thought, energy and order, the genius and the craftsman —ending with those inevitable seventeenth-century pairs, passion and reason, wit and judgement, nature and art. But such a marshalling of abstractions can be misleading. So arranged, the members of those pairs may seem more fully antagonistic than they really are; and such an account obscures how much Donne and Jonson had in common. We should remember that three love elegies perhaps written by neither were attributed by contemporaries to both. A sentence from Douglas Bush suggests succinctly why such confusion was possible: 'Both poets rebelled, in their generally different ways, against pictorial fluidity, decorative rhetorical patterns, and half-medieval idealism, and both, by their individual and selective exploitation of established doctrines and practices, created new techniques, a new realism of style (or new rhetoric), sharp, condensed, and muscular, fitted for the intellectual and critical realism of their thought.' Among a number of the things that Jonson said about Donne was the remark that he was 'the first poet in the world in some things'; and Donne addressed Jonson in a Latin poem as *Amicissimo et Meritissimo* and praised him as a unique kind of classicist, a follower of the ancients who dared to do new things. I think that each was correct in those judgements. (pp. 39-40)

Joseph H. Summers, "The Heritage: Donne and Jonson," in his The Heirs of Donne and Jonson, *Oxford University Press, 1970, pp. 13-40.*

M. THOMAS HESTER   (essay date 1982)

[Hester is an American aducator and literary scholar who has edited the John Donne Journal: Studies in the Age of Donne *since its founding in 1982—the year he also published* Kind Pitty and Brave Scorn: John Donne's "Satyres." *In the following excerpt from this work, he provides background for and an overview of Donne's* Satyres, *characterizing them as eloquent jeremiads composed during an era of apocalyptic religious zeal.]*

Despite the judgment of Ben Jonson and Alexander Pope that Donne's five **Satyres** are among "his best things" [see Additional Bibliography] with the notable exception of the third **Satyre** they are among his most neglected pieces. Even the third poem has received almost as much attention for the insight it supposedly provides about the poet's conversion (or apostasy) as for its intrinsic literary merit. One might rely on a critical cliché and contend that such a situation is surprising or unfathomable, but except for the fourth **Satyre** such neglect is understandable, given the extreme obscurity the poems manifest. We do have an excellent edition of the poems by W. Milgate, and several recent essays have begun to focus on Donne's considerable achievement in these poems. However, the **Satyres** as a whole have never received the critical attention given to the **Songs and Sonets,** the **Anniversaries,** and the **Elegies,** even though it has been pointed out frequently how those poems display the poet's mastery of satire.... Much too sophisticated to be apprentice pieces or early experiments, they disclose how, early in his career, Donne successfully met aesthetic, poetic, and moral problems and shed much light on his own opinion of his duty as Christian poet, fallen man, and religious devotee. Unique transformations of the norms and forms of formal verse satire, Donne's *Satyres* offer a unified, sequential examination of the problems of Christian satire, a creative shaping (or re-shaping) of the generic, conventional, intellectual, and biographical materials available to Donne in the 1590s.

One of the commonplaces of Donne criticism has been the emphasis on Donne the innovator and initiatior—Donne the first metaphysical poet, the first Renaissance meditative poet, the first formal verse satirist. Such nomenclature provides a valuable starting point for any analysis of his achievement. Indeed, it is central to this study of Donne as the most important and most original of the English formal verse satirists. But there is another Donne, another feature of his historical and personal situation to which attention should be directed. This is the position of Donne *at the end*—at the end of the sixteenth century, of one phase of Christian humanism, of a movement of English literary history. In fact, if we accept Jonson's evaluation, Donne had "written all his best pieces err he was 25 years old"[see excerpt dated 1618-19]—by 1598, the most probable date of composition for *Satyre V.* Such an end-of-the-age figure is well known to Donne readers, of course, as the English Elijah of the *Anniversaries* who saw the "new Philosophy cal[ling] all in doubt" and "all cohaerence gone" from the "old world" of morality and value. The concern of this study is with the first appearance in his poems of this jeremiadic "Trumpet," with Donne's first "invasion [of] this great Office" in the *Satyres*, those poems that belong chronologically, thematically, and, with the sudden reversal of his fortunes because of his marriage, biographically to the end of the century and to the end of one phase of Donne's career. This poet—or at least his persona, that "artful fabrication" who speaks the poet's poetic truths—is the figure who envisions the decay and destruction of order and value. Certainly he is always a Christian figure, acknowledging "the need and value of loving the imperfect and incomplete" and conceding that man is "necessarily finite, lacks omniscience, and therefore must fail in most of his endeavours"; Donne's satirist never loses sight of that eternal "cosmic tolerance for admitted failure [which] allows us to be comparably merciful to those who fail as we do." But this self-conscious awareness of his own fallen nature only reinforces his awareness of the precarious position of man in a providential universe, which is accentuated by his position at the end—at the end of the "golden age," at the end of the century, at the end of what many of his contemporaries insisted were "the last dayes." The search for and creation of a voice appropriate to such conditions is one of the central impulses of the *Satyres.*

Apocalyptic and millenarian fears and hopes abound at the end of centuries; but this fact, and our ability to turn such phenomena into historical commonplaces, cannot detract from the sincerity and urgency of the men and women who lived and wrote during such "last dayes." In a sense, in fact, the warnings and predictions of the soothsayers at the end of the sixteenth century were accu-

rate—if not in the apocalyptic or literal terms in which they were evoked, at least in terms of the development and directions of English art and civilization. The end was the beginning, the end of the golden age, the start of another period of magnificent creativity and art. And Donne's *Satyres*, like Donne himself at the time of their creation, at the end of his education and the beginning of his brief political career, stand on the cusp. The first English imitations of the ancient genre, the *Satyres*, by capturing the spirit, themes, and tensions—the rich complexities of that unique age of beginnings and endings, births and deaths—show Donne making his (poetic) beginning by focusing on the (apocalyptic) ending. To appreciate fully the stances, tensions, and generic complexities essential to these five poems, we must start at the end—at the end of the sixteenth century and the climate of opinion in which they were written. It is there that we find the bases for the genre and the persona Donne creates in the *Satyres.*

As recent criticism has confirmed, one of the cardinal rhetorical principles that the Renaissance inherited from the classics was the concept of decorum. Even the satire of the Renaissance, that genre least commented upon in the critical documents of the age, is better understood by cognizance of what the satirist understood "decencie demanded" or allowed of him. Alvin Kernan has documented, for example, the influence of one doctrine of decorum on English "savage" satire at the end of the sixteenth century; Annabel Patterson has suggested yet another. But Donne's poems, the most original, the "most consistent and ordered" verse satire of the period, seem little indebted to either of these concepts. There was, however, a broader and less exclusive concept of satirical decorum available to the Renaissance Christian satirist, a view of the requirements of the satirist that satisfied both the general rhetorical principles of verse satire and the ethical prescriptions of late sixteenth-century England.

This older and more comprehensive view of the features and limitations of the satirist was sanctioned by biblical example, patristic commentary, and sixteenth-century homiletic and critical opinion. It was verified, in fact, by the "first formal definition of satire in English literature," Thomas Drant's preface to his 1566 translation of Horace's *Satires*. Although this definition repeats in part the etymological confusion of *satira-satyros* that Kernan sees as the foundation of the "cankered muse" of Renaissance satire, Drant's defense of his inclusion of both the *Satires* of Horace and the *Lamentations* of Jeremiah in the same volume acknowledges the concept of satirical decorum that Donne's *Satyres* most fully enact. Both authors depict the satirist as a Christian "rebuker" whose earliest precedents were the Old Testament Prophets. And in accordance with the central rhetorical principle of *laus et vituperatio*, which Drant attempted to satisfy by offering the "chiding" of Horace with the "wayling" of Jeremiah, Donne's five poems provide a dramatic integration of these two concepts through their portrait of the satirist's gradual realization of the *ethos* his age identified as that of the Prophets. To this view of the satirist as a "zealous" prophet Donne's poems seem most fully indebted. Just as Donne, like Herbert, Crashaw, Vaughan, and Traherne after him, turns to the words, voices, themes, and stances of the biblical poets in his *Holy Sonnets* and *Divine Poems,* so he turns to biblical aesthetics in his earliest poetic creations in order to formulate a spokesman appropriate to the times in which he lived and wrote.

It is important to remember, at the same time, that the *Satyres* are imitations of the Latin genre. Most appraisals have quite correctly focused on them as the first example of "a sustained 'imitation' of the Latin genre" in English literature. Certainly, the exasperated indignation of Juvenal's "difficile est saturam non scribere" is echoed throughout the *Satyres*, and the rough asperity of Persius and the exhortative irony of Horace find their complements in the paradoxical encounters of Donne's persona with knaves and fools, as well as in his conversational style. Central throughout the *Satyres* is the adaptation, redaction, and accommodation of specific tenets and stances of Roman satire. Nevertheless, the speaker of these poems is not simply a Juvenalian "railer" in Elizabethan garb who modernizes the situations of Horace in the tones of Persius. He achieves a balance, an integration, to use his own words, of "Kinde pitty" and "brave scorn" not found in the Latin originals.

Sidney, Puttenham, and Wilson characterize the earliest Christian poets as prophets. And Renaissance documents concerned more specifically with satire—the annotations and *Artes poeticae* of Fabrini, Estienne, Robortellus, and Correa, for example—note specific analogies between the styles, techniques, and themes of the Roman satirists and biblical poets, especially the Old Testament Prophets. In the same way, the features of Donne's satirist in the *Satyres* accord with the Christian "zeal" that contemporary and traditional documents described as fundamental to the "satire" of the Prophets, and which they recommend in those times of "heinous enormities" Donne's five poems portray the satirist's instruction in the necessity, justice, and limitations (the decorum) of such zeal to the satirist in an "Age of rusty iron" and to fallen man in a providential universe.

Although often overshadowed temporarily by responses to military victories, sectarian disputes, or political intrigues, "it is not too much to say," Roy Battenhouse points out, "that the doctrine of divine Providence was the chief apologetic interest" of the sixteenth century. A single persistent and typically Elizabethan theory of Providence is difficult to formulate, however, except that it delineated God's attributes of Mercy and Justice in His continuing connection with His creation. At the end of the century, while acknowledging and agreeing that God's Justice is the "fullness" of his Mercy, influential voices insisted that a fuller understanding of and response to God's wrathful justice was necessitated by the alarming state of English manners and morality. (pp. 3-7)

However strongly the age earlier may have believed itself another golden age, and in spite of momentary exuberances over naval or political victories, warnings about impending doom and destruction temper English thought at the end of the century.

In search for remedies to forestall the doom, many in the age turned, quite naturally, to biblical guidances and examples. In their appeals for a more spirited assault against sin, what they concluded was needed immediately was the "godly zeal" of Old Testament Prophets, those exemplars whose "loving anger" was sanctified by the actions of Christ against the money-lenders and witnessed by the epistles of St. Paul. (p. 8)

The Church Fathers defended what the alarmed Elizabethans later called zeal on the basis of its power of reformation, its sanctification by biblical example, and its moral necessity. They agreed that such wrath, if initiated by a just cause, used out of love of goodness and hatred of sin, directed at sins rather than sinners, and aimed at moral reformation rather than personal vengeance, was "righteous" and "necessary."

The English poet, who in the apocalyptic climate at the end of the century, turned to verse satire, then, had a thoroughly Christian principle of satirical decorum on which to style his speaker. Patristic, homiletic, scholarly, and critical opinion—in addition to the example of the Prophets themselves—offered a "zealous" muse as well as a "cankered" muse to whom he could appeal. Donne's satirist speaks in the decorum of the former.

The outstanding feature and in many ways the abiding concern of the speaker of Donne's *Satyres* is with zeal, with his "anger meddled with and mixed with love." In one sense, the five poems present varying attitudes of the satirist as he self-consciously searches for a correct and satisfying balance of these two extremes. Topically, as John Shawcross points out, "the five satires pillory five universal dilemmas besetting man," but the initial and final concern of all five is with the concomitant hatred and charity of the satirist himself. This is not to suggest that the *Satyres* are concerned only with the education of the satirist; such a private concern cannot be separated from his commitment to his fellow man. Satire, or the satirist's understanding of his own duty, is always viewed as a relationship: as a duty to himself, his countrymen, and his God. In the *Satyres,* examination and analysis of the virtues of the active and the contemplative lives (in *Satyre I*), the widespread abuse of language and the Word (in *Satyre II*), the need for continual *wise doubt* and the integrated use of the rational faculties required of "our Mistresse faire Religion" (in *Satyre III*), the dangers of thoughtless visits to a hellish court peopled with informers (in *Satyre IV*), the "Officers rage and Suitors wretchedness" which perpetuate perversions of the law (in *Satyre V*) are each evaluated from the perspective of the demands which they place on the satirist's own zeal. The originality of the *Satyres,* then, lies not just in their focus on the satirist as a self-conscious penitent concerned with his complementary duties as fallen man and moral critic, but also in their application and elaboration of the decorum of the biblical satirists, the accommodation of a set of principles from biblical aesthetics to the moral and spiritual dilemmas of late sixteenth-century man.

Peter Medine [in the essay "Praise and Blame in Renaissance Verse Satire," published in *Pacific Coast Philology* (1972)] points out that the superiority of the *Satyres* results in part from Donne's facility in yoking the major criteria of verse satire—to praise and to blame—into "a coherent poetic design" by offering a persona who embodies "viable alternatives to the viciousness" he satirizes. The earliest (and crudest) attempt to fulfill this principle in the age was Drant's Englishing of Horace's satires, in which Drant appended a series of epigrams extolling virtuous examples to his rendition of the classical satirist's attacks on public vices. Similarly, in *Skialetheia* Everard Guilpin added praises of Lucretius and Epictetus to his attacks on perverse courtiers and vain women in order to fulfill this requirement. Even the most "cankered" satirist of the age, John Marston, integrated long praises of "reason," "Prudence," and "precepts of philosophy" into his otherwise pessimistic portraits of human viciousness and depravity to satisfy this tenet of satiric decorum. It is Donne's *Satyres* that most brilliantly fulfill this principle. Indeed, the constancy, charity, and self-knowledge of the contemplative scholar of *Satyre I* do offer a worthy contrast to the adulterous clothes, actions, and aims of the "fondling motley humorist" who tempts him to walk through the fashionable streets of London. In the same way, in the second *Satyre*, the satirist's legal and moral concern about the effects of "Good workes" and about his own capacity to bring about reformation through his own poem proposes an exemplary regard for the civilizing force of language in contrast to the mechanical, materialistic manipulation of words by parasitic frauds such as the poet-lawyer Coscus. Again, the satirist's meditative exertion of "all [his] Soules devotion"—the memory, understanding, and will of his rational soul—in the search for "true religion" provides a dramatic alternative to the adventurous abuses of memory, the sectarian abuses of understanding, and the secular manipulations of will that are scorned in *Satyre III*. The awareness of his own precarious position in the providential scheme and of the duty he owes to his "Mistresse Truth" displayed by the satirist in *Satyre IV* provides tacit condemnation of and a worthwhile option to the self-ignorance and disruptive libels he encounters in the Presence Chamber. Finally, the satirist's allegiance to "righteousnes" and his aspiration "To know and weed out . . . sinne" reveal a sense of moral responsibility in direct contrast to the officers' greed and the suitors' self-destructive capitulations to the present forms of legal injustice described in *Satyre V*.

The superiority of Donne's *Satyres* rests, however, not only on the successful integration of *laus et vituperatio* in each individual poem. As a five-act sequence—a *"book"* of *Satyres*, to use Jonson's description of them—the poems disclose the satirist's growing awareness of the nature and uses of Christian zeal. Sequentially, the *Satyres* portray the speaker's moral character (*I*), aesthetic development (*II*), spiritual awareness (*III*), and efforts to implement the lessons of that self-knowledge (*IV* and *V*). The first satire, for instance, endorses the scholar's "zealous" mockery of the humorist's inconstancy at the same time that it discloses the satirist's naive idealism and lack of self-criticism. The second delineates his development of a moral satirical criterion, based on his recognition that some sins deserve pity and others only hatred. But, at the same time, both poems intimate the limitations of his active Christian awareness. In the first he mistakes satire to be only the contemplative assertion of ideals to inconstant fools and thinks that his following the mercurial fop from his own study in order to reform him might be a "sin . . . against [his] conscience." Although the constant charity he shows for his "wild uncertaine" companion is not called into question, the fact that the scholar too is finally "ravish'd" by the "lechery" of the town (in a metaphoric sense, through the fop's betrayal-desertion of him) suggests that this virtue *alone* cannot sustain the satirist-reformer. In *Satyre II* he turns melancholically to sarcastic self-criticism because no discernible results are realized by his "Good workes." Having expressed his "hate [for] all this towne" and especially for the "excellently best" societal illness represented by fraudulent lawyers, he is able only partially to overcome his melancholy with the derisive and

cynical retort that at least he will escape the "vast reach of th' huge statute lawes" since he has spoken the mere truth. Although the speaker in both poems enacts viable alternatives to the foolishness and crimes he denounces, his own doubts about his satire outweigh his confidence in its therapeutic potential.

In the third *Satyre*, on the other hand, he realizes that the charity he offered the popinjay in *I* and the hatred he directed at Coscus in *II*—his own "Kinde pitty" and "brave scorn"—are justified. The "cure [for] these worne maladies" that he as a satirist seeks is, he realizes, actually the dynamic action of a mind in search for Truth and in open opposition to falsehood. The results of his efforts are best and only measured by eternal standards. Central in position and importance, this poem—as meditation and satire simultaneously—dramatizes the satirist's self-confirmation of the religious basis of his satire. It depicts his realization that the Christian "Sentinells" vigilant hatred of man's foes and the pilgrim's dynamic love of "Truth" are essential to both "true religion" and "wise . . . railing."

Satyre IV chronicles the continuation of the satirist's education, his acquisition of God-given knowledge, his fullest appraisal of his fallen inclinations and God's active wrath, and his attempts to implement that knowledge at the Elizabethan court. Having first visited the Presence Chamber out of mere curiosity (*absentia recti*) and suffered the punishment of God's "furious rod" in the form of a libellous *Inglese italianato*, the satirist fell into "a trance / Like his, who dreamt he saw hell." Enlightened by this trance and urged by his "precious soul" to return to the chamber, he sees that the court is indeed a hell, that he should feel pity for the suitors who go there, and that he must not fear that "huffing braggart, puft Nobility" if he is to fulfill his duty to his "Mistresse Truth." Having run from the court after his first visit for fear of "Becomming Traytor," he returns there after his vision, he admits, as a "Spie," therein initiating his obedience as a satirist.

That obedience is extended in the last *Satyre,* addressed to the wretched suitors who suffer from the injustice of the courts and to the lord keeper who has been commissioned to investigate their predicament. Similar to the first *Satyre* in situation, this final scene discloses the triumph of the satirist over his previous lack of knowledge about self and vocation. Now he is able to replace the recitation of abstract ideals with "accommodated" maxims that instruct a complaining suitor in the need for self-knowledge. Convinced of the validity of his satire, aware through his own experiences that the way to reformation lies through self-knowledge, the speaker of *Satyre V* dramatizes the active completion of his education in the *ethos* of prophetic "zeal" integral to the entire sequence. Now he is assured that he is "Authoriz'd . . . To know and weed out . . . sinne"—authorized publicly through his "service" to the queen's official and privately through the testing of his own moral confidence. Bolder and more confident than in any of the first four poems, the satirist exerts his energies finally to the instruction (and ridicule) of another fallen human being and laudatory advice to the lord keeper without rationalizations about the inevitable limitations of his helpfulness and without dissipating his energies in self-doubts. The meditative and public voices have merged completely here—"all things be in all"—to achieve a satisfying balance of "Kinde pitty" and "brave scorn."

The exemplary character of the satirist's zealous self-knowledge is suggested also by the mythic structure of the sequence. The dramatic portrait of his own journey from innocence (*I*), to darkness and despair (*II*), and finally to self-knowledge (*III*), suffering and God-given knowledge (*IV*), and obedience (*V*) duplicates the mythic or Christian structure of human history as it was delineated in such influential Christian humanist works as Erasmus' *Enchiridion*, the official *Book of Homilies*, and *The Book of Common Prayer*. As such, the satirist's own self-examination and zealous attitude provide the "easie wayes and neare" worthy of all men's imitation. Illustrative of the progressive regeneration of the speaker as satirist and as man, the sequential arrangement suggests that this self-awareness and zeal are the method and "cure" for "these worne maladies" on which the five *Satyres* focus.

In the third *Satyre* Donne's satirist offers the fullest defense of his zeal. His meditation on the dynamic use of the three powers of the rational soul begins with lines that read like a paraphrase of Becon's definition of the zeal of the Prophets:

> Kinde pitty chokes my spleene; brave scorn forbids
> Those teares to issue which swell my eye-lids;
> I must not laugh, nor weepe sinnes, and be wise.

Nowhere, in fact, is the affinity between the spirit of Donne's speaker and the Old Testament Prophets more pronounced than in this central poem.

This poem, which has proved so pivotal to critics concerned with Donne's early poetics, is equally useful for an understanding of the *Satyres*. Only once here does the merciful God of the New Testament appear. By and large, the God of Truth, the "Mistresse . . . worthy' of all our Soules devotion" of *Satyre III* is the Old Testament jealous God whose judgment is to be feared. Nine times is reference made to the Day of Judgment and to the punishment awaiting those who fail in their devotion. The certain fact that motivates the satirist here, demanding his "zealous" meditation on the need for "true religion" at the present time, is the surety of damnation for those who refuse "God himselfe to trust." In "Kinde pitty" and "brave scorn" the speaker of *Satyre III* finally evokes a vision of the sure Justice of God on "the last day" fully in the spirit and character of an Old Testament Prophet, and in line with contemporary homiletic warnings that such zeal is the moral antidote for the "worne maladies" of the day. Unlike the speaker in *Satyre I* who feared that his active satire might be a "sinne against [his] conscience" and the speaker in *Satyre II* who concluded that his satire was "bred" by the disregard of his own "Good workes," the speaker of *Satyre III,* in his final methaporic description and vision of the Mercy *and* Justice of the "Power" of God, finds a divine analogue to sanctify his own "Kinde pitty" and "brave scorn."

In the same vein, the initial question posed in *Satyre III*—whether "railing" can "cure these worne maladies" —is also central to all the *Satyres*. The structure and strategies of the satirist's progress is self-knowledge throughout the five poems and his final achievement of a working, divinely qualified balance between his hatred and charity suggest that "railing" can, as a balance of "Kinde pitty" and "brave scorn," be itself an exemplary attitude for all men. His examination of his own nature and genre shows

others whom he loves but whose sins he hates that the way to avoid damnation is through Christian zeal. Donne's *Satyres* thus provide a dramatization of his satirist's understanding of and conformity to the decorum of the earliest biblical reformers. If we dismiss the assumption that the internal debates about the nature of this speaker's utterances in these poems are symptomatic of Donne's own insecurity in this genre, it is possible to focus on these poems as a progressive examination and application of attitudes acceptable to the decorum of a Christian satirist. Such a reading does not deny that Donne's poems are classical imitations, but merely suggests that Donne has replaced the spokesman of Horace, Juvenal, and Persius with a speaker of Christian zeal. Transforming the forms and norms of Roman verse satire, the five *Satyres* provide a dramatic definition of what the age termed *zeal*—as the decorum of Christian satire and as integral to man's response to the grace of God. In accordance with the specific calls for reformation in a time of apocalyptic fervor and alarm, the *Satyres* portray a speaker whose meditative explanation of what "decencie demands" of him conforms to traditional and contemporary descriptions of the zeal of the Prophets. (pp. 10-6)

> *M. Thomas Hester, in his* Kinde Pitty and Brave
> Scorn: John Donne's "Satyres," *Duke University*
> *Press, 1982, 178 p.*

TERRY G. SHERWOOD   (essay date 1984)

[*Sherwood is a Canadian educator and literary essayist. In his* Fulfilling the Circle: A Study of John Donne's Thought *(1984), he stressed that "there can be no absolute separation between the importance of epistemological and psychological principles for Donne and his personal consciousness that infuses his works. That these principles are manifested in writings clearly enlivened by Donne's own experience simply adds convincing evidence of their importance in his thought. And the fact that these writings define the experience of consciousness according to shaping metaphysical forces makes them characteristic of Donne's thought in general." In the following excerpt from this work,* Sherwood examines Death Duell *as "the final part added to a consistent whole": a work that completes a life long cycle involving "Donne's own person as a factor in his works."*]

The event of *Deaths Duell* was remarkable even by the standards of Donne's day. He had been appointed to preach on 'his old constant day, the first *Friday* in Lent,' at Whitehall before the king. Though wasted by illness, Donne 'passionately denied' the requests of concerned friends that he not preach. His text was Psalm 68:20: *'And unto God the Lord belong the issues of death. i.e. from death,'* Isaak Walton captures a very special drama: 'Many that then saw his tears, and heard his faint and hollow voice, professing they thought Text prophetically chosen, and that Dr. Donne *had preach't his own funeral Sermon* [see excerpt dated 1640]. But it is not just the drama of a wasted, dying man who embodies his own words about death that is remarkable. Even more so is that the event of Donne's delivery and the sermon itself, taken together, represent a coherent and fulfilling conclusion to his life and thought.

The vivid sight of the dying man could have made the sermon itself anticlimactic if not for its own powerful effects. A forceful statement of omnipresent mortality and vivid images of putrefaction and vermiculation relentlessly aggravate fear of death. Donne's dying body becomes only the most immediate example of the principle of mortality and of the inevitability of material decay and putrefaction. . . . And the portrayal of the crucified Christ that concludes the sermon remains amongst the most powerful statements in Donne's religious prose.

To say that the sermon itself was not anticlimactic is not to say that it can have the same power for us as for the actual audience. Both the dying man and the artifact would have been important. Even for a spellbinder like Donne, his presence in the pulpit then would have been a rare moment; and in his very self-conscious staging of it can be found much of the intended effect on his audience. Walton's account of Donne's final days—his return from Essex to deliver the sermon, the delivery itself before the king and the Whitehall audience, his order that a life-size burial effigy be drawn prematurely, his contemplation of that drawing as his 'hourly object'—reveals parts of a whole. There is a consciousness of the interrelationship between his own person, the artifacts embodying or expressing it, and the communal Body including both person and artifacts. Familiar assumptions here reach back to Donne's beginnings. His abiding sense of the body as a legitimate medium of truth and of the human need to read it experience were revealed in the conception of the body as a 'book' as early as the love poetry in **'To his Mistris Going to Bed'** and **'The Exstasie'** and later in the verse letter **'To Sir Edward Herbert, at Julyers.'** The body's experience must be understood and known by an attentive reason. Likewise, we find the assumption that artifacts are surrogate bodies necessary for expressing truth. Such diverse works as **'The Canonization,' 'The Relique,'** *The Anniversaries*, the verse letters, and the *Devotions* reveal this assumption.

Frontispiece of Deaths Duell *(1632), reproducing the portrait of Donne in his burial shroud.*

Walton's nervous estimate of Donne's order for the burial effigy as showing 'a desire of glory or commendation . . . rooted in the very nature of man' is not the only interpretation that can be given of Donne's motives. In the *Devotions* Donne assumes that his own diseased body has significance for other members of the participating Body. This significance is embodied in the literary artifact, which must be considered rationally by members of Donne's audience just as Donne must consider the events of his immediate experience. In *Deaths Duell* Donne's own person is not explicitly expressed in the artifact, but it would have been tangibly present. As members of the same Body as Donne, his auditors could have participated, in a very immediate way, in the significance of his dying body. (pp. 193-94)

At bottom is operating the elemental bodily consciousness that . . . [is] one key factor in Donne's epistemology and psychology and which, in *Deaths Duell,* provokes the fear of physical death and dissolution of bodily identity. The imminence of Donne's own death would exacerbate that fear in members of his audience. The fearful appeal to this bodily consciousness is answered by the climactic image of the crucified Christ, with its assurance that through identification with death itself, in the pattern of Christ's suffering death, fear can be transformed into hope. Only through conformity to Christ that bends man's will to God's through penitentially crucifying sin, in humility, obedience, and patience, can one escape the fear of death. Donne's assurance of his own resurrection from sin

through conformity to Christ in the *Devotions* and Walton's account of his joyful assurance of salvation during the days before his death suggest that Donne would have viewed his own wasted body as an example of penitential conformity to Christ's suffering death. Thus, the vivid image of the dying man is fulfilled in the vivid depiction of the suffering God as its pattern. The audience is invited, implicitly, to participate in Donne as one exemplary member of the Body and, explicitly, to conform to the suffering and death of Christ the Head. In accordance with his Lenten purposes, 'Crucifying of that *sinne* that governes thee' to achieve conformity, Donne pulls tight the strings of bodily consciousness with his image of the suffering incarnate Word: 'There wee leave you in that *blessed dependancy*, to *hang* upon *him* that *hangs* upon the *Crosse,* there *bath* in his *teares,* there *suck* at his *woundes,* and *lye downe in peace* in his *grave,* till hee vouchsafe you a *resurrection*, and an *ascension* into that *Kingdome*, which hee hath *purchas'd for you*, with the *inestimable price* of his *incorruptible blood.* Amen. Only this palpable image of Christ can change bodily fears into hope through acceptance of the body's own necessary death and resurrection.

Donne keeps our attention on Christ's bodily suffering as, increasingly, the sermon, like the development of Donne's own thought, converges on the Cross. Divine love inspires Christ's freely given love:

> *Many waters quench not love,* Christ's tryed many; He was *Baptized* out of his *love,* and his love determined

not there; He wept over *Jerusalem* out his love, and his love determined not there; He *mingled blood* with *water* in his *agony* and that determined not his love; hee *wept pure blood*, all his blood at all his eyes, at all his pores, in his *flagellation* and *thornes (to the Lord our God belong'd the issues of blood)* and these *expressed*, but these did *not quench his love*.'

Love of Christ, in return, inspires penintential conformity in body and tripartite soul, thereby converting the forces of annihilation and recreating man the damaged goal of Creation. In the suffering of the Cross that pays sin's debt, God shows to man the pattern in body and soul that mortifies sin. Donne's emphasis upon the humanity of the Word, his very palpable physical and psychological suffering, brings the specifically human together with the larger metaphysical power of the Word. In the explicit conformity built on love, humility, obedience, patience, and acceptance of suffering and death, being is recreated. And Donne, in offering his own accomplished suffering to the audience, exemplifies this recreation for others, thereby, like Paul, fulfilling the suffering of Christ in his own flesh for the Body's sake.

Consistent with his earlier works, Donne stresses that this meeting of the personal and metaphysical occurs in time. Donne ends **Deaths Duell** at the end of his own circle with yet another meditation on time that places importance on the given moment. In the sermon the movement from fear to conformity with Christ, from death of the body to the resurrection of hope, recreates time. The sermon's initial weight on the omnipresence of death points to the negativity of fallen time: 'We celebrate our owne funeralls with cryes, even at our own birth, as though our *threescore and ten years life* were spent in our mothers labour, and our circle made up in the first point thereof. Similarly, the progression of fallen time is crippled and reversed: 'That which we call life, is but *Hebdomada mortium, a week of deaths,* seaven dayes, seaven periods of our life spent in dying, *a dying seaven times over,* and there is an end. *Our birth dyes* in *infancy* ,and our *infancy* dyes in *youth,* and *youth* , and the rest dye in *age,* and *age* also dyes, and *determines all.*

Against the degeneration of time through death, Donne, fittingly himself a dying man nearing his own last day, offers the model of Christ's last day. Gradually, the sermon conforms time itself to Christ, thereby re-informing time according to the Incarnate Word:

> Take in the *whole day* from the *houre* that *Christ received* the *passeover* upon *Thursday, unto* the *houre* in which hee *dyed* the *next day.* Make *this* present *day* in thy *devotion,* and consider what *hee did,* and remember what *you have done.* Before hee *instituted and celebrated* the *Sacrament,* (which was *after* the *eating of the passeover)* hee proceeded to that *act* of *humility,* to *wash his disciples feete,* even, *Peters, who* for a while *resisted* him; In thy *preparation* to the holy and blessed *Sacrament,* hast thou with a sincere *humility* sought a *reconciliation* with all the *world,* even with those that have been *averse* from it, and *refused* that *reconciliation* from thee? If so (and not else) thou hast spent that *first part* of this his *last day* in a *conformity* with him.

The day of Donne's sermon and the day before Christ's death are both special days. For Donne, it is his last sermon before an expected and welcome death, a point close to the Omega of his circle of time. For Christ, it is the pe-

riod of a single day immediately before his Crucifixion, likewise a point close to the Omega of his exemplary circle. The auditors, like Donne and Christ, must face the continuing possibility that each day may end their circles. Each day is a '*criticall* day' that must be regarded as potentially man's last to be brought into conformity with Christ's last day. Donne's visible conformity to Christ's pattern will dilate this particular moment in the respective lives of his listeners. Thus, **Death Duell** speaks to the immediate moment, to both individuals and to the communal Body, applying these special days of Donne and Christ. As in the **Devotions** Donne is speaking to members of the Body, the Church, invoking the image of Christ the Head; and he is spaeking to members of the Body, the Kingdom, here in the presence of its regal Heart. All members hear the same pattern for fulfilling time.

As elsewhere in Donne's works, time is fulfilled within the human soul. The reference points are psychological and epistemological; and the guiding conformity to Christ, which is so crucial in Donne's theology of participation, works within a larger within a larger conformity of the tripartite human soul to the tripartite God, In the *divisio* in preparation for 'these three considerations' of the three meanings of *exitus mortis* that make up the sermon, Donne establishes parallels to the three Persons of the Trinity:

> In all these three lines then, we shall looke upon these words; *First,* as the *God of power,* the *Almighty Father* rescues his servants from the jawes of death: *And then,* as the *God of mercy,* the glorious *Sonne* rescued us, by taking upon himselfe this *issue of death: And then* betweene these two, as the *God of comfort,* the *Holy Ghost* rescues us from all discomfort by his blessed impressions before hand, that what manner of death soever be ordeined for us, yet this *exitus mortis* shall be *introitus in vitam* our *issue in death,* shall be an *entrance into everlasting life.*

Similarly, the sermon works on all members of the tripartite Image in the human soul: on the reason in the frequent request that the auditors consider the matter of the sermon, especially the experience of Christ; on the will in the stimulation of love for Christ's loving sacrifice; and on the memory in the request that believers remember their own sinful actions in comparison with Christ's example. The recreation of time requires attentive efforts by the entire soul.

In the **Devotions** reason considers each moment in time according to the principles informing it. The same assumption in **Death Duell** makes conformity to Christ dependent on the soul's keen rational awareness. The audience is asked to consider the significance of moments in Christ's 'day' ending with his death. 'Make *this* present *day* that *day* in thy *devotion,* Tconsider what *hee did,* and remember what *you have done* Donne repeatedly points to the importance of considering the matter of the sermon, 'to consider with mee how to *this God the Lord belong'd the issues of death,* explicit sharpening the audience's rational attention. Implicitly, the audience is also being asked to consider the dying preacher standing before them, just as they are asked to consider his diseased body in the **Devotions.** The dramatic force of the given moment in Donne's works develops in these later works into a full-blown sense of temporal events as a form of communication from God to man, to be understood and known.

When Donne speaks of God as Logos, who necessarily proceeds logically, for whom a minute in time is a 'syllogisme he is emphasizing the rational dimension in that communication. The audience in **Death Duell** must consider not only Donne's spoken words, but also his presence in the pulpit as a form of temporal communication from God. This is necessarily the domain of reason's same bright attention emphasized throughout Donne's works as the condition for fulfilling temporal life. Reason must also attentively arbitrate the will's experience in love and examine anew what memory comprehends.

That Donne would expect the members of his audience to consider not only his words but also himself as part of the same event [bring us to a crucial matter in understanding Donne's works] namely, Donne's own person as a factor in his works. The complexities of Donne's nature have set off varied and, times, conflicting responses. Clearly, Donne was unsettled as a young man; it is nonetheless possible to determine those elements which dominate his essential nature even at that time. Merritt Hughes's clear warning against 'kidnapping' Donne in our own modern preconceptions still exhorts us to see Donne as he wished to be seen. Behind the restlessness and the chafing in Donne there was a yearning for constancy.... In Donne's restatement of Paul's joyous fulfilment of Christ suffering in his own flesh for the Body's sake, Donne expressed a Calling that, in the received forms of his Faith, fulfilled his yearning for constancy.

Walton's chronicle of Donne's final days, an account which his modern counterpart R. C. Bald regards as unexceptionable [see Additional Bibliography] suggests that Donne's faith was fulfilled in his death. But death does not compromise his abiding sense that the Body of Christ, the physical and spiritual community that contributes to the constancy of Donne's mature being, would continue to span heaven and earth after his death. Though Donne himself was spiralling closer to his circular God, whose mercy ever moved perpendicularly above the believer, he recognized even in his last acts the responsibility to other participating members. Donne's relationship to the community was not always so resolved, and his life on the circumference of his temporal circle was not always so fulfilled. In the third satire there is the incompleted search for a 'true religion, the injunction to 'doubt wisely' in a progress spiralling upward ('about must goe') to Truth on a 'huge' hill. In '**A Valediction: forbidding Mourning**,' its calmness a marked contrast to other love poems of Donne, is expressed the conviction that mutual love bonded by spiritual union can make an individual, private circle just. And in '**Goodfriday, 1613. Riding Westward**' he affirms the need for affliction to turn his sinful soul in its circular, westward movement back to its eastern origin, in conformity with the suffering Christ. However, in Donne's maturity, in his priestly Calling, he did achieve a personal assurance and constancy that fulfilled life along the circumference of his circle. In his assurance of his conformity with Christ, he offered his bodily presence to fulfil Christ's suffering for the sake of the communal Body. And in his literary works he embodied his sense of the epistemological and psychological immediacies that make up that confirmity.

To conclude, it is in the two major artifacts in his last remains, the sermon **Deaths Duell** and the death effigy in St Paul's, that we can find the final measure of the Calling that fulfilled his life. The sermon, although it now lacks the startling ambience centred in the dying man, still leaves its deep imprint on readers in the way it emboldens the problems of mortality and time. The death effigy likewise leaves its imprint, with its composed face accepting the inevitability of death. Donne would have appreciated time's witty justification of his personal value for the Body; the marble effigy remains, but the original building was destroyed by fire. Many modern readers would say that both the sermon and the effigy, like his other literary works, have outlasted the system of belief that inspired Donne. Yet it is not too fanciful to suggest—and we can perhaps appreciate this irony better than Donne—that his artifacts still inform a kind of Body in so far as they unite us in asking that we know and feel the large forces that shape us. That Donne's own works accomplish this successfully, often in the most immediate ways, make them a coherent and understandable achievement that can be said to help fulfill life on the circumference of time's circle. (pp. 195-200)

Terry G. Sherwood, in his Fulfilling the Circle: A Study of John Donne's Thought, *University of Toronto Press, 1984, 231 p.*

DENNIS J. McKEVLIN (essay date 1984)

[*In the following excerpt, McKevlin discusses Donne's efforts to reconcile the material and the spiritual aspects of life in his poetry.*]

In his essay "Meditative Action and 'the Metaphysick style'" [in *The Poem of the Mind* (1966)], Louis Martz proposes that "recent studies" by S. L. Bethell and Joseph Mazzeo suggest a closer reconsideration of Samuel Johnson's classic view of metaphysical poetry. Johnson's view, probably familiar to all, discovered the particular hallmark of metaphysical poetry to be the "combination of dissimilar images, or the discovery of occult resemblances in things apparently unlike" [see excerpt dated 1779]. "The most heterogeneous ideas," he goes on to say, "are yoked by violence together; nature and art are ransacked for illustrations, comparisons, and allusions." The "recent studies" alluded to in Martz' essay represent the independent research of Bethell and Mazzeo in the early 1950's, linking the theory of correspondences with the nature of metaphysical poetry. These critics [in *The Cultural Revolution of the Seventeenth Century* (1951) and *Aspects of Wit and Science in the Renaissance* (1931) respectively] suggest that a fruitful inquiry may be made on the basis of an examination of the theories of poetic wit develped during the seventeenth century by men like Baltasar Gracian and Emmanuele Tesauro. Bethell's investigation deals especially with human wit as the quasi-divine aptitude to apprehend analogies which the creator has left potentially inherent in nature and to express them in terms of the "urbanely fallacious argument." Mazzeo has named the theory which underlies such a process the "poetic of correspondences." The poetic of correspondences implies that there is, on the one hand, a network of universal analogies for the poet to perceive and to express in metaphor and, on the other hand, a supreme correspondence between the activity of the Creator and His living metaphor in the creative activity of man. (pp. 2-3)

Part of Donne's religious and intellectual heritage was, of course, this sense of basic unity between the human and the divine. The mystery of the Incarnation had reasserted the presence of the divinity in creation and, through the sacramental system, that presence had permeated earthly life. In Donne's era, however, the disruption of the medieval synthesis based upon faith and the fragmentation of the universal Church demanded that man assume a new attitude toward his universe and define the creative part which he was able to play in its shaping. "It is highly important for metaphysical poetry," Duncan writes [in his *The Revival of Metaphysical Poetry* (1969)], "that the system of correspondences both inspired further analogical reasoning and provided the methods and tools for it. Since correspondences were regarded as both literal and meaningful, logical analogy could be thought of as an instrument for discovering truth."

I am suggesting, therefore, that in the *Songs and Sonets* John Donne is conceptually creating the vision of a world of human love in which the divine and human are brought together analogously not through an appeal to faith or supernatural grace but through man's capacity to actualize the potentialities inherent in the system of universal correspondences. (p. 3)

Donne's *Elegies*, of course, deal with human love and in so doing they sometimes introduce a mixture of theology and carnality, and they involve the application of the system of universal correspondences; they are, in fact, sometimes similar in tone and subject matter to some of the lyrics in the *Songs and Sonets*. Their treatment of human love is, however, all too human. The glorification of physical love which can transform a soft bed into a hallowed temple, interpret a geographical map as a chart to the treasures of paradise, or raise a lover above the intrigues of the court is still bound within the confines of an earthly paradise. There is no development of the theme that the love between man and woman may lead to a union of the *human* and the divine.

Donne's religious poetry, on the other hand, often reflects the humble penitence and contemplation of a man who has resolved the conflict between matter and spirit and whose heart has come to rest in the love of the Creator. His images are, of course, still those of politics, was and earthly love because the religious poet still lives in the material world; they are, however, no longer used as guides in a search for union but as metaphors for a unity which man has already begun to experience. The web of universal correspondences is present in this kind of poetry, certainly, but it is seen as a reflection of the unity which its analogies had previously only implied. In religious poetry, moreover, the strong sense of individuality, commonly associated with the Renaissance, is necessarily diminished. (p. 101)

The world of the *Songs and Sonets* . . . lies midway between the merely physical love of man for woman and the love of man for God; it describes that love which is primarily rational and which effects a union analogous to the processions within the Trinity. In the *Songs and Sonets* Donne achieves in this manner, the conceptual union of the human and the divine. The world, of human love, the Restricted Maximum of Donne's vision, takes cognizance of both flesh and spirit and, by expressing them in proper proportion, brings about a resolution of opposites. By virtue of his participation in the *filiation Dei*, Donne has imaginatively restructured the universe, marred and disor-

ganized by fallen man's mistaken sense of values, around the focal point of rational love, restoring it to its preternatural balance.

The basis for Donne's perception of proper relationships is the system of universal correspondences which rests, in turn, upon the immanence of God in all creation. Thus all creation, in its lowest and its highest forms, is the fitting subject for the poetic expression of Donne's vision of reality. Through the urbanely fallacious argument, irrational love is presented in proper perspective. Rational love, however, in which man reaches his closest correspondence to divinity is the basis for the conceptual restructuring of the cosmos. For if divine activity is eternal, infinite, subsistent and creative, rational mutual love must participate relatively in these qualities as it is purified of imperfections. In the *Sermons* and the *Divine Poems* Donne expresses the search for direct union with God. In the *Songs and Sonets* he expresses, through the system of universal correspondences, the bliss of mutual human love which, in its analogy with the divine, brings together the individual, the cosmos and God; and this he achieves through an intellectual act which participates in the creative power of God. (p. 102)

> *Dennis J. McKevlin, in his* A Lecture in Love's Pholosophy: Donne's Vision of the World of Human Love in the "Songs and Sonets," *University Press of America, 1984, 115 p.*

DAVID M. SULLIVAN   (essay date 1987)

[*In the following excerpt, Sulllivan focuses on the death metaphor in the poem "Goodfriday 1613: Riding Westward."*]

East and west are the most important compass points in Donne's symbolic and poetic landscape. Images of maps appear frequently in his work, mostly in his *Divine Poems* and in his sermons. East is consistently associated with Christ and the Resurrection, west with death. These ideas are not unique to him. [In "'Good-friday, 1613. Riding westward' The Poem and the Tradition," published in *ELH* in 1961.] A. B. Chambers shows in some detail that a long line of Christian geographical symbolism, beginning with Zachariah and extending through the imaginative literature of the Church Fathers into the Renaissance, preceded him in making these same associations.

In the tradition and in Donne's poetry the map metaphor works like this: we are born in the east, and like the sun we are delivered into our grave in the west; but death means resurrection from death, the circle is completed by a kind of fiat, and west automatically becomes its opposite, the east, this time as the eternal joy of heaven. We can watch this symbolism working in one of Donne's finest religious lyrics, the **"Hymne to God my God, in my sicknesse"**:

> Whilst my Physitians by their love are growne
> Cosmographers, and I their Mapp, who lie
> Flat on this bed, that by them may be showne
> That this is my South-west discoverie
> *Per fretum febris,* by these streights to die,
>
> I joy, that in these straits, I see my West;
> For, though theire currants yeeld returne to none,
> What shall my West hurt me? As West and East
> In all flatt Maps (and I am one) are one,
> So death doth touch the Resurrection.

The "South-west discoverie," Clay Hunt says, "refers to the discovery of the navigational passage which the merchant explorers had sought for generations, an ocean passage to the Orient" [see Additional Bibliography]. He means the Straits of Magellan, the stormy passage the navigator discovered on his way west to the Pacific and the Philippines, where he died. In a similar way, the speaker knows, he must pass "through the strait of fever," as the Latin phrase has it, on his journey west and to death, whose "currants yeeld returne to none." But he joys to see his west because touching death he touches its opposite. "Take a flat Map," says Donne, "a Globe *in plano,* and here is East, and there is West, as far asunder as two points can be put: but reduce this flat Map to roundnesse, which is the true form, and then East and West touch one another, and are all one...." As Hunt puts it nicely,

> He does not regret that the currents will allow him no return from his passage, and he is not afraid to face the hardship and danger which he may expect as he goes farther into the West that now opens before him.... He thinks of the West (death) simply as the region that he must pass through to arrive at the East (resurrection and the joy of eternal life in heaven), the goal which all men have dreamed of and which truly adventurous men have actually sought.

It is in this general sense that the symbolism of **"Goodfriday, 1613. Riding Westward"** has traditionally, and rightly, been understood. So far so good. But "Riding Westward" was a colloquialism of Donne's time that meant literally "going to Tyburn"—going to hang on the Middlesex gallows, sometimes called Tyburn tree, located in the west end of London on the west bank of the Tyburn tributary. The speaker of this poem is a man condemned to die, and riding out, in no uncertain terms, to be executed. To appreciate the drama of this poem we must read it as it was understood by Donne's contemporaries, who would have recognized in it the elaborate conceit so highly dated that it has become lost since, and with it part of the poem's coherence and wit. (pp. 1-2)

I wish to cite this passage from the sermon ... that Donne preached upon Easter Day 1619, on this text from Psalms 89:48: "What man is he that liveth, and shall not see death?"

> Wee are all conceived in close Prison; in our Mothers wombes, we are close Prisoners all; when we are borne, we are borne but to the liberty of the house; Prisoners still, though within larger walls; and then all our life is but a going out to the place of Execution, to death. Now was there ever any man seen to sleep in the Cart, between New-gate, and Tyborne? between the Prison, and the place of Execution, does any man sleep? And we sleep all the way; from the womb to the grave we are never throughly awake; but passe on with such dreames, and imaginations as these, I may live as well, as another, and why should I dye, rather then another? but awake, and tell me, sayes this Text, *Quis homo?* who is that other that thou talkest of? *What man is he that liveth, and shall not see death?*

It pleased Donne to think of death as an execution. This idea is not necessarily a conceit: insofar as to be a Christian means to imitate Christ, it has an historical justification in the Crucifixion; and some correspondence, actual or symbolic, in the manner of dying, was, for Donne, both inevitable and good. Such a view of death, I am arguing,

is the controlling metaphor of **"Goodfriday, 1613. Riding Westward"** and a key to understanding it.

"Goodfriday" falls into two parts, and in each the meaning of death is different. It is first of all a dramatic poem: it records a change of mind, as the Holy Sonnets do frequently. The first part, which constitutes the bulk of the poem, ends with a series of rhetorical questions. While they are being asked, a change of heart occurs and the rider resolves to embrace the kind of death, literally or symbolically, that his religion and faith require.

As the poem opens, the rider betrays that he is dying a kind of spiritual death. Pleasure and business have taken over from devotion and the proper rule of his soul and are whirling him away from the risen Christ of the east, on whom the rider's attention is fixed, and toward the west, distancing him, as he perceives it, from his true faith. ... Chambers shows that Donne has reversed his cosmology. The primum mobile, in a tradition stretching far back into abtiquity, was always westward in motion. Its influence on the spheres, whose motions were naturally recalcitrant and desired to turn eastward, forced them to whirl westward with it. It was the same with the soul. The rational faculties of the soul were also, like the primum mobile, naturally "westward" in motion. They compelled the irrational faculties of the soul to whirl with them against the inclinations of their own baser nature. Whereas, in the traditional cosmology, it was natural for the rider to be carried toward the west, here Donne makes the motion of the first mover naturally eastward in direction in order to emphasize that death is the consequence of the rider's betrayal. Behind and above him in the east, the risen Christ hangs bloody, ragged, and torn. The speaker's predicament is that he cannot, or will not, turn his face to the east: he is afraid to die. ...

Though my interpretation of this poem, emphasizing the nature of punishment and expiation, is fundamentally different from that of Chambers, who analyzes it in terms of the nature of the soul, I agree fully with his observation that at this point the "westward journey ... becomes not a rational movement but a departure from the Christian path, a turning from light to enter the ways of darkness." I agree, too, that the rider, at once both Donne and Everyman, "must be pierced, must assume the 'rag'd and torn' apparel of God, and must then be scourged of the deformity thus put on"

The journey westward is both right and wrong. I am assuming that for Donne it is right because, as a follower of Christ, he is naturally, ineluctably, pursuing the path which Christ took as a mortal man—westward to death and execution. Of the inevitability of his end the rider is painfully aware. The journey is wrong, on the other hand, because he is at this moment afraid to meet his fate. Again, we must interpret the essential ambiguity of the poem in terms of Crucifixion. For the rider, the Crucifixion—his Tyburn, if you will—means both the agony of his physical death and his death to the pleasure and business of the world which have usurped the operation of his soul. For Donne and the poets of his time, the word "sun" could hardly pass from pen to paper without a thought that the reader would immediately check for a play on the well-worn tradition that associated sun with Son, by an effective cosmological analogy, as the two rulers of the heavens. When meditating on the agony of the Crucifixion, the speaker acknowledging that it made "the Sunne winke," he is only too conscious of the physical and spiritual pain he himself must undergo in order to die fully into his faith. Being able to behold the east means being able to make this leap, and he finds the thought of it excruciating:

> Could I behold those hands which span the Poles,
> And tune all spheares at once, peirc'd with those holes?
> Could I behold that endlesse height which is
> Zenith to us, and to'our Antipodes,
> Humble below us? or that blood which is
> The seat of all our Soules, if not of his,
> Made durt of dust, or that flesh which was worne
> By God, for his apparell, rag'd, and torne?
> If on these things I durst not looke, durst I
> Upon his miserable mother cast mine eye,
> Who was Gods partner here, and furnish'd thus
> Halfe of that Sacrifice, which ransom'd us?

In posing these questions, however, he becomes able to answer them. He finds that he can meet his religion on its own terms, for we find that in the next few lines, the second and concluding part of the poem, the speaker is anticipating his punishment with resolution and even eagerness:

> Though these things, as I ride, be from mine eye,.
> They'are present yet unto my memory,
> For that looks towards them; and thou look'st towards
>   mee,
> O Saviour, as thou hang'st upon the tree;
> I turne my backe to thee, but to receive
> Corrections, till thy mercies bid thee leave.
> O thinke mee worth thine anger, punish mee,
> Burne off my rusts, and my deformity,
> Restore thine Image, so much, by thy grace,
> That thou may'st know mee, and I'll turne my face.

When the speaker recognizes that his westward journey is good—"I turne my backe to thee, but to receive/ Corrections"—he accepts the destiny of Christ as man; and in this acceptance and awareness of it he becomes, as it were, fully awake: "was there ever any man seen to sleep in the Cart, between New-gate, and Tyborne? between the Prison, and the place of Execution, does any man sleep? And we sleep all the way; from the womb to the grave we are never throughly awake...." The rider is now "conscious." He now sees his death, physical and spiritual, as a punishment which redeems.

Christ is a military figure in this poem, at least inasmuch as Nature is "his owne Lieutenant." And Christ himself, of course, was the victim of a state execution, crucifixion being the punishment commonly reserved for traitors and slaves. He was a traitor by Roman law and paid with his life for the crime. In this sense, the rider is like Christ: for he also is, or was, a traitor, by virtue of his weakness to pleasure and business which he admitted at the outset. Hence his desire for punishment: to be redeemed from fire by fire. By a kind of irony it is Christ, however, who will become his executioner. The moment of his freedom becomes the moment of his ultimate captivity. The speaker resolves the dilemma of his western movement like this: he accepts the consequences of proceeding westward as necessary, even though they mean spiritual and eventually physical death. He accepts them because the punishment which is consequent upon his spiritual death will reform him, just as the fact of his physical death will mean eventually his resurrection. I believe that, for Donne, to turn

one's face to the east is possible only after death; for it is presumably only on Resurrection Day that Christ will reappear to the eyes. In making his plea for dissolution, the speaker finds some solace in what Chambers calls his "devotional memory." By this means, as a guide to repentance, the Christian can contemplate the spectacle of the Crucifixion by such imperfect means as are available to him.

When Donne rode westward on the day he composed this poem, as seems fairly certain, he was meditating on several important matters. He was about to enter holy orders—a step he had delayed until he could be sure his mind was set wholly on heavenly things. He was about to die, he must have felt, to a whole way of life. Perhaps it struck him as a strange coincidence, even as a kind of fate, that the eve of his conversion was Good Friday. The speaker of this poem, whether Donne or not, is a man sentenced to die. "That [Christ] was crucified with his face towards the West," says Sir Thomas Browne, "we will not contend with tradition and probable account..." This is the significance of the subtitle and such phrases as "carryed towards the West," "as I ride," and "punish mee." I do not believe that the poem dramatizes the meditations of a man actually being carted off to Tyburn, only symbolically, insofar as he is Everyman, and inasmuch as he is, in a minor key, by imitation, Christ himself, as I have tried to show. This poem records a crucial moment in the man's moral life when he becomes fully conscious of his dying, yet manages to meet it with humility and acceptance, though not without fear and tremblling. He accepts that to ride westward is not only inevitable but finally more good than bad, since that was the path Christ himself took, who suffered a real death, both before and during the execution, and who yet knew, paradoxically, that in his case, as in the case of all those who, like the rider, imitate Christ, death means life. (pp. 3-7)

> *David M. Sullivan, "Riders to the West: 'Goodfriday, 1613',"* in John Donne Journal: Studies in the Age of Donne, *Vol. 6, No. 1, pp. 1-8.*

WILLIS SALOMON   (essay date 1988)

[*Salomon is an American educator. In the following excerpt, he seeks to demonstrate that "Aire and Angels" is "an 'argument' for the relation between two context of Love: the 'metaphysical,' which defines amatory experience in terms of ultimates; and the 'rhetorical,' defines it in terms of concrete situations."*]

Donne's **"Aire and Angels"** presents certain interpretive problems, especially in its closing six lines. For some readers, the poems' ending cynically announces the "disparitie" between the love of men and women with an almost haughty air of masculine superiority. For others, however, the ending suggests not alienated gender relations, but perfect love. Each reading, I think, mishandles the ending, because neither considers the importance of the lightness of tone introduced into the poem with the announcement at line 26 of the "disparitie" between the love of men and women. This "lightness" results primarily from the speaker's return to the direct address of the beloved. Throughout the poem, the speaker involves himself with the problem of love's proper disposition. The return to direct address in the last six lines asserts in the poem the dynamic, experiential quality of active courtship after twenty-two lines of tortuous metaphysical invention. Approached in this way, **"Aire and Angels"** becomes neither simple cynicism nor elevated panegyric, but rather an "argument" for the relation between two contexts of love: the "metaphysical" which defines amatory experience in terms of ultimates; and the "rhetorical," which defines it in terms of concrete situations.

The relation of metaphysics and motive in **"Aire and Angels"** requires viewing the poem as a transaction between a purposeful speaker and the audience whom he addresses. For the speaker's reconciliation of amatory desire with the form of the universe is itself an attempt at amatory persuasion, and not only an attempt to define love. In the first stanza, the speaker directly addresses his beloved, whom he has perceived as "some lovely glorious nothing," that is, as an "angel." . . . Donne opposes her "spirituality" to her bodily presence as the addressee of courtly compliment. The speaker seizes on his idea of the lady's angelic transcendence and muses on how to bring her into corporeal being. One might easily tend, in the face of his argumentative assertiveness, to consider only its definitional logic. But doing so exclusively ignores the poem's primary tension between the substance of the speaker's argument and it's implied purpose. The speaker argues to a flesh and blood woman that her "nothingness," or incorporeality, must be embodied by means of his love. He compares this potential embodiment to the habitation by his soul of his body. But as the stock Petrarchan reference to the lady's physical appearance ("lip, eye, and brow") suggests, the body that love "must take" is hers; active courting forms the rhetorical situation here. In this way, the discussion of the lady's tenuous metaphysical existence obscures the speaker's concrete desire and its hoped-for consummation.

In the second stanza, however, we see that Donne does not simply intend to oppose metaphysical seriousness with the desires of the body:

> Whilst thus to ballast love, I thought,
> And so more steddily to have gone,
> With wares which would sinke admiration,
> I saw, I had loves pinnace overfraught,
> Ev'ry thy haire for love to worke upon
> Is much too much, some fitter must be sought;
> For, nor in nothing, nor in things
> Extreme, and scattring bright, can love inhere;
> Then as an Angell, face, and wings
> Of aire, not pure as it, yet pure doth weare,
> So thy love may be my loves sphaere;
> Just such disparitie
> As is twixt Aire and Angells puritie,
> 'Twixt womens love, and mens will ever bee.

The first eight lines question the possibility of an exclusively physical love. The last six lines of the poem could be expected to resolve these definitional problems. What makes **"Aire and Angels"** so interesting, however, is that the expectation of a definition of achieved, perfected love is subverted as the poem closes. The proportional metaphor of the closing passage plays on the concept of "puritie," the speaker's love being more "pure" than the lady's as an "angel" is more pure than its airy embodiment. In this way, Donne unifies the lovers as an emblem of love. But, at the same time, the optative force of "So thy love may be my love's sphaere" strongly suggests wooing, and it occurs as a direct address, a mode to which the poem

has returned after retreating into meditation. The possibility of amatory union is undercut by the closing reference to the continuing "disparitie" . . . "'twixt womens love and mens." In this way, Donne contrasts the ideal of love's union with the assumption that love must act on often contradictory impulses.

Thus the ending of **"Aire and Angels"** combines a conception of the lovers as "inhering" in each other with one that implies separation and acts on it. Dialectical reasoning foils the language of courtship, as the description of love's union in these last six lines is itself part of a courtly performance. But this is not to say that the poem ends simply as a disguised seduction argument. Donne pits the elaborate attempts to place love in the abstract against the more concrete implications of the poem's tone and mode of address. **"Aire and Angels"** does finally arrive at the definition of love sought by its complex dialectical turns. But that definition is the "disparitie" between men and women, the situation that motivated the speaker in the first place. The elaborate attempts at definition of love themselves attest to the "problem" they try to solve—that love relations constitute a continuing "disparitie" in which perfect union is more ideal than real. **"Aire and Angels"** in this way ends with a witty acknowledgment of the circumstances of its own genesis. But the announcement of this "disparitie" does not amount to cynicism at the end of the poem, because Donne shows how participation in love's ritual provides the fertile basis for the invention and scrutiny of a metaphysic of love. (pp. 12-14)

> *Willis Salomon, "Donne's 'Aire and Angels'," in* The Explicator *Vol. 46, No. 4, Summer, 1988, pp. 12-14.*

ADDITIONAL BIBLIOGRAPHY

Bald, R. C. *John Donne: A Life*. New York and Oxford: Oxford University Press, 1970, 627 p.
> Valuable detailed biography.

Bennett, Joan. "John Donne: 1571-1631" and "Donne's Technical Originality." In her *Four Metaphysical Poets: Donne, Herbert, Vaughan, Crashaw*, pp. 17-35, 36-57. Cambridge: Cambridge University Press, 1934.
> Surveys Donnes career and examines the poet's "most important innovations," his techniques.

Bewley, Marius. "Religious Cynicism in Donne's Poetry." *The Kenyon Review* 14, No. 4 (Autumn 1952): 619-46.
> Holds that the "Songs and Sonets, in their inculcation of an outrageous cynicism, in their abuse of religious imagery, in their distortion of scholastic philosophical concepts, in their cavalier employment of logic, represent many years in Donne's private guerrilla warfare against the dispositions of faith."

Bredvold, Louis I. "The Naturalism of Donne in Relation to Some Renaissance Traditions." *The Journal of English and Germanic Philology* XXII, No. 4 (1923): 471-502.
> A "study of the youthful Donne as a 'revolutionist in love,' . . . a more thorough analysis than has yet been presented of his audacious and singularly modern philosophy of that subject, and a discussion of some similar developments of thought in the Renaissance with which Donne may have been acquainted."

————. "The Religious Thought of Donne in Relation to Medieval and Later Traditions." In *Studies in Shakespeare, Milton, and Donne*, pp. 191-232. New York: Macmillan Co., 1925.

Examines "certain aspects of [Donne's] intellectual and religious experience, his mingled scepticism and mysticism, with the double purpose of tracing his religious development and of re-stating, with special emphasis on some hitherto neglected phases, his relation medieval thought."

Brodsky, Joseph. "Elegy for John Donne." *Triquarterly*, No. 3 (Spring 1965): 87-92.

Quiet-toned poem depicting Donne and all the world asleep in death, awaiting the dawn of the final resurrection.

Cathcart, Dwight. *Doubting Conscience: Donne and the Poetry of Moral Argument*. Ann Arbor: University of Michigan Press, 1975, 199 p.

Explores the questions of conscience evident in Donne's poems.

Coffin, Charles M. Introduction to *The Complete Poetry and Selected Prose of John Donne*, by John Donne, edited by Charles M. Coffin, pp. xvii-xxxvi. New York: Modern Library, 1952.

Short biography and critical overview.

Coleridge, Samuel Taylor. "Letters." In *Coleridge's Miscellaneous Criticism*, by Samuel Taylor Coleridge, edited by Thomas Middleton Rayor, pp. 139-45. 1936. Reprint. Folcroft, Pa.: Folcroft Press, 1969.

Comments upon the wit, tone, and vigor of several of Donne's letters.

Crofts, J. E. V. "John Donne." *Essays and Studies* 22 (1937): 128-43.

Approaches Donne as a man whose poetry reflected an age of decay and languor.

Doebler, Bettie Anne. *The Quickening Seed: Death in the Sermons of John Donne*. Edited by James Hogg. Salzburg Studies in English Literature under the Direction of Erwin A. Stürzl: Elizabethan and Renaissance Studies, vol. 30. Salzburg, Austria: Institute für Englishe sprache und literatur, Universität Salzburg, 1974, 297 p.

Studies the treatments of death in Donne's sermons and how they illuminate Donne's spiritual odyssey.

Dowden, Edward. "The Poetry of John Donne." In his *New Studies in Literature*, pp. 90-120. London: Kegan Paul, Trench, Trubner & Co., 1895.

A biographically based discussion of Donne's major poems.

Duncan, Edgar Hill. "Donne's Alchemical Figures." *ELH* 9, No. 1 (March 1942): 257-85.

Seeks "analyze the alchemical figures in Donne's poetry against a background of the theories and practices of alchemy as recorded in the compendious literature of the science current in the late sixteenth and early seventeenth centuries."

Eliot, T. S. "The Preacher as Artist." *The Athenaeum*, No. 4674 (28 November 1919): 1252-53.

Reviews *Donne's Sermons*, finding the sermons well selected and valuable while remarking on the qualities of Donne's development in this genre.

————. "The Metaphysical Poets" In his *Selected Essays,* pp. 241-50. New York: Harcourt, Brace & World, 1950.

Considered one of the signal works of twentieth-century poetry criticism, this study was markedly influential in stirring interest in Donne and his school. Eliot's essay, originally published in 1921 as a review of H. J. C. Grierson's *Metaphysical Lyrics and Poems of the Seventeenth Century*, essentially holds up to the twentieth-century reader the value of metaphysical poetry.

Fiore, Peter Amadeus, ed. *Just So Much Honor: Essays Commemorating the Four-Hundredth Anniversary of the Birth of John Donne*. University Park and London: Pennsylvania State University Press, 1972, 291 p.

Critical studies by such scholars as David Daiches, John T. Shawcross, Roger Sharrock, and William Empson.

Gardner, Helen, ed. *John Donne: A Colletion of Critical Essays*. Englewood Cliffs, N. J.: Prentice-Hall, 1962, 183 p.

Reprints key essays by such scholars as George Saintsbury, C. S. Lewis, Louis L. Martz, and J. B. Leishman.

Grant, Patrick. "John Donne's *Anniversaries*: New Philosophy and the Act of the Heart." In his *Literature and the Discovery of the Method in the English Renaissance*, pp. 77-101. London: Macmillan, 1985.

Close reading of the *Anniversaries*.

Guss, Donald L. *John Donne, Petrarchist: Italianate Conceits and Love Theory in the "Songs and Sonets"* Detroit: Wayne State University Press, 1966, 230 p.

Relates *Songs and Sonets* "to the dominant poetical tradition of Donne's time—that is, to Petrarchism."

Hoover, L. Elaine. *John Donne and Francisco de Quevedo: Poets of Love and Death*. University of North Carolina Studies in Comparative Literature, No. 61. Chapel Hill: University of North Carolina Press, 1978, 226 p.

Explores "the intellectual a well as the stylistic particularities that characterize the love poetry of two of the outstanding poets of the Baroque."

Hughes, Richard E. *The Progress of the Soul: The Interior Career of John Donne*. New York: William Morrow and Co., 1968, 316 p.

Traces Donne's life as an expression of "a mind discovering itself, and in the process standing as a dramtization of today's flight from loneliness and toward a fulfilling participatory experience."

Hunt, Clay. *Donne's Poetry: Essay in Literary Analysis*. New Haven and London: Yale University Press, 1954, 253 p.

Closely scrutinizes several poems and then proceeds to draw from them "some general conclusions and speculations about Donne's work and about Donne himself."

Husain, Itrat. *The Dogmatic and Mystical Theology of John Donne*. London: Society for Promoting Christian Knowledge, 1938, 149 p.

Examines in detail Donne's theology.

John Donne Journal: Studies in the Age of Donne I— (1982—).

Biannual periodical edited since its inception by Donne scholar M. Thomas Hester. Each issue carries scholarly essays on Donne's work and on that of such contemporaries as William Shakespeare, Ben Jonson, Inigo Jones, and George Herbert, as well as reviews of recent books on "the age of Donne."

Kermode, Frank. Introduction to *The Poems of John Donne*, by John Donne, edited by Frank Kermode, pp. xi-xxi. New York: Heritage Press, 1970.

General biographical and critical overview.

Lewalski, Barbara Kiefer. *Donne's "Anniversaries" and the Poetry of Praise: The Creation of a Symbolic Mode*. Princeton: Princeton University Press, 1973, 386 p.

Attempts "to identify and analyze some of the traditions and habits of . . . which gave rise to the *Anniversary* poems and their distinct symbolic mode."

Lewis, C. S. *English Literature in the Sixteenth Century, Excluding Drama*, pp. 469 ff. Oxford: Oxford University Press, Clarendon Press, 1954.

Harsh criticism of Donne's *Satyres, Elegies,* and verse *Letters,* but high praise for the *Songs and Sonets.*

Louthan, Doniphan. *The Poetry of John Donne: A Study in Explication.* 1951. Reprint. Westport, Conn.: Greenwood Press, 1976, 193 p.
> General reading of Donne's poetry.

Manlove, C. N. "Donne and Marvell." In his *Literature and Reality: 1600-1800,* pp. 3-15. New York: St. Martin's Press, 1978.
> Surveys the highlights of Donne's poetry, arguing that Donne "shows how much he is prepared to refuse the awkwardness and the multiple truth of the real world for the singleness of a mental one in his poetry."

Moloney, Michael Francis. *John Donne: His Flight form Medievalism.* Urbana: University of Illinois Press, 1944, 223 p.
> Biographical and critical study that seeks to trace in Donne's life and work reflections of an era of transition between the medieval age and "the naturalism of the New Age."

Mueller, William R. *John Donne: Preacher.* Princeton: Princeton University Press. 1962, 264 p.
> Close reading of Donne's sermons and identification of their stylistic characteristics.

Pinka, Patricia Garland. *This Dialogue of One: The "Songs and Sonnets" of John Donne.* University: University of Alabama Press, 1982, 193 p.
> Analyzes "the *Songs and Sonnets* through the personae in the poems."

Pope, Alexander. *Anecdotes, Observations, and Characters, of Books and Men. Collected from the Conversation of Mr. Pope, and Other Eminent Persons of His Time,* edited by Rev. Joseph Spence, pp. 22 ff. London: W. H. Carpenter, 1820.
> Very brief, scattered remarks on Donne's poetry.

Quiller-Couch, Sir Arthur. "John Donne." In his *Studies in Literature, first series,* pp. 90-100. Cambridge: Cambridge University Press, 1937.
> Short, admiring critical biography.

Richards I. A. "The Interactions of Words." In *The Language of Poetry,* pp. 65-87. Princeton: Princeton University Press, 1942.
> Examines Donne's *Anniversaries* and "A Valediction: forbidding mourning" to elucidate the way "through which words, by uniting, bring new beings into the world, or new worlds into being." Richards compares Donne's poems to selected poems by John Dryden, W. B. Yeats, and T. S. Eliot.

Roberts, Donald Ramsay. "The Death Wish of John Donne." *PMLA* LXII, No. 4 (December 1941): 958-76.
> Argues that Donne had a "positive wish to die" and "that it was persistent, even lifelong, and that a full understanding of this wish throws considerable light not only upon Donne's temperament and certain of his actions, but also upon certain aspects of his works and philosophy...."

Roston, Murray. *The Soul of Wit: A Study of John Donne.* Oxford: Clarendon Press, 1974, 236 p.
> Textual analysis of Donne's poetry. Roston argues "that the lively humour, the overt flippancy, the teasing reversals of argument, and the brash impudence of his libertine posing fulfil a central function in expressing with subtle tangetialism his own satisfaction with the scientism of his day."

Roussel, Roy. "Women and Fleas: The Argument of Seduction." In his *The Conversion of the Sexes: Seduction and Equality in Selected Seventeenth- and Eighteenth-Century Texts,* pp. 10-36. New York and Oxford: Oxford University Press, 1986.
> "Femocentric" study of "the experience of pleasure as a form of interruption" in Donne's poetry.

Saintsbury, George. Introduction to *Poems of John Donne,* Vol. I, by John Donne, edited by E. K. Chambers, pp. xi-xxxiii. London: George Routledge & Sons, 1896.
> Selective survey and generally glowing appraisal of Donne's poetry.

Sanders, Wilbur. *John Donne's Poetry.* Cambridge: Cambridge University Press, 1971, 160 p.
> Insightful interpretation of the poems and discussion of Donne's critical heritage.

Simpson, Evelyn M. *A Study of the Prose Works of John Donne.* Oxford: Oxford University Press, Clarendon Press, 1924, 367 p.
> Attempts "to give a clear and detailed account of the prose works of John Donne, and to show that a knowledge of these is essential to the right undrstanding of his life and character."

Smith, A. J. ed. *John Donne: Essays in Celebration.* London: Methuen & Co., 1972, 470 p.
> Studies of Donne's work by Barbara Hardy, Sydney Anglo, and D. W. Harding, among others.

Spencer, Theodore, ed. *A Garland for John Donne, 1631-1931.* Cambridge: Harvard University Press, 1931, 202 p.
> Essays on Donne's life and work by Mario Praz, John Hayward, John Sparrow, and several others. T. S. Eliot's contribution to this collection is excerpted above.

Spitzer, Leo. "Three Poems on Ecstasy (John Donne, St. John of the Cross, Richard Wagner)." In *Essays on English and American Literature,* by Leo Spitzer, edited by Anna Hatcher, pp. 139-79. Princeton: Princeton University Press, 1962.
> Takes up "The Extasie," along with poems by Wagner and St. John of the Cross, "in order to study the magic transformation which actual words of the particular language have undergone at the hands of the poets who have succeeded in making their inner experience a poetic reality for the reader."

Sprott, S. Ernest. "The Legend of Jack Donne the Libertine." *University of Toronto Quarterly* 19, No. 4 (July 1950): 335-53.
> Refutes the Long-held perception of Donne as "the witty talker, the glittering social star, and the reckless playboy."

Stampfer, Judah. *John Donne and the Metaphysical Gesture.* New York: Funk & Wagnalls, 1970, 298 p.
> Explication of Donne's poetry, seeking to apprehend its "peculiar personal poignance, one not of unfolding imagination, but in [Donne's] pinched immediate situation, in the poet's grasp for salvation, love, order, sexual fulfillment, against a crumbling universe of reference."

Stein, Arnold. *John Donne's Lyrics: The Eloquence of Action.* Minneapolis: University of Minnesota Press, 1962, 244 p.
> Attempts "to gain some insight into the integrity of Donne's poetic mind, and this purpose requires taking seriously two propositions: that Donne is a poetic logician endowed with a talent and love for the unity of imaginative form; and that Donne's poetry, though it is not simple, nevertheless deeply and persistently engages important problems which concern 'simplicity.'"

Summers, Claude J., and Pebworth, Ted-Larry, eds. *"Bright Shootes of Everlastingnesse": The Seventeenth-Century Religious Lyric.* Columbia: University of Missouri Press, 1987.
> Contains essays presented at a 1984 symposium by R. V. Young, Mary Ann Radzinowicz, M. Thomas Hester, and Claude J. Summers.

Symons, Arthur. "John Donne." In his *Figures of Several Centuries,* pp. 80-108. London: Constable and Co., 1916.
> Originally published in 1899 as a review of Edmund Gosse's *The Life and Letters of John Donne.* Symons provides a fa-

vorable general essay on Donne's poetry, arguing that Donne "forgot beauty, preferring to it every form of truth, and [that] beauty has revenged itself upon him, glittering miraculously out of many lines in which he wrote humbly, and leaving the darkness of a retreating shadow upon great spaces in which a confident intellect was conscious of shining."

Turnell, Martin. "John Donne and the Quest for Unity." *The Nineteenth Century* CXLVII, No. 878 (April 1950): 262-74.
   Discovers an affirmative answer to the following two questions: "Can we discover any single theme underlying the constant shift and change of mood in the *Songs and Sonets*? If so, is there any theme which is common to all [Donne's] best work?"

Tuve, Rosemund. *Elizabethan and Metaphysical Imagery: Renaissance Poetic and Twentieth-Century Critics.* Chicago and London: University of Chicago Press, 1947, 436 p.
   Study of imagery in the nondramatic poetry of the English Renaissance, with numerous references to Donne's poetry.

Unger, Leonard. *Donne's Poetry and Modern Criticism.* Chicago: Henry Regnery Co., 1950, 91 p.
   Examines signal works of modern Donne criticism (by Allen Tate, Cleanth Brooks, Rosemund Tuve, T. S. Eliot, and John Crowe Ransom, among others) that employ the term "metaphysical," surveying "some of the literature embraced by it, to make the category tighter and clearer, or else to discover that it is unfit for categorical pretension—at least beyond its historical origin."

Warren, Austin. "The Very Reverend Dr. John Donne." In his *Connections,* pp. 1-10. Ann Arbor: University of Michigan Press, 1970.
   Focuses on Donne in his roles as theologian and preacher.

Webber, Joan. *Contrary Music: The Prose Style of John Donne.* Madison: University of Wisconsin Press, 1963, 227 p.
   Examines Donne's prose "in the light of the traditions he knew" and shows "how and why he made of them what he did."

Williamson, George. "The Nature of the Donne Tradition." In his *The Donne Tradition: A Study in English Poetry from Donne to the Death of Cowley*, pp. 20-57. 1930. Reprint. New York: Noonday Press, 1958.
   Seeks to identify the characteristics of Donne's poetry, examining Thomas Carew's elegiac poem (see excerpt dated 1633) as a key to understanding it.

Yeats, W. B. Letter to H. J. C. Grierson. In his *The Letters of W. B. Yeats,* edited by Allan Wade, p. 570. London: Rupert Hart-Davis, 1954.
   Appreciative letter, written 14 November 1912 after obtaining a copy of Grierson's edition of Donne's poems. Yeats offers high praise to Donne.

Henry VIII

1491-1547

English essayist and lyricist.

Henry VIII—fixed in the popular imagination as the rotund monarch with the many wives, the man who virtually single-handedly initiated the English Reformation, the king responsible for numerous executions, including those of two wives and of England's premier man of letters, Sir Thomas More—is rarely thought of as an author. Yet he composed several songs: secular ballads celebrating love, friendship, and revelry, and religious masses and motets. He wrote a theological treatise, *Assertio septem sacramentorum (An Assertion of the Seven Sacraments)*, and may have been the author of *A Glasse of the Truthe*, a propagandist essay in favor of the king's divorce from Catherine of Aragon. Henry's small canon is completed by personal letters—most notably love letters to Anne Boleyn—and his annotations to and revisions of several important Reformation formularies of faith.

Henry was born at the royal palace at Greenwich, the second son of Henry VII and Elizabeth of York. While details of his education are lacking, the known facts of his elder brother Arthur's education and the evidence of Henry's own achievements and talents make its content and scope fairly certain. One of his principal tutors was the satirical poet John Skelton; under Skelton and others Henry received a thorough grounding in the classics, history, mathematics, languages (including Latin, Greek, and French), and music. The young prince also underwent rigorous physical training, excelling at riding, jousting, hunting, hawking, and archery. Ten-year-old Henry became heir to the throne in 1502 when Arthur, newly married to Princess Catherine of Aragon, unexpectedly died. As it was generally assumed that in due time Henry would wed Arthur's young widow, a papal dispensation was sought and received toward this end; Henry's father, however, repeatedly deferred the marriage. In 1509 Henry VII died and his son became Henry VIII of England. One of his first acts as king was to marry Catherine.

The early reign of "bluff King Hal" was famous for spectacle and ostentation but little active statecraft. Only seventeen at his accession, Henry found himself king of a politically stable and unusually wealthy realm, competently managed by ministers inherited from his father's reign. During these years, England's internal politics and foreign policy were dominated by Thomas Wolsey, who, starting as the royal almoner, rose during the first part of Henry's rule to become Archbishop of York and, in 1515 (also the year he was made a cardinal by Pope Leo X), Henry's lord chancellor. It was Wolsey who planned and orchestrated English statecraft, particularly foreign affairs, while Henry pursued his various amusements. (Henry did, on occasion, exercise royal control, but only sporadically, content for the most part to rely on his trusted Wolsey.) Thus was Henry, strikingly handsome and athletic in his youth, free to indulge his taste for the extravagant and his enthusiasm for sports, banquets, dances, tourneys, games, pageants, and revels of all kinds. Above all, Henry cherished music, becoming an enthusiastic patron of composers, musicians,

Henry VIII

and singers. He was himself an accomplished musician, excelling on the lute, organ, and virginals. During this early period of his reign, Henry composed several songs. Perhaps his best known is "Pastime with Good Company," a celebration of youth, companionship, and innocent pleasure. He also wrote love songs, including "Green Groweth the Holly," a lover's protestation of constancy to his lady. Among Henry's religious compositions are masses and the motets "O Lord the Maker of All Things" and "Quam pulchra es." In 1511 a son was born to Henry and Catherine; seven weeks later he died, the first in a series of infant deaths, stillbirths, and miscarriages that plagued the royal couple during the years of their marriage. Biographers and historians credit Henry's exuberance and love of chivalry and pageantry with his decision—the first major decision of his reign—to war with France. The first campaigns, starting in 1512, were indecisive, as indeed were all the many wars, and threats of war, that followed in the years to come. Thus Henry was chiefly occupied with foreign affairs during the early part of his reign, as England played an active role in the complicated power politics and shifting alliances of sixteenth-century Europe. Henry showed his love of splendor in one of the most spectacular events associated with his reign: his meeting with Francis I of France in 1520 at the Field of the Cloth of Gold near Guines, France. Henry and Catherine arrived at the rendezvous—intended as a grand show of amity between the two monarchs—with a retinue of five thousand. The field was resplendent with thousands of tents, pavilions, and a summer palace constructed specially for the event. For weeks, the notables of England and France celebrated their new-found (and, as it happened, short-lived) friendship with jousting and feasting.

Henry's first prose work, the Latin treatise *An Assertion of the Seven Sacraments*, was inspired by his indignation over German Protestant reformer Martin Luther's 1520 theological treatise, *De captivitate Babylonica ecclesiae praeludium (On the Babylonian Captivity of the Church, 1883)*. Luther's challenges to the Roman Catholic Church, begun in 1517 with the posting of his famous *Disputatio pro declaratione virtutia indulgentiarum (The Ninety-Five Theses, 1873)* in Wittenberg, had thrown all of Europe into a tumult as the Protestant revolt grew and the ecclesiastical status quo that had obtained for centuries was threatened. In *The Babylonian Captivity*, Luther struck at the very heart of Catholic orthodoxy, denying the sacramental nature of four of the seven Catholic sacraments: confirmation, marriage, ordination, and extreme unction. Henry, as an orthodox son of the church, a firm supporter of papal authority, and an amateur theologian, was appalled. *Assertion of the Seven Sacraments* is his refutation of a man he considered a dangerous, pernicious influence, an "infernal wolf." (Many contemporaries, including Luther himself, refused to believe that the book was really the work of the king, but most modern scholars agree that, though he may have received help in researching and organizing the work, *Assertion of the Seven Sacraments* is substantially Henry's.) Henry had the book sent to Rome, where it was presented to Pope Leo X in an elaborate ceremony. The pope was so impressed with Henry's championship of his cause that he granted an indulgence to every reader of the book and bestowed upon the king the honorific title Fidei Defensor, or Defender of the Faith. Henry, who had long coveted such an appellation (he was particularly piqued that Francis I was known as "Most Christian King"), received his new title—to this day used by British monarchs—with pride.

In general, the first fifteen years of Henry's reign were considered golden ones, characterized by bold forays into foreign affairs, and domestic tranquillity under the sponsorship of an intellectual and enlightened king. To the famous Dutch humanist Desiderius Erasmus, Henry's court was a mecca for the new learning, a haven for England's foremost men of letters, including Sir Thomas More, the noted author of *Utopia* (1516). In countless letters to friends and acquaintances, Erasmus praised the English king; in 1518 he wrote: "I would gladly move to a court like [Henry's].... The king is the most intelligent of the monarchs of our time and enjoys good literature.... The men who have most influence with [Henry and Catherine] are those who excel in the humanities and in integrity and wisdom.... What Athens or Stoa or Lyceum could one prefer to a court like that?"

Henry's personal life began to assume religious and political significance around 1525 or 1526. He and Catherine had produced no living children but the Princess Mary. Increasingly, Henry worried about the lack of a male heir

to succeed him. Along with this potential political crisis there existed a personal one: Henry had fallen in love with a young woman at court, Anne Boleyn, and was determined to marry her. Tentatively at first, Henry began to assert that it was against God's law, as stated in the book of Leviticus, for a man to wed his brother's wife, and thus his marriage with Catherine was invalid, papal dispensation or no; that Henry had no legitimate male heir was proof of God's displeasure with his incestuous liaison. Whether Henry sincerely believed this line of reasoning is uncertain. Many biographers surmise that, while at first he may have advanced his moral scruples purely for expediency, he eventually became truly convinced that his marriage was offensive to God. In 1527 the "King's Great Matter," as it came to be called, began in earnest. Over the next few years, Henry convened secret courts, sent urgent messages and learned ambassadors to Pope Clement VII requesting the dissolution of the marriage, assembled a phalanx of theologians and scholars to prove his case, appealed to the universities of Europe to find in his favor, and sparked an international debate on the issue. Theological disagreement centered around how the text in Leviticus was to be interpreted, especially in light of a seemingly contrary admonition in Deuteronomy, that it is a man's duty to wed his brother's widow, and the absorbing question of whether Catherine's short-lived marriage with the adolescent Arthur had ever been consummated (she insisted that it had not), and what bearing this might have on the case. The theological arguments became extremely abstruse, but in time the issue of the King's divorce began to take on an increasingly political cast. This is clearly shown in one pamphlet that was published in the king's defense, *A Glasse of the Truthe*. While the case for Henry's authorship of this work is not nearly so strong as that for *Assertion*, many scholars believe that Henry was full or partial author of it. In any event, he certainly agreed with the argument of *A Glasse of the Truthe*, which, in a dialogue between a lawyer and a divine, appeals to English patriotism in asserting that the pope was assuming excessive power, not only in issuing the original dispensation (invalid because it contradicted God's laws) but also in insisting upon the right to pronounce on Henry's case. That right, the author of *A Glasse* asserted, did not pertain to Rome; why should an English matter fall under Rome's jurisdiction? The case should be decided in England, and it should be decided in the king's favor for the good of England. Every English patriot should rally to the king's cause, for the begetting of a male heir for England hung in the balance.

Henry's countless embassies to Rome produced no definite results, nor even a definite signal of Clement VII's intentions. From England came several suggested solutions, including a plan for Catherine to enter a nunnery (foiled when she refused to do so) and the suggestion that Henry should be granted a papal dispensation for bigamy. In the meantime, Henry refused to see Catherine, sending her away and installing Anne Boleyn in her place. (Henry's love letters to Anne—nine in French, eight in English—date from this time, written during intervals they spent apart.) Anne was associated with a political faction which schemed for Wolsey's ouster; Henry, impatient with Rome's reluctance to grant him an annulment and inclined to blame Wolsey for it, withdrew his favor from the cardinal. Stripped of his office and much of his property, Wolsey was eventually arrested for "treason" but died of natural causes before his trial. He was replaced in office by Sir Thomas More. Henry's inconclusive wranglings with Rome continued, slowly ripening into the Henrician Reformation, as the king became increasingly determined to thwart papal authority and to gain control of the English church. In these endeavors, Thomas Cromwell emerged as Henry's principal policy maker. It was Cromwell who set in motion and supervised a propagandist campaign of pamphlets, sermons, plays, and popular pageants in support of Reformation ideas, and he who, with Henry's urging, was instrumental in inducing Parliament to pass a number of clerical reform laws, all of which had the effect of limiting ecclesiastical in favor of royal authority. This process culminated in 1532 in the so-called Submission of the Clergy, whereby the English clergy lost the right to independent legislation of clerical matters: all would now be subject to royal jurisdiction. More resigned the chancellorship the day after this legislation was enacted.

Meanwhile, Henry's divorce case was making no progress. Matters reached a crisis early in 1533 when it was discovered that Anne was pregnant; Henry married her secretly on January 25. Things moved quickly after that as Henry ceased dealing with Rome entirely and took matters into his own hands. Parliament decreed that cases were to be determined in the country of their origin without regard to any other authority. In May an English court, presided over by the Archbishop of Canterbury, Thomas Cranmer, declared Henry's marriage to Catherine invalid. (Clement responded by declaring Henry's marriage to Anne invalid and insisting, in vain, that Henry return to Catherine.) In September Anne gave birth, not to the male heir Henry so desperately wanted, but to a girl—Elizabeth. The following year Parliament passed the Act of Royal Supremacy, naming Henry supreme head of the English Church, subject to no authority under God. Henry's new supremacy was cemented by parliamentary laws and by numerous executions of opponents. The Act of Succession named Elizabeth heir to the throne (if sons should not be born), while the Princess Mary was disinherited (indeed, bastardized), as Henry's marriage to her mother was null and void. Many men, among them More and John Fisher, Bishop of Rochester, refused to take the compulsory oath to uphold the ecclesiastical supremacy of the king—and Parliament passed a law declaring this refusal to be treason, for which the penalty was death. More and Fisher were executed. (Both were canonized in 1935.)

The year 1536 was another watershed year in Henry's reign. Catherine died, forbidden to the last to see her daughter Mary. Anne was executed, condemned on charges of adultery. (She was not executed as Henry's wife, however, for a court headed by Cranmer declared the marriage invalid on the grounds that, because years before Henry had had an affair with Anne's sister Mary, the union was incestuous. So Elizabeth, in her turn, became a bastard.) Later that month Henry married Jane Seymour, formerly one of Anne's ladies-in-waiting. Henry began tentative negotiations to establish ties with the Lutheran princes of Germany and issued the first official statement of faith of the new ecclesiastical regime. This, *Articles Devised by the Kynges Highnes Majestie, to Stablyshe Christen Quietnes and Unitie amonge Us* (better known as the *Ten Articles*), closely followed Lutheran thought. Like subsequent Henrician formularies of faith,

the *Ten Articles*, though written by others, was subject to Henry's annotations and revisions. Also in 1536 began the dissolution of the monasteries, supervised by Cromwell. By 1540 English monasticism had been eradicated, with monastic lands and wealth reverting to the crown. In response to the dissolution of the monasteries, the divorce from Catherine, and the disassociation of the English Church from Rome, a series of uprisings, collectively known as the Pilgrimage of Grace, began in northern England in October 1536. This movement, according to J. J. Scarisbrick, "must stand as a large-scale, spontaneous, authentic indictment of all that Henry most obviously stood for." Although the participants, whose most notable leader was Robert Aske, tried to avoid open rebellion, emphasizing that they desired not to rebel against their king but to communicate with him, the Pilgrimage of Grace was forcefully extinguished and its leaders executed. This abortive uprising was the only organized domestic resistance to the religious and political upheaval of the Henrician Reformation.

In 1537 another English doctrinal prescription was published, *The Institution of a Christen Man* (popularly known as the *Bishops' Book*). In common with the earlier *Ten Articles*, the *Bishops' Book* is heavily influenced by Lutheran theology. Also in this year Henry's fervent hopes were finally fulfilled when Jane gave birth to a boy, Edward. Jane herself, however, died only days later. The year 1539 saw the passing of the Act of Six Articles, an orthodox statement of faith which seemed to reverse to some extent the trend toward Protestantism. At the same time, however, Henry was back in the marriage market and looking, on Cromwell's advice, toward a union that would cement ties with the German Lutheran princes. The choice for Henry's fourth wife finally settled on Anne of Cleves. At their first meeting, however, Henry found this new Anne not at all to his taste, though he reluctantly went through with the wedding early in 1540. But after six months of marriage his union with the "Flanders mare," as Anne was unflatteringly known, was dissolved on the grounds that Henry, not liking her, had not truly consented to the marriage and that this was proven by lack of consummation. (Another argument concerned a pre-contract apparently made on Anne's behalf several years before, but this argument does not appear to have been considered compelling even by those who made it.) Meanwhile, Cromwell was being hounded, as Wolsey had been, by political enemies who agitated for his downfall. Accused (though probably not guilty, according to historians) of heresy and treason, he was executed. On the day of Cromwell's death, Henry married nineteen-year-old Catherine Howard. She was condemned as an adulteress (on evidence historians generally find more convincing than that given in the Boleyn case) and executed in February 1542.

Thereafter, Henry increasingly returned his attention to affairs outside England, though these had not been completely neglected during the years of marital and religious turmoil. He had already, in the 1530s, legally incorporated Wales into the kingdom and laid the groundwork for his own royal rule in Ireland, achieved in 1541 when he was declared king by the Irish Parliament. Now he turned to Scotland (with no real success) and resumed the inconclusive squabbling with France that had characterized the early years of his reign. In 1543 there appeared the last of the Henrician formularies of faith, *A Necessary Doctrine and Erudition for any Christen Man*. This work, known as the *King's Book*, is more akin to Catholic orthodoxy than the theology of the *Bishops' Book*, testifying, as the earlier pattern of advance and retreat in the documents testified, that the Henrician Reformation—and Henry's own theology—was far from being a straightforward progression from Catholicism to Protestantism. Henry remained in many respects a traditionalist and was as suspicious of Protestant "heresy" as he was of Catholic "error." In fact, three years after his 1543 marriage to Catherine Parr, herself apparently an earnest Protestant, charges of heresy were brought against her with the king's compliance. Mysteriously, however, Henry chose not to impose any punishment and apparently lived amicably with this last Catherine for the remaining months of his life. He died in London in 1547. One of his principal biographers, Scarisbrick, has summed up his character and achievements thus: "Henry was a huge, consequential and majestic figure. At least for some, he was everything that a people could wish him to be—a bluff, confident patriot king who was master of his kingdom and feared no one. By the end of his long reign, despite everything, he was indisputably revered, indeed, in some strange way, loved. He had raised monarchy to near-idolatry. He had become the quintessence of Englishry and the focus of swelling national pride. Nothing would ever be quite the same after he had gone."

Henry has always excited interest for his fascinating personality and tumultuous personal life as well as for the momentous events of his reign. As an author, however, he is infrequently studied. Frequently, scholars treat his writings only in passing, or primarily as they relate to circumstances of Henry's life, the tenor of his thoughts, the progress of the Henrician Reformation, the political situation of his realm. Further, as Edmund Gosse has written, "the importance of Henry VIII's writings is considerably more anecdotal than positive": Henry's work is interesting chiefly, if not exclusively, because Henry VIII wrote it. This was true, to some extent at least, even in his own lifetime. *Assertion of the Seven Sacraments* was, in the words of Scarisbrick, "something of a best-seller" in its day, but doubtless much of its popularity was due to the prestige of its author and to the topicality of the Lutheran controversy. Another controversy fueled interest in *A Glasse of the Truthe*, which, like the earlier work, was praised or condemned along partisan lines. Subsequent critics, primarily historians of the Henrician Reformation and/or biographers of Henry, have generally agreed that both works are well written and convincingly argued productions of a competent amateur. Although the Reformation documents that Henry annotated and revised have not been the subject of "literary criticism" as it is generally understood, commentators find Henry's additions, deletions, changes, and marginal comments fascinating for the glimpse they afford of the king's theological and political beliefs. Similarly, Henry's letters are of interest as a window on his personal life. His only truly "creative" work, the songs, were highly popular and frequently performed at Henry's court. "Pastime with Good Company" quickly bacame a favorite throughout England, being sung in inns and alehouses, while the motets "O Lord the Maker of All Things" and "Quam pulchra es" became classics of English Church music. Modern critics of the songs, though few in number, affirm that Henry emerges from his musical age as a talented, competent composer and lyricist.

Certainly Henry's stature as one of England's most influential and intriguing monarchs enhances the value of his work. Just so, Henry's writings concurrently augment our vision of the king. While the historical significance of the king and the larger-than-life personality of the man must of necessity eclipse the writer, Henry's works are important testimonies to the mind and achievements of one of England's most famous—and infamous—monarchs.

PRINCIPAL WORKS

*Assertio septem sacramentorum adversus Martinum Lutherum hæresiarchon (essay) 1521

[*Assertio Septem Sacramentorum; or, An Assertion of the Seven Sacraments, against Martin Luther*, 1687; also published as *Defense of the Seven Sacraments against Martin Luther*, 1821]

*A Glasse of the Truthe: An Argument By Way of Dialoge, between a Lawyer and a Divine; That the Marriage of Henry VIII. with Catharine of Aragon Was Unlawful; and That the Cause Ought to Be Heard and Ordered within the Realm (essay) 1531

†Articles Devised by the Kynges Highnes Majestie, to Stablyshe Christen Quietnes and Unitie amonge Us, and to Avoyde Contentious Opinions, Which Articles Be Also Approved by the Consent and Determination of the Hole Clergie of this Realme [with others] (formulary) 1536

†The Institution of a Christen Man, conteynynge the Exposyton or Interpretation of the Commune Crede, of the Seven Sacramentes, of the .x. Commandementes, and of the Pater Noster, and the Ave Maria, Justyfication & Purgatory [with others] (formulary) 1537

†A Necessary Doctrine and Erudition for any Christen Man, Sette Furthe by the Kynges Majestie of Englande [with others] (formulary) 1543

Love-Letters from King Henry VIII. to Anne Boleyn (letters) 1714

Songs, Ballads and Instrumental Pieces Composed by King Henry the Eighth (songs) 1912

Miscellaneous Writings of Henry the Eighth, King of England, France & Ireland (essay, letters, songs, proclamations, and will) 1924

Henry VIII: Three Songs of His Own Composition (songs) 1936

Letters of King Henry VIII: A Selection with Other Documents (letters) 1937

*It has not been conclusively established that either of these essays is Henry's work. Most modern scholars believe that he is the primary, perhaps exclusive, author of *Assertion of the Seven Sacraments*. Establishing authorship of *A Glasse of the Truthe* is more problematic, and not all critics agree that Henry wrote it, even in part.

§While carried out under Henry's aegis, these works were not written by the king himself, though they contain his editorial marginalia and reflect, to varying degrees, his revisions. *Articles . . . to Stablyshe Christen Quietnes* is commonly known as *Ten Articles; The Institution of a Christen Man* as the *Bishops' Book;* and *A Necessary Doctrine and Erudition for any Christen Man* as the *King's Book.*

POPE LEO X. (essay date 1521)

[Leo X (born Giovanni de' Medici) was pope from 1513 until his death in 1521. It was during his pontificate that the German Protestant reformer Martin Luther began to challenge the doctrinal supremacy of the Roman Catholic Church. When Luther refused to recant his heresies, Leo excommunicated him; shortly thereafter, Henry wrote his denunciation of Luther, Assertion of the Seven Sacraments, *and sent the book to be formally presented to the pope. So pleased was Leo that he issued the following bull, in which he declares his appreciation of Henry's work and bestows upon the king the title of Defender of the Faith.]*

By the good pleasure and will of God Almighty, presiding in the Government of the Universal Church, though unworthy so great charge. We daily employ all our thoughts, both at home and abroad, for the continual propagation of the Holy Catholic Faith, without which none can be saved. And that the methods which are taken for repressing of such as labour to overthrow the Church, or pervert and stain her by wicked glosses and malicious lies, may be carried on with continual profit, as are ordered by the sound doctrine of the faithful, and especially of such as shine in regal dignity, we employ with all our power our endeavours and the parts of our ministry. And as other Roman bishops, our predecessors, have been accustomed to bestow some particular favours upon Catholic princes (as the exigencies of affairs and times required), especially on those who in tempestuous times and whilst the rapid perfidiousness of schismatics and heretics raged, not only preserved constantly in the true faith and unspotted devotion of the holy Roman Catholic Church, but also as the legitimate sons and stoutest champions of the same have opposed themselves both spiritually and temporally against the mad fury of schismatics and heretics.

So also we, for your Majesty's most excellent works and worthy actions done for us and this Holy See in which by divine permission we preside, do desire to confer upon your Majesty with honour and immortal praises that which may enable and engage you carefully to drive away from our Lord's flock the wolves, and cut off with the material sword the rotten members that infect the mystical body of Jesus Christ, and confirm the hearts of the almost discomforted faithful in the solidity of Faith. Truly when our beloved son John Clark, your Majesty's orator, did lately, in our consistory, in presence of our venerable brethren, cardinals of the sacred Roman Church, & divers other holy prelates, present unto us a book [*Assertion of the Seven Sacraments*] which your Majesty, moved by your charity (which affects everything readily and well), and enflamed with zeal to the Holy Catholic Faith, and fervour of devotion towards us and this Holy See, did compose as a most noble and wholesome antidote against the errors of divers heretics, often condemned by this Holy See & now again revived by Martin Luther. When I say he offered this book to us to be examined and approved by our authority, & also declared in a very eloquent discourse, that as your Majesty had by true reasons & the undeniable authority of Scripture & Holy Fathers, confuted the notorious errors of Luther, so you are likewise ready & resolved to prosecute with all the forces of your kingdom those who shall presume to follow or defend them. Having found in this book most admirable doctrine, sprinkled with the dew of divine grace, we rendered infinite thanks to Almighty God, from whom every good thing, and every perfect gift proceeds, for being pleased to fill with his grace, and to inspire your most excellent mind, inclined to all good, to defend by your writings his Holy Faith against the new broacher of these condemned errors; and to invite all other Christians, by your example, to assist and favour with all their power, the Orthodox Faith and Evangelical Truth, now under so great peril and danger.

Considering that it is but just, that those who undertake pious labours in defence of the Faith of Christ, should be extolled with all praise and honour: and being willing, not only to magnify with condign praise, and approve with our authority, what your Majesty has with learning & eloquence written against Luther, but also to honour your Majesty with such a title as shall give all Christians to understand, as well in our times as in succeeding ages, how acceptable & welcome your gift was to us, especially in this juncture of time. We, the true successor of St. Peter, whom Christ before his Ascension left as his Vicar upon earth, and to whom he committed the care of his flock, presiding in this Holy See, from whence all dignity and titles have their source, having with our brethren maturely deliberated on these things, and with one consent unanimously decreed to bestow on your Majesty this title, *viz:* Defender of the Faith. And as we have by this title honoured you, we likewise command all Christians that they may name your Majesty by this title; and in their writings to your Majesty that immediately after the word KING they add, DEFENDER OF THE FAITH. Having thus weighed and diligently considered your singular merits, we could not have invented a more congruous name, nor more wor-

Catherine of Aragon, first wife of Henry VIII.

thy your Majesty, than this worthy and most excellent title: which as often as you hear, or read, you shall remember your own merits and virtues. Nor will you by this title exalt yourself, or become proud, but according to your accustomed prudence, rather more humble in the Faith of Christ, & more strong and constant in your devotion to this Holy See, by which you were exalted. And you shall rejoice in our Lord, who is the giver of all good things, for leaving such a perpetual and everlasting monument of your glory to posterity, and shewing the way to others that if they also covet to be invested with such a title, they may study to do such actions and to follow the steps of your most excellent Majesty: whom with your wife, children, and all who shall spring from you, we bless with a bountiful & liberal hand; in the name of him from whom the power of benediction is given to us. And by whom Kings reign, and Princes govern, and in whose hands are the hearts of Kings.

Praying, and beseeching the most High, to confirm your Majesty in your holy purposes, and to augment your devotion: and for your most excellent deeds done in defence of his Holy Faith, to render your Majesty so illustrious & famous to the whole world, as that our judgment in adorning you with so remarkable a title, may not be thought vain, or light, by any person whatsoever. And finally, after you have finished your course in this life that he may make you partaker of his eternal glory. It shall not be lawful for any person whatsoever to infringe, or by any rash presumption to act contrary to this letter of our subscribing and command. But if anyone shall presume to make such attempt, let him know that he shall therefore incur the indignation of Almighty God, and of the Holy Apostles Peter and Paul. (pp. 34-7)

> *Pope Leo X, in a papal bull, in* Miscellaneous Writings of Henry the Eighth, *edited by Francis Macnamara, The Golden Cockerel Press, 1924, pp. 34-7.*

HENRY VIII   (essay date 1521)

[*In the following excerpt from his address to the reader of* Assertion of the Seven Sacraments, *Henry describes his reasons for defending the Church against Luther.*]

Although I do not rank myself among the most learned & eloquent; yet (shunning the stain of ingratitude & moved by fidelity & piety) I cannot but think myself obliged (would to God my ability to do it were equal to my good will) to defend my mother the spouse of Christ: which though it be more copiously handled by others; nevertheless I account it as much my own duty, as his who is the most learned, by my utmost endeavours to defend the Church, & to oppose myself to the poisonous shafts of the enemy that fights against her: which this juncture of time, & the present state of things, requires at my hand. For before, when none did assault, 'twas not necessary to resist. But now that the enemy (and the most wicked enemy imaginable) is risen up, who by the instigation of the Devil, under pretext of charity, stimulated by anger and hatred, spews out the poison of vipers against the Church & Catholic Faith; 'tis necessary that every servant of Christ, of what age, sex, or order soever, should rise against this common enemy of Christian Faith, that those whose power avails not, yet may testify their good will by their cheerful endeavours. (p. 40)

> *Henry VIII, "To the Reader," in his* Miscellaneous Writings of Henry the Eighth, *edited by Francis Macnamara, The Golden Cockerel Press, 1924, pp. 40-2.*

JEREMY COLLIER   (essay date 1708)

[*An English clergyman, Collier is chiefly remembered for his astringent attack on what he considered the licentiousness of the Restoration theater,* A Short View of the Immorality and Profaneness of the English Stage *(1698). In the following excerpt from his* Ecclesiastical History of Great Britain *(1708-14), he describes the intent and evaluates the success of* Assertion of the Seven Sacraments.]

[Henry VIII.] entered the lists against Luther, and published a book in defence of the seven sacraments [*An Assertion of the Seven Sacraments*]. Now because a royal divine, a king in controversy, is very unusual, I shall entertain the reader with part of the performance: it is dedicated to pope Leo X.

"In this address, your holiness may be surprised (says the king) to find a person bred to war and business of state, engage in a controversy of this nature, especially with a man that has spent his whole time in the improvements of learning." But notwithstanding his majesty owns himself somewhat unequally matched, yet the danger the Church was in by the spreading of heresy and schism, alarmed his zeal, and pushed him forward. That since the enemy appeared in the field, and overran the country with so much ravage and desolation, it was time to draw out against him. He was clearly of opinion, that no sincere Christian ought barely to look on, and stand neuter in the quarrel: and therefore, though his abilities were but moderate, he could not forbear engaging upon such motives. Besides, considering the circumstances of the case, he was willing to give the world a proof of his zeal for the Christian religion, and his regards to the holy see. And though his learning was but small, he hoped God would govern his pen and supply that defect. However, his majesty is pleased to say, he was not altogether unprepared for the contest. For being fully persuaded, that religion is the greatest support to the crown, and the best guide in civil administration, he had spent some time in that study. And that no part of learning entertained him better: and though the length of his progress had not been great, yet he hoped himself sufficiently furnished to inform the generality, and expose the fallacies in Luther's reasoning. It was in confidence of this issue that he had undertaken this dispute: that he had dedicated to his holiness to make the performance more public and serviceable. And that as his holiness had exerted his character, and disabled the heresy by the censures of the Church; so if either the prospect of interest, or the colours of argument, had still left an impression upon any persons, they might be convinced by counter-proof, and reasoned out of their mistake. That he chose to pitch upon this method, considering the nature of men was such that they had rather be led, than dragged. As to his success in the attempt, he should determine nothing, but refers that matter to his holiness; to whose censure and correction he likewise submits what he had written. (pp. 31-2)

As to the performance, the king seems to have the better of the controversy; and generally speaking to be much the sounder divine. Generally speaking, I say, his principles are more catholic, and his proofs more cogent. He seems superior to his adversary in the vigour and propriety of his style, in the force of his reasoning, and the learning of his citations. But then with due regard to his memory, it must be said his manner is not altogether unexceptionable: he leans too much upon his character, argues in his garter robes, and writes as it were with his sceptre. He gives rough language, sometimes treats Luther with contempt, and drives his invective pretty strong upon him. (p. 47)

> *Jeremy Collier, in an excerpt in his* An Ecclesiastical History of Great Britain, Vol. IV, *revised edition, William Straker, 1852, pp. 31-2, 47.*

JAMES ANTHONY FROUDE   (essay date 1856)

[*An English historian, Froude was the author of the influential, multivolume* History of England from the Fall of Wolsey to the Death of Elizabeth *(1856-70). Praised as the first comprehensive treatment of the Tudor period, the work is nevertheless faulted for Froude's evident bias in favor of the Reformation. In the following excerpt from this work, he views* A Glasse of the Truthe *as "a very picture of [Henry's] mind."*]

Henry's peculiar temper never allowed him to believe beforehand that a track which he had chosen could lead to any conclusion except that to which he had arranged that it should lead. With an intellect endlessly fertile in finding reasons to justify what he desired, he could see no justice on any side but his own, or understand that it was possible to disagree with him except from folly or ill feeling. Starting always with a foregone conclusion, he arrived of course where he wished to arrive. His *Glasse of Truth* is a very picture of his mind. "If the marshall of the host bids us do anything," he said,

> shall we do it if it be against the great captain? Again, if the great captain bid us do anything, and the king or the emperor commandeth us to do another, dost thou doubt that we must obey the commandment of the king or emperor, and contemn the commandment of the great captain? Therefore if the king or the emperor bid one thing, and God another, we must obey God, and contemn and not regard neither king nor emperor.

And, therefore, he argued, "we are not to obey the pope, when the pope commands what is unlawful." These were but many words to prove what the pope would not have questioned; and either they concluded nothing or the conclusion was assumed.

We cannot but think that among the many misfortunes of Henry's life his theological training was the greatest; and that directly or indirectly it was the parent of all the rest. If in this unhappy business he had trusted only to his instincts as an English statesman; if he had been contented himself with the truth, and had pressed no arguments except those which in the secrets of his heart had weight with him, he would have spared his own memory a mountain of undeserved reproach, and have spared historians their weary labour through these barren deserts of unreality. (pp. 269-70)

> *James Anthony Froude, "The Parliament of 1529: The King's Book," in his* History of England from the Fall of Wolsey to the Death of Elizabeth, Vol. I, *1856. Reprint by Charles Scribner's Sons, 1895, pp. 268-70.*

THE DIAL   (essay date 1907)

[*In the following excerpt, the anonymous reviewer comments on Henry's love letters.*]

A curious little book, fraught with interest both as a historical study and a human document, is the collection of the *Love-Letters of Henry VIII. to Anne Boleyn*. . . . A perusal of the letters shows Henry in the character of a fairly ardent though not passionate lover, with a strong tendency to moralize and to lay emphasis upon the practical rather than the sentimental aspects of his affection. There is nothing here to kindle Anne's cold heart, but much to assure her of her royal lover's devotion, and of his pious dependence upon divine Providence to bring their affairs to a happy issue. These emotions seem a little forced in view of the facts, and the colorless phrasing is due, possibly, to the fact that more than half of the letters were written in French. Besides, Henry lived before the dawn of the art of letter-writing. He evidently regards correspondence as a mere necessary means of communication, and does not dream of being personal or expansive in a letter. His scholarship shows only in a polished style and in chance bits of Latin; while of the wit and versatility that made Erasmus wonder, there is no sign. So there is nothing in these rather commonplace epistles to cause the most sensitive reader to raise a cry of confidence violated. And yet, as a work of a moral monster and a great king, the collection is not without a unique interest for modern readers, though most of that interest must be read between the lines.

> *A review of "Love-Letters of Henry VIII to Anne Boleyn," in* The Dial, *Vol. XLII, No. 495, February 1, 1907, p. 81.*

FRANCIS MACNAMARA   (essay date 1924)

[*The following excerpt is taken from Macnamara's preface (called "ingeniously irrelevant" by a reviewer in the* Dial*) to his edition of Henry's miscellaneous writings. Here, he spiritedly defends Henry's actions and character, reconciling the king's apparent inconsistencies.*]

The writings of Bluebeard? It sounds like a joke! Had this monster any thoughts beyond his appetites, and what value can they have for us to-day? Well, it is strange that Englishmen have so little curiosity as to that title of their kings [Defender of the Faith], which is stamped on every coin they carry in their pockets; they know that it was won by Henry VIII., and won at a time when theological discourse exercised the keenest intellects of Europe, yet of the work thus crowned they know nothing at all, and of the author only that he had six wives—or was it eight wives and was he Henry VI.? Pardon, they know also that he chopped off the heads of some of them! But grotesque as this knowledge may be, it somehow serves to keep Henry very much alive in the English mind: if we take a glance at that period of history, we see his father and his son but dimly in the mists of the past, while Bluebeard stands out between them, a bold figure in the full light of day. And it is a very warm light for such a cold-blooded monster to appear in! (p. 7)

The attitude of Englishmen towards this King of theirs may be described as one of amused bewilderment, not so much at any doings of his, as at the absence of hate or even disapproval in themselves; they find themselves much more inclined to love him, & do not know whether to be ashamed or not. All the world loves a lover, of course; but then that axe! Nor is this the only seeming contradiction in his character; those of us who reached the sixth form are aware that Henry VIII. established the English Church in independence of Rome, but also that he addressed to Rome a condemnation of Luther's revolt. It has generally been concluded either that his mind underwent an extraordinary change, or (as more credible) that his early professions were insincere; though what his motive was in the latter case is not suggested. But why then is Sir Thomas More not accused of insincerity, who within a like period of writing his *Utopia*, perhaps the most Protestant work in the English language, died a martyr for the Catholic Faith? The parallel is very remarkable, indeed the only way to get a true idea of Henry is to study him in relation to Sir Thomas More, so long his most intimate friend; they represent a perfect antithesis, and together seem to constitute a whole mind, as it were the two sexes in combination. While More was making his philosophic defence of liberty in the *Utopia*, Henry was defending religious discipline in his **Assertion of the Sacraments**; and when Henry was imposing his own supremacy on the Church, More was dying for the idea of individual submission. It would almost seem that in the interval not these men, but the world, had turned upside down, so that what at first had been philosophy was later religion; which would mean that the philosophic More & the religious Henry, both alike, could only maintain their characters by abandoning their early professions.

Nor is the turning upside down of the world such a fantastic notion as it sounds; it has a meaning which is not only very simply stated, but which is also the only possible meaning of the Protestant Reformation; for when it is found that forms no longer express the ideas with which they are identified, it is necessary for the sake of those ideas to reject the forms, meaning that the religious man will oppose all that to which the name of religion is attached—unless, in the words of Tennyson, 'faith unfaithful keep him falsely true.' Henry's **Assertion of the Sacraments** and More's *Utopia* were both written in a mediæval England, that is to say, before Luther's criticism of religious forms had possessed the English mind, and while religion so-called was still accepted as religion indeed; thus More as the philosopher stood for the relaxation of those forms, which Henry's religious mind delighted to insist on. Then came the idea of religion as faith in the inner light, in the spontaneous impulse of the individual rather than the traditional doctrine of the universal Church; and this being accepted, the religious Henry was only consistent in defying the faith he had defended, as was the philosophic More in maintaining the forms he had questioned.

To challenge Henry's sincerity without also challenging More's is plainly illogical, yet this is what is commonly done; the preposterous assertion being made, that Henry forced Protestantism on England, simply to gratify a lust for Anne Boleyn; as if any king could so tyrannise any people! The English were already proverbial in Europe for independence of mind, nor had Henry any armed force with which to impose his wishes on them; it would have been utterly impossible for him to pass the Act of Supremacy, had he not been giving expression to a strong feeling in the country. The difference in the judgment of history

Anne Boleyn, second wife of Henry VIII.

on the two men can only be due to the circumstance that More died a martyr; which seems to prove him a good man, in contrast to Henry who went on to live a libertine, apparently. (pp. 7-9)

But though sentiment, backed by moral training, disposes us to think of More as the good man, while we have no accepted standards by which to justify Henry, it is a fact that our vision of Henry is brighter; he seems to radiate light as a sun, and as a sun to hang self-supporting in space; while in contrast we see More as a dark & heavy groundling, a most virtuous man certainly, but still a man only. If the religious Henry pursued pleasure, and Luther came out of his monastery and took a wife, it was because God in the sixteenth century was in jovial mood; while More for the same reason wore a hair-shirt, in order as a philosopher to assert the free and independent dignity of man, the particular will opposed to the general. Again, if Henry kept the headsman busy, it was because God was impatient of obstructions in his road, having a new & mettlesome idea between the shafts of his chariot; an idea that was not to be reined in for any philosophic policeman, and so galloped over More as over the adulterous queens, in true Old Testament style.

His people always knew Henry as a lover, in spite of the dripping axe; indeed tradition is strangely obstinate on the point. There is a sceptre in existence, which antiquarians declare to be Scotch and of an earlier period; but just because there is a dove on the end of it, tradition persists in calling Anne Boleyn's sceptre. She whose head her lover took off is still the Queen of Love! The fact is that love is terribly moral, when it is concentrated on one person at a time; it was because Henry's love was of this kind that he was a Protestant and puritan, just as the King of France was a Catholic & formalist because he loved the sex at large. François premier was content to observe the form of marriage, while he took his pleasure with his mistresses; and so he had no divorce problem to bring him into conflict with the Pope. But Henry did not love primarily for pleasure, the passion of service was strong in this descendant of the Welsh serving-man; and such love is given not merely to the beauty of a woman, her external and transitory charm, it is given rather to the woman she shall grow into years hence, in a word, to her productiveness. Whatever qualities his wife might develop, Henry would bind himself to love & cherish; but in return she also must regard marriage as a service, her special duty being to give an heir to the throne of England. In this duty Catherine of Aragon failed, and Henry looked for another woman to perform it; but only after patiently enduring repeated disappointments, through miscarriages & deaths of sickly infants, during which this young & lusty King devoted himself to his wife with a romantic loyalty, such as was often sung of by mediæval troubadours, but never before was realised by any King in Christendom. (pp. 9-11)

Who is the great figure in our literature most resembling Henry VIII., what poet had three wives and wrote a book in favour of divorce? the puritan Milton! the least sensual of all Englishmen! Is it such a paradox, then, to call Henry VIII. a puritan; is not this rather the very character we should expect in the founder of English Protestantism? But if this argument serves to reconcile the axe with the dove, how did the puritan divorcer ever defend the sacramental idea of marriage? Why, it is just the sacramental character of marriage that Milton asserts! he would reject the outward and visible form for sake of the inward and spiritual grace, meaning a power in nature to hold people together, a lust of memory delighting in the familiar, at least as strong as the lust of sense delighting in the new. The law only arose to record this fact in nature, and so when the law becomes an imposition on nature its basis is gone; it is time then to seek the original idea of marriage at its source, nor will any shrink from the appeal to nature who have faith in the sacramental character of the form. This is the fundamental idea of the English Church, itself a divorce from universal Christendom; and so it is no accident that its establishment dates from the divorce of Catherine of Aragon. The Pope was truly infallible in the title he gave to Henry, but it was more in the divorce of Catherine than in the *Assertion of the Sacraments* that Henry proved his faith; the book was as it were the apprenticeship ofimitation, that every poet must serve before he can utter the creative word. Henry may be considered as saying first to the Pope, 'Certainly marriage is a sacrament,' and then as going on to say, 'For this very reason it takes more than the sexual act to constitute a marriage.'

This was the point on which Henry and Milton were at one, they would not admit that a marriage was necessarily valid, if the only ground of annulment allowed by the Canon Law was absent, namely unfitness of either party for sexual union. Nor were their own grounds of annulment so different from one another as they seem, for both amounted to a plea that the marriage was not made in heaven; which would mean consequently that the lust of memory was absent from the beginning, though neither used this phrase actually. Milton pleaded that in his marriage there was no companionship, no conversation of souls; but if that mysterious sense of affinity between persons is analysed, it is found to be a sense of common origin, such as makes the intimacy of brother and sister. Thus the pair are not only held together by memory, they are brought together by it in the first place; and it is only on this condition that the lust of memory will dominate the lust of sense, and marriage have its true sacramental character. Henry's plea was at bottom the same as Milton's, only he pointed to the evidence of facts rather than to a personal feeling; the fact that no son of his marriage had been reared seemed to him to prove that the marriage was not made in heaven. In support of this he could not only quote the Old Testament, but could point to the fact in nature, that a mating is only fruitful when there is identity of species; which is just another way of saying that without a common origin there can be no lust of memory, and consequently no true marriage. (pp. 13-14)

[If] Henry VIII. had merely stood for division of the Church, the ground would have crumbled beneath his feet; he had to find in that division an opposite idea of unity, if he was to confront Europe as the head of a whole nation, and command the sympathies of other nations. This idea had already been found for him, the mysterious idea of a unity born of division, and was formally represented by the mediæval Empire; which stood in opposition to the Church, the representative of unity produced normally by combination. The paradox of the Empire is not so difficult, if one considers that the idea of Empire is a self-sufficient whole, and that this can only be founded on self-sufficiency in the parts; the Holy Roman Empire had its roots in the feudal manor, the estate producing its own necessities, & growing rich by creating values rather than by importing those recognised. Thus it represented the genius of man, and stood as a great pyramid of natural rank; while the Church represented the gentleman against the genius, calling on the individual to submit himself to universal reason or humanity, our own watchword in the recent war. The imperial idea of genius is what the Germans opposed to ours when they talked of Kultur; there are only these two ideas in this or any other world, and they are set forth for us, the one in the Old Testament and the other in the New.

The gentleman is the average of all the specialities of genius; he is produced by combination in successive generations of the male with another the female, ever moderating the individual assertiveness of the original; whence the tenth earl is held to be a more perfect gentleman than the first, who was created for his genius. And so the Tudor dynasty, as a new creation, would naturally belong more to the party of the Empire than to that of the Church; though Henry VIII. only became conscious of this when he came to assert the individual genius of England against the universal humanity of the Church, a purely intellectual organisation by then. Again, as the Empire stood for temporal power, that is to say, for the spontaneous impulse of genius, for the King as the best man of his people at any moment, it was natural for Henry as the apostle of Time to address his appeal to the Emperor; he is only condemned by the standards of the Church, the cruel monster appears in the light of the imperial idea a scourge in the hand of God, who as creator is for ever ruthlessly destroying his own creations. The sacrifices which Henry claimed, the death of More for example, were such as the Divine Father claimed of his Son: and the Church of course was on the side of the Son, maintaining the philosophic idea of the New Testament against the religious idea of the Old, maintained by the Empire.

This should be enough to show that there was more than intrigue with big battalions in the letter which Henry addressed to the Emperor Charles V., in justification of his defiance of a papal summons; it might almost be called the charter of the British Empire. (pp. 16-17)

Henry's development is illustrated by the order of the works in this volume, which is roughly chronological. First comes the *Assertion of the Sacraments,* in which he maintains the indissoluble form of marriage, in an address to the Pope, as representing the rational discipline of individual impulse. Then come the love-letters to Anne Boleyn, in course of which he discovers in nature the inward & spiritual grace of marriage; these being followed by the songs, in which the new-born faith finds ecstatic utterance. Then comes the letter to the Emperor, in which he defies the authority of the Church, and rallies to the banner of spontaneous religion. Then come two proclamations to his people, in the first of which he exhorts them in their pleasure to prepare for war, the liberator of genius; and in the second of which he provides against the silting up of the Thames, that the operations of his beloved navy may not be interfered with. Finally there is his last will & testament, in which he confirms his life's work by establishing the succession on the child of Jane Seymour, the son in whom God had blessed his third marriage. If critics find that the character given to Henry in this preface is based on insufficient evidence, they will be only understating the case, for it is not based on evidence at all, but on direct perception of the man; this was indicated at the beginning, when we spoke of the light in which he appears. The method is that of legend rather than of history, the faculty is that used by the folk; it hardly requires an apology in these days, when history so often has to acknowledge the truth of folk-lore, which previously it had despised. (pp. 20-1)

> *Francis Macnamara, in a preface to* Miscellaneous Writings of Henry the Eighth, *edited by Francis Macnamara, The Golden Cockerel Press, 1924, pp. 7-21.*

SIR EDMUND GOSSE, C.B. (essay date 1925)

[*A distinguished English literary historian, critic, and biographer, Gosse wrote extensively on seventeenth- and eighteenth-century English literature. His commentary in* Seventeenth-Century Studies *(1883),* A History of Eighteenth Century Literature *(1889),* Questions at Issue *(1893), and other works is generally regarded as sound and suggestive, and he is also credited with introducing the works of the Norwegian dramatist Henrik Ibsen and other Scandinavian writers to English readers. In the following excerpt, he discusses the origin and purpose of* Assertion of the Seven Sacraments *and comments briefly on Henry's letters to Anne Boleyn.*]

Our regret that Henry VIII. disdained the use of the vernacular is increased by what we are told of the excellence of his Latin style. His biographers are unanimous in praising it, and Gairdner says that "if his arguments were mean, his Latin was king-like." Indeed, it was so far above the level of what kings were supposed to be capable of, that popular rumour attributed the composition of the [*Assertion of the Seven Sacraments*] to Richard Pace, Wolsey's right-hand man, who was supposed to inspire the King's foreign policy. But evidence is all against this legend, and Henry VIII. was quite clever enough to write his own thesis. (pp. 14-15)

The King's interest in dialectics, and his tentative attitude with regard to Rome, were awakened by the publication of a book which thrilled the whole of Christendom. He was already a Thomist, a practised student of the Schoolmen, although it is probable that their controversies presented themselves to his restless mind in a certain light of futility. But his zeal might have continued to be academic, if he had not been roused by his poet-laureate, Bernard Andree, to watch the movements in Germany of the new reformers and in particular of one Martin Luther, who had become the centre of rebellious activity.

Henry VIII. was finally drawn into the controversy which was revolutionising Europe, by the issue of Luther's famous *Babylonish Captivity of the Church,* a squib which blazed up into a volcano in 1520. The King, under suggestion from Andree and Wolsey, wrote to the Pope, Leo X., to tell him that he proposed to devote his leisure to "the defence of Christ's Church with his pen," and the Pope was enchanted, politically as well as ecclesiastically, at having found so brilliant a champion. (pp. 15-16)

It must be borne in mind in reading the *Seven Sacraments* that Henry VIII. had at this time developed no definite antagonism to the Papacy. In fact, he instinctively disliked the new-fledged Protestantism of Germany, and had formed no objection to the supremacy of Rome. But Luther had in the past three years greatly extended the scope and vehemence of his attacks, and had now reached a point where forgiveness was impossible, so that Henry VIII., who had watched the wrangling with Tetzel and even the burning of the bulls with indifference, perhaps indeed with some mischievous amusement, was genuinely alarmed at the attacks on the Roman interpretation of the Sacraments contained in Luther's latest work.

The *Babylonish Captivity* reduced the seven Sacraments by four, and retained only baptism, the Eucharist and penitence. There was, as Tunstal shudderingly said, "much more strange opinion in it, near to the opinions of Bohemia," that is to say, of Huss. Against this wave of the incoming tide of Reform, it must be confessed that the *Seven Sacraments* of Henry VIII. was no more effectual than was the mop of Mrs. Partington when she tried to stem the Atlantic. One of the King's most eminent admirers has frankly admitted that the book "reproduced, without novelty or energy, the old common-places of authority, tradition and general consent." The conservative world, indeed, was vastly delighted with it, but Luther was contemptuous. He compared the "Pharaoh of England" to a fat swine and a nettle-eating ass. How rude these theologians are to one another!

Marriage was one of the Sacraments rejected by Luther as being merely *de jure positivo,* ordained by the Pope and not binding on Christendom, and in view of the remarkable freedom with which Henry VIII. treated this Sacrament in later life, it is probable that the modern reader will turn to this chapter of his rather dreary book with more anticipation than to any other. Poor Queen Katharine had long been the victim of the indifference and the scorn of her tyrannical consort, but he had not yet formed the definite design of putting her away. He says:—

> Let us consider God the consecrator of this Sacrament. Has he not consecrated Marriage with his blessing, when he joined together our first parents? For the Scripture saith, "God blessed them, saying Increase and multiply." Whose blessing having operated in all other living creatures according to their several capacities; who shall doubt but that he has infused the force of spiritual grace into the spirit of man, who alone is capable of reason, unless he did believe that God should be so sparing of his blessings to man, whom he created after his own image, that having regard only to his body, he should omit the soul, that breath of life which he himself has breathed, and by which he was most represented, without imparting any part of that great blessing to it?

This seems a little confused in thought, but exemplary in sentiment. It is fair to admit that Henry VIII. to the end preferred a wife to a mistress, but whether in so doing he showed much reverence for the Sacrament of marriage, it must be left to the theologians to decide. (pp. 16-18)

We reach a very different order of ideas when we come to the letters addressed to Anne Boleyn. The character of this lady, still held so high in the eighteenth century, when Gray could write that,

> gospel-light first dawn'd from Boleyn's eyes,

has not worn well. We see in her a pretty young woman with little delicacy of instinct, and no strength of purpose. But the letters preserved in the Vatican by no one knows what strange chance, are curious documents. They contain no indication of time. . . . Anne's replies have all been lost, which is no great matter for regret. Henry's are downright and amorous, but not so outspoken as would be gathered from Brewer and others, who have been scandalised at the "gross allusions" in them. One cannot but feel pity for the girl who came to such a wretched end eight years later, in strict conformity, however, with Henry's famous Sacrament of Marriage. (p. 19)

> *Sir Edmund Gosse, "Bluebeard among the Authors," in his* Silhouettes, *William Heinemann Ltd., 1925, pp. 11-20.*

M. ST. CLARE BYRNE　(essay date 1936)

[*Byrne was an English author, playwright, and editor. The following excerpt is taken from her annotated edition of letters either written by Henry himself or composed at his command by secretaries. Here, Byrne discusses what she considers the forceful and distinctive prose style of the correspondence.*]

The only way to get any satisfaction out of these letters of Henry VIII is to read them. Dipping, skimming, gutting, tasting, and the various other processes that the skilled reader is accustomed to employ to circumvent Tudor long-windedness, will only produce boredom. There is nothing for it but to submit oneself to the intolerable

wordiness, immerse completely in the alien element, accept the whole preposterous convention. Read, word by word, and gradually ear and mind alike grow accustomed to the unendingly sustained rhythms, and the unfamiliar idiom begins to please. Despite their bewildering ramifications, sentences drive on and thrust through, with the strength and solidity of tree trunks half hidden beneath their abundant leafage. Apparent repetitions resolve into distinctness, impacting like hammer-blows.

All the vigour, the determination, the relentless pertinacity and the sheer force of the man speak eloquently in his style when it comes to its maturity. If some of the earlier letters are colourless and unremarkable, the later ones more than compensate in interest—especially, perhaps, those concerned with the Pilgrimage of Grace and the last phase of Scottish policy. There is an almost terrifying quality in the steady battering of the marshalled phrases, as week by week, month by month, year by year, these Scots letters, grim with implacable purpose, reiterate their demands.

Opinions vary about Henry's ability as a ruler. About the fixity of his aims, the strength of his will, and his capacity for concentration and hard work there can be no dispute. It is possible to dispute his wisdom, impossible to deny the power of the mind. And it is this power, this 'maistry', this concentrated will, that expresses itself more clearly than anything else in the style of his prose, and even in his very handwriting—highly individual, totally uncompromising, large, clear, steady and always unmistakably the same.

Power. Break it up into its components, and in Henry's case they will be energy and control. Look at his handwriting, and find them dominating the structure of every letter. Look at his alterations in a draft, and see the one breaking forth in long insertions, the other cutting down a superfluity of ambages with one ruthless stroke of the pen. Watch the vigorous exploration of fact and hypothesis throughout the intricacies of subordinate and co-ordinate clauses, and wait for the ramming home of the inexorable conclusion half a page away. Listen to the dignity and balance of the compacter sentence:

> This is no fashion for subjects, but rather after the fashion of war between prince and prince, which maketh us to marvel that they would thus blind us with fair words, calling us their natural and most dread sovereign lord under God, with desire of our mercy and pity, when nevertheless the effect of your said letters, in sundry points (as, in desiring hostages, a place indifferent, and abstinence of war for fourteen days after the meeting) showeth the contrary.

For us to-day 'eloquence'—so-called—too often connotes emptiness. Men fight shy of the complex and of the periodic sentence, having little skill in their construction and less confidence in the powers of concentration that may be looked for in their hearers or readers. But Tudor England loved and cultivated 'eloquentia' for all the graver concerns of life. It admired the sustained flight of declamation, found weight and purpose in the devices of rhetoric. Caught up in the excitement of discovering the magnificent possibilities of their own language, Tudor Englishmen are to be envied rather than patronized for the more extravagant delights of their prose. They *felt* about words. One word was not as good as another, and two were gener-

of the individual manner that time and again stamps a letter as indubitably Henry's. It would be unwise, however, to lay too much stress on tricks of style and turns of speech, cherished phrases and choice of words. The soundest evidence for their authenticity as the utterances of his mind is to be found in their clear and consistent revelation of an unmistakable personality—the personality of the real Henry. And the real Henry is not the popular Bluebeard, whose tendencies to matrimony have been greatly exaggerated; nor yet the bullying tyrant who muddled through, somehow, because he had the luck to secure clever ministers; but the King who has been described by his finest biographer as 'the most remarkable man who ever sat on the English throne'. (pp. xiii-xvi)

M. St. Clare Byrne, in an introduction to The Letters of King Henry VIII: A Selection, with a Few Other Documents, *edited by M. St. Clare Byrne, 1936. Reprint by Funk & Wagnalls, 1968, pp. ix-xix.*

C. W. C. OMAN   (essay date 1937)

[*An English historian and educator, Oman wrote* Warwick, the King Maker *(1891) and* On the Writing of History *(1939). In the following excerpt from a review of M. St. Clare Byrne's 1936 edition of Henry's letters and other documents, Oman relates the king's writings to his character and career.*]

This most interesting selection of letters [*Letters of King Henry VIII: A Selection with Other Documents*] is not intended to serve as an annalistic commentary on forty years of an eventful reign, but rather to form a basis for a psychological enquiry into the personality of 'the most remarkable man who ever sat upon the English throne.' To some he may appeal as the 'majestic lord who broke the chains of Rome'; to others he is 'a vast gloomy shadow thrown upon the screen of history.' The Editor leaves the reader his freedom of choice, after a perusal of this wonderful correspondence.

It is hard to believe that Henry VIII as a psychological study will ever exhaust the patience of students, though one may grow weary both of the details of his matrimonial infelicities and of the niceties of definition in 'the King's Religion,' which was thrust so ruthlessly upon his subjects. But to arrive at a conception of his individuality is an interesting line of enquiry, and his own letters provide one of the necessary approaches to that end. It is not always that the essential man can be discovered from his official, or even from his private, correspondence. Fortunately, Henry was an indefatigable user of the pen, and even official documents, which are so often meant to conceal rather than to reveal the underlying purpose of their writer, get a high value when it is possible to consult the original drafts, with all the interlineations and additions which the King put in with his own hand. Individuality emerges when we see precisely what His Majesty deleted and what he interpolated, when his secretaries laid before him the despatch, letter, or proclamation which they had drawn up after receiving his verbal instructions. Henry was an inveterate 'proof-reader,' and his scribes must have received back with a sigh anything that they had laid before him, knowing that it would have been well cut about, and perhaps modified in some unexpected fashion. (p. 88)

Princess Elizabeth, only child of Henry VIII and Anne Boleyn, who ruled England and Ireland as Elizabeth I from 1558 to 1603.

ally better than one. When his secretary presents him with 'Mahometans' Henry crosses it out and writes 'Turk'. His secretary writes 'A friend seeth sometimes in his friend's causes more than him that the matter toucheth.' Henry finds this bald, and emends to 'A friend seeth sometimes in his friend's causes, when they consist in diversity of matters, more, peradventure, than he to whom the matter toucheth near.'

Very few of Henry's letters are written in his own hand, with the exception of brief notes to Wolsey and the letters to Anne Boleyn. How far, in consequence, the language of diplomatic letters may be that of the ministers and secretaries who actually penned them, is open to dispute. No one, however, who consults the original documents, can fail to realize the concentrated attention and the personal supervision of detail that he gave, day by day, to his official correspondence. The nature and the extent of the alterations and additions that he was accustomed to make in his own hand demonstrate the close scrutiny to which even the most apparently formal draft was subjected before it was allowed to go forth under his bold signature.... Those who frequently wrote either for him or at his dictation, soon, I believe, caught 'the hang' of Henry's own style. Wriothesley writing for the King is not the same as Wriothesley writing personally.

I doubt if any one who is interested in such things can read ... he letters without becoming definitely conscious

[We] get from this collection . . . some conception of the many-sided activities of King Henry's mind, of the breadth of his intellectual interests, of his astounding mastery of detail, and of his marvellous self-confidence—not to say arrogance. Many students of history have been so overwhelmed by the discovery of the colossal capacity of the man that they have tended to accept him at his own valuation, and have failed to recognise that his whole life-work was a failure, and that his methods might be crudely described as a lesson in 'how not to do it.' His destructive work was unnecessarily ruthless; his constructive work was swept away immediately after his death by the group of unscrupulous satellites who had cowered before him when alive, and used their liberty, when he was gone, for designs of their own, of which he would not have approved.

The Editor has divided the vast bulk of Henry's correspondence into eleven sections, extracting from the thousand original documents, which might be in a rough way called his 'correspondence,' a limited number of the more important items—collected under the heads of War and Diplomacy, the 'King's Great Matter,' i.e. the Divorce question and the breach with Rome, Church reorganisation, internal administration, the Scottish policy, the question of the succession to the Crown, etc. In some ways the most interesting subsection is the packet of eight letters to Anne Boleyn, which (naturally) were holograph, and were not entrusted to any secretary. They produce on the whole a favourable impression, not being in courtly rhodomontade or mock-chivalrous diction, but, as the Editor observes, 'fired with a genuine affection, in which devotion and respect show a capacity for idealising the woman that he loved.' One longs—but fails—to find what were the precise causes of disillusion after marriage, which turned Henry into a Bluebeard. (pp. 89-90)

Henry's literary style is unmistakable, whether he is writing in English, Latin, or French. His secretaries may have drawn up screeds in the quasi-Ciceronian verbiage which was superseding mediæval Latin, or in the rather clumsy and many-claused English of the time, but His Majesty cut up the documents with so many of his own phrases and interlineations that they acquired a personal style. He was an excellent Latin scholar—Erasmus notes that the royal epistles which he received were in a distinct style, not in the hackneyed verbiage of scribes. Henry's Latin is as individual as his very characteristic English phraseology. The latter is, like so much writing of Tudor times, far too much given to parentheses and dependent clauses, till a sentence runs up to ten or eleven lines. But the effect is sonorous and trenchant, if generally permeated with his characteristic touch of arrogance.

The selection here printed illustrates the King's astonishing versatility and the pleasure which it gave him to display it. He could argue *de haut en bas* with Bishop Tunstal of Durham on the precise meaning of passages in the Fathers or the New Testament, with a complete mastery of texts. And no less could he instruct Ambassador Wooton on the exact limits, natural and political, of the county of the 'Boullongnois' (as he spelt it, one sees where the modern Cockney Boullong comes from). He was not aware that he was a very bad general: the 'Battle of the Spurs' was no credit to him, though a great discredit to his opponents the French commanders. But he was capable of shrewd military remarks, such as his observation to the Earl of Arran—his ally of the moment—that the Scots

must learn not all to dismount for battle, but to keep a good cavalry reserve. This much he had learnt from the lesson of Flodden. At Pinkie, a year after Henry's death, the Scots suffered once more from keeping to their old tactics, and fighting with vast masses of pikemen unsupported by any competent provision of cavalry.

Henry's love of detail emerges in curious side-issues. He could think out the order of the jousts, pageants, and ceremonies in which his soul delighted. When Lady Cobham is desired to take part in a royal procession, he dictates to her not only the colour of her horse, but the cut of her riding-habit, which shall be delivered to her by the Keeper of the Great Wardrobe. (pp. 91-2)

[His] ostentation was only a natural product of an all-pervading arrogance. Henry opined that he was set for great doings, and undoubtedly he made his mark on his times and his kingdom. The breach with Rome was certainly an epoch-making achievement. But other contemporary princes—the most notable case was Gustavus Vasa of Sweden—contrived to complete the rupture without leaving a land hideous with wrecked shrines, stakes, and gibbets, and utterly bankrupt. And the whole achievement got a degrading and sinister aspect from being mixed up with a purely personal affair, 'the King's Great Matter,' his determination to divorce his wife, Catherine of Aragon, with the Pope's consent if it could be procured, but if not in some other fashion. As the compiler of this collection points out, the question of the divorce was in Henry's mind long before he became besotted with the charms of his ill-chosen second wife. Nothing is more absurd than Gray's satiric line about Henry's seeing

> The Gospel-light first dawn in Boleyn's eyes.

He never saw the Gospel-light at all, being colour-blind to such illumination. And he remained a dogmatic Catholic to the end of his days, much enraged that the more conscientious of his unfortunate lieges could not comprehend what they called 'the King's Religion,' and either went to the block and the gallows for refusing to abjure papal jurisdiction, or else to the stake for cherishing heretical views as to the Real Presence in the Eucharist.

Henry loved to pontificate on matters religious. One of the most interesting examples of his love of definition and his tendency to interlineation is the text of the original draft for the *Act of Six Articles,* the six-thonged whip for Protestants, where the exact definition of Transubstantiation is tightened up by the King's personal additions to the text. He is set on excluding attempts at evasion by means of Consubstantiation, or other conceptions. And the proclamation against the bringing into the kingdom of 'naughty printed books' of Continental heretics is made more vicious by imposing on the lieges the duty of informing the Council if ever they should hap upon such volumes—i.e. every man is to become a government spy. Henry put in ten lines in his own hand to this effect.

A most disquieting specimen of the royal interlineation is to be found where the King inserts four lines of his own in the Act of Indictment against the Duke of Norfolk and his son Surrey. He stresses the clause in which these unfortunate noblemen are accused of aiming at power, by adding that they schemed to provide their master with 'a new harlot' from their own kin, 'thinking thereby to govern the realm by ruling the King.' It will be remembered that both Anne Boleyn and Catharine Howard had been of the Norfolk blood. The topic might surely have been left alone in a formal legal document—but its introduction is no more tactless than certain other of the clauses which cost the poetical but freespoken Surrey his head. It is curious to note that the monarch who accused the two Howards of this intended assault on his marital virtue, was actually on his death-bed when he penned these offensive lines. He must have known as well as did Norfolk and Surrey that his time of amours was over—the interlineation is as insincere as it is discreditable.

One of the documents which the Editor has printed with the King's personal phrases inserted in distinctive type among the rest of the verbiage of the despatch, is an extraordinary letter of directions for his ambassador Sir Thomas Wyatt, dated Oct. 16, 1538, giving him the arguments which he was to use to the Emperor Charles V about one of their many projected alliances. The terms are almost offensive and certainly most tactless:

> His Highness doubteth not that the Emperor considereth well that if it should please God to call him to his mercy (i.e. to end his life) the Imperial dignity is elective, and not likely to descend to his heir by succession, for that the Almains will be loth to have the Spanish nation ever their superior.... The Emperor's son, the Prince of Spain, is slenderly yet furnished with friends, for His Highness heareth of none that is joined with him which may in his minority stand him in friendly stead—which truly His Highness lamenteth.

Sir Thomas Wyatt is directed to 'signify' these untoward facts to Charles. We cannot envy him his task—these words are the King's own interlineation in his own handwriting; no secretary would have dared to pen them. Their import, however true, was certain to wound; it must have been an uncomfortable business to impress it on such a potentate as the Emperor. No doubt the ambassador softened the actual phrases, but it was the tactless argument that was offensive. No wonder that Wyatt is called on to 'require of the Emperor that he shall take these overtures in good part, and also promise, on the word of a prince, that he shall not disclose them to none but to such of his secret council as shall be sworn to the secrecy of the same.' This last claim is again of Henry's own interlineation. Can one wonder that Charles nourished a settled dislike for this candid relative? One hates those who talk about one's coffin.

If such were the words in which the King addressed the head of the Holy Roman Empire, it is not surprising to note that the phraseology of those addressed to mere relatives of his own was much more offensive. The letter which he caused Wolsey to send to his sister Margaret Tudor, Queen-Dowager of Scotland, in 1527, attracts attention not only by the brutality of some of its phrases, but by the irony of the fact that every word which Henry wrote to his sister might have been applied to himself with perfect accuracy within the next few years. Margaret, after securing a declaration of the nullity of her marriage to her second husband Angus, by what her brother calls 'a shameless sentence from Rome,' was on the point of marrying her third spouse, Henry Stuart, Lord Methven. This rather obscure young nobleman—whose title the King of England scornfully corrupted into 'Lord Miffen,' in his ostentatious ignorance of Scottish names, when writing at a

Jane Seymour, third wife of Henry VIII.

subsequent date, had no merits but his good looks, but Margaret (like her brother) had a very open heart. Accordingly Wolsey is made to write 'a most necessary message from your only especial and entirely beloved brother' to the effect that

> Your Grace behoves to fashion the estate of your life adverting the divine ordinance of inseparable matrimony, first institute in Paradise between man and woman, and now for no cause to be sundered except alone for adultery. Your Grace should soon perceive how synystrally (sic) you are seduced into damnable delusion, which persuades you to an unlawful divorce from lawful matrimony, directly against the ordinance of God, and utterly repugnant to man's law. For it is manifest that the causes alleged against the noble Earl of Angus [a "precontract"] are utterly surmised of malice. Notwithstanding if they had been of verity able to be instesyed, yet they were of no such urgent imputancy to make reasonable a divorce between him and Your Grace.

Now comes the most astounding piece of hypocrisy. Margaret had by Angus a daughter—that Countess of Lennox who was afterwards to be the mother of the unlucky Darnley—just as Henry had by Catherine of Aragon a daughter, the Lady Mary, afterwards to be Queen of England. The thoughtful uncle suddenly waxes lachrymose over the fate of his niece, if the Angus marriage is disallowed.

> Natural love to the fruit of your body, your most dear child and natural daughter, should provoke your Grace

after such a sort that it would relent and mollify a heart of steel, much more a motherly mind, which in Your Grace, nature enforcing the same, ought largely to be showed. Moreover, what change of conscience, yea, what danger of damnation, with perpetual infamy of your renown, slanderously to disdain with dishonour so goodly a creature, your own natural child procreate in lawful matrimony, as to be reputed baseborn. This can not be avoided unless Your Grace will (as in conscience ye are bound under peril of God's indignation) relinquish the adulterer's company.

What touching tenderness toward a niece aged twelve from the father of Mary Tudor, whom the author of those reproaches was to stigmatise as 'baseborn' in document after document within a few years! But circumstances alter cases when our own desires are concerned, and Henry's 'heart of steel' never seems to have considered the Lady Mary 'a goodly creature,' though years after he did speak of his younger daughter Elizabeth as 'endowed with virtues and qualities agreeable to her estate,' when he was proposing to marry her off for political purposes. This was after Elizabeth had, in her turn, been stigmatised as illegitimate for certain intervals of time. It is curious to make guesses as to whether her father ever looked over again, in his later years, the sermons on divorce which he preached to his erring sister in 1527. Probably he consigned them to oblivion, and shouldered the responsibility on to Wolsey—whose had been the pen that wrote these screeds, if not the brain that conceived them.

Altogether Henry's thirty years of correspondence north of Tweed with a series of regents, a peccant sister, a suspicious nephew, and a pack of greedy nobles, whom he very excusably styled 'a sort of wolves,' is a series of disappointments. Even a plan for getting possession of the young James V—who had spent so many of his earlier years in being kidnapped—came to nothing. The cream of this astonishing series of documents is a message sent in the King's name by seven members of the Privy Council to Sir Ralph Sadler, then in charge of Scottish negotiations (1543). The great enemy of Henry's plan for the marriage of his son prince Edward to the little Mary Queen of Scots was Cardinal Beton, the head of the Clerical party in Scotland. A powerful malcontent, the Earl of Cassilis, had written to Sadler offering to murder the Cardinal, 'if His Majesty would have it done, and would promise, when it were done, a reward.' To this obliging nobleman the Council make reply,

> His Majesty has willed us to signify that His Highness, reputing the fact not meet to be set forward expressly by His Majesty, will not deem to have to do in it, and yet (not misliking the offer) thinketh good that Mr Sadler should write to the Earl of the receipt of his letter containing this offer, which he thinketh not convenient to be communicated to His Majesty. Marry, to write to him what he thinketh of the matter, to say that if he were in the Earl of Cassilis' place, and were as able to do His Majesty good service as he knoweth him to be, he would surely do what he could for the execution of it, believing verily to do thereby acceptable service to the King's Majesty, and also a special benefit to the realm of Scotland, and would trust verily that the King's Majesty would consider his service, and you doubt not of his accustomed goodness to them which serve him.

The grammar of this disgusting document is as bad as its intention. But it obviously means that Henry does not

wish to appear as the actual instigator of the crime, but authorises Sadler to let the Earl know that His Majesty 'does not mislike the offer' and would reward its accomplishment with his wonted liberality. This is plain subornation of murder.... (pp. 92-7)

The reader of this selection of Henry's correspondence should peruse carefully... the King's final speech in Parliament (Dec. 24, 1545).... [In this speech], despite of all failures and misfortunes, there still emerges the essential self-complacency of the man. He is quite conscious of the 'notable qualities' that his subjects find in him, and of the 'perfect trust and confidence' which they put in him. He 'cannot choose but love and favour you, affirming that no prince more favoreth his subjects than I do you, and no subjects or commons more love and obey their sovereign lord than I perceive you do me.' Rising to the moral tone, he condemns those who live in adultery, 'lecherous and carnal persons,' and 'those who boast and brag'—whom he cannot but condemn as over proud. And lastly those who 'teach one contrary to another' in religion and 'sow in sermons debate and discord' are threatened with destruction—'I, whom God hath appointed his Vicar and high minister here, will see these divisions extinct, and these enormities corrected, according to my very duty, or else I am an untrue officer.' Obviously Henry cannot conceive that any one considers him 'a lecherous and carnal person,' or over-prone to arrogance, or a sower of discord in matters religious! Autolatry can go no further. (pp. 103-04)

> *C. W. C. Oman, "The Personality of Henry the Eighth," in* The Quarterly Review, *Vol. 533, July, 1937, pp. 88-104.*

PHILIP HUGHES (essay date 1950)

[*A distinguished English historian and Roman Catholic priest, Hughes was the author of* St. John Fisher *(1935) and* Rome and the Counter-Reformation in England *(1942). In the following excerpt from a work first published in 1950, he explicates the intent and argument of* A Glasse of the Truthe.]

The *Glasse of the Truthe* makes much of the fact that the pope's "unmete and unkind handling" of the king's marriage suit is the cause why this "hath hitherto had so long a delay". It invites the reader to consider what Sacred Scripture, "the counsels and ordinances of the Church universal, of the most ancient popes and other holy doctors' writings", have to say in support of the king's case; and for warrant that these are fairly cited the tract appeals to the known judgment of "so many approved universities".... [What] could be more popular than the argument which the tract repeats, again and again, that it is vital to the future well-being of England that the king should have a male heir, whatever the virtues of the princess who is heir apparent, and that it is the pope alone who now stands in the way, holding up, all these years, the hearing of Henry's case—and so, of course, blocking the new marriage which the king would make, and the resulting royal progeny of boys. Heirs male are the only solution, the tract insists, to the king's anxieties, the sole security for future peace in England. Whence it is not any longer to be borne that "this weighty and urgent cause... be longer differed or delayed by those which do but usurp to themselves an honour and vain glory contrary to many general councils, and their own laws also", as the tract will now prove.

The tract is written as a dialogue between a lawyer and a divine; and, as though to prepare men for Cranmer's approaching declaration that the marriage is null, it begins by saying, most untruthfully, that the king's cause is "laboured and vexed at Rome, from judge to judge, without end or effect"; whereas, had it been heard where it should have been heard, in the Archbishop of Canterbury's court, it should long since have been determined—and, the tract takes it for granted, in the king's favour. "All good English people", then, ought to detest the pope who has thus interfered with the natural course of the trial.

One principal hindrance to justice is the opinion of the canonists who allow the pope so much authority that, in the end, there is no law but the pope's will. Soon it will be a waste of time to worry about God's law—all that will matter will be to know, and perform, the papal will: a state of things agreeable to canonists, no doubt, who will then make great fortunes.

The two speakers then turn to discuss whether the Mosaic law set out in Leviticus is still binding on Christian men. This, they consider, is so obviously true that a prince and his people ought to refuse to believe what those who deny this put out as true in other matters—until they admit this to be true. If all princes would act in this way (against the pope) there would soon truly be "one flock and one shepherd": the principle that determines what is the truth being, in all cases, the plain declaration of Scripture with the assent of general councils and ancient saints and doctors.

"These be wonderful things to hear", says the lawyer. What unworthy subjects we are, to listen for a moment to those who malign the king's cause. Our duty is "to stick fastly and surely unto him". Patient he may be and seem, "though peradventure, he say little, yet may it fortune he marketh all"; and—a sinister hint, surely—wise men will begin to fear that to believe the slanderers who oppose the king's case is to be untrue to one's duty of allegiance. On the other hand, if all of us stand together against such slanderers "I think there should be rooted the greatest union between the head and the body that ever was seen or heard of".

The point is then raised of the pope's power to dispense with the divine law, and the divine declares that the ancient doctors and the moderns differ greatly in what they teach about this. Modern theologians, he says, have been infected by the lawyers' error "in wresting of Scripture for advancement of dignity". Then follows, to support the anti-papal intention of the tract, a long list of illustrious names from St. Augustine to St. Antonino of Florence, dead only seventy years before, and to Gabriel Biel whom the speakers might well have remembered; it includes more than one text from the False Decretals, and the scholastics quoted are, all but two, Franciscan doctors or Ockhamists. "No man can prove that the Pope may dispense with either the law of nature or the law of God", the divine concludes. It is the king's interpretation of Scripture which is right, the pope's wrong: "we ought clearly and wholly to believe this, and as true subjects to stick with our sovereign and prince, in this his just doing and laudable act".

The lawyer then sets out a long list of conciliar decisions to support his statement that the pope exceeded his powers when he transferred the king's case to his court at Rome. "How may the Bishop of Rome or any other primate be so bold as to break the canons?" he asks, and the divine echoes his sentiment: "Who could think that the Church of Rome, which indeed is but a daughter of the Church universal, might destroy the laws of her mother?" But in pushing his argument still further—that the pope is vowed to keep the canons, and that no other man can dispense him from that vow—the divine admits explicitly "he hath none superior in spirituality". The council of Constance is said to support this theory of the pope being bound by the canons, and Basel too; and again there is a great parade of names and texts, to the effect that the pope is bound to obey the rulings of general councils; and it is the testimony of all these that the king's case should have been decided at home by his own metropolitan. As for the pope's revocation of the case, "neither (the king) nor we will suffer so prejudicial an injury to be inferred to this realm, and so pernicious an example for all Christendom". The divine agrees that Englishmen will stand with the king rather "than put their necks under the yoke of the Pope, or his, at pleasure, laws"; and again there is a litany of saints quoted in approval—general statements, of course, in all cases, to the effect that we should obey God rather than man, and so forth. The lawyer, quoting Innocent IV and Panormitanus, now recalls a whole body of canonist discussion about the limitations on the powers of popes, the invalidity of papal commands and sanctions where to obey these involves sin, for example; and the divine gives instances of saints who conscientiously resisted the popes, and with them he cites Robert Grosseteste. These are the examples an Englishman will now follow if the pope proceeds either to excommunicate the king, or, by any threats, "to interrupt the justice of this cause".

The lawyer is not too happy about the divine's lighthearted treatment of that grave thing "the law", but the theologian insists that law ought to stand on the same basis as religion, "for the Church of God hath his foundation set upon a firm and steadfast stone of truth and faith, and not upon the mutable and wilful pleasure of Peter's successors". It is not man—as the lawyers would have it—but the Word of God, which is superior and "always permanent".

Very ingeniously the tract now introduces the question whether Catherine's first marriage had been consummated, and the lawyer shows how, by all the traditions of legal procedure, this must be taken as proved. The lawyer also says, very dishonestly (for he is obviously well informed), "I think the queen will never allege that matter, which hath not only no probability of truth but . . . a plain conclusion to the contrary". And then the theologian retails some of the evidence given at the Blackfriars trial, now four years since, to prove the consummation; and he tells a likely, but wholly untruthful, tale of the genesis of that dispensatory brief of Julius II, whose appearance, in the November of 1528, had routed all the plans of Henry and Wolsey. The lawyer sets out the legal case for the position that the marriage had indeed been consummated; and the theologian, admiringly, asks who can resist truth so evident, and then returns to what is the burden of the whole tract, that the good subject will be zealous and obedient to the king "according to (his) allegiance". How ungrateful and unnatural, for any man, to do otherwise than "offer to live and die in this his just cause and matter". And how terrible for all of us, says the lawyer, should the strong hand of the good prince fail us, should he die without a male heir!

What then is to be done?

First of all, it is parliament that must settle the matter, and before all else it must settle that it is in England that the case shall be decided, "for methinketh the succession of this realm ought not to be ordered by forreins"—a proceeding which would make them, "and not the king and his parliament", the rulers of the realm. Therefore "the king's highness and his parliament should earnestly press the metropolitans of this realm (their unjust oath to the pope notwithstanding) to set an end shortly to this", to think more to the kingdom "than to the ceremonies of the Pope's law", and not to refuse "when it shall be put to them, whosoever say nay, answering, when need shall be, according to their ancient and virtuous predecessors, 'Rather we ought to obey God than men'."

The tract ends with an outspoken claim that Henry's case is the case for morality and sexual decency, and that what the other side is asking for tends to "vice and uncleanness"; and it declares that even the distinguished personages who are opposing the king's case have themselves said that they would not recommend or advise any man to do such a thing as to marry his dead brother's widow. Is their opposition, then, really serious or sincere? Is it worth a loyal subject's consideration? And if subjects are not ready to do the king's cause justice, how can they expect the king to deal justly with them?

The *Glasse of the Truthe* is admirably written. . . . Within but a few months, at most, of its appearance from the press of the king's printer, the solution for which it hoped to prepare the popular mind was in train: the metropolitan had indeed disregarded his oath to the pope; Cranmer was judging the suit at Dunstable; Anne was acknowledged and crowned; parliament and convocation were confirming and ratifying all that was done; the pope and his law had been openly flouted; but to arrange the sex of the child Anne was bearing was a matter where none could avail—not even the lawyer and the divine. (pp. 248-53)

> *Philip Hughes, "Royal Supremacy—Achieved: July 4, 1533-July 6, 1535," in his* The Reformation in England: "The King's Proceedings,", *Vol. I, 1950. Reprint by The Macmillan Company, 1951, pp. 247-81.*

NEELAK SERAWLOOK TJERNAGEL (essay date 1965)

[*Tjernagel is an American educator and Lutheran minister who has written extensively on the Reformation. In the following excerpt from his study of Henry's relation to the early Lutherans, he evaluates the theology of* Ten Articles, *the* Bishops' Book, Six Articles, *and the* King's Book.]

The *Ten Articles* were published in 1536 with a preamble written by the king. He called dissent and discord a primary concern of his office as king and said that he had personally taken "great pains, study, labours, and travels" in the matter and had referred the religious issues to "our bishops and other of the most discreet and learned of our

clergy of this our whole realm" to agree upon "special points and articles; as well as such as be commanded of God, and are necessary to our salvation, and also divers other matters touching the honest ceremonies and good and politic orders. . . ."

The *Ten Articles* were divided into two equal parts, the first five being concerned with doctrine, the last with ecclesiastical usage. The first five articles drew heavily from the *Augsburg Confession*. With the exception of the second on original sin they parallel very closely the first seven of the *Wittenberg Articles*. The first article accepted the Bible and the three ecumenical creeds as the basis of English faith and practice. The fifth article, that on justification, stated that man is justified solely through the "mercy and grace of the Father, promised freely unto us for His Son's sake Jesus Christ, and the merits of His blood and passion," which are "the only sufficient and worthy causes thereof." Following this definition, there is an extended discussion of the relation of faith to good works. There is little in the second, third, and fourth articles that a Lutheran would have found exceptionable.

The last five articles reveal that, in spite of the willingness to accept the Lutheran view of the means of grace outlined in the first five articles, the English divines were not ready to conform to all the usages of Lutheran ecclesiastical polity and rejected the section of the *Wittenberg Articles* that had treated of those matters. The sixth article forbade the worship of images but advocated their use. With reference

The Great Bible of King Henry VIII.

to honoring and praying to saints, the two articles in question admitted that "grace, remission of sin, and salvation cannot be obtained but of God, only by the mediation of our Saviour Jesus Christ . . . yet it is very laudable to pray to saints in heaven everlastingly living."

Article 10 is noncommittal on the question of purgatory, saying of the dead that "the place where they be, the name thereof, and the kinds of pain there, also be to us uncertain by Scripture. . . ." The article does say that "as due order of charity requireth, and the Book of Maccabees, and divers ancient doctors plainly show . . . and forasmuch also as such usage hath continued in the Church so many years," prayers for the dead to commit them to God's mercy, and that "they may be relieved and holpen of some part of their pain" ought to be continued. The article demanded that abuses which had been advanced under the name of purgatory be put away.

The document in its totality included much of Lutheran theology. Only prayers to saints, prayers for the dead, and a modified view of purgatory ran contrary to the *Wittenberg Articles.* Melanchthon referred to it as something composed in confusion because it retained elements of Roman Catholic doctrine and practice. Nevertheless, Cranmer and his party had achieved a great deal in realizing a doctrinal formula that acknowledged the basic premises of Protestant thought. No more a definitive theological statement than the *Ninety-five Theses* of Martin Luther, the *Ten Articles* were authoritative in England for the next seven years. A compromise it may have been, but it is the first official acceptance of Protestantism in England in any form. (pp. 165-66)

Unlike the *Ten Articles,* the *Bishops' Book* was no mere doctrinal treatise; it was a practical handbook of faith and morals. Four fifths of the work was devoted to a discussion of the five chief parts of the catechism. These were the Ten Commandments, the Creed, The Lord's Prayer, and the sacraments of Baptism and the Lord's Supper. One fifth, or about 15 pages, consisted of short doctrinal articles on faith, the Ave Maria, free will, justification, good works, and prayers for souls departed. The last two articles, on justification and prayers for souls of the departed, were taken almost bodily from the *Ten Articles.* The last four sacraments, omitted from the *Ten Articles,* were included in this work.

The whole was far from being a finished theological treatise. It rather represented a compromise between the two English religious parties. It is clear, however, that its chief authors, Cranmer, Latimer, and Fox, much though they might lean toward the new learning, were not Lutherans. The work falls short of the fully matured Lutheranism of Robert Barnes or the Wittenberg reformers.

Yet, like the *Ten Articles,* the *Bishops' Book* drew its content from Lutheran sources. Where the *Ten Articles* had drawn from the *Augsburg Confession* by way of the *Wittenberg Articles,* this new book devised by the bishops was indebted in its contents to Luther's catechisms. Even its organization expresses its theology, though it does not follow the organization of the catechism itself. The first section, an exposition of the Apostles' Creed, covered 53 pages; the second, an exposition or declaration of the seven sacraments, ran to 48 pages. The third part was an exposition of the Ten Commandments, 47 pages long, and

the last an exposition of the Lord's Prayer, 25 pages, the Ave Maria, six pages, and justification and purgatory, taken verbatim from the *Ten Articles,* one page each.

The *Bishops' Book* divides the Creed into 12 articles. One example will suffice to show its debt to Luther's *Small Catechism:*

> *Small Catechism:* I believe that God has made me and all creatures; that he has given me my body and soul, eyes and ears, and all my limbs, my reason, and all my senses, and still preserves them. . . .

> *Bishops' Book:* I believe also and profess, that among his other creatures He did create and make me, and give unto me this my soul, my life, my body, with all the members that I have, great and small, and all the wit, reason, knowledge, and understanding that I have. . . .

The elaboration of the 12 articles is followed by "certain notes and observations necessary to be taught unto the people, for the better inducing of them unto the right understanding of the foresaid Creed." In this there is a repetition of the essential content of the first article of both the *Wittenberg Articles* and the *Ten Articles.* Luther's catechism had the merit of brevity; the *Bishops' Book* was so long that it failed to became a popular manual, in spite of Cromwell's repeated admonitions to the clergy to use it diligently for the edification of the people.

The exposition of the seven sacraments in the *Bishops' Book* was indeed a remarkable performance. It dared not forget that Henry VIII had once made a celebrated defense of the sacraments and that no document that ignored or rejected them could hope to get through Convocation or Parliament. So the issue was temporarily evaded under an exposition which, with the sole exception of extreme unction, conformed to every essential intent of Lutheran practice. Apparent concessions made in the body of the exposition were nullified by the closing remarks in favor of the special sacramental significance of the three sacraments that Luther had acknowledged. Later the English church was to follow the Continental trend of excluding penance also from the number of sacraments, which was finally limited to Baptism and Communion. (pp. 174-76)

The discourses on the Ten Commandments in the *Bishops' Book* give us a picture of the moral conditions, prevalent evils, and superstitions of the 16th century. A Protestant attitude toward relations between church and state is reflected throughout. Special emphasis was given to matters relevant in the changing religious scene of the time: Anabaptist attitudes toward law and property were dealt with in detail, warnings were issued against the abuse of religious images, and Sabbatarianism was disavowed in an admonition against being "over-scrupulous, or rather superstitious, in abstaining from bodily labour on the holyday." Two examples will suffice to show the similarity of the expositions of Luther and the *Bishops' Book* on the commandments:

> Remember that thou do sanctify and keep holy the Sabbath. *Luther's Large Catechism:* "The word holy day is rendered from the Hebrew word *sabbath* which properly signifies to rest. . . . Secondly, and most especially, that on such day of rest (since we can get no other opportunity) freedom and time be taken to attend divine service, so that we come together to hear and treat of God's Word. . . ."

Bishops' Book: "This word sabbote is an Hebrew word, and signifieth in English rest. So the Sabbath day is as much as to say the day of *rest....* Second... that besides this spiritual rest, (which chiefly and principally is required of us), we be bound by this precept at certain times to cease from all bodily labour, and give our minds entirely and wholly unto God, to hear and learn his word...."

Martin Luther concludes the explanation of the Ten Commandments in the *Small Catechism* with the words: "God threatens to punish all that transgress these commandments. Therefore we should dread His wrath and not act contrary to these commandments. But He promises grace and every blessing to all that keep these commandments." The *Bishops' Book* paraphrases the words as follows: "God threatens to punish all them grievously and extremely, yea to the third and fourth generation, which should transgress any of the said commandments: and contrary, how he promised to show mercy and give life everlasting to all them that should observe and keep the same...."

A portion of the paragraph in which the *Bishops' Book* makes the transition to the exposition of the Lord's Prayer reveals its grasp of the Lutheran theology of grace and good works:

> Although these laws and commandments of God teach us what is good, and what we should do to please God, yet they give not unto us strength and power to do the same; but all such strength cometh of God, by his singular grace and gift. And therefore, as Almighty God taught us by His prophet Moses what we should do, so He taught us by His Son Jesu Christ what we should ask. For as these Ten Commandments do teach us what is God's will, so the Pater noster teacheth us, that we should daily and continually pray to the Father in heaven, that it may please him to give us his help and grace to do his will....

The words of this statement on grace and works are general. So was the *Bishops' Book* as a whole, as indeed compromise documents must be. But the advantage was still on the side of Protestantism, and the book represents a progressive deterioration of Roman Catholic doctrine in England. (pp. 176-78)

Finally, it should be noted that it was a compromise between Roman Catholic and *Lutheran* theology. There is no evidence of an original or distinctive English theology in the *Bishops' Book*; neither is there evidence of any non-Lutheran Continental Protestantism. Where the *Bishops' Book* departed from Roman Catholic theology, it did so in Lutheran terms and in whole sequences of words and phrases borrowed from the writings of Luther and Melanchthon. (p. 178)

[The] *Act of Six Articles* was passed by Convocation and the House of Commons in the following terms:

> 1. First, that in the most blessed sacrament of the altar, by the strength and efficacy of Christ's mighty word, that being spoken, is present really the natural body and blood of our savior Jesus Christ, conceived of the virgin Mary, under form of bread and wine; and that after consecration there remaineth none other substance, but the substance of his foresaid natural body.
>
> 2. Secondly, that communion in both kinds is not necessary *ad salutem* by the law of God; and that it is to be believed, and not doubted of, but that in the flesh, under form of bread, is the very blood; and in the blood, under form of wine, is the very flesh, as well apart, as though they were both together.
>
> 3. Thirdly, that priests, after the order of priesthood received, as afore, may not marry by the law of God.
>
> 4. Fourthly, that vows of chastity or widowhood made by men or women, made to God advisedly, to be observed by the law of God; and that it exempteth them from other liberties of Christian people, which without that they might enjoy.
>
> 5. Fifthly, that it is meet and necessary that private masses be continued and admitted in this our English church and congregation, as whereby good Christian people (ordering themselves accordingly) do receive both godly and goodly consolations and benefits, and it is agreeable also to God's law.
>
> 6. Sixthly, that auricular confession is necessarily to be retained and continued, used and frequented in the church of God.

The whole act was ordered to be read in full by the clergy in all churches every three months. Death at the stake and confiscation of property was the penalty for speaking against transubstantiation, and no abjuration might excuse an offender. Loss of goods and imprisonment at the king's pleasure, with the death penalty for the second offense, were prescribed for heresy respecting the last five. The articles with the penal portion of the act became law on 28 June 1539. (pp. 197-98)

Wittenberg was shocked almost beyond expression by the act. To the Germans it was a betrayal of the mutual confidence that had been erected by the long series of negotiations between the two parties. Luther cried out against the king who had stripped the pope of his name and property in England but was perpetuating the pope's doctrine. (p. 199)

It was clear that [the bark of the *Act of Six Articles*] was worse than its bite. During the 8 years in which the act was law, 28 persons were executed in England for reasons of religion. One of these was executed for treason, 3 suffered under acts of attainder, 11 died for unspecified reasons, and 3 for religious offenses not related to the *Act of Six Articles*. That leaves only 10 who by the broadest stretch of the imagination can be said to have suffered the penalties of the "Bloody Act." The modern mind will deplore every one of those deaths and look with particular revulsion at the executions of a 15-year-old boy and a pious woman. Yet the number of executions falls far below the usual conception of the Tudor reaction in the reign of Henry VIII. The roster of the victims of the act proves that it was not devised to restore the Roman Catholicism that England had known before the reign of Henry VIII. (pp. 237-38)

The *King's Book* of 1543 does, however, suggest a return to the old religion in England. Its official title was *The Necessary Doctrine and Erudition of a Christian Man*. Its predecessor, the *Bishops' Book* of 1537, had been licensed for only three years, and its authorization had expired....
The new articles of religion, familiarly known as the *King's Book*, resulted from one of the last acts of Cromwell's life, the appointment of a commission of bishops and doctors to devise a new confession of faith. It was to

HENRY THE EYGHT

BY THE GRACE OF GOD KYNGE
of Englande, Fraunce, and Irelande, de-
fendour of the faythe, and in earthe of the
churche of Englande and also of Irelande,
supreme head, vnto all his faythful and lo-
uyng subiectes sendeth greetyng.

Ike as in the tyme of darkenes ⁊
ignorance, fyndynge our people seduced
and drawen from the trueth by hypocrisy
and superstition: we by the helpe of god
and his worde, haue trauayled to purge
and clense our realme from the apparant
enormities of the same, wherein by openyng of goddes
trueth, with settyng furth and publishyng of the scriptures, our labours (thankes be to god) haue not ben void
and frustrat: So nowe perceiuyng, that in the tyme of
knowledge, the deuill (who ceasseth not in all tymes to
vexe the world) hath attented to returne agayn, (as the
parable in the gospel sheweth) in to the house purged ⁊
clensed, accompanied with seuen worse spirites: and hypocrisy and superstition beyng excluded and put away,
we fynd entered in to some of our peoples hartes, an inclination to sinister vnderstādyng of scripture, presumption, arrogancy, carnal liberty, and contention: we be
therfore constrained for the reformation of them in time,
and for auoydyng of suche diuersity in opinions, as by
the sayd euill spirites myght be engendred, to set furth
with the aduise of our clergy suche a doctrine ⁊ declaration of the true knowledge of god and his word, with the
principall articles of our religion, as wherby all me may
A.ii. vniform-

Opening page of the King's Book *(1543).*

132

be the last doctrinal statement of the reign of Henry VIII. (pp. 242-43)

The **King's Book** of 1543 treated the same subjects as the **Bishops' Book** of 1537 except that it included an introductory article on faith and an article on free will. The earlier article on purgatory was little changed except for the title, which read "Prayers for Souls Departed" in the later work. Using the modern Lloyd edition for comparison, the **Bishops' Book** was 193 pages long, the **King's Book** 165. The portion on the Creed is reduced to one half the length of the earlier work, the sections on the Pater Noster and the Sacraments being only slightly reduced. A page and a half on justification in the **Bishops' Book** is enlarged to 12 pages under two heads, justification and good works.

The whole work represents the product of a lengthy deliberation by the bishops and doctors. In the records of the debate, conflicts between Protestantism and a Henrician conservatism are constantly in evidence. After approval by convocation of the clergy and by Parliament, it was printed with the king's approval on 29 May 1543. It was Protestant enough to secure the signatures of Cranmer and others, Catholic enough to win the approval of Stephen Gardiner, the ablest Catholic theologian in England.

We can be surprised only that in view of the mood which had been expressed in the **Six Articles,** and the debate that had preceded the approval of the book, it should have been so much like the **Bishops' Book.** Whole sections of that book were embodied in the new formula, the **King's Book** being little more than a revision of the former work.

We may take the word of a competent Roman Catholic scholar for the judgment that the **King's Book** was far from being a satisfactory statement of Roman Catholic doctrine. It was inadequate from the Roman point of view in its definition of the church, the sacraments, faith, justification, good works, and free will. Accepting the book as the reflection of the king's faith, Philip Hughes says [in Volume II of his *The Reformation in England* (1953)] that "Henry, whatever he is, is not a Catholic." Three years after the publication of the book, Henry issued a royal proclamation prohibiting the use of Tyndale's or Coverdale's translations of the Bible. The works of Frith, Tyndale, Wyclif, Joye, Roye, Fasile, Bale, Barnes, Turner, and Tracy were declared heretical, as well as any other "book or books containing matter contrary to the king's majesty's book called *A Necessary Doctrine and Erudition for any Christian man*."

For Cranmer and the Protestants the book was far from representing a complete loss of the substantial gains Protestant theology had made in England during the reign of Henry VIII. They accepted the document as the best they could get at the moment and were content to express their displeasure in it by neglecting to advocate its use. It was probably no more effective in reviving Catholic doctrine than the **Bishops' Book** had been in implanting Protestant theology. Both were too bulky to become popular.

The ineffectiveness of the **King's Book** before Henry's death was due to the fact that Cranmer remained archbishop of Canterbury. This meant that its use was not encouraged and that it did not become an important part of English religious life in the four years of its life. Whatever value the **King's Book** might eventually have had was nullified by the king's death in 1547. (pp. 243-45)

Neelak Serawlook Tjernagel, in his Henry VIII and the Lutherans: A Study in Anglo-Lutheran Relations from 1521 to 1547, *Concordia Publishing House, 1965, 326 p.*

J. J. SCARISBRICK (essay date 1968)

[*An English educator and historian, Scarisbrick won the* Yorkshire Post *award for best book of the year by a new author for his* Henry VIII. *Lacey Baldwin Smith, who later wrote his own biography of the monarch, called Scarisbrick's "by far the best biography of Henry VIII yet written." In the following excerpt from this work, Scarisbrick discusses the merits and effectiveness of* Assertion of the Seven Sacraments, *then surveys Henry's later theological "writings" —consisting primarily of annotations to works written by others—to trace the evolution of his religious tenets.*]

Henry first tried his hand at writing in the early months of 1518. We know little about the product except that it was finished by June of that year, that Wolsey had at first contested what Henry had written and then, to the author's delight, joined in the chorus of praise and declared the reasoning 'inevitable', and that, doubtless because the author soon tired, it never passed beyond manuscript stage. But it is a reasonable guess that, three years later, the piece was rescued from the oblivion that some may think it deserved and used to form the first two chapters of Henry's famous book—the chapters entitled "Of Indulgences" and "Of the Pope's Authority". Henry's first piece, therefore, was a very swift contribution to the controversy occasioned by Luther's attack on indulgences in late 1517, was set aside as soon as it was written and then emerged as the somewhat incongruous opening chapters of a work in defence of the seven sacraments. Such, at any rate, is a possible account of what happened.

His printed book, the **Assertio Septem Sacramentorum**, a lengthy treatise against Luther's *De Captivitate Babylonica* of 1520, appeared in the summer of 1521. By then, of course, Luther had been excommunicated and outlawed, but his creed was spreading fast and had begun to penetrate England. Several calls had come to Henry from Rome to exert himself against what was called a 'wicked pestilence', though probably few expected that he would produce a book. But such it was to be. (p. 110)

The Defence of the Seven Sacraments is not a piece of theology of the highest order. Estimates of it have varied enormously, but the truth surely is that its erudition is unremarkable (though it makes telling use of the Old Testament in particular), its grasp of Lutheranism defective, its exposition of Catholic teaching on the sacraments sometimes unimpressive and undoubtedly shot through with that semi- or crypto-Pelagianism against which, essentially, Protestantism protested. It left gaps which John Fisher, in a lengthy defence [*Defensio regis Angliae de fide Catholica adversus Lutheri Captivitatem Babylonicam* (1524)] of the king's book against Luther's riposte would later patiently, and tactfully, fill. Above all, it ran too easily into mere assertion and the jeering that is to be found in so many anti-Protestant works by Catholics, especially those of More and, to a lesser degree, of Fisher. In short, it is unlikely to have moved many convinced, informed Lutherans. Reading its rather conventional discourse on the sacraments and their all-too-mechanical operation (more wrong in tone than content, erring by omission rather than mis-statement), one pines for the sweep and fire of the *Babylonish Captivity* to which it was intended to reply.

But this is not to say that it was an ineffective book. On the contrary, it was one of the most successful pieces of Catholic polemics produced by the first generation of anti-Protestant writers. Simply because it was short and often unfair it would have engaged a wider audience than a ponderous professional work. It was a skilful piece of writing which made full use of the easy retort to Luther that one Augustinian hermit was neither likely suddenly to have discovered truth after centuries of darkness nor empowered by any authority to proclaim it. Henry's ecclesiology was not very strong, but the fundamental issue at stake, namely, the nature of the Church which Christ founded, comes out squarely. Finally, the book's greatest strength was the fact that its author was a notable king. Today it is its affirmation of the papal primacy, the condemnation of schism and the defence of the indissolubility of marriage which are remarked most obviously; but to so monarchical an age as his, Henry's book would have struck home even before it was read, simply because it was his. It could scarcely have been better calculated to bolster the humbler, perhaps uninformed, uncommitted Catholic—especially the lay Catholic—who fell away so easily. Wolsey was right to say that it should be sent not only to Rome but to 'France and other nations'; and Luther was right to reply to it violently.

But did Henry write it? This is yet another question which will never be answered completely. He did not write it entirely independently or with his own hand. Others gathered the materials and helped him throughout its composition. But he probably at least guided it through its final stages, when the time came to give shape to the whole work and place the pieces which others had made ready. In this limited sense it was his book. (pp. 111-12)

The book was an act of piety and perhaps of other things also. Henry wrote it because, doubtless, he believed wholly in the cause, because it would do good, because it would bring him acclaim and set him apart from his fellow kings, past and present. But the immediate reason why he wrote it was that Wolsey suggested that he should. We have the direct testimony of the king that he never intended any such thing 'afore he was by your grace moved and led thereunto'. Wolsey had sent him the copy of the *Babylonish Captivity* against which the king's book was aimed; he showed keen interest in its progress and carefully stage-managed its début; he was regarded by the pope as its architect; and later on, when the book was an embarrassment to him, Henry himself would say that he wrote it not of his free will, but at the instance of Wolsey and other bishops. Wolsey may well have been the prime mover for the same kind of reasons that Henry was the author. But had he an additional motive—to provide the king with an occupation which would help him endure the hardships of peace?

Henry's book was something of a best-seller. It went through some twenty editions and translations in the sixteenth century, in Antwerp, Rome, Frankfort, Cologne, Paris and Würzburg (among other places), besides England; and around it there quickly grew a sizable corpus of polemical writings.

By early 1522, two German translations had appeared—one by Hieronymus Emser (made at the request of Duke George of Saxony, Luther's persistent opponent), the other by Thomas Murner, at Strasburg. When the royal book thus penetrated his homeland, Luther quickly took up the pen and wrote a notoriously virulent reply, 'full of railing' and giving Henry about as thorough a lambasting as Henry had just aimed at him. The king's jeers that Luther had been wildly inconsistent in his theology and his attempt to dismiss him as 'a venomous serpent . . . infernal wolf . . . detestable trumpeter of pride, calumnies and schism' and the like, stung the latter to reply in kind and to trounce the king as 'deaf adder', 'miserable scribbler', 'fool', and worse. Henry himself made no response to this broadside, which took the form of a book in Latin and a slightly different version in German, but, instead, John Fisher and Thomas More took up the cudgels on his behalf: Fisher with a long defence of Henry's book which elaborated the latter and replied to the counter-attack point by point; More, under the pseudonym of William Ross, with an extremely vituperative harangue. In the same year, Thomas Murner came back into the story with a short tract, in German, cast in dialogue form and entitled *Whether the King of England or Luther is a Liar* —which, in turn, evoked a counter-blast from an anonymous Lutheran hand. Meanwhile Dr John Eck, already well known to Luther, had also written a defence of Henry's work, published in Rome in 1523.

There the contest rested until, in September 1525, Luther unexpectedly wrote a long letter to Henry in which he begged pardon for the abuse which he had poured on his head some three years before and offered to publish a full recantation. But this offer of an olive branch sprang from a complete misapprehension of what was really afoot in England. Luther had been persuaded by a false report passed on to him from Christian II, the exiled king of Denmark, that Henry had swung towards the Reformation, that Wolsey had tumbled and that it was now known that the *Assertio* was the work, not of Henry, but of 'that monstrous beast, hated by man and God . . . that pernicious plague and desolation of your majesty's kingdom', the cardinal of York, abetted by his fellow 'cunning sophists'. Armed with this false information, Luther penned his humble letter in which he offered his apologies and prepared to welcome Henry into the household of true believers.

He was, of course, rebuffed—with a long letter mocking him and his creed, decrying his marriage to the ex-nun Catherine von Bora, his attack on monasticism, his contemptuous remarks about Wolsey, and so on. But the reply took a curiously long time to be despatched. First, so it was said, it was delayed because Henry was on progress when Luther's letter arrived; then the latter was inexplicably mislaid, and, though Henry wanted his reply to be sent to the prince of Germany at once, Wolsey held up its despatch until a copy of Luther's piece could be appended to the king's screed. Hence it was not until late December 1527 that the reply reached Germany, over two years after Luther had opened the correspondence. Luther received a copy of Henry's response about Christmas time, *via* Duke George of Saxony, and was reported as saying that he had nothing further to say. But his opponents, especially Emser, quickly seized on his ill-judged letter and made full play both of his offer to recant and of Henry's firm rejection of him, with the result that he was driven to write another tract defending himself against their insinuations.

There the story of Henry's book and its aftermath effectively ended—in a rather desultory, inconclusive way. Three years later, however, Henry took the initiative and opened communications once more with the Lutheran world, when he turned thither for support for the divorce and began to discuss the possibility of a liaison with the Protestant princes. But, by then, times had changed. (pp. 113-15)

Between 1525 and 1547, it has been reckoned, some eight hundred separate editions of religious works were printed in English and a large proportion of these were of strongly Protestant hue—by such as Barnes, Coverdale, Richard Tracy, Becon, Taverner and Joye, as well as by the Reformers themselves, Luther, Melanchthon and Calvin. The first official statement of faith, the *Ten Articles* of 1536, followed the classical exposés of Lutheran theology, the *Augsburg Confession* and the subsequent *Apology*, almost verbatim for much of the way; and these two works were translated and printed in England in the same year by Taverner at Cromwell's behest and dedicated to him. The second formulary, the so-called *Bishops' Book* of 1537, again owed much to the *Apology* as well as to Luther's *Catechisms;* and its successor, the *King's Book* of 1543, though it retreated from the tempered Protestantism of the former works, still bore marked traces of the Reformation. That Henricianism was merely 'Catholicism without the pope' will not do. Though the repeated negotiations with Continental Protestantism were, on the whole, unhappy, and though Luther was eventually disappointed to find that, despite her early promise, England had not moved as fast or as far as he at one time expected, there can be no doubt that the Henrician Church took long strides towards the Reformers and that the English Protestantism which came to full flower in the next reign had many roots in this one. During Henry's reign, the English Church shifted a good way from the old orthodoxy. It moved erratically, now lurching towards Wittenberg, now pulling back—as diplomacy, the varying fortunes of jostling factions among the hierarchy, the king's own instincts and doubtless several other factors dictated. And over this strange evolution Henry himself presided. He was never a Lutheran; indeed, in some matters he was intransigently conservative. But that febrile, wayward mechanism, Henry's mind, was in ferment—exploring, questioning, seizing on novelties, often pushing far away from its theological past, juxtaposing new and old in a curious medley. (pp. 399-400)

In 1531 direct communication between Henry and Wittenberg, broken after the bitter exchanges of the 1520s, was restored when the king sent Robert Barnes to Luther to secure his approval of the divorce. (p. 400)

But Luther was a disappointment. . . . Luther's opposition to the royal divorce was absolute. (pp. 400-01)

Wittenberg's verdict, a certain amount of which ran remarkably, and ironically close to that of Fisher, Abel, their Spanish companions, and the rest of Catherine's supporters, was delivered to Henry by Barnes at Christmas-time 1531. Though it was a setback, it did not prevent the first of a series of exploratory embassies to the Lutherans eighteen months later—which would eventually mature into negotiations for a doctrinal and political union.

We cannot trace here in detail the complex story of the many embassies and their intricate theological negotiations, nor analyze the contents of the official statements of faith, especially the *Ten Articles* of 1536 and the *Bishops' Book* of the next year which owed so much to England's advances to the Lutherans. This has been done several times elsewhere—and our concern is, rather, with the evolution of Henry's own mind. (p. 401)

The Supreme Head [Henry], after his own fashion, had been intimately involved in the [negotiations with the Lutherans]. Doubtless with the encouragement of Cromwell and Cranmer, and doubtless with motives both profane and otherwise, he had followed closely the course of the innumerable embassies to and from the Continent, and perhaps occasionally thrust them onwards. He worked over at least some of the documents connected with the embassy which came from Wittenberg in 1538, scribbling in marginal corrections. He may have looked at Convocation's *Ten Articles* of 1536 and made a few, albeit very minor, corrections. He certainly studied its successor, the so-called *Bishops' Book,* very closely. Shortly after its publication in September 1537, he sent a long list of comments and criticisms to Cranmer—to which Cranmer made detailed reply. His annotations and Cranmer's counter-objections have survived and make intriguing reading. Nor were the remarks he addressed to the archbishop the sum total of his objections to the book. There survive two further documents containing his corrections to what had been written about the sacrament of Confirmation and

Anne of Cleves, fourth wife of Henry VIII.

prayers for the dead. Indeed, for one who was not addicted to writing and who, according to Cranmer, handed long works of theology to his courtiers for them to read for him, the hundred-odd often lengthy corrections and additions he made to the text of this sizable work must stand as a monument to his theological enthusiasm. Next, in a long reply to Tunstal in 1539 he set out his views on auricular confession and peppered the bishop's letter addressed to him with shrewd, hostile *marginalia*—as he had done to a paper by Latimer on Purgatory. He drew up the final text of the *Six Articles* of 1539. In 1540 he worked over a couple of the surviving replies of the bishops to searching questions concerning the sacraments, adding terse remarks beside their answers. Finally, there survive two documents containing about fifty of his corrections to the text of the *King's Book* of 1543. In short, when all these royal writings, most of them jottings and annotations, are put together, they amount to a considerable, if necessarily scrappy, *corpus*; and as their centrepiece stands Henry's most considerable effort, his corrections to the *Bishops' Book*.

Of course he remained himself even amidst theology. The Supreme Head could not always sustain his appetite for the sacred sciences against counter-attraction. On at least one occasion he had not gone very far with his work before he tired and his pen dropped from his hand, just as it had done years before when he was correcting Convocation's reform decrees; and on at least one occasion, when he was required to approve the *Bishops' Book* for publication, he did not even start to work. That book, which had been commissioned by the king, was finished in mid-July 1537. On the 20th of that month, Edward Fox, who had been closely involved in its compilation under Cromwell's aegis, wrote that it was ready except for a few notes on the Creed and asked to know the king's pleasure about its printing, and, in particular, whether it was to go out in his name or that of the bishops. He repeated this question four days later when he sent the last pages of the work to Cromwell. Despite his letters and despite an appeal from Latimer that the king should purge the book of any 'old leaven' before it was put forth, Henry did not read it. The book was printed with a grovelling episcopal petition as preface, begging the king to grant his approval, 'without the which . . . we knowledge and confess that we have none authority either to assemble ourselves together for any pretence or purpose or to publish any thing that might be by us agreed on and compiled', and asking Henry to make any correction which he saw fit, 'whereunto we shall . . . conform ourselves, as to our most bounden duty to God and to your highness appertaineth'; but their wish was not granted. Attached to this preface was the royal reply announcing that the king had not had enough time to 'overlook' the book but, being 'otherwise occupied', had but 'taken as it were a taste' of it. It therefore went out after Henry had done no more than flip over a few of its pages and without full royal approval. This strange episode has often been remarked, but never explained. Perhaps the explanation was that, at the time when he was required to work through the bishops' offering, Henry was absorbed in Jane Seymour and the approaching birth of her child, and the last thing which a love-sick expectant father wanted on his hands was a weighty theological treatise. Edward's birth and Jane's death left him with time to kill and a stomach for theology. It was then (about December 1537) that he read the book—some months after

it had been published—and found, after all, much that displeased him.

What emerges from the corpus of 'writings' which have been listed above? At times Henry was alarming. He took it upon himself to re-write the First Commandment so that it read 'Thou shalt not have, nor repute any other God, or gods, but me Jesu Christ'—a proposal which not only sent a shudder through Cranmer's obeisance to this vicar of God, his king, but clearly brought him as near an expletive as he had ever been. Henry corrected the *Bishops' Book* to imply that saints are mediators between man and Christ, and suggested that the Christian can pray only to Christ, not to God the Father. At times he was somewhat inept as, for example, when he persistently wrote of 'consecrating' sacraments, or crossed out a long section of notes after the passage on the Ten Commandments. Many of his corrections to the *Bishops' Book* and the *King's Book* were minor ones, the work of a rather enthusiastic pedant—and several times (as Cranmer vigorously protested) they obscured the sense of the passage, broke the flow of the argument or introduced irrelevance and redundancy.

Others of them are wondrously revealing of the royal view of all that is in Heaven and on Earth. Where the *Bishops' Book* stated that all men, rich and poor, 'the free and the bond' are equal in God's eyes, Henry cut down this egalitarianism with the proviso that the equality existed 'touching the soul' only. Where the book called upon the rich to succour the poor, he added the warning 'that there be many folk which had liever live by the graft of begging slothfully' and that these 'should be compelled by one means or other to serve the world with their bodily labour'. The bishops denounced such superstitions as believing in 'lucky' days or thinking it unlucky to meet 'in a morning with certain kinds of beasts, or with men of certain professions' and so on—and their words were crossed out by the king. They went on to denounce astrology, divination, palm-reading and the rest of the apparently ineradicable paganism of their fellow-men; but the king, who himself kept an astrologer at Court, promptly pruned the bishops' list of forbidden crafts and exempted astrology and 'physiognomy' from their prohibition—much to Cranmer's dismay. Where they prayed that we should impute adversity which befalls us to the will of God, not to the Devil or evil men, Henry altered the text to read, 'Make us when any adversity chanceth unto us that we may attribute it unto our desert'— a view of the human condition which drew from Cranmer a shocked lecture on God's inscrutable dealings with man. Where the bishops spoke sternly against 'uncleanly and wanton words, tales, songs, sights, touchings, gay and wanton apparel and lascivious decking', Henry reduced the censure to cover only 'uncleanly sights and wanton words'; and where they denounced 'surfeiting, sloth, idleness, immoderate sleep', he deleted all but the third—all of which was doubtless an honest antipathy to rigour. He crossed out the perhaps embarrassing allegations that a prince's duties towards his people include 'to provide and care for them, that all things necessary may be plenteous', and, perhaps even more significantly, where the book stated that princes might kill and coerce their subjects 'but by and according to the just order of their laws', he so altered the passage that it read that 'inferior rulers', as he called them, *i.e.* ministers of the crown, not princes, were limited by 'the just order of their laws'.

Throughout the annotations to the **Bishops' Book** Henry revealed what, to a Protestant at least, must look like strongly Pelagian tendencies. To put the same thing another way, he continually refuted the uncompromising statement of justification by faith alone which the book sustained and, indeed, upon which it was based, and he did so in a manner which was occasionally dubious even by Catholic standards. Faith for him was mere assent to revealed truth—*fides non formata*, as the scholastics called it; 'story faith', or 'faith in the mouth' as Tyndale and Cranmer called it (somewhat unfairly?)—not the 'lively', 'feeling' faith of the Reformers, which establishes a new, personal relationship between man and God and must, of its very nature, bring forth the fruit of good works, of steadfastness, obedience and joy (which is really what the Scholastics meant by *fides formata*). Time and again, therefore, Henry fell upon passages in the **Bishops' Book** where it affirmed the all-sufficiency of 'right Christian faith' and made corrections which Cranmer judged as unnecessary, misleading or downright erroneous. Where, for example, the book proclaimed that the Christian was the 'inheritor of his (*i.e.* God's) kingdom', Henry added 'as long as I persevere in his precepts and laws'; where it promised that we shall rise again, Henry added in parenthesis, after 'we', the words 'continuing a Christian life'. Man is by 'grace first called, and then by faith', he wrote; my faith will save me, 'I doing my duty'. One long passage on the meaning of faith he deleted and re-wrote; another he completely destroyed by the insertion of two words—the two words in italics in this quotation of the passage: 'The penitent must conceive certain hope and faith that God will forgive him his sins and repute him justified . . . not *only* for the worthiness of any merit or work done by the penitent but *chiefly* for the only merits of the blood and passion of our saviour Christ.' 'Only' and 'chiefly', with remarkable economy, turned upside down this statement of justification by faith alone. As has been said, Cranmer's comments on the royal corrigenda have also survived. To many of Henry's corrections Cranmer replied with a trenchant, even tart, directness which we hardly associate with the archbishop when addressing his king. Whenever he saw what he took to be the popish theology of works riding off Henry's pen, he unhesitatingly struck it down. He had already treated the king to a splendid discourse on the glory of the unfeigned faith of the Christian, a piece which deserves to be placed among the most prized of his remains; when he discovered what the king had done with his two additions, 'only' and 'chiefly', he hit back with the injunction, 'These two words may not be put in this place in anywise.'

It was the same with the **King's Book** six years later. Once more Henry struck at the root of Protestantism. Once more, when that book said that faith makes us members of the Mystical Body, he added 'as long as we so continue' in faith—and so on. It was not that he had not grasped what Cranmer was trying to tell him, but that he did not accept it. In a short paper by Latimer on Purgatory, which Henry read and annotated, the author at one point quoted St Augustine saying that a man goes to Heaven '*pro meritis bonis*'; and Henry has written in the margin, 'this text to *sic*, for 'doth' make against you in another of your opinions'. He clearly saw at least something of what was at issue, therefore, in the debate concerning faith and good works. But, to Cranmer's mind, he had not taken hold of the all-sufficiency of Calvary nor of man's total dependence on grace and of its efficacy. We have to be 'willing to return to God', he said, to 'conform our wills in this world to his precepts' and to 'join our wills to his godly motions' in a life of struggle and effort. Henry did not explicitly deny the rôle of grace, but it certainly seems that he instinctively thought of an order of *human*, unaided good works which, because they are naturally good, merit grace. We have to 'join our wills' to God's 'motions'—and this may easily become a doctrine of human works which share the labour of sanctification with divine grace as an equal partner. Christ is our 'sole redeemer and justifier', but he is also the 'chief and first mean whereby sinners attain the same justification'—the 'chief and first', not, therefore, the only mean. To Cranmer at least, Henry looked like a creature of his time, seemingly afflicted with a merit-theology which is no more truly Catholic than it is Protestant, but is, at root, a semi-Pelagianism which could threaten the whole redeeming mission of Christ.

The king's conservatism is no less evident than his perhaps impoverished understanding of the Redemption and of grace. In his hostile comments on Latimer's paper he showed how he clung to the doctrine of Purgatory; and his additions to the draft of the **Six Articles** of 1539 were all designed to secure greater rigidity. Though the original text of the first article had affirmed both the Real Presence and transubstantiation, the king made doubly sure of the latter by adding that, after consecration, there remained not only no substance of bread and wine, but also

Thomas Cardinal Wolsey, lord chancellor under Henry VIII from 1515 to 1529.

'none other substance but the substance of his (Christ's) foresaid natural body'. He expended the fifth article upholding 'private' masses to make it more explicit and binding. Where the second article had stated that communion under both kinds was not necessary 'by the law of God', he slipped in the addition that it was not necessary '*ad salutem* by the law of God'—which may not have added much, but gave the article a new precision. Vows of chastity, the fourth article had decreed, were to be observed 'by the law of God'; vows of chastity 'or widowhood', wrote the Supreme Head with that zeal for others' righteousness which rarely deserted him. Finally, as he worked over this draft, the king was no less vigilant in safeguarding his own station in life. In the preamble of the text he had been described rather laconically as 'Supreme Head . . . of this Church of England'; after he had finished with it his style ran 'by God's law Supreme Head . . . of this whole Church and congregation of England'.

But alongside stubborn conservatism lay an often startling radicalism. The king who stuck so fervently to transubstantiation, clerical celibacy and Purgatory, who took part in the procession of the Blessed Sacrament to the Altar of Repose on Maundy Thursday, received holy bread and holy water every Sunday, and daily used 'other laudable ceremonies', who hanged a man for eating meat in Lent and, had not his physician, Dr Butts, pleaded with him while he was with his barber, would have had the curate of Chartham in Kent whipped out of the country merely because the latter's congregation had publicly celebrated his acquittal of a charge of heresy, this king could also utter views which were as far removed from his Catholic past as some of the residue of that past was from the 'true religion' put out in the *Bishops' Book*. In the bitter wrangles which preceded the enactment of the *Six Articles*, the conservative bishops, led by Tunstal and Gardiner, fought Cranmer, Latimer and their fellows with tooth and nail. Several times Henry came down to the Lords to preside over the debates and 'confound' (so we are told) the radicals with his learning. At one point, however, when auricular confession was under discussion, the conservatives were apparently worsted, and after the debate Tunstal . . . wrote a long letter to Henry lamenting what had happened, setting out once more his argument that auricular confession, that is, confession to a priest, was necessary by the law of God, was *de iure divino*. When he received this missive, the king scribbled hostile comments in the margin such as 'false', 'this is an example, not a precept', 'all these authorities recommend, not command'. He then wrote a stinging riposte. Tunstal and Gardiner, it began, had been so fully answered the other day in the house of lords that it was surprising to receive this letter setting out the same argument and same texts again. Unless Tunstal was blinded by his own fancy, why did he now provoke the king, unskilled as he was, to make answer to him? He quoted St Chrysostom, but 'your author in this place furthereth you but little in your fallax argument . . . small reason is the ground of your fallax argument . . . you gather a wrong sense upon his words'. The other authorities did not prove the bishop's point—rather they proved Henry's, that auricular confession is not required either by reason or God's law—and 'I marvel you be not ashamed eftsoons to put them in writing'. 'I think that I have more cause to think you obstinate than you me', for Tunstal quoted Origen when the latter plainly meant that we must confess to God and said nothing about confessing to a

priest; he quoted Cyprian, and his words do not command us to confess, and so on.

Tunstal's attempt to swing the debate by this direct appeal to the king received rough handling and he lost his point. The sixth of the *Six Articles* reads 'auricular confession is expedient and necessary to be retained and continued, used and frequented in the Church of God'. The important thing is the omission. This time the words 'by the law of God' do not occur. Auricular confession is 'expedient' and hence its necessity is pragmatic only. Although it had not been dismissed as some may have wanted it to be, Henry had had his way and refused it the necessity of divine sanction which Tunstal and Gardiner argued for it. The point may seem trivial now, but it was significant then. What this article said about auricular confession was as hesitant as the words of that notoriously 'advanced' document, the *Ten Articles* of 1536. In 1539, therefore, the Protestant party salvaged something from the wreck.

In 1536 the official statement of faith spoke of three sacraments only. Next year, in the *Bishops' Book*, the missing sacraments were 'found again'—but with this proviso: that the sacraments of Baptism, Penance and the Altar had a higher 'dignity and necessity', by virtue of their manifest institution by Christ, than the other four. Thus were the factions among the clergy reconciled. But Henry dissented from their compromise. To the three 'first-class' sacraments, and at their head, he added Matrimony. The sacrament in which he was personally so extensively involved was to have primacy of place. The conservative counterattack had already won one victory by 'finding' the four sacraments which had been ignored in the previous year and now Henry would have that advance consolidated by lifting one of them to preeminence. But having thus given his support to the 'Catholic' party, he quickly went on to undo it by inflicting severe damage on the remaining three 'lesser' sacraments.

It is notorious to the historian of theology that the sacrament of Confirmation has been, and still is, the subject of considerable debate. Several questions have continually exercised the minds of theologians, medieval and modern, Roman Catholic and non-Catholic (and especially modern Anglicans among the latter), such as the evidence of its dominical institution, the necessity for its reception and the age at which it should be received. But the most vexatious matter of all has probably been to determine the exact relation between it and Baptism. In the main, medieval theologians, despite minor divergence of view, were agreed that Confirmation completed and perfected Christian initiation, that it brought an *augmentum ad gratiam*, not in the sense of merely intensifying the baptismal gifts, but also of 'sealing' and arming the adult Christian with the full presence of the Holy Spirit, that it did indeed carry Christian initiation to a stage beyond that of Baptism. This was how St Thomas, for example, had written; and this was how Henry, too, wrote in 1521. The *Assertio* had spoken in the boldest terms on Confirmation bringing 'perfect strength' to those regenerated in Baptism and of the 'sealing' and the full coming of the Holy Ghost. Sixteen years later Henry's mind was different. In his corrections to the *Bishops' Book*, which had spoken in an orthodox, though limited, manner to the effect that the sacrament causes us to be not only 'corroborated and established' in the graces of Baptism, but also to 'attain increase and abundance of the other virtues and graces of the Holy Ghost', the king consistently reduced Confirmation to the status of a sacrament which, in essence, *restored* the gifts of the sacraments already received—Baptism, Penance, the Eucharist and, presumably (since, curiously, he speaks of *four* sacraments) Matrimony. Though Confirmation bestows 'other graces of the Holy Ghost, as speaking of languages, prophesying and such others', primarily it merely confirms graces already bestowed. It is 'a restoration and new illumination of the graces given by the others (*sic*) iiii sacraments; a new restitution and restoration of graces granted by Christ to the iiii sacraments instituted by him', by which Christians are to be 'the better restored to their pristine state and established in the religion of a Christian man which they had before professed'. In 1540 the bishops were required to answer seventeen questions about the sacraments. One set of answers affirmed that the imposition of hands in Confirmation 'is grounded in Scripture'—against which opinion Henry scribbled the comment 'laying of hands being an old ceremony of the Jews is but a small proof of Confirmation'; and where it had been answered that the 'thing' of Confirmation, though not the name, is found in Scripture and the use of chrism something that 'hath been in high veneration and observed since the beginning', Henry had written, 'This answer is not direct and yet it proveth neither of the two points to be grounded in Scripture.' Three years later, when he came to correct the text of the **King's Book**, not only did the curious ideas about the effect of this sacrament which he had put forward in 1537 make a brief reappearance, but chrism was denied its adjective 'holy'. Clearly the king was sceptical about Confirmation and would allow it only a subsidiary place in the sacramental economy, and a position which, though not Protestant, was vulnerable to the assertion of, say, Wyclif and the Puritans, that this sacrament was 'superfluous'. However, none of what he wrote in 1537 came out in the book of 1543; and the latter spoke of '*holy* chrism', despite his correction. The theory of the Royal Supremacy was one thing; its practice another.

Henry was harsh also to the sacrament of Extreme Unction. He crossed out a long passage in the **Bishops' Book** which gave the traditional explanation, to be found also in the **Assertio,** of how the anointing was 'a visible sign of an invisible grace', conferred *ex opere operato,* just as, to Cranmer's dismay, he deleted the strongly Protestant statement that the anointing was 'an assured promise' that the sick man should be restored and his sins forgiven. And in 1540, when that same set of answers to the questionnaire on the sacraments asserted that 'Unction of the sick with prayer is grounded in Scripture', Henry wrote in the margin sharply 'then show where'. There is the same doubt, the same probing scepticism that we have met before—perhaps of a more thorough kind. Three years later, when the **King's Book** came to treat of this sacrament, what Henry had deleted in its predecessor was not restored. This time the king had his way.

But of all the sacraments, it was that of Holy Orders which suffered most.

What the **Bishop's Book** had to say about this sacrament was startling enough. In the first place it made no mention of the Mass among the functions of a minister and spoke only of his power 'to consecrate the blessed body of Christ in the sacrament of the altar'—by Catholic standards, a very inadequate statement. The word 'Mass' is used only

Catherine Howard, fifth wife of Henry VIII.

twice in the book, and then *en passant,* in the course of a short disquisition on Purgatory and on the fourth Commandment (to keep the Sabbath holy), where it survived probably more by chance than intention. Secondly, the book omitted all mention of the sacrament conferring an indelible 'character' on the recipient—a cardinal idea of Catholic theology, which the Reformers strenuously opposed. Thirdly, it consistently spoke of bishops and priests as though they were not specifically different. In the New Testament, it stated, 'there is no mention made of any degrees or distinctions in orders, but only of deacons or ministers, and of priests and bishops'; and the words 'priest' and 'bishop' were used indifferently throughout. 'Unto priests or bishops belongeth by the authority of the gospel to approve and confirm' candidates for benefices 'elected and presented unto them' (and notice 'elected'); the ministry set up by Christ and his apostles was given 'unto certain persons only, that is to say, unto priests *or* bishops whom they did elect, call and admit thereunto'; 'the said bishops *or* priests be but only his (*sc.* God's) instruments or officers'; 'for surely the office of preaching is the chief and most principal office, whereunto priests *or* bishops be called' and so on, repeatedly. Not only is the ministry defined in a strongly Protestant way, with preaching taking first place and ministration of the sacraments (and no more than this) second, but the specific distinction of order between priest and bishop is clearly denied, exactly as Protestant theology denied it. Moreover, at one point the book defined bishops and archbishops as 'superintendents or overseers' whose office was to 'oversee, to watch, and to look diligently upon their flock'; and, if those two terms were but direct translation of 'episcopus', they were also telling borrowings from the Lutheran vocabulary.

Henry went over this chapter of the book with the closest attention, making more corrections here than anywhere else. It is impossible that he did not perceive its strongly Lutheran drift. But he made no attempt to reverse it. He re-wrote the definition of the functions of the ministry, starting with 'authority to preach and teach the word of God', and spoke only of the clergy's power 'to consecrate sacraments'—an inappropriate verb which Cranmer quickly corrected. He inserted no reference to the Mass. He allowed the words 'superintendent' and 'overseer' to stand and introduced no specific differentiation of order between priest and bishop; and he who, years ago, had been the author of a work which condemned Luther for denying the indelibility of the 'character' of orders now made no effort to restate what, apparently, he had once proclaimed so earnestly. Further, he took pains to alter the text in more explicit favour of the Royal Supremacy. Where it had described how Christ set over the Church militant the governance of kings and princes and 'certain other ministers and officers' with spiritual duties to perform, Henry deleted 'other', so that the clergy no longer stood in seeming equality with their betters; and where the book instructed the clergy to preach to the people 'committed to their spiritual charge' about the iniquities of the bishop of Rome, Henry amended the text to read 'committed to our and their spiritual charge'. Where the book affirmed that 'it belongeth unto the jurisdiction of priests or bishops' to make rules concerning holy days, ceremonies and rites, Henry wrote instead that 'it is therefore thought requisite and right necessary' that the clergy should do these things. Where the book explained that the Fifth Commandment enjoined obedience not only to the spiritual father, 'by whom we be spiritually regenerated and nourished in Christ', but also to 'all other governors and rulers, under whom we be nourished and brought up, or ordered and guided', Henry removed the bouquet to the clergy and left the passage so that it urged obedience to natural parents 'and all other governors and rulers' only. Where the bishops recalled that Christ empowered the Apostles to 'elect, call and admit' their successors, 'that is to say, . . . bishops or priests', the Supreme Head put in the margin 'Note, that there were no kings Christian under whom they did dwell'. Most alarmingly of all, he put his pen through a passage exactly similar to one he deleted from the chapter on Extreme Unction.—*i.e.* that in which it was said that the sacrament of Orders is rightly so-called because it was instituted by Christ and consists of two parts, 'a spiritual and inward grace, and also an outward and a visible sign'. Once more this piece of traditional sacramental theology was removed. All that remained was the somewhat vague sentence that the sacrament 'was institute to the intent that the church of Christ should never be destitute' of ministers. 'It was institute' (Henry's formula) replaced the explicit statement of the sacraments' nature and dominical authority. Finally, wherever the words 'Holy Orders' appeared, he removed the adjective. Orders were to be no more 'holy' than was chrism.

Three years later (in 1540) came the questionnaires to the bishops on the sacraments. The questions themselves are of the greatest interest: they asked, for example, what the word 'sacrament' meant in Scripture and to the Fathers, whether it should be confined only to the seven sacraments, and what Scriptural authority there was for auricular Confession, Confirmation, Extreme Unction. Six of the seventeen questions concerned Orders. One asked whether the apostles 'in not having a Christian king among them, made bishops by that necessity, or by authority of God'; another whether bishops or priests were first and whether they 'were not two things, but both one office in the beginning of Christ's religion'; another whether bishops alone might make priests; another whether, on the evidence of the New Testament, both appointment and consecration were necessary, or whether a bishop was made solely by his appointment; another whether 'a prince Christian learned', who conquered infidels and had no clergy with him, could preach and teach the word of God; and the last whether, if all the clergy of a region died, the king thereof 'should make bishops and priests to supply the same'.

Some of these questions reopened disputes which had been present for some years. Some opened up matters with which we have already seen Henry deal. Some, particularly the last few quoted above, pushed enquiry into new territory.

The replies to these questions show that the feuds and disagreements between the factions had not abated. A number of the bishops reiterated the time-honoured formulae learned in the Schools. Others have evidently moved on. Cranmer, in particular, showed how far he had advanced. 'I know no cause why this word "sacrament" should be attributed to the seven only,' he said. The ceremonies of 'the committing of the ecclesiastical office' have 'no more promise of God' than those 'in the committing of civil office'; 'bishops and priests were . . . both one office in the beginning of Christ's religion'; a Christian king finding himself alone among infidels would be bound to preach the gospel and 'it is not forbidden by God's law' that he should 'make bishops and priests'.

Henry commented on two of these sets of replies. Some of his remarks we have already quoted when discussing his views on Confirmation and Extreme Unction. We must return to them now because they also throw further light on his attitude to the sacrament of Orders. One of the bishops' replies says that the making of a bishop is in two parts—appointment, which in the Apostles' time was by election (and is now performed by princes), and ordering. To this the king made a swift retort. 'Where is this distinction found? Now, since you confess that the Apostles did occupy the one part which now you confess belongeth to princes, how can you prove that ordering is only committed to you bishops?' In his replies, Cranmer came very near to bestowing the *potestas ordinis* upon the king. Civil and ecclesiastical ministers are equally sprung of royal appointment, he asserted; the prince who found himself alone among infidels would not be prohibited by God's law from ordaining a clergy. Henry seems to have been pushing to the same conclusion. If the Apostles performed one function in the making of a bishop (*i.e.* his election) which is known to belong now to princes, why should not the second part, consecration, belong to princes also? How can the bishops prove that their monopoly of ordering is not 'wrongly committed' to them? And when the same document says that the apostles, when they ordained, followed rules taught by the Holy Spirit and ordered 'by imposition of hands with prayer and fasting', Henry wrote

'*Ubi hic?*'—'where do you find this?' He was still as sceptical about this sacrament as he had been in 1537.

It would be unjust to place too much upon these marginal comments and jottings—particularly those which have just been quoted—and argue therefrom that Henry had arrived at a coherent, carefully-considered radicalism. Maybe he was not prepared to push all his ideas to their conclusion. He never made overt claim to the *potestas ordinis;* the **King's Book** did not contain all the corrections which he had made to the previous statement of faith. Nonetheless, it is clear that his mind was on the move, that he was toying with violent novelty, questioning and doubting much more of the Faith of his forefathers than merely the Roman primacy. The result was a highly personal admixture of new and old. Henry was his own theologian. Much of what he believed may have been uncompromisingly 'Catholic', but alongside a firm allegiance to transubstantiation, clerical celibacy, and the rest there was much of a very different colour. His ideas on Confirmation and Extreme Unction were not those of the Council of Trent, just as his ideas on Matrimony were not those of Luther. If he never accepted justification by faith alone, he certainly allowed, and himself put forward, the most heterodox views on the priesthood. Indeed, if there is any single thread to his theological evolution it is his anticlericalism. He who had persistently called the clergy his ministers and mere 'doctors' of the soul, and had thrust forward—against the clergy—the prince's claim to a cure of souls, now allowed the strongly Protestant description of the ministry in the **Bishops' Book** to stand, stripped the sacrament of Orders of its essential theology and its title of 'holy', and by 1540 was stabbing into it yet deeper. Furthermore, the deletions which he made in 1537 were not undone in 1543. The **King's Book** did not give back 'holy' to the sacrament of Orders, nor restore to it the exposition of its operations as a visible sign of an invisible grace, instituted by Christ. In that book the sacrament appeared as merely a gift 'given of God to Christian men . . . conferred and given to the apostles as appeareth in the Epistle of St Paul to Timothy'; and no more than the **Bishops' Book** did this one make a specific distinction between priest and bishop.

A belligerent anticlericalism which, wittingly or otherwise, had a strongly Protestant flavour went hand in hand with an unremitting, but strongly un-Protestant, insistence on clerical celibacy, from which Henry would not shift. He asserted it by proclamation, allowed it to do much to wreck the Anglo-Lutheran negotiations of 1538, reaffirmed it and . . . widened its compass in the **Six Articles** of 1539. Indeed, the latter lifted the prohibition of clerical marriage to a new level by declaring that what most would have judged to be a matter of ecclesiastical discipline only was forbidden 'by the law of God'—an addition which Henry himself made in the preamble of that act, where its authors had omitted it. (pp. 403-18)

[The] large discrepancies between the theological opinions which he expressed in the 1530s and what he had written years before in the **Assertio** are such clear evidence that his mind was on the move, discarding much of its past and venturing, however tentatively, into novelty. . . (p. 420)

J. J. Scarisbrick, in his Henry VIII, *University of California Press, 1968, 561 p.*

M. D. PALMER　(essay date 1971)

[*Palmer is an Australian-born English educator and historian. In the following excerpt from his* Henry VIII, *he describes and terms "hollow" the reasoning of* A Glasse of the Truthe.]

The necessity of nullifying his marriage to Catherine of Aragon and his desire to marry Anne Boleyn led Henry to make greater and greater claims for his own authority against that of the Pope. As he was a firm Catholic and wanted his subsequent offspring to be accepted as rightful heirs to the throne, he was keen to have papal approval for his remarriage, but the more unlikely this became, the more he was forced to question the Pope's jurisdiction in England. Finally he repudiated Papal authority altogether.

In the period between 1527 and 1532, Henry was first concerned with questioning the validity of Julius II's dispensation and then with the Pope's right to conduct the hearing of his case in Rome. Up to this point pressure had been brought on the Church in England, but no measures had been taken against the Pope. Direct pressure on Rome began with the Act in Conditional Restraint of Annates 1532, and it was accompanied by a propaganda campaign, which became more extreme, as pressure on the Papacy increased. Most of the books supporting Henry's case were published by the royal printer, Thomas Berthelet and therefore had some kind of official approval.

Thomas Cranmer, Archbishop of Canterbury, who gained favor with Henry by declaring his marriage to Catherine of Aragon null and void.

A considerable variety of books were published. Some were pamphlets aimed at a wide audience, like the anonymous *A Glasse of the Truth,* others like Fox's *De Vera Differentia* (1534) and Gardiner's *De Vera Obedientia* (1535) were written in Latin for the educated public both at home and abroad. Attempts to find English medieval treatises defending royal supremacy were vain as the only examples were those of Wycliffe and the Lollards which were heretical, but the gap was filled by translations of the works of Marsiglio of Padua, a fourteenth-century Italian, with the adverse chapters omitted. St German published a series of works between 1530 and 1535 which would have mainly appealed to lawyers. In addition to these, there were court writers like Thomas Starkey and Richard Morison, both of whom had been members of Reginald Pole's humanist circle at Padua, and managed to avoid being associated with Pole's opposition to Henry's remarriage.

There was no great coherence in the ideas that these writers put forward. Their main concern was to justify royal authority against that of the Pope and to commend passive obedience. It is, therefore, not to be expected that their statements on royal sovereignty would be utterly consistent. They were not very concerned about sovereignty nor were they particularly concerned about the exact distribution of power within the partnership of king and parliament. These matters only became important when parliament and king were trying to defend their position against each other in the seventeenth century. During Henry's reign, they agreed that the power of Church and Pope should be curtailed, and this was reflected in the books that were published. (pp. 45-6)

The divorce needed justification, but it did not receive it in published form until *A Glasse of the Truth* was published.... Previously Henry had been conducting a personal debate with the Pope in an attempt to persuade the Curia that Julius II had gone beyond his authority in issuing the original dispensation in 1505. One argument that Henry used was that the grounds given for the original dispensation were insufficient in that it was given only 'for preserving the peace between the crowns of England and Spain'. This argument was made untenable by the discovery of a second copy of the dispensation in Spain in 1528, which stated that it was for this 'and other reasons', and therefore this argument had lost all validity by [the time *A Glasse of the Truth* was published]. The other main contention was that Henry's marriage to Catherine broke the divine law and that the Pope could not release anyone from this. This point of view was still strongly defended [at this time] and a long list of ancient authors was given to justify the claim. A scriptural text was quoted as further evidence. Jesus said to the Pharisees, "Why do you break or transgress the commandment of God for your own traditions" (Matthew 15:3). The scriptures were not a sure basis of support for the king, because the condemnation of his marriage in Leviticus (Leviticus 20:21) is contradicted by the order in Deuteronomy that a man should marry his brother's widow if she is childless (Deuteronomy 15:5). The pamphleteer of [*A Glasse of the Truth*] explains this away by declaring that Deuteronomy referred to the Jews only and 'should not be but in a mystical sense observed by us Christian men'.

The hollowness of the arguments in *A Glasse of the Truth* reveals the insuperable task that Henry had undertaken in

questioning the authority of the Papacy to interpret the divine law. It was not only that to a papalist, a Pope could not be mistaken when he interpreted the canon law, but also that Julius II had many clear, recent precedents for issuing dispensations from the laws against marriages with kinsmen in the first degree collateral of affinity. There were also recent cases, where Popes had released Henry's relatives from marriages due to pre-contracts rather than to affinity, but the success of his sister Margaret in 1527 and his brother-in-law the Duke of Suffolk in 1528 in gaining release from their marriages, must have lulled Henry into thinking that it would not be difficult.

Had he taken sound legal advice in 1527, Henry would have seen that it was better to base his case on the insufficiency of Julius II's bull rather than on its illegality. Julius II's bull suggested that the marriage between Catherine and Arthur, which ended after five months with the death of Arthur from consumption, might have been consummated. The words *forsan consummatum* were used. This was important because a different kind of dispensation was needed for release from a mere contract without consummation than from a marriage that was both ratified and consummated. Only the latter created an impediment of affinity and it was from such an impediment that Henry VIII was released. If the impediment was of the former kind, which is called an impediment of public honesty, then a different dispensation from the one that Julius II had granted was needed. If he had argued, therefore, that the dispensation was valid but irrelevant to his particular case, there would have been no need to question papal authority. (pp. 46-7)

M. D. Palmer, in his Henry VIII, *Longman, 1971, 148 p.*

LACEY BALDWIN SMITH   (essay date 1971)

[*Smith is an American scholar whose historical and biographical studies include* Tudor Prelates and Politics, 1536-1558 *(1953) and* Elizabeth Tudor: Portrait of a Queen *(1975). His respected book* Henry VIII: The Mask of Royalty *(1971) differs from traditional biography in that "Mr. Smith's aim is not to tell us what Henry did," according to Thomas Lask, "but what kind of man it was who did it: what his values were, the nature of his thought and how these revealed themselves when combined with his character." In the following excerpt from this work, Smith comments on Henry's enthusiasm and intellect as they relate to* Assertion of the Seven Sacraments.]

As a result of his precipitate enthusiasms, Henry was destined to go through life eating his words. During the years when the King was a dutiful and eloquent son of the Church and was writing *The Defence of the Seven Sacraments,* Sir Thomas More warned him against overstating the theory of papal supremacy on the ground that popes were political figures with whom monarchs might some day find themselves in conflict. 'I think it is best therefore that the part be amended, and his authority more lightly touched.' Henry, however, would have no such politic half-measure. 'Nay, quoth his Grace, that it shall not. We are so much bounden to the See of Rome that we cannot do too much honour to it.' (p. 92)

Clearly the King was an enthusiast in all he did, in both the intensity with which he held a position and the lengths to which he was willing to go to sustain it. He wrote *The Defence of the Seven Sacraments* in a month; he informed Anne Boleyn that his study of the theological justification for his divorce involved four uninterrupted hours a day of intensive work and had caused 'some pain in his head'.... (p. 93)

Henry may have gone the whole way in his emotional commitments, but intellectually he rarely got more than half-way. In spite of his expertise, his extraordinary mastery of detail and his encyclopedic memory, he was not an intellectual. His mind was quick and its filing system neat and efficient, but compilation and cataloguing were largely substitutes for thinking. Whatever the theological merits of *The Defence of the Seven Sacraments* Henry never really answered Martin Luther because spiritually they had no common meeting-ground. Neither emotionally nor intellectually was the King equipped to comprehend the solitary nightmare of self-analysis which led the German monk to God. Typically Henry ignored the root and saw only the branches of Luther's argument. 'Why raises he this tumult?' The answer was direct and simple: to foster evil men who sought to escape punishment for their sins. The concept of faith based on despair without strict attention to good works and obedience to God's law was, for the English Moses, silly and dangerous. It was plain to all, the King explained, that there were 'ten to be found who sin in the too much confidence' of God's promise, for every 'one who despairs of obtaining pardon.' What Henry could not see was that God's Word when it enters man's heart has little to do with the theological niceties of the past. Luther was right: Henry Tudor's book was 'based on words of men and the use of centuries' about which the King was a specialist. The Defender of the Faith was always stronger when it came to ritualistic means than to spiritual ends. (pp. 93-4)

Lacey Baldwin Smith, in his Henry VIII: The Mask of Royalty, *Jonathan Cape, 1971, 328 p.*

G. R. ELTON (essay date 1972)

[*Elton is a German-born English historian. Among his many books are* The Tudor Revolution in Government: Administrative Changes in the Reign of Henry VIII *(1953) and* Wolsey *(1965). In the following excerpt from* Policy and Police: The Enforcement of the Reformation in the Age of Thomas Cromwell, *Elton discusses the success of* A Glasse of the Truthe *as a propagandist tract and considers its relation to the train of events leading to Henry's divorce from Catherine of Aragon.*]

The Glass of Truth acknowledged no author, but there are some firm hints that the King had a personal hand in it. (p. 176)

The **Glass of Truth** is a successful piece of propaganda—readable, clear, lively, short enough but seemingly full of meat. Its whole argument is directed very much by the theological and canonistic exposition one finds in [an earlier propagandist pamphlet, *The Determination of the Most Famous and Excellent Universities of Italy and France, That it Is Unlawful for a Man to Marry His Brother's wife and that the Pope Hath No Power to Dispense Therewith* (1531)], but where that was heavy and dull, though learned, the **Glass** provides a surface-skimming and popularised version of the official views on the Leviti-

cal law and the limitations of the pope's dispensing power. Newly added is the lengthy story of Prince Arthur's boasts about his wedding night which, intended to prove that the first marriage had been consummated, was originally obtained from witnesses for the legatine trial in 1529, and which now proved useful in cheering up a dry discourse. The dialogue form—between a theologian and a canon lawyer—makes possible both the breaking up of the argument into manageable chunks and a very useful pretence at debate, as though all opinions were given their chance before the conversation ends with a solemn approval of the King's case. The book is further made more attractive reading for its intended audience by having the theological and canonist arguments placed against a background of patriotic fervour and king-worshipping loyalty. The stress on the need for a male heir to save the realm from disaster, on the duty of obeying the King and of refusing to listen to the lying rumours which evil-wishers spread about him, especially the clangingly chauvinistic conclusion—all these show to whom the work is addressed. It was written to be read in England and to defend to Englishmen both the King's desire for a divorce and his refusal to submit to papal jurisdiction, and it does this work extremely well.

The book is as notable for what it does not say. There is not one word against the pope's headship of the Church, nor a single word of rudeness against one who is invariably referred to by his traditional title. All that is stated, again and again, is that the pope has no power to dispense from the law of Scripture and moreover no right to insist on provoking a case to Rome when, by the law of the Church, it should be heard in England. This was the line taken ever since Wolsey's failure in 1529 to hold his fellow-cardinal to a settlement in England. The tone of the book has nothing drastic or ominous in it, and to all outward appearance the **Glass** marks no change in English policy. However, there is one important qualification to this. The treatise does not confine itself to re-asserting the justice of the King's position; it also, very briefly, offers a solution for resolving the deadlock. Parliament, we are told, if it would exert its 'wits and good will', would soon find a way, and that way in effect should be an instruction to the 'metropolitans of this realm (their unjust oath made to the pope notwithstanding)' to bring the affair to a satisfactory conclusion. Not that this sort of talk was new, but it must be remembered that on previous occasions talk of Parliament had always ended in inaction as it was decided that there was nothing that Parliament could do to help. By contrast, some three months at the latest after the **Glass** was published, Cromwell was at work on the Act of Appeals by means of which Cranmer in May 1533 could issue a final sentence ending the marriage. A draft bill specifically empowering the archbishops to proceed fits the words of the **Glass** better than the Act of Appeals which in the winter of 1532 took its place (because it was decided to turn the settlement of the specific issue into the opening shot of the new revolutionary course of action), but either way Parliament would at last have shown itself able to intervene.

It is surely not extravagant, therefore, to see these future events forecast in the one positive proposal for action contained in the **Glass**. And from this it follows that the book was in measure intended to serve two purposes: to defend the justice of the King's demands, and to prepare the ground for the new and stronger line already decided

Catherine Parr, sixth (and last) wife of Henry VIII.

upon. The passage in the *Glass* makes real sense only in the light of what immediately followed and on the supposition that its authors knew what was coming forward next. Ever since Thomas More had resigned the great seal in May 1532, the radical policy espoused by Thomas Cromwell had dominated the Council; evidently, by the time that the *Glass* was being written, the decision to ignore Rome had already been taken, though possibly the decision that the moment for the declaration of a major break had come was still to be hammered out. But that the pope would not be allowed to stand any longer in the way of the Divorce is what those few words in the *Glass* discreetly indicate—as indeed does the very fact of the book's publication. (pp. 177-79)

G. R. Elton, "Propaganda," in his Policy and Police: The Enforcement of the Reformation in the Age of Thomas Cromwell, *Cambridge at the University Press, 1972, pp. 171-216.*

STEVEN W. HAAS (essay date 1979)

[*The following excerpt is from an essay in which Haas argues that Henry embraced the concept of the divine right of kings well before the Act of Royal Supremacy in 1534. Here, he adduces evidence from* A Glasse of the Truthe *to support this view.*]

[The thesis of *A Glasse of the Truthe*] is quite straightforward. The pope is guilty of over-stepping his authority by unreasonably delaying the divorce. The impartial and carefully considered decisions of both English and continental universities, as well as the holy scriptures and a long list of Church councils—especially Constance—have proved that papal action on this subject is too often without divine sanction. These 'facts' are revealed in a dialogue between a lawyer and a priest, who are both partisans of the king. The 'injustice' focussed upon by both speakers is the pope's delay of the divorce, which only postpones that day when Englishmen can enjoy a stable future insured by the birth of a male heir to the throne. All the futile challenges thrown up against the king's Levitical argument, especially that from Deuteronomy 25, are roundly criticized as irrelevant. Likewise, all of those rumours circulating in the countryside to the effect that Henry defies 'God's law' when he opposes the pope are mistaken and treasonable. Indeed, scriptural authority reveals that God's law is on the side of the king. The pope has no right to dispense with this divine law or the law of nature. The word of God requires that all subjects be loyal to their king, for he, not the pope, follows scripture.

One is perhaps most struck with the strong vein of nationalism that runs through the *Glasse*. Again and again, the loyal subject is reminded that Rome is a foreign power, and that the pope has no right to insist that Henry be called there for a decision on his divorce. Most assuredly, if the impasse is not overcome in short order it is even possible that parliament should handle the matter. It, rather than the pope, would surely decide the case on a basis of morality and justice, and these considerations are uppermost in the king's mind. (pp. 354-55)

[The] law of God as presented in . . . the *Glasse* is entirely promonarchical. The pope is accused of abusing God's law when he opposes Henry's Levitical arguments and requires that the king's case be tried in Rome. Hence, if any of Henry's subjects heed the rumours festering in the countryside which claim that the king is in contempt of God when he defies such papal assertions, they should realize that the pope, not Henry, was in violation of divine ordinance. In short, God's law is proclaimed by the *Glasse* to restrict the temporal sovereignty of the pope. Papal powers of dispensation and excommunication, in addition to legal jurisdiction, defy the sanction of scripture. Therefore it is a terrible delusion for the pope to assert that his word is equivalent to God's law. The conservatism of the royal cause is the issue here, and Henry had repeated recourse to the 'law of God' in this context throughout his dealings with the pope, Catherine and foreign ambassadors during 1531. Its attraction was that it placed the king alongside God, and the pope with mortals. The *Glasse* makes much of this distinction, as is exemplified in its claim that the pope ' . . . is but a man, and subjects must obey God rather than man'. The pope, not Henry, was hence the innovator and radical.

As in [William Tyndale's *Obedience of a Christian Man* (1528)], so in the *Glasse* does God's law demand that a loyal subject accept royal policy without question. Obedience to the king is equated with the law of God and of nature, piety and loyalty thus being one and the same. . . . Indeed, a subject in search of salvation had no choice but to 'sticke with' Henry, and to report all those misguided souls who dared commit a treasonable offence. . . . This assurance that divine favour would be gained by a watchful patriotism is strongly put in both the *Obedience* and the

Glasse. Likewise in the body and the conclusion of the *Glasse* a most familiar rationale for such a zealous loyalty is put forward. The first invocation warns the reader, 'For god commaundeth obedience to the prince, and so doth he not to the (demands) of the pope. . . . For it is farre out of order to breke theyn obedience thow owest to god, for thyn obedience towarde man (i.e. the pope)'. Lest the subject overlook or forget this stricture, he is soon reminded that:

> Wherfore since the truth favoreth our princes cause so moche: let us his subjectes (then) not omit neither our zele ne yet our obedience to him according to our allegiance: . . . nor our dutie to god in assisting the truth, as is the part and office of a trewe christian man . . . moche more, he (God) forbiddeth us in that (which) is against our prince and soveraine.

At this juncture, the central theme of the *Glasse* has been completed. While it is noteworthy that the remaining few pages do include two references to Parliament as the logical arbiter of the divorce, it is manifestly clear that these briefly put alternatives are but a postscript to the core of the text. Immediately following this speculation is a reaffirmation of the main theme, which concludes that 'Rather we ought to obey god than man, and thus this little treatise shall make his end'. (pp. 358-60)

> *Steven W. Haas, "Henry VIII's 'Glasse of Truthe'," in* History: The Journal of the Historical Association, *n.s. Vol. 64, No. 212, October, 1979, pp. 353-62.*

CAROLLY ERICKSON (essay date 1980)

[*An American historian, Erickson has written popular biographies of principal Tudor personalities, including* Bloody Mary *(1978),* The First Elizabeth *(1983), and* Mistress Anne *(1984). Like her others, her biography of Henry,* Great Harry, *is intended for the general reader rather than the scholar. Reviewer Christopher Hibbert described the book as "an admirable biography, graphic, judicious, carefully researched, skillfully constructed and full of those telling details that are an essential ingredient of the narrator's art." In the following excerpt from* Great Harry, *Erickson relates Henry's songwriting to his circumstances, describes the initial reception of his musical work, and examines the musical milieu of the era.*]

[In the early years of his reign] Henry himself was the foremost amateur musician [at court], and when he was not hunting or riding in the tiltyard he occupied himself with singing and dancing and playing the recorder, flute or virginal. He set poems to music too, and wrote masses and ballets in the Italian style for several parts. And with a candor characteristic of him Henry wove into his songs the thoughts that weighed on him in these years.

His songs defended the carefree, good times of youth—the recreations and innocent sport of a boy and his friends. They were fresh, bracing songs, vigorous and direct. But at the same time they sounded a cry of the heart.

> Youth will needs have dalliance,
> Of good or ill some pastance;
> Company me thinketh best
> All thought and fancies to digest,
> For idleness
> Is chief mistress
> Of vices all;
> Then who can say
> But pass the day
> Is best of all?

Behind the rousing verses was a plea for freedom and pleasure, and the argument, endlessly repeated, that innocent, "honest" pastimes counteracted the vices bred by idleness.

In part, this plea was a response to a chorus of critical voices. Although Henry himself insisted that his good times did not keep him from attending to affairs of state, and there is considerable evidence this was true, his principal advisers saw him as little more than an overgrown child. (pp. 57-8)

He was his own master. He might face the disapproval of his councilors, but whatever they thought of him, he was still their king. And the king's word was law.

It was this awesome realization, coupled with his awareness of his immaturity, that ran in Henry's thoughts at the outset of his reign and found expression in his verses. "With good order, counsel and equity, God lord, grant us our mansion to be!" he wrote. "For without their good guidance/Youth should fall in great mischance." He was unsure of himself; he was finding his way, a young man of firm conscience but slight experience set over sophisticated courtiers of uncertain morality and unmistakable inclinations to vice. "God and my right and my duty,/From them I shall never vary" Henry sang, insisting "I hurt no man, I do no wrong;/I love true where I did marry." But he knew as well as anyone that, if he chose, he could let his duty go, hurt whom he chose and cultivate wrongdoing, and betray Katherine with any woman who appealed to him—all without hindrance.

> For youth is frail and prompt to do,
> As well vices as virtues to ensue;
> Wherefore by these he must be guided
> And virtuous pastance must be therein used. (pp. 58-9)

If the courtiers were expected to keep Henry company and to share his amusements they were also an appreciative audience for his performances. They listened attentively while he sang and showed his virtuosity on the virginal, recorder, gitteron-pipe, lute-pipe, cornet and organ. They applauded his informal concerts on the organ and harpsichord—instruments he was said to practice on day and night. They sang the melodies he wrote to French verses about sorrowful partings, lovers' sufferings, and true love and overlooked the awkward rhymes he wrote himself:

> The daise delectable,
> The violett wan and blo;
> Ye ar not varyable;
> I love you and no mo.
>
> I make you fast and sure;
> It ys to me gret payne
> Thus longe to endure,
> Tyll that we mete agayne.

They were proud of his skill as an amateur composer whose best-known song, **"Pastime with Good Company,"** became a popular classic. His songs were sung in inns and alehouses as well as at court, and preachers incorporated them into their sermons. In 1521 servants in the royal household heard the king's almoner speak, taking as his text **"Pastime"** and another of Henry's songs, **"I love unloved."** His masses and motets, no worse than many others written by professional musicians, were sung in his chapel and elsewhere, and his instrumental music was played at banquets and as an accompaniment to court pageantry. (p. 110)

[In 1530 Henry was] at an extraordinary peak of creative power, not only intellectually but artistically. His mind ranged widely, and illumined everything it touched. He drew up visionary architectural plans. He commissioned painters, sculptors and master craftsmen to decorate his palaces and guided their work with craftsmanlike taste. He endowed colleges and patronized students and scholars. He returned with renewed fervor to composing love songs and instrumental pieces, writing two motets—**"O Lord the Maker of All Things"** and **"Quam Pulchra Es"**—that entered the enduring canon of English church music.

As a composer and performer Henry was a part of a broad transition in court music, from the highly professional and traditional style of the late Middle Ages, with its chivalrous basse-dances, its set forms and preference for the harp to a newer, more fluid Italianate style. Amateurs and professionals performed together the lively Italian pavanes and galliards, the amateurs learning from music-masters to read written notes and to follow the intricate patterns of part songs. The king had long been the most illustrious amateur musician in the country.... (p. 235)

Carolly Erickson, in her Great Harry, *Summit Books, 1980, 428 p.*

JASPER RIDLEY   (essay date 1984)

[*Ridley is a historical writer and biographer whose works include* Thomas Cranmer *(1962) and* Mary Tudor *(1973). Ridley has written of his work: "For me, the study of history and of the men and women who made it throws a fascinating light on the characters and behavior of individuals and of masses, and on the different types of human beings—the idealists, the power-politicians and the opportunists—who reappear in every century. I am interested in what is the same and what is different in the attitude of people in past and present generations. Though I enjoy research . . . , it is for me only a prelude to the writing, to attempting to bring alive the events of the past and to interpret the people of earlier centuries to my twentieth-century readers." In the following excerpt from his biography of Henry, Ridley describes the main points of* Assertion of the Seven Sacraments, *the work of "an intelligent amateur."*]

[Henry VIII's] *Assertion of the Seven Sacraments* was a short book of some thirty thousand words, written in Latin. . . . Very few of Henry's contemporaries believed that he had really written the book himself. Some thought that Wolsey had written it; others believed that More was the author. Luther was convinced that Edward Lee had written it. But according to More, though he and other theologians helped Henry with the research and contributed suggestions, Henry wrote the book himself.

Many modern scholars, like Henry's contemporaries, have refused to believe this; but though Henry was bored by

The deathbed of Henry as imagined hopefully by his supporters. Power is transferred smoothly to Prince Edward, while the Pope is overthrown.

state papers and disliked writing, and even reading, letters, he was fascinated by theological controversy. No one who reads his drafts and corrections of the articles of religion and doctrinal treatises which were issued in the last years of his reign should be surprised that he was already capable, fifteen years earlier, of writing *The Assertion of the Seven Sacraments*. When Pace arrived at Greenwich in April 1521, he found him avidly reading a copy of Luther's latest book which Wolsey had sent him. He took many hours off from hunting to sit in his closet studying the authorities which More, Fisher and Lee had assembled for him, and writing his book.

The style of the book also suggests that Henry was the author. It reads like the work, not of a professional theologian, but of an intelligent amateur. The quotations from Scripture and the patristic texts are kept to a minimum, and the arguments are put briefly, clearly, logically and forcibly. Although Henry denounces Luther with some vigour as 'this impious fellow', 'this new doctor', 'this little saint', 'the little monk', his language falls far short of the polemical insults which mark most of the anti-Lutheran tracts of the period.

After defending the practice of granting indulgences—it was wrong of Luther 'to excite men to confide in the riches of their own penitence and despise the treasures of Holy Church and the bounty of God'—Henry turned to the question of Papal supremacy. He treated it as being self-evidently true. 'I will not wrong the Bishop of Rome so much as troublesomely or carefully to dispute his right, as if it were a matter doubtful', for Luther 'cannot deny but that all the faithful honour and acknowledge the sacred Roman See for their mother, and supreme'. As regards the sacrament of the altar, Henry rejected Luther's insistence that the wine as well as the bread should be given to the congregation. He had no objection to the administration of the sacrament in both kinds, but put forward the orthodox view that, as this was an inessential matter, the present system of giving only the bread to the laity should continue, and no one should denounce it until the Church ordered otherwise. If Luther attached so much importance to carrying out the words of Scripture, why did he not insist that the Eucharist should only be administered at supper time?

How could Luther deny that marriage was a sacrament, merely because it was not stated to be so in the Bible? 'You admit no sacrament unless you read its institution in a book!' Marriage, wrote Henry, was the first of all sacraments to be instituted, because the first man, Adam, was married; and it was at a wedding that Christ performed his first miracle. 'If all generation out of wedlock is damnable, the grace of marriage must needs be great, by which that act (which of its own nature defiles to punishment) is not only purged, to take away the blemish; but is so much sanctified that, as the Apostle testifies, it becomes meritorious'. But why, asked Henry, 'search we so many proofs in so clear a thing? especially when that only text is sufficient for all, where Christ says "Whom God has joined together, let no man put asunder". O the admirable word! which none could have spoken, but the Word that was made flesh!'

Above all, Henry denounced Luther for encouraging sedition. He quoted with approval the passage from St Augustine: 'The power of the King, the right of the owner, the instruments of the executioner, the arms of the soldier, the discipline of the governor, and the severity of the good father, were not instituted in vain', and added: 'But I forbear to speak of Kings, lest I should seem to plead my own cause'. He went out of his way, in two places in his book, to refer to the superiority of men over women, which was so clearly laid down by Christian doctrine that even when a Christian woman had married an infidel husband, she was commanded by the Church to obey him.

In October, a beautifully bound copy of the book was presented to the Pope in Consistory by John Clerk, Henry's ambassador in Rome. The grateful Pope thanked Henry, his 'most dear son in Christ', who had formerly defended the Church with his sword and was now defending her with his pen; and in order to confirm Henry in his most holy purposes and to augment his devotion, he granted to him and his successors the title of 'Defender of the Faith'. He assured Henry that if anyone should ever try to deprive him of this new title, such a person would incur the indignation of Almighty God and of the holy Apostles, Peter and Paul [see essay dated 1521]. (pp. 127-29)

Jasper Ridley, in his Henry VIII, *Constable, 1984, 473 p.*

ADDITIONAL BIBLIOGRAPHY

Belloc, Hilaire. "King Henry VIII." in his *Characters of the Reformation*, pp. 26-45. 1936. Reprint. Freeport, N.Y.: Books for Libraries Press, 1970.
> Analyzes the character of Henry, "the author of that great disaster the English Reformation." Describing his subject as weak, selfish, capricious, and vain, Belloc concludes: "If the evil powers had had to choose their instrument, assigning to it the right proportions of violence and weakness, incomprehension, passion and the rest, they could hardly have framed a tool more serviceable to their hands than that which did—without full intention—effect the main tragedy in the modern history of Europe."

Bowle, John. *Henry VIII*. Boston: Little, Brown and Co., 1964, 316 p.
> Biography. Bowle assesses Henry in terms of his essential, decisive character trait of "opportunist realism."

Brewer, J. S., Gairdner, James, and Brodie, R. H., eds. *Letters and Papers, Foreign and Domestic, of the Reign of Henry VIII.* 22 vols. London: Longman & Co., 1862-1932.
> Prints the most important documents of Henry's reign. This collection is considered essential for the student who wishes to examine original source material.

Doernberg, Erwin. *Henry VIII and Luther: An Account of Their Personal Relations.* Stanford: Stanford University Press, 1961, 139 p.
> Examines the relationship of Henry and Martin Luther from the writing of *Assertion of the Seven Sacraments* to 1540. Doernberg acknowledges a bias against Henry and the Henrician Reformation but stresses that he strives for objectivity.

Hackett, Francis. *The Personal History of Henry the Eighth.* New York: Modern Library, 1929, 598 p.

Dramatic, "psycho-historical" biography. Hackett explains his method thus: "To be *then*-minded, to use imagination and intuition, to suggest life—this is the task of the psycho-historian. But no vividness excuses infidelity to the facts. . . ."

Harpsfield, Nicholas. *A Treatise on the Pretended Divorce between Henry VIII and Catharine of Aragon.* Edited by Nicholas Pocock. 1878. Reprint. New York: Johnson Reprint Corp., 1965, 344 p.

Harpsfield's spirited defense, written in the 1550s, of the validity of Henry's marriage to Catherine of Aragon. The author charges that Henry "(the more pity) did exasperate his fault with other greater faults, and after carnal adultery accumulated also spiritual adultery by schisms and heresies, to the utter undoing of his own and many a hundred thousand souls besides."

Herbert, Edward, Lord of Cherbury. "The Life and Reign of King Henry the Eighth: Together with Which Is Briefly Represented a General History of the Times." In his *"Autobiography of Edward Lord Herbert of Cherbury" and "The History of England under Henry VIII,"* pp. 109-748. London: Alexander Murray, 1870.

Reprints a 1649 biography of Henry, who, "with all his crimes, yet . . . was one of the most glorious princes of his time."

Jungman, Robert E. "'Pastime with Good Company' by Henry VIII." *Notes and Queries* 26, No. 5 (October 1979): 397-99.

Argues that in Henry's song the line "grugge so woll, but noon denye" is a "veiled reference to the relationsip between Anne [Boleyn] and the King in the latter months of 1530."

Maynard, Theodore. *Henry the Eighth.* Milwaukee: Bruce Publishing Co., 1949, 431 p.

Study of Henry's life and reign.

"Corrections of the *Institution of a Christian Man,* by Henry VIII., with Archbishop Cranmer's Annotations." In *Miscellaneous Writings and Letters of Thomas Cranmer, Archbishop of Canterbury, Martyr, 1556,* by Thomas Cranmer, edited by Rev. John Edmund Cox, pp. 83-114. Cambridge: Cambridge University Press, 1846.

Prints the *Bishops' Book,* showing Henry's annotations as well as Archbishop Thomas Cranmer's remarks on the king's revisions.

Pollard, A. F. *Henry VIII.* London: Longmans, Green and Co., 1925, 470 p.

Biography long considered the standard treatment of Henry.

Savage, Henry, ed. *The Love Letters of Henry VIII.* London: Allan Wingate, 1949, 112 p.

Reprints, introduces and annotates Henry's letters to his wives. The book also includes facsimile reproductions of the letters to Anne Boleyn.

Starkey, David. *The Reign of Henry VIII: Personalities and Politics.* London: George Philip, 1985, 174 p.

Useful, lavishly illustrated analysis of power politics in Henry's reign.

Stevens, John. *Music and Poetry in the Early Tudor Court.* Cambridge: Cambridge University Press, 1979, 483 p.

Reprints a comprehensive 1961 study of music and lyrics in early Tudor England. Henry's songs and ballads are referred to throughout and their texts reprinted in an appendix to the book.

Tree, Herbert Beerbohm. *Henry VIII and His Court.* London: Cassell and Co., 1911, 117 p.

Review of the principal characters and events of Henry's life and reign, "written as a holiday task . . . to offer an impression of the more prominent personages in Shakespeare's play" *Henry VIII* (1613).

Jan Kochanowski

1530-1584

Polish poet, translator, and dramatist.

Kochanowski is considered the first outstanding poet to
compose in Polish and a writer whose work has had an
enormous impact on the development of Slavic literature.
He created a distinct national literary style, transforming
his native speech into a sophisticated poetic language and
setting stylistic standards that dominated Slavic literature
from the Renaissance to the Romantic period. Kochanowski is best remembered for his *Psalterz Dawidów,* a
lyrical translation of *The Psalms of David,* still widely used
in Polish and Slavic churches, and for a work that has
been called a masterpiece of elegiac poetry, *Treny (Laments).* According to biographer David Welsh, Kochanowski wrote poetry that contains "a depth of felt experience which his successors failed to reach, just as they
could not match the lyricism of his songs, or the vitality
of his epigrams, or the orotund wealth of his psalms."

Because Kochanowski never provided good biographical
information about himself, scholars can only infer from
other sources many of the events and the chronology of
his life and work. Born in 1530 in Sycyna, a village in central Poland about one hundred miles from Cracow,
Kochanowski was raised in a well-to-do literary family (his
two younger brothers Mikolaj and Andrzej, and his nephew Piotr, were also well-known translators). After receiving his secondary education at Sieciechów Academy, he
entered the Cracow Academy in 1544. There he studied
philology and Greek and was commended for his command of Latin. Not surprisingly, Kochanowski's first epigrams rely heavily upon Latin and Greek examples. In
1547, due to his father's death as well as to an outbreak
of plague at the Academy, Kochanowski was forced to return home before completing his degree. The following
year, he embarked on over a decade of intermittent travels, visiting East Prussia, Italy, Vienna, Belgium, and
France. Scholars have noted that the poet's extended journeys, particularly his three-year sojourn in Italy, strongly
influenced his cultural development. While enrolled at the
University of Padua, then one of the four most advanced
intellectual centers in Europe, Kochanowski resumed his
study of philology and the classics, incorporating into his
poetry stylistic elements of such medieval Italian authors
as Petrarch and Dante. Perhaps the greatest factor influencing Kochanowski's development at Padua was his acceptance of humanism, a philosophy popular during the
Renaissance for its emphasis on the importance of the individual, interest in secular matters, and strong identification with classical literature and ideas. Kochanowski's humanist perspective colors much of his poetry and is best
evidenced in *Psalterz Dawidów.* In 1558 Kochanowski
journeyed to France, where he may have met Pierre Ronsard, a poet whose lyric style and literary philosophy, particularly his employment of the vernacular for even the
most elevated forms of poetry, Kochanowski greatly admired. Indeed, it was during his brief stay in France that
the Polish writer first began composing poetry in his native language.

Jan Kochanowski

In 1559 Kochanowski returned to Poland permanently.
He was made secretary to King Zygmunt I—a position he
held until approximately 1568. Popular at courts throughout Poland, the young poet began writing his numerous
Fraszki, witty short poems that address a variety of people
and subjects. While at court Kochanowski also composed
such political poems as "Zgoda" and "Satyr, albo Dziki
maz," two early pieces in which he assessed the Polish Republic and expressed concern regarding Polish relations
with Russia. Despite his public successes, the poet retired
in 1570 with his new wife to a country estate at Czarnolas.
There he began his translation of the Psalms and wrote his
most important works. In 1578, at the behest of Polish
chancellor Jan Zamoyski, Kochanowski produced his only
drama, *Odprawa poslow greckich (The Dismissal of the
Grecian Envoys).* This typically Renaissance tragedy,
based on the *Iliad* of Homer and the anonymous medieval
romance *The History of the Trojan War,* enjoyed modest
success. The following year Kochanowski completed what
is considered one of his most enduring works, the lyrical
Psalterz Dawidów. Several personal tragedies marked the
final years of Kochanowski's life at Czarnolas, culminating in the death of his three-year-old daughter, Orszula, in

1579. Despondent over the loss of his favorite child, Kochanowski composed *Laments*. In 1584, while preparing a complete edition of his works, Kochanowski died suddenly at the age of fifty-four.

Kochanowski was a prolific writer who composed fluently in both Latin and Polish. He drew on a variety of classical and contemporary sources, experimenting with numerous genres and stylistic elements. Included in his literary canon are epigrams, elegies, laments, lyric and political poetry, hymns, translations, one poetic drama, and an occasional prose piece. Adhering closely to the Antique motifs popular during the Renaissance, he blended his native idiom into classical frameworks. Kochanowski began his literary career composing in Latin and in the Vergilian tradition. Fully one third of his literary endeavors, the Latin works are comprised mainly of odes, elegies, and epigrams. Perhaps best known is *Lyricorum libellus*, a collection of twelve odes, that address religious topics and such public concerns as affairs of state, military victories, and national unity. Although now considered artistically inferior to his Polish poetry, Kochanowski's Latin works nonetheless reflect the poet's search to discover those genres and styles in which he later excelled.

Kochanowski's transition in 1558 to writing in Polish completely altered the development of Slavic poetry. Experimenting with stanzaic forms, metrical patterns, vocabulary, and syntax, Kochanowski molded his native tongue into a sophisticated literary language, demonstrating that the vernacular could adequately convey even the most erudite subjects. His success is best evidenced in three works: *Pieśni*, *Psalterz Dawidów*, and *Laments*. *Pieśni*, a collection of songs written over the course of almost twenty years, consists chiefly of lyrical translations or imitations of Horace's *Odes*, although some of the songs reflect the influence of Catullus, Propertius, and Petrarch. Treating a wide variety of subjects, both private and public, the various pieces in *Pieśni* range in theme from panegyric to erotic to pastoral. The smooth lyrical nature of Kochanowski's poetry and his command of the language are also evident in *Psalterz Dawidów*, considered by many scholars scarcely second to the original in beauty and artistry. Rather than attempt a literal translation of the Psalms of David, Kochanowski paraphrased the original—an artistic decision that gave him the freedom to utilize greater stylistic diversity and to incorporate familiar Polish elements through which he could more easily convey the fundamental motif of each psalm. Kochanowski combined stylistic elements from biblical, classical, and Polish literature in *Psalterz Dawidow*, creating a musical tone that influenced generations of Polish lyricists. Kochanowski's final masterpiece, *Laments*, chronicles a parent's attempt to accept the death of a child and is considered by far the most intimate and psychologically telling of his works. This collection of threnodies is of considerable interest not only for its expressive beauty, but also for the psychological insight the poems provide into a Renaissance thinker. A cycle of nineteen short poems, *Laments* is divided into two sections. In the first, the poet traces a cycle of grief, despair, and resignation over the loss of his daughter. In the second, he questions human faith and knowledge, eventually finding peace through his Christian beliefs. For the theme of *Laments* Kochanowski is indebted to Cicero, who, in *Tuscular Disputations*, also wrote on the loss of a daughter. Stylistically, the Polish poet drew on the works of such

classical authors as Ovid, Seneca, and Lucretius, and looked to the Psalms for inspiration, as well. Together, *Pieśni*, *Psalterz Dawidów*, and *Laments* have served as the source of much later Polish poetry.

During his lifetime, Kochanowski was a popular poet: his works were circulated in manuscript throughout Poland, and critics and readers alike recognized his artistic ability. He was therefore frequently commissioned by high-ranking officials to compose poetry for various occasions. The most popular of his works were *Laments* and *Psalterz Dawidów*. Both enjoyed a diverse readership, and many of the individual psalms, laments, and songs appeared during his lifetime in both Catholic and Protestant hymnals. In the century following his death, numerous reprints of Kochanowski's collected works evidenced the poet's enduring popularity. *Psalterz Dawidów* received perhaps the greatest amount of attention, with churches in Russia, Bohemia, Serbia, Hungary, Lithuania, Rumania, and Prussia adopting portions of the work into their services. Kochanowski's poetic style continued to dominate Polish literature until the nineteenth century when the Romantic poet Adam Mickiewicz supplanted the Renaissance poet as Poland's national literary hero. Although accorded a slightly lower rank in Polish literature after Mickiewicz's writing, Kochanowski's works are still read and treasured. Julian Krzyzanowski has thus assessed nineteenth- and twentieth-century Polish opinion of Kochanowski's place in the history of Slavic literature: "Jan Kochanowski has been universally acknowledged ... as the finest representative of the Polish civilisation in the period of the Renaissance and as the greatest national poet before the era of Romanticism."

Although the canon of criticism in Polish on Kochanowski is vast, few English assessments exist prior to the twentieth century. What little criticism has since appeared in English has favorably valued most of the poet's work, with critics concentrating upon *The Dismissal of the Grecian Envoys*, *Psalterz Dawidów*, and *Laments*. The merits of the poet's sole dramatic attempt have been variously assessed. While such critics as Czesław Miłosz consider *The Dismissal* "majestic in its clarity, equilibrium, and economy," other commentators support George Rapall Noyes's conclusion that the poet "had small dramatic talent." While fairly successful in its day, *The Dismissal* failed to establish a dramatic tradition in Poland and has rarely been performed in subsequent centuries. Kochanowski's poetry, however, has received almost universal acclaim from scholars writing in English. Commentators stress the importance of Kochanowski's poetry to the development of the Polish literary medium and scholars agree that the *Laments* and *Psalterz Dawidów* are by far his finest endeavors, poetry equal in lyric beauty to any composed by his European contemporaries. For his translation and adaptation of the Psalms, Kochanowski has been labeled the Pindar of Poland and scholars agree with Bruchnalski's opinion that *Psalterz Dawidów* "stands as one of the greatest achievements of Polish lyrical poetry in the course of four centuries. ... It captured the elements of poetry in the Psalms as it has never been captured by Polish translators before or since." Equally esteemed and universally considered an outstanding example of expressive elegiac poetry, the *Laments*, as Noyes judges, "convey to us the deep emotion of the bereaved father, and at the same time they satisfy our sense for beauty of form. ... Kochanowski's sincere grief, his fatherly love for his baby girl, after more than three centuries has not lost its power to touch our hearts."

Considered the founder of Polish poetry and the leading Polish literary figure for almost three centuries, Kochanowski contributed immensely to his nation's literary development. Utilizing existing classical poetic structures and helping shape the Polish literary language, Kochanowski established stylistic standards and poetic ideals that elevated Polish poetry to the level of its European contemporaries. As Bruchnalski has claimed, "The universality of [Kochanowski's] genius made him stand for centuries as the greatest poet of Poland—and the vitality of his work is such as to bridge successfully the gulf of time and to address a perennially fresh appeal to each succeeding generation."

*PRINCIPAL WORKS

"Pieśń o potopie" (poetry) 1558
"Pieśń" also published as "Czego chcesz od nas, panie?" (hymn) 1562
   ["The Greatness of God" 1881; also published as "A Song; or, What wilt Thou from us, Lord?" published in journal *The Slavonic and East European Review*, 1952-53]
"Satyr; albo, Dziki mąż" (poetry) 1564
"Zgoda" (poetry) 1564
Odprawa posłów greckich (drama) 1578
   [*The Dismissal of the Grecian Envoys*, 1918]
†"Pieśń świętojańska o sobótce" (poetry) 1579
   ["St. John's Eve," 1927]
Psałterz Dawidów [translator and adaptor] (psalms) 1579
‡*Lyricorum libellus* (verse) 1580
§*Treny* (poetry) 1580
   [*Laments*, 1920]
‖ *Fraszki* (verse) 1584
Jan Kochanowski (poetry, psalms, drama, songs, verse, hymns, prose) 1585
‖ *Pieśni* (songs) 1586
Dzieła wszystkie. 4 vols. (poetry, psalms, drama, songs, verse, hymns, prose) 1884-97
***Poems* (poetry, drama, verse) 1928

*Kochanowski was reluctant to have his works printed. Thus, scholars have had difficulty assigning accurate composition and publication dates to many of his works.

†Sections of this poem were first translated and published in *Specimens of the Polish Poets* (1827) and in *Poets and Poetry of Poland* (1881).

‡This collection of Latin odes was widely circulated in manuscript form beginning in approximately 1550.

§Laments I, VII, IX, X, and XIII were first translated and published in *Specimens of the Polish Poets*.

‖These verses were composed throughout Kochanowski's career and collected after his death. No complete translation of either *Fraszki* ("Trifles") or *Pieśni* ("Songs") exists, though several partial translations have appeared in various sources.

**This volume contains *Laments*, "St. John's Eve," *The Dismissal of the Grecian Envoys*, and two epigrams, "On His Linden" and "On His House at Czarnolas."

GEORGE RAPALL NOYES (essay date 1928)

[*Noyes was an American translator, essayist, editor, and academic. In the following excerpt from the introduction to his collaborative 1928 translation of Kochanowski's works, he identifies the Renaissance and classical sources in "St. John's Eve,"* The Dismissal of the Grecian Envoys, *and* Laments.]

Jan Kochanowski is at once the first great poet of Poland and the greatest of all Polish poets until the coming of the romantic period in the early nineteenth century. His work is the most perfect expression of the culture and refinement of the Renaissance as it manifested itself in Poland. (p. 1)

In Latin he was the equal of the best French and German humanistic poets of the time, though he does not rank with such masters as Bembo and Vida in Italy, or the Scotch Buchanan. In Polish, if we except an occasional lyric of an earlier period, he was the first author of verse that has beauty of form and is distinguished by true poetic feeling.

For some years after his return home Kochanowski lived the life of a wit and man of society, attached to the courts of various magnates and of the king himself. But despite his gay and even dissipated life, and despite the pagan influences of the Renaissance, he remained a devout Catholic and a man of deeply religious nature. His paraphrase of the Psalms [*Psałterz Dawidow*] is, next to the *Laments*, his most perfect work, and remains today the best poetic version of them in the Polish language: Kochanowski solved a problem to which no English poet has proved equal. (p. 3-4)

The fairest product of Kochanowski's genius as a writer of songs is his **"St. John's Eve,"** a poem in which he is close to the Polish country life that he saw about him, and comparatively independent of his classical models. On the eve of the festival of St. John the Baptist (June 24) the village folk in some portions of Poland still kindle bonfires, dance about them, and sing folksongs. These songs are sung mainly by women, and nearly always deal with love themes. The custom, now decadent, has been regarded as the relic of a pagan festival connected with the summer solstice. To this rite Kochanowski devoted a group of lyrics, informed, like the two lyrics that have just been mentioned, by the Horatian spirit. He drew inspiration from actual life, though he doubtless remembered that Tibullus and Propertius had mentioned similar festivals, and that Ovid in his *Fasti* had given a description of them. In its form and in its general character **"St. John's Eve"** owes nothing to any classical source: after four stanzas that describe the scene Kochanowski lets his maidens sing their songs as girls in Poland sang them.

How far these songs correspond to those that Kochanowski may himself have heard near his own home on a midsummer evening, is a question that cannot be answered with assurance, since no Polish folk poetry of the sixteenth century has been preserved to us. But this much is certain: the songs are not translations or imitations of any Greek or Latin originals, and in general they are dramatic, expressive of the feelings of the different girls rather than of the poet himself. (The exception is that of the Eleventh Maiden, whose praises of the fair Dorothea would be more appropriate to the lips of a youth, so that one may suspect in them a tribute to the charms of Kochanowski's future wife.) Hence it is fair to assume that in general type, and probably in the short eight-syllable verse, which is at present frequent in Polish folk poetry, they are of the same sort that were sung on the meadows of Czarnolas. The poet is of a different temper from a modern scientific student of folklore; he cares nothing for realistic truth of atmosphere. Neither does he, like the poets of the romantic school in the nineteenth century, strive to be faithful to the spirit of the folksong while giving to it a more artistic form. He is a man of the Renaissance. In "St. John's Eve" Latin fauns have strayed into Polish fields and a village girl, presumably by no means skilled in books, tells the story of Tereus, Progne, and Philomela. Her sisters occasionally use phrases taken from Latin models, though they are so well woven into the texture of the work that only a scholar can detect them. Like Horace, Kochanowski praises country delights with a touch of benignant condescension. Yet he is sincere; he has been impressed by the beauty of a popular custom and thinks it worthy of treatment in the style that he has developed by the study of classical poetry. In their songs his twelve maidens give a charming picture of Polish village life, a life of comfort and abundance, of simple pleasures and wholesome mirth.

On the other hand, *The Dismissal of the Grecian Envoys* is a Renaissance drama such as might have been written, whether in Latin or in the vernacular, almost anywhere in the Europe of the sixteenth century; only a few trifling details betray its Polish origin. In England it has parallels, for instance, in the *Gorboduc* (1561) of Sackville and Norton, and, more closely, in the *Samson Agonistes* (1671) of Milton. It is the first original tragedy in the Polish language, but did not, like similar works in contemporary France, prove the forerunner of a great dramatic literature. It was followed by no piece of a similar type until after a lapse of two hundred years; indeed the Polish drama as a whole is of small account until the end of the eighteenth century. (p. 5-6)

Kochanowski had many reasons for selecting as his own subject the demand for the return of Helen made by the Grecian envoys, Ulysses and Menelaus, and the rejection of it by the Trojan council.

From an artistic point of view this subject was not so satisfactory; it gave small opportunity for true dramatic development. And indeed Kochanowski had small dramatic talent. His tragedy is without hero or heroine around whom the action might center; its interest is historical, narrative rather than truly dramatic. Kochanowski puts in the mouths of his actors speeches that depict character well, though in very general terms. Paris the unprincipled, talented, attractive young gallant; Helen is a woman attached to her captor, yet condemning herself for yielding to him. Antenor the prudent counsellor and Cassandra the inspired prophetess are equally distinct figures. But of gradual development of character, of revelation of a complicated personality under the stress of emotion, the poet gives us hardly a hint. Kochanowski makes us forget his own shortcomings by the sustained dignity of his style, which is polished and reserved, animated by a truly classic spirit.

Like other learned dramatists of the sixteenth century, Kochanowski constructed his drama according to rules de-

rived from the practice of the Greek dramatists and of Seneca, and codified by such scholars as the great Italian humanist Julius Caesar Scaliger (1484-1558), in his *Poetics* (i. 9). His tragedy consists of a prologue (lines 1-29), five episodes or acts (lines 30-69, 94-169, 194-429, 436-481, 524-621), and an epilogue (lines 624-681). The acts are divided from one another by songs or speeches of the Chorus, which was an essential part of any ancient tragedy. It will be noted that only the third act contains over a hundred lines, and that the whole play is thus less than half the usual length of a Greek drama. Evidently Kochanowski had merely sketched in his work, intending to expand it later.... (p. 7-9)

To the unities of time and place, which prescribe that the action of a drama must not occupy more than a single day, and that the place represented on the stage should not be changed in the course of it, Kochanowski of necessity conforms through the presence of his Chorus on the stage. Certain traits of his style, such as his stichomythy, or arrangement of the dialogue in single lines, or symmetrical groups of lines (see lines 30-69) he imitates directly from the Greek dramatists. In his use of moral maxims (*sententiae*) he surpasses even Euripides and Seneca; nearly a fourth part of his play is composed of them: see for instance lines 38-49, 70-89. Here Kochanowski is an obedient pupil of Scaliger, who says that such maxims are "the columns or props of the whole tragic edifice." The humanists would have scorned the modern doctrine of "art for art's sake," if any man in their time had been witless enough to propound it; for them, as for Horace, moral instruction was one of the chief aims of poetry. In particular, Kochanowski suffuses his tragedy with the Greek idea of fatalism; a curse hangs over the race of Troy.

The main sources from which Kochanowski derived the material for his drama were Homer's *Iliad* and the *Trojan History* of Guido delle Colonne.... (pp. 9-10)

[Curiously] enough, *The Dismissal of the Grecian Envoys*, though it is an absolutely typical Renaissance drama, is in some ways akin to poems that Kochanowski, if he had known them, would have despised as barbarous. It is of course possible that Kochanowski knew Dares and Dictys as well as the Polish translation of Guido; in the case of Dictys there is some slight reason for such a supposition.

For developing details of his tragedy, for its style and its general tone rather than its plot, Kochanowski drew suggestions from a number of Greek and Latin writers: these are indicated in the notes to this volume. His use of Euripides as the model for the magnificent third ode of his Chorus is particularly worthy of attention.

Like other Renaissance poets, Kochanowski took no pains to avoid anachronisms. At times he gave a definitely Polish coloring to his work; his description of the tumultuous Trojan council suggests the Polish diet. Whether he meant his drama to have a bearing on contemporary politics may be doubted. But the last four lines of the play are certainly an utterance of the militarist Kochanowski, who desired for his country a vigorous foreign policy.

From *The Dismissal of the Grecian Envoys*, with its rigid, severely classical outlines, which at times smell of the lamp, one turns almost with surprise to the *Laments*. These are Kochanowski's highest achievement as a poet;

and well they may be, for they express his own heartfelt grief for the loss of his second daughter, his baby girl Ursula, who died, probably toward the close of 1579, at the age of thirty months. Yet, sincere though they be, the *Laments*, like the *Dismissal*, are nevertheless carefully developed according to the rules of Renaissance poetics, and they show an equally studied dependence on the style of the ancient poets, to whom, however, Kochanowski now joins the Bible as a source of inspiration. Milton expresses genuine emotion in his *Epitaphium Damonis*, though he writes in Latin; and in *Lycidas*, though he ornaments his poem with elaborate learning. Kochanowski was a poet of similar learned training. In the *Laments* he follows the precepts of Scaliger, who tells us that a dirge should consist of certain definite parts: praises of the deceased, proof of the loss sustained, grief, consolation, exhortations. (pp. 12-14)

For his division of his elegy into a series of poems, however, he had no ancient model. He may have been affected by the example of Petrarch's long series of sonnets and canzoni on the death of Laura, which includes a vision of the poet's dead mistress. But Petrarch gives merely variations on one theme rather than a history of the feelings called forth by the death of his beloved. Thus in the form of his work Kochanowski shows genuine originality.

For the ideas of the *Laments* Kochanowski is more indebted to Cicero than to any other classical author. After the loss of his much-loved daughter Tullia in the year 45 B.C., Cicero, in order to assuage his grief, by far the greatest of his whole life, buried himself in the study of philosophy, and during the next two years wrote in feverish haste his own philosophic treatises. It is then not surprising that Kochanowski expressly refers to him in the *Laments* and that he repeatedly borrows material from the *Tusculan Disputations*, in which Cicero sought to prove that the soul is immortal and that virtue, rising superior to pain and grief, is in itself sufficient to assure man happiness. But from ancient philosophy, which proves unable to console him, and which indeed was no sufficient prop to Cicero in his tribulations, the poet turns to Christian faith. The Bible is a source both of the style and of the substance of the *Laments*.

The *Laments* succeed one another in a carefully planned order. The first two are an introduction: the poet summons all the mourners of the world to help him mourn his lost daughter; he exclaims that, had he chosen to write verses for children, far better had they been cradle songs for the living rather than dirges for the dead! "Laments III-VIII" express simply and touchingly a father's grief; he tells of the charming nature of his daughter, of her talents, of her death, her burial, the desolation that she has left behind her. In "Laments IX-XI" the father's sorrow has become more poignant, passing into despair and doubt; his learning can offer him no solace. From this despair the poet partially recovers in "Laments XII and XIII," which resume the tone of "Laments III-VIII." "Laments XIV-XIX" describe how the father seeks and finds consolation for his grief. His search is at first vain, for it is in the world of ancient paganism ("Laments XIV-XVI"). From pagan philosophy he turns in "Lament XVII" to the Christian God for comfort. "Lament XVIII" is in spirit a psalm, or a prayer to God for mercy. And God grants his prayer. "Lament XIX" is not a dirge but a vision of Ursula, who is happy in her heavenly home. The poet's mother appears

to him, bearing Ursula in her arms, and utters words of Christian consolation, conceived, one must admit, in a somewhat Stoic spirit that shows Kochanowski to be still quite as much a philosopher as a mystic. But Christian faith has given him the relief that paganism refused.

Thus Kochanowski's *Laments* are not the immediate outpouring of a father's grief. Some small poems of a similar sort, found among his papers and printed after his death, may be of that character. But before writing the series that he himself published the poet had so far recovered from his loss that he was able to express his emotion with an elaborate art.

This art, however, is an art that conceals itself; as we read the *Laments* we are hardly conscious of their literary craftsmanship. The poems show their author's learning, but they do not force it on our attention. They convey to us the deep emotion of the bereaved father, and at the same time they satisfy our sense for beauty of form. Their polish of manner, provided that we ourselves are not destitute of literary cultivation, only heightens their appeal. Kochanowski's sincere grief, his fatherly love for his baby girl, after more than three centuries has not lost its power to touch our hearts.

Kochanowski's work is then that of a learned poet, who was at the same time a lover of his native Poland, and a man of deep and genuine feeling. The two *Epigrams* show his ideal of life, which, as his retirement to Czarnolas amply proves, was something more than a literary pose. *The Dismissal of the Grecian Envoys* exhibits the poet in his most intellectual mood, at work in a department of literature of which he was no master; here he depends for success on his imitation of classical technique and on his mastery of style. In "St. John's Eve" he celebrates a beautiful Polish popular custom, and is quite unconscious of any incongruity when he mingles with his folklore motifs some of his Latin learning. In the *Laments* he expresses his personal sorrow in a style of perfect harmony and dignity, with a *curiosa felicitas* like that of Horace, a felicity gained by diligence. Thus the poems translated in this volume illustrate with some adequacy the literary talent of the best poet who lived during what was once called "the Golden Age" of Polish literature. His writings still remain full of charm, however far they may have been surpassed by the more varied and more splendid romantic poetry that came into being in the half-century that followed Poland's loss of independence. The romantic poets of Poland, like those of other European countries, gave free rein to their own imagination; they relied on personal inspiration and strove to be independent and original. Kochanowski, on the contrary, was a pupil of the ancient masters, always striving to recreate their spirit in a form acceptable to his own age. But his long study would have been fruitless had he not been a poet by nature and a man of rich and varied personality. His spirit is both humanistic and universally human. (p. 14-17)

George Rapall Noyes, in an introduction to Poems by Jan Kochanowski, *edited by George Rapall Noyes, translated by Dorothea Prall Radin and others, University of California Press, 1928, pp. 1-17.*

W. BRUCHNALSKI (essay date 1930)

[*In the following excerpt, Bruchnalski assesses Kochanowski's contribution to the development of Polish poetry.*]

The outstanding anniversary in Poland this year will be that of Jan Kochanowski. Born four hundred years ago, his was for a long time the greatest name in the annals of Polish poetry. His activities opened up a new literary epoch for his country; and for nearly three centuries—before Mickiewicz turned literature into new channels and inspired it with new ideals—he continued to be unsurpassed for artistry. (p. 56)

In his works and in his life, he was fully representative of the best tendencies of his epoch, a true Humanist. Such he showed himself to be, above all, in his complete addiction to letters and literature. Here he entered the fields both of prose and poetry; and as a poet he shone unexcelled for centuries, a recognised master in all departments. In some he was a creative innovator, in others an absolute pioneer. His versatile genius sought expression both in Latin and Polish. If in the former case he was merely following the general practice of his times, his productions in the native tongue served to awaken to consciousness the forces of emotion and imagination latent in the nation. Polish poetry existed, it is true, before Kochanowski, but did not rise above the pedestrian level. He was the first poet of genius, the first who understood the meaning and practice of high artistry. Conscious of the excellence of his achievement, he felt entitled to boast "that he dared to rival poets reputed the greatest" and "had succeeded in climbing the rock of the fair Calliope, on which no Pole had yet set foot."

Polish, when he started to write, was still a language unbroken to fine literature, a somewhat vulgar medium. It clothed thoughts as an ill-fitting suit clothes a man. Kochanowski raised it from vulgarity to gentility, from the level of the coarse concrete to that of most delicate abstraction; refined it and enriched with ornaments of style, and made of it an instrument capable of expressing the subtlest shades of thought.

Thus he was the creator of artistic Polish and of artistic Polish poetry. This is the most important aspect of Kochanowski.

A pupil of the Renaissance, brought up in the atmosphere of classicism, he could not ignore the great contribution made by the epoch to European culture. Sharing contemporary European standards of literary good taste, he inevitably accepted the classical literary convention. In this submission, however, he brought the national literature, still in the first stage of its development, under the auspices of Greece and Rome, and helped it to establish contact with the treasures of classical culture.

With his intellectual curiosity, his steady interest in the new civilisation of South-Western Europe, his instinct for adaptation—with these qualities there also went a keen sense of the value of the fundamentally national elements. His appreciation of them led him to the striking departure of writing **"St. John's Eve."**

The universality of his genius made him stand for centuries as the greatest poet of Poland—and the vitality of his work is such as to bridge successfully the gulf of time and to address a perennially fresh appeal to each succeeding generation. (pp. 77-8)

W. Bruchnalski, "Jan Kochanowski (1529-1584)," translated by W. J. Chwalewik, in The Slavonic Review, Vol. IX, No. 25, June, 1930, pp. 56-78.

WIKTOR WEINTRAUB (essay date 1952)

[*Weintraub is a Polish editor, essayist, and academic. In the following excerpt, he rejects various suggested sources for Kochanowski's "What Wilt Thou from us, Lord?"*]

Jan Kochanowski began his literary activities by writing poems in Latin. His first Polish lyric was published in 1562, when he was already thirty-two. The poem which opened up a new period in the history of Polish poetry is thus the work of a mature writer, one of Kochanowski's masterpieces. It is a thanksgiving prayer composed in seven quatrains and, as it is entitled simply **"A Song"**, it is known usually by its opening words, **"What wilt Thou from us, Lord?"**

As the poem is short, perhaps it may not be inappropriate to give it here in a prose translation in order to give the reader some idea of its contents.

> 1. What wilt Thou from us, Lord, for Thy bounteous gifts, / what for Thy goodness which is measureless? / The Church will not contain Thee; everything is full of Thee: / Limbo and Sea and Earth and Heaven.
> 2. I know Thou needest not gold, as all the things are Thine / that man in the world calls his. / Thus, Lord, we praise Thee from our grateful hearts, / lacking a more fitting gift.
> 3. Thou art Lord of all the world, Thou didst build Heaven / and embroider it beautifully with golden stars; / Thou didst lay the foundations of the vast Earth / and cover its nudity with various herbs.
> 4. The sea, at Thy command, keeps to its shores, / fearful to cross its prescribed bounds; / the rivers hold great abundance of inexhaustible waters; / bright day and dark night observe their hours.
> 5. For Thee Spring brings forth different flowers, / for Thee Summer walks with a wreath of corn, / Autumn offers wine and various apples, / then slothful Winter rises for a meal prepared.
> 6. Through Thy grace nocturnal dew falls on the withered herbs, / and the rain quickly refreshes the parched corn; / from Thy hands all animals take their food; / and Thy bounty nourishes all.
> 7. O everlasting Lord, be praised now and for ever! / Thy grace, Thy goodness will have no end. / Keep us as long as Thou deignest on this lowly earth; / only let us be ever under Thy wings!
>
> (p. 412)

[It] would be difficult to find another 16th-century Polish poem so representative of the Renaissance ethos and the Renaissance style.

It is, no doubt, a religious poem, written in praise of God. But it is also a poem written in praise of this world, its magnificence, beauty and harmony. Of course, compared with God, the earth can be called 'lowly', nevertheless in its perfection it reflects God's greatness and benevolence. In Kochanowski's poem, God is being adored through His creation. The whole poem is infused with deep optimism.

Historians of literature, when dealing with this poem, have most often linked it with the Psalter. According to them, the poem partakes of the spiritual climate of the Psalter and was a paraphrase of *motifs* taken from the

Psalter. In order to prove this they would compare single stanzas or expressions from the poem with expressions from Kochanowski's verse-paraphrase *Psałterz Dawidow*.

Now, this procedure was methodically wrong for a very simple reason. Kochanowski's poetic paraphrase—his *magnum opus*—is of later date than the poem in question: it was published in 1579, and we can guess with a fair amount of probability that he did not start translating the psalms until some time about 1570.

In his paraphrase Kochanowski aimed at fidelity to the specific style of the Psalmist. Nevertheless, it is a free poetic paraphrase and it contains a number of amplifications. Thus, if we are to ascertain the extent to which our poem is dependent on the Psalter, we should compare it not with Kochanowski's own paraphrase, but with the Vulgate text, or we might mistake some of Kochanowski's own ideas, which he expressed in the poem and which later crept into his paraphrase of the Psalter, for signs of the influence of the Psalter.

A comparison of the poem with the Latin of the Vulgate text reveals that Kochanowski did borrow certain notions and expressions from the Psalmist, but only those that fitted in with his own ideas of God and His relationship to the world—ideas in many respects different from those informing the Psalter.

The God of the poem is exclusively one of goodness and benevolence, while the God of the Psalmist can be formidable and terrifying as well. There are in the Psalms some very rudimentary statements of the notion that God's might finds its expression in the order of natural phenomena, but more frequently the tokens of that might are miracles breaking the natural order of things: rivers flowing backwards, mountains melting, and so on. There is no place for miracles in the idea of God as expressed in our poem. Moreover, the beauty of the world is one of the main sources of Kochanowski's religious feeling. This aesthetic component of religious feeling can be surmised from some passages of the Psalms, but it never comes to the fore. And how strong it was in Kochanowski can be inferred from the fact that the amplifications in his poetic paraphrase of the Psalms are of just this aesthetic character. (pp. 413-14)

Moreover, the Psalms constantly speak of God in concrete terms, as of a person. In our poem there is only one discreet poetic image which suggests any personification, namely 'From Thy hands'. This image, of God's hands feeding the creatures of the earth, can be traced back to the Psalms (civ, v. 28), as well as the image 'under Thy wings' (see Psalm xci, v. 4). On the other hand, the expression 'everything is full of Thee' ('wszędy pełno Ciebie') would suggest that Kochanowski's idea of God contained a pantheistic tinge completely foreign to the Psalmist. We do, however, find in the Psalter a parallel to the enumeration which in Kochanowski's poem follows closely on that statement. Having said that 'everything' is 'full' of God, Kochanowski defines this 'everything' in the following line: 'Limbo, and Sea, and Earth, and Heaven.' This line can be compared with Psalm cxxxix, v. 8: 'Si ascendero in coelum, tu illic es; si descendero in infernum, ades' ["If I ascend up into the heaven, thou art there: if I make my bed in hell, thou art there"]. But while in the Vulgate the sense of this and the preceding line is that man cannot

hide from God and His wrath, in Kochanowski's poem the words become an amplification of the statement that God is omnipresent.

We have seen that Kochanowski made use of some of the poetic images of the Psalmist in order to express ideas about God and the world which are foreign to the Psalmist. For the source of Kochanowski's inspiration we must look elsewhere.

Stanislaw Windakiewicz, in his well-known book on Kochanowski (*Jan Kochanowski*, 1930), singled out another biblical text, the Book of Job, as this source. Windakiewicz, however, provides no arguments in support of his statement, which will not bear detailed examination. The considerations which do not allow us to admit that the poem was written in the spirit of the Psalmist oblige us also to reject the Book of Job as the source of Kochanowski's inspiration. (pp. 415-16)

Another attempt to find 'the source' of Kochanowski's poem was made in 1928 by Stanisław Dobrzycki. Dobrzycki was one of those scholars who had earlier tried to discover the inspiration of our poem in the Psalms and, in order to prove their theory, had compared it with Kochanowski's paraphrase. In 1928 he admitted that this was a 'mistaken method' and believed that he had found this source elsewhere, namely in the dialogue *Octavius*, written by Minucius Felix, one of the Fathers of the Church. *Octavius* tries to prove the existence of God on the evidence of the beauty and harmony of the world. The analogies between our poem and *Octavius* are striking both in general conception and in detail. Nevertheless it would be rather imprudent to claim, as Dobrzycki does, that Minucius Felix is 'the source' of our poem, as *Octavius* itself had a classical 'source' which was well known to Kochanowski.

Octavius is a Ciceronian dialogue. For the purposes of Christian apologetics Minucius Felix made use of the arguments Cicero put into the mouth of the Stoic Balbus in the second book of his *De natura deorum*. (p. 417)

It is not impossible that Kochanowski read *Octavius*, but we have no positive proofs that he did, and Minucius Felix by no means belonged to the most popular and widely read Fathers of the Church. As for *De natura deorum*, Kochanowski not only read it, but he was particularly familiar with this second book of the Ciceronian treatise.

Kochanowski was a classical scholar specialising in Cicero. He published his reconstruction of the text of Cicero's juvenile translation of *Phenomena*, a Greek astronomical poem by Aratus. Cicero's original translation has been lost; only some fragments of it have been preserved. In the second book of *De natura deorum* Balbus several times quotes Aratus's poem in Cicero's translation to corroborate his views. Kochanowski applied himself to the task of reconstructing the whole Ciceronian translation, substituting his own Latin version of the Greek poem for the missing passages. This translation, *M. T. Ciceronis Aratus ad Graecum exemplar expensus et locis mansis restitutus per J. Cochanovium*, was published as late as 1579. But we know that it was ready at an earlier date, for his friend A. P. Nidecki refers to Kochanowski's work on Aratus in the scholia to the second edition of his great four-volume collection of Cicero's *Fragmenta*, which appeared in 1565.

As became a humanist, Kochanowski had a great admiration for Cicero and his 'angelic pen' (for so he described Cicero's writings in his "*Laments*"). The Stoic ethics of the Polish poet had a Ciceronian tinge. *De natura deorum* must have been among his favourite books, and traces of its influence have been found in another of Kochanowski's poems.

Thus, Minucius Felix might be considered as 'the source' of Kochanowski's poem if we had in "**What wilt Thou from us, Lord?**" traits which we could refer to *Octavius*, but not to *De natura deorum*. Dobrzycki believed that such an instance was represented by the fifth stanza of the poem, dealing with the seasons. It is true that Balbus in the *De natura deorum* mentions the seasons only in the most general terms, while Minucius Felix refers to them in a way similar to Kochanowski's.... However, Dobrzycki himself invalidates his argument by quoting in the same article four lines from Ovid's *Metamorphoses* which in their imagery are closer to Kochanowski than the text of Minucius Felix.... (p. 418)

Moreover, such personification of the seasons belonged to the *loci communes* of Renaissance art, and to prove this it is enough to compare Kochanowski's stanza with old emblematic drawings representing the seasons. The seasons are depicted as four allegorical female figures. Spring is a woman with a wreath on her head, holding flowers in both hands and standing among flowers. Summer is a woman with a wreath on her head, holding in one hand a sheaf, in the other a torch. Autumn has a wreath of vine leaves on her head and holds a bunch of grapes in one hand and the horn of plenty, brimming over with fruit, in the other. Winter is portrayed as a woman sitting in a room; in front of her is a table with numerous dishes, and she is reaching out for one of them. The imagery of the poem conforms strikingly with these pictures. Only in these emblematic pictures do we find a representation of Winter which corresponds to Kochanowski's 'slothful Winter [who] rises for a meal prepared', while both Ovid and Minucius Felix here made use of different images.

Cicero's Balbus was a pantheist, as became a Stoic. He deified nature and worshipped God in the whole fabric of nature. One can find what is perhaps a reflection of the pantheistic idea of God in the opening lines of the poem where, addressing God, Kochanowski says 'everything is full of Thee' ('wszędy pełno Ciebie').

The subject of our poem—the beauty and harmony of the world as the source of the worship of God—is a recurrent *motif* in Kochanowski's poetry. We find it in two poems published after his death, as well as in a Latin philosophical elegy. It occurs also in his Polish translation of Aratus's *Phenomena*. While in his Latin reconstruction he tried faithfully to render the Greek original, in his Polish version he freely paraphrased the opening lines, dealing with the subject of God and man, and introduced *motifs* from the poem "**What wilt Thou from us, Lord?**" We have also seen that some ideas contained in this poem are reflected in his paraphrase of the Psalter. These things all make the poem the more representative.

The poem is representative of the spiritual climate of Kochanowski's age and of his attitude towards the world. It is an attitude typical of the Renaissance. We find it in the main current of Renaissance philosophy, which began

in the 15th century with Cusanus, was continued by the Florentine Academy and reached its apogee at the end of the 16th century in the work of Giordano Bruno. This convergence is far more important than analogies with any particular literary sources. It 'places' the poem and it explains why, when expressing his feelings, Kochanowski turned to this particular text of Cicero. (pp. 419-20)

We have seen that Kochanowski expressed in his poem some of the focal and most characteristic ideas of Renaissance philosophy. (p. 421)

The style of the poem is also typical of the Renaissance. It contains no telling, picturesque details. Its imagery points only to certain typical, generally accepted features such as the personification of the four seasons. We move in the world of generalities. The earth is covered with '*various* herbs'. Spring brings forth '*different* flowers'. '*All* animals' take their food from God's hand. The 'various apples' which Autumn offers should probably be understood simply as 'various fruits', in conformity with the Italian usage, where *pomo* means not only 'apple', but 'fruit' as well.

The principle behind the imagery is that of animisation or personification. In his paraphrase of the Psalms Kochanowski tried to render their peculiar emotional colouring, that of a man awestruck, or, when joyful, full of exaltation, almost of frenzy. Our poem, on the other hand, is pervaded by an even, serene optimism. The world, to be sure, is a magnificent spectacle, but images such as that of animals feeding out of God's hand or of the sky 'embroidered' with stars suggest a condition in which man can feel at ease.

The aura of generalities, of vastness and infinite dimensions is stressed by 'negative' epithets, starting with the negative prefix *nie*: 'wód nieprzebranych' ('inexhaustible waters'), 'nieobeszłej ziemi' ('vast earth'), 'nieśmiertelny Panie' ('everlasting Lord'). Similarly, God is throughout the poem described negatively, by verbs preceded by *nie*. The negative particle *nie* is thus repeated constantly in the poem, and the repetition is stressed by a device of sound instrumentation. (p. 422)

The verse form of the poem is of great regularity, even rigidity. In poetry written before the time of Kochanowski, such as Rej's or Bielski's, the rule was that one line must contain either a whole sentence or a distinct clause. *Enjambement*, or the carrying-over of a clause from one line to the next, was barred. Kochanowski stabilised two accents in the line: the accent that falls on the last syllable but one before the caesura and the accent that falls on the last syllable but one before the end of the line (in our poem, which is written in lines of thirteen syllables, these accents fall always on the sixth and the twelfth syllables). In this way he made the rhymes far more regular. While with his predecessors we find rather numerous instances of oxytonic words rhyming with paroxytonic, with Kochanowski this is exceptional. He thus freed the intonation of the clause from its previous function, which was to mark the end of the line. *Enjambement* is a common phenomenon in his poems. His reform gave to Polish verse a new flexibility, which was the result of free interplay between the constant elements (two accents, regular rhymes) and the changeable elements (the end of the clause) of the line. (pp. 422-23)

Wiktor Weintraub, "Kochanowski's Renaissance Manifesto," in The Slavonic and East European Review, *Vol. 30, No. 75, June, 1952 pp. 412-24.*

JERZY PIETRKIEWICZ (essay date 1953)

[*A novelist and essayist, Pietrkiewicz has translated the works of several English and Polish poets. In the following excerpt, he compares the dream sequences found in Kochanowski's* Laments, *Boccaccio's* Olympia *(c. 1361), and the anonymous fourteenth-century poem* The Pearl, *concentrating upon the artistic purpose of "Lament XIX" (the "dream" lament) and its relation to the cycle as a whole.*]

Kochanowski's **Laments** (*Treny*) is undoubtedly the most important cycle of poems in early Polish literature. Published in 1580, four years before the poet's death, the cycle has well served its elegiac purpose, preserving the memory of his thirty-month-old daughter Orszula. It contains nineteen compact Laments, some of them only fourteen lines long; all are numbered, and the last poem bears an explanatory subtitle, '**The Dream**' (*Tren XIX, albo Sen*). This Lament also strikes the reader with another disparity: being very long, it seems to weigh heavily upon the whole structure—158 lines out of a total of 586 lines in the cycle, indeed a puzzling disproportion.

These two facts, the use of the word 'dream' in its title and the length of the last Lament, are the starting points from which the whole argument of this essay will be evolved.

"Lament XIX" opens with conventional remarks about a restless night which is relieved, 'an hour before dawn', by sudden sleep, and at this point the poet's mother appears within his dream to console his sorrow, or rather to argue about Divine Providence, her monologue echoing the thoughts and phrases of the previous *Treny*. Her speech occupies practically the whole Lament (141 lines), whereas merely two lines are used to end the dream with an abrupt return to reality. The brevity of both its opening and its ending seems to have been responsible for the critics' neglect of the dream-formula employed by Kochanowski in this last Lament, to solve his artistic problem. For there was a problem to solve—a problem of structure rather than one of contents, and Polish scholars from Faleński and Nehring to Hartleb and Nadolski have wrestled with it, probing with different critical tools into the compact, yet elusive text of the cycle. The average reader, however, captivated by the striking directness of the three most lyrical Laments ("VI, VII, VIII"), follows the subsequent pattern of allusions with diminishing interest and reaches the final Lament, unprepared for its long, argumentative character. The frankest among readers admit that the Dream Lament is a disappointment, and it even bores the more impatient who have sought only in *Treny*. (pp. 388-88)

"Lament XIX" (or "Dream"), whether thought too long or too dry, achieves one and perhaps the most important artistic purpose: it holds the whole cycle together. It echoes many phrases from the previous laments, from those that bewail the loss as well as from those that describe the state of mind; but one should not be hasty in concluding that the final poem is merely repetitive and therefore tedious, as any overdrawn repetition. The best way of testing Kochanowski's method is to read the Dream Lament on two levels of reference, following the sequence of the dream and, at the same time, making cross-references to the whole cycle. Let us illustrate this double reading:

(1) In the dream Orszula is brought by Kochanowski's mother, the same *wdzięczna* Orszula whom we know as 'gracious' from the dedicatory prose epitaph onwards (II, VI, X, XIII). She appears as if she came to say her morning prayers with her father (*po pacioreczek do mnie przychodzita*, XIX, 7): this recalls "Lament XII" (*aż pierwej Bogu swoje modlitwy oddata*) and simultaneously refers to the time of the dream itself (*na godzinę przed świtaniem*, XIX, 3).

(2) She is dressed in a white night-gown (*giezłteczko*). Cf. "Lament VII", where *giezteczko* has a funeral connotation (shroud). The girl's eyes smile as they used to (cf. the laughing Orszula in "Lament VIII").

(3) At the beginning of her argumentative monologue, the poet's mother describes how his tears summoned her from the dwelling of the dead (*umarlych pokoje*, "XIX", 18), to which, in "Lament XIV", the poet desires to go with his Orphic lute (*aż do pokoja surowego Plutona*). Her consolation is to save his weakening health, undermined by sorrow: cf. the thought of health in "Lament XVII" (*kto przyjaciel zdrowia mego*, etc.).

(4) The dead should not be regarded as lost (*stracone*, "XIX", 25): here the mother rebukes the wailing queries that lead to doubt in "Laments X", "XI", "XII". This confirmation of life after death and of heavenly glories endows the little girl with new qualities, higher even than those of a future Sappho, for she 'among angels and eternal spirits' shines as the gracious morning star (*jutrzenka*, cf. lines 35-6). The whole passage is an authoritative answer to "Lament X", whose opening line 'My gracious Ursula, where have you vanished' begins a series of questions about her. Is she elevated above all the heavens, is she among the angels or in the Blessed Isles; does she drink from Lethe, or perhaps, owing to some blemish (*zmazeczka*), clean her soul in Purgatory.... After these questions, "Lament X" breaks into a cry of despair: 'Wherever you are, if you are ...' (*Gdzieśkolwiek jest, jeśliś jest*), and the poem ends with an entreaty that the dead girl should appear in any one of the three forms, *sen, cień, mara*. In the Dream Lament this wish is granted, and the visual presence of Orszula before the dreamer is audibly confirmed by his mother's speech.

(5) The speech unfolds its corrective argument, point by point, and from line 39 to 106 refers to that aspect of time (what might have been) which widened the framework of the epitaphic laments, projecting the thirty-month-old life into the bridal future ("VI", "VII"). The mother's reply is projected from a similar level of possibility, but its height can be measured only by Divine Providence. The trousseau and dowry (*wyprawa, posag*) are effectively contrasted in "Lament VII" with Orszula's little dresses and with her shroud, the bridal bed with her coffin. The dream apparition utters the word 'dowry', but in relation to a different possibility—that with her dowry Orszula might have bought herself a lord and suffered slights and scolding; that her marriage would have inflicted the pains of childbirth on her ("XIX", 57-60). This is certainly not a recapitulation of an earlier theme, but a correction, a voice of wisdom within the light of a heaven-sent vision. This light grows brighter when the praise of heavenly hap-

piness springs from the apparition's argument (*w niebie szczyre rozkoszy*, etc.).

Orszula's new dwelling place, illuminated by the majesty of the Creator, knows neither sickness nor old age: here 'death, fed on tears, has no freedom' ("XIX", 70). The peaceful knowledge of the causes of all things is the opposite of the poet's struggles with uncertainty ("XI", "XII"), and his mother, by proving the happy lot of Orszula, refutes the 'philosophical' Laments: hers is a one-sided debate as his has been in the previous poems of the cycle (e.g. his address to Cicero, "XVI"). Still, the dream monologue remains a debate with a now silent partner, whose objections, however, are recalled or alluded to by phrases and echoing words.

(6) The last fifty-nine lines of the Dream Lament contain references to the Bible, imprinting new significance on the psalmodic trend of the cycle ("XVII", "XVIII"), and here too, assertion rather than repetition establishes the links. Moreover, the earlier parts of the cycle (preceding "Laments XVII" and "XVIII") are not forgotten even in this final stage of composition . . . .The appeal to reason and self-cure (*rozumem ma uprzedzić, co insze czas goi*, "XIX", 148) is a logical outcome of the argument delivered from so high a level of authority. The God-sent apparition defeats the reasoning debater ("IX", "X", "XI", "XVI") by stronger reason that rests, like the questions and answers of the *Summa Theologica*, on Biblical quotations. *Jeden jest Pan smutku i nagrody* (The Lord of grief and reward is one)—this is the apparition's last reminder.

The whole of the last Lament, therefore, should be read against the previous parts of the cycle. By doing this we may perhaps acquire the author's bird's-eye view of the entire composition and humbly refrain in our criticism from imputing to Kochanowski various discrepancies in the structure of *Treny*.

The English reader of *Treny* will, no doubt, agree that Kochanowski's cycle bears some resemblance to the great 14th-century poem *The Pearl*. Alliteration, the stanzaic pattern, the rhyme-scheme and the links between the stanzas give *The Pearl* its perfect structural unity, whereas the division of *Treny* into nineteen sections of different length (only "XVI", "XVII" and "XVIII" are stanzaic) does not suggest a specific formal pattern. Yet the dream-formula, employed by the Polish poet in order to secure unity for his cycle, permits us to draw a parallel with *The Pearl*. (pp. 393-96)

Independently of each other both *The Pearl* and *Treny* have occasioned much controversy as to their literary character (e.g. is *The Pearl* pure allegory or should we look for autobiographical material in it?). The Polish *Treny* has been interpreted by lovers of biography as well as by diviners of classical sources, with the concomitant changes in the interpretation of Orszula. How easy it would be to treat her as a symbol, had *Treny*, like *The Pearl*, been anonymous. All the objections voiced against the Pearl as a real girl could equally well apply to Orszula. (pp. 396-97)

The main difference between the two works lies in the more precise character of the vision and the debate in *The Pearl*. The dreamer here is shown the glory of heaven, the procession of the innocents headed by the Lamb of God. He argues with the Pearl of his vision. The dream-formula

is fully developed and serves as the whole poem's framework. In *Treny* it is, one might say, projected from the last Lament on to the whole cycle.

But this incomplete use of the old device emphasises the complexity of *Treny* as a 16th-century elegiac cycle. The Dream Lament widens the cycle's ground of reference and indirectly restrains our speculations on the so-called Renaissance elements in Kochanowski's poetry. He was undoubtedly a modernist for his time, and any comparison of his poetic diction with that of his predecessor Rej (1505-69) reveals striking changes. Yet every true modernist must be a traditionalist, if the changes imposed by him on poetic diction are to survive a period of fashion. Kochanowski learnt much from the classics in his Italian student years and from his practice as a Latin poet. But the mediaeval Latin tradition should also be considered within the possible range of his wide interests, and here the parallel with *The Pearl* suggests another relevant point of similarity. The English poem has been discussed in relation to Boccaccio's eclogue on the death of his five-and-a-half year-old daughter. His *Olympia* (written *c.* 1361) consoles the mourning father by describing her happy life in Elysium and the elevation of her state after death (*nam numero sum juncta deum*, 142). Although the vision of the eclogue is not enframed in a dream-vision (in this very point the English poem and that of Boccaccio differ essentially), the dream-like state of mind is suggested in the words of Silvius, the unhappy father, and it is precisely in these words that the similarity with Kochanowski seems particularly relevant to our argument at the outset of this essay. (pp. 397-98)

The *Olympia* eclogue, when compared with both *The Pearl* and *Treny*, raises a new query in criticism, which shifts the problem of sources to a more immediate tradition. This immediate tradition cannot be ignored when we place the Polish poet against his native literature. By his great achievement as a verse translator of the Psalter (*Psałterz Dawidów*) Kochanowski linked his art with the earliest heritage of Polish written records. Not only the previous versions of the Psalter but the whole body of mediaeval Polish religious lyric must be taken into account as constant factors in the continuity of that national literature. We are therefore not surprised to find that it is in the penitential psalm-like Laments ("XVII", "XVIII") that Kochanoswki reaches the depths of his humility. His solution in *Treny* is not so much that of falling back on a worn-out formula, but rather a natural leaning against a firm construction: the dream-formula in the last Lament seems to be a conscious choice (hence the title "Dream"). This God-sent message, this set of unbroken answers to a series of questions, relates the dream-debate to the teaching of the Bible. The first line of "Lament XVII" (*Pańska ręka mię dotknęla* ["God hath laid his hand on me"]) draws its painful truth from the Book of Job (*manus Domini tetigit me*, ["the hand of God hath touched me"] "XIX", 21), and the whole of the Lament echoes its admonitions. The systematised comments on dreams by Macrobius may not fit the interpretation of Kochanowski's formula. The relations between *somnium* and *visio* as formulated in the Book of Job and quoted by St Thomas Aquinas in his *Summa Theologica* could hardly have passed unnoticed by such a devout student of the Bible as the poet of *Treny*. In the Book of Job (XXXIII, 15-16) we read: 'Per somnium, in visione nocturna, quando irruit sopor super homines, et dormiunt in lectulo; tunc aperit au-res virorum, et erudiens eos instruit disciplina' ["In a dream, in a vision of the night, when deep sleep falleth upon men in slumberings upon the bed; then he openeth the ears of men, and sealeth their instruction."]

It is this kind of dream revelation that an essentially Cath-olic poet would transform to his literary purposes and im-pose on the contemplative cycle of poems in order to fulfil his moral as well as his artistic task. The influence of the Bible was part of the same heritage. To draw a fixed line between earlier Polish literature and that of the Sigismund period, to which Kochanowski belonged, means attempt-ing a rigid division, and new literary contents do not nec-essarily imply a new literary form. The element of debate in *Treny* reminds one of the verse debate in full dress, written by Rej. . . . Its date, 1543, is accepted in histories of literature as a convenient point of departure from the Polish Middle Ages. (pp. 398-400)

There is no place here to summarise the editorial work on *Treny* with regard to their classical sources. I should like to end, however, with a brief note on the criticism of Kochanowski's structure and purpose.

Commentators have been tempted to speculate on the gen-esis of *Treny*. In the 19th century it seemed almost a natu-ral approach to so personal a work. On the surface the cy-cle is personal enough to be called a verse-memoir. Kochanowski dedicated *Treny* to his dead daughter, and her name echoes many times in this tomb-like edifice: she has become perhaps the most lyrical heroine of Polish lit-erature.

As soon as the hunt for autobiographical material began, however, the text refused to cooperate, and no relevant letter, no manuscript could be found to elucidate the cycle itself. (p. 401)

Another difficulty seems to be the changing style within *Treny*. The popular **"Lament VIII"** still remains one of the most integrated and fresh poems in Polish lyric, and no number of reprints in anthologies and school textbooks can alter this. Its first six lines fully deserve their fame:

> Wielkieś mi uczyniła pustki w domu moim,
> Moja droga Orszulo, tym zniknieniem swoim,
> Pełno nas, a jakoby nikogo nie było,
> Jedna maluczką duszą tak wiele ubyło.
> Tyś za wszystki mówiła, za wszystki śpiewała,
> Wszytkiś w domu kąciki zawżdy pobiegała . . .

(You have made my house empty indeed by thus van-ishing, dearest Ursula. Many of us are here, yet there seems to be no one, for so much has left with your little soul. You talked and sang for us all, you ran into all the corners of the house . . .)

In contrast to this direct elegiac emotion, the opening of **"Lament XIV"** relies on a well-known image, rich in liter-ary associations:

> Gdzie te wrota nieszczęsne, którymi przed laty
> Puszczał się w ziemię Orfeus, szukając swej straty?
> Żebych ja też tąż ścieżką swej najmilszej córy
> Poszedł szukać i on bród mógł przebyć, przez który
> Srogi jakiś przewoźnik wozi blade cienie . . .

(Where are those unfortunate gates, through which in years of old Orpheus descended into the earth, looking

for his loss? O, that I might along the same path seek my beloved daughter and cross that ford over which the grim boatman ferries the pale shadows . . .)

We find still different samples of style in the last group of Laments:

> Pańska ręka mię dotknęła,
> Wszystkę mi radość odjęła . . . (**"XVII"**)

(The hand of God has touched me; it has taken all my joy away.)

> My nieposłuszne, Panie, dzieci twoje,
> W szczęśliwe czasy swoje,
> Rzadko Cię wspominamy,
> Tylko rozkoszy zwykłych używamy. (**"XVIII"**)

(We, your disobedient children, O Lord, remember you rarely in moments of happiness, enjoying then only our habitual pleasures.)

This penitential Biblical tone, mounting up to the state of grace in the Dream Lament, justifies the visionary charac-ter of the final consolation. Yet the noticeable changes in style throughout the cycle encouraged the critics to exam-ine them in separate groups, setting the portrait of Orszula either against its mythological or its Biblical background. Hartleb's insistence on the epitaph (*nagrobek*) as the most solid and central structure within *Treny* did not prevent him from using the division method. Whatever division is proposed, whether into themes or into stages of composi-tion, the method must inevitably lead to new queries, thus further complicating the interpretation of the text.

Even if we accept the view that there was a turning point in the development of the cycle and that 'the poem about the dead daughter changed into an autobiographical work', in which the philosophising poet came into the foreground, this kind of argument destroys much of the recommended caution as regards the personal element in *Treny*: we are thrown back among the shadows of guess-work e.g. the Laments describing Orszula directly must have been written earlier, if there was to be any turning point in the development of the cycle, and so on. Was the poet then dissatisfied with his work and did he forestall his future interpreters by taking a long rest before his more 'philosophical' complaints? Such questions can be multiplied, and each of them, by implication, involves the character of the little girl. Who was she really, this thirty-month-old Orszula, shown now through tears and mytho-logical symbols, now through intellectual arguments and the dream-vision? If we try to reconstruct her portrait from what the text describes or suggests, we may put to-gether a set of poetic impressions, elusive at times, yet *po-etically* consistent. But if we do this, simultaneously rear-ranging the cycle to make it fit our conjectures, we are certain to be faced with various inconsistencies, and Orszula may disappear altogether in the clouds of mystery. (pp. 402-04)

Jerzy Pietrkiewicz, "The Mediaeval Dream-Formula in Kochanowski's 'Treny'," in The Sla-vonic and East European Review, *Vol. 31, No. 77, June 1953, pp. 388-404.*

MANFRED KRIDL (essay date 1956)

[A Polish historian and educator, Kridl has written several books on Polish literature, including his highly regarded anthology of nineteenth-century Polish literature. Literatura polska wieku XIX *(1923). In the following excerpt from a later work, he surveys Kochanowski's light poems, songs, and three masterpieces.* Psałterz Dawidów, Laments, *and* The Dismissal of the Grecian Envoys.*]*

Jan Kochanowski was the first Polish poet. A truly excellent poet, it may be said without exaggeration that he was the greatest in the Old Slavic world, and in Poland he remained the greatest until Mickiewicz—a comparison which bears out his exceptional significance in the history of Polish literature and culture. Kochanowski's work marks one of the peaks of Old Polish culture. (p. 62)

His early works were written in Latin, chiefly elegies modeled on Ovid, Tibullus, and Propertius. These poems, devoted to real or imaginary love, do not possess any outstanding significance. Besides Greek and Latin literature, Kochanowski undoubtedly studied both early and contemporary Italian and French literature, the works of Dante and Petrarch, as well as Ariosto, Ronsard, and other more modern authors. Perhaps Kochanowski found in these writers his own inspiration to write in the vernacular. It is said that while he was in France he met Ronsard, the great initiator of national poetry, and conceived at that time the Polish religious hymn **"Czego chcesz od nas Panie"** (**"What Do You Want from Us, O Lord"**), which begins with the words 'What do you want from us, O Lord, for all your generous gifts...' The story also tells how this hymn was sent to Poland, was read in numerous copies, and met with Rey's ardent praise. Whatever the case may have been, the fact remains that the hymn is among the most beautiful of Kochanowski's works, and some doubts have been expressed that it could have been written so early. But in poetic creation all kinds of 'miracle' are possible, and in this case all conjecture is fruitless, for only an authentic document could possibly resolve the question of the date of this work.

Judging by the subsequent development of Kochanowski's work, we may suppose that even during his stay abroad he laid the foundation for his 'literary program.' This program was generally in harmony with the trends of Ronsard's school, the so-called Pléiade, and it advocated among other things that poetry should be written in the vernacular but in classical style, so that national literature might be imbued with the spirit of the ancients and, at the same time, acquire a national character. It goes without saying that this whole conception of art was based on classical poetics. In this way western and southern Europe had absorbed and transmuted the inspiration of ancient culture, and Polish poetry had to follow the general example, if it was not to be a slave to classicism but become its independent heir and relive its inspiration in new historical conditions. By following the general process of the Renaissance, Polish poetry also acquired broader connections with European literature and gradually lost its provincial quality (how much provincialism there still is in Rey!) to become more universal. In order to accomplish this development in Polish poetry, a great poetic talent was necessary, and Jan Kochanowski became that talent. Thanks to his work, Polish poetry completely changed its character.... Kochanowski was the poet who gave his country pure poetry. His task as a poet is beautifully expressed in

"Muza" (**"The Muse"**), which begins with the famous line: 'To myself I sing and the Muses...'

With admirable brevity Kochanowski presents the eternal fate of poets who create for themselves and for art, without concern for profit or the opinions of those for whom 'rhymes' are merely empty sounds. At the same time, the poem reflects a profound conviction of the poet's own worth and his posthumous victory. Much later the Polish Romantic poet, Juljusz Słowacki, spoke in similar terms about his own poetry. (pp. 62-3)

Kochanoswki's most interesting and original works during [the Courtier] period are the ***Fraszki*** (***Trifles***, 1584), which he continued to write throughout his life. These are short poems on a variety of subjects, both light and serious. We find among them many anecdotes, various humorous stories, epigrams, epitaphs, portraits of friends, and descriptions of their adventures, among which love and wine occupy an important place. Many of these poems are devoted to women: confessions of love, compliments, arguments, and the like. They reflect courtly life, a gay and brilliant existence, and at the same time show a high social and cultural level as well as something of life in the cities and in the country. They are characterized now by a light-hearted *joie de vivre*, now by more profound reflection upon life. Kochanowski's wit is far more subtle than that of Rey, and in his writings he displays that indulgence with which wise men observe and accept their fellow men with their comic foibles as well as their vices and sins. (p. 64)

Their chief characteristic is their compactness, which catches the heart of the matter and emphasizes characteristic traits. The language has none of those superfluous words which Rey would often use simply for the sake of rhythm; it is fluid and free, but never vulgar. We may look at some examples in outline.

In the trifle intitled **"O doktorze Hiszpanie"** (**"The Spanish Doctor"**), an anecdote based on a *pointe*, a Spanish court doctor called Rosius leaves a very gay party in order to go to sleep. He does not, however, enjoy his rest for long; his companions quickly remember him, attack his quarters ('the doctor did not give way, but the door did') and force him to drink. Willy-nilly he gives in, until his head begins to swim. The trifle ends with the doctor's words: 'I went to bed sober, but I got up drunk.'

In another, **"O Kapelanie"** (**"The Priest"**), the queen wanted to go to Mass, but the priest was not found at home, 'for he was watching the wine pitcher.' As an excuse to the queen, who accuses him of oversleeping, the priest replies: 'I have not even gone to bed. What do you mean by long sleep?' A twoline epigram, **"Na nabożną"** (**"The Pious Woman"**), embodies one essential question: 'If you do not sin, as you say, my dear, why do you go to confession so often?' In one of the trifles, **"Do Miłości"** (**"To Love,"** there are several under this title), we find a faintly mythological concept of love combined with a complaint at 'the undaunted thought of the stubborn woman.' In another, **"Do paniej"** (**"To a Lady"**), the structure of which is based in part on a syntactical parallel, homage to a mistress in 'rhyme' is placed much higher than a sculpture in marble or gold, for 'the glory of poetic genius remains forever, It knows no damage and is not afraid of years.' In a witty, skilful, anaphorically constructed trifle, **"To a Girl"**, the poet assures a beautiful maiden that she should not avoid him, for, though his beard is grey, his heart is not so old, and in order to persuade her more effectively he mentions the analogy of garlic, which 'has a white head, but a green tail,' and the oak tree, 'whose leaves are pale, but who stands up firm because its root is healthy.'

The trifle, **"Do snu"** (**"To Sleep"**), touches on a different question, namely the mystery of sleep, which teaches man how to die and gives him 'insight into future life.' The soul's slumbering journey across the world and beyond it is expressed in a series of images of a metaphysical cast which contrast with the state of bodily rest. **"Na lipe"** (**"To the Linden Tree"**) is full of charm and a subtle feeling for nature. The linden tree itself speaks as a symbol of nature which gives calm and rest. The shade, the cool breeze, the song of birds, the scent of flowers and the whisper of leaves—these are motifs expressed in a subtle manner.

Kochanowski also wrote, during his career, what he called 'songs.' There is no basic thematic difference between these two genres, for the trifles were not concerned only with gay and ephemeral themes any more than the songs were limited to serious ones. However, the songs are generally in stanzaic form, and the lyrical element is more strongly emphasized in them.

Kochanowski's *Pieśni* (*Songs*) are found in four books which, like *The Trifles*, were published posthumously "(the first two books in 1585). The influence of Horace is to be found in all of them, and they include numerous translations or free adaptations of Horace's works. Kochanowski frequently paraphrases, but with equal frequency he borrows only Horace's idea, as from the odes *Aequam memento rebus in arduis* or *O nata mecum consule Mantio*, and he recreates it, making a Polish poem out of it; or again, he will take one detail and use it in completely original songs. But the Horatian spirit and mood pervade even the latter. There is praise of virtue, clear conscience, and the contentment they afford; there is a controlled hedonism in the desire for calm, happiness, and spiritual balance *(aequa mens)*; there is a belief in the mutability of fortune and the vanity of material things, and hence praise for moderation and contentment with whatever one has. In a word, it is the philosophy of a humanist who has experienced a great deal, observed the problems of men, is surprised by nothing, and intolerant of nothing. On the other hand, there is a great capacity for enjoying life, a deep interest in all its manifestations, and a sense of enjoying the moment, full of gayety and 'praise of the wine pitcher.'

The subjects of *The Songs* are varied. There are love songs, descriptive, patriotic, religious and contemplative poems, and others devoted to the family, to friends, to social life, and so on.

A few examples will give the reader at least some idea of Kochanowski's poetry in this genre. In the second song of the first volume, which begins with the words 'Serce roście patrząc na te czasy' ('The heart is edified, looking at our times . . .'), a descriptive element of a markedly lyrical sort is combined with the contemplative. The description concentrates on the contrast between recent winter and present spring. Before, there had been naked woods, snows reaching above the knees, ice on the rivers; now, trees and meadows are in bloom, there is growing corn, a west wind,

and the singing of birds. The heart is edified by this sight, and inner serenity and a clear conscience intensify the delight in nature. This mood of calm and contentment dominates the whole poem, which ends with an apostrophe to 'cheerfulness' or 'the good mind': 'Be with me, when I am sober or drunk'. Both the descriptive and the contemplative parts are composed of simple words, which create, however, expressive poetic images.

"Song III" of the same book '*Dzbanie mój pisany . . .*' ('Oh, my painted pitcher . . .') has a rhetorical structure; it is in the form of an oration to the pitcher as the symbol of a precious drink in which even philosophers indulge, and which makes everybody 'softer,' unveils secret thoughts, gives a sense of hope, and inspires courage. This song was one of the most popular of the sixteenth century and was frequently sung by the gentry.

In one form or another, the image of the pitcher appears in many of Kochanowski's songs. In **"Song IX,"** for example, it serves as a kind of ornament together with fiddles and lutes. The pitcher also colors the character of the philosophical reflections expressed in this poem; one should not worry excessively about the future, for we are all subject to the laws of Fortune; "everything is so strange in this poor world of ours, and he who wants to know everything will perish before he learns." Hence the moral: one should not boast of happiness, and one should bear unhappiness with fortitude. (p. 64-7)

The finest of Kochanowski's religious songs is the hymn already mentioned, **"What Do You Want from Us, O Lord."** It can be safely said that in this poem pure religious feelings of admiration, adoration, disinterested love, and delight in the Creator's work itself were expressed for the first time in Polish poetry in a way worthy of their aspiration. The Polish language shone with a new splendor and strength of expression. (p. 67)

The third and last period in Kochanowski's work, the one to which his greatest masterpieces belong: *Treny* (*The Threnodies*,) *Psałterz Dawidów* (*The Psalter of David*), and *Odprawa posłów greckich* (*The Dismissal of the Greek Envoys*), beside numerous minor works. Among the latter we should mention **"Pieśń Świętojańska o Sobótce"** (**"The Song of St. John's Eve"**), probably written in 1575; it describes the country fête, deriving from pagan times and preserved until very recent times, which is held on St. John's Eve in June. . . . **"St. John's Eve"** revealed for the first time to the Poles the beauty of their land; we found in Rey a eulogy for country life, but he emphasized the practical aspects of its existence. Although Kochanowski too looks at the country with the eye of a landowner, he can also see it as an artist. The work has a purely artistic character; it lacks any ethnographical particularities or folk influences.

One of the masterpieces of the Czarnolas period in Kochanowski's career, is his *Psalter of David*, published in 1579. This inspired work, of which innumerable translations into many languages have been made, had frequently been translated into Polish before Kochanowski. . . . The earliest translations in prose have only philological value, and the later translations in verse failed to come close to the original. Only Kochanowski's translation is a work worthy of the psalms themselves. Not knowing the Hebrew language, he took as his model the Latin adaptation by the

Scottish humanist, Buchanan, at the same time drawing upon contemporary Polish versions of the Psalter. His is not a literal translation, but a paraphrase in which the fundamental themes and motifs of the Psalms, and especially their spirit, are conveyed in a number of poems of various length, each poem corresponding to one Psalm. This is the work both of a philologist and artist. The simple sentences of the Hebrew original are frequently transformed into vivid poetic images, hence there is much amplification of the original text; Kochanowski's adaptation is thus considerably longer. He also frequently smoothes the elementary and crude force of the original and suits it to a more humanistic taste. The poet worked on the *Psalter* for eight years (1570-78).

What prompted him to assimilate *The Psalter* into Polish poetry? In the first place he found there one of the most profound expressions of the human soul, immersed in the contemplation of God and aspiring to union with Him. At the same time the psalms are penetrated by purely human feelings and thoughts, with all the fears, sadness, suffering, doubts and hopes common to all men. Kochanowski found there undoubtedly many of his own spiritual experiences symbolized and sublimated, as it is the case with any great poetry. He was excited by the poetic task of transferring that whole poetic world into the forms of his native tongue, that were about to be created by himself. How this was done, Mickiewicz testifies in his lectures on Slavic literature given in the Collège de France in the following words: 'In his translation of the Psalms [Kochanowski] is inspired, he has a noble and lucid style, a bold poetic rhythm, fluent and splendid phrases, and throughout a sacerdotal solemnity and the gravity of wisdom.' And, we should add, a thorough mastery of the verse and the stanza. We find in the psalms an immense wealth and variety with regard to the length of the line and the structure of the stanza (there are approximately 30 kinds), to rhythm and rhyme. The richness of Kochanowski's poetic devices makes the forms of earlier Polish poetry look poor by comparison. (pp. 68-9)

The second masterpiece of the Czarnolas period is Kochanowski's *Treny* (*Threnodies*, 1580). This genre, which laments the memory of the dear departed, was known in antiquity and was cultivated by Renaissance poets like Petrarch. Kochanowski's *Threnodies* are dedicated to the memory of his beloved daughter, Orszula, who died in her third year after a short illness. This shock provided the external impulse to write nineteen short poems, in which fundamentally the same motif appears through a series of extraordinarily rich variations. *Threnodies* tells a unique lyrical story of the suffering that can take possession of the whole human being. At the same time it is the picture of a mind which realizes that it has been overwhelmed by irrational forces, from which there is no escape, and attempts to understand its own inner processes. The poet's genius is shown in his ability to avoid monotony or repetition and to give new life to a theme, every nuance of which is thoroughly familiar and has been often described: the cries of despair and the first reaction to the shock; the prostration of grief; the gradual recovery of consciousness; the agonizing memories of the beloved child; the search for forgetfulness in the happy memories of the past, when the child was still alive; and then the renewed pangs of pain at the sudden sight of her clothes; bitter reflections on the collapse of his own philosophy of life, which had

been won with so much effort; and, finally, peace and resignation in his return to Christian faith.

Before the soul can reach this last stage of reconciliation and acceptance, it must pass through the inferno of suffering and doubt that penetrates to the very foundation of belief. The poet pictures the soul of a humanist, founded upon the ancient philosophies on which he has spent so many years of hopeful toil, and now suddenly confronted with a horror that shatters the edifice at a blow. The wisdom of the Stoics had taught him that a man may acquire happiness in a just balance of the spirit, so long as he considers the outside world as a game of blind forces unworthy of a truly wise man's attention. Thus he will not attach himself to the world and its affairs, and will not be moved by success or by failure, as is the case with the ignorant, the *profanum vulgus*. Raised above the vanity of this world, he will not be vulnerable to sudden despair or unseemly joy; he will preserve the detachment of spiritual balance, the *aequam mentem* through all the vicissitudes of life.

Kochanowski was certainly not a stoic philosopher in the strict sense of the word. But many traits fundamental to that wisdom had attracted him and allowed him to order his life for the sake of peace and contentment. His child's sudden death revealed to him the other side of life, the merciless, the cruel, the unintelligible and irrational side. And he shows us the heartrending, internal drama of a 'wise man,' made prey to all the instincts and feelings of this world—this unessential, despised world. He is a prey to the suffering which is the lot of every 'barbarian' who knows nothing of the nature of life and death. He shows us the humanist who weeps like a woman over the corpse of a small child, a child with no significance for the world; he presents a classical poet destined to describe lofty and exalted themes, possessed by such a small and unimportant object as a little girl.

Even his Christian faith in immortality is shaken by this cruel shock. In one threnody he wonders where his daughter's soul might rest after death. He reviews many possibilities, including the Christian answer, but he does not believe in any of them and fears that her soul may not exist at all.

These are the human and eternal perspectives of Kochanowski's *Threnodies*. Their literary expression is rich not only in qualities of the poet's own ingenuity but also in the best humanistic tradition. His wide reading in classical literature comes out in his many references to mythology; there are expressions borrowed from Horace, Ovid, and Catullus, and arguments from Seneca and Lucretius. (pp. 67-71)

We shall select several threnodies for more detailed analysis, in order to study more closely some characteristic aspects of their problems and their poetic art. The first threnody is a kind of introduction, in which the poet defines the chief problem of his work, calling upon all the tears, cries and sorrows of Heraclites and Symonides to help him in mourning for his beloved child. In the first four lines we have a wealth of expressions for grief: the weeping, tears, laments, complaints, sorrow, and despair. This is one motif of the poem, which is followed by the image of the child's sudden death compared with the death of a nightingale, which is devoured by a 'dragon' in front of the unhappy mother's eyes, while she tries in vain to defend her nestling. This vain defense evokes a reflection (the third motif) on the uselessness of despair before the irrevocable facts. 'All is vain,' cries the poet, 'who shall say which is easier, to overcome, or be overcome by grief.'

These three motifs form an organic whole which directly expresses the spiritual state of mind. The comparison employed in the second motif does not detract from this directness, because it possesses a symbolic character. The final reflection is strictly linked with the two preceding motifs.

The language operates mostly, though not exclusively, within abstract concepts, as in the initial enumerations. Remarks about the home and the 'charming girl' introduce concrete elements. The word 'all' (in one case even 'all and all') is repeated seven times, and it emphasizes the greatness of suffering which can be measured only against all the pains of the world. The numerous exclamations are in keeping with the general style of the poem.

The structure of "Threnody V" is based on a comparison of Orszula's death with the cutting off of a small olive tree by 'an over-zealous' gardener who is clearing the garden of weeds. The first part of the poem is devoted to a description of the olive tree which is suddenly cut off from further growth; the second to the similar death of the child. The work ends with an invocation to the evil Persephone. The description of the first part is expressed mainly in concrete terms with the aid of several personifications; among them we find a number of diminutives, which heighten the emotional tone of the description; the personifications emphasize the concept of the small tree as a living being. This device constitutes a link between the image of the death of the olive tree and that of the child.

The image of Orszula's death is generally conceived in the same way: she had grown under their parents' eyes, has scarcely risen from the ground; here a new motif appears, 'the contagious spirit of remorseless death,' which 'inspires' the child, who falls at her parent's feet.

The style reveals a truly classical quality of clarity and simplicity. Figures of speech are used in moderation. The combination of concrete and metaphorical elements does not obscure the meaning, but lends the language an emotional coloring. The expressions representing death are particularly striking.

"Threnody VIII" evokes in a penetrating way the atmosphere of emptiness in the home after the disappearance of the beloved creature. The house is full of people, but it seems 'as though it were empty; so much was lost with one little person.' This feeling of emptiness inspires memories of the child when she was still alive. Orszula appears, talkative, cheerful: 'you sang for everybody'; she was a busy, tender child, who never 'allowed her mother to worry or her father to think too much.' This characterization is closed with a variation from the first motif: 'Sorrow stares from every corner...'

Thus the principal motif of the poem is set in relief by the contrast between the past and the present. The style is particularly remarkable for the emotional weight of its highly condensed poetic formulations.

Amidst the wealth and variety of moods, experiences, and problems, "Threnody IX" occupies a place of special importance. An eternal problem is revealed in this twenty-line poem, which reaches beyond the loss of the child; it touches the mutual relationship of thought and life, of knowledge and nature, of intellect and mystery. This is the main motif of the first part where the poet grasps in a condensed way the essence of the philosophy of stoicism (probably not borrowed directly from its source, but rather through Seneca), as we explained above (p. 70). The second part of the poem, which is shorter, depicts the tragedy of 'an unhappy man' who wasted all his years to 'see the threshold' of this wisdom, and who is now hurled from the topmost steps.

The style is well suited to the subject and contains a variety of discursive elements. They are shown, for instance, in a number of condensed statements presenting the wisdom of the Stoics, carefully arranged in sequence, through sixteen lines. This accumulation of parallel statements, linked with each other in meaning and rhythm, lend the style a rather 'intellectual' character, though without making it less poetical. On the other hand, the metaphorical and figurative elements subdue the abstract tendency of the style.

"Threnody XI" is also contemplative in character and poses the theme of virtue and its effectiveness. The poem begins with an assertion that virtue is an insubstantial thing, a trifle; this is the principal motif, reinforced by two rhetorical questions ('Who has ever been saved by piety? Who has ever averted an evil chance by goodness?') and developed subsequently in the image of 'the unknown foe' who 'confounds human affairs, caring for neither the good nor the bad.' Another motif is then introduced: the limitation of the human mind; 'light dreams, ephemeral dreams,' are all its experience and knowledge of the world and God's secrets. This absolute pessimism finally produces a reaction, as the poet realizes that it leads him not only to the loss of all consolation but to that of his reason as well.

These three motifs blend, representing different aspects of the same problem: a conviction that evil is omnipotent, the hopelessness of any attempt to learn its causes, and the realization of the consequence of such a world view.

Among Kochanowski's stylistic devices, one should observe here the three repetitions of the word 'trifle' in the first two lines to emphasize the dominant theme. We find also the same vivid, forceful images that are in the other Threnodies, illustrating the attitude of the poet.

Finally the moral and religious crisis arrives ("Threnody XVIII"). The poet identifies himself with those who give God no thought in time of happiness, who forget the truth of the fact that everything comes from Him. There follows a series of moving pleas and prayers to God, contrition before His power, and hope of grace.

This Threnody is constructed in the form of a prayer, combining confessions and supplications. Several images develop the principal motif of the soul, lost in despair, which turns to God as to the source of both happiness and calamity. Here he confesses his own grievous sins, but preserves faith in God's infinite charity. These elements follow each other, yet they also grow out of one another, and thus constitute artistically an organic whole.

Kochanowski is also the author of the tragedy intitled *Od-prawa posłów greckich* (*The Dismissal of the Greek Envoys*). This work was written in 1578 for the celebration of the wedding of Chancellor Jan Zamoyski, and at his request. It was a work ordered, as it were, by a friend who could not be refused. The poet had too little time to create a fin-ished and polished play. That is why his tragedy remains little more than a sketch, though a sketch of unusual beau-ty. The subject is probably borrowed from Homer's *Iliad* (the poet was just then translating Book III of that work), but he was also assisted by the fantastic medieval ro-mance, *The History of the Trojan War*, and depicts a cer-tain episode in the conflict between Troy and Greece. (pp. 71-4)

Kochanowski's work is modeled on ancient tragedy in the style of Euripides and Seneca, and it follows the general pattern of humanist tragedy as it was then represented by Trissino and Jodelle. It has a single, unchanging scene (the square in front of the royal palace), choruses which give voice to sundry *sententiae*, and in its structure follows the principles set by the Greek masters. It contains a prologue (which in modern drama has been supplanted by exposi-tion), two episodes, relative to modern acts, and finally the *exodos* or *dénouement*. The chorus is heard after the prologue and after each of the episodes. The action is completed in one day. The play was performed at an aris-tocratic court in the presence of the king, by the youth of the gentry, as was the custom in the humanist tradition.

Although the subject was borrowed from foreign models, Kochanowski did not limit himself to what he found in them. Out of the familiar material, which was supple-mented with the Polish poet's own inventions, he created a new artistic unity. The value of *The Dismissal*, which may be called a kind of 'dramatic sketch,' does not lie in a tragic entanglement or in the presentation of great char-acters who struggle against fate; rather it is a competent presentation of a dramatically tense situation, occasioned by the arrival and dismissal of the Greek envoys. Kocha-nowski revealed an indisputable dramatic sense in his con-ception and execution of this situation. Several of the characters are firmly drawn, though only in outline, like Antenor, Aleksander (Paris), Kassandra, and the senators, and there is much dramatic life in such scenes as the de-liberations of the senators, the appearance of Kassandra, and her ominous prophecy about the fall of Troy. Some of the dialogues have a definite dramatic tone, as that be-tween Antenor and Paris where their different characters and opinions are set in conflict over Helen, while the cho-ruses move with a beautiful rhythm and verse. The poet's attempts to individualize the language of the various char-acters is also strongly felt. The play contains some inter-esting, though anachronistic, allusions to the disorder which reigned in the Polish Diet, to the insolence of some deputies who often terrorized the Diet and forced it into measures in their own favor, and to abuses of which the young gentry was guilty. The poet employs such expres-sions as 'the one God,' 'republic,' 'the peasant' and 'the peasant coat.' A clearly political tone, probably inspired by the king and his chancellor, is heard in the calls to war, which could only be understood as referring to Batory's intention of declaring war on Muscovy.

Kochanowski was above all a poet and an artist. Of the three intellectual movements of this time, only humanism influenced him decisively, shaping both his mind and his

art. Humanism gave him his most valuable qualities: his broad literary and artistic culture, his noble and refined morality, which he associated with a Christian faith, his clear, penetrating mind, highly sensitive but always guided by reason, and, most important of all, his art, modeled on classical masterpieces though it was as truly Polish as it was universal. Kochanowski was the first 'European' in the history of Polish literature, and his works belong to that realm of universal values which makes them a part of the heritage of world culture.

Kochanowski's poetic art adheres generally to the classical forms, with classical 'realism' and moderation, and is al-ways controlled in its realization of poetic devices. His po-etry abandons itself to no flights of fantasy that might lead it beyond the ordered forms of art, nor does it stoop to vulgar themes, for Kochanowski was always aware of the noble nature of his vocation. He never permitted himself to be drawn into literary innovations or revolutions, but he was never given to slavish imitation. He transformed foreign motifs and forms for his use, 'for himself and for the Muses.' The language he used was a distinctly literary language, the tongue of the educated class, raised to poetic dignity by new values of cadence, meaning, and vigor. It is always 'classical,' lucid, and noble, without exaggerated neologisms, but also without commonplace and prosaic expressions. A comparison with any of the usages of Rey reveals the nature of Kochanowski's achievement, which made of the Polish language a splendid instrument for po-etry. (pp. 74-6)

Manfred Kridl, "The Sixteenth Century: Human-ism and Reformation," in his A Survey of Polish Literature and Culture, *translated by Olga Scherer-Virski, Mouton, 1956, pp. 39-92.*

JOHN MERSEREAU, JR. (essay date 1962)

[*An American essayist and academic, Mersereau has written several studies on Russian and Slavic literature. In the fol-lowing excerpt, he points to four recurrent motifs in* La-ments *as indicative of Kochanowski's interpretation and ex-pression of grief.*]

Although written almost four centuries ago, the *Laments* of Jan Kochanowski remain one of Polish literature's most impressive masterpieces. Characterized by a profound lyr-icism and a high degree of technical perfection, this cycle of nineteen poems justly deserves to be included among the world's classics. The theme is an eternal one—man's reaction to death—and the treatment of this theme, de-spite its intensely personal character, achieves universali-ty. The *Laments* are not just the outpouring of a soul tor-mented by an unexpected bereavement; they present a pattern of grief and ultimate consolation which is as meaningful today as it was in the sixteenth century. (p. 37)

A rich critical literature has been produced concerning this work, whose multifold interpretations reveal its deep potential of meaning and evaluation. The cycle has been seen, to note but a few examples, as a philosophical dra-ma, a domestic document of the sixteenth century, and a poetic innovation representing a forward step in the legi-timization of autobiographical themes. The emotional qualities of the work have, of course, not been overlooked, but heretofore they have been accepted and appreciated with a minimum of analysis. However, it is precisely these elements of emotion, contributing so effectively to the lyrical power of the cycle, which are one of its most significant aspects. With his **Laments** Kochanowski has succeeded in verbalizing, in rendering in a communicable form, an emotion. His achievement is one of literature's most lucid and effective definitions of grief. (pp. 37-8)

How, indeed, does Kochanowski express his emotion? We are not concerned here with such traditional, and in reality vague, statements such as "I'm sad", "Woe is me", etc. Declarations such as these are far from conveying any specific feeling. What interests us here are the means by which the author exteriorizes his grief, the manner in which he gives expression to his mute feelings, thus representing to his readers in a concrete form his complex emotional state.

Before proceeding to a more detailed discussion of this matter, it is important to note the function of the structure of the work—the sequence of the component poems. There has been considerable scholarly attention devoted to the question as to whether or not the laments were actually composed in the order in which we know them. Some scholars have felt that the emotional content of certain laments indicates that they were written immediately following Ursula's death; others believe that those laments presenting the most vivid images of Ursula must necessarily have been written first. Their arguments are interesting, but they are, at best, academic. Kochanowski himself arranged the poems in the order in which they appear, and it would be an act of *lèse génie* to suspect that this arrangement was a haphazard one. The structure of the work proves just the contrary, for this structure plays an important role in achieving what the author must have intended to accomplish by his work: first, to express and exteriorize his grief, and second, to reaffirm the Christian precept "Thy will be done." With this latter theme are connected the six concluding laments ("**XIV-XIX**"), which are, as it were, a history of the author's search for and eventual discovery of consolation. In these final six laments, as elsewhere, the exposition and argumentation proceed logically, culminating in the dream which brings final consolation and, for the reader's benefit, the admonition towards which the whole work has gradually developed:

> . . . bear man's portion like a man;
> The Lord of grief and joy is one. ("**XIX**")

The structure has, however, a function in addition to the one connected with the logical progression of the work's philosophical tendency. Taken as a whole, the cycle leads the reader through the various states of the author's grief, from his initial formless misery to the final acceptance of the inevitability of his loss. Kochanowski shows that grief is not a static condition but an emotion in flux. He details the development of the emotion, giving a chronology of its various states.

The work opens with a poignant dedication:

> To Ursula Kochanowska
> a charming, delightful, extraordinary child
> who, having shown great promise of all
> maidenly virtues and attributes, suddenly
> and unaccountably in her infancy, to the
> great and unbearable grief of her parents,
> passed away. Written with tears by Jan
> Kochanowski, the unhappy father, for his
> darling daughter.

Thou art no more, my Ursula!

This touching dedication is more than a conventional gesture. It contains in their simplest form and most concise statement those elements which, reiterated and augmented by the content of the first two laments, will constantly be given new illumination and expression in the subsequent laments to create an objective picture of the poet's emotional state.

At the moment, however, we are concerned with the function of this dedication in the emotional chronology which the cycle presents. The cry of apparently unconsolable grief which closes the dedication, "Thou art no more, my Ursula", is the most immediate and general response to the bereavement. It is a spontaneous outburst, an echo of the sudden pain which comes with the comprehension that the child is dead.

The first lament takes us one step further. All is in vain: in vain he tried to save his daughter, in vain are his tears. "What then, by the living God, is not in vain on earth? All is in vain!" The despondency reflected in this lament develops into a mood of desperation in "**Lament II**," expressed by the cry: "Would that she had never seen this earth!" The quality of grief here almost achieves the character of an angry denial of what has been, a desire to reject the very existence of Ursula so that the pain of her loss might never have been experienced. In the third lament this element of desperation is replaced by a pervading gloominess. The knowledge that she is gone forever has intruded itself into the poet's consciousness: "But thou, my child, shalt ne'er return to me . . ." However, at the very end of this part one hears the first note of consolation: there is a possibility of meeting Ursula in afterlife. Following the initial moments of anguish, there has penetrated a ray of hope, which, gradually increasing in intensity, strengthened by reason and faith, by the final lament illuminates the poet's darkened spirit and provides consolation.

In the third lament, however, this release is but momentary, and in the fourth lament we are again faced with an image of grief. A new element emerges here: speculations on what might have been. There is a trace of self-pity—understandably, of course—in the poet's plaint that, God willing, Ursula might have outlived him, thus sparing him the burden of sorrow which he now bears. And again in the fifth lament, following a metaphoric description of Ursula's fate, the poet asks why he has been caused to pour out his tears: "Oh evil Persephone, how could you cause so many tears in vain to flow?" In the succeeding lament this thin note of plaintive self-pity is repeated in the poet's assertion that he has paid dearly in tears for the brief song of his little nightingale.

Having evolved from its initial anguish, through despondency, despair and gloom to self-pity, the poet's grief now loses some of its obsessive quality. Whereas previously the emotion was unrestrained and seemingly dependent only upon internal stimuli, Kochanowski now shows how, when the initial outpouring of grief has somewhat abated, the sufferer begins to respond to external stimuli. Thus, for example, the child's clothes provoke a sudden resurgence of the despondency evinced in the first lament. Or again, the house, lacking Ursula's presence, is oppressively empty, and "from every corner sorrow seizes one". An emotional condition at least partly held in check by reason ensues, broken only by brief relapses into despondency. The original emotional turbulence is succeeded by a mood of contemplation, and the poet is able to philosophize on the ineffectualness of wisdom in the face of personal disaster. But again, as he begins speculating on Ursula's state after death, he sinks into despair and calls to her to appear to him as a dream, a shade, or even in a nightmare.

Elements of self-pity intrude themselves into his subsequent philosophical generalizations on the vanity of man's pretensions to wisdom, and the poet complains bitterly of the sorrow which has robbed him both of his child and the peace of mind which, prior to her death, he believed wisdom had provided him. Finally, an admission to God of his sins and a prayer for mercy serve as a prelude to the last lament: after the poet's reaffirmation of faith he is permitted the dream in which the consoling image of Ursula, brought by his mother from paradise, appears before him and reconciles him completely with his fate.

Let us turn now to the problem of the means employed by the poet to arrive at his definition of grief. The discussion will be concerned for the most part with the content of the dedication and the first thirteen laments, for they embrace the area of the work in which the exteriorization and characterization of the emotional state primarily is accomplished.

Basically, Kochanowski's method is that of taking certain themes, motifs, and images suggested by the life and death of his child and combining these in various patterns to form the succession of laments. These elements, closely interwoven with references, allusions, paraphrases and philosophy of a Classical nature, are constantly given new expression and illumination to realize an objective picture of his grief.

Four motifs basic to the cycle appear in the dedication: the charming and talented child, death, the desolate parents, and destroyed hopes. Note particularly that each of these occurs also in one or both of the first two, introductory laments.

a) *the charming and talented child*:

> ("**I**")... and help me mourn my charming child...
> ("**II**")... to cry over the mute grave of my charming daughter...
> ("**III**")... my delightful infant.
> It is true that it [thy patrimony] could not compare
> With thy early reason, with thy fair qualities
> By which thy future virtues were already indicated.
> Thy words! thy rapture! thy charming bows!
> ("**VI**") My delightful little songstress! My Slavic Sappho.
> ("**X**") My charming child, where art thou lost?
> ("**XII**") *Almost the entire lament is a catalogue of her virtues.*
> ("**XIII**") My charming Ursula...

b) *death*:

The motif of death is not directly present in the dedication, although certainly suggested by the content. The motif proper appears in the two introductory laments, where death acquires the character of an active and terrible force, in place symbolized by Proserpine (Persephone), the queen of the underworld.

> ("**I**")... help me mourn my charming child,
> From whom ungodly death has parted me...
> ("**II**")... to cry over the mute grave of my charming daughter
> And to complain of the severity of harsh Proserpine.
> ... O pitiless, inexorable, implacable princess of fleeting shades.
> ("**IV**") Thou hast done violence to my eyes, ungodly Death,
> That I saw die my own beloved child!
> ("**V**")... breathed upon by the infectious breath
> Of pitiless Death, she fell dead at our feet. O evil Persephone,
> How could you make so many tears in vain to flow?
> ("**VI**") Suddenly pitiless Death frightened thee,
> My charming, precious chatterbox.

The effect of this motif of pitiless Death is strengthened by recurrent imagery in which Ursula is metaphorically presented as an unripe fruit shaken by death ("**IV**"), a young olive shoot cut from the parent root by a careless gardener (the entire "**Lament V**"), as an ear of corn which falls before the harvest ("**XII**"). The contrast between the charming child and implacable death finds expression also in the image of Ursula as a tiny nightingale birdlet destroyed by a pitiless serpent ("**I**") or as a little nightingale whose song is suddenly stilled through fear of Death ("**VI**").

c) *desolate parent or parents*:

This motif appears first in the dedication, whence it is carried over to the first lament. Here the poet calls upon Heraclitus and Simonides to bring their laments and tears to help him mourn his daughter. Henceforth the motif is not as extended as in the first lament:

> ("**II**")... she left them [her parents] in grievous affliction.
> ("**III**") How greatly grieved I am today...
> ("**IV**")... at her death I could never be more mournful,
> More sad, nor more troubled than I now am.
> ("**VI**") But the mother, hearing the parting so mournful,
> Must have had a good heart to have lived through such grief.
> ("**VII**") *The entire lament is connected with this motif, as it describes the feelings of the parents who intended to give their daughter a wedding dress and dowry but had rather to give her a shroud and a lump of clay as a pillow.*
> ("**XII**") No father loved his daughter more than I,
> None more than I has mourned.
> ("**XV**") *This lament is devoted primarily to the fate of Niobe, which the poet sees as paralleling his own.*

The motif of the desolate parents is closely tied to the theme of the impossibility of consolation. The poet touches upon this theme in the third lament: "But thou, my child, shalt ne'er return to me, nor e'er assuage my grief!" and again in "**Lament VIII**": "From every corner sadness seizes one, and in vain the heart seeks consolation."

d) *destroyed hopes*:

In the dedication it is indicated that Ursula had shown great promise "of all maidenly virtues and attributes...." Her death has spelled the destruction of the hopes her parents had in her and in their own future happiness through her. This motif is continually strengthened in the poems that follow:

> ("**I**")... help me mourn my charming child,

From whom ungodly death has parted me
And of a sudden deprived me of all my consolation.
("II") My delightful little songstress! My Slavic Sappho!
Who was to inherit not only my earthly portion
But also my lute.
Already thou hadst shown such promise . . .
("XII") And along with you I bury also hope . . .
("XIII") Thou hadst kindled great hopes in my heart,
Then of a sudden didst thou abandon gloomy me
And take with thee all consolation.

As the poet's grief undergoes transformation from its original mute state into an intellectual formulation, ideas inspired by his affliction continually recur and serve as themes for his discourse and speculation. Among these, the theme of the vanity of man's acts and his intellectual pretensions is foremost. In the first lament we read: "'It is vain to weep,' you friends perchance do say. What then, by the living God, is not vain on earth? All is vain! We grope for what is soft but everywhere are pinched! The life of man is naught but vanity." The second lament repeats this gloomy, grief-inspired theme: "The vanity of it. Whatever fate pursues one, it causes either our gloom or gladness." This theme receives its most forceful statement in the eleventh lament, which is devoted entirely to a declaration of the vanity of virtue, wisdom, and piety as a protection against the slings of fate. Again in the sixteenth lament this theme receives further development: the poet shows that Stoic wisdom is a pretense, for it does not protect when misfortune strikes. "O deluded people, O insane pride! How easy it is to display one's wisdom when life is according to our desires and our heads are still whole."

This theme serves a two-fold purpose. It reflects one aspect of the mental condition of the person stricken by grief, indicating the despair that seizes him when his only armaments are philosophical sophistries; further, it prepares the way for the introduction of that new element which will bring relief to the poet: confidence in the wisdom of God. Misfortune has revealed the vanity and bankruptcy of all human wisdom. Man's only recourse is to accept his fate as the will of God and trust that God knows best. And, as we know, after Kochanowski declares this resignation and trust he is permitted a glimpse of Ursula, brought to him from paradise by his mother.

The intensity of the emotion of grief is largely dependent on the value the sufferer places upon the lost object, and Kochanowski was aware of this. Thus, no small part of his cycle is devoted to an exposition of the virtues and charms of Ursula. Significantly, the virtues which the author ascribes to his daughter are quite different in a qualitative sense from those Kochanowski enumerates in his other laments connected with the passing of important figures from Polish social or political life. They are more personal and, if you will, more daring, for Ursula's charming babble and childish antics are put on a level with the achievements of men of state. But it is just this personal element which makes the cycle so poignant, and the reader—at least the modern one—is far more deeply touched by the father's enthusiasm for the childish innocence of his daughter than by his "official" adulation of the civic or social accomplishments of celebrated personages.

The degree of the parents' grief is further revealed by the method of contrast: juxtaposed to the images of Ursula's death ("Laments I, IV, V, and VII") her burial ("Laments VII and XIII"), the gloom pervaded house and the deso-

late parents are the glimpses of the idyllic life at Czarne Lasy when Ursula was alive. The scenes of that happy and tranquil existence become part of the emotional bridge between the reader and the poet. We begin to appreciate what this life must have been, we sense its fulness and charm, and we do so not because the poet insists upon these qualities but because an image of this life has been created which speaks for itself. Then the reader is made to suffer vicariously at the child's death-bed, he must stand beside the parents at the grave. with increasing clarity the shock of the bereavement which has destroyed the idyl is rendered evident, and the intensity of the father's grief is more meaningfully conveyed.

The spontaneous quality and emotional power of the *Laments* have led many commentators to term it an improvisation. Perhaps it was. But this should not be interpreted to mean that the work lacks organization or disciplined execution. A poet of Kochanowski's talents might well have improvised this cycle avoiding the pitfalls of formlessness and disorder. In any case, it is evident that the emotional effect of the work has been achieved by a subtle application of devices governed by the author's intellectual formulations for the expression of his grief.

The literature of the world presents many examples of demonstrated grief which have the power to "infect" the reader, to stimulate a sympathetic emotional response. But rarely does one encounter such a precise expression of grief as in the *Laments*, such a clear representation of its variations in quality and intensity. Through the agency of his art, Kochanowski has rendered a subjective experience in an objective form: emotion has achieved definition. (pp. 38-45)

John Mersereau, Jr., "Jan Kochanowski's 'Laments': A Definition of the Emotion of Grief," in Studies in Russian and Polish Literature: In Honor of Wactaw Lednicki, *edited by Zbigniew Folejewski and others, Mouton & Co., 1962, pp. 37-45.*

RAY J. PARROTT, JR. (essay date 1969)

[*Parrott is an American essayist, translator, and academic. In the following excerpt, he examines the mythological and classical allusions in Kochanowski's portrayal of his daughter in* Laments.]

[Kochanowski] wrote many fluent Latin lyrics during his early period. But it is his later, Polish verse which has secured his prominence as the creator of Polish poetry as an art. His major achievements are the short classical tragedy, *The Dismissal of the Grecian Envoys*, his *Songs, Epigrams,* paraphrase of David's *Psalms*, [*Psalterz Dawidow*], and the *Laments* on the death of his little daughter Ursula. As yet, very little scholarship in Engligh has been devoted to Kochanowski.

[It] is my intention to focus on those mythological allusions, and those classical allusions, which have an immediate, symbolic function in the *Laments* per se.

Specifically, I would like to examine the function of these allusions as they bear on thematic development, the depiction of the deceased child, Ursula, and Kochanowski's expression of grief in the *Laments*.

It might be well to pause first, though, and pose the question of what these mythological and classical allusions "meant" to the late sixteenth century Polish reader. Or, phrased somewhat differently, what general assumptions prompted Kochanowski to employ a wide array of these allusions in his *Laments*. (p. 4)

Two central motives must have lain behind Kochanowski's conception of the cycle of *Laments*. (It goes without saying that they are not a spontaneous outpouring of grief.) He obviously wanted to dramatize the personal experience of grief over the death of his child Ursula. Beyond this he had a didactic intent implicit in the structural organization of the cycle: he sought to illustrate that ultimate consolation lay only within a Christian reponse, i.e. faith—as opposed to a rational response—to the child's premature death. In a concluding act of faith he would trust to God's wisdom rather than human ratiocination.

However, it is apparent that no reader could respond in kind to Kochanowski's grief, at least not through the *Laments'* denotative impact. Yet it is the poet's precise intent to evoke not merely a sympathetic response, but a similar response—to actualize his grief upon the reader. To realize this sense of grief as fully as possible, Kochanowski must appeal to some commonly shared experience. He must seek some frame of reference through which the reader can "perceive" the poet's experience, and respond in kind. Thus it is that Kochanowski turned to mythological and classical allusions among other poetic devices. In a very real sense he resurrects another commonly shared "reality" in realizing his emotions upon the reader. These allusions could be expected to evoke a specific response in the sensitive reader; they would grant that larger frame of reference through which he could empathize with the poet's grief, the poet's conceptual depiction of Ursula, and the thematic implications of the *Laments* as a whole.

In a cycle of poems running to some 586 lines, scarcely two dozen obvious mythological and classical allusions certainly do not tell the entire story. Even including the attested textual correspondences previously mentioned—correspondences which themselves certainly grant a larger frame of reference to the *Laments*—the sum of all classical allusion remains slight in the context of the entire cycle. Nevertheless, their accumulative effect is singularly appreciable. Clearly, Kochanowski was aware of their capacity to arouse a specific, appropriate response in the reader within a given frame of reference. They do not intrude in the cycle; rather they complement the variety of poetic devices which the poet employed to achieve his thematic intent and a lyricism of grief.

In his article "Jan Kochanowski's *Laments:* A Definition of the Emotion of Grief", John Mersereau, Jr. [see excerpt dated 1962] has shown how the poet "exteriorizes" his expression of grief in the cycle through a variety of poetic devices. It is my aim to illustrate how Kochanowski employed a variety of mythological and classical allusions to achieve not only a portion of this expression of grief, but also in part to actualize Ursula's "portrait" and the thematic structure of the *Laments*. Naturally some symbolic overlapping is occasioned by most of the allusions. Such instances will be considered to have a primary and secondary significance and will be treated mainly on the former level of meaning.

The Latin epigraph to the *Laments,*

> Tales sunt hominum mentes, quali pater ipse Juppiter auctiferas lustravit lumine terras. (For the mind in men upon earth goes according to the fortunes the Father of Gods and Men, day by day, bestows upon them.)

occasions the first mythological allusion in the cycle. It derives from the *Odyssey* and has a dual significance. It relates directly to the poet as the first point of reference to be considered in this study, and expresses the theme of the transitory quality of human fortune. This is apparent in that, in Homer, the epigraph is preceded by the passage:

> Of all creatures that breathe and walk on the earth there is nothing more helpless than a man is, of all that the earth fosters; for he thinks that he will never suffer misfortune in future days, while the gods grant him courage, and his knees have spring in them. But when the blessed gods bring sad days upon him, against his will he must suffer it with enduring spirit.

The premature death of Ursula had caught Kochanowski unawares. The "blessed gods" seemingly had favored him with an idyllic life at his estate Czarnolas and Ursula had provided much of the charm in her parents' life. Thinking that "he will never suffer misfortune in future days," the poet was plunged into an abyss of despair by the child's sudden death, bearing this sorrow "with enduring spirit." Throughout the succeeding sixteen laments Kochanowski seeks an answer from the gods, as it were, as to why this unexpected fate has befallen him.

Thus the allusion to Jupiter, the father of the gods and men, and in turn to Homer's *Odyssey,* immediately evokes a larger context; a context, moreover, essential to the intensification of the poet's image of grief and the larger thematic pattern of the conflict between a rational, pagan Wisdom and the Christian faith which ultimately grants the poet consolation. (I will return to this theme subsequently, particularly as it bears on the passage just cited. But first, I would like to carry the implications of the mythological allusions bearing on the poet a bit further.)

The opening lines of the first "**Lament**" mark the first instance of a classical allusion which carries an obvious, symbolic overtone.... In summoning Heraclitus and Simonides to grieve with him, Kochanowski implicitly compares himself to them and emphasizes the depths of his sorrow by invoking two names synonymous with grief in the classical tradition.... In doing this Kochanowski not only adds a dimension to his grief by calling up an illustration more vivid and striking than his own pen could furnish, but the evocation serves to reiterate the thematic kernel of the epigraph. Thus Kochanowski has "set the stage" against which the remaining laments in the cycle must be viewed. By alluding to the classical tradition he implicitly raises his own cycle of *Laments* to the level of this tradition. This, in turn, unquestionably gives them greater force, lending them an evocative power beyond the immediate presentation.

In the fourth "**Lament**" Kochanowski again compares his grief to perhaps *the* classical symbol of grief, Niobe. Niobe arrogantly had boasted of her superior procreative powers to those of Leto, the mother of Apollo and Diana. Having seven sons and seven daughters, Niobe felt herself powerful enough to defy the gods and called upon the people of Thebes to worship her instead of the less fertile Leto. But, as Edith Hamilton points out in her *Mythology,* "Insolent words uttered in the arrogant consciousness of power were always heard in heaven and always punished." To punish Niobe for the affront to their mother, Apollo and Diana killed all her children. Watching her children die, Niobe herself turned into stone from grief. Then she was borne by the wind to Mount Sypilus, destined to eternally shed tears of grief. The passage explicitly equates Kochanowski's grief with that of Niobe's:

> A przynamniej tymczasem mogłem był odprawić
> Wiek swój i Persefonie ostatniej się stawić,
> Nie uczuwszy na sercu tak wielkiej żałości,
> Której równia nie widzę w tej tu śmiertelności.
> Nie dziwuję Niobie, że na martwe ciała
> Swoich namilszych dziatek patrząc skamieniała.

> (And at least in the meantime I might have left this life And presented myself to the last of the goddesses, Persephone, Not having felt such great sorrow in my heart To which I see nothing to campare it with in this world. I do not wonder that Niobe turned to stone While looking at the dead bodies of her dearest children.)

Niobe has a recurrent symbolic function in the *Laments:* she serves both to point up the depths of Kochanowski's despair at the loss of his child, and, secondarily, she reiterates the omnipresent theme of Death. Interestingly enough, Kochanowski extends the comparison between himself and Niobe to their respective children. In the fifteenth "**Lament**" he likens the death of Niobe's children to flowers falling before a keen sickle:

> Takie więc kwiaty leżą kosą podsieczone.

> (Thus like flowers lying severed by a scythe.)

And in the fifth "**Lament**" Kochanowski had likened Ursula to a young olive shoot cut off by a weeding gardner:

> Jako oliwka mała ... ostre ciernie lub rodne pokrzywy
> Uprzątając sadownik podciął ukwapliwy.

> (As if a little olive shoot ... cut by a zealous gardener clearing out sharp thorns or fertile nettle-weeds ...)

Later in the fifteenth "**Lament**" Kochanowski again evokes the symbol of Niobe in her stony grief as a parallel to his own. He fears that he, too, might turn to stone unless his sorrow is calmed.... The theme of death, of course, again is secondarily reinforced.

A further classical allusion which symbolizes perhaps Kochanowski's deepest despair in the cycle, is the reference to Brutus in the first line of the eleventh "**Lament**." The poet, together with Brutus, momentarily doubts the merit of even virtue in life.... Professor Noyes cites in the notes to his *Poems by Jan Kochanowski* that the poet errs in attributing these remarks to Brutus. The poet's faulty memory aside, what is important is the unquestionably premeditated use of a classical allusion to echo the poet's thoughts on a personal level. This serves both to intensify the reader's image of Kochanowski's mental state, and to heighten the reader's emotional response by equating the poet's thoughts with so foremost a classical figure as Marcus Junius Brutus. On a second level of meaning it implicitly attacks Cicero's stoic philosophy in the *Tusculan Disputations.* That is, Kochanowski is beginning to reject Cicero's view that "the soul is immortal and that virtue, rising superior to pain and grief, is in itself sufficient

to ensure Man's happiness." Virtue is nonsense; his grief has not abated!

The final mythological allusion which directly relates to the image of the poet is that of Orpheus in the fourteenth "**Lament**".... The implication is obvious: Kochanowski ponders whether he, too, might pursue and retrieve his daughter Ursula as Orpheus had sought his wife Eurydice centuries earlier.... Thus, through the use of mythological and classical allusions, Kochanowski has succeeded in identifying his mental anguish with a series of classical figures who experienced similar grief. This poetic association, again, reinforces his own image of grief to an empathic degree for the reader. The reader "perceives" and can empathize with the poet's emotion of grief through the common medium of the mythological or classical allusion. Heraclitus, Simonides, Niobe, and Orpheus: these names evoke a specific response in the sensitive reader acquainted with the rich classical and mythological traditions, and serve to realize Kochanowski's grief upon the reader through a transferral of associations.

The thematic implications touched upon in the foregoing will be examined subsequently. Prior to this, though, I would like to suggest certain associations arising out of the juxtaposition of mythological and classical allusions with the child Ursula.

Jerzy Pietrkiewicz's article "The Mediaeval Dream-Formula in Kochanowski's *Treny*" [see excerpt dated 1952-53] illustrates, beginning with the *Laments'* dedication, how the reader is led to expect "an uncommon elegiac cycle about an uncommon child." The very existence of the *Laments* suggests the exceptional abilities and promise of the child Ursula.

An important means of emphasizing Ursula's talent—latent and realized—is the use of some strikingly appropriate mythological and classical allusions. Those allusions create only a part of the child's "portrait;" on the other hand they are a significant ingredient in the total image produced. They lend credence to Kochanowski's idealized portrait by relating the child to a revered classical tradition; the child's stature is elevated by equating her abilities with those of the gods, etc.

The first classical allusion directly related to Ursula is that of the nightingales in the first "**Lament**." The serpent of Death, attracted to the birds' nest by their singing, attacks and devours all the little songsters.... According to Professor Noyes, the snake symbol is adapted from the *Iliad,* and Kochanowski substituted *nightingales* for *sparrows* in the "**Lament**" in obvious allusion to Ursula's gift of song.

The second allusion implicitly related to Ursula has already been mentioned: the comparison of the child to a young olive shoot in the fifth "**Lament**." The image created obviously serves to underscore the child's potential talent, a talent destroyed before it even blossomed. It has been pointed out that the comparison is a frequent classical illustration. What is particularly striking about the comparison, though, is that the olive is not indigenous to Poland. Such a comparison, certain to strike the Polish reader, thereby increases the overall impact of the allusion. The association also implicitly links Ursula with the lands of classical antiquity, further connecting her with the larger frame of meaning afforded by the classical traditions. And, yet again, the theme of Death is reiterated.

In the sixth "**Lament**" Kochanowski likens Ursula to Sappho, the Greek lyric poetess who lived on the island of Lesbos at the turn of the seventh and sixth centuries B.C. Moreover, he again poses the image of the nightingale songstress in further emphasizing the child's lyrical potential. . . . An additional, indirect amplification of Ursula's lyrical gift can be seen in the fifteenth "**Lament**." (XV, 1-6). Kochanowski bids Erato, the muse of love poetry, to quiet his grief. The quality of lyricism usually associated with love poetry and the reference to the lute which Ursula had been destined to play, would seem to represent a reiterative correlation to the child's exceptional lyrical talent. The allusion is not a direct correspondence; the immediate effect, however, seemingly serves to complement those qualities heretofore ascribed to the child.

Every mythological and classical allusion which is associated with the theme of Death obviously, albeit indirectly, refers to the child Ursula. But the effect in such instances does not serve to point up the child's conceptual portrait, rather simply the state of death. Therefore I will treat them subsequently as a means for intensifying theme in the *Laments*.

It goes without saying that Death is one of, if not the primary theme in the *Laments*. (Variations of the theme are, of course, possible. "Man's reaction to Death," "How can Man respond to Death?" or "How can Man endure Death?" could and have been suggested as the main theme in the *Laments*. However, for my purposes such distinctions are immaterial.) Accordingly, nearly three-fourths of the allusions in the cycle directly or indirectly emphasize this theme. The sum of these Death allusions—in fact, the sum of all the mythological and classical allusions—plays an even larger thematic role: that is, the aggregate represents the very matrix of that pagan Wisdom structurally and thematically juxtaposed to Christian faith in the total work. It is true that classical and mythological allusions can be found in the last three *Laments*; indeed classical philosophy is curiously intertwined with Christian philosophy in the arguments for "Christian" consolation in the final "**Lament**". By and large, though, biblical allusions occupy the center of the thematic stage in these final *Laments*. Significantly enough, very few biblical allusions are employed in the first sixteen *Laments*. Thus, in a very real sense the structural division between pagan Wisdom and Christian faith which can be observed in the entire cycle is complemented by classical and biblical allusions respectively. That this was a concious act on the part of the poet seems self-evident.

Proserpine, or Persephone, is the most consistently evoked synonymic symbol of Death. She was the wife of Pluto and they reigned respectively as the king and queen of the realms of the dead. Kochanowski alludes to her in the second, fourth, and fifth *Laments* respectively:

. . . I skarżyć się na srogość ciężkiej Prozerpiny.

(. . . And complain about the severity of grim Proserpine.)

Wiek swój i Persefonie ostatniej się stawić . . .

(My life and presented myself before Persephone, the last of the goddesses.)

. . . O zła Persefono, Mogłażeś tak wielu łzam dać up-

łynąć płono?

(Oh evil Persephone,
How could you will such a flow of tears?)

In setting up a pattern of recurrent allusions to the theme of Death, however, one really should begin with the invocation to Heraclitus and Simonides in the first "**Lament**," Simonides, the poet of lamentations, in particular could be said to establish this pattern of recurrent, symbolic allusions. The allusions to Persephone follow, and reference to Niobe also functions to intensify the theme in the fourth "**Lament**" (iv, 17-18).

Conventional references to the child's death recur in the sixth through ninth *Laments* as Kochanowski relates of her death, burial, the state of desolation she has left behind, and his own state of despair respectively.

In the tenth "**Lament**" Charon, the ferryman who "bore the souls of the deceased over the river of Acheron" in the underworld, is alluded to in reiteration of the theme. . . . (pp. 8-17)

The final mythological allusions to the theme of Death are in the fifteenth "**Lament**." Here Kochanowski bids Phoebus Apollo, the god of archery, prophecy and music, and his sister Diana (Artemis) to slay Niobe (nieszczęsna matko) as well and end her unavailing sorrow. The allusion, of course, calls forth the past references to Niobe and the death of her fourteen children for the reader, thereby raising the Death theme to a final crescendo. . . . (p. 18)

Consistent with Christianity's principle of a Life-affirming death, there are no mythological or classical allusions to death after this fifteenth "*Lament*" Biblical and Christian allusions come to the fore in the seventeenth, eighteenth, and the final "Dream" *Lament*.

The recurrent, symbolic death pattern effected by the foregoing allusions seems self-explanatory and little need be added in explication.

The final, thematic allusion to be treated in this study occurs in the sixteenth "**Lament**." This "**Lament**" marks the real turning-point in Kochanowski's philosophical struggle between pagan Wisdom (Rationality) and Christian Faith. It is the poet's final effort to reconcile his grief through pagan philosophy. Failing in this, Kochanowski turns to Christianity for his ultimate consolation.

The poet polemicizes with Cicero's (Arpinie) Stoic philosophy, especially the latter's notion of bearing all pain and grief "with enduring spirit." The very crux of the polemic, though, lies in the thematic conflict between Christian faith and pagan Rationality. Through the first sixteen *Laments* Kochanowski has sought an answer in pagan philosophy which would calm his despair for the death of Ursula. He sought consolation through Man's faculty for reasoning, and, as we know, found that wisdom typified by the mythological and philosophical allusions of the classical, rational tradition [was] useless. In the face of an overpowering emotion of grief, Man alone is simply unavailing. Faith in God, in the correctness of His judgement, and the secure knowledge that Ursula was happy in the Kingdom of Heaven alone bring Kochanowski to a state of consolation; "to (a) final acceptance of the inevitability of his loss." Thus the *Laments* end on a note of Christian consolation.

Drawing upon classical myths and tradition as an artistic nucleus, Kochanowski was able to intensify not only his own image of grief, but also the idealized portrait of his daughter, and the seminal themes of Death and Christian faith versus pagan Rationality. Unquestionably other symbolic overtones could be dredged up with the aid of the less obvious mythological and classical allusions in the cycle of *Laments*. On the other hand, the foregoing hopefully serves to illustrate Kochanowski's poetic awareness of the classical traditions, and his ability to infuse this material into the *Laments* in a highly meaningful and effective way. (pp. 18-19)

> Ray J. Parrott, Jr., "Mythological Allusions in Kochanowski's 'Laments'," in The Polish Review, Vol. XIV, No. 1, Winter, 1969, pp. 3-19.

DAVID WELSH (essay date 1974)

[*Welsh was an English translator, essayist, and academic. In the following excerpt from his critical study of Kochanowski, he compares the poet's Polish translation of the Psalms of David to the English version of the Psalms by Sir Philip Sidney.*]

Kochanowski spent almost a decade rendering the *Book of Psalms* into Polish. First printed in 1575 or 1578, his psalms [*Psalterz Dawidów* went into numerous editions. Indeed, for over a century, the Psalms remained his best-loved work. Set to music, they continue to be sung in Polish churches, both Catholic and Protestant, to the present day. In quantity, they amount to almost a third of Kochanowski's total output in Polish.

As with most of Kochanowski's poetry, we know little about the circumstances under which he worked on the immense task (one hundred and fifty psalms altogether, divided into five parts)....

The work has been described as his "poetical laboratory," in which he experimented with a great variety of stanza patterns, meters, rhymes, and vocabulary. But what prompted Kochanowski the humanist to choose the Psalms for translation? With their often high-flown songs of praise, thanksgiving, supplication and imprecation, with audacious, sometimes bizarre imagery, echoing with the name of forgotten desert tribes and containing prophecies and visions—the Psalms were poetry of a kind far removed from Renaissance ideals of poetry. (p. 50)

Kochanowski approached his task as a humanist, not as a theologian or composer of a prayer book. As his poetry demonstrates, he was supremely confident of the value of poetry in human life. Medieval scholasticism had no place in his work. His poetry does not concern itself with dogma. God, or the Supreme Being as Kochanowski sometimes calls Him, was not the jealous figure of dread of the Old Testament, but (as witness the **"Song"** already described) a Being whom man venerates and worships. But, like his contemporary Erasmus of Rotterdam, whose writings Kochanowski knew, he was reluctant to investigate the "mysteries of God," such attempts being beyond the competence of man. (p. 51)

[The] most "poetic" English rendering of the Psalms is generally conceded to be that of Sir Philip Sidney, completed after his death by Mary, Countess of Pembroke, his sister. Sidney's versions constituted an entire school of English versification, just as Kochanowski's in Polish. Both writers demonstrated in their respective languages a remarkable ability to integrate meaning with stanza form, and both clearly thought in terms of form rather than content.

Sidney's *Psalms* were not printed until the nineteenth century, but the work was circulated in a large number of manuscript copies—like so much poetry, including some of Kochanowski's—and was well known to John Donne, among others.

Though Kochanowski and Sidney were contemporaries, they obviously did not know each other's work (even though Sidney paid a brief visit to Poland in the 1570's). Yet, in addition to the general similarities noted above, both versions share certain stylistic traits. Both poets knew that the Psalms had originally been composed in "measured verse," which justified poetic renderings, as distinct from the prose of the other books of the Old Testament. Indeed, this fact was a prime difficulty when poets set about versifying the Psalms. As they were intended for chanting, or singing, a particularly rich, even orotund effect was required, marked by strength, fullness, and richness. Kochanowski achieved this style in several ways—through epithets of various kinds in particular. The metrical patterns were also carefully chosen; in the "historical narrative" Psalms, such as no. 78, giving an account of the Exodus and crossing of the Red Sea, Kochanowski used thirteen-syllabic lines—a meter that became traditional in Polish poetry when an elevated or epic style was called for. Sidney also chose his meters carefully.... (pp. 52-3)

A feature of the style of the Old Testament as a whole is the frequent use of emphatic negatives, in sharp contrast to the teachings of Christ which are expressed as positives. Kochanowski's Psalms also abound in negatives, usually epithets describing God, who is said to be "immeasurable" (*niezmierzony*) in Psalms 13, 54, 60, 71, 90, 97, and 130; elsewhere He is "infinite" (*nieprzeżyty*), "unconquered" (*niezwalczony*), "immortal" (*nieśmiertelny*), "unalterable" (*nieodmieniony*), "incomprehensible" (*niepojęty*), and so forth. Professor Julian Krzyżanowski lists over sixty negative epithets used by Kochanowski, most now obsolete (not all are from the Psalms, however). The effect of such epithets used frequently is to stress the remoteness of the Old Testament God.

But negative epithets are not used exclusively in describing God: we find other examples, such as "inexpressible mercy" (*niewyslowione milosierdzie*), "irreproachable judge" (*sędzia nienagoniony*), "inescapable bow" (*łuk nieuchroniony*), and others. Sidney shared this predilection with Kochanowski, writing "undefiled hartes," "undying rhymes," "unworn wheels," "unstedfast change," "unthralled," and the like. Both poets knew that Aristotle had recommended elevating a description in epic poetry by listing attributes the person or thing described did *not* possess.

Another kind of epithet, also deriving from classical epic poetry, was the compound, much favored by poets of the Renaissance. Ronsard, for instance, believed the duty of patriotic French poets was to "manufacture new words on the pattern of Greek and Latin originals ... thereby making their own language the equal of foreign tongues." English poets imitated the fashion; Spenser writes "sea-shouldering whales," Sidney used "scorne-gold hair" and "life-giving lights." Kochanowski likewise coins "swift-feathered bird" (ptak prędkopióry), "sea-flying vessels" (okręty morzolotne), "Thou the many-powerful" (Ty wielowładny), "all-fertile year" (rok wszytkorodny), and "high-flying sun" (słońce gorolotne). Such inventions were a novelty in Polish poetry of the sixteenth century, but were soon adopted by other writers (as were other of Kochanowski's innovations in prosody and vocabulary). The compound epithet remains a feature of Polish poetry until the end of the Age of Enlightenment (1796).

A third sort of epithet characteristic of Kochanowski's Psalms and indeed much of his poetry as a whole is best described as "neutral," not drawing attention to itself. The sky is "lofty" (wysoki), slavery "heavy" (ciężka), weeping "inconsolable" (nieutulony), tyrants "cruel" (okrutni), a harp "gilded" (złocona), and gifts "generous" (szczodre). As with the compound epithets, the neutral epithets, too, were used frequently in eighteenth-century Polish poetry (as they were by English contemporaries, including Alexander Pope). The effect was always to neutralize or "dampen" too ebullient lines. As with other stylistic devices, the eighteenth-century usage was yet another way of reacting against the stylistic excesses of the Baroque.

Kochanowski uses nearly five hundred epithets of various kinds in his Psalms, of which one hundred and thirty do not occur elsewhere in his other poetry. This suggests he was using them for special effects of grandeur, cultivating archaisms for the purpose, and using elevated turns of speech, without the colloquialisms so frequent in the Polish epigrams.

Yet another characteristic feature of Kochanowski's style in the Psalms (shared by Sidney) was the copious use of synonyms, or near synonyms, usually in groups of three. A few examples out of many must suffice: "the complaints of wretched people / And inconsolable weeping, and heavy sighing" (ludzi nędznych narzekanie / I płacz nieutulony, i ciężkie wzdychanie), "the sentences of the Lord are all rightful, /All eternal / all just" (Wyroki Pańskie wszytki są prawdziwe, / Wszytki stateczne, wszyvki sprawiedliwe).... To be sure, both Kochanowski and Sidney may have introduced such tricolons (groups of three words or phrases) for metrical purposes or for rhyme; even so, they also indicate a new feeling for the wealth of their own vernaculars.

As might be expected, Kochanowski occasionally saw fit in his version of the Psalms to make a few small alterations, to make the texts sound somewhat less strange to his Polish readers by introducing purely Polish elements. He did not go as far as Górnicki had done a few years earlier in his *Polish Courtier*, but his restraint was due to the fact that the Psalms were, after all, Holy Writ, and therefore unusual closeness to the original was essential. *The Courtier* was a secular book, and the text could be altered, especially to make it more accessible to what Górnicki called "the domestic Pole" (Polak domowy).

So Kochanowski makes only a few minor changes; the Biblical "bulls of Bashan" become wolves, the "cedars of Lebanon" appear as oak trees, and the birds of the Psalmist are defined as "sparrows." Similarly, wild goats become the more familiar roe deer, though Kochanowski retains camels, and saw no need to alter the phrase "as for the stork, the fir trees are her dwelling-place," since both bird and tree were familiar. (pp. 53-5)

Kochanowski's *Psalms* demonstrated that a vernacular language was a suitable medium for the most elevated poetry. In this way, Kochanowski's work contributed to the upsurge of national awareness which appeared all over Europe in the sixteenth century. (p. 56)

David Welsh, in his Jan Kochanowski, *Twayne Publishers, Inc., 1974, 160 p.*

HENRIK BIRNBAUM (essay date 1975)

[*Birnbaum is a German essayist, editor, and academic. In the following excerpt, he compares Kochanowski's poetic expression of grief in* Laments *with that of the Old Icelandic poet Egil Skallagrimsson in his tenth-century work,* Sonatorrek.]

Much has been written about Jan Kochanowski, the first great master of verbal art in Polish, and his most personal and lyrical work, *Treny*, a cycle of poems occasioned by the death of his infant daughter Orszula. In the view of most connoisseurs the *Laments* represent the highest achievement of the Czarnolas poet, nearing fifty when struck by fate and consequently writing his sequence of dirges. (p. 85)

While the formal perfection of the Polish Renaissance poet's *Laments* has been widely acknowledged, the question of whether or to what degree these elegiac poems express genuinely spontaneous feelings continues to be a matter of controversy also among the unqualified admirers of Kochanowski's artistic accomplishment. Thus, his *Treny*, abounding in literary echoes and allusions, has frequently been characterized as an instance of obligatory poetic hyperbolism (especially in view of the tender age of merely two and a half of the beloved deceased, the aging poet's first-born or possibly second child), as a—to be sure, supremely performed—exercise in an established and much emulated literary genre, or even as little more than a "literary convention". On the other hand, Kochanowski's highly lyrical poems have also been referred to as an "elementary outburst of grief". Perhaps Julian Krzyżanowski has come closest to a fair judgment when he pointed out (in his *Treny Jana Kochanowskiego*, 1967) that it is precisely the unique ability of combining these two facets—personal, deeply experienced sorrow and its appropriate poetic expression, conforming with the conventions of the prevailing (or, to be exact, revived) literary style of the period—that have made this cycle of *Laments* the unequaled (while soon and often imitated) masterpiece of its kind, as alive today as when it was written nearly four centuries ago. Yet there can be little doubt that it is in particular the genuine, heartfelt grief and emotion of merciless bereavement, defeating and breaking through, as it were, all attempts at conventional philosophizing and rationalization on the part of the poet-father, that have contributed the most to making Kochanowski's *Treny* a piece of poetry of timeless, universal appeal, speaking directly also to the modern reader.

The literary sources and archetypes for the *Laments* have been thoroughly searched and researched and today, as in earlier years, only the proper assessment of the Czarnolas poet's degree of originality (or lack thereof) as compared to his models remains at issue. Thus, as was pointed out by G. R. Noyes in the Introduction to his 1928 English edition of Kochanowski's poetry (translated by him in collaboration with others), [see excerpt dated 1928] the Polish poet in his *Treny* "follows the precepts of Scaliger, who tells us (*Poetics* iii. 121) that a dirge should consist of certain definite parts: praises of the deceased, proof of the loss sustained, grief, consolation, exhortations. . . . In offering consolation (*Poetics* iii. 122) the precepts of the philosophers should be used, but they should be varied and expressed in figurative language, that they may not appear commonplace. Examples are of more avail than arguments." As further suggested by Noyes, "Kochanowski may have been guided solely by ancient examples", of which there were indeed plenty, ranging from Simonides in the 6th century B.C. to Ausonius in the 4th century A.D., "rather than by Scaliger's formal rules". In addition, Kochanowski may also have been influenced by earlier neo-Latin poets, in particular Janus Pannonius (1434-1472) who had written a sequence of elegies lamenting the death of his mother Barbara. It has been established that Kochanowski was acquainted with Pannonius' poetry, some of which he even paraphrased. Further, granted that Kochanowski may have been influenced by the example of Petrarch in dividing his elegy into a sequence of poems (cf. the long series of sonnets and *canzoni* bemoaning the death of Laura), the structured account of the development of his feelings, brought about by the passing of his beloved child, must be considered entirely Kochanowski's own. Once the attempts to reconstruct a different original order of the individual *Laments* (contemplated by Hartleb for example) proved futile, it may be said that in the form and composition of his *Treny* the Polish Renaissance poet has shown considerable originality.

It has been pointed out on more than one occasion that for many of the philosophic ideas of the *Laments* Kochanowski was indebted to Cicero more than to any other author of classical antiquity. Cicero also had lost a much-loved daughter, Tullia, and it was to ease his grief and find consolation in spiritual matters that the Roman thinker and politician had withdrawn to work intensely on his philosophic writings of which, in particular, the *Tusculanae Disputationes* is telling evidence. It is only natural, therefore, that explicit references to Cicero and his work found their way into Kochanowski's poems of mourning. . . . But just as all philosophical arguments had not been sufficient to lend strength and comfort to Cicero, so Jan of Czarnolas in the last three *Laments* turns to religion, to his Christian faith, for consolation. Controversial, to some extent, is the impact of the Bible, especially the Book of Psalms (whose translation, or rather Polish adaptation, titled **Psałterz Dawidów**, had been completed by Kochanowski only shortly before he undertook to write his *Treny*) and the New Testament, as it becomes apparent toward the end of his cycle of elegiac poems. In "**Tren XVII**" and "**XVIII**", the poet humbles himself before the Lord, imploring Him to grant him mercy and help, and in the concluding, longest, and perhaps most enigmatic "**Tren XIX**" (subtitled *albo Sen*), the poet's deceased mother appears to him with his lamented daughter in her arms paraphrasing the words of the Gospel. . . . Yet, as Czesław Miłosz has keenly observed, "paradoxically, his mother restores, to a certain extent, the validity of Stoic reasoning . .

. Since he knew how to bring solace to other people in similar misfortunes, she advises him now: 'Master, cure yourself.' From the consolation we may infer that a certain precarious balance between Christian faith and antique philosophy has been regained by the author, who thereby remains true to his Renaissance ideals." Finally, also the question of whether his brand of Christianity, at this stage in his life, was in conformity with the official dogmas of the Roman Catholic Church has been a matter of much debate.

While truly the chef d'oeuvre of the leading poet of Slavic Renaissance literature, Kochanowski's *Treny* is, as was indicated, firmly embedded in a long and rich tradition, allowing for many meaningful comparisons of this cycle of elegiac poems both with its formal and thematic predecessors in world literature (in addition to juxtaposing the Orszula poems with Kochanowski's own earlier exercises in epicedial poetry, e.g. his elegy "**O śmierci Jana Tarnowskiego**" of 1561) and its specifically Polish imitations and literary echoes.

However, being itself a high-quality piece of world literature by dint of its formal perfection, its philosophic-religious ideas, and its emotional depth, Kochanowski's elegiac sequence can be meaningfully compared not only with its ascertainable genetic models and archetypes but also with literary works for which the *Laments* themselves served as an example and source of inspiration. The comparison may well be extended beyond the narrower scope just referred to, to include other masterpieces of world poetry for which, while displaying a thematic affinity with Kochanowski's poems, no genetic relationship in terms of any direct literary influence can be proven or, in some instances, even conceived. A fine example of the methodological yield of such a typological (rather than genealogical) juxtaposition of Kochanowski's *Treny* with a historically unrelated piece of literature can be found in J. Pietrkiewicz's article on the medieval dream-formula in the Polish poet's elegiac cycle [see excerpt dated 1952-53]. Thus, while at least theoretically there could indeed have existed a relationship of direct influence between Kochanowski's dirges and Boccaccio's eclogue "Olympia", written ca. 1361 on the occasion of the death of the Italian poet's young daughter, even though it seems that the kinship between these two poetic works is perhaps rather limited to some particular *loci communes* suggesting common (viz., classic) sources of literary borrowing, it seems, on the other hand, entirely inconceivable to assume a genetic connection between Kochanowski's *Laments* and the exquisite Middle English poem "The Pearl" by an anonymous writer of the 14th century. Yet *Treny* undeniably bears some resemblance to "The Pearl", as aptly shown by Pietrkiewicz with regard to a few striking analogies as well as some less obvious but therefore no less typical points of coincidence, granted also substantial differences and disagreements obtaining between the Middle English and Polish poems.

A further such typological parallel of thematic and genre-conditioned resemblance could be drawn between Kochanowski's *Treny* and another historically altogether unrelated threnody, likewise undoubtedly belonging to the treasure of world literature—Egil Skallagrímsson's major Old Icelandic poem *Sonatorrek* (meaning approximately 'Irreparable Loss of Sons'). To my knowledge no such comparison has ever been made (at least in print) despite the fact that, granted certain obvious and fundamental differences and incomparabilities, a collation of these poems, too, could yield some interesting and revealing observations bearing on the function of poetry per se and on some invariable universals underlying literary typology. (pp. 85-91)

Superficially the resemblance between *Treny* and *Sonatorrek* is obvious. Both are poems by mourning fathers, written on the occasion of the death of their respective favorite children, the infant Orszula in the case of Kochanowski, Bödvar, drowned in the prime of his life, in the case of Egil. Both poets were themselves no longer young men when struck by the ordeal, Kochanowski close to fifty, Egil about or just past that age.... Yet the apparent differences between the two poets and their particular walks of life are, of course, also significant: first of all, Egil was mourning the death of an eighteen-year-old son while Jan of Czarnolas bemoaned the loss of a thirty-month-old baby girl. Moreover, Egil, a figure of the Norse Early Middle Ages, was deeply rooted in paganism and his gods were the deities of the Old Germanic pantheon, Odin foremost among them. [There] is no reason whatsoever to think that Egil had any knowledge of classical antiquity and its culture. By contrast, Kochanowski, the overshadowing figure of Polish Renaissance literature, had studied in Kraków, Königsberg, and Padua and was widely traveled, having extended his journeys not only to Germany and Italy but also to France. No doubt he was one of the best read men of his time in Poland, himself writing refined Polish and at the same time cultivating an elegant style in his Latin poetry. It is a matter of record that Kochanowski was thoroughly conversant with classic, especially Roman, authors and poets, Cicero and Horace being his favorites. Intimately familiar with, and deeply influenced by, the vitality and ideology of pagan classical antiquity, especially as distilled in its Stoic brand, Kochanowski was nonetheless an ardent believer in Christianity (his more than formal attachment to official Catholicism remaining, to be sure, an issue of some controversy), and in no other of his writings has the clash between his enlightened Stoic philosophy and his transrational Christian faith, but also the eventual reconciliation of the two, found such powerful expression as in the sequence of poems written on the occasion of the death of his daughter.

On the formal side, there are, naturally, points of divergence but also of agreement in the poems of the two mourning fathers. *Sonatorrek*, like the other remarkable longer poem, *Arinbjarnarkvila*, composed by Egil shortly afterwards, is written in the *kviluháttr* meter, a sort of regulated Eddic *fornyrlislag*, consisting of eight-line stanzas of alternating three- and four-syllable unrhymed verse. This was a formally much less demanding verse form than *dróttkvætt*, the preferred meter of Skaldic poetry. In other words, when turning to personal themes filled with subjective emotionalism (and, incidentally, testifying at the same time to Egil's monumental egocentricity), the Icelandic *skald* chose a relatively unsophisticated poetic form, sharply contrasting with the traditional, rigorously patterned forms of Baroque-like Skaldic verse. (pp. 91-3)

If, on the whole, the poetic form of the Old Icelandic *skald*'s most lyrical and revealing poem, conveying its universal human message also to the modern reader of a thousand years later, is relatively simple (though, using a largely veiled language, hardly straightforward or easily in-

terpreted in every detail), at least by comparison to other specimens of highly mannered Skaldic poetry, the same is not true of Kochanowski's poetic reckoning with, and ultimate submission to, his God where the discipline and dignity of the model Renaissance man occasionally seems threatened with being overpowered by his feelings of bereavement and despair. Yet it may be a matter of literary interpretation whether the no doubt particularly exquisite and sophisticated form of *Treny* is to be thought of as purely a reflection of the Polish poet's need to match the strength of his emotions by an adequate linguistic expression or whether, on the contrary, the very ability of elaborating a highly elegant and perfect poetic form, so masterfully demonstrated, does not suggest a certain emotional distance, if not detachment, from the immediate subject matter at hand. Perhaps here, again, a correct interpretation ought not to be sought in a clear-cut either/or answer but can rather be found in the direction of a both/and solution. Most probably, Kochanowski, while deeply shaken by the loss of his beloved Orszula, had regained sufficient spiritual balance—the virtue par excellence of the Stoics—to work, and work intensely, on the formal perfection of the dirges lamenting her death. No one can deny, however, that traces of the poet's being on the verge of losing that balance are to be found in the *Laments* themselves.

Among the formal devices used by Kochanowski to enliven and lend some inner, syntactic-metric tension to the regular, often isosyllabic verse patterns by which the Renaissance poets expressed their yearning for esthetic harmony, equilibrium, and clarity (Kochanowski himself being the foremost exponent of isosyllabism in the history of Polish versification), *enjambement* and irregular (mobile) *caesura* accentuate the interplay between narrative-reflective and lyrical passages and function to mark emotional shock.... "**Tren XVII**" echoes the pious, though pained submissiveness of the somewhat monotonous and uncomplicated psalmodic language of the Bible (so familiar to Kochanowski from his work on *Psalterz Dawidów*) and perhaps also that of medieval hymnody.... The poetic syntax of Kochanowski's *Treny* is by and large more simple, with a preference for paratactic constructions, compared to the heavy architectonics of his earlier court poetry. Occasionally an element echoing the lyrics of folk songs can be perceived, as is also the case with some other of his poetry, notably the "Pieśń świętojańska o Sobótce", written during that last period of creativity symbolized by the linden tree of Czarnolas.... The high artistic quality in *Treny* is achieved throughout by the poet's extraordinary ability to bring the linguistic form of each *Lament* closely in tune with its particular content. Thus, only where Stoic philosophy (*Mądrość*) or Cicero himself are invoked and reminiscences of classic antiquity otherwise alluded to (as in "**Tren IX**" and "**XVI**") does the syntactic structure become accordingly more complex, hypotactic, with multiple clause embedding.

The thematic resemblance and the external circumstances under which *Sonatorrek* and *Treny* were composed as well as, *mutatis mutandis*, some of the formal devices used (or, for that matter, refrained from) by the two poets in writing their most personal, lyrical poems may suffice to suggest some comparative comments, in particular as it is precisely these very masterpieces that have secured both the pagan *skald* of the Early Middle Ages and the Stoic-Christian poet of the Renaissance a place in world literature. There are, however, some additional considerations of a more general nature that would seem to warrant a comparison of these elegies—to be sure, in generic and typological rather than in genetic literary terms.... (pp. 94-6)

Even if there is no reason to doubt that the loss of their children was a most shattering experience for the two poet-fathers, the poems in which they expressed their sorrow are not primarily monuments commemorating their deceased progeny but rather testimonies to the psychology of the poets' own coping with their bereavement: *Sonatorrek* and *Treny* may indeed be considered documents of the sublimation of grief through the power of poetry. And, moreover, their elegies were couched in a style and linguistic form masterfully complying with the norms and devices of the prevailing poetic systems of their respective periods and models. (p. 96)

> *Henrik Birnbaum, "The Sublimation of Grief: Poems by Two Mourning Fathers," in* For Wiktor Weintraub: Essays in Polish Literature, Language, and History Presented on the Occasion of His 65th Birthday, *edited by Victor Erlich and others, Mouton, 1975, pp. 85-98.*

CZESŁAW MIŁOSZ (essay date 1983)

[*A celebrated Polish poet, essayist, and novelist, Milosz was awarded the Nobel Prize for literature in 1980. In the following excerpt, he illumines some of Kochanowski's minor poetry, noting the poet's "polonizing" of ancient motifs in* The Dismissal of the Grecian Envoys.]

Until the beginning of the nineteenth century, the most eminent Slavic poet was undoubtedly Jan Kochanowski.... Kochanowski set the pace for the whole subsequent development of Polish poetry. In his work, the language reached maturity, and today he is considered a classic of Polish syllabic verse. It is rather difficult, though, to present a precisely drawn portrait of Kochanowski. In his poetic work he was discreet to the point of secretiveness about his personal adventures, and it is that work which remains today our only biographical source. The very character of his poetry adds to the difficulty. At first glance there is nothing striking or extraordinary about it; classical, limpid, it is simply an act of perfect ordering of the language. It flows naturally, so to speak, without any apparent effort; one might call it a pure "breathing" of Polish, and in this respect analogies can be found between Kochanowski and the French poets of *La Pléiade*. Also, both drew from the same Latin and Italian sources. (p. 60)

Kochanowski's poetry ripened slowly, as a result of his extensive studies and life experience. There was nothing in him of a precocious genius. Perfectly bilingual, he composed his first poems in Latin during his stay in Italy. But in Paris he was already writing in Polish. From that city he sent his famous song of gratitude to God: **"What Do You Wish, O Lord, In Return For Your Bounteous Gifts?"** Later on, he employed both languages. His literary models were Latin and Greek poets, above all, Horace. (pp. 61-2)

Longer poems of humorous, satirical, or simply didactic nature do not occupy a prominent place among Kochanowski's works, though as his tribute paid to these genres, so popular at that time, they are interesting. **"The Game**

of Chess" ("Szachy", published around 1564) was the first attempt in Polish to write a humorous epic, or heroicomic, poem. It was written under the obvious influence of a Latin poem by an Italian humanist, Vida. Kochanowski, unlike his model, places the action not on Olympus, but (and the detail is amusing) at the royal court of Denmark. A kind of novelette in verse about a battle on a chessboard and two young men who compete for the hand of a beautiful princess, it is presented with a considerable amount of true humor.

Poems like **"Harmony"** (**"Zgoda,"** 1564), **"The Satyr, or The Wild Man"** (**"Satyr albo Dziki Mąż,"** 1564), **"The Banner, or Homage from Prussia"** (**"Proporzec albo Hold Pruski,"** 1569) can be defined as journalism in verse which rather faithfully expresses contemporary political concerns, formulated along the lines of official court views. In the first of the poems mentioned, a personified Harmony addresses the Poles, advising them to end their quarrels, especially those between religious denominations. The Satyr in the poem of that title serves a similar admonitory purpose; in particular, he, as an inhabitant of Poland (and a baptized one, we may presume), complains of the devastation of nature provoked by the economic boom: as a consequence of the intense cultivation of land and the high volume of exports required to buy foreign luxuries, forests are being destroyed. The Satyr reproves the citizens who are losing their chivalrous virtues and who believe that gold will protect them from their enemies, and this at a time when the country's outlying provinces are being devastated by the Tartars, and the Muscovite despot has not only taken Polotsk but claims that Halich (Galicia) belongs to him by "natural law." The Satyr adds: "I would rather uphold your side because the Muscovite despot has never paid much heed to constitutions." Nor are concerns of education alien to the Satyr. Though Kochanowski himself spent many years in Italy, his Satyr considers studies abroad too expensive, advising instead substantial endowment of Kraków University as the necessary first step toward creating a Polish institution which could rival the Sorbonne.

"The Banner" is a tableau representing the ceremony of homage paid by the prince of East Prussia in 1525 to the king of Poland in recognition of the latter's sovereignty over that province. A banner held at that ceremony provides the point of departure for the poem. One side of the standard depicts the history of Polish-Lithuanian relations with the Teutonic Order. The reverse side pictures, we learn, the entire history of the Slavs, beginning with the Amazons who landed in Scythia, then migrated toward the north over the river Don and founded two Sarmatias (Poland and Russia). The poem ends with an appeal to the king to continue the policy which had produced the union of Poland and Lithuania and a common victory over the Teutonic Order. The tableau posseses a certain hieratical grandeur.

Kochanowski's journalistic works were addressed mainly to voters and members of the Diet. They are written in thirteen-syllable verse with a caesura occurring after the seventh syllable—the so-called Polish Alexandrine. Kochanowski also displayed his civic interests in Latin poems, such as the one he composed in answer to a violent satire on the Poles written by a French poet, Desportes, who had come to Poland with Henry Valois, the Polish king-elect. Kochanowski's poem was entitled **"Gallo croci-**

tanti" (translatable as either "**To a Crowing Gaul**" or "**To a Crowing Cock**").

Some of his public political pronouncements are also significant. (pp. 62-3)

A short occasional poem was called in Kochanowski's time in Italy a *frasca* (literally, "little twig"); thus a collection of his short poems in this genre, published in 1584, received the name *Fraszki*. All of them are distinguished by conciseness of form and concentration of material, but their character varies from anecdotes, humorous epitaphs, and obscenities to pure lyricism. Combined, they form a sort of very personal diary, but one where the personality of the author never appears in the foreground, as if the poet took pleasure in confounding his future biographers. (p. 64)

A certain philosophy is clearly traceable throughout all of Kochanowski's songs, namely, an affirmation of the Renaissance principle of the individual as an autonomous subject meditating upon the human condition and establishing his own relationship with the universe. A Christian attitude is fused with the Horatian *carpe diem* so popular among the poets of the Renaissance. If Kochanowski consciously competed with Horace, he succeeded not only in completely "Polonizing" the motifs which he drew from the ancient poet, but in preserving the sensuous quality of his native language, rooted as it was in the physical world and very far from any classical dryness. Conscious that he was creating a Slavic poetry which could rival works in Latin, the poet presumes:

> About me Moscow will know and the Tartars
> And Englishmen, inhabitants of diverse worlds.
> The German and the valiant Spaniard will be acquainted
>   with me
> And those who drink from the deep Tiber stream.

> O mnie Moskwa i będą wiedzieć Tatarowie,
> I różnego mieszkańcy świata Anglikowie;
> Mnie Niemiec i waleczny Hiszpan, mnie poznają,
> Którzy głęboki strumień Tybrowy pijają.

The main value of the songs lies in their tone of serenity, their quiet affirmation of existence—a bucolic tone so typical, for a long time, of Polish poetry. Mythological deities, if they appear, have Slavic faces, and satyrs inhabit, undoubtedly, Polish forests. Some songs are related to events of the moment, and there is no lack of political topics. (p. 66)

Kochanowski's songs reveal him as a man who sought an equilibrium between his quiet country life, on the one hand, and a preoccupation with public affairs, on the other. A recurring image is that of evening, glowing logs in a fireplace, a jug of wine. The changing seasons provide a background for the poet, whose moods harmonize with those of nature. The *Songs* includes his earliest and his latest poems, and one of them has already been mentioned—"**What Do You Wish, O Lord, In Return For Your Bounteous Gifts?**"

"*The Dismissal of the Grecian Envoys*" is the finest specimen of Polish humanist drama. (p. 68)

Kochanowski wrote the tragedy at the peak of his artistic maturity—a few years before the death of his daughter, when he produced his best poetry in the *Laments*. It seems that only after some hesitation he finally settled on a subject suitable for a wedding feast. The work could not be a bloody tragedy. He had intended to translate Euripides' *Alcestis* but dropped the idea almost as soon as he started. The war of Troy had been popular in medieval Europe as a literary motif, and its popularity lasted into the Renaissance. Horace had advised dramatic poets to choose themes from the *Iliad*, and Kochanowski knew Horace well.... [He] finally chose an episode preceding the war.... *The Dismissal* is neither a tragedy of passions nor a tragedy of a revealed fate. We can hardly say that his characters are heroes. They are necessary initiators of action, while the true hero is a collective one: the Trojan state. The messengers arrive with offers of peace on condition that Helen be restored to her husband. A group of wise statesmen led by Antenor is for fulfilling the Greeks' demand, but a faction led by Alexander (Paris), Helen's abductor, wins the majority through skillful demagoguery at a council presided over by King Priam (and in its deliberations similar to the Polish Diet). Our feeling of impending doom is enhanced by a reference to the traditional story of Troy, which the viewer knows in advance, and by Cassandra's vision, which confirms our knowledge. Yet the fatal outcome is due not to an inexorable fatality but merely to stupidity and demagoguery. The tragedy centers about those characters who understand what is at stake but who cannot reverse the trend. Thus, one can say that it is the very futility of human passions which provokes horror and pity. Perhaps the most pitiable are those who are unaware, like Alexander, Helen, and Priam (a weak man and a constitutional monarch like the Polish kings).

For its construction the play follows the rule of Renaissance poetics based on Horace and codified by the French theoretician of Italian origin, Scaliger. Thence, the division into five "epeisodia" or acts. The plot proceeds from the exposition to the announcement of the catastrophe and finally to the catastrophe itself. The action which takes place beyond the stage is related in dialogue: a messenger, for instance, reports on the deliberations of the council; the future is shown through a vision of Cassandra; and the first step of fulfillment is announced by an officer who brings the news of the Greek attack. A chorus of Trojan maidens, like a detached voice of judgment, delivers three long speeches: the first is on the folly of youth; the second, on the responsibility of rulers; the third and most interesting is an apostrophe to the boat used by Alexander (Paris) on his trip to Greece.

Kochanowski uses blank verse of thirteen or eleven syllables, and in this we see the trace of his years in Italy. The first Italian tragedy modeled after Greek tragedy was written in the first half of the sixteenth century by a patrician from Vicenza, Trissino. In his theoretical writings Trissino advocated the use of *verso sciolto* (unrhymed verse) as more "natural" in tragedy. *Verso sciolto* wandered from Italy to England in the same century, where, adapted to the rhythmical needs of English, it became known as "blank verse." And this is what Kochanowski adapted to Polish in *The Dismissal*. Following the natural tendency of the language, his verse, both in dialogue and in choruses, is syllabic. The third chorus, however, mentioned above, is somewhat of an exception. In it he attempted to mold his native tongue into a form duplicating the qualities of Greek verse. (The first line is a translation from Euripides.) Greek versification, of course, is based upon entirely different principles, but thanks to the poet's struggle, what we receive is a daring and beautiful poem. Together with Cassandra's lament, it is the highlight of the play. Kochanowski, by basing the pattern of versification on the count of syllables combined with dactylic and trochaic feet, produces in that chorus a syllabotonic verse.

The Dismissal, so majestic in its clarity, equilibrium, and economy, nevertheless remained an exception in old Polish literature. Humanist tragedy, which had reached such perfection in Kochanowski, was not destined to develop further either quantitatively or qualitatively. (pp. 68-71)

> *Czeslaw Milosz, "Humanism and Reformation: The Sixteenth Century and the Beginning of the Seventeenth Century" in his* The History of Polish Literature, *1969. Reprint, Second edition, by University of California Press, 1983, pp. 25-110.*

ADDITIONAL BIBLIOGRAPHY

Coleman, Marion Moore. "Jan Kochanowski." In his *Polish Literature in English Translation: A Bibliography*, pp. 42-6. Cheshire, Conn.: Cherry Hill Books, 1963.
> Comprehensive bibliography of English translations of Kochanowski's works made between 1827 and 1960.

Giergielwicz, Mieczslaw. *Introduction to Polish Versification.* Philadelphia: University of Pennsylvania Press, 1970, 209 p.
> Examines Kochanowski's use of and contribution to several forms of Polish verse.

Gömöri, G. "*The Dismissal of the Grecian Envoys* and Bornemisza's *Magyar Elektra.*" *The Slavonic and Eastern European Review* 60, No. 1 (January 1982): 16-24.
> Compares Kochanowski's *Grecian Envoys* to Péter Bornemisza's *Magyar Elektra* (1558?), measuring the influence of such classic authors as Sophocles, Seneca, and Euripides.

Noyes, George R. "Jan Kochanowski: 'The Founder of Polish Poetry'." In *Great Men and Women of Poland*, edited by Stephen P. Mizwa, pp. 66-80. New York: Macmillan Co., 1942.
> Surveys the career of Kochanowski, noting his motivations for writing and the sources he drew from for his style and subject matter.

Ulewicz, Tadeusz. "The Portrait of Jan Kochanowski in the Encyclopaedias of Non-Slavic Countries: A Critical Survey." *The Polish Review* XXVII, Nos. 3-4 (1982): 3-16.
> Surveys the critical and biographical attention paid to Kochanowski by the major encyclopedias of several countries, including France, England, Germany, Italy, Greece, and Spain.

———. "The European Significance of Jan Kochanowski from the Renaissance to the Romantics." *Cross Currents: A Yearbook of Central European Culture* 3 (1984): 151-75.
> Traces Kochanowski's influence upon writers and cultures in Slavic countries over a period of three centuries.

Aemilia Lanyer

1569-1645

(Also Emilia; also Lanier) English poet

A minor seventeenth-century English poet, Lanyer contributed to the limited canon of literature by female writers of the Shakespearean age with *Salve deus rex judæorum*, a small volume of poetry considered unique for its feminist recasting of Christ's Passion. Attempting to revise misogynistic interpretations of Christian belief, Lanyer revealed a keen intellect in her argument for women's essential role in perpetuating Christianity. Only recently rediscovered, Lanyer's work provides valuable historical and sociological insight into Elizabethan England.

Lanyer's life is briefly sketched both in *Salve deus* and in the notebooks of Simon Forman, an astrologer who cast her horoscope. Born at Bishopsgate in 1569, she was the illegitimate daughter of an Italian court musician, whose mismanagement of family funds and death in 1576 necessitated her employment at a young age. While working as a maid in the household of Susan Wingfield, countess of Kent, Lanyer appears to have gained the initial academic background that would eventually include a strong working knowledge of the Bible, Classical literature, and the poetry of such contemporaries as Mary Sidney, countess of Pembroke—an impressive scholarly display for any Elizabethan woman, much less one of such modest means and social standing. Sometime during her teenage years, presumably while in attendance upon the countess of Kent, Lanyer met and became the paramour of Lord Henry Carey Hunsdon, first cousin to Queen Elizabeth. Well-kept by Hunsdon, Lanyer, through his connections, became acquainted with the aristocratic ladies to whom she would later appeal for patronage. Upon becoming pregnant in 1592, Aemilia was discarded by Hunsdon and married off to a court musician and gentleman soldier, Alphonso Lanyer. Their union was unhappy and they were separated periodically due partly to Alphonso's extended military excursions, but also, apparently, by design. During one such separation, Aemilia resided for a short period with Margaret Clifford, countess of Cumberland, at the Berkshire estate of Cookham. Clifford's influence proved crucial to Lanyer's development as a poet, for while at Cookham Lanyer received additional academic tutelage and experienced a religious conversion, becoming devoutly Protestant. Indeed, Lanyer attributed her literary endeavors and the religious nature of her subject matter to the behest of the countess, whose patronage may have made it possible for *Salve deus* to be published in 1611. Not surprisingly, Clifford is the central female character of *Salve deus*: the dedication, "To the Ladie Margaret," relates her preparation to assume the role of a bride of Christ, almost one-quarter of the title poem addresses the countess's numerous Christian virtues, and "The Description of Cooke-ham" recounts the poet's remembrance of her idyllic life at the Berkshire estate. In 1613, some time after Aemilia had left Cookham, Alphonso died, leaving his wife to engage in multiple lawsuits concerning potential revenue from his estate. Aside from a brief record noting Lanyer's unsuccessful attempt to establish a school for young women in 1617 and a court petition indicating her involvement in financial litigation in 1635, little else is known of her life between the publication of *Salve deus* and her death in 1645 at age seventy-six.

Salve deus rex judæorum, Lanyer's only known work, is a poetic reinterpretation of Christ's Passion that emphasizes the role Christian women have played in upholding social morality throughout history. Composed of eleven dedications, the title poem, and a short country-house poem, *Salve deus* is intended solely for women: Lanyer made no attempt to address a male audience, concentrating instead upon enlightening women of all classes to the essential nature of their Christian mission. The dedications, addressed to potential patronesses and typical of Tudor literature, emphasize the exemplary characteristics of each noble woman. The title poem reinterprets biblical history beginning with Adam and Eve, meditating on the Passion, death, and resurrection of Christ, and concluding with commentary on the state of Christianity in contemporary England. Asserting that Christ chose women to continue his work on earth, Lanyer contrasted the failures of Adam, the apostles, and the male sex in general, with the virtues of the redeemed Eve, the Virgin Mary, and the daughters of Jerusalem. Central to Lanyer's fusion of biblical history with an ideal contemporary society is her admonition of Clifford and other contemporary noble women to prepare to assume honored positions as brides of Christ. *Salve deus* concludes with the elegiac poem "The Description of Cooke-ham," in which Lanyer painfully acknowledges the discrepancy between her dream vision of an ideal Christian world of women (based upon her experience at Cookham) and the reality of the imperfect world of men to which she must return.

Virtually no criticism on Lanyer's work exists prior to the 1970s. Upon its publication in 1611, *Salve deus* appears to have attracted little or no attention, and Lanyer was all but forgotten for over three centuries until her work was rediscovered in 1973 by A. L. Rowse. Claiming that Lanyer was the Dark Lady alluded to in Shakespeare's sonnets, Rowse theorized that *Salve deus* was written as an angry rebuttal to Shakespeare's portrait. This hypothesis, which was quickly refuted by other Shakespeare scholars, brought Lanyer's life and work to light, but also shifted initial attention away from the work itself. Hence the small body of criticism that now exists on *Salve deus* which has examined the poet's interpretation and presentation of Christian mythology, her technical competence, and the potential sociological value of her work. In general, critics deem Lanyer's feminist portrayal striking and, as Barbara K. Lewalski concludes, "[of] considerable intrinsic interest as a defense and celebration of good women." Lanyer's poetic talents, however, have been variously assessed. While critics praise her work as occasionally brilliant in imagery and acknowledge her basic command of rhyming and iambic pentameter, she is considered but a modestly skilled poet. Most commentators concur with Lewalski's opinion that " 'The Description of Cooke-ham' is the gem of the volume," and also with Rowse's assessment that "she was too facile and fluent: she wrote too much, she padded out what she had to say—it [the volume] would have been more effective if shorter." Scholars have begun not only judging the artistic merits of *Salve deus,* but assessing the work's value as a potential source of historical insight, as well.

One of the rare breed of Elizabethan women writers who composed from an even rarer feminist perspective, Lanyer, through her work, has provided interesting insight into her age, raising numerous literary and sociological questions. Scholars consider *Salve deus* worthy of much further critical study, for its artistic merits, for the exceptional nature of its feminist appeal, and for its value as a historical document.

PRINCIPAL WORK

Salve deus rex judæorum (poetry) 1611

EMILIA LANYER   (essay date 1611)

[*In the following dedication "To the Vertuous Reader" (1611), Lanyer expresses her moral and social reasons for composing* Salve deus rex judæorum.]

Often have I heard, that it is the property of some women, not only to emulate the virtues and perfections of the rest, but also by all their powers of ill speaking, to ecclipse the brightnes of their deserved fame: now contrary to their custome, which men I hope unjustly lay to their charge, I have written this small volume, or little booke, for the generall use of all virtuous Ladies and Gentlewomen of this kingdome; and in commendation of some particular persons of our owne sexe, such as for the most part, are so well knowne to my selfe, and others, that I dare undertake Fame dares not to call any better. And this have I done, to make knowne to the world, that all women deserve not to be blamed though some forgetting they are women themselves, and in danger to be condemned by the wordes of their owne mouthes, fall into so great an errour, as to speak unadvisedly against the rest of their sexe; which if it be true, I am perswaded they can shew their own imperfection in nothing more: and therefore could wish (for their owne ease, modesties, and credit) they would referre such points of folly, to be practised by evill disposed men, who forgetting they were borne of women, nourished of women, and that if it were not by the meanes of women, they would be quite extinguished out of the world, and a finall ende of them all, doe like Vipers deface the wombes wherein they were bred, onely to give way and utterance to their want of discretion and goodnesse. Such as these, were they that dishonoured Christ his Apostles and Prophets, putting them to shamefull deaths. Therefore we are not to regard any imputations, that they undeservedly lay upon us, no otherwise than to make use of them to our owne benefits, as spurres to vertue, making us flie all occasions that may colour their unjust speeches to passe current. Especially considering that they have tempted even the patience of God himselfe, who gave power to wise and virtuous women, to bring down their pride and arrogancie. As was cruell *Cesarus* by the discreet counsell of noble *Deborah,* Judge and Prophetesse of Israel: and resolution of *Jael* wife of *Heber* the Kenite: wicked *Haman,* by the

divine prayers and prudent proceedings of beautiful *Hester*: blasphemous *Holofernes,* by the invincible courage, rare wisdome, and confident carriage of *Judeth*: and the unjust Judges, by the innocency of chast *Susanna*: with infinite others, which for brevitie sake I will omit. As also in respect it pleased our Lord and Saviour Jesus Christ, without the assistance of man, beeing free from originall and all other sinnes, from the time of his conception, till the houre of his death, to be begotten of a woman, borne of a woman, nourished of a woman, obedient to a woman; and that he healed women, pardoned women, comforted women: yea, even when he was in his greatest agonie and bloodie sweat, going to be crucified, and also in the last houre of his death, tooke care to dispose of a woman: after his resurrection, appeared first to a woman, sent a woman to declare his most glorious resurrection to the rest of his Disciples. Many other examples I could alleadge of divers faithfull and virtuous women, who have in all ages, not onely beene Confessors, but also indured most cruel martyrdome for their faith in Jesus Christ. All which is sufficient to inforce all good Christians and honourable minded men to speak reverently of our sexe, and especially of all virtuous and good women. To the modest sensures of both which, I refer these my imperfect indeavours, knowing that according to their owne excellent dispositions, they will rather, cherish, nourish, and increase the least sparke of virtue where they find it, by their favourable and best interpretations, than quench it by wrong constructions. To whom I wish all increase of virtue, and desire their best opinions. (pp. 77-8)

Emilia Lanier, "To the Vertuous Reader," in her The Poems of Shakespeare's Dark Lady: Salve Deus Rex Judaeorum, *Jonathan Cape, 1978, pp. 77-8.*

A. L. ROWSE   (essay date 1978)

[*An English historian, poet, and critic, Rowse is the author of numerous studies of Elizabethan history and literature, many of which have been highly controversial for their untraditional approach to conventions of historical and literary scholarship. At the same time, Rowse's works have been praised for their lively prose style and exhaustive knowledge of social and political life in Elizabethan England. In the following introduction to his 1978 reprint of Lanyer's work,* The Poems of Shakespeare's Dark Lady, *Rowse proclaims Lanyer the dark lady of Shakespeare's sonnets, assessing the effectiveness of* Salve deus *as a rebuttal to Shakespeare's defamatory portrait.*]

[Emilia Lanier is] a fair poet, far superior to the Queen, for example, who wrote antiquated doggerel. In fact, except for Sidney's sister, the Countess of Pembroke, Emilia is the best woman poet of the age. This is not saying much, but it is to be observed that she has an easy natural command of iambic pentameter—all her verses are in that measure—and she has no less easy a command of rhymes. Her defect indeed is that she was too facile and fluent: she wrote too much, she padded out what she had to say—it would have been more effective if shorter.... (p. 17)

On the other hand, she reveals herself a highly educated woman, well read in the Bible and the classics patronised by the Renaissance. She has a gift for words—quite exceptional to anyone acquainted with the comparative illiteracy of even famous Elizabethan women, Lady Ralegh, Bess of Hardwick, Mary Fitton, or others of the Queen's ladies-in-waiting. Very few women in the age—only notoriously well educated ones like Mary Sidney or the Cooke sisters—could rival her. She has complete power of expression, if verbose and redundant; occasionally she uses rare words, or has an apt and memorable turn of phrase, even a moving line, for all her rhetorical exaggeration in keeping with her temperament.

In versification she is close to Samuel Daniel. . . . (pp. 17-18)

[So strong is Emilia's] personality, her egoism and sense of self that it comes through in every line she writes and makes it easy to read her character.

Her prose address is a piece of rampant feminism, like nothing else in the age—though a strong assertion of feminism runs all through the poems too, culminating in a passionate defence of Eve and putting the blame for eating the fatal apple on Adam! It is obvious that something personal had aroused her anger. Shakespeare's Sonnets had been published, though not by him, in 1609, with their unforgettable portrait of the woman who had driven him 'frantic-mad', dark and musical, tyrannical and temperamental, promiscuous and false, a powerful and overbearing personality, quite well known, of bad reputation. (Perhaps those Sonnets were intended as a warning to the young patron for whom they were written: he certainly did not fall under her spell as his susceptible poet had done—though she told Forman that she had been 'favoured . . . of many noblemen' and received great gifts. This was exaggeration typical of her, and of her poems). The portrait was defamatory enough. The very next year, 1610, her book was announced, and in 1611 published.

In her angry prose riposte she reproved women for speaking ill of their own sex and spreading scandal about them. All women do not deserve to be blamed, and they should leave this to 'evil disposed men who—forgetting they were born of women, nourished by women, and that, if it were not by the means of women, they would be quite extinguished out of the world and a final end of them all—do like Vipers deface the wombs wherein they were bred.' Emilia was certainly a good hater, *à l'italienne*. Women were to take no notice of the imputations laid upon them by men other than to use them to their own benefit, as spurs to virtue. She then cites the wise and virtuous women from the Old Testament who had brought down the pride and arrogance of men. Cruel Sisera had been done in by Jael; wicked Haman overthrown by beautiful Esther, Holofernes by the courage of Judith, the unjust Elders by chaste Susanna.

Moreover, it had pleased Jesus Christ to be begotten of a woman, born of a woman, nourished by and obedient to a woman; he healed pardoned and comforted women. In his last agony he took care to make disposition of a woman; after his resurrection he appeared first to a woman. We notice, however, the tell-tale fact that, in all her long poem, there is no mention of Mary Magdalen, the repentant prostitute. The emphasis is all on virtue and chastity—wearisomely so; it is in character for her to go on and on about it, to be emphatic and to exaggerate. Virtuous women have been confessors and martyrs in all ages; it therefore becomes honourably minded men 'to speak reverently of our sex' and cherish virtue where they find it,

putting the best interpretation upon it rather than give it 'wrong constructions'.

We see that Emilia has been personally piqued by something, as also that she is supercilious about others, ready to be censorious and to lay down the law.

We are not concerned with the religious or even the poetic aspect of her poems, we are concerned with the personal; we are looking for information about her. Fortunately, she is such an egoist that there is plenty of it—she herself stands in the forefront of almost every line—but we could wish for more information about other people. The dedicatory poems do at any rate give us some information about the great ladies she knew, and some she didn't know. (pp. 20-1)

The poem to Lady Anne Clifford, at this time Countess of Dorset, is interesting for the oblique light it throws on Emilia herself in what she says about birth. . . . What difference was there when the world began, when all sprang from one woman and one man:

> Then how doth Gentry come to rise and fall?
> Or who is he that very rightly can
> Distinguish of his birth, or tell at all
> In what mean state his ancestors have been,
> Before some one of worth did honour win?

Emilia might well, with her own illegitimacy, argue that, and we may regard much of her moralising as but sour grapes. (pp. 23-4)

To the long religious poem [*Salve deus rex judaeorum*] Emilia appended "The Description of Cooke-ham", where she had evidently passed happy summer days with the Countess and her daughter, Lady Anne, as a girl. The poem is in pentameter again, which Emilia falls into with natural ease, but this time in rhymed couplets. It provides a rare enough example of an Elizabethan topographical poem, with a rapturous response to the beauty of the landscape, if somewhat marred by a too prolonged example of the pathetic fallacy. (p. 31)

[Emilia's] book was received with stony silence. It may have achieved its purpose in reaping some reward from the dowager Countess—that would have been in keeping with current usage. But there is no evidence that any of the great ladies took any notice of the too obviously sycophantic poems with their clamorous assertions of virtue unrewarded, and hints to relieve. Few copies of the book can ever have been printed for so very few have survived. (p. 33)

It certainly is a most precious boon that we have been left this rare work by that extraordinary woman: in it we hear the acutely personal voice and read the character of Shakespeare's Dark Lady at last. (p. 37)

> *A. L. Rowse, "Introduction: Shakespeare's Dark Lady," in* The Poems of Shakespeare's Dark Lady: Salve Deus Rex Judaeorum *by Emilia Lanier, Jonathan Cape, 1978, pp. 1-38.*

EMRYS JONES (essay date 1979)

[*Jones is a British essayist and academic. In the following excerpt, he refutes A. L. Rowse's dark lady theory (see ex-*

cerpt dated 1978) while separately considering the historical and sociological value of Lanyer's work.]

Emilia Lanier *could* have been Shakespeare's mistress, but there is no evidence whatever to link her with him (as opposed to Lord Hunsdon), and it is only on Dr Rowse's say-so that her poems . . . are entitled *The Poems of Shakespeare's Dark Lady*. In this context, his description of himself as 'the cautious historian' strikes a distinctly odd note.

Emilia Lanier's book was printed in 1611, and is made up of a long poem *(Salve Deorum Rex Iudeorum)*, a verse **"Description of Cooke-ham",** and dedicatory poems to influential court ladies, including Queen Anne, Princess Elizabeth, and several countesses. The main item, a religious poem of 1,870 lines, is a meditation on the life of Christ. What is slightly surprising is that Emilia Lanier, though a negligible poet, proves to be a competent verse rhetorician, She has a decent verbal style, uses the poetic and mythological commonplaces with a modest skill, and shows a resourceful metrical variety (couplets, quatrains, sixains, rime royals and ottava rimas). Particularly striking is the outspoken feminism she voices at every opportunity—'She might be a precursor of Women's Lib', as Dr Rowse rather predictably puts it [see Additional Bibliography].

Her title-page singles out a section called "Eves Apologie in defence of Women" for, according to Emilia, women have had a raw deal from men throughout history, and Adam was far more to blame for the Fall than Eve. In a short prose address **"To the Vertuous Reader,"** she again speaks out on behalf of women against the injustice and tyranny of men. This feminist slant gives the whole volume a sharp flavour of personality.

Emilia Lanier's writings, both prose and verse, have sociological value, and her name will undoubtedly figure in future volumes of 'women's studies'. (She has, in fact, already been noticed in Juliet Dusinberre's *Shakespeare and the Nature of Women* (1975). There were so few women writers in Shakespeare's England that it is good to know about her.

But instead of being content with bringing these poems to our notice, Dr Rowse insists on pressing his Dark Lady case. Shakespeare's sonnets were published in 1609, just over a year before these poems, and he tries hard to find links between the two books. He believes, in fact, that the sonnets actually provoked Emilia's poems and that her indignant defence of women is 'a violent reaction to the defaming portrait of her' that appeared in the sonnets. I can see nothing in favour of this view. The high-minded piety of the preface and the poems, though feminist in expression, seems to call for a quite different kind of explanation. We need to know more about feminism among Shakespeare's contemporaries. Nor is Dr Rowse on strong ground when, looking for Dark Lady characteristics, he calls her description of Christ 'sensuous, not to say sexy'. Every detail in her description is, in fact, transcribed—with irreproachable piety, I should have thought—from the Song of Solomon. Dr Rowse should not have missed this, since Emilia herself says as much in a marginal note: 'A briefe description of his beautie upon the Canticles'. Nonetheless, despite the absence of Shakespearian connections, despite, too, the lack of intrinsic poetic interest, we should feel indebted to him for a reprint

which throws some unexpected light on its period. (pp. 28-9)

Emrys Jones, "Dark Feminist?" in The Listener, *Vol. 101, No. 2592, January 4, 1979, pp. 28-9.*

ALIKI BARNSTONE AND **WILLIS BARNSTONE** (essay date 1980)

[*Aliki Barnstone is an American poet, essayist, and editor. Her father, Willis Barnstone, is a poet, translator, editor, and novelist. In the following excerpt from their collaborative text,* A Book of Women Poets: From Antiquity to Now *(1980), they briefly assess Lanyer's work.*]

As an accomplished poet, [Emilia Lanier's] long work *Salve Deus Rex Judaeorum* is a dexterous work of historical and biblical events in which she reveals and argues the virtue of Eve, Deborah, Judith, Esther, Susanna, as well as Cleopatra with whom she had full sympathy. Her work, recognized only now with the publication of Rowse's edition of her collected poems, is compelling both artistically and for its original, independent, and lucid thought.

Aliki Barnstone and Willis Barnstone, "Emilia Lanier," in A Book of Women Poets from Antiquity to Now, *edited by Aliki Barnstone and Willis Barnstone, Schocken Books, 1980, p. 435.*

ALIKI BARNSTONE (essay date 1981)

[*In the following excerpt, Barnstone contrasts Lanyer's feminist representation of the myth of Eden with Andrew Marvell's ideal of a pre-Eve Eden as revealed in his "The Garden" and "Damon the Mower."*]

In Andrew Marvell's "The Garden" we see the multiple exiles created by the myth of Eden. Marvell the man is exiled from the first Garden accompanied by his mate whom he blames for his banishment. He aspires to return to the lost earthly paradise when he "walked without a mate" and was therefore pure. In his aspiration woman suffers a double exile: from man and from "that happy garden-state" of perfection, which means not only from Eden but from its master, God. Ultimately, the Genesis lesson of "The Garden" implies the separation and therefore exile of body from spirit, and of woman and man from the earth.

"The Garden" is Andrew Marvell's dream of the perfect state of man—in which woman and her alluring imperfections do not exist. He creates two gardens: one of permissible sensuality where the grass, which in the "Damon the Mower" poems represented woman, sin, and death, can somehow be enjoyed without moral conflict; and one of meditation, transcendence, and union with God. Although he has created a misogynous garden, which, as Frank Kermode writes [in his 1967 edition of Marvell's selected poetry], has "sensual delight free of sexual pursuit, the satisfaction of the senses against that of the mind," Marvell's language belies him. He uses the language of Eros, entrapment, and physical ecstasy in the same manner as in the "Mower" poems, where he is overtly speaking of his fear of the female body and of the grass which is flesh. . . . Marvell is incapable of evoking the full experience of the earth (which in Genesis was also corrupted by the Fall) without bringing in women and undertones of sin. (pp. 147-48)

For Marvell, God's very creation of Eve—"It is not good that the man should be alone. I will make him a help-mate" (Gen. 2:18)—is a regrettable mistake: He claims: "After a place so pure, and sweet / What other help could yet be meet!" Yet his views reveal those shadowy fears of blame and punishment pronounced in the Bible, in which Eve is the major culprit. (p. 148)

Emilia Lanier (1569-1645), the first important woman poet in the English language and, according to A. L. Rowse "Shakespeare's dark lady," seeks to subvert the meaning of the myth of Eden in order to redeem women in the name of Eve, and to bring harmony and equality to women and men. In her long poem, *Salve Deus Rex Judae-orum*, she refutes all the main attitudes about womanhood found in both Marvell and his source, the Bible, which she courageously reinterprets. In the preface **"To the Vertuous Reader"**, [see excerpt dated 1611], she states that she

> has written this small volume, or little booke, for the generall use of all virtuous Ladies and Gentlewomen of this kingdom.... (p. 149)

First, Emilia Lanier admonishes women not to fall into the trap of self-hatred by affirming the established male attitudes toward women. Secondly, she recalls the foolish-ness of "evill disposed men" who lack "discretion and goodnesse" by denigrating women who, as mothers, save the race from extinction. After a defense of the virtue of childbearing (as opposed to its accursed state in Genesis), she goes on to praise other virtues and catalogues the ac-complishments of women of biblical and secular history. Men have tried "the patience of God himself, who gave power to wise and virtuous women, to bring down their [men's] pride and arrogancie." Most of her poems are ad-dressed to noble women. In the preface she lists some of their qualities as well as the villainies of their male coun-terparts... But she does not limit herself to men's villai-nies; she provides a model for an harmonious exchange between women and men. This confidante, who comforts and in comforted by women, is Jesus Christ... Lanier's greatest defense of and praise for women, however, is in the section of *Salve Deus Rex Judaeorum* titled "Eve's Apologie in Defence of Women." While arguing within the confines of Christian faith, she not only upsets the tradi-tional interpretation of the garden myth in Genesis, in which woman is blamed for evil, mortality, and knowl-edge, but she questions how innocent "poore *Eve*" could even be capable of guilt, since God is omnipotent and all Good.... Invoking the problem of evil, she indicts not only the Serpent and Adam the surrogate lord (whom she actually refers to as Lord) but God himself. In each stanza she says that Eve's sin is small compared to that of Adam, who, by name and powers, is throughout associated with God. By this association, God is the author of Evil as well as Good. Moreover, she transforms Eve's fault into virtue, for Eve brings both knowledge and love to man. (pp. 151-52)

Lanier's emphasis on the value that men place on knowl-edge and on their debt to Eve for the gift of that knowl-edge is significant, for, as E. M. W. Tillyard states in *The Elizabethan World Picture*, though sin and death were in-troduced to the world through knowledge, the way to sal-

vation is also through knowledge. The rationale for this contradiction, as Tillyard explains, is: "By the Fall man was alienated from his true self. If he is to regain true self-knowledge he must do it through contemplating the works of nature of which he is a part."

After her defense of Eve's excess of love and "faire hand" of knowledge, Lanier says that compared to Eve's small sin of disobedience, man's sins toward women—cruelty, enslavement, and tyranny—are greater as the sun is great-er than a "little starre." Finally, she makes a plea for liber-ty and equality. In a world of correspondences, in the di-vine cosmic hierarchy, stretching from God to the lowest pebble, women were inferior to men as men inferior to an-gels. To ask for equality between the sexes was to chal-lenge the divine order; to invite the sin of chaos. As John Fortescue [quoted in Tillyard's book] wrote, "Hell alone, inhabited by none but sinners, asserts its claim to escape the embraces of this order." And, indeed, Lanier's ideas were not popular.... Lanier extolls the virtue of child-bearing, making a stand for the "cursed" body of woman and for the life force. By contrast, when Marvell wishes to return to an Eden before Eve, his is a wish for a monastic, almost lifeless, world without progeny or human love—the sterile world of his silver bird, devoid of mutability.... (pp. 152-53)

Eden represents a time of immortality (of eternity) and in-nocence before knowledge (or before the birth of the ego or individuality) and can be seen as an embryonic state. Marvell's "pre-worldly abode," his embryonic state, ex-cludes the presence of a mate who would destroy his gar-den paradise by introducing sexual knowledge, birth, mor-tality, and mutability. He would exclude the "fatal apple of discord," the apple of knowledge, and the consequent expulsion from Eden, all of which constitute the birth of consciousness and conflict. For Emilia Lanier, it is pre-cisely the moment of expulsion, the mutability, the birth pains, and the freedom and equality of a real Eve which receives her praise. She accepts the post-Edenic state on earth and persistently seeks justice for Eve, for women, and reconciliation between women and men, and so con-travenes the edict: "Your yearning shall be for your hus-band / yet he will lord it over you" (Gen. 3:16). As a result of her vision and experience of the circumstances of wom-en, she reinterprets Genesis (abusing orthodox interpreta-tion) in order to redeem and esteem women in their post-Edenic world. (p. 154)

> *Aliki Barnstone, "Women and the Garden: An-drew Marvell, Emilia Lanier, and Emily Dickin-son," in* Men by Women, *edited by Janet Todd, Holmes & Meier Publishers, Inc., 1981, pp. 147-67.*

BETTY TRAVITSKY (essay date 1981)

[*In the following excerpt, Travitsky questions critical assess-ments of* Salve deus *that regard it primarily as a religious work.*]

Although superficially Lanier's work [*Salve deus rex ju-dæorum*] may seem to be a religious poem lacking propor-tion, a careful reading serves to establish its cohesion and good sense. She states that her purpose in writing is to "applie my Pen to write [the] ... never dying fame," of the countess of Cumberland, her former employer and the mother of Anne Clifford. Therefore, the countess is Lanyer's center of interest, but she enhances her praises for the countess and enlarges her theme by depicting her as an example of feminine virtues. These virtues are set forth in accounts of Eve, the daughters of Jerusalem, and the Virgin Mary, as well as in tales of less exalted women and in repeated praises of the countess. Christ's passion is recounted, however briefly, because it is a subject in which the countess is interested and because she approves time spent on it; it is introduced into the poem in relation to the countess, who is a model of godliness, who will enjoy eternal bliss because of the sacrifice of Christ. Once one appreciates the fact that the subject of this poem is the commendable qualities of women such as the countess of Cumberland, then the account of the life of Christ and the supportive materials concerning commendable women fall into perspective. Once the poem's axis is so established, the amount of attention given these subjects is reasonable.

Similarly, a shorter piece, appended to the main poem, has a legitimate place within such a frame. This piece is **"A Description of Cookeham,"** a residence of the countess in which Lanyer lived when she was in her service; the emphasis in this description is on Cookeham's conduciveness to meditation and withdrawal from earthly things.

Finally, Lanyer's smooth style and skillful paraphrasing of biblical texts should be noted, and this writer should be placed on the periphery of the group of women writers who composed defenses of women. (p. 97)

> *Betty Travitsky, "Secular Writings," in* The Paradise of Women: Writings by Englishwomen of the Renaissance, *edited by Betty Travitsky, Greenwood Press, 1981, pp. 89-113.*

BARBARA K. LEWALSKI (essay date 1985)

> [*Lewalski is an American essayist and academic. In the following excerpt, she explicates* Salve deus, *illuminating Lanyer's attempt to reverse traditionally negative perceptions of women in Christian mythology.*]

A volume of religious poems published in 1611, **Salve Deus Rex Judaeorum,** was written by a gentlewoman who identified herself on her title page as "Mistris Aemilia Lanyer, Wife to Captaine Alfonso Lanyer, servant to the Kings Majestie." Since published women poets were so very rare in Elizabethan and Jacobean England, the volume invites attention on that score alone. But beyond this, it has considerable intrinsic interest as a defense and celebration of good women and of Lanyer herself as woman poet. It has also some real, if modest, poetic merit. (p. 203)

Salve Deus Rex Judaeorum, for all its diversity of subject matter, is governed by certain unifying themes and concerns. It is set forth as a comprehensive "Book of Good Women," fusing religious devotion and feminism so as to assert the essential harmony of those two impulses. Lanyer does not imitate Boccaccio, or Christine de Pizan, or Chaucer—but she does employ several poetic genres and verse forms with considerable facility to celebrate good women. Given Lanyer's questionable past, her evident concern to find patronage, and her continuing focus on women, contemporary and biblical, we might be tempted

to suppose that the ostensible religious subject of the title poem, Christ's Passion, simply provides a thin veneer for a subversive feminist statement—but that conclusion would be wrongheaded. Lanyer is a woman of her times, and her imagination is governed by its terms. She appears to be sincerely, if not very profoundly, religious, and she presents Christ's Passion as the focus for all the forms of female goodness—and masculine evil—her poems treat. Her good women meditate upon and imitate this model, and as poet she interprets her experience of life in religious categories.

The first section of the book, the dedications, sets up a contemporary community of good women. Most of the dedicatees were linked through kinship or marriage with the staunchly Protestant faction of Robert Dudley, Earl of Leicester, which promoted resistance to Spain, active support of Protestantism on the Continent, continued reform in the English church, and patronage of the arts, especially Christian poetry. Lanyer's dedications continually emphasize the descent of virtue in the female line, from virtuous mothers to daughters: Queen Anne and Princess Elizabeth, Margaret and Anne Clifford, Catherine and Susan Bertie, Katherine Howard and her daughters. The author positions herself among these women, describing her book as the glass which shows their several virtues, and inviting them to receive and meditate upon Christ their Bridegroom here depicted.

The extraordinary virtue and merit she discerns in these ladies also redounds upon herself as poet, justifying her in undertaking what is "seldome seene, / A Womans writing of divinest things" (**"To the Queenes most Excellent Majestie,"**). Aemilia's several apologias for her poetry excuse it as faulty and unlearned by reason of her sex, but her disclaimers seem closer to the *humilitas* topos than to genuine angst. She continually proclaims her poems worthy of attention for the virtue and divinity they manifest: the implication is that a woman poet may write worthily since all these women are seen to be so worthy.

The first dedication (in six-line pentameter stanzas rhymed *ababcc*) honors Queen Anne for embodying the qualities of Juno, Venus, Pallas, and Cynthia, and for attracting Muses and Artists to her throne. Lanyer calls the queen's particular attention to "*Eves* Apologie, / Which I have writ in honour of your sexe," and concludes with a defense of her poems' worth as deriving from nature rather than from learning and art. . . . (pp. 207-08)

The sonnet-like poems to Princess Elizabeth and the Lady Arabella (dedications two and four) emphasize their learning: Lanyer offers her own "first fruits of a womans wit" to Elizabeth, whose "faire eyes farre better Bookes have seene"; and she apostrophizes Arabella as "Great learned Ladie . . . / so well accompan'ed / With *Pallas*, and the Muses." The third dedication (in seven-line pentameter stanzas rhymed *ababcc*) is addressed **"To all vertuous Ladies in generall"**; it praises all who are ladies-in-waiting to Queen Virtue, companions of the Muses, and Virgins waiting for the Bridegroom. The fifth dedication (in the same verse form as that to the queen) praises the Countess of Kent as the glass displaying all virtues to the young Aemilia, and as a heroic follower of Christ even in infancy when her staunchly Protestant mother, Catherine Bertie, Countess of Suffolk, fled England with her family during Queen Mary's reign. . . . (pp. 208-09)

The next dedication is given special importance by its central position, its length, its verse form unique in this volume (four-line pentameter stanzas rhymed *abab*), and its genre: it is a dream vision narrative entitled **"The Authors Dreame to the Ladie Marie, the Countesse Dowager of Pembroke."** In it Lanyer recounts a dream visit under the conduct of Morpheus to the Idalian groves where she finds the Countess of Pembroke enthroned in Honor's chair, crowned by eternal Fame, and receiving tribute from various classical representatives of art, beauty, and wisdom: the Graces, Bellona, Dictina, Aurora, Flora. Under the countess' aegis the strife between Art and Nature is resolved, and all the company join to sing the countess' psalm versions. (p. 209)

Morpheus then reveals the lady's name, indicates that she spends all her time "In virtuous studies of Divinitie," and (continuing Lanyer's argument concerning the equality or superiority of women in moral and spiritual matters) ranks the countess "far before" her brother Sir Philip Sidney "For virtue, wisedome, learning, dignity." Dismayed upon awakening from her vision, Lanyer resolves to present her own "unlearned lines" to that lady, expecting that she will value these "flowres that spring from virtues ground" even though she herself reads and writes worthier and more profound books. . . . The poem is well conceived, well made, and charming, testifying by its length and art to the importance of the Countess of Pembroke as model for Lanyer's conception of herself as learned lady and poet.

The later dedications are again epistolary in form. That to the Countess of Bedford (in seven-line pentameter stanzas rhymed *ababbcc*) identifies Knowledge, wielded by Virtue, as the key to her heart, and emphasizes, like Johnson's epigram, her "cleare Judgement." The dedication to the Countess of Cumberland—distinguished as the book's primary patron and audience by the fact that only this dedication is in prose—offers the Passion poem as a worthy text for the countess' meditations in that its subject "giveth grace to the meanest and most unworthy hand that will undertake to write thereof." Also, describing the poems as a mirror of the countess's "most worthy mind," it claims that their art can extend the life of both dedicatee and author: these poems "may remaine in the world many yeares longer than your Honour, or my selfe can live, to be a light unto those that come after."

The dedication to the Countess of Suffolk (in six-line, pentameter stanzas rhymed *ababcc*) praises her as "fountaine" of all her husband's blessings, and, with continuing emphasis upon the female community, urges the countess to guide her "noble daughters" in meditations based upon Lanyer's Passion poem. In this dedication Lanyer eschews apologies for her poetic vocation and poetic achievement, claiming that both are God-given. She was led by her birth-star "to frame this worke of grace," and is enabled to do so by God himself: "his powre hath given me powre to write, / A subject fit for you to looke upon."

The final long dedication to Anne, Countess of Dorset (116 lines, in eight-line pentameter stanzas rhymed *abababcc*) presents her as the worthy heir to her mother's excellencies and virtues, contrasting a female succession grounded upon virtue and holiness with the male succession through aristocratic titles. In this verse epistle, uniquely, Lanyer presumes to teach proper moral attitudes

and conduct to her subject, as if privileged to do so by former familiarity. Intimating (perhaps) that Anne should continue such familiarity despite the differences in their rank, and evidently alluding to the fact that Cumberland's will alienated his estates and the titles they carried from his daughter (against the terms of the entail), Lanyer compares the worthlessness of aristocratic titles to the "immortall fame" which "faire virtue" wins. . . . The dedication ends by begging Anne to excuse any insufficiency in her poem arising from "wants, or weaknesse of my braine," since her subject, Christ's Passion, is beyond any human art.

If these dedications as a group portray a contemporary community of learned and virtuous women with the poet Aemilia their associate and celebrant, the prose **"Epistle to the Vertuous Reader"** [see excerpt dated 1611] confirms and extends that community, offering the book "for the generall use of all virtuous Ladies and Gentlewomen of this kingdome." The epistle is a remarkable contribution to the so-called *querelle des femmes*, that ongoing controversy over women's inherent worthiness or faultiness which produced a spate of writing, serious and satiric, from the Middle Ages through the seventeenth century and beyond. Lanyer first lectures those women who "forgetting they are women themselves . . . speake unadvisedly against the rest of their sexe," and she urges them to leave such "folly" to "evill disposed men." With considerable passion she denounces those men who, "forgetting they were borne of women, nourished of women, and that if it were not by the means of women, they would be quite extinguished out of the world, and a finall ende of them all, doe like Vipers deface the wombes wherein they were bred"—associating such men with those who "dishonoured Christ his Apostles and Prophets, putting them to shamefull deaths." Marshalling biblical evidence with rhetorical force and flair, she claims that God himself has affirmed women's moral and spiritual equality or superiority to men. . . . In clipped, forceful phrases, she cites further evidence to the same point from the singular honors accorded to women by Christ. . . . (pp. 210-13)

Lanyer's long poem on Christ's Passion (in eight-line pentameter stanzas rhymed *abababcc*) constitutes the second part of her volume. The account of the Passion emphasizes the good women who played a major role in that event, and it is presented from the vantage point of women, past and present. Not only is the Passion narrative interpreted through the sensibility of Lanyer as woman poet, it is also enclosed within descriptions of the Countess of Cumberland as exemplary image, imitator, and spouse of the suffering Saviour. As poetic interpreter, Lanyer treats her material variously, sometimes relating events, sometimes elaborating them in the style of biblical commentary, sometimes meditating upon images or scenes, often apostrophizing participants as if she herself were present with them at these events.

The conceptual scheme of this poem is of primary interest; stylistically, it is uneven. Lanyer uses rhetorical schemes—especially figures of sound, parallelism, and repetition—with considerable skill; her apostrophes often convey strength of feeling; she can describe and sometimes dramatize a scene effectively. There are few striking images or metaphors, but her allusions are usually appropriate and her language straightforward taking on at times colloquial directness. Her greatest fault is slackness—padding lines and stanzas to fill out the metrical pattern.

The Passion poem begins with a long preface addressing the Countess of Cumberland. The first nine stanzas propose to immortalize her in verse, and recall the solace she has found for her many sorrows in the beauties of Cookham and the love of God. Stanzas 10 to 18 comprise an embedded psalmic passage praising God as the strong support of the just and the mighty destroyer of all their enemies, with obvious (and later overt) application to the much wronged Margaret Clifford. Lanyer perhaps intends the passage as a gesture of discipleship to the Countess of Pembroke, as it echoes or paraphrases a melange of psalm texts, chiefly Psalms 18, 84, 89, and 104.... (pp. 213-14)

Stanzas 19 to 33 identify the countess as one of those just who are specially beloved and protected by God, and praise her for abandoning the delights of the court to serve her heavenly king in rural retirement. This section includes a dispraise of beautiful women—Helen, Cleopatra, Rosamund, Lucretia, Matilda—whose beauty led them or their lovers to sin or ruin; by contrast, the countess' inner beauty of grace and virtue made Christ the husband of her soul, and his death "made her Dowager of all."

This statement leads into Lanyer's proper subject, the Passion.... Proposing like many of her contemporaries to render sacred matter "in plainest Words" so as not to distort it, she prays God to "guide my Hand and Quill."

Her account of the Passion is part commentary or meditation on the biblical story and part apostrophe—a poetic figure which often intensifies emotion and creates an effect of immediacy. The first section begins with Christ's prayers and subsequent capture in the Garden of Gethsemane. Using apostrophes to poignant effect, Lanyer conveys Christ's profound isolation even from his beloved apostles:

> Sweet Lord, how couldst thou thus to flesh and blood
> Communicate thy griefe? tell of thy woes?
> Thou knew'st they had no powre to doe thee good,
> But were the cause thou must endure these blowes.

The emphasis throughout his section is on the sins and failures of Christ's own apostles. Peter declared that his faith would never fail, but Christ knew Peter would deny him three times. Christ implored the apostles to wait and watch with him, but they slept. The Apostle Judas proved to be "A trothlesse traytor, and a mortall foe." Peter offended Christ and the laws by drawing his sword against Christ's enemies. Turning then to the "accursed crew" of Scribes and Pharisees who apprehended Christ, Lanyer castigates them with a fine flourish of parallelism and antithesis:

> How blinde were they could not discerne the Light!
> How dull! if not to understand the truth,
> How weake! if meekenesse overcame their might;
> How stony hearted, if not mov'd to ruth:
> How void of Pitie, and how full of Spight,
> Gainst him that was the Lord of Light and Truth:
> Here insolent Boldnesse checkt by Love and Grace,
> Retires, and falls before our Makers face.
> Here Falshood beares the shew of formall Right,
> Base Treacherie hath gote a guard of men;
> Tyranny attends, with all his strength and might,
> To leade this siely Lamb to Lyons denne.

The section ends by reverting to the disciples' failures: "Though they protest they never will forsake him, / They do like men, when dangers overtake them." This formulation begins Lanyer's sharply drawn contrast between the weak and evil men in the Passion story and the good women who play a role in it.

The second section focuses upon yet more wicked men, Christ's several judges—"wicked *Caiphas*," "Proud *Pontius Pilate*," "scoffing Herod." It begins by describing Christ through a series of epithets—George Herbert's technique in "Prayer I".... Then Lanyer addresses a lengthy apostrophe to Pilate, explicitly contrasting good women with these weak and evil men. Ranging herself with Pilate's wife whom she takes as the representative of womankind, Lanyer pleads with Pilate to spare Christ, relating that plea to a remarkable apologia pronouncing Eve guiltless of any evil intention in the Fall.... She presses that argument, claiming that Eve's "harmeless Heart" intended no evil at all, that her fault was only "too much love, / Which made her give this present to her Deare." All the guilt of the Fall belongs to Adam, who was strong, wise, and undeceived. Moreover, any faults which women might have inherited from Eve are far outweighed by the guilt and malice of men, epitomized in Pilate.... (pp. 214-17)

The third section presents the procession to Calvary, the Crucifixion, and the Resurrection, again contrasting the responses of good women and evil men to these events. The journey scene is described with considerable dramatic effectiveness.... A lengthy apostrophe to the daughters of Jerusalem follows, contrasting their tears and their efforts to beseech mercy for Christ with their menfolk's cruelty.... Then Lanyer locates herself with the mother of Jesus as observer and mourner at the crucifixion, and in an extended passage meditates upon Mary's role in the Redemption and her exaltation as "Queene of Womankind".... (pp. 217-18)

Lanyer's baroque description of the crucifixion itself is not without poetic force and religious feeling:

> His joynts dis-joynted, and his legges hang downe,
> His alabaster breast, his bloody side,
> His members torne, and on his head a Crowne
> Of sharpest Thorns, to satisfie for pride:
> Anguish and Paine doe all his Sences drowne,
> While they his holy garments do divide:
> His bowells drie, his heart full fraught with griefe,
> Crying to him that yeelds him no reliefe.

But the emphasis on good women continues.... (pp. 218-19)

A long coda to the Countess of Cumberland, which parallels the long prologue, expatiates upon the many forms in which Christ appears to the countess as she practices the works of mercy, and portrays her in Canticles imagery as Christ's Spouse. It also proclaims her superiority to the worthy women of history. She is more noble and more faithful to her spouse than Cleopatra was, since "she flies not from him when afflictions prove" and she dies not one death for love but a thousand. She also surpasses the famous women who fought and conquered with the sword. (p. 219)

At this juncture we find a sensuous and not ineffective baroque passage expatiating upon the sweetness of Christ's grace and love:

Sweet holy rivers, pure celestiall springs,
Proceeding from the fountaine of our life;
Swift sugred currents that salvation brings,
Cleare christall streames, purging all sinne and strife.
Faire floods, where souls do bathe their snow-white wings,
Before they flie to true eternall life:
Sweet Nectar and Ambrosia, food of Saints,
Which, whoso tasteth, never after faints.

Such sweetness "sweet'ned all the sowre of death" to the first martyrs—St. Stephen, St. Lawrence, the Apostles Andrew and Peter, and John the Baptist. The praise of these male saints as chief of the martyrs and confessors by whom "our Saviour most was honoured" provides some counterweight to the massive wickedness Lanyer lays to men's charge throughout the poem. But it is a small gesture. Lanyer concludes her poem by declaring that the Countess of Cumberland follows in the footsteps of these martyrs, folding up "all their Beauties" in her breast.

The final poem, **"The Description of Cooke-ham"** is the gem of the volume. In 210 lines of pentameter couplets it sustains a gentle elegaic tone and contains some lovely pastoral description. The poem presumably executes the Countess of Cumberland's charge, reported in *Salve Deus* as not yet fulfilled, to write "praisefull lines of that delightfull place," the "*Paradice*" of Cookham. Whether Lanyer's poem was written before or after "Penshurst," it was conceived on very different lines. It is a valediction—a farewell by the author and by the residents (the Countess of Cumberland and her daughter) to an Edenic home, perhaps in specific reference to the countess' permanent departure to those residences she would occupy as a widow.

This poem also embodies but gives mythic dimension to Lanyer's dominant concerns: the Eden now lost is portrayed as a female paradise inhabited solely by women—the countess, her young virgin daughter Anne, and Aemilia Lanyer. In keeping with the Edenic myth Lanyer (who is twenty years older than Anne Clifford) describes herself as a constant participant in Anne's sports, as if they had been young girls together at Cookham. Located in Berkshire a few miles from Maidenhead, the area is still a beauty spot, with extensive frontages on the Thames, rich woodlands, lush meadows, picturesque scattered hamlets, and high hills in the west—which however do not afford a prospect into thirteen shires, as Lanyer's poem asserts.

The elegaic tone is established in the opening lines, as Lanyer bids farewell to the place she associates with her conversion and the confirmation of her vocation as poet. . . . (pp. 219-21)

Then begins the description of the estate, as it responds to the arrival and departure of its mistress in terms of the seasonal round. The house itself is barely mentioned, but the estate becomes a *locus amoenus* as each part decks itself out in all its spring and summer loveliness for her arrival. . . . Other aspects of nature contribute to the welcome with an obsequiousness analogous to that of the Penshurst fish and game offering themselves to capture, but Lanyer's tone carries no hint of Jonson's amused exaggeration. . . . (p. 221)

Like that other Eden the focus of interest in this place is a "stately Tree." This oak surpasses all its fellows in height

and also incorporates qualities of other trees: it is straight and tall "Much like a comely Cedar" and it has outspread arms and broad leaves "like a Palme tree," veiling the sun and fanning the breezes. Seated by this tree the countess enjoys regal honors and delights: "Hills, vales, and woods, as if on bended knee" salute her, and the prospect of "thirteene shires" (if not of all the world) is "fit to please the eyes of Kings." However, this tree offers no temptation, only contentment and incitement to meditate upon the creatures as they reflect their Creators' beauty, wisdom, love, and majesty. Elsewhere in the woods the countess meditates on the Scriptures, "Placing his holy Writ in some faire tree," and in her daily life at Cookham she follows in the spiritual footsteps of the greatest Old Testament saints. (p. 222)

The next passage is a complaint that Lanyer can no longer associate with Anne Clifford, now Countess of Dorset, because "Unconstant Fortune" has placed too great a social divide between them. While the passage gives vent to Lanyer's discontent with her station, and makes a transparent bid for further attention from Anne, it is thematically appropriate. The social constrictions attending Anne's nobility by birth and marriage are set off against the natural associations, dictated solely by virtue and pleasure, in Edenic Cookham, "Whereof depriv'd, I evermore must grieve."

Next, Cookham's grief at the ladies' preparations for departure is described in a notably effective passage in which pathetic fallacy fuses with the seasonal change from autumn to winter. . . . The countess' gracious leavetaking of all the beloved creatures and places on the estate culminates in the charge to Lanyer to preserve them in poetry. Then the scene declines into sentimentality as Lanyer portrays herself stealing the farewell kiss the countess bestows on the noble oak.

The final passage echoes the imagery of the opening passage, as all the beauties of the *locus amoenus* wither in desolation. . . . (p. 222-23)

In sharpest contrast to Jonson's "Penshurst" which celebrates a quasi-Edenic place whose beauty and harmony are centered in and preserved by its lord who "dwells" permanently within it, Lanyer's country-house poem portrays the destruction of an idyllic place when its lady departs. Cookham takes on the appearance of a ravaged Eden after the first human couple is expelled. But here it is a female pair—or rather trio—who depart: the countess called away by her "occasions"; the virgin daughter to her marriage; Lanyer to social decline. Offering her poem as "This last farewell to *Cooke-ham*" Lanyer suggests strongly that none of them will return to this happy garden state, in which women lived without mates, but found contentment and delight in nature, God, and female companionship. Though of uneven quality, **"The Description of Cooke-ham"** is an attractive poem presenting a sustained imaginative vision. . . .

Despite its artistic flaws, Lanyer's volume is worthy of attention for the charm of the **"Cooke-ham"** poem and for its quite remarkable feminist conceptual frame. The patronage poems present a female lineage of virtue from mother to daughter, a community of good women extending from Catherine Bertie, Protestant fugitive in Mary Tudor's reign, to the young Anne Clifford, heir to the

"Crowne / Of goodness, bountie, grace, love, pietie" long worn by her mother, the Countess of Cumberland. The Passion poem extends this community back to biblical times, portraying women as Christ's truest apostles and followers. In the "**Cooke-ham**" poem a female Eden suffers a new Fall when the structures of a male social order force its women inhabitants to abandon it. In sum, the fundamental Christian myths—Eden, the Passion, the Community of Saints—are here revised, with women at their center. (p. 224)

> *Barbara K. Lewalski, "Of God and Good Women:*
> *The Poems of Aemilia Lanyer," in* Silent but for
> the Word: Tudor Women as Patrons, Transla-
> tors, and Writers of Religious Works, *edited by*
> *Margaret Patterson Hannay, The Kent State Uni-*
> *versity Press, 1985, pp. 203-24.*

ELAINE V. BEILIN (essay date 1987)

[*Beilin is an American essayist and academic. In the following excerpt from her book* Redeeming Eve (1987), *she analyzes* Salve deus *and Lanyer's attempt to inspire her sex by
portraying "Christian virtue in living women."*]

The impetus to glorify virtuous women, whether manifested in Mary Sidney's consecration of Elizabeth or in Joanna Lumley's and Elizabeth Cary's idealization of fictional heroines, was crucial to the development of women's poetry. In creating such images of beneficent feminine power, these women writers justified their own literary endeavors: whether in the person of a Virgin Queen or a feminine type of Christ, a redeemed Eve who spoke and acted wisely and well authorized their own virtuous intentions as writers. By ransoming women's knowledge and speech from the suspicion of subversion and shrewishness, they could themselves attempt more as writers and gently woo an audience to read their works. Nowhere is this process more evident than in the work of Aemilia Lanyer, the first woman seriously and systematically to write epideictic poetry, the poetry of praise, about women.

Until Lanyer wrote *Salve Deus Rex Judaeorum*, the Renaissance praise of virtuous women, both as real people and as ideal figures, was almost entirely in the hands of men and so had accrued many conventions appropriate to men addressing women. Dominant were the language of courtship and the assumption that the woman praised was an exception to her sex. Often, male praise evolved from the poet's own amorous, political, religious, economic, or poetic interests rather than from the woman herself. Even the trend which Barbara Lewalski has called "the Christianization of the poetry of praise," while it might alter the virtues for which the lady was praised, did not ultimately focus on the woman's spirituality but on the poet's. (pp. 177-78)

Aemilia Lanyer probably wrote *Salve Deus Rex Judaeorum* a few months before Donne began his first poem on Elizabeth Drury, the "Funerall Elegie." While both poets were concerned with the ideal Christian woman, it is important to distinguish Donne's praise (and Jonson's too) of the Christian woman from Lanyer's, because Lanyer's work evolves from a quintessentially feminine poetic consciousness. Whereas Donne and Jonson developed their images of virtuous women "as *Poets* use," hoping to reveal a truth

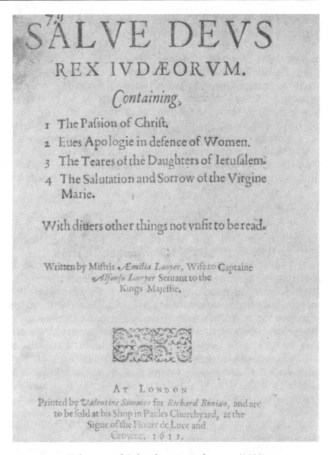

Title page of Salve deus rex judæorum (1611).

about human nature (and revealing much about the poet himself), Lanyer wrote specifically to praise women, and more precisely, to redeem for them their pivotal importance as Christians.

To accomplish her task, Lanyer called upon her considerable knowledge of English poetry, her scriptural reading, and a familiarity with traditional debate material on the woman question. Whether or not she had read the works of other women writers—she does refer to Mary Sidney's Psalms—like many of her predecessors, she found particular value in the feminine allegories of Scripture. The parable of the wise virgins and the Song of Songs provided images central to Lanyer's attempts to place women at the heart of Christianity, and she developed their potential with new intensity and completeness.

To this point, the only other feminine work of praise to develop the image of the brides of Christ was an elegy on Marguerite de Navarre, published in 1551 and written by Anne, Margaret, and Jane Seymour, the three young daughters of Edward Seymour, Duke of Somerset and Anne Stanhope, both ardent Reformers.... (p. 179)

The sisters and their subject, Marguerite, share a virtue which promises salvation after death, or "a second life." By so praising the great woman—and of significance for English Protestants, a woman identified with the French Reformation—the Seymours glorified feminine virtue and glimmeringly suggested the lines that Aemilia Lanyer would later develop to praise the whole sex.

As shadowy as Aemilia Lanyer's life may be today, as a writer she emerges with the color and sound of a vivid personality. Claiming to be motivated by misogynist disparagement of women, in her one published work, *Salve Deus Rex Judaeorum*, Lanyer presents a single-minded, fervent argument for the importance of woman's virtue. Viewing women's history from Eve to the present, Lanyer represents her sex as the heroic protectors of the Christian spirit. In her work, she infuses the image of the true Christian woman, already so important to women writers, with a dramatic new scope. Ranging from Genesis to Gethsemane to the present, her generous imagination successfully unites the most sacred moments of Scripture with figures of contemporary life.

Establishing women's spiritual prominence demands a poetry of praise rooted in women's qualities, and this Lanyer creates more fully and skillfully than any writer before her, partly by extending the conventional exempla to invent her own panegyrics for contemporary ladies, and partly by exploiting imagery representing women's continued reception of God's grace. But Lanyer's devoted praise of women, from her apology for Eve to her encomia for the Countess of Cumberland, does not derive solely from anger or even a desire for justice. Rather, it evolves from her own piety and her poetic calling as a Christian visionary who yearns for a world greatly different from the one she knows. Continually, her poem opposes the fallen, ungodly world with a vision predicated upon Christian ideals, manifested first by Christ himself, and then by women—the Virgin and the Daughters of Jerusalem in the past, and women like the Countesses of Pembroke and Cumberland in the present. Although she has been censured for exaggerating women's qualities and toadying to the great, Lanyer is better understood as a millenarian advocating the establishment on earth of God's will through the particular agency of women. But while her poem begins optimistically enough with the symbols of triumph and communion, and proceeds to celebrate women at the heart of Christian doctrine, it concludes when she painfully recognizes the vast gulf between human wishes and their realization. (pp. 180-81)

Lanyer's poetry reveals that she was ardently Protestant, knew Scripture well, and drew on both Christian and classical tradition to mix scriptural narrative, meditation, and theological allegory with pastoral, encomium, and elegy. While she refers to misogynist tracts and knew their traditional rhetorical devices, as well as those of women's defenders, the core of her argument evolves not from repeating and reversing the old terms of the woman question, but from her admiring portraits of living women praised as the descendants of a redeemed Eve, the daughters of Jerusalem, and the Virgin. In Lanyer's poem, the image of the brides of Christ assumes a new prominence as a way of declaring women's spirituality. By praising such women as the Countesses of Kent, Cumberland, and Pembroke, Lanyer attempts to realize Christian virtue in living women, to warn misogynists of their impiety, and to inspire other women. Particularly in her treatment of the Countess of Cumberland, Lanyer merges her Christian vision and her concept of ideal womanhood.

Salve Deus Rex Judaeorum is divided into three parts: more than 800 lines dedicating the work to Queen Anne, Princess Elizabeth, seven other virtuous ladies, and **"To all Vertuous Ladies in generall"**; the poem of over 1800

lines, *Salve Deus Rex Judaeorum*, divided into four parts, "The Passion of Christ," "Eves Apologie in defence of Women," "The Teares of the Daughters of Jerusalem," and "The Salutation and Sorrow of the Virgine Marie"; and a poem of 211 lines, **"The Description of Cooke-ham,"** an early example of a country-house poem. These three divisions overlap and interweave in theme and image, creating an integrated vision: the dedications present the essential Christian virtues in the figures of contemporary ladies; *Salve Deus* narrates the central experience of their lives, Christ's passion, and justifies the importance of women to Christianity; **"The Description of Cooke-ham"** is an elegy for a feminine, Christian paradise.

Although she composed on the well-explored subject of Christ's Passion, Lanyer's particular perspective results in a distinctive poem. Like other such poems, Lanyer's "Passion" embraces both encomium and elegy, but it also becomes the model for both the subject and form of her poetry on women. In her direct praise of Christ, Lanyer actually reveals Him as the true source of feminine virtue.... In **"The Description of Cooke-ham,"** she echoes both the death and resurrection (temporal loss and consolation in immortality) of Christian elegy. As a result, her superficially digressive poem develops along single lines of thought, imagination, and execution, all emanating from meditation on the meaning of Christ's life and death. Continually, Lanyer emphasizes this integrity by repeating images of Christ the bridegroom and the Christian triumph, and by developing the Countess of Cumberland's multiple functions as imitator and bride of Christ, patron of Christian poetry, and divine mother-figure.

The dedications may seem at first to be the most dubious part of Lanyer's work, sounding to twentieth-century ears like fulsome, self-serving flattery of potential patrons. Like readers of Jonson's "To Penshurst" or "Elegy on Lady Jane Pawlet," the reader of so much praise must wonder why Lanyer presents her subject as such a paragon of virtue. But seeking to answer that question leads to the poem's central purpose: to reveal the ultimate reality behind the virtuous life, or as Lanyer proposes, "To write of Christ, and of his sacred merits...." In her dedications, Lanyer concentrates on the spiritual gifts of women, expressing her intention most clearly in the image of the wise virgins prepared for the bridegroom who will indeed come in the central section of her poem. Unlike many defenders of women, Lanyer implies that her dedicatees are precedents for other women, not mere "blazing comets," and as she intends her "little booke for the generall use of all virtuous Ladies and Gentlewomen of this Kingdome," she also designs her "commendation of some particular persons of our owne sexe" to prove that "all women deserve not to be blamed." Indeed, this is an understatement, because Lanyer attempts to eradicate centuries of blame with a burst of encomium. In the dedication, each woman's spirituality dominates her portrait, and she joins an ideal gallery devoted solely to Christian virtue.

The persona Lanyer creates to perform this task also emerges in the dedications as a humble soul, apparently self-deprecating like other women writers, yet wholly dedicated to her important task. In the first dedication to the queen, she refers to herself as "dejected," "feeble," "rude," and "unpolished," and continually describes herself as a troubled unfortunate tied to a miserable world, yet yearning for the "happy rayne" of the next. Linked closely to this traditionally Christian affliction is the confession of her inability as a writer, particularly as a divine poet.... But by redefining the inability topos as human inadequacy before God, Lanyer can identify the poet as a true Christian and underscore the piety of her attempt to praise Christ and to clarify the nature of women.

Exerting negative influence are, she implies, both men who defame women and male poets.... Naming the source of her creativity as Nature, Lanyer seeks to circumvent the "Art," the conventions and rhetoric with which men commonly represent women.... Like her contemporaries, the poet defines Nature as what God gives humankind, the prime essence, as opposed to Art, what mankind does to nature, the imitation that is often false. Just as she seeks to redefine women's spirituality, the poet wishes to find her poetic voice "At the well head [where] the purest streames arise." This poet, accurately perceiving how she is blocked from masculine Art, wants to create a feminine "natural" poetry not to be judged by men's standards but to be read, delighted in, and used by women. Lanyer does not mean to abandon literary tradition: her poem, although it diverges from masculine conventions of praise, cannot reject all precedents. Instead, mixing form and genre, Lanyer forges a new context and direction for poetry about women.

One of the important aspects of Lanyer's work is the inclusiveness by which she tries to interest a wide feminine audience in its long spiritual history. Not only does *Salve Deus* narrate the Passion, but it turns to the past to exonerate Eve and to the future to praise the Countess of Cumberland. Likewise, in her dedications, she embraces the first lady of the body politic, the queen, "all vertuous Ladies in generall," seven prominent aristocratic women of her day, and the anonymous "Vertuous Reader," thus implying a whole commonwealth of women—or city of ladies—learned and virtuous, to whom she may appeal.

Beginning appropriately with the most prominent, Lanyer addresses Queen Anne, and by themselves these 27 stanzas might seem to conform to the style of florid overstatement common to Renaissance dedications:

> For you have rifled Nature of her store
> And all Goddesses have dispossest
> Of those rich gifts which they enjoy'd before....

But in the context of the whole, this language conforms to the poet's exalted style when she considers the qualities of virtuous women. Contributing to this heightened manner are three images drawn from conventional rhetoric, yet used to dignify and enhance women's spirituality. The triumph, the mirror, and the feast appear continually in the dedications, and reinforcing one another, they express the elevation of each woman's virtue.

First, Queen Anne appears in triumph. Like "great Eliza" before her, she displaces the goddesses in the Judgement of Paris and wins the golden ball, gaining State and Dignities from Juno, Wisdome and Fortitude from Pallas, and "all her Excellencies" from Venus.... Holding up a mirror "where some of your faire Virtues will appeare," the poet invites the queen to behold the source of true royalty, "that mightie Monarch both of heav'n and earth / He that all Nations of the world controld," he who is "Crowne and Crowner of all kings." In the Passion of Christ that will pass through the mirror, Anne will view "through a glass

darkly" the reality of Christian virtue which her own virtues imitate, as do those of the other great ladies whom the poet asks to gaze into the "dim," but true steel.

The third and most important image that Lanyer introduces is that of the feast, to which the queen is "the welcom'st guest." Designating it as a Passover feast...the poet recalls the Last Supper and its symbolic promise of resurrection. In subsequent dedications, the other virtuous ladies are also bidden to "grace this holy feast" until the poet has completed a female communion: all the seats are for virtuous ladies who act as the new apostles attending Christ. No other image in the poem expresses so powerfully Lanyer's conviction of the unity of women with the central doctrines of Christianity. To ask the Countess Dowager of Kent of the Countess Dowager of Pembroke or the Countess of Dorset to come "unto this wholesome feast" is to praise them as exemplary Christians in the context of a religious poem which will examine the very roots of faith. If this is mere flattery, one suspects that it would not please women of such piety as Margaret Russell or Mary Sidney.

Lanyer separates her praise of the queen and a brief dedication to her daughter, the Princess Elizabeth, from the dedications to the other seven women with a dedication **"To all vertuous Ladies in generall."** While continuing the image of the triumph, the poet concentrates on representing such ladies as the wise virgins well prepared for their bridegroom, Christ. Although this parable had appeared regularly in women's writing, in her dedications and in her praise of the Countess of Cumberland, Lanyer exploits the full poetic force of lover and beloved. The fate of virtuous ladies in poetry had always been to exist as the idealized, and often deceased, beloveds of male poets who were principally interested in finding their own way to heaven. But in this poem, these living women, because of their own virtues, have a direct relationship with Christ, their only lover.... As Lanyer develops the metaphor expressing the direct communion of virtuous women with the resurrected Christ, she simply circumvents masculine poetry which treated such figures as extraordinary or as mediators for the poet. Her poetry insists that this is woman's true nature. Appropriately, in the final stanzas of this dedication, Lanyer alters the function of Fame who usually heralds the achievements of great men in the world. Instead, Fame commends the "very best" of these ladies to the poet's particular notice, and their "glorious Trophies" will be a litany of womanly virtue.

Lanyer's ensuing subjects of praise are no less than the most prominent noblewomen in England, all of whom she lauds for their learning and virtue: Lady Arabella Stuart; Susan Bertie, Countess Dowager of Kent; the Countess Dowager of Pembroke; Lucy Harington Russell, Countess of Bedford; Margaret Russell, Countess Dowager of Cumberland; Katherine Knyvet, Countess of Suffolk; Anne, Countess of Dorset. (pp. 182-88)

The virtues of the Countess of Pembroke, to whom the longest and central dedication is addressed in the form of a dream-vision, are first expressed by a parade of mythological figures whom the countess greets and subsumes: the Graces (gifts of God), Minerva (Wisdom and Chastity), the Muses (who with "Harps and Vialls in their lilly hands" are distinctly angelic), Bellona ("a manly maid which was both faire and tall"—Fortitude and Wisdom),

Dictina (Chastity), and Aurora (Beauty). In her presence, Art and Nature are encouraged to dwell together in a new union, for in this pastoral setting of woods, flowers, and a sacred spring, Nature inspires Art to sing "holy hymnes." Perhaps recalling Mary Sidney's "Lay of Clorinda," Lanyer reiterates that Nature is the source of feminine Art. More precisely, she implies that women accurately translate Nature, God's book, into sacred poetry.... Her knowledge, which she uses to illuminate God, and her wisdom, which produces harmony, the "heavenli'st musicke ... That ever earthly eares did entertaine," qualify the Countess of Pembroke as a divine poet. Lanyer, attempting to relocate the source of feminine virtue in God rather than in man, creates in her dream-vision a centerpiece of feminine beauty, wisdom, and harmony more immediately potent than conventional symbols because of its attachment to a living woman writer.

Although she had disclaimed learning, Lanyer repeatedly raises the subject of knowledge in her poem. As we have seen, feminine knowledge posed problems for both men and women writers, but Lanyer's positive emphasis on women's learning, knowledge, and wisdom as attributes contributing to their spirituality and virtue foreshadows her impassioned defense of Eve. Well beyond her peers, she asserts the power of knowledge and still continues to praise it as a feminine virtue.

In each of these dedications, the poet apostrophizes the lady, asking her to meditate upon the Passion and to ready herself to accept Christ as her lover.... Lanyer confirms that the spiritual virtues, those conventionally assigned to women, have their source and perfect expression in Christ.

In her final prefatory address, a prose piece "**To the Vertuous Reader**," [see excerpt dated 1611], Lanyer clearly articulates her purpose in praising women. Castigating women who criticize other women and the "evill disposed men" who defame them, Lanyer identifies the latter as those who also "dishonoured Christ his Apostles and Prophets, putting them to shamefull deaths." Insisting that the same hatred produces both misogyny and anti-Christian deeds leads the poet to the positive association of women and the Christian faith. Not only have "wise and virtuous women" been God's scourges to punish evil men, but most important, they surrounded Christ in his ministry.... Advocating the restoration of women to their rightful place necessitates not only praise of great ladies, but a recitation of the deeds of Christ and of women, to show how the one imitates the other. This task Lanyer fulfills in the second part of her work, the poem, *Salve Deus Rex Judaeorum*.

Lanyer organized *Salve Deus* to unite women's piety with the principal story of Christianity. Of the 230 stanzas, the central 123 (stanzas 42-165) relate the main events of the Crucifixion drawn from Scripture; woven in and around this narrative is extended praise of God and Christ and a related series of seven encomia on the Countess of Cumberland. Indeed, fully one quarter of the stanzas praise the Countess, a number that might seem inappropriate to a poem on Christ's Passion had the dedications not already established the links between God and woman. The Countess's spiritual life is sketched in her stanzas: her understanding, her contempt for the world, her love of God

and his creation, her devotion to the Bridegroom, her imitation of Christ, and her apotheosis.

Notably, Lanyer's encomia do not celebrate the military deeds, power, or public virtue appropriate to men, but the piety, humility, charity, faith, patience, and constancy of women. The Countess of Cumberland, who played little part in the politics and powermongering of the day, who, unlike some great ladies, influenced no great actions, who patiently endured her afflictions, who retired from court to country—surely the most uneventful life for encomium—appears instead as the perfect Christian. Her great drama is the Passion of Christ itself, and to Lanyer her participation in it surpasses any possible worldly achievement.

Why Lanyer chose the Countess of Cumberland as the pivotal personality in the poem may relate to the protection the countess gave the poet in her youth.... The countess seems to have inspired a ... veneration in Lanyer, who presents her as a perfect Christian, a living woman to admire and emulate. Not only will she appear as a bride of Christ, but also as a mother-figure similar to the Virgin Mary and as an inspirer of divine poetry.

Adapting the conventions of praise to the entirely spiritual qualities of her subject, in her first address to the countess, Lanyer strikes the theme that will echo throughout the poem: how the countess's life subjects earth's temporary afflictions to heaven's immortal beauties. The poet exalts the countess by placing her in succession to the now-canonized Elizabeth.... The countess appears here and later as one who has suffered, but her afflictions actually prepare her for glory at the Day of Judgment when "thou as the Sunne shalt shine; or much more cleare." Because the countess possesses a truly Christian soul, meditating on her brings the poet to contemplate God's power and justice which must reward the righteous and punish sinners.... The deep division between good and evil, between the "blest" countess and the godlessness around her, thematically unites the poet's praise of the lady and her praise of Christ to which the poem is progressing.

The second encomium on the countess pursues her rejection of the world, founded on her "constant faith" which scorns equally "base affliction" and "prowd pomps." Her retirement from court to country represents her "leaving the world, before the world leaves thee" and reveals the countess as "the wonder of our wanton age," serving heaven's king before earth's. Her life teaches others to love virtue rather than the world, "that great Enchantresse."

That the countess's praiseworthy attributes are not her beauty or position, but her gifts of character, her spiritual virtues, leads Lanyer to a topic often considered by male poets, an "Invective against outward beauty unaccompanied with virtue." Physical beauty, "that pride of Nature" brings only danger for it causes men to "seeke, attempt, plot and devise, / How they may overthrow the chastest Dame." Lanyer's examples range from Helen of Troy and Lucrece to Cleopatra, Rosamund, and Matilda, all betrayed by their outward beauty. But like the martyred Matilda, the countess is filled with the grace of God who is the "Husband" of her soul and "dying made her Dowager of all; / Nay more, Co-heire of that eternall blisse." In this third encomium, which establishes the primacy of the spirit, she figures as the bride of Christ, one of the faithful whom he died to save, bringing the poet to her central meditation on the Passion.

To praise fully the Christian soul, Lanyer must return to its source, Christ Himself, and it is at this point in the poem that she clearly dedicates herself as a divine poet.... Fully aware of the authority vested in "most holy Writ," she insists her language will not venture beyond the limits of doctrine; nor does she seek poetic fame, but rather writes for God's glory, "in plainest words to showe, / The Matter which I seeke to undergoe." Like other Reformist writers who chose the "plainest words" to convey scriptural truth, Lanyer's "unworthy" persona wants a crystal-clear style to convey Christ's story. Thus, she asks God "t'illuminate my Spirit," announcing her vocation as a preacher of the Word, guided by divine inspiration.

Lanyer's insistence that she will adhere strictly to doctrine rationalizes her feminine perspective on the Passion, for although Christ is the central hero of the next 123 stanzas, he is surrounded primarily by women; by the visionary wife of Pilate, by a redeemed Eve, the Daughters of Jerusalem, the Virgin Mary, and the Countess of Cumberland. Through her vivid retelling of Scripture, Lanyer makes her case for women's essential place in Christianity.

The narrative begins on the dark night in the garden of Gethsemane, and adhering closely to the gospels, Lanyer feelingly recreates the betrayals and the torments of Christ that ultimately lead to human redemption. She particularly details how the disciples abandon Christ: protesting that they will never forsake him, "They do like men, when dangers overtake them." Although "men" may well be the generic term here, it recalls men's betrayal of women earlier cited, and in light of Lanyer's subsequent praise of the Daughters of Jerusalem, her intention may well be to criticize the sex. She deepens the disciples' disgrace by passionately praising Christ, listing His names and attributes, from "beauty of the World, Heavens chiefest glory," to "Water of Life," "Guide of the Just," and "Ransomer of Sin." Here Lanyer reveals the source of all praise in her work and contrasts His glory with the cruel behavior of the judges, particularly Caiaphas and Pontius Pilate.

Just before the drama of Pilate's decision, in a vivid and arresting passage, Lanyer introduces the voice of his wife who pleads with her husband not to condemn Christ, specifically because such a fault far overshadows Eve's sin.... This section, balanced between blame for men, particularly Adam, and praise for Eve and her daughters, shows how Lanyer assigns the sexes distinct characteristics, as did the patristic commentators, but by contrast exploits that tradition to redeem women and to refurbish them as Christians. The defense of Eve relies on the classic definition of woman as the lesser creature, one who "was simply good, and had no powre to see." Her "undiscerning Ignorance and Weaknesse" allowed the serpent to deceive her, although her pure heart intended no ill. Adam, by contrast, must accept blame, because he had strength and knew God's commandments even before Eve was created. While Lanyer follows traditional interpretation in admitting Eve's deception, she insists that Eve sinned "for knowledge sake" but that Adam sinned for the worse motivation, only because "the fruit was faire." Deliberately omitting any rationale for Adam, such as St. Augustine's admission of Adam's "social love" for Eve, Lanyer intends through Pilate's wife, to exonerate Eve

"whose fault was onely too much love, / Which made her give this present to her Deare." And in an ironic twist, Pilate's wife remarks, "Yet Men will boast of knowledge, which he tooke / From Eves faire hand, as from a learned Booke." Thus locating the origin of all knowledge in a woman's act, even if it does corroborate her inherent weakness, Lanyer attempts to undermine the male stranglehold on learning by suggesting that men owe it all to women.

More important, in the moral realm, Lanyer distinguishes between Eve's simplicity and the malice with which Pilate will betray Christ. Although Eve is blameworthy, Pilate's deed will be the worst sin of all time, so bad that men can no longer declare themselves superior to women, and "your fault beeing greate, why should you disdaine / Our beeing your equals, free from tyranny?" Almost imperceptibly, the voice of Pilate's wife merges into the poet's, as Lanyer vigorously attacks Pilate, using traditional material to bolster her case for women.... As a representative man, Pilate can bring no credit to his sex, precisely serving Lanyer's enthusiastically biased purpose.

Sharply contrasted to this extended vituperation is the description of Christ going to His death, His attributes humanly mirrored in the "teares of the daughters of Jerusalem" and in "the sorrow of the virgin Marie." Christ professes "virtue, patience, grace, love, piety"—a list already familiar to readers to treatises on women's education, but here placed firmly in context at the very heart of Christian doctrine. The lesson of the Cross is "how by suffering he could conquer more / Than all the kings that ever liv'd before," a doctrine that exalts spiritual strength over physical might, and that in Lanyer's view gives women their particular prominence. She represents this idea in the poem by immediately introducing the weeping women, the only ones in the multitude to pity Christ and to receive from their Lord, Love, and King "mercie, grace, and love." ... [Again] the poet exalts womankind in her praise of [the Virgin] Mary, extended in an apostrophe of over fourteen stanzas to include all the main events of Mary's life.

Mary's stature derives from her essential femininity as "Mother of our Lord," and "most beauteous Queene of womankind." Although the Virgin had long been an important image for Christian women, Lanyer avoids Catholic doctrine but still designates Mary as a shining example for her sex. She asserts an acceptably Protestant role for the Virgin as the archetypal true Christian woman: chaste, obedient, humble, pious.... Like Christine de Pisan's Virgin, she appears as the supreme example of a woman empowered by chastity in a male world.

Through Mary, Lanyer moves to her depiction of Christ's death, vividly painted and decried. And at this most painful and dramatic moment, Lanyer turns again to the Countess of Cumberland, inviting her as the "Spouse of Christ" to view the Passion with "the eie of Faith," to feel both grief and joy as "thy Love" dies, "his count'nance pale, yet ... sweet." By summoning the countess here, the poet makes her an analogy to the Virgin Mary, an example to all women, and brings her into complete sympathy with the love and self-sacrifice of Christ.

The narrative proceeds with the effects of the Crucifixion on earth, the descent from the Cross, the Entombment, and the coming of the Marys to discover the Resurrection. Lanyer's allegory at this point reminds her readers of the female imagery attached to the Church. . . . While this image is fundamental in Christian theology, in this context it is notable that the Church and the ideal woman possess many of the same qualities and that both belong to patriarchal systems that mirror each other: the marriage of Christ to the Church is the model for human marriage. But the only "human" marriage Lanyer celebrates here is that of the countess and her Bridegroom, Christ, a marriage that attempts radically to redefine the importance of female spirituality. Most naturally, Lanyer turns to the Canticles as a source of imagery, for the Song of Songs had long been allegorized as the love of Christ and the Church, or Christ and the individual soul, or even Christ and the Virgin Mary. (pp. 189-99)

The traditional Christian allegory of the Song of Songs opens up a source of imagery to Lanyer that allows her more literally to glorify a Christian woman as the particular beloved of Christ, not only because of her spiritual beauties but for what she does in the world—caring for others and dispensing charity. Praise devolves on her not only for contemplating the Passion, but for her *gestae*, for performing works of mercy. (p. 200)

From the beginning of the poem, Lanyer felt sure of the countess's immortality, here expressed in the most exalted imagery. Now ending her work, the poet reveals that the countess's "excellence hath rais'd my sprites to write," that she has inspired a poem on immortality and enabled the poet to overcome her insufficiency. In this respect, the countess again acts as a mother-figure, giving birth and nurture to poetry itself. (p. 201)

Nature had a significant function in the dedications to *Salve Deus*. In her dedication to Queen Anne, Lanyer had quite conventionally described Nature as the creation of God and as the source of Art; but it was also the "Mother of perfection" and Lanyer particularly claimed its protection for her own work. In her praise of the Countess of Pembroke, she had created a perfect natural setting, a woodland spring where Art and Nature existed equally in "sweet unitie," and she had designated it as the place where the countess's holy Psalms might appropriately be sung. In the last part of her poem, "The Description of Cooke-ham," Lanyer retrieves these earlier allusions in a poem that transforms a literary landscape into a redeemed Eden inhabited by three women: the countess, her daughter, and the poet. The countess's presence blesses the landscape, her daughter, and the poet, who is enabled to write her poem in praise of divine virtue. Again, Lanyer draws an analogy between nature sanctified by a godly woman and the creation of art. The poem is, however, retrospective, a farewell to Cookham, and so its prevailing tone is elegiac. It seems that the vision of paradise, of a redeemed nature, is at best momentary, and when her redeemed Eve withdraws, the landscape and the poet must alter radically.

Implicitly comparing the pastoral landscape to Eden, Lanyer composes a parable of the Fall: at first, the landscape reflects an earthly paradise, but a special one where the female virtues flourish; however, unnamed outside forces, represented by Fortune, inevitably bring change, and the type of those virtues, the countess, must leave. Unlike the poet's exalted mood at the end of *Salve Deus*

when she celebrated the countess's virtue from a celestial perspective, the mood here suits the insufficiency of the world to sustain grace, and in the last part of "The Description," both Nature and the poet mourn the passing of such perfection, the poet hoping that at least its memory may live for future ages in the poem itself.

From the beginning of the poem, Lanyer couches her description of Cookham as a farewell, both to the source of her poetic inspiration and to a place of pleasure, grace, and virtue. But the place's pleasures, she reminds the countess, are as "fleeting worldly Joyes that could not last: / Or as divine shadowes of celestial pleasures, / which are desir'd above all earthly treasures." These images dominate the poem, urging the reader to see the beauty of this world as a testament to its Creator, and yet to recognize the evanescence of the earthly realm. From the beginning, too, the countess, "Mistress of that Place," represents the source of grace; through the course of the poem, Lanyer clarifies its Christian foundation, which echoes the first two parts of *Salve Deus* by imaging the beneficent and nurturing influence of the countess upon the landscape and its occupants, her daughter and the poet. Her departure defaces and desolates the setting and leaves the poet to mourn, suggesting the spiritual death of a world devoid of such grace and virtue.

"The Description of Cooke-ham" combines the poetic traditions of the *locus amoenus*, pastoral, and praise of a patron; it offers a serious challenge to Jonson's "To Penshurst" as the first English example of a country-house poem. Like Jonson, Lanyer recalls classical precedents and creates an idealized and moralized landscape as part of her praise. She, however, proceeds beyond encomium to a vision of absence and loss because earth cannot possess the Edenic perfection of virtue represented by the countess. (pp. 201-03)

Because she is a vessel for God's grace, when the countess withdraws, she leaves behind an unregenerate world, filled with images of death. Cookham without the countess reflects a world without God's love and grace to redeem it. While *Salve Deus* drew an ideal picture of a world blessed by women's Christian virtue, "The Description of Cooke-ham" shows not only the ideal but the misery of its absence.

Only in the poet's "unworthy breast" will the countess's virtues live on, "tying my heart to her by those rich chaines." And when the poet dies, it may be only her poem that memorializes the Edenic Cookham. In her final lines, Lanyer does not offer much hope that her exultant vision of woman's Christian virtue will hold sway in the fallen world.

"The Description of Cooke-ham," like the dedications and *Salve Deus Rex Judaeorum*, is a poem densely packed and intensely written. As avowals of the importance of feminine virtue, the three works succeed not through reasoning, but through the poetry of faith and revelation. And poetry is central to Lanyer's piety and her attempts to establish the spiritual preeminence of women. Only by availing herself of a rich range of poetic forms, images, and allusions could she create a canvas large enough to impress and convince her readers. Her great centerpiece, the Passion of Christ, serves as both doctrinal and poetic pattern for the rest of the poem, presenting as it does the archetypal subject of praise, the image of perfect virtue. By her mix of genres, Lanyer achieves an effect similar to that of a monumental triptych: the large central panel conveys the crucial doctrine by revelation of a divine event; each side panel relates that divine image to the human landscape and to particular lives.

In this light, Lanyer's adherence to a "natural" poetry can be more fully understood. Having found that male "Scholers" "by Art do write," she identified the source of her own work as Nature. Considering that she must use conventional poetic forms and figures, her meaning may not at first be clear. Both poetically and philosophically, Lanyer wished to circumvent masculine thinking and writing about women, and to return to what she envisioned as the source. To redeem women, she claimed the innocence of the first woman, and identified feminine virtue with Christ's virtues. To alter the traditional separation between woman and God, as a poet she mixed genres, interrupted sequence, and juxtaposed high matter with low. As a result, her poem cannot easily be classified according to conventional kinds. In other words, in following Nature as the source of her Art, the poet used what she needed at the moment to convey her doctrine, whether it was encomium, narrative, or elegy, or whether she wished to move from a Christian's love for Christ to Cleopatra's love for Antony in one stanza. If this far from seamless method does violence to Renaissance poetic decorum, and may even annoy the modern reader, Lanyer gains the power of surprise and drama in her attempts to reach and teach her audience. One may view her as she conveys herself at the beginning as a naive writer "of slender skill," and "all unlearned," or by contrast, as a fit contemporary of John Donne and Ben Jonson. The poet who married the Countess of Cumberland to her bridegroom, Christ, with the language of Canticles, and who may be responsible for initiating the country-house poem in English, is, after all, a woman who, despite her disavowals, did not fear to tread where angels walked. (pp. 206-07)

Elaine V. Beilin, "The Feminization of Praise: Aemilia Lanyer," in her Redeeming Eve: Women Writers of the English Renaissance, *Princeton University Press, 1987, pp. 177-207.*

ADDITIONAL BIBLIOGRAPHY

Mahl, Mary R., and Koon, Helene, eds. "Aemilia Lanier." In their *The Female Spectator: English Women Writers before 1800*, pp. 73-5. Bloomington and London: Indiana University Press, 1977.
    Brief biographical sketch of Lanyer.

Rowse, A. L. Introduction to his *Shakespeare's Sonnets: The Problems Solved*, pp. ix-xxv. London: Macmillan Press, 1984.
    Asserts Lanyer's place in Shakespeare's sonnets as the Dark Lady, labeling her "the outspoken feminist of the age."

Schoenbaum, S. "Shakespeare, Dr. Forman, and Dr. Rowse." In his *Shakespeare and Others*, pp. 54-79. Washington: Folger Shakespeare Library, 1985.
    Considers and then rejects Rowse's Dark Lady theory, concluding she was but "another dark lady."

George Lyttelton (First Baron Lyttelton of Frankley)

1709-1773

English poet, prose writer, and historian.

Popularly dubbed "Good Lord Lyttelton" for his personal and political probity, Lyttelton was a prominent English citizen, statesman, author, and literary patron. Although his works include both prose and poetry, he has been most readily associated with a single elegy, *To the Memory of a Lady Lately Deceased: A Monody.* While Lyttelton was the literary colleague of Henry Fielding and Alexander Pope, among other prominent figures of the day, his own literary achievements were surpassed by those of his contemporaries, and he has been relegated to but a small place in the history of English literature. Nevertheless, the integrity, forthrightness, and versatility evident in his works—characteristics here wholly representative of his time—have established Lyttelton, in the words of an anonymous critic, as a man "whose character is to be estimated by the combined excellence of his various gifts and talents."

The author was born the eldest son of Sir Thomas Lyttelton in Hagley, Worcestershire. He was educated at Eton and at Christ Church, Oxford, distinguishing himself as a scholar although, like many young gentlemen of his day, he did not take a degree from the university. After leaving Oxford he enjoyed the traditional grand tour of the continent and, upon returning to England, saw his first significant verse, *The Progress of Love, in Four Eclogues*, published in 1732, followed in 1735 by the prose work *Letters from a Persian in England to His Friend at Ispahan.* But Lyttelton, like others in his family, chose to pursue a political, not a literary, career. He became equerry and subsequently secretary to the Prince of Wales and was elected to Parliament, joining the ranks opposing First Minister Robert Walpole. Lyttelton, a staunch Whig, quickly achieved mixed prominence in the House of Commons both as leader of the opposition and for his unsophisticated candor—candor that, coupled with Lyttelton's awkward appearance and distracted demeanor, drew waggish and even sneering remarks from the press and from his peers. Thought by many to have been the butt of Lord Chesterfield's epithet "respectable Hottentot" (though this identification has since been debated), Lyttelton was often lampooned in this sort of vein. Indeed Chesterfield, in a letter to his son underscoring the importance of social elegance, depicted Lyttelton in a portrait calculated to discourage imitation: Lyttelton "does not know his most intimate acquaintance by sight, or answers them as if they were at cross purposes. He leaves his hat in one room, his sword in another, and would leave his shoes in a third, if his buckles, though awry, did not save them." Chesterfield added, however: "I sincerely value and esteem him for his parts, learning and virtue: but, for the soul of me, I cannot love him in company." Still, though eventually losing the preferment of the Prince of Wales, Lyttelton discharged the responsibilities of several elevated positions in addition to his duties in Parliament and managed to exert influence as a member of the small but powerful political faction known as the Cobhamites. Although he opposed repealing the Stamp Act and favored a mailed-fist policy

George Lyttelton

with the increasingly troublesome American colonies, Lyttelton also urged a reduction in the size of Britain's standing army in 1739 and spoke against the parliamentary privilege of writing and publishing seditious libels in 1763.

In 1742, while closely enmeshed in politics, Lyttelton married Lucy Fortescue, with whom he had a son and two daughters. According to Samuel Johnson, who included the author in his celebrated *Lives of the English Poets*, Lyttelton "appears to have lived in the highest degree of connubial felicity" for five years before his wife died in childbirth. Lyttelton's loss was not only keenly felt but eloquently transmitted in his best-known work, the *Monody*, published in 1747. In the same year, having resolved doubts entertained from his youth and thus turning from deism to Christianity, he also published *Observations on the Conversion and Apostleship of St. Paul in a Letter to Gilbert West.* Although he remarried two years later, Lyttelton was unable to regain the domestic contentment he had previously known, so the union soon ended in separation. After his father's death, Lyttelton inherited a baron's title and a sizable estate. In 1756 the peerage was conferred upon him and, thereafter removed from political turbulence, he sat in the House of Lords. Throughout his remaining years at Hagley Park, the rural retreat that afforded him great pleasure, Lyttelton entertained such notables as Pope, Fielding (who dedicated *Tom Jones* to him), William Shenstone, and James Thomson, serving not only as host but as a generous patron to the last-named author as well. Leisure also enabled Lyttelton to resume his literary endeavors without interruption. His *Dialogues of the Dead* was published in 1760 and *The History of the Life of King Henry the Second and the Age in Which He Lived*, a protracted effort which underwent much revision and ran to four volumes, was completed and published two years before his death.

Unless he intended it slyly, Samuel Johnson apparently exempted the *Monody* from his otherwise trenchant estimation of Lyttelton's writings in his *Lives of the English Poets*, remarking only that the author, after his first wife's death, "solaced his grief by writing a long poem to her memory." The *Monody*, however, survives not merely as an expression of personal loss but also, according to S. C. Roberts and others, as "a monument of eighteenth-century domesticity." In it, Lucy Fortescue represents the very beau ideal of wife and mother, a woman who is gentle, modest, virtuous, and who, preferring a quiet country life to the dissipations of city or court, is utterly content to augment her husband's happiness. The piece combines Lyttelton's warm feeling for external nature with classical and pastoral allusions. Though such allusions are commonplace in much eighteenth-century verse, some critics of Lyttelton's work have strongly censured his use of them in the *Monody*. The poet Thomas Gray, Lyttelton's contemporary, found such trappings obtrusive where the simpler (and, to Gray, underrepresented) elements of nature, sorrow, and tenderness should preside. A later critic, John Wilson Croker, challenged what he termed the outward "felicity of composition" in the poem, questioning the work's very "depth of grief" and concluding that "it no doubt existed in [Lyttelton's] heart, but it did not flow through his pen." On the whole, however, the *Monody* has been deemed a moving expression of private grief, an effective adaptation of the traditional pastoral elegy.

Lyttelton patterned *Letters from a Persian in England* after Charles-Louis de Secondat Montesquieu's *Lettres persanes* (1721; *Persian Letters*, 1722), which had earlier been instrumental in popularizing the reportial pseudo-foreign letter as a legitimate genre in France and England. In Lyttelton's epistolary piece Selim, a Persian in England, relates to his friend Mirza, in Ispahan, his observations on the social, political, and intellectual phenomena of the country in which he is a visitor. The *Letters* understandably became a showcase for Lyttelton's own perceptions of contemporary affairs. While most critics, including Johnson, have allowed for the author's youth in their overall evaluations of the work, they have not excused his inconsistent narrative technique. As Rose Mary Davis has observed, Selim "is not very Persian. Lyttelton is less adroit than his French model at keeping the disguise on: and sometimes it falls off entirely, and we meet face to face the young Englishman at the threshold of his political career." Because of similarities in structure, Lyttelton's *Letters* has been frequently compared with Oliver Goldsmith's *Citizen of the World* (1762), nearly always to the advantage of Goldsmith's work. Yet the *Letters* retains the interest of commentators thanks to its colorful glimpse into the conditions of another time and its equally memorable profile of Lyttelton as eighteenth-century social satirist and reformer.

The *Dialogues of the Dead*, which Johnson termed "rather effusions than compositions," also relies heavily on precedent, borrowing from works of Lucian, François Fénelon, and Bernard Le Bovier de Fontenelle. The piece unites continents and centuries to present fanciful conversations among prominent individuals on issues ranging from systems of sovereignty to literary trends and gastronomic tastes. The *Dialogues*, like the *Letters*, serves as a vehicle for Lyttelton's own views. Its philosophical solemnity—couched frequently in platitudes—is not unrelieved by satiric wit and even whimsical humor, especially where lighter topics are treated. The *Dialogues* was well received upon its appearance in 1760, although critics past and present have faulted its conspicuous authorial intrusion.

While the *History of Henry the Second* was recommended as "a learned and honest book" by Robert Southey, it has nonetheless been overwhelmingly determined, as Austin Dobson has noted, Lyttelton's "*magnum opus*—great by its quantity rather than its quality." Better than a decade in the writing and several years in revision and printing, the voluminous *History* is grounded in painstaking scholarship. However, because of the author's anxiety to gratify punctillious critics, it largely disintegrates into a recitation of colorless facts. Ironically, Lyttelton's *History* has been most roundly disparaged by those whom he especially endeavored to please.

In Johnson's *Lives of the English Poets*, Lyttelton is depicted as "a man of literature and judgement" who devoted "part of his time to versification." By his diversification Lyttelton exemplified ideals fundamental to his time. He today remains a figure who, while credited with certain literary accomplishments, is remembered less for these than for his thorough embodiment of the age in which he lived.

PRINCIPAL WORKS

Blenheim (poetry) 1728
The Progress of Love, in Four Eclogues (poetry) 1732
Advice to a Lady (poetry) 1733
Letters from a Persian in England to His Friend at Ispahan (fictional letters) 1735
Observations on the Conversion and Apostleship of St. Paul, in a Letter to Gilbert West (religious tract) 1747
To the Memory of a Lady Lately Deceased: A Monody (poetry) 1747
Dialogues of the Dead (fictional dialogues) 1760
The History of the Life of King Henry the Second and of the Age in Which He Lived. 4 vols. (history) 1767-71
The Works of George Lord Lyttelton (poetry, prose, and history) 1774
Memoirs and Correspondence of George, Lord Lyttelton (prose and letters) 1845

DAVID HUME (letter date 1754)

[*Hume was an eighteenth-century Scottish philosopher whose theories concerning the nature of knowledge and ideas constitute a significant contribution to philosophical speculation. Such works as* An Enquiry concerning Human Understanding *(1748) and* An Enquiry concerning the Principals of Morals *(1751) remain highly influential philosophical treatises. In the following excerpt from a letter written in 1754 to the Abbé Le Blanc, Hume offers a brief, balanced assessment of* Henry II *and of Lyttelton's literary work in general.*]

Sir George Lyttelton, who is an Author of Taste, has wrote the **Reign of Henry the Second;** & it will be publishd the Winter after the next. The Period is not interesting, nor is Sir George's Genius very strong, tho' it be polish'd. Notwithstanding the Expectations of the Public, this may prove but a middling Production. But he is a man of Rank & Figure, which encreases his Vogue. His Poetry is better than his Prose. (p. 209)

> *David Hume, in a letter to Jean-Bernard Le Blanc on October 24, 1754, in his* The Letters of David Hume, Vol. I, *edited by J. Y. T. Greig, Oxford at the Clarendon Press, 1932, pp. 206-09.*

GEORGE EDWARD AYSCOUGH   (essay date 1776)

[*In the following excerpt from a dedication prefacing the third edition of* The Works of George Lord Lyttelton *(1776), Ayscough, Lyttelton's principal publisher, endorses the writings of Lyttelton, particularly his juvenilia.*]

Every line of these tracts **The Works of George Lord Lyttelton** conveys the most useful instructions and admonitions to mankind, and are calculated to aid the great causes of publick and private virtue.

If it should be asked, Why I chose to publish the juvenile letters of his lordship [George Lyttelton], written during his travels through France and Italy? Perhaps it would be sufficient to answer, Because they are replete with profitable and entertaining accounts of the political transactions of those times, together with the most sensible and pertinent remarks on the state of Europe at that period. But I shall further add, that I have stronger and more weighty reasons for their publication, not only because they are the produce of the best of *heads*, but because they are effusions from the best of *hearts*; and because they are the early and wonderful proofs of his generosity, piety, and above all his filial reverence; and may be justly deemed the first ebullitions of virtues, which, being afterwards matured by age and experience, extended their beneficent influence over mankind in general, and were more immediately felt by the inhabitants of this free country. (pp. vi-viii)

> *George Edward Ayscough, "To the Right Honourable Thomas, Lord Lyttelton, Baron of Frankley,"* in The Works of George Lord Lyttelton, Vol. I, *edited by George Edward Ayscough, third edition, J. Dodsley, 1776, pp. v-ix.*

SAMUEL JOHNSON   (essay date 1781)

[*Johnson is one of the outstanding figures in English literature and a leader in the history of textual and aesthetic criticism. Popularly known in his own day as the "Great Cham of Literature," Johnson was a prolific lexicographer, essayist, poet, and critic whose lucid and extensively illustrated* Dictionary of the English Language *(1755) and* Prefaces, Biographical and Critical, to the Works of the English Po-*

ets *(10 vols., 1779-81; reissued in 1783 as* The Lives of the Most Eminent English Poets) *were new departures in lexicography and biographical criticism, respectively. As a literary critic he was neither a rigid theorist nor a strict follower of neoclassical rules, tending instead to rely on common sense and empirical knowledge. Basically skeptical in all matters but religion and always ready to shift his argument's ground if necessary, he had in his criticism one criterion in mind: the power of a work to please and instruct. At his best a direct and pungent prosodist, Johnson was a perceptive and acute judge of works' defects as well as merits, but because of his forceful style his listings of defects are often more memorable than his extensive general praise. In the following excerpt from* Lives of the English Poets, *originally published in 1781, Johnson appraises Lyttelton's representative writings.*]

[George Lyttelton] was a very early writer, both in verse and prose. His **Progress of Love**, and his **Persian Letters**, were both written when he was very young; and, indeed, the character of a young man is very visible in both. The Verses cant of shepherds and flocks, and crooks dressed with flowers; and the **Letters** have something of that indistinct and headstrong ardour for liberty which a man of genius always catches when he enters the world, and always suffers to cool as he passes forward. (p. 465)

Politicks did not . . . so much engage him as to withhold his thoughts from things of more importance. He had, in the pride of juvenile confidence, with the help of corrupt conversation, entertained doubts of the truth of Christianity; but he thought the time now come when it was no longer fit to doubt or believe by chance, and applied himself seriously to the great question. His studies, being honest, ended in conviction. He found that religion was true, and what he had learned he endeavoured to teach, by **Observations on the Conversion of St. Paul**; a treatise to which infidelity has never been able to fabricate a specious answer. (p. 467)

Lyttelton published his **Dialogues of the Dead**, which were very eagerly read, though the production rather, as it seems, of leisure than of study, rather effusions than compositions. The names of his persons too often enable the reader to anticipate their conversation; and when they have met, they too often part without any conclusion. He has copied *Fénelon* more than *Fontenelle*.

When they were first published, they were kindly commended by the *Critical Reviewers*; and poor Lyttelton, with humble gratitude, returned, in a note which I have read, acknowledgements which can never be proper, since they must be paid either for flattery or for justice. (p. 468)

His last literary production was his **History of Henry the Second**, elaborated by the searches and deliberations of twenty years, and published with such anxiety as only vanity can dictate. (p. 469)

Lord Lyttelton's Poems are the works of a man of literature and judgement, devoting part of his time to versification. They have nothing to be despised, and little to be admired. Of his **Progress of Love**, it is sufficient blame to say that it is pastoral. His blank verse in **Blenheim** has neither much force nor much elegance. His little performances, whether Songs or Epigrams, are sometimes spritely, and sometimes insipid. His epistolary pieces have a smooth equability, which cannot much tire, because they are short, but which seldom *elevates* or *surprizes*. But from this censure ought to be excepted his *Advice to Belinda*, which, though for the most part written when he was very young, contains much truth and much prudence, very elegantly and vigorously expressed, and shews a mind attentive to life, and a power of poetry which cultivation might have raised to excellence. (pp. 471-72)

Samuel Johnson, "Lyttelton," in his Lives of the English Poets, *Vol. II, Oxford University Press, London, 1906, pp. 465-72.*

ROBERT SOUTHEY   (letter date 1805)

[*A late-eighteenth and early-nineteenth-century English man of letters, Southey was a key member of the so-called Lake School of poetry, a group which included the celebrated authors William Wordsworth and Samuel Taylor Coleridge. Southey's poetry consists mainly of short verse, ballads, and epics, many of which are notable for their novel versification and meter. His prose writings—which are generally more highly praised than his poetry—include ambitious histories, biographies, and conservative social commentaries. Today Southey is primarily remembered as a conservative theorist and as the biographer of such figures as Horatio Nelson, Thomas More, and John Wesley. In the following excerpt from a letter to his friend John May, he recommends Henry II as a reliable chronicle of English history.*]

Of English history we have little that is good;—I speak of modern compilers, being ignorant, for the most part, of the monkish annalists. Turner's *History of the Anglo-Saxons* ought to be upon your shelves. . . . so much new information was probably never laid before the public in any one historical publication; Lord Lyttelton's *Henry II.* is a learned and honest book. Having particularised these two, the 'only faithful found,' it may safely be said, that of all the others those which are the oldest are probably the best. What Milton and Bacon have left, have, of course, peculiar and first-rate excellence. (p. 341-42)

Robert Southey, in an extract from a letter to John May on August 5, 1805, in his The Life and Correspondence of Robert Southey, *Vol. II, edited by Rev. Charles Cuthbert Southey, second edition, Longman, Brown, Green, and Longmans, 1850, pp. 340-42.*

THE GENTLEMAN'S MAGAZINE   (essay date 1845)

[*In the following excerpt, an anonymous critic presents Lyttelton as a comprehensive, rather than superior, figure of his time.*]

[To] form a due estimate of his character, Lyttelton's talents and acquirements in literature are to be added to his political knowledge, his parliamentary experience, and his powers as a calm and argumentative debater. He is one of those persons whose character is to be estimated by the combined excellence of his various gifts and talents. In no branch of natural endowments or acquired knowledge did he stand in the foremost ranks among his contemporaries. As a statesman he was not distinguished; to the higher branches of oratory he did not aspire; and his poetry, though bearing marks of elegance and refinement, of a taste cultivated and formed on the best and purest models, has little in it that can satisfy more than casual perusals; but his *Conversion of St. Paul*, and his *History of Henry the Second*, are the firmest and strongest monuments to his fame. The reasoning of the former treatise is ably and elegantly conducted through a series of sound and well-connected arguments; and the latter is one of the most learned histories we possess in our language. It is not to be compared to the brilliant pages of Hume and Gibbon, or to the expanded eloquence of Robertson; it is formed upon a different model, and with other views; it displays great research, great knowledge of the laws and constitution of the country, of the history of the times it treats of, and it has received the valuable testimony to its excellence from the most able and impartial judges. (p. 443)

A review of "Memoirs and Correspondence of George Lord Lyttelton, from 1734 to 1773," in The Gentleman's Magazine, *n.s. Vol. XXIV, November, 1845, pp. 443-60.*

[JOHN WILSON CROKER]   (essay date 1846)

[*Croker made extensive contributions to the periodical the* Quarterly Review, *the most prominent conservative Tory organ of the early nineteenth century. While Croker was a noteworthy critic of literature and historical writings, he had a greater role in guiding the political direction of the* Quarterly Review. *Croker, who was First Secretary of the Admiralty and a friend to Tory leaders in government, so effectively channeled the government's views into the* Review *that, from 1830 to 1850, the journal was considered the voice of the old Tory party. After 1850, editors of the* Review *gradually tempered its political partisanship. In the following excerpt, Croker furnishes a predominantly perfunctory overview of Lyttelton's literary career.*]

At Eton is said to have been written . . . [Lyttelton's] *Soliloquy of a Beauty in the Country,* with an easy flow of verse and pleasantry, much, we think, beyond the ordinary powers of a schoolboy:—

Oh! what avails it to be young and fair,
To move with negligence—to dress with care?
What worth have all the charms our pride can boast,
If all in envious solitude be lost?
Where none admire, 'tis useless to excel,
Where none are beaux, 'tis vain to be a belle. . . .

This is lively, and although too obviously modelled on Pope, it has here and there a touch of reality that we suspect may have been furnished by the domestic scenes of Hagley. (pp. 225-26)

At Oxford [Lyttelton] continued to cultivate his literary taste, which, however, as with most young authors, expended itself in imitations—beyond the feeble elegance of which Lyttelton, indeed, never rose; nay, his earlier works are, we think, positively better than his last. Pope was then in the zenith of his deserved fame, and naturally the 'cynosure of *labouring* eyes,' and accordingly we find in the front of Lyttelton's poems, after the manner of Pope's Pastorals—the *Progress of Love, in four Eclogues*, addressed respectively to Pope—to Dodington ('who had himself written some very pretty love-verses, which have not been published')—to Edward Walpole, we presume a schoolfellow or fellow-student—and his own uncle Lord Cobham. This economical prodigality of adulation, by which the oil of dedication is spread over the largest possible surface, seems to have begun by Pope in his *Moral Essays,* and was followed by Lyttelton and by the greater names of Young and Thomson, who did little honour either to themselves or their patrons by these *allotments* of panegyric. Lyttelton's birth and station relieve him from the imputation of any unworthy motive; he was proud to be the friend and imitator of Pope, and was not sorry to gratify his private feelings by a public record of his friendships. His addresses to his friends are—unlike the sickening adulation of Young—short, inoffensive, and not inappropriate, but the eclogues themselves we abandon to Johnson's general and special condemnation of all such 'mock pastorals'—only adding that they would be still worse if they approached reality. Damon and Delia, crooks and flowers, are merely tiresome—Roger and Sukey, and the details of nearly the lowest and least intellectual scale of human life, would be intolerable; but we need not pursue this topic—we are in no danger of seeing the revival of either class of bucolics, and have done with authors who confessed to being 'sillier than their sheep.' (pp. 227-28)

In the ***Persian Letters,*** as in all his other works, Lyttelton is but an imitator:—the idea, the name, and some of the details are borrowed from the *Lettres Persannes* of the President Montesquieu—then in high repute. Johnson, impressed perhaps with the idea that they were written by an Oxonian of eighteen, treats them slightingly as too 'visibly the production of a very young man.' They would not, it is true, thirty years later, have added much to the fame which Lyttelton had, rather by his rank than his writings, attained; but they are, we think, no contemptible production even for the age of twenty-five; and they may still be read with amusement and some information as to the manners of the time. (p. 229)

Towards the close of his residence at Oxford, in the winter of 1727, he seems to have produced his blank—peculiarly blank—verses on ***Blenheim Castle,*** towards the due celebration of which he invokes the assistance of Minerva—patroness of arms and arts—who, in that double capacity, assisted Marlborough in winning the battle and Vanbrugh in building the house—while for the description of the park he relies on 'Thalia, Sylvan maid!' and likens the Duke himself to Alexander the Great. Amidst such common-places, one passage, though not original, is at least nursing. The old Whig Sibyl, Sarah, Duchess of Marlborough, reminds him of the gentle fascinations of Eve in Milton's Eden:

———But not alone
In the calm shades of honourable case
Great Marlbro' peaceful dwelt: indulgent heaven
Gave a companion of his softer hours,
*With whom conversing he forgot all change
Of fortune and of state;* and in her mind
Found greatness equal to his own, and loved
Himself in her.

                                              (pp. 230-31)

In 1742 Lyttelton married Miss Lucy Fortescue—the sister of Lord Clinton—of whom it may be said that she is remembered, after a lapse of a century, by a poem which is itself forgotten. She died in child-birth, of her third child, in 1747; and 'Lyttelton,' said Johnson, in the first edition of his *Life, 'solaced himself'* by writing a long poem to her memory. We agree with Mr. Phillimore that this awkward phrase was probably meant as a sneer, which Johnson afterwards softened into *'solaced his grief;'* but in spite of all the scanty approbation which Mr. Phillimore has picked up here and there on fragments of this celebrated ***Monody,***

we cannot persuade ourselves that it exhibited either much felicity of composition or much depth of grief. Not that we question his sorrow for his amiable young wife: it no doubt existed in his heart, but it did not flow through his pen; and the monody is on the whole in an exaggerated tone of devotion to her memory, which his early and unfortunate re-marriage with Miss Rich renders almost ludicrous. Even in an ordinary case, a re-marriage after so short an interval as a couple of years does seem to derogate a little from the tenderness and delicacy of a sincere grief—but he who calls in the public, with such peculiar solemnity, to be witnesses and admirers of his excess of sorrow, engages himself, under pain of ridicule, to a longer and more ascetic mourning. Mr. Phillimore quotes as praise, Campbell's opinion that 'the kids and fawns of the monody do not quite extinguish all appearance of sincere feelings.' Slender praise!—but worse than the 'kids and fawns' are, to our taste, *Petrarch and Laura,* and particularly that almost comic comparison, spread through two long stanzas, of the inferiority of Petrarch's loss, because, first, these Italian lovers had not been, as Mr. and Mrs. Lyttelton fortunately were, united in holy wedlock; and secondly, their 'mutual flames' had not been 'crowned with such dear pledges' as the connubial felicity of Hagley—Laura's eleven children having all been, no doubt, the legitimate offspring of her jealous husband, M. de Sade! This is bad enough; but there is an expression in one of his letters that strengthens our suspicion that his grief was more ostentatious than delicate. Dr. Doddridge (to and from whom this collection [***Memoirs and Correspondence of George, Lord Lyttelton, 1734 to 1773***] contains eighteen or twenty prosy letters) had addressed to Lyttelton some awkward and blundering effusions of condolence, in which the good man mentions, as constituting a kind of companionship in affliction, that his own wife, 'dear Mrs. Doddridge,' though 'looking *pure well,'* 'had been lately *alarmed* by the appearance of small-pox in Northampton:' in return to which twaddle Lyttelton assures the Rev. Doctor that he partakes his uneasiness for his—Doddridge's—'*Lucy*'—'your *Lucy!'* Could the grief be profound that so trivialized—so prostituted, we may almost say, a beloved name? We dare say Mrs. Doddridge (whose Christian name happened to be *Mercy*) was an excellent person, but that a man of taste and feeling, who it seems had never seen her, should have called her—*à propos* of an alarm about the small-pox in Northampton—by the hallowed name of his own 'late espoused saint,' so fondly beloved, so suddenly and so recently lost—seems to us stranger than even the comparison to *Laura.* (pp. 251-52)

Mr. Phillimore is, as usual, unlucky in his criticism. We know not why he should say that the ***Persian Letters*** and the ***Dialogues*** were written after the French model, according to the *fashion of the day*—the *days* being near thirty years asunder, and, neither, we think, more addicted to French models than earlier or later days. Nor can we discover what he means by saying that the ***Dialogues of the Dead*** are written on an *entirely French model:* they are no more on the French model than on the Greek. They imitate Lucian, as the two Frénchmen [Fénelon and Fontenelle] also did; but they are as thoroughly English, and as little French, as such a work can be; and the last paragraph of his eulogy, which supposes that all the variety of speakers have but *one style,* is no very great compliment, and has perhaps too much of truth in it. He complains, too, of Johnson's *'criticism'* on this work in these terms:—

Dr. Johnson's dislike of Lyttelton has been often mentioned, and it is visible in his *criticism* on this work. "That man," he said, "sat down to write a book to tell the world what the world had all his life been telling him." Must not this be the case with most books which are the fruit of reading, meditation, and experience of life?—and in what lies the intended sting of this remark?

Now this is unfair both to Johnson and Lyttelton: this *criticism* is not to be found where Mr. Phillimore's mention would lead us to look for it—in Johnson's *Life* of Lyttelton, where his judgment, though in our opinion below the merit of the work, is still favourable, and has none of the absurdity of the passage quoted by Mr. Phillimore; which passage is, in fact, nothing more than the recollection of a Dr. Maxwell of a remark made by Johnson in conversation thirty years before, and which, like several others of Dr. Maxwell's anecdotes, there is good reason to suspect of having been inaccurately remembered. Johnson of all men never could have stated as censure what would be in fact the highest praise of such a work—that it was produced by an accurate observation of mankind. On the whole, we are glad for once to adopt and indeed to carry a little higher Mr. Phillimore's approbation of the **Dialogues of the Dead,** of which we think that not merely 'some,' but most, if not all, 'are ingenious and amusing, as well as instructive'—the production of a well-stored and well-regulated mind—conceived with judgment, and executed with taste.

As to Lyttelton's largest work, the **History of Henry II.,** the letters now published prove that there was some reason for Johnson's short and contemptuous account of it—that 'it was elaborated by the searches and deliberations of twenty years, and published with such anxiety as only vanity can dictate.' It appears from a letter to Pope, that he had already made so much progress in it in 1741 as to hope to conclude it within two or three years. It was not, however, till 1764 that the first three volumes were published, and it was not completed till 1771; and it appears that his vanity was gratified by the approbation which an early communication of his volumes procured from some of his eminent and noble friends—Horace Walpole, Warburton, Lord Chesterfield, Lord Hardwicke.... Walpole repaid the confidence by a compliment that must have satisfied any vanity:—

I twice waited on you in Hill-street, to thank you for the great fa-your of lending me your **History,** which I am sorry I kept longer than you intended; but you must not wonder. I read it with as great attention as pleasure: it is not a book to skim, but to learn by heart, if one means to learn anything of England. You call it the **History of Henry II.**—it is literally the history of our Constitution, and will last much longer than I fear the latter will; for, alas! my Lord, your style, which will fix and preserve our language, cannot do what language cannot do—reform the nature of man.

Walpole's opinion, if here sincerely given, has not been ratified by posterity. The **History** is little read, and not even consulted as much as its laborious diligence deserves: but the period is too remote, and the subject too voluminously treated, for popularity; and the style, which Walpole so much extols, seems diffuse and flat to the taste of an age formed on the dazzling brilliancy of Gibbon, or the clearer and more mellowed colouring of Hume. (pp. 259-61)

[John Wilson Croker], *"Phillimore's 'Lord Lyttelton',"* in The Quarterly Review, *Vol. LXXVIII, No. CLV, June, 1846, pp. 216-67.*

W. J. COURTHOPE   (essay date 1905)

[*Courthope was an English educator, poet, literary critic, and biographer whose most notable work is his six-volume* History of English Poetry (1895-1910). *Described by Stuart P. Sherman as a confirmed classicist in poetical theory, he reacted against Romantic theory and practice and advocated a return to the heroic couplet and the satiric poetry characteristic of the age of Alexander Pope, whose collected works he edited. Courthope's criticism tends to center on the extent to which authors reflected the English character and traditions that had enabled the British empire to arise from the institutions of the Middle Ages. In the following excerpt from his* History of English Poetry, *Courthope briefly assesses Lyttelton's status as a poet of his age.*]

[Lyttelton's] place among the English poets is due much more to the influence which he exercised on others, through his taste and character, than to his original productions. Lord Waldegrave says of him:—

Sir George Lyttelton was an enthusiast in religion and politics; absent in business; not ready in a debate: and totally ignorant of the world.

It might have been added that he was also an enthusiast in literature. Full of generous feeling, he had not enough of original thought to let his personality penetrate through the forms of conventional expression. He is always an imitator; yet his work is of interest, as showing how strongly the social tendency to "nature-worship" was influencing Englishmen of education and accomplishment, who had been brought up within the strict limits of classical reserve. The following pathetic stanza from his **Monody,** which was much admired by Gray, may illustrate this remark:

In vain I look around
O'er all the well-known ground,
My Lucy's wonted footsteps to descry!
Where oft we used to walk,
Where oft in tender talk
We saw the summer sun go down the sky.

Nor by yon fountain's side,
Nor where its waters glide
Along the valley can she now be found,
In all the wide-stretched prospect's ample bound:
No more my mournful eye
Can aught of her espy,
But the sad sacred earth where her dear relics lie.

And in the lines addressed **To Mr. West at Wickham,** we see Lyttelton's appreciation of the "simplicity" praised by Shenstone, expressed without Shenstone's artificiality:—

Fair nature's sweet simplicity
With elegance refined,
Well in thy seat, my friend, I see,
But better in thy mind.
To both from courts and all their state
Eager I fly, to prove
Joys far above a courtier's fate,
Tranquillity and love.

(pp. 377-78)

W. J. Courthope, "The Early Romantic Movement in English Poetry," in his A History of English Poetry, Vol. V, *Macmillan and Co., Limited, 1905, pp. 360-420.*

AUSTIN DOBSON (essay date 1910)

[*Dobson, an English verse-writer and man of letters, wrote
a number of biographical prose works showing a close
knowledge of eighteenth-century society and literature. He is
best remembered for his series* Eighteenth Century Vignettes (1892-96) *and for his own* Poems on Several Occasions (1889). *In the following excerpt originally published in
the* National Review *in 1910 and included in Dobson's* Old
Kensington Palace and Other Papers, *Dobson surveys Lyttelton's major works.*]

[Lyttelton] wrote **Persian Letters** (after Montesquieu); he
wrote **Dialogues of the Dead** (after Lucian); both of which
found an honourable place in Harrison's *British Classicks.*
He wrote a compact and closely-reasoned pamphlet on the
Conversion of St. Paul; he wrote an extraordinarily conscientious and laborious **History of Henry II**. He also composed a sufficient number of minor poems to secure his
admission to those wonderful *Lives of the Poets* which tolerated Stepney and Fenton while they gave grudging
praise to Milton and Gray. He was the patron and friend
of Fielding and Thomson; he was 'ironed' by Chesterfield,
and he was libelled by Smollett. These things—it is submitted—are distinctions which should serve to justify
some passing inquiry into his personality as a man of letters. (pp. 174-75)

[Lyttelton's eclogues, **The Progress of Love**] are not their
poet's masterpieces; and belong distinctly—as much as
their model, Pope's own *Pastoral*—to the artificial
growths of Parnassus. One can well imagine old Johnson
blinking scornfully into that sham Arcadia, with its Delias
and Damons. They 'cant,' he says, 'of shepherds and
flocks, and crooks dressed with flowers' [see excerpt dated
1781]—things which, to be sure, were never to be encountered in Fleet Street. Lyttelton is far better in the **Advice
to a Lady**, of a year earlier. This is full of good sense, although the superior tone assumed by 'mere man,' if approved by Dorothy Osborne or Mary Evelyn, would
scarcely commend itself in the present day:

> Let e'en your *prudence* wear the pleasing dress
> Of care for *him*, and anxious *tenderness.*
> From kind concern about his weal or woe,
> Let each domestick duty seem to flow.
> The *household sceptre* if he bids you bear,
> Make it your pride his *servant* to appear:
> Endearing thus the common acts of life,
> The *mistress* still shall charm him in the *wife*,
> And wrinkled age shall unobserv'd come on,
> Before his eye perceives one beauty gone;
> E'en o'er your cold, your ever-sacred urn,
> His constant flame shall unextinguish'd burn.

From the last couplet the poet evidently expected the pattern spouse to predecease her husband, an arrangement
which would scarcely have found favour with Mrs. Bennet
of *Pride and Prejudice.* Johnson justly praises the **Advice to
a Lady**, but it is not difficult to understand how its somewhat tutorial note prompted the witty summary, or 'pocket version,' of Lady Mary Wortley Montagu:

> Be plain in dress, and sober in your diet:
> In short, my deary, kiss me and be quiet.

Unless we class Lyttelton's letters as prose works, his earliest published effort in this way was a 'little treatise' entitled **Observations on the Life of Cicero,** which appeared in
1731, and passed through two editions. Joseph Warton,
who knew the author, thought highly of this essay; and indeed, preferred its 'dispassionate and impartial character
of Tully,' to those later and more pretentious volumes of
Conyers Middleton which Lord Hervey so carefully
purged of 'low words and collegiate phrases.' But Lyttelton's first prose production of importance is the **Letters
from a Persian in England to his Friend at Ispahan.** These,
some of which, from a sentence in his opening letter to his
father, must have been sketched before he went abroad,
are avowed imitations of Montesquieu, whom he had
known in England previous to 1734, and to this date the
majority of them probably belong. According to Warton,
in later life their author felt they contained 'principles and
remarks which he wished to retract and alter,' and he
would willingly have withdrawn them from his works. But
not lightly is the written word recalled: and the booksellers
did not let them die, for all their evidences of that 'spirit
of Whiggism' which his continental experiences of arbitrary power had confirmed, and which made him, on his
return, the favourite of the Prince of Wales and the sworn
foe of his father's patron, Walpole. In general, they present much the same features as most of the imitations
prompted by Montesquieu's famous book. The author visits the various places of amusement, marvels at the sensuous effeminacy of the Italian Opera, the brutalities of the
bear-garden, the forlorn condition of the poor debtor, the
craze for cards, the prevalence of intrigue, the immorality
of stage plays—and so forth. Other letters deal with political corruption, the humours of elections, the inequality of
Parliamentary representation, the apathy of the clergy.
Some of the points raised are still in debate, as the functions of the House of Lords and the shortcomings of a too-
exclusively-classical education. In the thirty-eighth letter
there is an illustration, which, whether borrowed or not,
has become popular. Speaking of the supplies granted by
the Commons to the Government, it is said 'that when
these gifts are most liberal, they have a natural tendency,
like plentiful exhalations drawn from the earth, to fall
again upon the place from whence they came.' Elsewhere,
there is a compliment to Pope: 'We have a *very great poet*
now *alive*, who may boast of one glory to which no member of the French Academy can pretend, viz., that he never flattered any man *in power*, but has bestowed immortal
praises upon *those* whom, for fear of offending men *in
power*, if they had lived in France, under the same circumstances, no poet would have dared to praise.' Pope must
have recollected this when, two years later, he spoke, in
the *Imitations of Horace*, of 'young Lyttelton' as 'still true
to Virtue and as warm as true.' It is perhaps a natural
thing to contrast the **Persian Letters** with the later *Citizen
of the World*; and to wonder why one is forgotten and the
other remembered. The reason is not far to seek. If Goldsmith's book had been no more than the ordinary observations of an intelligent and educated spectator, it would
scarcely be the classic it remains. But the *Citizen* has humour and fancy and genius, of which there is nothing in
Lyttelton. His portraits of his father (letter xxxvi), and of
Bishop Hough of Worcester (letter lvi), already celebrated
in the 'Epistle to Ayscough,' are filial and friendly; but

they are not the 'Man in Black,' or the unapproachable 'Beau Tibbs.' The most to be said of the **Persian Letters** is, that they are common-sense comments on contemporary ethics, politics, and philosophy; and that, for so young a man, they are exceptionally mature. (pp. 181-85)

[Of Lyttelton's **Monody**], the best latter-day report must be that; like the obsequious curate's egg, it is 'excellent in parts.' Gray, a critic from whom, in any age, it is difficult to differ, regarded it as at times 'too stiff and poetical,' by which latter epithet he no doubt meant to deprecate the employment, in a piece aiming above all at unfeigned expression, of classical accessory and conventional ornament. Nature and sorrow, and tenderness, are the true genius of such things'—he wrote unanswerably to Walpole; and these he found in some degree . . . . (p. 187)

With the death of Mrs. Lyttelton has sometimes been connected her husband's next prose work, the pamphlet entitled **Observations on the Conversion and Apostleship of St. Paul**; and it is perhaps not an unreasonable conjecture that his bereavement should have turned his thoughts in more serious directions. . . . Warburton might it 'the noblest and most masterly argument for the truth of Christianity that any age had produced'; while Johnson declared, with equal fervour, that it was 'a treatise to which infidelity had never been able to fabricate a specious answer [see excerpt dated 1781]. (pp. 188-90)

By his father's death in 1751 he became Sir George; and five years later, with the break-up of the Newcastle ministry, he was created Baron Lyttelton of Frankley, near Hagley. This ends his official life as a politician; and his chief literary productions during the seventeen years which remained to him were three in number. The first is a couple of letters, included in the third volume of his works, describing a visit to Wales in 1756, and addressed to that notorious Archibald Bower whose dishonest *History of the Popes* was exposed by Goldsmith's 'scourge of impostors,' Dr. Douglas. Lyttelton, however, if he did not believe Bower, seems to have thought better of him than most people, and could never be induced to disown him. The chief merit of the letters is their note of genuine enthusiasm for natural beauty. The **Dialogues of the Dead,** his next work, is avowedly reminiscent of Lucian, Fénelon and Fontenelle; but it is his best effort, for all that Walpole profanely called it *Dead Dialogues,* and despite Landor and the admirable 'New Lucian' of the late Henry Duff Traill, may still be read with interest. What particular faint praise Johnson intended to convey by saying that the dialogues are 'rather effusions than compositions' [see excerpt dated 1781] must depend on some subtle distinction between pouring and mixing which escapes us; but they are certainly fluent and clear, and could only have been 'effused' by a writer of exceptional taste and scholarship. Today some of the shades evoked are more than shadowy. But it is still good to read of the 'Roi Soleil' discoursing with Peter the Great on their relative systems of sovereignty; to listen to staunch old Chancellor Oxenstiern upbraiding Christina of Sweden for abdicating the throne of Gustavus Adolphus in order to consort with a parcel of painters and poetasters; or to admire at Apicius and the epicure Dartineuf (Dodsley's master and Pope's ham-pie 'Darty') comparing the merits of Juvenal's muraena with those of the Severn lamprey, and smacking ghostly lips over the 'apolaustic gulosities' of Lucullus and Æsopus the player. Dartineuf and Apicius are finally lamenting that

they had lived too early for West Indian turtle, when they are roughly recalled by Mercury to the virtues of Spartan 'black broth' and an appetite. As might be expected, several of the dialogues turn upon literary topics. There is an edifying discourse between 'Dr. Swift' and 'Mr. Addison,' touching the curious freak of fortune which made one a divine and the other a minister of State, with some collateral digression on their relative forms of humour; there is another between Locke the dogmatizer and Bayle the doubter. Virgil and Horace interchange compliments until they are interrupted by the creaking pedantries of Scaliger, who has to be summarily put in his proper place by a reminder from the wand of the shepherd of souls. But the longest and ablest colloquy is between Boileau and Pope, who review the literature of their respective countries. This was a theme in which Lyttelton was at home. What is said of Shakespeare and Molière, of Milton and Pope's *Homer,* of the true function of history, of the new French *comédie mixte* ["hybrid comedy"], is undeniable, while the sentiment with which Pope winds up might stand for a definition of intellectual *entente cordiale* ["hearty understanding"]. 'I would have them [the French] be perpetual competitors with the English in manly wit and substantial learning. But let the competition be friendly. There is nothing which so contracts and debases the mind as national envy. True wit, like true virtue, naturally loves it own image, in whatever place it is found.' (pp. 190-93)

Lyttelton's *magnum opus*—great by its quantity rather than its quality—was his long-incubated **History of Henry II** . . . What Johnson calls his 'ambitious accuracy' made him employ a 'pointer' or punctuating expert, at increased cost to himself, and with the astounding result that the third edition comprised no fewer than nineteen pages of errata. It may be that some of this meticulous desire to be correct was prompted by fear of Smollett and the *Critical Review;* but it was obviously subversive of spontaneity, and could not fail to attract the persiflage of mockers like Walpole. 'His [Lyttelton's] **Henry II** raises no more passion than Burn's *Justice of Peace,* this reader said; and he had earlier expressed the opinion that the dread of present and future critics rendered Lyttelton's works 'so insipid that he had better not have written them at all.' To Lyttelton, nevertheless, he praised the first instalment. In 1771 the book was finished, the first three volumes having then gone into three editions, which indicates a certain popularity. The two leading historians, however, were not enthusiastic. Hume sneered at it; and Gibbon, who reviewed it in the *Mémoires littéraires de la Grande Bretagne,* says in his *Autobiography,* that it was 'not illuminated by a ray of genius.' But in his published notice, while refusing to the author the praise due to Robertson and Hume, he gives him the credit of being a '*bon citoyen* ["good citizen"], a '*savant très éclairé*' ["brilliant scholar"] 'and an '*écrivain exact et impartial* ["painstaking and impartial writer"]. 'Possibly the modern school of historians would do greater justice to Lyttelton's minute and painstaking method. Hallam quotes **Henry II** repeatedly; and the author of the *Short History of England* calls it a 'full and sober account of the time.'

As a politician and statesman, Lyttelton was naturally well known to many prominent contemporaries. But to speak here of Pitt or Bolingbroke—of Warburton or Horace Walpole—would occupy too large a space; and it must suffice in this connection to single out three or four exclusively literary figures to whom he stood in the special light either of intimate or patron. With Pope, who praised him more than once in print, he had been acquainted before the Grand Tour; and Pope . . . had corrected his *Pastorals.* When later Lyttelton, succeeding Bubb Dodington, became the Prince of Wales's secretary, Pope was gradually drawn into the Leicester House circle. Both the secretary and his royal master made frequent visits to Twickenham; and there were records, on urns and garden seats, of Pope's sojourns at Hagley. One of these described him as 'the sweetest and most elegant of English poets, the severest chastiser of vice, and the most persuasive teacher of wisdom.' As far as one can gauge Pope's complex nature, he seems to have been genuinely attracted to his young admire. (pp. 195-98).

Another visitor to Lyttelton's Worcestershire home was the genial and indolent author of *The Seasons,* for whom he cherished a regard even greater than that which linked him to the pontiff of the eighteenth-century Parnassus. . . . With Lyttelton's aid he corrected *The Seasons* for the new edition of 1744, adding, in 'Spring,' a description of Hagley, an address to Lyttelton, and references to that 'loved Lucinda,' whom, two years earlier, Lyttelton had brought home to his father's house. Lyttelton it was who procured for Thomson the sinecure appointment of Surveyor-General of the Leeward Islands; and . . . it was under Thomson's roof that the *Conversion of St. Paul* was penned. Whether Lyttelton was responsible for eight out of the nine lines describing Thomson in the 'Castle of Indolence' is doubtful; but it is certain that the poet depicted his Hagley host in the stanza beginning

> Another guest there was, of sense refined,
> Who felt each worth, for every worth he had;
> Serene yet warm, humane yet firm his mind,
> As little touched as any man's with bad:
> Him through their inmost walks the Muses lad,
> To him the sacred love of nature lent,
> And sometimes would he make our valley glad—
>
> (pp. 198-200)

> *Austin Dobson, "Lyttelton as Man of Letters," in his* Old Kensington Palace and Other Papers, *Chatto & Windus, 1910, pp. 173-206.*

LAWRENCE F. ABBOTT (essay date 1926)

[*In the following excerpt, quoting extensively from* Persian Letters, *Abbott emphasizes Lyttelton's far-reaching satire of eighteenth-century English life.*]

The *Persian Letters* throw some light on the reasons why their author was known as "the good Lord Lyttelton." They were manifestly prompted by the *Lettres persanes* of Montesquieu. Montesquieu's letters purport to have been written by two Persians of distinction traveling in Europe, and they satirize the abuses of Church and State in France. Lyttelton's letters are supposed to be the comments of a Persian gentleman, temporarily residing in England, on the follies of English society. Lord Lyttelton was a devout upholder of Christianity, and Dr. Johnson applauded some of his arguments in defense of the faith as unanswerable. One of his letters criticising the theater of his day may be quoted, therefore, without apology, in spite of the frankness of its language. It might be written, in a little more restrained form perhaps, of some of the Broadway farces of the present time:

> As I now understand English poetry well, I went last night with some friends to see a play. The principal character was a young fellow who, in the space of three of four hours that the action lasted cuckolds two or three husbands, and debauches as many virgins. I had heard that the English theater was famous for killing people upon the stage, but this author was more for propagating than for destroying.

> There were a great many ladies at the representation of this modest performance; and though they sometimes hid their faces with their fans (I suppose for fear of showing that they did not blush) yet in general they seemed to be much delighted with the fine gentleman's heroical exploits. "I must confess," said I, "this entertainment is far more natural than the opera [in a previous letter he had criticised the artificiality and affectation of the newly introduced Italian opera]; and I do not wonder that the ladies are moved at it." But if in Persia we allowed our women to be present at such spectacles as these, what would signify our bolts, our bars, our eunuchs? Though we should double our jealousy and care they would soon get the better of all restraint, and put in practice those lessons of the stage which it is so much pleasanter to act than to behold.

The stage is by no means the only object of the visiting Persian's satire. He criticises marriage settlements and divorce. Having proposed marriage to a very pretty girl, and being acceptable both to the young lady and to the mother, he found that he must make a prenuptial settlement on his inamorata, or "a great independent allowance in case her husband and she should disagree." Whereupon he withdrew exclaiming: "No, by Hali! I will never wed a woman who is so determined to rebel against her husband that she articles for it in the very contract of her marriage!"

In the domain of politics this supposititious Persian speaks some sound sense which he would be likely to repeat if he could return to literary life and comment on recent events in Pennsylvania:

> I have seen them constantly busied in passing laws for the better regulation of their police, and never taking any care of their execution; loudly declaring the abuses of their government, and quietly allowing them to increase!

> I have seen them distressed for want of hands to carry on their husbandry and manufactures; yet permitting thousands of their people to be destroyed or made useless and hurtful to society, by the abominable use of spirituous liquors!

> I have seen them make such a provision for their poor, as would relieve all their wants if well applied; and suffer a third part of them to starve, from the roguery and riot of those entrusted with the care of them!

> But the greatest of all the wonders that I have seen, and which most of all proves their infatuation, is that they profess to maintain liberty by corruption.

Altogether these *Persian Letters,* written by an Englishman nearly two hundred years ago, make interesting reading on this side of the Atlantic today. (pp. 404-05)

> *Lawrence F. Abbott, "A Forgotten Classic," in* The Outlook, *Vol. 143, No. 12, July 21, 1926, pp. 404-05.*

S. C. ROBERTS (essay date 1930)

[*An English author, scholar, and secretary at the Cambridge University Press from 1922 to 1948, Roberts's primary literary interests were in Dr. Samuel Johnson and Sir Arthur Conan Doyle's Sherlock Holmes. In the following excerpt, he surveys Lyttelton's principal writings.*]

George Lyttelton's education—Eton and Christ Church—contains no surprises. Of his Eton verses (and even Johnson admits that they were so much distinguished as to be recommended as models to his schoolfellows) one rather remarkable example survives. It is the *Soliloquy of a Beauty in the Country* and the manner is, of course, the manner of Mr Pope:

> Ah, what avails it to be young and fair,
> To move with negligence—to dress with care?
> What worth have all the charms our pride can boast
> If all in envious solitude be lost?
> Where none admire, 'tis useless to excell;
> Where none are beaux, 'tis vain to be a belle.
>
> (p. 4)

[Of other pieces,] Johnson says, with characteristic good sense, that "they have a smooth equability which cannot much tire, because they are short, but which seldom elevates or surprises" [see excerpt dated 1781]. From this general criticism however he excepts the *Advice to Belinda*:

> Be good yourself, nor think another's shame
> Can raise your merit, or adorn your fame.
> Prudes rail at whores, as statesmen in disgrace
> At ministers, because they wish their place.

There we have lines redolent of the century of Pope and Swift, of Fielding and Smollett. But in a moment we come to this:

> Seek to be good, but aim not to be great,
> A woman's noblest station is retreat.

It is the pen of George Lyttelton, but the voice is the voice of Charles Kingsley.

It was as inevitable that Lyttelton should enter into political life as that he should have proceeded upon the Grand Tour. (pp. 7-8)

The personality of Lyttelton offered plentiful material for literary, as well as pictorial, caricature; according to Birkbeck Hill, he was Chesterfield's "respectable Hottentot" and Horace Walpole wrote:

> Absurdity was predominant in Lyttelton's composition: it entered equally into his politics, his apologies, his public pretences, his private conversations. With the figure of a spectre and the gesticulations of a puppet, he talked heroics through his nose, made declamations at a visit, and played cards with scraps of history or sentences of Pindar. He had set out on a poetical love plan, though with nothing of a lover but absence of mind and nothing of a poet but absence of meaning. Yet he was far from wanting parts; spoke well when he had studied his speeches and loved to reward and promote merit in others.
>
> (pp. 9-10)

Before he became prominent in politics, Lyttelton was already known as a poet. Besides the early poems which have been already quoted he published in 1732 a composition entitled *The Progress of Love*, in four eclogues, and

the *Persian Letters* were also begun at a very early age. To the year 1747 belong two more intimate works. At the age of 32 Lyttelton had married Lucy Fortescue. This lady, as we should expect, was the ornament and joy of her husband's life. In Lyttelton's own words:

> He, only he, can tell, who, match'd like me,
> (If such another happy man there be)
> Has by his own experience tried
> How much the wife is dearer than the bride.

But as Johnson curtly remarks, "Human pleasures are short; she died in childbed about five years afterwards and he [Lyttelton] solaced his grief by writing a long poem to her memory". Johnson's reference is to the once celebrated monod [*To the Memory of a Lady Lately Deceased: A Monody*], now known only by the conventionally chilly comments of the historians of literature. Nevertheless, it is in itself a monument of eighteenth-century domesticity and it received genuine praise for its elegiac tenderness from no less an authority than Thomas Gray:

> O shades of Hagley, where is now your boast?
> Your bright inhabitant is lost.
>
> (pp. 10-11)

Lyttelton made a characteristic excursion into theological literature. Having "in the pride of Juvenile confidence, with the help of corrupt conversation, entertained doubts of the truth of Christianity", he afterwards re-established his convictions and published a work entitled *Observations on the Conversion of St Paul*. Lyttelton's method of apologetic is worth noting. Either, he says, Paul must have been an impostor, who said what he knew to be false; or he was an enthusiast who by the force of an overheated imagination imposed on himself; or he was deceived by others; or what he says about his conversion did really happen and therefore the Christian religion is a divine revelation. Theology apart, one definition is worth quoting: "Now these are the ingredients of which enthusiasm is generally composed; great heat of temper, melancholy, ignorance, credulity, and vanity or self-conceit".

This is an admirably clear exposition of the eighteenth-century point of view. Enthusiasm today is catalogued among the virtues, especially if it be so strong as to outlive youth. It connotes a certain temperamental ardour, an eagerness for fresh experience, a belief in the value of life. The common text-book *cliché* about the eighteenth-century mistrust of enthusiasm is based on a confusion of meanings. It did not suppress the spirit of courage and of adventure: it even felt wistfully towards the spirit of romance. Fielding was called an enthusiast for righteousness. Boswell, in the modern sense of the word, was one of the greatest enthusiasts in history.

Lyttelton's *Persian Letters* were, as Johnson is careful to emphasise, the work of a very young man. They have, he says, "something of that indistinct and headstrong ardour for liberty which a man of genius always catches when he enters the world and always suffers to cool as he passes forward". It was not really the precocity which Johnson hated; it was the Whiggishness of the precocity. In form, the *Letters* are a fairly close imitation of Montesquieu; and granted that they thereby lose something of spontaneity, granted that they do not come under the category of the Hundred Best Books, they still remain a considerable achievement for a boy in the early twenties—indeed, though they were not published until 1735, it appears from a letter written by Lyttelton to his father that the writing of them was begun some seven years before. There are plenty of dull pages in them, though on the other hand, as Lyttelton's Victorian biographer is careful to point out, the letters "are not without occasional indelicacy both of thought and expression". But if they are nothing else, the letters are interesting as giving the Whig moralist's view of the social conditions of the time. Had Lyttelton lived a century earlier he might well have been prominent amongst the character-writers. (pp. 12-14)

Many of the letters are devoted, like those in Goldsmith's *Citizen of the World,* to a satirical review of fashionable follies. Though the delicate charm of Goldsmith is lacking, Lyttelton has a certain austere humour: Selim, the supposed Persian visitor, is bored by the opera. He finds it very far from inflaming him to a spirit of faction and much more likely to lay him asleep. "Ours in Persia", he says, "sets us all a-dancing; but I am quite unmoved with this." "Do but *fancy* it *moving*", replies his friend, "and you will soon be moved as much as others. It is a trick you may learn when you will, with a little pains: we have most of us learnt it in our turns."

But Lyttelton is not merely the social satirist—he quickly reveals the spirit of the humanitarian reformer as well: bear-gardens, debtors' prisons, gaming-houses, mercenary marriages, political corruption—all these are treated with an ethical solemnity far removed from that spirit of detachment which is the mark of the true essayist. (pp. 14-15)

Taken as a whole, the **Persian Letters** are thoroughly eighteenth-century and thoroughly English—ethical, didactic, insular. (p. 16)

It is characteristic of Lyttelton's literary quality that his two most considerable prose works were frankly works of imitation. He was a well-read gentleman and could wield a fluent pen; but of creative imagination he had nothing. Like every good Whig, he aspired towards better things; of originality he was suspicious. So, in his preface to the **Dialogues of the Dead** he writes in the true eighteenth-century manner:

> Lucian among the ancients and among the moderns Fenelon archbishop of Cambray and Monsieur Fontenelle have written **Dialogues of the Dead** with a general applause ... And sometimes a new dress may render *an old truth* more pleasing to those whom the mere love of novelty betrays into error ... Indeed one of the best services, that could now be done to mankind by any good writer, would be the bringing them back to *common sense;* from which the desire of shining by extraordinary notions has seduced great numbers, to the no small detriment of morality, and of all real knowledge.
>
> (p. 17)

Lyttelton's immortality, like his own literary inspiration, is largely borrowed. His works are unread, his biography unreadable; yet no one can approach the literature of the eighteenth century without meeting his name. At an early stage of his career he became a patron of literature and much might be written of his friendship with Shenstone and James Thomson. But the most famous of his protégés was Henry Fielding. Fielding and Lyttelton were at school together and their friendship was true and lasting. The

dedication of *Tom Jones* to Lyttelton was no merely formal compliment. It was Lyttelton who suggested the writing of the book and it was at a party in the country, of which Pitt and Lyttelton were members, that the novel was first read in manuscript. Unfortunately there was no Boswell present to record the comments made. Fielding's dedication is perhaps the best, and certainly—even when allowances are made for the hyperbole inevitable in such compositions—the most permanent, tribute to the character of George Lyttelton. There is real gratitude in it, for Fielding had received real benefits; and there is one paragraph in particular which has a special significance in relation to Lyttelton the moralist:

> From the name of my patron, indeed, I hope my reader will be convinced, at his very entrance on this work, that he will find in the whole course of it nothing prejudicial to the cause of Religion and Virtue; nothing inconsistent with the strictest rules of decency, nor which can offend even the chastest eye in the perusal. On the contrary, I declare, that to recommend Goodness and Innocence hath been my sincere endeavour in this history.

Here is a familiar and highly characteristic passage in relation not only to Lyttelton but to the essentially moral outlook of the eighteenth century. (pp. 20-1)

Morality, sense of duty, respectability, domesticity ... were neither the invention nor the prerogative of the Victorian Age. The outlook of George Lyttelton (the Good Lord Lyttelton) upon the world was, indeed, tinged with the ethical respectability which is commonly associated with the Victorians.

Add to this ... a real enthusiasm for literature, a certain power of oratory and a genuine piety, and you have the Good Lord Lyttelton. Awkward, angular and—it is to be feared—lacking a sense of humour, he fell short of greatness and came perilously near to being a prig. To read his works is to experience the sensation of a curious blend of Horace Walpole and the Prince Consort. (p. 23)

> *S. C. Roberts, "An Eighteenth-Century Gentleman," in his* An Eighteenth-Century Gentleman and Other Essays, *Cambridge at the University Press, 1930, pp. 1-23.*

ANANDA VITTAL RAO (essay date 1934)

[*In the following excerpt, Rao appraises Lyttelton's major works.*]

The **Progress of Love** is a pastoral poem in four parts written in the heroic couplet, after the manner of Pope, its main theme being Love—in the four stages of Uncertainty, Hope, Jealousy, and Possession. The four eclogues are respectively dedicated to Pope, Dodington, Edward Walpole and Lord Cobham.

Johnson's review of this poem is very short and almost pertinent, but it is manifestly unjust. "The verses," he wrote, "cant of shepherds and flocks, and crooks dressed with flowers." "Of his **Progress of Love,** it is sufficient blame to say that it is pastoral." The intolerance of the latter statement is typical of the attitude Johnson assumed towards the pastoral as a poetic form. Speaking of such a generic classification of literature Sir Edmund Gosse says,

"A poem is a good or a bad poem. It is no business of the critic to condemn it because it is an eclogue or a pindaric ode, or to patronise it because it is a ballad or a moral idyll."

It is true that there is no outstanding merit in the *Progress of Love.* Having regard, however, to the period in which it was written, and the extreme youth of the author, it is easy to appreciate the poetry of this piece. In ease and dignity of verse, it is not much behind Pope's pastorals. There is no personal allusion or religious satire or didactic motive behind the poem, just as there is neither the idealism nor the imagination of the Elizabethan poets to give it vigour and life. In places, its personifications and hackneyed allusions to Cynthia, Pan and Phœbus, to the Naiads and Nymphs, give the poem a depressing air of artificiality.... (pp. 25-6)

The only excuse, perhaps, for such things is the fact that it was the normal habit among poets to indulge in them, not excluding Pope or even Gray.

There is, however, a certain freshness and vigour about the descriptions in the poem, a freshness which one does not often come across in the too easy elegance of similar verses in Pope's *Hylas and Aegon.* (pp. 26-7)

Lyttelton seems to have been at this time strongly influenced by Milton's poetry. There is, indeed, in the depiction of... [his] natural scenery..., a distinctly recognizable strain of reminiscence from... lines from *L'Allegro*.... (pp. 27-8)

To some extent, Lyttelton imitated Pope's manner too. Thus the smartness of the following passage has a ring of the more brilliant and clever lines in Pope's poetry:

> Ah no! the conquest was obtained with ease;
> He pleased you, by not studying to please.
> His careless indolence your pride alarmed;
> And had he lov'd you more, he less had charmed.

However, it is not always as above; in a few places, the *Progress of Love* has natural force and simplicity. (p. 29)

Blenheim, the other poem written at Oxford, was published in 1728. Twenty-three years before, two greater poets than Lyttelton had attempted the same subject in verse—John Philips in *Blenheim* and Addison in *The Campaign.* Lyttelton's effort cannot stand comparison with either poem, whether in point of description or vigour of style. In one respect, Lyttelton follows Philips—in the adoption of blank verse and the imitation of Milton's *Paradise Lost.* As seen before, Lyttelton was, about the time, much under the influence of Milton's poetry. Whether he was directly influenced by Philip's poem it is not easy to decide. Though all the three poets extol Marlborough, Addison and Philips describe the actual battle and the campaign, whereas Lyttelton describes more the palace of Blenheim. To the high tribute he pays to the Duke for his military prowess, Lyttelton adds an eulogy of the Duchess for her constant love. (p. 30)

Blenheim is not a spontaneous effort of Lyttelton's pen. Miltonisms are much in evidence and they do not enhance the merit of the poem. Phrases like 'chief of confederate hosts' and similes in the manner of Milton are in frequent use. The poem begins with an invocation to Minerva and Thalia, the Sylvan Muse. Then follows a description of Blenheim Castle, with the conventional dryads and nymphs. The comparison of Marlborough with the heroes of classical history, such as Lucullus, Cæsar and Alexander, is in the approved style, and sets the stamp of immaturity on the verses. Adulation and ecstatic praise are heaped on the devoted head of the Duke. Patriotism is another incentive to the poet. (pp. 30-1)

The *Persian Letters* number about seventy-eight in all. Lyttelton had obviously read and taken as his model the *Lettres Persanes* of Montesquieu, the English translation of which was first published in 1722. It is probable the *Turkish Spy* and Defoe's *Tour through England* also led him to the choice of his theme, but there can be little doubt that Montesquieu was his immediate inspiration. Dr. Anderson says the letters were 'an imitation of those of Montesquieu, whom he had known in England;' Austin Dobson also suggests, probably on the strength of Anderson's statement, that Lyttelton had known the French author in England previous to 1734. (p. 70)

While Lyttelton is avowedly inspired by Montesquieu, and has the latter's licentiousness of description in the story-interludes, he is in no sense a slavish imitator. There are occasional touches of vigour and originality; Lyttelton lacks no doubt the delicate mockery and the masterly satire of his model. However, for a young man, barely twenty-five, the expression of sane and forcible views on the problems of State and Society, and the entertaining sketches of individual characters in the *Persian Letters* have remarkable quality and merit. The imitation of Montesquieu is plain enough in the similarity of themes—the mock epitaph on the businessman in Lyttelton, and the diner-out in the French author, the strictures on the Law Courts, and the madness of proselytism, the plea for tolerance, the analysis and dissection of political parties, their leaders and their aims, of the Government and political history of each country, the Troglodytes, the coffee-house haunters and so forth. A detailed examination is thus unnecessary. The fact of his imitation is by no means a discredit to Lyttelton. Goldsmith, far superior to Lyttelton in his gracefulness, humour and touch of genius, is, in his material and outward form, equally imitative of Montesquieu in the *Citizen of the World,* and even of Lyttelton, in some respects, as will be shown later. The ability of Lyttelton lies in his adaptation of Montesquieu's scheme to English life, customs and politics, in the boldness, originality, and frankness of his views. His style has no marked distinction or quality; it is not cumbrous, it has a rough strength, but at the same time it has neither the sweet grace nor the easy flow of the style of his Irish successor in the *Chinese Letters.*

In the Preface, or 'Letter to the Publisher,' Lyttelton states his object in giving to the world the observations of a Persian, 'so foreign and out of the way.' "As there is a pleasure in knowing how things *here* affect a foreigner, though his conceptions of them be ever so extravagant, I think you may venture to expose them to the eyes of the world; the further because it is plain the man who wrote them is a lover of liberty, and must be supposed more impartial than our own countrymen, when they speak of their own admired customs and favourite opinions." The letters are all supposed to be written by Selim, a traveller from Persia came to stay in England, to his friend Mirza at Ispahan to gratify the latter's thirst for knowledge. He promises to apply himself, 'principally to study the English Government.' Moreover, "Whatever in the manners of this people appear to me to be *singular* and *fanatical,* I will also give thee some account of . . . . ."

In accordance with his first object, Selim devotes a number of the letters to a description of the growth of society, political institutions, and government, and the history of the English constitution. The Troglodytes cover about ten letters and their history is given "to shew by what steps, and through what changes, the original good of Society was overturned, and mankind became wickeder and more miserable in a state of Government, than they were when left in a state of nature." The growth of law and equity is said to have risen from that of property and individual wealth. "From this (property) grew up a thousand mischiefs—pride, envy, avarice, discontent and violence." The multiplicity of laws is severely condemned. "If subtleties and distinctions are admitted to constitute right, they will equally be made use of to evade it: and if justice is turned into a science, injustice will soon be made a trade." From law, Lyttelton turns to religion, and describes its vicissitudes, the oligarchy of priests, and the rise of dogmatism. He deals next with the 'divine right of Kings,' and the unenviable increase of luxury and corruption in an absolute monarchy. As Goldsmith does later, Lyttelton laments that a 'thousand wants were created every day, which nature neither suggested nor could supply.' Commenting on the influx of foreign doctors and quacks come to cure the ailments of the wealthier members of Society, who revelled in surfeit, Lyttelton remarks acidly: 'The only advantage was, that those who had learned to live at a great expense, now found the secret of dying at a greater.' The history of the Troglodytes ends with a well-drawn picture of Lyttelton's Utopia and the gospel of Whiggism. (pp. 71-3)

Three of the letters deal with the elections and election scenes in England. The prevalence of bribery, corruption, drunkenness, and disorder come in for a full share of the young Whig's satire. "When I came to the town where I was to lodge, I found the streets all crowded with men and women, who gave me a lively idea of the ancient Bacchanals. Instead of ivy they carried oaken boughs, were exceedingly drunk and mutinous, but at the same time, mighty zealous for religion." "I asked if they had no laws against corruption. Yes, said he, very strong ones: but corruption is stronger than the laws. If the magistrates in Persia were to sell wine, it would signify very little that your law forbids the drinking of it." A well-deserved commentary on the Peachums and the trading justices of Lyttelton's day.

While Lyttelton's comments on the law's delays and vexations, and the corruption in administration, are bitter and provokingly severe, he is not blind to the essential virtues of the English nation and the legal guarantees of the rights of Englishmen. (pp. 75-6)

The Italianate Englishmen, who, though the dullest fellows in their country, become perfect virtuosi after foreign travel, come in for a good deal of ridicule. So also the Society lady, with her receptions and protégés; and the parasites that hover in fashionable saloons, "fellows, who without a grain of sense or merit, make their way by reciprocally complimenting one another. They neither *bark nor bite,* but *cringe and fawn;* so that neither good

manners nor humanity will allow one to kick them out, till at last they acquire a sort of right by sufferance." (p. 77)

At the Opera, the Persian comments on the lack of taste and decency in some of the actors. He is astonished to hear his neighbour tell him that there is the party spirit even in music. "It is a rule with us to judge of nothing by our senses and understanding; but to hear and see and think, only as we chance to be differently engaged." The Persian then complains that he is quite unmoved by the music; his neighbour's reply is worth quoting:—"Do but *fancy* it *moving,* and you will soon be moved as much as others. It is a trick you may learn when you will, with a little pains; we have most of us learnt it in our turns."

The brutality of the bear-garden is another theme touched upon. "The pleasure was, to see the animals worry and gore one another, and the men give and receive many wounds." A Frenchman watching, the spectacle disapproves of the 'sanguinary disposition' of the English exhibited in their loud and excited approval of the entertainment! Then there is an amusing description of the frequent card-parties that eighteenth century Society so often indulged in. (p. 78)

The Persian has cynical views on the so-called 'platonic love,' and is shocked to learn of the mercenary considerations behind marriage. He tries to marry an Englishwoman, and hearing of all the stipulations about jointure and allowance, he cries out, "No . . . by Hali—I will never wed a woman who is so determined to *rebel* against her husband, that she *articles* for it in the very contract of her marriage." (p. 79)

On the educational system of the day, with its undue insistence on the classics, Lyttelton is severe. "The whole purpose of their education is to acquire some Greek and Latin words; . . . if they are backward in this, they are pronounced dunces." "It were far better," Lyttelton suggests, "that they should learn to speak English with grace and elegance, and be thoroughly acquainted with their own national history and political constitution." The Persian, commenting on the great number of English youths who got no benefit from foreign travel, but only learnt newer fashions and vices, says: "Were I to go to Persia, with an English coat, an English footman, and an English *cough,* it would amount to just the improvement made in France by one half of the youth who travel thither. Add to these a taste for music, with two or three terms of building and of painting,—and you are an accomplished gentleman." (p. 80)

The Persian Letters must have created a sensation when it was first published. It became immediately popular, for there were four editions in one year and a fifth in 1744. After Lyttelton's death it was reprinted in Harrison's British Classics and it was thrice translated into French, in 1735, 1761 and 1775. The secret of Lyttelton's success in England was his almost novel design, the boldness of his opinions and the freshness of treatment. No doubt, twenty-five years later Goldsmith eclipsed him completely in the *Chinese Letters*; yet Goldsmith himself must have probably been indebted to Lyttelton in his material. A close reading reveals a similarity of themes dealt with by the authors, and in the descriptions of the gambling parties and the law courts, in his views on the expenses and delays of law-suits, and the mercenary nature of the marriage bond, Goldsmith followed in the steps, not of Montesquieu so much as of Lyttelton. (p. 81)

The humour, fancy and genius of Goldsmith accomplished a far greater work on the coarse material that Lyttelton gave than the *Persian Letters*. Lyttelton's style has none of the easy grace and felicity of Goldsmith's; if it is plain, it is not without vigour and strength, and is tolerably good without any particular distinction. There are a few good illustrations and figures of speech in the letters, of which one has become popular and has been often quoted. (p. 82)

The *Monody* is written in the form of a long irregular ode, more or less pseudo-Pindaric, composed of nineteen stanzas of unequal length; the lines vary in their syllables, and the consequent variety adds a certain charm and beauty to the elaborately lyrical verse. The poem breathes the sincere grief of an afflicted husband and father; the recollection of married happiness, and of Lucy's sweet presence in the Hagley woods, the loneliness of the children, the grace and accomplishments of Lucy, all these are conjured up by the poet; and send him to bitter weeping, and almost despair in divine justice. But the poem ends in a calm spirit: God's mercy is great and we dare not question His will.

The *Monody* is excellent in parts for its poetic imagination and simple expression of grief. At times, however, the strained effort at poetry is too obtrusive to be overlooked; pomp and profusion in words spoil the effect. The poem is thus uneven in merit. There are a few reminiscences of Milton's *Lycidas,* which the poet evidently had in mind as a model. . . . [There] is a long list of classical and mythological names, introduced with some skill, but without half the music and effect that are created by Milton's extraordinary skill in the use of names in *Lycidas*. Milton generally uses the decasyllabic verse, whereas Lyttelton uses lines of varying length. Although the *Monody,* as a personal elegy, possesses some distinction, it can bear no comparison with *Lycidas* with its exquisite harmony, its perfection of verbal finish, and its beautiful music. The faults of the *Monody* are, as has been said before, its unevenness, and occasional lapses into a florid diction, unsuitable to the elegy of personal grief. It is equal in merit to Tickell's elegy on Addison, though it has not the stateliness and dignity of the closing lines in the latter, but is perhaps, both in passionate feeling and felicity of expression, superior to Pope's "Elegy in Memory of an Unfortunate Lady."

The pastoral element in the *Monody* is more pronounced than it ought to be. . . . In some places, Lyttelton's pastoralism is at its worst, and Horace Walpole, seizing on them, had very little good to say of the poem: but Gray could not bring himself to condemn the *Monody* in this fashion. He admired "six good prettyish lines" in the well-known fourth stanza, but disapproved of the more florid portions of the poem. "I am not totally of your mind," he wrote to Walpole in November, 1747, "as to Mr. Lyttelton's elegy, though I love kids and fawns as little as you do. If it were all like the fourth stanza, I should be excessively pleased. Nature and sorrow and tenderness are the true genius of such things: and something of these I find in several parts of it (not in the orange tree). Poetical ornaments are foreign for the purpose, for they only show a man is not sorry . . . and devotion worse; for it teaches him, that he ought not to be sorry, which is all the pleasure of the thing." Gray's criticism is mostly just, but

there is no doubt that he liked the poem, in spite of its 'kids and fawns.' 'He called Lyttelton 'a gentle elegiac person,' and in another letter he wrote, "Have you seen Lyttelton's *Monody* on his wife's death? There are parts of it too poetical and stiff: but others are truly tender and elegiac as one would wish." (pp. 146-49)

Observations on the Conversion and Apostleship of St. Paul, was written by Lyttelton for converting Thomson to belief in the Christian revelation. (p. 151)

The aim of the book was to demonstrate the divine origin of the Christian revelation, and Lyttelton bases all his arguments on the account of the conversion and apostleship of St. Paul as given by the saint himself, and on his sermon to King Agrippa. Lyttelton examines the evidence in the Epistles of St. Paul, and successfully proves to the reader that St. Paul was neither an impostor, nor an enthusiast, the dupe of his own heated imagination, nor a dupe of clever people practising deception on him. From this, Lyttelton infers that the epistles are true, as also the account of St. Paul's conversion. Lyttelton finally concludes that the Christian religion, on the score of St. Paul's conversion alone, is a divine revelation. (p. 152)

Johnson warmly commends the book, and calls it a "treatise to which infidelity has never been able to fabricate a specious answer." Warburton described it as the "noblest and most masterly argument for the truth of Christianity that any age has produced." Doddridge, the Nonconformist divine, wrote that it was "the most compendious yet unanswerable demonstration of Christianity proposed in a clear, elegant and nervous manner." Lyttelton's father, a devout Christian, read the treatise with infinite pleasure and satisfaction. "The style is fine and clear, the arguments close, cogent and irresistible."

While there is little exceptional literary merit in the book, the *Observations on St. Paul's Conversion* is a masterly presentation of the arguments in favour of Christianity as a revealed religion. It became widely popular, and ran into seven or eight editions in the author's lifetime, was frequently reprinted in England and America by religious Societies, even till the end of the last century, and was translated into French twice, by l'Abbé Guénée in 1754 and by Jean Deschamps in 1758. (p. 155)

[*The Dialogues of the Dead*] were admittedly written on the model of "Lucian among the Ancient and among the Moderns, Fénelon, Archbishop of Cambray, and Monsieur Fontenelle." The influence in England of Lucian, the pioneer and master of this literary form, became very marked after the Renaissance, as can be seen from the works of Erasmus, More and others, and the indebtedness to him, in some respects, of the Elizabethan dramatists. The immediate predecessors of Lyttelton were Prior and Fielding in England, and Fénelon and Fontenelle in France. Lyttelton's *Dialogues* are in most ways superior to those of the English writers before him who imitated Lucian. Though not a pioneer, he was the first to write the *Dialogues* in an interesting and lively way, bringing to bear upon the book his sound knowledge and classical learning.

Lyttelton gives his plan, in brief, in the preface. "It sets before us the history of all times and all nations, presents to the choice of a writer all characters of remarkable persons, which may best be opposed to or compared with each other and is perhaps one of the most agreeable methods that can be employed, of conveying to the mind any critical, moral, or political observation, because the *dramatic* spirit, which may be thrown into them, gives them more life. And sometimes a *new dress* may render *an old* writer more pleasing." Lyttelton then warns the reader naïvely that "the dead are often supposed, by a necessary fiction, to be thoroughly informed of many particulars, which happened in times posterior to their own, and in all parts of the world." He also protests that he is a good Christian, and says that he has kept Mercury, Charon, and others in his ***Dialogues*** as "only the sports of a poetical pen."

Lyttelton succeeded in his intention, and the ***Dialogues*** are even today interesting and enjoyable reading. Austin Dobson justly says "that despite Landor, and the admirable *New Lucian* of Henry Duff Trail, they may still be read with interest," and that "they still yield a faded pleasure to the reader" [see excerpt dated 1910]. While they are, in a few places, heavy and dull, on the whole, the general quality is remarkably good.

The imitation of Fénelon in many of the dialogues is evident in the theme and in the manner of treatment. In the comparison of the policy and conduct of the government of kings and statesmen, of the principles of strategy and military skill by famous warriors and generals, in the question of the application of ethical ideas to politics, in the plea for pacifist governments for the nations—in all these, Lyttelton is obviously reminiscent of Fénelon. Lyttelton, however, though avowedly didactic in his Preface, is actually far less so in the ***Dialogues*** than Fénelon, who is almost always homiletic. They could not have been otherwise, written as they were by the Archbishop for the instruction of the young Duke of Burgundy. Lyttelton is far more lively and amusing; he is more after Fontenelle, Fénelon's master, in this respect. Lyttelton's ***Dialogues*** have thus, in a sense, their own distinction and originality.

There are altogether twenty-nine dialogues in the book, excluding the three written by Mrs. Montagu. Lyttelton's favourite method is to pit one member of a class against another, the contrast or similarity between whom is a matter of great interest, worthy of being threshed out,—in all classes,—kings, philosophers, critics, historians, poets, warriors, tyrants and so forth. There are other dialogues where there is greater variety and more entertaining material. It will be useful now to turn to a few individual dialogues.

In 'Plato and Fénelon,' the two, after mutual compliments, (Plato delivering himself still in 'poetical style') discuss the depravity of taste in Fénelon's age among the writers and poets. Plato asks how this evil came about. Fénenelon notes that the same decay took place among the Romans after the age of Augustus, and ascribes it to "an immoderate love of *wit,* of *paradox,* of *refinement.*" "The works of their writers (the moderns), like the faces of their women, must be painted and adorned with artificial embellishments to attract their regard. And thus the natural beauty of both is lost." Lyttelton seems to dwell here with reproach on the tendency of the poets of his age to seek mere brilliance. 'Mr. Addison—Dr. Swift' is one of the best in the book, and contains a just comparison of the wit and humour of each writer. Dr. Swift starts well: "Surely, Addison, Fortune was exceedingly inclined to play the fool

when she made you a *minister of state* and me a *divine.*" The conversation gradually turns into a heated argument about the merits of each author's writings and his wit. Swift claims a special gift of wit from nature. "Wit is like grace; it must be given from above." At the critical moment, Mercury appears and the two disputers agree to refer the point to the God of Wit. The divine Hermes is hailed by Addison over a question of precedence. But Mercury greets Swift first in a hearty fashion, and he is so engrossed with the Dean, that the neglected Addison remarks that the dispute is decided in Swift's favour. Mercury, however, hastens to reassure him, and tells him not to be discouraged. "Sir Roger, Will Honeycomb, Will Wimble and twenty more characters are drawn with the finest strokes of unaffected wit and humour in your admirable writings. Allowing that in the force and spirit of his (Swift's) wit he has really the advantage, how much does he yield to you in all the elegant graces: in the fine touches of delicate sentiment; in developing the secret springs of the soul; in showing the mild lights and shades of a character; in distinctly marking each line and every soft gradation of tints, which would escape the common eye, Swift was able to do nothing that approaches this. He could draw an ill face or caricature a good one, with a masterly hand; but that was all in his power." Swift is then rebuked for his harsh and rough satire. "Satire, like antimony, if it be used as a medicine must be rendered less corrosive. Yours is often rank poison. But I will allow that you have done some good in your way."

'Ulysses—Circe' gives Lyttelton's style at its best—short simple sentences, bright and graceful. Circe asks the Wise Wanderer why he will not stay in her earthly paradise, and what draws him back to Thrace. Ulysses answers: "The pleasure of virtue; the supreme happiness of doing good. Here I do nothing. My mind is in a palsy; all its faculties are benumbed. I long to return into action—toils and cares fright me not. They are the exercises of my soul; they keep it in health and in vigour. Give me again the fields of Troy rather than these vacant groves. There would I reap the bright harvest of glory; here I am hid, like a coward, from the eyes of mankind. The image of my former self haunts and upbraids me—it even intrudes itself into your presence, and chides me from your arms." Later, Circe asks him why he prefers the mortal Penelope, his wife, a mortal grown old—to herself, the immortal Circe, of unfading youth. Ulysses answers: "With all your pride of immortal beauty, you are not so powerful a charmer as she. You feel *desire,* and you give it: you have never felt *love* nor can you inspire it. How can I love one who would have degraded me into a beast? Penelope raised me into a hero." (pp. 287-92)

'Virgil—Horace—Scaliger' is a bright little dialogue where Scaliger's pedantry, harshness and arrogance as a critic, are fully exposed before the great poets, who fool him to their heart's content, aided by the ever-mischievous Mercury. Scaliger receives humbly 'the mortification of truly knowing himself.' The 'longest and ablest colloquy,' however, as Austin Dobson calls it, is the dialogue between Pope and Boileau. The literary criticism in the piece is exceptionally good, and discloses advanced views. (p. 293)

The ***Dialogues of the Dead*** raised protests from two different quarters. Voltaire indignantly complained of his having been called an exile, in the dialogue between Pope and

Boileau where they discuss French and English writers. (p. 298)

The other objection came from the Methodists. John Wesley took exception to Mercury's speech referring to *The Tale of a Tub* in 'Addison—Swift.' "But Martin (Luther), they tell me, has lately spawned a strange brood of Methodists, Moravians, and Hutchinsonians, who are madder than ever Jack was in his worst days." Wesley, while he 'could heartily subscribe to a greater part' of the 'ingenious book,' could not naturally take the reflection on the Methodists as a trifling speech put in Mercury's mouth, rather than as Lyttelton's personal opinion. "I would ask any one who knows what good breeding means, is this language fit for a nobleman or a porter? But let the language be as it may, is the sentiment just?. . . . . Why should a good-natured and a thinking man thus condemn whole bodies of men by the lump? In this, I can read neither the gentleman, the scholar, nor the Christian. . . . " (pp. 302-03)

The *Dialogues of the Dead* are, on the whole, even to-day enjoyable and readable. Some of them are undoubtedly dull, as the personages Lyttelton introduced are more ancient and vague than they were in his own day. The rest are full of life and spirit, they are sensible and well written, the style is uniformly good, and the opinions sound. The general scholarship and classical learning of the writer are also well employed. On the other hand, the dramatic element, which the author strove for, is not often present. The dialogues, moreover, have not the fine delicacy of sentiment, the imagination, and the classic beauty of the *Imaginary Conversations* of Landor. Horace Walpole spitefully attacked them, calling them 'Dead Dialogues.' Johnson grudgingly admits that 'they were very eagerly read,' and at the same time remarks queerly that they were 'the production rather of leisure than of study, rather effusions than compositions.' The answer to the learned Doctor is best given by Austin Dobson. "What particular dispraise," he writes, "Johnson intended to convey by saying that the dialogues are 'rather effusions than compositions,' must depend on some subtle distinction between pouring and mixing which escapes us; but they are certainly fluent and clear, and could only have been 'effused' by a writer of exceptional taste and scholarship." Of Lyttelton's prose works, there can be little doubt that the *Dialogues of the Dead* is his best production, and one well worth a reprint. (pp. 304-05)

The *History of Henry II* is a long account in four volumes of a single reign and a single king, with a short introduction concerned with the earlier period. It possesses no literary distinction: its style, though not displeasing, is uniformly unimposing. There is, however, little doubt that considered as pure history, the result of painstaking research and zeal for accuracy, it is worthily done. In a letter to Dr. Warton, of 15th August, 1767, Lyttelton explains why in the effort to be correct, it was difficult for him to escape dulness. "I could have made it more amusing if I would have treated it more superficially; but if the historic muse will search for truth among the ruins and cells of Gothic antiquity, some dust and cobwebs will stick to her, and she will not look so fine as if she had been only gathering flowers or straining cream." It was natural, therefore, that Walpole, while praising the book inordinately in its early days, should sneer later that 'it raises no more passions than Burn's *Justice of the Peace':* that Gibbon should

call the book 'that voluminous work, in which sense and learning are not illuminated by a single ray of genius.' Hume hated his 'Whiggery and Piety,' 'qualities,' he remarks sarcastically, 'so useful both in this world and the next.' To Johnson, as has been shown before, the book savoured of the 'vilest Whiggism' and was equally repugnant. Other critics looked upon it more dispassionately. Southey called it 'a learned and honest book'; which was just what it was meant to be. Gibbon, in his actual review, of nearly thirty pages written in French, was more just than in the *Autobiography. . . .* Hallam quoted the book often in his work, and called it 'a full and sober account of the time.' Thus the usefulness, accuracy, and value of the researches Lyttelton made are admitted now, and would appeal to the modern historian, in an age when specialization is so keenly sought after. To the general reader, it can have no interest at all; the period is too remote, and the volumes too bulky to induce any one to read the *History of Henry II.* (pp. 310-12)

Lyttelton's intellectual attainments were considerable. He was no genius, in the essential sense of that oft-used word. He was a good scholar, well versed in the classics of Rome and Greece, as well as those of England. His *Dialogues of the Dead* shows his classical learning; even his Parliamentary speeches are interspersed with reminiscences of happy hours with the ancients. *The History of Henry II* is a tribute to his industry and capacity for research. He possessed powers of imagination, not considerable, yet beyond the average writer of his day, as the *Persian Letters* reveal. His poems are not the weak effusions of a persevering versifier. The *Monody* is an exquisite poem in spite of its flowery imagery in parts. Tenderness, pathos and simplicity mark this personal elegy, and render it noteworthy in the poetry of his period. Lyttelton was a deeply religious man, with very sincere convictions and liberal sentiments. While he believed in full in the truth of the Christian faith, he was no narrow bigot, bound down to creeds and dogmas. He could never brook intolerance or a blind hatred of other faiths, and insistence on the superficial formalities and ceremonials of religion seemed to him the root cause of religious trouble.

In many ways, Lyttelton must have been a unique figure in his social circle. He was a devout admirer of virtue and high thinking; he was sincerely religious in his bent of mind; yet he was not morose or homiletic. He was a sound scholar, and remained one, without adding self-conceit to learning; he was humble, and would talk affably to the poorest author or divine. He moved in a society of county aristocrats, prominent politicians, and peers; yet rarely did he affect the foppishness and frivolity of his circle. (pp. 329-30)

An estimate of Lyttelton as a writer is necessary before the conclusion of this . . . [essay]. It is not easy to judge the position of Lyttelton among the English poets. If true poetry can be inspired only by deep emotion and lyrical feeling, by a vivid imagination or a haunting passion for Beauty, Lyttelton has few claims to poetry. It is not true to say of him, as of even greater poets in his age, that he wrote because the urge within for self-expression was irresistible. If, on the other hand, simple grace, harmony and smoothness in verse, a capacity to love Nature in her calm moods, and elegance in epistolary verse, are sufficient to create poetry, Lyttelton must be considered a poet. There are undeniable limitations to this claim; he was imitative, and then, he did not write much poetry. But even the few songs, the **Monody**, and the prologue to Thomson's *Coriolanus,* entitle him to a worthier consideration than he has had during the last one hundred years. The corrections in Thomson's *Seasons* also show an exquisite taste, and a simplicity, caught as it were from the classics that Lyttelton loved so well. He is no doubt conventional and imitative; in his early days his master was Pope. Later, perhaps, it was Thomson. He attempted different kinds of verse, blank and rhymed, songs and odes, the heroic couplet and the ballad style. In general, however, his poetry can be called pastoral and elegiac. A few of his poems are reminiscent of Milton. In spite of imitation, however, it is easy to see from his poems that he contrived to be, in a vague manner, individual in his expression. Lyttelton's poetry is, again, of interest, in the words of Professor Courthope, as "showing how strongly the social tendency to 'nature-worship,' was influencing Englishmen of education and accomplishment, who had been brought up within the limits of classical reserve."

In English prose, Lyttelton stands on the same level as in poetry. He is an imitator of Montesquieu, Lucian and Fénélon, but he borrowed only the form and the manner. The material was his own, and it was largely moulded by his taste and scholarship in the **Dialogues,** and by his power of clear thinking and satiric description in the **Persian Letters.** He has a genuine love of literature, and his literary criticism is almost unexceptionable and surprising in his generation. The **Letters** written to Bower during the journey in Wales show that he possessed a spontaneous love of Nature, and a mind remarkably free from the prevailing indifference to the real beauty of landscape and scenery. Lyttelton's style is, on a few occasions, vigorous and effective, and has quality; in general, it is clear and correct, but has no pretension to any special distinction.

We have considered in detail Lyttelton's contribution to English literature. Time has unquestionably reduced its value and importance. The verdict of his own and the succeeding generation was entirely in Lyttelton's favour. The age that followed has brushed him aside; the judgment may not be just, but it is not surprising, when greater writers are sharing the same sorry fate. To the student of literature, however, Lyttelton is still an interesting figure in the age of Pope and Johnson, both as the author of the **Dialogues of the Dead,** and the **Monody,** and as the last and one of the greatest of noble patrons of literature in England. (pp. 331-33)

> *Ananda Vittal Rao, in his* A Minor Augustan: Being the Life and Works of George, Lord Lyttelton, 1709-1773, *The Book Company, Ltd., 1934, 387 p.*

JOHN HAYWARD (essay date 1934)

> [*In the following excerpt, Hayward provides a capsule summary of Lyttelton's career and importance.*]

Although there is nothing particularly memorable about George Lyttelton . . . , there is so much in his life and writings characteristic of the society to which he belonged, that he will always be remembered as a type when he is all but forgotten as an individual. In his life, which was exemplary but undistinguished, as well as in those mildly

agreeable but uninspired effusions which comprise his **Collected Works,** he epitomized the cultured existence of an eighteenth century Whig gentleman. In both, he went further than many of his more famous contemporaries towards achieving the French ideal of the *honnête homme* ["honest man"]. . . .

The best that can be said of Lyttelton as a statesman is that he was incorruptible; the worst, that he was unimaginative, absent-minded and long-winded—"a pompous old Grandee," according to Horace Walpole, who snatched every opportunity for holding his uncle's enemy up to ridicule.

As a patron of letters it was another matter. Lyttelton used his personal prestige and his public position to encourage and support professional writers. Grave but amiable, he enjoyed playing Maecenas to the minor Augustans. Thomson composed part of his *Seasons* at Hagley and submitted the manuscript to his host for correction, an action which the latter unwisely interpreted after the poet's death as permission to alter and rewrite much of the poem. Fielding, who dedicated his *Tom Jones* to him, Joseph Warton, Mallet. West and Shenstone were among the many men whom Lyttelton assisted in various ways. Pope, who needed no assistance from anyone, was one of his closest friends, and so, too, were Garrick and Dodsley, whose famous anthology benefited from his supervision. When in London, Lyttelton was a passionate *salonnier* and was such a constant visitor at Mrs. Montagu's in Hill Street that a more than literary sympathy was suspected between them. At Hagley he was no less passionately attached to the prevailing craze for landscape gardening in the picturesque style, and incurred the jealousy of his friend and neighbour, Shenstone, who could never design a prospect without Lyttelton going one better. . . . He introduced Nature into his domains with the same feeling as he had introduced her into his pastorals, a feeling that trembles with the first intimations of the romantic revival. He died as the sun was rising on a new age, enthroned on his good works and supported by all the deities who had attended his cradle, though not before he had paid for the correctness of his own life with the mortification of seeing his son, who was to become the "Wicked Lord Lyttelton," wasting his substance in riotous living. He lies buried along with so many of the minor Augustans he had patronized, and amongst whom he is not to be counted the least, in the great mausoleum of *Johnson's English Poets.*

> *John Hayward, "Good Lord Lyttelton," in* The Spectator, *Vol. 153, No. 5539, August 24, 1934, p. 261.*

ROSE MARY DAVIS (essay date 1939)

> [*In the following excerpt, Davis discusses the origin and structure of* Letters from a Persian *and* Dialogues of the Dead, *including a brief critical history of each work.*]

[Lyttelton's] **Letters from a Persian** grew out of the vogue of the pseudo-foreign letter in France and England, which began with the translation into French in 1684 of the *Turkish Spy* of G. P. Marana. In 1711 the *Réflexions morales, satiriques et comiques sur les Moeurs de notre Siècle of* J. F. Bernard first used this type of letter as a vehicle of the critical spirit of the eighteenth century, and in 1721 the *Lettres Persanes* of Montesquieu gave the *genre* a place in literature and vastly increased its popularity. Lyttelton's letter to his father in 1728 transmitting the first draft of his work, shows that his acquaintance with this work preceded the first translation by Ozell, which appeared in 1730. This early draft must have been revised before publication, as the printed version contains references to events which happened as late as 1734. The idea, title, and form of the book were obviously borrowed from Montesquieu.

All of Lyttelton's letters are written from Selim, the Persian in England, to Mirza, his friend in Ispaham, in contrast to the variety secured by the numerous correspondents in Montesquieu's work. The writer is not very Persian. Lyttelton is less adroit than his French model at keeping the disguise on: and sometimes it falls off entirely, and we meet face to face the young Englishman at the threshold of his political career, for example, when the Persian, supposedly without previous knowledge or experience of the organization of English law, reasons, as in Letter XXVII (revised edition), on the limitations of the House of Lords as a judicial body.

Although Lyttelton's Persian, like his French model, exhibits a lively interest in the social, political, and intellectual phenomena of the country in which he is a visitor, his views coincide with those of Montesquieu only on such general topics as the freedom of women, religious toleration, and the superiority of a mild over a despotic form of government. His various portraits of eccentrics were probably inspired by the *Lettres Persanes*, especially the epitaph of his "man of business." The best bit of characterization and of satire in Lyttelton's book is found among this group, the portrait of the "good-natured man," whose good nature was limited to a willingness to get drunk with his friends, even against his own inclination, when they demanded it of him.

The most important use of material suggested by the *Lettres Persanes* is found in the story of the Troglodytes, which Lyttelton continued from the point where Montesquieu left it. The story in Montesquieu grows out of an inquiry made by the Persian, Mirza, of his friend, Usbec, as to whether happiness comes from the pleasures and satisfactions of the senses or from the practice of virtue. Usbec dresses his reply out as a parable, the story of the Troglodytes, a small nation, dwelling in Arabia. He portrays this people as living in a state of nature, first, a natural state of vice, which eventually brings about the extinction of the whole race with the exception of two families, who continue in a natural state of virtue. As their numbers increase they wish to choose a venerable old man of their number as their king. He is grief-stricken at the request and accuses the people of being weary of virtue, which they are obliged to sustain by their own efforts, and of wishing to substitute obedience to a prince, whose laws will be less rigid than the moral code which they have imposed on themselves.

Lyttelton, taking up the story at this point, traces the growth of the evils, attending upon organized society and government. A defensive war led to the growth of militarism, social inequality, laws, and legislation, until finally the development of religious intolerance and of the theory of the divine right of kings was interrupted by defeat in offensive warfare. The growth of luxury and ease led to that

of unnecessary learning. When it was proposed to establish and endow an academy for philosophers, a wise counsellor, opposing the project, remarked that the children of the Troglodytes "come into the World, extremely knowing in the Course of the Planets, and the Nature of the Soul; but the Manners of the World, and the Heart of Man they know nothing of." Lyttelton, agreeing with his friend, Pope, that the proper study of mankind is man, took the opportunity to attack the belief in the virtue of a recluse and contemplative life as an end in itself. The change from an absolute to a limited monarchy, and the growth of party divisions, is traced to the point where the king, chafing under the restrictions on his power, was counselled by one of his senators to fix it "on a sure and lasting basis" by trading on the vices of his subjects and setting "private interests against public." In this way he might make himself superior to all restraint without disturbing the "*nominal securities*" which the people have set up. The king's advisor promises, if entrusted with the management of affairs, to extinguish every spark of the spirit of liberty. And here with Sir Robert Walpole about to take the helm the history of the Troglodytes ends. In Lyttelton, as in Montesquieu, it illustrates the eighteenth century preoccupation with the origins of society and government.

The Persian in England comments on some of the lesser social phenomena in this Hogarthian world, such as the Italian opera, bear-baiting, gambling, and the loose morals portrayed in the fashionable drama. He is free in his criticism of the debtors' prison, the discarding of old soldiers who have fought well, but are not handsome enough to appear in a review, the exclusive emphasis on classical studies in education, the censorship of private letters, the borough system, and the conduct of the parliamentary election, of which he is a spectator on his travels through the country. The Persian, after informing himself on English history, writes an account of it to his friend, outlining the development of the English constitution from Saxon times through the reigns of Elizabeth and the Stuarts, and tracing the substitution of corruption for the royal prerogative.

Several sketches of individuals are of interest. Lyttelton portrays the ideal English nobleman as one who is "a strenuous assertor of the privileges of the people," and "at the same time desirous to preserve the just rights of the crown" with "an estate that might set him above dependance," so that he might employ his superfluities in charity, while he should "claim no *privilege* that might exempt him from the strictest rules of justice; and afford his *protection* not to men *obnoxious to the law*, but to every virtue and useful art." The Persian is so much impressed by the virtue and disinterestedness of the venerable John Hough, Bishop of Worcester, that were Mahometism not so rooted in his heart, he might have been made a convert to Christianity.

Selim ends his series with high compliments to the English people, praising their good sense, sincerity, good-nature, politeness, industry, and valor. Their faults are newly introduced, and so

> contrary to the genius of the people, that one would hope they might be easily rooted out. They are undoubtedly, all circumstances considered, a very *great*, a very *powerful*, and *happy* nation; but how long they shall *continue so*, depends entirely on the *preservation of their liberty*.

It is to the constitution of their government that they owe all their blessings, and its preservation depends upon "a firm union of all honest men, justice upon public offenders, national and private frugality." The author's desire to give more praise than blame to his native country serves considerably to dilute the satirical effect of the letters as a whole. (pp. 38-42)

Phillimore remarks that these letters "are not without occasional indelicacy both of thought and expression; and were on this account, as well as that of their extreme political opinions, a subject of regret to Lyttelton in after-life." Although the work is by no means exceptionally coarse judged by the standards of the time, the excision of a few passages in the revised edition might possibly be attributed to a desire to refine the original. In the story of the Troglodytes a rather ferocious attack on men of learning is softened and considerably abridged; a passage in the letter on the fate of old soldiers, which might be taken as advocating that they should be left free to plunder captured towns was omitted; several passages which might seem to imply disrespect for the person of the King were also omitted; and there were numerous minor changes in the direction of improving and polishing the style.

Lyttelton transmitted to the Rev. William Warburton the new edition of the **Letters from a Persian**, to which he had made "considerable corrections," but had added nothing "new, or particularly applicable to these times, being resolved to have no paper war to carry on against the Court writers or any body else." Unless he had "entirely changed the plan of the book, which is and must be of a *critical* nature," he could not make it more free from the objections raised at its first publication. (pp. 42-3)

The early editions of the **Letters from a Persian** were treated by current periodicals as a manifesto of the Opposition to the ministry. They were favorably noticed by the *Craftsman*, and at about the same time attacked by the *Free Briton*, as an "*Invective against the Constitution of this Kingdom*," whose author makes "all his Observations subservient to the little Interests, and Spite of an *Anti-ministerial Cabal*."

The most important fact about the **Letters from a Persian** for the student of English Literature is their influence on Goldsmith's *Citizen of the World*, which first appeared in 1760. Thus Lyttelton's youthful essay stands as a kind of connecting link between two works which have an established place in literature—the *Lettres Persanes* and the *Citizen of the World*.

Johnson described the **Letters from a Persian** as exhibiting "the character of a young man" and "something of that headstrong ardour for liberty which a man of genius always catches when he enters the world, and always suffers to cool as he passes forward" [see excerpt dated 1781]. Warton relates that Lyttelton shortly before his death told him that he had determined to throw the **Persian Letters**, "his first juvenile performance," out of the projected edition of his collected works, "in which he said there were principles and remarks that he wished to retract and alter." Warton, however, advised him that he could not prevent the booksellers from inserting these letters in his works.

Later critics have tended to be kind to the **Letters from a Persian**, in spite of their obvious immaturity. The acrimonious John Wilson Croker calls them "no contemptible production even for the age of twenty-five; and they may still be read with amusement and some information as to the manners of the time" [see excerpt dated 1846]. He takes issue with Phillimore's view that the political opinions expressed are extreme; from his own Tory point of view, he sees nothing "that a moderate Whig should in after life seriously regret." (pp. 43-4)

Lord Lyttelton's **Dialogues of the Dead** are generally recognized as constituting his chief claim to literary distinction. (p. 310)

In his preface the author has briefly outlined the history of the literary form which he had chosen as a vehicle for his reflections and conclusions on many topics: "Lucian among the ancients, and among the moderns Fénelon, archbishop of Cambrai, and Monsieur Fontenelle, have written *Dialogues of the Dead* with a general applause."

Lucian had many imitations, but the use of the form in eighteenth century England was inspired chiefly by two French writers of the late seventeenth century, Fontenelle, whose *Dialogues des Morts*, appeared in 1683, and Fénelon, later Archbishop of Cambrai. The latter appointed in 1689 preceptor to the young Duke of Burgundy, grandson of Louis XIV, wrote his Dialogues for the instruction of his pupil, and his purpose was moral and didactic.

Lyttelton was also primarily concerned with the instruction of the young. His preface concludes with the hope that his book "may induce our young gentry (for whose service it is more particularly intended) to meditate on the subjects treated of in this work:" Conscious that such a purpose made inevitable the use of a good deal of platitudinous material, he put his own apology and justification into the mouth of Fénelon, who admits that it has been objected to his own dialogues

> that most of them are too full of *common-place morals*. But I wrote them for the instruction of a young prince: and one cannot too forcibly imprint on the minds of those who are born to empire the most simple truths; because, as they grow up, the flattery of a court will try to disguise and conceal from them those truths, and eradicate from their hearts a love of their duty, if it has not taken there a very deep root.

To Fénelon, he represents Plato as paying tribute in Elysium, saying that his *Dialogues des Morts*

> breathe the pure spirit of virtue, of unaffected good sense, of just criticism, of fine taste. They are in general as superior to your countryman Fontenelle's, as reason is to false wit, or truth to affectation.

Lyttelton was, however, probably as familiar with the work of Fontenelle as with that of Fénelon, and while it is not easy to point to specific illustrations of the influence of the latter, it is likely that to him may be due Lyttelton's occasional departures from the obvious and platitudinous into more than his usual sublety.

The first edition contained twenty-five dialogues, the largest single group that had been written in English up to that time, with three additional ones written by Mrs. Montagu. The four added in the fourth edition brought the total as they stand in Lyttelton's collected works up to thirty-two, twenty-nine of which are by him. The distribution of his interests is rather well indicated by the fact that of the twenty-nine, fifteen are given to problems of statecraft, eight to literature and philosophy, and six to moral and personal problems. The characters are drawn from the fields of classical and modern history, literature, and philosophy.

A good deal of the material in the dialogues is derived from sources indicated in footnotes. The author most frequently cited is Plutarch, and among the other names which appear are those of Pliny, Machiavelli, Suetonius, Sir William Temple, St. Evremond, Bayle, Seneca, Voltaire, Xenophon, Rabelais, Thucydides, Shakespear, Robertson, Hume, and Livy. But we have here the reflections of a man not only widely read, but also widely experienced. Between conflicting views expressed by the speakers, it is usually not difficult to determine which side the author is on, especially where the problem in hand is one of any weight, and among opinions in matters of government, aesthetics, philosophy, and morals, for the most part typical of the age in which he lived and of the class to which he belonged, we may find some clues to his individuality.

Though the book was not, like Fénelon's, intended for a future ruler, no less than ten of the twenty-nine dialogues are between persons who as kings, consuls, governors, prime ministers, or military dictators have ruled over states. The problems of the philosopher who has in charge the education of a future ruler are discussed by Plato in two of the dialogues. "It is indeed," he tells Fénelon,

> the peculiar misfortune of princes that they are often instructed with great care in the refinements of policy, and not taught the first principles of moral obligations, or taught so superficially, that the virtuous man is soon lost in the corrupt politician.

And to Diogenes he justifies his complaisance at the court of Dionysius by the plea that

> whoever will serve mankind, but more especially princes, must compound with their weaknesses, and take as much pains to gain them over to virtue, by an honest and prudent complaisance, as others do to seduce them from it, by a criminal adulation.

If we examine the conclusions reached on questions pertaining to government, we find that the blend of reforming zeal and flippancy in the *Letters from a Persian* has given way to a sober advocacy of tried and established principles. The first dialogue of the series, that in which Lord Falkland and Mr. Hampden agree in the true English spirit of compromise that both sinned by excess, sets forth a list of Lyttelton's aversions in matters of government. He was against the use of the royal prerogative and against democracy; against excessive party spirit and "religious fury," with their almost inevitable outcome of civil war.

In two dialogues, that between Marcus Portius Cato and Messala Corvinus and that between Marcus Brutus and Pomponius Atticus, the question discussed is that of the relative desirability of compromise with a government of which one cannot approve or of retirement. Lyttelton remained always consistently against the idea of retreat, philosophical or otherwise, from the life of action. Ulysses desires to abandon Circe that he may return to a life of action and the employment of his talents; Queen Christina

confesses to Chancellor Oxenstiern that there is no lasting happiness except in "the consciousness of having performed our duty in that station, which it has pleased the divine Providence to assign to us." And Plato, reproving Diogenes, cites the teachings of Socrates:

> that the business of true philosophy is to consult and promote the happiness of society. She must not therefore be confined to a *tub* or a *cell*. Her sphere is in senates, or the cabinets of kings.
>
> (pp. 310-13)

It is Plato also, in his dialogue with Fénelon, who warns of the "enervating ease and softness of luxury" as the prelude to servitude:

> when all sense of public virtue is thus destroyed, will not fraud, corruption, and avarice, or the opposite workings of court-factions to bring disgrace on each other, ruin armies and fleets without the help of an enemy, and give up the independence of the nation to foreigners, after having betrayed its liberties to a king?
>
> (pp. 310-13)

The importance to a nation of encouraging learning and the arts is emphasized repeatedly. Oxenstiern will not excuse Christina for abdicating to devote herself to literary pursuits, since she might have indulged her tastes in a way compatible with her royal responsibilities:

> For a prince to encourage and protect arts and sciences, and more especially to instruct an illiterate people, and inspire them with knowledge, politeness, and fine taste, is indeed an act of true greatness.

Of the essays given to literary criticism, that between Addison and Swift contains one remark which has become famous. "Surely, Addison," says Swift in opening the dialogue, "Fortune was exceedingly inclined to play the fool . . . when she made you *a minister of state* and me *a divine.*" A friendly argument between the two as to which excelled in wit is interrupted by Mercury, who, hailing Swift, at first overlooks Addison. But when Swift takes this as the answer to their question, Mercury remarks that

> Apollo perhaps would have given a different judgement. I am a wit, and a rogue, and a foe to all dignity. Swift and I naturally like one another . . . But allowing, that in the force and spirit of his wit he has really the advantage, how much does he yield to you in all the elegant graces; in the fine touches of delicate sentiment; in developing the secret springs of the soul; in shewing the mild lights and shades of a character; in distinctly marking each line, and every soft gradation of tinge, which would escape the common eye:

The longest and most interesting of the dialogues is that between Pope and Boileau. Since Lyttelton permits his characters in Elysium to admit their faults freely, we have some of his own reservations on Pope's character. Pope says of himself and Boileau:

> We both were too irritable, and too easily hurt by offences, even from the lowest of men. The keen edge of our wit was frequently turned against those whom it was more a shame to contend with than an honour to vanquish.
>
> (pp. 315-16)

The two speakers discuss in turn Shakespeare, Molière, Corneille, Racine, Milton, Dryden, the Restoration dramatists, the French *comédie larmoyante,* La Fontaine, Prior, Spenser, Thomson, Waller, Cowley, and Voltaire, with passing references to Homer, Euripides, Sophocles, Menander, Lucan, Virgil, Longinus, Jonson, Fletcher, Tasso, Ariosto, Dante, Camoens, St. Evremond, Sarrazin, and Voiture. The list is interesting as a kind of syllabus of Lyttelton's own readings, but since he had been personally acquainted with Pope, many of the critical opinions expressed may be derived from the latter.

Of Shakespeare, he says

> No other author had ever so copious, so bold, so *creative* an imagination, with so perfect a knowledge of the passions, the humours, and sentiments of mankind. He painted all characters, from kings down to peasants, with equal truth and equal force. If human nature were destroyed, and no monument were left of it except his works, other beings might know *what man was* from those writings.

But the usual eighteenth century reservation is made on the mixture of tragedy, comedy, and farce in the same play, which the author explains by the taste of the times in which Shakespeare wrote. Shakespeare is equal to Molière in "comic force," but "in the fine and delicate strokes of satire, and what is called *genteel comedy*" he is "greatly inferior." (pp. 316-17)

He deplores the licentiousness of Restoration comedy, but regards the writers of *comédie larmoyante* as inferior to Molière. The Comic Muse now "weeps over vice, instead of shewing it to mankind, as I think she generally ought to do, in ridiculous lights."

To Spenser he grants "a force and beauty in some of his *images* and *descriptions,*" equal to any in Homer, Virgil, Tasso, Ariosto, and Dante:

> But he had not the art of properly *shading* his pictures. He brings the minute and disagreeable parts too much into sight; and mingles too frequently vulgar and mean ideas with noble and sublime. Had he chosen a subject proper for *epic poetry,* he seems to have had a sufficient elevation and strength in his genius to make him *a great epic poet:* but the allegory, which is continued throughout the whole work, fatigues the mind, and cannot interest the heart so much as those poems, the chief actors in which are supposed to have really existed....
>
> (pp. 317-18)

Lyttelton was not without fear of the corrosive effects of analysis and reason. When Locke and Bayle discuss the relative merits of the philosophy which dogmatizes and that which merely doubts, Locke argues that

> It would be better then to be no philosopher, and to continue in the vulgar herd of mankind, *that one may have the convenience of thinking that one knows something....* What opinion ought I to have of a physician, who should offer me an eye-water, the use of which would at first so sharpen my sight, as to carry it farther than ordinary vision; but would in the end put them out

Locke's further remarks, in the light of recent discoveries in physics, might serve as a warning to the dogmatizers in science:

> Can you seriously think, that, because the hypothesis of your countryman, Descartes, which was nothing but an

ingenious, well-imagined romance, has been lately exploded, the system of Newton, which is built on experiments and geometry, the two most certain methods of discovering truth, will ever fail: or that, because the whims of fanaticks and the divinity of the schoolmen cannot now be supported, the doctrines of that religion, which I, the declared enemy of all enthusiasm and false reasoning, firmly believed and maintained, will ever be shaken?

In another dialogue, true religion is defined as "the perfection of reason," and fanaticism as "the destruction of reason." Nevertheless Lyttelton puts into the mouth of Plato an argument which he had formerly used in the *Observation on the Conversion and Apostleship of St. Paul,* that the use of religious pageantry solely to confound the multitude may be justified:

> Wise men have endeavored to excite an awful reverence in the minds of the vulgar for external ceremonies and forms, in order to secure their obedience to religion and government, of which these are the symbols.

But Lyttelton would make no truce with enthusiasm, and thereby incurred a reproof from John Wesley, who objected to Plato's lament that Fénelon should have been influenced by "the *reveries* of a madam Guyon, a distracted enthusiast," and was even more offended by a remark on the *Tale of a Tub* in the dialogue between Addison and Swift: "Martin, they tell me, has lately spawned a strange brood of Methodists, Moravians, Hutchinsonians, who are madder than ever Jack was in his worst days." Of this, Wesley inquires whether it is

> language for a nobleman, or a porter? ... What a pity is it, that so ingenious a man, like many others gone before him, should pass so peremptory a sentence in a cause which he does not understand!

The dialogues are not of an unrelieved solemnity, although even Lucian and Rabelais discuss the function of satire somewhat gravely. "Plain good sense," according to Rabelais, "like a dish of solid beef or mutton, is proper only for peasants; but a ragout of folly, well dressed with *a sharp sauce of wit,* is fit to be served up at an emperor's table."

Perhaps Lyttelton's most effective use of satire in the dialogues is in that between an English duellist and a North American savage, in which the savage, although he has killed his enemies with their women and children, objects to getting into Charon's boat with a man who admits having killed his countryman and friend.

In lightest vein is the dialogue between the two Epicures, Apicius and Darteneuf. Their argument about the comparative delicacies eaten in ancient and modern times is interrupted by Mercury, who knows of two men who had more pleasure in eating than either of them:

> ... one was a Spartan soldier, and the other an English farmer.... Labour and hunger gave a relish to the *black broth* of the former, and the *salt beef* of the latter, beyond what you ever found in the *tripotanums* or *ham pyes,* that vainly stimulated your forced and languid appetites, which perpetual indolence weakened and constant luxury overcharged.
>
> (pp. 320-22)

The *Dialogues* were well received. It was reported that the whole of the first impression was sold off in two hours. As might be expected Mrs. Montagu and Mrs. Carter were enthusiastic, and on May 7, Chesterfield acknowledged a complimentary copy:

> You have applied history to its best use, the advantage of morality; you have exposed vice and folly, but with so noble a hand that both fools and knaves must feel that you would rather correct than execute them.

Horace Walpole, on the other hand, referred to the *"Dead Dialogues"* and called the style "a mixture of bombast, poetry, and vulgarisms." Gray inquired of Mason what he thought of Lyttelton and Mrs. Montagu "with their secondhand Dialogues of the Dead." Apparently Lord Bath was not enthusiastic either, for in October, Lyttelton wrote to Mrs. Montagu that he presumed Lady Hervey really liked the **Dialogues** and that "Lord Chesterfield's warmth in their Praise has secured her vote in their favour, in spite of Horace Walpole and of Lord Bath."

Reviews were on the whole favorable. Lyttelton's old enemy, Smollett, wrote in the *Critical Review* that

> the hand of a master is too visible in every page to escape the most undiscerning. A distinguishing judgment, delicacy of sentiment, propriety of thought, and purity of diction, recommend this little performance at the first glance. Yet, to speak our opinion freely, we think the dialogues too abruptly introduced and the *personae* characterized rather by the writer than by their own conversation.... Upon the whole, we have not lately seen a work of more entertainment and real instruction, where sound sense, and a lively imagination, are more happily united, or where the erudtion of the scholar is more agreeably tempered with the feeling, the taste, and the sentiments of a gentleman.

According to Dr. Johnson, "poor Lyttelton with humble gratitude, returned, in a note which I have read, acknowledgments [of this favorable review] which can never be proper, since they must be paid either for flattery or for justice" [see excerpt dated 1781]. (pp. 322-23)

These dialogues inspired a number of imitations. Besides John Brown's *Additional Dialogues* in 1760 and Archibald Campbell's *Lexiphanes* in 1767, there appeared in 1762 an anonymous volume of *New Dialogues of the Dead,* included by the *Dictionary of National Biography* in a list of works wrongly ascribed to Lyttelton. A preface to the work states that the favorable reception recently given to Lord Lyttelton's similar work has encouraged the author to publish his own dialogues. *Dialogues of the Living,* 1762, also anonymous, contains a dialogue on comedy between Lord Lyttelton and Mr. Hurd. The second edition of a translation of Lucian, by John Carr, which appeared in 1774 was dedicated to Lyttelton's memory. Thomas Francklin's translation of Lucian, 1781, has an introductory dialogue between Lucian and Lord Lyttelton in the Elysian Fields. In reply to Lyttelton's statement that he endeavored to come as nearly to him as he could, Lucian says that he was "on the whole tolerably successful; though, to say the truth . . . you are rather too grave to be quite *Lucianic,* too polite to be merry, and too wise to be very entertaining." (p. 325)

Rose Mary Davis, in her The Good Lord Lyttelton: A Study in Eighteenth Century Politics and Culture, *Times Publishing Company, 1939, 443 p.*

HOXIE NEALE FAIRCHILD   (essay date 1939)

[*An American educator, Fairchild is the author of numerous essays and books on literary and religious subjects. His major works include* The Noble Savage: A Study in Romantic Naturalism *(1928), which is a lengthy discussion of the depiction of the unspoiled primitive life in literature and its relationship to romantic naturalism, and a six-volume study,* Religious Trends in English Poetry *(1939-68), which traces religious thought and feeling in English poetry from the eighteenth to the twentieth century. In the following excerpt from the latter work, Fairchild characterizes several facets of Lyttelton's verse.*]

The statement that [George Lyttelton] became more orthodox and less sentimental with advancing years need not imply that he was at any time either wildly romantic or ardently pious. During the 1720-1740 period he seems to have regarded formal creeds with cool aristocratic indifference but without eagerness to "écraser l'infâme" ["crush squalor"]. Free from any tinge of libertine mockery, his verse rather often appeals from the Church to what he imagines to be a loftier moral standard:

> To error mild, to vice alone severe,
> Seek not to spread the law of love by fear.
> The priest, who plagues the world, can never mend.
> No foe to man was e'er to God a friend:
> Let reason and let virtue truth maintain,
> All force but theirs is impious, weak, and vain.

As we should expect of a supporter of the Prince of Wales, Lyttelton's favorite virtue is patriotism. From love of country, however, his ideals readily expand to a more general love of mankind:

> Happy is He, and He alone, who knows
> His Heart's uneasy discord to compose;
> In gen'rous love of others' good to find
> The sweetest pleasures of the social mind;
> To bound his wishes in their proper sphere,
> To nourish pleasing hope, and conquer anxious fear:
> This was the wisdom ancient sages taught,
> This was the sov'reign good they justly sought;
> This to no place or climate is confin'd,
> But the free native produce of the mind.

These lines, somewhat incongruously addressed **To my Lord Hervey,** combine the stoicism of "ancient sages" with a more sentimental view of the joys of benevolence. Herein they are characteristic of "the good Lord Lyttelton." Both in his life and in his writings he retained much of the balanced, unenthusiastic Augustan spirit; but he was also in some degree a Man of Feeling. Though an important figure in political affairs, he never ceased to be an unworldly, absent-minded, and awkward benevolist. Sharp-witted people like Hervey, Chesterfield, Horace Walpole and Smollett were inclined to sneer at him; but Thomson was his protégé, Joseph Warton his domestic chaplain, and Glover, James Hammond, and Shenstone his close friends.

In his poems, though not strikingly pre-romantic, Lyttelton is hardly an orthodox neoclassicist. **Blenheim** is written in Miltonic blank verse and includes a reverent tribute to Chaucer. His conception of love is unusually earnest and idealistic. He likes external nature, and has some ability to describe it. In the familiar **Monody** his memories of his dead wife are closely associated with the scenes amidst which she moved:

O shades of Hagley, where is now your boast?
Your bright inhabitant is lost.
You she prefer'd to all the gay resorts
Where female vanity might wish to shine,
The pomp of cities, and the pride of courts.
Her modest beauties shun'd the public eye:
To your sequester'd dales
And flow'r-embroider'd vales
From an admiring world she chose to fly . . . . (pp. 396-97)

But when his beloved wife died in 1747, Lyttelton found small comfort in reason, virtue, patriotism, and benevolence. . . .

No doubt, however, his personal tragedy made Lyttelton's religious feelings deeper and more urgent. For the remainder of his life he was a sensible, sober, mildly evangelical Christian. He persuaded himself that his treatise on St. Paul had converted Thomson, and after the poet's death he set about preparing an edition of his friend's poems in which every unorthodox passage was to be revised or deleted. Patrick Murdoch, the "little, round, fat, oily, man of God," had the honesty and good taste to dissuade his lordship from carrying out this plan.

The piety of Lyttelton's later years, however, is not reflected in his verse: he ceased to be a poet and began to be a Christian almost simultaneously. The fact is not much to be lamented, for to judge from the treatise on St. Paul his religion was not of the poetically inspiring sort. (p. 398)

Hoxie Neale Fairchild, "Sentimentalism—Mild Cases," in his Religious Trends in English Poetry: Protestantism and the Cult of Sentiment, 1700-1740, Vol. I, *Columbia University Press, 1939, pp. 361-423.*

ADDITIONAL BIBLIOGRAPHY

Chew, Samuel C. "An English Precursor of Rousseau." *Modern Language Notes* XXXII, No. 6 (June 1917): 321-37.

Posits that some of the doctrines of Jean-Jacques Rousseau are traceable to Lyttelton's *Letters from a Persian.*

Davis, Rose M. "'The Correspondents'." *PMLA* LI, No. 1 (March 1936): 207-20.

Investigates the authenticity of letters which purportedly passed between Lyttelton and his daughter-in-law, and which were anonymously published as a novel, *The Correspondents, an Original Novel; in a Series of Letters,* in 1775.

Review of *The Correspondents, an Original Novel; in a Series of Letters,* by Lord Lyttelton? *The Gentleman's Magazine* XLV (August 1775): 371-72.

Leaving their authenticity questionable, reprints from *The Correspondents* letters written ostensibly by Lyttelton and his daughter-in-law.

Johnson, Franklin P. "Lyttelton." *Philological Quarterly* VII, No. 3 (July 1928): 309-10.

Briefly comments on one of Lyttelton's unpublished, more obscure verses.

Pitcher, Edward W. 'Lyttelton, Goldsmith, and 'The Story of Zelis'." *The Papers of the Bibliographical Society of America* 74, No. 3 (1980): 259-62.

Minimizes the indebtedness of Oliver Goldsmith's *The Citizen of the World* to Lyttelton's *Letters from a Persian.*

Jean Paul Marat

1743-1793

(Born Jean Paul Mara) Swiss-born French journalist, essayist, and novelist.

Self-styled "L'Ami du Peuple" ("Friend of the People") after the best-known title of his incendiary journal, Marat was one of the foremost proponents of radicalism during the French Revolution. His frenzied attacks on oppressors of the poor and calls to the masses to overthrow their tyrannizers unleashed the headlong violence with which the Revolution and his periodical *L'ami du peuple; ou, Le publiciste parisien, journal politique, libre et impartial* (*Friend of the People*) have become synonymous. Yet modern critics and historians have discerned a complex individual beneath the straightforward sobriquet "Friend of the People," one whose philosophies were informed as much by his ego as by outrage at the condition of his countrymen and whose long-term reputation as a man exclusively good or evil warrants more objective scrutiny.

Little is known of Marat's early years. He was born at Boudry in the principality of Neuchâtel, Switzerland. While a young man, he studied medicine in Bordeaux and Paris and was later awarded an honorary degree from the University of St. Andrews. He established thriving practices in France and England and published numerous treatises on scientific, philosophical, and political topics, among them his *Essay on the Human Soul* in 1772 and a more comprehensive effort in the same vein, *A Philosophical Essay on Man*, the following year. These were succeeded by *The Chains of Slavery* in 1774, written to stir British citizens to press for social and political reform on the occasion of a parliamentary election. From 1777 to 1783, he also held the post of physician to the bodyguard of the comte d'Artois (later Charles X of France). Despite his lucrative profession and the respectful recognition given his continuing scholarship, however, Marat was dissatisfied with the level of honor accorded him and bitterly disappointed when he was not elected to the prestigious Académie des Sciences.

With the Revolution in 1789, open social unrest in France enabled Marat to vent certain views already introduced in his writings, and he devoted himself to the *Friend of the People*. In this journal, Marat denounced not only monarchist despotism but the wealthy aristocracy that was supplanting it. He exhorted the masses to depose the rich, put to death their most powerful constituents, and elect a dictator (himself) sympathetic to the common welfare. When Marat gained a sizable following, his enemies tried unsuccessfully to suppress him. He was condemned by the Paris court of the Châtelet for abetting the attack on Versailles and in 1790, the year his *Plan de législation criminelle* was published, the Châtelet ordered his arrest, but he escaped to England for several months. Over the next two years he was compelled at times to publish his journal underground with the aid of many supporters. By 1792 France was ripe for the type of violence Marat craved so deeply. With the dissolution of the monarchy in August of that year and the lynching of officials known as the September Massacres, the populace gained the ascendancy. Marat emerged from

Marat

hiding, the rigors of which had damaged his health, to play a conspicuous part in revolutionary activities. He joined the Paris committee of police and surveillance and was elected to the National Convention (the legislative body that succeeded the Legislative Assembly in September 1792) as a deputy.

Marat meanwhile maintained his journalistic diatribes, changing the name of his paper to *Le journal de la République française* when a republic was decreed. Despite his championing the lower classes, Marat had little confidence in their ability to govern themselves, and so he continued to campaign for a dictatorship and to advocate purges of political undesirables. A member, and eventually president, of the extreme left-wing faction known as the Montagnards, he seemed dangerously radical to all but a few of his closest associates. To his opponents, particularly members of the moderate Girondin party, whom he viciously attacked in his *Journal*, Marat appeared monstrous. After the Girondins secured control of the Convention during the early months of 1793, they attempted to arrest Marat, who once more sought asylum before emerging in April of that year to clear himself of several serious charges. With Girondin force thus stalemated, Marat exploited his growing influence with the masses by having several Girondin officials arrested. At this juncture, however, he was too ill to profit from such a victory: his health had severely deteriorated from prolonged periods of living in underground hiding places, and he was able to obtain relief from a burning skin disorder only under a regimen of medicinal baths. Nevertheless, he conducted a vigorous crusade in his *Journal* against the resurgent Girondins all the while. In July 1793 Charlotte Corday, a young Girondin sympathizer, stabbed Marat to death in his bath. Although initially buried in state and celebrated with flowery odes and addresses—Marat's memorial address was delivered by the Marquis de Sade—Marat was burned in effigy four months after his death. For decades, strong division characterized estimations of the man and his work, with some commentators embracing Marat as a savior and others reviling him as a bloodthirsty madman. In the last century, commentators have approached Marat with more detachment, concluding that he must remain an individual of whom the world can entertain no single definitive notion.

Although the author was an avowed disciple of such consummate philosophers as Charles-Louis de Secondat, Baron de la Brède et de Montesquieu and Jean-Jacques Rousseau, J. M. Thompson and other commentators have noted a dearth of systematic thought in Marat's own writings. Nowhere has this been deemed more apparent than in the work best known as *Friend of the People*. Here Marat routinely slandered officials on the basis of hearsay alone, dramatizing particular issues by means of innuendo and attempting to ignite public furor by any expedient—though he wryly admitted: "[My] hand would wither rather than write another word if I really thought that the people were going to do what I tell them to." While his concern for the people was genuine, its expression was often charged with contempt for the ignorance and apathy bred of unrelieved poverty. Marat scarcely believed that the masses were capable of instituting his directives—fragmented as these directives were and at times all but buried beneath what has been termed classic megalomania—but he knew that the explosiveness of these injunctions would be his most powerful aid in rousing the lower class to revolution. While some commentators have found flashes of astounding political insight in the *Friend of the People*, most critics agree that the work is for the most part devoid of a consistent methodology or the capacity for practical application. Those rare critics who have treated the *Friend of the People* from an aesthetic point of view have concurred that Marat's prose (written hastily and under adverse circumstances) lacks the refinement of that of such contemporaries as Camille Desmoulins and Maximilien François-Marie-Isidore de Robespierre. To this general determination, however, Samuel Bernstein has added an accolade any journalist might covet: "If the sentences were not eloquent, they were at least energetic, swift-moving, vibrating, and crowded with facts."

Despite their secondary stature, several of Marat's other works are valued as reflections of the author's scope and, more significantly, the derivative nature of his political thought. Seldom mentioned by critics are *Les aventures du jeune Comte Potowski* (*Adventures of the Young Count Potowski*) and *Les lettres polonaises* (*Polish Letters*), believed to have been written when Marat was in his thirties but not published until after his death. These works were modeled respectively after Rousseau's *Nouvelle Héloïse* (1761; *Eloisa*, 1761) and Montesquieu's *Lettres persanes* (1721; *Persian Letters*, 1722). Both are epistolary pieces, the first the romance of a Polish noble separated from his fiancee by civil war and family differences, the second a travel narrative related by Prince Kamia to his friends in Poland. Of the *Adventures*, Norman Hampson has noted briefly that its "passionate language has a curious coldness and the whole thing reads like a literary exercise." Louis R. Gottschalk has claimed that the *Polish Letters*, though "a better piece of writing . . . are dull in comparison with Montesquieu's work [*Persian Letters*]. But they are an important key to the development of their author's *Weltanschauung*." Gottschalk has identified certain sentiments—for example, Marat's intolerance of private property and admiration of the English constitution—that are introduced by Prince Kamia in the *Polish Letters* but considerably expanded in Marat's political writings, especially *The Chains of Slavery* and *Plan de législation criminelle*. While these last-named volumes furnished a springboard for the somewhat more comprehensive ideology (if Marat's views can be thus collectively termed) contained in the *Friend of the People*, they are themselves wholly representative of Marat's thought. Although *The Chains of Slavery* borrows a depiction of a primitive, uncorrupt state of nature from Rousseau, it is primarily a savage attack on despots who exploit public resources for their own gain. The work concludes by expressing Marat's fundamental disbelief in traditional political and economic means to effect change. Both Rousseau and Montesquieu provide precedents for *Plan de législation criminelle*. This call for redefining criminal behavior and punishment has been commended by Hampson despite its essential incongruity in "trying to squeeze both Montesquieu and Rousseau between the shafts of the constitutional coach." Hampson has added of Marat that "his political theories were of the most rudimentary kind."

Over time Marat's standing in the history of ideas and of literature has elicited wildly diverse reactions. The man and his works have been worshipped and denounced with fervor and passion. More recently, the two have been submitted to comparatively impartial criteria. In spite of the vagaries of reputation, however, Marat himself remains a fascinating figure even to those commentators opposed to his philosophies or critical of the ultimate value of his writings. Marat has come to be regarded as an undisciplined, often unprincipled catalyst—if but one of many such dissidents during his time, yet one who significantly shaped the Revolution. Nevertheless, Hampson has reminded those who do not distinguish between the blood Marat demanded and that which was actually spilled: "To a considerable extent, the conclusions that Marat welcomed were ones to which more thoughtful and more honourable revolutionaries were inexorably driven. He was the Mephistopheles to their Faust."

PRINCIPAL WORKS

An Essay on the Human Soul (essay) 1772
A Philosophical Essay on Man, Being an Attempt to Investigate the Principles and Laws of the Reciprocal Influence of the Soul on the Body (essay) 1773
The Chains of Slavery, a Work Wherein the Clandestine and Villainous Attempts of Princes to Ruin Liberty Are

Pointed out, and the Dreadful Scenes of Despotism Disclosed, to Which Is Prefixed an Address to the Electors of Great Britain, in order to Draw Their Timely Attention to the Choice of Proper Representatives in the Next Parliament (essay) 1774

Offrande à la patrie; ou, Discours au Tiers État de France (essay) 1789

*Le publiciste parisien, journal politique, libre et impartial. Par une société de patriotes, et rédigé par M. Marat, auteur de l'"Offrande à la patrie," du "Moniteur," et du "Plan de constitution," etc. (journal) 1789

Plan de législation criminelle, ouvrage dans lequel on traite des délits et des peines, de la force des preuves et des présomptions, et de la manière d'acquérir ces preuves et ces présomptions durant l'instruction de la procédure, de manière à ne blesser ni la justice, ni la liberté, et à concilier la douceur avec la certitude des chatimens, et l'humanité avec la sûreté de la société civile (treatise) 1790

†Les aventures du jeune Comte Potowski (novel 1847; also published as *Un roman de cœur, par Marat, l'ami du peuple, publié pour la première fois, en son entier, d'après le manuscrit autographe et précédé d'une notice littéraire, par le bibliophile Jacob*, 1848

Œuvres de Marat (l'ami du peuple) receuillies et annotées par A. Vermorel (essays and treatises) 1869

‡Éloge de Montesquieu, présenté à l'Académie de Bordeaux le 28 Mars 1785 par J. P. Marat, publié avec une introduction par Arthur de Brezetz (prose) 1887

§Polish Letters, by Jean Paul Marat, Translated from the Original Unpublished Manuscript, Issued by the Bibliophile Society for Members Only (novel) 1904

La correspondance de Marat (letters) 1908

*Marat's signature work was published under this title for only five days. From 1789 to 1792, it assumed its most familiar heading, *L'ami du peuple; ou, Le publiciste parisien, journal politique, libre et impartial*. It appeared under *Le journal de la République française, par Marat, l'ami du peuple, député à la Convention nationale* from 1792 to 1793, after which it was alternately called *Le publiciste de la République française* and *Observations à mes commettans*. Its title at the author's assassination in 1793 was *Le publiciste de la République française, par Marat, l'ami du peuple, député de la Convention, auteur de plusieurs ouvrages politiques*.

†The composition date for this work has been fixed in the early 1770s.

‡This work, though not published until more than a century later, was submitted in competition to the Academy at Bordeaux in 1785.

§The composition date for this work has been fixed in the early 1770s.

JEAN PAUL MARAT (speech date 1793)

[*In the following excerpt from his famous speech delivered in 1793, Marat defends himself against the accusations leveled by the Convention.*]

Citizens, Members of the Revolutionary Tribunal: If Roland the patron of the clique of the Girondists had not wasted the public property in misleading the people and perverting the public mind; if the faction of statesmen had not flooded the whole republic with infamous libels of the Commune, the municipality, the sections, the committee

of surveillance, and, above all, directed against the deputation of Paris; if they had not so long laid their heads together to defame Danton, Robespierre, and Marat; if they had not ceaselessly represented me as a factionist, an anarchist, a drinker of blood, an ambitious man, who looked for supreme power under the title of tribune, triumvir, and director; if the nation, completely undeceived, had recognized the perfidy of these impostures; if their guilty authors had been branded, I would have resisted the arbitrary acts brought against me under the title of "Decree and Act of Accusation," by a perfidious faction, which I had so often denounced as almost wholly composed of royalists, traitors, and plotters. I would moreover have waited till the constitution had been reinforced by the return of patriotic deputies, before presenting myself at the tribunal, and thus have overwhelmed the vile wretches who are persecuting me to-day with such odious rancor.

If, therefore, I appear before my judges, it is only to rise triumphant and confound imposture; it is to unseal the eyes of that part of the nation which is already led astray on my account; it is to go out a conqueror from this imbroglio, to reassure public opinion, to do a good service to the fatherland, and to strengthen the cause of liberty.

Full of confidence in the enlightenment, the equity, and the civic spirit of this tribunal, I myself urge the most rigorous examination of this affair. Strong in the testimony of my own conscience, in the rectitude of my intentions, in the purity of my civic spirit, I want no indulgence, but I demand strict justice. (pp. 79-80)

The "Act of Accusation" is . . . null and void, in that it is diametrically opposed to the fundamental law, which has not been and which cannot be repealed. It is null and void in that it attacks the most sacred right that belongs to a representative of the people.

I am quite aware that this right does not include that of plotting against the state, of attempting any enterprise against the interests of liberty, of attacking the rights of citizens, or of compromising public safety, but it certainly allows a citizen to say, write, or do anything that accords with the sincere purpose of serving the country, of procuring the general welfare, and causing the triumph of liberty. It is so essentially inherent in the functions of the nation's representatives that without it it would be impossible for the faithful to defend the fatherland and themselves against the traitors who would oppress and enslave them.

The patriots of the Constituent Assembly so thoroughly felt the necessity of making the representatives inviolable and unassailable, capable of struggling with impunity against the despot and completing the revolution, that they hastened to consecrate this right by the famous decree of June 23, 1789, before they had even constituted themselves the National Assembly.

They felt so thoroughly that this right was inherent in every public function, that they stretched it to cover every judicial body, every administrative body, and even all citizens united in a primary assembly.

Without this inalienable right could liberty maintain itself a moment against the machinations of its conspiring enemies? Without it, how, in the midst of a corrupt senate, could a small number of deputies, invincibly attached to the fatherland, unmask the traitors who seek to oppress it or put it in fetters?

Without that essential right, how could a small number of far-seeing and determined patriots foil the plots of a numerous faction of schemers? One may judge of this by what happens to us. If the faction of statesmen can under false pretext attack me, expel me from its convention, hale me before a tribunal, hold me in captivity, cause me to perish; to-morrow under other pretexts it will attack Robespierre, Danton, Callot-d'Herbois, Panis, Lindet, Camille, David, Audoin, Laiguelit, Meaulle, Dupuis, Javougues, Granet, and all the other courageous deputies of the convention. It will restrain the others by terror. It will usurp the sovereignty. It will call to its side Dumouriez, Cobourg, Clerfayt, its accomplices. Supported by Prussians, Austrians, and "Emigrants," it will reestablish despotism in the hands of a Capet who will cut the throats of all the known patriots, and it will endow the first employments with the treasures of the state. The decree of accusation issued against me for my political opinions is therefore an attack on national representation, and I do not doubt that the convention, with its quota filled by the return of patriotic commissaries, will soon feel its dangerous consequences, its ill-boding results, and will blush that it should have been decreed in its name, and will hasten to repeal it as destructive of all public liberty.

The act of accusation is not only absurd in that it violates all constitutional liberty and attacks national representations, it is still more so in that the committee, contrary to all principle, turns the convention into a criminal tribunal, for it makes it pronounce without shame an iniquitous judgment, in deciding, without preliminary examination of a single document, without even having placed in question if such writings are mine, that I am found to have provoked murder and pillage, to have called up a power that threatens the sovereignty of the people, dishonored the convention, incited its dissolution, etc.

But what will appear incredible is that the committee calls down, without ceremony, without shame, and without remorse, capital punishment on my head, and cites articles of the penal code, which, according to it, condemned me to death. I doubt not that such is the object they have in view. How many statesmen have been tormented with despair of keeping me in prison, smothering my voice, and restraining my pen? Did not one of them, the atrocious Lacaze, have the impudence to ask the convention, as Dumouriez and Cobourg asked of the faction, that I should be outlawed? So that the act of accusation is a veritable "verdict rendered," which has only now to be executed.

Finally, this act is a tissue of lies and fabrications. It accuses me of having incited to murder and pillage, of setting up a "Chief of State," dishonoring and dissolving a convention, etc. The contrary was proved by the simple reading of my writings. I demand a consecutive reading of the denounced members; for it is not by garbling and mutilating passages that the ideas of an author are to be learnt, it is by reading the context that their meaning may be judged of.

If after the reading any doubts remain, I am here to remove them. (pp. 82-3)

> *Jean Paul Marat, "Defense against the Charges,"*
> *in* The World's Great Speeches, *edited by Lewis*

Copeland, second edition, Dover Publications Inc., 1958, pp. 79-83.

F. BOWEN-GRAVES (essay date 1874)

[*Bowen-Graves was an English barrister and historical essayist. In the following excerpt he exonerates Marat, whom he believes has received "more concentrated hatred, disgust, and abhorrence than has probably fallen to the lot of any other individual of modern times."*]

In 1773, just a hundred years ago, there was published in London the first work of an author who up to the age of thirty had lived in complete obscurity, but was destined before his life closed to accumulate on his head more concentrated hatred, disgust, and abhorence than has probably fallen to the lot of any other individual of modern times. The work was called *A Philosophical Essay on Man*, and the author was Jean Paul Marat.

Writers upon the Revolution when speaking of this man, have agreed in presenting us with a picture of the most repulsive object that their imagination could conceive. The Marat of their pages is a sort of fabulous monster, a portent rather than a man. The dictionary of invective has been exhausted to find epithets sufficiently choice. Such Englishmen as have any ideas on the French Revolution beyond hearsay take them probably, for the most part, from Carlyle. From the perusal each carries away in connection with Marat, a general notion of phantasms, obscene spectra, bullfrogs, and dog-leeches. If he turns to the French historians he finds equal violence, equal vagueness. The Revolution of which they are so proud needs, they seem to think, a scapegoat. Why admit that its evils and its violence were a necessary part of it? Better surely, if we can, to regard them rather as separable accidents; and to that end let us take an individual, small of stature and ugly, and kind on his back the sins of the people, and send him away into the desert with all decent expressions of repugnance: that being done, we can turn with clear consciences to the comfortable meditation upon the stainless glories of our nation. And if the sins imputed to him be contradictory and mutually exclusive of each other, why, so much the more monstrous his character. Let him be, as occasion serves, a cold-blooded calculator or a raging maniac, a profligate Lothario in Madame Roland's eyes, or fanatically ascetic in M. Michelet's, for Lamartine the incarnation of anarchy, for Quinet the apostle of Caesarism.

There are in M. Chevremont's collection a hundred and fifty portraits of Marat, and no two, it is said, are alike. Of all the writers who have inveighed against him, no two have described the same character. The consequence is that the world in general has no more idea of what he really was than what he really looked like; and this, though he was the author of a score of volumes on physics, philosophy, and politics, and of nearly a thousand numbers of a newspaper. (p. 43)

Marat's life was devoted almost absolutely to the *Ami du Peuple*, of which he was from the outset the editor after the first month the sole author, and in a few more the printer and publisher. Anything more unlike what we now-a-days understand by the word "newspaper" it is difficult to imagine. In outward from it considerably more resembled a tract. Sometimes eight, sometimes twelve, sometimes sixteen small octavo pages; on one day in large type, with the last sheet or two almost blank; on another in small type, crammed to the last inch; sometimes beginning in large and then changing half way to small, to enable the writer to compress within his limits his flood of language,—full of typographical errors, wrong dates, mistakes in names, and inaccuracies of every kind; hardly any of what we should call news, perhaps an analysis of the last debate in the Assembly, with Marat's commentary on it, perhaps entirely filled by a single article on some question of the day, or crowded with letters to the editor denouncing some court intrigue, some official malpractice, some arbitrary sentence of the Châtelet,—such was the form in which this extraordinary journal was hawked every morning about the streets of Paris. (p. 48)

Open a single number of the *Ami du Peuple*, and it is sure to be interesting. Either the unshrinking logic of the argument, or the clearness of insight into a political situation, or the penetrating estimate of individual character, or the ungovernable passion of an invective against some oppression of the weak, some treacherous intrigue, fascinates the attention. Read a dozen at a sitting and they are sure to be dull. There is immense repetition. Marat hammers and hammers at the same proposition with a pertinacity which is effective enough in a newspaper, but which is intolerable in a volume. There is hardly, from first to last, a spark of humour. Satire is banished as a thing unclean. Of a style like that of Camille Desmoulins, in political writing, Marat always disapproved. "Satirical writers," he says, "attack indeed the tyrant, but not tyranny. . . . The want of decency likewise prejudices the cause of the public. Gross invectives indispose peaceable men, scandalise well-bred men, and alienate all those cool patriots who are tied but by a thread to the cause of liberty." From coarseness of expression the *Ami du Peuple* is absolutely free. It is not in Marat's paper, but in the *Aeles des Apôtres*, and such like of the royalist. Peltier Champcenetz, Rivarol, or Suleau, that ones finds the rivals of Hébert and his *Père Duchesne*.

The characteristic of the journal which perhaps first strikes the eye, and certainly produces in the end the greatest weariness, is the constantly recurring denunciation. One's first impulse is to toss the volume away as rubbish, and believe, with M. Michelet, that the author "vents accusations dictated at random by his dreams." A little study of Marat's views shows that the question is not to be so easily disposed of. Denunciation, whether of questions of individual oppression, or of treason to the State, was with him not so much a passion as a principle. His theory of suspicion was deliberately formed and expressed over and over again with unhesitating precision. "Liberty can never be established," he says, "unless the principle is recognised that the humblest citizen has the right to attack, expose, and denounce every agent of authority whose conduct is illegal, equivocal, or suspicious." Denunciation is to be looked upon not as a means of curing or of avenging an evil, but primarily at least, and essentially as a preventive. Conclusive proofs are almost always at the time unattainable—to wait for them would nine times out of ten be to wait till the plot has been put in execution, and the denunciation, as a preventive measure, stultified. (p. 49)

[The] *Ami du Peuple* is by no means the kind of publication with which one might expect a demagogue to gain the ear of Paris. It exists on anything rather than flattery of its readers. In many respects, indeed, the stamp of its author's mind was absolutely antipathetic to the people he addressed. Of the wit, satire, epigram of the French, he is . . . all but destitute. He has no sympathy with their light-hearted vanity; their frivolity drives him to despair; their theatricality he cannot endure. For their displays in the Champ de Mars, and their altars, and their allegorical gods and goddesses, and all the mummery which was as dear to Robespierre as to Hébert and Chaumette, Marat has profound contempt. It is as impossible to imagine his marching after the Dictator's sky-blue coat in adoration of the Etre Suprême, as to picture him prostrating himself before Reason, incarnate in Madame Momoro. He speaks his mind to the people in language fully as severe as that which he bestows upon principalities and powers. Take the first few numbers of the paper. "Frivolous people," is almost the first thing one sees, "you are blinded by your vanity." "People of egoists," it goes on next day, "who act only from self-interest, who consult only their passions, and with whom vanity is the only motive power. . . . A nation, without intelligence, without morals, without virtues, is not made for liberty." Nor does he shrink, where justice or wisdom seem to call for it, from downright antagonism to the popular movement. (p. 55)

[Through the] years of struggle in which the bourgeoisie was winning its place and power from the aristocracy, the people, with that simple faith so grand and so sad to look back upon, were starving, enduring, fighting, dying to win the battle for others. Marat, with his clear, deep insight, saw on the one hand this "exploitation" of the working class, on the other the absence of a true representative and leader, either sprung from the ranks of the people or living their life. This life, then, he felt called upon to live. In no other way could his words come straight from the heart—the cry of human wretchedness from one who felt and sympathised, not merely from sensitiveness of imagination, but from the bitterness of contact and experience. Into this life he threw himself with an intensity of purpose which made him seem less a man than a personified idea. That which brought him home to the hearts of the poor, which gave him his fascination over David the painter and Fabre the poet, which even to us, steeped in the prejudices of a century's middle-class respectability and middle-class literature, makes him an object of such powerful attraction is this,—that in him there was, as it were, concentrated—in all its weakness and all its strength, in its despair and in its faith, in its passionate hatred and its deep tenderness, in its hideousness and in its strange beauty, in its degradation and its grandeur—the whole force of human suffering.

The life he chose he had lived to the end without wavering. He had entered into it professing no vague liberal, or socialist, or revolutionary principles, which may be turned to anything according to the exigencies of the hour, but with his programme in his hand, with his *credo* definitely formulated, and its conclusions worked out in detail. From his *Plan of a Constitution,* and *Criminal Legislation,* there was no room to doubt, and from the practical consequences of those theoretical treatises he never shrank. In a time of general corruption and general suspicion, his character had remained untarnished. One popular idol after another had fallen dishonoured. Mirabeau had been bought, Dumouriez had been a traitor, the name of Brissot had been dragged through the mire, that of Danton even had not escaped, but on Marat, as on Robespierre, no shadow of stain had fastened. Vague accusations, hurled random by the royalist press, had glanced off him without a mark, not because he had put them by with affected scorn, or had challenged proofs which might have been already destroyed, but because he had said, and it had been enough to say, "Name the side, the party, to whom I have been sold, and name too the services I have done them for their money." (pp. 72-3)

One can hardly help wondering what might have been the difference in the course of the Revolution if Marat had lived. Would the Terror have been more terrible, as M. Quinet thinks? or would there have been a terror at all? Of this one thing we may be sure, that a difference there would have been; for Marat living would have rendered Robespierre impossible. But, indeed, it is idle to conjecture what he might have done or become, when it is so difficult to come at the truth of what he did and was. The generation that knew him has passed away, and with them the love and gratitude they bore him; and the literary champions of vested interests have taken sufficiently good care that similar sentiments shall not easily recur. Until that future comes for which he toiled, his name will remain a byword: as, indeed, why should it not, considering that it is the condemnation of the present. (p. 74)

F. Bowen-Graves, "Marat," in The Fortnightly Review, Vol. XV, No. LXXXV, January 1, 1874, pp. 43-74.

HIPPOLYTE ADOLPHE TAINE (essay date 1884)

[*Taine is often considered the founder of the sociological school of literary criticism. Although today his formula of "race-milieu-moment" has been severely criticized, Taine had a profound impact on the sociological criticism of the nineteenth century, and even on the development of Marxist critical thought in the twentieth. Taine argued that a work of literature can be totally understood as a product of three influences: race, moment and milieu. By "race" Taine meant the combined physical traits and specific mental habits of a certain nationality of people, such as the French, the English, and so on. Today, especially after the abuse of the term by the Nazis during their rise to power, race seems a weak and constricting foundation for judging literary works. It is unclear for most critics what Taine meant by the term "moment," but it is generally assumed that it is either the sum of race and milieu, or simply the milieu of a particular time. The term "milieu" is the only one of the three that is still useful to critics. It includes, according to Taine's definition, not only the physical environment but also political and social conditions. Though a writer's milieu might have a profound impact on his or her style of writing, most modern critics see it as only one aspect contributing to the direction of an individual's creative work, and by no means an adequate explanation for the greatest works of art in world history. That Taine saw it as the major force in matters of art and literature has only detracted from his standing in the history of literary criticism. In the following excerpt from his three-volume La révolution (1878-84; The French Revolution, 1878-85), he seeks to establish Marat as a madman.*]

Three men among the Jacobins, Marat, Danton and Robespierre, merited distinction and possessed authority:—owing to a malformation, or distortion, of head and heart, they fulfilled the requisite conditions.—Of the three, Marat is the most monstrous; he borders on the lunatic, of which he displays the chief characteris-

tics—furious exaltation, constant over-excitement, feverish restlessness, an inexhaustible propensity for scribbling, that mental automatism and tetanus of the will under the constraint and rule of a fixed idea, and, in addition to this, the usual physical symptoms, such as sleeplessness, a livid tint, bad blood, foulness of dress and person, with, during the last five months of his life, irritations and eruptions over his whole body. Issuing from incongruous races, born of a mixed blood and tainted with serious moral commotions, he harbors within him a singular germ: physically, he is an abortion, morally a pretender, and one who covets all places of distinction. His father, who was a physician, intended, from his early childhood, that he should be a savant; his mother, an idealist, meant that he should be a philanthropist, while he himself always steered his course towards both summits. "At five years of age," he says, "it would have pleased me to be a schoolmaster, at fifteen a professor, at eighteen an author, and a creative genius at twenty," and, afterwards, up to the last, an apostle and martyr to humanity. "From my earliest infancy I had an intense love of fame which changed its object at various stages of my life, but which never left me for a moment." He rambled over Europe or vegetated in Paris for thirty years, living a nomadic life in subordinate positions, hissed as an author, distrusted as a man of science and ignored as a philosopher, a third rate political writer, aspiring to every sort of celebrity and to every honor, constantly presenting himself as a candidate and as constantly rejected,—too great a disproportion between his faculties and ambition! Talentless, possessing no critical acumen and of mediocre intelligence, he was fitted only to teach some branch of the sciences, or to practise some one of the arts, either as professor or doctor more or less bold and lucky, or to follow, with occasional slips on one side or the other, some path clearly marked out for him. "But," he says, "I never had any thing to do with a subject which did not hold out.... great results for myself, and show my originality, for I cannot make up my mind to treat a subject over again that has been well done, or to plod over the work of others."—Consequently, when he tries to originate he merely imitates, or commits mistakes. His treatise on *Man* is a jumble of physiological and moral commonplaces, made up of ill-digested reading and words strung together haphazard, of gratuitous and incoherent suppositions in which the doctrines of the seventeenth and eighteenth centuries, coupled together, end in empty phraseology.... His *Optics* is the reverse of the great truth already discovered by Newton more than a century before, and since confirmed by more than another century of experiment and calculation. On *Heat* and *Electricity* he merely puts forth feeble hypotheses and literary generalisations; one day, driven to the wall, he inserts a needle in a piece of rosin to make this a conductor, in which piece of scientific trickery he is caught by the physicist Charles. He is not even qualified to comprehend the great discoverers of his age, Laplace, Monge, Lavoisier, or Fourcroy; on the contrary, he libels them in the style of a low rebellious subordinate, who, without the shadow of a claim, aims to take the place of legitimate authorities. In Politics, he adopts every absurd idea in vogue growing out of the *Contrat-Social* based on natural right, and which he renders still more absurd by repeating as his own the arguments advanced by those bungling socialists, who, physiologists astray in the moral world, derive all rights from physical necessities. "All human rights issue from physical wants. If a man has nothing, he has a right to any surplus with which another gorges himself. What do I say? He has a right to seize the indispensable, and, rather than die of hunger, he may cut another's throat and eat his throbbing flesh. . . . Man has a right to self-preservation, to the property, the liberty and even the lives of his fellow creatures. To escape oppression he has a right to repress, to bind and to massacre. He is free to do what he pleases to ensure his own happiness." It is plain enough what this leads to. —But, let the consequences be what they may, whatever he writes or does, it is always in self-admiration and always in a counter sense, being as vain-glorious of his encyclopædic impotence as he is of his social mischievousness. Taking his word for it, his discoveries in Physics will render him immortal. . . . Anterior to his treatise on **Man**, moral and physical relationships were incomprehensible. "Descartes, Helvetius, Haller, Lecat, Hume, Voltaire, Bonnet, held this to be an impenetrable secret, 'an enigma.'" He has solved the problem, he has fixed the seat of the soul, he has determined the medium through which the soul communicates with the body.—In the higher sciences, those treating of nature generally, or of human society, he reaches the climax. "I believe that I have exhausted every combination of the human intellect in relation to morals, philosophy and political science." Not only has he discovered the true theory of government, but he is a statesman, a practical expert, able to forecast the future and shape events. He makes predictions, on the average, twice a week, which always turn out right; he already claims, during the early sessions of the Convention, to have made "three hundred predictions on the leading points of the Revolution, all justified by the event." In the face of the *Constituants* who demolish and reconstruct so slowly, he is sufficiently strong to take down, put up and complete at a moment's notice. "If I were one of the people's tribunes and were supported by a few thousand determined men, I answer for it that, in six weeks, the Constitution would be perfected, the political machine well agoing, and the nation free and happy. In less than a year there would be a flourishing, formidable government which would remain so as long as I lived."—If necessary, he could act as commander-in-chief of the army and always be victorious: having twice seen the Vendeans carry on a fight he would end the war "at the first encounter." "If I could stand the march, I would go in person and carry out my views. At the head of a small party of trusty troops the rebels could be easily put down to the last man, and in one day. I know something of military art, and, without boasting, I can answer for success."—On any difficulty occurring, it is owing to his advice not having been taken; he is the great political physician: his diagnosis from the beginning of the Revolution is always correct, his prognosis infallible, his therapeutics efficacious, humane and salutary. He furnishes the panacea and he should be allowed to prescribe it; only, to ensure a satisfactory operation, he should himself administer the dose. Let the public lancet, therefore, be put in his hands that he may perform the humanitarian operation of blood-letting. "Such are my opinions. I have published them in my works. I have signed them with my name and I am not ashamed of it. . . . If you are not equal to me and able to comprehend me so much the worse for you." In other words, in his own eyes, Marat is in advance of everybody else and, through his superior genius and character, he is the veritable saviour.

Such are the symptoms by which medical men recognise immediately one of those partial lunatics who may not be put in confinement, but who are all the more dangerous; the malady, as they would express it in technical terms, may be called the *ambitious delirium*, well known in lunatic asylums. Two propensities, one an habitually perverted judgment, and the other a colossal excess of self-esteem, constitute its sources, and nowhere are both more prolific than in Marat. Never did man with such diversified culture, possess such an incurably perverted intellect. Never did man, after so many abortive speculations and such repeated malpractices, conceive and maintain so high an opinion of himself. Each of these two sources in him augments the other: through his faculty of not seeing things as they are, he attributes to himself virtue and genius; satisfied that he possesses genius and virtue, he regards his misdeeds as merits and his crotchets as truths. —Thenceforth, and spontaneously, his malady runs its own course and becomes complex; next to the ambitious delirium comes the *mania for persecution*. In effect, the evident or demonstrated truths which he supplies should strike the public at once; if they burn slowly or miss fire, it is owing to their being stamped out by enemies or the envious: manifestly, they have conspired against him, and against him plots have never ceased. First came the philosophers' plot: when his treatise on **Man** reached Paris from Amsterdam, "they felt the blow I struck at their principles and had the book stopped at the custom-house." Next came the plot of the doctors, who "ruefully estimated my enormous gains. Were it necessary, I could prove that they often met together to consider the best way to destroy my reputation." Finally, came the plot of the Academicians; "the disgraceful persecution I had to undergo from the Academy of Sciences for two years, after being satisfied that my discoveries on Light upset all that it had done for a century, and that I was quite indifferent about becoming a member of its body . . . Would it be believed that these scientific charlatans succeeded in underrating my discoveries throughout Europe, in exciting every society of savants against me, and in closing against me all the newspapers!" Naturally, the would-be-persecuted man defends himself, that is to say, he attacks. Naturally, as he is the aggressor, he is repulsed and put down, and, after creating imaginary enemies, he creates real ones, especially in politics where, on principle, he daily preaches insurrection and murder. Naturally, in fine, he is prosecuted, convicted at the Chatelet court, tracked by the police, obliged to fly and wander from one hiding-place to another; to live like a bat "in a cellar, underground, in a dark dungeon;" once, says his friend Panis, he passed, "six weeks on one of his buttocks" like a madman in his cell, face to face with his reveries.—It is not surprising that, with such a system, the reverie should become more intense, more and more gloomy, and, at last settle down into a *confirmed nightmare;* that, in his distorted brain, objects should appear distorted; that, even in full daylight men and things should seem awry, as in a magnifying, dislocating mirror; that, frequently, on the numbers (of his journal) appearing too blood-thirsty, and his chronic disease too acute, his physician should bleed him to arrest these attacks and prevent their return. (pp. 121-27)

The "Friend of the people" has merely rascals for adversaries. Praise of Lafayette's courage and disinterestedness, how absurd! If he went to America it was because he was jilted, "cast off by a Messalina;" he maintained a park of artillery there as "powder-monkeys look after ammunition-wagons;" these are his only exploits; besides, he is a thief. Bailly is also a thief, and Malouet a "clown." Necker has conceived the "horrible project of starving and poisoning the people; he has drawn on himself for all eternity the execration of Frenchmen and the detestation of mankind."—What is the Constituent Assembly but a set of "low, rampant, mean, stupid fellows?"—"Infamous legislators, vile scoundrels, monsters athirst for gold and blood, you traffic with the monarch, with our fortunes, with our rights, with our liberties, with our lives!"—"The second legislative corps is no less rotten than the first one."—In the Convention, Roland, "the officious Gilles and the forger Pasquin, is the infamous head of the monopolisers." "Isnard is a juggler, Buzot a Tartuffe, Vergniaud a police spy."—When a madman sees everywhere around him, on the floor, on the walls, on the ceiling, toads, scorpions, spiders, swarms of crawling, loathsome vermin, he thinks only of crushing them, and the disease enters on its last stage: after the ambitious delirium, the mania for persecution and the settled nightmare, comes the *homicidal mania*.

With Marat, this broke out at the very beginning of the Revolution. The disease was innate; he was inoculated with it beforehand. He had contracted it in good earnest, on principle; never was there a plainer case of deliberate insanity.—On the one hand, having derived the rights of man from physical necessities, he conluded "that society owes to those among its members who have no property, and whose labor scarcely suffices for their support, an assured subsistence, the wherewithal to feed, lodge and clothe oneself suitably, provision for attendance in sickness and when old age comes on, and for bringing up children. Those who wallow in wealth must (then) supply the wants of those who lack the necessaries of life." Otherwise, "the honest citizen whom society abandons to poverty and despair, reverts back to the state of nature and the right of forcibly claiming advantages which were only alienated by him to procure greater ones. All authority which is opposed to this is tyrannical, and the judge who condemns a man to death (through it) is simply a cowardly assassin." Thus do the innumerable riots which the dearth excites, find justification, and, as the dearth is permanent, the daily riot is legitimate.— On the other hand, having laid down the principle of popular sovereignty he deduces from this, "the sacred right of constituents to dismiss their delegates;" to seize them by the throat if they prevaricate, to keep them in the right path by fear, and wring their necks should they attempt to vote wrong or govern badly. Now, they are always subject to this temptation. "If there is one eternal truth of which it is important to convince man, it is that the mortal enemy of the people, the most to be dreaded by them, is the Government." —"Any minister who remains twice twenty-four hours in office, when it is not impossible for the cabinet to operate against the Government is 'suspect.' "—Bestir yourselves, then, ye unfortunates in town and country, workmen without work, street stragglers sleeping under bridges, prowlers along the highways, beggars without fuel or shelter, tattered vagabonds, cripples and tramps, and seize your faithless mandatories!—On July 14th and October 5th and 6th, "the people had the right not only to execute some of the conspirators in military fashion, but to immolate them all, to put to the sword the entire body of royal satellites leagued together for our destruction, the whole herd of traitors to the country, of every condition and degree." Never go to the Assembly "without filling your pockets

with stones and throwing them at the impudent scoundrels who preach monarchical maxims; I recommend to you no other precaution but that of telling their neighbors to look out." "We do not demand the resignation of the ministers—we demand their heads. We demand the heads of all the ministerialists in the Assembly, your mayor's, your general's, the heads of most of the staff-officers, of most of the municipal council, of the principal agents of the executive power in the kingdom."—Of what use are half-way measures, like the sack of the hotel de Castries? "Avenge yourselves wisely! Death! Death! is the sole penalty for traitors raging to destroy you! It is the only one that strikes terror into them. . . . Follow the example of your implacable enemies! Keep always armed, so that they may not escape through the delays of the law! Stab them on the spot or blow their brains out!"—"Twenty-four millions of men shout in unison: If the black, gangrened, archi-gangrened ministerialists dare pass a bill reducing and reorganising the army, citizens, do you build eight hundred scaffolds in the Tuileries garden and hang on them every traitor to his country—that infamous Riquetti, Comte de Mirabeau, at the head of them—and, at the same time, erect in the middle of the fountain basin a big pile of logs to roast the ministers and their tools!"—Could "the Friend of the people" rally around him two thousand men determined "to save the country, he would go and tear the heart out of that infernal Mottié in the very midst of his battalions of slaves; he would go and burn the monarch and his imps in his palace, impale the deputies on their benches, and bury them beneath the flaming ruins of their den."—On the first cannon shot being fired on the frontier, "it is indispensable that the people should close the gates of the towns and unhesitatingly make way with every priest, public functionary and anti-revolutionist, known machinators and their accomplices."—It would be wise for the people's magistrates to keep constantly manufacturing large quantities of strong, sharp, short-bladed, double-edged knives, so as to arm each citizen known as a friend of his country. Now, the art of fighting with these terrible weapons consists in this: Use the left arm as buckler, and cover it up to the arm-pit with a sleeve quilted with some woollen stuff, filled with rags and hair, and then rush on the enemy, the right hand wielding the knife."—Let us use these knives as soon as possible, for "what now remains to us to end the evils which overwhelm us? I repeat it, nothing but executions by the people."—The Throne is at last down; but "be careful not to give way to false pity! . . . No quarter! I advise you to decimate the anti-revolutionist members of the municipality, of the justices of the peace, of the members of the departments and of the National Assembly."—At the outset, a few lives would have sufficed: "five hundred heads ought to have fallen when the Bastille was taken, and all would then have gone on well." But, through lack of foresight and timidity, the evil was allowed to spread, and the more it spread the larger the amputation should have been. With the sure, keen eye of the surgeon, Marat gives its dimensions; he has made his calculation beforehand. In September, 1792, in the Council at the Commune, he estimates approximatively forty thousand as the number of heads that should be laid low. Six weeks later, the social abscess having enormously increased, the figures swell in proportion; he now demands two hundred and seventy thousand heads, always on the score of humanity, "to ensure public tranquillity," on condition that the operation be entrusted to him, as the summary, temporary justiciary.— Save this last point, the rest is granted to him; it is unfortunate that he could not see with his own eyes the complete fulfilment of his programme, the batches condemned by the revolutionary Tribunal, the massacres of Lyons and Toulon, the drownings of Nantes.—From first to last, he was in the right line of the Revolution, lucid on account of his blindness, thanks to his crazy logic, thanks to the concordance of his personal malady with the public malady, to the precocity of his complete madness alongside of the incomplete or tardy madness of the rest, he alone steadfast, remorseless, triumphant, perched aloft at the first bound on the sharp pinnacle which his rivals dared not climb or only stumbled up. (pp. 129-33)

> *Hippolyte Adolphe Taine, "The Governors," in his* The French Revolution, Vol. III, *translated by John Durand, Henry Holt and Company, 1885, pp.121-289.*

LOUIS R. GOTTSCHALK (essay date 1927)

[*Gottschalk was a noted American educator and historian who wrote numerous works on national revolutions in general and the Marquis de Lafayette in particular. In the following excerpt from his first book, a biography of Marat, he surveys Marat's career as a revolutionist, noting his importance as a prototypical modern revolutionary.*]

It is not difficult to imagine what would have been the result if Marat had obtained the coveted seat in the Academy. During the years preceding the Revolution, instead of being a man nursing a grudge, he would have gone on living contentedly in the prestige thus bestowed upon him. Had he taken any part in the Revolution at all, then, it would probably have been in the moderate and contained manner that characterized the activities of Academicians such as Bailly, Condorcet, and Lavoisier. There is every reason to believe that he would have been entirely conservative and well-satisfied with the world, and not a sensitive soul touched to the quick by an alleged injustice. As things actually were, however, the Revolution offered him a new outlet for his pent-up *amour de la gloire.* Subconsciously, or perhaps even consciously, he now turned whatever genius he had, or thought he had, from science, which had proved sterile, to the opportunities offered by the impingements of events culminating in the French Revolution. (pp. 30-1)

[From] the very beginning Marat took an active, though not prominent, part in the revolutionary movement. During the period between the *Arrêt du Conseil* of July 5, 1788 and the *Lettres Royales* of January 24, 1789, he was, he informs us, dangerously ill and daily expecting to breathe his last. To have died without having had a share in the prologue of the Revolutionary drama, without having given expression to his *amour de la gloire* in the new field of opportunity, would have been a miserable death indeed. And so he put forth what he expected to be his last efforts in the composition of a work dramatically entitled *Offrande à la Patrie.* Although this was published in February 1789, it seems to have been written before the *Lettres Royales* of January 24.

In this pamphlet the writer indicated that he shared the feeling of hopeful expectation that prevailed about him. Louis XVI, he declared, was a good king, characterized by "his love for his people, his zeal for the public welfare."

The noble monarch, roused by the mismanagement of his ministers and the infidelities of the nobility and the clergy, had turned to his people for guidance. For love of him France must put forth her best efforts to meet the emergency: "Blessed be the best of kings!" And Necker, the much hated and feared Necker of later days, was now no less esteemed. For the moment he was "the great statesman, equally distinguished for the sagacity of his views and the spotlessness of his career, whose talents have called him to the administration of finances." With such a king and such a minister, Marat took it for granted that the government of France ought to be monarchical.

He had studied his Montesquieu very carefully, however, and was entirely convinced of the necessity of keeping the legislative, judiciary, and executive branches of the government separate and distinct. He wanted the legislative power, of course, to belong exclusively to the Estates-General, but, on account of the complexity of a great kingdom such as France, he felt that they ought to exercise this power only in questions of national and general interest. The king's province was to act as the executive power, which was to include the administration of the laws and of internal affairs, jurisdiction over foreign policy, and the making of appointments. The judicial power he wished to see confided to a hierarchy of tribunals, of which the court of last resort in both civil and criminal cases was to be the King's Council. This first court of justice of the realm was also to try impeachments upon the indictment of a committee from the Estates-General, the king having no power to pardon or to prevent the trials of officials under impeachment. By making the branches of the government independent of each other in this way, Marat hoped to create a system of checks and balances which would prevent the accumulation of too much power in any one of the three departments.

Marat believed that, together with these regulations for the trichotomy of governmental powers, the fundamental laws of the kingdom ought to include a declaration of the rights of man. Among these rights of man he emphasized especially the freedom of press, which, when censored, favored the despotism of the Academy; the right of habeas corpus; a more equitable court procedure, which should include trial by jury, public sessions of courts, and lawyers at government expense for the poor; no exemption from taxation, which should be in proportion to wealth; the abolition of hunting rights; and a more just and humane criminal code. There was very little of an original nature in Marat's book. These were popular demands that he was only one among thousands to agitate for.

His conception of the fundamental laws of France would have provided for little better than a slightly limited despotism, in view of the tremendous powers left by it in the hands of the king and the restricted sphere of legislation granted to the Estates-General. Marat, however, disciple of Rousseau as well as of Montesquieu as he was, had not repudiated his belief in the sovereignty of the people. He was beginning to conceive of the sovereignty of the people as the great mass of peasants and workers, who now, on the eve of a colossal revolution, were enjoying the support of the financiers, the newly created nobles, the curés, and the men of letters. He implied that these higher classes were not of the people, but merely allied to it temporarily, and that there was imminent danger of their being detached from it by the enemies of the Third Estate. However, this alliance of classes,

Jacques-Louis David's painting, Death of Marat *(1793).*

tion. On July 14, the Hôtel des Invalides and the Bastille were attacked. The former fell without offering any telling opposition. The other was taken only after a bloody struggle; the commander and a few soldiers of the garrison were massacred after its surrender. This event caused the King to recall Necker and to dismiss the troops who had been mobilized at Versailles. On July 17 he went himself to Paris, there to put on the tricolor cockade as a token of submission. The Paris mob had prevented reaction. (p. 43)

The events of the Fourteenth of July had given impetus to the work of the National Assembly on the proposed constitution. As it became more and more evident that the first Committee of the Constitution under the leadership of Mounier was intending to give to France a document modeled upon that of England, Marat's old feeling regarding the imperfection of that instrument of government returned and found expression in letters that he sent to the most famous of the Constituents. He claimed to have written twenty such missives, but there is only one extant today, affixed to his French edition of the *Chains of Slavery*, under the title of *Tableau des vices de la Constitution anglaise*. It is dated August 23, 1789. In it Marat spoke against the plan of Mounier's committee, maintaining that the English constitution had several vices and emphasizing especially the influence of the king upon legislation. With like purpose in mind he began his first journal which was entitled *Le Moniteur patriote*. But though this periodical ran to forty numbers, Marat was associated with only its first issue.

As time passed, the date for the report of the Committee of the Constitution drew constantly nearer. The questions that exercised the Assembly and the people of Paris most were whether there should be an upper house in the legislature and whether the king should have the right to veto legislation. An affirmative answer to both of these questions would strengthen the aristocracy greatly; a negative one might destroy it entirely. If Marat was to make his views on the constitution count for anything, it behooved him to put them before the public speedily. This he did in a work named *La Constitution ou Projet de déclaration des Droits de l'homme et du citoyen, suivi d'un Plan de constitution juste, sage et libre*, which appeared toward the end of August 1789. The author had evidently intended the book to be published earlier. At any rate, in the preface, he apologized for its late appearance, claiming that it had been ready for the press three weeks earlier, but that printers and police regulations had interfered with its immediate issue. It was frankly intended to influence public opinion and the vote of the Assembly upon the proposals of Mounier.

Here Marat shows himself to have been an eclectic political philosopher, building his theories again upon what pleased him most especially from Montesquieu and Rousseau. From the latter he took once more the theory of the sovereignty of the people that he had used before. Members of the state, he wrote, engage in a social contract for their mutual interest. Taken individually, therefore, the people are subjects; taken collectively, they are the sovereign. As sovereign they are entirely independent of every human power, their acts are law, and they are the only true legislature. However, for reasons of practicality, the people act through representatives. Birth alone gives every citizen the right to share in the selection of these represen-

which made up the body of the nation, was for him the only true sovereign; from it alone emanated all legitimate authority. He looked to it, and more particularly to the upper strata of it, to take the direction of the Revolution into its own hands and, co-operating with the King, to achieve a reformation of French society and government that should be for the benefit of the entire nation. The kingship, he repeated, was instituted only to force observance of the laws; the king himself was subject to them. If the government should refuse to accept the constitution that was about to be proposed, the nation had the right to resort to decisive means to force it to do so by refusing all aid to the state, by preventing the levying of taxes, and by meting out justice to offenders on its own authority. In the last analysis, therefore, Marat felt that the body of the people was the judge of what the constitution ought or ought not to be. He was confident, however, that no duress of any nature would have to be exercised upon the "wise and virtuous ministry" of France. (pp. 36-9)

[In July, 1789,] the conservative or court party, led by the Queen and Marat's one-time patron, the Count of Artois, induced the all too easily influenced King to gather an armed force at Versailles with the intention of using it against the National Assembly. On July 11, Necker, the leader of the liberal faction in the Royal Council and the idol of the French people, was dismissed. In fear that the revolutionary movement which was meant to benefit them would be suppressed, the Paris populace, for the first time, took an active part in the political drama of the Revolu-

tatives. The national senate, thus chosen by universal suffrage, becomes the central authority of the state, but its decrees do not become law until they have been sanctioned by the people; and lest it should grow too powerful, its individual members are subject to recall and punishment. Thus Marat appeared to advocate a unicameral legislature, subject to the direction and good-will of its constituencies. The army, too, he argued, ought to be faithful first to the people and then to the king; it ought to be a national militia under the orders of municipal magistrates rather than an armed force dependent upon and bound by oath to the ruler.

To strengthen this doctrine of the sovereignty of the people, Marat borrowed from Montesquieu the theory of the separation of powers, which he likewise had advocated before. Like most of the political writers of his day, he considered France too large and its administration too complex to be adapted to anything but a monarchical form of government. Care must be taken, however, to circumscribe the power of the monarch, so as to prevent him from becoming tyrannical. Arguing again that even in England the legislative and executive branches were not sufficiently separated, he urged that the defects of the English constitution be avoided—that the king be deprived of all means of influencing elections, that the legislature be permitted to convene and adjourn of its own accord without the intervention of the executive, and that no one who should sit in the law-making body be allowed to accept any office from the crown until after the lapse of ten years.

As we have seen, Marat had championed these limitations upon the royal prerogative before, but in this work he insisted upon others here suggested for the first time. He wished to take all significance from the right of veto, which he formerly had been willing to grant to the king. Now he wanted it to be merely a formality, the king consenting as a matter of course to every bill that had been passed by the legislature. Furthermore, in order to prevent the executive power from exerting too great an authority over the judiciary, Marat thought that the right to nominate judges ought to belong to the municipalities. His purpose in thus limiting the influence of kings was "not to demand of them that they do good" but to "make it impossible for them to do harm."

Eloquent as were some of these expositions, his most appealing tones were reserved for a plea for greater social justice. The misery of the poor and unfortunate still moved Marat. He saw them, often the victims of circumstances and mischance beyond their control, striving in vain to better their humble lot or resigning themselves in utter despair to their wretchedness. By nature, he cried, they were born subject to certain needs and from these needs alone they derived their rights to satisfaction. Should society deny them these rights, they might justly obtain them by force. To preserve their own lives and to resist oppression they might even take the lives of others. Therefore, to maintain peace, society ought to forbid by law the growth of conspicuous inequalities of wealth. Society owed to its members who owned no property a means of subsistence, while, on the other hand, those who possessed only their physical necessities, if so much, owed nothing to society. It was from those who had more than enough that the state ought to collect its revenue. He even went so far as to avow that where marked differences in wealth existed, a part at least of the property of the rich, often become opulent through intrigue and dishonesty, ought to be consfiscated for the amelioration of the condition of the needy.

This book presented with greater thoroughness the familiar line of reasoning that Marat had already developed; and along with it occurred repetitions of the same contradictions that he had previously been guilty of. For example, while seeking to circumscribe the royal power, he left to the king not only the right to issue administrative ordinances, which were to have effect as long as the legislature allowed, but also the prerogative of appointing his ministers, who, however, were not to retain office in the face of public opinion. Again, while declaiming against the injustice of private wealth, he maintained that the right of private property was a necessary factor in civil liberty; and while declaring that birth alone gave one the right of suffrage, he believed that women and children ought to take no part in political affairs since they are adequately represented by the heads of the family. Moreover, he declared that where the worth of candidates for office was equal, the representatives of the people ought to be elected from the richer classes of citizens, their fortunes being a guarantee of their good behavior. In other words, he was not a socialist in any modern sense of the word, although he did perceive, as he already had even before the Revolution, that the unequal distribution of wealth was unjust and reprehensible.

Up to this point the general tenor of Marat's early publications had become successively more radical and his political philosophy more definite and organized, but it was evident that he was still expectant of a revolution which should take place without any violent change in the government of France. He wished that the power of the king should be limited, but that France should continue to be a monarchy in more than name alone. The monarch, to be sure, was to be enlightened, to undertake measures for the welfare of the poor, to seek to better the condition of his subjects, but he was still to be left tremendous powers that he might use for evil as well as for good. Whatever reform was to take place, then, was to seep down from above and not to rise from below.

This conception of the Revolution was continued in the first issues of the *Ami du Peuple*.... Convinced of the necessity of a paper which would keep the electorate informed of the latest political developments, he originally wanted the electoral assembly to undertake its publication. Being unable, however, to persuade his colleagues to take such a step, he soon withdrew from that body in order to devote himself to the task alone. At first the heading of the journal led one to suspect that it was sponsored by a "society of patriots," but after a few issues had appeared, Marat openly avowed his sole responsibility for it. He soon projected his personality into the *Ami du Peuple* so completely that for contemporaries and for posterity he himself became known as the Friend of the People and his identity became inseparable from that of his journal. The prospectus of the leaflet made its appearance early in September 1789. The journal resembled in substance our American editorial page rather than a modern newspaper, seldom running to more than eight octavo pages and almost never giving the news except as a basis for editorial opinion. The first regular number was issued on September 12. Its title at the beginning was *Le Publiciste parisien*, but after the first five editions it took the more descriptive name of *L'Ami du Peuple.* (pp. 44-9)

It appears, then, that until September 1789 Marat held many of the ideas conventionally mouthed by the majority of the contemporary intelligentsia. Although, as a liberal monarchist, he desired to restrict the king's power, he had no wish to see monarchy actually abolished or even rendered *fainéant.* Marat's position at this juncture was unsettled and shifting. Consistency is, after all, a virtue of the unimaginative mediocre and Marat was not that. But through all his inconsistencies the bourgeois approach to political philosophy is easily discernible. His appeal is to the middle class; he has not yet conceived of the revolution as a popular movement. "One might say," declares Jaurès, "that he called the proletariat to the rescue only in despair at seeing the normal plan of the Revolution disrupted by the stupidity of the moderate bourgeoisie." It is this "despair at seeing the normal plan of the Revolution disrupted by the stupidity of the moderate bourgeoisie" —despair at what Marat soon was able to persuade himself was the counter-revolution—that henceforth troubled the suspicious spirit of the newborn Friend of the People and determined his future development. (pp. 50-1)

[Marat's] writings of the early revolutionary period were of a moderate character, similar to a myriad of other works and possessing no distinguishing features. If, as he claimed, his *Offrande à la patrie,* published on the dawn of the Revolution, was crowned by a patriotic society, that is an indication less of its intrinsic merit or influence than of the fact that such societies were very numerous and not over-discriminating in approving brochures of a patriotic spirit. It was not until the establishment of his daily journal that Marat became a figure of importance in the French Revolution. This is shown by the sudden increase in the amount of attention devoted to him by the Paris Commune and the National Assembly, the numerous attempts to arrest him, and the counter measures of the Cordeliers to protect him. But it was not his political philosophy that caused this alignment for and against him; it was his attacks upon Necker, Lafayette, Bailly, and other alleged counter-revolutionaries. It was his destructive invective and not any constructive ideology that won him both his enemies and his friends.

Yet, by this time he was beginning to set forth a definite political program. He advocated the formation of revolutionary clubs, but prematurely—when a few pioneers, such as the Breton Club, already existed, but before they were ready to become an active part of the political machinery of the Revolution. The clubs that eventually were formed developed gradually, largely as a matter of political exigency, and were not the product of any deliberate attempts at artificial cultivation such as Marat had advocated. By the time the clubs had begun to be a factor in politics, Marat had already gone on to another demand—the revolutionary tribunal. Again he was ahead of the times. The idea of a judicial body created for the express purpose of punishing political offenders did not seize the popular imagination for three more years. And in the meantime Marat had begun to support still another project—the dictatorship. This, however, was the least popular of all his political schemes. Marat himself admitted that he had been unable to obtain any support in preaching it and that he was entirely alone among all the thinkers of the Revolution in championing it. And yet it

is his chief contribution to revolutionary philosophy—the theory which he advocated longest and most consistently. Admission of its unpopularity was tantamount to admission of the unpopularity of his whole scheme of political philosophy. Of his constructive policies, therefore, there remains only his support of the revolutionary committees, such as the Committee of Public Safety, which was the only plan that he advocated opportunely and successfully. This idea, however, was not his; he was but one of many to champion it and, as has been shown, there is good reason to believe that he recommended it only because it came nearest to a realization of his dictatorship program, which had become too obnoxious to the people at large for him to continue openly as its exponent.

These are the several phases of Marat's constructive politics. They entitle him, to be sure, to generous credit for his political insight, but the fact nevertheless remains that they did not appeal to the minds of his dearly-beloved people. It was his attacks and not his proposals that won their support. It was because he constantly feared counter-revolution and threw himself bodily upon it wherever he beheld it that he became known as a whole-hearted supporter of the Revolution. He made prediction upon prediction of disastrous conspiracies that were afoot to overthrow the achievements of recent years, for prediction was a form of accusation. (pp. 172-74)

But it was not by attacks and predictions alone that Marat showed himself the devotee of the Revolution. He had suffered for it more than any other. Everybody knew (Marat took care that they should learn) of the seven or more attempts to arrest him, of his frequent hiding in unwholesome places, of the seriousness of the resultant illness, of his having lost all his wealth in the service of the people and their Revolution. He announced, perhaps with some truth, that he had lived for a period of nine months on only bread and water in order to furnish the expenses of printing his pamphlets and papers; that "for more than three years [this was in 1793] he had not taken a quarter of an hour of recreation" so that he might give more time to his country's needs; that he "watched day and night" over the safety of the people. But whether true or not, these statements, repeated with literally hundreds of others of a similar tenor to readers who were probably as gullible as newspaper-readers have ever been, had a telling effect. Their admiration and confidence grew: if he had devoted his life to them, they would be no less willing to devote their lives to him.

When once he had deserted his bourgeois notions, Marat deliberately cultivated the favor of the lower classes. The phrase *Ami du Peuple,* which he now used not only to describe his journal but also as a title that accompanied his signature even on official papers, had been chosen advisedly. But his program of labor and social reform, though derived from a sincere conviction of the injustice of the economic organization of society and probably emphasized in order to win for him the support of the populace, was no more heeded than his political program. More profitable than this was his deliberate imitation of the dress of the lower classes. Contemporary portraits and memoirs bear witness to his unkempt clothes and uncouth manner. He who had once had a marquise for a mistress was now a *sans-culotte,* wore his shirt open at the neck, a bandage around his head, and pistols in his belt.... Marat himself realized very well why he was popular. In his first interview with Robespierre, when the Incorruptible protested against his virulent addresses, Marat replied:

> Learn that my reputation with the people rests, not
> upon my ideas, but upon my boldness, upon the impet-
> uous outbursts of my soul, upon my cries of rage, of de-
> spair, and of fury against the rascals who impede the ac-
> tion of the Revolution. I am the anger, the just anger,
> of the people and that is why they listen to me and be-
> lieve in me. These cries of alarm and of fury that you
> take for empty words are the most naïve and most sin-
> cere expressions of the passions that devour my soul.

Such, indeed, were the reasons for the esteem in which
Marat was held, an esteem which in part was cultivated
and in part was the natural result of his political sympathies. It was not due to his ideas or to his program, but to
his character, his language, his attacks, his apparent sincerity and devotion to the cause of the Revolution.
(pp. 174-78)

Such then was the career of Jean Paul Marat, son of a
teacher of languages, doctor to the body-guard of the
Count of Artois, friend of the people, and Nemesis of the
Girondins. It is a career that presents many curious contrasts. While a physician who devoted unremunerated
years to the cause of pure science, he sold patent medi-
cines; while a conservative seeking a title of nobility and
preaching that a good king is the finest creation of a
friendly Providence, he had urged a more equitable distribution of property; while a radical protesting against privileged orders and ruling aristocracies, he had favored a dictatorship; while a demagogue clamoring for hundreds and
thousands of heads, he had exerted every effort to save
three of the impeached Girondins; and while a hard and
relentless pursuer of the enemies of the Revolution, he
had met his death at the hands of one who had hoped to
gain access to him because she claimed to be unhappy.
The essence of true greatness—the ability to mould
events—was not his; he was moulded by events. Some are
born to radicalism; Marat had radicalism thrust upon him.
Force of circumstances outside of his control alone had
changed him from a well-paid, complacent servant of the
nobility into the leading spirit of the popular movement of
his time. It was not a movement that he had created but
one at the head of which he had placed himself after it already existed and had become vigorous.

Throughout it all he retained, amidst his fiery attacks and
denunciations, enough of the old conservative instinct to
make him cling to the monarchy until it had itself lost all
footing, and to make him distrust all popular enterprises
unless they had leaders who stood above the populace. He
knew the strength of the people and desired it to be employed in their own behalf, but lacked confidence in them.
He was not a democrat. He loved the common folk but
did not respect them, as one loves an erring and misguided child. The keynote of his whole revolutionary creed,
therefore, had been his cry for the concentration of power
in clubs, tribunal, dictator, committee. He wished to insure the people's welfare through the aid of others, to
reach a radical end by conservative means. But the people
of his day trusted and followed him, unable to examine
the program he preached for the attention required by his
passionate, volcanic, melodramatic personality. And that
is why revolutionaries since his time have seen in him an
apostle of freedom and a martyr of liberty, without sharing his distrust of the common people, without adopting

his policy of the undemocratic concentration of power in
the hands of one or very few at most. But whether to
friend or foe, his devotion to the cause of revolution has
counted for all, the details of his political theories for
naught. Detached from that devotion and that cause, he
may perhaps appear to be the homicidal maniac he has
sometimes been depicted, but it is well to remember that
the explosive atmosphere of revolutions generally tends to
produce some plain-spoken soul whose uncompromising
sincerity, whatever its conscious or unconscious basis, recognizes no legitimate obstacle in the way of success for the
cause he champions. (pp. 194-95)

> *Louis R. Gottschalk, in his* Jean Paul Marat: A
> Study in Radicalism, *1927. Reprint by The Uni-
> versity of Chicago Press, 1967, 225 p.*

J. M. THOMPSON   (essay date 1929)

[*Thompson was an English clergyman and historian who
wrote numerous works on the New Testament and on the
French Revolution, focusing especially upon French revolutionary leaders. In the following excerpt, he presents the po-
lar perceptions entertained of Marat.*]

Marat approaches the Revolution—an ingenious, conceited, cantankerous little man, his pockets swollen with
press-cuttings and unpaid bills, and his head full of his
great grievance against the French Academy, which will
not admit that he knows more about optics than Sir Isaac
Newton. And perhaps it was the festering of this grievance
into a 'persecution complex' which turned the lively and
not unsociable scientist into the sour recluse and cynical
'friend of the people' who from his cellar castigated in
turn every phase of the Revolution.

In 1788 Marat wrote his first revolutionary pamphlet, and
called it *Offrande à la Patrie*; and this was soon followed
by others dealing with the Constitution, the Rights of
Man, and the faults of the British system of government.
But pamphleteering was a middle-class method, and Marat seems to have wanted, from the first, to get into close
touch with the common people. He was to be seen reading
aloud from Rousseau's *Contrat Social* at the street-
corners. And early in September, 1789, he began to issue
the small eight-paged journal which, under the name of
Ami du Peuple (in September, 1792, *Journal*, and in
March, 1793, *Publiciste de la Révolution française*) appeared, with some intervals, almost every day until his
death. The motto of this paper under the monarchy was
one that Marat had already borrowed from Rousseau—*vitam impendere vero*—'truth or death.' He began
it, he says, in 'a severe but honest tone, that of a man who
wishes to tell the truth without breaking the conventions
of society'; but soon, finding that the deputies and officials whom he censured did not mend their ways, he 'felt
that it was necessary to renounce moderation, and to substitute satire and irony for simple censure.' When this too
failed, he came to think that nothing would succeed but
force, and preached the extermination of all who supported the old *régime*, or opposed the new order of liberty.
Marat was gifted with a fatal clairvoyance, unredeemed by
any touch of toleration. His doctor's eye diagnosed disease
everywhere. He had an unrivalled knowledge of the pa-
thology of politics. He denounced in turn each National
Assembly and almost every leader of the people. And as

he flattered himself that his scientific discoveries were original and epoch-making, so it became a matter of pride with him to point out treachery where others had never suspected it, and to represent himself as the saviour of the country from unprecedented disasters. Besides, it is demoralizing to anyone to be expected to denounce something or somebody once a day; and Marat's criticisms were often quite irresponsible. Barbaroux—doubtless an enemy—describes an occasion on which he and a friend visited Marat. 'We found the great man writing his journal. He was in a hurry: the printer was calling for copy. You should have seen the casual way in which he composed his articles. Without knowing anything about some public man, he would ask the first person he met what he thought of him, and write it down. "I'll ruin the rascal," he would say.' Such methods naturally brought Marat many attacks. But the prophet liked being a martyr, and kept up the pose of a hunted man, hiding in attics and cellars, long after any danger of arrest had passed. It increased his prestige, and the circulation of his paper.

Mere denunciation does not make a prophet; and in his constant castigation of error Marat might have lost the power of speaking the truth. He was saved by a more amiable characteristic—a genuine care for the poor. After August, 1792, he chose a new motto for his paper—*Ut redeat miseris, abeat fortuna superbis*—or 'Let us tax the rich to subsidize the poor.' Marat was never a Communist. He thought equality of property an impracticable ideal. But he believed that society ought to compensate the poor for their loss of natural rights—liberty, equality, and the rest—by a system of public philanthropy that could provide them with work, pay them adequate wages, supply them with cheap food, and look after their sick. His socialism, like Robespierre's, was of the old-fashioned kind that would leave the rich man in his castle and the poor man at his gate, but would tax the superfluities of the one to relieve the necessities of the other. But though Marat is a 'friend of the people,' and an enemy of all aristocrats, financiers, and profiteers, he has no illusions as to the unfitness of the crowd for liberty or self-government, and is as ready to denounce them as their oppressors. 'O Parisians!' cries this new St. Paul on the Areopagus, 'you frivolous, feeble, and cowardly folk, whose love of novelty is a mania, and whose taste for greatness is a passing fancy; you who have a rage for liberty as though it were a new fashion in clothes; you who have no inspiration, no plan, and no principles; who prefer clever flattery to wise advice, fail to recognize your true champions, and trust the word of any casual stranger; who surrender to your enemies on their word of honour, and pardon the most perjured traitor on the first whisper of remorse; you whose projects and plans of vengeance are always made upon the spur of the moment; who can always produce an isolated effort, but are incapable of sustained energy; you whose only incentive is vanity, and whom nature might have formed for the highest destinies, if she had only given you judgement and perseverance—must you always be treated as grownup children?' Marat must have realized before long that the crowd was no more likely to be reformed by abuse than the politicians. But he had made the discovery on which more than one popular preacher has built up a reputation, that the crowd enjoys being abused. He said once, in a moment of frankness, to Basire, 'I put up my price for the public, my friend, because I know that they purchase my wares; but my hand would wither rather than write another word if I really thought that the people were going to do what I tell them to.'

Accordingly it is a mistake to look in Marat's writings, as some of his admirers do, for a system of thought. One idea, and one only, seems to string together the pearls of his invective, and to give to his expression of proletarian class-feeling something of the consistency of a political programme. This is the notion of a dictatorship. He had read in his classics the history of such tyrants as Polycrates of Samos, and Dionysius of Syracuse. He knew that democracy in the Greek cities grew out of tyranny, and tyranny out of proscription, executions, and the spoiling of the propertied classes. He believed that it was by the same road that the Paris people—it was characteristic that he hardly thought of the countryside as part of the problem—would achieve their rights. And this was why, with the clear-headedness of a fanatic, and the callousness of a medical man, he never shrank from proclaiming the last article of his creed—'I believe in the cutting off of heads.' The fantastic numbers of heads which he is said to have demanded, ranging on various occasions from 500 to 270,000, might give the impression that he was not serious; but this would be to forget that he was an editor, with a shrewd sense of the publicity value of big figures, and not a cold mathematician: that he was not a blood-thirsty man, but a thwarted idealist, whose imagination ran to see vengeances from which his eyes would have turned away. The Marat who organized the massacres of September, 1792, was the same who, a few years before, excused himself, on grounds of sensitiveness, from attending a postmortem. (pp. 168-72)

Though everything was done to obliterate Marat's memory, the legend of him lived on. Or rather, two legends. For to some he remains a monster, with 'a soul compounded of blood and dirt,' and Charlotte Corday seems a heroine, as noble as she was beautiful; whilst to others he appears as a single-minded philanthropist, and a prophet of modern socialism. In his death, as in his life, he is divided. We are haunted by the Siamese ghost of Marat I and Marat II. Is there any critical operation that can cut them apart, and yet keep them alive?

Napoleon made a sensible remark. 'I like Marat,' he told Gourgaud, 'because he is honest: he always says what he thinks.' If a man really does that, he is likely to give the impression of being two persons, at least, and is perhaps fortunate if he can retain any identity. We purchase consistency at the price of many evasions of the issue, and by accepting many opinions at second-hand. Marat's strength, both for good and bad, lay in his refusal to believe or to do anything at second-hand—to be anything but his own inconsistent self. In the careful and vivid study of Marat by his friend Fabre d'Églantine—it is the best that we have of him—this simplicity is described as the clue to his whole character. 'It characterized alike his person, his thought, his words, and his acts. In everything his insight explained things by their most natural causes; in everything his genius had recourse to the most simple means; that was why he nearly always appeared extravagant to men who were slaves of habit and prejudice, followers of routine, and the real or pretended dupes of the social hypocrisy and duplicity of the present time.' We may add that, as Marat was sincere in a world of hypocrites, so he was courageous in a society of cowards. But simplicity is not enough. It makes fools as well as saints;

it turns sincere men into fanatics, and courageous men into criminals. And when it is combined, as it was in Marat, with a strong dramatic instinct and a 'persecution complex,' its results may be quite incalculable.

All that history can hope to do, in any case, is to describe the resulting character. Even that is, with Marat, almost impossible. His speeches and books merely tell us his opinions; his portraits, for what they are worth, show us his appearance—nothing more; his letters throw practically no light on his real self; contemporary memoirs are often vivid, but seldom intimate or fair. The historian would give up all these sources of information for half an hour's talk with someone who knew Marat.

If he were a hundred years old he might have had such an opportunity. The historian and politician, J. W. Croker, was in Paris in 1837 or 1840, buying from the bookseller Colin, who had been Marat's printer, that great collection of papers and pamphlets which is now in the British Museum. Colin told him that Marat's sister, Albertine, was still living in Paris, and 'she is as like her brother,' he added, 'as one drop of water is like another.' Croker went to see her. 'She was very small,' he says, 'very ugly, very sharp, and a great politician.' Another writer, Esquiros, who saw her about the same time, said, 'The creature before me *was* Marat. In her correct, precise, and vehement vocabulary I recognized all the ideas and even the expressions of her brother. The woman seemed less the sister of Marat than his shade.'

That is as near as we shall ever get to the real Marat. (pp. 183-85)

> *J. M. Thompson, "Marat," in his* Leaders of the French Revolution, *D. Appleton and Company, 1929, pp.163-85.*

J. MILLS WHITHAM   (essay date 1930)

[*Whitham was an English man of letters. Among his many works, he wrote two studies of revolutionary France:* Biographical History of the French Revolution *(1930) and its companion volume,* Men and Women of the French Revolution *(1933). In the following excerpt from the former, he offers an evocative and sympathetic portrait of the author.*]

Marat, like Saint-Just, had his execrators and his worshippers. Men denounced him as an ulcerous low fellow who incited the people to widespread murder and rapine; others revered him as a martyr who spent life and forfeited happiness in a consummate philanthropy. He raved against the servitude of labouring men and workless men, compassionate for the sect or faction he chose to represent exclusively, attacking royalists and traitors, commercial plutocrats, profiteers, war-contractors, and the sober liberals, as if they were so many rotted branches of one huge overshadowing tree. His life-story was a mesh of obscurities and contradictions, wisdom and follies, science and perhaps quackery, pity and fury; yet always he claimed to be the Friend of the People, and his hankering for democracy flamed even at moments when he scolded the people almost as angrily as he scolded the aristocracy of wealth and all well-fed bourgeois, shouting for a dictatorship in the name of the People he professed to love and strove incessantly to help. The Revolution had begotten and killed Saint-Just: Marat was reborn in it. Much of his pre-Revolution struggle for existence passed in thick shades, vague in outline; the rest of his days took colour from smoky red glare; and his hoarse grumblings and anathemas were heard at any time in streets, at crossways, in Assemblies and Committees, or from the many cellars and lairs to which he ran for cover and safety, hue and cry at his heels. (p. 243)

His first published work, *An Essay on the Human Soul,* printed in England, 1772, an anatomical and mystical treatise, pleased and bewildered a noble lord; by whose influence Marat had offer of work abroad in connection with the Russian Embassy. He declined, afraid of the Russian climate, he said; in fact, not ready to exile himself among barbarians, certain there must be triumphs for him and his gifts in a hub of civilisation. His work, expanded in two volumes, appeared a year later as *A Philosophical Essay on Man;* a challenge to Helvétius, serious enough to provoke a sharp retort from Voltaire when translated by Marat into French.

His next work, *The Chains of Slavery,* in which, as he wrote, the clandestine and villainous attempts of Princes to ruin liberty were exposed, drew the praiseful attention of English democrats, added political virtue to his equivocal fame as a *savant,* led to persecutions, if he spoke truth; to journeys here and there, and much renown among the radical and workmen's Clubs in the north country. (p. 245)

He translated Newton's *Optics,* opposed to Newtonian theory, vain in these matters; and soon his inveterate habit of railing, and the beginnings of persecutional mania, fouled his track. He fought orthodox science and the vested interests of the Academy, unable to tolerate even the least criticism, braving ridicule, yet sore, hypersensitive, nervously diseased, beating himself against impregnable defences; for the scientific walls of Jericho did not fall when he issued command. At the eve of the Revolution, public favour had left him, gone elsewhere in the dance for new excitements and heroes. He had spent his money on ceaseless experiment, shattering his health, and lived in a painful obscurity, having resigned in temper or been dismissed from the Comte d'Artois' household. No one seemed to know precisely how or where he existed; a would-be reformer, prey to an invincible sadness, a philosophic despair, after failure to prove the imagined power of his genius to an ungrateful world; yet at work on his experiments and driven to and fro over Europe, half-starved, enflamed in mind and nerves by many real and many fictitious affronts; now in conflict with all Academies and constituted authorities, for they had reviled him, made an outcast of him, destroyed his opportunity to save the world alike from the curse of autocratic governments and more autocratic tyrants in Science and Philosophy. Marat had lived in a very midnight of bitterness and dejection, and looked toward death as a profound relief, overwhelmed by the pain of the world and the futility of endeavour, and oppressed by a cosmic dread.

There was much folly, a taint of madness, woven in the strange, haunted psychology of Marat, and perhaps he behaved like a rogue under the whip of circumstance, scorched by the lava in his veins; all joy withered in him, his features woe-bitten, haggard, drawn painfully, eyes staring, apprehensive, dangerous. Here was a man at war with Society, quivering for revolution and the hideous usage of Terror in his pity for other human outcasts, aggravated by the torment of his own life and the evil and wretchedness surrounding him. And he was stored as no other of his day with a piercing invective about to fly out and set his awaiting, combustible world on fire.

He was in Paris at the end of 1788, physically a wreck, bedridden, unfriended, expecting soon to die in poverty and loneliness; and he revived once more, judging the political situation with the uncanny foresight peculiar to him and never long absent from him. He began a fresh series of polemical writings, continued with but few intermissions until the day of his death, usually indifferent to science at this calamitous stage, ignoring derisive Academies, aware that greater issues were at stake, a new arena having opened miraculously for him in which he would battle for a wider humanity, and progress to a glory hitherto denied to him.

His first shot in the fray sounded with the pamphlet, *Offrande à la patrie*, and the announcement to citizens that Privilege was doomed. He spoke of impudent ministers decried for their ineptitude, aviled by their thievery, abhorred for their excesses, and now under the ban of an indignant, long-suffering public; for they had been traitors to their master and to the country and had led the State to a verge of ruin. He bemoaned the woes of the people and called on them to demand their rights. The true Marat torrent was at last in spate. A second broadside asked for union, and prudence; a third warned the people against the besetting French malady of infatuation. They must use severity in a choice of representatives for the States General, enlightenment and virtue being indispensable qualities in a deputy.

He left his bed, galvanised into life and hope and aim, strong enough to stand at the crossways and declaim passages from Rousseau's *Contrat Social;* and, rightly or wrongly, he claimed a popular and defensive share in the taking of the Bastille. Then he had the notion of a journal in which he could speak directly and each day to the people; and after preliminary and abortive effort, and a hectic search for supplies, he began to issue *L'Ami du peuple*, in September, with its motto, "Truth or Death." The first numbers were considered scandalous, as he admitted in his proud delight; but, he said, he had reason for attacking the National Assembly. How dare he use moderation when enemies at home and abroad were seeking to throttle liberty! Enemies must be exterminated. His audacity grew as the early struggles of the Revolution took shape. He saw in himself the watch-dog of Paris, having to bark by a duteous necessity, and day by day, sounding alarms and menacing all authority. He encouraged mobs, approving any violence on the part of a people cheated and driven by governmental impostors and taskmasters; and he denounced all repressive measures as so many insults to the Rights of Man and the ideals of liberty, equality, and a universal brotherhood. In his opinion, nature had offered abundant provision, and anyone deprived of such provision had the imprescriptible right to rob those who were stuffed with more than their just portion. Men must kill to save themselves, and devour the palpitating flesh of their victims; they were entitled to oppress, enchain and massacre in order to avoid oppression. He qualified his dictums only by restricting the Rights of one man inasmuch as they encroached on the Rights of another.

Marat spoke of liberty and believed in equality. The rich had suppressed the poor. Now the poor must bring the rich to their own level of hardship and want as an initial step to a flat social level of modest happiness. He was a thwarted idealist; and in his failure to solve problems calmly and by reason, he stamped on them and roared, paradoxical, bizarre. He partly excused his gospel of violence, arguing that folk were brutalised by and saturated with misery and would give ear only to extravagant counsel and gross invective; therefore as a good journalist he used the means likely to fix attention, though he confessed he would rather his hand withered than that the people should do as he bade them. He was occupied with the care of their salvation, prepared to adopt any method whereby he could protect them from reversion to thraldom; and always he would be their incorruptible, brave defender.

Marat's journalism was spurred by the condition of Paris, the Court and ministers, the weak and inactive democracy of the moderates; and assuredly by the fevers of his mind and the torment of his body. (pp. 247-50)

Marat had written that in his fifth year he longed to be a schoolmaster, at fifteen a professor, at eighteen an author, at twenty a genius consecrating himself to glory, then sacrificing himself to his country. He said he had exhausted the whole range of the human spirit, morals, philosophy, science, politics, extracting the best from all; that meanwhile he found his most tender pleasure in meditation, in those tranquil moods when the spirit admiringly contemplates the magnificent spectacle of nature, seeming to hear itself in the silence, weighing in the balance the happiness and the grandeur of humanity, piercing in its restless curiosity the sombre future, searching for Man beyond the tomb as far as eternal destiny. He may have believed himself at times when he prattled in this exhaustive fashion, and he gave no rest to his encyclopædic, flogged brain, actually tormented to solve the riddle of life and to shape an evangel for the betterment of a world stricken with pain. Truth and justice, he repeated, were his earthly divinities, and he estimated men by their personal qualities, not by success, respecting wisdom and admiring his notion of right. He convinced a multitude of his sincerity in these matters, and of his indignation against enemies and his pity for the oppressed; and his dramatic talents, his own trumpeted public and private virtues, were imposed on himself and his contemporaries, and led to his apotheosis.

No doubt he was a frustrated idealist and a romantic, soured with early failures, confronted with scorn, a prey to despair; and in the pursuit of glory he thought he had abundant genius and the power to save men, and wrought himself to distraction in the effort to crush; for he had been thwarted in his will to create. His audacity equalled his vanity in the latter years, and the Revolution afforded him an opportunity to exercise one and the other, carried him to a pitch of notoriety that must have invigorated him even when he was distraught and when the majority of reasonable men avoided him.

Fabre d'Églantine, the creator of the fanciful revolutionary Calendar with its *Brumaire, Frimaire, Thermidor, Fructidor*, the old names for the months having been judged unworthy of the new France, wrote that simplicity was the key to Marat's character, defining his thought, words, acts; that always his insight accounted for things by their most natural cause and his genius had recourse to the most simple means; consequently he appeared extravagant to men who were the slaves of habit and prejudice, followers of routine, submissive to social cant and the prevalent humbug of the day. That too may have been partly true as the measure of the man. He had the simplicity of a child in his affections and sensibilities; and now and again he had the simplicity of an unmuzzled beast in his relation to opponents of himself and of the people. Always he lived in a state of nervous fever, and, toward the end, of physical agony; and his skill as a journalist saturated crowds with his own passion, and meant death. He said he belonged to no party, being a party in himself; and at a time when creative ideas were usually ignored in the stress and lunacy of war, his system of thought, if it could be named system and thought, turned to destruction, his rhetoric to vituperation, his imagination to blood, englutting the scientist, the philosopher, the theosophist, often the humanist, the lamentable sum-total parading itself with a grim and unconscious irony in praise of equality and freedom.

Revolution nurtured such a man. (pp. 263-64)

> *J. Mills Whitham, "Marat and the Sansculottes," in his* A Biographical History of the French Revolution, *1930. Reprint by The Viking Press, 1931, pp. 243-65.*

SAMUEL BERNSTEIN (essay date 1941)

[*Bernstein is an American essayist who has written many works on Marxism, political revolutions, and labor-management crises from a decidedly partisan perspective. In the following excerpt from an essay originally published in 1941, he sympathetically sketches Marat's career as a revolutionary.*]

Popular leaders make history and are made by it. They are sharp-eyed men, generous and human. They see through people and events like X-rays, dig beneath the surface to detect the relation of things, their movements and their consequences to individuals and the community. Their perspectives are large. If they at times look to the rear it is not to nourish on the promises of yesterday, but to learn from the past, its errors and its merits, its knavery and sublimity. They are like stalwart oaks, with roots deep down in their country. They are of the people, yet freed from common vices and conventions. That is perhaps why their visions are far and their judgments prophetic.

Robespierre and Marat were two such men. The first was a parliamentarian, legalistic, cautious and acute; the second was a journalist, relentless, trenchant and astute. Each valued the other's services to the French Revolution. Robespierre saw Marat as "a fine citizen, a zealous defender of the people's cause"; Marat considered Robespierre "the patriotic orator," "the Aristides of the century," "loyal to liberty." Contemporaries draped them with obloquy.

They hated Marat, in particular. If they portrayed Robespierre as treacherous and gory, they placed Marat among the demented, the diseased, and the criminal. And historians, accepting their estimates, have poked fun at his gestures, his features and his small stature. Perhaps a clue to their aversion was his defense of the have-nots, his never-ending warnings, like siren-blasts, against conspiracies of reaction, and his call to the lowly to be the sentinels of the

nation as well as its governors. His ascendancy over them mounted steadily during the first four years of the Revolution until he fairly symbolized their objectives. By the time of his assassination, in 1793, they looked upon him as "The Friend of the People." (p. 9)

Marat had been in Paris thirteen years before the start of the Revolution. It is safe to assume that none of the signs of the decaying old régime escaped him. The conflict between those who desired to retain feudal relics and those who championed reforms produced a vast literary crop, most of it ephemeral. This was the golden age of pamphleteers, each proudly bequeathing to the nation his special remedy. Though occupied with scientific research, Marat could not be silent while society was in convulsion. The reform movement probably brought to mind the John Wilkes affair in England, of which he had been an eyewitness. The movement at any rate carried him along, and in February 1789, appeared anonymously his *Offrande à la patrie,* addressed to the Third Estate of France. It marked Marat's début as a participant in the Revolution.

The language of the pamphlet was fairly restrained, but underneath it was the suggestion that the people should take over the government. Marat praised the king, for in February, 1789, the French monarch was held in deep respect. But he called on the king to abandon the feudal class and join the people, for the people, he said, were "the strength and wealth of the state." The people should be firm in demanding reforms. If the government refused to sanction them then the people should boycott it, even refuse to pay taxes. Even now, in this early pamphlet, Marat foresaw that the resistance of the privileged orders would bring civil war and invite foreign intervention.

The pamphlet, appearing among so many others, probably did not have many readers, but did not go unnoticed. It was published at the expense of a patriotic society, implying that Marat already had connections with a political organization. And it caused a small polemic. Marat replied with a second pamphlet that was bolder than the first. He charged his critics with apathy and timidity. In the last analysis such critics amounted to very little in times of crisis. Reform was unavoidable, he held, but the king could not be trusted to introduce it, for he had no interest in the people's happiness. Only a national assembly could free the nation. The people should not expect anything from the privileged and monopolists, warned Marat, but trust instead to their own courage "to break their chains." (pp. 11-12)

Once the Parisians had shown the capacity to safeguard the National Assembly against reaction, a large and influential portion of its deputies started back. Their new, ill-clad defender dismayed them. Besides, reports from the countryside told of peasants' risings against their feudal lords. The insurgents were erasing feudal barriers, razing *châteaux*, and burning records. This threat to property rights persuaded the legislators to abolish personal services, but they left standing the onerous feudal dues that the peasants could redeem. Under the circumstances the Assembly proceeded to stabilize conditions by erecting a new political framework.

Marat published his own constitutional plan toward the end of August 1789. He proposed a constitutional monarchy. The monarchical form, however, was but a wrapper for a design to secure the people's happiness. People would be taxed according to their ability to pay. Above all, society had to guarantee to each of its members what Jefferson had broadly described as "life, liberty and the pursuit of happiness." Marat was rising to the defense of 15,000,000 Frenchmen whom hunger and poverty, he said, were wearing out. "I know," he wrote, "that I am exposing myself to danger by pleading fervently the cause of these unfortunates, but fear will not halt my pen." Marat's program was as distant from socialism as were Rousseau's and Jefferson's and Robespierre's. For in common with them he aimed at a society of small owners, in which property was "the fruit of labor, industry and talent." Where wealth was unequally divided, Marat argued, society owed the working people food and shelter, care during illness and old age and education for their children. Marat's project evoked no response from the constitution framers.

Events were pressing. The Assembly showed signs of bogging down under the influence of conservative deputies, enamoured of the conservative English government. The *jacquerie* was continuing in the rural areas. Were it not for public charity and the opening of workhouses for the unemployed, the cities, too, might have been turbulent. Marat felt the time was propitious for the launching of a paper. Through an arrangement with a book-dealer he was able to begin publication of *The Friend of the People*.

Marat considered himself "the people's sentinel." Perhaps no other phrase so accurately epitomized the history and content of his newspapers. *The Friend of the People* and its successors were designed to keep the people on the alert, to focus attention on ineptness and treachery in the governing group, to disclose the internal enemy and its foreign ties, to prevent the new rich class from appropriating the gains of the Revolution that the plebeians had secured by their fighting, and finally to strip the new masters of all make-believe and expose them as no better than the old. Naturally, the paper had many enemies. Its influence even among the lowly, penetrated with difficulty during the first two years of the Revolution. There were times when Marat regarded himself as a voice in the wilderness, and he would then prophesy that the people's political backwardness would permit reaction to triumph. But when the effervescent Parisians showed signs of stirring, his optimism returned.

He mastered the art of adapting the style to the purpose of the paper. Form and content seem to have melted into each other. The liberal Camille Desmoulins indulged in witticisms that sometimes lapsed into the sophomoric. Robespierre was as meticulous about his paragraphs as he was about his breeches. Marat, however, neither aimed to amuse nor stopped to correct the rhythm of his phrases. Forced to produce a daily issue under extremely trying conditions, he wrote rapidly. If the sentences were not eloquent, they were at least energetic, swift-moving, vibrating, and crowded with facts. In contrast to contemporaries who sought precedents and exemplars in classical antiquity Marat kept his footing firmly in the present, and attempted to settle vital issues within the limits prescribed by conditions.

Always Marat put his trust in the people. Despite their lethargy and their faith in the ruling upper middle class, especially in the first two years of the Revolution, he prodded them almost daily, reminding them to be vigilant, predicting their favorite leaders would betray them, and persistently charging that counter-revolutionists were plotting the restoration of the old régime. Marat was aware of the force of tradition; he knew the effect of poverty in making men support decadent practices. But his stay in England and events in France had also taught him that the people could be irresistible for furthering the advance of mankind. Consequently even in his greatest despondency and bitterness he never lost faith in them.

The early numbers of the paper examined critically the National Assembly. It had no plan of work; it was occupied more with royal prerogatives than with the people's needs. Its deputies were either silent or verbose, but concluded nothing. Its composition, moreover, made it incapable of reforming the nation. Marat cited the case of the feudal dues. The purpose behind the concessions of the feudal classes was to pacify the rural areas. The reforms adopted were therefore deceptive, for the peasants had to pay for the seignorial rights. None of the proclaimed sacrifices of the landlords could either bring prompt relief to the starving population or reform the state. The truth was, Marat said, the changes were superficial. Their aim was to paralyze the reforming spirit of the nation. He concluded by demanding the election of a new assembly from which the feudal classes and their allies would be excluded.

The paper was equally critical of the Parisian municipal government. It contained too many highly paid officials of the old school; it functioned secretly; it had erected a wall between itself and the people; it protected speculators and monopolists; it had surrounded itself with "a throng of venal intriguers;" and it was selling adulterated bread to the poor. But the small folk, who were nine-tenths of the capital's inhabitants, he said, were shorn of their rights, excluded from the National Guard and perpetually occupied with the struggle against starvation.

Dauntless criticism earned Marat persecution. Apart from posters denouncing him, his printer was intimidated and the distribution of his paper hampered. A municipal councilor, moreover, sued him for libel. He fled to Versailles, went into hiding, secretly attended sessions of the National Assembly and escaped arrest only because the police agents happened to be his readers and admirers. Returning to the capital he discovered that a spurious *Friend of the People* was circulating. Still in clandestine existence, he resumed the publication of his paper after an interruption of almost a month. The police discovered his whereabouts, invaded the printing shop and confiscated an issue. Thus began his hunted life.

He continued along the course he had charted. His aim was to "unmask traitors, remove from public office the covetous . . . the cowardly, the inept and incompetent," instruct "the poor who have always been subjected and oppressed, and inspire them with a consciousness of their rights." Then, "no human power can stand in the way of the infallible march of the Revolution." The people "will smash the rule of the wealthy just as they have shattered that of the nobility."

Before the meeting of the Estates General in May 1789, Marat had called for the unity of the entire Third Estate to defeat the feudal aristocracy. Once victory over the old order was attained, he began to suspect that the upper middle class was preparing to halt the advance of the Revolution, even achieve the sort of compromise with the feudal class the English had reached in 1688. Suspicion turned to conviction as he studied the doings of the National Assembly and the municipal governments. Only the people, he concluded, could be relied on to complete the Revolution. Their risings had led to the triumph of its first stage. If kept on the qui vive, he reasoned, they would push the Revolution to other stages. Marat was impatient with those who grew "compassionate over the merited punishment of a few profligates. But I see only the misfortunes, the calamities and the disasters of a great nation that . . . has been enchained, pillaged . . . oppressed and massacred for centuries. Who has more sense, humanity and patriotism, they or I? They endeavor to lull the people to sleep, while I strive to awaken them. They feed them opium, but I pour *aqua fortis* into their wounds. I shall continue to pour it until the people have completely regained their rights and become free and happy."

Marat pursued this course until his death in 1793. Compromise would be equivalent to betrayal; or to use his own manner of expression: "A fool can pretend to please everyone in normal times; but only a traitor can claim to do so during a revolution." There were periods when he was a victim of discouragement and despair, particularly in the first two years of his revolutionary life. These spells derived in the main from a want of response to his agitation. For Marat, at this time, was a prophet without disciples. (pp. 13-16)

Marat had little popular following from 1789 to 1791. Even so, his writings, especially his paper, were read by almost four thousand persons, according to one estimate. Also, the *Orateur du peuple,* edited by one of his disciples, shared his ideas. Individuals and organized groups at this time already looked upon him as a leader. For example, in February 1791, when the Cordeliers Club learned of the possible suspension of Marat's paper for lack of support, it formally declared that the disappearance of "the patriot, Marat," from the political scene "would be a public calamity, that his silence would be a general misfortune and the surest sign of the coming ruin of the state." The Club urged him to continue the defense of the people's cause and pledged its membership "to protect his person as well as to disseminate his doctrines."

Marat seems to have won admirers in the second half of 1791. Readers sought his advice, confided in him, and protested against counter-revolutionary officials and policies. They addressed him in the most laudatory terms: "our prophet," "the great magician of the century," "the most zealous partisan of the Revolution," the "true defender of the needy class." Workers communicated to him their complaints against employers.

The fast moving events changed Marat from a comparatively neglected journalist into a people's hero. The royal family, discredited by its attempted flight, the need to buttress the king's position, the outbreak of war only to be followed by defeats, and the invasion of France, these factors and others deriving from them were calculated to give Marat a vast audience. The comeback staged by reaction in 1793, and the civil war resulting from it, threatened the Revolution with extinction. People recalled Marat's earlier warnings and sought his political wisdom as revolutionary France organized itself to meet the challenge of feudal Europe. When the assassin's knife struck him down, he was at the apogee of his fame.

Evaluations of Marat have seldom been free from partisanship. For he articulated the popular aspirations in one of the greatest revolutions of history. He discovered quickly after its start that it could neither be fought with rose water nor its triumph be assured by preaching homilies. If his enemies hated him intensely he hated them as much. He neither expected quarter nor gave it, for he had dedicated himself to a cause in which the issues were sharply drawn and fought over bitterly. Whether Marat wins or alienates sympathies, he must be appraised as a political man who kept pace with history when it moved at a fast tempo. His writings and doings, if examined calmly in their extraordinary setting, are extremely impressive for their penetrating judgments and prophetic insights. (pp. 24-5)

> *Samuel Bernstein, "Marat, Friend of the People,"*
> *in his* Essays in Political and Intellectual History,
> *Paine-Whitman Publishers, 1955, pp. 9-25.*

NORMAN HAMPSON (essay date 1983)

[*Hampson is an English educator and historian. In the following excerpt, he provides an overview of the author's work and then examines the* Friend of the People.]

[Marat's] sympathy for the plight of the poor (if not for their political competence) was probably genuine enough, but he had no idea what to do about it—beyond encouraging them to revolt against whomever happened to be in power. His constitutional proposals were in line with radical democratic thinking in 1789 and a good many of them were to be implemented by the Constituent Assembly.

All sovereignty resided in the people, who collectively embodied the general will and 'can never want what is bad for them, sell or betray themselves'. If this suggests that Marat had certainly understood his Rousseau, his assertion that the civil rights of citizens were 'even more sacred than the fundamental laws of the state' could be interpreted as pointing in the opposite direction. The electorate was entitled to impose imperative mandates on its delegates but, like Montesquieu, Marat thought this unwise, except in the case of fundamental laws. All legislation, however, should be subject to referendum. Like Montesquieu and unlike Rousseau, Marat praised the way things were done in England, whose government was 'the most celebrated for its wisdom'. He approved of the personal inviolability of the king, as professed across the Channel. Both king and Ministers were somehow responsible to the people, although Marat did not explain what this meant in practice. In one place he said that Ministers should be elected, the accused allowed counsel and treated as innocent until they had actually been convicted. Taxation should be proportionate to wealth, with indirect taxation adjusted to fall very heavily on such luxuries as servants, horses and carriages. Arguing that France had nothing to fear from her enemies unless she herself adopted an aggressive foreign policy, he wanted the army reduced to 60,000, with a militia of 200,000 disposing of its own artillery and stationed in all the major towns. The consent of the civil authorities should be required before troops were used against civilians. Despite the fact that 'public matters are scarely within the range of ordinary people', all heads of families should have the vote, although, as usual, he advised them to elect 'men from the wealthiest class of citizens, whose fortune becomes a guarantee of their integrity'. On the subject of the clergy he was more violent and less realistic. 'The veil is rent, the mystical shadows in which they wrapped themselves are dispersed by the torch of reason.' . . . Apart from those in charge of monastic finances, there was not a monk who would not jump at the chance of leaving the cloister, if offered a small pension.

It was all rather a jumble, which was not surprising since he was trying to squeeze both Montesquieu and Rousseau between the shafts of the constitutional coach. On the one hand he attacked those who professed 'a stupid respect for the institutions of our fathers, the ancient usages of the kingdom . . . Why should we play at patching up an edifice that threatens to crush us in its fall and bury us beneath its ruins, when we can build anew?' On the other, he commended England as a model, still praise Louis XVI and thought that nobles and clergy were hastening to prove themselves citizens. He professed to detest 'licence, disorder, violence and irregularity', but said that the sufferings of the poor were all due to their pitiless exploitation by the agents of central and local government, who could only be tamed by the threat of revolt. He himself was probably hesitating over his choice of rôle, divided between the optimism of that unforgettable spring of 1789 and his deep-rooted convictions about eternal social war and the villainy of governments. If the latter won neither Montesquieu nor Rousseau would count for much. (pp. 127-28)

To begin with, Marat seems to have seen his revolutionary rôle as that of adviser to those in power. He sent a presentation copy of his *Offrande à la patrie* to Necker, 'that great statesman . . . distinguished both by his wisdom and his integrity'. On 29 September 1789 he said that he had already written a score of letters to the Constituent Assembly. If that of 23 August is typical, these were unlikely to have had much effect: ostensibly about the danger of copying the British constitution, this letter consisted mainly of Marat's version of the British government's attempts to suppress *The chains of slavery* in 1774. He went on writing to the Assembly for quite a while, letting the deputies know, in May 1790, that he had been 'born with an inclination towards study' etc., etc. In this authorised version of his career he admitted that when he had returned to France 'the kind of censor's rôle that I had played in England seemed too dangerous', which rather weakened his claim to have been 'the apostle and martyr of liberty'. No one took any notice of him.

His respectful letters to the Assembly were rather different from the one that he wrote to the Paris Commune on 25 September 1789, ordering it to purge itself of its less worthy members—he was particularly worried about 'men without any situation, living in furnished rooms and without any means of support apart from their work.' 'I am the eye of the people; you are at most its little finger.' 'The incorruptible defender of the rights of the people', he alone had saved liberty during the July crisis. This did not make any impression on the Commune.

Since no one was disposed to listen to his advice, he founded a newspaper of his own. The prospectus described it as the creation of a society of *patriotes*, which al-

lowed Marat to refer to 'the purity of views, the breadth of knowledge and well-earned success of the political works of the editor, a zealous citizen who for a long time neglected his own reputation, the better to serve his country, and whose name will be inscribed amongst its liberators'. This excellent man had saved Paris on the night of 14 July by halting single-handed 'several regiments of German cavalry' that were trying to move into Paris while its feckless inhabitants were still celebrating the fall of the Bastille. His paper, with the uninspiring title, **Le Publiciste Parisien**, carried Rousseau's device: *Vitam impendere vero*, and its editor promised his readers 'freedom without licence, energy without violence and good sense without excess'. All the other aspiring editors promised much the same thing.

Marat began moderately enough, but on 16 September he changed his title to **L'Ami du Peuple**. This was a stroke of genius: the paper *was* Marat and he was soon using the title to refer either to it or to himself. The tone changed too. On the following day he told his readers, 'We make a great song and dance when a few villains whose extortions have ruined whole provinces, fall beneath the blows of the populace [sic], in legitimate revolt, and we keep silent when the satellites of the Prince go in for the military butchery of thousands of his subjects'. It had not taken long for Marat to find his style and his message was scarcely to alter during the next four years. The tone of the paper did fluctuate: when he was living in the open he was relatively moderate; when he went underground—as he did in November 1789 to avoid prosecution for a libel directed against the wrong man—he became violent. He was on the run for most of the time. This was no doubt unpleasant, perhaps even dangerous, but it gave him a freedom to defy the law that was denied to his competitors. It may also have had an effect on his mental stability. The violence of his writing varied both with the political situation and with his own state of mind as well. The king's flight in 1791 brought on a particularly vicious paroxysm, when he demanded the shaving of Marie Antoinette's head, the burial alive of imaginary armies of invading *émigrés* and the impaling of the majority of deputies. Where verbal ferocity is concerned, one can easily concede his claim to have been unique.

The issues of 18-20 September contained a *discours au peuple* that was a kind of profession of faith. The French were a frivolous people whose liberation in 1789 had been a temporary accident. Paris in particular was the home of luxury and vice. The provinces were marginally less corrupt, 'But what can one expect from an egoistic people that acts only from self-interest, lets its passions dictate to it and responds only to vanity? Let us not deceive ourselves: a nation witout understanding, without *moeurs*, without *vertus*, is not made for liberty.' The cardinal mistake of the Parisians was not to have taken advantage of their lucky victory, in order to exterminate their enemies. This had allowed 'them' to recover and to win over the majority of the deputies. As a result, 'You are further from happiness than ever'. Bad as things already were, in the future they could only get worse, and all this was due to people neglecting Marat's warnings. 'What regrets you would have spared yourselves if you had followed the wise advice that the **Ami du Peuple** gave you nine months ago [i.e. in the **Offrande**].' 'There is only one way to save the state, that is to purge and reform the National Assembly, to expel with ignominy all its corrupt members ... to convene [to a new assembly] only men distinguished by their enlightenment and their virtues, and to supply it with a detailed plan of action, in accordance with a well organised constitutional plan.' A footnote explained that this was no other than his own work, published in the previous month. What he wrote during the next four years amounted to little more than variations on these themes.

Throughout the revolution Marat's attitudes were the product of a megalomania so monstrous that it sometimes struck people as funny. When he said to his fellow-deputies in the Convention, on 4 October 1792, 'You can't prevent the man of genius from projecting himself into the future. You don't understand the man of learning whose knowledge of the world anticipates events.... Where would you be if I had not prepared public opinion....' the general hilarity must have taken him by surprise for he was a totally humourless man.

He was the only one of the people's defenders who had never been deceived (22 December 1790), the only one capable of judging men, who had never relaxed his guard but always immolated himself for the salvation of the people (20 April 1791). 'I believe I have exhausted just about all the combinations of morals, politics and philosophy that the human spirit has devised, to arrive at the best conclusions' (14 January 1793). Turning on his political allies in the Convention, he told them, 'I am not like you, only born yesterday, where liberty is concerned. I sucked in love of liberty with my mother's milk and I was free forty years ago when France was still peopled only by slaves' (1 March 1793). If he really started at ten, he must have been a kind of political Mozart. His delight in proclaiming his own virtues and giving his readers the edifying story of his life became even more of an obsession with him in 1793. By then he was seriously ill and perhaps concerned to get the record straight before he died. A month before his assassination he wrote that his energetic contribution to the revolution would be a source of 'profound reflection' to posterity which would be amazed, both by his firmness, courage, etc., and by the fact that no one took any notice of him (17 June 1793). (pp. 193-96)

It was understandable if the thought of so much talent running to waste sometimes made him sad, or even bitter. 'Poor people! You tremble at the dangers your defender runs. A thousand swords of steel are suspended over his head at every moment. But he will never abandon you. Strong in the purity of his heart, when the fatal moment comes he will fly to his execution with the joy of a martyr' (16 January 1790). There were times when he could not help losing his patience. 'Perish then, stupid and cowardly citizens, since nothing affects you. And you, their unfortunate defender, die of grief at the sight of your powerless efforts. Why force yourself once again to pull back your unworthy compatriots from the edge of the abyss? No, it is not with a people of vile slaves that one can make a nation of free men' (16 January 1791). (p. 197)

The question that immediately arises is how one is to account for Marat's influence when the evidence for his paranoia is so overwhelming. Where the politicians were concerned, the extent of that influence is easily exaggerated. One Montagnard deputy, Thuriot, said in the Assembly 'There is no one here who can let himself be influenced by Marat or believe that he influences the

Early portrait of Marat which depicts him as a violent revolutionist.

Convention'. Another, Levasseur, said much the same thing in his memoirs. Marat himself complained a good deal, towards the end of 1792, that he was completely isolated. Things changed in the following spring, when the quarrel between Montagnards and Girondins reached a new intensity and the Montagnards had to defend anyone who was attacked by their opponents. Marat was then too useful as a hatchet-man for his services to be rejected. Unlike Robespierre and Saint-Just, he rarely offered any constructive suggestions about policy but confined himself to exposing plots and denouncing individuals. At the time, he did not appear to stand for anything very much. Things became different when his murder by Charlotte Corday made him a genuine victim, if not exactly the martyr he had always pretended to be. He was now irreproachable, canonised by the Cordelier Club, and as the revolution itself entered the bloody impasse of 1794 he made posthumous converts.

His most faithful clientele had always come from the streets. Dutard, an observer employed by the Minister of the Interior, summed this up with his usual intelligence. The *petit peuple* could not condemn Marat for things like the September massacres, without condemning themselves. 'They don't respect him, they even think he is slightly mad, but whether because his predictions have sometimes come off, or because of his opposition to parties that the people themselves hate, or because their idea of his integrity (the people's god) had earned him supporters, he has won their protection.' If Marat prided himself on one quality above all others, it was on his ability to smell out plots and to expose counter-revolutionaries, which may have impressed those whose political education was on the rudimentary side. He did have some undeniable—and well-publicised—successes. Since he denounced virtually everyone in office, the law of averages was bound to guarantee him that. (pp. 198-99)

When he wanted, he could be a shrewd, even a statesman-like observer. Like Mirabeau, he understood how the destruction of the intermediate bodies so dear to Montesquieu had potentially increased the power of the central government (16 December 1790). Unlike almost everyone else, he foresaw the danger of a breach with the Church. 'This is perhaps the only occasion since the taking of the Bastille when you need moderation in dealing with the enemies of your peace. One should not violate consciences and no power on earth can tyrannise over souls' (9 January 1791). He consistently opposed the abolition of noble titles: 'Instead of waiting for reason to do its work, the Assembly has barbarously undermined a stately edifice, built by glory and respected by time' (25 September 1791). Burke could scarcely have put it better. He had quite an acute understanding of the king's character and behaviour (1 October 1791). He could have made his reputation as a different kind of journalist but, as he told Robespierre at what may have been their only meeting, his influence was not due to his 'close analysis', but to 'the frightful public scandal' that his paper created, 'to the effusions of my soul, the outbursts of my heart, my violent denunciation of oppression, my violent attacks on the oppressors, my accents of grief, my cries of indignation, fury and despair' (3 May 1792).

Beneath the emotional self-indulgence, there is a clue here to the real reason why Marat stood out from the anonymous mass of journalists who made the revolution such a bonanza for the printing trade. He alone offered a coherent alternative to the orthodox interpretation of the revolution. What had happened in 1789 was not the reaffirmation of the rule of law but its defiance by force (23 February 1791). 'To what do we owe our liberty if not to popular insurrection?' (10 November 1789). This had been a lucky accident: 'The people rose in revolt and the other classes joined in only to prevent plundering' (12 April 1791). There was no conversion of the more conservative, no compromise and no national regeneration. The Enemy (it was never very clear whether this meant the king, his ministers, the nobility and upper clergy or the wealthy in general) immediately set about recovering the ground they had lost. They quickly bought the majority in both the Constituent and Legislative Assemblies. Indeed, since it led to the bribery of almost all men of talent, the revolution had corrupted *moeurs* rather than regenerated them. 'We are at war with the enemies of the revolution . . . Concern for the salvation of the *patrie* and our own safety therefore makes it imperative that we treat them as traitors and exterminate them as base conspirators' (21 May 1791). Whatever good had been done had been achieved by force. 'Follow its work and you will see that the Assembly has only been pushed into action by popular revolt. It was revolt that subjugated the aristocratic faction in the Estates General, against which the arms of the philosophers and the king's authority had fought in vain' (11 November 1789). It was therefore absurd to protest against 'those popular executions to which you owe

the revolution and the only good laws that ever came out of the National Assembly' (26 September 1790). Official law was the weapon of the enemy. The people's reply, which was equally legitimate, was mob violence. 'The government is the mortal, the eternal enemy of the peoples' (31 December 1789). Marat was never quite sure whether this was an unchangeable law of nature or whether the French revolution might not offer an escape from the endless cycle of revolt, new tyranny and further revolt. Since princes were always the enemies of their subjects, 'any Minister who has been in office for some time is necessarily suspect' (21 December 1789). 'To imagine that a Minister could be a *patriote* is folly; to pretend that he actually is one is madness' (28 June 1790). On the other hand, if the right action were taken, everything would be possible. The purge of the Assembly 'would release the springs of plenty and bring back peace and happiness at a stroke' (25 September 1789). 'A few guilty heads paraded in the streets from time to time would have kept the senate in a state of holy terror . . . already the reign of justice would have been established; alarms would have given way to peace, competition would have released the springs of abundance and you would already have been free and happy' (20 October 1790).

Marat then found himself faced by the contradiction that has afflicted a good many subsequent revolutionaries: how was a degraded people, corrupted by centuries of servitude, to sustain the effort needed for its liberation? It was not until 1790 that he found the answer, during his stay in England. 'The only way to restore order is to nominate for a time a supreme dictator, to arm him with public force and to hand over to him the punishment of the guilty . . . A few heads struck off will check the public enemies for a long time and will preserve a great nation from the horrors of poverty and civil war for centuries.' There was not much doubt about who the man should be. Once he had got hold of this idea, Marat repeated it over and over again, until it got him into trouble in the early days of the Convention. The job specification varied: sometimes three days would have been enough; in his own case, life-tenure would be necessary to preserve the benefits he could bring. Sometimes the leader's function was to draft a constitution or to win the war; more often it was to organise the slaughter of counter-revolutionaries—the fatal omission that had ruined the work of July 1789. (pp. 202-04)

No one else followed Marat in his bloodier fantasies. If the treatment he recommended was a prescription for anarchy and civil war, his diagnosis of why the revolution had failed to fulfil the expectations of 1789 was another matter. Beneath Marat's lies, slander and hysteria there was enough truth in his version of events to make it sound as plausible as the official interpretation. The constitutional compromise that almost everyone professed was one in which few believed. When most people hoped for the best without really expecting it, Marat successfully predicted the worst. To the extent that he contributed to the atmosphere of hatred and fear—and his appeals to the mob to lynch political leaders were unlikely to increase their attachment to the revolution—he may have given events a push along the road, but it was a road they would almost certainly have taken in any case. His own resolute pessimism may have been due to paranoia but pessimism is an even safer bet during a revolution than in normal times.

By the spring of 1794 everyone was trapped in a suffocating atmosphere of terror and hysteria—which was *not* due to the pressure of external events, since the war was going well—and Marat's view of things began to seem more credible. Saint-Just, who had not previously paid him much attention, began bringing his name into one speech after another and took over the *Maratiste* argument that all France's ills were the product of conspiracies that could have been prevented by more violent repression in the past. He even suggested to his colleagues on the Committee of Public Safety that they should appoint a dictator. This raises the disquieting question of whether *Maratisme* should be considered, not as the aberration of an individual, but as the natural destination of anyone who tried to adapt Rousseauist principles to the circumstances of revolution.

So far as Marat himself was concerned, his political theories were of the most rudimentary kind. All his life he retained an extraordinary veneration for Montesquieu. On 4 July 1791 he wrote that, if he had still been alive, he was the only man who would have made a suitable tutor for the Dauphin. And yet it would be difficult to think of a single idea of Montesquieu's that Marat accepted. Temperamentally, he was much closer to Rousseau, 'the most mortal enemy of absolute power' (28 December 1790), 'the sage whose virtues I respect even more than his talents' (4 July 1791). He shared Rousseau's contempt for the decadence of urban society, especially that of Paris, 'the sewer of all the vices' (5 February 1791), 'the only rotten part of France' (12 October 1791), 'the most corrupt [city] in the whole of Europe, the most venal and the most worthless' (27 July 1791). Like Rousseau, he loved to abuse his readers for their effeminacy, sharing his dislike of society women. The French were unworthy of democracy which was only possible in a free society like that of Sparta, some of the Swiss cantons, the United States and—a picturesque touch—San Marino. Marat obviously considered himself to be on a par with his two heroes. When Desmoulins reminded him of Voltaire's review of *De l'homme*, Marat replied that Voltaire had criticised Montesquieu and Rousseau too. He thought that the three of them would have been slumming it if they had been sentenced to the Pantheon.

When it came to offering theoretical guidance to his readers, Marat's thoughts were few and predictable. Democracy was inconceivable in France, 'a nation of vile egoists, without *moeurs*, energy or soul, men corrupted by soft living and vice, old slaves, consumed by their passion for gold and always ready to sell themselves to any master who could pay them. . . . Even if the poorest part of the population is healthy, without any resources how can it bring the rest of the nation to subscribe to this healthy form of government?' (7 July 1791). Not merely did those he was inclined to described as the 'plebs' or the 'populace' have no political power; they were also 'bad at judging things, they rarely see things as they are . . . because of their lack of understanding' (8 November 1790). For their enlightenment they needed journalists—but not too many, for Marat had the true revolutionary's suspicion of the media. Royalist journalists should be lynched and only a few *patriote* papers allowed. Eventually he thought that one would be enough (25 April 1792). One political party would be sufficient too. If the Assembly were composed of honest men, 'it would be neither expedient nor necessary

to allow the minority to protest against laws, or even to record their objections or negative votes, since men of good sense and pure intentions can never take decisions contrary to the national interest' (20 May 1793).

There could, of course, be no question of parliamentary sovereignty in the abstract. It was all a question of who was right. The intimidation of deputies by the public was 'a crime when all those who speak are enlightened and well-intentioned. But it is a good deed when they are factious conspirators' (25 January 1791). The poor did not know how to vote (and they were disfranchised in the 1791 election) and the rich voted only to protect their privileges. It was no wonder if the Convention was worse than the Legislative Assembly and that had been worse than the Constituent (26 November 1792). The laws of war applied as much to the deputies as to anyone else. They must be lynched as soon as they failed to do their duty (15 September 1792).

There is a kind of logic to all this. If the revolution was an actual war, it made sense to argue that 'liberty exists only for the friends of the *patrie*, chains and torments for its enemies' (6 March 1791). If the Assembly was controlled by the Enemy it was natural to argue that its laws were not morally binding on the other side. Marat dressed this up in rather fancy language: 'The law must be the expression of the general will, but of an enlightened will, based on the rules of eternal reason; a law that is obviously unjust is no law, even if it is endorsed by the whole nation' (10 January 1793). The obvious question is who was to decide that it was unjust if the whole nation agreed with it, and the answer is presumably either God or Marat. Since we are all against sin—at any rate as a general proposition—it is pleasant to denounce injustice and to demand righteousness of our governors, and how could one criticise a man who was doing precisely that, unless one had something to conceal. This line of argument may have commended itself to some of Marat's 'plebs'. What he was actually doing was to locate the general will within his own person. Some members of the revolutionary government were to do much the same in 1794.

One might have expected the People's Friend to have paid a fair amount of attention to improving their living conditions. Behind his posturing, verbal barrages against the vicious and corrupt rich and rather patronising sympathy for the virtuous and benighted poor, there was some awareness of actual problems and some genuine sympathy for real people. He knew and he was less inhibited than most of the revolutionaries in admitting, that for the urban poor, life had become more difficult since 1789. He saw that alcoholism was in part the response to grinding and unpleasant work for low wages (14 June 1790). He repeated his old arguments: the one originally derived from Montesquieu, that the poor were entitled to a decent livelihood (27 October 1790) and the assertion that 'those without property, who can claim no employment, who derive no benefit from the social pact' had no *patrie* (24 November 1789). It was when he came to explain why this should be and what could be done about it, that the trouble began. In one mood he reverted to his old pessimism: almost all wealth was the product of violence, favour or fraud (18 November, for 19 November 1789; *Ami du Peuple* No. 52). The rich were incorrigible, but intelligent self-interest, reinforced by judicious intimidation, might induce them to palliate by their philanthropy what the state was powerless to cure (18 November 1789, 28 February 1793). If not, the poor might demand the 'agrarian law': in other words, the redistribution of land (27 October 1790). In a fit of temper, he said this would advance the cause of enlightenment. Generally, however, he was a violent opponent of anything more than the traditional restraints on the grain trade. Price controls were 'the height of folly and wickedness' (12 February 1793). 'No doubt the blind multitude was bound to enthuse over the doctrine of perfect equality' (25 September 1791). He told his readers that he himself had reassured the Swiss banker, Perregaux, that he was a firm opponent of 'strict equality' (3 March 1793). He was not very keen on other people supping with bankers, and six months later Perregaux seems to have been acting as a secret British agent. It is tempting to think of how Marat could have used such 'evidence' against someone else. (pp. 205-08)

He had no clear or consistent economic principles. Despite a passing reference to the virtues of competition, he opposed the abolition of the old guilds on the ground that consumers would suffer if there was no control over bad workmanship. 'When every workman can work for himself, he stops wanting to work for anyone else. If desire for betterment is divorced from desire for a reputation for good work, one can say goodbye to good faith. Look at the endless development of the passion for gain that torments all classes in big cities.' His solution was in the best Rousseauist tradition and would have delighted Mme de Wolmar: craftsmen should be made to serve an apprenticeship of six or seven years under masters responsible for their good conduct. Those distinguished by their skill and *sagesse* should eventually be helped to set up in business for themselves—but they would have to repay the money advanced if they had not married within three years. 'The only way to make society prosper is to reward talent and good conduct. It is nature's will that the ignorant should be guided by those with knowledge and men without *moeurs* by respectable people' (16 March 1791). Those who have welcomed Marat as a preacher of class war have not read him very carefully.

What emerges from all this is that Marat was perhaps rather more aware than men like Robespierre and Saint-Just of the poor as people with problems and not just as an abstract category of the population. Unlike Saint-Just, he never seems to have thought at all seriously about economic policy and he fitted everything into a simplistic view of the world where all problems could be solved by the revolt of the poor under the leadership of men like himself and the intimidation—but not the expropriation—of the rich. The *petit peuple* might be 'the only healthy part of the nation' but this was only because 'they have neither the time nor money to deprave themselves and so have to remain close to nature' (7 October 1790). This must have prompted the thought that it might be kinder to leave them that way and from time to time Marat did ask himself why he went on working so hard to save men who were not worth the trouble. (p. 210)

As always, one is left wondering how far Marat believed himself. He certainly manufactured evidence. When Desmoulins reproached him for this he replied 'How do you know that what you took to be false news was not a text that I needed to parry some fatal thrust and achieve my purpose?... To judge men you always need positive, clear and precise evidence... the general current of affairs is

enough for me' (5 May 1791)... He may or may not have believed the curriculum vitae that he invented for himself. He was careless about facts and self-contradictions and took liberties with the truth but it defies plausibility to believe that he was merely writing for effect. It does not matter very much, except with regard to his own reputation. To a considerable extent, the conclusions that Marat welcomed were ones to which more thoughtful and more honourable revolutionaries were inexorably driven. He was the Mephistopheles to their Faust. (pp. 214-15)

Norman Hampson, "Marat" and "Marat II," in his Will & Circumstance: Montesquieu, Rousseau and the French Revolution, *1983. Reprint by University of Oklahoma Press, 1983, pp. 107-28, 193-215.*

ADDITIONAL BIBLIOGRAPHY

Acton, John Emerich Edward Dalberg-Acton, Lord. *Lectures on the French Revolution*, pp. 93ff. Edited by John Neville Figgis and Reginald Vere Laurence. London: Macmillan and Co., 1920.
> Study of the Revolution. In mentioning the author in conjunction with other French revolutionaries, Acton terms Marat "the most ghastly of them all."

Belloc, Hilaire. *Robespierre: A Study*, pp. 220ff. New York: G. P. Putnam's Sons, 1928.
> Scattered references to Marat in a biography of his contemporary and fellow revolutionary, Maximilien François-Marie Isidore de Robespierre.

Béraud. Henri, "Marat." In his *Twelve Portraits of the French Revolution*, translated by Madeleine Boyd, pp. 117-32. Boston: Little, Brown, and Co., 1928.
> Biographical sketch of the author which attempts to plumb the adulation and hatred he inspired.

Carlyle, Thomas. "Charlotte Corday and Marat." In *Essays of the Past and Present*, edited by Warner Taylor, pp. 54-9. New York: Harper & Brothers, 1927.
> Interpretative reenactment of Marat's murder which decidedly champions Charlotte Corday.

Catteral, R. C. H. "The Credibility of Marat." *The American Historical Review* XVI, No. 1 (October 1910): 24-35.
> Attempts to discredit Marat on the alleged circumstances of the publication of *The Chains of Slavery*.

Fishman, W. J. "Jean-Paul Marat." *History Today* XXI, No. 5 (May 1971): 329-37.
> Comprehensive biographical portrait which provides some little-known details of Marat's earlier years.

Gottschalk, Louis R. "The Criminality of Jean Paul Marat." *The South Atlantic Quarterly* XXV, No. 2 (April 1926): 154-67.
> Refutes the theory advanced by Sidney L. Phipson in his biography *Jean Paul Marat His Career in England and France before the French Revolution* (1924) that Marat was both a convict and fugitive from the law during a period of medical practice in England.

Hampson, Norman. "A Power Hungry Patriot." *The Times Higher Education Supplement*, No. 475 (11 December 1981): 11.
> Accounts for Marat's success as a revolutionary.

Madelin, Louis. *Danton*, pp. 29ff. Translated by Lady Mary Loyd. New York: Alfred A. Knopf, 1921.

Scattered references to Marat in this biography of his fellow revolutionary Georges-Jacques Danton.

Scherr, Marie. *Charlotte Corday and Certain Men of the Revolutionary Torment*, pp. 10ff. New York: AMS Press, 1970.

Brief references to Marat throughout a colorful biography of Corday.

Soboul, Albert. "Religious Sentiment and Popular Cults during the Revolution: Patriot Saints and Martyrs of Liberty." In *New Perspectives on the French Revolution: Readings in Historical Sociology*, edited by Jeffrey Kaplow, translated by Orest Ranum and Robert Wagoner, pp. 338-50. New York: John Wiley & Sons, 1965.

Essay published originally in French in 1957 cites Marat's martyrdom as representative of "the specifically religious nature" of cults spawned by the French Revolution.

Weiss, Peter. *The Persecution and Assassination of Marat as Performed by the Inmates of the Asylum of Charenton under the Direction of the Marquis de Sade*. Translated by Geoffrey Skelton. London: John Calder, 1965, 124 p.

Dramatic depiction of an imaginary encounter between Marat and his contemporary, Comte Donatien-Alphonse-François de Sade, the French marquis and novelist whose criminal debauchery and sexual offenses eventually resulted in his incarceration in the insane asylum of Charenton. In a note on the historical background of the play, Weiss states that he bases the encounter solely on the fact that it was Sade who delivered the memorial address at Marat's funeral (primarily to extricate himself from the immediate danger of the guillotine). However, Weiss does reproduce many of Marat's actual sentiments, creating "the conflict between an individualism carried to extreme lengths and the idea of a political and social upheaval."

Marie de l'Incarnation

1599-1672

(Born Marie Guyart; also Guyard) French-born Canadian autobiographer, essayist, epistler, and religious writer.

Marie was one of the principal female religious writers of seventeenth-century France and foundress of the Ursulines of Quebec. She is best known for two spiritual autobiographies, *La relation autobiographique de 1633* ("The Relation of 1633") and *La relation autobiographique de 1654* ("The Relation of 1654"). These works, which are considered models of candidness and perspicacity, recount the emergence and growth of Marie's personal relationship with God. Marie is also known for her extensive correspondence, letters in which she chronicled convent life in New France and noted major events in the development of the Quebec colony. Her works are therefore valued for the light they throw on Christian spirituality as well as for their record of an important chapter in North American history.

Information concerning Marie's life is drawn chiefly from her two *Relations* and from a biographical work compiled by her son, Dom Claude Martin, titled *La vie de la Vénérable Mère Marie de l'Incarnation* (1677). She was born Marie Guyart in Tours, France in 1599, the daughter of Florent Guyart, a master baker, and Jeanne Michelet, a descendant of the noble Babou de La Bourdaisière family. Instructed at home and at a local school, she was given the education of a typical French tradesman's daughter of the period: the fundamentals of reading and writing, augmented by regular infusions of Roman Catholic teaching. At age seven Marie saw the Lord in a dream. "Will you be mine?" he asked her. "Yes," she replied, marking the first step in a spiritual pilgrimage that was to last her entire life. Immediately she began regular communication with God, telling him her "personal matters" and meditating on sermons she heard in the parish church. By age fourteen she had decided upon the life of the cloister, but her mother, sensing in Marie a cheerful humor and worldly temperament, steered her toward marriage instead. Considering marriage unacceptable to her constitution, Marie nevertheless married master silk-maker Claude Martin in 1617, resolving to make the best of the situation. Two years later Martin died, leaving Marie with a six-month-old son bearing his father's name and a bankrupt business. Marie is comparatively silent about this period in her life, but it is known that she returned to her parents' house, resisted heavy pressure to remarry, and went into seclusion in an upper room. There she read spiritual works and communed with God, preparing herself for a life of religious service whose course had yet to be revealed.

On 24 March 1620, the vigil of the Feast of the Incarnation, Marie, then 20 years old, underwent her first mystical experience. Overcome in the streets of Tours by a vision of the foulness, the utter repugnance, of her sins and imperfections, she saw herself immersed in the Lord's blood, a sinner of the worst kind. Henceforth she was "so greatly changed" that she "no longer knew" herself. She resolved once again to commit herself to the religious life, but practical concerns, including settling her late hus-

Marie de l'Incarnation

band's debts, occupied her first. Later she responded to the plea of her sister's husband, Paul Buisson, to manage his business and household affairs for a time. Marie performed this task brilliantly for several years, demonstrating a remarkable talent for business which was to prove invaluable in her later work. Now 27 and with a son who had just turned eight, Marie followed the advice of Dom Reymond de Saint-Bernard, a member of the Order of Feuillants, and entered the novitiate of the Ursulines of Tours, leaving young Claude, for whom she retained a deep and abiding love, in her sister's care. (Marie later admitted that in her separation from her son she "had suffered a living death." The pain was therefore the worse when Claude, accompanied by a band of sympathetic schoolboys, stormed the convent, crying out: "Rendez-moi ma mère! Je veux avoir ma mère!"—"Give me back my mother! I want to have my mother!") Marie became an Ursuline nun and took her vows in 1633, taking the name Marie de l'Incarnation. In her new role, Marie's managerial skills were soon evident: she was made assistant mistress of novices and a teacher of Christian doctrine. But she felt that her mission lay elsewhere, in a new land upon some "further shore." One day God took her in a dream to a vast and foggy country where "the silence that was there made part of its beauty." Later the Lord told her: "It was Canada that I showed you; you must go there to build a house for Jesus and Mary." On 4 May 1639 Marie, accompanied by a small contingent of Ursulines and Hospitallers, sailed for the New World, arriving in Quebec on 1 August.

Quebec proved virgin territory for the missionaries, and Marie put her business and organizational skills to use at once. At first the nuns lived roughly, but by 1642, owing chiefly to Marie's tremendous industry, they were installed in a massive stone convent—a wonder for New France. This situation was short-lived, however: the first of several fires destroyed the building within months. To bolster the Ursuline mission financially, Marie plunged herself into all manner of economic matters, especially the development of mineral and salt mines and the export of porpoise oil. She never lost sight, however, of the primary purpose of her mission: the Christian education of native Indian girls. To Marie's immense satisfaction, the number of pupils increased steadily. By the time of her death in 1672, Marie had trained over one hundred "delights" of her heart and "brightest jewels" in her crown—such were the pet names she settled on her students. Nor did Marie neglect the adult Indians, for whom she wrote an Iroquois catechism and performed many services. All the while she was cheered by reports from her son, with whom she corresponded frequently, finding special satisfaction in his election as superior of the Benedictines of Saint-Maur in 1652 and assistant to the superior-general of his order in 1668. Marie's 33 years in Quebec were never easy: she worked tirelessly for the mission, suffering terrible depredations from the very people to whom she had devoted her life. Yet, linked as it was with the early history of New France, Marie's apostolic life was always rich in incident and interest—a fact well borne out in *The Relation of 1654* and in Marie's many letters. At her death she left a legacy of religious service that continues to this day in the house she founded in Quebec.

It is estimated that Marie wrote dozens of discrete treatises and nearly 13,000 letters in her lifetime; of these, but a few have survived, including about 200 letters (most of which are known only through Dom Claude's *Vie*) and fewer than ten other works. Marie's best-known writings are by far the two *Relations*. *The Relation of 1633* was prepared at the request of Father de La Haye, rector of the Collège d'Orléans, when Marie was still in the convent at Tours. In it Marie sets out details of her religious life and mystical initiation. This work was kept secret during Marie's lifetime and did not see print until 1677, when fragments of it were included in Dom Claude's *Vie*. *The Relation of 1654* is longer than the first and adds much to our knowledge of Marie's religious life. It was prepared on the order of her spiritual adviser at the time, Father Jerome Lalement, as both a history of Marie's spiritual development and as a record of the growth of the Quebec mission. Some critics rank this work very high in the canon of Western mysticism, focusing as it does on Marie's firsthand experience of divine love. Marie sent this *Relation* to her son, who requested elaboration of many points and statements. She answered him with a *Supplément* (also known as *Mémoire complémentaire*) in 1656, but only bits of this work have survived. During her residence in Quebec Marie carried on a huge correspondence of both an official and personal nature. Sometimes she wrote as a businesswoman, seeking funds for the convent; at other times she reported on the progress of the mission, recounting its successes and setbacks; at still others, in letters to her son and other intimates, she opened her heart to reveal her deepest thoughts about life in the spirit. Some of the letters are comparatively polished, others merely drafts written in haste while the mail ship prepared to weigh anchor. Yet most—those written at leisure and under pressure alike—are filled with topical news: colorful descriptions of local events, detailed accounts of the natural wonders of New France (nearly always related secondhand, for Marie remained cloistered in Quebec), exciting portraits of acquaintances, and reflective surveys of the colony's growth. As such, the letters are a valuable source for early Canadian history. Moreover, they are remarkable for their smooth, unmannered prose and customary spontaneity, even in official correspondence: an expression of the writer's boundless curiosity and eagerness to share her experiences with others.

Marie's surviving minor works are practically unknown to critics writing in English. *Lettres de conscience* is a short collection of letters written to Dom Raymond between 1622 and 1634, probably the most intense mystical period for Marie. The letters treat spiritual matters and discuss the nature of prayer and God's love. *Exposition succincte du "Cantique des cantiques"* is the only extant lecture by Marie. One of a series of talks on the mysteries of the Christian faith, the Psalms, and the Song of Songs, it was delivered to novices in Tours. "I could not keep silent," Marie wrote concerning the lecture, "and I found it very easy to present my thoughts to my sisters who were all astonished to hear me speak in this way." Marie conceived *L'école sainte; ou, Explication familière des mystères de la foy* as a simple and direct catechism. It was written between 1633 and 1635 for the young religious of Tours and appears to have been used to good effect: Father Pierre F. -X. de Charlevoix recognized it as one of the finest catechisms in French. Under the title *Retraites de la Vénérable Mère Marie de l'Incarnation*, Dom Claude published a series of his mother's *relations d'oraison* ("prayer thoughts") in 1682. These *relations* are Marie's private notes on prayer compiled for her spiritual adviser. Finally, there are a few surviving examples of epithalamia written "to dissipate the fervor of the spirit." Considered remarkably candid and considered, they treat God's love as Marie experienced it herself.

Marie's works have never been widely known among critics writing in English, but they have long been esteemed among the French and by Quebecers. The importance of Marie's mission, particularly the value of a written record of it, was recognized early. Dom Claude rushed his mother's two *Relations* into print, furnishing them with a lengthy introduction and extensive critical apparatus. Within a few years of her death Marie was regularly venerated as a saint and objects connected with her were treasured as relics. François de Laval, first bishop of Quebec, wrote of her in 1677: "Her life, ordinary on the outside but very regular and animated by a completely divine inner nature, was a living rule for her entire community. Her ardour for saving souls and especially for the conversion of the Indians was so great and so far-reaching, that it seemed as if she bore them all in her heart, and we do not doubt that she contributed greatly by her prayers to obtaining from God the blessings which He has showered on this new-born Church." This affirmation of Marie's talents is typical of the many that followed, emphasizing as it does Marie's overriding dedication to her mission and complete faith in God. Before the turn of the century, by which time *Retraites* and *L'école sainte* were numbered among the works in print, Marie's career had won the acclaim of French bishop and writer Jacques-Bénigne Bossuet. Styling Marie the "Teresa of the North," he commented on the form and content of the two *Relations*, declaring: "Tout y est admirable"—"Everything there is admirable." Throughout the eighteenth-century Marie was the subject of several short studies and at least one substantial one, *La vie de la Mère Marie de l'Incarnation, institutrice et première supérieure des ursulines de la Nouvelle-France* (1724) by Father de Charlevoix. Around the middle of the eighteenth century Marie's reputation was to be made known to the Holy See, but circumstances surrounding the Treaty of Paris, by which France lost Canada to England, blocked proceedings for the time being. The issue was revived in 1867—coincidentally the year in which Francis Parkman published a study containing an extensive but mixed review of Marie's spiritual career. By 1875, when the Hurons of Lorette testified to the veneration in which they held Marie, proceedings relating to canonization were under way. In 1877 the cause was officially introduced; in 1882 the process of absence of cultus was held; in 1891 the reputation of sanctity was scrutinized; the writings were examined in 1895; validation of the processes was confirmed in 1897; and Pius X confirmed Marie's heroic virtues in 1911. In 1980 John-Paul II proclaimed Marie "Blessed." Meanwhile, critics continue to study Marie's works. Since the early twentieth century Marie's writings have been available in scholarly editions, and commentators have examined them as history, spiritual autobiography, works of pure mysticism, and for gleanings of religious sentiment. Further, the language, diction, and prose style of the *Relations* have been discussed in several studies published in French, and a range of biographical material has been made available in English. Today Marie is recognized as a woman of virtue and accomplishment who contributed much to mystical theory and the early history of French Canada. "One of the sublimest and most finely balanced contemplatives the Church has ever known," according to James Brodrick, Marie bears witness to the power of faith and missionary devotion to duty in New France.

PRINCIPAL WORKS

*La vie de la Vénérable Mère Marie de l'Incarnation, première supérieure de la Nouvelle-France, tirée de ses lettres et de ses écrits (autobiography and letters) 1677
[*The Autobiography of the Venerable Marie of the Incarnation*, 1964]
Lettres de la Vénérable Mère Marie de l'Incarnation (letters) 1681
[*Word from New France: The Selected Letters of Marie de l'Incarnation*, 1967]
†Retraites de la Vénérable Mère Marie de l'Incarnation, religieuse ursuline, avec une exposition succincte du "Cantique des cantiques" (essays and lecture) 1682
L'école sainte; ou, explication familière des mystères de la foy pour toutes de personnes qui sont obligées d'enseigner la doctrine chrétienne (catechism) 1684

Lettres de la Révérende Mère Marie de l'Incarnation (née Marie Guyard), première supérieure du monastère des ursulines de Québec. 2 vols. (letters) 1876
Lettres historiques de la Vénérable Mère Marie de l'Incarnation sur le Canada (letters) 1927
Écrits spirituels et historiques. 4 vols. (autobiography, essays, and letters) 1929-39

*This work, compiled by Dom Claude Martin, contains extracts from *La relation autobiographique de 1633* ("The Relation of 1633") and *La relation autobiographique de 1654* ("The Relation of 1654").

†The second part of this work, *Exposition succincte du "Cantique des cantiques,"* is also known as *Entretien spirituel sur l'épouse des "Cantiques."*

MARIE DE L'INCARNATION   (essay date 1654)

[*In the following prologue of* The Relation of 1654, *Marie describes the origin and purpose of this, her second autobiography. The spiritual director to whom she refers is Father Jerome Lalemant, S. J., Marie's director from 1645 until 1672. In 1656 Marie said of him: "This great servant of God has been for me another Dom Raymond of St. Bernard [an earlier director much esteemed by Marie], and my soul feels itself bound to him in its pursuit of the ways of God."*]

I have been ordered by him who holds the place of God in the direction of my soul to put down in writing, insofar as I can, the graces and favors which the Divine Majesty has given me by means of the gift of prayer He has been pleased to grant me. I will, then, undertake this task for God's honor and greater glory, in the name of the most adorable Word Incarnate, my heavenly and divine Spouse.

> *Marie de l'Incarnation, "Prologue," in her* The Autobiography of Venerable Marie of the Incarnation, O.S.U.: Mystic and Missionary, *translated by John J. Sullivan, S.J., Loyola University Press, 1964, p. 1.*

MARIE DE L'INCARNATION   (letter date 1654)

[*In the following excerpt from a 1654 letter to her son, Marie explains the circumstances surrounding the composition of* The Relation of 1654.]

Please don't think that these notebooks that I am sending you [***The Relation of 1654***] have followed any predetermined order as more mature works would do. Whenever I took up my pen to begin, I hardly knew a word I was going to write; but while writing, the spirit of grace led me so that I wrote whatever He pleased . . . there have always been so many interruptions and I have had to work amid all the distractions of domestic affairs.

> *Marie de l'Incarnation, in a letter to Dom Claude Martin on August 9, 1654, translated by Mother Denis Mahoney, in* Marie of the Incarnation: Mystic and Missionary *by Mother Denis Mahoney, O.S.U., Doubleday & Company, Inc., 1964, p. 299.*

FRANCIS PARKMAN (essay date 1867)

[Parkman is recognized as one of the greatest historians America has yet produced. His multivolume France and England in North America *(1865-91), which treats the struggle between France and England for control of North America, is celebrated for its probing scholarship, consummate narrative skill, and unified construction. In the following excerpt from part two of the work,* The Jesuits in North America in the Seventeenth Century *(1867), Parkman traces Marie's spiritual development, noting the value of her writings as a record of the French mission in Quebec.]*

There was another nun [among the ursulines of Tours] who stood apart, silent and motionless,—a stately figure, with features strongly marked and perhaps somewhat masculine; but, if so, they belied her, for Marie de l'Incarnation was a woman to the core. For her there was no need of entreaties; for she knew that the Jesuits had made her their choice, as Superior of the new convent. She was born, forty years before, at Tours, of a good *bourgeois* family. As she grew up towards maturity, her qualities soon declared themselves. She had uncommon talents and strong religious susceptibilities, joined to a vivid imagination,—an alliance not always desirable under a form of faith where both are excited by stimulants so many and so powerful. Like Madame de la Peltrie, she married, at the desire of her parents, in her eighteenth year. The marriage was not happy. Her biographers say that there was no fault on either side. Apparently, it was a severe case of "incompatibility." She sought her consolation in the churches; and, kneeling in dim chapels, held communings with Christ and the angels. At the end of two years her husband died, leaving her with an infant son. She gave him to the charge of her sister, abandoned herself to solitude and meditation, and became a mystic of the intense and passional school. Yet a strong maternal instinct battled painfully in her breast with a sense of religious vocation. Dreams, visions, interior voices, ecstasies, revulsions, periods of rapture and periods of deep dejection, made up the agitated tissue of her life. She fasted, wore hair-cloth, scourged herself, washed dishes among the servants, and did their most menial work. She heard, in a trance, a miraculous voice. It was that of Christ, promising to become her spouse. Months and years passed, full of troubled hopes and fears, when again the voice sounded in her ear, with assurance that the promise was fulfilled, and that she was indeed his bride. Now ensued phenomena which are not infrequent among Roman Catholic female devotees, when unmarried, or married unhappily, and which have their source in the necessities of a woman's nature. To her excited thought, her divine spouse became a living presence; and her language to him, as recorded by herself, is that of the most intense passion. She went to prayer, agitated and tremulous, as if to a meeting with an earthly lover. "O my Love!" she exclaimed, "when shall I embrace you? Have you no pity on me in the torments that I suffer? Alas! alas! my Love, my Beauty, my Life! instead of healing my pain, you take pleasure in it. Come, let me embrace you, and die in your sacred arms!" And again she writes: "Then, as I was spent with fatigue, I was forced to say, 'My divine Love, since you wish me to live, I pray you let me rest a little, that I may the better serve you'; and I promised him that afterward I would suffer myself to consume in his chaste and divine embraces."

Clearly, here is a case for the physiologist as well as the theologian; and the "holy widow," as her biographers call her, becomes an example, and a lamentable one, of the tendency of the erotic principle to ally itself with high religious excitement.

But the wings of imagination will tire and droop, the brightest dream-land of contemplative fancy grow dim, and an abnormal tension of the faculties find its inevitable reaction at last. From a condition of highest exaltation, a mystical heaven of light and glory, the unhappy dreamer fell back to a dreary earth, or rather to an abyss of darkness and misery. Her biographers tell us that she became a prey to dejection, and thoughts of infidelity, despair, estrangement from God, aversion to mankind, pride, vanity, impurity, and a supreme disgust at the rites of religion. Exhaustion produced common-sense, and the dreams which had been her life now seemed a tissue of illusions. Her confessor became a weariness to her, and his words fell dead on her ear. Indeed, she conceived a repugnance to the holy man. Her old and favorite confessor, her oracle, guide, and comforter, had lately been taken from her by promotion in the Church,—which may serve to explain her dejection; and the new one, jealous of his predecessor, told her that all his counsels had been visionary and dangerous to her soul. Having overwhelmed her with this announcement, he left her, apparently out of patience with her refractory and gloomy mood; and she remained for several months deprived of spiritual guidance. Two years elapsed before her mind recovered its tone, when she soared once more in the seventh heaven of imaginative devotion.

Marie de l'Incarnation, we have seen, was unrelenting in every practice of humiliation; dressed in mean attire, did the servants' work, nursed sick beggars, and, in her meditations, taxed her brain with metaphysical processes of self-annihilation. And yet, when one reads her *Spiritual Letters,* the conviction of an enormous spiritual pride in the writer can hardly be repressed. She aspired to that inner circle of the faithful, that aristocracy of devotion, which, while the common herd of Christians are busied with the duties of life, eschews the visible and the present, and claims to live only for God. In her strong maternal affection she saw a lure to divert her from the path of perfect saintship. Love for her child long withheld her from becoming a nun; but at last, fortified by her confessor, she left him to his fate, took the vows, and immured herself with the Ursulines of Tours. The boy, frenzied by his desertion, and urged on by indignant relatives, watched his opportunity, and made his way into the refectory of the convent, screaming to the horrified nuns to give him back his mother. As he grew older, her anxiety increased; and at length she heard in her seclusion that he had fallen into bad company, had left the relative who had sheltered him and run off, no one knew whither. The wretched mother, torn with anguish, hastened for consolation to her confessor, who met her with stern upbraidings. Yet, even in this her intensest ordeal, her enthusiasm and her native fortitude enabled her to maintain a semblance of calmness, till she learned that the boy had been found and brought back.

Strange as it may seem, this woman, whose habitual state was one of mystical abstracton, was gifted to a rare degree with the faculties most useful in the practical affairs of life. She had spent several years in the house of her brother-in-law. Here, on the one hand, her vigils, visions, and penances set utterly at nought the order of a well-governed family; while, on the other, she made amends to her impatient relative by able and efficient aid in the conduct of his public and private affairs. Her biographers say, and doubtless with truth, that her heart was far away from these mundane interests; yet her talent for business was not the less displayed. Her spiritual guides were aware of it, and saw clearly that gifts so useful to the world might be made equally useful to the Church. Hence it was that she was chosen Superior of the convent which Madame de la Peltrie was about to endow at Quebec.

Yet it was from heaven itself that Marie de l'Incarnation received her first "vocation" to Canada. The miracle was in this wise.

In a dream she beheld a lady unknown to her. She took her hand; and the two journeyed together westward, towards the sea. They soon met one of the Apostles, clothed all in white, who, with a wave of his hand, directed them on their way. They now entered on a scene of surpassing magnificence. Beneath their feet was a pavement of squares of white marble, spotted with vermilion, and intersected with lines of vivid scarlet; and all around stood monasteries of matchless architecture. But the two travellers, without stopping to admire, moved swiftly on till they beheld the Virgin seated with her Infant Son on a small temple of white marble, which served her as a throne. She seemed about fifteen years of age, and was of a "ravishing beauty." Her head was turned aside; she was gazing fixedly on a wild waste of mountains and valleys, half concealed in mist. Marie de l'Incarnation approached with outstretched arms, adoring. The vision bent towards her, and, smiling, kissed her three times; whereupon, in a rapture, the dreamer awoke.

She told the vision to Father Dinet, a Jesuit of Tours. He was at no loss for an interpretation. The land of mists and mountains was Canada, and thither the Virgin called her. Yet one mystery remained unsolved. Who was the unknown companion of her dream? Several years had passed, and signs from heaven and inward voices had raised to an intense fervor her zeal for her new vocation, when, for the first time, she saw Madame de la Peltrie on her visit to the convent at Tours, and recognized, on the instant, the lady of her nocturnal vision. No one can be surprised at this who has considered with the slightest attention the phenomena of religious enthusiasm.

On the fourth of May, 1639, Madame de la Peltrie, Marie de l'Incarnation, Marie de St. Bernard, and another Ursuline, embarked at Dieppe for Canada. In the ship were also three young hospital nuns, sent out to found at Quebec a Hôtel Dieu, endowed by the famous niece of Richelieu, the Duchesse d'Aiguillon. (pp. 174-81)

It was three years later before the Ursulines and their pupils took possession of a massive convent of stone, built for them on the site which they still occupy. Money had failed before the work was done, and the interior was as unfinished as a barn. Beside the cloister stood a large ash-tree; and it stands there still. Beneath its shade, says the convent tradition, Marie de l'Incarnation and her nuns instructed the Indian children in the truths of salvation; but it might seem rash to affirm that their teachings were always wise or useful, since Father Vimont tells us approv-

ingly, that they reared their pupils in so chaste a horror of the other sex, that a little girl, whom a man had playfully taken by the hand, ran crying to a bowl of water to wash off the unhallowed influence.

Now and henceforward one figure stands nobly conspicuous in this devoted sisterhood. Marie de l'Incarnation, no longer lost in the vagaries of an insane mysticism, but engaged in the duties of Christian charity and the responsibilities of an arduous post, displays an ability, a fortitude, and an earnestness which command respect and admiration. Her mental intoxication had ceased, or recurred only at intervals; and false excitements no longer sustained her. She was racked with constant anxieties about her son, and was often in a condition described by her biographers as a "deprivation of all spiritual consolations." Her position was a very difficult one. She herself speaks of her life as a succession of crosses and humiliations. Some of these were due to Madame de la Peltrie, who, in a freak of enthusiasm, abandoned her Ursulines for a time, . . . leaving them in the utmost destitution. There were dissensions to be healed among them; and money, everything, in short, to be provided. Marie de l'Incarnation, in her saddest moments, neither failed in judgment nor slackened in effort. She carried on a vast correspondence, embracing every one in France who could aid her infant community with money or influence; she harmonized and regulated it with excellent skill; and, in the midst of relentless austerities, she was loved as a mother by her pupils and dependents. Catholic writers extol her as a saint. Protestants may see in her a Christian heroine, admirable, with all her follies and her faults. (pp. 185-86)

Francis Parkman, "Devotees and Nuns," in his The Jesuits in North America in the Seventeenth Century: France and England in North America, *Part Second, 1867. Reprint by Little, Brown, and Company, 1896, pp. 167-87.*

THE HURONS OF LORETTE   (letter date 1875)

[In the following excerpt from a postulatory letter sent to Pius IX in 1875, the Hurons of Lorette, recognizing Marie's services to their ancestors, request for her the honors of beatification.]

We, the chiefs and braves of the Huron nation . . . on our knees before Your Holiness present to you a precious perfume, the perfume of the virtues of Reverend Mother Mary of the Incarnation. . . . She it was who called us from the depths of our forests to teach us to know and adore the true Master of life. Through her we learned to be meek. . . . Our mothers have kissed the imprint of her feet. With her hand she marked on our hearts the sign of the Faith and the Faith remained graven on our hearts. . . . Many a moon has passed since that first dawning of the true light upon us. Our nation, then great, is now threatened with complete extinction, but, Holy Father, we beg you to receive with the last wish and the last breath of the Huron Tribe the testimony of its profound gratitude to Reverend Mother Mary of the Incarnation.

The Hurons of Lorette, in an extract from a letter to Pope Pius IX in 1875, in The Month, *Vol. CLXXV, No. 908, February, 1940, p. 105.*

M. M. MAXWELL SCOTT (essay date 1913)

[*In the following excerpt, Scott discusses the literary and historical value of Marie's correspondence.*]

The history of Quebec during the mid-seventeenth century] may be said to be also the history of Mère Marie and her companions, so intimately are they connected. Her letters home [*Lettres de la Vénérable Mère Marie de l'Incarnation*] are very valuable to the historian, and her literary style is worthy of the great period in which she lived. Mère Marie kept up an affectionate correspondence with her sisters, the nuns at Tours and other friends, but, above all, with her son, whom she was never to see again in this world. In 1641 Dom Martin entered the Benedictine Congregation of Saint Maur, and became distinguished for his great virtues and learning. His mother's joy when his vocation was decided was intense, and it was owing to her maternal love and respect for his priestly character that we possess some record of her interior life and the great graces bestowed upon her. Dom Martin would not be gainsaid in his desire for her confidence and under obedience to her Confessor, she complied with his wishes.

Among the Venerable Mother's general correspondence we find interesting references to current events in France, and even to those in England. For instance, on one occasion she speaks of her prayers for Charles I and his family. She and her community prayed and did penance, she tells us, for Louise de la Vallière, whose aunt had been one of Mère Marie's novices, and there is a letter of thanks to Mère Angélique Arnauld, for her gifts to the Quebec convent, and an affectionate allusion to the late "precious death" of St Jane Frances de Chantal. (p. 102)

The Venerable Mother's letters home give us some charming pictures of the Indians who flocked to the convent. We see the "chiefs and captains," who kneel before her and ask her to teach them how to pray. To one of them who had forgotten his good resolutions she said, "Well, are you going to give up your faults? Do you love God? Do you believe in Him? Do you wish to obey Him?" "Oh! that is settled," was the reply, "I love God, and I wish to obey Him in future. . . . I am exceedingly sorry to have offended Him Who made us all." Some of these poor men were most fervent. "When I hear the good Charles, Pigaronich-Noël, Négabamat or Trigalier speak," she says, "I would not leave them to listen to the first preacher in Europe. I find in their discourses such a confidence in God, such a faith and ardour, which causes admiration and devotion. They are even ready to give their lives for Jesus Christ, though Indians fear death exceedingly. Some time ago Pigaronich said to me, 'I do not live now for the beasts as I did before, nor for fur robes, I live and I am for God. When I go hunting I say to Him, "Great Captain Jesus, Jesus, do what You wish with me. Even if You stop the game and it does not come within my reach, I will always hope in You. If You wish me to die of hunger, I am content."'" (p. 105)

The Venerable Mother's life was one of unceasing work, as long as her health permitted and when she was ill all her sufferings were offered for her beloved Indians. (p. 109)

M. M. Maxwell Scott, "The Teresa of Canada (1599-1672)," in The Dublin Review, Vol. CLII,

Nos. 304 & 305, first & second quarter, 1913, pp. 93-110.

HENRI BREMOND (essay date 1923)

[*Bremond was a French historian and literary critic. He is known chiefly for his multivolume* Histoire littéraire du sentiment religieux en France depuis la fin des guerres de religion jusqu'à nos jours *(1916-33), a study of the religious element, especially mysticism, in French literature. In the following excerpt from Volume VI,* La conquête mystique: Marie de l'Incarnation, Turba Magna, *he offers a capsule description of Marie's mysticism.*]

Willy nilly, we bring [the mystics] down to our own level. We place them in an intellectual, a sentimental, a literary setting which not only is not theirs, but which in some fashion is the negation of theirs . . . In fact, the admiration which we profess for a Teresa and a Mary of the Incarnation is in inverse ratio to their real greatness. The higher they are raised up, the more they escape us. When they seem to us to touch the utmost summits of lyricism, they are only at the stammering stage of the first years. Where ours comes to an end their true sublimity has its beginning.

Henri Bremond, in an excerpt in "The Saint Teresa of the New World: II," in The Month, Vol. CLXXV, No, 908, February, 1940, p. 91.

AGNES REPPLIER (essay date 1931)

[*Repplier was a distinguished American biographer and essayist best known as a master of the familiar essay. A devout Roman Catholic, she chronicled the lives of early North American Catholics, including Marie de l'Incarnation. In the following excerpt from her full-length study of Marie, she examines Marie as mystic, challenging Francis Parkman's contention (see excerpt dated 1867) that Marie was guilty of spiritual pride.*]

Francis Parkman, while admitting Mère Marie's intelligence, and her supreme executive ability, accuses her of "an enormous spiritual pride" [see excerpt dated 1867]. It is a grave accusation, and one as difficult to refute as to prove. Spiritual pride is doubtless visible to the eyes of God as are all our other sins; but it is a trifle hard for us to distinguish it by the light of ordinary evidence. Perhaps the old counsel, "If we would really know our hearts, let us impartially review our actions," is as good a rule as we can find; and, judging by her actions, Mère Marie's spiritual life was sound to the core. Saint Gregory says that humility of soul is the mystic's safeguard. Mère Marie was at all times a mystic; therefore it behooved her to be humble. Parkman had the profound distaste for mysticism that was characteristic of his generation. He pronounced it "insane," which is a satisfactory definition of any phenomenon of which we disapprove.

Charlevoix, dealing with this enigmatic but supremely important phase of Mère Marie's life, is both intelligible and reasonable. He quotes the rule laid down by the fathers of the Church, which says very simply that the faithful may (note there is no "must") believe that the secret elevation of the soul is by the grace of Heaven, provided that the mystic's life corresponds in the eyes of men with such a grace, and that there is no sign of self-esteem or of mental weakness. This is the common language of theologians. "The human soul has a natural capacity, but no exigency, and no positive ability, to reach God otherwise than by analogical knowledge. But God permits some souls to feel his sensible presence which is mystical contemplation. In such an act there is no annihilation or absorption of the creature into God; but God becomes intimately present in the created mind."

The danger of such individual experience is the tendency of the devout soul to become a law to itself. This is why Saint Theresa warned her nuns that they must never allow the illumination of prayer to decide for them anything concerning their duties, work, responsibilities, or routine. The rule of the order was the rule for them—and for her. Once when she was frying fish for the convent dinner a sudden ecstasy of contemplation wrapped her round. Its sweetness was overwhelming, but it did not distract her attention from the matter in hand. Her business was to fry the fish, and she fried it.

Charlevoix says that while there is certainly no obligation to believe that Mère Marie's mysticism was a genuine and a holy thing, such a belief is reasonable because there is no discordant note in her life or in her writings. "All was seemly in her behavior, all was sane in her advice." "To the fervor of the mystic," comments a recent historian, "she joined that strong sense of the actual which marked

Odo of Cluny, and Bernard of Clairvaux." This was evidenced in the discipline of her convent, in the hold she had upon the rulers of Quebec, in the unfailing success with which she carried through every measure she undertook, in the temporal as well as in the spiritual wisdom of her axioms and her rules. There was in her a solidity of judgment, a clear and practical intelligence. If she habitually contemplated the heavens, she walked the earth with firm and sure steps. Moreover, she had a great and salutary regard for the judgment of others, and this is always a safeguard. Wisdom would not die with her, and she knew it.

There was no radical change in Mère Marie during the long years of her cloistered life. She met altered circumstances with altered efforts, and sometimes with an altered point of view. Her horizon widened, and her interests widened with it. Her responsibilities grew heavier, and her administrative ability grew stronger with experience. But from first to last she never lost the supreme quality of the mystic—a sense of personal relation with God. Parkman, who was much displeased with her life in Tours, and much pleased with her life in Quebec, came to the conclusion that she was a reformed character, and amiably commended her reformation.

> Marie de l'Incarnation, no longer lost in the vagaries of an insane mysticism, but engaged in the duties of Christian charity and the responsibilities of an arduous post,

The Ursuline Monastery, Quebec. The house built by Marie de l'Incarnation in 1651 is at the center, facing the belfry.

displayed an ability, a fortitude, and an earnestness which command respect and admiration. Her mental intoxication had ceased, or recurred only at intervals; and false excitements no longer sustained her.

It is hard to think of anybody less sustained by excitements false or real than this balanced and decorous woman, who from early youth manifested the same traits that distinguished her later years. There were no doubt alternations of light and shadow in her spiritual as well as in her temporal life, moments of joy and moments of depression. Mutability is the order of existence. But at all times and under all circumstances she was self-controlled, of a still and grave demeanor, and endowed with a capacity for affairs. A poor young widow who was so useful in the conduct of business that her relatives deplored and resented the loss of her services, must have been as good a supervisor at thirty as at sixty. If there dwelt any illusions in her soul, they certainly were not fostered by idleness.

Mère Marie's letters [*Lettres de la Vénérable Mère Marie de l'Incarnation*] begin with her life in New France. Before that time her compositions were purely religious, and were written either for the use of her novices in Tours, or at the suggestion of her confessor, who seems to have considered that the best way to clarify thoughts and impressions was to set them down in the lucidity of words. But when transplanted to Quebec, letter writing became an important part of her daily duties. How was she to raise money for her convent, her school, her little savages, her needy pensioners, save by enlisting the sympathies of the wealthy and distinguished? In later years, when begging was no longer imperative, she kept on writing about her adopted country because the keenness of her own interest found delight in awakening and gratifying the interest of others. There is something inspiriting in this animated concern for all that went on about her, and there is enlightenment in her carefully considered verdicts.

Take, for example, her final tribute to Argenson. Mère Marie was well aware on what grounds he and Laval had fallen out so bitterly. Her sympathy as a friend and her loyalty as a nun were enlisted on the prelate's side; but nothing could blind her to the courage and capacity of the governor. When this courage and this capacity were questioned in the dark days of Indian warfare, she championed him against all criticism. When he was recalled to France, she wrote these well-considered words in his behalf:

> M. Argenson had much to bear from discontents who censured him for refusing to risk an attack upon Quebec by withdrawing its garrison for active fighting. He saw himself powerless to protect the length and breadth of New France with the scanty forces at his command, and he could not leave the towns at the mercy of the Iroquois. He was compelled to make all decisions for himself, as he stood in need of wise and loyal counsellors. He was of a generous mind, and singularly patient under criticism. He came often to the convent, and never let pass an opportunity of doing us a kindness. We talked much about public affairs. His successor, M. d'Avaugour, says frankly that he cannot understand how the country has been so well looked after with a meagre income and an inadequate army.

The rules prescribed by Mère Marie for her nuns were moderate, her counsels prudent and kind. She discountenanced self-imposed asceticism, having need of healthy workers, and rightly considering that the climate of Quebec, the poverty of the convent, and the restricted food supply provided all the austerity of which they stood in need. The business of keeping warm in winter time was one of supreme importance. If the braziers failed to affect the frozen chapel air, the nuns said their prayers in the community room or in bed. But if forced to endure cold, they were expected to endure it uncomplainingly, and as a matter of course. They were not the only people shivering in New France.

The one approach to impatience noticeable in Mère Marie's writings is her distaste for great talkers. Habitually silent, she forgot that many excellent and useful people are habitually talkative, and that allowance must be made for this harmless and not altogether unnatural idiosyncrasy. Even edifying speech wearied her if it lasted long. "Too many words are fatal to religious devotion," she wrote. "The heart and the mouth do not open simultaneously." A bustling haste was also little to her liking: "Our hurry to be done with one thing so as to begin another means the ruin of both." Inevitably she was drawn to contemplation as the purest form of prayer: "It is said that contemplation is idleness, and in a fashion this is true; but it is idleness alive to every impression of divine grace. The highest life consists of spiritual nearness to God and the active practice of duty." One is reminded of Joubert: "*Vivre, c'est penser et sentir son âme.*" To find time for this ennobling leisure as well as for hard systematized work is to leave nothing unenjoyed or undone.

Mère Marie was fundamentally humorless. There is an occasional caustic quality in her writings which relieves their intense seriousness. Her advice to her nuns, to "Bear with man for the sake of God," covers a great deal of ground. Her comment upon an invoice of marriageable girls, that they were "mixed goods," "*une marchandise mêlée,*" was as near an approach to humor as her letters can show. Of Saint Theresa's daring wit, of the flashing speech, keen as a blade, which distinguished Saint Basil of Cappadocia and Saint Thomas Aquinas, there is no vestige, nothing to indicate that they would have even carried a message to her mind. Her language, always unadorned, seems now and then preternaturally calm, considering the things she has to tell. She notes the death of the Mohegan captive who gave warning of the threatened invasion of the Iroquois in words so matter of fact, "after disposing of him in the usual way, that is by burning," that the baldness of the statement lends an added horror to the deed. It must be remembered that burning a prisoner of war was in the nature of a compromise on the part of the Algonquins. They could not understand the squeamishness with which the missionaries regarded the old and respected custom of prolonged torture; but they had substituted the stake as a comparatively merciful measure.

If Mère Marie's letters lack the lightness of touch which would have made them as delightful as they are informative, they are often couched in very engaging language. She writes to the superior of the Ursulines at Dijon, suggesting that, as they have but little money to spare, they might be all the more generous with their prayers: "It would be a deed well worthy of your piety to try with the help of your religious to gain a hearing from God, that He may be kindly disposed to the poor savages of New France." A gentle and irresistible petition.

Charlevoix tells two characteristic stories of Mère Marie when she was still Mme. Martin, attending to her brother-in-law's business, and filling her scanty leisure with works of charity. A poor little shopkeeper of Tours had been accused of dishonesty. Everybody save the young widow believed him guilty; and when she pleaded for him, and proclaimed her belief in his innocence, the judge reprimanded her for risking her fair name and the respect in which she was held by such ill-advised partisanship. Nevertheless the man was later on cleared of the charge; and so deep was the impression made by her courageous stand that humble folk, who rightly fear the law, looked upon her as their champion against injustice.

The other tale is of a woman, also belonging to the lower class, whose son had committed an unnamed crime, and who was wrought up to such a pitch of sorrow and rage that she passed from one convulsion of fury into another. Mme. Martin, who had been called in by the frightened neighbors, tried in vain to quiet her with kind and gentle words. The wretched mother, past all control, heard nothing, saw nothing, but shrieked and tore at herself and at her clothing like the mad creature that she was. Then the visitor suddenly flung out her strong arms and clasped the swaying woman to her breast. Close, close she held her until the beat of her own heart, steady as a pendulum, quieted the throbbing heart pressed close to it. The firm will imposed itself upon the infirm will. The frantic sufferer grew silent, passive, and pitiful. The hour of dementia was over.

It is inevitable that commentators on Mère Marie's life should compare her to that great mystic and great executrix, Saint Theresa. Père Emery, author of *L'Esprit de Sainte Thérèse,* has gone out of his way to indicate the resemblance; and Bossuet unhesitatingly alludes to the Ursuline nun as the "Theresa of the North." The comparison is, nevertheless, in kind, not in degree. Saint Theresa is one of the high lights of hagiography. Her field was wider than Mère Marie's, her task harder, her mind keener, her personality more magnetic. She has stamped herself upon the history of her church. The work of reformation was her work. She did not destroy what she undertook to reform, which is always an easy thing to do. She preserved it, bettered and purified, which is exceedingly difficult. Her figure attracts and holds attention because of her vivifying and cleansing blitheness of spirit. She possessed the quality of distinction which Matthew Arnold says "corrects the world's blunders, and fixes the world's ideals."

One may be a great poet without nearing Shakespeare, and a great statesman without rivaling Pitt. Mère Marie resembled Saint Theresa inasmuch as her piety was equalled by her capacity for work. She had the same talent for administration, albeit it was exercised within narrower bounds. Her outward life was normal, and was regulated by the rules of her order. Her inner life, noble and sustained, bore fruit in her steadfast perseverance, and in her cheerful acceptance of circumstance. She had one advantage over her prototype. She was a pioneer. She had risked what in her day was the great adventure, and she had a chance to impose her personality upon a new country and a savage people. Character is the great force in human affairs, and her reliability made her a guide in doubt and a bulwark in difficulties. What Anatole France calls "*la douceur impérieuse des saintes*" was the weapon with which she fought her battles, established her authority, and be-

came a living principle in the keen, hard, vivid, friendly, and dangerous life of New France. (PP. 275-87)

Agnes Repplier, in her Mère Marie of the Ursulines: A Study in Adventure, *Doubleday, Doran & Company, Inc., 1931, 314 p.*

JAMES BRODRICK (essay date 1940)

[*In the following excerpt, Brodrick extols Marie's Frenchness and praises her literary style.*]

It is a delightful occupation if, like most delightful occupations, quite superfluous, to praise France. Frenchmen themselves have done it so deftly and persistently that irate foreigners (*d'outre Rhin*) have been moved to inquire, "Is God a Frenchman?" Boasting is part of their charm, because there is nothing selfish in it, but only the exuberance of their love for *la belle France.* All the best people have "boasted," including our Lady and St. Paul, who has bequeathed to us a small theology of the subject. Any man who belongs to the true European tradition also belongs to France, and might adapt a famous apostrophe to express his gratitude:

O France, my country, city of the soul,
The orphans of the heart must turn to thee!

For France humanized and Christianized on our behalf the splendid but too masculine Roman inheritance, infusing into it the best womanly qualities until it lost its hard lines and became gracious and gay and tender. Have not nearly all the most human and lovable saints been French, from Paulinus, the poet of friendship, to Teresa, the Little Flower whose fragrance has sweetened the whole earth? But of all the great sons and daughters of the Church's Eldest Daughter none better illustrates the many-sided genius of France than the Venerable Mary of the Incarnation. She boasts herself with charming *naïveté* of her "talent pour le négoce" ["business acumen"]. In the opinion of the best judges she was one of the sublimest contemplatives the Church has ever known. Her range of human experience was far greater than the great St. Teresa's, for she was wife and mother as well as nun, and she achieved what both St. Teresas could only dream of, by crossing the Atlantic as the pioneer nun missionary of Christendom. Four centuries and a year ago it was an unheard and undreamt of thing in the Church for a nun to be a missionary. All nuns were enclosed, in the strictest legality of the term, and one might as well try to move a mountain as to dislodge the canon of the code which kept nuns firmly at home. The holy projects of St. Angela Merici and Mary Ward foundered on that particular rock, but Mary of the Incarnation somehow sailed round it and off to the Red Indians of New France, while all the bishops of Old France blessed and applauded. Marie's whole life was a ravishing paradox. French of the French, as Abbé Bremond delighted to emphasize, "vraiment notre Thérèse, une Thérèse de chez nous, française de tête et de cœur, jusqu'au bout des ongles" ["truly our own Thérèse, a Thérèse from our house, French from head to heart, right down to her fingertips"], she has yet a universal appeal.

At a time like the present, when the bastard mysticisms of Nazi-ism and Communism are endeavoring to black-out heaven itself, this great, true mystic brings its light and peace and beatitude to our doors. Part of her quintessential Frenchness was to be lucid, and none more clearly than she or with more poetic charm had described the holy mysteries of the soul's ascensions to God. Until recently it was not easy to acquire her matchless **Relations** or her letters [*Lettres de la Vénérable Mère Marie de l'Incarnation*], but now the Benedictines of France are bringing out a splendid edition of both, which make the finest war-time reading that any man more concerned to lift up his heart than to bury his head could desire. (pp. 47-8)

It was Bossuet, with his genius for a comprehensive phrase, who christened Mary of the Incarnation the St. Teresa of Canada. As a great adventuring soul, an explorer into God, Marie yields hardly at all to Teresa, and, though she had not the Spanish Saint's marvellous literary power and fecundity, she wrote many a page on the beatitude and martyrdom of the soul under the action of divine love worthy to rank with the finest in the classics of mysticism. But their beauty and sweetness are no more to be described than the tints of a sunset or the perfume of a rose. They have to be experienced, to be read and savoured in the lovely old French of which she was a natural master. Her style, as Bremond well says [in *Histoire littéraire du sentiment religieux en France depuis la fin des guerres de religion jusqu'à nos jours*, Vol. VI: *La conquête mystique: Marie de l'Incarnation Turba Magna* (1923)], did not take the veil when she became an Ursuline. It made no vow of poverty and kept to the end the tang of Touraine. But while the style may be the man, it is certainly not the mystic, which is a reason for giving here some other words of the same eminent and charming historian. Speaking of the mystics in general, he says:

> Willy nilly, we bring them down to our own level. We place them in an intellectual, a sentimental, a literary setting which not only is not theirs, but which in some fashion is the negation of theirs... In fact, the admiration which we profess for a Teresa and a Mary of the Incarnation is in inverse ratio to their real greatness. The higher they are raised up, the more they escape us. When they seem to us to touch the utmost summits of lyricism, they are only at the stammering stage of the first years. Where ours comes to an end their true sublimity has its beginning [see excerpt dated 1923].

That daunting judgment is absolutely fair. In heaven we shall all be mystics, thanks to Purgatory, but until then we inevitably tend to shy away from what is most divine in the saints and to grasp at the human ties and touches of nature which makes them our kin. With the poets we find easy symbols of the beauty of their holiness in flowers and starlight and music, but before God they are much more like flashes of lightning or the tremendous pageant of the sea. (pp. 91-2)

Marie's correspondence with Dom Raymond on the subject of her and his Canadian aspirations drew from Abbé Bremond some of his joyous pages. He was a critic by no means easy to please, and he had a hawk's eye for anything the least banal, artificial or cock-a-hoop in the people whose characters he so brilliantly analysed. But Marie swept him completely off his feet, and filled him with a love and reverence that just managed to stop short this side idolatry. Fearful lest his readers might miss in their haste some delicate nuance of irony, so gentle and so devastating, some exquisite touch of femininity, some sally of

mischievous humour always in ambush for Reverend Father Sobersides when he walked abroad with his bell, book, and candle, Bremond italicized these charmingly human ebullitions in the letters of his heroine. (p. 97)

[When one thinks of Mary of the Incarnation one] is inevitably reminded of Marie de Sévigné, for whose honour a thousand pens, including this leaky one, would leap from their clips. But adorable though she was, she is not in the same class as our Marie, who, equally gay, equally interested in the tragi-comedy of life around her, equally the foe of the solemn and lachrymose, counted the whole world well lost for the privilege of breaking her royal heart to save a few poor Red Indians. (p. 105)

> *James Brodrick, "The Saint Teresa of the New World: I" and "The Saint Teresa of the New World: II," in* The Month, *Vol. CLXXV, Nos. 907 and 908, January and February, 1940, pp. 47-56; 91-105.*

MOTHER M. ALOYSIUS GONZAGA L'HEUREUX (essay date 1956)

[*In the following excerpt, L'Heureux reviews criticism of Marie's works and examines the mystical content of her writings.*]

Of all the theologians and mystical writers who have pondered over or examined the writings of the Venerable Mother Marie of the Incarnation, O.S.U., there are few who have not been impressed, indeed, fascinated by the logic of her thought and the clearness of her language.... Bossuet's oft-quoted "Tout y est admirable" ["Everything there is admirable"], written to Madame Cornuau in a letter dated June 1, 1695, referred to the form as well as to the content of the **Relations,** excerpts of which he had found in [Dom Claude Martin's] *Vie de la Vénérable Mère Marie de l'Incarnation.* (p. 1)

[The] critical judgments of the erudite Benedictine [Dom Albert Jamet], who to this day remains the foremost authority on the doctrine of the Venerable Marie of the Incarnation, are worthy of consideration. Although at times the language of Venerable Mère Marie is disarmingly simple, even ordinary, yet many a scholar has been perplexed in the presence of such words as *correspondance, respir, retour, tendance,* etc., and very few have ventured to define them. In a manner unparalleled, however, Dom Jamet is conversant with the depth of meaning and the plenitude of significance language had in Venerable Mère Marie's mystical experience. With his masterly erudition, he comments lengthily [in his 1930 edition of Marie's *Écrits spirituels et historiques*] on the historical and semantic value of words, though at times even he may dismiss problemwords with the conventional "comme disent les mystiques" ["as it is said by the mystics"]. In the course of a series of lectures in religious psychology delivered at the University of Fribourg, M.-T. Pénido unraveled more than one knotty problem, and declared that the Venerable Mère Marie's mystical itinerary is "d'une complexité inouie et presque déconcertante" ["of an almost unheard of and nearly disconcerting complexity"]. (pp. 3-4)

What are those qualities of clearness, of lucidity, and of precision which a modern writer [James Brodrick] has called "a part of Mother Marie's quintessential Frenchness" [see excerpt dated 1940], and which, added to so many superior gifts, natural and supernatural, have evoked from the initiate sentiments of appreciation and admiration? How then explain the scarcity of translations of her works, especially in English? Could it be that the theological and psychological precision of earlier analyses has not struck deep enough into the veins of what Ferdinand de Saussure would call [in *Cours de linguistique générale* (1931)] her "parole," her individual expression? There were moments when even Claude Martin called upon his Mother to clarify some difficult passage of her letters, though he more often averred that they needed no commentary. (p. 5)

In 1620, the Gallican Church, accepting the Tridentine reforms after much hesitation and against the will of Louis XIII, was giving the world an example of Catholic revival. (p. 121)

Though we find in the style of the **Relation** several of the characteristic traits of the later and more classical writers of the 17th century, it appears to us that the spirituality of the Venerable Mother, deep, luminous, active (because mystical), belongs to this epoch of Louis XIII, and that the mystic, if not the writer, finds her place alongside the protagonists of the Catholic counter-reform, very near the author of the *Traité de l'Amour de Dieu*.

Indeed, while Olier and Condren were devoutly engaged in the worship of the divine priesthood of Christ; while Bérulle drew from his contemplation of the Word Incarnate the inspiration to prepare holy and cultured priests for the Church; while, with the encouragement of M. Vincent, he was laying and consolidating the foundation of the Oratoire, and Jean Eudes and his disciples were devoting themselves to a closer study of Holy Scripture, Marie Guyart Martin of Tours, the very young and destitute widow of a silk dealer, was also engaged in the mystical contemplation of the Word, and later as Marie de l'Incarnation, in her cloister of Tours, was privileged to receive an infused knowledge of the significance of the Scriptures. In the humble Ursuline nun, whether exercising the function of a classroom teacher or of mistress of novices, whether interpreting the Canticle to her "consoeurs" ["sisters in religion"] or writing her autobiography in the solitude of her convent cell, we contemplate "lapensée française en travail" ["French thought at work"]. But in that "pensée" there was the ineffable whispering of the Holy Ghost, whose name appears so frequently in her writings, and though then seemingly the light under the bushel, she was to become a few years hence, in the hand of Providence, a glowing torch to enlighten the savage tribes of Canada as well as a brilliant beacon on the path of the heroes and apostles, her contemporaries in the Church of the New World. (p. 122)

[While] we would not imply that Venerable Marie's mysticism should be termed "eclectic," neither would we connect her with any existing school of spirituality. We heartily subscribe to Dom Jamet's statement as to her "uniqueness," yet we cannot see her isolated from her age and milieu, albeit in the splendor of mystical summits. As we indicated . . . , hers is "la pensée française en travail," illumined, adorned with the all-pervasive action of divine Life, flashing the light and love of that Life on those about her. It was naturally impossible for her not to absorb a certain amount of the spirituality of her time. Often at a loss to find words to translate her own experiences, she

could not but welcome the aid of books which came under her hand. And thus it happened . . . that in the **Relations** we sometimes find the Spanish thought in Berullian externals. (p. 145)

The life of our great French mystic extends over seventy-two years of the "grand siècle," thirty-nine of which were spent in her own country. While we may not claim for her the literary power and fecundity of the writers of that age, and still less of the prince of tragedy, yet we cannot deny that her two autobiographies, depicting now the beatitude, now the martyrdom of her soul under the action of God, are veritable dramas, some lines of which ring with an emotion akin to Racinian pathos. (p. 153)

> *Mother M. Aloysius Gonzaga L'Heureux, in her* The Mystical Vocabulary of Venerable Mère Marie de l'Incarnation and Its Problems, *1956. Reprint by AMS Press, 1969, 193 p.*

REVEREND JAMES BRODRICK, S.J.   (essay date 1962)

[In the following preface (dated 1962) of Fr. John J. Sullivan's 1964 edition of The Relation of 1654, *Brodrick considers Marie's achievement as a mystic and writer.]*

Venerable Marie of the Incarnation, Bossuet's "St. Teresa of Canada," is very little known among Catholics at large. This is a great pity, for she was one of the most attractive of profound mystics, and dared to be humorous even when treating of the high things of God. Like St. Teresa, she possessed immense practical ability and managed a large transport system with all the competence, but infinitely more of the humanity, of a modern tycoon. Marie went beyond Teresa in her experience of life, for she was a married woman with a son who became a famous Benedictine, and she was the first strictly speaking missionary nun of modern times.

Her letters make as joyous reading any day as those of Madame de Sevignè, and her **Relations** of her mystical experiences, written only at the express commands of her spiritual directors, are among the great documents of mystical literature. But all her works, though published in our time in many tomes of impeccable scholarship, have remained in their charming old Tourangeau French, inaccessible to the ordinary reader.

To the best of my knowledge, Father Sullivan is the first to provide an English translation of the 1654 **Relation**, which is indeed an autobiography. His pioneering work will bring joy, not only to all Ursulines of the English-speaking world, but to every serious student of the ways of God with great and privileged souls. They are unaccountable ways, for Marie was compelled to crucify all her maternal instincts and to abandon her boy, aged eleven, to become an Ursuline nun. Nearly forty years later the wound was still unhealed, and she wrote from her heroic post at Quebec to Claude, then one of the brightest ornaments of the learned Benedictine Congregation of St. Maur:

> Know once again that in separating from you I subjected myself to a living death. The Spirit of God was inexorable to the tender love which I felt for you. . . This divine Spirit was pitiless to my feelings. His voice urged unceasingly with a holy impetuosity which allowed me

no repose. In parting from you it seemed as if my soul
was being wrenched from my body, with intensest pain.

The extraordinary stages of Marie's missionary vocation
are told in [the *Relation of 1654*], and it is as moving a
story of suffering and heroism, lit up by unconquerable
gaiety, as any in the love dialogue between human beings
and God. (pp. vii-viii)

> *Reverend James Brodrick, S.J., in a preface to*
> The Autobiography of Venerable Marie of the In-
> carnation, O.S.U.: Mystic and Missionary, *trans-*
> *lated by John J. Sullivan, S.J., Loyola University*
> *Press, 1964, pp. vii-viii.*

JOHN J. SULLIVAN, S.J.   (essay date 1962)

[*In the following excerpt, Sullivan reviews criticism of* The
Relation of 1654 *and comments on the origin, form, and intent of the work.*]

Mystic and missionary! Venerable Marie of the Incarnation was preeminently both one and the other. Pope Pius
XII, in his allocution of December 8, 1950, to the first International Congress of Religious Men, tells us that "St.
Francis Xavier and St. Teresa of Avila are brilliant proofs
of the fact that the most active zeal can be closely associated with the quest for the riches of the interior life."
There are, of course, many notable examples in the history
of Christian spirituality of the entire compatibility of intimate union with God and an intense exterior apostolate,
of contemplation and action; and the name of Venerable
Mother Marie of the Incarnation deserves a place very
high on the list.

For, on the one hand, Venerable Marie enjoyed the highest degrees of infused contemplation over a very long period of years. Indeed, "in the opinion of the best judges she
was one of the sublimest contemplatives the Church has
ever known," as Father James Brodrick, S.J., the distinguished English hagiographer, remarks in his article on
Venerable Marie in the *Month* for January 1940 [see excerpt dated 1940]. And as he notes in the preface to [*The
Autobiography of Venerable Marie of the Incarnation, O.
S.U., Mystic and Missionary*], Venerable Marie's *Relations*
of her mystical experiences are among the great documents of mystical literature [see excerpt dated 1962]. And
this eminent mystic was also a missionary who journeyed
to New France in 1639.

In the judgment of Dom Albert Jamet, O.S.B., the learned
editor of the critical edition of the writings of Venerable
Marie, her *Relation of 1654* is "a capital document in the
field of mystical literature." Writing in *Etudes* for January
5, 1931, Father Lucien Roure, S.J., observes that Venerable Marie's *Relations* are marked by a spontaneity, an accent of sincerity, a surety of analysis and psychological fi-
nesse in the exposition of the most complex states of the
soul and of the highest divine communications, which
place these works in the first rank of mystical literature.
(pp. xv-xvi)

But Mother Marie of the Incarnation was also the pioneer
nun missionary of the Church. Her missionary apostolate
among the Indians at Quebec extended over the last thirty-two years of her life, from August 1639 until April
1672. And what a truly remarkable apostolate it was! Here

was a woman who, during her missionary labors, was associated in some measure and degree with the North American martyrs, St. Isaac Jogues, St. John de Brebeuf, St. Gabriel Lalemant. Here was a woman whose zeal for souls
caused her at the age of forty to study and master the very
difficult Algonquin and Montagnais languages, and at the
age of fifty to study and master the equally difficult Huron
tongue. And that same zeal for souls caused Venerable
Marie to compose a Huron catechism, three Algonquin
catechisms, an Iroquois catechism, a French-Algonquin
and Algonquin-French dictionary, and an Iroquois dictionary. For thirty-two years she labored to teach the faith to
the daughters of the savages. The fruitfulness of her missionary apostolate is reflected in this excerpt from a letter
written by the chiefs of the Huron tribe to Pope Pius IX
about two hundred years after her death, a letter which
contained a petition for her beatification: "Reverend
Mother Marie of the Incarnation called us from the depths
of our forests to teach us to know and adore the true Master of life. She took our hearts in her hand and placed
them before the Eternal God like a basket of fruit gathered
by herself. . . . With her hand she marked our hearts with
the sign of the Faith, and that Faith has remained engra-
ven in our hearts. . . . Holy Father, we beg you to receive
. . . of the Huron Tribe the testimony of its profound gratitude to Reverend Mother Marie of the Incarnation" [see
excerpt dated 1875]. Truly, Venerable Marie was preeminently mystic and missionary!

In the light of the above data we can readily understand
the role assigned to Venerable Marie by the distinguished
French theologian, the late Father Jules Lebreton, S.J., in
his work *Tu Solus Sanctus*. In this study of the principal
orientations of Christian mysticism—that is, the contemplative, the apostolic, and the reparative, as illustrated in
the lives of eminent mystics—Father Lebreton singles out
the life and writings of Venerable Marie as illustrative of
the apostolic orientation of mysticism.

Yes, the life of Venerable Mother Marie of the Incarnation proves with a very special clarity the compatibility of
contemplation and action, of an intense interior life and
an absorbing exterior apostolate.

Among the numerous writings of Venerable Marie are two
Relations, that of 1633 and that of 1654, both of which are
an account of her life, especially her interior life, written
at the order of her spiritual director. The *Relation of 1654*
is undoubtedly her masterpiece.

A word about the origin of the critical edition of this *Relation* prepared by Dom Jamet. In reluctant response to the
earnest and persistent petition of her son, then a Benedictine monk, Venerable Marie sent him this account of her
life which she had written with her own hand. This he
used as the basis of the *Life* of his mother, which was published five years after her death, in 1677. This same *Relation of 1654*, whether the original manuscript or a copy of
it, also served as the basis of the life of Venerable Marie
written some years later, in 1724, by Father P. F. X. de
Charlevoix, S.J. Nothing is known as to the fate of the
original manuscript of the *Relation of 1654*. Up until recent times the only witnesses to that *Relation* were the
printed lives mentioned above, especially that by Venerable Marie's son, Dom Claude Martin. (pp. xvi-xviii)

The *Relation of 1654* is not a scientific treatise on the
higher states of prayer; rather, it is a highly personal docu-

The tomb of Marie de l'Incarnation, Ursuline Monastery, Quebec.

ment, an account of God's very intimate dealings with Venerable Marie's soul, an account of her own interior life. External events are mentioned, yes; not, however, for their own sake but only insofar as they are necessarily involved in the account of her interior states. The *Relation* is marked by certain evidences of hastiness of composition, such as repetitions, faults of cohesion, occasional omission of words, laconic concision. But at the same time it is characterized by a charming simplicity, naturalness, spontaneity, directness, and unction.

A letter which Venerable Marie sent to her son at the same time as the manuscript enables us to see the reasons for its style, for any defects in its composition. She writes [see excerpt dated 1654]:

> Don't think that these pages I'm sending you has been premeditated in order to observe a certain plan in them, as is the case with works which have been carefully prepared. Such a procedure was impossible for me in the state of soul wherein God keeps me at present, and the path along which His Divine Majesty now leads me does not permit of my observing any method in what I write. When I take up my pen to begin, I don't have in mind a single word of what I'm going to write, but as I write along the Spirit of grace who guides me causes me to put down what is in keeping with His own good pleasure. He it is who caused me to begin writing and to carry it through, always with many interruptions and in the midst of great distractions occasioned by our domestic affairs.

In yet another letter to her son she indicates the reason for the brevity of treatment of some parts of the *Relation:*

> There are many things—and I can say that most of them are of this nature—which it would be impossible completely to describe, and all the more so inasmuch as God's interior dealings with my soul involve graces so intimate and impressions so spiritual of union with Him in the center of my soul that they cannot be expressed. And futhermore, there are certain communications between God and the soul which would strike people as incredible if one who experiences them were to manifest them exteriorly as they transpire interiorly...
> This is in part the reason for my repugnance to write of these matters... The older one grows, the more incapable one is of writing about these experiences, for the spiritual life simplifies the soul in a consuming love in a manner so extraordinary that one no longer finds the terms wherewith to speak of such things. (pp. xviii-xix)

Venerable Marie repeatedly affirms her inability to express satisfactorily her spiritual experiences; indeed, her inability to put them into words at all. Some of the features of the composition of the *Relation of 1654,* as well as the sublimity of much of its subject matter, will of course make for difficulties of translation. Obviously a translation which made very clear the sublime experiences which Venerable Marie herself could express only very obscurely would by that very fact be suspect. The very transcendence of those experiences makes them ineffable, so that any attempt to express them verbally must necessarily leave them shrouded in obscurity for the listener or reader. (pp. xix-xx)

Peharps an attentive reading of the autobiography of Venerable Marie of the Incarnation will persuade the reader that the early biograper... [Father Pierre Francis X. de Charlevoix, S.J.] was not far from the truth when he wrote, "History presents us with few women who can compare with the illustrious Marie of the Incarnation." (p. xxi)

> *John J. Sullivan, S.J., in an introduction to* The Autobiography of Venerable Marie of the Incarnation, O.S.U.: Mystic and Missionary, *translated by John J. Sullivan, S.J., Loyola University Press, 1964, pp. xv-xxi.*

MARY DENIS MAHONEY, O.S.U. (essay date 1964)

[*In the following excerpt, Mahoney examines Marie's mysticism and comments on her prose style.*]

It would need a flamboyant mystic indeed, so one would think, to stand out in the jostling crowd of *beati* that thronged the spiritual highways of the seventeenth century. For mysticism in the France of the Medici was very much *à la mode*. It was "the thing"—one might say the fashion, and what Frenchman wants to be out of fashion? Consequently mystics abounded, both false mystics and true. Mistress and servant, soldier and statesman, all alike experienced supernatural dreams, divine touches, interior locutions. Into such an environment was born Marie Guyart who was to become one of the greatest mystics of this extraordinary mystic age.

And yet, although there is much that is unusual about the paths God destined for Marie, there is little that is flamboyant about her. The various manifestations verging on hysteria which characterised so many contemporaries are singularly lacking in Marie. The extraordinariness of her graces is matched only by the extraordinariness of her response—a response vital, faithful and, above all, remarkably controlled. Even in the face of an imminent ecstasy Marie maintains that poise and balance which is one of her most individual characteristics. If she stands out from her contemporaries, it is not because she is more colourful but rather because she is more tranquil, with that delicate poise of spirit which so aptly fits her for her mystic graces.

Wife, widow, cloistered religious, missionary—Marie passed through all these states in turn, states which in God's providence did not contradict each other but prepared and reinforced her vocation. God would have all; God would be all. And in establishing His absolute dominion over her soul, He led her in great zig-zag lines which only a soul made docile by faith would have followed.

Her conscious entrance into the mystic way occurred on the vigil of the feast of the Incarnation in the year 1620. Marie was at that time a widow of twenty, harassed by the demands of a failing business and the care of her child who was less than a year old. It was in order to settle some business matters that she walked eastward along the busy streets of Tours on that memorable morning. As she walked, suddenly, without warning or explanation, the visible world fell away from her eyes, and to the eyes of her soul there appeared a world of spirit, so true, so terrible, so utterly real that until the end of her life the impression was never effaced from her heart. There she stood, stock-still in that busy street, while her first great mystical experience swept over her. (pp. 277-78)

When she came to herself, she found a new creature, so strong had the divine action been upon her. All that she had ever thought herself to have done for God, all that had appeared to her to be love for Him was ashes beneath her feet, while within her burned a flame which left no portion of her body free from the anguish of love. In her bewilderment she adds, "And what is more incomprehensible, this mercilessness seems sweet."

We are singularly fortunate in possessing Marie's own account of this initial grace and of the many others that follow it. Living as she did in the age of memoirs and diaries, it is not surprising to find that at least twice during her lifetime her confessors (Père Raymond de St. Bernard, a Feuillant Father, and Père Jérôme Lallemant, a Jesuit) ordered her to write accounts of her spiritual life. These accounts, in addition to several hundred letters and some miscellaneous spiritual notes, provide the source for the extensive life of Marie completed by her Benedictine son, Dom Claude, shortly after her death. Marie's prose, like everything else about her, slips the bonds of artificial convention and frees itself from the "ornamental flowerets," from the "emblems and allegories" which decorated much of the religious prose of her day. But, unfortunately, she leaves much unsaid; she wrote under obedience, despite great repugnance, and with the sole purpose of satisfying her directors concerning her spiritual life. Such a purpose naturally excludes the details of daily life, and the biographer who attempts to piece together Marie's exterior life must often walk cautiously amid conjecture.

And yet in the realm of the spiritual, Marie's memoirs leave little to be desired. Her limpid prose, at once free and strong, is extraordinarily adequate for the task before her. She possesses a singular gift for descriptive expression and analogy, and also an ability for objective analysis which enables her not only to describe what has happened to her but also to evaluate and classify it. When, then, Marie labels this vision of the Precious Blood as the day of her "conversion," we must concede its importance even while hesitating over the meaning of the word "conversion." That this was in any way a turning from sin to virtue is manifestly false; Marie's life had always been one of unswerving fidelity to God. Her son Claude himself explains it [in his *Vie de la Vénérable Mère Marie de l'Incarnation*] as his mother no doubt meant it: "By this conversion we must understand the firm resolution which she took to think no longer of the world with its cares and hopes in order to give herself wholly to God and to live solely for His Love." (pp. 279-80)

[The] direct operation of the Spirit within her neither frightened nor puzzled her. She accepted it without question as she continued throughout her life to accept both the graces and privations which God lavished upon her. In an age which bristled with spiritual directors, Marie kept her own counsel. It was neither pride nor diffidence which caused her to act thus, but the clear-eyed candour of a child who saw no problem in carrying out with loving fidelity what God so obviously asked of her. Although she was overwhelmed with grace and enveloped in mystic prayer, no mention of any of this was made to her director. The Holy Spirit was her only guide. She felt no need for any other. (p. 280)

Mary Denis Mahoney, O.S.U., "Venerable Mary of the Incarnation," in Spirituality through the Centuries: Ascetics and Mystics of the Western Church, *edited by James Walsh, S.J., P. J. Kene-*ᵈ˟ ℓ. *Sons, 1964, pp. 277-92.*

ADDITIONAL BIBLIOGRAPHY

Brodrick, James, S. J. "Venerable Marie of the Incarnation." In his *A Procession of Saints*, pp. 168-95. New York: Longmans, Green and Co., 1949.
    A biographical sketch, focusing on Marie as "one of the sublimest and most finely balanced contemplatives the Church has ever known."

Browne, P. W. "The Oldest Institutions of Learning for Women in North America." *The Catholic Educational Review* 30 (February 1932): 87-99.
    Detailed account of Marie's founding of the Ursuline monastery in Quebec.

Chabot, Marie-Emmanuel, O.S.U. "Biographies: Guyart." In *Dictionary of Canadian Biography: 1000 to 1700*, Vol. I, pp. 351-59. Toronto: University of Toronto Press, 1979.
    Considers the form and content of Marie's principal works, noting especially the light they shed on the author's character and on daily life in seventeenth-century Quebec.

Laval, Bishop François de. Letter to Dom Claude Martin. In *Dictionary of Canadian Biography: 1000 to 1700*, Vol. I, p. 356. Toronto: University of Toronto Press, 1979.

An elegiac tribute written in 1677. Laval assesses Marie's character and describes her achievements as a missionary.

Mahoney, Mother Denis, O. S. U. *Marie of the Incarnation: Mystic and Missionary*. Garden City, N. Y.: Doubleday & Company, 1964, 421 p.
    A full-length biography of Marie, based on her letters and spiritual notes.

———. "Ven. Marie of the Incarnation." In *New Catholic Encyclopedia*, Vol. IX: *Ma to Mor*, edited by the Editorial Staff of the Catholic University of America, pp. 219-20. New York: McGraw-Hill Book Company, 1967.
    Surveys Marie's career as the first woman missionary to the New World, noting the value of her works as a source for seventeenth-century Canadian history.

Marshall, Joyce. Introduction to *Word from New France: The Selected Letters of Marie de l'Incarnation*, by Marie de l'Incarnation, edited by Joyce Marshall, pp. 1-33. Toronto University Press, 1967.
    A biographical sketch of Marie, noting the historical value of her letters.

Ronayne, Charles F. "A Study in Adventure." *The Saturday Review of Literature* VII, No. 39 (18 April 1931): 745.
    Reviews Agnes Repplier's *Mère Marie of the Ursulines* (see excerpt dated 1931), concentrating on Marie's "supreme executive ability."

Schmidt, Josef. "Marie de l'Incarnation's Spirituality—A Disturbing Proximity?" *Monastic Studies* 17 (1986): 209-17.
    Examines Marie's spiritual and literary career as a "fascinating mixture of unconventional conventionality."

Molière

1622-1673

(Pseudonym of Jean Baptiste Poquelin) French dramatist.

Molière is widely recognized as the greatest comic writer of seventeenth-century France and one of the foremost dramatists in world literature. In such masterpieces as *Le Tartuffe (Tartuffe), Dom Juan (Don Juan)*, and *Le misanthrope (The Misanthrope)* he set precedents that completely altered the focus and purpose of comedy, introducing realism to the French stage and elevating comic drama from farcical buffoonery to an important forum for social and religious criticism. Molière thus profoundly influenced the development of modern comedy and established comic drama in France as a legitimate literary medium, equal to tragedy in its ability to portray aspects of human nature.

Molière devoted his life to the theater, achieving remarkable literary and financial success in his career. Born in Paris and christened Jean Baptiste Poquelin, he was the eldest of six children of a well-to-do bourgeois who held a prestigious royal appointment as *valet de chambre* and *tapissier*, or upholsterer, to Louis XIII. Jean Baptiste was apprenticed in his father's trade but showed little inclination for the family business. According to his first biographer, Jean Le Gallois de Grimarest, the boy's interest in acting was sparked by his grandfather, who had a passion for the theater and occasionally took his grandson to see productions at the famous Hôtel de Bourgogne. Jean Baptiste's fascination with the stage likely increased while he attended one of the best secondary schools in Paris, the Jesuit Collège de Clermont, where he studied and perhaps acted in classical dramas by such authors as Terence and Plautus. (His later work shows evidence of his debt to these authors, to whom he has frequently been compared.) It is also thought that at Clermont he studied philosophy under the prominent mathematician and Epicurean philosopher Abbé Pierre Gassendi. After leaving Clermont, Jean Baptiste studied law briefly before inheriting his father's position at court. In 1642, possibly while traveling as *valet de chambre* to Louis XIII, he met and became romantically involved with Madeleine Béjart, a young actress. She and her family strongly influenced Jean Baptiste: in 1643 he formally renounced his royal appointment, sacrificing a highly respectable bourgeois living to pursue a theatrical career. Within one year he adopted the stage name of Molière (possibly out of respect for his father's desire to avoid being associated with the theater, which was then deemed disreputable) and together with the Béjarts established the troupe l'Illustre Théâtre (The Illustrious Theater), in which he acted and of which he eventually became director and stage manager. But numerous expenses, the troupe's general inexperience, and Molière's particularly bad tragic acting prevented the company from successfully competing with the professional troupes at the Hôtels de Bourgogne and de Marais, bringing on collapse in July 1645. Despite being sued for bankruptcy and temporarily imprisoned for the theater's debts, Molière continued to actively pursue his theatrical career, touring the provinces with the Béjarts as strolling players. During this crucial thirteen-year apprenticeship Molière

Molière

wrote his first plays—*La jalousie de Barbouillé (The Jealousy of Le Barbouillé), Le médecin volant (The Flying Doctor)*, and *L'étourdi (The Blunderer)*—all short adaptations of Italian farces in the tradition of the commedia dell'arte.

Upon returning to Paris in 1658, the thespians, though by then well seasoned, were still unsuccessful as tragedians; their premier Parisian performance of Pierre Corneille's *Nicomède* (1651) left audiences unimpressed. The accompanying farce, however, Molière's *Le dépit amoureux (The Amorous Quarrel)*, was greeted with overwhelming enthusiasm, and the production earned them both the favor of Louis XIV and the privilege of sharing a theater with the famous Italian performers of Scaramouche. Within one year Molière gained lasting recognition with *Les précieuses ridicules (The Affected Ladies)*, a one-act comedy of manners satirizing two foolish provincial ladies who imitate the artificial social graces and overrefined manners of the Parisian upper class. Molière's portrayal of pretentiousness in high society was so accurate that it outraged numerous aristocrats who believed themselves the targets of the dramatist's parody. Molière thus earned the first of many influential enemies; thereafter, his life and plays were almost always at the center of controversy. After the

257

successful production of *Sganarelle; ou, Le cocu imaginaire (The Imaginary Cuckold)* in 1661, Molière wrote *Dom Garcie de Navarre (Don Garcia of Navarre)*, a heroic tragedy that failed dismally, convincing him to relinquish his ambition of writing tragedy. The following year he married Armande Béjart, a twenty-year-old coquette (thought to be either the sister or daughter of Molière's former mistress, Madeleine Béjart) ill suited to the reputedly serious nature of her forty-year-old husband. The union was unhappy and was marked by periodic separations. The extent to which Molière's marital experiences affected his dramas is still debated, but the problems of marriage, especially between older men and much younger women, became the subject of many of his plays. Armande's uncertain parentage and rumored infidelities became the subject of hostile pamphlets and malicious gossip by Molière's enemies, who, in the controversy following the production of his next play, *L'école des femmes (The School for Wives)*, accused him of incest and labeled him a cuckold. Written within a few months of his marriage, *The School for Wives* concerns the schemes of a middle-aged man to create a wife incapable of cuckolding him by raising her from girlhood in complete ignorance and innocence. Although it was Molière's greatest commercial success, the play was severely criticized as immoral and sacrilegious and its author was castigated for failing to conform to formal dramatic rules. Molière responded to the acrid allegations with two one-act plays, *La critique de "L'école des femmes" (The "School for Wives" Criticised)* and *L'impromptu de Versailles (The Impromptu of Versailles)* (his only direct acknowledgments and refutation of the negative literary and personal criticism levelled against him), in which he defended his dramatic technique and satirized his enemies.

Charges of impiety plagued Molière throughout his career, culminating in the controversy surrounding his most renowned work, *Tartuffe*. First performed in a three-act version in 1664, *Tartuffe* reveals the intrigues of Tartuffe, a hypocritical spiritual advisor who attempts to gain control over an entire household by manipulating one man. Molière's daring exposure of the vices of false *dévots* and the hypocrisy of certain practices condoned by the Catholic church sparked perhaps the most important censorship battle of seventeenth-century France. *Tartuffe* was condemned as sacrilegious by people of almost every religious persuasion including the Jesuits and Jansenists— dominant rival factions of the Catholic church—as well as the influential underground society, Compagnie du Saint Sacrement (Society of the Holy Sacrament) which boasted such powerful and prestigious members as Molière's former patron, Armand de Bourbon, Prince de Conti. These disparate sects all believed themselves the targets of Molière's satire—persuasive evidence of the misunderstandings the play fostered. Although *Tartuffe* was extremely popular with audiences and was acclaimed by Louis XIV, the Archbishop of Paris issued a decree threatening to excommunicate anyone who performed, attended, or even read the play. In the midst of the controversy, Molière produced *Don Juan*, a cynical recasting of the legend of the irreligious libertine who embraces hypocrisy and commits unpardonable sins. *Don Juan*'s sensitive subject matter invited further censorship from outraged church officials, who had the play suppressed after only fifteen performances. In 1667, Molière submitted a five-act revision of *Tartuffe* called *L'imposteur* in which he renamed

Tartuffe Panulphe, secularized the hypocrite's priestly mien, and subdued the overtly religious trappings of the play. Molière's attempt to pacify angry church officials was unsuccessful, however, and he thus turned to Louis XIV, petitioning him more than once for an official reprieve. In one such appeal, Molière expressed his conviction that comedy could have a legitimate social and critical value: "I believe that I can do nothing better than attack the vices of my time with ridiculous likenesses; ... hypocrisy is, without doubt, one of the most common, the most disagreeable, and the most dangerous of these." His pleas were unsuccessful, as Louis was reluctant to oppose powerful religious interests. The King's personal support of Molière was unfailing, however, and it is possible that without his royal favor and protection, the dramatist might well have been executed for heresy. It was not until 1669—after the bulk of political and religious power had shifted away from his most adamant opponents—that Molière was permitted to perform publicly the final version of the play. Following the controversy surrounding *Tartuffe*, Molière reverted on several occasions to writing less consequential farces. Plagued with recurrent illnesses throughout his career due primarily to exhaustion from overworking, the dramatist was diagnosed a hypochondriac by angry doctors whose profession he had parodied, and slandered by such envious rival playwrights as Le Boulanger de Chalussay in *Elomire hypocondre* (1671). Ironically, Molière died of a lung disorder in 1673 following the fourth performance of his final comedy, *Le malade imaginaire (The Imaginary Invalid)*, in which he played the role of the hypochondriac. Molière's conflicts with the Church continued even in death. Denied both the ministrations of a priest and interment in consecrated ground because of his profession, he was granted but a serviceless funeral and that only after Louis XIV intervened on his behalf.

As a dramatist, Molière sought above all to entertain. He wrote: "I should like to know if the golden rule is not to give pleasure and if a play achieves its purpose has not been following the correct path?" Molière's view of comedy gradually evolved, however, to embrace the belief that "the business of comedy is to present, in general, all the defects of man and principally of our country." His dramatic canon, comprising over thirty plays, ranges from slight farces imitative of the Italian commedia dell'arte to highly sophisticated comedies comparable to tragedy in their portrayal of the complexities and contradictions of human nature. His mature plays, variously termed comedies of manners, of character, and of observation, combine criticism of seventeenth-century French society with penetrating insight into human nature. Commentators agree that Molière's strength as a dramatist lies in his diverse, insightful characterization rather than in his plots, a number of which have been deemed unoriginal, contrived, and awkward. Portraying recognizable characters acting in real life situations and using a simpler, more natural language than that hitherto utilized by writers of farce or tragedy, Molière exposed artificiality and vice in society. His plays frequently depict a specific character flaw in its extreme—for example, the obsessive avarice of Harpagon in *L'avare (The Miser)*—or pillory a social institution, as in the merciless ridiculing of members of the medical profession in *The Imaginary Invalid*. Though frequently exaggerated types, such characters are nonetheless multidimensional: people whose prototypes, readily discovered in seventeenth-century France, are universal representatives as well. Juxtaposed with such monomaniacs as Alceste in *The Misanthrope* are such *honnêtes hommes* and *raisonneurs* as Alceste's rational counterpart, Philinte, who add balance and serve to restore social harmony and equity at the play's conclusion. Molière thus created complex characters whose actions and perceptions are both entertaining and illustrative of the human capacity for vice and virtue. Though often extremely critical, even caustic, Molière's comedies are considered good-natured, and commentators note that they are surprisingly free of bitterness. Indeed, critics generally agree that rather than wishing to destroy existing social structures, Molière intended to point out specific, willful vices in hopes that society might eventually correct itself. This goal, along with Molière's desire to make audiences laugh, resulted in a legacy of dramas of human nature considered by critics and audiences alike both extremely comical and universally revealing.

As Molière's comic vision premiered an entirely new dimension of French comedy, his works were inevitably at the center of critical controversy. His striking introduction of realism onto the French stage, beginning with *The Affected Ladies* and *The School for Wives*, brought to the fore the longstanding debate over the role of comedy in literature. Most, if not all, seventeenth-century French writers and critics deemed comedy intrinsically inferior to tragedy as a dramatic vehicle for exploring man and society. Moreover, Molière's satirical realism invited evaluation of his works based on their potential religious and social impact. At the forefront of the negative critics were religious leaders who deemed Molière a dangerous revolutionary and denounced his works as a threat to public morality. Ironically, he was also defended by critics on moral grounds for the same perceived revolutionary spirit, and he was praised by contemporary writers as a much-needed reformer. Other detractors included traditionalists who condemned Molière on purely literary grounds, faulting his occasional deviation from classically inspired dramatic rules to write plays with fewer than five acts or to compose in free verse or prose rather than exclusively in alexandrines. Attempts to discredit Molière in either a professional or personal capacity had little effect on his theatrical success, however. His plays were extremely popular and, despite claims by critics that he was merely a mediocre *farceur*, rival playwrights and companies soon began almost uniformly imitating his dramatic style. In England, Molière's presence was marked by imitation and evaluation, with many English critics ranking him beside Ben Jonson. That most Restoration dramatists were familiar with his works is evidenced in the nearly forty plays that appeared prior to 1700 in which such authors as John Dryden, William Wycherley, Aphra Behn, and Thomas Shadwell adapted, translated, or borrowed freely from his comedies. The extent to which Molière's comedies actually influenced the development of English Restoration drama is still debated, but that his works received extensive scholarly and public attention is undisputed. Molière's positive reputation in England continued to flourish during the eighteenth century. In France, however, public and critical opinion of his works declined drastically. Throughout the eighteenth century there, his works were often severely criticized or ignored altogether, though he still retained a small following. No longer heralded as the master of comedy, Molière was frequently relegated to the position of a vulgar, bourgeois writer of farces. His natural style was judged too simplistic for the refined theatergoer; thus, his plays were resoundingly rejected in favor of the more elegant, contemporary comedies of Pierre Marivaux and Nivelle de la Chalussée. Nonetheless, scholars continued to cite him as the source of all French comedy, advising aspiring dramatists to study his technique.

In the early nineteenth century, during the French Restoration, Molière's comedies regained preeminence among dramatic critics and enjoyed a tremendous resurgence of public popularity. His plays were by far the most frequently performed of the era, as he was considered by the neoclassicists the purest representative of the classical theater of the age of Louis XIV. Ironically, Romantic critics also valued Molière's works, seeing in his dramas a revolutionary, almost tragic, individualism that transcended rigid classicism. Esteemed by the two predominant literary movements of the Restoration, Molière and his comedies were exempted from the negative criticism directed at almost every one of his contemporaries. Critics of the socialist and humanitarian schools praised him as well, perceiving in his dramas a potential vehicle for moral and social reform. Commentators surmise that this almost universal admiration may have been, at least in part, a reaction against the most influential nineteenth-century detractor of Molière, the German critic August Wilhelm von Schlegel. In a series of lectures delivered between 1809 and 1811, Schlegel dismissed Molière's work as unoriginal and unenduring: "The classical reputation of Molière still preserves his pieces on the stage, although in tone and manners they are altogether obsolete. . . . The originals of the individual portraits of Molière have long since disappeared." Schlegel's condemnation united the many French critics who strongly opposed the German scholar's valuation, evoking nationalistic feelings and fostering extensive Molière studies that included scientific compilation of documents pertaining to his life and career as well as detailed attempts to establish Molière as the exponent of such philosophies and dogmas as skepticism, epicureanism, humanism, rationalism, or libertinism. In their efforts to examine and present every aspect of Molière's life and work, several critics collaborated to create the semi-anecdotal journal *Le moliériste*, a monthly review published between 1879 and 1889 devoted entirely to Molière studies. While providing an important forum for debate in Molière studies, *Le moliériste* has been discredited by subsequent scholars as being, in many instances, tantamount to a journal of hero worship. While occasionally extreme, the "moliéromania" of nineteenth-century France played an important role in securing Molière's reputation as one of the immortals of dramatic literature—a reputation that was fixed as early as 1835 by C. A. Sainte-Beuve in his *Portraits littéraires*: "In poesy, in literature, there is a class of men beyond comparison, even among the very first; not numerous, five or six in all, perhaps since the beginning, whose characteristic is universality, eternal humanity, intimately mingled with the painting of manners and morals and the passions of an epoch. . . . Molière is one of these illustrious witnesses."

Twentieth-century scholars have addressed a number of issues concerning Molière and his works, and the majority of critical assessments have been positive. In general, scholars have continued the objective scholarly work instigated by such nineteenth-century scholars as Sainte-Beuve, Ferdinand Brunetière, and Gustave Larroumet, probing in virtually every literary, scientific, and historical aspect of the dramatist and his work. Several valuable critical biographies by noted scholars, including Gustave Michaut, Brander Matthews, and John Palmer, appeared in the early part of the century, treating important historical and sociological questions. More recent studies have explored and analyzed the psychology of such renowned characters as Tartuffe, Don Juan, and Alceste. While scholars still seek philosophical, ethical, and religious messages in Molière's comedies, critical interest has, in many instances, shifted away from assessments of Molière's didactic intent toward purely aesthetic examinations of his comic technique, as exemplified by Will G. Moore's pioneering work, *Molière: A New Criticism* (1949). Variously considered a blasphemer, a moralist, a stinging social satirist, and a writer of pure comedy, Molière has, as Alvin Eustis notes, "borne a different message for each successive generation since his own." Heralded by critics of every century as the father of modern comic drama, Molière is esteemed for the universality of his comic portraits. As Matthews concludes, "Molière is in many ways . . . the embodiment of certain dominant characteristics of the French people. . . . But he is more than French, for his genius transcends the boundaries of race; it has the solid elements of the universal and the permanent."

*PRINCIPAL WORKS

La jalousie de Barbouillé (drama) 1645?
  [*The Jealousy of Le Barbouillé*, 1876]
Le médecin volant (drama) 1645?
  [*The Flying Doctor*, 1876]
L'éstourdy; ou, Le contre-temps (drama) 1653; also published as *L'étourdi*, 1888
  [*Sir Martin Mar-All*, 1714; also published as *The Blunderer; or, The Counter-plots*, 1732]
Le dépit amoureux (drama) 1656
  [*The Amorous Quarrel*, 1714]
Les précieuses ridicules (drama) 1659
  [*The Affected Ladies*, 1714]
Sganarelle; ou, Le cocu imaginaire (drama) 1660
  [*The Imaginary Cuckold*, 1714]
Dom Garcie de Navarre; ou, Le prince jaloux (drama) 1661
  [*Don Garcia of Navarre; or, The Jealous Prince*, 1714]
L'école des maris (drama) 1661
  [*A School for Husbands*, 1714]
Les fâcheux (drama) 1661
  [*The Impertinents*, 1714; also published as *The Bores*, 1875]
L'école des femmes (drama) 1662
  [*A School for Women*, 1714; also published as *The School for Wives*, 1732]
La critique de "L'école des femmes" (drama) 1663
  [*"The School for Women" Criticised*, 1714; also published as *"The School for Wives" Criticised*, 1875]
L'impromptu de Versailles (drama) 1663
  [*The Impromptu of Versailles*, 1714]
Le mariage forcé (drama) 1664
  [*The Forced Marriage*, 1714]
La Princesse d'Élide (drama) 1664
  [*The Princess of Elis, being the Second Day of the Pleasures of the Inchanted Island*, 1714]
Le Tartuffe (drama) 1664; also performed as *L'imposteur*, 1667 and *Le Tartuffe; ou, L'imposteur*, 1669 [revised versions]

  [*Tartuffe: or, The Hypocrite*, 1714; also published as *Tartuffe: or, The Imposter*, 1732]
Dom Juan; ou, Le festin de pierre (drama) 1665
  [*Don John; or, The Libertine*, 1714; also translated as *Don Juan; or, The Feast with the Statue*, 1875]
Le médecin malgré lui (drama) 1666
  [*The Forced Physician*, 1714; also published as *The Doctor in Spite of Himself*, 1915]
†*Le misantrope* (drama) 1666; also published as *Le misanthrope*, 1851
  [*The Misantrope; or, Man-Hater*, 1714; also published as *The Misanthrope*, 1819]
Amphitryon (drama) 1668
  [*Amphitryon; or, The Two Sosias*, 1714]
L'avare (drama) 1668
  [*The Miser*, 1714]
George Dandin; ou, Le mary confondu (drama) 1668
  [*George Dandin; or, The Wanton Wife*, 1714]
Monsieur de Pourceaugnac (drama) 1669
  [*Monsieur de Pourceaugnac; or, Squire Trelooby*, 1704]
Le bourgeois gentilhomme (drama) 1670
  [*The Gentleman Cit*, 1714; also published as *The Bourgeois Gentleman*, 1972]
Les fourberies de Scapin (drama) 1671
  [*The Cheats of Scapin*, 1714; also translated as *The Rogueries of Scapin*, 1876]
Psiché [with Pierre Corneille] (drama) 1671
  [*Psiché*, 1714; also published as *Psyche*, 1732]
Les femmes savantes (drama) 1672
  [*The Learned Ladies*, 1714]
Le malade imaginaire (drama) 1673
  [*The Hypocondriack*, 1714; also published as *The Imaginary Invalid*, 1876]
The Works of Mr. de Molière. 6 vols. (dramas) 1714
The Dramatic Works of Molière. 6 vols. (drama) 1875-76
The Plays of Molière in French with an English Translation. 8 vols. (dramas) 1902-07

*Most of the English translations of Molière's plays were first published in the 1714 collection *The Works of Mr. de Molière*. A few first appeared in *The Dramatic Works of Molière* (1875-76).

†The English translation of this work was originally published in the journal *Monthly Amusement* in 1709.

JEAN LORET (poem date 1660)

[*A French journalist, Loret wrote and published a series of verse gazettes,* La muse historique, *chronicling current events from 1650 to 1665. In the following excerpt from* La muse historique *(1660), he commends Molière's productions of* The Blunderer *and* The Affected Ladies *for Louis XIV and the prime minister, Cardinal Jules Mazarin.*]

The players of His Highness the Prince
Had a good day not long since,
For the Cardinal, as it befell
Who had not been feeling well,
When pain gave him interval
Bade them, not into the hall,
But the better to content him
In his own room—they present him
Nothing at all of your tragic stuff
But two comedies pleasant enough,
L'Étourdi, to wit, as it is called,

Which often has held me enthralled,
And the Marquis de Mascarille
Who is only a marquis at will—
Wherein every line of the play
Holds something to make one feel gay
And many folk very high placed
Found both plays were quite to their taste
And by his particular care
For the author, good Molière,
This most generous Eminence
Made bestowal, in recompense
Tc him and to all who are in his
Troupe, of a handful of guineas. . . .

(pp. 110-11)

Jean Loret, in an extract from a poem in The
Latin Genius *by Anatole France, translated by
Wilfrid S. Jackson, 1924. Reprint by Gabriel
Wells, 1924, pp. 110-11.*

JEAN DE LA FONTAINE (letter date 1661)

[*French fabulist, poet, and translator, La Fontaine is considered one of the outstanding French classical authors. Although he composed over 240 poems and had been called
the greatest lyric poet in seventeenth-century France, he is
best remembered for his numerous fables, many of which
are still widely read in France. In the following excerpt from
a letter written in August 1661 to François de Maucroix, La
Fontaine, in commemorating a court performance of* The
Bores, *extols Molière's style.*]

This writer's [Molière's] style
Charms, at the moment, all the Court.
His name is known to all, in short,
By now it's left e'en Rome behind.
It gives me joy, he's to my mind.
For was he not our whilom choice,
When we agreed, with single voice,
In France once more should *find* abode
The style and taste that Terence showed?
Plautus is naught but a buffoon,
And never was it such a boon
Before the boards to sit awhile;
For now no longer need we smile
At jaded tricks we used to see,
Found good *in illo tempore.*
For now has Fashion changed her ways.
Jodelet [Paul Scarron] is no more the rage
And nothing now received as good
But follows Nature's every mood.

(pp. 115-16)

*Jean de la Fontaine, in an extract from a letter to
Maucroix in August, 1661, in* The Latin Genius
*by Anatole France, translated by Wilfrid S. Jack-
son, 1924. Reprint by Gabriel Wells, 1924, pp.
115-16.*

MOLIÈRE (essay date 1663)

[*The presentation of* The School for Wives *in 1662 engendered fierce protest; the popular play was attacked as irreligious, immoral, and crude. Molière replied to his critics in
1663 with a play* "The School for Wives" Criticized, *from
which the following excerpt is taken.*]

(ÉLISE *is discovered. Enter* URANIE.)

URANIE. How's this, my dear cousin? No one has come
to call?

ÉLISE. Not a soul.
URANIE. Really, it's surprising that we've both been
alone all day.
ÉLISE. I'm surprised too, cousin Uranie. This is hardly
our custom. Your house, thank God, is the ordinary ref-
uge of all the loafers of the court.
URANIE. The fact is, the afternoon has seemed very long.
ÉLISE. As for me, I have found it very short.
URANIE. Well, cousin Élise, intellectuals love solitude.
ÉLISE. Thanks for the compliment; but you know I'm
hardly an intellectual.
URANIE. I like people around, I admit.
ÉLISE. So do I; but I like certain people. And we have to
endure so many tiresome callers that I enjoy being
alone. (p. 97)

(*Enter* GALOPIN.)

GALOPIN. Madame, Madame Climène has come to call
on you.
URANIE. Good heavens! What a visit!
ÉLISE. You were just complaining about being left alone.
Heaven is punishing you. (p. 99)

(*Enter* GALOPIN, *ushering in* CLIMÈNE)

CLIMÈNE Oh, please, darling, have a chair brought for
me, quickly!
URANIE. (*to* GALOPIN) A chair here, quick!

(GALOPIN *brings a chair, and exits.*)

CLIMÈNE. Ah, dear God!
URANIE. What's the matter?
CLIMÈNE. I'm ready to drop!
URANIE. But what's wrong?
CLIMÈNE. My heart fails me!
URANIE. Is it the vapors?
CLIMÈNE. No.
URANIE. Do you want to have your stays unlaced?
CLIMÈNE. Oh, dear, no. Oh!
URANIE. What's your trouble, then? And when did it
strike you?
CLIMÈNE. More than three hours ago. I caught it in the
Palais-Royal Theatre.
URANIE. How's that?
CLIMÈNE. I've just seen, for my sins, that wretched trav-
esty, *The School for Wives*. It made me so sick at my
stomach, I'm still weak. I don't think I'll get over it for
a fortnight.
ÉLISE. It's amazing how one can fall sick without a mo-
ment's warning.
URANIE. My cousin and I, I don't know what we're
made of. We saw the play day before yesterday, and we
both came back sound and healthy.
CLIMÈNE. What? You saw it?
URANIE. Yes; and we listened from one end to the other.
CLIMÈNE. And it didn't drive you almost into convul-
sions, darling?
URANIE. I'm not so delicate, thank God. Personally, I
think the play would be more likely to cure people than
to make them sick.
CLIMÈNE. Good heavens, what are you saying? Can such
a proposition be advanced by a person with a pittance
of common sense? Can one with impunity bite one's
thumb at reason, as you are doing? And in the last analysis, can there be a spirit so starved of wit that it can
relish the insipidities which season that comedy? As for
me, I admit that I found in it no smallest grain of the
true Attic salt. The "children begotten through the ear"
seemed to me in the most detestable taste; the "cream
tart" made me positively sick at my stomach; and at
"the husband's stew" I almost vomited!

ÉLISE. Bless me, how neatly you put it! I would have said that the play was a good one; but your eloquence is so persuasive, you phrase things in such an agreeable way, that I have to accept your judgment, in spite of myself.

URANIE. For my part, I'm not so ready to yield; and, to give my honest opinion, I think this play is one of the most amusing the author has done.

CLIMÈNE. Really, such talk makes me sorry for you! I cannot endure such obscurity of discernment in you. Can a virtuous person find any charm in a play which forever keeps modesty in a state of alarm, and constantly befouls the imagination?

ÉLISE. Oh, I like the way you put things! How sharp you are in criticism, madame! How I pity poor Molière to have you for an enemy!

CLIMÈNE. (*to* URANIE) Believe me, my dear, you must positively revise your judgment. For the sake of your reputation, don't go telling people that you liked the play.

URANIE. I don't really know what you found in it that wounds modesty.

CLIMÈNE. Alas, everything! I maintain that a decent woman couldn't see it without confusion, so many were the filthy, dirty things I noticed.

URANIE. You must have special gifts for discovering obscenities, for I didn't observe any myself.

CLIMÈNE. You just won't admit noticing them, assuredly; for all the obscenities are there, please God, and perfectly bare-faced. There isn't the slightest veil to disguise them, and the boldest eyes are appalled by their nudity.

ÉLISE. (*admiringly*) Ah!

CLIMÈNE. (*simpering*) He, he, he!

URANIE. But anyway, please point out one of those obscenities.

CLIMÈNE. Oh, dear! Is it necessary to point them out?

URANIE. Yes. I'm just asking for one passage which shocked you so much.

CLIMÈNE. Do I need any other than the scene with that Agnes, when she says what the young man has taken?

URANIE. Well, what's dirty about that?

CLIMÈNE. Ah!

URANIE. But, please—

CLIMÈNE. Oh, fie!

URANIE. Still, what—

CLIMÈNE. I have nothing to say.

URANIE. As for me, I see nothing wrong in it.

CLIMÈNE. All the worse for you.

URANIE. All the better for me, I should say. I look at the side of things that is shown to me; I don't turn them over to look for what one isn't supposed to see. (pp. 100-03)

CLIMÈNE. Well, the fact is, when you see that play you have to be blind, and pretend not to see what it means.

URANIE. You mustn't try to see meanings which aren't there.

CLIMÈNE. Oh, I insist the smut is there; you can't dodge it.

URANIE. And I just don't agree.

CLIMÈNE. What! Decency is not clearly offended by what Agnes says in the part we were speaking of?

URANIE. No, really. She doesn't say a word which isn't perfectly decent; and if you want to imagine that something else is understood, you are the one who is indecent, not she, because she is just speaking of a ribbon which has been taken from her.

CLIMÈNE. Oh, ribbon, ribbon all you like; but that "my—" where she stops isn't put in for nothing. That "my—" gives you some strange thoughts. That "my—" is furiously scandalizing. No matter what you say, you can't defend the impudence of that "my—."

ÉLISE. It's true, cousin Uranie; I am on madame's side against that "my—." That "my—" is impudent to the highest degree. You're quite wrong to defend that "my—."

CLIMÈNE. It has a most intolerable lubricity.

ÉLISE. What was that word, madame?

CLIMÈNE. Lubricity, madame.

ÉLISE. Oh, bless me, lubricity! I don't exactly know what it means, but I think it is perfectly lovely. (pp. 103-04)

(GALOPIN *appears at the door, with the* MARQUIS *crowding him.*)

GALOPIN. Stop, sir, please!

MARQUIS. You don't know me, evidently.

GALOPIN. Oh, yes, I know you; but you can't come in!

MARQUIS. What a lot of noise, little lackey!

GALOPIN. It isn't proper to try to come in in spite of people.

MARQUIS. I want to see your mistress.

GALOPIN. She's not at home, I tell you.

MARQUIS. There she is in the room!

GALOPIN. That's true, there she is; but she's not at home.

URANIE. What's all this?

MARQUIS. It's your lackey, madame, who is playing the fool.

GALOPIN. I tell him you're not at home, madame, and he keeps on trying to come in.

URANIE. And why do you tell the gentleman I'm not at home?

GALOPIN. You scolded me the other day for telling him you were at home. (pp. 105-06)

MARQUIS. Your little lackey, madame, is scornful of my person.

ÉLISE. He's very wrong, surely.

MARQUIS. Perhaps I am paying for my ill demeanor, which is getting de meaner and de meaner! Ha, ha, ha, ha!

ÉLISE. With time, he will learn to recognize the right people.

MARQUIS. What were you discussing, ladies, when I interrupted you?

URANIE. The new play, *The School for Wives.*

MARQUIS. I've just left the theatre!

CLIMÈNE. Well, monsieur, please tell us how you found it.

MARQUIS. Absolutely intolerable.

CLIMÈNE. Oh, I'm delighted to hear it!

MARQUIS. It's the most wretched thing ever seen. Why, what the devil! I could hardly get a seat. I was nearly smothered at the entrance, and I never had my feet so stepped on. Look at the state of my knee ruffles and ribbons!

ÉLISE. Clearly, *The School for Wives* is quite impossible. You are quite right in condemning it.

MARQUIS. I don't think there's ever been such a bad play.

(*Enter* DORANTE.)

URANIE. Oh, here is Dorante! We were waiting for him.

DORANTE. Don't stir, please; don't interrupt your conversation. You're discussing a subject which has been the principal theme in all the houses in Paris for the last four days; and nothing is more amusing than the variety of opinions expressed. For in short I have heard some people condemn the play for the same things that others esteem the most.

URANIE. Monsieur le Marquis has just been speaking very harshly of it.

MARQUIS. That's true. I find it detestable; *morbleu*, detestable as detestable can be; what you might call detestable.

DORANTE. And for my part, my dear Marquis, I find the judgment detestable.

MARQUIS. What, Chevalier, you wouldn't propose to defend that play?

DORANTE. Yes, I propose to defend it.

MARQUIS. *Parbleu!* I guarantee it's detestable.

DORANTE. The guarantee is not absolutely iron-clad. Tell me, please, Marquis, why the play is—what you say?

MARQUIS. Why it's detestable?

DORANTE. Yes.

MARQUIS. It's detestable, because it's detestable.

DORANTE. After that, there's no more to be said; the case is settled. But still, inform us; tell us the faults of the play.

MARQUIS. How do I know? I didn't even take the trouble to listen. But anyway, damme sir, I know I've never seen anything so bad. And Dorilas, who was next me, agreed with me.

DORANTE. There's an authority; you are well seconded.

MARQUIS. All you needed was to listen to the continual roars of laughter from the pit. I don't need any other proof that the play is worthless.

DORANTE. So, Marquis, you are one of the gentlemen of fashion who won't admit that the pit has any common sense, and who would be sorry to join in its laughter, even at the best joke on earth? (pp. 106-07)

MARQUIS. So, Chevalier, now you're the defender of the pit! *Parbleu*, I'm delighted, and I shan't fail to inform it that you're one of its friends! Ha, ha, ha, ha, ha, ha!

DORANTE. Laugh all you like. I'm in favor of good sense, and I can't bear the cranks and crotchets of all our Marquises de Mascarille. It makes me furious to see those people who deliberately make themselves ridiculous in spite of their rank; who boldly decide everything and talk about everything, without knowledge; who cry out in delight at the bad parts of a play, without stirring at the good parts; who, similarly, when they see a painting or hear a concert, blame and praise everything wrongly; who pick up somewhere the technical terms of the art they're criticizing, and always mispronounce and misuse them. Eh, *morbleu!* My good sirs, when God hasn't given you knowledge about something, keep quiet; don't make your hearers laugh; and reflect that if you don't say a word, maybe people will think you're profound. (pp. 108-09)

URANIE. Ah, here is the celebrated author, Monsieur Lysidas! Just at the right moment! (*Enter* LYSIDAS) Monsieur Lysidas, take a chair, and sit down there.

LYSIDAS. Madame, I've come a little late; but I had to read my play at the home of Madame la Marquise—you know, I told you about her. And the applause was such that I was kept an hour longer than I expected.

ÉLISE. Applause has a magical power to detain an author. (p. 110)

[URANIE. Let's] learn the opinion of Monsieur Lysidas.

LYSIDAS. On what subject, madame?

URANIE. On *The School for Wives*.

LYSIDAS. Ha, ha!

DORANTE. What do you think of it?

LYSIDAS. I have nothing to say. You know that among us authors, we must speak of one another's works with great circumspection.

DORANTE. Yes, but just among us here, what do you think of the play?

LYSIDAS. I, sir?

URANIE. Yes, give us your honest opinion.

LYSIDAS. I think it's very fine.

DORANTE. Positively?

LYSIDAS. Positively. Why not? Isn't it in fact very fine indeed?

DORANTE. Umm. You're a sly devil, Monsieur Lysidas. You don't say what you think.

LYSIDAS. I beg your pardon!

DORANTE. Good Lord, I know you! Don't pretend to me!

LYSIDAS. I, sir?

DORANTE. I can see clearly that your praise of the play is only out of courtesy; at the bottom of your heart, you agree with many people who think it's very bad.

LYSIDAS. He, he, he!

DORANTE. Come, admit that the play is really terrible.

LYSIDAS. It is true that it is not much approved by the connoisseurs.

MARQUIS. 'Pon my soul, Chevalier, you're caught! You're paid off for your mockeries! Ha, ha, ha, ha!

DORANTE. Go right ahead, my dear Marquis.

MARQUIS. You see we have the scholars on our side.

DORANTE. It is true, Monsieur Lysidas' judgment carries weight. But Monsieur Lysidas will permit me not to surrender, even for that; and since I have been so bold as to defend myself against the opinions of Madame Élise, he cannot take it ill if I oppose his views. (pp. 111-12)

LYSIDAS. Molière is very fortunate, monsieur, to have so warm a defender. But to come to the point, the question is whether or not the play is a good one; and I am ready to indicate a hundred evident faults in it.

URANIE. It's a funny thing about you playwrights, that you always condemn the big successes, and you say nothing but good about the plays no one goes to. You show an invincible hatred for the first lot, and a hardly conceivable affection for the second.

DORANTE. It is very noble to take the part of the afflicted.

URANIE. Please, Monsieur Lysidas, point out these faults, which I didn't notice.

LYSIDAS. Those who know their Aristotle and their Horace immediately recognize that this play sins against all the rules of the art.

URANIE. I must admit that I am not familiar with those gentlemen, and I don't know the rules of the art.

DORANTE. You make me laugh with your rules, which you are always blasting in our ears, to confound the ignorant. To hear you talk, one would think that these rules of art are the greatest mysteries in the world; and yet they are only a few obvious observations that common sense has made, regarding what can diminish one's pleasure in such productions. And the same common sense which made these observations long ago readily makes them over again every day, without any help from Horace and Aristotle. I should like to know if the great rule of all rules is not merely to give pleasure, and if a play which has attained this end has not taken the right course. Do you think that the entire public is mistaken about these matters, and that every man is not a judge of his own pleasure?

URANIE. I have noticed one thing about those gentlemen; those who talk the most about the rules and know them better than anybody write plays that no one admires.

DORANTE. That shows, madame, how little one should be concerned about their endless involved disputes. For in short, if people don't like the plays which observe the rules and if they do like the plays which don't observe the rules, then necessarily there must be something wrong with the rules. So let's not worry about those quibbling regulations which they want to impose on public taste, and when we see a play let's consult only the effect it makes on us. Let us confidently enjoy those works which actually grip us and touch our hearts, and let's not seek out arguments to prevent our finding pleasure in them.

URANIE. As for me, when I see a play, I only want to know if I am touched and moved. And when I have been really amused, I don't begin wondering if I was wrong, and if Aristotle's rules forbade me to laugh.

DORANTE. That's like a man who might find a sauce delicious, and who would then try to find out if it was good by looking it up in *Le Cuisinier français.*

URANIE. That's true; and I wonder at some people's hairsplitting about things which we ought to feel for ourselves.

DORANTE. You are right, madame, to find those mysterious distinctions peculiar. For if they are justified, we are forced not to believe ourselves; our own senses must be slaves of authority. And even to our food and drink, we can no longer dare to call anything good without the approval of the experts.

LYSIDAS. In short, sir, your only argument is that *The School for Wives* is a success; you don't care at all whether it follows the rules, provided—

DORANTE. Wait a minute, Monsieur Lysidas; I don't grant you that. I do say that the great art is to please, and that since this play has pleased those for whom it was written, I think that's sufficient, and there's not much reason to bother about the rest. But even so, I maintain that it does not offend against any of the rules you're talking of. I have read about them, please God, as well as the next man; and I could readily demonstrate that perhaps we have no play in the theatre more regular than that one is.

ÉLISE. Courage, Monsieur Lysidas! If you draw back, we are lost!

LYSIDAS. What, sir! The protasis, the epitasis, and the peripetia—

DORANTE. Oh, Monsieur Lysidas, don't smite us with your big words! Please don't be quite so scholarly. Humanize your speech, and speak so as to be understood. Do you think that a Greek name gives more weight to your argument? And don't you think it would be just as effective to say the exposition as the protasis, the plot development as the epitasis, and the resolution as the peripetia?

LYSIDAS. They are artistic terms which it is quite permissible to use. But since the words offend your ear, I shall explain myself otherwise, and I shall ask you to reply categorically to three or four remarks I shall make. Can one endure a play which sins against the very definition of a play? For in short the word "drama" comes from a Greek word meaning "to act," indicating that the essential of this sort of poetic composition lies in action. And in this particular play there is no action; everything consists in the recitals which either Agnes or Horace makes.

MARQUIS. Aha, Chevalier!

CLIMÈNE. That is very keenly observed; he has put his finger on the weak spot.

LYSIDAS. Is there anything so unhumorous, or, to say it outright, anything more vulgar, than some of the phrases at which everyone laughs; especially the "children through the ear"?

CLIMÈNE. Very good.

ÉLISE. Ah!

LYSIDAS. The scene where the two servants in the house delay in opening the door, isn't it tiresomely long, and entirely out of place?

MARQUIS. That's true.

CLIMÈNE. Certainly.

ÉLISE. He's right.

LYSIDAS. Doesn't Arnolphe give his money too readily to Horace? And since he is the ridiculous character, should he be given the action of a worthy man?

MARQUIS. Good. Excellent point.

CLIMÈNE. Admirable!

ÉLISE. Marvelous!

LYSIDAS. The sermon to Agnes and the maxims she reads, aren't they grotesque, and thus shocking to the respect we owe to the holy mysteries?

MARQUIS. Well said!

CLIMÈNE. That's the way to talk!

ÉLISE. Nothing could be better!

LYSIDAS. And that Monsieur Delafield, who is presented to us as an intelligent man, and who seems so serious in many places, doesn't he descend to an excessively low level of comedy in the fifth act, when he explains to Agnes the violence of his love, with that extravagant rolling of the eyes, those absurd sighs, and those idiotic tears which make everyone laugh?

MARQUIS. Egad! It's marvelous!

CLIMÈNE. A miracle!

ÉLISE. *Vive* Monsieur Lysidas!

LYSIDAS. I leave out a thousand other things for fear of boring you.

MARQUIS. *Parbleu,* Chevalier, now you're in a nice fix!

DORANTE. Well, let's see.

MARQUIS. You've found your match, faith!

DORANTE. Perhaps.

MARQUIS. Answer, answer, answer, answer!

DORANTE. Gladly. He—

MARQUIS. Go on and answer, I beg you.

DORANTE. Then let me alone. If—

MARQUIS. By Jove, I defy you to answer!

DORANTE. Of course, if you talk all the time.

CLIMÈNE. Please, let's hear his arguments.

DORANTE. Firstly, it is hardly true to say that the whole play consists of recitals. Many actions do take place on the stage, and the recitals themselves are actions, in accordance with the nature of the subject; all the more since these recitals are made innocently to the person concerned, who thus falls constantly into a confusion of mind which amuses the spectators, and who, at each new revelation, takes all the measures he can to ward off the calamity he fears.

URANIE. To me, the beautiful thing about *The School for Wives* is just those perpetual confidences of Horace. And what seems to me very funny is that an intelligent man, who is warned of everything by the simple girl he loves and by an infatuated rival, can't for all that avoid what happens to him.

MARQUIS. Mere bagatelle, mere bagatelle.

CLIMÈNE. Weak reply.

ÉLISE. Poor argument.

DORANTE. As for the "children through the ear," that is only funny as echoed by Arnolphe; and the author did not put that in as a joke in itself, but only as a means of characterizing the man. The phrase points up his mental twist, since he reports a silly little triviality of Agnes' as the funniest thing in the world, which gives him almost inconceivable joy.

MARQUIS. Not much of an answer.

CLIMÈNE. Hardly satisfactory.

ÉLISE. Nothing at all.

DORANTE. As for the money he gives so freely, not to mention that the letter from his best friend is a sufficient guarantee, there's nothing incompatible in a man's being ridiculous in certain things and a worthy man in others. And as for the scene with Alain and Georgette in the house, which some have found too long and too forced, there is certainly good reason for it. Just as Arnolphe has been caught, during his absence, by the naïveté of his beloved, when he returns he is kept at his own door for a long time by the simplicity of his servants, so that he may be punished constantly by the very precautions which he thought would save him.

MARQUIS. As reasons, they don't amount to much.

CLIMÈNE. Just whitewash.

ÉLISE. Really pitiful.

DORANTE. And as for the moral admonitions which you call a sermon, it is certain that really religious people who heard them didn't find that they profaned our holy mysteries. And clearly the words "hell" and "boiling caldrons" are well justified by Arnolphe's monomania and by the simplicity of the girl he's talking to. And as for the amorous transport of the fifth act, which is accused of being too excessive and too farcical, I should like to know if that isn't a proper satire of lovers, and if the most serious and sober gentlemen, on such occasions, don't do things—

MARQUIS. 'Pon my word, Chevalier, you would do better to say nothing.

DORANTE. Very well. But still, if we should look at our own selves, when we are very much in love—

MARQUIS. I won't even listen to you.

DORANTE. Please do listen to me. In moments of violent passion—

MARQUIS. (*sings*) La, la, la, la, lare; la, la la, la, la la.

DORANTE. What—

MARQUIS. La, la, la, la, lare; la, la la, la, la, la.

DORANTE. I don't know if—

MARQUIS. La, la, la, la, lare; la, la, la, la, la, la.

DORANTE. It seems to me that—

MARQUIS. La, la, la, la, lare; la, la, la, la, la, la.

URANIE. Our dispute is really funny. I think someone could make a little play of it. That wouldn't be bad as an afterpiece to **The School for Wives**.

(pp. 117-23)

Molière, "The Critique of The School for Wives," in his Eight Plays by Molière, translated by Morris Bishop, The Modern Library, 1957, pp. 96-123.

PIERRE ROULLÉ (essay date 1664)

[*Roullé, a French clergyman and essayist, was one of Molière's most vehement detractors in the controversy surrounding Tartuffe. In the following excerpt from his Le roi glorieux du monde (1664), he roundly condemns both play and author.*]

A man, or rather a demon in flesh and habited as a man, the most notably impious creature and libertine who ever lived throughout the centuries, has had the impiety and abomination to bring forth from his devilish mind a play [**Tartuffe**] ready to be rendered public, and has had this play performed on the stage, to the derision of the whole church.... He deserves for this sacrilegious and impious act the severest exemplary and public punishment; he should be burned at the stake as a foretaste of the fires of hell in expiation of a crime which is a treason against heaven and calculated to ruin the Catholic religion by censuring and counterfeiting its most religious and holy practice, which is the conduct and direction of souls and families by means of wise guides and pious conductors. His Majesty, having severely reproached him, though moved by a strong indignation, has, in the exercise of his ordinary clemency, in which he imitates the essential gentleness of God ... pardoned the devilish hardihood of this creature in order to give him time to devote the rest of his life to a public and solemn penitence; but, to keep this licentious and wicked composition from public sight and view, His Majesty has ordered the author, on pain of death, to suppress, tear up, stifle and burn all that he has set down, and to do nothing in the future so infamous and so unworthy, or to produce anything to the light of day so

insulting to God and so outrageous to the church, religion, and the holy sacraments.

Pierre Roullé, in an extract from "Le Roi Glorieux du Monde," in Molière by John Palmer, 1930. Reprint by Benjamin Blom, Inc., 1970. p. 335.

NICOLAS BOILEAU-DESPRÉAUX (poem date 1664)

[*Boileau-Despréaux was a seventeenth-century French poet and critic known for the wit and brilliance of his satires and epistles and the humor of his mock-heroic epic, Le lutrin (1683). An ardent advocate of neoclassical literary theory, which informs his influential L'art poétique (1674; The Art of Poetry, 1683), and a harsh detractor of mediocre French writers, Boileau acquired a reputation as "the legislator of Parnassus," or codifier of French neoclassical critical doctrines. Molière's friend, Boileau frequently wrote to praise the dramatist's work or to defend it from detractors; on other occasions, however, his judgments were less favorable. For other samples of Boileau's views of Molière, see the excerpts by Boileau (1683) and Pierre Bayle (1702). In the following excerpt from "Satire II: To M. de Molière," originally published in 1664, he satirically begs Molière to teach him the art of rhyming.*]

Unhappy those who wou'd to Sense confine
Their Writings, and with Genius Method join;
Fools write with Ease, are ne'er for Rhimes perplext,
Nor ever in the Choice of Phrases vext.
Such, ever fond of what they last brought forth,
Admire themselves, and wonder at their Worth;
While Wits sublime their utmost Fancy stretch,
To gain the Summit they but seldom reach;
Disgusted still, themselves, at what they write,
With Pain they read, tho' others with Delight.
They scarce, what all the World applaud, will own,
And wish for their Repose it was undone.

You then, who see the Ills my Mose endures,
Shew me a Way to Rhyme, a Way like yours.
But least I shou'd in vain your Care implore,
Teach me then, dear *Moliere*, to Rhyme no more.

(p. 154)

Nicolas Boileau-Despréaux, "Satire II: To M. de Moliere," in his The Works of Monsieur Boileau Made English, Vol. I, E. Sanger & E. Curll, 1712, pp. 150-60.

ARMAND DE BOURBON, PRINCE DE CONTI (essay date 1666?)

[*Conti was a prominent French nobleman and general. An avid theatergoer, he was one of Molière's earliest and most enthusiastic patrons; while in the provinces, the prince gave Molière's troupe a pension and the honored title of comédiens du Prince de Conti. In 1656, however, after a near-fatal illness, Conti experienced a religious conversion, retiring from public life to write theological treatises and becoming an adamant opponent of the theater. In one of several tracts denouncing public amusement, Les sentiments des peres de l'eglises sur la comedie et les spectacles (1666?; The Sentiments of the Fathers Relating to Plays and Public Shews, 1711), he declared: "If Tragedies and Comedies are Representations of Crimes, and of irregular Passions, they are Bloody, Lascivious and Impious; for the Representation of an Enormous Crime, or of a Shameful thing, is not better than what it represents," and: "Tis not strange then that such People should be possess'd by the Devil.... Indeed how*] *many Examples have we of others, who communicating with the Devil by going to Plays, have fallen from GOD? for no Man can serve two Masters."* In the following excerpt from The Sentiments, *Conti directly attacks Molière and his 1665 production of* Don Juan.]

Can there be more open teaching of atheism than in the **Festin de Pierre**, where, after putting the most horrible impieties into the mouth of a witty atheist, the author commits the defence of God's cause to a lackey whom he makes utter, on its behalf, every kind of impertinence? And finally he seeks to justify his comedy, so crammed with blasphemy, under cover of a squib which he offers as the ridiculous implement of Divine vengeance.

> *Armand de Bourbon, Prince de Conti, in an extract in* The Latin Genius *by Anatole France, translated by Wilfrid S. Jackson, 1924. Reprint by Gabriel Wells, 1924, p. 122.*

NICOLAS BOILEAU-DESPRÉAUX (poem date 1683)

[*In the following excerpt from a poem written in 1683, Boileau acknowledges Molière's genius while negatively criticizing those who failed to appreciate Molière during his lifetime.*]

Death only can consummate Worth defend,
From Wrong and Envy, which with Life will end.
A Poet dead; good Sense his Writings weighs,
And sets the lawful Price upon his Plays.
E're MOLIERE lay in charitable Dust,
How few were to his Muse and Merit just?
Coxcombs and Fools wou'd scarce for Sense allow,
Those Strokes that are so much commended now.
As soon as a new Piece of his was play'd,
New Fools were anger'd, and new Criticks made.
  Ign'rance and Error, like false *Marquee*'s Drest,
Defam'd his Wit and his best Plays deprest.
Most Fault was found, where most his Genius shone,
So wise, so just, was our indulgent Town.
This Lord, wou'd have the Scene be more exact,
And that, is tir'd before the Second Act.
The Reason is, she fears the Picture's known,
And takes Offence, because so like his own.
Another vindicates the *Bigot*'s Cause,
And fain against the Bard wou'd arm the Laws.
The Court he Sacrifices to the Pit,
The Marquis raves, and damns his fancy Wit
But when the Sisters cut the fatal Thread,
And rank'd him with the Number of the Dead,
Than strait his Conduct and his Wit were best,
And now they firmly stand the Crittick's Test.
With him was *Comedy*, they cry'd, interr'd,
And scarce the Ancients are to him preferr'd,
His Death was to the Buskin such a blow,
'T has ne're recovered, since it fell so low.

(pp. 76-7)

> *Nicolas Boileau-Despréaux, "Epistle VII to Monsieur Racine," in his* The Works of Monsieur Boirleau-Despréaux, Vol. II, *E. Sanger & E. Curll, 1711, pp. 75-82.*

ADRIEN BAILLET (essay date 1686)

[*A French devotional writer, compiler, biographer, and critic, Baillet is remembered for his biography of René Descartes (1691) and scholarly treatments of the works of a variety of authors in his* Jugemens des sçavans sur les

principaux ouvrages des auteurs (1685-86). In the following excerpt from John Ozell's 1714 partial translation of Jugemens, *Baillet begrudgingly acknowledges the positive criticism of Molière's works by other scholars while providing his own review. René Rapin, a seventeenth-century French Jesuit to whom Baillet frequently refers, was a noted Latin poet and humanist. Baillet voices his negative opinion of Molière more forcefully in another section of* Jugemens (*see second excerpt by Baillet dated 1686*).]

It must be confess'd no Body ever receiv'd of Nature more Talents than Monsieur *de Moliere* did, to railly all Mankind, to find out the Ridiculous of the most serious Things, and to expose it with Finenes and Simplicicy to the Eyes of the Publick; in this consists the Preheminence that is allowed him over all the Modern Comick Writers, over those of ancient *Rome*, and over those of *Greece* it self.

In order to outdo those others, he thought himself obliged to take a Path different from theirs; he particularly bent himself to study the Genius of the Grandees, and what we call the *Beau Monde*; whereas the others often confin'd themselves to the Knowledge of the Populace. The ancient Poets, says Father [René] *Rapin* [in his *Réflexions sur la poétique d'Aristotle et sur les ouvrages des poètes anciens et modernes* (1674)], had only Valets for their Buffoons; but *Moliere*'s Buffoons are Marquisses and Persons of Quality. Others in their Plays have been content with mimicking the common ... Life, but *Moliere* has mimick'd all *Paris* and the Court. That same Father pretends that *Moliere* is the only Man amongst us that ever discover'd those Strokes of Nature which distinguish and make him known. He adds, that the Beauties of his Portraits are so natural, that they are intelligible to the grossest Apprehensions; and that his Talent of raillying was backt by that of Mimicking. (p. 241)

[As] capable as *Moliere* was, 'tis said he did not thoroughly understand the Rules, and that only the People's Love cou'd have absolved him from an infinite Number of Faults which he committed; it might likewise be said that he did not much mind *Aristotle* and other Masters, provided he hit the Taste of his Spectators, whom he acknowledg'd for his sole Judges.

Father *Rapin* says that the Contrivance of his Comedies is always defective in something, and that his Unravelings are not successful.

It must be own'd he spoke very good *French*, translated tolerably well from *Italian*, was no ill Copier of his Authors; but it may not be upon good Grounds to say he had not the Gift of Invention, nor a Genius for fine Poetry, tho' even his Friends agree that in all his Pieces, the Comedian had a greater share than the Poet, and that their chief Beauty lay in the Action.

(p. 245)

> *Adrien Baillet, in an extract from "Judgments of the Learned," in* The Works of Mr. de Moliere, Vol. V, *translated by John Ozell, 1714. Reprint by Benjamin Blom, Inc., 1967, pp. 241-45.*

ADRIEN BAILLET (essay date 1686)

[*In the following excerpt from Ferdinand Brunetière's 1898 partial translation of* Jugemens, *Baillet cites Molière as one of the chief enemies of organized religion. For a more schol-arly treatment by Baillet, see the preceding excerpt dated 1686.*]

[M. Molière] is one of the most dangerous enemies that the age or the world has raised up against the church, and he is the more formidable as he still makes after his death the same havoc in the heart of his readers as he made in his lifetime in that of his spectators.... Gallantry is not the only science to be learned in the school of Molière, but also the most ordinary maxims of licentiousness against the true sentiments of religion, whatever the enemies of bigotry may say, and we can assert that his *Tartufe* is one of the least dangerous to lead us to *irreligion*..., the seeds of which are scattered in so cunning and hidden a way in most of his other pieces, that we may affirm that it is infi-nitely more difficult to resist its influence there than where he openly and indiscriminately ridicules the bigoted and the devout. (pp. 120-21)

> *Adrien Baillet, in an extract from "Jugements des Savants," in* Brunetière's Essays in French Litera-ture, *translated by D. Nichol Smith, T. Fisher Un-win, 1898, pp. 120-21.*

DOMINIQUE BOUHOURS   (poem date 1686?)

[*A seventeenth-century French Jesuit, Bouhours was a gram-marian and man of letters. In the following memorial poem, probably first published in 1686 in Adrien Baillet's* Juge-mens des sçavans sur les principaux ouvrages des auteurs, *he deems Molière a great moral reformer and reproves the French for failing to appreciate him.*]

> Ornament of the Stage, Incomparable Actor,
> Charming Poet, Illustrious Author,
> 'Twas you whose Wit
> Has cured the Extravagance of the Marquisses.
> 'Twas you whose Mummery
> Has repress'd the Pride of the arrogant Citizens.
>
> Thy Muse in ridiculing the Hypocrite
> Has reclaim'd the false Devotees:
> The Affected Lady by thy Raillery
> Sees her false Merit:
> The Enemy to Mankind,
> And the Countryman that admires every thing,
> Have not read your Works in vain;
> Both are instructed by what they thought wou'd only
>   divert'em.
>
> In short, you reform both Town and Court;
> But what was your Reward?
> The *French* will in time be ashamed
> Of their Ingratitude.
> They wanted a Comedian
> To polish them;
> But *Moliere*, your Glory wou'd be compleat,
> If amongst their other Faults which you so well describe,
> You had reproved them for their Ingratitude.

> *Dominique Bouhours, in a poem in* The Works of Mr. de Moliere, Vol. V, *translated by John Ozell, 1714. Reprint by Benjamin Blom, Inc., 1967, p. 242.*

PIERRE BAYLE   (essay date 1702)

[*Bayle was a French philosopher and critic whose liberal Protestantism in an age of religious dissent and persecution*

compelled him to spend much of his life in exile. Although the author of numerous works, it is upon his Dictionnaire historique et critique (1697; rev. ed., 1702; The Dictionary Historical and Critical of Mr. Peter Bayle, 1710) *that his reputation rests. Composed of brief, pithy biographical arti-cles that frequently excluded major figures to address ob-scure names, the* Dictionary *contains Bayle's unabashed opinions and reflects his fundamental skepticism on all is-sues. The* Dictionary *was influential, particularly in France, in shaping subsequent encyclopedic studies. The French crit-ic Ferdinand Brunetière has avowed that to "forget Bayle or to suppress him is to mutilate and falsify the whole history of ideas in the eighteenth century." In the following excerpt from the translation of the second edition of his* Dictionary, *Bayle determines Molière's rank among the ancients, imag-ining the dramatist's response to Nicolas Boileau-Des-préaux's negative criticism of his work in* L'art poétique (1674; The Art of Poetry, 1683).]

[*Many are of opinion that [Molière's] plays exceed or equal the noblest performances of that kind in ancient Greece and Rome.*] Mr. [Charles] Perrault displeased many people by contradicting those who say, that no modern author can be compared with Homer and Virgil, Demosthenes and Cicero, Aristophanes and Terence, Sophocles and Euripi-des.... I think I may say that among the productions of the pen, there are few things, wherein so many people have acknowledged the superiority of our age, as in the comical pieces. Perhaps the reason of it is, that the beau-ties and niceties of Aristophanes are not known to all those who are sensible of Moliere's wit and charms; for it ought to be granted, that in order to pass a right judgment upon the comic Poets of Greece, it were necessary to be throughly acquainted with the faults of the Athenians. There is a ridicule common to all times and people, and a ridicule peculiar to certain ages and nations. Some scenes of Aristophanes, which appear dull to us, did, per-haps, wonderfully please the Athenians, because they knew the fault he ridiculed. Perhaps, it was a fault alto-gether unknown to us, a ridicule consisting in some partic-ular facts, and in a transient and common taste of that time, of which we can have no notion, though we are able to read the originals.... Moliere is not liable to this incon-veniency, we know what he aims at, and easily discover whether he describes well the ridicule of the age we live in; when he succeeds in any thing, it cannot escape us. Nay, he seems to be more copious than Aristophanes and Ter-ence, as to those thoughts and nice railleries, of which all ages and polite nations are sensible. This is a very consid-erable prerogative; for it cannot be said, that our age has not a true relish of the fine passages of the Latin Poets. If you shew some thoughts of Horace, Ovid, Juvenal, &c. to ingenious ladies in old French, if you translate them faith-fully, though never so coarsely, they will tell you that those thoughts are fine, delicate, and nice. There are some beau-ties of wit in fashion at all times: one would think that Moliere is more copious in that respect than the ancient comic Poets. He has some beauties that would vanish away in a translation, or in a country of a different taste from that of France; but he has many others that would be preserved in all sorts of translations, and approved what-ever the taste of the readers might be, provided they un-derstood the essence of a good thought. (pp. 741-42)

· · · · ·

[*Mr Boileau ... found fault with him for humouring too much those that sat in the pit; which is a reasonable cen-*

sure in some respects, but unjust in the main.] Moliere was dead when Mr Boileau praised him in one of his Epistles [see excerpt dated 1683], as much, or more, than in the satire he had inscribed to him [see excerpt dated 1664]. It is therefore a great piece of injustice to say, that he praised him out of policy, and for fear of being bantered by him upon the stage, if he should say nothing to his advantage, or if he should venture to criticize him. But, will some say, he criticized him when he had nothing to fear, and therefore the suspicion entertained of him seems to be well grounded. I am not of that opinion; I believe that if he had made his *Art Poëtique* in Moliere's life-time, he would have inserted in it the censure contained in the following verses. It was, in a manner, essential to his subject; there is in it a very judicious observation, which should be an inviolable rule, if comedies were only made to be printed; but because they are chiefly designed to appear on the stage in the presence of all sorts of people, it is not just to require they should be adapted to Mr Boileau's taste. These are his words.

Etudiez la Cour, & connoissez la ville,
L'une & l'autre est toûjours en modeles fertile.
C'est par là que Moliere illustrant ses écrits
Peut-être de son Art eût remporté le prix;
Si moins ami du peuple en ses doctes peintures,
Il n'eût point fait souvent grimacer ses figures,
Quitté pour le bouffon, l'agreable & le fin.
Et sans honte à Terence allié Tabarin.
Dans ce sac ridicule où Scapin [in *The Cheats of Scapin*]
  s'envelope,
Je ne reconnois plus l'Auteur du *Misanthrope.*

Study the court, and know the city well:
So shall your various characters excel.
It was by this that Moliere in his plays
Perhaps, as victor, might have claim'd the bays;
If he, to please the rabble of the town,
Had not sometimes affected the buffoon;
Preferr'd low farce and drollery to wit,
And more like Tabarin than Terence writ.
In that same bag which Scapin doth enclose,
The author of the *Misanthrope* I lose.

He blames Moliere for endeavouring to please, not only men of a nice judgment, but also the common people. Moliere had some reasons for it, and might have said what Arlequin answered in a like case. 'Those jests, said I to him, (to Arlequin) are pleasant enough in your plays; it is pity they are not equally good. I own it, replied he, but they please several young people, who come to our playhouse only to laugh, and who laugh at any thing, and very often without knowing why. Our plays are frequently acted before such people, and if our jests were not suited to their capacity, our house would be very often empty. I am sorry, said I to him, that you have almost left your old pieces off; they were well approved by men of sense, they contained many things of good use in morality, and I dare say, that your stage was a place where vice was so effectually ridiculed, that every body found himself inclined to love virtue meerly out of reason. Should we act none but our old pieces, replied he, our play-house would be little resorted to, and I will tell you what Cinthio formerly told St Evremond, that good actors would be starved notwithstanding their excellent plays.' It ought to be observed, that players are at great charges, and that plays are no less designed for the diversion of the people, than for the diversion of the senate; and therefore they must be adapted to the taste of the public, in order to bring a numerous audience; for without that although they were a perfect compound of ingenious, nice, and exquisite, thoughts, the actors would be ruined by them, and they would be of no use to the people.

This is what may be said . . . against those who censure Moliere. . . . (p. 744)

Pierre Bayle, "Poquelin," in his The Dictionary Historical and Critical of Mr. Peter Bayle: M-R, *Vol. IV, edited by Des Maizeaux, second edition, J. J. and P. Knapton and others, 1737, pp. 740-45.*

JEAN LE GALLOIS DE GRIMAREST? (essay date 1705)

[*A French man of letters, Grimarest wrote the first biography (1705) of Molière, the factuality of which has frequently been questioned. In the following excerpt taken from John Ozell's 1714 edition of Molière's works and believed to have been originally published in Grimarest's biography, Molière is extolled as a master of prose comedy, though it is noted that "all his plays are not equally beautiful."*]

It may justly be said that *Moliere* was a happy and inimitable Genius, and that never any Man better follow'd the Precept which requires that Comedy shou'd instruct at the same time that it diverts. In rallying Men for their Faults, he taught them how to correct them; and perhaps the Follies he has condemn'd might have reign'd even till now, if the Portraits, which he drew after Nature, had not been so many Mirrors, in which those he ridiculed saw their own Imperfections. His Raillery was fine, and he turn'd it in so artful a Manner, that as Satyrical as 'twas, those who were the Subjects of it, were so far from taking Offence, that they themselves laugh'd at the Ridiculousness he had shewn in 'em. (pp. xvii-xviii)

The Inclination he had to Poetry made him apply himself to read the Poets with a Particular Application. He was a perfect Master of them, and particularly of *Terence.* He had chosen him as the most excellent Model he cou'd follow, and never did any Body imitate him so well as he did. Those who conceive the Beauty of his *Miser* and *Amphitryon,* affirm that he has outdone *Plautus* in both of 'em. (p. xviii)

All his Plays are not equally beautiful; but it may be said that in the worst of 'em there are Strokes which cou'd not proceed from any but a great Master; and that those which are look'd upon to be the best, as the *Misantrope,* the *Tartuffe,* the *Learned Ladies,* &c. are Master-pieces that cannot be sufficiently admired.

That which caused this Inequality in his Works, some whereof are not much regarded in Comparison of the others, is, that he was obliged to confine his Genius to certain Subjects, which were prescribed to him, and to work very hastily, either by the King's Command, or because of the Necessity of the Affairs of his Company; yet this did not lessen the extreme Application and the particular Study he bestow'd upon all the great Parts that he himself acted in his Plays. Never did Man enter so well as he into the natural Action of the Stage. He has exhausted all the Subjects that cou'd furnish him with any thing; and if the Criticks were not all satisfied with the Unravelling some of his Plays, so many Beauties prepossess'd the Minds of the Audience in his Favour, that such slight Faults were easily pass'd over. (p. xxv)

Jean Le Gallois de Gimarest? in a preface to the Works of MR. Moliere, Vol. I, translated by John Ozell, 1714. Reprint by Benjamin Blom, Inc., 1967, pp. xvii-xxix.

JOHN DENNIS   (letter date 1720)

[*An English dramatist, critic, and poet, Dennis was one of the leading literary theorists of Restoration London. His most important critical works are* The Advancement and Reformation of Modern Poetry *(1701) and* An Essay on the Genius and Writings of Shakespeare *(1712). In the following excerpt from a letter written in 1720 to Henry Cromwell, Dennis assesses the characters and dialogue of* Tartuffe, *according this play and* The Misanthrope *extremely high praise.*]

Moliere's Characters in his *Tartuffe* are Masterpieces, mark'd, distinguish'd, glowing, bold, touch'd with a fine yet a daring Hand; all of them stamp'd with a double Stamp, the one from Art and the other from Nature: No Phantoms but real Persons, such as Nature produces in all Ages, and Custom fashions in ours. His Dialogue too is lively, natural, graceful, easie, strong, adapted to the Occasion, adapted to the Characters. In short, 'tis by this Comedy and by the *Misanthrope* that *Moliere* perhaps has born away the Prize of Comedy from all Persons in all Ages, except *Ben. Jonson* alone. (p. 408)

John Dennis, in a letter to Henry Cromwell on June 14, 1720, in his The Critical Works of John Dennis: 1711-1729, Vol. II, *edited by Edward Niles Hooker, The Johns Hopkins Press, 1943, pp. 407-09.*

FRANÇOIS MARIE AROUET DE VOLTAIRE   (poem date 1733)

[*A French philosopher and man of letters, Voltaire was a major figure of the eighteenth- century European Enlightenment. As a man of diverse and intense interests, Voltaire wrote prolifically on many subjects and in a variety of genres, always asserting the absolute primacy of personal liberty. Voltaire's most valuable contribution to literature is usually considered his invention of the philosophical* conte, *or tale, in which the story is a vehicle for an ethical or philosophical message; the most famous of these* contes *is the highly regarded* Candide *(1759). The following excerpt is taken from Voltaire's 1733 poem* Le temple du goût, *which describes the poet's fanciful, satirical journey to the literary "temple of taste." Here, he imagines an encounter with Mol-ière, "the great painter" of human nature.*]

I saw the inimitable Molière, and I made bold to accost him in these terms:

> Terence the sage, and the polite,
> Could well translate, but could not write;
> His elegance is cold and faint,
> He could not Roman manners paint:
> You the great painter of our nation,
> Have drawn each character and station;
> Our cits with maggots in their brain,
> Our marquises as pert as vain,
> Our formal gentry of the law,
> All by your art their likeness saw;
> And you would have reformed each fault,
> If sense and virtue could be taught.

(pp. 67-8)

François Marie Arouet de Voltaire, "The Temple of Taste," in The Works of Voltaire: A Contemporary Version, *Vol. X, edited by Tobias Smollett, translated by William F. Fleming, revised edition, E. R. Du Mont, 1901, pp. 40-69.*

CHARLES DIBDIN   (essay date 1800)

[*Dibdin was an English songwriter, dramatist, autobiographer, novelist, and essayist. In the following excerpt from his multivolume history of the English drama, he compares Mol-ière to the ancients, discussing the author's innovations and limitations as a reformer.*]

The rank MOLIERE held in literature has been long estimated and decided. We have nothing to do but to compare his works with whatever we know of, perfect and admirable, in the ancients, and we shall find him in every point of view rising greatly superior to them all. He has all the pointed severity of ARISTOPHANES, without his wickedness and his malignity; he has to the beauty, the fidelity, the portraiture of MENANDER, added higher and more finished graces of his own; he has the nerve and strength of PLAUTUS without his grossness and his obscenity; and he has a thousand times more elegance from nature and genius, assisted by philosophic observation, than TERENCE.

Nature, and the absurdities of the age in which he lived, supplied him with an inexhaustible source of materials. Comedy took a new form in his hands, and became a scourge for the vices and follies of all ranks, to the truth of which all were implicitly obliged to subscribe; and there can be but little doubt, if he could have written independantly, and have been independantly attended, but he would have carried comedy, true comedy as correct as it can be defined, to a higher degree of perfection than any author has done either before or since.

MOLIERE, however, was a reformer; and reformers in any way dare not innovate all at once. Could he have done this, he would have written no dialogue in verse, he would have made his characters at once speak the language of nature. But there are higher crimes to accuse him of. Pure morality would probably have been laughed at by a people full of intrigue and given up to every licentiousness; on this account, and I most sincerely believe on no other, did MOLIERE introduce his naive and natural humour, his strong remarks, and his sterling truths, through mediums which neither his heart nor his understanding at all times approved.

To make children ridicule their parents, deride their observations, laugh at their age, and insult their infirmities, are circumstances true comedy should reject with contempt; to introduce adultery, and endeavour, by subtle devices and insinuating persuasion, to imprint on young minds a love of vice, is revolting to true comedy; to recommend knavery, by giving it a fashionable air, and permitting it at last to triumph over simplicity and honesty, has nothing to do with true comedy; "but," says a French author, "MOLIERE, though truly honourable, was an actor and a manager. It was therefore necessary he should think of the receipt of the house, and this receipt too often imposed silence on his veracity, and of course diminished his real glory. It was necessary to make the pit laugh. Oh that so great a genius should be sunk to so low a degree of humiliation."

If, however, vice, through MOLIÈRE, became at times winning and seducing, he did not fail at other times to expose it to contempt and ridicule; but, whenever he did so, it was sure to raise him up a host of enemies. This, in his dependent situation . . . , gave him throughout his life a thousand vexations, and induced him sometimes to conform to the age rather than revolt against it. In short, when he considered himself merely as a poet, he fell into the errors of poets; when as a philosopher, he shone with all the truth of a moralist, and the dignity of a man. (pp. 374-77)

> *Charles Dibdin, in his* A Complete History of the English Stage, *Vol. I, Charles Dibdin, 1800, 386 p.*

AUGUST WILHELM SCHLEGEL   (lecture date 1811)

[*Schlegel was a German critic, translator, and poet. With his younger brother, Friedrich, he founded the periodical* Das Athenäum (1798-1800), *which served as a manifesto for the German Romantic movement. He is perhaps best known for his translation of Shakespeare's works into German and for his* Über dramatische Kunst und Literatur (1809-11; Lectures on Dramatic Art and Literature, 1815). *In the following excerpt from one of his lectures, a notoriously unfavorable assessment of Molière, he examines and refutes the claims of French critics who consider Molière "the unrivalled Genius of Comedy."*]

Molière has produced works in so many departments, and of such different value, that we are hardly able to recognize the same author in all of them; and yet it is usual, when speaking of his peculiarities and merits, and the advance which he gave to his art, to throw the whole of his labours into one mass together. (p. 305)

Without travelling out of France, he had opportunities of becoming acquainted with the *lazzis* of the Italian comic masks on the Italian theatre at Paris, where improvisatory dialogues were intermixed with scenes written in French: in the Spanish comedies he studied the ingenious complications of intrigue: Plautus and Terence taught him the salt of the Attic wit, the genuine tone of comic maxims, and the nicer shades of character. All this he employed, with more or less success, in the exigency of the moment, and also in order to deck out his drama in a sprightly and variegated dress, made use of all manner of means, however foreign to his art: such as the allegorical opening scenes of the opera prologues, musical intermezzos, in which he even introduced Italian and Spanish national music, with texts in their own language; ballets, at one time sumptuous, and at another grotesque; and even sometimes mere vaulting and capering. He knew how to turn everything to profit: the censure passed upon his pieces, the defects of rival actors imitated to the life by himself and his company, and even the embarrassment in not being able to produce a theatrical entertainment as quickly as it was required by the king,—all became for him a matter for amusement. The pieces he borrowed from the Spanish, his pastorals and tragi-comedies, calculated merely to please the eye, and also three or four of his earlier comedies, which are even versified, and consequently carefully laboured, the critics give up without more ado. But even in the farces, with or without ballets, and intermezzos, in which the overcharged, and frequently the self-conscious and arbitrary comic of buffoonery pre-

vails, Molière has exhibited an inexhaustible store of excellent humour, scattered capital jokes with a lavish hand, and drawn the most amusing caricatures with a bold and vigorous pencil. All this, however, had been often done before his time; and I cannot see how, in this department, he can stand alone, as a creative and altogether original artist: for example, is Plautus' braggadocio soldier less meritorious in grotesque characterization than the ***Bourgeois Gentilhomme?*** We shall immediately examine briefly whether Molière has actually improved the pieces which he borrowed, in whole or in part, from Plautus and Terence. When we bear in mind that in these Latin authors we have only a faint and faded copy of the new Attic Comedy, we shall then be enabled to judge whether he would have been able to surpass its masters had they come down to us. Many of his shifts and inventions, I am induced to suspect, are borrowed; and I am convinced that we should soon discover the sources, were we to search into the antiquities of farcical literature. Others are so obvious, and have so often been both used and abused, that they may in some measure be considered as the common stock of Comedy. Such is the scene in the ***Malade Imaginaire***, where the wife's love is put to the test by the supposed death of the husband—an old joke, which our Hans Sachs has handled drolly enough. We have an avowal of Molière's, which plainly shows he entertained no very great scruples of conscience on the sin of plagiarism. (pp. 306-08)

And even when in his farcical pieces Molière did not lean on foreign invention, he still appropriated the comic manners of other countries, and more particularly the buffoonery of Italy. He wished to introduce a sort of masked character without masks, who should constantly recur with the same name. They did not, however, succeed in becoming properly domiciliated in France. . . .

As the Sganarelles, Mascarilles, Scapins, and Crispins, must be allowed to retain their uniform, that every thing like consistency may not be lost, they have become completely obsolete on the stage. The French taste is, generally speaking, little inclined to the self-conscious and arbitrary comic, with its droll exaggerations, even because these kinds of the comic speak more to the fancy than the understanding. . . . And, in fact, the French comic writers have here displayed a great deal of refinement and ingenuity: in this lies the great merit of Molière, and it is certainly very eminent. Only, we would ask, whether it is of such a description as to justify the French critics, on account of some half a dozen of so-called regular comedies of Molière, in holding in such infinite contempt as they do all the rich stores of refined and characteristic delineation which other nations possess, and in setting up Molière as the unrivalled Genius of Comedy.

If the praise bestowed by the French on their tragic writers be, both from national vanity and from ignorance of the mental productions of other nations, exceedingly extravagant; so their praises of Molière are out of all proportion with their subject. Voltaire calls him the Father of Genuine Comedy; and this may be true enough with respect to France. According to La Harpe, Comedy and Molière are synonymous terms; he is the first of all moral philosophers, his works are the school of the world. Chamfort terms him the most amiable teacher of humanity since Socrates; and is of opinion that Julius Caesar who called

Terence a half Menander, would have called Menander a half Molière.—I doubt this. (pp. 308-09)

[Comedy] is an applied doctrine of ethics, the art of life. In this respect the higher comedies of Molière contain many admirable observations happily expressed, which are still in the present day applicable; others are tainted with the narrowness of his own private opinions, or of the opinions which were prevalent in his age. In this sense Menander was also a philosophical comic writer; and we may boldly place the moral maxims which remain of his by the side at least of those of Molière. But no comedy is constructed of mere apophthegms. The poet must be a moralist, but his personages cannot always be moralizing. And here Molière appears to me to have exceeded the bounds of propriety: he gives us in lengthened disquisitions the *pro* and *con* of the character exhibited by him; nay, he allows these to consist, in part, of principles which the persons themselves defend against the attacks of others. Now this leaves nothing to conjecture; and yet the highest refinement and delicacy of the comic of observation consists in this, that the characters disclose themselves unconsciously by traits which involuntarily escape from them. To this species of comic element, the way in which Oronte introduces his sonnet, Orgon listens to the accounts respecting Tartuffe and his wife, and Vadius and Trissotin fall by the ears, undoubtedly belongs; but the endless disquisitions of Alceste and Philinte as to the manner in which we ought to behave amid the falsity and corruption of the world do not in the slightest respect belong to it. They are serious, and yet they cannot satisfy us as exhausting the subject; and as dialogues which at the end leave the characters precisely at the same point as at the beginning, they are devoid in the necessary dramatic movement. Such argumentative disquisitions which lead to nothing are frequent in all the most admired pieces of Molière, and nowhere more than in the **Misanthrope**. Hence the action, which is also poorly invented, is found to drag heavily; for, with the exception of a few scenes of a more sprightly description, it consists altogether of discourses formally introduced and supported, while the stagnation is only partially concealed by the art employed on the details of versification and expression. In a word, these pieces are too didactic, too expressly instructive; whereas in Comedy the spectator should only be instructed incidentally, and, as it were, without its appearing to have been intended.

Before we proceed to consider more particularly the productions which properly belong to the poet himself, and are acknowledged as master-pieces, we shall offer a few observations on his imitations of the Latin comic writers.

The most celebrated is the **Avare**. The manuscripts of the *Aulularia* of Plautus are unfortunately mutilated towards the end; but yet we find enough in them to excite our admiration. From this play Molière has merely borrowed a few scenes and jokes, for his plot is altogether different. In Plautus it is extremely simple: his Miser has found a treasure, which he anxiously watches and conceals. The suit of a rich bachelor for his daughter excites a suspicion that his wealth is known. The preparations for the wedding bring strange servants and cooks into his house; he considers his pot of gold no longer secure, and conceals it out of doors, which gives an opportunity to a slave of his daughter's chosen lover, sent to glean tidings of her and her marriage, to steal it. Without doubt the thief must afterwards have

been obliged to make restitution, otherwise the piece would end in too melancholy a manner, with the lamentations and imprecations of the old man. The knot of the love intrigue is easily untied: the young man, who has anticipated the rights of the marriage state, is the nephew of the bridegroom, who willingly renounces in his favour. All the incidents serve merely to lead the miser, by a gradually heightening series of agitations and alarms, to display and expose his miserable passion. Molière, on the other hand, without attaining this object, puts a complicated machine in motion. Here we have a lover of the daughter, who, disguised as a servant, flatters the avarice of the old man; a prodigal son, who courts the bride of his father; intriguing servants; an usurer; and after all a discovery at the end. The love intrigue is spun out in a very clumsy and every-day sort of manner; and it has the effect of making us at different times lose sight altogether of Harpagon. Several scenes of a good comic description are merely subordinate, and do not, in a true artistic method, arise necessarily out of the thing itself. Molière has accumulated, as it were, all kinds of avarice in one person; and yet the miser who buries his treasures and he who lends on usury can hardly be the same. Harpagon starves his coach-horses: but why has he any? This would apply better to a man who, with a disproportionate income, strives to keep up a certain appearance of rank. Comic characterization would soon be at an end were there really only one universal character of the miser. The most important deviation of Molière from Plautus is, that while the one paints merely a person who watches over his treasure, the other makes his miser in love. The love of an old man is in itself an object of ridicule; the anxiety of a miser is no less so. We may easily see that when we unite with avarice, which separates a man from others and withdraws him within himself, the sympathetic and liberal passion of love, the union must give rise to the most harsh contrasts. Avarice, however, is usually a very good preservative against falling in love. Where then is the more refined characterization; and as such a wonderful noise is made about it, where shall we here find the more valuable moral instruction?—in Plautus or in Molière? A miser and a superannuated lover may both be present at the representation of Harpagon, and both return from the theatre satisfied with themselves, while the miser says to himself, "I am at least not in love;" and the lover, "Well, at all events I am not a miser." High Comedy represents those follies which, however striking they may be, are reconcilable with the ordinary course of things; whatever forms a singular exception, and is only conceivable amid an utter perversion of ideas, belongs to the arbitrary exaggeration of farce. Hence since (and it was undoubtedly the case long before) the time of Molière, the enamoured and avaricious old man has been the peculiar common-place of the Italian masked comedy and *opera buffa*, to which in truth it certainly belongs. Molière has treated the main incident, the theft of the chest of gold, with an uncommon want of skill. At the very beginning Harpagon, in a scene borrowed from Plautus, is fidgetty with suspicions lest a slave should have discovered his treasure. After this he forgets it; for four whole acts there is not a word about it, and the spectator drops, as it were, from the clouds when the servant all at once brings in the stolen coffer; for we have no information as to the way in which he fell upon the treasure which had been so carefully concealed. Now this is really to begin again, not truly to work out. But Plautus has here shown a great deal of ingenuity: the excessive anxiety of the old man for his pot of gold, and all that he does to save it, are the very cause of its loss. The subterraneous treasure is always invisibly present; it is, as it were, the evil spirit which drives its keeper to madness. In all this we have an impressive moral of a very different kind. In Harpagon's soliloquy, after the theft, the modern poet has introduced the most incredible exaggerations. The calling on the pit to discover the theft, which, when well acted, produces so great an effect, is a trait of the old comedy of Aristophanes, and may serve to give us some idea of its powers of entertainment.

The *Amphitryon* is hardly anything more than a free imitation of the Latin original. The whole plan and order of the scenes is retained. The waiting-woman, or wife of Sosia, is the invention of Molière. The parody of the story of the master's marriage in that of the servant is ingenious, and gives rise to the most amusing investigations on the part of Sosia to find out whether, during his absence a domestic blessing may not have also been conferred on him as well as on Amphitryon. The revolting coarseness of the old mythological story is refined as much as it possibly could without injury to its spirit and boldness; and in general the execution is extremely elegant. The uncertainty of the personages respecting their own identity and duplication is founded on a sort of comic metaphysics: Sosia's reflections on his two *egos*, which have cudgelled each other, may in reality furnish materials for thinking to our philosophers of the present day.

The most unsuccessful of Molière's imitations of the ancients is that of the *Phormio* in the **Fourberies de Scapin**. The whole plot is borrowed from Terence, and, by the addition of a second invention, been adapted, well or ill, or rather tortured, to a consistency with modern manners. The poet has indeed gone very hurriedly to work with his plot, which he has most negligently patched together. The tricks of Scapin, for the sake of which he has spoiled the plot, occupy the foremost place: but we may well ask whether they deserve it? The Grecian Phormio, a man who, for the sake of feasting with young companions, lends himself to all sorts of hazardous tricks, is an interesting and modest knave; Scapin directly the reverse. He had no cause to boast so much of his tricks: they are so stupidly planned that in justice they ought not to have succeeded. Even supposing the two old men to be obtuse and brainless in the extreme, we can hardly conceive how they could so easily fall into such a clumsy and obvious snare as he lays for them. It is also disgustingly improbable that Zerbinette, who as a gipsy ought to have known how to conceal knavish tricks, should run out into the street and tell the first stranger that she meets, who happens to be none other than Geronte himself, the deceit practised upon him by Scapin. The farce of the sack into which Scapin makes Geronte to crawl, then bears him off, and cudgels him as if by the hand of strangers, is altogether a most inappropriate excrescence. Boileau was therefore well warranted in reproaching Molière [see excerpt by Bayle dated 1702 for Boileau's comment] with having shamelessly allied Terence to Taburin, (the merry-andrew of a mountebank). In reality, Molière has here for once borrowed, not, as he frequently did, from the Italian masks, but from the Pagliasses of the rope-dancers and vaulters.

We must not forget that the **Rogueries of Scapin** is one of the latest works of the poet. This and several others of the

same period, as **Monsieur de Pourceaugnac**, **La Comtesse d'Escarbagnas**, and even his last, the **Malade Imaginaire**, sufficiently prove that the maturity of his mind as an artist did not keep pace with the progress of years, otherwise he would have been disgusted with such loose productions. They serve, moreover, to show that frequently he brought forth pieces with great levity and haste, even when he had full leisure to think of posterity. If he occasionally subjected himself to stricter rules, we owe it more to his ambition, and his desire to be numbered among the classical writers of the golden age, than to any internal and growing aspiration after the highest excellence.

The high claims already mentioned, which the French critics make in behalf of their favourite, are principally founded on the **Ecole des Femmes**, **Tartuffe**, **Le Misanthrope**, and **Les Femmes Savantes;** pieces which are certainly finished with great care and diligence. Now, of these, we must expressly state in the outset, that we leave the separate beauties of language and versification altogether to the decision of native critics. These merits can only be subordinate requisites; and the undue stress which is laid in France on the manner in which a piece is written and versified has, in our opinion, been both in Tragedy and Comedy injurious to the development of other and more essential requisites of the dramatic art. We shall confine our exceptions to the general spirit and plan of these comedies.

L'Ecole des Femmes, the earliest of them, seems to me also the most excellent; it is the one in which there is the greatest display of vivacious humour, rapidity, and comic vigour. As to the invention: a man arrived at an age unsuitable for wedlock, purposely educating a young girl in ignorance and simplicity, that he may keep her faithful to himself, while everything turns out the very reverse of his wishes, was not a new one: a short while before Molière it had been employed by Scarron, who borrowed it from a Spanish novel. Still, it was a lucky thought in him to adapt this subject to the stage, and the execution of it is most masterly. Here we have a real and very interesting plot; no creeping investigations which do not carry forward the plot; all the matter is of one piece, without foreign levers and accidental intermixtures, with the exception of the catastrophe, which is brought about somewhat arbitrarily, by means of a scene of recognition. The *naïve* confessions and innocent devices of Agnes are full of sweetness; they, together with the unguarded confidence reposed by the young lover in his unknown rival, and the stifled rage of the old man against both, form a series of comic scenes of the most amusing, and at the same time of the most refined description.

As an example how little the violation of certain probabilities diminishes our pleasure, we may remark that Molière, with respect to the choice of scene, has here indulged in very great liberties. We will not inquire how Arnolph frequently happens to converse with Agnes in the street or in an open place, while he keeps her at the same time so carefully locked up. But if Horace does not know Arnolph to be the intended husband of his mistress, and betrays everything to him, this can only be allowable from Arnolph's passing with her by another name. Horace ought therefore to look for Arnolph in his own house in a remote quarter, and not before the door of his mistress, where yet he always finds him, without entertaining any suspicion from that circumstance. Why do the French critics set such a high value on similar probabilities in the dramatic art, when they must be compelled to admit that their best masters have not always observed them?

Tartuffe is an exact picture of hypocritical piety held up for universal warning; it is an excellent serious satire, but with the exception of separate scenes it is not a comedy. It is generally admitted that the catastrophe is bad, as it is brought about by a foreign means. It is bad, too, because the danger which Orgon runs of being driven from his house and thrown into prison is by no means such an embarrassment as his blind confidence actually merited. Here the serious purpose of the work is openly disclosed, and the eulogium of the king is a dedication by which the poet, even in the piece itself, humbly recommends himself to the protection of his majesty against the persecutions which he dreaded.

In the *Femmes Savantes* raillery has also the upper hand of mirth; the action is insignificant and not in the least degree attractive; and the catastrophe, after the manner of Molière, is arbitrarily brought about by foreign means. Yet these technical imperfections might well be excused for the sake of its satirical merit. But in this respect the composition, from the limited nature of its views, is anything but equal throughout. We are not to expect from the comic poet that he should always give us, along with the exhibition of a folly, a representation also of the opposite way of wisdom; in this way he would announce his object of instructing us with too much of method. But two opposite follies admit of being exhibited together in an equally ludicrous light. Molière has here ridiculed the affectation of a false taste, and the vain-gloriousness of empty knowledge. Proud in their own ignorance and contempt for all higher enlightenment, these characters certainly deserve the ridicule bestowed on them; but that which in this comedy is portrayed as the correct way of wisdom falls nearly into the same error. All the reasonable persons of the piece, the father and his brother, the lover and the daughter, nay, even the ungrammatical maid, are all proud of what they are not, have not, and know not, and even what they do not seek to be, to have, or to know. Chrysale's limited view of the destination of the female sex, Clitander's opinion on the inutility of learning, and the sentiments elsewhere advanced respecting the measure of cultivation and knowledge which is suitable to a man of rank, were all intended to convey Molière's own opinions himself on these subjects. (pp. 309-15)

The *Misanthrope*, which, as is well known, was at first coldy received, is still less amusing than the two preceding pieces: the action is less rapid, or rather there is none at all; and there is a great want of coherence between the meagre incidents which give only an apparent life to the dramatic movement,—the quarrel with Oronte respecting the sonnet, and its adjustment; the decision of the law-suit which is ever being brought forward; the unmasking of Celimene through the vanity of the two Marquisses, and the jealousy of Arsinöe. Besides all this, the general plot is not even probable. It is framed with a view to exhibit the thorough delineation of a character; but a character discloses itself much more in its relations with others than immediately. How comes Alceste to have chosen Philinte for a friend, a man whose principles were directly the reverse of his own? How comes he also to be enamoured of a coquette, who has nothing amiable in her character, and who entertains us merely by her scandal? We might well

say of this Celimene, without exaggeration, that there is not one good point in her whole composition. In a character like that of Alceste, love is not a fleeting sensual impulse, but a serious feeling arising from a want of a sincere mental union. His dislike of flattering falsehood and malicious scandal, which always characterise the conversation of Celimene, breaks forth so incessantly, that, we feel, the first moment he heard her open her lips ought to have driven him for ever from her society. Finally, the subject is ambiguous, and that is its greatest fault. The limits within which Alceste is in the right and beyond which he is in the wrong, it would be no easy matter to fix, and I am afraid the poet himself did not here see very clearly what he would be at. Philinte, however, with his illusory justification of the way of the world, and his phlegmatic resignation, he paints throughout as the intelligent and amiable man. As against the elegant Celimene, Alceste is most decidedly in the right, and only in the wrong in the inconceivable weakness of his conduct towards her. He is in the right in his complaints of the corruption of the social constitution; the facts, at least, which he adduces, are disputed by nobody. He is in the wrong, however, in delivering his sentiments with so much violence, and at an unseasonable time; but as he cannot prevail on himself to assume the dissimulation which is necessary to be well received in the world, he is perfectly in the right in preferring solitude to society. Rousseau has already censured the ambiguity of the piece, by which what is deserving of approbation seems to be turned into ridicule. His opinion was not altogether unprejudiced; for his own character, and his behaviour towards the world, had a striking similarity to that of Alceste; and, moreover, he mistakes the essence of dramatic composition, and founds his condemnation on examples of an accidentally false direction.

So far with respect to the famed moral philosophy of Molière in his pretended master-piece. From what has been stated, I consider myself warranted to assert, in opposition to the prevailing opinion, that Molière succeeded best with the coarse and homely comic, and that both his talents and his inclination, if unforced, would have determined him altogether to the composition of farces such as he continued to write even to the very end of his life. He seems always to have whipped himself up as it were to his more serious pieces in verse: we discover something of constraint in both plot and execution. His friend Boileau probably communicated to him his view of a correct mirth, of a grave and decorous laughter; and so Molière determined, after the carnival of his farces, to accommodate himself occasionally to the spare diet of the regular taste, and to unite what in their own nature are irreconcileable, namely, dignity and drollery. However, we find even in his prosaic pieces traces of that didactical and satirical vein which is peculiarly alien to Comedy; for example, in his constant attacks on physicians and lawyers, in his disquisitions upon the true correct tone of society, &c., the intention of which is actually to censure, to refute, to instruct, and not merely to afford entertainment.

The classical reputation of Molière still preserves his pieces on the stage, although in tone and manners they are altogether obsolete. This is a danger to which the comic poet is inevitably exposed from that side of his composition which does not rest on a poetical foundation, but is determined by the prose of external reality. The originals of the individual portraits of Molière have long since disappeared. The comic poet who lays claim to immortality must, in the delineation of character and the disposition of his plan, rest principally on such motives as are always intelligible, being taken not from the manners of any particular age, but drawn from human nature itself. (pp. 316-18)

> *August Wilhelm Schlegel, "Lecture XXI," in his* Lectures on Dramatic Art and Literature, *edited by Rev. A. J. W. Morrison, translated by John Black, revised edition, 1846. Reprint by George Bell & Sons, 1902, pp. 304-38.*

[SIR WALTER SCOTT] (essay date 1828)

[*Scott was an enormously popular historical novelist whose works exerted a profound influence on early nineteenth-century European literature. In the following excerpt, he compares Molière with Shakespeare and determines the probable sources of Molière's genius.*]

[The] universal sense of the humorous renders such a complete master of comedy as Molière the property, not of that country alone which was honoured with his birth, but of the civilized world, and of England in particular, whose drama has been enriched by versions of so many of his best pieces. (p. 308)

[We] can scarcely hesitate to assign the first place amongst the comic writers of any age or nation [to Molière]. (p. 309)

[We] willingly take some general view of the character of Molière as an author, in which we feel it our duty to vindicate for him the very highest place of any who has ever distinguished himself in his department of literature. His natural disposition, his personal habits, his vivacity as a Frenchman, the depth of his knowledge of human nature, his command of a language eminent above all others for the power of expressing ludicrous images and ideas, raise him to the highest point of eminence amongst the authors of his own country and class, and assure him an easy superiority over those of every other country.

Our countrymen will perhaps ask, if we have forgotten the inimitable comic powers of our own Shakespeare. The sense of humour displayed by that extraordinary man is perhaps as remarkable as his powers of searching the human bosom for other and deeper purposes. But if Johnson has rightly defined comedy to be "a dramatic representation of the lighter faults of mankind, with a view to make folly and vice ridiculous," it would be difficult to show that Shakespeare has dedicated to such purposes more than occasional and scattered scenes, dispersed through his numerous dramas. The *Merry Wives of Windsor* is perhaps the piece most resembling a regular comedy, yet the poetry with which it abounds is of a tone, which soars, in many respects, beyond its sphere. In most of his other compositions, his comic humour is rather an ingredient of the drama, than the point to which it is emphatically and specially directed. . . . It must also be remembered, that the manners in Shakespeare (so far as his comedy depends on them) are so antiquated, that but for the deep and universal admiration with which England regards her immortal bard, and the pious care with which his works have been explained and commented upon, the follies arising out of the fashions of his time would be entirely obsolete. (pp. 345-46)

The scenes of Molière, however, are painted from subjects with which our own times are acquainted; they represent follies of a former date indeed, but which have their resemblances in the present day. Some old-fashioned habits being allowed for, the personages of his drama resemble the present generation as much as our grandmothers' portraits, but for hoop petticoats and commodes, resemble their descendants of the present generation. Our physicians no longer wear robes of office, or ride upon mules, but we cannot flatter ourselves that the march of intellect, as the cant phrase goes, has exploded either the *Malade Imaginaire*, or the race of grave deceivers who fattened on his folly. If, again, we look at Molière's object in all the numerous pieces which his fertile genius produced, we perceive a constant, sustained, and determined warfare against vice and folly,—sustained by means of wit and satire, without any assistance derived either from sublimity or pathos. It signified little to Molière what was the mere form which his drama assumed: whether regular comedy or comédie-ballet, whether his art worked in its regular sphere, or was pressed by fashion into the service of mummery and pantomime, its excellence was the same,—if but one phrase was uttered, that phrase was comic. Instead of sinking down to the farcical subjects which he adopted, whether by command of the king, or to sacrifice to the popular taste, Molière elevated these subjects by his treatment of them. His pen, like the hand of Midas, turned all it touched to gold; or rather, his mode of treating the most ordinary subject gave it a value such as the sculptor or engraver can confer upon clay, rock, old copper, or even cherry-stones.

It is not a little praise to this great author, that he derived none of his powers of amusement from the coarse and mean sources to which the British dramatic poets had such liberal recourse. This might, and probably did, flow in part from the good taste of the poet himself, but it was also much owing to that of Louis XIV. Whatever the private conduct of that prince, of which enough may be learned from the scandalous chronicle of the times, he knew too well *son métier de Roi* ["his position as King"], and what was due to his dignity in public, to make common jest with his subjects at any thing offensive to good morals or decorum. Charles II., on the other hand,—

> A merry monarch, scandalous and poor,—

had been too long emancipated by his exile from all regal ceremonial, to lay his sense of humour under any restraints of delicacy. He enjoyed a broad jest, as he would have done an extra bottle of wine, without being careful about the persons who participated with him in either; and hence a personal laxity of conduct which scandalized the feelings of Evelyn, and a neglect of decency in public entertainments, encouraged by the presence of the sovereign, which called down the indignation of Collier. Some comparatively trifling slips, with which the critics of the period charge Molière, form no exception to the general decorum of his writings.

Looking at their general purpose and tendency, we must be convinced that there is no comic author, of ancient or modern times, who directed his satire against such a variety of vices and follies, which, if he could not altogether extirpate, he failed not at all events to drive out of the shape and form which they had assumed.

The absurdities of *L'Etourdi*, the ridiculous jargon of the *Précieuses*, the silly quarrels of the lovers in the *Dépit Amoureux*, the absurd jealousy of husbands in *L'Ecole des Maris*, the varied fopperies and affectations of men of fashion in *Les Fâcheux*, the picture of hypocrisy in the *Tartuffe*, the exhibition at once of bizarre and untractable virtue, and of the depravity of dissimulation in the *Misanthrope*, the effects of the dangers of misassorted alliances in *George Dandin*, of the tricks of domestics in *Les Fourberies de Scapin*, of the pedantic affectation of learning in *Les Femmes Savantes*, of the dupes who take physic and the knaves who administer it in the *Malade Imaginaire*, —all these, with similar aberrations, exposed and exploded by the pen of a single author, showed that Molière possessed, in a degree superior to all other men, the falcon's piercing eye to detect vice under every veil, or folly in every shape, and the talons with which to pounce upon either, as the natural prey of the satirist. No other writer of comedy ever soared through flights so many and so various.

We have said that the comedy of Molière never exhibits any touch of the sublime; and from its not being attempted in those more serious pieces, as *Don Garcie* and *Mélicerte*, where a high strain of poetry might have been struck to advantage, we conceive that Molière did not possess that road to the human bosom. One passage alone strikes us as approaching to a very lofty tone. Don Juan, distinguished solely by the desperation of his courage, enters the tomb of the Commander, and ridicules the fears of his servant when he tells him that the statue has nodded in answer to the invitation delivered to him by his master's command. Don Juan delivers the same invitation in person, and the statue again bends his head. Feeling a touch of the supernatural terror to which his lofty courage refuses to give way, his sole observation is, *"Allons, sortons d'ici"* ["Let's go, let's leave here"]. A retreat, neither alarmed nor precipitated, is all which he will allow to the terrors of such a prodigy.

In like manner, although we are informed that Molière possessed feelings of sensibility too irritable for his own happiness in private life, his writings indicate no command of the pathetic. His lovers are always gallant and witty, but never tender or ardent. This is the case, not only where the love intrigue is only a means of carrying on the business of the scene, but in *Le Dépit Amoureux*, where the ardour of affection might have gracefully mingled with the tracasseries of the lovers' quarrels; and in *Psyché*, in which it is to be supposed the author would have introduced the passionate and pathetic, if he had possessed the power of painting it. Nor do any of his personages, in all the distresses in which the scene places them, ever make a strong impression on the feelings of the audience, who are only amused by the ludicrous situations to which the distresses give rise. The detected villainy of Tartuffe affects the feelings indeed strongly, but it is more from the gratification of honest resentment against a detected miscreant, than from any interest we take in the fortunes of the duped Orgon.

Neither did Molière ornament his dramatic pieces with poetical imagery, whether descriptive or moral. His mode of writing excluded the "morning sun, and all about gilding the eastern horizon." He wrote to the understanding, and not to the fancy, and was probably aware moreover that such poetical ornaments, however elegant when under

the direction of good taste, are apt to glide into the opposite extreme, and to lead to that which Molière regarded as the greatest fault in composition, an affectation of finery approaching to the language of the *Précieuses Ridicules*. (pp. 346-49)

In what, therefore, it may be asked, consisted the excellence of this entertaining writer, whose works, as often as we have opened a volume during the composition of this slight article, we have found it impossible to lay out of our hand until we had completed a scene, however little to our immediate purpose of consulting it? If Molière did not possess, or at least has not exercised the powers of the sublime, the pathetic, or the imaginative in poetry, from whence do his works derive their undisputed and almost universal power of charming? We reply, from their truth and from their simplicity; from the powerful and penetrating view of human nature, which could strip folly and vice of all their disguise, and expose them to laughter and scorn when they most hoped for honour and respect; also from the extreme *naiveté* as well as force of the expressions which effect the author's purpose. A father consults his friends about the deep melancholy into which his daughter is fallen: one advises to procure for her a handsome piece of plate, beautifully sculptured, as an object which cannot fail to give pleasure to the most disconsolate mind. The celebrated answer, *vous êtes orfèvre, Monsieur Josse* ["You are a goldsmith, Mr. Josse"], at once unmasks the private views of the selfish adviser, and has afforded a measure by which all men, from Molière's time to our own, may judge of the disinterested character of such friendly counsels. This short, dry, sudden and unexpected humour of Molière, seconded as it always is by the soundest good sense, is one great proof of his knowledge of his art. The tragic may be greatly enlivened by some previous preparation, as the advance of a mighty host with its ensigns displayed has, even at a distance, an effect upon the nerves of those whom it is about to assail. But wit is most successful when it bursts from an unexpected ambush, and carries its point by surprize. The best jest will lose its effect on the stage, if so much preparation is employed as leads the spectator to anticipate what is coming, as it will suffer in society if introduced with the preface of "I'll tell you a good thing!" In this species of surprize Molière surpasses every writer of comedy, but the jest at which you laugh springs as naturally out of the subject, as if it had been obvious to your apprehension from the very commencement of the scene. A brief sentence, a word, even an exclamation, is often sufficient to produce the full effect of the ludicrous, as a spark will spring a mine, in the place and time when the explosion is least suspected. The most unexpected means in the hands of this great artist are also the most certain; and you are first made sensible of what he has aimed at, when you admire his arrow quivering in the centre of the mark.

The depth and force of Molière's common sense is equally remarkable in displaying his own just and sound opinions, as in exposing the false taste and affectation of others. Ariste, Philinte, and the other personages of his drama, to whom (as the ancients did to their choruses) he has ascribed the task of moralizing upon the subject of the scene, and expressing the sentiments which must be supposed those of the author himself, have all the firmness, strength, and simplicity proper to the enunciation of truth and wisdom; and much more of both will be found within the precincts of Molière's works, than in the formal lessons of men of less acute capacity. (pp. 349-50)

Some readers may be disappointed, that after pronouncing Molière the prince of the writers of comedy, we should have limited the talents by which he attained such preeminence to the possession of common sense, however sound, of observation however acute, and of expression, however forcible, true and simple. It is not, however, by talents of a different class from those enjoyed by the rest of humanity that the ingredients which form great men are constituted. On the contrary, such peculiar tastes and talents only produce singularity. The real source of greatness in almost every department is an extraordinary proportion of some distinguishing quality proper to all mankind, and of which therefore all mankind, less or more, comprehends the character and the value. A man with four arms would be a monster for romance or for a show; it is the individual that can best make use of the ordinary conformation of his body, who obtains a superiority over his fellow-creatures by strength or agility. In a word, the general qualities of sound judgment, clear views, and powerful expression of what is distinctly perceived, acquire the same value, as they rise in degree above the general capacity of humanity, with that obtained by diamonds, which in proportion to their weight in carats become almost inestimable, while the smaller sparks of the same precious substance are of ordinary occurrence, and held comparatively in slight esteem. (p. 351)

[Sir Walter Scott], "Molière," in The Foreign Quarterly Review, *Vol. II, No. III, February, 1828, pp. 306-51.*

JOHANN WOLFGANG VON GOETHE   (essay date 1828)

[*Goethe was a German writer who is considered one of the greatest figures in world literature. A genius of the highest order, he distinguished himself as an artist, musician, and philosopher who contributed richly to his nation's literature. Excelling in all genres, Goethe was a shaping force in the major literary movements of the late eighteenth and early nineteenth centuries in Germany. His two-part drama* Faust *(1808, 1832; translated as* Faust, *1823, and Goethe's "Faust": Part II, 1839) is ranked beside the masterpieces of Dante and Shakespeare. In the following excerpt from an essay originally published in 1828, he comments on the spirit of Molière and* The Misanthrope.]

Examine the **Misanthrope** carefully and ask yourself whether a poet has ever represented his inner spirit more completely or more admirably. We can well call the content and treatment of this play "tragic." Such an impression at least it has always left with us, because that mood is brought before our mind's eye which often in itself brings us to despair, and seems as if it would make the world unbearable.

Here is represented the type of man who despite great cultivation has yet remained natural, and who with himself, as well as others, would like only too well to express himself with complete truth and sincerity. But we see him in conflict with the social world, where one cannot move without dissimulation and shallowness.

Johann Wolfgang von Goethe, "Molière's 'Misanthrope'," translated by Randolph S. Bourne, in his Goethe's Literary Essays: A Selection in English,

edited by J. E. Spingarn, Harcourt Brace Jovanovich, 1921, p. 212.

ATTICUS [PSEUDONYM OF ISAAC D'ISRAELI]   (essay date 1833)

[*Although probably most famous as the father of novelist and British prime minister Benjamin Disraeli, Isaac D'Israeli was an essayist who wrote several interesting and important works on eighteenth-century literature. His criticism is considered of particular value because of his access to documents and understanding of traditions now lost. In the following excerpt, he illustrates Molière's gradual development from a good dramatist to a great comic artist.*]

Moliere was a creator in the *art of comedy*—and although his personages were the contemporaries of Louis the Fourteenth, and his manners, in the critical acceptation of the term, local and temporary, yet his admirable genius opened that secret path of Nature, which is so rarely found among the great names of the most literary nations. Cervantes remains single in Spain; in England, Shakspeare is a consecrated name; and centuries may pass away before the French people shall witness another Moliere.

The history of this comic poet is the tale of powerful genius creating itself amidst the most adverse elements. We have the progress of that self-education which struck out an untried path of its own, from the time Moliere had not yet acquired his art, to the glorious days when he gave his France a Plautus in his farce, a Terence in his composition, and a Menander in his moral truths. But the difficulties overcome, and the disappointments incurred, his modesty and his confidence, and, what was not less extraordinary, his own domestic life in perpetual conflict with his character, open a more strange career, in some respects, than has happened to most others of the high order of his genius. (pp. 429-30)

It is a remarkable feature, though not perhaps a singular one, in the character of this great comic writer, that he was one of the most serious of men, and even of a melancholic temperament. One of his lampooners wrote a satirical comedy on the comic poet, where he figures as Moliere hypochondre. Boileau, who knew him intimately, happily characterised Moliere as le Contemplateur. This deep pensiveness is revealed in his physiognomy.

The genius of Moliere, long undiscovered by himself, in its first attempts in a higher walk did not move alone; it was crutched by imitation, and it often deigned to plough with another's heifer. He copied whole scenes from Italian comedies, and plots from Italian novelists: his sole merit was their improvement. The great comic satirist, who hereafter was to people the stage with a dramatic crowd who were to live on to posterity, had not yet struck at that secret vein of originality—the fairy treasure which one day was to cast out such a prodigality of invention. His two first comedies, **L'Etourdi** and **Le Dépit Amoureux**, which he had only ventured to bring out in a provincial theatre, were grafted on Italian and Spanish comedy. Nothing more original offered to his imagination than the Roman, the Italian, and the Spanish drama; the cunning adroit slave of Terence; the tricking, bustling *Gracioso* of modern Spain; old fathers, the dupes of some scape-grace, or of their own senile follies, with lovers sighing at cross purposes. The germ of his future powers may, indeed, be discovered in these two comedies, for insensibly to himself he had fallen into some scenes of natural simplicity. In *L'Etourdi,* Mascarille, "le Roi des Serviteurs," [the King of Servants"], which Moliere himself admirably personated, is one of those defunct characters of the Italian comedy no longer existing in society; yet, like our Touchstone, but infinitely richer, this new ideal personage still delights by the fertility of his expedients and his perpetual and vigorous gaiety. In *Le Dépit Amoureux* is the exquisite scene of the quarrel and reconciliation of the lovers. In this fine scene, though perhaps but an amplification of the well-known ode of Horace, *Donec gratus eram tibi,* Moliere consulted his own feelings, and betrayed his future genius.

It was after an interval of three or four years that the provincial celebrity of these comedies obtained a representation at Paris; their success was decisive. This was an evidence of public favour which did not accompany Moliere's more finished productions, which were so far unfortunate that they were more intelligible to the few; in fact, the first comedies of Moliere were not written above the popular taste; the spirit of true comedy, in a profound knowledge of the heart of man, and in the delicate discriminations of individual character, was yet unknown. Moliere was satisfied to excel his predecessors, but he had not yet learnt his art.

The rising poet was now earnestly sought after; a more extended circle of society now engaged his contemplative habits. He looked around on living scenes no longer through the dim spectacles of the old comedy, and he projected a new species, which was no longer to depend on its conventional grotesque personages and its forced incidents; he aspired to please a more critical audience, by making his dialogue the conversation of society, and his characters its portraits. (p. 432)

Tormented by his genius, Moliere produced *Les Précieuses Ridicules.* . . . The success of the comedy was universal; the company doubled their prices; the country gentry flocked to witness the marvellous novelty which far exposed that false taste, that romance-impertinence, and that sickly affectation, which had long disturbed the quiet of families. Cervantes had not struck more adroitly at Spanish rhodomontade.

At this universal reception of the *Précieuses Ridicules,* Moliere, it is said, exclaimed—"I need no longer study Plautus and Terence, nor poach in the fragments of Menander; I have only to study the world." It may be doubtful whether the great comic satirist, at that moment, caught the sudden revelation of his genius, as he did subsequently in his *Tartuffe,* his *Misanthrope,* his *Bourgeois Gentilhomme,* and others. The *Précieuses Ridicules* was the germ of his more elaborate *Femmes Savantes,* which was not produced till after an interval of twelve years.

Moliere returned to his old favourite *canevas,* or plots of Italian farces and novels, and Spanish comedies, which, being always at hand, furnished comedies of intrigue. *L'Ecole des Maris* is an inimitable model of this class.

But comedies which derive their chief interest from the ingenious mechanism of their plots, however poignant the delight of the artifice of the *denouement,* are somewhat like an epigram, once known, the brilliant point is blunted by repetition. This is not the fate of those representations

of men's actions, passions, and manners, in the more enlarged sphere of human nature, where an eternal interest is excited, and will charm on the tenth repetition.

No! Moliere had not yet discovered his true genius; he was not yet emancipated from his old seductions. A rival company was reputed to have the better actors for tragedy, and Moliere resolved to compose an heroic drama, on the passion of jealousy, a favourite one on which he was incessantly ruminating. *Don Garcie de Navarre, ou le Prince Jaloux,* the hero personated by himself, terminated by the hisses of the audience.

The fall of the *Prince Jaloux* was nearly fatal to the tender reputation of the poet and the actor. The world became critical; the Marquises, and the Précieuses, and recently the Bourgeois, who was sore from *Sganarelle, ou le Cocu Imaginaire,* were up in arms; and the rival theatre maliciously raised the halloo, flattering themselves that the comic genius of their dreaded rival would be extinguished by the ludicrous convulsed hiccough to which Moliere was liable in his tragic tones, but which he adroitly managed in his comic parts.

But the genius of Moliere was not to be daunted by cabals, nor even injured by his own imprudence. *Le Prince Jaloux* was condemned in February 1661, and the same year produced *L'Ecole des Maris* and *Les Facheux.* The happy genius of the poet opened on his Zoiluses a series of dramatic triumphs.

Foreign critics, Tiraboschi and Schlegel [see excerpt dated 1811], have depreciated the Frenchman's invention, by insinuating, that were all that Moliere borrowed taken from him, little would remain of his own. But they were not aware of his dramatic creation, even when he appropriated the slight inventions of others; they have not distinguished the eras of the genius of Moliere, and the distinct classes of his comedies. Moliere had the art of amalgamating many distinct inventions of others into a single inimitable whole. Whatever might be the herbs, and the reptiles thrown into the mystical cauldron, the incantation of genius proved to be truly magical.

Facility and fecundity may produce inequality, for on these occasions the poet wrestles with Time; but when a man of genius works, they are imbued with a raciness which the anxious diligence of inferior minds can ever yield. Shakspeare, probably, poured forth many scenes in this spirit. The multiplicity of the pieces of Moliere, their different merits, and their distinct classes—all written within the space of twenty years—display, if any poet ever did, this wonder-working faculty. The truth is, that few of his comedies are finished works; he never satisfied himself, even in his most applauded productions. Necessity bound him to furnish novelties for his theatre; he rarely printed any work. *Les Facheux,* an admirable series of scenes, in three acts, and in verse, was "planned, written, rehearsed, and represented in a single fortnight." Many of his dramatic effusions were precipitated on the stage; the humorous scenes of *Monsier de Pourceaugnac* were thrown out to enliven a royal fête.

This versatility and felicity of composition made everything, with Moliere, a subject for comedy. He invented two novelties, such as the stage had never before witnessed. Instead of a grave defence from the malice of his critics, and the flying gossip of the court circle, Moliere found out the art of congregating the public to "the quarrels of authors." He dramatised his critics. In a comedy without a plot, and in scenes which seemed rather spoken than written, and with characters more real than personated, he displayed his genius by collecting whatever had been alleged to depreciate it; and *La Critique de l'Ecole des Femmes*, is still a delightful production. This singular drama resembles the sketch-book of an artist, the croquis of portraits—the loose hints of thoughts, many of which we discover were more fully delineated in his subsequent pieces. With the same rapid conception, he laid hold of his embarrassments to furnish dramatic novelties as expeditiously as the king required. Louis XIV. was himself no indifferent critic, and more than once suggested an incident or a character to his favourite poet. In *L'Impromptu de Versailles*, Moliere appears in his own person, and in the midst of his whole company, with all the irritable impatience of a manager who had no piece ready. Amidst this green-room bustle, Moliere is advising, reprimanding, and imploring his "ladies and gentlemen." The characters in this piece are, in fact, the actors themselves, who appear under their own names; and Moliere himself reveals many fine touches of his own poetical character, as well as his managerial. The personal pleasantries on his own performers, and the hints for plots, and the sketches of character which the poet incidentally throws out, form a perfect dramatic novelty. Some of these he himself subsequently adopted, and others have been followed up by some dramatists without rivalling Moliere. The Pigaro of Beaumarchais is a descendant of the Mascarille of Moliere; but the glory of rivalling Moliere was reserved for our own stage. Sheridan's *Critic, or a Tragedy Rehearsed*, is a congenial dramatic satire with these two pieces of Moliere, and it is not improbable was suggested by them.

The genius of Moliere had now stept out of the restricted limits of the old comedy; he now looked on the moving world with other eyes, and he pursued the ridiculous in society. These fresher studies were going on at all hours, and every object was contemplated with a view to comedy. His most vital characters have been traced to living originals, and some of his most ludicrous scenes had occurred in reality before they delighted the audience.... The memorable scene between Trissotin and Vadius, their mutual compliments terminating in their mutual contempt, had been rehearsed by their respective authors, the Abbé Cottin and Menage. The stultified booby of Limoges, *Monsieur de Pourceaugnac*, and the mystified millionaire, *Le Bourgeois Gentilhomme*, were copied after life, as was Sganarelle, in *Le Médecin malgré lui*. The portraits in that gallery of dramatic paintings, *Le Misanthrope,* have names inscribed under them; and the immortal *Tartuffe* was a certain Bishop of Autun. No dramatist has conceived with greater variety the female character; the women of Moliere have a distinctness of feature, and are touched with a freshness of feeling. Moliere studied nature, and his comic humour is never checked by that unnatural wit where the poet, the more he discovers himself, the farther he removes himself from the personage of his creation. The quickening spell which hangs over the dramas of Moliere is this close attention to nature, wherein he greatly resembles our Shakspeare, for all springs from its source. His unobtrusive genius never occurs to us in following up his characters, and a whole scene leaves on our mind a complete but imperceptible effect.

The style of Moliere has often been censured by the fastidiousness of his native critics, sometimes as *bas* and *du style familier*. ["low" and "plain"]. This does not offend the foreigner, who is often struck by its simplicity and vigour. Moliere preferred the most popular and naïve expressions, as well as the most natural incidents, to a degree which startled the morbid delicacy of fashion and fashionable critics. He had frequent occasions to resist their petty remonstrances; and whenever Moliere introduced an incident, or made an allusion of which he knew the truth, and which with him had a settled meaning, this master of human life trusted to his instinct and his art.

This pure and simple taste, ever rare at Paris, was the happy portion of the genius of this Frenchman. (pp. 434-37)

> Atticus [*pseudonym of Isaac D'Israeli*], "The Genius of Moliere", in The New Monthly Magazine, Vol. XXXVII, No. CXLVIII, April, 1833, pp. 429-40.

C. A. SAINTE-BEUVE (essay date 1835)

[*Sainte-Beuve is considered the foremost French literary critic of the nineteenth century. Of his extensive body of critical writings, the best known are his lundis—weekly newspaper articles that appeared every Monday morning over a period of two decades, in which his knowledge of literature and history was evident. While Sainte-Beuve began his career as a champion of Romanticism, he eventually formulated a psychological method of criticism. Asserting that the critic cannot separate a work of literature from the artist and from the artist's historical milieu, Sainte-Beuve considered an author's life and character integral to the comprehension of his work. This perspective led to his classification of writers into what he called familes d'esprits, or "families of the mind." Though he usually treated his subjects with respect, he dealt harshly with several, notably François Chateaubriand and Honoré de Balzac. In the twentieth century, Sainte-Beuve's treatment of Balzac provoked the ire of Marcel Proust and inspired* Contre Sainte-Beuve *(1954;* By Way of Sainte-Beuve, *1958), in which Proust contested the validity of Sainte-Beuve's analytical method. Other twentieth-century critics praise Sainte-Beuve's erudition and insight but question his biographical approach. They consider him a historian of manners, a psychologist, and a moralist. In the words of René Wellek, "Sainte-Beuve should be described as the greatest representative of the historical spirit in France," who, at his best "preserves the delicate balance needed to save himself from relativism or overemphasis on external conditions." In the following excerpt from a study of Molière first published in French in 1835, Sainte-Beuve acknowledges what he sees as Molière's exceptional transcendence of his age, providing as well an appreciative critical survey of Molière's plays.*]

In poesy, in literature, there is a class of men beyond comparison, even among the very first; not numerous, five or six in all, perhaps, since the beginning, whose characteristic is universality, eternal humanity, intimately mingled with the painting of manners and morals and the passions of an epoch. Facile geniuses, strong and fruitful, their principal trait lies in this mixture of fertility, firmness, and frankness; it is knowledge and richness at the foundation; true indifference to the employment of means and conventional styles, every framework, every point of departure suiting them to enter upon their subject; it is active production multiplying through obstacles, the plenitude of art, obtained frequently without artifices or retarding apparatus. (p. 87)

It is to modern times and the Renaissance that we must turn for the men whom we are seeking. Shakespeare, Cervantes, Rabelais, Molière, with two or three later of unequal rank, and that is all; we can characterise them by their resemblances. These men had divers and thwarted destinies; they suffered, they struggled, they loved. Soldiers, physicians, comedians, captives, they found it hard to live; poverty, passions, impediments, the hindering of enterprises,—they endured all. But their genius rose above their shackles and, without resenting the narrowness of the struggle, kept its neck from the collar and its elbows free. . . . [Thus] these rare geniuses, of grand and plastic beauty, —beauty inborn and genuine,—triumph with an easy air under the most opposing conditions; they develop, they assert themselves invincibly. They do not develop merely by chance and at the mercy of circumstances, like such secondary geniuses as Ovid, Dryden, or the Abbé Prévost, for instance. No: their works, as prompt, as numerous as those of minds that are chiefly facile, are also entire, strong, cohering to an end when necessary, perfected again and again, and sublime. But this perfection is never to them the solicitude, sometimes excessive, the constantly chastened prudence of the studious and polished school of poets, the Grays, Popes, and Boileaus, poets whom I admire and enjoy as much as any one, and whose scrupulous correctness is, I know, an indispensable quality, a charm, and who seem to have taken for their motto, Vauvenarque's admirable saying: "Clearness is the varnish of masters." In the very perfection of the superior poets there is something freer, bolder, more irregularly born, incomparably more fertile, more independent of ingenious fetters; something that goes of itself, that sports; something that amazes and disconcerts the distinguished contemporary poets by its inventive resources, even in the lesser details of their profession. It was thus that Boileau, among his many natural causes for surprise, cannot refrain from asking Molière where he "found rhymes." (pp. 88-90)

Although [Molière] chiefly grasped the comic side, the discordances, vices, deformities, and eccentricities of mankind, seldom touching the pathetic side, and then only as a passing accessory, yet, when he does so, he yields to none, even the highest, so much does he excel in his own manner and in every direction from freest fancy to gravest observation, so amply does he occupy as king all the regions of social life that he chooses for his own.

Molière belongs to the age in which he lived by his picturing of certain peculiar oddities and the presentation of customs and manners, but he is, in fact, of all ages; he is the man of human nature. To obtain the measure of his genius nothing serves better than to see with what facility he fastens to his century and detaches himself from it; how precisely he adapts himself to it and with what grandeur he can issue from it. The illustrious men, his contemporaries, Boileau, Racine, Bossuet, Pascal, are far more specially men of their time, of Louis XIV's epoch, than Molière. Their genius (I speak of the greatest of them) bears the hall-mark of the moment when they came, which would, probably, have been quite other in other times. . . . . [Molière] was far more independent of [his age], although he paints it more to the life than any one. He adds to the lustre of that majestic aspect of the great century; but he is neither stamped by it, nor confined to it, nor narrowed to it; he proportions himself to it, he does not inclose himself within it. (pp. 91-2)

[The] farther we advance in the period called that of Louis XIV the more we find literature, poesy, the pulpit, the stage, taking on a religious and Christian character; the more they evidence, even in the general sentiments they express, a return to belief in revelation, to humanity as seen *in* and *by* Jesus Christ. This is one of the most characteristic and most profound features of that immortal literature. The seventeenth century rose *en masse* and made a dike between the sixteenth and the eighteenth centuries, which it separates.

But Molière,—I say it without conveying either praise or moral blame, and simply as a proof of the freedom of his genius,—Molière does not come within this point of view. Although his figure and his work appear and stand forth more than all others in this admirable frame of the great epoch of Louis the Great, he stretches and reaches forward, backward, without, and beyond; he belongs to a calmer thought, more vast, more unconcerned, more universal. The pupil of Gassendi, the friend of Bernier, of Chapelle, and of Resnault is directly connected with the philosophy and literature of the sixteenth century; he had no antipathy against that century and what remained of it: he entered into no reaction, religious or literary, as did Bossuet, Racine, Boileau, and three-fourths of Louis XIV's century. He is of the posterity of Rabelais, Montaigne, Larivey, Regnier, of the authors of the *Satyre Menippée;* he has, or would have had, no difficulty in coming to an understanding with Lamothe-le-Vayer, Naudé, or even Gui Patin, that carping personage, doctor of medicine though he was. (pp. 94-5)

I do not, by any means, intend to say that Molière, in his work or in his thought, was a decided free-thinker; that he had any system on such subjects, or that (in spite of his translation of Lucretius, his free jesting, and his various *liaisons*) he did not have a foundation of moderate, sensible religion, such as accorded with the custom of the times, a religion which reappeared at his last hour, and had already burst forth with such strength from Cléante's lips in *Tartuffe*. No; Molière the wise, an Ariste of calm propriety, the enemy of all excesses and absurdities of mind, the father of that Philinte whom Lélius, Erasmus, and Atticus would have recognised, had nothing of the licentious and cynical braggadocio of the Saint-Amants, Boisroberts, and their kind. He was sincere in being indignant at the malicious insinuations which, from the date of the *École des Femmes,* his enemies cast upon his religion.

But what I want to establish, and which characterises him among his contemporaries of genius, is that he habitually saw human nature in itself, in its universality of all periods; as Boileau and La Bruyère saw and painted it often, I know, but Molière without mixture such as we see in Boileau's *Épitre sur l'Amour de Dieu*, and La Bruyère's discussion on Quietism. He paints humanity as if it had no growth; and this, it must be said, was the more possible to him, painting it, as he did especially, in its vices and blemishes: tragedy evades Christianity less easily. Molière separates humanity from Jesus Christ, or rather he shows us the one to its depths without taking much account of the other. In this he detaches himself from his century. In the famous scene of the Pauper he gives, without a thought of harm, a speech to Don Juan which he was forced to suppress, such storms did it raise: "You spend your life in praying to God and you are dying of hunger; take this money; I give it you from love of humanity." The beneficence and the philanthropy of the eighteenth century, that of d'Alembert, Diderot, and Holbach, are in that saying. And it was Molière who said of the Pauper when he brought back the gold piece that other saying, so often quoted, so little understood, it seems to me, in its gravest meaning,—a saying that escaped from a habit of mind essentially philosophical: "Where must virtue needs go niche itself!"—*Où la vertu va-t-elle se nicher!* No man of Port-Royal or its congeners (note this well) would have had such a thought; the contrary would have seemed to him more natural, the poor man being, in the eyes of the Christian, an object of special mercies and virtues. It was he, too, who, talking with Chapelle of the philosophy of Gassendi, their common master, said, while disputing as to the theory of atoms, "Never mind the morality of it." Molière belongs simply, as I think, to the religion, I do not say of his Don Juan or of Epicurus, but of Chremes in Terence: *Homo sum*. We may apply to him in a serious sense Tartuffe's speech: "A man . . . a man, in short!" This man knew frailties and was not surprised by them; he practised good more than he believed in it; he reckoned upon vices, and his most burning indignation was uttered by a laugh. He considered this sad humanity as an old child now incurable, to be corrected a little, but, above all, to be soothed by amusing it.

To-day, when we judge of things from a distance and by clear results, Molière seems to us much more radically aggressive against the society of his time than he thought he was: this is a danger we should guard against in judging him. (pp. 95-8)

The moment when Molière came upon the scene was exactly that which suited the liberty that he had, and that which he gave himself. Louis XIV, still young, supported him in all his bold and free endeavours, and protected him against whoever attacked him. In *Tartuffe,* and also in the tirade of Don Juan against advancing hypocrisy, Molière foresaw with his divining eye the sad end of a noble reign, and he hastened, when it was with great difficulty possible and when it seemed to be useful, to denounce with pointed finger the growing vice. (p. 99)

Molière was so thoroughly *man* in the freest sense, that he obtained, later, the anathemas of the haughty and so-called reforming philosophy just as he had first won those of the ruling episcopacy. On four different counts—*l'Avare, Le Misanthrope, Georges Dandin,* and *Le Bourgeois Gentilhomme*—Jean Jacques will not listen to wit, and spares him no more than Bossuet did.

All this is simply to say that, like Shakespeare and Cervantes, like three or four superior geniuses through the course of ages, Molière is a painter of human nature to its depths, without acceptance or concern about worship, fixed dogma, or formal interpretation; that in attacking the society of his time he represented the life of the greater number; and that in the midst of established manners and morals, which he chastised to the quick, he is found to have written of mankind. (pp. 100-01)

Molière . . . began his career by the practice of life and passions before painting them. But it must not be thought that his inward existence had two separate and successive parts, like that of many eminent moralists and satirists—a first part, active and more or less ardent; then, the fire subsiding from excesses or from age, a second part of sour,

biting observation, disillusion, in short, which harks back to motives, scrutinises, and mocks them. That is not at all the case with Molière, or with any of the great men endowed, to his degree, with the genius that creates. Distinguished men who go through this double phase, reaching the second quickly, acquire, as they advance, only a shrewd, sagacious, critical talent, like M. de La Rochefoucauld, for example; they have no animating impulse nor power of creation. Dramatic genius, that of Molière in particular, has this that is singular about it: its method of proceeding is wholly different and more complex. In the midst of the passions of his youth, of hot-headed, credulous transports like those of the mass of men, Molière had, even then, in a high degree, the gift of observing and reproducing, the faculty of sounding and seizing hidden springs which he knew how to bring into play to the great amusement of every one; and later, in the midst of his complete, sad knowledge of the human heart and its divers motives, from the height of his melancholy as a contemplative philosopher, he still preserved, in his own heart, the youth of active impressions, the faculty of passions, of love and its jealousies—a sacred heart indeed! Sublime contradiction, and one we love to find in the life of a great poet; an indefinable assemblage which corresponds with what is most mysterious in the talent of dramatic comedy; I mean the painting of bitter realities by means of lively, easy, joyous personages who all have natural characters; the deepest probing of the heart of man exhibiting itself in active and original beings, who translate it to the eye by simply being themselves! (pp. 105-06)

Though [*L'Étourdi*] is only a comedy of intrigue imitated from the Italian imbroglios, what fire already in it! what flaming petulance! what reckless activity thrilling with imagination in Mascarille! whom the stage up to that time had never known. No doubt Mascarille, such as he first appears, is only the son in direct line of the valets of Italian farce and ancient comedy, one of the thousand of that lineage anterior to Figaro: but soon, in the *Précieuses Ridicules,* he will individualise himself, he is Mascarille the marquis, a wholly modern valet in the livery of Molière alone. The *Dépit amoureux,* in spite of the unlikelihood and commonplace conventionality of its disguises and recognitions, presents, in the scene between Lucile and Éraste, a situation of heart eternally young, eternally renewed from the dialogue of Horace and Lydia; a situation that Molière himself renews in *Tartuffe* and in the *Bourgeois Gentilhomme* with success always, but never surpassing in excellence this first picture; he who knew best how to scourge and ridicule shows how well he knew love.

The *Précieuses Ridicules,* acted in 1659, attacked modern manners to the quick. In it Molière abandoned Italian plots and stage traditions to see things with his own eyes, to speak aloud and firmly, according to his nature, against the most irritating enemy of all great dramatic poets at their outset—affected and finical pedantry, the shallow taste of the alcove, which is mere distaste. (pp. 109-10)

After the rather coarse, but honest, spice of the *Cocu imaginaire,* and the pale but noble essay of *Don Garcie,* Molière returned, in the *École des Maris,* to the broad road of observation and truth with gaiety. Sganarelle, whom the *Cocu imaginaire* showed us for the first time, reappears and is developed in the *École des Maris;* Sganarelle succeeds Mascarille in Molière's favour. Mascarille was still young and a bachelor; Sganarelle is essentially a married man. Derived probably from the Italian stage, employed by Molière in the farce of the *Médecin volant,* introduced upon the regular stage in a rôle that has a little of the Scarron about it, he naturalises himself there as Mascarille had done. The Sganarelle of Molière in all his varied aspects, valet, husband, father of Lucinde, brother of Ariste, tutor, poetaster, doctor, is a personage who belongs to Molière, as Panurge to Rabelais, Falstaff to Shakespeare, Sancho to Cervantes; he is the ugly side of human nature embodied; the aged, crabbed side, morose, selfish, base, timid, by turns pitiful or humbugging, surly or absurd. At certain joyous moments, such as that when he touches the nurse's bosom, Sganarelle reminds us of the rotund Gorgibus who, in turn, brings back the goodman Chrysale, that other jovial character with a paunch. But Sganarelle, puny like his forefather, Panurge, has left other posterity worthy of both of them, among whom it is proper to mention Pangloss, not forgetting Victor Hugo's Gringore. In Molière, facing Sganarelle at the highest point of the stage, stands Alceste: Alceste, in other words, all that there is most serious, most noble, loftiest in comedy; the point where ridicule comes close to courage, to virtue. One line more, and the comic ceases; we reach a personage purely generous, almost heroic and tragical. Sganarelle possesses three-fourths of the comic ladder, the lower by himself alone, the middle he shares with Gorgibus and Chrysale; Alceste holds the rest, the highest—Sganarelle and Alceste; in them is all of Molière.

Voltaire says that if Molière had written nothing but the *École des Maris* he would still be an excellent writer of comedy. Boileau cannot witness the *École des Femmes* without addressing to Molière (then attacked on all sides) certain easy stanzas in which he extols the "charming naïveté of the comedy, which equals those of Terence supposed to be written by Scipio." Those two amusing masterpieces were separated in their production by the light but skilful comedy-impromptu called *Les Fâcheux,* written, learned, and represented in fifteen days for the famous fête at Vaux. Never did the free, quick talent of Molière for making verse show more plainly than in this satirical comedy, especially in the scenes of the piquet and the hunt. The scene of the hunt was not in the play at its first representation; but Louis XIV, pointing with his finger to M. de Soyecourt, a great huntsman, said to Molière: "There is an original you have not yet copied." The next day the scene of the huntsman was written and acted. Boileau, whose own manner of writing the play of the *Fâcheux* preceded and surpassed, thought of it, no doubt, when he asked Molière, three years later, where he "found his rhymes." The truth is, Molière never sought them; he did not habitually make his second line before the first, nor did he wait half a day or more to find in some remote corner the word that escaped him. His was the rapid vein, the ready wit of Regnier, of d'Aubigné, never haggling about a phrase or a word even at the risk of a lame line, a clumsy turn, or, at worst, an hiatus—a Duc de Saint-Simon in poesy; with a method of expression always looking forward, always sure, which each flow of thought fills out and colours. (pp. 111-13)

[To] the hour of his death in 1673, Molière never ceased to produce. For the king, for the Court, and for fêtes, for the pleasure of the public at large, for the interests of his company, for his own fame, and for posterity, Molière multiplied himself, as it were, and sufficed for all. Nothing

hypercritical in him, nothing of the author in his study. True poet of drama, his works are for the stage, for action; he does not write them, so to speak, he plays them. His life as a comedian of the provinces had been somewhat that of the primitive popular poets, the ancient rhapsodists, the minstrels and pilgrims of Passion; these went about, as we know, repeating one another, taking the plots and subjects of others, adding thereto as occasion demanded, making little account of themselves and their own individual work, and seldom keeping "copy" of that which they represented. It was thus that the plots and improvisations in the Italian manner which Molière multiplied (we have the titles of a dozen) during his strolling years in the provinces were lost, with the exception of two, the *Médecin volant* and the *Barbouillé.* (pp. 113-14)

Molière, the most creative and the most inventive of geniuses, is the one, perhaps, who has imitated the most, and on all sides; this is still another trait which he has in common with the primitive popular poets and the illustrious dramatists who followed them. Boileau, Racine, André Chénier, poets of study and taste, imitate also; but their method of imitation is much more ingenious, circumspect, and disguised, and it chiefly bears on details. Molière's method of imitating is far freer, fuller, and at the mercy of his memory. His enemies attacked him for stealing half his works from the old bookstalls. He lived, during his first manner, on the traditional Italian and Gallic farce; after the *Précieuses* and the *École des Maris* he became himself; he governed and overtopped his imitations, and, without lessening them much, he mingled them with a fund of original observation. The river continued to float wood from its banks, but the current was wider and more and more powerful. What we must carefully recognise is that Molière's imitations are from all sources and infinitely varied; they have a character of loyalty, free and easy as they are, something of that primitive life where all was in common; although usually they are well worked-in, descending sometimes to pure detail: Plautus and Terence for whole tales, Straparolo and Boccaccio for subject matter, Rabelais and Regnier for characters, Boisrobert, Rotrou, and Cyrano for scenes, Horace, Montaigne, and Balzac for simple phrases—all are there; but all is transformed, nothing is the same. In a word, these imitations are for us chiefly the fortunate summary of a whole race of minds, a whole past of comedy in a new, superior, and original type, as a child beloved of heaven who, with an air of youth, expresses all his forbears.

Each of Molière's plays, following them in the order of their appearance, would furnish matter for a long and extended history; this work has already been done, and too well done by others for me to undertake it; to do so would be merely copying and reproducing. Around the *École des Femmes,* in 1662, and later around *Tartuffe* battles were fought as they had been round *The Cid* and were to be around *Phèdre;* those were the illustrious days for dramatic art. The *Critique de l'École des Femmes* and the *Impromptu de Versailles* sufficiently explain the first contest, which was chiefly a quarrel of taste and art, though religion slipped in àpropos of the rules of marriage given to Agnes. The *Placets au Roi* and the preface to *Tartuffe* show the wholly moral and philosophical character of the second struggle, so often and so vehemently renewed afterwards.

But what I wish to dwell on here is that, attacked by big-ots, envied by authors, sought by nobles, valet to the king, and his indispensable resource in all his fêtes, Molière, troubled by passion and domestic jars, consumed with marital jealousy, frequently ill with his weak lungs and his cough, director of a company, an indefatigable actor him-self while living on a diet of milk,—Molière, I say, for fif-teen years was equal to all demands; at each arising neces-sity his genius was present and responding to it, keeping, moreover, his times of inward inspiration and initiative. Between the duty hurriedly paid at Versailles and at Chan-tilly, and his hearty contributions for the laughter of the *bourgeoisie,* Molière found time for thoughtful works des-tined to become immortal. For Louis XIV, his benefactor and supporter, he was always ready; *L'Amour médecin* was written, learned, and acted in five days; the *Princesse d'Élide* has only the first act in verse, the rest is in prose, for, as a witty contemporary of Molière said, "Comedy had time to fasten only one buskin, but she appeared when the clock struck, though the other buskin was not laced." In the interests of his company he was sometimes obliged to hurry work; as he did when he supplied his the-atre with a *Don Juan,* because the actors of the hôtel de Bourgogne, and also those of Mademoiselle, had theirs, and the statue that walked was a town marvel. But these distractions did not keep him from thinking of Boileau, of strict pledges, of himself, and of the human race, in the *Misanthrope,* in *Tartuffe,* in the *Femmes Savantes.* The year of the *Misanthrope* is, in this sense, the most memorable and the most significant in Molière's life. (pp. 116-19)

Molière has been lauded in so many ways, as painter of manners and morals and human life, that I wish to indi-cate more especially a side which has been brought too lit-tle into light, or, I may say, ignored. Until his death, Molière was continually progressing in the *poesy* of come-dy. That he progressed in moral observation and in what is called high comedy—that of the *Misanthrope, Tartuffe,* and the *Femmes Savantes*—is too evident a fact, and I shall not dwell upon it; but around and through that de-velopment, where reason grew firmer and still firmer, and observation more and more mature, we ought to admire the influx, every rising and bubbling, of the comic fancy, very frolicsome, very rich, very inexhaustible, which I dis-tinguish strongly (though the boundaries be difficult to de-fine) from the rather broad farce and the Scarronesque dregs in which Molière dabbled in the beginning. How shall I express it? It is the difference between some chorus of Aristophanes and certain rash outbreaks of Rabelais. The genius of ironical and biting gaiety has its lyric mo-ments also, its pure merriment, its sparkling laugh, redou-bled, almost causeless in its prolonging, aloof from reality, like a frolic flame that flutters and flits the lighter when the coarse combustion ceases—a laughter of the gods, su-preme, inextinguishable. This is what many minds of fine taste, Voltaire, Vauvenargues, and others, have not felt in appreciating what are called Molière's latest farces; and Schlegel [see excerpt dated 1811] should have felt it more. He who mystically celebrated the poetic final fireworks of Calderon ought not to have been blind to these rockets of dazzling gaiety, these auroras at an opposite pole of the dramatic universe. *Monsieur de Porceaugnac,* the *Bour-geois Gentilhomme,* the *Malade imaginaire,* witness in the highest degree to this sparkling, electrifying gaiety which, in its way, rivals in fancy the *Midsummer Night's Dream* and the *Tempest.* Pourceaugnac, M. Jourdain, Argant,

they are the Sganarelle element continued, but more poet-ic, freer from the farce of the *Barbouillé,* often lifted, as it were, above realism. (pp. 120-21)

In that order of minds which includes, through divers ages and in divers ranks, Cervantes, Rabelais, Le Sage, Fiel-ding, Beaumarchais, and Walter Scott, Molière is, with Shakespeare, the most complete example of the dramatic and, properly so-called, creative faculty. Shakespeare has, above Molière, pathetic touches and flashes of the terri-ble—Macbeth, King Lear, Ophelia—but Molière redeems in some respects this loss by the number, the perfection, the continual and profound weaving together of his princi-pal characters. In all these great men evidently, but in Molière more evidently still, the dramatic genius is not an outside extension, expansion of a lyrical and personal fac-ulty, which, starting from its own interior sentiments, toils to transport them outwardly and make them live, as much as possible, under other masks (Byron in his tragedies, for instance); nor is it the pure and simple application of a faculty of critical, analytical observation, which carefully exhibits in the personages of its composition the scattered traits it has collected. There is a whole class of true dram-atists who have something lyrical, in one sense almost blind, in their inspiration; a warmth, a glow, born of an inward vivid sentiment, which they impart directly to their personages. (pp. 130-31)

Hardly was he dead, before Molière was appreciated on all sides. We know the magnificent lines of Boileau, who rose in them to eloquence [see excerpt dated 1683]. Molière's reputation has since shone ever higher and incontestable. The eighteenth century did more than confirm it,—it pro-claimed it with a sort of philosophical pride. Our own young century, accepting that fame and never calling it in question, made use of it, at certain times, as an auxiliary, as an arm of defence or condemnation. But later, compre-hending it in a more equitable manner, comparing it, ac-cording to philosophy and art, with other renowns of neighbouring nations, it has better understood and re-spected it. Constantly enlarging in this way, Molière's rep-utation (marvellous privilege!) has reached its true mea-sure, has equalled truth, but has not passed beyond it. His genius is henceforth one of the ornaments, one of the claims of the genius of humanity itself. Among the great world-fames that survive and last there are many that maintain themselves afar, so to speak; whose names last better than their works in the memory of mankind. Mo-lière is of a smaller number, whose life and works are sharers in all the possible conquests of the new civilisa-tion. Reputations, future geniuses, books, may multiply; civilisations may transform themselves hereafter, but five or six great works have entered inalienably the depths of human thought. Every coming man who can read is one reader the more for Molière. (pp. 139-40)

> *C. A. Sainte-Beuve, "Molière (1622-1673)," in his* Portraits of the Seventeenth Century: Historic and Literary, *translated by Katharine P. Worme-ley, G. P. Putnam's Sons, 1904, pp. 85-140.*

HENRI VAN LAUN (essay date 1875)

> [*Van Laun was a Dutch translator, educator, and essayist whose texts on English dramatic literature were widely read in the nineteenth century. In the following excerpt from the*

preface to his translation of Molière's works, he provides a general discussion of Molière's characters, his use of language, and how the plays may be classified.]

I think it will be generally admitted that Molière is the greatest comic poet France has produced, and that he is equal, if not superior, to any writer of character-comedies on the ancient or modern stage. His plays may be divided into six classes or groups:—*First*, the small dramatic poems or pastorals, such as **Psyché, les Amants magnifiques, la Princesse d'Élide, les Fâcheux, Mélicerte, la Pastorale comique**, and **Amphitryon**, which he wrote for court festivals, by order of Louis XIV.; *Second*, his farces, written to suit the taste of the less refined, such as **les Fourberies de Scapin, le Bourgeois-gentilhomme, la Comtesse d'Escarbagnas, Monsieur de Pourceaugnac, le Médecin mal-gré lui, George Dandin, le Sicilien, l'Amour Médecin, le Mariage forcé, Sganarelle**, and **les Précieuses Ridicules**,—and yet, notwithstanding their absurdity, attracting the higher classes by their witty descriptions of grotesque characters; *Third*, his comedies—**l'Etourdi, l'École des Maris, l'École des femmes, l'Avare, Don Garcie de Navarre, le Dépit amoureux**, and **le Malade imaginaire**—in each of which the principal object seems to have been to bring into prominence one particular vice or folly, with all its necessary consequences; *Fourth*, those splendidly conceived plays, **Don Juan, les Femmes savantes, Tartuffe**, and **le Misanthrope**, which pourtray humanity in all its aspects; *Fifth*, those critical short pieces, **la Critique de l'École des femmes** and **l'Impromftu de Versailles**, in which, with masterly acumen, he defends his own plays and attacks his adversaries; and *Sixth*, those early attempts of his comic muse, **le Médecin volant** and **la Jalousie du Barbouillé**, which gave ample promise of what he afterwards became.

It is always difficult to state when a playwright has taken from any other author, for the saying, *"Je prends mon bien partout où je le trouve"* ["I take my goods where I find them"], has covered, and still covers, a multitude of literary sins. Moreover, Molière possessed a power of absorption and assimilation which enabled him so to vivify the materials he borrowed that they became new creations of incomparable value. In this sense, to take an idea or a mere thought from another author can hardly be called an imitation; and though Molière, in his first two or three plays, translated several scenes from Italian authors, he has scarcely ever done so in his latter pieces. To mention which of his comedies I consider, or rather which are generally thought, the best, would be difficult, where everything is so eminent; for in all his plays characters will be found which demonstrate his thorough knowledge of nature, and display his genius. To discover these little peculiarities in which the specific difference of character consists; to distinguish between what men do from custom or fashion, and what they perform through their own natural idiosyncracy; to select, unite, and draw these peculiarities to a dramatic point, demands real genius, and that of the highest order.

Generally Molière's satire is directed against hypocrites, against quacks, against the affectation of learning amongst ladies, and against snobbishness. If I were to enumerate, however, all the characters our author has created, I should arrive at the sum total of all human passions, all human feelings, all human vices, and at every type of the different classes of society. In *l'Avare* sordid avarice is represented by *Harpagon*, and want of order and lavish prod-

LE

FESTIN

DE

PIERRE,

COMEDIE.

Par J. B. P. DE MOLIERE.

Edition nouvelle & toute differente de celle qui a parû jusqu'à present.

A AMSTERDAM.

M. DC. LXXXIII.

First-edition title page of the work better known as Don Juan.

igality by his son *Cléante*; in **le Festin de Pierre** the type of shameless vice is *Don Juan, Donna Elvira* displays resignation amidst love disgracefully betrayed, *Mathurine* primitive and uncultivated coquetry, and *Mons. Dimanche* the greed of a tradesman who wishes to make money. *Tartuffe*, in the comedy of that name, represents hypocrisy and downright wickedness. *M. Jourdain*, a tradesman who has made money and who imitates a nobleman, is, in **le Bourgeois-gentilhomme**, no bad specimen of self-sufficient vanity, folly, and ignorance; whilst *Dorante*, in the same play, is a well-copied example of the fashionable swindler of that period. In **le Misanthrope**, *Alceste* pourtrays great susceptibility of tenderness and honour, *Célimène*, wit without any feeling, and *Philinte*, quiet common sense, amiability, intelligence, instruction, knowledge of the world, and a spirit of refined criticism. This is also displayed by *Chrysalde* in **l'École des Femmes**, by *Béralde* in **le Malade imaginaire**, and by *Ariste* in **l'École des Maris;** whilst *Sganarelle* in the latter play is an example of foolish and coarse jealousy. *George Dandin*, in the comedy of that name, is a model of weakness of character and irresolution, *Angélique*, an impudent and heartless woman, and her father, *Monsieur de Sotenville*, the coarse, proud, country squire of that age. *Argan*, in **le Malade imaginaire**, represents egotism and pusillanimity; *Vadius* and *Trissotin*, in **les Femmes savantes**, pedantic foolishness and self-conceit; *Agnès*, in **l'École des Femmes**, cunning as well as ingenuity; and *Aglaure*, in **Psyché**, feminine jealousy. Finally, *Nicole, Dorine, Martine, Marotte, Toinette*, and *Lisette* personify the homely servant-girls, who, possessing plain, downright common-sense, point out the affectation and ridiculous pretensions of their companions and superiors; whilst *Claudine*, in *George Dandin,* Nérine, in *Mons. de Pourceaugnac*, and *Frosine*, in the *Avare*, represent the intriguant in petticoats,—a female *Mascarille.* (pp. i-iii)

Another not less remarkable faculty of Molière is that the language his personages employ is precisely suited to them. It varies according to their age, character, rank, and profession, whilst the very sentence becomes long or short, stilted or tripping, pedantic or elastic, finical or natural, coarse or over-refined, according as an old or young man, a marquis or a citizen, a scholar or a dunce, has to speak. It can be said of Molière, more than of any other author we know, that he always employs the right word in the right place.... Even his peasants speak correctly the dialect of the province or county Molière gives them as the land of their birth; all his creations bear proofs of his genius in an incisiveness of expression and clearness of thought which no other writer has equalled.

Molière has written some of his comedies in prose, others in verse,—and in verse that has none of the stiffness of the ordinary French rhyme, but which becomes in his hands a delightful medium for sparkling sallies, bitter sarcasms, well sustained and sprightly conversations. He has also managed blank verse with wonderful precision,—a rare gift among French authors. The whole of *le Sicilien*, the love scenes of the *Avare*, the monologues of *Georges Dandin*, and certain scenes of *le Festin de Pierre*, are written in this metre.

Molière's plays have been translated into every language of Europe, and some of them even into the classical tongues; they have found admirers wherever intellectual beings are congregated; they have been carefully conned and studied by literary men of every age and clime; and Goethe himself read some of these comedies every year. (pp. iv-v)

Molière wrote his plays to be represented on the stage, and not to be read in the study only; that therefore we must recall, on reading him, the change of voice, the step, the smile, the gesture, the twinkle of the eye or movement of the head in the actor. Thus we are never tired of perusing him; he never cloys; we can remember all his good sayings, quote them, study him again and again, and every time discover fresh beauties.

A remarkable characteristic of Molière is that he does not exaggerate; his fools are never over-witty, his buffoons too grotesque, his men of wit too anxious to display their smartness, and his fine gentlemen too fond of immodest and ribald talk. His satire is always kept within bounds, his repartees are never out of place, his plots are but seldom intricate, and the moral of his plays is not obtruded, but follows as a natural consequence of the whole. He rarely rises to those lofty realms of poetry where Shakespeare so often soars, for he wrote, not idealistic but character-comedies; which is, perhaps, the reason that some of his would-be admirers consider him rather commonplace. His claim to distinction is based only on strong common sense, good manners, sound morality, real wit, true humour, a great, facile, and accurate command of language, and a photographic delineation of nature. It cannot be denied that there is little action in his plays, but there is a great deal of natural conversation; his personages show

that he was a most attentive observer of men, even at court, where a certain varnish of over-refinement conceals nearly all individual features. He always makes vice appear in its most ridiculous aspect, in order to let his audience laugh at and despise it; his aim is to correct the follies of the age by exposing them to ridicule. (pp. vi-vii)

Henri Van Laun, in a preface to The Dramatic Works of Molière, Vol. I, *translated by Henri Van Laun, William Paterson, 1875, pp. i-xviii.*

MATTHEW ARNOLD   (essay date 1879)

[*Arnold is considered one of the most influential authors of the later Victorian period in England. While he is well known today as a poet, in his own time he asserted his greatest influence through his prose writings. Arnold's forceful literary criticism, which is based on his humanistic belief in the value of balance and clarity in literature, significantly shaped modern theory. In the following excerpt from an essay originally published in 1879, he compares Molière as a comic poet with Shakespeare as a tragedian, deeming Molière a great "theatre-poet" and noticing what he considers the artificiality of his poetic form.*]

Molière is by far the chief name in French poetry; he is one of the very greatest names in all literature. He has admirable and delightful power, penetrativeness, insight; a masterly criticism of life. But he is a comic poet. Why? Had he no seriousness and depth of nature? He had profound seriousness. And would not a dramatic poet with this depth of nature be a tragedian if he could? Of course he would. For only by breasting in full the storm and cloud of life, breasting it and passing through it and above it, can the dramatist who feels the weight of mortal things liberate himself from the pressure, and rise, as we all seek to rise, to content and joy. Tragedy breasts the pressure of life. Comedy eludes it, half liberates itself from it by irony. But the tragedian, if he has the sterner labour, has also the higher prize. Shakespeare has more joy than Molière, more assurance and peace. *Othello*, with all its passion and terror, is on the whole a work animating and fortifying; more so a thousand times than *George Dandin*, which is mournfully depressing. Molière, if he could, would have given us Othellos instead of George Dandins; let us not doubt it. If he did not give Othellos to us, it was because the highest sort of poetic power was wanting to him. And if the highest sort of poetic power had been not wanting to him but present, he would have found no adequate form of dramatic verse for conveying it, he would have had to create one. For such tasks Molière had not power; and this is only another way of saying that for the highest tasks in poetry the genius of his nation appears to have not power. But serious spirit and great poet that he was, Molière had far too sound an instinct to attempt so earnest a matter as tragic drama with inadequate means. It would have been a heart-breaking business for him. He did not attempt it, therefore, but confined himself to comedy.

The *Misanthrope* and the *Tartuffe* are comedy, but they are comedy in verse, poetic comedy. They employ the established verse of French dramatic poetry, the Alexandrine. Immense power has gone to the making of them; a world of vigorous sense, piercing observation, pathetic meditation, profound criticism of life. Molière had also one great advantage as a dramatist over Shakespeare; he wrote for a more developed theatre, a more developed society. Moreover he was at the same time, probably, by nature a better *theatre-poet* than Shakespeare; he had a keener sense for theatrical situation. Shakespeare is not rightly to be called, as Goethe calls him, an epitomator rather than a dramatist; but he may rightly be called rather a dramatist than a theatre-poet. Molière,—and here his French nature stood him in good stead,—was a theatre-poet of the very first order. Comedy, too, escapes, as has been already said, the test of entire seriousness; it remains, by the law of its being, in a region of comparative lightness and of irony. What is artificial can pass in comedy more easily. In spite of all these advantages, the *Misanthrope* and the *Tartuffe* have, and have by reason of their poetic form, an artificiality which makes itself too much felt, and which provokes weariness. The freshness and power of Molière are best felt when he uses prose, in pieces such as the *Avare*, or the *Fourberies de Scapin*, or *George Dandin*. How entirely the contrary is the case with Shakespeare; how undoubtedly is it his verse which shows his power most! But so inadequate a vehicle for dramatic poetry is the French Alexandrine, that its sway hindered Molière, one may think, from being a tragic poet at all, in spite of his having gifts for this highest form of dramatic poetry which are immeasurably superior to those of any other French poet. And in comedy, where Molière thought he could use the Alexandrine, and where he did use it with splendid power, it yet in a considerable degree hampered and lamed him, so that this true and great poet is actually most satisfactory in his prose. (pp. 220-23)

Matthew Arnold, "The French Play in London," in his *Irish Essays and Others, Smith, Elder, & Co.,* 1882, pp. 208-43.

FERDINAND BRUNETIÈRE (essay date 1898)

[*An influential French critic of the latter half of the nineteenth century, Brunetière taught for many years at the prestigious École normale supérieure and edited and contributed frequently to the popular journal* Revue des deux mondes. *Conservative and classical in his tastes, Brunetière opposed the aesthetics of Romanticism, Impressionism, and Naturalism. His most important contribution to literary criticism is his Darwinian-based theory of the evolution of genres, which he explicated in his* L'évolution des genres dans l'histoire de la littérature *(1890). In the following excerpt, Brunetière describes Molière's philosophy of human nature, focusing on* Tartuffe *as it reveals the dramatist's attitude toward religion.*]

I know it is difficult to make oneself understood, and I willingly admit that whoever does not succeed in doing so has himself to blame. But really, with every allowance for my own incompetence, I would never have believed it would have been so hard to convince certain Frenchmen—dramatic authors, professors, journalists, and lecturers—that Molière would not be Molière had he not thought sometimes; that there is something more in him than a classic Labiche; and that after seeing the *École des Femmes* or the *Malade imaginaire*, and laughing heartily at Arnolphe or the worthy Argan, we still carry away with us something to think over for a long time. For having dared to say so, indeed, I find that I am reminded on all hands of the false modesty which is expected of the commentator, and I would have required to treat Molière as a merry-andrew or buffoon, in order not to cause alarm among

those who will on no account allow their notion of him to be disturbed; or rather, according to their view, it is in this way that he will now have to be treated. (p. 66)

[We] forget that he would be dead, like so many others who none the less did not fail to amuse the good folk of their time, had there been nothing more in his work than in theirs; and that, since we must possess for the understanding of the *École des Femmes* or *Tartufe* what is ironically called "enlightenment" and "intellect," which are quite unnecessary for the appreciation of *La Cagnotte*, this is just the reason why he is Molière.

I shall lay stress at the outset on this remark. Nobody now is unaware that the subject of the *École des Femmes*, which was borrowed by Molière from Scarron, is essentially the same as that of the *Folies amoureuses* and the *Barbier de Séville*. There is the same situation, the same intrigue, the same dénouement. There are the same characters too; Bartholo, Albert, or Arnolphe, it is still the same guardian who is duped; Rosine, Agathe, or Agnès, it is still the same artless girl who makes game of him; Almaviva, Éraste, or Horace, it is still the same lover who lends his aid, young, resourceful, and triumphant. Yet, in whatever esteem we hold Beaumarchais or Regnard, they are not Molière, neither in build nor in class, nor perhaps in species, and though it is possible to prefer them to him, we never venture a comparison.... [The] verses of Molière have not in general the elegance and ease, the grace and facility of those of Regnard: that his style, though more *podded* perhaps, to use Sainte-Beuve's happy expression, is yet not so lively, smart, or clever, nor its air so free and sprightly. And who will refuse to admit that, if the plot of the *Barbier de Séville* is not better than that of the *École des Femmes*, it is at least in a way more *implex*, as used to be said, more ingenious, richer in surprises, above all nearer our modern taste? From Molière to Beaumarchais, during the insensible decadence of all the other parts of the dramatic art, one alone has been perfected, and this is precisely the intrigue; and the comedy of Beaumarchais marks the principal epoch in this progress.

Since, then, it is neither by the complexity nor the ingeniousness of the intrigue, nor by quality of style, nor novelty of invention, that Molière is as superior to his first model as to his imitators, what is there left, and what conclusion is to be drawn? There is left this, that it is by the depth of the penetration with which he has drawn his characters; by the truth of an imitation of life which could not succeed but from a certain manner, at once personal and original, of seeing, understanding, and judging life itself; in one word, by the reach, or, in another, by the philosophy of his work.

It is this philosophy which, in the following pages, I shall try to define and characterise. Not that I wish, as may be suspected, to ascribe to the author of the *Fourberies de Scapin* what is called a connected system. I shall not forget that I am speaking of a dramatic author, and that *Tartufe*, the *École des Femmes*, and the *Malade imaginaire* are primarily comedies. But what I shall not forget also is that Molière thinks; and since he makes me think, I wish to know on what? Since he forces me to reflect on certain questions, I wish to know what precisely these questions are. Since he has put them, I wish to know how he has decided them. And if these questions do still concern us, and are still of living interest, I wish to know, in short, how far

I am myself for or against Molière. His comedies are not exactly *theses*, but they are not very far from being so. They have more connection with the *Fils naturel* than with *Adrienne Lecouvreur*, or with the *Ami des Femmes* than with *Mademoiselle de Belle-Isle*. Nothing could be more unlike anecdotes stretched over five acts. In this sense, the philosophy of Molière may be said to be Molière himself, and I shall endeavour to show that, properly understood, it is Molière in his entirety.

It does not appear that he took any trouble to disguise his philosophy, nor consequently is it difficult to recognise or to name. *Naturalistic* or *realistic*, what the comedy of Molière always preaches, by its faults as much as by its merits, is the imitation of nature; and its great lesson in aesthetics and in morality, is that we must submit, and, if we can, conform to nature. By this, by the endeavour after a faithful imitation of nature, is to be explained the subordination, in his plays, of the situations to the characters; the simplicity of the intrigues, the most of which are only "scenes of private life"; the unsatisfactoriness of the dénouements, which, from the very fact that they are not dénouements, bear a closer resemblance to life, where nothing begins or ends. By this also is to be explained the quality and the depth of the comic art of Molière. For if, among the many ways of provoking laughter, Molière knew too well his triple business of author, actor, and manager to despise or overlook any of them, not excepting the easiest and commonest, there is yet one which he prefers, and this way consists in making merry over habits or prejudices which are conquered by the all-powerfulness of nature. And by this still, by his confidence in nature, is to be explained also, and above all, the character of his satire, since he directed it only against those whose fault or absurdity lay in disguising, falsifying, corrupting, restraining, or endeavouring to coerce nature.

In the same way he never inveighed against licentiousness or debauchery; he never inveighed against ambition: he never seems even to have had the intention of attacking them. These are vices which are instinctive and conformable to nature: they are self-confessed, and sometimes even vaunted. What more natural in a man than to wish to raise himself above his fellows, unless it be to play with the pleasures of life? But, on the other hand, "précieuses" of every sort and absurd marquises, ageing prudes and grey-haired gallants, bourgeois people who would be gentlemen and matrons who dabble in philosophy, sextons or great lords who cover "their fierce resentment under the cloak of heaven's interest," the Don Juans and Tartufes, the Philamintes and Jourdains, the Arnolphes and Arinoés, the Acastes and Madelons, the Diafoiruses and Purgons—these are his victims. They are all those who disguise nature, who, to distinguish themselves from her, begin by leaving her, and who, flattering themselves on being stronger or cleverer than she is, have had the pretensions to govern her and reduce her to their sway.

On the other hand all those who follow nature, true nature, the Martines and Nicoles, his Chrysale and Madame Jourdain, Agnès, Alceste, and Henriette, with what sympathy have they not always been treated? "Such are his people, such is the way to act." They show themselves just as they really are; and by nothing but showing themselves they bring into prominence the universal and somewhat mean complacency of Philinte, the fierce egoism of Arnolphe, the stupidity of M. Jourdain, the pretentious sim-

pering of Armande, or the solemn affectedness of her mother Philaminte. Is the lesson not clear enough? On the side of those who follow nature, on the side of the former, are also truth, good sense, honesty, and virtue; on the other side are absurdity, pretension, stupidity, hypocrisy—that is to say, on the side of those who defy nature, who treat her as an enemy, and whose doctrine is to fight and triumph over her. (pp. 67-72)

I shall pass rapidly over his first pieces: *L'Étourdi, Le Dépit amoureux, Les Précieuses ridicules, Sganarelle, L'École des Maris*. Not that, if we look at them closely, we can fail to see the thought of Molière and the liberty of his banter already giving promise of greater boldness. If the *Dépit amoureux* and the *Étourdi* are only canvases in the Italian manner, on which Molière is content to trick out the arabesques of his fancy—more brilliant, more lively, more witty too perhaps, at that time while youth had not yet left him, than in the ceremony of the *Bourgeois Gentilhomme* or the *Malade imaginaire*—the *Précieuses ridicules* and the *École des Maris* are already a spirited and a well-ordered attack on all those who designed, as we have said, to disguise or deck out nature. Their very succession seems to me instructive. Instead of asking M. de Mascarille simply to sit down, perhaps you say to him, with the Misses Gorgibus, "Satisfy the desire which this chair has to embrace you"? Then you are quite ridiculous, as you are not at all natural. You are, however, only ridiculous. But, instead of overstraining nature and making her, if possible, as ridiculous as we are, perhaps we aim at forcing, cramping, and regulating her? Let us be on our guard. We meet the fate of the Sganarelle of the *École des Maris* and his Isabelle, and we are not only ridiculous, but begin to be dull, harsh, and offensive. First proof or first sketch of Arnolphe, this Sganarelle differs from him only in being treated less seriously, in the style of Scarron, if I may say so, rather than in the great style of Molière. Now let us come to Arnolphe, and speak of the *École des Femmes*. It is the first in date of the great comedies of Molière, that which first placed him in the position he still continues to occupy alone, and, because its intrigue is more amusing, its language more frank, and its philosophy more optimistic, I know several of his devotees who will even now have it to be his masterpiece.

Recently we have heard the amusing proposal that we should talk of the *École des Femmes* as if Molière had entitled it the *Suite de École des Maris* ["Sequel to the School for Husbands"]. It is equally probable that if the *Misanthrope* was entitled the *Mariage fait et défait* ["Marriage Made and Unmade"] we would not see in it what we do see, and what we have at least the right to wish to see, no more than in *Tartufe*—which should rather have been called the *Imposteur*—if Molière had entitled it, for example, *Une Famille au temps de Louis XIV* ["A Family in the Time of Louis XIV"]. This is a curious way of reasoning. To justify Bossuet from the reproaches made against his *Discours sur l'Histoire universelle*, may we not also propose to speak of it as if he had entitled it *Observations sommaires sur l'Histoire de quelques Peuples anciens!* But titles which have no value when the authors have not cared to give them, as for example *Monsieur de Pourceaugnac*, have a value when, like the *École des Femmes*, they signify something of themselves; and—I am no doubt very naive to say so, but it is worth saying—since there are some who hold an opposite opinion.

What then is the "school for wives" according to Molière, and what is the lesson to be derived from his comedy? There is nothing more evident. The "school for wives" is love, or rather it is nature; and the lesson, which is plain enough, is that nature alone will be always stronger than all we can do to thwart its wish. Brought up "in a small convent, far from all experience," Agnès has nothing for her but to be youth, love, and nature.—It even seems that there is a certain element of unfeelingness in her, not to say of simple perverseness, which I should mistrust if only I was Horace!—More natural and less learned, less lively, too, than the Isabella of the *École des Maris*, she has not and never will have the playful grace of the Henriette of the *Femmes savantes*. As for Arnolphe, Molière himself has been careful to inform us, in speaking of him, "that it is not incompatible for a person to be ridiculous in certain things and an honest man in others." He is not, moreover, an old man, as he seems generally to be imagined, and many people believe themselves young at his age. What he has against him is, then, merely his wish to force nature, and he is foolish, ridiculous, and contemptible only in this point. I say nothing of Horace: among the lovers of Molière's repertoire, there is none more insignificant, whose merit more strictly reduces itself to that of his "flaxen peruke," who is, moreover, more worthy of Agnès. He is young like her, as he is simple, and like her he is nature itself. What could be clearer? And without passing the limits of his art, without preaching on the stage, how could Molière have told us that we do not change nature in her essence; that whoever tries to pays for it dearly; and that consequently the beginning of all our evils is the desire to make the attempt.

For, as to those who refuse this interpretation of the *École des Femmes*, I should be curious to know how they explain the effect it produced and the outburst of resentment which followed. Would the very indecent double meaning of the ribbon scene and the joking about "hell's caldrons" have been sufficient? Yes, if you will, and on the condition that they signify something else and more than they really do. But, in reality, what contemporaries thought was that comedy, which had, till then, with the Corneilles, Scarron, and Quinault, confined itself to providing amusement by devices in turn ludicrous and romantic, had now, with Molière, puffed itself up, if I may say so, with quite another ambition, and had, for the first time, in the *École des Femmes*, touched indirectly on the great question which then divided men's minds. They recognised in the *École des Femmes* an aim which went further. It seemed to them in short that this poet was overstepping his limits, that he was extending the sphere of his art even to those objects to which it should remain a stranger, and that he was haughtily leaving behind his rôle of "public entertainer." They endeavoured to silence him. Molière replied to them one after the other with the *Critique de l'École des Femmes*, the *Impromptu de Versailles*, and *Tartufe*.

As he had written the *Critique de l'École des Femmes* in answer to the pedants and prudes and people like his Lysidas and Climène who "censured his finest work," as he had written the *Impromptu de Versailles* to avenge himself on the comedians of the Hôtel de Bourgogne, who did not scruple to attack even his private life, so Molière seems at first to have thought of *Tartufe* only to reply to those, and at the same time to carry fire and sword into their camp, who accused him of indecency and, above all, of impiety in his *École des Femmes*. (pp. 88-93)

Tartufe is first and foremost a reply and an attack. To make no mistake about it, it is sufficient to remember that, before appearing for the first time in the month of May 1664, *Tartufe* was separated from the *École des Femmes*, which was represented for the first time in the winter of 1662, really by an interval of only fifteen or sixteen months—the time necessary to write it!—and by two or three pieces, which are precisely the *Critique de l'École des Femmes*, the *Impromptu de Versailles*, and the *Mariage forcé*. If the first two are sufficiently well known, we must say of the third that Molière doubtless saw in it—as it was expressly written for the king, and in haste—a means of paying his court and of ranging on his side the all-powerful master on whom his adversaries depended as well as he. A clever courtier indeed was Molière; this is a point we must remember; and poor Corneille himself has no humbler dedication than that of the *École des Maris* to the king's brother: "There is nothing so superb as the name I put at the head of this book, and nothing meaner than that which it contains."

This preliminary remark may already throw some light on the true meaning of *Tartufe* and Molière's intentions. It shows at least that *Tartufe*—very different in this respect from *Amphitryon*, for example,—is an act as much as a work: a work of combat, as we would now say, and an act of declared hostility. But against whom? This is the point. For it is no use repeating that Molière himself declared that it was only against "false coiners of devotion." ... (pp. 93-4)

Molière, in writing *Tartufe*, attacked Jansenism, and in Jansenism, as we shall now see, religion itself.

This would never be doubted but for the accepted custom of considering in *Tartufe* only Tartufe himself; and when Tartufe only is considered there is no trouble in showing that he really is Tartufe and a hypocrite. "The traitor is to be plainly seen through his mask; he is recognised at once in his true colours; and the rolling of his eyes and his honeyed tones impose"—only on Madame Pernelle, an old fool, and her son Orgon. Tartufe sweats hypocrisy: all the meaner lusts are concentrated in him as it were to make him a monster of moral deformity; however comic he be, he inspires fear, and disgust perhaps even more than fear; to touch him we would wish a pair of tongs; and on meeting him on our way we would take care not to run up against him, for fear of befouling ourselves. The intention here is manifest beyond doubt. Tartufe is the satire or caricature of hypocrisy; the expressions he uses could not for a moment deceive anybody; and if one were to dare to offer any criticism on Molière, it would be, with La Bruyère, that he has painted him in too crude colours. But what is to be made of the other characters, and of Orgon in particular, who is undoubtedly of distinct importance, for we must remember that it was not the character of Tartufe, but of Orgon, which Molière interpreted in his piece, just as he acted Arnolphe in the *École des Femmes*, Alceste in the *Misanthrope*, and Harpagon in the *Avare*? And it is really on Orgon, as much as on Tartufe, that the whole piece turns; it is he who keeps the stage from the first act to the last, while Tartufe appears only at the third; and for a clear understanding of affairs, it is from him consequently, as much as from Tartufe, that we must ask Molière's secret.

Now Orgon was by no means a simpleton, and Dorine, from the first act, took great care to tell us so. "During our troubles he acted like a man of sense and displayed some courage in the service of his prince." His house was free and hospitable, and the presence of a mother-in-law had brought neither disorder nor trouble. A good husband, a good father, a good master was Orgon: he was also a good citizen. A faithful and sure friend, he was chosen from among twenty others to be entrusted with a matter on which depended a friend's honour, liberty, and life. "But since he has taken so strongly to Tartufe, he has become a perfect dolt." That is to say, since he met him, all his former good qualities had turned into as many faults. Instead of being the indulgent husband of a young wife, he had become indifferent and crotchety; the tender father had changed into a domestic tyrant; the man of honour into an unfaithful guardian. What is this to say—for Orgon is sincere, his devotion is true, and not for a moment is he made to appear as a dishonest man, and still less as a hypocrite—what is this to say but that as much as he advances in devotion, so much does he advance towards inhumanity? Now, "he could see brother, children, mother, and wife die, without troubling himself one whit," as he said while hitting his nail on his teeth; and Tartufe alone accomplished this work, not the Tartufe, let it be understood, who covets his wife while marrying his daughter, but the Tartufe who can barely be seen, he whose lessons teach only, according to the language of Christianity, no heed of the things of this world, self-denial, and the pure love of God.

These words put us on the track of what Molière attacks in religion; the point is delicate enough, but it is important to mark it. (pp. 99-101)

[What] he does not like in religion is that which is opposed to his philosophy, the principle on which all religion worthy of its name reposes, the constraint, in short, which it places on us. While all around him, not only the Jansenists, but the Jesuits also, are teaching that human nature is corrupted in its substance; that we carry in ourselves our most dangerous enemies, and that these are our instincts; that in following their impulse we run of our own accord to eternal damnation; that there is no hope of safety but in keeping a tight rein on them; that the life of this world has been given us not to be used, and that nature is a perpetual source of combat, struggle, and victory over herself,—Molière believes, as we have shown, precisely the reverse. He believes "that we must refuse our body or our senses nothing which they desire of us in the exercise of their powers or natural faculties"; he believes that in following our instincts we obey the wish of nature; and, of nature, he believes that one cannot tell if there is more insolence and pride, or stupidity and folly, in wishing to live not merely apart from her, but in opposition to her.

Is the contrast not evident or even glaring? Will it not be granted that it is the moral constraint which is the foundation of religion—and had alone been so since the appearance of Calvinism and Jansenism—which Molière attacked in his *Tartufe* under the name of hypocrisy? Did he not wish to show us that in teaching us to "set our hearts on nothing," religion taught us to neglect, not so much ourselves as these "human sentiments" which give life its value? Did he not wish to show, in short, that pious people, whether sincere or hypocritical, are always dangerous; that in proposing for the efforts of men an end which is

unattainable, they dissuade them from their true duties; and that in preaching, as they do, the contempt and dread of this world, they turn us from the object of life, which is first of all to live?

Here it is, I know, that the sayings of Cléante are appealed to:

> There is false devotion as there is false bravery: and as we never find that the truly brave are those who make much noise where honour leads them, so the good and truly pious, in whose footsteps we should follow, are not those who pull so many long faces.

But, to appeal to these lines, it would first be necessary to show that they, and the speeches of Cléante generally, are the expression of the true thought of Molière. Now this cannot be, no more than Molière can be held answerable for the Alceste or the Philinte of his *Misanthrope;* and when, too, the Chrysalde of the *École des Femmes* is mentioned in this connection, we forget, if this good fellow really spoke in the name of Molière, what is the strange advice which Molière would thus have given us, and that it would justify the most violent passages of the *Maximes sur la Comédie.*

Indeed the "raisonneurs" of his plays do not act the part of the chorus of the ancient comedy; they express a part of his thought only, that which he believes most in accordance with the prejudices of his public; and their speeches are but a bait for the pit. And so what is the distinction Cléante endeavors to establish between the sincere and the hypocritical in religion? The hypocritical, to him, are all those who make a show, if I may say so, who act openly in some way or other, who do not conceal their devoutness as a weakness or a crime. But the sign of the sincere is to show no devoutness, to be content to be devout in themselves, and, provided they live a good life, to let others live as they wish. In other terms still, the mark of true piety, for Cléante, is to be concerned only with piety. As soon as religion aims at raising itself into a guide for life, he begins to suspect it, as he also says, of ostentation and insincerity. And this is why, were a new demonstration needed of Molière's intentions, it would be found in the speeches and rôle of that character whom we are told to consider his interpreter.

So had he really wished to shelter his *Tartufe* from malevolent interpretations, I shall not have the impertinence to say how he ought to have set about it, but it is not Cléante whom he would have chosen to speak in his name; it is Elmire, the wife of Orgon, whose tractable and sincere devotion he would have opposed to the devotion, sincere too, but extravagant, of her booby of a husband. It is she, since he has entrusted her with unmasking Tartufe, whom he would likewise have entrusted with expressing his respect for these sentiments of which the language of Tartufe is only a sacrilegious parody, she, and not Cléante, who takes no part in the action, who speaks only behind the scenes, and who could easily be taken out of the piece without being missed.

So at least has he done in the *Misanthrope*, where the sincere Eliante decides between Alceste and Philinte, and fills, between the coquettishness of Célimène and the prudery of Arsinoé, the part of nature and truth. So also has he done in the *Bourgeois Gentilhomme*, and so in the *Femmes savantes*, where it is not the old fellow Chrysale, nor his brother-in-law Ariste, nor even perhaps Clitandre, but Henriette in especial, who incarnates his true thought.

But the Elmire of *Tartufe* is only a pleasant woman, to whom every religious idea may be said to appear a stranger, who cannot find any of the necessary words to reply to the gross declaration of Tartufe. "Others would perhaps take it in a different fashion; but she wishes to show her discretion"; and since, moreover, her virtue is not the less unimpeachable for it, what is this to say but that by nature "men that are free have an instinct and spur that prompteth them unto virtuous actions, and withdraws them from vice"? In her difficult situation as the young wife of an old husband, as the mother-in-law of a grown-up girl and a grown-up man, to avoid giving any handle to slander and to remain thoroughly honest, Elmire had only to follow her nature, and had not the least need of correcting or conquering it, even of trying to bring it to perfection.

Contemporaries — and their impressions must be trusted—made no mistake about it; and five days after the first performance of *Tartufe*, the *Gazette de France*, in the issue of 17th May 1664, declared the piece "absolutely injurious to religion, and capable of producing very dangerous effects." Molière, now that he had the support of the king, showed his boldness by replying with his **Don Juan.** He did better still; he profited by the quarrels of his adversaries; he had the tact to persuade the Jesuits that his *Tartufe* was a retort to the *Lettres provinciales*, and to persuade the Jansenists that it was the continuation or redoubling of these *Lettres*. It is Racine who tells us, in the oft–cited sentence, that "the Jansenists said that the Jesuits were represented in that comedy, but the Jesuits flattered themselves that it was aimed at the Jansenists." And, indeed, when Tartufe comes upon the stage, speaking the verse:

Laurent, put by my hair-shirt and my scourge;

as also when he says, in offering his handkerchief to Dorine:

Go hide thy bosom, for I hate the sight,

it seems as if it were a Jansenist who spoke. On the other hand, was it not the Jesuit who was represented in his turn when Tartufe ardently explained to Elmire "the art of rectifying the evil of the act by the purity of the intention"? (pp. 102-07)

[Molière] is praised for having better understood, in spite of fanatics, if there were any at his court, the true interests of religion than all the people of sincere and deep religion who were about him. It was they who made the mistake in thinking themselves attacked and wounded by *Tartufe*. They did not understand Molière. In distinguishing false devotion from the true, "the mask from the person," and "the false money from the good," they did not see the service which that "reforming comedy" rendered to the cause of religion. But Louis XIV saw it, since he was, as it were, outside of and above the dispute; he is praised for having had the courage to join in it; and we, to-day, pretend to see even better what he saw so well. (p. 110)

[What] pleases us in *Tartufe* is just Molière's effort to separate morality from religion. We have no need of a rule of good life, and certainly not of a rule outside of and above nature: this is what *Tartufe* teaches clearly enough, and this is what we like in the usual interpretation. We are very pleased to see all those who labour to correct their nature fall, like Orgon and his mother, into absurdity and folly; and, on the other hand, we admire, in the honesty of Elmire and the good sense of Dorine, the beauty of our indifference. But it would be time also to recognise that this is the opposite of religion. It would be time above all to acknowledge that, if it is the opposite, the truly pious people have the right to feel hurt by *Tartufe;* that if the wound has not closed for two hundred and fifty years, there is no doubt that it was deep; that the hand which made it meant to make it; that therefore it was not only false devotion, but also true, which Molière meant to attack; and that it was for the gain of nature that he meant to destroy the religion of effort and moral constraint. (pp. 111-12)

Ferdinand Brunetière, "The Philosophy of Molière," in his Brunetière's Essays in French Literature, *translated by D. Nichol Smith, T. Fisher Unwin, 1898, pp. 66-133.*

GEORGE SAINTSBURY (essay date 1907)

[*Saintsbury has been called the most influential English literary historian and critic of the late nineteenth and early twentieth centuries. His numerous literary histories and studies of European literature have established him as a leading critical authority. Saintsbury adhered to two distinct sets of critical standards: one for the novel and the other for poetry and drama. As a critic of novels, he maintained that "the novel has nothing to do with any beliefs, with any convictions, with any thoughts in the strict sense, except as mere garnishings. Its substance must always be life not thought, conduct not belief, the passions not the intellect, manners and morals not creeds and theories. . . . The novel is . . . mainly and firstly a criticism of life." As a critic of poetry and drama. Saintsbury was a radical formalist who frequently asserted that subject is of little importance and that "the so-called 'formal' part is of the essence." René Wellek has praised Saintsbury's critical qualities: his "enormous reading, the almost universal scope of his subject matter, the zest and zeal of his exposition," and "the audacity with which he handles the most ambitious and unattempted arguments." In the following introduction to A. R. Waller's translation of Molière's works, Saintsbury deems Molière the "Master of the Laugh." Lytton Strachey takes exception to this view in the excerpt dated 1907.*]

So infinite has been the writing about [Molière] that I should not be surprised to find (though I never actually saw or heard of such a thing) that some one had written something like the following dialogue in one of his own most popular styles. 'Is Molière a strictly original writer?' 'Not at all.' 'Does he not borrow from Plautus, Terence, the Italians, the Spaniards, his French predecessors, Cyrano, Scarron, everybody, in the most barefaced manner?' 'Certainly.' 'Is it not the fact that even the *lune toute entière* and *Que diable allait-il faire dans cette galère?* and even *Mes gages!* are not his own inventions?' 'It is most true.' 'Does he respect the decencies of the stricter and nobler comedy?' 'He does not care a scrap about them.' 'Has he any romantic touches?' 'Hardly any.' 'Is his language quite unexceptionable in propriety?' 'Very much the reverse.' 'Is he careful in construction, and does he pay particular attention to probable and neatly adjusted *dénouement*?' 'He is and does exactly the contrary.' And so it might go on for as many pages as the patterns in his own plays fill.

As to the charges, direct and indirect, of plagiarism, it cannot, at this time of day, be necessary to say much. It is practically acknowledged by all critics whose opinion is of the slightest value that such charges are only valid against *bad* writers—that the good writer may 'take his property' (in Molière's own attributed and very likely genuine words) where he finds it. But another charge or class of charges, less fully outlined in the above dialogue, requires ampler dealing. From the very first the keen eye of professional jealousy saw that the word to use against Molière was *farce*. 'Farce' is the critical *tarte à la crème* ["cream tart"]. And, as sometimes happens in such cases, the defenders have played into the hands of the attack by exhibiting a sort of nervous 'confession and avoidance' of it. We find, implied or expressed in apologies of Molière ('I didn't know the Bible wanted an apology,' as a king of England whom stupid people call stupid remarked), something like this: 'Well! the *Précieuses* and the *Bourgeois Gentilhomme* and *M. de Pourceaugnac*, and a number of the smaller pieces *are* rather farcical; but pray do think of *Tartuffe* and *Le Misanthrope*!' Then, exaggerating this nervousness still farther, they try to make of these two masterpieces, if not also of *Don Juan*, something like tragedies, to throw a tragic air over Molière's whole career, to lament his necessity of writing roaring farces for the city and wishy-washy entertainments for the Court. Nay, one may strongly suspect that the anxiety about his private life has something of a similar motive.

Now it may go near to be feared shortly that all this is partly due to that old leaven of human nature, Cant, and partly to the less noisome but half-ludicrous and half-pathetic tendency of the same nature to look behind the curtain which is the picture, to 'seek for noon at fourteen hours,' and generally to make a dupe and a gull of itself. Why should it be so difficult to take Molière for what he is—the Master of the Laugh? and so tempting to make him something else—a great poet, a great moralist, a fashioner of terrible tragedies under comic veils? I believe (If I could only put it in his own words!) I could hit pretty well on what his own thoughts in the matter would be, and a famous passage it would make! In the English sense Molière is hardly a 'poet' at all—he had no occasion to be so, though he is an admirable versifier in his own easy way (*not* easy to do), and the mingled awe and admiration with which the French regard the tricks he plays with the stiff language and prosody of their classic tongue make a very funny mixture. As for his morality, it is practically never bad and seldom if ever careless; but he does not make it his first or his direct object in all cases. And for the tragic or comic turn—it might be well to look into that matter carefully before deciding it. The end of *Don Juan* is not in the least burlesqued in itself, and it is only dulness that sees burlesque even in Sganarelle's comment on it; but it is part of the donnée—of the material furnished to the author, not by him. If *Tartuffe* had ended at the point which its first representation reached,—the close of the Third Act (and there are some reasons for doubting whether the two last were not an afterthought) it would not be much less comic and it would be considerably less tragic. Nor would some people, though they might regret the table scene, weep much for the loss of the end, which is one of Molière's most violent introductions of the *Rex ex Machina*.

But *Le Misanthrope*? May it be permitted to doubt whether Molière really intended to excite all the admiring sym-

pathy which has been bestowed on Alceste? Without that sympathy he remains an admirable comic figure, but he becomes hardly more of a tragic one than Malvolio, for whom also some respectable persons have tried to excite it. He is a 'man of honour' no doubt, but he is also, if one may dare to say so, a 'fool of honour,' and not a very amiable one. It is quite evident that wounded vanity, and impatience at not having it all his own way with Célimène, are quite as much at the bottom of his conduct as virtuous disapproval of the ways of society; his proposal to Éliante after he has as he thinks been jilted by Célimène (in the first, not the second case) is a very bad compliment to her, and doubtfully the act of a gentleman. Although Oronte is an ass—a very delightful ass and one of a numerous tribe—Alceste is both a prig and a boor in his dealings with him: and I really wonder why Acaste and Clitandre, who, though coxcombs, appear to have been 'men of spirit and honour,' did not give their worships the Marshals of France another job for his rudeness. That Molière saw all this, and meant it to be seen, I am perfectly sure. Indeed, one of the best suggestions ever made on this much-discussed play is (it is, I think, M. Despois' in one of his posthumous notes) that he definitely meant to present Philinte as a mellowed and rationalised Alceste, Alceste as a Philinte who has not got over the first fermentation. At any rate he meant Alceste himself to be laughed at quite as much as to be sympathised with, if not a good deal more. Here I am certain: and in *Tartuffe* I rather think he originally at least intended to dwell more on the rascality than on the villainy of Tartuffe, and on the folly of Orgon more than on either. To attempt, therefore, to separate the final causes of his work into Pure and Applied Laughter seems to be a mistake; and to attempt further, as the good Riccoboni did, to justify the very 'farces' themselves, and rank them according to their greater or lesser dose of seriousness, seems a greater one, in fact an idle absurdity. One step more, and you come to the seventeenth-century objection that he had the impudence to write a whole five-act piece, *L'Avare*, in prose (you might, it seems, write three in it but not five), or the grave protest made some century ago by Auger, the unlucky original of Daudet's *L'Immortel*, that the dancing of the cooks who bring in the Bourgeois Gentilhomme's supper is improbable. But the part to be allotted to seriousness in his theatre generally is, I admit, a much more difficult question and not to be settled offhand. You must read Molière long, and you must read him not in scraps or separate plays, but continuously, before you really apprehend his essence.

For it is not an essence of style and form, as Milton's is almost wholly and Dante's to a great extent. It is not an essence of craftsmanship like Dryden's, or Racine's, or, in a lesser way still, Pope's. It is not the power of creating a special less or more limited world of his own, like (in very different ways) the essence of Spenser, or Ariosto, or Balzac, or Dickens. It is not quite—though it comes nearer to these—the power of investing everything with actual life, which belongs to Shakespeare supremely, and to Scott, Thackeray, Fielding, in different ways and degrees. It does not exactly transform everything by passing it through a bath of burlesque irony like Rabelais, or romantic irony like Cervantes, or indignant irony like Swift. It only asks everything which suggests itself 'Can you help me to make men laugh?' and if so, it takes the thing and makes it do this. With the rest it *n'a que faire*, as the French phrase goes. It has no business for them; they may be excellent things for other artists and other methods, but not for it and for *him*.

To this mistress-method Molière was never false, except in the one instance of **Don Garcie de Navarre**, which practically does not count, for he abandoned it soon as a play, he never printed it, and he put it in the stock-pot for **Le Misanthrope**, where one may venture to think that it proved itself rather a dangerous ingredient. Elsewhere, I believe, he was always true to it, and it always brought him luck. But it dispensed him from some things which, in other methods, may be justly demanded. Literal originality was one, for if you can get a new laugh out of old jokes, why not? It dispensed him from the formal *dénouement*, though it may be observed (and it is an interesting comment on Aristotle's dislike and distrust of 'character') that the great character-mongers—Shakespeare sometimes, Scott and Thackeray almost always, Fielding perhaps more than is sometimes allowed—are apt to 'huddle up' their actions. It made him, to some of the grave and precise, distractingly miscellaneous in his choice of means—pantomime, horseplay, philosophical instruments of the **Pourceaugnac** and **Malade Imaginaire** type, impossible arabesques of incident and decoration, a whole dream-world of incongruities.... If it was his mistress he was its master—the Master of the Laugh. (pp. xxxix-xlv)

There may be people who have to apologise to themselves for enjoying it by extolling the darker parts of **Tartuffe**, the more serious ones of the **Misanthrope**, the ingenious but slightly overdone philosophisings of the **Femmes Savantes**, and Clitandre's rather too long and rather too earnest snubbings of Trissotin. Let this not be our way, and while quite appreciating these more serious things, let us prefer, without shame or shuffle, the lovers' quarrels and makings-up of the **Dépit Amoureux** (reproduced more than once); the **Précieuses Ridicules**, entire and perfect from rise to drop of curtain; the myriad shapes of bore in **Les Fâcheux**; the pendant-contrast of Isabelle (who is a minx) and Isidore (who is not) in **L'Ecole des Maris** and **Le Sicilien**; the sufferings and humours of the various Sganarelles, including the king of them all, that admirable wood-cutter, whom Molière, taking him from an amusing but ordinary Fabliau, made a person for ever in **Le Médecin Malgré Lui**. Let us be a little sorry for Arnolphe (for, after all, he behaves like a gentleman to Horace, who does not behave like a gentleman to him), but at the same time feel that he, like Malvolio rather ill-treated, is like Malvolio a thoroughly comic character, and reflect that it is not at all impossible that Agnes (who again is a minx) will avenge him on Master Horace after all. Let us be truly thankful for Moron and the bear (how Shakespeare would have liked them!) in that **Princesse d'Élide** which so few people trouble themselves about; and recognise, humanely but not sentimentally, that George Dandin 'l'avait voulu'; and rejoice in **Don Juan** and **L'Avare** from beginning to end; and think scorn of any one who thinks scorn of M. de Pourceaugnac and Madame d'Escarbagnas. Let us put the **Bourgeois Gentilhomme** in the very highest place possible for the broader comedy.... Let us welcome Trissotin and Vadius and Armande and Belise and Henriette (Philaminte is a little too odious, and not quite comic enough—*we* can beat her with Lady Catherine de Burgh). And so let us come to that astonishing 'farce,' as they call it, wherein Molière caught up the sum of his method and uttered it once for all and last of all, with such a triumph of learn-

ing, such a prodigality of humour, such a treasury of knowledge of human nature, as have rarely been combined elsewhere, and as almost necessitated the application of the old rhetorical figure of turning out the medal and breaking the mould. (pp. xlvi-xlviii)

> *George Saintsbury, in an introduction to* The Plays of Molière in French: 1655-1656, *Vol. I, edited and translated by A. R. Waller, John Grant, 1907, pp. xi-xlviii.*

LYTTON STRACHEY (essay date 1907)

[*Strachey was an early twentieth-century English biographer, critic, essayist, and short story writer. He is best known for his biographies* Eminent Victorians *(1918),* Queen Victoria *(1921), and* Elizabeth and Essex: A Tragic History *(1928). Critics agree that these iconoclastic reexaminations of historical figures revolutionized the course of modern biographical writing. Strachey's literary criticism is also considered incisive. In the following excerpt from a 1907 article in the* Spectator, *he extols Molière as a dramatist with the ability to "combine the polished brilliance of the classic with the romantic sense of humanity." In the course of his remarks, Strachey refutes George Saintsbury's characterization of Molière as primarily "the Master of the Laugh" (see excerpt dated 1907).*]

Englishmen have always loved Molière. He is one of the very few French writers whom we can explore without the uneasy feeling of being in a foreign country; we are at home with him, and he, we feel, is at home with us. We have, too, given solid proof of our admiration, for there is no other foreign author whom we have imitated so much. Ever since he wrote he has dominated our comic stage. 'The frippery of crucified Molière,' as Pope put it, has always been the stock-in-trade of the hack English playwright; and some of the most famous scenes of Sheridan and Congreve have been 'lifted' almost bodily from the author of the **Misanthrope** and the **Femmes Savantes**.... 'Translating Molière,' says Mr Meredith, 'is like humming an air one has heard performed by an accomplished violinist of the pure tones without flourish.'... (pp. 121-22)

[The] quality of Molière's genius shows itself nowhere more clearly than in his exquisite precision. Whatever his point may be—and one might compile an infinite gradation of his points, ranging from the broadest buffoonery to the subtlest psychological crux—he can seize it and make the best of it with the same unerring exactitude, the same undeviating certainty of touch. Mr Meredith's metaphor of the 'pure tones without flourish' is no empty one, for Molière's best phrases have precisely the rich simplicity of the *virtuoso*. He can call up with a common sentence a whole universe of reverberating suggestion and pervasive irony. '*Nous avons changé tout cela!*' ["We have changed all that"]—It is the epitome of all the cranks of the world. He can make a bad pun the instrument of eternal mockery.... To read one of his scenes is to watch some wonderful cook at work over a delicious dish—keeping it on the simmer while each savoury ingredient is dropped in: the oil, the olive, the salt—and then at the psychological moment whipping it off the fire, and setting it before you done to a turn. In short, Molière's workmanship is essentially classical. It is true that his construction is apt to be weak; the action of his plays is too often 'huddled up', as Professor Saintsbury says [see excerpt dated 1907]...;

but the pervading spirit of his work is none the less that very spirit of precision, finish, and refinement which informs all that is most characteristic in the art of his countrymen. But it is the great distinction of Molière that he is not only a classicist, but something else besides. The weakness of the classical ideal lies in its tendency towards the narrow and the confined—towards a perfection which is only perfect because it has excluded and ignored so much. Pushed to its extremity, it produces a Voltaire—the most consummate of artists, dancing in a vacuum on the tight-rope of his own wit; and its antithesis is to be found among the dramas of the romantic Elizabethans, whose looseness, vagueness, disorder, and irregularity are redeemed by the image of large and tumultuous life which those very qualities have brought into being. The marvellous achievement of Molière was to combine the polished brilliance of the classic with the romantic's sense of humanity. He is as definite, as witty, as complete as Voltaire himself; and yet his pages are throbbing with vitality; his characters stream across them in all the freshness and in all the variety of life; his world is the great world—the world of Shakespeare and Cervantes, of Balzac and Scott.

But if this combination of breadth and refinement is the distinctive feature of Molière's art, what is the distinctive feature of Molière himself? What, to use Professor Saintsbury's expression, is the 'essence' of Molière? . . . Professor Saintsbury discusses the question, and discusses it with all his usual vivacity and learning; everything that he says is interesting; and it is only to be regretted that so much of what he says should be also a little perverse. . . . Most modern critics have laid stress on the serious side of Molière's mind; Professor Saintsbury has taken up *l'opinion contraire*, and argues forcibly that Molière was at heart a laugher, and nothing more. He was 'the Master of the Laugh'. His 'essence' simply 'asks everything which suggests itself, "Can you help me to make men laugh?" and if so, it takes the thing, and makes it do this. With the rest it *n'a que faire*, as the French phrase goes.' Surely that is as paradoxical as any of the exaggerated statements about Molière's sole value lying in his tragic power. No one in his senses will doubt for a minute that Molière was indeed 'the Master of the Laugh'. But was he (as Professor Saintsbury declares) master of nothing more? Was he not also the Master of the Smile? Is not that, in fact, his true 'essence'? Laughter is the expression of a simple emotion; but a smile (no less than a tear) is an intellectual thing; and Molière's greatest work is intellectual to an intense degree. The distinction is nowhere more plainly visible than in one of the best known of all his comedies—*Le Bourgeois Gentilhomme*. The latter half of that delightful piece is a cataract of rollicking buffoonery, which leaves one with aching sides, gasping for breath. Professor Saintsbury's words exactly fit it; Molière has taken the foolish tradesman playing the *grand seigneur*, and has covered him with such enormous ridicule, has plunged him into such preposterous predicaments, that men will laugh over him till the end of time. And if Molière's sole object had been to do that—to draw the greatest possible quantity of laughter from his subject—all that was necessary was to write the whole play on the same pattern and the thing was done. But that was not his sole object, for the earlier scenes present a complete contrast to the later ones; it is not their laughableness that makes them valuable, but their psychology. The Monsieur Jourdain whom we love and know, the Monsieur Jourdain whom Molière has

drawn for us so exquisitely, so subtly, so sympathetically—at him we can hardly laugh at all, at him we must perpetually smile. And who can doubt that a creation such as that is really a finer and a greater achievement than the most triumphant evocation of the most Olympian laughter? Professor Saintsbury, indeed, is forced into strange extremes by his theory, for he has to do his best to turn each of Molière's most profound and complex character-studies into something funny, something that will 'help to make men laugh'. He has to make excuses for Don Juan (who is never even ridiculous); he has to shuffle aside Tartufe (who is nearly always horrible); he has to forget Harpagon altogether.

> Hélas! mon pauvre argent! mon pauvre argent! mon cher ami! on m'a privé de toi; et, puisque tu m'es enlevé, j'ai perdu mon support, ma consolation, ma joie; tout est fini pour moi, et je n'ai plus que faire au monde.
>
> [Alas! my poor money! my poor money! my dear friend! they have deprived me of you; and, now that you are taken away from me, I have lost my support, my consolation, my joy; all is finished for me, I have no longer any concern with the world].

That is despair; and despair, surely, is no laughing matter. Over the *Misanthrope* Professor Saintsbury fights a gallant fight; but it is impossible to believe that any reader who is acquainted with that wonderful drama will be convinced by his arguments. For, indeed, there is no escaping the fact that in the *Misanthrope* at least Molière is not only supremely gay and supremely brilliant, but supremely melancholy too. The play is a tragedy in the truest sense of the word, though there is no 'sceptred pall' in it, no Shakespearean imagination, no Sophoclean grandeur; it is the tragedy of actual life. Its climax does not come in death, but in a lady leaving a room. And when that happens, when at the last, amid the silence of the little *salon*, Célimène, without a word, turns round and passes out for ever from our sight—who does not feel the same quality of anguish, the same poignancy of desolation, as that which fills us when King Oedipus goes forth into the darkness, or Cordelia dies? (pp. 122-26)

> *Lytton Strachey, "Molière," in his* Spectatorial Essays, *1964. Reprint by Harcourt Brace Jovanovich, 1965, pp. 121-26.*

AUSTIN DOBSON   (poem date 1910)

[Dobson, an English poet and man of letters, wrote a number of biographies showing a close knowledge of eighteenth-century society and literature. He is best remembered for his series Eighteenth Century Vignettes *(1892-96) and for his* Poems on Several Occasions *(1889). In the following poem* "La bonne comedie" *(1910), he deems Molière a master of* "true comedy".]

Les Précieuses Ridicules allèrent aux nues dès le premier jour. Un vieillard s'écria du milieu du parterre: "Courage, Molière! voilà de la bonne comédie!" (Notice sur Molière.)

[The *Affected Ladies* went to the skies from the first day. An old man cried out from the pit: "Courage, Molière! This is a good comedy!" (Notice on Molière.)]

True Comedy *circum praecordia ludit* ["plays around the heart"]
It warms the heart's cockles. 'Twas thus that he viewed it,
That simple old Critic, who smote on his knee,
And named it no more than he knew it to be.

"True Comedy!" Ah! there is this thing about it,
If it makes the House merry, you never need doubt it:
It lashes the vicious; it laughs at the fool;
And it brings all the prigs and pretenders to school.

To the poor it is kind; to the plain it is gentle;
It is neither too tragic nor too sentimental;
Its thrust, like a rapier's, though cutting, is clean,
And it pricks Affectation all over the scene.

Its rules are the rules ARISTOTLE has taught us;
Its ways have not altered since TERENCE and PLAUTUS;
Its mission is neither to praise nor to blame;
Its weapon is Ridicule; Folly, its game.

"True Comedy!" — such as our POQUELIN made it!
"True Comedy!" — such as our COQUELIN played it!
It clears out the cobwebs; it freshens the air;
And it treads in the steps of its Master, MOLIÈRE!

(pp. 598-99)

Austin Dobson, "La Bonne Comédie," in his Collected Poems, *ninth edition, Kegan Paul, Trench,
Trübner & Co. Ltd., 1913, pp. 598-99.*

BRANDER MATTHEWS (essay date 1910)

[*An American critic, playwright, and novelist, Matthews
wrote extensively on world drama and served for a quarter
century at Columbia University as professor of dramatic literature; he was the first to hold that title at an American
university. Matthews was also a founding member and president of the National Institute of Arts and Letters. Because
his criticism is deemed both witty and informative, he has
been called "perhaps the last of the gentlemanly school of
critics and essayists" in America. In the following excerpt,
he evaluates several aspects of* The Learned Ladies, *including the effectiveness of its humor, its central message, the
truthfulness of its character delineation, and its style.*]

In the *Femmes Savantes* we have the ultimate model of
high comedy—a type of play which must be excessively
difficult of attainment if we may judge by its extraordinary rarity in the dramatic literature of every language,
ancient and modern. By high comedy we mean a humorous play which is sustained by a worthy theme and in
which the action is caused by the clash of character on
character. The *Femmes Savantes* is even more absolutely a
comedy than *Tartuffe*, since that superb play threatens at
one moment to stiffen into drama and almost into tragedy. It is ampler in its theme than the *Avare* and the *Bourgeois Gentilhomme*, where the interest is centered on the
presentation of every aspect of a single character. If not so
significant in its thesis as the *Misanthrope*, it is better built
and more adroitly adjusted to the demands of the theater,
where the desires of the crowd must always be considered.

The *Femmes Savantes* is also one of the most original of all
its author's plays. The loftier and the larger Molière's
comedy the less he borrows. When he was composing a
farce, he was content to go to others, sometimes for his
plot and sometimes for his episodes; he was willing
enough to take the *Fourberies de Scapin* from the Latin
and the *Etourdi* from the Italian. But the indefatigable industry of his countless commentators has not enabled
them to indicate the actual sources of the *Femmes Savantes*
or of *Tartuffe*, even though it has permitted them to point
out a few suggestions here and there in the works of his
predecessors and his contemporaries by which he may

have profited. It is when Molière is at his best that he
owes least to others. He was then looking, not at what had
already been set on the stage, but at what was going on in
the society by which he was surrounded. He was drawing
directly from nature, and he was not disposed to take his
material ready-made from the hand of another. He had no
need to copy anything but humanity itself.

Molière seems to have given a longer time to the composition of the *Femmes Savantes* than he was able to bestow on
any other of his later plays. Apparently he had begun to
compose this comedy several years before it finally appeared in the theater. It was prepared at leisure, even if its
preparation was more than once interrupted by a call to
produce other plays for which there was an immediate demand either from the king or from the company. And perhaps this preoccupation with a more ambitious work may
account for the perfunctory carelessness with which the
Comtesse d'Escarbagnas was dashed off and for the reckless swiftness of the *Fourberies de Scapin*. The *Femmes Savantes* is spaciously conceived, solidly constructed, and
highly finished. Evidently the author had allowed it to rip-
en slowly; and when at last he chose to bring it before the
public it was free from all evidences of haste.

It is a five act comedy in verse; and it was first acted at
the Palais-Royal in March, 1672, less than a year before
Molière's death. It is the last of Molière's nobler comedies;
and in it he handled again, on an ampler scale, the subject
he had lightly treated in the earliest play written after his
return to Paris. In the *Précieuses Ridicules* he had killed
the vogue of the romance-of-gallantry, as one of his masters in comedy, Cervantes, had killed the vogue of the ro-
mance-of-chivalry. Yet the spirit which animated the *précieuses* was not dead, and it had manifested itself anew in
fresh forms in the thirteen years since Molière had first attacked it. In these new manifestations he detected a menace to society far more dangerous than he had discovered
in the older affectations. It was with delight that he returned to the assault, not with another little play, like the
Précieuses Ridicules, amusingly sustained by the artifices
of farce, but with a compactly planned comedy of fuller
import, devoid of fantastic exaggeration and direct in its
portrayal of character.

In the *Femmes Savantes*, as earlier in *Tartuffe*, in the *Avare*
and in the *Bourgeois Gentilhomme*, Molière lays his story
in a single family. An easy-going citizen, Chrysale (played
by Molière himself) has a wife, Philaminte, who is educated beyond her intelligence. There are two daughters, Armande, the elder, who takes after her mother, and Henriette, the younger (played by Molière's wife), who has
simpler tastes and more commonplace desires. Chrysale
has a brother Ariste, who is the embodiment of common
sense, and also a sister Bélise, an absurd old maid, who
holds with Philaminte and who believes herself to be
sought by several suitors. A most presentable young man,
Clitandre (acted by La Grange), had paid his attentions to
Armande, only to be rebuffed by her scorn for anything so
mundane as matrimony, whereupon he transferred his affections to Henriette. In the midst of this family group
there is another outsider, Trissotin, whom the learned ladies have made a pet of, because he appears in their eyes
as the embodiment of the wit they admire and of the
learning they adore.

The art of comedy is largely the art of contrasting characters so that each shall make the other more salient and more significant; and in none of his plays has Molière shown himself a more skilful artist than in this. The weak-willed Chrysale is set over against the firm and resourceful Ariste. The pedantic and platonic Armande is set by the side of the charmingly natural Henriette. The over-educated Philaminte is shown engaged in controversy with her ignorant servant, Martine. And Clitandre, who has the easy courtesy of a man of the world, stands in juxtaposition with the pretentiously arrogant Trissotin.

The art of comedy also calls for dexterity in the conduct of the plot, for certainty of exposition and for cumulative interest in the episodes as they succeed one another. Here also Molière is seen at his best; and the opening passages of the play take us as swiftly into the full current of the story as the opening episodes of *Tartuffe*, than which there could be no higher praise. The action is engaged in the very first scene by a colloquy between the two sisters, in which Armande reproaches Henriette with the younger's willingness to marry a discarded admirer of the elder. She ends by asking whether Henriette is absolutely convinced that her lover has conquered his earlier affection. Henriette thereupon summons Clitandre to declare himself and to decide between them; and the young fellow, to the warm dissatisfaction of the elder sister, makes it plain that his heart is now given irrevocably to the younger. And the spectators cannot help feeling that Armande will thereafter do all in her power to prevent the course of true love from running smoothly.

In the second act we make the acquaintance of Chrysale, to whom Ariste declares the desire of Clitandre to wed Henriette. But when the more or less hen-pecked husband discloses this matrimonial project to his strong-willed wife, he is told that she has made another arrangement. She is determined that Henriette shall marry Trissotin. This prodigy of wit and wisdom has not pretended to be in love with the girl; but he is willing enough to wed her because both of her parents are wealthy. When Ariste hears of the match proposed by Henriette's mother, he upbraids her father with his weakness in yielding; and at last he arouses in Chrysale a spirit of manly resistance. The worthy burgher resolves to assert himself for once. He sends for a Notary to draw up the marriage-contract of Henriette and Clitandre; and he is fearless in proclaiming that the young couple shall be made happy that very day.

When Aristotle laid down the principle that every play ought to have a single story of a certain importance in itself, and that it ought also to set forth the beginning and the middle and the end of this single story, he was unwittingly testifying to the convenience of a three-act form, one act containing each of these necessary parts of the plot. And even when the dramatic poets have felt compelled to fill out the larger framework of five acts, they have been able to do this only by subdividing one of these necessary parts between two acts. This is what Molière has done in the *Femmes Savantes*. In his first two acts we see only the beginning of the story, in which the characters are set before us sharply and in which our interest is keenly aroused in what is to follow. Molière had also to divide the ending of his story between the fourth and fifth acts. It is in the third act that he gives us the swift succession of effects for which we have been prepared by the earlier acts and which make us eager for the later acts.

In this middle act we behold the learned ladies assembled. We see them purring with extravagant delight as the complacent Trissotin reads aloud two of his empty and labored little poems. We look on while Trissotin introduces his friend, Vadius, who knows as much Greek as any man in France. We gaze with joy at the quarrel that soon arises between the two parlor-poets, who get hotter and hotter in the violence of their objurgations until they almost come to blows. We are shown the angry withdrawal of the unvanquished Vadius, leaving Trissotin to the consolation of his trio of female admirers. And we look on while Philaminte tells Henriette that she is to accept Trissotin as her husband. The girl protests in vain; but when her mother has left the stage to be succeeded by her father, she finds sudden encouragement. Despite the warnings of Armande, Chrysale announces to Henriette that she shall be married at once to Clitandre.

After all the bustling comedy-scenes of this third act, the fourth may seem a little thinner in substance, partly because it is mainly a preparation for the end of the play. Armande embittered by jealousy seeks to set her mother even more strongly against Clitandre, who comes in just in time to overhear her insidious attack. He defends himself; and at that Armande declares that she will now accept the suit she formerly rejected. Since he is not satisfied with a purely platonic relation, she will take him for her husband. But Clitandre has to decline, as he is now sincerely in love with Henriette. And after an amusing and rather personal passage of arms between Clitandre and Trissotin, we see Chrysale still resolved that his younger daughter shall wed the man of her choice.

In the fifth act Henriette pleads with Trissotin to renounce his suit, telling him plainly that her heart is given to Clitandre; but the self-seeking pretender refuses to withdraw. When the Notary arrives to draw the marriage contract, Chrysale designates Clitandre as the future husband, and Philaminte sets forward Trissotin. Finally, the mother suggests that if Clitandre must marry one of her daughters, he can have Armande, at the same time that Trissotin marries Henriette. Chrysale is weakening a little when Ariste arrives with two letters, one to Philaminte announcing the loss of a lawsuit, which will greatly diminish her fortune, and the other to Chrysale, declaring that his bankers have defaulted, which will sadly reduce his wealth. And thereupon Trissotin promptly withdraws, unwilling to marry a poor girl. Clitandre persists in his suit; and then Ariste confesses that the bad news is only a device of his own to expose the mercenariness of Trissotin. And now that all opposition is withdrawn, Chrysale valiantly orders the Notary to proceed with the marriage contract.

Slight as may be the story of the *Femmes Savantes* it is sufficient to sustain satisfactorily the interest of the spectators; and it is developed in a sequence of situations unsurpassed in effectiveness of humor and in exquisite truthfulness of character-delineation. No single episode in all Molière is at once more vigorously amusing and more truthful than the quarrel between Trissotin and Vadius. Nothing is more characteristically comic than Philaminte's protest to the Notary, against the barbarity of the legal terms in which the marriage contract is drawn. No character has a more opulent humor and a more vital humanity than Chrysale, the weak-willed but well-meaning husband. And the comedy as a whole has a unity of intent and a harmony of tone which Molière was rarely able to attain, forced as he often was to relieve a somber theme with episodes of an almost farcical vivacity. From the rise of the curtain in the first act to its final fall on the fifth, the play is kept consistently on the highest plane of comedy.

In no other play has Molière gathered together a more entertaining collection of characters, sharply individualized and eternally true to life. The success of the play was immediate; and it has been enduring, for its thesis is as pertinent to-day as it was two centuries and a half ago, and its characters have a permanent appeal. Philaminte and Armande are prototypes of the perennial blue-stocking; and we can find them in our own time perorating in culture-clubs and attending conventions to the neglect of their household duties. Their vocabulary may be different nowadays; but their attitude is the same. They may not be devoted to Greek, they may not be enchanted by petty little poems, they may not be striving to reform the language; but they have changed only their outer garments, and this disguise does not prevent our recognizing them at once as old acquaintances. It would be easy to pick out in the twentieth century not a few women who are thrusting themselves forward in drawing-rooms and on the platform, and who are as affected as the Bélise and as pretentious as the Philaminte that Molière presented in the seventeenth century. And it might not be difficult to find a few who are as ignorant and as foolish.

And Trissotin flourishes to-day in America and reveals himself as complacently self-satisfied as he did in France under Louis XIV. He may wear a coat of another color, but he has not transformed his character. He may have transferred his interests to more modern topics; but his method is unmodified and his manners also. He is as vain and as superficial as ever; and he is still surrounded by a little group of admiring women, open-mouthed and empty-headed. (pp. 287-96)

Keenly as Molière has perceived and presented the folly of Bélise and the absurdity of Philaminte, he is subtler in his portrayal of the more perverted Armande, the prurient prude, who pretends to put the pleasures of the mind above those of the senses, while allowing us to suspect that her own thoughts dwell unduly and unpleasantly on more material things. Molière had a plentiful lack of liking for a young woman who paraded her false delicacy and her platonic shrinking from the realities of matrimony and of motherhood. He sees in this type a dangerous detachment from duty, and he does not disguise his indignation. Possessed as he is by the social instinct and believing as he does in the necessity of being natural, he could not but detest the theories which Armande proclaims. He perceives clearly enough that if these theories should prevail, the family would disintegrate. Therefore he holds them to be threatening to society.

He makes his own attitude plain by contrasting the etherealized views of Armande with the practical common sense of Henriette. No dialogue in all his comedies is more carefully written or more thoroughly thought out than the opening scene of the *Femmes Savantes*, in which Armande and Henriette reveal themselves unconsciously. The elder sister is characterized with a full understanding of her individuality; but it is the younger sister who has the author's sympathy and whom he portrays with a caressing touch. Henriette is nature itself and straightforward simplicity; she is essentially womanly; she has a wholesome

charm and a feminine grace. Perhaps it is not too much to say that Henriette embodies Molière's ideal of the French girl, just as Rosalind may represent Shakspere's ideal of the English girl. And the contrast of the two characters is as instructive as it is interesting; it affords us an insight into the divergent attitude of the two races toward woman as a wife and as a mother. The Frenchman does not idealize woman as the Englishman is wont to do, for Shakspere is ever and always poetic, whereas Molière deals with the prose of life, even if he has to express himself in rimed alexandrines. As the type of maidenly ignorance of Molière gives us Agnès, where Shakspere presents us with Miranda; and as the representative of all that is most attractively feminine he depicts Henriette, where Shakspere has imagined Rosalind. The love-affair of Clitandre and Henriette is not romantic and it has no hectic flush of romanticism; it is a solid affection, founded on sympathy of taste and of character; but it is quite as likely to result in durable happiness as the more poetic wooing of Orlando and Rosalind.

If it is appropriate to apply a modern term to this masterpiece of comedy, it might be described as a problem-play. It is a picture of manners and a gallery of portraits; but it has also its thesis, as the *Ecole des Maris* had and the *Misanthrope* also. As we sit in the theater while its successive scenes are acted before us, we are forced to reflect upon the higher education of woman, or at least upon the effect produced on the social organization when women undertake a rivalry with men in the attaining of learning. (pp. 296-98)

Molière is too completely a dramatist to set on the stage any single character as the mouthpiece for his own opinions. It is his duty as a dramatist to let the persons in his play express the sentiments by which they are severally animated. In fairness to the characters he has created he must permit them to speak for themselves and to proclaim their beliefs each in his own fashion. Even Chrysale, the character that Molière himself impersonated, cannot be held necessarily to voice his own opinions on the question at issue. And yet in the course of the comedy Molière manages to have one or another of the speakers say the things which he wants the audience to hear and which he holds it necessary to have said by some one, if the whole subject is to be presented at full length. Sometimes one of these needful remarks is made by Chrysale and sometimes by Ariste. Both Clitandre and Henriette take part in this expression of the opinions that have to be put forth. And now and again it is the rustic Martine who takes her part in the discussion and who drops words of unexpected wisdom.

As a result, it is not difficult to arrive at Molière's own views on the thesis he has propounded, even though he has put into his play no single character charged with the utterance of his personal opinions. If we want to discover what Molière himself thinks we need not scrutinize what any one of his characters happens to say; we have only to consider the comedy as a whole and to weigh the total impression it leaves upon us. What Chrysale may declare at one moment or what Martine may put forth at another, what Philaminte or Bélise may assert—these things are useful enough in their place; but the truth is not in any one of them. It is what all the characters say, it is what they do, it is what they are—these are the things which tell us what Molière's own attitude is. This attitude is clearly shown by the single fact that the learned ladies are all of them more or less foolish, and that Trissotin, the man whom these foolish women foolishly admire, is also foolish. It is even more evidently disclosed by the added fact that the most sympathetic character, Henriette, is in revolt against the pretentiousness of her mother and her aunt and her sister.

Although Molière himself broke away early from his father's house, and although his own home was not happy, he is ever the defender of the family from foes within and without; and he thinks that everything is dangerous which may tempt a woman to disregard her household duties. His belief is that woman is completely filling her place in the world when she is simply a wife and a mother. He thinks that women fail to do the best they can for themselves when they turn aside from this noble function, and when they despise and neglect the privileges of wifehood and of motherhood to assert arrogantly an equality with men, instead of being satisfied with the superiority which men have generally conceded to them. He is of opinion that a woman will have a full life and will best accomplish that for which nature intended her, only when she is satisfied with her place in the household and when she joys in being the mother of children whom she has the pleasure of bringing up. If her life is thus filled to overflowing, she will have little leisure for rivalry with man in the acquisition of knowledge and in the advancement of learning. Therefore Molière cannot help perceiving that the pretension of women to intellectual equality is too often but a barren affectation. And for pretentious affectations of every kind Molière had only contempt and scorn.

In the *Femmes Savantes*, as perhaps in no other of his comedies, can we discover the abiding influence of Montaigne, which is as direct and at times as powerful as that of Rabelais. It is in *Monsieur de Pourceaugnac* that the indebtedness to Rabelais is most clearly revealed, in its hearty humor and in its exuberant fun-making. Both Rabelais and Montaigne were governed by the social instinct and they saw man as a member of society. Moreover they both believed in nature, as they each understood it, and they were prompt to plead in its behalf. In spirit Molière was akin to both of them; and he had nourished himself on their works. His indebtedness to them is deeper than any chance reproduction of casual passages, here and there, in one play or another; it extends to his philosophy, to his attitude toward life as a whole, to his feeling for the larger problems of existence.

In the *Femmes Savantes* we can discover as well that Molière had found his profit also in the study of another of his predecessors. Nisard declared that he could detect the influence of Descartes in some of the comic dramatist's most beautiful passages, "in that logic of dialogue so free in its turns and yet so serried." And it is perhaps in this play that these passages are most abundant, in the opening scene between the two sisters, for example, and in the later scene when Clitandre explains to Armande why he has transferred his affection to Henriette. Molière's style was suppler than ever in this comedy, more substantial, more warmly colored. Perhaps *Tartuffe* and the *Misanthrope* are the only other plays of his which really rival the *Femmes Savantes* in literary merit. His style is never academic; it has ever the savory directness of popular speech; it always unites clearness of thought to intensity of expression.

Purists and pedants have found fault with his manner of writing as they have with Shakspere's, and to as little purpose. Neither the English dramatist nor the French aim at empty propriety of phrase; their sentences are always animated and tingling with the emotion of the moment. In their hands the language is molten and malleable and they bend words to their bidding, often forcing a phrase to carry more meaning than it had ever borne before. Especially is Molière's a style intended for oral delivery. It is meant not for the eye of the single reader in the library, but for the ears of the audience assembled in the theater. More than one speech which may seem trailing and tortuous to the linguistic critic, falls trippingly from the tongue of the actor. And it was the actor whom Molière had ever in mind. His lines were written primarily for delivery on the stage and only secondarily for perusal in the study. They have the free and flexible rhythm of the spoken word, so different from the more balanced construction which befits a style intended only for the reader. Molière was an actor himself and he knew the needs of the actor. If we may accept the testimony of Coquelin, who reincarnated most of the parts Molière prepared for his own acting, even the longest of these parts is not physically fatiguing to the actor, however difficult any one of them may be to impersonate adequately.

The unfailing brilliance of the dialogue of the *Femmes Savantes* is never external; it is achieved by no explosive epigram; it is not the result of merely picking clever sayings from a notebook and pinning them into the conversation at a venture. But if there is no trace of artificial crackle and rattle like that which at once pleases and provokes us in the comedies of Congreve and of Sheridan, and which we cannot help suspecting to have been elaborated at leisure, there is in this comedy of Molière's a constant play of wit of a more truly intellectual kind. The French dramatist's humor is more solidly rooted in truth and more luxuriant in its flower; and his wit is less specious and more pervasive. The whole play is bathed in wit and swims in wit; and this wit is rather in the thought than in the phrasing. It is the wit of the intelligence, and not of the vocabulary only.

French critics have distinguished three forms of witticism, of the humorous stroke proper to comedy. One is the witticism itself, pure and simple, existing for its own sake, as serviceable in one scene as another; and for this inexpensive effect Molière has no liking. Another is the speech that evokes laughter because it expresses essential character; and a third is the phrase which comes spontaneously as the culmination of a situation, and which is funny only because it is spoken by that particular character at that particular moment. The dialogue of Molière's comedies is studded with humorous strokes of these two latter classes. Indeed, he had the gift of hitting on the sentence which combines the two, expressing character at the instant that the situation culminates. Such is the parting shot of Vadius as he challenges Trissotin to meet him face to face—"at the bookseller's." Such is Chrysale's sudden "my sister," by which he seeks to suggest that he has been addressing to Bélise the daring speech that he suspects Philaminte is ready to resent.

Molière does not condescend to the empty glitter of the clever sentence, which is extraneous to the immediate purpose of the scene; and he also eschews that bandying of sharp personalities which often degenerated into sheer vulgarity of retort in the Restoration dramatists, and which is not as infrequent as might be wished in Shakspere. There is delicate fencing in the interview of the two sisters; there is sharp rapier-play in the duel between Clitandre and Trissotin; and there is rougher saber work when Vadius and Trissotin turn on each other. But even in the encounter between these two thin-skinned and quick-tempered men there is no hint of the seeming brutality which we discover in the cut-and-thrust repartee of Beatrice and Benedick, and which suggests rather the boxing-glove than the fencing-foil. In Molière's comedy the characters, however irritable or exacerbated, abide by the rules of the sport and they do not hit below the belt. They preserve the courtesy of the school of arms, with the self-respect which implies respect for others. (pp. 298-304)

> *Brander Matthews, in his* Molière: His Life and His Works, *Charles Scribner's Sons, 1910, 385 p.*

W. P. KER (essay date 1922)

[*Ker was a noted Scottish scholar of medieval literature and an authority on comparative European literature and the history of literary forms. In the following excerpt from an essay first published in 1922, he evaluates Molière as a comic dramatist, centering on* The Misanthrope.]

To begin with, let the Devil's Advocate have his say. Molière's enemies provide him with arguments; Molière's best friend among the poets, Boileau, admits some of their charges, particularly that of clowning and buffoonery [see Bayle excerpt dated 1702 for Boileau's comment]. . . . It is not a charge that can be lightly evaded, and it is not far-fetched or hypercritical. It is there all the time, and the English reader need not be primed with Meredith's *Essay on Comedy* [see Additional Bibliography] in order to see the difference between Scapin and the Misanthrope. Is it worth while, when Don Juan is on the scene, to get a laugh out of the blow which is meant for Pierrot and lands on Sganarelle? Not even the *Misanthrope* is safe: the scene with Alceste's stupid servant at the end of the fourth act is noted by the corrector as rather too elementary for the finest of all comedies in the world.

The finest? Yes; and so fascinating that true believers, who of course are true lovers, will swear, as they follow it, that it is the only play in the world—here at last the quintessence, the eternal Idea, not in abstraction, but full of the life and movement of pure comedy, nothing omitted, nothing lost, nothing left over for other comic poets to attempt. This frame of mind, which is worship, may of course be misunderstood; it is going too far, says the sober critic. After all, there are other plays in the world, and Congreve's Millamant is not discountenanced in comparison with Molière's Célimène. But to the true believers this is irrelevant: they have found in the *Misanthrope* the end of their quest for the very essence of comedy; here they are at home, triumphant. And here, naturally, the noise of the adversary is silenced—his censures and complaints not refuted, simply ignored. (pp. 350-51)

Molière in his critical remarks on his challengers says many things very quietly and shortly that sum up and dispose of long, large, and tedious controversies. Thus on the dramatic unities (in the *Critique de l'Ecole des Femmes*) [see excerpt dated 1663]: "These are easy notes made by good sense to secure the pleasant effect of the play, and

good sense is capable of the same at any time without recourse to Horace or Aristotle. *Je voudrois bien savoir si la grande règle de toutes les règles n'est pas de plaire*" ["I should much like to know whether the grand rule of all rules is not the art to please"]. The result of this on the Abbé d'Aubignac and other patrons of the unities is like the simple speech in *The Emperor's New Clothes*: "The Emperor has nothing on." Hear what the innocent child says! (pp. 351-52)

Matthew Arnold, it is true, in his essay on the French Play in London (when the Comédie-Française came here in 1879), thinks that Molière ought to have been a tragic poet, and that he was put off by the weakness of French tragic verse [see excerpt dated 1879]. The critic, with his favourite device of quotation, has no difficulty in contrasting the effect of the French tragic Alexandrine with that of Shakespeare's blank verse, or in proving that the rhythms and rhymes of *Hernani* leave him cold. It may be admitted that Molière's verse in heroic drama—that is, in *Don Garcie de Navarre*—makes little attempt to do better than the ordinary conventional style, and does not scruple to repeat "vos divins appas" ["your divine Charms"] and similar customary phrases, which make one think of the notary's eloquence in a later most admirable French comedy: "Daignez, Mademoiselle, corroborer mes espoirs!" ["Deign, Mademoiselle, to corroborate my hopes!"]. But Matthew Arnold's objection to French verse leads him too far when he finds *Tartuffe* and the *Misanthrope* actually suffering from their burden of rhyme. "The freshness and power of Molière are best felt when he uses prose, in pieces such as the *Avare* or the *Fourberies de Scapin* or *George Dandin*." The freshness and power of Molière's prose who would deny? But it is going too far to find his genius better expressed in *L'Avare* or in *George Dandin* than in the two great rhyming comedies; to find in the verse of Alceste and Célimène constraint and artifice. M. Rigal is surely more plausible when he detects in Racine the pupil of Molière, using for tragedy the natural easy mode of dialogue which is the poetry of Molière. There is no need, for the present, to say more on this point: what is really important is that Molière did not think less highly of his dramas because they were not tragical; that he saw and appraised truly the right task of the comic poet. . . . It is not that the lovers of comedy are hard to please: contrariwise, they find true comedy everywhere—in fragments and patches and medleys. What they do not find, or hardly, is the perfect work, where the Muse herself conducts the orchestra, and nothing is flat, superfluous, or grating. The *Misanthrope*—some would add *Tartuffe*, and some *Les Femmes Savantes*, but the *Misanthrope* surely—has this place. Here is what is meant by comedy.

The persons are few, but no one notices this as a defect or a lowering of vitality. There are enough for the whole world of good society to be represented there. It is the comedy of good manners, like not so very many: not like *Tartuffe*, or *L'Ecole des Femmes*, or *L'Avare*. One other play of Molière's, *Les Femmes Savantes*, keeps to the true world: without are *bourgeois* and peasants. But *Les Femmes Savantes* is the play of good manners in a different sense from the *Misanthrope*: it is narrower in scope, being more definitely satirical and depending on "humours" more occasional and transitory than the eternal contradiction, the immortal harmony of Alceste and Célimène. The scene of Trissotin and Vadius is all very well in its way, but it is rather mechanical and caricatural: it is not out of place in *Les Femmes Savantes*, though that play, in the main, is more subtle than this scene: but there is no room in the *Misanthrope* for any such exhibition. In the *Misanthrope*, it is true, the sonnet of Oronte belongs to the world of *Les Précieuses* and of *Les Femmes Savantes*, but it is not introduced to show up the faults of fashionable taste: that is a secondary thing: its real purpose is to bring out Alceste's uncompromising sincerity. We are gainers by the way in hearing the lovely old verse of Alceste's ballad. . . . But the theatrical value of this lies in Alceste's refusal to be conventionally polite, and in his disgust at Philinte's conventional compliments.

The characters in the *Misanthrope*, as usual in comedy (and not infrequently in real life also), fall into contrasting pairs—Alceste and Célimène, Alceste and Philinte, Célimène and Arsinoé. Philinte, the good-natured, easy-going man of the world, has to argue with his friend's stubborn principles to prove that truth is not always convenient. Arsinoé, a very valuable person, a prude in the old as well as the later sense of the word, well deserving her place in the comedy, puts out her cold malignity against the more lively and brighter mischief of the spirit of Célimène. Part of the play, indeed most of it, is in the old fashion of debates and contentions—the mode from which, as Mr. Neil showed us in his edition of the *Knights*, all comedy is descended. Now contrasts and debates on the stage are dangerous; they may look too much like got up things, not imaginative, but merely calculated contrasts. The way to cure this is to use imagination to fill up the abstract outlines. And there is another way, well understood by Molière and nowhere more excellently employed than here, and that is to let the surrounding world, the fashion of life common to all the characters, have its right proportion in the story. Atmosphere counts for as much in the *Misanthrope* as in the "Meniñas" of Velasquez: the people on the stage are not, as many of the Elizabethan *dramatis personae* are, hard-shelled individual atoms of humanity, moving in worlds unrealised, without any visible means of subsistence. The fashion of the age is one of the antagonists of Alceste, but it is much more than an object to be railed at for complacent and undiscriminating flattery. It is much more than that, and more than Alceste recognises. If he himself were not in that world, living as part of it along with Célimène, Philinte, Oronte, Arsinoé, and a few marquises, his proud soul would be nothing to us; and it is Molière's great success that he has kept this world alive, along with and through his characters.

Are the friends of Molière to be judged according as they judge Célimène? It is a very delicate question, and indeed it must not be pressed. The facts of the case are considerably against the lady; she is, if not perfidious, at any rate not scrupulously sincere, and she speaks with a cruel tongue. Are we to accept the obvious judgment, and congratulate Alceste on being well rid of her? Possibly not.

The historians of Molière tell us that the comedy of Alceste and Célimène followed the heroic comedy of *Don Garcie de Navarre*, and used over again some of the drama of jealousy that had failed to impress the public in its original shape. *Don Garcie* undoubtedly was a failure, and as a failure it is often allowed to remain unnoticed. But there are some strong scenes in it, and they have their bearing on the *Misanthrope*. Don Garcie is not Alceste; he is simply the humour of jealousy dressed up for an heroic Span-

ish play; with just enough human life to serve for a contrast to the noble lady Done Elvire. Elvire in the heroic comedy is not a counterpart of Célimène, except that she has a half reasonable man to deal with: Elvire is much less amusing than Célimène, being no more than true heart and good sense. But in her treatment of Don Garcie, since the problem is not unlike what Célimène has to face, we can to some extent make out what Molière had at the back of his mind. He does not tell us everything about Célimène, and the partisans of that lady may be justified in believing that she is worth fighting for. And it may be said here that generally those who refuse to take the ordinary view of Beatrix Esmond will be found, with as much wisdom or the want of it, on the side of Célimène. Done Elvire gives them some encouragement. She has to talk to a man, Don Garcie, who is jealous perpetually and on all sorts of occasions: she explains to him that it will not do, most admirably; and, contrary to the usual practice of elegant females in drama, she does not take the first opportunity of misunderstanding her lover, nor even the last occasion, when she might have broken with him for ever and incurred no blame. What would she have said if Don Garcie had been of the same mind as Alceste? Clearly she would have told him a truth or two, plainly but with no bitterness; she would not have let him go; neither would she have accepted his lodge in a wilderness as a feasible scheme of a happy life. She would have seen the vanity of the creature, have felt that his emulation of the noble savage was really selfish, a touch of the egoist; and since Alceste, though suffering from "the distempered devil of self," is a right sort of man, he would have come round. Molière, it is proved, had not forgotten Don Garcie when he wrote the *Misanthrope*; if Célimène at the end does not talk like Done Elvire, it is not that Molière thinks she has no case to defend. What Alceste exacts from his wife to be is more than Done Elvire would have yielded, we are sure of; and that being so, we refuse to think the worse of Célimène on account of Alceste's indignation.

The English ("tardy, apish nation" though they may be) need not be altogether discontented when they review their transactions with Molière. . . . John Dennis was one of the first Englishmen to see the Alps "with a delightful Horrour, a terrible Joy," and one of the first to praise Molière [see excerpt dated 1720]:

> For *Molière's* Characters in his *Tartuffe* are Masterpieces, mark'd, distinguish'd, glowing, bold, touch'd with a fine yet daring Hand . . . ['Tis] by this Comedy and by the *Misanthrope* that Molière perhaps has born away the prize of Comedy from all Persons in all Ages, except Ben Jonson alone.

"Ben Jonson alone" we may find unnecessary, but this is proof of Dennis's good faith. His strong language is not careless or indiscriminate, nor is his regard for Ben Jonson merely literary or antiquarian. . . . Happily there is no compulsion laid on us to compare Molière with Ben Jonson, nor with Shakespeare either. (pp. 352-59)

Shakespeare seems to have been left free to choose his subjects and vary his methods as he thought fit. Molière has very little freedom: he is hindered in *Tartuffe*, an invention of his own; he is hindered in *Don Juan*, which was anyone's subject, as hackneyed as Punch and Judy. He is dependent on the Court, and is called on for *comédies-ballets*; he has to please the parterre, and he gives them (not all grudging) the thumpings of Sganarelle and the mockery of Medicine. Terence is translated to Tabarin (the zany of a mountebank), as Boileau complained; the *Phormio* of Terence to the *Fourberies de Scapin.* And this near the end, close upon *Les Femmes Savantes.* To the last of his days, and he died in the *Malade Imaginaire,* he kept the old talent for all the fun of the fair, and with all his irritability and nervous ill-temper he never seems to have found anything wrong in it, anything degrading in a change from high to low comedy. He had his great disappointments; not to speak of the *tracasseries* ["bickering"] about *Tartuffe* and the *Festin de Pierre,* he must have been hurt at the failure of *Don Garcie de Navarre,* at the poor success of the *Misanthrope.* But does he ever complain of anything that is required of him for the King's entertainment? Never, except incidentally when he has not enough time to invent, compose, rehearse, and stage what is wanted. Nor is there want of spirit in the compulsory pieces. *Les Fâcheux* is not a play; it is a hurried set of odd characters, satire rather than comedy. Nothing in Molière is livelier, though you may hesitate whether the greatest and therefore the most amusing bore is the hunting man or the gentleman who insists on your hearing his hand at piquet, all of it, to the end.... The French stage in the House of Molière has never discouraged the more obvious sort of comedy, and it is really part of the spirit of Molière that he should have agreed with the groundlings in their easy laughter, as well as with the quality in their finer shades.

"Courage, Molière! voilà la bonne comédie!" ["Courage, Molière! This is a good comedy!"]

That was the voice of the people, they say, after *Les Précieuses Ridicules.* It was a good opinion, though the cry of "Courage!" was not needed for one of the bravest spirits that ever lived. This essay is written to salute his memory on his birthday, with a grateful sense that "la bonne comédie" finds inexhaustible variety of meaning in his works, and, further, that when all is said, the people of this island, which gave shelter to Saint-Evremond in his exile and a hearty welcome to the Comédie Française at a later date, may fairly ask leave to praise the author in whom they see more clearly than in any other the spirit and soul of France. (pp. 360-62)

W. P. Ker, "Molière," in his Collected Essays of W. P. Ker, Vol. I, *edited by Charles Whibley, Macmillan and Co., Limited, 1925, pp. 350-62.*

JOHN PALMER (essay date 1930)

[*A British novelist, drama critic, and mystery writer (under the pseudonym of Francis Beeding), Palmer was a respected man of letters. In the following excerpt from his biography of Molière, he discusses Molière's handling of character in* The School for Husbands.]

L'Ecole des Maris is a play with a thesis. Ariste and Sganarelle, two elderly brothers, have been entrusted with the education and future destiny of Léonor and Isabelle. Ariste is in favour of a reasonable indulgence. Sganarelle is the advocate of an unreasonable repression. The brothers expect to marry their young wards. Ariste secures the affection and esteem of Léonor and will continue as her husband to allow her the liberties which he is confident she will not abuse, whereas Sganarelle by his severities and

suspicions drives Isabelle into the arms of a rival. (pp. 196-97)

Ariste develops his theme at length. Good company, balls, plays and other diversions—these help to form and enliven the mind. The best of all schools is the world. Finally, to the amazement and scandal of his brother, he affirms that he will be as faithful to his views after marriage as before and Sganarelle predicts for him the fate that in the sequel befalls himself. Sganarelle intends to look better after his wife. Dressed in good plain serge, with a black dress for festal occasions, she shall keep the house, look to its affairs and mend her linen.

There has been a good deal of high writing concerning the doctrines of Ariste. Certain critics have found here a whole philosophy of nature: let the young grow as they please; honour and virtue being spontaneous and from the heart will of themselves be triumphant. There is, however, very little philosophy of nature in *L'Ecole des Maris,* though there is abundance of commonsense such as Molière invariably applies to all matters of social conduct. The less, indeed, we say of nature in this connection, the better. Marriage between a man of sixty, for Ariste is alas! a sexagenarian, and a girl of eighteen is an arrangement which nature might be expected to regard with at most a qualified approval, and it should be observed that nature, if she prompts Léonor to marry Ariste for his kindness and instructs her in all the honourable virtues, also teaches Isabelle to be something of a minx. We readily forgive her ingenious duplicities; they are a legitimate defence against the tyranny of her guardian. But the critics who have read this play as an ode in celebration of the simple virtues of the human heart, would have done better to observe that Isabelle owed to nature and to nature alone a genius for complicated intrigue rarely equalled upon any stage. There is, in fact, just enough, but no more, of the philosophy of nature in Ariste to correct the lack of it in Sganarelle. Ariste expressly allows that nature in the young must be corrected, but corrected in such a way that virtue does not inspire them with reprobation and fear. He is advocating not licence but a reasonable freedom.... He stands for the conduct of an average man in a reasonably ordered society.

L'Ecole des Maris is a genuine comedy of character. Though the incidents of the play tend to farce, and the character of Sganarelle, who retains a generic name inherited from the comic old men of the Italian theatre, inclines at moments, towards the fantastical, neither the subject of the comedy nor the veracity of its portraiture is for a moment compromised. The extravagant absurdity of Sganarelle towards the close of the play is a logical consequence of the fixed ideas and emotions by which he is from first to last inspired. The situations in which he becomes involved are extravagant, but their extravagance is an expression of his own distorted inspiration. He becomes continuously more egocentric, and his gullibility arises in every case from a blind preoccupation with his own interests and desires. Molière here first reveals his comic genius at the full. The comedy of Sganarelle is a sublimation of the comedy of the drunken man, a source of infinite delight to his sober fellows because he has ceased to be one of them and is now a being, set apart, with a surprising logic and a procedure peculiar to himself. Unsuspectingly he acts as go-between between Isabelle and his rival, conveys their messages, fosters their intrigue, and finally himself conducts her to the arms of her lover—a figure of farce in his conduct, but saved for comedy by the fact that the ease with which he is deceived is due to the strongest and most persistent passion of his nature. He misleads himself more than he is misled. His egoism is so monstrous that it becomes at times pathological, and it is precisely at such moments that the genius of the author transforms what might so easily have been an exaggeration of farce into a profound and genuine stroke of character. The climax of the farce is also a climax of comic delineation. Turn, for an example, to Act II, Scene 14. Sganarelle, tremulous with delight at the fancied discomfiture of his rival falls, apparently, into a sudden pity for the young man: ... That is the *coup de génie*—a supreme touch. The drunken egoist embraces in his rival an embodiment of his own triumph; his sudden sympathy is due to a vivid sense of the defeat which he believes himself to have successfully escaped. The pity of the egoist for others is never more than a vicarious compassion for himself.

Molière's Sganarelle, to the careless eye a figure of farce, is, indeed, the first of his masterpieces of comic portraiture. It survives the most modern tests. The creator of Sganarelle knew nothing of complexes which are now a commonplace of popular psychology, but for those whom it amuses to apply modern terminology to a classical subject, Sganarelle of *L'Ecole des Maris* is an excellent victim. His attitude to society, apparently so insolent, is due to a constitutional diffidence. His contempt for the amenities of human intercourse is sheer timidity. His aggressive misanthropy is mere avoidance. The scheme whereby he seeks to win a wife who shall be entirely devoted is inspired by a persistent sense of his own inferiority. He rails at virtues in others in which he instinctively feels himself to be deficient, and the malicious joy which he feels in his own apparent triumph is sheer reaction from his normally downcast condition. His brief intoxication, when he thinks himself beloved of Isabelle, is the new wine that bursts the wineskin of a temperament fundamentally unexpectant of success in any form. In the manner of his kind he harps continually on the misfortunes and disabilities of others—his brother's age or the infidelities of his neighbour's wife—merely to keep his spirits up. He must be seeking continually to prove himself the better man, and this is no more than an anxiety to assert a superiority which he feels to be constantly in peril. His resolute disregard of fashion, culminating in his proud declaration that those who find him ill to look upon have only to shut their eyes, is the defiance of a nervous distemper.

Note how the skill of the practical man of the theatre in dealing with an audience, so strangely lacking in *Don Garcie*, is in this play apparent at every turn. Observe especially the care he takes to prevent our delight at Sganarelle's discomfiture being impaired by any compassion for his undoing. Sganarelle is as odious in defeat as in prosperity. He brings about his disgrace by the eagerness with which he desires to exult over the disgrace of his brother. He has a genius for the mean word and is inspired by an egoism so monstrous that our sympathy is at every turn estranged. Even the gentle Ariste declares at the last that no one can pity a man who rejoices so spitefully in the misfortunes of others.... (pp. 197-200)

Ariste, even when he believes himself to be deceived, remains true to his principles. He is disappointed, but there is no rancour or malice in the man, and he does not regret the generosity which has been, so he imagines, so ill repaid. Sganarelle is equally consistent. He cannot learn from his misfortunes. He has put his system to the test, and it has failed. But the failure, instead of convincing him of his error, merely confirms it. The fault lies not in himself or his opinions, but in the wickedness of the sex in general and of Isabelle in particular.... (p. 201)

L'Ecole des Maris completely obliterated the failure of *Don Garcie*. The Italianate author of the early farces, who with *Les Précieuses Ridicules* had begun to discover the true comedy in a satire upon contemporary manners, was now revealed as a dramatist with definite views, who could deal wisely and finely with problems of conduct and character. He had passed from the brilliant sketching of an external fashion to a serious study of social behaviour. He had thus entered upon that perilous enterprise of dealing with the accepted moral conventions of his day in the light of his own individual ideas and temperament which was to involve him in bitter and continuous controversy to the day of his death. (pp. 207-08)

John Palmer, in his Molière, *1930. Reprint by Benjamin Blom, Inc., 1970, 518 p.*

PERCY ADDISON CHAPMAN (essay date 1937?)

[*Chapman was an American essayist and educator. In the following excerpt from his posthumously published* The Spirit of Molière *(1940), he explicates the themes of jealousy and cuckoldry in* The School for Wives.]

[Based] on the *Précaution Inutile* of Scarron, the *Ecole des Femmes* is a further exploitation of the theme of the *Ecole des Maris*. True enough, Arnolphe is a wealthy Parisian bourgeois with houses in town and estates in the country—the fullest portrait that Molière has yet attempted of a contemporary figure. The plot turns on the fact that one of these estates carries with it a title, and at the beginning of the play Arnolphe is shown as desirous of assuming it and of being called Monsieur de la Souche. Yet this respectable bourgeois, who was far from abnormally susceptible to noble ambitions, is still Sganarelle. In him, even much more than in his predecessor of the *Ecole des Maris*, cuckoldry has become a fixed idea. He sees it everywhere. Gleefully he seeks for evidence of it amongst his friends and acquaintances. Nothing rejoices him so much as a tale of marital infidelity, and for him the inevitable result of marriage, as marriages are ordinarily made, is horns. All the observation of his forty-two bachelor years (he is pointedly shown to be forty-two) has led him to this conclusion. In his own case, we discover as he talks with his friend Chrysalde in the opening scene of the play, he has found a way to avoid them. He has adopted a little girl whom he had taken from the hands of a country nurse at the age of four, he has had her brought up in a convent in utter ignorance of the "facts of life," so that—perhaps from looking in her convent at pictures of the Annunciation—she thinks that children are "born by the ear"; he has recently shut her up in one of his town houses under the guard of a simple-minded peasant couple, and tomorrow he will marry her. She will be entirely his. All she knows in life he will have taught her. He has found a means of satisfying completely what La Rochefoucauld calls "the secret desire of possessing what one loves."

No better theatrical convention could be found, it would seem, to stress the inhuman absurdity of such a design, in a world where men live together in society, than to bring it out from the recesses of the house where it was conceived and to air it in a public square where people come and go about their affairs. It may be shown as colossally heroic and gloriously monstrous when an Italian prince of the Renaissance shuts up his beloved in a dark mysterious castle hidden among mist-covered marshes, as in the story told by Stendhal. Solitude and power are necessary if such a scheme is to be taken for a moment seriously. "Secret desires" of that sort are of the kind that men ordinarily situated must keep to themselves. If they become known, they will lead—not to disaster, there are no disasters in public squares—but to ridicule.

Something of the sort must have been the idea of this comedy as Molière conceived it. But the public square of comedy, good "stylization" as it was, proved an inadequate setting for the presentation of a probable human episode such as the "rules" required. The whole play is a tissue of improbabilities. It is improbable that people should come out of their houses to discuss their most private affairs in the street, and yet Molière's plot requires that almost the entire action be composed of the discussion of private affairs.

The story is briefly as follows. To Arnolphe comes young Horace, the son of an old friend who has been away for years. Horace announces his father's speedy return to Paris, but confides to Arnolphe that in the meanwhile he needs money. Arnolphe without hesitation presents him with his purse, and then learns what Horace is to do with it. He is in love. . . . But the person in question is precisely the young Agnes whom Arnolphe is guarding and intending to marry. Horace knows her as the ward of a certain "de la Zousse, ou Source," whom he does not connect with Arnolphe.

On this misunderstanding the whole plot turns. Arnolphe, instead of enlightening his young friend as to the identity of the object of his affections, encourages him to pursue his design, and then makes every effort to see to it that the design is frustrated. This line of conduct in itself smacks more of the farce than of life. However, young Agnes, whom love draws to Horace at first sight, discovers within herself a brain and will of her own. Every obstacle that Arnolphe puts in the path of the young lovers is thus turned as it were by the power of love itself, and Agnes finally walks out of the house and joins her lover. This is, of course, no good ending for a comedy, and Horace immediately turns the ward of Monsieur de la Souche over to his friend Arnolphe for safe-keeping until he shall have seen his father and gained his consent to marry her. The father shortly arrives with a friend who has been for years in America (favorite haven of the *deus ex machina* of Renaissance comedy), but whose daughter, left in France, they arranged long ago for Horace to marry. It then appears that this daughter is the very Agnes, ward of Arnolphe, about whom the play has revolved, and the end comes with the latter's discomfiture and the satisfaction of all the rest.

None of the events of the comedy is shown to the audience. The stage represents the front of the house in which Agnes is kept under the guard of Alain and Georgette, and her acquaintance with Horace begins as she is sitting on

Engraved handbill produced for early performances of The School for Wives.

her balcony, and he bows to her from the square below. Yet the audience learns of this meeting, first when Horace tells Arnolphe of it, and later, in delicious detail, when Agnes in all innocence recounts it herself to her suffering guardian. Then, Arnolphe having instructed the servants to refuse the young man admittance, and Agnes to repel his advances, and having posted himself to see that his orders are carried out, Horace again walks beneath the balcony, and is received by a "grès," that is, a stone which Agnes throws in his direction. Of this episode, however, which, like the first, could have taken place on the stage itself, the audience learns only when Horace recounts it to his "friend" Arnolphe as a good joke on Monsieur de la Souche: for to the stone was attached a note, read aloud by Horace, in which Agnes avows her love for him and her ignorance of proper conduct under the circumstances with an innocence, a sweetness and a frankness which are at the same time exquisite and unspeakably comic. So the play goes. Whether the events take place in Agnes' room, in the garden at the rear of the house, or in the public square itself, the audience is appraised of these through conversations which are held in the most unlikely place imaginable for them.

The meetings of the characters, their entrances and exits, their accounting for their presence outside the house, are all managed with an obvious, though not unskillful, awkwardness. At the very center of the play, for example, is a scene in which Arnolphe, seated, to Agnes, standing, preaches a veritable sermon upon the relations between husband and wife:

> Du côté de la barbe est la toute puissance
>
> [All authority is on the side of the beard].

and then has Agnes read aloud a series of stanzas called "Les Maximes du mariage, ou les Devoirs de la femme mariée" ["The Maxims of Marriage, or The Duties of the Married Woman"]. If ever there was a scene for the closet, it would seem to be that one. Yet Arnolphe, by calling to his servants for "un siège au frais ici" ["a chair out in the open"], as if to profit by the cool of the evening, makes in a way acceptable the picture of the enthronement of the husband and the humility of the wife in that very public square which amplifies the absurdity of any such conception of marital relationship.

In other words, there is here a sort of conflict between the traditional stylization of comedy and the equally traditional plot of the comedy of intrigue based on events, and, on the other hand, the real interest of classical comedy as it was developing, which, like that of all classical drama, lay in qualities of character and in psychological reactions as revealed through conversations. The plot is a romantic love story, yet the play lies in the characters of Arnolphe and Agnes opposed to each other. Horace is a mere conventional young lover who is presented to the audience as of no interest, however interesting he may be to the heroine. The events merely seem to add one trait after another to the two main characters. The action is the effect of love: love unrequited in Arnolphe, love encouraged in Agnes. Manners are not forgotten, that is, pictures of contemporary Parisian life; but they are brought in incidentally as illustrating the characters' preoccupations, mainly in the discussions between Arnolphe and Chrysalde upon the generality of marital woes. It is a question whether this aspect of the *Ecole des Femmes* is important enough to justify its being looked upon as the first French comedy of manners. It does not indeed turn as much upon manners as did the *Fâcheux*. Making a plot was one thing, painting manners another.

Agnes in this play frees herself from her guardian and joins her lover as does the Isabelle of the *Ecole des Maris*. But whereas the latter is represented as being thoroughly mature and sophisticated, an adept at dissimulation and of an extraordinary inventiveness, in Agnes her utter innocence and truthfulness are only matched by her ignorance. She talks of her feelings at the approach of Horace with the same candor that she shows in telling of the fleas that bother her at night (oh, heroines of romance, what would you say of this?). Whereas Isabelle knows that Sganarelle is repulsive and Valère attractive, Agnes has never heard of love and is all obedience and sweetness toward Arnolphe at the same time that a new and unsuspected feeling is drawing her toward Horace. Far from realizing that she must trick her guardian in order to escape from him, she is easily led to believe that Arnolphe will respect her inclination for Horace and favor her union to him, and she is only undeceived when he himself has made his opposition too brutally evident.

For her, vice has no more meaning than virtue:

> Je m'entends point de mal dans tout ce que j'ai fait....
> Le moyen de chasser ce qui fait du plaisir?

> [I have not intended any harm in all I have done....
> How can one chase away what gives pleasure?]

Some critics have been inclined to see back of this line all its philosophical consequences, and to make of Molière, not only a thorough "libertine" and epicurean, but also a precursor of the hedonistic philosophers of the eighteenth century. It would perhaps be safer merely to see in Agnes a figure of innocence, purity, naturalness, of young love—the first "ingénue" in fact, but lacking the aura with which much romantic writing would have surrounded her. She is presented with a sort of cruel completeness and with no attempt to veil the physical and social implications of love. No sacredness is here attached to innocence and purity, and Agnes is represented as welcoming the caresses of her lover with as much candor as his impassioned declarations. The most shocking scene in the play to many contemporaries was that in which she tells Arnolphe of the visit made her in his absence by Horace.... [Whatever] images arise in the spectator's mind are of a sort to present together the sweetness of innocence and the gestures of lust. It is, of course, the spirit of the farce, which looks life in the face. But your farceur is usually careful never really to arouse in his audience the feeling of what innocence and purity are—there were no women in the farces of Molière's childhood. That he should dare to do so in this play is evidence of the depths to which comedy was penetrating. We are far, here, from the delicacy of the *Fâcheux*. Indeed it confirms ... that, the more Molière worked upon a comedy, the less able he was to remain within the bounds of taste as it existed in his time.

What is true of the figure of Agnes is even more so of that of Arnolphe. After Mascarille, this is the longest part that Molière wrote for himself, and, in contrast to the "emperor of rascals," is perhaps the most grotesquely ridiculous. No more "playing heroes" for Molière. This was an awkward part, full of asides and lengthy monologues, which, however, had shown themselves effective with the public, even if disapproved by the critics of drama. It was a complex one, too. Arnolphe is not only the Sganarelle of the *Cocu* and the *Ecole des Maris*, but in him to vanity is added a real love for his ward. Love, that is, if such a name can be given to the desire to possess entirely. It is such love as could exist in a world where self-love alone would be observed as a reality. As a matter of fact, Arnolphe, from the beginning, is presented as the sort of man for whom society is, to put it mildly, suspicious.... That Chrysalde, Arnolphe's "good friend," should be a cuckold would cause in him only satisfaction and a sense of superiority.... In him the sin of presumption and of "suffisance" fairly cries out for a fall. Such a design as he has upon Agnes is mad, such a design is odious, such a design is contrary to the essential requirements of life in society—it is unspeakably absurd. So does the exposition present this figure, unsympathetic, condemned in advance, deserving of punishment.

The trouble is, however, that mad, odious, anti-social, absurd as Arnolphe's desire may be made to appear, it is none the less only too human.... The longing for complete possession ... is, alas! too close to the human heart and to the secret of success in living not to excite sympathy after all. The spectator at this play—especially perhaps the modern spectator—is constantly on the point of exclaiming: "Poor Arnolphe!" A recent reviewer calls Agnes a "cruel child." Molière, going even deeper into the character of his cuckold, has endowed him not only with the desire to possess, but also and at the same time the desire to be loved. Whenever his fixed idea is not involved, he is represented as a man capable of disinterested friendship and of arousing friendship. He is no mere grotesque, as is Sganarelle. He is a man, with much good to him but with a weakness. Such is, it will be remembered, Aristotle's requirement for the hero of tragedy.

On returning from the country, Arnolphe expects the household to be overjoyed at seeing him, but his two country bumpkin servants are so simple-minded that, far from showing him any affection, they are too innocent even to show respect. Looking for devotion and met with neglect, Arnolphe changes from the benevolent master to the violent tyrant, and the hilarious farce scene thus provoked sets the tone for the ensuing changes in his feelings for Agnes. . . . (pp. 122-32)

As he sees his ward slipping from him, Arnolphe has come to realize more and more what the possession of Agnes means to him, and is reduced to plead with her in a way which, grotesque though it is, is none the less the expression of real suffering:

Enfin à mon amour rien ne peut s'égaler:
Quelle preuve veux-tu que je t'en donne, ingrate? . . .
Je suis tout prêt, cruelle, à te prouver ma flamme.

[In short, my love is without compare:
What proof do you wish me to give you, ungrateful
    one? . . .
I am quite ready, O cruel one, to prove to you my love].

But when she answers:

Tenez, tous vos discours ne me touchent point l'âme;
Horace avec deux mots en ferait plus que vous

[Stay, nothing you say touches my heart;
Horace could do more in two words than you],

he is thrown into the extreme of violence:

Ah! c'est trop me braver, trop pousser mon courroux! . . .
Mais un cul de couvent me vengera de tout.

[Ah! You try my anger too far, and affront me to
    much! . . .
But a far off convent shall avenge everything].

The convent was of course the traditional alternative to marriage for the recalcitrant girl. Molière's "cul de couvent," by analogy to "cul de basse-fosse," meaning the deepest of dungeons, is one of those twists of language by which he drives home the absurdity of desire when ill-directed. It brings out in a flash the contrast between the ferocity of authority and the gentleness of love, assimilating as it does a convent, which should be a refuge and a reward, to a prison, place of punishment and restraint.

What is to be said as to the relation between the theme of jealousy and cuckoldry to be found in the *Ecole des Femmes* and the plays preceding it, and Molière's own personal experience? For moderns eagerly looking in an artist's work for revelations of his own life and circumstances, it is easy to leap upon the parallel between Arnolphe, aged forty-two, Agnes in her teens, and Molière, aged forty, Armande half as old, just as in the *Ecole des Maris*, the older

and successful guardian, Ariste, is similar to Molière, whereas the younger guardian, Sganarelle, is not. (pp. 133-34)

Quite evidently this series of comedies [on jealousy and cuckoldry], is even more the result of observation of life than it is a reflection of emotional experiences. More than that, Sganarelle and even Arnolphe are types of farce far more than they are individuals. They are as old as French art. The problem of Arnolphe is that of Panurge, on which Rabelais spends an entire book, and the differences inMolière's treatment from Rabelais' are far more explicable through an examination of their two worlds than of their personalities. For Rabelais, the main problem was knowledge, for Molière, it is society. Rabelais' cure for cuckoldry—as for everything else—was "trink," Molière's is renunciation by the male of the hope which he derives from the authority granted him by custom. Such is the lesson that the two "schools" teach. In the first, the older lover wins by kindness, the younger loses by selfishness. In the second, it is the older lover who is the grotesque, and it is youth which wins or rather nature. The idea of the first play, borrowed from Mendoza, shows the generous spirit triumphing, in spite of the handicap of age, the ungenerous spirit losing in spite of advantages. This is the atmosphere of the serious play of Molière's youth, but not that of comedy. High moral qualities excite less enthusiasm, in 1662, than in the days of Rodrigue and Auguste, because they inspire less confidence. People flocked to the Palais-Royal, to roar at Arnolphe, as a score of years before they had flocked to the Marais to be stirred and uplifted by the heroes of tragedy. The *Ecole des Femmes* marks a deepening, it is true, in Molière's work, and for this it would be hazardous to allege that his experience was in no way responsible. But still more it marks a further progress in comedy. (pp. 135-36)

Percy Addison Chapman, in his The Spirit of Molière: An Interpretation, *edited by Jean-Albert Bédé, Princeton University Press, 1940, 250 p.*

JOHN GASSNER (essay date 1940)

[*Gassner, a Hungarian-born American scholar, was a great promoter of American theater, particularly the work of Tennessee Williams and Arthur Miller. He edited numerous collections of modern drama and wrote two important dramatic surveys,* Masters of Modern Drama *(1940) and* Theater in Our Times *(1954). In the following excerpt from* Masters of Modern Drama, *he assesses the levels of wit, social criticism, and characterization found in Molière's comedies.*]

Molière was no reformer of the militant stamp; although he was the intellectual superior of most men of his generation, he was a true son of the age. Indignation was not in good taste when the predominant ideal of French society was reasonableness. Moreover, a display of bad temper in the theatre would not have been consonant with the viewpoint of a man who made irrationality and excess the butt of his wit. He never roared like Jonson; he simply laughed.

His comic method was accordingly sure and neat. Most of his plays were written in the formal Alexandrine couplets with general adherence to the unities of time, place, and action. Even when he had more than one plot in hand, his story remained lucid and its events were scrupulously balanced. His style was playful even when most terse, and restrained even when most playful, for his laughter at its best was, without ceasing to be laughter, "nearer a smile"; it was, in short, "humor of the mind." A unique talent for grace and flexibility, for the deft use of the fencer's foils, is a prerequisite for this kind of humor, and it is little wonder that Molière seems rather commonplace and vacuous when his glinting lines are dulled in English translations.... Rarely is his limber and pirouetting, yet direct and manly, manner captured in English.... Underlying this style is a culture or a refinement of manners not equally dispensed to every creature, and a "gaiety of disposition" which Voltaire rightly attributed to all masters of laughter. (Even if, being human, they too must on occasion experience anger and despair.) There is something rare in such a disposition, despite the assumption that any fool can laugh. As a matter of fact, fools can't; they can only guffaw.

It is a mistake to believe that such a style is an easy accomplishment; actually, in Molière's case, it was the product of a process of refinement and it was attained only after many essays in the more easily acquired art of horseplay. It is equally a mistake to imagine that it is synonymous with superficiality. Actually the smile of the truly civilized artist is "something overcome"—a triumph of spirit over error or failure. And this was particularly true of Molière whose private life was unhappy and whose personal outlook was distinctly critical. Nor is his smile at all reminiscent of the frozen expression of some pre-Attic statue. It was instinct with tenderness for natural people, young lovers, and sensible persons of all classes. He had real humanity—he had feeling without sentimentality.Molière succeeded, both as a dramatist and as a showman, by astutely combining wit, criticism, and appealing characterization.

Only in never sentimentalizing the latter and in retaining his equanimity when his characters are calculating or stupid did he maintain that intellectual flavor which gives high comedy its clean sharpness. He possessed a fundamental humanity, but he expressed it best in comedy that is as "pure" or "high" as it can be made without approaching inhumanity. He was rarely neutral in issues involving hypocrisy, unreason or denial of healthy instinct; he is not found neutral in his comedies when Tartuffe is triumphing and when miserly or fatuous old men strive to frustrate youthful love. That is the basis of such a neat judgment as John Palmer's that "Justice in the comedies of Molière is always done. There is no intrusion of the man of feeling or prejudice to mar the even tenor of his comic way." Only with respect to this balanced approach to humanity are Bergson's words that "laughter is incompatible with emotion" true of Molière. (pp. 287-88)

Molière essayed tragedy and tragic acting and would have liked to succeed in these departments. His life and career reveal a rounded personality and not a disembodied intellect. Surely, the modern theatre's second universal genius is not the cerebral wart that some of his admirers discover in their eulogies. He merely allowed intelligence to dominate the emotions. (p. 288)

John Gassner, "Molière and the Comedy of Society," in his Masters of the Drama, *Random House, 1940, pp. 286-314.*

MARTIN TURNELL   (essay date 1947)

[*Turnell was an English translator and essayist who wrote widely on French literature and made significant translations of the works of Jean-Paul Sartre, Guy de Maupassant, Blaise Pascal, and Paul Valéry. In the following excerpt from his* The Classical Moment: Studies of Corneille, Molière, and Racine *(1947), Turnell uses* The School for Wives *to substantiate his opinion that Molière's characters are "comprehensive [studies] of the complexities and contradictions of human nature."*]

A great imaginative writer naturally draws on his own experience for his work, but there is no evidence for the view that in the *École des maris* Molière was attempting to explore the prospects of his forthcoming marriage or that Arnolphe in the *École des femmes* is "a portrait of the artist." In both plays the emphasis falls on *école*, on education for marriage. The *École des maris* is a charming comedy in which Molière contrasts two different ways of bringing up young women—the narrow, jealous method of Sganarelle which leads to deception and disaster, and the tolerant and reasonable spirit of Ariste who lets Léonor go her own way, marries her with her own consent and no doubt lived happily ever after.

L'École des femmes is not among Molière's supreme achievements, but it marks an immense step forward. For here in essentials and for the first time we find the mature Molière. The maturity is nowhere more apparent than in the transformation of Sganarelle into Arnolphe, the first of the great comic characters. When Arnolphe declares: ...

> Afin que les soupçons de *mon esprit malade*
> Puissent sur le discours la mettre adroitement,
> Et, lui sondant le coeur, s'éclaircir doucement.
>
> [Now, may my unhappy suspicions be
> set at rest! I will sound her [Agnes's]
> heart as cleverly as I can, and
> try to make the conversation reveal the truth.]

he not only sounds a fresh note, he also looks forward to [Philinte's] warning to Alceste:

> Non, tout de bon, quittez toutes ces incartades,
> Le monde par vos soins ne se changera pas;
> ...que *cette maladie*
> Partout où vous allez, donne la comédie.
>
> ["Come, seriously, leave all those rude freaks.
> The world will not change for all your meddling...
> This complaint of yours is as good as comedy"].

The critical words are *mon esprit malade* and *cette maladie*. For all Molière's principal comic characters are *malades*. More than any other great comic writer of the time he realized that comedy is essentially a serious activity. His work is a study of some of the chief social maladies not merely of his own, but of all time, seen against the background of a stable order. In this play it is jealousy, in *Tartuffe* religious mania and in *le Malade imaginaire* the cult of ill-health. The ravages of the *maladie* are very extensive. It undermines the natural human faculties and encloses the victim in a private world of his own disordered imagination. One of the fundamental traits of the *malade* is a fanatical desire to impose the standards of this private world on society, as Alceste tries to "change the world" and Arnolphe tries to bring up Agnès according to his own unbalanced theories:

Dans un petit couvent, loin de toute pratique,
Je la fis élever selon ma politique,
C'est-à-dire ordonnant quels soins on emploierait
Pour la rendre idiote autant qu'il se pourrait.

[In a little solitary convent I had the girl brought
up according to my own ideas: that is to say, I
told them what means they should employ to
make her as simple as possible].

This sinister declaration, this open attempt to destroy a woman's natural faculties, shows to what extent the *malade* has become a menace to the community. The remedy lies in collective action, in the destruction of the anti-social tendencies by laughter and the introduction of sane values into the comic world. This brings us to the *honnête homme* who makes his first appearance in the *École des femmes*. Chrysalde is not of the stature of Cléante or Philinte, and his view that it doesn't matter whether you are a *cocu* or not as long as you take your misfortune like a gentleman is crude in comparison with their urbane, polished discourses on *la juste nature* and *la parfaite raison*; but in spite of his shortcomings he does stand for a norm of tolerance and good sense.

I have never felt convinced by the theory of certain French critics that Molière's characters are in some sense abstractions, that he shows us the Jealous Man, the Hypocrite, the Misanthrope or the Miser, while a modern novelist like Balzac shows us a particular miser in a particular French province in the nineteenth century. There is a clear distinction between Shakespearean comedy and Jonson's "comedy of humours." It seems to me that Molière is closer to Shakespeare than he is to Jonson, and that so far from probing more deeply into human nature thanMolière, Balzac bears a striking resemblance to Jonson. Classical comedy certainly imposed limitations, but what is remarkable is that in spite of these limitations Molière managed to present such a comprehensive study of the complexities and contradictions of human nature. Argan is not merely a *malade imaginaire*, he is mean and cruel and cheerfully prepared to sacrifice his daughter's happiness in order to secure free medical advice for himself. In the *Femmes savantes* what really interests us in Armande is not her ridiculous intellectual pretensions, but the angry frustration of the sexually acquisitive woman.

The *École des femmes* is primarily a study of jealousy, but Arnolphe is no more a simple case than Molière's other characters. The originality of Molière's approach is well brought out by Ramon Fernandez [see Additional Bibliography] when he suggests that the point of the play lies in the transformation of the *homme-père b! into the homme-mari* ["man-as-husband"]. It is true that Arnolphe loves his ward as a husband while she can only love him as a father, but this is not the whole of the problem. It must not be thought that the prominence given to cuckoldry is a light-hearted borrowing from traditional French farce or that Molière's treatment of it has anything in common with Wycherley's in his crude adaptation of the play. Arnolphe's anxiety to "create" a wife who will be faithful to him springs from a primitive but deep-seated fear of being a cuckold. There is no need to dwell on the psychological implications of this fear which is so pervasive that it turns jealousy into a form of sexual mania. When Arnolphe declares:

Je veux pour espion, qui soit d'exacte vue,
Prendre le savetier du coin de notre rue
Dans la maison toujours je prétends la tenir,
Y faire bonne garde, et surtout en bannir...
Tous ces gens qui sous main travaillent chaque jour
A faire réussir les mystères d'amour.

[I will employ the cobbler who lives at the corner of our
street as a spy. I intend to have her always in the
house, and to keep strict watch there. Above all I will
banish... all those people who dabble everyday of their
underhanded lives in forwarding love-intrigues].

the crux of the passage lies in the lurid *mystères d'amour*, and the words gain their effect from the contrast with the normal life of the *quartier* which Molière evokes with his characteristic skill. For in Arnolphe's disordered imagination the whole of this world is undermined by the subterranean activities of the purveyors of love, as the whole of his personality is undermined by his mania. When in another place he cries:

Et cependant je l'aime, après ce lâche tour
Jusqu'à ne me pouvoir passer de cet amour.
Sot, n'as-tu point de honte? Ah! je crève, j'enrage,
Et je souffletterais mille fois mon visage.

[and yet I love her, in spite of this mean trick, love
her to distraction. Fool, have you no shame? Ah! I shall go
mad, go mad, I could slap my face a thousand times].

there is no mistaking the voice. It is the voice of all Molière's great comic characters, the voice of impotent, exasperated denunciation of a world which they cannot "change" and in which they have no place.

The voice also explains one of the secrets of Molière's art. "His characters," wrote Paul Bourget, "are, so to speak, composed in two layers. The first consists of the peculiarities which make them ridiculous, the second of the authentic human material.... At certain moments in the play, the first layer bursts apart and reveals the second."

Although this comment suggests that there is something a little mechanical about the construction of Molière's characters and underestimates, perhaps, the extent to which their peculiarities are rooted in their personality, it underlines one important factor. In the central passages in the comedies there is a sudden eruption of subterranean instincts into the world of everyday experience, and it is this that gives Molière's work its special resonance. At such moments the mind of the spectator is suspended between two impulses—pity and laughter—which superficially appear to exclude one another, and comedy is felt to be a continual oscillation between what one writer has lately called *la vie tragique* and la vie *triviale*. It is not, however, an alternation between tragic and comic emotions. The two are fused into a single new emotion which differs from them both and is proper to comedy. Life is suddenly perceived under a twofold aspect and this is the core of the comic poet's experience.

It is not the tranquil homilies of Chrysalde which place Arnolphe's *maladie* in its true perspective, but the simple words of Agnès, as she speaks of her love for Horace:

Il jurait qu'il m'aimait d'une amour sans seconde,
Il me disait des mots les plus gentils du monde,
Des choses que jamais rien ne peut égaler,
Et dont, toutes les fois que je l'entends parler,
La douceur me chatouille et là-dedans remue
Certain je ne sais quoi dont je suis toute émue.

[He swore he loved me better than anyone else had ever been loved, and said the prettiest things imaginable to me, things which none can equal and which, every time I heard them spoken, thrilled me with pleasure. I felt something, I know not what it was, that coursed through me].

In these lines, in which we seem to catch the very tone of the girl's voice and which derive much of their force from the contrast with Arnolphe's overwrought declarations, we see the healthy, natural human feelings asserting themselves, expressing themselves in spite of a lack of adequate concepts on the part of the speaker. It is the ruin of Arnolphe's horrifying *politique*. (pp. 54-8)

> Martin Turnell, "Molière," in his The Classical Moment: Studies of Corneille, Molière and Racine, *1947. Reprint by Greenwood Press, 1971, pp. 44-132.*

W. G. MOORE (essay date 1949)

[*An English essayist and educator, Moore was a well-known scholar of French literature whose contributions to Molière studies have been highly praised. In the following excerpt from his* Molière: A New Criticism *(1949), Moore discusses the figurative masks worn by Molière's characters in* The School for Wives, Tartuffe, *and* The Misanthrope *in an attempt to determine whether such masks can be considered indicative of his views on the principles of comedy. Brian Nicholas assesses and rejects Moore's views of the character Tartuffe in his excerpt dated 1980.*]

The peculiar feature and symbol of the dramatic tradition in which [Molière] was trained was the mask.... Assuming for a moment that his plays show cases of social habit as a kind of mask covering human nature, should one say more than this? What is the connexion between Molière's skill in portraying assumed attitudes (masks) and the comic vision that is the dynamic and formative element of his work? In other words, has the mask anything to do with the principle of comedy as Molière imagined it? The question might be settled without difficulty if we were agreed what that principle is, but ... we must proceed from the mask to the comedy rather than fit the mask to a presupposition of the comedy.

It is obvious, to begin with, that many comic effects can be obtained by the juxtaposition of the real and the assumed. This is a frequent source of comedy in ordinary life and one would not expect a trained comedian, whose business it was to distil comedy from any kind of situation, to pass it by. What the valet really thinks of his master is of course very different from what he can say in his presence. The comic dramatist arranges a situation in which the two views clash and amuse by the abruptness of the contrast. Thus Sganarelle:

> Mon maître est un fourbe, il n'a dessein que de vous abuser, et en a bien abusé d'autres, c'est l'épouseur du genre humain, et ... (apercevant Don Juan). Cela est faux; et quiconque vous dira cela, vous lui devez dire qu'il en a menti. Mon maître n'est point l'épouseur du genre humain, il n'est point un fourbe, il n'a pas dessein de vous tromper, et n'en a point abusé d'autres. Ah, tenez, le voilà; demandez-le plutôt à lui-même.

[My master is a knave. He only intends to ruin you as he has ruined so many others; he marries the whole sex and ... (He sees Don Juan.) It is false, and you can tell whoever told you it that he lies. My master does not marry the whole sex, he is not a knave, he does not intend to deceive you, and he has never ruined others. Oh! stop, here he is, ask him himself, if you like].

The valet may be released from his mask of discretion not by the absence of his master, but by freedom to speak his mind. Harpagon is curious to know what people think of him, and Maître Jacques reluctantly consents to tell him, only to be beaten and told to 'learn how to speak'. It is amusing, and liberating, to see the mask of convention removed, because in real life this rarely happens.

But discretion imposed by social status is a simple form of mask. What of that imposed by one's views, attitude, temperament? We meet many people whose behaviour is dictated by an idea, a way of looking at things. The seventeenth century called this 'imagination' and saw in it, in Pascal's words, an enemy of reason, which it dominates and subdues, to the extent of establishing within man 'a second nature'. On this point Pascal and Molière seem to be in ... agreement.... Molière has animated for us these people who get things wrong and who live in a world of their own, the hypochondriac, for example, or the miser. Even his titles emphasize their delusion: *Le Cocu Imaginaire, Le Malade Imaginaire.* Is not Jourdain of this family also, the bourgeois who apes the gentry, who imagines himself a man of quality? And in such plays we are given hints of a real man other than the mask of his delusion. Argan thinks he is ill and weak because he believes his doctors, but when he forgets what they say he is strong and shows that he can do what he will never admit he can do. Harpagon is at times an inhuman miser with no thought for people, at others a human being sensitive to lack of affection.

These are cases of human nature covered by a mask which is unconscious. But we meet yet another category, whose policy it is to play a part, rogues, schemers, charlatans. The doctors do not get things wrong; they lead others wrong; they are not deceived but deceivers. They assume a mask of omniscience for their own profit. Arnolphe is a tyrant, Tartuffe a hypocrite, Don Juan a libertine, each for his own ends. But here surely the simile of the mask breaks down; in these cases is not the mask the man? Yet here again they have other qualities which they are anxious to hide, which are not assumed but almost completely suppressed. Arnolphe is timid, Tartuffe sensual, Don Juan is warm-hearted as well as calculating. They are clever, but not clever enough to take us in all the time. Is not their cleverness a mask, the more dramatic for being imposed by their own will? If this is so, Molière has turned the mask into a symbol of much more than a vice or defect that adheres to a man. It is a symbol of cleverness, art, skill on which a man prides himself, but which may well run counter to his real self. The struggle to keep the mask in place, to achieve one's end, becomes a struggle between art and nature, craft and habit, intelligence and character. If such be Molière's principle of comedy, is it not nearer poetry than realism?

These points may be tested by scrutiny of such a play as *L'École des Femmes.* Arnolphe is a man with a plan of which he is proud, and which is inhuman to the point of involving the stultification of a human being. He speaks of his ward, to whom his plan has denied a proper education, in the most impersonal and callous terms. He has indeed all the marks of the crank, filled with the persuasion that he is right, that no one can teach him anything, that by his ingenuity he has solved a problem that has perplexed the world for centuries. The plan is, in a word, the School for Wives. It sets out to ensure fidelity in the wife by making her unattractive and completely dependent upon her husband. Furthermore, Arnolphe has not only skill and confidence; he has luck; he holds all the cards and is even informed by his opponent of each step taken or contemplated by the other side. Nevertheless his plan fails. Why? Many reasons might be given. No doubt because things are so arranged that the other side (whom we as spectators want to see victorious) are allowed, for our pleasure, to be so. But why do we sympathize with them, or rather, why has the dramatist so put the position that we all do want Arnolphe to be defeated? We might say that we 'naturally' side against him. He is trying to interfere with nature, and nature defeats him. The famous letter written by Agnès is a poignant document: 'Comme je commence à croire qu'on m'a toujours tenue dans l'ignorance, j'ai peur de mettre quelquechose qui ne soit pas bien' ["I begin to see that I have always been kept in ignorance, and I am therefore afraid I shall write something which may not be right"]. Who can read this powerful description of an awakening natural faculty without sympathy? The struggle within and behind the play is one between artifice and nature.

But what happens to Arnolphe? He is beaten, but does he admit his error, and reform, or think out a better plan? Some contemporaries were scandalized at the end of the play, and denied that he was a comic figure at all. To leave him tricked and cheated, even though he deserved to lose, what is comic about this? The answer is, nothing. The comedy of the play does not consist wholly, or even chiefly, in the fact that nature has been lucky enough to outwit art. That would come to little more than *Schadenfreude*. There is another Arnolphe than the crank. The crank is inhuman, but Arnolphe falls in love; in no grand way, certainly; it is a kind of sensual calf-love, but it is no part of his plan; it is a feeling quite opposed to the plan and which he obviously had not reckoned upon at all. When he is in power he says, parodying the heroes of Corneille,

Je suis maître, je parle; allez, obéissez

[I am master, I say; go, obey],

as one might talk to a dog. This is the tone of the Maxims of Marriage which he pontifically makes Agnès read in order that she may fully realize her wifely duty. Yet in a later scene we find him on his knees professing that he will do anything for her, that she need make no promises, nor even be faithful:

Tout comme tu voudras tu pourras te conduire

[You shall do everything you like].

The mask is off. The man who was going to prove that a woman could be made so unattractive that no one would entice her away from her husband has fallen for the creature he tried to stultify. Instead of a confident tyrant we see a grovelling silly lover, and see him with pleasure, not because we rejoice that his scheme has come to nothing, for perhaps we never took it seriously, but because we

have been led to glimpse the reality beneath the mask. This is not pretty, but it is at least real, and human, and unpretentious.

The play has been called a study of jealousy and I cannot think the claim will be taken seriously. These impossible and farcical situations would invalidate any serious study of jealousy. Beside *Othello* this play would seem a bungler's work. But as a comedy, constantly opposing the natural to the assumed and unnatural, the play is alive, no bungling but an admirably graded sequence of conflicts, leaving a single aesthetic impression. With its aesthetic we are not for the moment concerned, but with the principle of the mask that lies near its centre.

A similar vision of normality, disturbed by the cunning of an impostor, is found in a greater and more famous comedy, **Tartuffe**. It is remarkable that for many people this great play has ceased to be a comedy at all; it is often read as if it were a realistic satire. No one could deny that sinister forces are here suggested in powerful fashion. The mask of hypocrisy is an almost perfect fit, and ensures a steady increase of power to the wearer. It is probable that in a first three-act version of the play the mask was never removed and was completely successful. But that hypocrisy is a mask there should be no doubt. The sub-title of **L'Imposteur** settles the question. The play is about a man who gives himself out to be what he is not; he wears the mask of piety and that is not in itself a comic proceeding, unless or until it be shown to be . . . a mask, and not the man.

This elementary contrast within the man who plays a part is surely a basic feature of the role of Tartuffe. The part he plays is of vital importance to him. It assures his wellbeing and his domination over his fellows. It is the mask of a pious attitude, ascetic, world-renouncing, sanctimonious: 'Couvrez ce sein que je ne saurais voir' ["Go hide thy bosom, for I hate the sight"]. But this part is not kept up all the time. We see more than the mask, at times, when for one reason or another he is not hypocritical but sincere. In any judgement of the part it would seem vital to ask when the mask falls. Can anything be deduced from the alternation of hypocrisy and sincerity? In the case of a classical dramatist this may reveal the dramatic purpose. The mask falls at four points of the action, twice with Orgon and twice with Elmire. Nowhere else in the play, as far as I can see, does Tartuffe pretend to be other than a holy man. These four points of the action are worth close scrutiny.

The first is the famous third scene of the third act. 'Mon sein n'enferme pas un coeur qui soit de pierre' ["My breast does not contain a heart of flint"]; with this statement the hypocrite seems to me to be leaving his role. It is the first of a series of ambiguous statements, which are true of his real nature as well as of the mask he has assumed. The point is more evident when he says: 'Ah, pour être dévot je n'en suis pas moins homme.' ["Ah! I may be pious, but I am none the less a man"]. He intends surely to convey by this that humanity is not incompatible with piety. But his statement is true of himself as a natural and evil man: that his piety has not (in the least) affected his humanity, a statement which as a lover he may sustain, but which as an ascetic he would not. The same double echo is heard in a moment: 'Mais Madame, après tout, je ne suis pas un ange' ["But, after all, Madame, I am not an angel"]. From this Tartuffe proceeds to something which is not ambiguous at all, to an avowal of sharp practice and trickery which he would not for the world have anyone but Elmire overhear. . . . This is the complete avowal, by the *masqué,* that his mask is a mask. It may not be funny; it is deeply comic.

The second glimpse of Tartuffe's sincerity seems to me even more instructive for the aesthetics of this play. Three scenes later Tartuffe, accused of seducing his employer's wife, pleads guilty, as indeed he was. His statements are all true. . . . How can one escape the comedy of hearing, from one whose profession and practice it was to disguise the truth, 'la vérité pure' ["the pure truth"]? With extreme ingenuity Molière forces his impostor into a second situation where he can drop the mask, a situation quite different from the first. For here to tell the truth is not the result of natural, animal desire; it is the fruit of policy. To tell the truth in that context is the highest and most successful deception. He is not believed. So he can assume the mask once more and cover his own advantage with the will of heaven:

> La volonté du Ciel soit faite en toute chose.

> [The will of Heaven be done in all things].

It is, I suppose, highly unlikely that the first version of the play contained a second interview between Tartuffe and Elmire. There must have been strong reasons for making the impostor walk a second time into an obvious trap. Before we assume a weakness on the part of the dramatist let us note what is gained by the repetition. The force of the satire is not increased. The character of Orgon is not affected. But the impostor is this time not only completely exposed by his words, but actually discovered beyond hope of justification. The mask is, so to speak, almost torn off his face. To the objection that a clever scoundrel would have foreseen and avoided a second encounter there is a plain answer. That Tartuffe does not foresee it is a feature of his character; it is the final proof that he was not in that connexion wise, cautious, or cunning any longer; that, in a word, he was infatuated. Once again the impostor is sincere, sincere in his hesitation, in his professions of pleasure at her words which he longs to hear. . . . Sincere also in his application to her of religious terms describing the happiness he may never have really felt before God but does actually feel before her, and sincere above all in his gross sensuality, that demands more than words, what she calls 'les dernières faveurs' ["the last favors"] and he 'des réalités' ["the realities"]. This is the real world in which he moves, and having admitted it he scoffs at morality:

> Si ce n'est que le Ciel qu'à mes voeux on oppose,
> Lèver un tel obstacle est pour moi peu de chose.

> [If Heaven is the only thing which opposes my wishes
> I can easily remove such an obstacle].

To fear God is a ridiculous fear; casuistry can cover anything. Sin does not count when concealed. . . . The new morality is to follow one's director blindly:

> Vouz n'avez seulement qu'à vous laisser conduire

> [You have only to allow yourself to be led].

In the following scene there is a final glimpse of the real man. When his pious excuses are cut short he claims that he is master of the house, in the eyes of the law, that he will be a match for all of them, and thus (picking up the mask again) avenge heaven. In his last scene the mask is slightly adjusted to that of the good citizen. He regards as his first duty the good of the State. It is of some aesthetic importance to note that he ends, as he began, by provoking Dorine's pungent comment, 'L'imposteur'.

If the foregoing analysis be sound, we are faced in this play with a character at once more profound and more comic than has been made clear. There is, to begin with, no doubt of its realism. The author himself had in a significant stage-direction to call attention to the fact that his impostor was a scoundrel. He is indeed a sinister figure, 'escroc cherché par la police' ["a crook searched for by the police"] as Vedel says, whom we fear rather than laugh at. (pp. 40-8)

The view that *Tartuffe* is a comedy does not imply any softening of the character of the impostor. We may admit him to be a sinister figure, but we should at the same time notice that Molière has stressed this aspect far less than others. As a dangerous man he is kept in the background and hardly ever seen at work. As a contrast in and to himself he is exhibited in an endless variety of pose. Molière was apparently not satisfied with the contrast in the nature of an impostor, that his acts are at variance with his professions. He carries the contrast to a much deeper level, to situations which force the impostor to be himself, to drop the mask, as we have shown. It is vital to notice how close is the connexion between Tartuffe's sincerity and his undoing. He is unmasked, not primarily by others, not by Damis, or the police, but(in our eyes, and it is after all for the audience that the dramatic spectacle is staged) by himself. More than this, he is not unmasked by his slips, or by a faulty technique, but because, and whenever, he wants to be. His scheme, in fact, of being an impostor will not work. At times he does not want it to work. Where intellectual ends are involved it works to perfection; where more elementary and more human ends are involved, such as the satisfaction of his animal desires, the scheme does not work at all; it breaks down, because he is too human to allow it to work. . . . Tartuffe fails, as M. Michaut [see Additional Bibliography] has made clear, precisely because he was over-confident of his powers, because he reckoned without his appetites. . . . It is not far from such a conception to discovery of the comic principle lying at the root of such a character. Is it so much a 'malheur' ["misfortune"] that Tartuffe's human nature escapes his calculation? Is this not the real nerve of the play?

A third example should stand beside the two already analysed if the evidence is to have its full weight. But the character and situation of Alceste need not be described at length as the relevant points can be briefly made clear. The subject of the play, as its latest editor has remarked, is comparable to that of *Tartuffe*: 'l'hypocrisie religieuse conduit tout droit à l'hypocrisie sociale' ["religious hypocrisy leads right to social hypocrisy"]. There are many things in *Le Misanthrope* beside any symbolism of the mask, but it is noteworthy that this man who claims to base his case upon reason, who in his assertions of principle is a tiresome doctrinaire, is not only unreasonable but bad-tempered, selfish, brusque. He is, in fact, very far from the man he thinks he is or that he blames others for not being. His views, his doctrine, are in sharp contrast to his nature, his mood, his real situation. The contrast is pointed by his engagement to a lady of whose views he is most critical. He admits that she is not his type:

> Il est vrai, ma raison me le dit chaque jour;
> Mais la raison n'est pas ce qui règle l'amour
>
> [It is true my reason speaks to me each day;
> but reason does not always rule love].

Tartuffe, one remembers, made much the same admission:

> Un coeur se laisse prendre et ne raisonne pas.
>
> [The heart surrenders without reasoning].

This parallel is not fortuitous. The role of love in these comedies is so similar as to warrant our close attention. Each of three main characters is betrayed, as he would call it, by the same agency. His plan is ruined by the fact of his falling in love. It is curious not only that their roles should have much in common but that the agency of their failure should be the same. A comic trick? No doubt, and one that Molière had seen and had used before. In the old farce one would laugh with the lovers against the pedants or tyrannical guardians. But the proceeding here gathers (as do so many others in Molière's work) its full sense and power by being perfectly motivated. The motivation is not very hard to discover. Is not love a symbol for what is not the mask but the man, for nature, as opposed to art? It is contrary to idea and policy; it is unpremeditated and even in a sense unwelcome. The lover curses his luck that he should be in love. But it is beyond human power to control; it is an instinct, not an idea.

Comedy founded on this antagonism of the wits and the instinct is deeply founded in human nature. For normal human nature includes both the feelings and the ideas, brain and heart, reason and instinct. Molière presumed in his audience a normal balance of the two elements. But the deceiver, or the fool, or the doctrinaire prides himself on his wits, his ideas, his reason. He leaves his instinct out of the reckoning; he adopts a mask of intelligence. But instinct will be revenged and returns unexpectedly; the mask has to fall.

Such a view of human nature is, as one would expect from a 'comédien', different from both the Christian and the rationalist interpretations current in Molière's day. It agrees with the Christian psychology of Pascal, who said . . . that rationalism is a simplification. But to many Christians it would seem pagan in its assumption of normality and balance. It might seem inspired by that humanism of the Renaissance which regarded all the instincts as right. This is why Molière was regarded as a libertin, 'peut-être le seul agressif' ["perhaps the only aggressor"] said Perrens. The difficulty is that in the plays no conclusions are drawn; a picture is presented. The picture seems to me to fit neither the Christianity of Bossuet nor the worship of nature, which for Brunetière [see excerpt dated 1898] was Molière's philosophy. It is a picture of contrast within the autonomous personality. The power of will and of wit is checked by what most people think the inferior power of instinct and sense. Men are shown as inhuman in their worship of power and intellect; they are human only in their baser instincts. But for his gross sensuality Tartuffe would be a robot. What Christians call our lower nature is

seen as saving our superior qualities. But perhaps we should not be too easily alarmed. All depends on what conclusions are drawn. Molière is doing no more than present a picture of normality. . . . The pride of the over-clever and the over-confident is severely handled in his drama, as in that of Racine. But his vision of normality includes instincts as a corrective. Did La Rochefoucauld not admit as much when he wrote that 'l'homme croit souvent se conduire lorsqu'il est conduit' ["man often thinks he leads when he is led"]. (pp. 48-52)

> *W. G. Moore, in his* Molière: A New Criticism,
> *1949. Reprint by Oxford at the Clarendon Press,*
> *1968, 147 p.*

ALLARDYCE NICOLL (essay date 1949)

[*Called "one of the masters of dramatic research," Nicoll is best known as a theater historian whose works have proven invaluable to students and educators. Nicoll's* World Drama from Aeschylus to Anouilh *(1949) is considered one of his most important works; theater critic John Gassner has described it as "unquestionably the most thorough* [study] *of its kind in the English language* [and] *our best reference book on the world's dramatic literature." Another of his ambitious theater studies is the six-volume* A History of English Drama, 1660-1900 *(1952-59), which has been highly praised for its perceptive commentaries on drama from the Restoration to the close of the nineteenth century. Nicoll was also a popular lecturer on Shakespearean drama and the author of several studies of Shakespeare's works. In addition, he was the longtime editor of* Shakespeare Survey, *an annual publication of Shakespearean scholarship. In the following excerpt from* World Drama from Aeschylus to Anouilh, *Nicoll surveys and evaluates Molière's dramatic career.*]

All the comic authors of the second half of the seventeenth century . . . fade into insignificance when we turn to Jean-Baptiste Poquelin, who, under the name of Molière, stood forward in this time as one of the greatest masters in the art of comedy that the world has known. (P. 318)

Before *L'étourdi* it is possible, even likely, that Molière had written one or two short farces; if so, we have a suggestion of their style in two pieces, *La jalousie du Barbouillé* (*The Jealousy of Le Barbouillé*) and *Le médecin volant* (*The Flying Doctor*), first published in 1819 from an early manuscript. Clearly based on the style of the *commedia dell' arte*, yet displaying affinities with medieval farce, they well illustrate the manner in which their author may have served his apprenticeship, drawing strength and assurance from the popular French tradition, and enlivening that with material taken from Italian sources. The former play introduces to us a jealous fool, Le Barbouillé, married to Angélique. At a loss to know what to do, he consults a doctor, who, refusing to listen to him, gives him a long discourse on his own merits. In the end, thinking to trap his wife as she returns home late from a party, he is himself locked out of his house and severely chided by Angélique's father. Equally slight is the plot of *Le médecin volant*. Here also a doctor appears, but in this case a pretended one. Gorgibus, father of Lucile, does not wish his daughter to marry Valère, whereupon the young man's servant, Sganarelle (played by Molière himself), takes upon him to dress as a doctor, and, despite his ridiculous patter, completely dupes Gorgibus and is thus enabled to effect the union of the lovers. . . . The title of the farce comes from the fact that in the course of his intricate deception Sganarelle is forced to impersonate not only the doctor, but also his own supposed twin brother—all of which necessitates his flying on and off the stage in disguise and out.

For the longer and more pretentious comedy of *L'étourdi* Molière passed from the *commedia dell' arte* to the *commedia erudita*, choosing for inspiration *L'inavvertito (The Indiscreet Man)*, by Nicolò Barbieri, already used by Quinault for his *L'amant indiscret*. The plot is little more than a series of episodes. Lélie is in love with Célie, and in order to win her agrees that his servant, Mascarille, should indulge in a series of stratagems. To the disgust of this witty and ingenious rogue, however, Lélie destroys plot after plot by his blunderings. Sometimes he wrecks his servant's plans through ignorance of what is being arranged, sometimes through excessive honesty, sometimes through his own love obsession. There is an undoubted advance here upon the style of the short farces, but dramatic intricacy is lacking, the characters are as yet only surface-drawn, and there is no sign of that comedy of social criticism which later was to prove Molière's greatness.

After the series of episodes in this play we move to a mass of complication in *Le dépit amoureux (Lovers' Spite*; acted first at Béziers in 1656), another work based on an Italian comedy—*L'interesse (Self-interest)*, by Niccolò Secchi. Although it can hardly be esteemed to show an advance upon *L'étourdi*, individual scenes exhibit a widening of the author's dramatic skill. Such episodes, for example, are the lovers' quarrels, which are the core of the play, and the scene in which Albert tries in vain to get the attention of the pedant Métaphrase. . . . (pp. 318-20)

Towards the end of the year 1658 Molière brought his company to Court and won royal favour with a repertoire of farces, his own and others'. To those he added, in 1659, *Les précieuses ridicules (The Affected Ladies)*—also a farce, but a farce with a mighty difference. Here for the first time the individual style of the author becomes apparent, for *Les précieuses ridicules* is in essence a social comedy. The externals of the plot are not unlike those of many earlier plays—the disguising of a witty servant—but in this case the servant's masquerading has a different dramatic purpose. When Mascarille parades as a marquis it is not in order to cheat an old man and win a lady for his master, but to expose the absurd affectations of the ladies themselves. In the cult of preciosity, fed by the interminable romances of the time, Molière saw an object well worthy of the laughter of social comedy; he sought to entertain, and to reform through entertainment. The Marquis has himself carried directly into the house, and the girls at once are infatuated with his elegant hauteur and languid grace. "My dear," says Cathos, "we should call for chairs"; "Almanzor," replies Madelon to her page, "convey me hit her at once the appliances of conversation." To cover her mistake in thus vulgarly alluding to chairs, Cathos turns to the Marquis: "For pity's sake," she begs,

> do not be inexorable to that armchair which for the last quarter of an hour has stretched out its arms to you; satisfy the desire it has of embracing you.

The attack on what was then a fashionable diversion of Parisian Society soon had various ladies of the Court protesting violently, and, although Molière assured them that he was but aiming his shafts at absurd provincials, he found that the hornets' nest he had aroused suggested the taking of more cautious steps for at least the immediate future. In *Sganarelle, ou le cocu imaginaire (Sganarelle; or, The Cuckold in his own Imagination)* he accordingly produced an innocuous, and a highly successful, farce in which the citizen Sganarelle thinks his wife unfaithful and yet cannot rouse up courage enough to seek vengeance on her supposed lover. He considers the claims of honour, lets prudence calm his rage, and then, with anger once more rising, comes to his final conclusion. He will address himself to some manly action:

> Yes, my blood is up, I will revenge myself on the scoundrel, I will be no coward! And to begin with, in the heat of my passion, I am going to tell every one everywhere that he is living with my wife.

After a somewhat unfortunate excursion into the field of tragi-comedy (*Don Garcie de Navarre*) the actor-dramatist once more swung back to social comedy in *L'école des maris (The School for Husbands)*, the first truly great comedy from his pen, and one destined for a lengthy career. Although lacking the ease and organic structure of some of his later works, this comedy, based on Terence's *Adelphi* and on Lope de Vega's *Discreta enamorada*, exhibits clearly the qualities that give him his real title to fame—the development of a social comedy in which excesses are ridiculed wittily, good sense is enthroned, and the golden mean is made the prize of man's endeavour. Externally this comedy is, like Ben Jonson's, classically realistic; like the English dramatist, Molière endeavours to present in imaginative terms deeds and language such as men do use; yet there is an essential difference between the two. Jonson bent all his energies to the creation of satire, and the things he satirized were those follies that touched him nearly; for Molière the task was to shed comic laughter on follies he deemed inimical to the social structure. Jonson was ego-centred; Molière's orientation was towards the society to which he belonged.

The School for Husbands is somewhat mechanically planned, but Molière's typical approach is well exemplified in its scenes. The two main characters are set before us at the very beginning—Ariste, who argues that one should bow to the ways of society, and Sganarelle, his brother, who churlishly insists on the expression of his own individuality. "We should always fall in with the majority," says Ariste, "and never cause ourselves to become conspicuous. All excesses are offensive, and every truly wise man ought not to display affectation either in his dress or his language, but willingly follow the changing customs of his time." These two men are revealed in relation to their wards, Isabelle in the charge of Sganarelle and Léonore in the charge of Ariste. Where the socially amenable Ariste allows Léonore her freedom, the puritanically individualistic Sganarelle insists on imposing his will upon Isabelle. The greater part of the play is devoted to showing how this girl, irked by the restrictions imposed upon her, eventually tricks her guardian and marries Valère, while at the end Léonore expresses her willingness to marry Ariste, whose kindness has won her heart. Poor Sganarelle, the misanthropist, is left alone cursing the female sex and the more strongly confirmed in his misanthropy.

Following *The School for Husbands* came the rather slight sketch entitled *Les fâcheux (The Bores)*, which formed a *comédie-ballet* presented before the King in 1661. *L'école des femmes (The School for Wives)* soon followed, and in this Molière made a notable advance in his comic art. The serious element is over-pronounced in *The School for Husbands*: brilliant as are many of the scenes, the play is written to a thesis. Far greater freedom and more liveliness in the character delineation animate its successor. The difference between the two comedies may be realized when we contrast the Ariste and Sganarelle of the one with the other's Chrysalde and Arnolphe. Basically they represent the same types, but here the types are made richer and more delicately humanized. Arnolphe is also a surly individualist, but instead of having a philosophy on which his actions are dependent, he is presented as an ambitious, self-confident egotist. Similarly, Chrysalde appears not as a mouthpiece for a particular view of life, but as a good-humoured, cynical man of the world. (pp. 320-23)

The play immediately made a stir, and there were not wanting moralists and literary critics who attacked its contents and its style, whereupon Molière made dramatic history and added to his stock of comic scenes by penning the first play upon a play—*La critique de l'école des femmes (The School for Wives criticized)* [see excerpt dated 1663]. Climène, a *précieuse*, feels faint with disgust after seeing it; Uranie protects it against her strictures; Élise satirically agrees with Climène; a marquis thinks it must be altogether silly because it has proved so popular; the poet Lysidas feigns to praise, but easily allows himself to reveal his belief that such pieces are not true comedies. Into the mouth of Dorante Molière has put his own defence. He argues that the general applause given to the drama is a testimony to its value and to good sense, that the "rules of art" cannot be taken as definitive laws. "I should like to know," he remarks, "whether the greatest rule of all rules is not to please, and whether a piece which has gained that end has not followed the right road."

The controversy continued. Edmé Boursault gave to the Hôtel de Bourgogne his *Le portrait du peintre, ou la contre-critique de l'école des femmes*, whereupon Molière replied with *L'impromptu de Versailles (The Impromptu at Versailles)*, in which his actors are gathered together for a rehearsal. Here, again, Molière seems to have been making dramatic history: the play within the play was a well-known device, but this seems to be the first "rehearsal" piece on record. Ironically he hits out at the style of acting at the Hôtel de Bourgogne. Once more a single individual, Brécourt, is introduced to put forward the claims of common sense. The comic author does not present satirical portraits, he argues: "The business of comedy is to represent in a general way all the defects of men, and particularly those of our own age"—and consequently he ought to remain free from the strictures of those petty individuals who fail to see that in his work is to be found a corrective for society

Immediately after these plays came a couple of slight *comédies-ballets—Le mariage forcé (The Forced Marriage)* and *La Princesse d'Élide (The Princess of Elis)* both acted in 1664, the one at the Louvre and the other at Versailles. Neither deserves much attention, although the former—which shows Sganarelle anxious to marry, and then, having seen his future wife's flirtatious propensities, at the end aghast at the thought of the wedding—is written with verve and gaiety.

A third time Molière was asked during this year to contribute in the diversion of the Court, but instead of these two flimsy shows his chief offering to the gorgeous spectacle at Versailles, entitled the *Plaisirs de l'île enchantée*, was the first version of his deepest and his bitterest comedy, *Tartuffe, ou l'imposteur (Tartuffe; or, The Impostor)*. We cannot tell precisely, of course, what relationship this bears to the drama we now possess, but the fact that, after its Court performance, it was not again given until 1667, and then was forbidden public representation until 1669, suggests that basically it contained the same material as that with which we are now familiar.

Here was the most complete fusion of comedy and purpose. From the portraits of folly Molière now turns to vice. Tartuffe is a sensual, self-seeking hypocrite who trades on credulity. Fastening upon the dull-witted Orgon, he insinuates himself into his household and threatens to bring it to complete disaster. Only his own lust and his over-confidence, brought to betrayal by the innate honesty of Orgon's wife, result in his unmasking, discomfiture, and punishment. Technically the comedy is a true work of genius. For two entire acts Tartuffe himself does not appear before us, yet a powerful impression of his personality is built up through the references to him on the part of the other characters: thus the looming character of his personality comes upon us with the greater force, while his eventual entry is made the more impressive. In the first scene the bigoted Madame Pernelle, mother of Orgon, gives him praise, while his true nature is hinted at in the words of Damis, her grandson, and the maid, Dorine. The whole family is set before us in inimitably etched lines, so that we are thoroughly acquainted with their personalities before ever the main figure appears—and his appearance is effectively contrived. Dorine, the maid, is on the stage when he enters. Catching sight of her, he immediately turns to his servant:

> TARTUFFE. Laurent, lock up my hair-shirt and my scourge, and pray Heaven ever to enlighten you with grace. If anybody comes to see me, say that I am gone to the prisons to distribute my alms.... (*Turning to* DORINE) What is it you want?
>
> DORINE. To tell you—
>
> TARTUFFE. (*taking a handkerchief out of his pocket*) Ah! Heaven! before you speak to me, take this handkerchief, pray.
>
> DORINE. What's the matter?
>
> TARTUFFE. Cover this bosom, of which I cannot bear the sight. Such objects hurt the soul, and are conducive to sinful thoughts.

Almost at once we see him making love to Élmire, Orgon's wife; Damis, her son, tells his father, and Tartuffe shows his genius by refusing to deny the specific accusation; instead, he piously declares that he is "a wicked, guilty, miserable sinner," and, when Orgon angrily turns on his son, magnanimously chides his patron:

> Ah! let him speak; you blame him wrongfully, and you would do better to believe what he tells you. Why should you be so favourable to me in this instance? Do you know, after all, what I am capable of doing? Do you, brother, trust to the outward man; and do you think me good, because of what you see? No, no, you

are deceived by appearances, and I am, alas! no better than they think. . . .

His unmasking comes only when Orgon is persuaded to listen while he makes further love to Élmire and seeks speciously to argue that she may without sin lie with him because of "the purity of the intention." Even then he is not defeated and almost succeeds in ruining Orgon, who is saved only by direct intervention of the King.

There is an atmosphere here closely akin to that of Jonson's *Volpone*, but, whereas in the English play there is hardly a worthy character among all the *dramatis personae*, and whereas all these *dramatis personae* are exaggerated caricatures, Molière's domestic interior, although treated idealistically, is true to life, and good shines among the bad. Madame Pernelle is the typical old bigot, Orgon the besotted fool, Élmire the wife who would rather suffer inconveniences than have trouble in the house, Dorine the keen-eyed little maid, Damis the honest youth who has not tact enough to make his honesty known. In reading *Volpone* we are not concerned with the interests of society; in *Tartuffe* Molière seeks to arouse laughter that he may warn his fellows of an insidious danger.

Tartuffe was a hypocrite: in *Don Juan, ou le festin de pierre (Don Juan; or, The Banquet of Stone)* Molière delineated the atheist for whom no conventional morality has any meaning, the brave soul whose daring leads him to disaster. There is a mood of continual dissatisfaction about his hero; like Faust, although in another way, he seeks for the unattainable. . . . Accompanied by the timorous Sganarelle, he is revealed in diverse aspects, in the end—like Tartuffe—donning the garb of the hypocrite in order to effect his purposes, and after this final evil being consumed in hell-fire, while Sganarelle, true to the spirit of comedy, can think only of the money owed him and now lost to him for ever:

> Oh! my wages! my wages! His death is a reparation to all. Heaven offended, laws violated, families dishonoured, girls ruined, wives led astray, husbands driven to despair, everybody is satisfied. I am the only one to suffer. My wages, my wages, my wages!

An apparently more joyous play followed—*L'amour médecin (Love is the Best Doctor)*, acted in 1665 as part of an elaborate *comédie-ballet*—but the bitter tone apparent in the two dramas immediately preceding cannot quite be concealed by its gaiety. The plot is a simple one. Lucinde, daughter of Sganarelle, pretends illness in order to further her love-affair with Clitandre. Four pompous doctors are called in to attend her, and spend most of their time in boring talk about the social aspects of their profession. Eventually Clitandre dresses as a physician, declares that Lucinde's trouble is mental, and persuades Sganarelle that she must be humoured:

> CLITANDRE. However, as one must flatter the imagination of patients, and as I see in your daughter signs of distress of mind that would be dangerous if prompt remedies were not administered, I have made use of her own fancies and have told her that I was here to ask her of you in marriage. Then her face changed in a moment, her complexion cleared up, and her eyes brightened. If you keep up that delusion in her for a few days, you will see that we shall save her. (pp. 324-28)

L'amour médecin was followed by what many critics regard as Molière's greatest play, *Le misanthrope*, in which his

comic view of life becomes darker and his consideration of man more philosophic. Basically this is a study in the opposition in the human being between his own individuality and his needs as a social animal. The central figure is Alceste, a character akin to the individualist of *L'école des maris*, but more intimately and effectively delineated. The empty politenesses that accompany social life arouse his anger and annoyance; why, he asks, should he praise a wretched sonnet on which his opinion is requested or bow and smile to a man whom he has no intention of seeing again? To his own disgust he finds himself emotionally attracted by the young widow Célimène, a gay, flirtatious coquette, and the greater part of the comedy is occupied with tracing his repulsion to her follies and his paradoxical desire to possess her. Contrasted with him is the good-humoured, complacent Philinte, who, while recognizing the absurdities of the world, is prepared to accept its manners and to comply with its conventions. The two sides of the picture are presented with scrupulous balance. Alceste is undoubtedly a figure that stirs in us both admiration and sympathy; compared with Célimène, he possesses an honesty and integrity wholly worthy. Yet the individualist is an ever-potent menace to his companions; the only logical course for him and for the society to which he belongs is to have him sent out in loneliness to a desert. This, indeed, is the end of Alceste. Célimène's frivolity has been amply demonstrated, but even a realization of her pettinesses cannot kill the love for her he has in his heart: he consents to forgive her, on condition that she will follow him into the solitude where he has vowed to live. "What!" cries Célimène, "renounce the world before I grow old, go and bury myself in the wilderness?" Alceste argues with her:

> But if your love answers to mine, what can be to you all the rest of the world; are not all your desires centred in me?
>
> CELIMENE. Solitude at twenty years of age frightens me. I do not find in my heart greatness and self-denial enough to yield to such a fate; if the gift of my hand can satisfy your wishes, I am willing; and marriage—

This offer Alceste indignantly rejects, and the play ends with his departure, while Philinte and Éliante prepare for their common-sense wedding, and Célimène retires, no doubt to capture other hearts. These characters are sensible, yet to the very conclusion the balance is preserved: there is a moving quality in the hero's final words:

> As to myself, betrayed on all sides and crushed with injustice, I will escape from a gulf where vice triumphs, and look in all the earth for a desert place where one may be free to be a man of honour.

Laughter, gay and uninhibited, comes again in *Le médecin malgré lui (The Doctor in spite of Himself)*, in which a woodcutter, Sganarelle, is mistakenly forced to act as a physician. . . . (pp. 329-30)

Many plays were still to follow, although some, such as *Le Sicilien, ou l'amour peintre (The Sicilian; or, Love the Painter)*—an anticipation of the *opéra-comique*—may be disregarded. *Amphitryon*, except for the vivacious part of Sosie (written for himself), does not add much to the body of his work, and *Georges Dandin, ou le mari confondu (George Dandin; or, The Baffled Husband)*, although replete with verve, is little more than an elaboration of *La jalousie du Barbouillé*, with development of character and the provision of a firmer social background.

In *L'avare* (*The Miser*), as in *Amphitryon*, Molière sought his theme among the plays of Plautus, selecting for this purpose the *Aulularia*. Although this play is superior to [*Amphitryon* and *George Dandin*], it betrays a falling off from the brilliance of *Tartuffe* and *Le Misanthrope*. The miser, Harpagon, is rather farcically conceived, and the plot tends to be confused. One has the double impression that Molière, unlike Ben Jonson, is not at his happiest in dealing with miserliness and that his skill of hand is declining. What is of interest, however, is the manner in which the French dramatist has departed from his original by associating the old man with a large household instead of leaving him an isolated recluse. Within that household, too, there is one person, Maître Jacques, who is a masterpiece of comic portraiture. He is both cook and coachman, and keeps two coats ready for his assumption of either of his two duties. A somewhat stupid but good-willed fellow, he provides much of the laughter of the play.

A *comédie-ballet* entitled *Monsieur de Pourceaugnac* followed in 1669—a merry record of the painful adventures suffered by a provincial lawyer among the professional sharks of Paris. In this piece Molière experimented upon, and considerably improved, the comic-opera style already tried in *L'amour médecin*. The mediocre *Les amants magnifiques* (*The Magnificent Lovers*) was of the same character, as was also the joyous *Le bourgeois gentilhomme* (*The Bourgeois Gentleman*), produced during the same year. The picture painted of M. Jourdain is superb. A middle-class shopkeeper who has amassed a small fortune, he determines to figure in the world of Society. He enters in dressing-gown and nightcap, having been told that in this wise aristocrats hold their morning levees; amid the dancing- and music-masters whom he has summoned to instruct him he meanders along in simple-minded delight. Soon the professional teachers are at each others' throats, each claiming the superiority of his own subject, until the exponent of philosophy, flying at his companions, remains lord of the stage. "*Nam sine doctrina vita est quasi mortis imago*," declares the philosopher. "You understand this, and you have no doubt a knowledge of Latin?" "Yes," replies M. Jourdain; "but act as if I had none. Explain to me the meaning of it." "The meaning of it is that 'without science life is an image of death'." "That Latin is quite right," says M. Jourdain. A ludicrous lesson follows, and rises to a culmination in Jourdain's famous discovery that he has been speaking prose all his life without knowing it. Into this world of the fantastically real the Turkish episode at the end fits with perfect harmony: M. Jourdain is made a Mamamouchi by a group of men disguised to hoodwink him, and the play ends with the simple, foolish, and rather pathetic little shopkeeper thoroughly pleased with himself and entirely ignorant of the figure of fun he has become.

In *Les fourberies de Scapin* (*The Tricks of Scapin*) a return is made to that admixture of *commedia dell' arte* and native farce with which Molière began his work, with Scapin keeping the scenes in constant movement by his skilful impostures. Provincial pretensions are satirized in the rather slight *La Comtesse d'Escarbagnas*, and then, somewhat surprisingly after these efforts, comes the magnificent *Les femmes savantes* (*The Learned Ladies*). Here the theme is that of education for women. Central in the picture is the pedantic Philaminte, the middle-aged wife of the honest bourgeois Chrysale, who neglects her home for the sake of philosophy. She has two daughters, Armande, a prudish *précieuse*, and the common-sense Henriette. Clitandre is the lover, once the wooer of Armande, but, disgusted by her affectations, now the avowed adorer of her sister. Philaminte deems him too unlearned to marry one of her daughters, preferring the wit Trissotin. On this basis the comedy proceeds. Armande professes repugnance at the thought that Henriette can even dream of marriage—although secretly and almost unknown to herself she is consumed with jealousy. Poor Chrysale tries from time to time to put in a word, but the masterful Philaminte ever bears him down. One hilarious occasion occurs when the maid Martine is being dismissed. Chrysale tentatively inquires the cause, but is soon forced to berate the girl without knowing why: he eventually discovers that she has been guilty of using a word disapproved of by a famous grammarian. Towards the very conclusion of the drama, when Philaminte seems certain to compel Henriette to marry Trissotin, a *deus ex machina* appears in the person of Chrysale's brother, Ariste, who falsely announces that the family has lost all its money: Trissotin immediately backs out of his pretensions to Henriette, while Clitandre nobly offers the household all he possesses. Anticipating many a later sentimental heroine, Henriette now refuses to wed Clitandre, because she would not burden him with their poverty, when Ariste reveals the fact that his news was merely a device to expose Trissotin. The last words are spoken by Chrysale, anxious at last to assert his authority: turning to the notary, he bids him, "Execute my orders and draw up the contract in accordance with what I said."

The brilliance of this comedy cannot be denied, and yet that last sentimental note is troublesome: it is an indication that a new world is approaching. Molière's own career, however, was now near its end. Suffering from a disease he knew would soon bring his end, he ironically penned his last comedy, *Le malade imaginaire* (*The Imaginary Invalid*), at the fourth performance of which he collapsed and died. Argan here is a hopeless hypochondriac who surrounds himself with doctors and apothecaries, and it is his person who dominates in the play. Opposed to him is the gay maid Toinette, whose frank enjoyment of life and refusal to think of the morrow provides a vivid contrast to his dark thoughts. A further foil is established in Argan's brother, Béralde, who, mocking the hypochondriac's fancies, counsels a visit to the theatre to see some of Molière's plays. It is in this scene that Béralde quotes the author himself as saying that he will have nothing to do with the doctors:

> He is certain that only strong and robust constitutions can bear their remedies in addition to the illness, and he has only just strength enough to endure his sickness.

Thus closed Molière's career. During its course he had succeeded in creating a comic world which places him among the greatest of comic playwrights. Building from the individual, yet concerned with the presentation of types, he wrote plays in which an inimitable gallery of memorable portraits is placed before us. His fundamental attitude is one of common sense; frankly he accepts the world, and strives to show that excesses of all kinds are fatal to the even tenor of social life. Although his plays include many farces, and even his darkest comedy contains much of hilarity, his greatest power lies in his skill in arousing what has been called "thoughtful laughter," where a smile takes the place of the guffaw and in the mind is left a dominant concept. Logical proportion, avoidance of extremes, honest acceptance of the facts of life, the application of reason to social affairs—these were the messages which Molière constantly preached to his fellows even as he contributed richly to their entertainment. (pp. 331-34)

Allardyce Nicoll, "Molière and the Comedy of Manners," in his World Drama from Aeschylus to Anouilh, *George G. Harrap & Company Ltd., 1949, pp. 316-34.*

GEORGES POULET (essay date 1950)

[*Poulet has been described as an existentialist critic who in his most important work attempts to reconstruct an author's "consciousness," or relation to, and understanding of, time and space, nature and society. A key element of his early criticism was his belief that every author lives in an isolated world defined by individual consciousness and so cannot be understood in terms of generalizations about an era or period. The task of the critic is to enter this individual consciousness and define it. In his later work, however, Poulet has come to see individual consciousnesses as united in an all-embracing spirit of a time, and he often discusses writers in terms of the widespread characteristics of an age. In the following excerpt from a work first published in 1950, he discusses the theoretical bases of Molière's comedy.*]

"I find," says Molière,

> that it is much easier to speak loftily of high feelings, to defy fate in verse, to reproach destiny and abuse the gods, than it is to enter properly into the ridicule of men.... It is a strange enterprise, that of making honest men laugh.

An enterprise strangely difficult, in fact, for the precise reason Molière gives us; for if, in tragedy, it is easier to speak loftily of high feelings, that is because such feelings are at one and the same time expressed and experienced. There is no separation between the author and his character; not even between the character and the spectator. When the hero "defies fate," his mood and his audacity are ours. There is established a kind of subjective identity which makes of the author, the character, and the public one single feeling being. The tragic moment is easy of achievement because it is a moment lived by a unique person who expressly manifests what everyone feels.

All else is the comic moment. The difficulty which that implies is that it is not "given" to enter directly into the person of the character. Far from entering into his being, it is a matter of "entering into ridicule of him." And to enter upon ridicule is precisely the contrary of entering into a being; it is to withdraw from him: it is to put the person in the position of an object one sees, and not a being with whom one feels. It is to pose an object, instead of *being* a subject.

The "strange enterprise" which permits the creation of a comic moment is thus the very opposite of the unitive consciousness which forms the tragic moment. It has for its province the consciousness of a disunion between the author and his public, on one side, and the character in the play, on the other. On the one side, *us;* on the other,

him. And whatever the feelings of this *him*, they succeed in touching only our external senses and presenting manifestations of a person with whom it is impossible for us to identify ourselves, but with whom it is necessary to confront ourselves. The comic character is the triple object of our attention, our judgment, and our feeling.

And first of all it is the object before our senses. As such, it is only what it appears to be. It is a face, a voice, some gestures. It is its actions and nothing more. That is what Molière himself declares:

> Let not anyone tell me that all the feelings which I attribute to men ... are not felt as I describe them; for it is only in the occasion itself that it seems as if one has them or not; and not even then does anyone discover that he has them; it is just that one's actions make us suppose necessarily that one has them.

These are words which can have been written only by someone who from instinct puts himself in the very situation in which the comic genius must put himself. It is not permissible in this situation to *feel oneself* experiencing the feelings of the character; one can only *attribute* them to him; and what is more, one can only attribute them to him on the *occasions* when he seems to have them; and their existence is perceived only because the character *acts* in such a way as to make one necessarily suppose that he has such feelings.

Thus the starting point of the comic art of Molière is situated in the *occasion*, in which a being is comprehended only through his actions.

And, in fact, did not the theater of Molière begin by being exactly that, and nothing more than that? A comedy of actions and gestures which did not "imply" anything else: the *Médecin volant;* the *Jalousie du Barbouillé?*

But this starting point is only a point without duration. A deed, a gesture, is still not a complete action, it is not a thing that endures, it is an instantaneous manifestation. In the comic art of Molière there is first of all the actual presence of a certain demeanor which is immediately clear to the spectator.

But in the instant in which the demeanor of the object is understood by the spectator, the latter grants to the object the particular being which the object's demeanor makes the spectator necessarily suppose it possesses. He no longer sees only the object under the sensible appearance of its deeds, but as a being distinct from himself, which consequently requires a judgment on the part of his reason, and which provokes a reaction on the part of his sensibility.

Every object, every being distinct from us, is judged by us. And this judgment, says Molière, is a judgment of conformity. Our "essential reason" decides whether, in the moment in which it performs its deed, the performer fails to conform himself to the rules and order connected with a truth, which has a permanent value. Thus the judgment of reason implies a curious transfiguration of the object; for if, on the one hand, its nonconformity is situated in the instant in which it arises, on the other hand it is a nonconformity only in connection with what transcends all instants. From the point of view of the eternal reason, the instantaneous manifestation of an eternal nonconformity is itself eternal. It is *sub specie aeternitatis*. What is unreasonable is eternally unreasonable.

But with the judgment of reason there is associated another judgment which is at bottom that of our sensibility. Because, says Molière:

> although Nature made us capable of knowing reason by following it, still, well aware that if there were not some visible mark attached to it which would render this knowledge easy, our frailty and our indolence would deprive us of the effect of so rare an advantage, she wished to give to reason some sort of exterior form recognizable from without. . . . Ridicule is the external and visible form which Providence has attached to all that is unreasonable. . . .

This form is a "cause of joy," a "matter of pleasure." It is basically the immediate reaction of our being as we confront the deed which falls immediately under our senses. The instant it is perceived by our "essential reason" as incompatible with eternal principles, it is immediately felt by our "apparent reason" to be contrary to propriety. What is perceived as ridiculous is that which is perceived as an incongruous hiatus in the uninterrupted line of our customary experience. We say to ourselves: we are not accustomed to seeing gentlemen act like this.

This ridicule is the immediate perception of a sudden perturbation in the order of human duration. And, seen from this angle, it is no longer a permanent thing depending upon abstract reason alone. It presents itself in duration and appears there under the form of a moment which breaks up this duration. Ridicule is a moment of rupture.

But rupture in the object, not in ourselves. It is because of this that the moment of rupture in Molière is so different from the moment of rupture in Corneille. Indeed, in Corneille the action by which the hero breaks with antecedent duration is a deed in which we adhere; it is an act of the will, a tragic act, to which we give consent. In Molière, on the contrary, the action by which the character is dissociated from the continuous duration of good usage is a deed by which he forces us simultaneously to dissociate ourselves from him. The instant he breaks with the order of things, we re-associate ourselves more closely with it. Thus the action of the character becomes absolutely isolated and, by consequence, inoffensive. It is a perturbation in the order which does not menace the order. The discontinuity it creates is localized in the single object which causes it. It is as if in following a well-defined path one saw someone stumble in it. Hence the simultaneous existence of two kinds of duration for the mind: the duration of the order in which one participates and which lasts; and the instant of disorder which is limited to the object and which interrupts time.

Thus the comic is the perception of an ephemeral and local fracture in the middle of a durable and normal world.

Let us imagine a seducer who one day is suddenly made to seem ridiculous: "These *first instants*," says Molière,

> are of important consideration in these matters; they produce almost the same effect as a long duration, because they always *break* the chain of passion and the course of the imagination, which ought to hold the soul attached, from beginning to end, to an amorous venture, in order for it to be successful. . . .

But, in a certain sense, any relationship of a character to ourselves is a venture in seduction; any character, by the sole fact of his presence, tries to catch our sympathy. This is the case with the philosophy teacher when he praises moderation, or with Chrysale when he pretends to assert his authority. But when immediately afterward, in one of those "first instants which almost have the effect of a long duration," Chrysale yields before Philaminte, and the philosophy teacher to the impulse of anger, so in this precise moment the chain of our adherence finds itself broken. Our feeling is reversed. Suddenly we no longer feel *with* the character; we feel *against* him.

But we *feel* all the same. If ridicule is indeed, as Molière says, the coldest of all our feelings, it is none the less authentically a feeling. It is at once judgment and feeling. That is why Molière declares in the *Critique* that "the best way to judge is to abandon oneself to things." "Let us not consider in a comedy," he says, "what effect it is having on us. Let us abandon ourselves in good faith to the things that seize us by the entrails. . . ." And again: "When I see a comedy, I look only to see if things touch me."

But to abandon oneself to things, to let oneself be touched by them, is to react instantaneously in the order of sensibility. The comic genius operates, then, directly on the moment. Like the painter of frescoes, he knows his matter is "pressing" and wishes ". . . without compliance/That a painter come to terms with his impatience,/Treat it in his own way, and *with a sudden stroke/Seize the moment* it gives into his hand."

The comic spirit is a seizure of the instantaneous.

But then the question arises, the same question as for the theater of Corneille: how shall we make a comedy out of the comic instant? How shall we prolong our laughter? How shall we give a temporal value to a character whom our rational judgment has assigned to a kind of negative eternity, and who "touches" our judgment of sensibility only in the lightning flash of the instant?

There are two Molierean universes: the one of customs; the other of passions. The first is a durable universe. It is the universe of persons of good sense, of spectators, of gentlemen. A sort of connivance unites them and situates them in a constant duration which is not at all on trial and which is not at all in peril.

But there is another universe, that of the passions, which in itself is not less tragic in Molière than in Racine. It is a universe in which one is in incessant tension, in ceaseless agitation, in a perpetual renewing of the same desires. (pp. 293-96)

There is [a] . . . rhythm of passion in Molière. A perpetual reincarnation of the hungry desire, the generation in a closed cycle of passion triumphant and passion frustrated—such is the essentially repetitive process by which Molière's characters continually manifest themselves in duration. For him . . . the life of the soul is a flame which perpetually renews its form. A precarious, spasmodic duration, always under the menace of an instantaneous explosion; a duration essentially tragic. (pp. 296-97)

Molière does not take type as a starting point; he does not adopt the "realist" conception of an abstract being in more or less concrete finery. No, he comes to give his characters the value of types by the constant repetition of essential traits. The character becomes generalized as the play advances, by reason of the fact that, incessantly returning to strike our attention, the same traits are finally found to be retained at the expense of secondary traits; as if from an infinity of misers, one extracted little by little the idea of the exemplary miser, the paragon who represents them all. (p. 297)

From this point of view there is no temporal movement in the plays of Molière. It is the same repetitive duration as in the drama of passion from which it eliminates the tragic. But in eliminating the tragic it eliminates movement also. It becomes a mere static repetition in which there is progress only in the pattern of the character and in the estimate we form of him. An historical progress, which has a place only in the order of knowledge, of abstraction even. In proportion as the character becomes more typical, he passes little by little from the actual to the absolute. He becomes the eternal example of an eternal unreasonableness.

Thus, if the resemblance, if the perceptible repetition were not there to reawaken within us in each instant the feeling of ridicule which those so decisive "first instants" had brought to birth there, the character would become completely detached from all temporality and all reality and would run the risk of falling into a schematic intemporality. There exists in this regard a veritably Proustian text of Molière's which marvelously lights up the subtle play of the "intermittences" of ridicule and of the "irregular progresses" of the comic. In the *Lettre de l'Imposteur*, speaking of Panulphe, that is to say of Tartuffe, he says this:

> The excessive ridicule of the manners of Panulphe makes it certain that every time they are presented to the spectator on some other occasion they will assuredly seem to him ridiculous.... The soul, naturally avid of joy, will necessarily be delighted at the first sight of things that it once conceived as extremely ridiculous, and *will renew in itself the idea of the very lively pleasure it tasted that first time.*

Thus each time we notice a new comic manifestation of character, "we shall be first of all struck by the memory of that first time," and this memory, mingling itself with the present occasion, will "fuse the two occasions into one."

Thus to the objective repetition of the course of passion there is joined the subjective repetition of the feeling it provokes in us. The character repeats himself, and we begin to laugh again, and in beginning to laugh again we accord to him once more the freshness of actuality. The comic art of Molière is eternal in two ways: first in the manifestation of a reason, which makes an eternally valid judgment upon human deportment; and then in that of the sensibility, which never ceases to make us feel this deportment eternally present and living. (pp. 297-98)

Georges Poulet, "Molière," in Perspectives in Contemporary Criticism: A Collection of Recent Essays by American, English, and European Literary Critics, *edited by Sheldon Norman Grebstein, Harper & Row, Publishers, 1968, pp. 293-98.*

J. D. HUBERT (essay date 1962)

[*Hubert is an American essayist and academic. In the following excerpt from his* Molière and the Comedy of Intellect, *he discusses the ultimate destruction of the literary illusions internalized by Cathos and Magdelon in* The Affected Ladies.]

In the autumn of 1659, Molière, then thirty-eight years old, produced his first masterpiece, a one-act farce in prose, *Les Précieuses ridicules*. Not only did this short play suffice to establish his reputation and his fame, but it set forth, almost in the manner of a manifesto, his conception of literature in general and of comedy in particular. The farce recounts how two suitors avenge their rude reception by two provincial maidens, besotted by stories of love and adventure. Many a writer before and after Molière has achieved success by describing the strange effects which literature can produce on mediocre minds. We do not intend, however, to compare the foolish Magdelon and her equally silly cousin Cathos to Cervantes' magnanimous Don Quixote, whose brains had been addled even more than theirs by countless novels of chivalry.... Don Quixote definitely possesses the lofty imagination of his creator; and so does the heroic Dorante, the protagonist of Corneille's *Le Menteur*. Obviously, Cathos and Magdelon belong to an inferior species, for their readings and their imagination serve merely to feed their vanity and their affectation. Their inner world, like that of Flaubert's Emma Bovary or the heroine of Maupassant's "La Parure," consists almost exclusively of clichés, of *idées reçues*, of all the banalities and dregs of third-rate literature.

As readers, Molière's *précieuses* differ from Madame Bovary in at least one important respect: whereas Emma practically sells her soul to make life conform to the picture-book romanticism of her childhood, Magdelon and Cathos merely deny the outside world in favor of the make-believe universe of current best-sellers. Even the platitudes which they so blithely exchange with the valet Mascarille, disguised as a marquis, deal almost entirely with literature.... (pp. 16-17)

In rejecting La Grange and Du Croisy as suitors and in preferring the glitter of their disguised servants, the two girls actually show a preference for bad literature over good. Mascarille especially, in dress, manner and expression, is the very incarnation of the salon literature that Molière and his friend Boileau so cordially despised. In fact, La Grange, who stages the play within the play that will soon destroy Magdelon and Cathos, knows immediately what sort of bait to use: "Je vois ce qu'il faut être pour en être bien reçu" ["I see what one must be in order to be well received by them"]. Characteristically, Molière uses the word "être," whereas a dramatist of an earlier period might have preferred in this particular instance the term "paraître" ["to appear"]. But in Mascarille, there can be no demarcation between appearance and essence, affectation and profound personality, public and private image. Divested of his bravery, he stands revealed to our two *précieuses* as a fraud. Indeed, the two porters, who had carried him on stage in a sedan chair, had, in spite of their lack of education and polish, immediately recognized him as such. Mascarille, in his parting words, ambiguously reproaches his erstwhile admirers their lack of regard for "la vertu toute nue" ["naked virtue"]. And until Du Croisy and La Grange had burst upon the scene, poor Mascarille had embodied for Cathos and her cousin the most desirable features of Parisian literary circles, and his aura had conformed to their every expectation. In the play within the play, arranged by La Grange, but so sincerely performed by Mascarille and Jodelet, Molière has thus externalized a certain type of bad taste.

Molière does much more than attack the unenlightened public whose tastes conform with those of the two girls, for he satirizes the writers and even the actors—those of the Hôtel de Bourgogne—they most admire. Magdelon and Cathos have devoured the interminable novels of Madeleine de Scudéry, as no doubt many of the spectators present themselves had done. But our two *précieuses* have obviously gone much further than any other reader in their rejection of all forms of behavior that do not rigidly follow the pattern of their favorite fictional characters. Molière chose as a perfect foil for the two maidens an obvious nonreader, Gorgibus. To contemporary spectators, he must have seemed just as ridiculous as his daughter and niece, for he behaves as though he had spent his entire existence in some sort of backwoods whose denizens did not even suspect the existence of literature, let alone of preciosity. To Gorgibus' conventional attitude concerning marriage, Magdelon opposes ideas just as conventional if somewhat more fashionable. . . . She apparently wishes to substitute a purely literary convention for a social one, and the expression "dans les formes" ["according to rule"] reveals the rigidity of her code. She strikes us as a strange sort of pedant, as grotesque in her way as Métaphraste or

Handbill produced for early performances of The Affected Ladies.

all the doctors and notaries who will follow in her footsteps. As Magdelon proceeds with her long speech, she transforms these conventions into a rigid, systematic and almost obsessive pattern of behavior. . . . She thus reduces the stuff and nonsense of contemporary novels to a set of absolutes, that she considers binding in day to day existence. By this reduction, she tends to exclude the reality of human feelings as well as the eventualities of a normal life.

Cathos and Magdelon do not, however, confine their preciosity to literature, but indulge in every conceivable form of artificiality. La Grange had defined their type as a cross between a *coquette* and a *précieuse*. Indeed, they use, in spite of their youth, vast quantities of make-up, as though they wished to transform their countenances into a fixed and permanent mask. Old Gorgibus, at least, conveys that impression. . . . With all this pomade, they must look something like Jodelet, who paints his face white in the manner of a clown. The lard mentioned by Gorgibus represents the sordid matrix of their affectation, of their ethereal prudery. The two girls, like any self-respecting *précieuses,* are of course prudes and probably Platonists to boot. Cathos especially expresses her horror of nature in the raw, of undisguised reality: "Comment est-ce qu'on peut souffrir la pensée de coucher contre un homme vraiment nu?" ["How can one endure the thought of lying by the side of a man entirely unclothed?"] But does Cathos really hate sex or do her words merely echo the distorted idealism of some members of the *précieux* set? Such hatred might explain why the two maidens wish to escape to a purely imaginary universe. . . . But why look for hidden motivations in a satirical comedy of manners? After all, everything Magdelon and Cathos say or do reflects dramatically and even structurally their ambition to replace the world they live in by literature. These two essentialists might formulate their *cogito* as: "I read, therefore I am." And because they read the wrong sort of books, they must fall for the nonsense of a valet who prides himself on his wit and his creative powers: he who lives by literature, will perish by literature.

Les Précieuses ridicules has, since its first performance, given rise to a controversy. Did Molière intend to satirize a poor imitation of preciosity or the thing itself? Professor Antoine Adam [in his *Histoire de la littérature française au XVIIe siècle* (1952-56)] has shown that Molière definitely had in mind Madeleine de Scudéry and her coterie. In fact, La Grange, at the very beginning of the farce, expresses his opposition to the whole movement: "L'air précieux n'a pas seulement infecté Paris, il s'est aussi répandu dans les provinces, et nos donzelles ridicules en ont humé leur bonne part" ["The craze for culture has not only infected Paris but has also spread into the country, and our ridiculous damsels have taken their fair share of it"]. La Grange's strong words—whether or not they express the author's own viewpoint—definitely cast an unfavorable light on preciosity itself, and not only on Cathos and Magdelon. Subsequent scenes will show that La Grange had some justification in referring to preciosity as a contagious disease. Molière, however, attacks the movement in a devious manner, for he flays two vain females who have succumbed to the outward manifestations of preciosity rather than the actual way of life that prevailed at the Hôtel de Rambouillet. And the author uses indirection of a similar kind to make fun of the rival comedians of the Hôtel de

Bourgogne, for instead of attacking them directly, he makes Mascarille admire them for their artificiality. Mascarille, played by the author himself, even denigrates the acting of Molière and his company "... ils ne savent pas faire ronfler les vers, et s'arrêter au bel endroit" ["they don't know how to make the verses speak, or to pause at a fine passage"]. The author will use this same technique in *L'Impromptu de Versailles,* damning his rivals with the exaggerated praise of fools. Pascal, only a few years earlier, had perfected this effective weapon in order to harass the Jesuits. By using indirection against Madeleine de Scudéry and the Hôtel de Bourgogne, Molière could transform into accomplices even fairly staunch admirers of *Le Grand Cyrus* and of Montfleury, for he knew that no one in the audience could possibly identify with such idiots as Magdelon, Cathos, and Mascarille. This explains the general enthusiasm that greeted the farce at its first performance, attended, if we can believe Ménage, by many members of the *précieux* set, who applauded as much as everyone else.

In this as well as in most of his subsequent plays, Molière chooses as victim a gullible or even dedicated person whose tribulations serve to devaluate the system of values in which he or she believes. Normally, this clever method does not obscure the issue, even though it helps protect the author. Sometimes, for instance in *Dom Juan,* we can scarcely determine the playwright's actual intentions, and interpretation must become a form of conjecture and speculation.

Systematic deflation characterizes *Les Précieuses ridicules.* Cathos and Magdelon imitate a certain conception of preciosity, in the same manner that Mascarille and Jodelet ape two quite different aspects of aristocratic behavior, or that Don Quixote strives to live up to the outmoded, but still admired, ideal of knight errantry. Deflation, in this farce, thus takes the form of parody and caricature: Cathos-Aminthe replaces Catherine-Arthénice of Hôtel de Rambouillet fame, while the two footmen perform the parts of noblemen and wits. Molière cleverly attributes to the four principals, in a most exaggerated form, the actual shortcomings of real *précieuses* and genuine aristocrats. He pokes fun at Mascarille in precisely the same manner that, in *Le Misanthrope,* he will satirize the "petits marquis" whose blue blood is above suspicion. Molière cruelly chastises a relatively poor imitation, but in so doing he deals a tremendous blow at current affectations.

One cannot insist too strongly on the general aggressiveness of the play, on its inherent cruelty. Cathos and Magdelon, by identifying life with the vicissitudes of fiction, have tried to protect themselves from the dull hazards of day to day existence. As they wish to live in an illusory world and indulge their silly vanity, it is fitting that an illusion of a different sort should shatter their dream and bring them down to earth. In thus pulverizing their fondest illusions, their hopes of a brilliant future in Parisian literary and aristocratic circles, Molière actually destroys their very being. The beatings which La Grange and Du Croisy will publicly administer to their servants provide only a slight and purely external indication of the tortures that the two would-be *précieuses* are undergoing at the same moment, almost to the point of annihilation. The more they suffer, the more ridiculous they seem, and the more the audience laughs at them. Freud spoke the truth

when he described certain types of laughter as a form of aggression.

Molière very nearly lends a tragic dimension to this cruel destruction of illusion by means of the dramatic device of tragic irony. (pp. 17-22)

Molière, even more frequently than in his two previous plays, amuses the audience with the idea of theatrical illusion. Our *précieuses* are performing their parts to the best of their ability in a play intended to bring about their complete destruction. And at the end, they will suffer mainly as spectators from the absurdity of their own performance. Molière reminds us more than once of this paradox.... Moreover, the author plays with the idea of theatrical illusion by attributing Jodelet's whitened countenance to a recent illness.... In *Le Dépit,* Gros-René had referred to his bulkiness in much the same manner. However, such devices take on added significance in a farce dealing with the annihilation of literary illusions. Molière, for that reason, insists several times on the purely histrionic quality of the trick played by the infuriated suitors. He stresses, moreover, the idea of entertainment, indispensable to the performance of a farce, for Mascarille does not hesitate to hire musicians who transform the play into a ludicrous ballet. Thus, the cruel destruction of illusions coincides with the triumph of the theater, where good literature takes the place of trash. (pp. 22-3)

> *J. D. Hubert, in his* Molière & the Comedy of Intellect, *1962. Reprint by Russell & Russell, 1971, 275 p.*

JAMES DOOLITTLE (essay date 1962)

[*In the following excerpt, Doolittle analyzes the relationship of natural human dignity, rationality, and social institutions in Molière's plays, dividing the dramatist's career into two distinct thematic phases.*]

Plot in any play implies conflict of some kind. In Molière the conflict invariably takes place between human nature and something else. The something else is always recognizable because it is always logical, always rationally consistent with itself. For Harpagon, for example, a dollar is worth 100 cents, no more, no less; the sum of the enemas and other medicaments of *Le Malade imaginaire* adds up to medical beatitude; to call M. Jourdain *Monseigneur* or *votre grandeur* is to send him to his conception of paradise as surely as Orgon expects to get there by renouncing his humanity and aping the pious system of words and gestures of his friend Tartuffe.

If these very logical characters receive their comeuppance, it is not for lack of logical procedure on their part. On the contrary, their logic is impeccable; the trouble is that they start from a false premise, the premise, in every case, that human nature is a reasonable or logical phenomenon. That Molière did not think human nature a logical phenomenon is abundantly demonstrated by every play in his theatre.

To define Molière's concept of human nature is not part of my purpose here. It is part of my purpose, however, to repeat that for Molière the notion of human nature carries with it an inseparable attribute which we may call "dignity," and that for him dignity can neither be attained to nor preserved by logical means. One may go a step further and suggest that a Molière character who rigidly adheres to systematically logical procedure in his thoughts and behavior is thereby annulling his dignity and making himself ridiculous. Such is the situation of every comic hero, every victim of Molière's laughter, that is, in the canon of his plays. Reason, twenty-four-hour-a-day rationality, is incompatible with human nature, human dignity, and he who guides his every word and move thereby sooner or later finds himself the butt of human ridicule, deprived of his dignity.

Molière's victims are rationalists; they are logicians who proceed faultlessly from a fallacious premise through one or three or five acts to their ultimate discomfiture, of which in many cases they are made aware, and of which in all cases the audience is made aware. Orgon is freed of Tartuffe, M. Jourdain becomes a *mamamouchi*, Argan receives his medical degree, Harpagon gets his cherished money back. These characters are presumably happy when they leave the stage; the fact remains that in the eyes of the audience they are still fools or dupes or scoundrels, and it is the audience that matters. And then there are others who are not so happy at their final exit: Arnolphe, Alceste, George Dandin, Pourceaugnac. Each of these has been brought face to face with the failure of his logic as a means to success and happiness; and though the extent to which the lesson has been learned by any one of them may be debatable, the fact is that, be he happy or not, wiser or not, we have seen the desires and ambitions of each of these characters frustrated because he would not allow its due to the illogical phenomenon of human nature.

My principal concern here is with the premises upon which Molière's victims base their logic. These premises fall into two categories. Conveniently enough, these categories occupy two nearly equal chronological divisions of Molière's Paris career. From 1659 until his death in 1673 he produced thirty-one plays. The mid-point of this career is marked by the presentation, in successive years, of three masterpieces: *Tartuffe, Dom Juan, Le Misanthrope.* It is *Dom Juan,* produced in 1665, which, as I see it, stands at the beginning of the second phase of Molière's dramatic practice.

The first phase is perhaps best exemplified by *L'Ecole des femmes.* . . . (pp. 153-55)

Considered superficially or logically, there is nothing intrinsically wrong about either Arnolphe's objective or his methods. Generally speaking, a faithful wife seems to be a good thing to have, and it is a common notion that one's reason is the best instrument for the solution of one's problems. Arnolphe's downfall occurs because his reasoning is based upon a faulty or partial premise, and also because his objective is in fact not the fulfillment of his dignity (which would require his respect for the dignity of Agnès as well) but the satisfaction of his vanity, of his desire to show that he is different from and superior to other people.

This scheme of things, this way of conducting a play, occurs in all of Molière's plays. In all of them the essential situation consists of objectives conceived in and rendered desirable by passions, these objectives being pursued by means which are rationally devised and employed with rigid logic. The initial premise may be, and usually is, ill-

judged, ill-chosen, or at odds with human nature, and hence doomed to failure. That the objectives sought may be, and often are, eminently desirable from any dispassionate point of view does not alter the fact that it is because of their passions that the characters look upon them as being desirable, or, to put it perhaps more accurately, that the stated objectives—a faithful wife, scientific eminence, a pious character, the practice in society of complete sincerity, and so forth—are so many pretexts or masks disguising a vain, egotistical desire to show oneself to be better than other men, superior to one's own humanity or to humanity in general.

We observe that, while this scheme is common to all the plays of Molière, it is utilized in two different ways, one of them in the plays presented before *Dom Juan,* the other in the remainder. Before *Dom Juan,* the objectives and the means of the principal characters are such as would be appropriate to virtually anyone in comparable circumstances. Arnolphe's desire not to be a cuckold is shared, at least theoretically, by any prospective or actual husband, including Arnolphe's friend Chrysalde; Arnolphe is distinguished from these others, not by the nature of his desire, but by its intensity. The social ambition of the *précieuses* Cathos and Madelon is neither reprehensible nor in any way different from that of numerous young ladies in any time; it is not the ambition of Molière's *précieuses* which is ridiculous, but rather their misunderstanding of the nature of its fulfillment. The jealousy of Dom Garcie de Navarre is particularized only by the courtly heroic tradition which governs its expression; his princess Elvire behaves, not like a coquette, but simply like any civilized lady who is unwilling to be dominated by a boor. And so on. *Dom Juan,* in short, is preceded on the list by a baker's dozen of plays, outstanding among them *Les Précieuses ridicules, L'Ecole des femmes, Tartuffe,* and also the gloomy failure *Dom Garcie de Navarre.* In the details of form, plot, and conduct, these four plays differ a good deal, to be sure, from one another. At the same time the rights and wrongs of the matter, in every case, are amply clear to the audience and to most of the characters as well; there is not the slightest difficulty in distinguishing the fools from the sensible people. As in our horse opera, one can always tell the good guys from the bad guys, except that, *Tartuffe* apart, there are no villains, morally speaking, before *Dom Juan.* Indeed, Molière goes out of his way to inform us in these plays that his fools are decent people, their foolishness notwithstanding.

The name role of *Tartuffe* introduces a genuine villain. But he is not a genuine human being. Tartuffe is not a man; he exhibits no inconsistency with himself; he is all black. He is not a character but a puppet or mask—a mask beautifully and subtly contrived, to be sure, but inhuman precisely because he so perfectly embodies pious gestures for impious purposes. It is not in *Tartuffe* but in *Dom Juan,* that the humanity of the hypocrite is made manifest, that the causes, human and other, which can turn an imperfect man into the perfect criminal that Tartuffe is are illustrated and set in place, to form the matrix, so to speak, in which such criminal perfection may be conceived.

Dom Juan provides, I believe, the key to Molière's subsequent practice. As a creation of comic character, Dom Juan is scarcely less enigmatic than Célimène or Alceste; since, however, his actions and words are uttered upon a much larger variety of subjects than those of his predecessors, it is possible to perceive with somewhat greater clarity a consistent pattern underlying them.

Whatever else Dom Juan may be, he is always and everywhere a nonconformist; thus his independence is expressed almost exclusively in terms of a willful violation of institutional conventions. No other Molière play contains such a variety of institutional conventions. No other Molière cast contains representatives of so many classes and professions. Peasant, commoner, lackey, merchant, hermit, brother, wife, ghost, statue; the claims of religion, law, science, rank; of the honor of soldier and nobleman, of filial duty, reason, passion, heaven, earth, hell—all of these enter into the fabric of this remarkable play. Dom Juan's constant effort is to assert his independence of all of them. His constant desire is to flout authority of whatever kind, less for any profit that he may thereby obtain than for the sheer joy of flouting authority.

In marrying his Elvire, for example, Dom Juan has not only adapted the trappings of marriage to his own peculiar purpose; he has also violated the sanctity of a convent and induced Elvire to abjure her duty to her monastic condition, her family, and her fiancé (whether the fiancé is divine or human is a question which Molière leaves unanswered). Before the play is over, Elvire has called Dom Juan to account on the basis of duties by turns marital, chivalric, and religious, each time to the vast amusement of her unrepentant husband, who entertains himself also by mocking, deadpan, the heroic efforts of Elvire's noble brothers. Each of his conquests, accomplished or intended, must be made in the face of institutional obstacles. These women are protected not only by their share of natural modesty but much more formidably by contractual engagements. Dom Juan is delighted by feminine beauty, to be sure, but feminine beauty considered as an object, not of contemplation or worship, but of action, as something to be conquered.

What is true of his view of the love of women characterizes also his attitude toward other social relationships, toward religious and scientific institutions. He exhibits, with complete frankness, the utmost scorn for the attitudes, the gestures, and the jargon whose use is presumed to show that the user adheres faithfully to these institutions. Dom Juan has only contempt for those people who knowingly or unknowingly accept the consecrated word and gesture for the reality of an action originating in belief. For him, only the man whose exterior represents exactly that man's inner conviction seems worthy of respect. The only such character in this play is the poor hermit; all the others utilize appearances, not as expressions of their inner truth, but as disguises for it. In each case Dom Juan unerringly penetrates the hypocritical disguise, and for so doing he is of course punished by death and damnation, the sentence being executed by the most completely conventional and respectable character of all—the statue.

Dom Juan is not a particularly funny character; we do not laugh at him. But we do laugh with him. His function is to penetrate the disguises of his interlocutors and to laugh at the incongruity between the mask and the reality of each of them. Thus, although he is not a comical character, he functions precisely as does a comedian, a creator of comedy, a Molière. Dom Juan is amused, pursued, oppressed, and finally destroyed by the acolytes of institu-

tional respectability. And this, with variations only in degree, is the situation, at least potentially, in nearly every subsequent play. Here the success and happiness of the heroes are menaced less by individual characters themselves than by characters, and events also, representing one or more of the institutions of society, science, and religion.

Tartuffe is the first play to introduce the words and gestures, the external aspect, of an unmistakably identifiable and very respectable institution as constituting a menace to the dignity of decent human nature. But the basic design of *Tartuffe* is identical with that of most of the earlier plays: there is a single character whose mistakenly conceived obsession threatens the desires and the well-being of his fellow characters, all of whom are cognizant of his error. And the error is always an error of judgment, not one of moral delinquency.

With **Dom Juan** two important alterations appear. The first is the presentation of characters who are guilty of varying degrees of moral corruption. The second is the employment of established institutions as corrupting agents. By this I do not mean institutional appearances, as used by Tartuffe; I mean the substance underlying the appearances—the institutions themselves. Thus in the plays beginning with **Dom Juan** it is often difficult to distinguish with certainty between right and wrong, between the good guys and the bad guys. Dom Juan, for instance, is no model of virtue by any standard, but then the purity of his antagonists is doubtful also. The moral dilemmas arising in *Le Misanthrope* are simply insoluble. *George Dandin* presents the most completely villainous cast in Molière, yet there is a good deal to be said in defense of both the hero and his wife. The Bourgeois and Pourceaugnac are both victimized by scoundrels more intelligent than they, but it is their own snobbery and greed which make this possible.

The corruption of all these characters originates and is expressed in terms of one or more of the institutions that I have mentioned. Science is represented either by pedantry or, more often, by medicine. Religion, after the bitter experience of *Tartuffe*, appears only in **Dom Juan** and, safely disguised as astrology, in *Les Amants magnifiques*. The institution most frequently utilized is a social one, the convention of distinction of rank. (pp. 155-60)

The view of institutions as oppressors of human dignity may be clarified . . . by some comparisons between plays occurring before and after the critical moment represented by **Dom Juan**. Certain of the later plays are developments or *reprises* of earlier ones. Thus, for example, *Les Précieuses ridicules* is echoed and elaborated in *Les Femmes savantes; Dom Garcie de Navarre* has its counterpart in *Le Misanthrope; La Princesse d'Elide* comes to full bloom in *Les Amants magnifiques*. In these pairings the distinction between the earlier member and the later one is the same: none of the conflicting elements in the earlier one are specifically institutional, whereas in the later one the institution has become the indispensable element.

For instance, both Euryale of *La Princesse d'Elide* and Sostrate of *Les Amants magnifiques* are in love with their princesses. Sostrate is opposed far less by his lady than by his inferiority in rank; to this obstacle, furthermore, Molière adds another more formidable one in the hostility of the astrologer Anaxarque. There is no hint anywhere in *La Princesse d'Elide* of dishonesty or other corruption; Anaxarque, on the other hand, sets the whole weight of his combined religious and scientific authority against Sostrate because each of Sostrate's rivals, both of them princes by the way, has sought to procure the astrologer's favor by bribery.

The *précieuses* Cathos and Madelon speak and act according to their mistaken notion of the ways of the kind of society to which they aspire to be admitted. The *femmes savantes,* on the contrary, emulate with exactness the speech, behavior, and tastes of a well-defined and limited group, that of the pedants. Mascarille and Jodelet are frankly pretending to be what they are not; Trissotin and Vadius are genuinely the pedants that they claim to be. The only vice of the *précieuses* is stupidity; in *Les Femmes savantes,* by contrast, Trissotin, Armande, Bélise, and Philaminte are all guilty of self-interested dissimulation, of hypocrisy.

Dom Garcie de Navarre and his princess Elvire are virtuous heroes in the Cornelian tradition. Dom Garcie is cursed with a streak of jealousy which Elvire does nothing whatever to provoke, as Dom Garcie himself acknowledges. Alceste is jealous too, of course; but his jealousy is first of all justified to some extent by the behavior of Célimène; secondly, it is only one of a number of traits in an extraordinarily complex character whose fundamental component is a domineering egotism disguised as a virtuous concern for sincerity. Alceste is doubtless unaware of his hypocrisy; one may say that in him hypocrisy is sublimated into the misanthropy which manifests itself in the constant denigration of all things which are not itself; and among these things the most prominent are the institutional gestures of polite social conduct. It is true that the vice of Alceste, like that of Dom Garcie, originates within himself; unlike that of Dom Garcie, it is deliberately fostered and inflamed by the behavior of others, behavior for which Alceste is not responsible. I should say that in the earlier play Dom Garcie is manifestly wrong and his fellow characters manifestly right; in *Le Misanthrope* Alceste and his society together are simultaneously right and wrong. While one can agree that Alceste carries his opinions and his actions too far, one cannot so easily declare that his announced principles are wrong, that his misanthropy is his fault alone and not justified to a considerable extent by the conventional conduct of the society in which he lives. Célimène too is vastly different from Dom Garcie's Elvire, who is utterly right from start to finish, correct, frank, loving, and very dull. As to Célimène, who can say? One of the most enigmatic of characters, she is also one of the most charming.

From this comparison it should be clear that, in the later member of each pair of plays, Molière utilized institutional customs and concerns which do not occur at all in the earlier member. And he uses them to threaten or actually to destroy the personal dignity, happiness, or well-being of most of the individuals involved. Institutional conventions, the logical application of their codified rules and regulations, are set in opposition to human happiness and dignity.

Previous to *Dom Juan,* society, its principles, customs, beliefs, usages, are viewed as the proper criteria for good judgment and right conduct. This notion, abundantly obvious in the earlier plays themselves, is carried over into the great critical pieces: *La Critique de l'Ecole des femmes* and *L'Impromptu de Versailles,* in which the judgments of

cultivated (and hence institutionalized) people overwhelmingly prevail against the narrow opinions of rule-mongering pedants, a few prudes, and one's jealous professional rivals. What happens after *Tartuffe* is not precisely a reversal; rather the authority of all socially respectable institutions is cast with that of the prudes and the pedants into the scales against the expression and maintenance of what, for Molière as for any other authentic artist, must be the indispensable subject and final justification for his art, the illogical phenomenon which also justifies human existence, namely, human dignity.

It would, I think, be moronic to regard Molière in any sense as a revolutionary. There is nowhere in his theatre the slightest suggestion that existing institutions should be altered or eliminated; but there is everywhere, and especially after *Dom Juan,* the implication that any man who deserves the title of man must be the master and not the servant of institutions. This is not to say that I would make of Molière a systematic thinker or philosopher, social or otherwise. Molière was an artist, and thus by definition independent of institution and system and intellectualism alike. Like Pascal, he seems to have believed that reason is indeed something, but it is not everything. Like Pascal, he was aware that it takes no more than a buzzing fly to dethrone man from his reasonable lordship of this world. Unlike Pascal, Molière came to see in the systematic observance of institutional gestures not the means to wisdom but the annihilation of dignity. (pp. 161-64)

> *James Doolittle, "Human Nature and Institutions in Molière's Plots," in* Studies in Seventeenth-Century French Literature: Presented to Morris Bishop, *edited by Jean-Jacques Demorest, Cornell University Press, 1962, pp. 153-64.*

LIONEL GOSSMAN   (essay date 1963)

[*Gossman is a Scottish essayist and educator. In the following excerpt from his book* Men and Masks: A Study of Molière *(1963), he analyzes* The Misanthrope, *examining Alceste's extensive use of masks.*]

To all appearances, Alceste is a seeker after authenticity in a world profoundly marked by inauthenticity. Looking around him, he sees every one of his fellow men, including his best friend Philinte, bound over to others. Their behavior, their judgments, their whole lives are inauthentic in Alceste's view, entirely determined by the public of others before whom they parade a mask that constantly changes and adapts itself according to circumstances. Life is a vast comedy in which each man plays as many parts as he has friends and enemies. At no point is a man truly himself. Appearances, Alceste complains, do not reveal reality; they hide it. Alceste would transform this world of falsehood and illusion into a world in which appearance mirrors reality:

> Je veux qu'on soit sincère, et qu'en homme d'honneur,
> On ne lâche aucun mot qui ne parte du coeur.

> [I would have you be sincere, and, like a man of honor, not let slip any word save that which comes from the heart].

The inauthenticity of these noble aspirations is revealed, however, at the very beginning of the play. Alceste is not concerned with his own honesty and sincerity, which he would have us accept unquestioningly. He is concerned only with the honesty and sincerity of others, and it is for them that he is constantly laying down the law. "Je veux" ["I want"] is never far from his lips. Alceste is deeply disturbed by the insincerity of others because he cares a great deal what people think of him and feel toward him. Although he affects to despise their judgments and to reject their advances, there is nothing he longs for more than to be esteemed and loved by others, and not by one or two others, but by all others. Furthermore he is not content to be esteemed and loved, he longs to be esteemed more highly than anyone else and loved more wholeheartedly. He suffers from the polite formality of the compliments addressed to him, not because they are meaningless to him, but because they mean so much to him, not because they are insincere, but because he so desperately wants them to be sincere.... (pp. 67-8)

Because he cares so deeply what others think of him, Alceste wants to be sure that they really think what they say. He cannot have this certainty, however, for not only is no one prepared to give it, no one can give it. Just as he wants the love of Célimène, which he cannot be sure of, and turns down Eliante, Alceste craves the admiration and esteem of the very people whom he accuses of insincerity. He desires whatever escapes him and only what escapes him. What is given to him is never what he wants, only what is withheld. He cannot, consequently, be given what he wants. He can only try to seize it by trickery or violence. Alceste and those he complains of on account of their "insincerity" are thus seen to belong to the same world. While they refuse to reveal themselves, he desires only what is concealed, while they resist, he attacks. The changing appearances of others confound, as they are intended to do, all attempts to "see through" them. Only those can be balked, however, who make the attempt.

Desiring as he does the complete approbation of others, Alceste longs to see into every heart, so that he can be sure of his place in the esteem of others. Inevitably, whatever he cannot see is experienced by him as a menace. He senses that what lies beyond the limit of his vision is the freedom of others, and it is precisely by this freedom that he feels constantly threatened. Anxious to have himself recognized by others as superior and absolute, he affects indifference to their opinions, but in his heart he is constantly interrogating them and constantly being frustrated by the answers. He loudly protests his uprightness, sincerity, and independence, but when this evokes the compliments and respect that it was intended to, he finds that the gold has turned to ashes before his eyes, for he cannot believe the compliments that are paid to him. He who sets himself up to be an absolute in the eyes of others finds another absolute when he looks into theirs, he who would look on others as objects finds himself reflected as an object in theirs. Not surprisingly, he experiences the whole world as an infernal web of lies and deceit:

Je ne trouve partout que lâche flatterie,
Qu'injustice, intérêt, trahison, fourberie.

[I find nothing but base flattery,
injustice, self-interest, deceit, roguery].

Alceste's world is made up of innumerable atoms which are absolute and relative at the same time. Absolutes for themselves, they find that they are relatives for others; the relativeness of others for them, on the other hand is transformed into an absoluteness the moment an attempt is made to grasp and hold it. Alceste cannot tolerate this situation. He refuses to find himself in the same boat with everybody else; he wants to be above all others; unfortunately, however, only they can set him above them, and this they will not do. "Je veux qu'on me distingue" ["I wish to be loved for myself"], Alceste cries in petulant rage, but his words resound in a terrifying void. In this cry of need the supposed misanthrope ... acknowledges his utter dependence on the humanity he despises, his total infatuation with that which he professes indifference to. What he craves is the love and recognition of those whom he scorns, what he longs for is to be adored by those very "gens à la mode" ["fashionable people"] from whom he ostensibly turns away in disgust. But he wants this adoration to be real, not conventional. The world which refuses to adore Alceste, to doff the mask and reveal itself to him in its defenseless nakedness, is at once the object of his desire and the enemy to be humiliated. (pp. 68-70)

Even Alceste's relations with his closest friend are poisoned by his unbridled desire to be superior, and by the terror of inferiority that accompanies it. He finds no confidence and no repose in friendship; *all* others are rivals and enemies for him. He must, therefore, affirm his superiority, regain, as he imagines, the upper hand, by affecting to be indifferent to Philinte, to the extent that—what delight!—he finds the impeccably masked Philinte running after him, pleading to be allowed to defend himself, begging for a gracious word or look, for this is how Alceste interprets Philinte's concern for him.

Alceste desperately needs Philinte. His rejection of him is as much a pose as his frequently repeated threats to abandon the world. At the same time as he turns away, he is constantly looking over his shoulder, as it were, to make sure that Philinte is still there. But precisely because he wants Philinte's recognition of him as a being different from and above every other being, he cannot bear Philinte's freedom to accord or to refuse this recognition. Alceste can never have been on terms of real friendship and trust with Philinte, and his own remark about having only affected friendship is truer than he himself imagines when he makes it. He wants Philinte to believe that he has only pretended to be his friend. He himself, however, really believes that he was Philinte's friend. His remark about having only pretended to be his friend is, in his own mind, a deliberate lie, which he tells to "protect himself." In fact Alceste's very lack of trust, his very need to "protect himself" reveals that he is incapable of friendship, just as he will later be shown to be incapable of love. As soon as he becomes aware of Philinte as a person independent of him, an otherness and a freedom, he sees in him no longer a friend, but an enemy and a rival. To this would-be absolutist every otherness is a menace.

Alceste is in an intolerable position. He craves genuine and sincere recognition from others, not the conventional respect of the mask. This recognition can be given, however, only by a free subject. It would no longer be worth anything to Alceste if it were not freely willed by the giver. Yet the freedom which is the condition of the recognition he desires is inevitably experienced by him as a menace, since freedom to give must mean also freedom not to give. What Alceste requires is an impossible contradiction—a freedom that is not free. The absolute freedom of others confounds his own claim to absoluteness by making him relative with respect to them. Others must therefore be brought to recognize his absoluteness and to admit their own dependence. Alceste's need of the recognition of others thus places him, the would-be absolute, in the strictest dependence on others. He is obliged to woo the world in order to wrest from it a recognition that, if he were truly the absolute he claims to be, he would not have to ask for. Alceste must conceal this dependence from others and from himself, by affecting to despise the world, by *presenting himself* as the absolute he claims to be. His sincerity, his disgust, and his indifference are thus the *poses* of an independence he does not in fact possess, while the sincerity he demands from others is the indispensable condition of the recognition he desires from them. All the contradictions in Alceste's behavior can be traced back to this fundamental and initial imposture. (pp. 71-2)

It is not that society is put out by Alceste's nonconformism, or that it laughs at him because he is different. It laughs at him because he is the same but pretends to be different. Great comedian that it is, the world recognizes the comedian in Alceste, and it laughs because it sees in him a comedian *who acts as if he were not one, and who is completely trapped by his role.*

Alceste's frantic coming and going, his wooing of the world, and his resentment of it are manifested at the deepest level in his relation with Célimène.

As Alceste himself presents it, his love for Célimène is so great and so absolute that it can be realized only through the exclusion from it of all that is contingent, of all that has value in the eyes of others alone.... His love for Célimène, Alceste protests, is pure giving; it is its own beginning and its own end, for it is independent of anything beyond itself, the pride of conquest, the charm of wit, the advantage of wealth.

Many critics—notably Arnavon and Bénichou—have justly observed that the love of this champion of sincerity is darkly tainted with fanatically possessive egoism. Alceste does not dream of a situation in which all contingency and public approval or disapproval would be abolished in the simple and pure equality of love. On the contrary, he needs the judgment and the values of others in order to manifest his "love"... and he needs the contingent in order to make himself the absolute for Célimène that he wants to be. It is through Célimène's destitution—a destitution in terms of the values of others: money, prestige, power—that he hopes to become the very ground of her existence ("Vous voir tenir tout des mains de mon amour" ["to see you owe everything to my love"]). Just as he is hardly concerned with his own sincerity but greatly concerned with the sincerity of others, Alceste does not want to love, but *to be loved*. The language he speaks is the language of power, not the language of love.

The tyrannical aspect of Alceste's "love" does not escape Célimène, who retorts drily to his strange declaration: "C'est me vouloir du bien d'une étrange manière" ["This is wishing me well in a strange manner"]. Her insight is justified at the end of the play. If there was ever a time for Alceste to prove the constancy and purity of his love, this was it. Célimène at the end of the play is as destitute as he could have wished. But Alceste does not want or know how to give love. He wants only to be loved, to be preferred absolutely. Rounding on Célimène harshly and cursing his love for her, he brutally lays down the conditions on which alone she can redeem herself in his eyes... ...Célimène replies that she cannot renounce the world. She offers Alceste her hand in marriage, however, only to find herself interrupted by an irate "lover" who rejects her offer in insulting terms.... (pp. 72-5)

The contradictoriness and inauthenticity of Alceste's position is mercilessly exposed in this scene. By stipulating that Célimène must withdraw to a desert place with him, Alceste is attempting to realize *literally* his goal of complete and utter domination. In his desert he would *in fact* be the whole world for Célimène. If Célimène had accepted, however, Alceste would no longer have wanted to go with her. This is one reason for the alacrity with which he accepts her refusal. Alceste can desire Célimène only as long as she is an "enemy," a freedom to be reduced to slavery. Had she accepted his offer, he would have ceased to "love" her, since, having renounced her freedom, she would no longer be in a position to give it up for him. Like Dom Juan, Alceste cannot find the recognition and admiration he longs for in the love of a devoted mistress. At the same time, he cannot accept her offer of marriage, for marriage, as Jupiter made amply clear in *Amphitryon*, does not constitute a sufficient abandonment by the beloved of her freedom. Alceste's "love" for Célimène is such that he can neither accept her as free, nor accept her as unfree. If she is free he does not possess her freedom, and if she is unfree she no longer has any freedom for him to posess. Alceste is condemned by the very nature of his desire to desire indefinitely without satisfaction. In the debased romantic parlance of recent times, he is "in love with love."

As we discover the true nature of Alceste's "love" for Célimène, we also discover the true nature of his supposed spontaneity and sincerity. Alceste's love for Célimène is not an inconsistency or "comic flaw" as has sometimes been held, not at least in the sense in which it has been described as one. The fact that reason does not determine love in no way contradicts the position Alceste *professes* to hold; it is, on the contrary, essential to it. When Philinte compares Eliante favorably with Célimène and expresses surprise that Alceste does not choose the former rather than the latter, since Eliante is in every way a more "suitable" match than Célimène..., Alceste's reply is no banal comment on the irrationality of passion, it is a rejection of the level on which Philinte is discussing love. From the point of view of prudence and advantage, Philinte is no doubt right..., but, Alceste observes, the realm of love like that of justice lies beyond reason (read: the calculating reason) and it is not governed by interest. "Mais la raison n'est pas ce qui règle l'amour" ["Reason plays no part in the bestowing of love"], he says, and he might have added: "nor ought it to." Alceste cannot admit that reason ought to govern love, for reason in the sense of "sagesse," the shrewd accommodating of ends, means, and interests, is precisely what Alceste ostensibly rebels against in the world of his fellow creatures. Nothing is more opposed to the "sincerity" he advocates than careful calculation of advantages and disadvantages. Alceste's own description of his love for Célimène as passing reason is thus entirely consistent with the position he claims to hold and the free, natural, spontaneous, and sincere person he claims to be.

At the same time, however, Alceste appreciates that his infatuation with the worldly and sophisticated Célimène must appear strange to his public. People must inevitably wonder what he, the bluff and uncompromising champion of simplicity and sincerity, finds so attractive in this cultivated and self-conscious society lady. . . . To justify his behavior and conceal his real motives, from himself as well as from others, Alceste must despise Célimène at the same time as he "loves" her, he must present his love as at once *irrational*—an enslavement, unworthy of him—and *super-rational*—a manifestation of his perfect freedom and a higher emotion than anything his contemporaries, with their mean calculations, can possibly achieve. Like the Romantic lovers who were to succeed him, he swithers ambiguously between both these presentations of his relation to Célimène in an attempt to make both seem true at the same time. This explains why the words "*la raison n'est pas ce qui règle l'amour*" have so often been taken as an expression of his shame at the totally irreducible and uncontrollable fact of love. The ambiguity of Alceste's attitude to his love for Célimène is understandable. On the one hand, he must posit his love as transcending the cunning calculations of his fellowmen, as absolute, coming from the heart, sincere and free. In this sense his love acts as a mark of his superiority. At the same time, however, he must appear to despise Célimène, in order to show that he is not really the slave that he seems to be. He must remind his audience that he is superior even to his own desire. His love must be shown to be at once super-rational, the free creation of his own sincere and spontaneous nature, and irrational, not consented to, beneath him.

In reality, Alceste's love for Célimène is neither super-rational (above all reason and all explanation) nor irrational (below all reason and explanation). It is quite simply a peculiar and contradictory fascination which goes by the name of love in the vocabulary of the Alcestes of the world. It *can* be explained, and the explanation reveals that far from being the sincere and spontaneous being he says he is, Alceste is as calculating as anyone else.

It is precisely because Célimène is the most sought after and *worldly* of women (to all *appearances* the most unsuitable for Alceste) that he falls in love with her. It is not Célimène that Alceste loves or desires. She is irrelevant *as a person* to his "love." It is the world that he seeks to reach and possess through her. To have at his feet this woman whom all the world admires and courts would be to win the recognition of the world for himself. Alceste's love is entirely mediated by those very "gens à la mode" for whom he so loudly protests his contempt. He "loves" Célimène because she has what he wants—the admiration of the world—and cannot admit he wants, without at the same time admitting that he is not the free, frank, and independent person he wants to be admired as. The object of his desire is thus also his unavowed rival, and this *for the very same reason* that she is the object of his desire. While he protests his love for Célimène, Alceste must therefore conceal the real reason for this love by affecting to deplore her participation in the "false" society of the *gens à la mode* and to despise her charms and her popularity. The final break with Célimène strikingly illustrates the ambiguity that characterizes Alceste's entire relationship with her from the beginning. Alceste calls on witnesses to observe how superior and disinterested his love is compared to the love of the elegant suitors who have

abandoned Célimène, while at the same time he affirms before them his own contempt for it as unworthy of him. . . . Having once proved how different his love is from that of Célimène's frivolous and calculating suitors, however, Alceste is only too quick to use her unwillingness to follow him to his desert as an excuse to drop her. Célimène without her suitors can have no attraction for Alceste.

Those who fall for Alceste's argument about the irrationality of passion are his dupes. Alceste cannot accept in the front rank of his own consciousness, or admit to others, that his whole life is pure posturing before others, that he who claims to be sincere and spontaneous is as preoccupied with the public as anybody and as mediated by it as those whom he charges with acting parts for others. Is he not, after all, the only person in the world who does not posture, whose emotions spring directly from the heart and who speaks nothing but what he really thinks and feels? Alceste uses the myth of the irrationality of passion to hide from others and from himself a character that is every bit as cold and ungenerous as the characters of those he criticizes for their coldness and lack of generosity. (pp. 755-9)

Alceste's life is in an important sense a life not of participation but of demonstration. This is one way in which he differs from the tragic heroes of Racine. The scandalous contradiction between the ideal and the real, between being and appearance, between the world of absolute values and the world of contingent opportunities is at the heart of seventeenth-century tragedy. There is never any danger, however, that Alceste will share in the sombre destinies of Racine's heroes. His world is far removed from theirs. He does not stake his destiny, as Junie or Andromaque or Monime does, on living an authentic life in a world of inauthenticity. The inauthenticity of the world is not a menace to him; on the contrary, it is the very source of all his satisfactions. It provides the basis for his own superiority and he spends his time not in a real struggle to reach authenticity, but in endless efforts to have his superiority recognized by the very world of inauthenticity which he affects to detest. The absence of value in the world becomes, with Alceste, a matter for personal self-congratulation. Far from threatening his existence, the world of lies and deceit founds it. He exhausts himself in theatrical gestures, because all his wrestling with the ideal and the real, all his disgust with the world's falseness, however painfully experienced subjectively, is, objectively viewed, nothing but vain, ineffectual, and deeply inauthentic posturing. He does not really suffer because life is full of pretense and selfishness, because men have made their lives so vain and stupid. He suffers because he cannot bear to be like others and because others refuse him the adulation which he wants from them.

In the end he is so divorced by his monstrous vanity from any authentic participation in human affairs that he is unable to function normally in the world. . . . He acts out his role so intensely that he becomes the prisoner of his own theatricality. Incapable, as we have seen, of any form of real communication with others, either in love or in friendship, he loses all contact with the real world. His entire being is demonstrative. . . . For the abstract satisfaction of proving—as he imagines—that the world is not fit to judge him, he is willing to sacrifice the justice of his cause. But just as Alceste is not really interested in Célimène herself, he is not really interested in justice. He claims to refuse the kind of justice that can be had in the world because it is not absolute justice; in reality, however, he is anxious to place himself beyond all possible justice, beyond good and beyond evil, to have himself recognized as an absolute that no relative—no other—*can* judge. In his frenzied efforts to achieve this recognition Alceste, rather like George Dandin in a later play, rushes joyfully toward self-destruction. (pp. 80-3)

> Lionel Gossman, in his *Men and Masks: A Study of Molière,* The Johns Hopkins Press, 1963, 310 p.

FRANCIS L. LAWRENCE (essay date 1968)

[*Lawrence is an American essayist and educator. In the following excerpt from his* Molière: The Comedy of Unreason, *a study of Molière's minor plays, he discusses* The Princess of Elis, *arguing that the drama has been unfairly neglected.*]

Through the centuries *La Princesse d'Élide* has been neglected by critics who have some justification since, in appearance at least, it was first neglected by Molière. Composed expressly for a festival at Versailles, "Les Plaisirs de l'Isle enchantée," it concerns the courtship of a princess who scorns love and marriage. Euryale, prince of Ithaca, seeing that two other suitors who offer their love and services are retarding rather than advancing their interests, decides to pretend a coldness equal to that of the princess. Her pride aroused, the princess attempts to inspire with love the only indifferent man she has met. In the process, she falls in love with him, and when an extension of his stratagem leads her to believe that he loves her cousin, the princess reveals her change of sentiment so clearly that the prince confesses, to their mutual satisfaction, that his only object has been to win her heart. The princess' fool, Moron, is the prince's ally throughout the plot and carries on an unsuccessful love affair with a cold shepherdess. Like so many of the pieces ordered for court entertainment the play was written in a great rush. Having composed a first act in verse Molière was forced to break off midway through scene one of the second act to complete the remainder in prose. The play ran for twenty-five performances in Paris from November 9, 1664, to January 4, 1665. Then it closed never to be presented again in town during Molière's lifetime, though it was played successfully on several occasions at court, always in its original hybrid form.

The general consensus among critics has been that the play is a mediocre and unsuccessful piece that Molière did not consider to be worth the trouble of reworking. Hubert dismisses it as "purely spectacular." Fernandez [see Additional Bibliography] enters a mild but signally unfair complaint that the comedy does not turn out to be an embodiment of the genius of England's greatest Renaissance dramatist or France's eighteenth century master at badinage and delicate amorous psychology.... On the other hand, the Spanish play that was Molière's source, Moreto's *El Desdén con el Desdén,* has been called, to quote a relatively conservative admirer [Mabel M. Harlan, in *The Relation of Moreto's "El Desdén con el Desdén" to Suggested Sources* (1924)], "one of the outstanding half-dozen plays of the *siglo de oro.*" The obvious implication, one that remarkably few have hesitated to draw, is that the

changes Molière made in the play impoverished the Spanish author's masterpiece. All in all, posterity has had hardly a good word to say for *La Princesse d'Élide.* That is the more extraordinary since another of Molière's works in the *galant* vein, *Dom Garcie de Navarre,* has recently been the subject of vigorous efforts at rehabilitation. The curious fact is that *La Princesse d'Élide* needs no desperate effort of rhetoric and ingenious interpretation to justify it. A cursory reading shows it to be a competent, amusing play; brief consideration of the conditions under which it was played reveals that the reports of its demise are greatly exaggerated; and a comparison with its source indicates that if literary history is to continue to rate the Spanish comedy so highly, then some effort at tardy justice must be made for its imitation which is, in many aspects, a distinct improvement on the original. (pp. 107-08)

In view of Molière's habitual conduct as an author, it is hardly surprising that he did not bother to rewrite the portion of the play he had been obliged to put down in prose. Of all Molière's works we know of only one that may have been revised — the *Tartuffe* which had its first showing in three acts during the same festivities for which *La Princesse d'Élide* was composed. In spite of extensive speculation on the nature of those three original acts, nothing authorizes us to assert positively either that the five-act *Tartuffe* we possess is a substantially revised, different play or that it represents simply the completion of the unfinished piece with, perhaps, a few minor changes. Even in this unusual, pressure-ridden case it is uncertain that Molière did in fact change more than a word here or an emphasis there of his original concept for the play. Molière's moving finger, like Shakespeare's, having writ, passed on. The editions of both playwrights are the cherished occupational despair of their honest editors since neither the Englishman nor the Frenchman apparently cared how the works were published. Far from submitting carefully reworked editions, they allowed their plays to be printed with shocking typographical errors. Whatever changes Molière might have made over the years are presumably transmitted by the La Grange and Vinot edition of 1682, but, in an edition made nine years after Molière's death, there can be no guarantee that every change comes from the hand of the playwright and the alterations of 1682 are, on the whole, unexceptional.

The appearance that Molière treated *La Princesse d'Élide* cavalierly then is deceptive. If it remained in its original state, so did the rest of his work. If it was confined to court performances, it was not that only Louis XIV liked it. Only Louis XIV could afford it.

Molière's adaptation of Moreto's *El Desdén con el Desdén* is more in the nature of a transformation since he tampers freely with the plot devices, wholly eliminates the ill-assorted mixture of vulgar and Gongorist punning that characterizes the style, and adds a low comic love subplot. Molière's princess, like Moreto's, scorns love, but whereas Moreto's Diana does so for the rather effete reason that her constant studies warn her against it, Molière's princess—who is given no proper name—is a Diana in fact. She imitates the goddess in loving only the chase and forest. Molière gives her a vigorous characterization in an early scene. She turns an icy gratitude on two suitors who have just humiliated her and deprived her of her kill by "rescuing" her from a huge boar.... The arrangement that brings the three noblemen to the presence of the scornful heroine also differs in the two plays. In Molière's work, the three princes have been invited by the Prince d'Elide to participate in the hunt, races, and other games. He hopes that his daughter will fall in love with one of his guests, and the princes of Messena and Pylos have already declared themselves her suitors. Nevertheless there is enough elasticity in the situation to permit Euryale, prince of Ithaca, to maintain that he too scorns love and participates in the races only for the honor of winning. The arrangement in Moreto's play is, by contrast, embarrassingly awkward. All three nobles are in Barcelona specifically and avowedly for the purpose of courting Diana. The hero, Carlos, explains to Diana that he feels an even greater aversion to love than she does. He joins her other two suitors in courting her not because like them he loves her, but because he feels it to be his duty as a gentleman.... (pp. 109-11)

If the imagination boggles at Moreto's original concept of gentlemanly duty, it is strained to the breaking point by the situations he contrives in the second act of which Molière wisely omits the greater part. The first contrivance that Molière suppressed is a love game in which partners are chosen by the selection of colored ribbons. Diana arranges to have Carlos as her partner and he vacillates from tepid compliments to vehemently sincere love-making, back to insult as he assures her that he is only fulfilling his duty in the game. For a second episode, in which the hero wanders through a private garden pretending not to notice the princess, Molière in the interests of *vraisemblance* ["verisimilitude"] describes the singing and dancing of the princess as having taken place before rather than during the garden incident. Euryale is spared the grotesque simulation as well as the downright rudeness attributed to Carlos (he is said to have denied hearing her because it sounded like school children singing and he did not care to remain). Another rather disquieting feature of the Spanish piece that Molière omits is a by-play between Carlos and his servant, in which the servant forcibly restrains Carlos from noticing Diana by holding a dagger to his master's throat.

The most significant addition that Molière made to the plot of his play was a typically *molièresque* development of the servant's part into a parody on the actions of his masters. Pontilla in Moreto's play is the conventional Spanish *gracioso* and functions as a tool in the love intrigue between Carlos and Diana which is the only action of the play. Molière's Moron is a much more developed character. In himself, he is that engaging mixture of conceit and frank practical cowardice that recalls at its origin, the *miles gloriosus,* and at its apotheosis, Falstaff. Moron parodies the aristocratic boar hunt in which the princess is rescued from a maddened beast by two courageous princely suitors. The buffoon had the first encounter with the boar and saved himself in a very practical fashion:

MORON. J'ai jeté tout par terre et couru comme quatre.

ARBATE. Fuir devant un sanglier, ayant de quoi l'abattre! Ce trait, Moron, n'est pas généreux....

MORON. J'y consens; Il n'est pas généreux, mais il est de bon sens.

[MORON. I threw everything on the ground and ran like anything.

ARBATE. You ran away before a boar, though you had weapons to kill him! That was not a valiant act....

MORON. I agree; it was not courageous, but it was common sense.]

On hearing the princess reproach her rescuers, Moron directly opposes his attitude in the face of danger to the princess' imitation of a hunt goddess. He marvels that the well-timed death of that ugly beast vexes her: "O! comme volontiers j'aurois d'un beau salaire/ Récompensé tantôt qui m'en eût su défaire!" ["Oh, how willingly would I have pensioned anyone who would have rid me of him just now!"] By the aristocrats' standards, Moron is a coward; by Moron's standards, the aristocrats are fools.

The love affair between Moron and his cruel shepherdess, Philis, is a shadow moving in advance of the central love interest. Like Moron's burlesque hunt before the real one, scenes of Moron and Philis lightly prefigure, in comic distortions, what is to come in the relationship between Euryale and the princess. Moron attempts to learn to sing in order to please his difficult love (Troisième Intermède); Euryale is captivated by the vocal talent the princess displays to conquer him. Philis silences Moron to hear his rival; the princess tells Euryale that she has fallen in love with the Prince of Messena. Philis sings with another shepherdess a troubled speculation on the good or evil of love that redoubles the inquietude of the princess. It immediately precedes her public display of her love for the prince.... Even a farcical gesture Moron makes, pretending to stab himself as a compliment to Philis (Quatrième Intermède), is reproduced by Euryale in the final love scene. When the princess has all but admitted her love for him, Euryale confesses his amorous ruse.... (pp. 111-13)

More significant than all these reflections is the second perspective on the entire theme of courtship and disdain offered in the attitudes of Moron and Philis. To the whole polite fiction of the respectful high-born lovers who hold that, with all their merit, they are unworthy of their beloved is opposed the low-born, pusillanimous Moron who cannot see how anyone could resist his suit: "Est-ce qu'on n'est pas assez bien fait pour cela? Je pense que ce visage est assez passable et que pour le bel air, Dieu merci, nous ne le cédons à personne" ["Am I not handsome enough for that? I think my face is surely passable, and, as to fine manners, thank Heaven, I yield to none."] Obviously no man courts without having a good opinion of himself and his chances. Moron is a braggart, but the aristocratic conventions cannot escape some contamination. The approach of low comic characters to situations that prefigure those of the main, high plot places the *généreux* plot and characterization in an equivocal perspective even before they emerge. On the woman's side, the cold, teasing indifference of Philis as she toys with her lovers is a telling caricature of the princess' hardness of heart. The princess would prefer a comparison with Diana, but Philis is the nearest parallel.

At this point in Molière's development, then, as the greatest of his comedies were beginning to appear, the most casual product of his hand bears the imprint if not of his genius at least of his consummate technical skill. The result is not anything so hard, so fixed, cut and dried as satire. Certainly it would not have been beyond Molière to satirize *galanterie* at an elaborately contrived royal festival of *galanterie.* He was, after all, at the same time presenting *Tartuffe* and stirring up the powerful religious cabals which were composed of the sort of people who neither enjoyed nor approved of comedy. The court, on the other hand, did appreciate comedy and Molière appreciated the court. William Empson defines parodies as "appreciative criticisms"; Molière could with perfect safety have launched a much broader, less subtle appreciative criticism of *galanterie*. What he did instead was to toy with the central situation of the conventional *galant* work whether poem, play, or novel: the pursuit of a cold woman. In *La Princesse d'Élide* the same object is exposed from two sides—the Moron-Philis aspect and the Euryale-princess aspect—so that an ironic light bathes both sides of the double perspective. (pp. 113-14)

> *Francis L. Lawrence, in his* Molière: The Comedy of Unreason, *Tulane Studies in Romance Languages and Literature, 1968, 119 p.*

HALLAM WALKER (essay date 1971)

[*Walker is an American educator and essayist. In the following excerpt from his* Molière *(1971), he explicates the theme of Molière's last play,* The Imaginary Invalid.]

As a culmination of a theatrical career devoted to the creation of an illusion of living action, Molière's final comedy, *Le Malade imaginaire,* could not have struck a more fitting note. In a farce about a hypochondriac intent upon achieving an illusion of vitality and health, the doomed playwright wrote the last of his works which would give him his only triumph over death, the immortality of the great artist.

This comedy about "the imaginary invalid" caps a series of "medical" plays in which the doctor is portrayed as the destroyer of life and health, a figure whose verbal and material magic give him a peculiar power over the gullible. The character was ideally suited to the purposes of an author who delighted in exploiting the acceptance of such illusory notions for reality, so from 1659 on, medicine and doctors are frequently satirized. *Le Médecin volant* was followed by *L'Amour médecin, Le Médecin malgré lui,* and by the part of *Dom Juan* in which Sganarelle is disguised as a doctor. Then too, *Monsieur de Pourceaugnac* has heavy satire of medicine, so that the final comedy is very much a reprise of earlier material. Extending the satire in depth and resuming so many things observed throughout his works, *Le Malade imaginaire* moves far beyond its predecessors in medical farce and stands as a remarkable example of the style of noble farce.

It is so great an irony that the playwright-actor should have died in the role of the hypochondriac that one cannot help commenting on this supreme instance of the interplay of truth and fancy, yet it is not justifiable to conclude that this indicates an extension of showmanship into his very existence and that he planned to exploit his own fate. All hint of the macabre is driven in flight before the affirmation of health, life, and love in this "comedy mixed with music and dance," as the writer described his play. (pp. 167-68)

This comedy, like the others, is predicated not upon originality of subject or handling but upon a regrouping of essential parts, and thus we see a plot framework of deluded egomaniac, the tyrant father, threatening and disrupting his family for his own ends. The customary young couple is prevented from marrying until an ingenious ruse conceived by a witty servant controls the title figure. The old friends are all on stage, for Argan is the father, Toinette the maid, Angélique the daughter, and Cléante the gallant suitor. Not to be forgotten are the reasoning brother, Béralde, the scheming second wife, Béline, and they are joined by the farce types of doctors and lawyer, the Diafoirus, father and son, Monsieur Purgon, and Maître Bonnefoi. The ironic names, suggesting "purges" and "good faith," are completed by that of Fleurant, the apothecary, whose "flowery" name belies his chief function as enema giver. The stock types immediately place us in the world of commedia dell'arte in which such business as repetition of humorous lines and gestures is fundamental. With the rules of the game clearly established, Molière can then proceed to devise analogies and variations on his theme, and his control through style will make for an impression of rightness and balance. Music and dance will have integral functions expressive of the central idea, and there is little from his repertory of techniques which does not come into play. The comedy is in prose, but by now we perceive that the true poetry of his theater is not dependent upon the use of Alexandrine verses but rather upon the poetic expressiveness with which the various parts are used in relation to each other and to the whole effect. The production of symbolic sense by all means at the command of the dramatist is the touchstone for judgment of the poetic worth.

The informing idea toward which all aspects of *Le Malade imaginaire* should direct our attention must obviously involve illusions about health or some similar neurosis. The key verb would be "to live" and furthermore, in the notion of Argan, "to live forever" by medical magic. The typically Molièresque twist is that the character who is so intent upon living should dwell as if in suspended animation, bound to his rest and cures. In contrast to this idea, the true magic life—joy in the present moment—is stressed by the young lovers and by Toinette. The message of natural happiness is presented by Béralde as well, and the grasping Béline also expresses her version of present joy through her wish for gold to buy happiness. The wife is a transitional sort of character, thematically speaking, since she is partly one of the group of leeches who live by exploiting illness and death, the doctors and lawyer. They profit from Argan's mania which has made living a hollow mockery by purging and medicating the body until he is nothing but an evacuating, embalmed bag of flesh, to use Béline's terms of description. To go on living, he feels he must limit himself to a deathlike imprisonment; chaining himself to a cane, chair, or toilet. The morbid preoccupation with the chance of demise has led him to reject his true healthy nature and take on the stench of death. Molière shows occasional flashes of normal strength on the part of Argan, in order to illuminate the aberration.

So consistently does the author develop a theme in this manner that one may say that an aspect of his style is the use of great paradoxes of the sort, the endless, striking contrasts of truth and its distortions, of fact and fancy, of knowledge and ignorance. There can be no greater paradox than a light comedy about fear of death, but the mastery of Molière comes to the fore as he creates this very thing. He starts the comedy with the title character ruminating (he is visceral in his mode of thought) upon his medical treatments even as he is waiting for a purge to take effect. He uses his wealth to buy health through medication, but he remains an economical bourgeois and tallies his bills carefully. The reading aloud of prescriptions "to refresh the entrails of Monsieur" has an incantatory effect upon him, but he is still fastened to his toilet chair and must call for the servant to rescue him. When there is no answer, he rings and shouts for her in despair, exclaiming as if to announce the theme of the work: "They are going to leave me to die here!" Toinette counters this by out-yelling him, showing her nature as healthy and vigorous, and she resorts to physical actions both to mock him and ultimately to show him some sense. Action is the proper means to combat the absurd fixity of mind and body of Argan, not to mention the languishing surrender of the daughter to her father's tyranny. Argan has decided to marry Angélique to Thomas Diafoirus to have a doctor in the family; hypochondria and bourgeois thrift being thus wed.

The death-life contrast is extended throughout all parts of the play, and to it may be connected analogous thematic contrasts. Love should be life at its fullest, but the romance of Angélique and Cléante is pretty feeble until aided by Toinette. Forced marriage to Thomas has given the word a fatal connotation for the girl, and she is furthermore threatened by her stepmother with banishment to a deathlike existence in a convent if she disobeys. The static must be fought by the active, and Toinette constantly tries to rouse ire if not good sense. Toinette: "I know you. You are naturally good." Argan: "I'm not at all good, and I'm mean when I want to be." Nature asserts itself when she provokes her master into chasing her briskly around the chair, bandishing his cane in wrath. Another paradox is the strange combination within Argan of will to command with desire for protection, for from Béline he wants to hear, "Come, come, my poor little boy" and to be coddled in a sort of infantilism. The process of paradoxes and twists of nature will be continued as the notary discourses on how to flout justice and do the children out of the inheritance and the doctors work harm with their supposed cures.

Act I was originally followed by an interlude of song and dance in which a merry Polichinelle routine restored some tone of healthy gaiety after the introduction of the mentally sick Argan and his morally sick household. Act II begins with a series of "bright" and "dark" scenes designed to alternately express hope and despair in keeping with the theme and plot of the play. Toinette introduces Cléante as a substitute music master for Angélique's singing lesson, and the couple exchange vows while singing a pastoral under the nose of Argan, a ruse like that of *Le Sicilien*. This light note counters the "dark" one of the entrance of the black-robed doctors who suggest vultures around the dying man, yet the patent idiocy of Thomas Diafoirus and the pride of his father are hilarious despite the blackness of the medical satire. The young people sing of their determination "to die rather than consent to separation," giving a light bit of counterpoint on the ideas of life and death. Much of the scene is structured on contrasts between words and actions, a familiar process, and this is summarized by the speech of Toinette, mocking Thomas: "It will be wonderful if he cures as well as he talks."

There follows a scene in which Argan pries from his young child, Louison, the fact that a young man has been visiting Angélique, and the inclusion of this, Molière's only use of a child character, is significant. The contrast of warped age and natural youth is basic, of course, but the little girl is an accomplished faker who uses the most effective weapon against her father by playing dead when he hits her. He is immediately reduced to abject self-pity by her sham, then furious at being tricked. The efficacy of the ruse has been shown, and it will be repeated later with Argan playing dead to deceive Béline and hear her reactions. Stage illusions on life and death could not be embodied more succinctly. The second act ends on a bright note as Béralde introduces a troupe of Gypsy dancers who do a Moorish ballet to help cure the hypochondriac, singing of the joys of youth and love.

Le Malade imaginaire has but three acts, a fact which may make for increased unity of action. At the start of Act III, Argan seems to have responded to the treatment by his brother, and he even forgets to walk with his cane, but any attempts to combat his mania with reason are met with resistance. Through Béralde Molière expresses the idea that nature is the sure guide and cure, defending his comedies as just making fun of the "ridiculousness in medicine." The brother keeps the apothecary from administering a treatment to Argan with the result that the doctor, Purgon, enters in a rage to warn and curse the patient for disobedience. Like a witch doctor he condemns the victim to suffer a series of diseases and death, "lientery, dysentery, dropsy, and deprivation of life." Argan, completely reduced by such an incantation, says, "Good Lord! I'm dead," but Béralde counters, "You are mad.... Pinch yourself a bit, come to yourself, and don't let imagination run away with you.... The principle of life is within you."

The last act is composed of scenes which bring together violent extremes like the folly of Argan at the curse and the lively vigor of Toinette's ruses, for the servant next enters to announce the arrival of a distinguished doctor, to be played by herself. The robe and title suffice to fool the hypochondriac who solemnly ponders the medical advice from Toinette to cut off an arm to give vigor to the other. Pretense and disguise will be turned to good advantage as Argan is persuaded to simulate death in order to see the faithful grief of Béline, criticized as avaricious by Béralde. Death, or the feigning of it, thus becomes the means for restoration of Argan to some contact with real life; "Isn't there any danger in playing dead?" he inquires uneasily. Béline's delight at his "demise" opens his eyes to her schemes, and the genuine grief of Angélique, fooled by the same trick, shows her real love for her father. The corpse-like Argan springs to life and agrees to the marriage of his daughter and Cléante, apparently showing that light has returned to his darkened mind, but the hypochondria is incurable. Since the external features of medicine work the magic he craves, it is suggested that he himself become a doctor and minister to his ills. The mad logic appeals to him, so the play ends in a burlesque ceremony of the conferring of the degree of doctor. Comic ballet brings together words, music, and dance to sum up Argan's fantastic illusions, and Latin doggerel serves the same purpose as the "Turkish" language of the *mamamouchi* ceremony. The title character is duped for his own good and that of everyone else, since there is no other means to save him.

The final dance is introduced by the statement that carnival time authorizes such revelry and masking, so the play ends on a note of joyous freedom and vitality which contrasts with the closed, sick-chamber atmosphere of the start. It is as if Molière were reminding us that "it is always Mardi Gras before Lent" and that life's pleasures should be celebrated before one gives attention to death. The device is not "*Memento mori*" or "think of death" but rather "remember to live." The sense of the play is so basic that these common expressions are not out of place as statements of theme, nor can there be any other real theme in true comedy. *Le Malade imaginaire* is a full development, by the best theatrical means at Molière's command, of the concept of joyous living and of the "imaginary" obstacles to such living erected by men's fancies. (pp. 168-73)

> *Hallam Walker, in his* Molière, *Twayne Publishers, 1971, 192 p.*

ROBERT McBRIDE (essay date 1977)

[*McBride is an Irish literary critic, essayist, and educator. In the following excerpt from his book* The Sceptical Vision of Molière, *he investigates the religious and moral tension of* Don Juan, *deeming Sganarelle the real hero of the play.*]

In my analysis of [*Dom Juan*], I propose to devote as much attention to Sganarelle as to Dom Juan. It is probably true to say that most critics have concentrated largely on the eponym, doubtless because Molière's treatment of the *libertin* was considered to indicate clearly his intention in writing the play, and also because he seems at first sight to enjoy a manifest superiority over the other protagonists. But it is important to note that the role of the valet was played by Molière himself, whereas La Grange played the part of the hero; and in many respects it is the valet who, like Orgon in *Tartuffe*, provides the key to Molière's attitude towards his *libertin*. . . . It is also noteworthy that out of twenty-seven scenes in the play, Sganarelle is on stage for twenty-six of them. This represents the single greatest innovation by Molière in his treatment of the legend; in the other French versions, the valet appears merely as the stock character of farce, whose function is to add set pieces of comedy to the melodrama. At all times he is nothing more than an episodic and subservient type, whereas in Molière's play he has an importance at least equal to that of Dom Juan.

The role of Sganarelle is not only central to the comedy; in his opening speech on the virtues of 'tabac' ["tobacco"] he illustrates the main theme of the play. It is not just another proof of the play's incoherence . . . ; the valet's burlesque reasoning exemplifies that subtle transmutation of trivial reality (here *tabac*) into an object worthy of veneration, which illustrates the basic paradox at the heart not only of the most elementary type of comedy . . . but also of the philosophy of *Tartuffe*. Sganarelle has a natural penchant for argumentation, but what is even more important to note in this scene is the skilful manipulation of appearances and reality, which not only forms the basis of his nature, but also defines his paradoxical relationship with his master. For Sganarelle is simultaneously engaged in the service of Dom Juan *and* in satirizing him to others. After having told Gusman the unpleasant truth about his master, he then adds that 's'il fallait qu'il en vînt quelque

chose à ses oreilles, je dirais hautement que tu aurais menti' ["if any of it should reach his ears I should flatly declare you lied"]. Dom Juan is the catalyst who provokes criticism and acquiescence, truthfulness and lying on Sganarelle's part, and the instantaneous conversion of the one into the other. Without having seen his master, we glimpse the element that links his valet to him; this is none other than Sganarelle's nature, which is grounded on the expedient conversion of appearances into reality and vice versa.

Their ambivalent relationship is fully illustrated in their first dialogue in the second scene, when Dom Juan tries to elicit his valet's reaction to the abandonment of Elvire. . . . When Sganarelle expresses his suspicion that some new infatuation has been responsible for the Dom's latest infidelity, he is asked again for his reaction to such a state of affairs. . . . The truth is that Dom Juan is not at all interested in Sganarelle's answers as such, for his questions are more quizzical than purposive. He certainly does not envisage any possible change of his conduct depending on Sganarelle's response. The valet's answer is equally as paradoxical as his master's question—'Assurément que vous avez raison, si vous le voulez; on ne peut pas aller là contre. Mais si vous ne le vouliez pas, ce serait peut-être une autre affaire' ["Undoubtedly you are right, if you have a mind to it. But if you were not inclined to it, it might, perhaps, be another matter"]—and is born of his instinctive fear of his master . . . and of the fundamental characteristic of his own nature, his predilection for argument, which was noted above. Right and wrong depend apparently for him not on any objective principle, but on his master's will. But Dom Juan sees the expediency of such an answer; nothing less than an unambiguous and *truthful* reply from Sganarelle will satisfy him. Thus liberated from his fear of reprisals for being honest, Sganarelle can now express his utter disapproval of the Dom's recent actions. The latter has now achieved what he planned in his initial question: having isolated for a brief moment the true Sganarelle, that is to say the valet too deeply steeped in traditional moral beliefs to share the libertine notions of his master, he can now afford himself his principal pleasure of overthrowing Sganarelle's absolute condemnation of his conduct. He achieves this by a brilliant rationalization of his own *libertinage* and his argument proceeds in three successive stages: 'Quoi? Tu veux qu'on se lie à demeurer au premier objet qui nous prend . . .' ["What! Would you have a man bind himself to remain with the first object that attracts him . . ."]. To be faithful to one's fiancée is to cut oneself off from all objects of beauty, to die in one's youth; constancy and fidelity are therefore only the prerogative of fools, who blind themselves to the fact that beauty has the right to charm us wherever we are; it is therefore unjust to refuse to recognize the beauty and merit of others by withholding one's affections.

Dom Juan is not at all concerned with a moral justification of his conduct, but is merely content to demonstrate to his bewildered valet that reasons can be effortlessly adduced against the traditional moral standards of fidelity, honour and chastity, which thereby lose that absolute character with which Sganarelle has invested them. He does not even trouble himself to set these reasons in opposition to those of his valet; they are incidental to his objective of creating doubt in the mind of Sganarelle about the moral code by which people are supposed to live. (pp. 83-5)

Sganarelle cannot argue with him now on the plane of reason; all he can do is to point to the indubitable fact that his master has *not* succeeded in making the reality of evil evaporate.... Dom Juan does not like to be reminded of this unpalatable fact, or of Sganarelle's warning 'que les libertins ne font jamais une bonne fin' ["that free-thinkers never come to a good end"]. At this point in the play, he would seem to illustrate the principle of the comic, the *disconvenance* ["incongruity"] which, according to the *Lettre sur la Comédie*, can be seen in contradictory actions proceeding from the same source. It is therefore the dramatist's function to engineer scenes in which such *disconvenance* manifests itself to the spectator. But in the case of Tartuffe, the hypocrite has himself taken over the role of the dramatist as he exploits mischievously the contradictions in language and reason to an extent which threatens to afford him immunity from comedy. Dom Juan is also one of these superior characters whose behaviour is grounded on his ability to manipulate at will the principles by which society coheres. He has triumphantly 'proved' the basis of his morality to Sganarelle, at least in reason and in theory. But how profound is his assurance of the *rationale* of the code which he professes? Does it command complete assent from his will and emotions as well as from his theory of *libertinage*? His reply in this scene to Sganarelle's warning about the disastrous end of *libertins* is highly revelatory in this respect: 'Holà, maître sot, vous savez que je vous ai dit que je n'aime pas les faiseurs de remontrances' ["Stop, master fool, you know I have told you I do not like makers of remontrances"]. This sharp reaction to his valet's homily is certainly proof that his self-assured impunity from traditional moral scruples is purely verbal, and not emotional. It is surely supremely comic that the *libertin* who prides himself on being able to persuade others that black is white and that white is black, should give the impression that he has so succumbed to his own verbal virtuosity as to affect disbelief in the supernatural, of which he seems nonetheless to have an emotional conviction! But he is doubly comic in this scene in his remonstrance to his valet; for has he not repeatedly asked Sganarelle to give him his true opinion about his conduct? Now he says that he has previously warned Sganarelle of his dislike of 'les faiseurs de remonstrances!' Does he then seek mere approval from his valet? No, because he has just refused the latter's compliant acquiescence. He can only threaten to impose silence on his valet by force, as Sganarelle is used to emphasize the one weakness in the *libertin* credo. Sganarelle manages however to prolong his satire of Dom Juan's disbelief, by deftly employing the tactic of the *libertin* against him. He does this by reverting to oblique condemnation.... The *libertin* who delights in providing specious reasoning to justify himself is the victim of Sganarelle's speech, which can always be defended on the grounds that it is concerned with others, and not with Dom Juan. *A bon entendeur salut* ["If the shoe fits, wear it"].

It is opportune then to raise the question of Molière's attitude to Dom Juan in this scene. It is obviously impossible to identify the author's views solely with one protagonist, since each makes use in turn of the comic principle which is the basis of Molière's comic art. But the fact remains that Dom Juan, in spite of his self-assured appearances, fits into the same comic framework here as does Orgon; the latter is profoundly comic to the extent that he presumes to overstep the bounds of human nature by his overweening desire to know the unknowable. Dom Juan does precisely the same thing in this scene; the basis for his libertine behaviour can only be the absolute denial of divine retribution in an after-life, and it is such a denial which promises to free him from the scruples of traditional morality. Yet Dom Juan can never be absolutely freed from the weakness of human nature (i.e. those emotions and passions which combine to keep such belief in a supernatural after-life alive). If he could be assured in all equanimity of the truth of such a denial, it would be unnecessary for him to react so testily to Sganarelle's moralizing. Sganarelle's function in this scene and in the rest of the play is to bear out the impossibility of such a denial by provoking answers from his master which suggest a loss of libertine composure on his part. (pp. 85-7)

The second scene of this Act is ... of great significance, because it is what Sganarelle says and does here which seems to provide the best insight into Molière's attitude towards his *libertin's* actions in the rest of the play. It is the valet, with his apparently weak arguments and innate pusillanimity, who will best expose the libertine pose of Dom Juan. It is, I believe, a basic misunderstanding of the importance of the role of Sganarelle that has largely contributed towards confusion concerning Molière's intentions. We find, for example, that B. A. Sieur de Rochemont anticipates much later criticism when he objects that Molière ought to have entrusted the defence of morality and religion to a character equal in argument to Dom Juan. The author of the *Lettre sur les Observations* answers this charge effectively by saying that had Molière replaced Sganarelle by someone more obviously suited to theological debate, the play would no longer be a comedy but a 'conférence sur le théâtre' ["discourse on the theater"]. Sganarelle has certainly much in common with his master, notably a remarkable dexterity in juggling with the values of appearances and reality. But to suggest, as recent criticism has done, that he is nothing more than a *coquin* ["rogue"] enslaved by Dom Juan, is to confuse his use of the comic principle (the manipulation of appearances and reality which offers both the only way of escape from domination by his master and the triumph of the comic spirit over the *libertin*) with the morality of that principle. In other words, we are surely intended by Molière to enter into complicity with the comic hero (whether he be Sganarelle or Dom Juan), without stopping to consider the morality of his actions. The conclusion of such critics as A. Adam is that since neither protagonist is edifying, the intention of Molière must remain rather dubious. But in fact Molière is merely using the apparent gross inferiority of the valet as a veil beneath which his satire of the *libertin* here is all the more complete and damning. There is no doubt that this satire gains in pointedness by astute deflection rather than by direct application. This is not to say that Sganarelle is the 'âme simple et pure' ["simple and pure soul"] which J. Arnavon made him out to be, standing against the villainy of his master. He is rather the character in the play who reflects *par excellence* the strength and ultimately the weakness of the *libertin* in the eyes of Molière.... (p. 88)

In the following scene Elvire arrives to confront Dom Juan with his act of infidelity towards her. His avowal of surprise at seeing her parallels the moments in *Tartuffe* whenever the mask of 'l'âme de toutes la mieux concertée' involuntarily falls to expose the real face behind it. The *li-*

bertin is disconcerted here because Elvire has penetrated the aristocratic decorum surrounding his infidelity, and he can therefore only ask his valet to present the reasons for his departure to her. Sganarelle's garbled answer 'Madame, les conquérants, Alexandre et les autres mondes sont causes de notre départ' ["Conquerors, Alexander and other worlds, Madam, are the causes of our departure"] exposes the comic side to the Dom in this scene. The *libertin* who prides himself on the coherence (whether simulated or real) of his actions, is dependent on the incoherence of his valet's inventiveness. Elvire underlines his manifest confusion, by suggesting to him the role he ought to play in such a situation. In order to re-establish in the eyes of others the myth of his coherence, a paradox of the most extreme kind is required to justify his confusion. This is duly supplied when we hear the sinner reply in saintly terms worthy of his great *confrère*, Tartuffe,'. . . que je n'ai point le talent de dissimuler, et que je porte un coeur sincère ["I have not a talent for dissimulation: my heart is sincere"]. He is correct verbally, for he scrupulously refuses the role of the hypocritical *galant* which Elvire has suggested to him. Instead, he substitutes the higher, more intangible form of deception which consists precisely in telling the truth; the infidelity which Elvire has suspected is perfectly true, but he gives the wrong reasons for it, rationalizing his action by pretexting 'un pur motif de conscience' ["a simple scruple of conscience"]. He knows that she is not deceived by this stratagem, just as Tartuffe knows that Cléante has not succumbed to his casuistical reasons for appropriating Orgon's *donation*. But both also know that, objectively, their fictitious 'obedience' to the divine will nullifies for the moment the accusation of deceit brought against them. Such an intellectualization of their position gives them the necessary time and freedom to manoeuvre. Elvire, like Cléante, can do nothing against such consummate evasiveness, but as a last resort she imprecates divine retribution for his actions. Apparently the meeting with Elvire has ended in the Dom's victory; yet as she invokes heaven for a second time, Dom Juan can do no other than divert his thoughts from the possibility of punishment to his most recent project of seduction. In reality, however, there is here more than a hint of the loss of composure and self-assurance discernible in the previous scene, on which the comic aspect of the *libertin* is based.

In the scenes with the *paysannes* ["countrywomen"], 'we see an illustration of the code elaborated by the Dom in Act I, the 'donjuanism' which he summarized in two points: 'la beauté me ravit partout où je la trouve' [" beauty delights me wherever I find it"], and 'je ne puis refuser mon coeur à tout ce que je vois d'aimable' ["I cannot refuse my heart to any lovely creature I see"]. To follow this instinctive desire to conquer each new beauty is the principle that governs his nature, and in each of his manifestations of passion the Dom is sincere, because he follows the imperious call of that nature. But in order to be sincere to such a credo, he must, by his very nature, be insincere to the individual to whom he spontaneously avows his love, because his sincerity has a purely relative value and is predestined to be transferred continually to someone else. (pp. 88-90)

Dom Juan's enslavement to the senses has been seen as providing a comic contrast with his self-confessed awareness of what he is doing. This is in fact yet another facet of the paradox of lucidity and cecity which make up his nature; but whereas the contrast may be said to exist in theory in this scene, in the theatre we have at this point an overwhelming sense of his ability to appear simultaneously as what he is and what he is not. It is this total paradox underlying his nature which is emphasized here, rather than one particular aspect of it. For Dom Juan is so much a prisoner of his paradoxical nature, that he must be sincere and insincere at one and the same time. Sganarelle, in a mocking comment, shows that he does indeed understand perfectly the truth of his master's nature (as he had said to Gusman in Act I, Sc. 1): when the Dom protests that he is different from all the other plausible courtiers of whom the *paysannes* have heard, and that he will certainly marry Charlotte, he unwisely invokes Sganarelle's testimony to him. . . . For Charlotte, marriage is the ultimate and unimpeachable proof of a suitor's sincerity; to Sganarelle's practised eye, marriage is but the culmination of the insincerity of a master whom he has described as 'un épouseur à toutes mains' ["a suitor at all hands"]. Sganarelle once again allows us to glimpse momentarily his superiority over his master, as he indirectly exposes for all to see (but not Charlotte!) that true side to the Dom's nature which he is here at pains to hide.

The dialogue between the two *paysannes* and the Dom in Scene 4 provides an excellent example of the way in which the latter manipulates appearances and reality. Called upon to declare unequivocally his love for the one or the other (having promised marriage to both), he extricates himself with a virtuosity which matches perfectly the ballet-like sequence of *répliques*. He begins his defence with a lie to each *paysanne*. To Mathurine he says that Charlotte wished to marry him, but that he could not because of betrothal to her. He tells the corresponding lie to Charlotte. He follows this with a second lie to each in turn, pretexting that 'no amount of persuasion will convince her that she is wrong.' Having convinced each of the blind obstinacy of the other in maintaining that he promised to marry her, he can now afford to hazard the truth in jest. He tells each in turn to wager that the other will maintain that he promised to marry her. He has succeeded in diverting attention temporarily from himself, as both now start to quarrel with each other, but the stratagem threatens to rebound on him as both coalesce in pressing him for a definite answer. Dom Juan once again escapes with a masterly échappatoire ["evasion"]: each, he tells them, has an inner assurance either of the truth or of the error of the claim she makes. It is therefore superfluous for him to try to add to such certainty. He himself inadvertently sums up the principle which has governed the entire dialogue and which he has exemplified so well when he says that 'Tous les discours n'avancent point les choses' ["All the talk will not forward matters"]. Words, he seems to tell the very people whom he has just deceived by his *belles paroles* ["beautiful words"], can only possess relative certainty, because their latent and unsuspected meanings can be exploited so easily.

Once again Dom Juan has, to all appearances, secured a resounding triumph of resourcefulness and plausibility. But the last word in the *imbroglio* belongs again to Sganarelle, as he gives a kind of glossary of 'donjuanism' to the *paysannes* at the end of this scene. He profits from his master's momentary absence to tell them the truth about him, a truth which the Dom partially overhears as he comes back to fetch his valet. . . . Having instantaneously converted his negative criticism into positive attributes, Sganarelle can now explain carefully to his master that the world is full of calumny, and that the *paysannes* are to disbelieve everything adverse about him. The Dom's own technique of evasion by paradox has again been surreptitiously turned against him; and he, like his victims in this scene, has no means of redress against someone who can convert the unpleasant truth into its opposite with such impeccable ease. We admire Sganarelle for his irreproachable *tour de force*, and at the same time share the ironic perspective into which Molière has placed Dom Juan's frustrated attempt at seduction.

The discussion in Act III, Sc. 1, between master and valet on medicine and on the existence of heaven, hell and retribution in afterlife, has been integrated by Molière into the framework of the legend, and gives the play a philosophical character quite out of keeping with the two French versions. Once again it is the role of the valet which seems to me to provide the key to the significance of this controversial scene. Tradition has viewed the credulity and *naïveté* of the valet as nothing more than a butt for the cynical atheism of his master. (pp. 90-2)

It is not difficult to see how such a view of the valet's role leads to the conclusion that this scene represents another disquieting triumph for the Dom's scepticism over the well-intentioned but hopelessly inadequate Sganarelle. But such an interpretation tends to overlook the fact that Sganarelle is made to express these naïve views first and foremost for the purpose of comic dialogue; it is important to take into account the extent to which this exigency influences the mode of expression of his ideas, before accepting them literally as a solemn formulation of his own creed. Just as he has previously argued in this scene, in an (unsuccessful) attempt to stimulate a response from his master, that doctors are effective because they manage to kill suffering patients more rapidly than the disease, so he now moves away from medicine to the one subject which he feels can be guaranteed to unloose his master's opinion, religion. Here, therefore, as elsewhere throughout the play, he acts primarily as an ironic and burlesque spectator of his master, both eliciting his opinions and sitting in comic judgement on them. When he has catechized Dom Juan, and has made the not unexpected discovery that the *libertin* professes disbelief in heaven, hell and immortality . . . , he reacts with simulated and pious concern. (p. 92)

Of course he does not intend to convert him, any more than he intends to believe in the 'moine bourru ["peevish monk"]. But since he has exhausted his store of questions on orthodox matters of faith, he resorts to such traditional superstitions to provoke the Dom's exasperated reaction. Eventually he is successful in prompting a sceptical retort from his master: 'Je crois que deux et deux font quatre, Sganarelle, et que quatre et quatre font huit' ["I believe that two and two make four, Sganarelle, and that four and four make eight"]. This *boutade* ["witticism"] has been seen as furnishing one of the articles of Molière's own beliefs; but it is surely impossible either to attribute this to Molière, given the comic context in which it occurs, or to see it as the formalized credo of the *libertin*. Dom Juan is both curiously amused and vaguely irritated by Sganarelle's buffoonery, and he takes the line of least resistance to the importunate questioning which his cavalier riposte offers to him. But hoping to silence the valet by this lapi-

dary remark, he merely provides him with the pretext he has desired so avidly for his discourse on the harmony of man's being, which he takes as proof of his divine origin. The fact that part of his bizarre argument is probably a burlesque version of Pierre Gassendi's treatise on man can scarcely be taken as an indication that Molière shares the philosopher's view about the nature of things. Nevertheless the central part of Sganarelle's argument does seem to indicate the verdict of comedy on the *libertin's* beliefs: 'Il faut avouer qu'il se met d'étranges folies dans la tête des hommes, et que, pour avoir étudié, on est bien moins sage le plus souvent' ["It must be admitted it [religion] puts strange follies into men's heads and that one is seldom wiser after having studied it carefully"].

This is no less than a summary of that *folle sagesse* ["insane wisdom"] which was, in **Tartuffe**, comedy's conclusion on Orgon's futile attempt to pronounce dogmatically on things which elude the grasp of man. Dom Juan's conduct is based upon such a belief which, although diametrically opposed to that of Orgon, is rooted in the same kind of dogmatism which consists in asserting that a nonempirical proposition is absolutely true or untrue. Rather than dismiss peremptorily the existence of the supernatural, it is better, say Sganarelle and the so-called *raisonneurs*, to be wise within the bounds permitted by our human condition. This will therefore exclude any pretence to absolute knowledge, and will most certainly include a degree of *folie*, which is nothing else than the modest confession of one's own ignorance about such transcendent matters. Sganarelle well illustrates such wisdom, by arguing empirically about the relationship between cause and effect, and then choosing to fall grotesquely on his face just as he reaches the climax of his argument for the harmonious functioning and interaction of the human organs. (pp. 92-3)

Sganarelle's deliberate fall is symbolic not only of his knowledge of what can and cannot be achieved by human wisdom, but also of the futility of trying to prove the improvable. (p. 93)

I do not believe that this scene, or indeed the play as a whole, allows us to say anything of a more specific nature than this about its treatment of religious beliefs. . . . Molière's views in this scene [are] neither solely with Sganarelle, nor with Dom Juan, although Sganarelle's views have more in common with *la docte ignorance* ["the learned ignorance"] of scepticism than Dom Juan's presumption. This is confirmed by the fact that the valet, although apparently imbued with less intelligence than his free-thinking master, nevertheless glimpses the contradictory essence of man's nature, namely that it is compounded of reason and unreason at the same time. Seen in this light, is it not the *inhuman* Dom Juan who is comic inMolière's eyes in this scene, and not Sganarelle after all?

The following scene in which *Un Pauvre* plays a central role, is no less ambiguous than the previous one. Although the equivalent scene exists in Dorimond and Villiers (Dom Juan stops a *Pèlerin*, and forces him to forfeit his religious habit), there is a complete absence of the overtly tendentious features of Molière's scene, where Dom Juan commits sacrilege as he offers the hermit money on condition that he swears an oath. His Dom Juan is here no longer just the *libertin* whose independence of religion incites him to maltreat a religious. More obviously than hitherto in Molière's play, he assumes the role of evil incarnate, a Mephistopheles who issues an unequivocal challenge to the good man to recognize the supremacy of an ethic based on self-indulgence and expediency over self-abnegation and moral principle. The hermit resists Dom Juan's temptation to swear in order to gain the proffered *louis d'or* ["gold coins"], acceptance of which would imply dissatisfaction with the impoverished state that providence has allowed him. Does such a result represent the triumph of good over evil? . . . [The] implications of the scene seem more complex than such a straightforward judgement would allow. (p. 94)

Molière here crystallizes dramatically the general problem of the play, and also returns in a more forceful and insistent manner to one of the principal preoccupations of *Tartuffe*; to all appearances innocence, goodness and devoutness suffer on earth, whereas the *libertin* Dom Juan prospers with impunity. (p. 95)

I do not think that Molière's answer to the problem raised in this scene is to be found either in the faithful endurance of the *Pauvre* or the truculent incredulity of Dom Juan, but rather in the philosophical vision which imagines and dramatizes such an encounter. In their opposition, the two characters symbolize the kind of question and answer about providence that has always taken place in the minds of those people who have found it difficult, as the author of *Tartuffe* and *Dom Juan* apparently found it difficult, to accept the proposition that 'Just are the ways of God; and justifiable to Men.' Molière is raising such a question, and leaving it without a categorical answer, for such an answer appears to be unobtainable. This tentativeness on his part does not mean that we cannot discern the general tendency of his thought in the dramatic movement of the scene. It is clear that as the dramatist and spectator see this scene, the *Pauvre* is utterly defeated by the Dom's probing scepticism which points out the manifest discrepancy between his fervent praying and his abject state—he is defeated, that is to say, *objectively* and as far as human logic is concerned. He can only 'justify' this discrepancy between his faith and his penury by trusting blindly in the kind of subjective conviction which Milton's lines express so well:

> All is best, though oft we doubt,
> What th'unsearchable dispose
> Of highest wisdom brings about.
> 　　　　(*Samson Agonistes*, ll. 1745-7)

To what extent does Molière use Dom Juan to illustrate the problem behind the creation of the scene? There are sufficient indications throughout the play to show that his *libertin* posture is treated in a comic or an ironic way for us to know that Molière does not entirely approve of his ideas; certainly there is not the slightest sign that Molière approves in any way of his actions towards the *Pauvre*. But Molière has *permitted* Dom Juan to go with impunity to the furthest limits of provocative impiety and odious conduct towards the *Pauvre*, not presumably because he approves of his attitude, but because he wishes to place the more urgently before us the ineluctable fact that all too frequently those who live without due regard for sanctity or piety or humanity do indeed flourish, whereas those whose lives are spent in devotion and selflessness, although infinitely more admirable than the Dom Juans and Tartuffes of this world, are inexplicably exposed to suffer their ridicule. (p.p. 95-6)

In the scene with the *Pauvre* and in the encounter with Elvire's brothers, Dom Juan does not appear in a comic light; in those scenes he is exempt from comic irony within the universe of the play, as Molière uses him to demonstrate firstly the strong objections to a belief in a controlling providence operative in human affairs, and secondly, the indefinable nature of the *libertin*-hero which can elude facile attempts to situate it in a precise moral category. But in Scene 5 of this Act Dom Juan and Sganarelle only are on stage—an indication that the Dom's attitude will once more be put into an ironic perspective by his valet. As they find themselves in front of the tombstone of the *Commandeur* whom the Dom has killed, the statue lowers its head. The naïve valet is nevertheless sufficiently openminded to admit that he *does* see the *Commandeur* move. It is only the stubborn preconception of the *libertin*, that he *will* not and therefore *cannot* permit the supernatural to have an objective existence, which makes him persist in denying the valet's observation. Above all, he is intent on keeping up the myth of his own superiority over the rest of humanity in Sganarelle's eyes. He is comic here because although he is convinced that he is superior to everybody, he cannot (because he will not) see what even the meanest creature can see plainly. He whose boast is that he lives by his senses will not accept the irrefutable evidence which they offer to him!

In the following scene, Sganarelle repeatedly stresses to Dom Juan the manifestation of the supernatural '. . . que nous avons vu des yeux que voilà' ["What we saw yonder with our own eyes"]. The comic aspect of Dom Juan refusing to assent to such a physical sign of the reality of the supernatural is now underlined in his reaction to Sganarelle's renewed warning about divine retribution. His threat to the valet is certainly the most violent and terse which he has yet uttered. . . . Once more the self-assured free-thinker can only have recourse to physical threats as he seeks to keep up his image in front of Sganarelle—and once more Sganarelle eludes adroitly his attempt to dominate him completely by a *réplique* which barely conceals its irony under its compliance: 'Fort bien, Monsieur, le mieux du monde. Vous vous expliquez clairement; c'est ce qu'il y a de bon en vous, que vous ne m'allez point chercher des tours; vous dites les choses avec une netteté admirable' ["Perfectly, monsieur, perfectly. You explain yourself clearly. It is a good feature in you that you never beat about the bush, you say things with an admirable plainness"]. (pp. 98-9)

From the end of Act IV onwards, the importance of the supernatural elements of the play is much more evident than hitherto: the first appearance of the Commander's statue at supper follows closely on the warnings of imminent retribution given by Dom Louis and Elvire in Scenes 4 and 6. The reality of divine retribution becomes increasingly inevitable as the Dom appears more and more successful in inverting and perverting the basic human values of filial affection and fidelity; there is only one more step for him to take before he divests himself completely of every human attribute, and he crosses this when he feigns religious conversion to his father. This paradox in his own behaviour is brought about not merely for sacrilegious and libertine reasons, but rather because he knows that it corresponds to an objective inversion of moral values which has taken place in the world at large: '. . . l'hypocrisie est un vice privilégié, qui, de sa main, ferme la bouche à tout le monde, et jouit en repos d'une impunité souveraine' ["hypocrisy is a privileged vice, which, with its own hand, shuts everyone's mouth and peacefully enjoys a sovereign impunity"]. These lines crystallize the most extreme confusion of truth and falsehood within the character and the play; in fact they go beyond mere confusion and point to the more permanent paradox of the fusion of truth and error, symbolized by the deference shown to hypocrisy by those who are at the same time aware that it is grounded in falsehood. Formerly, whilst Dom Juan had been able to invest untruth with the appearance of truth, he had only been able to do it long enough to deceive Elvire, the *paysannes* and Sganarelle for a time: he could not do it permanently, because such a situation would automatically have meant the defeat of the forces of morality and good within the play, and the virtual end of the drama. But at this point of the play, no such conflict of good and evil is possible, according to the words of Dom Juan, because society at its worst is composed of hypocrites and scheming rogues, and at best, of those who acquiesce tacitly in the deceptions practised by the numerous Dom Juans in their midst, as well as of those who, like Dom Louis and Elvire and her brothers, penetrate the mask of deception but cannot ensure that its wearer is brought to justice. It is as though Dom Juan's specious inversion of values had been suddenly extended to embrace everyone, and all the moral values of society, neutralizing the forces of good.... But although everyone has suffered a morally adverse effect from their encounter with Dom Juan, forcing them to contradict in some degree the moral codes by which they profess to live, such a conclusion would be in direct contradiction with the dramatic situation of the play. Dom Juan has not, at this point, triumphed; he has just been denounced by Dom Louis, by Elvire, and is still being pursued by Dom Carlos and Dom Alonse. If human retributive justice fails, there is still the certainty of a dramatic conflict between the divine representative of goodness and truth, the statue, and Dom Juan, the hypocrite. The suspension of the human drama, so strongly implied in Dom Juan's words and actions here, in turn implies that his creator was himself brought to the point where he saw no real opposition to his *libertin.*

Molière has thus permitted Dom Juan to push his deception to its farthest limit (religious hypocrisy), and the *libertin,* like his predecessor Tartuffe, knows the impunity such hypocrisy affords him from human retribution. He illustrates this as he takes refuge in casuistry in front of Dom Carlos. The paradox of Dom Juan the unassailable *libertin-dévot* must therefore call forth a *dénouement* responsible for a still greater paradox—namely, that of the defeat of the *libertin,* who cannot be defeated from within the universe of the play. The supernatural *dénouement* implies the recognition by Molière of the Dom's invincibility (or rather the invincibility of his subterfuge), and is thus necessarily and logically motivated by the evolution of Dom Juan's character.... [The] *dénouement* becomes both the only possible ending to the play and, in the vision of the playwright, at least the symbol of the reaffirmation of justice over falsehood if not of his actual belief in such a possibility. (pp. 102-03)

Molière takes care to alienate the *libertin* progressively from the ties and responsibilities which bind him to his fellow-men: he has nothing but scorn for those in distress, like the *Pauvre:* he does not pay his debts to his social in-

feriors; he seduces and marries as he pleases; he abandons Elvire whom he has abducted from a convent; he rejects the natural bonds of filial affection; he puts religion to his own perverse ends. If he sets himself above the values by which his fellow human beings live, he seeks in his Promethean independence to reject their God in order to take his place himself. His refusal to admit God's existence (thereby admitting the existence of someone greater than himself) is a transposition onto the plane of myth of his refusal to consider his fellows as anything other than instruments to do his pleasure. By intensifying the moral flaw of the *libertin* in such a way, Molière has made his final attitude towards Dom Juan perfectly clear. (p. 104)

In conclusion, it would seem that **Dom Juan** is a much less impious play than it has frequently been considered to be. Written during the fierce polemics surrounding **Tartuffe,** it has owed its impious reputation as much to the controversial circumstances of that play as to the sceptical aura of the legendary figure of Don Juan. Yet the view of W.G. Moore, on the other hand, to the effect that there is nothing in the conclusion of the play to show that Molière did not agree with Pascal in his condemnation of the *libertin* is arguable if in my view an overstatement. Molière's last word on his subject would appear to be at once more ambiguous and nuanced than either of these views.

Nuanced and ambiguous, because the real hero of the play is Sganarelle and not, after all, Dom Juan, in spite of contrary appearances. It may well be said, as seventeenth-century critics did in fact say, that the opinions of the valet are equally if not more subversive from a religious point of view than those of his master—but this does not take into account the comic principle which underlies and shapes the attitude of the protagonists. All the burlesque and extravagant postures of Sganarelle are only of importance to the extent that they elicit or provoke some kind of response from Dom Juan. Their *raison d'être* is, therefore, dramatic before it is moral. Sganarelle provides Molière with a means of acquiring distance from the *libertin,* in a way that would make identification with what the latter says and does totally impossible. How could the author of the defiant postures which Dom Juan strikes accept them seriously, and without reservation, when they are inevitably satirized almost simultaneously by the unassailable irony of Sganarelle? Even though Molière may conceivably have assented mentally to some of Dom Juan's opinions, how could he ever divorce them from the caustic corrective supplied instantaneously by the comic vision? The converse is also true—if he is detached sufficiently from his *libertin* to view him in Sganarelle's ironic perspective, he is also sufficiently detached from the valet to see him as a character playing a part in a comedy assigned to him by his creator. And as the creator of the play, he sees the individual comedies which they play consciously or unconsciously, as well as the comedy of their mutual relationship. In his creative detachment he perceives the manifest inability of the Dom to disprove or to refute definitively the existence of the supernatural: his every reaction to its intimations betokens a man who would like to dogmatize about it, and who does indeed in a certain limited way, but who lacks that ultimate rational proof to secure his assumption and his existence as a *libertin.* Sganarelle also seeks to ground his existence rationally, attempting to prove the immortality of the soul and the existence of God. The *folie* of the first issues in inhumanity, and he comes to grief. The *folie* of the second issues in extreme humanity in all its ignorance of metaphysical matters, and survives. He does survive because the comic vision springs from the refusal to accept one's strictly finite and creaturely nature, and emphasizes man's need to disabuse himself about the limitations of humanity. (pp. 105-06)

Robert McBride, in his The Sceptical Vision of Molière: A Study in Paradox, *Barnes & Noble Books, 1977, 250 p.*

BRIAN NICHOLAS (essay date 1980)

[*Nicholas is an English educator and essayist. In the following excerpt, he weighs comic and satirical aspects of the character Tartuffe. In doing so, he questions W. G. Moore's view of Tartuffe as a pure comic character (see excerpt dated 1949).*]

The satirical intentions of *Tartuffe* have been hotly debated for three hundred years. It has been widely criticized (or welcomed) as an anti-religious play; and though Michaut argued vigorously for the absence of any strong satirical intention [see Additional Bibliography], his interpretation obliged him to relegate Tartuffe to the status of an agent in Orgon's comedy, to see Molière as having (at any rate before he was provoked by his enemies) little more ideological interest in the impostor than in the parallel figures of Scapin in *Les Fourberies* or Angélique in *George Dandin*. To fit Tartuffe to a definition of the 'pure' comic character would restore him to the importance which the title of the play indicates and would be a clinching achievement for the critical approach which Moore proposed [see excerpt dated 1949]. I should like to suggest that, for all the interest of his discussion, the question seems to me to remain open, and the figure of Tartuffe to be as problematical as ever.

Perhaps, in dealing with comedy, a preliminary apology and a remark on terminology are needed. There is always a risk of absurdity, away from the theatre and away from particular actors and audiences, in discussing why we laugh at things, still more in adjudicating whether we *ought* to laugh at them. I use the word 'comic', therefore (as I think Moore does), not in any *a priori* sense, but to indicate a common denominator of many of Molière's comic butts. Generalizing from our actual experience of these laughable figures we may say that the comic character is usually stupid and self-contradictory, or at least a good deal less clever and consistent than he thinks he is. He is not witty, but the object of others' wit, dominated by the audience and illuminated by the author's putting him in situations where his contradictions, inadequacies, and lack of self-criticism find concentrated dramatic expression. The attention of the audience is directed *into* the comic character's mentality. Its interest is intrinsic, not allusive. By a 'satirical' figure (and here my definition must be based on the normal use of the term in the disputed interpretations of Molière) I mean a character whom the author uses primarily as an instrument, in order to point *outwards* towards moral or social attitudes and behaviour with which the audience are already familiar and which can be attacked by exaggeration and readily recognizable allusion. The satirical figure may have comic elements, but the fact that we laugh in his presence does not prove

this decisively: we may be laughing either at ideas and images evoked through him, or *with* him at the objects of his misdeeds.

Even these broad distinctions are probably over-schematic, but they are necessary as working tools and they do not, I hope, seriously conflict with Moore's own use of the terms. The problem for discussion, then, is: to which of these categories does Tartuffe more appropriately belong?

Moore's arguments for Tartuffe as a comic character, though they are spread among the various chapters of his book, can be divided into two main groups: those which are derived from structural considerations and those which are based on detailed analysis of Tartuffe's speech.

The essence of the broader argument is that *Tartuffe* is structurally comparable with *L'École des femmes* and *Le Misanthrope*, in that Tartuffe, Arnolphe, and Alceste all make claims to dominate the world and manage their own lives, and are all undone by an element—love or sensual temptation—which they have left out of account. 'Each of three main characters is betrayed, as he would call it, by the same agency.' Other critics have noted that the immediate cause of Tartuffe's downfall is his attempted seduction of Elmire, without concluding that this is the central theme of the play and hence that Tartuffe is a pure comic character. I think they may be justified.

There is a considerable difference in presentation between *Tartuffe* and the other two plays. That pretension and inner contradiction are central themes in the latter is stated from the start. Philinte calls attention to the anomalous nature of Alceste's love and the audience is alerted to its comic possibilities. We see Arnolphe constantly measuring himself against the evolving situation, expressing a certainty of superiority and final victory which we are ready to hold against him when he eventually fails. In *Tartuffe* the situation is quite different. Though two acts are used to prepare Tartuffe's entry, they are not primarily used to set up this sort of comic potentiality. An attack is mounted on him and fun is made of Orgon. We are certainly eager to see Tartuffe—but he is not presented to us as a pretentious character riding for a fall. On the contrary, the main feeling as expressed by Dorine and Damis is one of exasperation at the apparent impossibility of ever dislodging the impostor. A common feature of Molière's comedies, as Moore remarks, is that the central characters are warned that they will be laughed at (as Orgon is by Cléante). Damis is on the whole too bitter to take pleasure in Tartuffe's contradictions—hardly in a mood to read a 'most joyful litotes' into Tartuffe's 'je ne suis pas un ange' ["I am not an angel"]. Dorine may point out these contradictions to Orgon with some relish—but she sees them not primarily as aesthetic spectacle but as weapons for her sarcastic assault on her master's infatuation. At any rate we are very far here from the smiling expectancy of Chrysalde or the benevolent but still amused solicitude of Philinte, which alert the audience to the imminence of comic trouble for the protagonists.

Nor does the eventual appearance of Tartuffe seem to herald the comedy of exposure. It has often been remarked that we never see Tartuffe alone, and this has many implications for the interpretation of the play. One of them is that we are not aware of what his precise intentions are in exploiting Orgon's household. He *might* have conceived a plan of being a consummate hypocrite, consciously aimed at a perfectly-acted show of asceticism, carefully put himself on guard against the dangers that Elmire represented for his plan. We can imagine a play in which he expressed his aims much as Arnolphe does and where we could take comic delight in the incompetence with which he goes about realizing them. Then indeed comedy of character would be present from the start; and by the same token the play would be largely freed from the suspicion of subversiveness, since Tartuffe would be mocked for his inability to understand and simulate even the externals of piety.

However, though this could be the presentation, it is not in fact the one that Molière chose. We know nothing of Tartuffe's precise intentions, or of his estimate of himself, and therefore have no term of comparison against which to judge his performance. *Is* he trying to be the perfect hypocrite and failing? The fact that he is grossly transparent to the sensible characters does not settle the issue. The important point is that Orgon is convinced by even this show, and once Tartuffe is established in the household there is no very urgent need to impress others. We have, indeed, no proof that the seduction of Elmire is not also part of his plan, so that the notion of his being unexpectedly tripped up by his own sensuality remains speculative. Dorine has mentioned her suspicions in the first act and they are confirmed almost immediately Tartuffe appears—he is exposed in advance as far as the sensible characters are concerned, and henceforth his *dramatic* function (we may perhaps agree with Michaut here, if not on his valuation of Molière's interest in the character as a whole) is in large part as an agent in the exposure of Orgon's stupidity. Certainly, as Michaut himself conceded, there is one moment when Tartuffe figures as the classic comic dupe: as he advances towards Elmire at the climax of the seduction scene. Moore implies that such isolated admissions should logically lead Michaut and Brunetière to a general comic interpretation. But even here there is another, and perhaps even a more important, focus of comic interest: we are concerned with the effect of the experiment on Orgon as well as with Tartuffe's self-destruction. The scene might be compared with that of the feigned death in *Le Malade imaginaire*—and we would not describe this scene as the exposure of Bélise, whose character, once again, the sensible members of the household have been aware of from the start.

The argument, then, for Tartuffe as the comically pretentious but unsuccessful impostor, the man who, as it were, has a wager with the audience which he loses, seems to me still unproven; and the arguments of those critics who see him as freer, more dangerous, and (even if immediately transparent) less securely dominated by the audience or any of the characters than comic butts of the type of Arnolphe and Alceste, have perhaps more cogency than Moore allows.

Let us now turn to Moore's analysis of Tartuffe's self-revelation through speech. This is a detailed application of the 'mask' theory, whereby Molière's central comic procedure is to strip off the masks that his characters wear to the world, by putting them in positions where they say more than they mean to, or speak truer than they know. Tartuffe's speech is 'an alternation of hypocrisy and sincerity', and the comedy arises from the unconscious ambiguity of his language and his failure to keep up his part all the time.

For Moore the mask falls four times during the play—'nowhere else ... does Tartuffe pretend to be other than a holy man':

(i) The first occasion is in Act III, Scene 3: 'the hypocrite seems to be leaving his role' in the speech beginning 'Mon sein n'enferme pas un cœur qui soit de pierre' ["My breast does not contain a heart of flint"] ... to the promise of 'De l'amour sans scandale et du plaisir sans peur' ["love without scandal, pleasure without fear"], which is no longer even ambiguous but 'an avowal of sharp practice', 'the complete avowal, by the *masqué*, that his mask is a mask. It may not be funny. It is deeply comic.'

(ii) This involuntary self-revelation is contrasted with 'a 'situation quite different from the first' but similarly comic—Tartuffe's mock self-accusation to Orgon in Act III, Scene 6. Moore comments: 'How can one escape the comedy of hearing, from one whose profession and practice it was to disguise the truth, "la vérité pure" ' ["the pure truth"]?

(iii) The second scene with Elmire (IV, 5) offers another example of artifice invaded by nature, culminating in lines like 'Lever un tel obstacle est pour moi peu de chose' ["I can easily remove such an obstacle"], where Tartuffe openly 'scoffs at morality'.

(iv) There is a 'final glimpse of the real man' in the following scene when Tartuffe claims that he is master of the house, but he soon resumes the mask of piety, promising to 'venger le ciel qu'on blesse' ["to avenge an offended heaven"].

The conclusion is that Tartuffe is a comic character because 'as a dangerous man he is kept in the background and hardly ever seen at work. As a contrast in and to himself he is exhibited in an endless variety of pose'. For Moore, it should be stressed, there is no question but that Tartuffe is a total rogue and impostor; Molière's achievement lies in having extracted the comic possibilities from his consciously criminal behaviour.

The place of example (ii) seems questionable here, since in this case, most clearly, Tartuffe is the agent of Orgon's comedy; telling the truth is a form of conscious deception rather than self-revelation. Moore of course recognizes this, but he still claims that we have here 'a new discovery in dramatic ambiguity'. And though the claim of ambiguity is modified ('Molière attains that razor-edge of language which ... it is not quite right to call ambiguity ... the clarity is perfect'), his conclusion is nevertheless that 'the principle at work here is dramatic irony', that the example illustrates the way in which Molière 'makes his puppets say what, on reflection, they would not say'. The implication is that this example is parallel to the one on which this part of the discussion ends—Argan's 'Je ne suis pas bon, je suis méchant quand je veux' ["I am not good, I am bad when I want"] (*Le Malade imaginaire*), which is certainly a deeply true statement that a character is dramatically forced into making.

Now there seems to be a case for saying that a significant distinction is blurred here—a blurring apparent in Moore's sentence: 'With relentless dramatic skill Molière forces his rogue into a situation where he can and must show forth this paradox'. 'Forces', 'must show forth', suggest the comedy of self-revelation, '*can* (show forth)' shows the situation in its (truer?) light as a well-taken opportunity. On the assumption that Tartuffe is a pure impostor his speech is surely different in kind from that of an Argan or an Alceste. It is a tactical weapon dictated by circumstances, sometimes, admittedly, very pressing ones, but as long as it is effective the question of what Tartuffe would do 'on reflection' hardly arises. . . . A criminal Tartuffe would not be wounded, or enlightened, if the implications of his 'self-revelation' were picked up . . . ; he is working with a borrowed personality and knows the real truth already. There may be surface verbal humour here, but surely not comedy of character: that is to say, our attention is not directed critically towards the inner consciousness of the character in such a way as to distract us from any satirical reference that may be present (say, to certain perversions of Christian humility) or from our primary awareness of Orgon as comic butt.

To sum up, the wit and resourcefulness of this speech, on Molière's part and on Tartuffe's, is not in question, but its validity as evidence in the case for a comic Tartuffe seems to depend on our accepting rather inclusive definitions of dramatic irony and comic ambiguity as they relate to character.

The case for the comic Tartuffe cannot of course be answered by calling this one example into question. We could, however, go further and ask whether the other three examples of 'mask-dropping' are really different in kind from this one. Is Tartuffe in fact most accurately described as 'leaving his role' at various points during the interviews with Elmire?

If we look at the long speeches in the first interview we find strongly-argued and eloquent pieces of rhetoric. Tartuffe's eating habits may let him down, but in many ways he is an accomplished performer. He is carried away, but only as the orator is carried away; and the achievement is the more impressive when we remember—still on the assumption that Tartuffe is the total impostor—that the history of the progress of his passion must be pure invention. . . . Surely this is not an avowal that 'the mask is a mask'; it is not an abdication of hypocritical practice but an attempt to extend its field of effectiveness. (pp. 753-58)

Moore's analysis commits him to seeing a sharp distinction between Tartuffe's stance and state of mind in examples (i) and (ii) quoted above. But the formulae 'Ah! pour être dévot, je n'en suis pas moins homme' ["Ah! I may be pious but I am none the less a man"] and 'Mais, madame, après tout je ne suis pas un ange' surely already anticipate the argumentative technique of 'Mais la vérité pure est que je ne vaux rien' ["But the simple truth is that I am worthless"]. There seems a case for saying that they proceed from a similar state of consciousness and evoke a similar response in us, a response not best described as a sense of their being involuntary acts of self-definition and self-betrayal.

A second objection might be that there *are*, indisputably, and despite a general homogeneity, variations of tone within Tartuffe's speech. But to admit this does not seem to me necessarily to lead to a comic interpretation. Indeed an argument *against* this interpretation is perhaps afford-

ed by the most extreme of these shifts. One point where Tartuffe unequivocally quits the dignified for the confidential manner is in his remark to Elmire about Orgon, 'C'est un homme, entre nous, à mener par le nez' ["He is a man to be led by the nose"]. Here, if anywhere, the mask is dropped, and this would presumably rank as a culminating point in the comedy of self-revelation. Yet a possible reaction to this shift might be to feel that it jars slightly, even seems mildly *invraisemblable* ["improbable"] coming from Tartuffe as we have predominantly known him. Do we not perhaps experience here not so much an involuntary shift on Tartuffe's part from hypocrisy to sincerity, as a shift on Molière's part from a fairly serious to a grossly caricatural portrayal—of a satirical type? We shall almost certainly (given the situation) feel that it is good for a laugh; but, if there is any question of miscalculation, I suspect we shall feel that it is on Molière's part rather than Tartuffe's. Certainly the jar would seem to be the *less* artistically acceptable in the measure in which we are still looking for a comic treatment comparable with that of Alceste. For in high comedy even the self-revealer will have some sort of internal consistency, and will reveal himself through the normal texture of his speech rather than through gross departures from it.

The likelihood, I feel, is that we accept gratefully here the sort of shift which might be disruptive to the coherence of a character like Alceste. This is perhaps because we have been conditioned throughout the play to a range of humorous effects superimposed on the fairly homogenous texture of Tartuffe's lofty casuistry. These exaggerated effects are present from Tartuffe's first appearance — earlier, in fact, if we remember Dorine's account of his appetite. Indeed, to return to structural considerations, the movement of the first scene with Elmire is perhaps too precipitate to be appropriately described as character comedy. Gross effects intrude very early, with the famous exchange: 'Ouf! vous me serrez trop.—C'est par excès de zèle' ["Oh! you squeeze me too hard.—It is from excess of zeal"]. This is good knock-about fun, perhaps with an allusive element. But if we were to posit that Molière had spent two acts setting up the potentialities of Tartuffe as a substantial comic butt, we might feel he had failed to sustain the promise by knocking him down so summarily in the third. From the start, in fact, we are conscious of Tartuffe as something intermittently more farcical, more obviously manipulated by the author than the high comic character. And a part of our aesthetic pleasure in his speech surely derives from this manipulation. To return to Moore's example of 'De l'amour sans scandale et du plaisir sans peur': do we register this as self-revelation, a frank avowal of criminality? Or would we not perhaps prefer a different account? Are we not primarily aware, in that triumphant final alliteration, of the virtuoso artist putting the crowning touch on a satirical portrait, compressing into one epigrammatic line the ultimate in impudent casuistry? Again, we could say that this is not Tartuffe's nature playing tricks with his speech, but Molière manipulating it for his own ends.

What precisely those ends were I do not want to discuss in this paper. I want only to suggest that on *internal* grounds alone there is a case for rejecting an exclusively (or even predominantly) 'pure' comic interest on Molière's part. In fact the satirical interpretation may do better justice to Molière's achievement, for if our expectations are not those of character comedy we shall be able to accommodate the minor discontinuities more easily. Admittedly the case in part rests on a very fine distinction; as the example of 'De l'amour sans scandale...' shows, *satire*, through exaggeration, of the enterprising casuist uses techniques and situations very similar to those needed for the exposure of a *comic* over-confidence. To try to clinch the distinction would perhaps involve resort to an unrealistically analytical approach to the sources of laughter. At least, however, it may be possible to prove a difference of emphasis—in *Le Misanthrope*, dominantly towards the exploration of a coherent consciousness, in *Tartuffe*, towards the exploitation of a character for broader purposes and in a more free-ranging way.

I have tried so far to argue against the comic interpretation of *Tartuffe* in the terms in which Moore proposes it. But I should not wish to return to a dogmatic reassertion of the purely satirical reading of a Brunetière [see excerpt dated 1898]. I should like to conclude by suggesting that there may well be a case for an alternative, or complementary, reading of the play in which Tartuffe has, at least fitfully, comic features, but that such a reading will not imply a dilution of the satirical interpretation—rather in fact the opposite.

It is impossible to overlook the numerous surface resemblances between Tartuffe's speech and that of other Molière characters. The parallel between his 'Mais la vérité pure est que je ne vaux rien' and Argan's 'Je ne suis pas bon, je suis méchant quand je veux' has already been mentioned. One might also compare (rhythmically and verbally) his

> L'amour qui nous attache aux beautés eternelles
> N'étouffe pas en nous l'amour des temporelles

with Armande's rationalization in *Les Femmes savantes*:

> Cet empire que tient la raison sur les sens
> Ne fait pas renoncer aux douceurs des encens

Or, indeed, 'Ah, pour être dévot...' with Alceste's belated recognition:

> ...que c'est à tort que sages on nous nomme,
> Et que dans tous les cœurs il est toujours de l'homme.

The use of such parallels to prove the comic Tartuffe was rejected above on the assumption that the utterances of Tartuffe and the other characters proceeded from very different states of consciousness and represented different uses of speech. This was to argue with Moore on his own premises, which involve acceptance of Tartuffe's character being that of a pure, conscious impostor. We might however put the case the other way round: set aside (especially in so far as they depend on authorial assurances) our notions of what Tartuffe is 'really' like, and regard the parallels themselves as weighty evidence for a similarity of kind between him and the other characters. What would be the implications of such an approach—and how far could it be justified?

Are characters as different as Argan, Armande, and Alceste essentially of one family—and does Tartuffe belong to that family? Implicit in my rejection of the comic Tartuffe was perhaps also dissent from some of the emphases of Moore's 'mask' conception. Despite its variations and refinements this approach very much stresses the existence of two 'layers' to character—an appearance and a reality—and exposure of pretence as a prime function of comedy. In such a scheme *l'imposteur* would seem to be the very prototype of the comic character. The mask theory has valuable applications—particularly... in the case of figures like Alceste and Arnolphe, whose declared pretensions are belied by their conduct. It has obvious links with another theory of comedy which has proved fruitful in the study of Molière—that of Bergson. Nevertheless, the stressing of conscious pretensions or pretence, of the *removable* mask as a source of comedy, marks a shift of emphasis from Bergson's notion of comic automatism (which would have more accurately described the old 'fixed-mask' character that Moore sees Molière as having transformed and revivified). Bergson's automatism suggests in the comic character a sort of total self-absorption (or total absent-mindedness) which, when it issues in moral action, has none of the attributes of imposture, but rather those of its opposite: sincerity.... It might be that, far from being the archetypal comic character, an impostor would be the odd man out in Molière's work. There is room for discussion about the extent to which Argan and Armande are best described as frauds or self-deceivers. But even if they are frauds there is an important minimal sense in which they are 'sincerely' identified with their *personae*: if they do not totally believe in it themselves, they expect others to do so—and are genuinely annoyed when they do not. Their vanity is deeply involved in the attempt to present themselves as serious and consistent characters.

There is a case for saying that the bulk of the comedy results from the preposterousness of such claims, and that even when he is dealing with 'impostors' it is this self-deceiving area of their personality that most engages Molière's attention. Argan's 'Je ne suis pas bon' is in a sense involuntary self-revelation. But is it best described as showing the reality beneath the mask? Perhaps Argan does not even want to claim to be good. What he wants is to evade interrogations on the point, to claim the right to be tyrannical yet to be respected. The comedy arises from his misapprehension about the sort of behaviour and self-definition which are consistent with securing the respect which he thinks he deserves. This is militant self-vindication run mad. In the same way the remark of Armande quoted above, though it takes the form of a concession, is anything but concessive in spirit; it is not a momentary failure to keep up a part, to keep the mask in place (still less, of course, a frank 'avowal that the mask is a mask'); rather it is an aggressive and totally characteristic remark intended to enhance a case which the audience dismisses as untenable. Again, what is revealed is not so much a reality beneath a façade as a total unitary absurdity, and the comedy derives not from a disruption of the normal texture of the character's speech but from that normal texture itself. With Alceste, again, the admission that there is 'de l'homme' in everyone gains its comic effect precisely from the fact that it is not made in humility; it is still an aggressive stricture on the rest of the world, an accusation of holding 'à tort', about the human race, a belief which only Alceste ever held—and about himself. Time after time we see the fixed character in a self-justifying posture that is haughty or aggressive or tyrannical; and it is surely the posture itself, not something revealed underneath it, that is comic. Certainly this massive self-satisfaction is the product of a sort of bad faith, and the characters are well aware of the precariousness of their

situation. But they are something more complex than impostors; in every case the self-deceiving posture, the *persona*, is the essential man. It is perhaps significant that the
attempt to 'unmask' Argan in *Le Malade imaginaire* is
pretty half-hearted, though Toinette succeeds in making
him do what many an invalid could do under pressure.
What seems to engage Molière's attention more is the *naturalness* with which the hypochondriac rallies, after his
momentary apprehension at Toinette's threatening list of
desirable amputations, to despatch her with the inveterate
invalid's apology.... Is there really a truer reality 'underneath' such a surface? Can a hypochondriac be defined as
a healthy man wearing the mask of illness? Certainly,
when he is alone, Argan is nowhere near admitting he is
a fraud, and Armande's behaviour makes it reasonable to
infer that she has a similarly serious view of herself.

If this emphasis is sound, the inclusion of Tartuffe in the
category of Alceste, Argan, and Armande would seem to
depend on his being much more involved in his role than
the notion of the impostor suggests; he would be comic in
proportion as he moved towards a 'sincere' (if self-
interested) belief in his own *persona*. 'Ah, pour être dê-
vot...', 'Mais la vérité pure...' would be comic if they
were felt neither as the product of miscalculation, of a momentary and involuntary lapse into sincerity, nor yet (the
satirical interpretation) as parody forms of daring casuistical gambits, but as characteristic and still fundamentally
assertive expressions of the whole personality. The parallel
with Alceste's protestation about the quality of his love
would then be exact; each character would be seriously
putting forward a truth about himself as self-enhancing,
and having it interpreted by the audience as self-
condemning. The completely comic Tartuffe, as Mauriac
acutely noted [in *Journal* (1934)], would be the sincere but
degenerate Christian, still defiantly trying to assert the
tenability of his position, resorting... to a desperate casuistry in order to reconcile his conduct with his principles;
and his position in the household would be less that of the
criminal intruder than that of the touchy and self-
righteous moral tyrant: he would be nearer to Orgon himself than to Scapin.

Is there any justification at all for such a reading of Tartuffe's character? Attempts at a comic interpretation before Moore have often invoked a certain sort of sincerity
in the hypocrite (a fundamental sincerity, not the disruptive sincerity of Moore's reading). On the whole, such critics are fittingly tentative, and one would not wish to defend the extreme position of Coquelin [given in an 1884
French edition of *Tartuffe*], whose portrait of Tartuffe as
the totally sincere but perverted mystic is in any case
something of a *jeu d'esprit*. What seems worth proposing
is that these interpretations have at least some basis in the
text and in the assumptions of Molière's comic philosophy
as a whole, and that they are not necessarily the products
of an imported anti-clericalism as Michaut maintained.

Discussion of the 'real' nature of a fictional character
whom we never even see alone is highly dangerous; at
most we can only register the images of him that the play
offers and see whether they allow or perhaps invite broader inferences. It certainly seems safe to assert that *at times*
Tartuffe is a far less simple character than the impostor
whom we see donning the mask.... On that first appearance, if anywhere, we see the unambiguous criminal at
work—but there are scenes where he seems nearer to total

involvement in his role, to that 'minimal sincerity'... [of]
Argan and Armande.

Let us consider, for example, the scene in which Cléante
remonstrates with him over the proposed ejection of
Damis. Here we see Tartuffe defending an untenable position; but surely it would be an inaccurate account of our
response to say that we feel that we are in the presence of
a pure impostor calculatingly deploying well-rehearsed (if
hastily mobilized) sophistries. Do we not feel that Tartuffe
is *genuinely* annoyed at being opposed...? This impression of self-righteousness rather than imposture is aided
by the fact that Cléante takes him seriously, not openly ac-
cusing him of criminality but rather putting forward his rival view of what Christian charity demands in the situation. The structure of the scene recalls that of many other
ideological debates in which reason and moderation face
obstinacy and self-delusion, and find them impenetrable:
the discussions between Béralde and Argan, between
Chrysalde and Arnolphe, and, most significant perhaps,
elsewhere in *Tartuffe* itself, between Cléante and the 'sincere' bigot Orgon. In all these cases the position disapproved of by the moderate is linked with the character defect of self-interest and self-deception; and that character
defect expresses itself through the built-in defence mechanism of physical retreat: Harpagon, Argan, Bélise, Armande, all have their equivalent of Tartuffe's 'certain de-
voir pieux' ["certain pious duty"]. What do they say to
themselves when they have made their escape? Argan
mutters to himself about his household's lack of sympathy

LE TARTVFFE

Engraved handbill produced for early performances of Tartuffe.

and the high cost of medicine; it was perhaps a justified sense of an *air de famille* ["family resemblence"] between Tartuffe and this sort of character which led Coquelin to picture the solitary Tartuffe not chuckling over his successful roguery but praying fervently to the casuist's God to make Elmire look a little more kindly on the demands of his condition as 'un homme' ["a man"]. Might it not be perhaps that the pull of his normal preoccupation with the comically self-absorbed led Molière into producing a character more problematic than he initially intended? Such a supposition would help to square two incontrovertible historical facts: Molière's repeated protestations of ideological innocence and the equally vigorous objections that the character has raised.

I do not want here to test the validity of such a reading against the text of *Tartuffe* as a whole. I am concerned only to suggest that the extent to which Tartuffe is a quintessentially Molièresque comic character will probably be in proportion to his involvement in his role; and to remark that such an identification, rather than diminishing the satirical emphasis, greatly increases it. This point is of course open to discussion, but it has on the whole been common ground in the polemics about the play. It was not for nothing that Molière felt the need to repeat emphatically that Tartuffe was an impostor,... and critics who have maintained Molière's ideological innocence have likewise felt the need to vindicate his claim to be attacking conscious imposture. For it is in the generalizing implications of a 'sincere' Tartuffe that subversiveness would lie. The suggestion that it is possible, perhaps even psychologically commonplace, for someone other than a mere criminal to talk and act like Tartuffe, that he differs only in degree from large categories of the truly religious, leads to an implied devaluation of a whole cast of mind, a whole moral stance in society. It tends to connect the holding of certain views almost automatically with the possession of certain character defects.

How far Molière intended to make generalizing psychological suggestions is a tricky point, but it is the fate (and the privilege) of powerful imaginative creations not to be able to avoid doing so in the minds of some readers. We should look hard at the text before drawing such inferences; but equally we should not deny them if they are manifestly there. (pp. 758-64)

Whatever Molière's declared or conscious intentions, the evidence of the text is powerful on this point. We have already noted Cléante's serious disagreement with Tartuffe over what 'l'intérêt du ciel' dictates in a particular situation. Tartuffe's other arch-enemy, Dorine, provides a similar sort of attack on Tartuffe's position, whether it be real or feigned. Indeed, the ultimate subversiveness of the play might be that there is a certain nonchalance about the whole question of hypocrisy and sincerity. Dorine has not thought much beyond the certainty that, whatever his motives, the man who objects to a few ribbons and 'une visite honnête' ["an honest visit"] is absolutely undesirable. As Bénichou notes, [in *Morales du grand siècle* (1948)], her objections to Tartuffe are somewhat random, even mutually contradictory: she is equally glad to attack his severity as though it were genuine, or to accuse him of hypocrisy. It is surely significant that Molière entrusted the case for the prosecution to such a figure—and the more revealing since his alleged aim in the first two acts was to clear up just this risk of ambiguity. Perhaps, again, the conscious

aims gave way to less clearly-formulated intentions; and Voltaire, who admired the play so much, might have been right to see in it an anticipation of his own attitude to *l'infâme*—an attitude in which the sincerity with which his opponents hold their views is given scant attention. The standards of judgement are quite different—and sincerity is not enough.

This is to get a long way from pure comedy, but not, I think, from the immediate implications of the text. The interdependence of comedy and 'ideas' is perhaps worth reasserting in the present critical situation. Not that Moore or any other recent critic (with the possible exception of Bray [in *Molière, homme de théâtre* (1954)] denies that there are philosophical implications in Molière's work or that it transmits a view of life. Nevertheless, there has been a tendency to suggest (and for students to infer) that the aim of (faire rire) ["causing laughter"] can be considered as a self-contained, almost a technical theatrical activity and that questions of ideas can be 'postponed'. This is surely unrealistic. What is laughable, above the level of the simplest farce, is determined by the interaction between the moral views of the author, his audience, and posterity. The allusiveness of *Tartuffe* is too insistent to be postponed; and explanation of the force of those allusions must be a factor in adjudicating between the comic and satirical interpretations. At the same time one would not want to return to a dominantly historical approach; I have tried to suggest in these pages that, on *internal* and comparative grounds alone, there is a case for questioning what at times seems to have risked becoming (through no fault of its proponents) an accepted orthodoxy. (pp. 764-65)

Brian Nicholas, "Is Tartuffe a Comic Character?" in The Modern Language Review, *Vol 75, Part 4, October, 1980, pp. 753-65.*

JAMES F. GAINES (essay date 1984)

[*Gaines is an American essayist and educator. In the following excerpt from* Social Structures in Molière's Theater, *he evaluates* The Miser *in terms of seventeenth-century bourgeois society.*]

All social groups must come to grips with problems and tensions within their own boundaries as well as with intergroup confrontations. The survival of the bourgeoisie in seventeenth-century France, torn by bouts of internal strife, depended on a deceptively delicate balance of social engagements and reciprocal gifts, exchanges of children and wealth that were institutionalized in the form of marriages and dowries.... We of the twentieth century, who are accustomed to viewing the emerging bourgeoisie through a glass darkened by merchant villains like Dickens's Ebenezer Scrooge and Uriah Heep, Balzac's Baron Nucingen and his accomplice Du Tillet, or Flaubert's Monsieur Lheureux, may too easily forget how essential compromise and reciprocity were to the bourgeois clans during the insecure era before the appearance of organized capitalism and the self-made man. Fernand Braudel's theories about the ancien régime's overriding concern with "material life" and "capital before capitalism" help to put in a proper perspective the force of mutual dependency in the thought of Molière's fellow citizens.

The divine and secular approbation of social relations evoked by Domat found its most perfect expression in the rite of marriage, which provided for a contractual blending of family fortunes in the form of dower and dowry, as well as for the continuation of the lineage through another generation. (pp. 169-70)

[It] would be unreasonable to expect universal observation of even a mutually beneficial standard such as the code of bourgeois reciprocity; the system of exchange contained, and may even have encouraged, a certain number of disruptors—individuals who attempted to destroy the balance of familial alliance for egotistical ends. The phenomenon of imbalance appears to some degree in many of Molière's plays, often in combination with other structural failures. For example, the *précieuses ridicules*, Cathos and Magdalon, refuse to accept bourgeois reciprocity. So do Sganarelle of *L'Ecole des maris* and Arnolphe of *L'Ecole des femmes*. Yet, it was not until 1668 that a five-act play, *L'Avare*, was devoted particularly to the struggle between reciprocity and imbalance.

The words spoken by *L'Avare*'s protagonist, Harpagon, at the end of a desperate soliloquy on the theft of his buried gold, are most revealing: "Je veux faire pendre tout le monde; et si je ne retrouve mon argent, je me pendrai moi même après" ["I will hang the whole world; and if I do not find my money, I will then hang myself"]. These utterances express the miser's lonely struggle against a society he can neither understand nor control. They guarantee Harpagon a prominent place in the pantheon of greed, along with such other literary creations as Shakespeare's Shylock, and Le Sage's Turcaret. Yet, Molière takes care to show that, unlike Shylock who extends credit to Venetian merchants, or Turcaret, who farms the king's taxes, Harpagon is not a professional usurer and has no institutional justification for his avarice. Rather than serving the monarch or the business community, he preys upon gullible heirs and seeks to gobble up their patrimonies. Compared to the nonprofessional miser on whom he is based, Euclion in Plautus's *Aulularia*, Harpagon is far more active and dangerous; for Euclion accidentally discovered his gold in a fireplace and passively continued to hide it, but Harpagon seeks to enlarge his treasure by illicit means. From Boisrobert's *La Belle Plaideuse* Molière derived the striking scene of a father arranging to lend at usurious rates to his own child. When angered, Shylock is content to pursue his creditor Antonio in the courts, and Turcaret quells his rage by smashing china; but Harpagon nearly leaps into the audience in his frenzied persecution of those who took his treasure. Molière thus invites the reader to inquire whether his miser's pattern of behavior can be of any benefit to household, family, or state, or whether it threatens, on the other hand, to destabilize the bourgeois world reflected in the play.

Among the numerous status indicators in *L'Avare*, the key to establishing Harpagon's condition as a distinguished burgher is the large sum of money he has hidden in his garden, 10,000 écus, or about 30,000 livres tournois—enough money to buy a political office in the sovereign courts, to establish an attractive dowry, or to pay about one hundred servants' salaries for a year. A messenger who arrives in the third act with further business propositions leads one to suspect that the 30,000 livres may represent only a fraction of Harpagon's cash reserves, which

in turn make up, according to Pierre Goubert's research, less than ten percent of most bourgeois fortunes.

As befits his standing, Harpagon has a house, a carriage and team, and numerous servants, including his son's valet La Flèche, Maître Jacques the cook-coachman, the maid Dame Claude, two lackeys named La Merluche and Brindavoine, and most important of all his *intendant* Valère. The services of the latter were required only in a large estate with diverse business interests and farmland, for his duties included dealing with the tenant farmers and signing sharecropping leases, as well as auditing the accounts of the *maître d'hôtel*. The existence of a nearby farm is suggested by the arrival of a *cochon de lait* ["sucking-pig"] in act five, an event that the bloodthirsty Harpagon misinterprets, for he believes at first that it is the robber who is to be split open, grilled, broiled, and hung. It was common bourgeois practice to invest heavily in property in the nearby countryside and to stipulate that part of the rent be paid in kind in order to furnish the larder.

These social indicators tend to depict Harpagon as a member of the middle bourgeois stratum, which produced many magistrates and other public officers.... *Officier* or not, Harpagon is identified with the upwardly mobile segment of the bourgeoisie that yearned for nobility. He has clearly risen above the precarious level of the struggling artisan. Even those for whom immediate *anoblissement* was impossible would attempt to "live nobly" from the interest on conventional investments, to avoid any dishonorable activity, and to hope that, with the passage of time, their descendants might, through the accumulation of offices and marriage alliances, elevate themselves to the *état* ["state"] of nobility.

Molière's audience would expect a man in Harpagon's position to be absorbed with the concerns of his lineage. The son had to be provided with a legal or financial office or with a commission in the army, as well as with a dower for marriage. Even more crucial was the daughter's dowry money, which might well claim the major share of the patrimony. Not only would this sum be the bride's only sure resource in case of need, but the quality of son-in-law it attracted, and his chain of alliances, might also have a decisive effect upon the rise of the family. (pp. 170-73)

Having determined as nearly as possible from the status indicators in *L'Avare* the social identity of Harpagon and the normative concerns that Molière's contemporaries would have associated with this level, one must return to the text to appreciate the nature of the miser's transgressions. According to the master plan explained in the first act, Harpagon's son, Cléante, is betrothed to an old widow, his daughter, Elise, to the ancient Anselme, and the miser himself is to wed the young Mariane. The obvious danger in this design is that none of the couples is very likely to produce offspring, thus threatening the survival of the lineage in an age when, as most demographers would agree, nature was given free rein to produce all the births biologically possible. Harpagon has no doubt arranged these sterile unions to protect his hoarded gold from the claims of potential heirs. (pp. 173-74)

Relying on what he supposes to be absolute parental authority, Harpagon intends to compel Cléante and Elise to follow his plans, although marriage required the consent of *both* parents and children, and unilateral compulsion was denied legality by jurists.... The miser cannot envision the possibility that two families may both gain through the reciprocal gift of their children and their fortunes, the exchange of their genetic and economic identities. Any provision for the welfare of the youngsters must, in his view, subtract from his personal wealth, if not from his very identity. Thus, he must live by the outlandish credo of refusal, "sans dot" ["without dowry"], which sounds like a death knell for the future of his family.

It is not surprising that the miser is just as inadequate in the role of suitor as in the role of father. He shows none of the lighthearted generosity that his son demonstrates, and instead of an elegant contract feast, he orders disgusting, inedible dishes.... Whereas most men would seek to regale their lady, he orders the servants to pour the wine sparingly. Rather than to escort her to some gallant entertainment, such as the theater, he offers to take her as far as the fair, which is free. In his overwhelming fear of giving anything away, Harpagon ironically chooses in Mariane a partner who will bring him nothing in return, except an imaginary 12,000 livres annually in spared expenses.... (pp. 174-75)

Harpagon's relationship with his servants shows that his obsession with hoarding money has discredited him beyond the boundaries of the family unit. Master-servant associations depended to a great extent on decorum and esteem, but as La Flèche says of Harpagon, "Il aime l'argent, plus que réputation, qu'honneur et que vertu" ["he loves money more than reputation, honour and virtue"]. The valet mocks the miser, who, he says, will not even give a person good-day, but only lend it. When the servants show him the holes in their threadbare clothes, he advises them, "Rangez cela adroitement du côté de la muraille, et présentez toujours le devant au monde" ["Always manage to keep that side of you to the wall, and show people your front only"]. It is true that he scarcely takes better care of his own physical appearance, judging by the obsolete ruff and quaint hat he wears. This fear of the movement of money surpasses thrift and constitutes a wasteful neglect, for Harpagon would rather see his people deteriorate like his decaying carriage and unshod horses than to restore them to a state congruent with his *condition*. The dowries, apprenticeships, and other rewards that many masters bestowed on their servants are unknown to the miser. Instead he subjects the staff to constant humiliations, such as the insults he hurls at La Flèche, "maître juré filou, vrai gibier de potence" ["you arrant thief, you cursed gallow bird"], and the hilarious close inspection of the valet's pants. Sarcastic Maître Jacques speaks for all the servants when, disappointed that Harpagon pulls a handkerchief from his pocket instead of a reward, he sneers, "Je vous baise les mains" ["I thank you kindly"]. As with his children, Harpagon shirks paternalistic responsibilities toward his servants and crassly exploits them.

Harpagon's patterns of irresponsible misbehavior seem impervious to any lessons of reform; he is certainly one of Molière's most "unreconstructed" characters, to use Robert J. Nelson's terminology [see *Molière: A Collection of Critical Essays,* edited by Jacques Guicharnaud, in the Additional Bibliography]. Without some extraordinary measures for survival, his lineage seems doomed to wither and die, for he is in a position to deny his approbation for any normal bourgeois marriage. It is in this light that one must judge the antiauthoritarian reactions of La Flèche, Valère, and Cléante. La Flèche explains that he robs Harpagon not for personal gain, nor to recoup the servants' rightful wages, but as a moral example to combat the miser's perversions.... Valère's deception of his master through the disguise that permits him to woo Elise clandestinely is counterbalanced by the suitor's deserving actions. He has earned Elise's love by giving her the precious gift of life when he saved her from drowning. His generosity and her gratitude developed into "cet ardent amour que ni le temps ni les difficultés n'ont rebuté" ["ardent love which neither time nor difficulties discouraged"].

The force of natural reciprocity that draws the young people together is thus identified as a sort of bourgeois "cri du sang" ["call of the blood"]. Cléante's motives in helping Mariane are typical of this spirit of good will: "Figurez-vous, ma soeur, quelle joie ce peut être que de relever la fortune d'une personne que l'on aime; que de donner adroitement quelques petits secours aux modestes nécessités d'une vertueuse famille" ["Just think how good it would be to increase the comfort of those we love, to give a worthy family some slight aid"]. Contrast these sentiments with those of Harpagon, who says of the girl: "... je suis résolu de l'épouser, *pourvu que j'y trouve quelque bien*" ["I have resolved to marry her, provided I find she has some means"] emphasis added). The miser is quick to reproach his son for indulging in un-bourgeois luxury.... Yet, it is the son who is the true guardian of the family's social identity. When Harpagon is exposed engaging in usury in act two, Cléante reminds him that such conduct constitutes derogation for anyone claiming to live nobly... .. This ban rested on the fact that since 1560 *roturiers* ["plebeians"] holding offices exempt from the *taille* were treated like nobles in matters of derogation and were forbidden even from engaging in commerce; furthermore, all lenders were expressly forbidden to loan to "fils de famille" ["young men of good family"]. Indeed, it seems that Harpagon's activities extend far beyond this one incident of derogation, for La Flèche declares that he doesn't recognize any of the furniture mentioned in the promissory note and that it must come from a secret warehouse associated with other loans.

In the third act, Clèante's generosity once again confronts Harpagon's avarice, as both seek to woo Mariane. It would seem that Harpagon should have the upper hand, since he enjoys the advantages of money and authority, but he ruins his opportunity to impress the young lady by scrimping on the entertainment and by failing to conceal his coarseness. Speaking of his daughter, he cannot resist the urge to use rustic proverbs: "Vous voyez qu'elle est grande; mais mauvaise herbe croît toujours" ["You see how tall she is; but rank grass grows apace"]. Cléante, on the other hand, quickly demonstrates a command of refined conversation when he upstages his father and compliments Mariane.... Cléante further emphasizes his own virility and Harpagon's decrepitude by putting the old man's diamond ring on Mariane's finger. In a gesture that demonstrates his willingness to share and his sophistication as a lover, he makes her keep it, insisting, "Il est en de trop belles mains" ["It is in hands too beautiful"].

On witnessing this, Harpagon erupts in a series of curses. The son, wise and worldly, has stolen the center of attention, proving his mastery of the social ritual of courtship. The more the old man rages, the more Cléante urges Mariane that she must keep the ring. Molière underscores Harpagon's impotence by stressing his inability to share with his betrothed or even to articulate a reasonable response to his son's gallant rivalry. The only recourse he has at the end of the scene is to send his valet to collect the leftovers of the feast, of *cadeau*, that Cléante had secretly arranged for Mariane. (pp. 175-78)

The miser and his fellow characters differ noticeably in the degree of trust they have in society. Although the young people rebel against Harpagon to the extent that they secretly meet with their lovers, they retain enough confidence in social conventions that they never attack the principle of paternalism or seek to wed without fatherly permission. Both Cléante and Valère admit to their passions when the truth becomes necessary.... It is significant that Harpagon misunderstands this openness, assuming that Valère is a thief, since gold is the only thing the miser considers worthy of devotion. For this sociopath, "de tous les humains l'humain le moins humain" ["of all the human beings the least human"], all life becomes the occasion for fear and larceny; he thus fails to appreciate the return of his strongbox by his son.... Harpagon is alienated from both the generous and the needy and lacks faith in all segments of the social network.

The dénouement of *L'Avare* resolves all questions of social disparity by reorganizing a new clan around old Anselme. ... He withdraws all plans of marriage in favor of his son's future role as family leader. After all, the recovery of his long lost heir removes from his shoulders any responsibility for beginning another family and obviates his motives for marrying Elise. At the same time, his riches replenish Mariane's dowry and eliminate the need for her to choose a husband on the basis of support. For the sake of bourgeois reciprocity, he is obliged to make several petty concessions to Harpagon's avarice, including paying the legal officers and purchasing a wedding suit for the miser, but this is a small price to pay for removing the only obstacle to the double marriage. Valère, his status and fortune restored, may now totally discard his *intendant* disguise and marry Elise. Mariane, freed from poverty, can accept the proposal of Cléante rather than that of his disagreeable father. In a fitting twist of reciprocal irony, Harpagon's children, who seemed at the beginning of the play to be too well placed in the hierarchy for their loved ones, are finally in a position to benefit greatly from their alliance.

Critics since the eighteenth century have followed the example of Riccoboni in arguing that the ending of *L'Avare* is immoral because it fails to punish adequately either Harpagon or his antagonists, a charge based mainly on the financial crimes of usury and burglary and on the children's disobedience. However, even La Flèche realized that Harpagon's gold was not the central issue of the play when he exclaimed, "Que nous importe que vous en ayez ou que vous n'en ayez pas, si c'est pour nous la même chose!" ["What does it matter to us whether you have any or you have not? It is all the same to us!"] The morality of fleecing a Shylock or a Turcaret in the name of comic example is at best debatable; the chastisement of Harpagon is never an issue, for sums of wealth are overshadowed by the forms of social solidarity that they are meant to represent. The *scène de reconnaissance* and the advent of Anselme mark the triumph of conscious mutual responsibility over the monomaniacal money interests of the pro-

tagonist. Having removed his opposition to the marriages, he can do no further harm and is free of others as others are free of him. As Anselme's new clan leaves the stage to sign the contracts that will solemnly bind them together, Harpagon heads for a lonely rendezvouz with his *chère cassette* ["dear money-box"]. (pp. 178-80)

> *James F. Gaines, in his* Social Structures in Molière's Theater, *Ohio State University Press, 1984, 283 p.*

DOROTHY F. JONES (essay date 1987)

[*Jones is a Canadian essayist and educator. In the following excerpt, she approaches* George Dandin *through a study of the play's plot, theme, and imagery.*]

In *George Dandin*, says Harold Knutson, "we behold... a total inversion of the comic myth: loathing, not love, links man and woman, marriage is present bondage instead of future bliss; parental authority, represented here in the ludicrous Sotenville couple, has prevailed in its most crass form.... And in a genre whose purpose is to celebrate life, the last words sound a vague threat of suicide...." [see Additional Bibliography]. I should like to take these remarks a step further, considering them in light of the religious tradition within which Molière wrote. In so doing, I suggest that an even deeper ironic and parodic dimension will emerge in the play, reflected in its action, its themes, and its imagery. (p. 100)

"The sexual union of man and woman... becomes the image for the full metaphorical relationship of God and man," as Northrop Frye puts it. In the action of traditional comedy, two lovers are brought together by a movement towards unity which culminates at the end of the play in their wedding, symbol of communion and new life. Such a movement is obviously absent in *George Dandin*. What replaces it? For many critics, including Knutson, the action of the comedy is instead characterized by a circular rhythm, with each act merely another in a string of defeats for Dandin.... "Even the energetic forward thrust of comedy has been tamed to a sterile, predetermined, cyclical movement," says Knutson. "Nor is there a reversal to bring the cycle to a true halt.... Dandin will have his ups and downs indefinitely."

I suggest, on the contrary, that what replaces the movement towards marriage in the play is a movement towards separation. The play shows us the "inverse of the comic myth" not merely because the couple is already unhappily married at the beginning, but because the action itself moves towards solitude rather than unity, towards rupture rather than reconciliation. The "mortifications" of Act I and the "déplaisirs" ["displeasures"] of Act II become, as the *Livret* of 1668 said, the "comble des douleurs" ["ultimate pain"] of Act III. From the point of view of the couple, something does happen between the beginning and the end of the comedy: things go from bad to worse. And if marriage is the paradigm for the relationship between God and human beings, worse is very bad indeed.

Act I begins with Dandin's regret over his marriage, continues with his discovery of his wife's potential infidelity, and concludes with their first meeting onstage, a scene in which neither speaks to the other and their hostility is expressed indirectly. Dandin insults his wife by insulting

Claudine, while Angélique lies to her husband by addressing Clitandre.

Act II provides an honest encounter—the only one of the play— between husband and wife, but it is the honesty of warfare become open. Angélique denies she has really married Dandin ("ce sont eux [mes parents] proprement qui vous ont épousé" ["strictly speaking you married them [my parents]"]), claims the right to independence, and seizes it in her increasing involvement with Clitandre. The confrontation ends with an ironic repetition of their marriage vows, now only become weapons in a duel:

> DANDIN. Je suis votre mari, et je vous dis que
> je n'entends pas cela.
> ANGÉLIQUE. Je suis votre femme, et je vous dis que
> je l'entends.
>
> DANDIN. I am your husband, and I
> cannot approve such goings on.
> ANGÉLIQUE. I am your wife, and I
> tell you that I do approve of them.

The thrashing with which Dandin threatens his wife at the end of this scene comes . . . when Angélique beats her husband. The verbal conflict thus becomes physical.

Physical, too, is the evocation in Act III of the marriage bed which Angélique leaves to join Clitandre ("Mon mari ronfle comme il faut, et j'ai pris ce temps pour nous entretenir. . . . " ["My husband is snoring beautifully, so I have taken the opportunity to meet you again . . ."]). Each spouse now demands separation from the other. Angélique's plea for pardon from her husband has been variously interpreted. But, sincere or not, it is rejected, and the last hope for reconciliation between the pair vanishes. As the comedy ends, Dandin is planning to take the final step into solitude to break the marriage bond, through death, the ultimate separation.

Angélique's involvement with Clitandre, the counterpart to the rupture of the marriage, takes on a deeper meaning if one recalls that adultery is the biblical symbol not merely of marital betrayal but of the breaking of a right relationship with God. . . . The character of Clitandre has been interpreted variously in productions of the play. But even the kindest critics, those who see him as representing for Molière's audience the aristocratic ideal, have not argued that he is the true lover with whom Angélique will find the happiness lacking in her marriage. Indeed, the abortive nature of their relationship is expressed structurally by Clitandre's disappearance from the stage in the middle of Act III — this, despite the tradition of assembling all the characters onstage for the dénouement. Francis Lawrence's view of the play as "a drama of courtly love seen through the reverse side of the glass" is useful here. Lawrence suggests that Angélique is expecting her husband to behave in the tradition of the courtly lover, and Dandin, the "unwilling shepherd," is unable to do so. But it never occurs to Lawrence—nor should it—to suggest that Angélique, that "pauvre mouton" ["poor sheep"], as Claudine calls her, would find the right shepherd in Clitandre. Instead, her relationship with him is shown in the play to be rooted in illusion, colored by her naive dreams of the glories of court life. . . . Seduced by Clitandre or not, in her pursuit of this paragon Angélique is worshiping a false god.

Dandin's isolation at the end of the comedy is merely the deepest expression of the theme of solitude which replaces, in this play, the happy involvement of two lovers. The comedy begins and ends with a monolog, and the hapless hero is physically alone onstage for five out of twenty-three scenes. In contrast, for example, Harpagon, Argan, Pourceaugnac have only one solitary scene each, while Alceste, that hater of humankind, never appears by himself at all. Peacock notes [see Additional Bibliography] that "in a comparatively short play" Dandin "has been given eight soliloquies and numerous aparté ["asides"]— aparté which remind us that, even in the presence of others, Dandin remains essentially alone. Contemporary directors (Roger Planchon, Guy Rétoré) have made much of the fact that, in marrying, Dandin has rejected his class. But his solitude goes even deeper. . . . "A man shall leave his father and mother and cleave unto his wife," says the book of Genesis (2:24), thus underlining the primary intimacy of the marital relationship. Dandin has indeed left behind all human ties. Among the cast of characters, for him there is no family, no friend, even no confidant. And, to replace them, there is no wife to cleave unto. The marriage, which should supersede other relationships, is, ironically, merely a source of deeper loneliness.

The use of language is another of the ways in which the theme of solitude is expressed in the play. We are in the world of Babel. Communication is garbled, deliberately or accidentally. Messages have two meanings (Angélique, I), are conveyed to the wrong people (Lubin, I, III); gestures contradict words (Angélique, II), words contradict feelings (Dandin, I, III). Language serves not to unite, to "communicate," but to dominate and deceive. (pp. 100-03)

One of the most powerful expressions of the theme of solitude in the comedy is the image of the house and the door, expressed in setting, text, and staging. There are a surprising number of textual references to houses and doors. . . . But the most striking example of this image is not verbal but gestural, the famous door scene of III, 6, where each spouse in turn bars the door to the other. The same *jeu de scène* appears in Molière's sources, notably his own *Jalousie du Barbouillé*, but takes on an added dimension in the context of *George Dandin*. Norbert Elias points out that while the bourgeois founds a "family," the aristocrat founds a "house." In marrying Angélique, Dandin has sought the right of entry to the "maison de Sotenville" and perhaps even more significantly to "celle de la Prudoterie . . . , maison où le ventre anoblit, et qui, par ce beau privilège, rendra vos enfants gentilhommes", as his mother-in-law reminds him. When Angélique locks her husband out of the house, the gesture dramatizes the failure of this attempt to enter the aristocracy. If, in archetypal terms, one also sees the house as a feminine symbol, Angélique's rejection takes on an added dimension.

While this house belongs to Dandin, he is in fact rarely in it, only twice in the entire comedy, and only once with Angélique, at the moment she is leaving him to meet Clitandre. In contrast, the interloper Clitandre spends half of Act II in the house closeted offstage with Dandin's wife, while the lonely husband hovers onstage outside his own front door. Dandin's complaint to his in-laws at this state of affairs is a fine example of the house as symbol of the breach of marital unity. . . . From the beginning of the play, Dandin expresses the troubles of his marital life in terms of the disruption of his house: "Ma maison m'est effroyable maintenant, et je n'y rentre point sans y trouver quelque chagrin" ["My house is now hateful to me: I never enter it without finding something that annoys me"]. The house is thus presented not only as a symbol of marital unity, but as the center of Dandin's own life, a privileged space now destroyed by the arrival of his wife. This fact lends special force to the door scene of Act III: Dandin enters his house to make sure his wife remains outside. (pp. 103-04)

Just as the marriage in *George Dandin* is the inverse of the happy union symbolizing true life, the house and door have an equal ironic value. Both husband and wife shut the door on the possibility of real communion with each other, each pushing the other into the "outer darkness" of separation and solitude.

Dandin's own solitude has yet another dimension. He is isolated by a sense of guilt.... "The dominant mood of *George Dandin* is remorse," comments Knutson. This is certainly true of the first act, from the *mea culpa* of the first scene—"George Dandin, George Dandin, vous avez fait une sottise la plus grande du monde" ["you have committed the greatest folly in the world"]—to the famous "Vous l'avez voulu, vous l'avez voulu" ["you would have it, you would have it"] of Scene 7. As the play continues, Dandin attempts to shift his guilt to Angélique: if *she* will dishonor him, he can perhaps stop blaming himself. (pp. 104-05)

Knutson speaks perceptively of "Dandin's general feeling of expiation" and the "specific humiliations" he endures. But the expiation is never complete. What Dandin really needs is forgiveness, and the punishments he receives in each act are so many parodies of pardon. The farcical beating of Act II recalls the ecclesiastical discipline of flagellation, and in Acts I and III, in an echo of the rite of penance, he "confesses" and gives "satisfaction" to Clitandre and to Angélique, at the direction of his priestly father (in-law), M. de Sotenville. The ceremony of Act III, as Couton points out [in a 1971 French edition of Molière's works], is the "amende honorable" described by Furetière: the guilty person was forced to kneel in public.... Ironically, there is a moment of truth within this final parody. Forced to beg his wife's forgiveness for "l'extravagance que j'ai faite" ["the folly I have committed"], Dandin adds in an honest aside, "de vous épouser" ["in marrying you"]. But forgiveness is not forthcoming. (p. 105)

Angélique's situation at the end of the comedy is equally unhappy. Confronting her husband in Act II, she claimed she was free to enjoy Clitandre's attentions because she had been married against her will, and "je prétends n'être point obligée à me soumettre en esclave à vos volontés!" ["I do not pretend to be obliged to submit, like a slave, to your will"]. This honest rebellion, rather than her subsequent pursuit of Clitandre, is her truest moment of freedom. Bought and sold like an object, she is here involved in a live relationship, however hostile, with her husband. The marriage she calls death is painfully alive. But at the end of the play all has changed. She is committed to a world of deceit in her game with Clitandre (and his probable successors). Moreover, she is isolated not only from Dandin but from her parents. Her confrontation with them in Act III, paralleling her earlier duel with Dandin, begins as her only truthful exchange with her father and

mother in the entire comedy. It ends on a tone of such total capitulation that Angélique seems to choose for herself the role of object that others have assigned to her.... With this submission, Angélique chooses silence over honest protest, cuts herself off from both husband and family, and consigns herself to the lonely world of lies. Only the grotesque Sotenville, in their final line, are left to evoke the happy nuptials which normally conclude comedy.... "Et nous, mamour, allons nous mettre au lit" ["As for us, my dear, let us return to bed"].

To the isolation of Angélique and Dandin from each other is added a further separation. Sin is separation from God. And in the closing scene of the comedy, Dandin, unreconciled with his wife or himself, prepares to take the final step away from his Creator by taking his own life. (pp. 105-06)

Dandin's marriage remains unredeemed and uncelebrated. The True Vine is replaced by Bacchus, the true Shepherd by the "bergers et bergères" ["shepherds and shepherdesses"] of pastoral convention, and the audience, like Dandin, is simply invited not to take things too seriously. The broken marriage is unhealed, the issues are unresolved by any "comic redeemer," in Knutson's phrase, and all one can do is forget the whole thing. The play thus becomes, through its full dénouement, a *divertissement* in the truest Pascalian sense, a failure to fully confront the human condition and thus be open to a genuine celebration of life and grace. (pp. 108-09)

Dorothy F. Jones, "Religious Parody in Molière's 'George Dandin'," in Symposium, *Vol. XLI, No. 2, Summer, 1987, pp. 100-09.*

JEAN-MARIE APOSTOLIDÈS   (essay date 1988)

[*In the following excerpt, Apostolidès discusses social and religious implications of Harpagon and Don Juan in* The Miser *and* Don Juan.]

Molière's theater presents a gallery of dangerous personalities whose maladjustment threatens the security of a new institution, the nuclear family. These individuals are often delinquent fathers, rebellious sons, or bachelors whose ambition has turned them into criminals. These characters are dangerous because they are appealing, and they are captivating because they play on social contradictions, moving back and forth from one system of values to another. Instead of finding the "golden mean," they behave unacceptably, either by exchanging too much and in an unorthodox manner, or by refusing to exchange altogether. By excess or by default, they imperil the fragile balance in the model of the *honnête homme*.

Two of Molière's plays, *The Miser* and *Don Juan*, will put us in a better position to understand the mechanisms of simulation. In both cases, the main character is unable to unite the different values that divide his world, and consequently he favors some values to the detriment of the others. The social group reacts to these transgressions, but, in doing so, they come to regard the dangerous individual as sacred. The latter is not understood in his identity with the others but rather in his difference. The stage makes it possible to ostracize this individual by giving him the mask of a monster (Harpagon) or even that of a devil (Don Juan). (pp. 478-79)

• • • • •

Harpagon is a seventeenth-century miser, that is to say, a usurer. He makes money work for what it will yield, and, on this account, he is one of the most important precapitalist figures in French theater. However, Molière portrays him from a moral standpoint and is interested less in the social mechanisms that favor the usurer than in the disastrous effects of this practice on Harpagon's family. Harpagon is a widower of about sixty, the father of two children he hopes to marry off, and he has a fairly large number of servants, at the head of whom is a steward named Valère. Unlike most of the leading bourgeois characters Molière puts on stage who use their fortune to monopolize an imaginary capital of honor, Harpagon assumes his bourgeois ignominy and wants instead to augment his usurious and commercial capital. He is detached from traditional values. He is not impressed by nobility, he spurns family conventions, and he entertains solely financially advantageous relations with others. He is a father in name only and considers himself rather an individual with no attachments, someone to whom everyone is a potential rival or enemy. With his own son, he finds himself involved first of all in a relationship of amorous rivalry, later in the relationship of usurer to borrower. The monetary tie takes the place that should belong to the affective tie, and Harpagon even tries to get rid of his children with the least possible expense: "without dowry!" For their part, the children dream only of running away from home. At least Cléante does; he wants to start a family with Marianne far from his childhood milieu: "I'm determined to run away with my beloved and take whatever fortune Heaven may vouchsafe us."

If we accept Henri Bergson's definition of comedy— *"Something mechanical encrusted on the living"* —Harpagon presents himself as an adding machine. As soon as he enters into contact with someone, he does not perceive who that person is, but rather what he owns. With a surprising degree of precision, he can say how much what someone has can yield under any given circumstances. The energy that drives Harpagon is not expressed in affective or amorous behaviors but is converted directly into money. Since he feels neither love nor hate, he does not understand these feelings in others, whom he treats as abstract forces to be turned into profit.

This inversion of values that dehumanizes human beings likewise humanizes things, at least the most essential thing: money. Harpagon treats it as if it possessed a soul, since, according to him, money is the energy that sustains the world. When his cash box is taken from him, he is deprived of his vital energy; this is why he yells that a murder has taken place. In his delirium, he calls his money his "beloved," his "consolation," his "joy." When later there is a quid pro quo between him and Valère (Valère is speaking of women, and Harpagon, of money), the misunderstanding can be prolonged only because gold has been humanized: Harpagon cannot imagine that anyone could be attached to anything else. In Valère, who flatters him constantly, he recognizes his own character traits, the same obsession with possession. Indeed, Harpagon dreams of a world without loss, without waste, a world where it would be possible to accumulate ad infinitum, without expending any energy. In this sense, he already embodies a certain "capitalist" spirit for which everything represents progress, and linear time points to an ever-larger conquest,

to an ever-more-dominant rationality. And since Harpagon identifies his existence with gold, he thinks he will live indefinitely since he spends only the bare minimum necessary to restore his ability to calculate.

This obsessive fear of spending is characteristic of the behavior of a miser. There is no scrap, no rag that cannot serve as currency, as one can note in the list of assorted objects that Harpagon slips into the terms of his loan agreement unbeknownst to his borrowers and which he requires them to sell as a substitute for a part of the principal. These cast-offs of aristocratic and bourgeois wealth have lost their use value for Harpagon, who reassigns them a reduced exchange value and puts them back into circulation in usurious exchange. But the refusal of any expenditure, any loss, amounts to repression and comes out as absolute loss, that is, death. In no other play by Molière does death have a stronger presence than in *The Miser*. It is the reverse of the wish for total accumulation, the other symptom of Harpagon's folly. The myth of Midas enables us to understand: like the legendary king, the usurer transforms everything he touches into gold but in doing so he loses his life. His children flee from him, his servants lie to him and steal from him, his horses, reduced to skeletons, are of no use to him. Every relationship that is not monetary is struck with sterility. Verbal or affective exchanges are reduced to an illusion due to the dominance of the exchange of money. The only sincere wishes are death wishes: Cléante promises his father will die within eight months, Frosine advises Marianne not to sign the marriage contract except on the condition that Harpagon will die soon, and she herself wishes that he rot in hell. In his answers to these wishes, Harpagon expresses delight at the thought that he will see his children buried. In this comedy where human beings are reified by the relationship to money, death is only the final consequence of their transformation into abstract things, quantifiable and negotiable.

The only characters who retain a bit of humanity, even though they themselves are treated as merchandise, are Master Jacques, among the servants, and Elise, among the children. If the coachman-cook shows some tenderness for his master, the miser's daughter is undoubtedly more complex than she appears. Her age is not given, but she is so sensible that she must be about thirty. She has in fact taken on the mother's role. Although she no doubt loves Valère sincerely, she cannot bring herself to act, that is, to flee the house. She encourages her fiancé to keep his mask. Despite the promise of marriage that he has gotten her to sign, she holds to the status quo: "I must confess I am concerned about the outcome," she confides. She treats her father considerately, never criticizes him openly, unlike her brother, and cannot even bear for anyone to criticize him in her presence. When Valère tries to do so, albeit with restraint, he has to apologize for having offended her. As we learn at the beginning of the play, Elise is of a melancholy temperament. Her fears concern not only her father but her fiancé as well. When Valère talks about going to find his parents, a move which would provide an avenue of escape from a difficult situation, Elise holds him back: "Oh no, Valère. Do not go away, I beseech you! Stay and give your whole attention to gaining my father's confidence." She encourages him in his role as a hypocritical financier who not only indulges the boss' whims but above all follows his example.

By imitating Harpagon's behavior, Valère acquires the same power in Harpagon's family as Tartuffe does in Orgon's, and sometimes he even uses practically the same phrases as Tartuffe. As for Elise, she acts like an Elmire who has succumbed to the hypocrite's charm. If she owes her life to her father, does she not owe it just as much to the lover who saved her from drowning? And does her affection not have as its origin the debt that she cannot repay in any other way? Elise justifies her indecision by conjuring up to Valère the inevitable disappointment that marriage brings; she fears, she says, "the cruel indifference with which men so often requite an innocent love too ardently offered them." And, in the face of her lover's protests, she voices an opinion that puts all men in the same category: "you all talk like that. Men are all alike in their promises." In short, she wants to be the eternal fiancée, because marriage would bring about an affective loss. She makes a fetish of absolute love, perhaps because it is of Oedipal origin, but mostly because she does not want to tap the sentimental capital it represents. Like her father, but in the domain of libidinal economy, Elise fears loss, the deterioration of feeling and death. By refusing to consummate the marriage, she keeps absolute love (and her virginity) like a treasure.

This interpretation of Harpagon's daughter helps us understand the father. Just before the play begins, two parallel and independent events have taken place in the household: first, the promise of marriage between Elise and Valère, and second, the settlement of a long-standing obligation: a debtor came to repay Harpagon the considerable sum of 10,000 pounds. With no time to invest this gold, the miser buried it at the far end of the garden. During the course of the play, he keeps going to check on it and ends up having it stolen. Even though Harpagon generally puts his money to work, here he contemplates it. He takes it out of circulation and momentarily suspends its double value of usage and exchange. The gold becomes his fetish, his God, a hieratic object he literally adores. He treats it the way his daughter treats love, as an absolute. Ordinarily, when money works, it gets used up in the process of circulation; the owner must separate himself from it and make it take risks so that it will yield. Here, Harpagon cannot bring himself to do so, and prefers the phantasm of economic omnipotence (the fact that money theoretically permits a multitude of purchases among which one must choose) to the loss due to a particular investment.

We find the same structure in the libidinal economy. The period of engagement is the short time when the woman is taken out of circulation yet remains "un-consumed," suspended between use and exchange.... We can now appreciate the full force of the quid pro quo that structures act 5: the fiancée and the cash box are equivalent objects for two men, one of whom "has ingratiated himself in the favor" of the other, that is, Valère and Harpagon. The fetishism of the monetary sign and absolute love are a single deviation, in the double domain of monetary economy and libidinal economy. This deviation corresponds to a fixation on the sign of exchange (gold/love), to a refusal of loss, a mocking return to the sacred, which the characters are unable to mourn.

•　•　•　•　•

All exchangers are epitomized in Don Juan, who surpasses the type and attains the dimensions of a myth. On two oc-

casions during the course of Molière's play, allusion is made to the clothes Don Juan is wearing, first by Sganarelle, then, after the drowning, by Peter: "A regular gentleman, 'e be—gold lace on his clothes from head to foot." With the gold, Don Juan sports ribbons the color of fire ("There bain't no part of 'em, even their shoes, that don't be a-loaded down with 'em.") What we know about Sganarelle's costume, from the postmortem inventory of Molière's personal effects, proves that he wears clothes matching those of his master. Don Juan appears under the double sign of gold and of fire, and it is through these two emblems that we will interpret him. (pp. 480-85)

[The protagonists of ***Don Juan***] appeal to Christian values to judge Don Juan. All of them refer to the ethics of the Gospel to condemn the seducer, to condemn the man that broke the oaths traditionally binding men together. Upon seeing the multiple transgressions perpetrated by Don Juan, the clan delegates Don Louis as its chief, who judges the guilty party and sanctions the rupture the seducer himself had sought: "You claim descent from your ancestors in vain. They disown you." Don Juan causes yet another rupture by destroying the bipolarity that is the foundation of traditional society, that of the sacred and of the profane. In abducting Elvira, he violates the convent and commits sacrilege by putting the inside world in contact with the outside. Then, having married the nun, he breaks the bonds of marriage once again to devote himself to new conquests. This act, his claim to rival God Himself, is the heinous crime, the sin for which there is no forgiveness. He feels strong enough to taunt his Creator by stealing a virgin consecrated to Him.

According to a religious interpretation of the world, Don Juan assumes a diabolical role. He tempts each of the characters in turn, traps them with fallacious words. Those who enter into contact with him find themselves being offered, in exchange for their salvation, valorized things they cannot acquire without transgressing Christian morals. To each person, Don Juan proposes new values which not only cannot be offered by the religious universe, but whose acquisition could very well weaken long-standing solidarities. The first victim of the seduction is of course Sganarelle, who gave himself to the devil not only in the hope of a reward (his wages) but also because the light emanating from the evil angel has dazzled him and because he has made Don Juan his captivating model. Don Juan plays the seducer with women too, by making them glimpse a richer life, affectively or materially. The only character of the play who does not succumb to the devil is Francisco, the destitute pauper who has put his absolute trust in Heaven. Don Juan asks him to swear, that is, to commit a mortal sin, in divine as well as human law. He proposes to the pauper to exchange his soul for a gold louis and repeats the temptation three times while making the coin shine in his hand. And Francisco, poverty notwithstanding, and with an unparalleled dignity, refuses what he considers to be a fool's bargain: "No sir, I'd rather starve."

Nevertheless, it is by another aspect of his personality that Don Juan appears as the incarnation of the devil. At a time when everyone possesses sufficient grace (the Jesuits maintain it against the Jansenists), he is the exception. He accepts damnation voluntarily. He is the damned par excellence, he to whom Lucifer has granted his "grace," an infernal grace that is the negative of God's. From the beginning of the play to the end, from Sganarelle to the Specter of the last act, from the sublunar world to the celestial universe, everyone and everything comes to warn Don Juan of the risks his soul runs. He pays no attention and denies everything until the last moment. Not only does he refuse the gift of prophecy that emerges from his entourage (Sganarelle, Elvira, and Don Louis prophesy in turn), but also he ridicules the miracles God has allowed to happen, the transgressions of the order of things that He has accepted to convert the infidel. Whether before the miracle of the statue, three times repeated, or faced with the apparition of the Specter, Don Juan dismisses Heaven's grace. He returns God's own gifts to Him in order to owe Him nothing: "those who reject Heaven's mercy bring down its wrath" is the final judgment uttered by the statue of the Commander while he transmits the divine Fire. During five acts, the flight of the hero is crossed by many hands held out to him, that of Sganarelle who tries to convert him, of Elvira and Don Louis who attempt to put him back on the straight and narrow, of Peter who pulls him out of the water, and even the hand held out by Monsieur Dimanche to obtain his money. Don Juan refuses these various extended hands and only takes hold of those who can lead him into hell. (pp. 485-86)

Molière's play should first be read from a Christian perspective because the religious pole unifies all the divided social structures, that of the family, of politics, or of exchange. Each of the protagonists comes to condemn Don Juan, but Heaven alone is powerful enough to execute the sentence. Whereas in other comedies by Molière the threatened characters do not have much difficulty in driving away the *pharmakos* (scapegoat), in **Don Juan** they are all scattered, split up, and do not communicate among themselves except through the intermediary of the hero. Don Juan restores the unity of the world, but against him, and only in the theological meaning of the play. He is marked with the *minus* sign and permits the coherence of the divine word by the promise of Fire. It is the progressively stronger assurance of his eternal damnation that solidifies the values of the group; God needs the devil to manifest His existence to the world.

The first universe is religious, structured around two poles, the sacred and the profane; it is placed under the sign of Fire. The second universe, superimposed on the first, is secular, egalitarian, and no longer hierarchical. Don Juan does not wear the sign *minus* there, but rather the *plus* sign. Gold has succeeded Fire. All of the characters of the drama are conscious of the coexistence of the two universes and of the tug-of-war between them, engendered by their opposite values. The temptation to which Don Juan submits them consists precisely in his proposing to be their intermediary, allowing them to pass from one universe to the other, from the religious world to that of the market. And if, with the exception of the pauper, each gives in to a greater or lesser degree, it is because each one's confidence in Christian values has already been shaken. (p. 487)

Don Juan's power to change his fellow human beings recalls the power of gold when it comes into contact with objects: he transforms people into merchandise, he attributes a quantifiable value to them, and he makes them circulate. This process of market transformation manifests itself in his relationships as seducer with women. What he says about them boils down to this: all women are equal

and cannot be distinguished except by the time required to conquer them. As with merchandise, it is the quantity of time spent to *produce* them that determines their value. What differentiates Elvira from Charlotte is the seduction time, since it takes Don Juan several weeks to seduce the former but only a quarter of an hour to persuade the latter to marry him. The difference between people is no longer qualitative but quantitative and thus measurable. All women are inherently desirable, for they are, in Don Juan's eyes, merely transitory incarnations of the abstract Woman he seeks to reproduce, an imaginary being invented by his calculating desire. Beyond concrete, carnal individuals, with their qualities and their faults, above all with their vile or noble essences, their common or aristocratic blood, Don Juan searches for the common denominator. This is the reason all women seem lovable to him and that he dreams of passing from one to another as if he were making perpetual rounds.

Don Juan does not transfer his desire onto gold as Harpagon does; rather, he is the incarnation of that desire, which looks like precious metal to him. It never wears out, it is never used up, and the seducer thinks he has enough love for all the women in the world. In fact, he is able to go so quickly from one to another because he does not wear them out, nor does he wear himself out. He transforms them into merchandise, but this metamorphosis is carried out for the benefit of others. As far as he is concerned, he is careful not to consume them entirely; he sizes them up, evaluates them, compares them, seduces them, and abandons them. Above all, he interferes in the lives of couples, that of God and Elvira, of Peter and his Charlotte, of the young engaged couple we glimpse, just as the serpent came between Adam and Eve. He gleans his pleasure in passing, before sending the transformed lovers back to each other. He extracts, as it were, an erotic surplus value by prohibiting the free exchange of desire, by opposing any amorous behavior in which he does not take part. For him, there is no pleasure except in a love triangle in which he mimics the desire of the other. His pleasure seems to derive from anticipation, at the mere sight of requited love. Hence he does not exhaust the use value of the women he transforms into marketable objects; he only uses what is necessary to determine their exchange value, that is to say, to fix their price. Then, once the women are uprooted from their universe, Don Juan puts them into circulation and takes no more interest in them. He has succeeded in freeing them from their essence and in endowing them with a new value, an erotic value, which will subsequently permit a free seduction of new partners.

As a figure of gold, Don Juan plays in the economic universe the same role the devil plays in the theological universe. He is a transforming force, wearing the *minus* sign in one world, the *plus* sign in the other. He is a counter-God who frees beings from the weight of tradition, he is the very principle of movement. He becomes something of an alchemist and achieves the synthesis at which Harpagon fails. His contact with women gives them another value, no longer linked to who they are but to what they own, no longer qualitative but quantitative; he gives them a price and thus enables their general exchange, under a "perverse" system in which the market economy imposes its model on the libidinal economy. The play is structured around this double universe. In both worlds, it is a matter of conversion. The group tries to convert Don Juan to

Christian values, while the seducer converts women to erotic and market values. But, since no one speaks the same language, they cannot understand each other. Only Sganarelle, the pivotal character of the play, is able to use the double language, which is why he can switch so easily from religious values to those of his master. He is the universal translator, the one who attempts a halfhearted osmosis between the two worlds with incompatible values.

At the end of the comedy, Heaven learns accounting, and Don Juan agrees to speak the language of religion. Gold and Fire, emblems of the two contradictory universes, grow closer in the fifth act. . . . [Communication] between two universes occurs through the sacrifice of the negative. For Don Juan to attain the level of myth, he must be eliminated. His annihilation will make possible the movement from the Christian feudal world to the market world, which is still ours today. Modernity begins with the solemn sacrifice of this Antichrist, who thereby attains exemplary status and enters the pantheon of contemporary gods. By offering his hand to the statue of the Commander, Don Juan sanctions the fusion of the contradictory values he incarnates. (pp. 488-90)

> *Jean-Marie Apostolidès, "Molière and the Sociology of Exchange," translated by Alice Musick McLean, in* Critical Inquiry, *Vol. 14, No. 3, Spring, 1988, pp. 477-92.*

ADDITIONAL BIBLIOGRAPHY

Alsip, Barbara W. "Myth and Fairy Tale in Molière's *La Princesse d'Élide*." *Papers on French Seventeenth Century Literature* 10, No. 18 (1983): 221-32.
Compares the princess in *The Princess of Elis* to mythological and fairy tale figures to illustrate her initial inability to become an adult.

Besant, Walter. "Molière." In his *The French Humorists from the Twelfth to the Nineteenth Century*, pp. 310-57. Boston: Roberts Brothers, 1874.
Anecdotal relation of Molière's life and works.

[Blaze de Bury, Marie P. R. S.] "Molière." *The Edinburgh Review* LXXXII, No. CLXV (July 1845): 172-202.
Analyzes Molière's plays under four categories: small dramatic poems or pastorals; farces and pasquinades; comedies of vice or folly; and plays of human nature and the heart.

Bowen, Barbara C. "Some Elements of French Farce in Molière." *L'esprit créateur* VI, No. 3 (Fall 1966): 167-75.
Determines the extent to which French farce influenced Molière's comic view.

Brody, Jules. "*Don Juan* and *Le Misanthrope*, or The Esthetics of Individualism in Molière." *PMLA* 84, No. 3 (May 1969): 559-76.
Argues that Don Juan and Célimène preserve their roles as non-comic characters by imposing their individuality upon the world.

Bulgakov, Mikhail. *The Life of Monsieur de Molière*. Translated by Mirra Ginsburg. New York: Funk & Wagnalls, 1970, 259 p.
Humorous fictionalized biography written in the 1930s.

Chatfield-Taylor, H. C. *Molière: A Biography*. New York: Duffield & Company, 1906, 466 p.
Critical biography concerned mainly with those comedies (including *The School for Wives, Tartuffe*, and *Don Juan*) whose public reception and response directly affected Molière's personal and professional lives.

Coe, Richard N. "The Ambiguity of Dom Juan." *Australian Journal of French Studies* I, No. 1 (January-April 1964): 23-35.
Refutes the long-established opinion that Don Juan's character lacks unity.

Cornett, Patricia L. "Doubling in *Amphitryon*." *Essays in French Literature*, No. 9 (November 1972): 16-29.
Examines the dual relationships of Sosie and Amphitryon and Jupiter and Mercury to illuminate the "ultimate relationship dramatized in the play, that of the human and the divine."

De Selincourt, Aubrey. "Molière." In his *Six Great Playwrights*, pp. 74-104. London: Hamish Hamilton, 1960.
Explicates Molière's plays, calling the dramatist a civilized writer whose comic focus is the anomalies of human character.

Doolittle, James. "Bad Writing in *l'Avare*." *L'esprit créateur* VI, No. 3 (Fall 1966): 197-207.
Offers a thematic explanation for the "bad writing" of the first two scenes of *The Miser*. Doolittle argues that Molière intended to "exhibit the nefarious contagion of Harpagon's mania which is visible in the play's other roles."

"Molière." *The Edinburgh Review* CCXI, No. 431 (January 1910): 85-110.
Explores Molière's philosophy, comparing him with noted French men of letters and concluding that Molière is the "foremost figure of all French literature."

Eustis, Alvin. *Molière as Ironic Contemplator*. The Hague: Mouton, 1973, 231 p.
Evaluates the role of irony in Molière's life, work, and ideology.

Fellows, Otis E. *French Opinion of Molière: (1800-1850)*. Providence, R.I.: Brown University, 1937, 125 p.
Well-documented study of nineteenth-century public and scholarly thought on Molière.

Fernandez, Ramon. *Molière: The Man Seen through the Plays*. Translated by Wilson Follett. New York: Hill and Wang, 1958, 212 p.
1929 interpretation of Molière's life in terms of his works.

Forehand, Walter E. "Adaptation and Comic Intent: Plautus' *Amphitruo* and Molière's *Amphitryon*." *Comparative Literature Studies* 11, No. 3 (September 1974): 204-17.
Discusses Molière's "process of adaptation" of Plautus's play, concluding that Molière's version is both lighter and less philosophical.

France, Anatole. "Molière." In his *The Latin Genius*, pp. 95-130. New York: Gabriel Wells, 1924.
Biographical sketch that includes poems and commentary by such contemporaries of Molière as Jean Loret, Jean de La Fontaine, Le Boulanger de Chalussey, and Armand de Bourbon, Prince de Condé.

Fraser, R. D., and Rendall, S. F. "The Recognition Scene in Molière's Theater." *The Romanic Review* 64, No. 1 (January 1973): 16-31.
Examines Molière's complex manipulation of the conventional recognition scenes in *The Blunderer, The School for Wives*, and *The Bourgeois Gentleman*.

Grivelet, Michel. "Shakespeare, Molière, and the Comedy of Ambiguity." *Shakespeare Survey: An Annual Survey of Shakespearean Study and Production* 22 (1969): 15-26.
    Examines the ambiguity of identity in *Amphitryon* and Shakespeare's *Comedy of Errors* (1594).

Gross, Nathan. *From Gesture to Idea: Esthetics and Ethics in Molière's Comedy.* New York: Columbia University Press, 1982, 159 p.
    Examines the ethical values of *Tartuffe, Don Juan, The Misanthrope, George Dandin,* and *The Bourgeois Gentleman.*

Guicharnaud, Jacques, ed. *Molière: A Collection of Critical Essays.* Englewood Cliffs, N.J.: Prentice-Hall, 1964, 186 p.
    Essays by several twentieth-century authorities on Molière, including Gustave Lanson, Will G. Moore, Ramon Fernandez, Lional Gosman, and H. Gaston Hall.

Gutwirth, Marcel. "The Unity of Molière's *L'avare*." *PMLA* 76, No. 4 (September 1961): 359-66.
    Asserts that audience response to *The Miser* results from the "formidable scope of its theme—nothing less than a head-on confrontation with the primal comic myth of a narrowly averted victory of Death over Life."

Hall, H. Gaston. *Molière: "Tartuffe".* Great Neck, N. Y.: Barron's Educational Series, 1960, 63 p.
    Explicates structural and stylistic elements in *Tartuffe,* providing important background and historical information.

Hammer, Carl, Jr. "Molière's *Tartuffe* and Goethe's *Grosskaphta*." *Romance Notes* XVIII, No. 3 (Spring 1978): 368-74.
    Compares Goethe's work with Molière's, noting that Goethe borrowed heavily from the French dramatist.

Henry, Patrick. "Paradox in *Le Misanthrope*." *Philological Quarterly* 65, No. 2 (Spring 1986): 187-95.
    Uses *The Misanthrope* to demonstrate the persistence of Renaissance aesthetics in French classical theater.

Hope, Quentin M. "Dramatic Techniques in *Les précieuses Ridicules*." In *Renaissance and Other Studies in Honor of William Leon Wiley,* edited by George Bernard Daniel, Jr., pp. 141-50. Chapel Hill, N.C.: The University of North Carolina Press, 1968.
    Discusses Molière's use of experimental dramatic techniques involving timing, rhythm, recurring phrases, and topical satire in *The Affected Ladies.*

———. "Place and Setting in *Tartuffe.*" *PMLA* LXXXIX, No. 1 (January 1974): 42-9.
    Argues that place and setting contribute significantly to Molière's dramaturgy.

Howarth, W. D., and Thomas, Merlin, eds. *Molière: Stage and Study.* Oxford: Oxford University Press, Clarendon Press, 1973, 293 p.
    Collection of nineteen essays in French and English. Essayists include Jacques Guicharnaud, J. D. Hubert, and H. Gaston Hall.

Hubert, Judd. "Molière: The Playwright as Protagonist." *Theatre Journal* 34, No. 3 (October 1982): 361-71.
    Metadramatic interpretation of Molière's work, arguing that Molière manipulated the functions of authorship.

Hugo, Victor. "Preface to Cromwell." In *Prefaces and Prologues to Famous Books,* edited by Charles W. Eliot, pp. 337-87. New York: P. F. Collier & Son, 1938.
    Contains a brief, appreciative reference to Molière as the author who "occupies the topmost pinnacle of our drama, not only as a poet, but also as a writer."

Jagendorf, Zvi. "Molière's Denouements." In his *The Happy End of Comedy: Jonson, Molière, and Shakespeare,* pp. 78-110. Newark: University of Delaware Press, 1984.

Examines recognition scenes in several of Molière's plays.

Johnson, Roger, Jr.; Neumann, Editha S.; and Trail, Guy T., eds. *Molière and the Commonwealth of Letters: Patrimony and Posterity.* Jackson: University Press of Mississippi, 1975, 873 p.
    Useful reference source for students of Molière. Includes examinations of Molière's influence upon later writers, critical analyses of the plays, discussions of the staging of the dramas, and a continuation of Paul Saintonge's *Fifty Years of Molière Studies: A Bibliography, 1892-1941* (1942) (see citation below).

Kennedy, William J. "Comic Audiences and Rhetorical Strategies in Machiavelli, Shakespeare, and Molière." *Comparative Literature Studies* 21, No. 4 (Winter 1984): 363-82.
    Traces the literary history and development of comedy by studying the responses of sixteenth- and seventeenth-century audiences to *La mandragola* (1518), *Twelfth Night* (1601-02), and *The Miser.*

Ker, William Paton. "Molière and the Muse of Comedy." In his *The Art of Poetry: Seven Lectures, 1920-1922,* pp. 117-37. Oxford: Oxford University Press, Clarendon Press, 1923.
    Compares Molière's prose with his verse, questioning whether he was a poet in the true sense.

Kierkegaard, Soren. "The Immediate Stages of the Erotic or the Musical Erotic." In his *Either/Or,* Vol. 1, pp. 43-135. Princeton: Princeton University Press, 1944.
    Compares Molière's portrayal of the Don Juan legend unfavorably to Mozart's *Don Giovanni.*

Knutson, Harold. *Molière: An Archetypal Approach.* Toronto and Buffalo: University of Toronto Press, 1976, 208 p.
    Archetypal interpretation (one that includes "a focal point of several related disciplines—psychology, anthropology, philosophy, criticism itself") of selected themes in Molière's plays.

Konstan, David. "A Dramatic History of Misanthropes." *Comparative Drama* 17, No. 2 (Summer 1983): 97-123.
    Examines the double natures, values, and paradoxes of the misanthropes of Menander, Shakespeare, and Molière.

Lancaster, Henry Carrington. *A History of French Dramatic Literature in the Seventeenth Century.* 2 vols. Baltimore, Md.: The Johns Hopkins Press, 1936.
    Divides Molière's plays into three parts, providing a critical analysis with an overview of seventeenth-century French political and social thought.

———. "The Comedies of Molière." In *Literary Masterpieces of the Western World,* edited by Francis H. Horn, pp. 164-84. Baltimore: The Johns Hopkins Press, 1953.
    Biographical and critical survey.

Lawrence, Francis L. "The Ironic Commentator in Molière's *Dom Juan.*" *Studi Francesi* XII, No. 35 (January-April 1968): 201-07.
    Interprets *Don Juan* through the relationship between Don Juan and Sganarelle.

Lewis, D.B. Wyndham. *Molière: The Comic Mask.* London: Eyre & Spottiswoode, 1959, 214 p.
    Critical biography containing summaries of Molière's plays.

Machan, Helen W. "Molière: The Universal and Timeless Aspects of His Comedies." *Kentucky Foreign Language Quarterly* IV, No. 3 (1957): 136-45.
    Characterizes Molière's humor as founded on truth and humanity and describes the human traits Molière treats comically in his plays.

Marsi, Jean-Denis. "*Les Fâcheux:* A Study in Thematic Composition." *The USF (University of South Florida) Language Quarterly* 22, Nos. 1-2 (Fall-Winter 1983): 27-9.

Studies the dramatic structure of *The Bores.*

Matthews, Brander. "The Modernity of Molière." *Outlook* 131, No. 1 (3 May 1922): 35-6, 39-40.
  Praises the permanence and universality of Molière's plays.

McBride, Robert. "The Sceptical View of Marriage and the Comic Vision in Molière." *Forum for Modern Language Studies* V, No. 1 (January 1969): 26-46.
  Examines the comical and skeptical structures of the marriages in Molière's plays as evidence of the dramatist's philosophy and comic insight.

McGalliard, John C. "Chaucerian Comedy: *The Merchant's Tale,* Jonson, and Molière." *Philological Quarterly* 25, No. 4 (October 1946): 343-70.
  Compares Chaucer and Molière, noting that Chaucer "anticipated the great comedy of character" of Molière.

Meredith, George. "Essay: On the Idea of Comedy and of the Uses of the Comic Spirit." In his *The Works of George Meredith: Vol. XXIII,* pp. 3-55. New York: Charles Scribner's Sons, 1910.
  General theoretical discussion of comedy containing frequent references to Molière.

Merrill, Robert V. "Molière's Exposition of a Courtly Character in *Don Juan.*" *Modern Philology* 19 (1921-22): 33-45.
  Considers the development and exposition of Don Juan, studying as well his relation to contemporary courtly standards.

Michaut, Gustave. *La jeunesse de Molière.* Paris: Hachette, 1922, 255 p.
——. *Les debuts de Molière a Paris.* Paris: Hachette, 1923, 252 p.
——. *Les luttes de Molière,* Paris: Hachette, 1925, 247 p.
  A biographical trilogy in French by a respected authority on Molière's life.

Le Moliériste 1-10, Nos. 1-120 (1879-89).
  A French monthly review, edited by Georges Monval, devoted exclusively to Molière studies.

Murry, J. Middleton. "Congreve and Molière." In his *Pencillings,* pp. 203-12. New York: Thomas Seltzer, 1925.
  Compares Congreve and Molière as dramatists, refuting the critical view that the former is superior to the latter.

Nurse, Peter H. "The Role of Chrysalde in *L'école des femmes.*" *The Modern Language Review* 56, No. 2 (April 1961): 167-71.
  Assesses Chrysalde's role as *raisonneur* in *The School for Wives.*

Nurse, P[eter] H. "Molière and Satire." *The University of Toronto Quarterly* XXXVI, No. 2 (January 1967): 113-28.
  Maintains that Molière's comedies include positive and coherent ethical frameworks.

Peacock, N. A. "The Comic Ending of *George Dandin.*" *French Studies* XXXVI, No. 2 (April 1982): 144-53.
  Argues that *George Dandin* is essentially comic, not tragic, because the play's ending is "a parody of the traditional tragic denouement."

Perry, Henry Ten Eyck. "The Height of French Comedy: Molière." In his *Masters of Dramatic Comedy and Their Social Themes,* pp. 150-98. Cambridge, Mass.: Harvard University Press, 1939.
  General, comprehensive survey of Molière's dramatic career. Perry concludes that Molière "must be considered as the greatest writer of thoughtful comedy in the history of the theater."

Regosin, Richard L. "Ambiguity and Truth in *Le Misanthrope.*" *The Romanic Review* LX, No. 3 (October 1969): 265-72.
  Examines the language of *The Misanthrope,* focusing upon such repeated images as "combat and trial" to explicate the metaphorical structures and dramatic motifs of the play.

Riggs, Larry W. "Language and Art as Merchandise in *Le Bourgeois Gentilhomme.*" *The USF (University of South Florida) Language Quarterly* XVII, Nos. 1-2 (Fall-Winter 1978): 15-19, 32.
  Discusses M. Jourdain's interpretation of identity in *The Bourgeois Gentleman.*

——. "Esthetic Judgment and the Comedy of Culture in Molière, Flaubert, and Beckett." *French Review* 54, No. 5 (April 1981): 680-89.
  Examines Molière's interpretation and use of language, defining the central conflict of his comedies as the search for "a conclusive self-realization."

Romero, Laurence. *Molière: Traditions in Criticism, 1900-1970.* Chapel Hill: North Carolina Studies in the Romance Languages and Literatures, 1974, 176 p.
  Useful bibliography of Molière studies, with an essay on the "roots of the traditions."

Saintonge, Paul. *Fifty Years of Molière Studies: A Bibliography, 1892-1941.* Baltimore, Md.: The Johns Hopkins Press, 1942, 313 p.
  Enumerative Molière bibliography, surveying textual and aesthetic criticism published between 1892 and 1941. The bibliography was continued in 1944 by Saintonge and R. W. Christ (see citation below) and by Roger Johnson, Jr. and others in *Molière and the Commonwealth of Letters: Patrimony and Posterity* (see citation above).

——. "Theme and Variations." *L'Esprit Créateur* VI, No. 3 (Fall 1966): 145-55.
  Claims Molière used standard plots but varied them so greatly that he achieved "a structure which was all variation and no theme."

Saintonge, Paul, and Christ, R. W. "Omissions and Additions to *Fifty Years of Molière Studies.*" *Modern Language Notes* LIX, No. 4 (April 1944): 282-85.
  Updates Saintonge's *Fifty Years of Molière Studies: A Bibliography, 1892-1941* (see citation above) to the year 1944, adding over forty new entries by English and French critics.

Schwartz, I. A. "Molière and the Commedia dell'arte." In his *The Commedia dell'arte and Its Influence on French Comedy in the Seventeenth Century,* pp. 79-108. Paris: Librairie H. Samuel, 1933.
  Examines the influence of the commedia dell'arte upon Molière's dramas.

Shaw, David. "Egoism and Society: A Secular Interpretation of Molière's *Dom Juan.*" *Modern Languages* 59, No. 3 (September 1978): 121-30.
  Argues against the idea that *Don Juan* is based upon Molière's personal views of Christianity.

——. "*Les Femmes Savantes* and Feminism." *Journal of European Studies* 14, No. 53 (March 1984): 24-38.
  Refutes the claim that *The Learned Ladies* is an antifeminist play.

Short, J. P. "The Comic Worlds of Molière." *Studi Francesi* 88 XXX, No. 1 (January-April 1986): 30-7.
  Discusses the imaginary worlds created by Molière's characters.

Simon, John. "Laughter in the Soul: Molière's *Misanthrope.*" *The Hudson Review* 28, No. 3 (Autumn 1975): 404-12.

Language and character analysis of *The Misanthrope.*

Singer, Irving. "Molière's Dom Juan." *The Hudson Review* XXIV, No. 3 (Autumn 1971): 447-60.
    Argues, against the traditional view, that Don Juan is not a hypocrite like Tartuffe, but rather a character who challenges hypocrisy.

Smith, Horatio. "Molière." In his *Masters of French Literature*, pp. 1-57. New York: Charles Scribner's Sons, 1937.
    Examines the nuances of Molière's writing in light of the dramatist's adaptable nature.

Stendhal [pseudonym of Henri Beyle]. "On the Morality of Molière." In his *Racine and Shakespeare*, translated by Guy Daniels, pp. 60-75. New York: The Crowell-Collier Press, 1962.
    Accuses Molière of immorality insofar as he "filled one with a dread of not being like everybody else." Stendhal particularly criticizes *The Learned Ladies* for ridiculing the intelligence of women.

Stoll, Elmer Edge. "Molière and Shakespeare." *The Romanic Review* XXXV, No. 1 (February 1944): 3-18.
    Cites similarities between the two dramatists.

Szogyi, Alex. "Aesthetic Structures (Molière and Chekhov)." *Proceedings of the 8th Congress of the International Comparative Literature Association*, edited by Béla Köpeczi and György M. Vajda, pp. 591-99. Stuttgart: Kunst and Wissen, 1980.
    Posits a fundamental similarity between Molière's work and that of nineteenth-century Russian dramatist Anton Chekhov, arguing that both authors adapted "a personal expression in which the vision is tragic but the expression of it is deeply comic."

Wadsworth, Charlotte B. "Molière's Debt to Montaigne." *Modern Language Quarterly* 8, No. 3 (September 1947): 290-301.
    Asserts that Molière borrowed heavily from Michel de Montaigne's *Essais* (1580-95), especially for ideas expressed through *raisonneurs* in the dramas.

Wheatley, Katherine E. "Molière Now and Then." *Forum (Houston)* 11, Nos. 2, 3 (Summer-Fall 1973; Winter 1974): 21-31.
    Deems Molière's acting ability the key to the original success of *The School for Wives*, noting that later actors have misinterpreted the roles and relationship of Agnes and Arnolphe, thus failing to convey the Molièresque irony which made his productions so popular.

Wilcox, John. *The Relation of Molière to Restoration Comedy.* 1938. Reprint. New York: Benjamin Blom, 1964, 240 p.
    Debates whether the ideas and spirit of Molière influenced English Restoration drama.

Zolbrod, Paul G. "Coriolanus and Alceste: A Study in Misanthropy." *Shakespeare Quarterly* XXIII, No. 1 (Winter 1972): 51-62.
    Compares Shakespeare's *Coriolanus* (1607-08) and *The Misanthrope*, focusing upon the central relationships within each play.

(Sir) Thomas More

1478-1535

(Also wrote under pseudonyms Ferdinandus Baravellus and Guilielmus Rosseus) English essayist, biographer, poet, epigrammatist, epistler, and dialogue writer.

An English saint and humanist, More is considered one of the greatest minds of the sixteenth century. His literary reputation is based chiefly on *Utopia*, an imaginative travel narrative describing an ideal state governed by reason. He is also known as the author of an important series of anti-heretical polemics as well as major devotional works. Yet More is celebrated above all as a man of exemplary character and virtue. Immensely accomplished in many fields, he excelled as a statesman and counselor of Henry VIII. Loyal as he was to the king, however, More could not see his way to approving Henry's divorce from Catherine of Aragon or the king's repudiation of papal jurisdiction in England in favor of his own. More's act of conscience—his refusal to bend to the king's authority—cost him his life, and he is esteemed today as a Roman Catholic martyr. But as martyrs go, More is comparatively human, for in the words of More critic Anthony Kenny, "the scholar, the martyred public servant, and the controversial prose writer are not three different, conflicting personalities, but a single, consistent human being."

More was born in London in 1478 (a few scholars say 1477), the only surviving son of Sir John More, then a barrister, and Agnes Graunger More, Sir John's first wife. More attended St. Anthony's School in Threadneedle Street before being sent at age twelve or thirteen to live in the household of John Morton, archbishop of Canterbury (later cardinal) and lord chancellor. Even as a boy More distinguished himself for character and brilliance, causing the archbishop, who predicted that More would prove to be a "marvellous man," to send him to study at Oxford in about 1492. At the university More made friends with humanists Thomas Linacre and William Grocyn, two of the original conduits of the classically inspired New Learning just then emerging in England. More survived in Oxford on a meager allowance from home, scarcely able to indulge in the usual amusements of university students. This left ample time for study, and More soon became skilled in the classics, French, history, mathematics, and music. Yet, possibly under pressure from his father, who may have sensed his son's inclination toward an unremunerative academic career, More withdrew from the university after only two years to begin law studies in London at New Inn. By 1496 he had been admitted to Lincoln's Inn as a student, and soon after he was called to the outer bar and then made a bencher. More's unusual abilities as lecturer, scholar, and advocate were instantly recognized both inside and outside the legal community. He tackled complicated legal issues, translated epigrams from the Greek anthology, and began writing Latin and English verse. His growing reputation won him the acquaintance of William Lilly, John Colet, and other distinguished men of letters, most notably the Dutch humanist Desiderius Erasmus, who remained a lifelong friend and intimate correspondent.

(Sir) Thomas More

In 1499 More experienced the first of a series of strong spiritual longings. Intent upon becoming a priest, he took lodgings near the London Charterhouse in order to participate in the religious observances of the Carthusians. He wore a hair shirt, scourged himself mercilessly, and deprived himself of sleep. Yet suddenly, after four years of living this way, More abandoned his ascetic practices to embrace secular society anew. Scholars have offered a variety of explanations for More's change of plan, but it seems clear at least that More found celibacy intolerable and was eager to make a name for himself outside the cloister. Hence his return full-time to the bar, where he shone more brilliantly than ever before. In 1504 More was elected to parliament. Soon he successfully opposed Henry VII on a money matter, thereby becoming an object of the king's indignation. This led More to retire to a friend's house in Essex for a time, apparently out of concern for his personal safety. The next year he married Jane Colt, the daughter of his Essex host. The couple settled in Bucklersbury, London, where More delighted in domestic life and engaged in literary pursuits in his spare time. In 1509 he hailed the coronation of Henry VIII with joyous Latin verse. Jane died in 1511, after bearing four children. More remarried less than a month later; then he and his new wife, Alice Middleton, removed to Crosby Place, London. Meanwhile, More prospered handsomely, advancing professionally and politically. He was sent to Flanders in 1515 to settle a thorny commercial dispute and to Calais on similar business in 1517. The interim saw the publication of *Libellus vere aureus nec minus salutaris quam festiuus de optimo reip, statu, deque noua Insula Vtopia* (*A fruteful and pleasant worke of the beste state of a publyque weale, and of the new yle called Vtopia*), commonly known as *Utopia*, in 1516. This work greatly enhanced More's European reputation. In 1520 More attended Henry VIII at the Field of the Cloth of Gold. Thereafter he rose in the king's estimation and was entrusted with ever greater responsibilities. Although Henry was extraordinarily familiar with More, often dining with him privately and visiting him at the Chelsea mansion he had had built around 1524, More never deluded himself about the king's true motives and feelings. "If my head should win [the king] a castle in France," he told his son-in-law William Roper in 1525, "it should not fail to go."

More's days at court were marked by political and religious controversy. With the spread of Protestantism in Europe, More found himself in the midst of a debate on which depended the fate of the Roman Catholic Church in England. In polemic after polemic More set out what he considered the errors of the Protestant reformers, defending Church doctrine assiduously while admitting (to a degree) certain infractions and abuses among the clergy. At first Henry showered More with praise for his efforts, for the king himself was originally a fierce opponent of heresy. In time, however, More's views of the Church no longer suited the king's purposes. With his growing belief that Queen Catherine would bear him no male heir, Henry began to look for a way out of his marriage, considered irrevocable and permanent in the eyes of the Church. Pope Clement VII refused to grant an annulment, and no amount of effort would change the pope's mind. Henry was enraged: his longserving lord chancellor, Cardinal Thomas Wolsey, was stripped of his offices and honors in 1529 for failing to persuade the pope to come over to Henry's side; relations between the Crown and Rome were severed; and Henry, denying the pope's supremacy in matters concerning religion in England, went ahead with the divorce anyway and assumed the pope's spiritual and temporal authority by making himself supreme head of the English church. More succeeded Wolsey as lord chancellor, but his tenure was not long: he resigned in 1532. The English clergy acquiesced for the most part to Henry's plan, but opposition remained, most visibly in More's refusal to uphold the divorce or accept the Act of Supremacy acknowledging the king's claimed authority. More never denied Henry's claim; rather, he remained silent, trusting that a legal maxim, that under the law silence must be construed as consent, not opposition, would protect him. It did not. More was imprisoned in the Tower of London in 1534 and interrogated relentlessly in an effort to make him sign the document. He was deprived of his property, saw his family endure harsh consequences for his refusal, and suffered both physically and psychologically during his imprisonment. Still he remained resolute: he would not sign. A trial was held, false evidence was presented, and More was convicted of high treason. The sentence was death. More was beheaded at Tower Hill on 6 July 1535, "simply because," according to Dom David

Knowles, "he would not admit that a lay ruler could have jurisdiction over the Church of Christ." A few days after the execution, word of More's death reached Europe in the so-called "Paris Newsletter." This account of More's last moments bears witness to his two allegiances: "He spoke little before his execution. Only he asked the bystanders to pray for him in this world, and he would pray for them elsewhere. He then begged them earnestly to pray for the King, that it might please God to give him good counsel, protesting that he died the King's good servant but God's first." More's head was fixed upon London bridge. He was beatified by Leo XIII in 1886 and canonized by Pius XI in 1935, the four-hundredth anniversary of his death.

More's literary works generally complement the various phases of his career. His early writings are chiefly humanist in character; the works of the middle period are controversial, anti-heretical polemics; and the later writings, a few of which were composed during More's confinement in the Tower, are almost entirely devotional. More's humanist works exemplify the spirit of the Renaissance, an age of discovery and rediscovery fashioned after a belief in the humanizing value of the Greek and Latin classics. The extent of More's literary activity before 1510 or so—the period of More's evolving humanism—is not clear, but it is known from a 1503 "Lamentation for the Death of Queen Elizabeth" and congratulatory Latin verses on the coronation of Henry VIII that More tried his hand at poetry on occasion. Indeed, he may have done so often and well, for according to the nineteenth-century biographer John, Lord Campbell, "at the University More distinguished himself very much by the composition of poems, both in Latin and in English." It has also been claimed—this time by Erasmus himself—that More wrote comedies in his youth, but if he did, none has survived. More's earliest substantial literary excursion, *The Lyfe of Johan Picus, Erle of Myrandula*, is an adaptation of the Latin biography by G. F. Pico. More considered the Italian scholar Giovanni Pico della Mirandola, who is the subject of *The Lyfe*, to be the consummate Renaissance thinker, and he plainly stated his admiration of Pico's vast learning and boundless curiosity in the work. *The Lyfe* was followed in about 1513 by a second biography, *The History of King Richard III*. This study of the contrasting moral and ethical tempers of Edward IV and Richard III exists in Latin and English versions, was never finished, and remained in manuscript until after the author's death. The theme of *Richard*, the insidiousness of overpowering greed and self-interest, proved the springboard for More's most celebrated work, one now considered the paradigm of English humanism: *Utopia*. Both *Richard* and *Utopia* contain commentary on political matters, and both treat the problems of counseling princes. More wrote Book II of *Utopia* during the 1515 embassy to Flanders. Here he described an imaginary state governed by reason, an enlightened pagan community in which goods are owned in common and are available to all as needed. This state contrasts markedly with the divided one described in Book I, which was written in England in 1516 and appears to contain criticism of current English social conditions. The second book is sometimes considered the more successful of the two. Erasmus, for one, believed this to be the case, but he did not fault More for this circumstance. Writing of *Utopia* to Ulrich von Hutten in 1519, Erasmus commented: "The recognizable unevenness of style results from the manner and method of its composition. [More] wrote the second book at a leisurely pace, and then recognizing the need for it, hastily added the first." More used the fictional traveler Raphael Hythloday as a mouthpiece in *Utopia*: Hythloday describes his foreign experiences, faulting private interest in public life and promoting a pure, pre-Marx form of communism. Critics are at odds about More's intentions in *Utopia*. According to C. S. Lewis, "all seem to be agreed that it is a great book, but hardly any two agree as to its real significance: we approach it through a cloud of contradictory eulogies." In fact, the range of critical responses to *Utopia* is tremendously diverse: some commentators see the work as an expression of More's own political views; others consider it little more than a witty exercise; while still others view it as essentially medieval in character and hardly progressive. All acknowledge, however, the work's status as the ancestor of an entirely new literary genre, the Utopian romance.

More's anti-heretical writings grew out of the turbulent religious climate of the early sixteenth century. An incipient English Protestantism, combined with growing domestic and European support for the religious views of Martin Luther, challenged the authority of the Church of Rome everywhere, and More was charged with the task of defending Catholic positions in England. He began his work in earnest in 1523 with *Ervditissimi viri Ferdinandi Barauelli opus elegans, doctum, festiuum, pium, quo pulcherrime retegit, ac refellit insanas Lutheri calumnias*, a pseudonymous essay commonly known as *Responsio ad Lutherum*. Here More attacked Luther's response to Henry VIII's defense of the Church in *Assertio septem sacramentorum* (1521). It is not known whether More volunteered to write the defense or whether the job was forced upon him. In either event, critics agree that More was the perfect man to debate Luther in print: he knew his subject thoroughly; wrote Latin prose skillfully and with ease; was able both to sink to the level of vulgarity commonly employed by Luther and, when the occasion warranted it, rise to define the nature of the Church in elegant and precise terms; and knew how to temper grave seriousness with light humor—a skill that helped endear all classes of readers to More's argument. According to Thomas Stapleton, a sixteenth-century biographer of More, the *Responsio* met with much favor in some quarters and was recognized as "a serious and solid defence of the true faith against the impudent attacks of Luther." In 1529 More published the first, and according to most critics the best, of his vernacular polemics, *A dyaloge of syr Thomas More knyghte, one of the counsayll of oure souerayne lorde the kyng and chancellour of hys duchy of Lancaster, wherin be treatyd dyuers maters*. In this dialogue, which More conceived as a denunciation of the English reformer William Tyndale, the author and a messenger debate Reformation theology. More was particularly concerned with establishing the authority of the Church in matters concerning faith, doctrine, and the liturgy, and he discussed Tyndale's translation of the New Testament at length. More's next vernacular polemic was *The Supplycacyon of soulys, Made by Syr Thomas More knyght councellour to our souerayn lorde the Kynge and chauncellour of hys Duchy of Lancaster, agaynst the Supplycacyon of Beggars*, a response to Simon Fish's *Supplicacyon for the Beggers* (1529). In *The Supplycacyon* More defended the Church against Fish's charge that clerical extravagance leads to increased pover-

ty and suffering among beggars. Commentators have faulted this work as overly discursive and noted that it lacks the irony and insight of the 1529 dialogue. Next More took on Tyndale again in a work published in two parts, *The confutacyon of Tyndales answere* and *The second parte of the confutacion of Tyndals answere*. Unlike More's earlier controversial writings, this highly ironic essay has no real narrative structure. Rather, More simply set out quotations from the reformers' works and refuted them. Nevertheless, the confutations have some dramatic interest, padded as they are with bawdy tales and off-color exempla. Two other of More's vernacular polemics, *A Letter of syr Thomas More knyght impugnynge the erronyouse wrytyng of John Fryth agaynst the blessed sacrament of the aultare* and *The answere to the fyrst parte of the poysened booke, whych a namelesse heretyke hath named the souper of the lorde*, complement the English works already described but have a narrower compass. The *Reply to Frith* challenges the Lutheran John Frith's claim that transubstantiation is impossible, while *The answere to the fyrst parte* also treats the question of the real presence of Christ in the Eucharist, but with a bit more passion. Critics consider these two works structurally and thematically inferior to More's earlier efforts at controversy, having as they do a jadedness about them that tends to undermine the polemical stance.

More's best-known devotional works are *A treatice vpon the Passion of Chryste* and *A dialoge of comfort against tribulacion*. The composition date of *A treatice* is uncertain, but it is known that at least a portion of the English section (More also wrote a Latin continuation titled *Expositio passionis domini*) was written before More's imprisonment. *A Treatice* is both meditative and didactic: it aims to stimulate profitable thought concerning the Passion of Christ. Hence it is prefaced with theological instruction, scriptural illustrations, admonitions against pride, and a discourse on the nature of the sacraments. Although the treatise is decidedly medieval in conception, form, and intent, commentators have noted traces of the humanism that imbues so much of More's work, especially in the many allusions to the classics in the *Expositio* section. More's *Dialogue of Comfort* is considered a masterpiece of English religious literature and the finest of his contemplative writings. Written during More's first months in the Tower, it is a reasoned, ordered, and polished exposition of the power of faith. The dialogue is set in Budapest during the 1528 Turkish invasion and takes the form of a debate between young Vincent and his aged uncle Anthony, the former seeking consolation from the latter during this troubling time. The two exchange thoughts and tales about the nature of tribulation, agreeing in the end that we are all prisoners in a world of pain, waiting to die at any time. The life well lived, then, is the one that anticipates death, for such a life will lead to union with Christ. The *Dialoge* is one of More's most esteemed works and has been described as the foundation of English post-medieval devotional literature.

More's critical reputation may be summed up succinctly: the man is greater than the writer. Nevertheless, according to R. W. Chambers, with the beheading of More, "all learning felt the blow and shrank." Thus More touched religion, politics, and scholarship alike, leaving a mark that has grown with time. Days after More's execution, efforts were begun to promote the statesman as a Catholic martyr. Word of his death quickly reached the Continent, where he was hailed as a man of exemplary faith, piety, and learning. Charles V himself deeply lamented More's demise, noting that "if we had been master of such a servant, of whose doings ourself have had these years no small experience, we would rather have lost the best city of our dominions than have lost such a worthy councillor." In England, open commendation of More was of course impossible given the political climate, but relics, manuscripts, and letters were gathered by More's Chelsea family circle, especially by More's daughter Margaret Roper, wife of William. In 1557 William wrote the first comprehensive biography of his father-in-law. It did not contain substantial commentary on More's literary works, but Roper praised the man in lavish terms, providing valuable insight into More's character while portraying him as a man of wit, intelligence, good humor, and endless mirth. In 1558 Nicholas Harpsfield wrote the first biography of More to comment at length on the literary works. Although not published until the present century, Harpsfield's study helped set the tone for future evaluations of More the writer: a zealous and disciplined man, eminently fair by nature and champion of truth. The reign of Mary Tudor (1551-58) saw a brief respite in the persecution of Catholics in England, allowing publications of More's collected English works in 1557. This edition appears to have had a wide circulation and likely helped reinforce More's growing reputation as, in the words of Robert Whittington, "a man of an aungels wyt & syngler lernyng." Nevertheless, commentary on More remained strongly partisan throughout the sixteenth century. Edward Hall, a staunch supporter of Henry VIII's political agenda, wrote of More in 1547: "I cannot tell whether I shoulde call him a foolishe wyseman, or a wise foolishman." This sort of ambivalence continues to color evaluations of More today.

Serious criticism of More's literary works alone began early. The first edition of *Utopia* contained letters from leading scholars testifying to the literary merits and social importance of the work. In 1517, the humanist Guillaume Budé wrote regarding *Utopia*: "In his history [*Utopia*] our age and those which succeed it will have a nursery, so to speak, of polite and useful institutions; from which men may borrow customs, and introduce and adapt them each to his own state." Decades later, Stapleton saw in *Utopia* More's "incomparable and almost superhuman wit." Indeed, virtually none of the early commentators found significant fault with *Utopia*. All praised it as a highly imaginative, carefully reasoned model of an ideal state, even if a few early readers failed at first to recognize—as some indeed did—that Utopia existed only in More's mind.

Recently, critics have found themselves less united in their judgments than they once were. Some commentators have noted a disparity between the Catholic More and the Utopian More, with a few Catholics arguing that *Utopia* is a jeu d'esprit, a lighthearted joke. Socialists, on the other hand, have seen the work as an early prototype of refined communist theory. Most scholars agree, however, that the work is serious in most respects and more than just a communist diatribe, that it is designed to circumscribe right behavior from wrong. Yet this leaves the essential nature of good and bad behavior at issue—a matter on which there appears to be little agreement. In the words of Anthony Kenny, "to begin to understand the book—ironic as it is in parts—it is enough to know that it is a product of

the energetic drive for reform characteristic of the best Catholic scholars before the Protestant Reformation made their advocacy of change more qualified and more cautious."

More's other works have always been less known than *Utopia*, but a few of them hold important places in the history of English thought and letters. *The History of King Richard III* is the ultimate source of Shakespeare's *Richard III* (1594?) and the model of the official Tudor view of this period of history. In fact, More's Richard—a cunning, treacherous usurper of the crown, the force behind the murder of the boy princes in the Tower—is, by way of Shakespeare, one of the most celebrated characters in world literature. *A dialog of comfort* is considered a seminal piece in the history of English prose. Its style and sentence structure are at once traditional and progressive, mixing classical syntax and diction with native English elements. On account of this work and others More has been called "the father of English prose." More's controversial writings remain essential sources for the study of Reformation thought and politics. For as the adversary of leading theologians in an age of religious upheaval, More was at the center of earthshattering disputes that are still with us. Today More's works, major and minor alike, are being explored from numerous angles. Scholars have probed More's writings for evidence of women's place in sixteenth-century English society; examined Tudor notions of pleasure as evidenced in *Utopia*; attempted to elucidate More's views concerning private property; compared More with William Langland and Edmund Burke as reforming conservatives; and traced the influence of More's writings on later thinkers. In the end, most commentators would agree with More's friend Colet, who claimed of More: "While the island abounds in distinguished intellects it contains but one true genius."

That More was a genius has never been doubted by serious commentators. His *Utopia* has always been hailed as a great work, and his controversial and devotional writings retain places of honor in the histories of their genres. In 1517 Budé wrote of More: "He is a man of the keenest discernment, of a pleasant disposition, well versed in knowledge of the world." More made his mark in literature, theology, and statecraft. He knew more of the world than most men, but he chose to leave the world rather than live with a circumstance he found repugnant. In the words of Richard Whittington, he was "a man for all seasons."

PRINCIPAL WORKS

**The Lyfe of Johan Picus, Erle of Myrandula, a grete lord of Italy, an excellent conning man in all sciences, and verteous of lyuing* [translator] (biography) 1510

Libellus vere aureus nec minus salutaris quam festiuus de optimo reip. statu, deque noua Insula Vtopia authore clarissimo Thoma Moro (prose) 1516
  [*A fruteful and pleasaunt worke of the beste state of a publyque weale, and of the newe yle called Vtopia*, 1551]

†*A mery gest how a sergeaunt wolde lerne to be a frere* (verse) 1516

‡*Epigrammata clarissimi disertissimqve viri Thomae Mori Britanni, pleraqve e Graecis versa* (poetry) 1518; published in *De optimo reip. statu, deqve noua insula Vtopia*

[*Certain Select Epigrams Translated Out of the Works of Sir Thomas More* (partial translation), 1659]

Thomae Mori epistola ad Germanum Brixium: qui quum Morvs in libellum eius, quo contumeliosis mendacijs incesserat Angliam (essay) 1520

Ervditissimi viri Ferdinandi Barauelli opus elegans, doctum, festiuum, pium, quo pulcherrime retegit, ac refellit insanas Lutheri calumnias [as Ferdinandus Beravellus] (essay) 1523; also published as *Eruditissimi viri Guilielmi Rossei opus elegans, doctum, festiuum, pium, quo pulcherrime retegit, ac refellit insanas Lutheri calumnias* [revised edition, as Guilielmus Rosseus] 1523

A dyaloge of syr Thomas More knyghte, one of the counsayll of oure souerayne lorde the kyng and chancellour of hys duchy of Lancaster, wherin be treatyd dyeurs maters (dialogue) 1529; revised edition, 1530

The Supplycacyon of soulys, Made by Syr Thomas More knyght councellour to our souerayn lorde the Kynge and chaunceller of hys Duchy of Lancaster, agaynst the Supplycacyon of Beggars (essay) 1529

The confutacyon of Tyndales answere made by syr Thomas More knyght (essay) 1532

The apologye of syr Thomas More knyght (essay) 1533

The debellacyon of Salem and Bizance (essay) 1533

A Letter of syr Thomas More knyght impugnynge the erronyouse wrytyng of John Fryth agaynst the blessed sacrament of the aultare (essay) 1533

The second parte of the confutacion of Tyndals answere (essay) 1533

The answere to the fyrst parte of the poysened booke, whych a namelesse heretyke hath named the souper of the lorde (essay) 1534

The Boke of the Fayre Gentylwoman, that no man shulde put his truste, or confidence in, that is to say, Lady Fortune (prose and poetry) 1540

§*Kyng Edward the fifth* (biography) 1543; published in *The Chronicle of John Hardyng*

‖*The Tragical doynges of Kyng Richard the thirde* (biography) 1548; published in *The Vnion of the two noble and illustrate famelies of Lancastre & Yorke*

A dialoge of comfort against tribulacion, made by Syr Thomas More Knyght, and set foorth by the name of an Hungarien (dialogue) 1553; revised edition, 1573

#*A treatice vpon the Passion of Chryste* (essay) 1557; published in *The Workes of Sir Thomas More Knyght*

**The Workes of Sir Thomas More Knyght, sometyme Lorde chauncellour of England, wrytten by him in the Englysh tonge* (essays, biographies, poetry, dialogues, epigrams, letters, and prose) 1557

Thomae Mori, Angliae ornamenti eximii, Lucubrationes, ab innumeris mendis repurgatae: Vtopiae libri II. Progymnasmata. Epigrammata. Ex Luciano conuersa quaedam. Declamatio Lucianicae respondens. Epistolae (essays, poetry, epigrams, prose, and letters) 1563

Epistola, in qua non minus facetè quàm piè, respondet Literis Joannis Pomerani (essay) 1568

††*A Brief Fourme of Confession, Instructing all Christian folke how to confesse their sinnes* (essays and prayers) 1576

Dissertatio epistolica, de aliquot sui temporis Theologastrorum ineptijs (essay) 1625

Epistola Thomae Mori ad Academiam Oxon. (essay) 1633

The Correspondence of Sir Thomas More (letters) 1947

The Yale Edition of the Complete Works of St. Thomas More. 14 vols. (essays, biographies, poetry, dialogues, prayers, epigrams, letters, and prose) 1963-

Sir Thomas More: Neue Briefen (letters) 1966

*The date of the first printing of this work is disputed.

†This work was probably written in 1503.

‡This work was first published in the third edition of *Utopia*.

§A corrected text of this work was published in 1548 as *The pitifull life of kyng Edward the v.* in *The Vnion of the two noble and illustrate famelies of Lancastre & Yorke*. The first authoritative text was published as *The Historie of King Edward the fifth* in 1577 in Raphael Holinshed's *Laste Volume of the Chronicles of England, Scotlande, and Irelande*.

‖This work was written in about 1513 and exists in both an English and a Latin version. A very corrupt text of the English version was published in 1543 in *The Chronicle of John Hardyng*. The first authoritative text of the English version was published as *The History of King Richard the thirde* in 1557 in *The Workes of Sir Thomas More Knyght*. The Latin version, *Historia Richardi regis*, was published in 1565 in *Thomae Mori Angli... Omnia, quae hucusque ad manus nostras peruenerunt, Latina Opera*.

#A Latin continuation of this work was published as *Expositio passionis domini* in 1565 in *Thomae Mori Angli... Omnia, quae hucusque ad manus nostras peruenerunt, Latina Opera*. The Latin version was translated as *St. Thomas More's History of the Passion* in 1941.

**This work contains the fragment known as *The Four Last Things*, begun by More in 1522.

††This work contains selections from More's devotional works.

THOMAS MORE (letter date 1516)

[*In the following excerpt from a letter written to his friend Erasmus in December 1516, More relates his satisfaction at the favorable reception yet afforded* Utopia.]

Master [Cuthbert] Tunstal recently wrote me a most friendly letter. Bless my soul, but his frank and complimentary criticism of my commonwealth [in **Utopia**] has given me more cheer than would an Attic talent. You have no idea how thrilled I am; I feel so expanded, and I hold my head high. For in my daydreams I have been marked out by my Utopians to be their king forever; I can see myself now marching along, crowned with a diadem of wheat, very striking in my Franciscan frock, carrying a handful of wheat as my sacred scepter, thronged by a distinguished retinue of Amaurotians, and, with this huge entourage, giving audience to foreign ambassadors and sovereigns; wretched creatures they are, in comparison with us, as they stupidly pride themselves on appearing in childish garb and feminine finery, laced with that despicable gold, and ludicrous in their purple and jewels and other empty baubles. Yet, I would not want either you or our friend, Tunstal, to judge me by other men, whose character shifts with fortune. Even if heaven has decreed to waft me from my lowly estate to this soaring pinnacle which, I think, defies comparison with that of kings, still you will never find me forgetful of that old friendship I had with you when I was but a private citizen. And if you do not mind making the short trip to visit me in Utopia, I shall definitely see to it that all mortals governed by my kindly rule will show you the honor due to those who, they know, are very dear to the heart of their king.

I was going to continue with this fascinating vision, but the rising Dawn has shattered my dream – poor me! – and shaken me off my throne, and summons me back to the drudgery of the courts. But at least this thought gives me consolation: real kingdoms do not last much longer.

Thomas More, in an extract from a letter to Erasmus on December 4, 1516? in More's "Utopia" and Its Critics, *edited by Ligeia Gallagher, Scott, Foresman and Company, 1964, p. 80.*

GUILLAUME BUDÉ (letter date 1517)

[Budé was a distinguished sixteenth-century French humanist. He corresponded widely with leading thinkers of the age, acted as mentor to François Rabelais, and was instrumental in reviving interest in the classics throughout Europe. Celebrated as he is for his intellectual achievements, he is perhaps best remembered for his love of lavishness: he lived so luxuriously, so extravagantly, that visiting scholars were left aghast by the costly magnificence surrounding him. In the following excerpt from a 1517 letter to his English friend Thomas Lupset, a classicist then resident in Paris, Budé favorably reviews Utopia, *noticing the importance of the work as a model for beneficial living.]*

I owe you many thanks, my learned young friend Lupset, for having sent me Thomas More's *Utopia*, and so drawn my attention to what is very pleasant, and likely to be very profitable, reading. (p. 81)

[More] is a man of the keenest discernment, of a pleasant disposition, well versed in knowledge of the world. I have had the book by me in the country, where my time was taken up with running about and giving directions to workpeople (for you know something, and have heard more, of my having been occupied for more than a twelve-month on business connected with my country-house); and was so impressed by reading it, as I learnt and studied the manners and customs of the Utopians, that I well-nigh forgot, nay, even abandoned, the management of my family affairs. For I perceived that all the theory and practice of domestic economy, all care whatever for increasing one's income, was mere waste of time.

And yet, as all see and are aware, the whole race of mankind is goaded on by this very thing, as if some gadfly were bred within them to sting them. The result is that we must needs confess the object of nearly all legal and civil qualification and training to be this: that with jealous and watchful cunning, as each one has a neighbour with whom he is connected by ties of citizenship, or even at times of relationship, he should be ever conveying or abstracting something from him; should pare away, repudiate, squeeze, chouse, chisel, cozen, extort, pillage, purloin, thieve, filch, rob, and – partly with the connivance, partly with the sanction of the laws—be ever plundering and appropriating. (p. 82)

As for the island of Utopia, which I hear is also called *Udepotia*, it is said (if we are to believe the story), by what must be owned a singular good fortune, to have adopted Christian usages both in public and in private; to have im-

bibed the wisdom thereto belonging; and to have kept it undefiled to this very day. The reason is, that it holds with firm grip to three divine institutions: – namely, the absolute equality, or, if you prefer to call it so, the civil communication, of all things good and bad among fellow-citizens; a settled and unwavering love of peace and quietness; and a contempt for gold and silver. Three things these, which overturn, one may say, all fraud, all imposture, cheating, roguery, and unprincipled deception. Would that Providence, on its own behalf, would cause these three principles of Utopian law to be fixed in the minds of all men by the rivets of a strong and settled conviction. We should soon see pride, covetousness, insane competition, and almost all other deadly weapons of our adversary the Devil, fall powerless; we should see the interminable array of law-books, [the work of] so many excellent and solid understandings, that occupy men till the very day of their death, consigned to bookworms, as mere hollow and empty things, or else given up to make wrapping-paper for shops.

Good heavens! what holiness of the Utopians has had the power of earning such a blessing from above, that greed and covetousness have for so many ages failed to enter, either by force or stealth, into that island alone? that they have failed to drive out from it, by wanton effrontery, justice and honour?

Would that great Heaven in its goodness had dealt so kindly with the countries which keep, and would not part with, the appellation they bear, derived from His most holy name! Of a truth, greed, which perverts and sinks down so many minds, otherwise noble and elevated, would be gone from hence once for all, and the golden age of Saturn would return. In Utopia one might verily suppose that there is a risk of Aratus and the early poets having been mistaken in their opinion, when they made Justice depart from earth, and placed her in the Zodiac. For, if we are to believe Hythloday, she must needs have stayed behind in that island, and not yet made her way to heaven.

But in truth I have ascertained by full inquiry, that Utopia lies outside the bounds of the known world. It is in fact one of the Fortunate Isles, perhaps very close to the Elysian Fields; for More himself testifies that Hythloday has not yet stated its position definitely. It is itself divided into a number of cities, but all uniting or confederating into one state, named Hagnopolis; a state contented with its own customs, its own goods, blest with innocence, leading a kind of heavenly life, on a lower level indeed than heaven, but above the defilements of this world we know, which amid the endless pursuits of mankind, as empty and vain as they are keen and eager, is being hurried in a swollen and eddying tide to the cataract.

It is to Thomas More, then, that we owe our knowledge of this island. It is he who, in our generation, has made public this model of a happy life and rule for leading it, the discovery, as he tells us, of Hythloday: for he ascribes all to him. For while Hythloday has built the Utopians their state, and established for them their rites and customs; while, in so doing, he has borrowed from them and brought home for us the representation of a happy life; it is beyond question More, who has set off by his literary style the subject of that island and its customs. He it is who has perfected, as by rule and square, the City of the

Hagnopolitans itself, adding all those touches by which grace and beauty and weight accrue to the noble work; even though in executing that work he has claimed for himself only a common mason's share. We see that it has been a matter of conscientious scruple with him, not to assume too important a part in the work, lest Hythloday should have just cause for complaint, on the ground of More having plucked the first flowers of that fame, which would have been left for him, if he had himself ever decided to give an account of his adventures to the world. He was afraid, of course, that Hythloday, who was residing of his own choice in the island of Udepotia, might some day come in person upon the scene, and be vexed and aggrieved at this unkindness on his part, in leaving him the glory of this discovery with the best flowers plucked off. To be of this persuasion is the part of good men and wise.

Now while More is one who of himself carries weight, and has great authority to rest upon, I am led to place unreserved confidence in him by the testimony of Peter Giles of Antwerp. Though I have never made his acquaintance in person – apart from recommendations of his learning and character that have reached me – I love him on account of his being the intimate friend of the illustrious Erasmus, who has deserved so well of letters of every kind, whether sacred or profane; with whom personally I have long corresponded and formed ties of friendship.

Farewell, my dear Lupset. Greet for me, at the first opportunity, either by word of mouth or by letter, Linacre, that pillar of the British name in all that concerns good learning; one who is now, as I hope, not more yours than ours. (pp. 84-6)

Greet More also once and again for me, either by message . . . or by word of mouth. As I think and often repeat, Minerva has long entered his name on her selectest album; and I love and revere him in the highest degree for what he has written about this isle of the New World, Utopia.

In his history our age and those which succeed it will have a nursery, so to speak, of polite and useful institutions; from which men may borrow customs, and introduce and adapt them each to his own state. Farewell. (p.86)

> *Guillaume Budé, in a letter to Thomas Lupset on July 31, 1517, in More's 'Utopia' and Its Critics, edited by Ligeia Gallagher, Scott, Foresman and Company, 1964, pp. 81-6.*

ERASMUS (letter date 1519)

[*A Dutch humanist, Erasmus is considered one of the greatest thinkers of the sixteenth century. He wrote extensively on the burning political and social issues of his time, although he never took a decided stand on the Reformation. He knew More personally—the two first met in England in 1499, fully thirty years before More succeeded Wolsey as Lord Chancellor— corresponded with More when they were apart, and promoted More's works and reputation on the Continent. Their friendship was, according to E. E. Reynolds, one that "quickly passed into legend." In the following excerpt from a 1519 letter to the German humanist Ulrich von Hutten, written in response to the recipient's request for a biographical sketch of More, Erasmus commends More's character and erudition, noting as well the intent and style of Utopia.*]

Most illustrious Hutten, you are not alone in the sympathetic understanding, this near-passion, which you bear the talented Thomas More. Many others are moved by the qualities of erudition and true humor which you note in his writing, and in your case the admiration is fully returned. The great pleasure he takes in your work is enough to inspire one to jealousy. It must be an instance of that wisdom of Plato which is the most desirable, possessing as it does a capacity to fire man beyond that of even the most exalted external beauty. Sight is not the exclusive province of the body; the mind's eye too is susceptible to what the Greeks epitomized as love at first sight. Thus it is that men who have never actually exchanged a single word or glance can sometimes become affectionately attached to one another. The appreciation of beauty varies according to the individual and this is true, too, of taste in mind and person— some afford us a relish which others simply cannot inspire; it is as though like minds shared a special affinity.

Your request for a complete picture of More leaves me wishing that my ability to draw him (at full length) could do honor to your sincere entreaty. Time spent in considering so wonderful a friend can only be pleasurable. But it is not every man who can catch the complete More and he may well be particular about the artist for whom he sits. Truly, I cannot imagine More an easier subject than Alexander the Great or Achilles, for his claim to immortality can be no less than theirs. The artistry of an Apelles is here called for, while my strokes, I fear, more closely approximate those of Fulvius or Rutuba, gladiators both. Yet I will attempt a rough sketch based upon the recollection of my intimacy with him during my visits. If you ever chance to encounter him while on foreign service, I fear you will quickly discover what a talentless artist you have charged with this task; you will denounce me as a jealous blindman for offering such a meager account of so many merits. (p. 287)

There is no occurrence, however grave, in which [More] is unable to find some delight. The quickness of the bright and learned fires his admiration, while the folly of the dull and unlearned often affords simple amusement. The wonderful flexibility of his taste allows him to tolerate even jesters. The light banter of his own wit encompasses the fair sex, extending even to his own wife. Another Democritus, you could call him, or more properly, a new Pythagorean philosopher, easily surveying the confusion and commerce of the marketplace. (pp. 289-90)

He had plunged into literature early in life and even in his youth pursued both Greek letters and philosophy. Instead of applauding these efforts, his father, a lawyer by profession, cut off his allowance and nearly disinherited the boy for abandoning the traditional family profession. Now the relationship of law to true learning is extremely vague, but its study does yield both position and the truest path to fame and fortune among Englishmen. Certainly, no mean number of their peers derive from its ranks, and excellence in the field is held to be possible only after years of intense devotion. His inclination toward the finer things could hardly dispose our young friend to undertake such study. In spite of all this, his acuteness and intellectual capacity enabled him to master the subject thoroughly, even after his excursion into the schools, and he quickly surpassed those preoccupied solely with the law in both earnings and volume of practice.

The Sacred Fathers, too, received a share of his attentive energy. While still a young man he delivered well-attended lectures on Augustine's *De Civitate Dei.* Old men and priests neither disdained nor regretted their lessons from the young layman. He concentrated diligently upon such religious disciplines as vigils, fasts, and prayers, also, for he was considering the priesthood. This display of wisdom contrasts favorably with the common practice of plunging headlong into an exacting vocation without the precaution of prior trials. He nearly took orders, but the attractions of marriage proved so strong that he determined to be a chaste husband rather than a lewd priest. (p. 290)

He sat for some years as a civil judge in his native city of London. This is a prestigious post involving few duties (meeting as it does only on Thursdays and only before dinner). No judge has disposed of so many cases or surpassed his unimpeachable integrity. It was even his practice to waive the fixed three-shilling fee customarily assessed against both parties to a suit. Such conduct earned him an enviable reputation in the city. It was his decision to rest content in this situation, offering as it did both dignity and protection from public hazard.

He had several times been pressed into service on embassies and his skill in these missions has so impressed King Henry VIII that that monarch could not sit still until he had dragged More to his court. I must say, literally, "dragged" because no one has ever been as eager to get into court as More was to stay out of it. That prince, however, was intent upon establishing about him a circle of learned, serious, intelligent, and honest men, and his most insistent choice was More, with whom he is now so close that he can hardly endure his absence.

There is no wiser counselor for grave matters nor is there an easier companion in pleasant conversation. More provides discreet handling of delicate situations, offering mutually satisfactory solutions. And the man cannot be bribed. What a boon for the world if only Mores were installed as magistrates! (pp. 291-92)

Let us consider those studies which drew More and myself together. Poetry was the chief concern of his early years. He then struggled to perfect his prose style, working in every form. The results of this endeavor are familiar especially to such as you who always have his books in your hands. Declamations were his favorite exercise, especially those on unresolved subjects, which presented the most intricate challenge to the mind.

Thus, while yet a lad he undertook a dialogue in defense of Plato's principle of complete community, including wife-sharing! He framed a reply to Lucian's *Tyrannicide,* requesting me to provide the opposition, so that he could check his development in that type of writing. In his *Utopia,* he proposed to illustrate the source and spring of political evil, with a special eye toward the England which he knows so well. The recognizable unevenness of style results from the manner and method of its composition. He wrote the second book at a leisurely pace, and then recognizing the need for it, hastily added the first.

He is an unparalleled extempore speaker, marrying the most apt thought to the most felicitous language. His mind seizes and foresees all that is at issue, and his completely furnished memory quickly provides whatever ma-

terial is needed. One strains one's imagination to envision a sharper disputant, and he often beards the most distinguished theologians in their own dens. John Colet, possessed of a sharp and incisive judgment, is given to saying that while the island abounds in distinguished intellects it contains but one true genius. (pp. 292-93)

Here, then, is my poor portrait, whose subject shames its artist. You will be even unhappier with it should you chance to meet its subject firsthand. I have at least undone your accusation of neglect and undercut your criticism about the brevity of my letters, though even this one seemed short in the writing and will, I trust, not seem overlong in the reading either; our More's sweetness will see to that.... (pp. 293-94)

> *Erasmus, in an extract from a letter to Ulrich von Hutton in 1519, in* The Essential Thomas More, *edited by James J. Greene and John P. Dolan, New American Library, 1967, pp. 286-94.*

ROBERT WHITTINTON (essay date 1520)

[*Whittinton (or, more commonly, Whittington) was a Tudor grammarian. He is best known as the author of* Vulgaria Roberti Whitintoni Lichfeldiensis et de institutione grammaticulorum Opusculum *(1520), a Latin grammar for boys that is valued today as a mirror of sixteenth-century manners and school life. It is likely that Whittinton knew More personally, if not intimately, through a Court preferment. In the following excerpt from* Vulgaria, *Whittinton sets out four phrases about More to be used as exercises in Latin grammar. The last phrase, concerning More's mental character, is the source of the famous characterization of More as "a man for all seasons."*]

Moore is a man of an aungels wyt / & syngler lernyng. Grammaticus loquendi modus. Morus est vir diuini ingenij / & singularis (vel egregie) eruditionis. Oratorius. Morus est vir mirando ingenio / et prestantissima eruditione. Historicus.
Morus est vir preclarus ingenio / et eruditione. Poeticus. Morus est vir prestans ingenij. &c.
Modus oratorius est venustior ceteris / & frequentior: quare huic sepius est innitendum nisi historias scribas / aut poemata.
He is a man of many excellent vertues (yf I shold say as it is) I knowe not his felowe.
Est enim vir claris virtutibus (vt facessat assentatio) qualem haud noui alterum.
For where is the man (in whome is so many goodly vertues) of y¹ gentylnes / lowlynes / and affabylyte.
Ubinam est vir (in quo tante coruscant virtutes) ea benignitate. comitate. ea denique affabilitate.
And as tyme requyreth / a man of meruelylous myrth and pastymes / & somtyme of as sad grauyte / as who say. a man for all seasons. (p. 64)

> *Robert Whittinton, "Vulgaria Roberti Whitintoni Lichfeldiensis," in* The Vulgaria of John Stanbridge and the Vulgaria of Robert Whittinton, *edited by Beatrice White, Kegan Paul, Trench, Trubner & Co. Ltd., 1932, pp. 31-128.*

THOMAS MORE (epitaph date 1532)

[*More wrote his own epitaph, two versions of which are known to have survived. One, in Latin verse, is inscribed on the More tomb in Chelsea old church. The other, in prose, More sent to Erasmus in 1532. According to R. W. Cham-*

bers, "that More wished his prose epitaph . . . to have wide currency among his humanist friends is shown by his having sent a copy to Erasmus—which meant publication." In this prose epitaph, printed below, More offers a succinct self-evaluation.]

Thomas More was born of an honest but undistinguished family in London; he concerned himself to a certain extent in literary efforts; in his youth, after several years as an advocate in the law courts, and having held the office of Under-Sheriff in his native city, he was admitted to the court of the invincible king, Henry VIII, the only king ever to have merited by pen and sword the title of Defender of the Faith; he was received at court, elected to the king's council, knighted, appointed Undertreasurer, Chancellor of Lancaster, and finally Chancellor of England by special royal favor. During this time he was elected Speaker of the House of Commons; in addition, he served as royal ambassador at different times and in a variety of places, the last of which was at Cambrai as an associate and colleague of Cuthbert Tunstall, at that time Bishop of London and soon thereafter Bishop of Durham, a man whose peer in learning, wisdom, and virtue is seldom seen in this world today. There he witnessed as ambassador, to his great joy, the renewal of a peace treaty between the supreme monarchs of Christendom and also the restoration of a long-desired world peace, which peace may the Lord confirm and perpetuate. Such was his conduct while holding these offices that his excellent sovereign at no time found fault with him; he was neither disdained by the nobility nor unpleasant to the populace; rather he was a molester of thieves, murderers, and heretics. His father, John More, was a knight selected by the king as a member of a group of judges known as the King's Bench; he was affable, pleasant, innocent, mild, merciful, honest and upright. Though advanced in age, he was exceptionally vigorous for his time of life; having witnessed the elevation of his son to the chancellorship of England, he considered his stay on earth complete and willingly departed this world for heaven. The son had throughout the lifetime of the father been compared with him and was called the young More, a fact that he found agreeable; now with the loss of his father, as he considered his four children and eleven grandchildren, he began in his own mind to grow old. This feeling was increased by a chest ailment that appeared soon thereafter as a sign of advancing age. Sated with the transient things of this life, he resigned his office, and through the incomparable kindness of the most indulgent prince, may God favor his undertakings, he finally arrived at what had been, almost since childhood, the object of his desires, to have the last years of his life free to gradually retire from mundane affairs and meditate upon the eternity of the life hereafter. He then arranged for the construction of this tomb as a constant reminder of ever approaching death and had the bones of his first wife transferred here. Lest he may have erected this tomb in vain while yet living, and lest he tremble with fear at the thought of advancing death instead of going forth to meet it gladly with a longing for Christ, and that he may find death not really a death for himself but rather the door to a happier life, I beg you, kind reader, pray for him while still he lives and when he is dead. (pp. 285-86)

> *Sir Thomas More, "More's Epitaph," in* The Essential Thomas More, *edited by James J. Greene and John P. Dolan, New American Library, 1967, pp. 285-86.*

SIR THOMAS MORE (essay date 1533)

[*In the following excerpt from his* Apology, *More explains why he wrote his controversial works and defends himself against charges that he handled his critics unfairly.*]

So well stand I not (I thank God), good reader, in mine own conceit, and thereby so much in mine own light, but that I can somewhat with equal judgment and an even eye behold and consider both myself and mine own. Nor I use not to follow the condition of Aesop's ape, that thought her own babes so beauteous and so far passing in all goodly feature and favor, nor the crow that accounted her own birds the fairest of all the fowls that flew.

But like as some (I see well) there are that can somewhat less than I, that yet for all that put out their works in writing, so am I not so blind upon the other side but that I very well perceive very many so far in wit and erudition above me, that in such matter as I have anything written, if other men, as many would have taken it in hand as could have done it better, it might much better have become me to let the matter alone than by writing to presume anything to meddle therewith.

And, therefore, good reader, since I so well know so many men so far excel and pass me in all such things as are required in him that might adventure to put his works abroad, to stand and abide the judgment of all other men; I was never so far overseen as either to look or hope that such faults as in my writing should by mine oversight escape me, could by the eyes of all other men pass forth unspied, but shortly should be both by good and well-learned perceived, and among so many bad brethren as I wist well would be wroth with them, should be both sought out and sifted to the uttermost flake of bran and largely thereupon controlled and reproved.

But yet against all this fear this one thing recomforted me, that since I was of one point very fast and sure that such things as I write are consonant unto the common Catholic faith and determinations of Christ's Catholic Church, and are clear confutations of false, blasphemous heresies by Tyndale and Barnes put forth unto the contrary, any great fault and intolerable should they none find, of such manner, sort, and kind as the readers should in their souls perish and be destroyed by, of which poisoned faults mine adversaries' books be full.

Now will I begin with that point that I most esteem. For of all the remnant of his opponents against him may I little count. But surely loath would I be to misrehearse any man's reason against whom I write, or to rehearse him slenderly. And in that point undoubtedly they see full well themselves that they say not true. For there is no reason that I rehearse of Tyndale's or of Friar Barnes' either but that I use the contrary manner therein that Tyndale useth with mine. For he rehearseth mine in every place faintly and falsely too, and leaveth out the pith and the strength and the proof that most maketh for the purpose. And he fareth therein as if there were one that, having day of challenge appointed in which he should wrestle with his adversary, would find the means by craft to get his adversary before the day into his own hands, and there keep him and diet him with such a thin diet that at the day he bringeth him forth feeble, faint, and famished and almost hunger starven, and so lean that he can scant stand on his legs; and then is it easy, ye wote well, to give the sely soul a fall. And yet when Tyndale hath done all this, he taketh the fall himself.

But every man may well see that I never use that way with Tyndale nor with any of these folk; but I rehearse their reason to the best that they can make it themselves, and I rather enforce it and strength it of mine own than take any part of theirs therefrom.

And this use I not only in such places as I do not rehearse all their own words (for that is not requisite in every place), but I use it also in such places besides, as of all their own words I leave not one syllable out. For such darkness use they purposely, and Tyndale in especially, that except I took some pain to set out their arguments plainly, many that read them should little wit what they mean. . . .

Howbeit, glad would I have been if it might have been much more short, for then should my labor have been so much the less. But they will, if they be reasonable men, consider in themselves that it is a shorter thing and sooner done to write heresies than to answer them. For the most foolish heretic in a town may write more false heresies in one leaf than the wisest man in the whole world can well and conveniently by reason and authority soil and confute in forty. Now when that Tyndale not only teacheth false heresies, but furnisheth his errors also with pretense of reason and Scripture, and instead of reason sometimes with blunt subtleties and rude riddles too, the making open and lightsome to the reader the dark writing of him that would not by his will be well perceived, hath put me to more labor and length in answering than some men would per adventure have been content to take.

And I sometimes take the pains to rehearse some one thing in divers fashions in more places than one, because I would that the reader should in every place where he fortuneth to fall in reading have at his hand, without remitting over elsewhere, or labor of further seeking for it, as much as shall seem requisite for the matter that he there hath in hand. And therein the labor of all that length is mine own, for ease and shortening of the reader's pain.

Now come I to them that say I handle Tyndale and Frith and Barnes ungoodly and with uncomely words, calling them by the name of heretics and fools, and so use them in words as though the men had neither wit nor learning; whereas it cannot be denied (they say) but that they be such as every man knoweth well have both.

As for wit and learning, I nowhere say that any of them have none, nor I mean no further but for the matters of their heresies. And in the treating of those they show so little wit or learning either that the more they have, the more appeareth the feebleness of their part and the false-hood of their heresies, if they have any great wit or any great learning indeed, and then for all that, in the defend-ing of those matters with such foolish handling so shame-fully confound themselves.

Howbeit of very truth, God, upon such folk as having wit and learning fall wilfully from faith to false heresy, sho-weth his wrath and indignation with a more vengeance in some part than (as some doctors say) he doth upon the devil himself. For (as divers doctors hold opinion) the fiends be fallen from grace, and therefore have lost their glory, yet God hath suffered them to keep their gifts of na-

ture still, as wit, beauty, strength, agility, and such other like. (pp. 224-27)

[They] that would have builded up the Tower of Babylon for themselves against God had such a stop thrown upon them that suddenly none understood what another said, surely so God upon these heretics of our time that go busi-ly about to heap up to the sky their foul, filthy dunghill of all old and new false, stinking heresies, gathered up to-gether against the true Catholic faith of Christ, that him-self hath ever hitherto taught his true Catholic Church; God, I say, who, when the apostles went about to preach the true faith, sent down his own Holy Spirit of unity, concord, and truth unto them with the gift of speech and understanding, so that they understood every man and ev-ery man understood them, hath reared up and sent among these heretics the spirit of error and lying, of discord and of division, the damned devil of hell, which so entangleth their tongues and so distempereth their brains that they neither understand well one of them another, nor any of them well himself.

And this that I here say, who so list to read my books shall find it so true and so plainly proved in many places that he shall well see and say that this is the thing which in my writing grieveth this blessed brotherhood a little more than the length.

And, therefore, where they find the fault that I handle these folk so foul, how could I other do? For while I de-clare and show their writing to be such (as I needs must, or leave the most necessary points of all the matter un-touched), it were very hard for me to handle it in such wise, as when I plainly prove them abominable heretics and against God and his sacraments and saints very blas-phemous fools, they should wene that I speak them fair.

But I perceive well that these good brethren look that I should rebuke the clergy and seek out their faults and lay them to their faces and write some work to their shame, or else they cannot call me but partial to the priests. How-beit, by this reason they may call me partial to the laymen too. For I never used that way neither toward the one nor the other. I find not yet such plenty and store of virtue in myself as to think it a meetly part and convenient for me to play, to rebuke as abominable, vicious folk anyone's honest company, either spiritual or temporal, and much less meet to rebuke and reproach either the whole spiritu-alty or temporalty, because of such as are very stark nought in both. (pp. 228-29)

[Look] at my **Dialogue,** my **Supplication of Souls,** and both the parts of the **Confutation,** and ye shall clearly see that I neither have used toward the clergy nor toward the tem-poralty any warm, displeasant word, but have forborne to touch in special either the faults of the one or of the other. But yet have I confessed the thing that truth is: neither part to be faultless. But then, which is the thing that offen-deth these blessed brethren, I have not letted, furthermore, to say the thing which I take also for very true, that as this realm of England hath had hitherto, God be thanked, as good and as laudable a temporalty, number for number, as hath had any other Christian region of the quantity, so hath it had also, number for number, compared with any realm Christened of no greater quantity, as good and as commendable a clergy, though there have never lacked in any of both the parts plenty of such as have always been nought; whose faults have ever been their own, and not to be imputed to the whole body, neither of spiritualty nor temporalty, saving that there have been peradventure on either part, in some such as by their offices ought to look thereto, some lack of the labor and diligence that in the re-forming of it should have belonged unto them, which I de-clare always that I would wish amended, and every man specially labor to mend himself and rather accustom him-self to look upon his own faults than upon other men's.... (pp. 230-31)

Now come I to the last fault that the brethren find in my books. For as for one more that was showed me within this seven night, I not so much esteem as to vouchsafe to answer, that is, to wit, where they reprove that I bring in among the most earnest matters, fancies and sports and merry tales. For as Horace sayeth, a man may sometimes say full soth in game. And one that is but a layman, as I am, it may better happely become him merrily to tell his mind than seriously and solemnly to preach. And over this I can scant believe that the brethren find any mirth in my books. For I have not much heard that they very merrily read them.

And therefore, good Christian readers, as for such further things as I have in my said preface [to *Confutation of Tyn-dale's Answer*] promised, I propose to pursue at some oth-er further leisure. But first I think it better to bestow some time upon another thing, and leaving for a while both de-fense of mine own faults and finding of other men's in writing, think better to bestow some time about the mend-ing of mine own in living, which is a thing now for many men more necessary than is writing. For of new bookmak-ers there are now more than enough. Wherefore that all such as will write may have the grace to write well, or at the least wise none other purpose than to mean well, and as well writers as others to amend our own faults and live well, I beseech almighty God to grant us, and that all folk spiritual and temporal in this world living, and all good Christian souls departed hence and yet not out of pain, may for grace every part pray for other, and all the blessed, holy saints in heaven, both here for grace and there for glory, pray to God for us all. Amen. (pp. 235-36)

> *Sir Thomas More, "The Apology of Sir Thomas More," in* The Essential Thomas More, *edited by James J. Greene and John P. Dolan, New Ameri-can Library, 1967, pp. 223-36.*

EDWARD HALL (essay date 1547?)

[*An English historian and lawyer, Hall was one of Henry VIII's most committed supporters and an unrelenting cham-pion of the house of Tudor. He was under-sheriff of London at the time of More's execution and may have been present at the scaffold. Because of his strongly partisan position, most commentators consider Hall a hostile witness in mat-ters relating to More. In the following excerpt from his his-tory of the reign of Henry VIII, he acknowledges More's eru-dition while questioning his wisdom.*]

[More was] a manne well learned in the toungues, and also in the Common Lawe, whose wytte was fine, and full of imaginacions, by reason wherof, he was to muche geven to mockinge, whyche was to his gravitie a great blemishe. (p. 158)

[He] was lorde Chauncelor of England, and in that tyme a great persecutor of suche as detested the supremacy of the byshop of Rome, whiche he himselfe so highly favored that he stoode to it till he was brought to the Skaffolde on the Tower hyll where on a blocke his head was striken from his shoulders and had no more harme. I cannot tell whether I shoulde call him a foolishe wyseman, or a wise foolishman, for undoubtedly he beside his learnyng, had a great witte, but it was so myngled with tauntyng and mockyng, that it semed to them that best knew him, that he thought nothing to be wel spoken except he had minis-tred some mocke in the communicacion.... (p. 265)

> *Edward Hall, "The Twenty-First Year" and "The Twenty-Eighth Year," in his* Henry VIII, *T. C. & E. C. Jack, 1904, pp. 150-76, 268-78.*

WILLIAM ROPER (essay date 1557)

[*An English biographer, Roper is remembered for a single literary work:* The Mirrour of Vertue in Worldly Greatness; or, The Life of Syr Thomas More Knight. *As a boarder and later as More's son-in-law, Roper was a member of the More household for sixteen years. There he became his father-in-law's confidant and grew to know him intimately—"no one man living ... of him and of his doings understood so much as myself," Roper claimed. Roper set down his remem-brances and impressions of More in 1557, more than twenty years after his father-in-law's death. As the first full-length biography of More and as a firsthand account,* The Life *is valued for the light it sheds on More's character and for the glimpses it provides of More's mind. The following excerpt is in two parts. In the first, Roper praises More's eloquence and learning. In the second, conceived by Roper as the work's epilogue, Roper records Charles V's assessment of More's character as related to Sir Thomas Elyot. According to James Mason Cline, "Roper desired that this final epi-sode should, after the manner of a saint's legend, draw up the separate energies of all others within itself, and by its single impact express the whole life of More."*]

This Sir Thomas More, among all other his virtues, was of such meekness that if it had fortuned him with any learned men resorting to him from Oxford, Cambridge, or elsewhere, as there did divers—some for desire of his ac-quaintance, some for the famous report of his wisdom and learning, and some for suits of the Universities—to have entered into argument (wherein few were comparable unto him) and so far to have discoursed with them therein that he might perceive they could not without some inconve-nience hold out much further disputation against him; then, lest he should discomfort them—as he that sought not his own glory, but rather would seem conquered than to discourage students in their studies, ever showing him-self more desirous to learn than to teach—would he by some witty device courteously break off into some other matter and give over.

Of whom, for his wisdom and learning, had the King such an opinion, that at such time as he attended upon his Highness, taking his progress either to Oxford or Cam-bridge, where he was received with very eloquent orations, his Grace would always assign him—as one that was prompt and ready therein—*ex tempore* to make answer thereunto. Whose manner was, whensoever he had occa-sion either here or beyond the [seas] to be in any universi-ty, not only to be present at the reading and disputations there commonly used, but also learnedly to dispute among them himself. Who, being Chancellor of the Duchy, was made ambassador twice—joined in commission with Cardinal Wolsey; once to the Emperor Charles into Flanders, the other time to the French king into France. (pp. 28-9)

• • • • •

[Soon after Sir Thomas More's] death came intelligence thereof to the Emperor Charles. Whereupon he sent for Sir Thomas Elyot, our English Ambassador, and said unto him: "My Lord Ambassador, we understand that the King, your master, hath put his faithful servant, and grave, wise councillor, Sir Thomas More, to death." Whereunto Sir Thomas Elyot answered that he understood nothing thereof.

"Well," said the Emperor, "it is too true. And this will we say, that if we had been master of such a servant, of whose doings ourself have had these many years no small experience, we would rather have lost the best city of our dominions than have lost such a worthy councillor!" Which matter was by the same Sir Thomas Elyot to myself, to my wife, to Master Clement and his wife, to Master John Heywood and his wife, and unto divers other his friends accordingly reported. (p. 86)

> *William Roper, in his* The Lyfe of Sir Thomas Moore, Knighte, *edited by James Mason Cline, The Swallow Press, 1950, 120 p.*

NICHOLAS HARPSFIELD   (essay date 1558)

[*Harpsfield was an English essayist, theologian, and biographer who is remembered as a staunch champion of Roman Catholicism. For his religious beliefs he was imprisoned in* the Fleet *in 1559, where he appears to have remained until his death in 1575. Earlier, around 1558, Harpsfield wrote what proved to be one of the major biographies of Thomas More:* The Life and Death of Sir Thomas More, Knight. *Although not published until 1932, this work circulated widely in manuscript and was instrumental in promoting More's reputation as a Catholic martyr. Harpsfield's* Life of More *is avowedly based on William Roper's* The Mirrour of Vertue in Worldly Greatnes; or, The Life of Syr Thomas More Knight *(see excerpt dated 1557); indeed, Roper wrote his work for Harpsfield's benefit, believing Harpsfield to be the man best qualified for the role of "official" biographer of More. Here, Harpsfield offers a highly favorable overview of More's major works.*]

[It remayneth nowe] that we speake somewhat of [Sir Thomas More's] bookes, whereby he hath consecrate his woorthy name to immortalitie in this transitorie worlde to the worldes ende. And I doubt not, for his great paines and trauell therein, especially for Gods sake, to whom he had his principall respect, he hath receaued his condigne reward in the celestiall worlde that neuer shall haue ende. Whereof some are written in latin onely, [some in English onely], some certaine in both tonges. (p. 100)

Among other his latine bookes are his **Epigrammes,** partly translated out of greeke, partly so wittily and pleasauntly deuised and penned of his owne, as they may seeme to be nothing inferiour or to yelde to any of like kinde written in our dayes; And perchaunce woorthy to be sett and compared with many like wryters of the olde [forerun] dayes. These **Epigrammes**, as they be learned and pleasaunt, so are they nothing byting or contumelious.

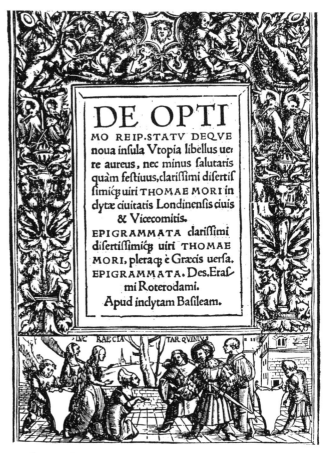

Title page of the March 1518 edition of Utopia, *the first to contain More's* Epigrammata.

Howbeit certaine merie conceyted Epigrammes that he made of Germanus Brixius, a frenche man, vntruely and falsely setting forth and aduauncing the valiant doinges of the frenche captaine, Herueus, by the Sea against the englishe men, so incensed the saide Brixius, albeit the thinges that Sir Thomas More wrate were true, and yet written in the time of hostilitie and warre, that he wrote a very spitefull booke against the saide Sir Thomas More, and so farre forgott himselfe that he went about, as farre as in him laye, to bring him in discredite with king Henry the eight as one that was the kinges enemie. And so when the kinges were at peace, Brixius longe after beganne with Master More his newe and cruell warre. His booke he intituled *Antimorus,* which Master More aunswered [in **Epistola ad German. Brixium.**] And albeit he had a great deale the better hande against Brixius, and that not onely by censure and judgement of Erasmus, Brixius great frende, but many other learned men Brixius frendes also, yet at the desire of Erasmus, and vpon sight of his letters, he stayed all his bookes, newly printed, from further sale, and recouered into his handes some copyes that his frendes had, to supresse them. So much of Brixius, which I haue the sooner planted in here because I knowe Master More is herein by some Protestant*es* noted and slaundered.

He wrote also most elegantly and eloquently **The Life of Kinge Richarde the Thirde**, not only in englishe, which booke is abroade in printe, but corrupted and vitiated, but in latine also, not yet printed. He did not perfect and finish the same booke, neyther any sithens durst take vpon him to sett his hande to the penne to finishe it, [either] in the one or other tonge, all men being deterred and driuen from that enterprise by reason of the incomparable excellencie of the saide worke; As all other painters were afraide in the olde time to supplye and perfect the image of Venus painted, but imperfectly, by Apelles, for his excellent workmanshipp therein.

But the booke that beareth the pricke and price of all his other latine bookes of wittie inuention, for prophane matters, is his *Utopia*. He painteth me it forth so liuely and so pleasauntly, as it were an exquisite platforme, paterne and example of a singuler good common wealth, as to the same neyther the Lacedemonians, nor the Athenienses, nor yet, the best of all other, the Romanes common wealth, is comparable; [full] pretily and probably deuising the said common wealth to be in one of the countreys of the newe founde landes declared vnto him at Antwerpe by Hithlodius, a Portingall, and one of the Sea companions of Americus Vespusius, that first sought out and founde these landes; such an excellent and absolute state of common wealth that, sauing the people were vnchristned, might seeme to passe any state and common wealth, I will not say of the olde nations by me rehearsed, but euen of any other euen in our time.

Many great learned men, as Budaeus and Johannes Paludanus, [seemed to take the same storie as a true storie. And Paludanus] vpon a feruent zeale wisshed that some excellent diuines might be sent thither to preache Christes Gospell; yea, then were here amonge vs at home sundry good men and learned diuines very desirous to take that voyage, to bring that people to Christes fayth, whose maners they did so well like vpon. And surely this saide iollye inuention of S*ir* Thomas More seemed to beare a good countenaunce of truth, not onely for the credite M*aster* More was in with the worlde, but euen for that about that time many straunge and vnknowen nations and many conclusions were discouered, such as our forefathers did neither knowe nor beleeue; it was by most certaine experience found, especially by the wonderfull nauigation of *nauis* called Victoria that sayled the world rounde about, that shippes sayle bottome to bottome, and that there be Antipodes, that is to say, that walke foote against foote; which thing Lactantius and others doo flatlye denye, laughing them to scorne that did so write. Againe, it is certainly founde that there is vnder the Zodiacke (where Aristotle and others say that for the immoderate and excessiue heate is no habitation) most pleasaunt and temperate dwelling and the most fruitfull countreys of all the world. These and other considerations cause[d] many wise, learned men nothing lesse to mistrust that this had beene nothing but an inuentiue drifte of S*ir* Thomas Mores owne imagination and head, but tooke it for a very sure knowen story. Wherein they were deceaued by M*aster* More, as wise and [as] well learned as they were; as Zeu[x]is the Painter was in the olde time, notwithstanding he painted grapes so liuely and exquisitely that the birdes came to picke vpon them as vpon very grapes in deede. But when Parrhasius, another exquisite Painter, had shewed him a certaine table, wherin he had painted a vaile or curtin: "Take away," quoth Zeu[x]is, "this vaile and curtin, that I may see your painting it selfe." Wherat Parrhasius fell vpon a great laughter, saying: "Yesterday thou didst deceaue the birdes, but this day I haue deceaued thee, as cun-

ning a painter as thou art." For in deede it was no curtaine, but a table so artificially painted that it seemed to Zeu[x]is a very curtaine.

In this booke, among other thinges, he hath a very goodlye processe howe there might be fewer theeues in Inglande, and a meruailous inopinable probleme of sheepe: that whereas men were wont to eate the sheepe, as they doo in other countreys, nowe contrarywise sheepe in Inglande pitifully doo deuoure man, woman and childe, houses, yea, and Townes withall.

And like a moste thankefull man, he maketh honorable mention of Cardinall Morton, Archbisshopp of Caunterbury and Lorde Chauncellour of Inglande, In whose house . . . him selfe in his tender youth was brought vp; Albeit it be by the dissembled name of the saide Hithlodius, whom he imagineth to haue bene in Inglande, and to haue beene acquainted with the saide Cardinall.

And as this booke in his kinde is singuler and excellent, conteyning and prescribing a common wealth farre passing the common wealthes deuised and instituted by Licurgus, Solon, Numa Pompilius, Plato and diuers other; so wrate he in another kinde and sort a booke against Luther no lesse singuler and excellent [*Responsio ad Lutherum*]. King Henry the eight had written a notable erudite booke against Luthers booke *de captiuitate Babilonica*, most euidently and mightily refuting his shamefull, vile heresies against the Catholike faith and Christes holy Sacramentes; which did so greeue and yrke Luther to the very hart, that hauing no good substantiall matter to helpe himselfe withall, he fell to scoffing and sawcie iesting in his aunswere to the king*es* booke, vsing almost nothing els throughout his aunswere but the faire figure of rhetorike called sawce mallepert, and playeth the very varlett with the king. To whom S*ir* Thomas More made a Replye, and so doth discipher and open his wretched, vile handlinge of the sacred Scripture, his monstrous opinions, and manifest and manifolde contradictions, that neyther he nor any of his generation durst euer after putt penne to the booke to encounter and [re]ioyne with his Replye. In the which aunswere, beside the deepe and profounde debating of the matter it selfe, he so dresseth him with his owne scoffing and iesting rhethoricke as he woorthelye deserued. But because this kinde of wryting, albeit a meete cover for suche a cupp, and very necessary to represse and beate him with his owne follye, according to Scripture, *Responde stulto secundum stultitiam eius*, seemed not very agreable and correspondent to his saide grauitie and dignitie, the booke was sett forth vnder the name of one Gulielmus Rosseus onely, suppressing his owne name.

He made also in latine another proper and wittie Treatise [*Epistola contra J. Pomeranum*] printed against a certaine epistle of John Pomerane, one of Luthers standerdbearers in Germanie.

And after he was shutt vp in the towre, he wrote a certaine exposition in latine vpon the passion of Christe [*Expositio passionis Domini*], not yet printed, which was not perfited, and is so plainly and exquisitely translated into Englishe by his foresaide Neece, mistris Bassett, that it may seeme originally to haue beene penned in Englishe by S*ir* Thomas More himselfe.

Some other thinges he wrate also in latin which we praetermitt, and will nowe somewhat talke of his englishe workes; w*hich* all, beside the translation of John Picus, erle of Mirandula [*The Life of Pico della Mirandula*], and the foresaide life of king Richarde, and some other fewe prophane thinges, concerne matters of religion for the most part.

The first booke of this sort was his booke[s] of dialogues [*A Dialogue Concernynge heresyes and matters of religion*], made by him when he was Chauncello*ur* of the duchie of Lancaster: which bookes occasioned him afterwarde (as, according to the olde prouerbe, one busines begetteth another) to write diuers other thinges; for whereas he had amongst many other matters touched and reproued Wil*li*am Tindalls adulterate and vitiate translation of the newe Testament, Tindall, not able to beare to see his newe religion and his owne doinges withall to haue so fowle an ouerthrowe as S*ir* Thomas More gaue him, after great and longe deliberation and consultation with his euangelicall brethre*n*, tooke in hande to aunswere some part of his saide dialogues, especially touching his foresaide corrupt translation. But what small woorshipp he wanne thereby, i[t] is eathe for euery man to see, that with indifferent affection will vouchsafe to reade S*ir* Thomas Mores Replye [*Confutation of Tyndales Answere*]. . . . taste. (pp. 100-08)

[Now] we will note vnto you the integritie, the sinceritie and vprightnes, the good and gratious nature and disposition, of the saide S*ir* Thomas More in his wryting, not onely against Tindall, but generally against all other Protestantes. First then it is to be considered in him that he doth not, as many wryters doo against the aduersaries, and all the Protestantes doo against him and other Catholikes, writhe and wrest their wordes to the woorst, and make their reasons more weake and feeble then they are; but rather enforceth them to the vttermoste, and often times farther then the partie himselfe doth, or perchaunce could doo. And was of this minde, that he saide he woulde not lett while he liued, wheresoeuer he perceaued his aduersarye to say well, or himselfe to haue saide otherwise, indifferently for both to say and declare the truth. (p. 108)

Here is nowe farther to be considered in his wrytinges that he neither hunted after praise and vainglory, nor any vile and filthy gaine or worldly co*m*moditie; yea, so that inuenomed and poysoned hereticall bookes might be once suppressed and abolished, he wisshed his owne in a light and faire fire also. (p. 109)

[In 1532] S*ir* Thomas More wrate a letter [*Aunswere to Frithes Letter agaynst the Blessed Sacramen of the Aulter*] impugning the erroneous wryting of John Frith.

And whereas after [that] he had geuen ouer the office of the Lorde Chauncello*ur*, the heretikes full fast did write against him, and founde many faultes with him and his wrytinges, He made a goodly and a learned *Apologie* [See excerpt date 1533] especially of that they layde to his charge of the slender recitall or misrehearsing of Tindall and Barnes argumentes, and sheweth that they were calumnious slaunders, and that himselfe vsed Tindall and Barnes after a contrary and better maner then they vsed him: "for he rehearseth" S*ir* Thomas Mores

> argumentes in euery place faintlye and falsely too, and leaueth out the pithe and the strength and the proufe that moste maketh for the purpose; And he fareth therein as if there were one that hauing day of challenge appointed, in which he should wrestle with his aduersarye,

would finde the meane by crafte to gett his aduersarye before the day into his owne handes, and there keepe him and dyet him with such a thinne dyet, that, at the day, he bringeth him foorth feeble, faint and famished, and almost hunger starven, and so leane that he can scant stande on his legges; and then is it easie, ye wote well, to geue the silly soule a fall.

And yet when Tindall had "done all this, he taketh the fall himselfe." But euery man maye well see that S*ir* Thomas More neuer vseth that way with Tindall, nor with any of those folke, but rehearseth their reason to the best that they can make it themselues, and rather inforceth and strengtheth it (as we haue before declared) of his owne, then taketh any part of theirs therefrom.

Whereas nowe farther they founde fault with the length of his bookes, he wryteth, among other thinges, that "it is litle meruaile that it seeme longe and tedious vnto them to reade it ouer within, whom it yrketh to doo so muche as looke it ouer without, and euerye way seemeth longe to him that is wearie [ere] he beginne." "But I finde," saith he,

> some men againe to whom the reading is so farre from tedious, that they haue read the whole booke ouer thrise, and some that make tables thereof for their owne remembraunce, and that suche men as haue as muche witt and learning both, as the best of all this blessed brotherhood that euer I heard of. (pp. 122-24)

About this time there was one that had [made] a booke "of the diuision of the spiritualtie and temporaltie," of the which booke the brethren made great store, and blamed S*ir* Thomas More that he had not vsed in his wryting suche a softe and milde maner and such an indifferent fasshion as the saide person did. By occasion whereof S*ir* Thomas More discourseth vpon the saide booke (the autho*ur* whereof pretended to make a pacification of the foresaide diuision and discorde), And openeth many faultes and folyes and heynous false slaunders against the Clergie, craftily and smoothly, vnder an holy [collusion] and pretence of pacification, in the saide bookes. To the which S*ir* Thomas Mores discourse there came an aunswere afterwarde in printe vnder the tytle of *Salem and Bizance*. To the which S*ir* Thomas More replyed, and so dressed this pretie, politike pacifier that he had no lust, nor any man for him, to incounter afterwardes with the saide S*ir* Thomas.

The pretie, pleasaunt, wittie declaration of the tytle of the saide booke (because it is seldome and rare to be gotten) I will nowe, gentle Reader, set before thine eyes. The said tytle is framed in this sort: *The debellation of Salem and Bizance, sometime two great townes, which being vnder the great Turke, were betweene Easter and Michelmas last passed, this present yere of our Lorde 1533, with a meruailous metamorphosis enchaunted and turned into two englishe men, by the wonderfull inuentiue witt and witchcrafte of Sir John Somesay, the pacifier, and so by him conueyed hither in a dialogue, to defende his diuision against the Apologie of Sir Thomas More, knight. But nowe being thus, betweene the saide Michelmas and Alhalloutide next ensuing, in this debellation vanquished, they be fledd hence and vanished, and are become two townes againe, with those olde names chaunged, Salem into Jerusalem, and Bizance into Constantinople, the one [in] Greece and the other [in] Siria, where they may see them that will and winne them that can. And if the pacifier conuey them hither againe, and tenne such other townes with them, embattailed in such dialogues, Sir Thomas More hath vndertaken to put himselfe in [the] aduenture alone against them all. But and if he lett them tary still there, he will not vtterly forsweare it, but he is not much minded as yet, age nowe so comming on, and waxing all vnwildie, to goe thither and geue the assault to such well walled townes, without some such lustie companie as shal be somewhat likely to leape vp a little more lightly.*

This is the tytle of the foresaide booke. And that in very deede the saide S*ir* Thomas More hath most valiantly discomfited the pacifier, and ouerthrowen his two great townes, may easily appere to such as will vouchsafe to reade the saide S*ir* Thomas More his aunswere, The circumstances and particularities whereof to rehearse, would make our present Treatise to growe too bigge. (pp. 127-29)

Nowe haue we beside other excellent and fruitfull bookes of his which he made being prisoner in the towre, as his three bookes *Of Comfort against Tribulation, A Treatise to Receaue the Blessed Sacrament Sacramentally and Virtually Both A Treatise Vpon the Passion,* with notable introductions to the same. He wrote also many other godly and deuout instructions and prayers.

And surely, of all the bookes that euer he made, I doubt whether I may preferre any of them to the saide three bookes, yea, or any other mans, eyther heathen or christian, that haue written (as many haue) eyther in the greeke or latine of the saide matter. And as for heathen, I doo this woorthie man plaine iniurie, and doo so much abase him in matching and comparing him with them, especially in this point, seing that [though] they were neuer otherwise so incomparable, [they] lacked yet and knewe not the very speciall and principall grounde of comfort and consolation, that is the true fayth in Christe, in whom, and for whom, and his glory, and from whom, we must seeke and fetche all our true comfort and consolation. Well, lett them passe, and lett vs then further say, that as the saide S*ir* Thomas More notably passeth many learned christians that haue of the same matter written before, so lett vs adde that it may well be doubted, all circumstaunces well considered and weighed, if any of the residue may seeme muche to passe him, or to be farre preferred afore him. There is in these bookes so wittie, so pithie, and so substantiall matter for the easing and remedying and patiently suffring of all maner of griefes and sorowes that may possibly incumber any man, by anye maner or kinde of tribulation, whether their tribulation proceede of any inwarde temptation of our ghostly enemy the deuill, or by any outwarde tentation of the world threatning to spoyle and bereaue vs of our goodes, landes, honour, of our libertie and freedome, by greeuous and sharpe imprisonment, or finally of our life withall, by any painefull and exquisite cruell death; Against all which he doth so wonderfully, so effectually, and so strongly prepare, defence and arme the Reader, that a man cannot desire or wish any thing of more efficacie or importance thereto to be added. In the which bookes his principall drifte and scope was to stirre and prepare the mindes of englishe men manfully and couragiously to withstande, and not to shrinke at, the imminent and open persecution whiche he fore[sawe], and immediatly folowed, against the vnitie of the Churche and the catholike fayth of the same. Albeit full wittily and wisely, that the bookes might the more safely goe abrode, he doth not expressly meddle with those matters, and

couloureth the matter vnder the name of an Hungarian, and of the persecution of the Turke in Hungarie, and of a booke translated out of the Hungarians tonge into the latin, and then into the englishe tonge.

Of these bookes there is then great accompt to be made, not onely for the excellent matters comprised, and moste wittily and learnedly handled therein, but for that also they were made when he was most straightly inclosed and shutt vp from all company in the towre. In which sort I doubt whether a man should finde any other booke of like woorthines made by any christian. And yet if anye suche be to be founde, and suche as this, much soone should yeeld and geue place to the same; yet surely, there is one thing wherein these bookes of S*ir* Thomas More by an especiall prerogatiue surmounte, or els I am deceaued, all other of this sort, and that is, that they were for the moste part written with none other penne in the worlde then with a coale, as was also his Treatise vpon the passion; w*h*ich copie, if some [men] had, they might and would more esteeme then other bookes written with golden letters, and woulde make no lesse accompt of it then St Jerome did of certaine bookes of the learned martyr Lucian written with his owne hande, that perchaunce he happed [vpon], and esteemed them as a pretious iewell.

And yet is there one thing that in the valewing and prysing [of] these bookes I esteeme aboue all other, and that is, that in these bookes he is not, as many great clerkes in their bookes sometime are, like to a whetstone, that being blunt and dull it selfe, whetteth and sharpeth other thinges; it was not so with this man; for albeit he wrote these bookes with a deade blacke coale, yet was there another and a most hott burning coale, suche a one, I say, as touched and purified the lippes of the holy prophete Esaias, that directed his hande with the deade coale, and so inflamed and incensed his heart with all to heauenwarde, that the good and wholsome instructions and councell that he gaue to other men in his bookes he himselfe shortly after, in moste patient suffring of the losse of his goodes, landes, of imprisonment, and of death withall, for the defence of Justice and the catholike fayth, experimented and woorthely practised in himselfe.... (pp. 132-35)

Nicholas Harpsfield, in his The Life and Death of Sir Thomas Moore, Knight, Sometimes Lord High Chancellor of England, *edited by Elsie Vaughan Hitchcock and R. W. Chambers, Oxford University Press, London, 1932, 400 p.*

SIR PHILIP SIDNEY (essay date 1586?)

[*Sidney was a sixteenth-century English poet, essayist, critic, and romance writer. As a personality he epitomized the beau ideal of the Elizabethan courtier: brilliant, loyal, flattering, learned, poised. As a writer he is remembered chiefly for three works, all of which were published posthumously: the pastoral prose romance* The Countesse of Pembrokes Arcadia *(1590); the sonnet sequence* Astrophel and Stella *(1591); and the critical essay* The Defence of Poesie *(1595; originally* Apologie for Poetrie*). In the following excerpt from the last-named work, he considers More's vision of a commonwealth in* Utopia.]

[Even] in the most excellent determination of goodness, what philosopher's counsel can so readily direct a prince, as the feigned Cyrus in Xenophon; or a virtuous man in all fortunes, as Aeneas in Virgil; or a whole commonwealth, as the way of Sir Thomas More's *Utopia*? I say the way, because where Sir Thomas More erred, it was the fault of the man and not of the poet, for that way of patterning a commonwealth was most absolute, though he perchance hath not so absolutely performed it. For the question is, whether the feigned image of poetry or the regular instruction of philosophy hath the more force in teaching: wherein if the philosophers have more rightly showed themselves philosophers than the poets have attained to the high top of their profession, as in truth

> Mediocribus esse poetis,
> Non dii, non homines, non concessere columnae;

it is, I say again, not the fault of the art, but that by few men that art can be accomplished. (pp. 33-4)

> *Sir Philip Sidney, "Examination I," in his* A Defence of Poetry, *edited by J. A. Van Dorsten, Oxford University Press, London, 1966, 112 p.*

THOMAS STAPLETON (essay date 1588)

[*A staunch recusant, Stapleton was born in July, 1535, the very month of More's execution—"as if," according to Thomas Fuller, "divine providence had purposely dropped from heaven an acorn in place of the oak that was felled." He left England for the Continent soon after the accession of Elizabeth I. During his long exile he wrote lives of St. Thomas the Apostle, St. Thomas à Becket, and More, publishing the three at Douai in 1588 as* Tres Thomae *("Three Thomases"). The More portion of the work, praised by T. E. Bridgett as "by far the best Life of More," is valued as both a history and work of devotion, although scholars have noted that it is marred somewhat by occasional factual errors. In the following excerpt from the* Life of More, *Stapleton reviews More's major writings, citing the opinions of contemporary commentators and offering his own views of the merits of More's literary endeavors.*]

Now we shall try to speak of [More] as a literary man, of his attainments, his studies, his love of books, his labours, and his successes. . . . [In his youth] he diligently exercised himself in writing and speaking, and gained fame as a poet, an orator, and a philosopher. Before he entered upon his public career it is not surprising that a man of such talents, having time upon his hands, could not bear to be idle. But in such a constant pressure of business as the appointments he held involved—and added to this he was married and had the care of a family—who could have expected that he would have been able to do any literary work of importance? For the Muses love leisure and have the greatest abhorrence for the clamour of the tribunals and the bustle of the Court. Such is our sluggishness that they demand almost undivided allegiance. More's natural bent was entirely to a literary life, and often did he bewail the multitude of business he had to attend to, and the constant interruptions to which he was subject. Thus he writes, after finishing the *Utopia*, to his friend, Peter Giles of Antwerp:

> Whiles I do daily bestow my time about law matters: some to plead, some to hear, some as an arbitrator with mine award to determine, some as an umpire or a judge, with my sentence to discuss. Whiles I go one way to see and visit my friend: another way about mine own private affairs. Whiles I spend almost all the day abroad among others, and the residue at home among mine

own; I leave to myself, I mean to my book, no time. For when I am come home, I must commune with my wife, chat with my children, and talk with my servants. All the which things I reckon and account among business, forasmuch as they must of necessity be done: and done must they needs be, unless a man will be stranger in his own house. And in any wise a man must so fashion and order his conditions, and so appoint and dispose himself, that he be merry, jocund, and pleasant among them, whom either nature hath provided, or chance hath made, or he himself hath chosen to be the fellows and companions of his life: so that with too much gentle behaviour and familiarity, he do not mar them, and by too much sufferance of his servants maketh them his masters. Among these things now rehearsed, stealeth away the day, the month, the year. When do I write then? And all this while I have spoken no word of sleep, neither yet of meat, which among a great number doth waste no less time than doth sleep, wherein almost half the lifetime of man creepeth away.

This being so, what time remained for study? He answers immediately:

> I therefore do win and get only that time which I steal from sleep and meat. Which time because it is very little, and yet somewhat it is, therefore have I once at the last, though it be long first, finished *Utopia*; and have sent it to you, friend Peter.

Ordinarily, indeed, More did not give more than four or five hours to sleep. He used to rise at two and devote himself to study and prayer until seven. The rest of the day he gave to business. Thus he was able to write . . . very many works, Latin and more especially English. He wrote the *Utopia*, if we may believe John Paludanus, while yet a youth, but it would be more correct to call him a young man at the time. For he wrote it on his return from an embassy to Flanders, as he states in the Preface. But it is clear he had not yet been summoned by the King to the Court, from the fact of the King's offering him a pension at the close of the embassy. . . . In fact, he wrote the *Utopia* in 1516 when he was thirty-three. (When he suffered in 1535 he was fifty-two years of age.)

Of the excellence of [*Utopia*] it is not necessary for me to speak, for it is in everyone's hands and has been translated into French, Italian, and Flemish; but I will transcribe the opinions of some famous scholars. William Budé in a letter to Thomas Lupset thus writes [see excerpt dated 1517]:

> We owe the knowledge of Utopia to Thomas More, who has made known to the world in this our age the pattern of a happy life and a perfect rule of good behaviour. Our age and future ages will have this history as a precious source of noble and useful laws which each one may take and adapt to the use of his own State.

John Paludanus of Cassel in a letter to Peter Giles writes as follows:

> You may see in Utopia, as in a mirror, all that pertains to a perfect commonwealth. England certainly has many excellent learned men. For what may we conjecture of the rest if More alone had performed so much, being, first, but a young man, and, then, so fully occupied with public and domestic business, and, lastly, practising a profession quite other than literature?

Peter Giles in a letter to Jerome Busleyden, Provost of Aire, thus speaks of the *Utopia*:

So many miracles meet here together that I am in doubt which I should most admire, the extraordinary fidelity of his memory which could record almost verbatim so many matters heard but once

(for Giles had to give his support to the fiction),

or his wisdom in pointing out the sources—utterly unknown for the most part—of actual evils and potential benefits for the State, or the force and ease of his style which, with such pure Latinity and such eloquence, has treated of so many matters, although he is so much distracted both with public and domestic affairs.

I will add now the weighty judgement of Jerome Busleyden, a member of the Council of the Emperor. After reading the *Utopia* he wrote to More thus [see Additional Bibliography]:

In the happy description of the Utopian commonwealth there is nothing lacking which might show most excellent learning and the highest skill in human affairs. For so varied is your learning, so wide and accurate your knowledge of affairs, that whatever you write is the fruit of valuable experience, and whatever you wish to convey is expressed most eloquently: a marvellous and rare happiness, indeed, all the rarer in that, to the envy of the many, it is possessed but by the few. Few indeed they are who have the sincerity, the learning, the integrity, and the influence needed to enable them to contribute so dutifully, so honourably, and so prudently to the common good as you have succeeded in doing. You have willed to benefit, not only yourself, but all nations of the world: you have made all men your debtors. You could have bestowed no more worthy or useful gift upon mankind than by depicting, as you have done, the perfect state, with ideal customs and laws. The world has never seen wiser, more perfect, or more desirable institutions. In their excellence they leave far behind them the famous and much-lauded states of Sparta, Athens, and Rome.

Further on he makes a very wise observation, and praises the fact that

the State of Utopia as depicted by More labours not so much in making laws as in forming the most upright magistrates so that, according to their pattern, their evident integrity, their exemplary manners, and the clear mirror of their justice, the whole state and true government of every perfect commonwealth may be framed.

Paul Jovius also speaks of this renowned book in the following terms:

The fame that More has won by his *Utopia* will never die. For he describes most eloquently how in the land of that happy nation the State is governed by most wholesome laws and enjoys a rich peace. Since he loathed the corrupt manners of this wicked age, his purpose was to show by a pleasant fiction the right path to a blessed and most happy life.

Certainly no one who reads this masterpiece, the *Utopia*, can fail to agree with Budé, Erasmus, Cochlaeus, Rhenanus, Busleyden, Tunstall, Cardinal Reginald Pole, Paludanus, Hutten, Vives, Grapheus, Zasius, and all other readers of the work in their verdict that More had an incomparable and almost superhuman wit. In invention no work could be more happy, apt, and clever; in expression none more worthy, rich, and elegant; in its teaching of life and manners none more sound, earnest, and wise. The reader never tires of the book, and cannot finish it without the greatest profit to himself if he reads it with attention and a desire to learn.

Almost at the same time he wrote in Latin the history of Richard III, King of England [*The History of Richard III*]. He wrote it only to practise his pen; he never finished it or revised it; but yet it lacks neither polish nor elegance of style. He had written it in English at an earlier date, with greater fulness of detail, and with yet more eloquence.

In 1523 the foul-mouthed Luther issued a foul book against Henry VIII's book on the Sacraments. More published a reply to Luther's abuse [*Eruditissimi viri Guilielmi Rossei opus elegans*], and though it best to answer his rudeness and scurrility in the same style. Luther should be overwhelmed with filth like that with which he had covered the King, so that finding his intemperate language used against himself he might lose the pleasure which no doubt he had found in uttering it. But as at that time More was a knight and a member of the King's Council he was conscious that rudeness and vulgarity were unbefitting his position: consequently he allowed the book to go out, not in his own name, but in that of William Ross. As a man of that name about this very time went on a pilgrimage to Rome and died in Italy, even the English themselves were quite ready to believe him to be the author. The book is a serious and solid defence of the true faith against the impudent attacks of Luther, besides being extraordinarily clever and witty. As to his answering abuse with abuse, in the last lines of the book he explains that he did it with great reluctance, but was forced to it.

Although Luther has given himself wholly over to the powers of evil and has become hardened in his schism, yet he should determine with himself to take at least some account of good manners, so that he may claim the authority of a dogmatiser rather than a low buffoon of a heretic. For if he is willing to enter upon a serious discussion, if he will withdraw his lies and false accusations, if he will have no more to do with folly, rage, and the Furies who hitherto have been his all-too-familiar spirits, if he will cleanse the filth with which he has so vilely befouled his tongue and his pen, then there will not be wanting disputants who will treat with him as seriously as the matter demands. But if he goes on with his scurrility and madness as he has begun, with his calumnious attacks, his inept folly, his stupid rage and his vulgar buffoonery, if he will use no language but that of the sewer . . . then, let others do what they will, we will decide, from this time forth, either to drag out the madman from his stronghold and show him in his true colours, or to leave our raving friend with all his Furies . . . covered with his own filth.

These are his last words to Luther, and in them he smears Luther's lips with dainties fit for such a rogue and gives him a sweet morsel suited to his palate. Certainly this book, as Cochlaeus says, "with great cleverness and play of wit, and with violent diatribe, was a most complete refutation of Luther's book. It cast back in his teeth all his infamous lies, so that he dared to utter no further word." Whereas generally Luther was very busy with his pen and ready to reply to any who attacked him, after he had read Ross, he became more dumb than a fish.

More wrote, also, against John Pomeranus a letter of admirable clarity [*Epistola in qua . . . respondent literis Pomerani*], which has been printed separately.

These are almost all the Latin works, at any rate among those that have survived, that he wrote while still at liberty. For when he was in prison, he wrote a long treatise on the Passion of our Lord, of which the latter part is in Latin and printed among his Latin works, although the earlier and by far the larger part is in English. But of this, more hereafter.

Now I will mention what he wrote in English either in controversy with heretics or on subjects of devotion.... He wrote his *Life of Richard III* while practising as a lawyer in London. When he was summoned to the Court and to the Council of the King, although he had an extraordinarily busy life, yet he found time to write very many works. When he was knighted, in the King's Council, and Sub-Treasurer of the realm, he wrote a treatise of remarkable piety and learning on the *Four Last Things*, but the greater part has perished. Later on the heretics began to come into England from Belgium, as More notes in a letter to Erasmus. "All the heresies," he writes, "found shelter in Belgium, and thence their books were sent into England." Although More at the time was a much-occupied man, as a member of the King's Council and Chancellor of the Duchy of Lancaster, yet he found time to write four books of dialogues on the subjects then in controversy. The work is lengthy, detailed, and learned: it treats fully of the Invocation of the Saints, Pilgrimages, Relics, etc.: it proves by many arguments which is the true Church and that the Church is infallible.

After he had finished the *Dialogues* he dealt with an heretical pamphlet which had appeared under the title of *The Supplication of Beggars*, and which advised the King that the best, and indeed the only, means for the relief of the poor and for provision for the other needs of the State was to confiscate at least three-quarters of all ecclesiastical and monastic property. Against this pamphlet, which was not a supplication but a libel, More wrote, the year after the Dialogues, a complete reply, entitled *The Supplication of Souls*. In this book he speaks in the person of the souls in purgatory, for whose relief, by prayers and masses, ecclesiastical and monastic revenues were, in large part, founded: he defends the Church's teaching on Purgatory and prayers for the dead; and he proves that if monasteries were destroyed and the property of the Church confiscated, the King's power would be lessened and the number of beggars increased, as experience, the teacher of fools, afterwards proved.

When, later on, Tyndall, that heresiarch who afterwards suffered at Vilvorde in Brabant the just penalty of his impiety, attacked More's *Dialogues,* the latter, although then Lord Chancellor, wrote a long work to refute him [*The Confutation of Tyndale's Answer*]. Of the nine books into which this refutation is divided, three were written while he was Chancellor, six after he had resigned. In the single year which intervened between his resignation and his imprisonment he wrote also, against the Sacramentarian John Frith, a book on the True Presence of the Body and Blood of Christ, then an *Apology* and a defence of that *Apology* under the title of *The Debellation of Salem and Bizance*. Finally he wrote in five books *An Answer to the ... Book which a Nameless Heretic hath named: The Supper of the Lord*. In prison he wrote *A Dialogue of Comfort against Tribulation*, in three books—a work of great beauty, full of piety and learning, which hardly has an equal amongst works of the kind. There, too, he wrote *A Treatise Histori-*

cal containing the Bitter Passion of our Saviour Christ, according to the four Evangelists, beginning at the text "The feast of unleavened bread was at hand" and continuing as far as the words "They laid hands upon Jesus." At that point hands were laid upon him, by the increased strictness of his confinement, so that all further opportunity of writing was denied him. This lengthy treatise is written with careful detail and is full of the deepest piety.

All the English works of More were published in one large volume in the reign of Queen Mary [*The Works of Sir Thomas More Knyght*]. When I read the greater portion of this volume thirty years ago, I found More to have been a most diligent student of the Holy Scriptures, and to have had a considerable acquaintance with the Fathers and even with the disputes of the Schools. His quotations, even if not very numerous, are always forthcoming where needful and always to the point. They are drawn from Augustine, Jerome, Chrysostom, Cyril, Hilary, Bernard, and Gerson. We know that afterwards, when difficulties arose with the King, in self-defence he alleged that he had spent seven years in the study of the Fathers in order to get to know their view of the Pope's Primacy.... For the present it is enough to remark what a store of patristic learning a man of his attainments and extraordinary memory could thus obtain. For even though he was reading with one special object in view, who can doubt that he would have noted, by the way, many passages that bore on modern heresies. I have come to the conclusion, in reading through his works, that he paid special attention to the study of dogmatic theology. For when he speaks of grace, free will, merit, faith, charity and other virtues, original sin and even predestination, he is so guarded and exact in his statements that a professional theologian could scarcely speak more accurately. That he had carefully read St Thomas is proved by a story told by John Harris, his secretary. Once a pamphlet recently printed by a heretic was brought to More's notice while he was travelling by water from his home at Chelsea to London. When he had read a little he pointed out with his finger some passages to Harris. "The arguments," said he, "which this villain has set forth are the objections which St Thomas puts to himself in such and such a question and article of the Secunda Secundae, but the rogue keeps back the good Doctor's solutions." I myself once heard him arguing with Father Alphonsus, of the Friars Minor, who had been confessor to Queen Catharine, the first wife of Henry VIII. He was defending the opinion of Scotus on attrition and contrition as safer and more probable than the opinion of Occam. It might well appear astonishing that a man whose whole life was filled with the affairs of public life and the Court, who was, too, well versed in general literature, should not only have dipped into scholastic theology, but have been thoroughly familiar with it.

More's English controversial works did great good at the time and were read and reread three or four times by many serious scholars, some of whom drew up "tables" of the work as an aid to memory, as he himself had occasion to note. Afterwards they were reprinted in the reign of Queen Mary and were of the greatest use during the restoration of Catholicism that then took place. For during that bright interval, which by the great mercy of God was granted to us between the two periods of schism, nothing more powerfully strengthened and promoted the Catholic cause than the numerous works of More in English, edited with great care and labour by William Rastell.... Many other works of More, however, both Latin and English, perished in the bitter persecution which befell his household after he was taken away from it...: those that we have were, so to say, snatched from the flames and preserved by the special care of his friends. For immediately after his death, More's large and valuable library, together with the rest of his furniture, was sacked by Thomas Cromwell, the Keeper of the King's Seal, and a fit tool for a tyrant. More's untiring energy is shown by the fact that all that he composed for publication during his whole life, English and Latin works alike, was written by his own hand, as he was unwilling to rely on the industry of another. (pp. 30-9)

> *Thomas Stapleton, in his* The Life and Illustrious Martyrdom of Sir Thomas More, *translated by Philip E. Hallett, Burns, Oates & Washbourne, Ltd., 1928, 235 p.*

GILBERT BURNET (essay date 1715)

[*Burnet was an English cleric and author. He was successively chaplain to Charles II, adviser of William of Orange, and bishop of Salisbury. He is best known for his posthumously published* History of My Own Times *(1724-34), a work that has been described by Angus Ross as "a lively eyewitness account, written with a quaint egotism by a quick rather than a profound mind." In the following excerpt from* The History of the Reformation of the Church of England, *first published in 1679 and later revised by the author for publication in 1715, he notes a contrast between the tone and purpose of* Utopia *and More's later, controversial writings in English.*]

[Thomas More] was a man of rare virtues and excellent parts: in his youth he had freer thoughts of things, as appears by his *Utopia*, and his Letters to Erasmus; but afterwards he became superstitiously devoted to the interests and passions of the popish clergy: and, as he served them when he was in authority, even to assist them in all their cruelties; so he employed his pen in the same cause, both in writing against all the new opinions in general, and in particular against Tindal, Frith, and Barnes; as also an unknown writer, who seemed of neither party, but reproved the corruptions of the clergy, and condemned their cruel proceedings. More was no divine at all; and it is plain to any, that reads his writings, that he knew nothing of antiquity, beyond the quotations he found in the canon law, and in the master of the sentences; (only he had read some of St. Austin's treatises;) for upon all points of controversy, he quotes only what he found in these collections: nor was he at all conversant in the critical learning upon the scriptures; but his peculiar excellency in writing was, that he had a natural easy expression, and presented all the opinions of popery with their fair side to the reader, disguising or concealing the black side of them with great art; and was no less dexterous in exposing all the ill consequences that could follow on the doctrine of the reformers; and had upon all occasions great store of pleasant tales, which he applied wittily to his purpose. And in this consists the great strength of his writings, which were designed rather for the rabble, than for learned men. (pp. 711-12)

> *Gilbert Burnet, "Book III," in his* The History of the Reformation of the Church of England, Vol.

I, *new edition, 1715. Reprint by Oxford at the University Press, 1829, pp. 361-727.*

JONATHAN SWIFT (essay date 1736)

[*An eighteenth-century Anglo-Irish essayist, poet, historian, and autobiographer, Swift is considered the foremost prose satirist in the English language and one of the greatest satirists of all time. He is best known as the author of* Travels into Several Remote Nations of the World, in Four Parts, by Lemuel Gulliver, First a Surgeon, and Then a Captain of Several Ships *(1726; this work is commonly known as* Gulliver's Travels*), a complex study of human nature and the moral, philosophical, and scientific thought of the age. In the following excerpt from his 1736 essay "Concerning That Universal Hatred, Which Prevails against the Clergy," Swift praises More's character while impugning Henry VIII. Commenting on this very passage, R. W. Chambers later wrote in* Thomas More *(1935): "Dean Swift did not give testimonials recklessly." Countering Chambers's assessment, Richard Marius claimed in his 1984 biography of More: "At times, as when Chambers justifies his snow-white estimate of More's character by quoting the praise of Jonathan Swift, he is simply silly."*]

I have been long considering and conjecturing, what could be the causes of that great disgust, of late, against the clergy of both kingdoms, beyond what was ever known till that monster and tyrant, Henry VIII, who took away from them, against law, reason, and justice, at least two-thirds of their legal possessions; and whose successors (except Queen Mary) went on with their rapine, till the accession of King James I. That detestable tyrant Henry VIII, although he abolished the Pope's power in England, as universal bishop, yet what he did in that article, however just it were in itself, was the mere effect of his irregular appetite, to divorce himself from a wife he was weary of, for a younger and more beautiful woman, whom he afterwards beheaded. But, at the same time, he was an entire defender of all the Popish doctrines, even those which were the most absurd. And, while he put people to death for denying him to be head of the Church, he burned every offender against the doctrines of the Roman faith; and cut off the head of Sir Thomas More, a person of the greatest virtue this kingdom ever produced, for not directly owning him to be head of the Church. Among all the princes who ever reigned in the world there was never so infernal a beast as Henry VIII, in every vice of the most odious kind, without any one appearance of virtue.... (p. 301)

> *Jonathan Swift, "Concerning That Universal Hatred, Which Prevails against the Clergy," in his* The Prose Works of Jonathan Swift, D.D.: Writings on Religion and the Church, Vol. III, *edited by Temple Scott, George Bell and Sons, 1898, pp. 299-304.*

SHARON TURNER (essay date 1828)

[*Turner was an English man of letters who wrote pioneering studies of Old English literature. In the following excerpt from his* History of the Reign of Henry VIII —*but one work in Turner's multivolume "The Modern History of England" series—he suggests that More's literary reputation has been enhanced by the circumstances and manner of his death.*]

In beheading More and Fisher, whatever were their faults, Henry only exalted to immortality, and to his own depreciation, two men, who, without this termination of their lives, might never have enjoyed it. There was little in either that without their harsh fate would have survived their contemporaries. Fisher was a worthy, but not a strong-minded man, and his literary works are of small value, and are now never, by any accident, consulted. More, who counteracted, if he did not curtail his own *Utopia*, and whose other writings degrade him for their feebleness, their bigotry, their scurrility, and their persecuting tendency, below the educated men of his day, would have sunk into oblivion, except as a punster, as a worthy pattern of the domestic virtues, and as one who had been fond of literature, and had been famed for it, but who, in its most important department, was also its unsparing persecutor; if the oppressive violence of his death had not imparted that sympathy and sanctity to his memory, which the human heart liberally bestows on the victims of power, who unite firmness of principle with moral rectitude and intellectual cultivation. (pp.394-95)

> *Sharon Turner, "Chapter XXVII," in his* The History of the Reign of Henry the Eighth: Comprising the Political History of the Commencement of the English Reformation, Vol. II, *third edition, Longman, 1828, pp. 354-97.*

SIR JAMES MACKINTOSH (essay date 1846)

[*Mackintosh was a nineteenth-century English essayist, philosopher, and historian. In the following excerpt, he comments on the language, style, and intent of selected works by More.*]

As if it had been the lot of More to open all the paths through the wilds of our old English speech, he is to be considered also as our earliest prose writer, and as the first Englishman who wrote the history of his country in its present language. The historical fragment [*The History of King Richard III*] commands belief by simplicity, and by abstinence from too confident affirmation. It betrays some negligence about minute particulars, which is not displeasing as a symptom of the absence of eagerness to enforce a narrative. The composition has an ease and a rotundity (which gratify the ear without awakening the suspicion of art) of which there was no model in any preceding writer of English prose.

In comparing the prose of More with the modern style, we must distinguish the words from the composition. A very small part of his vocabulary has been superannuated; the number of terms which require any explanation is inconsiderable: and in that respect the stability of the language is remarkable. He is, indeed, in his words, more English than the great writers of a century after him, who loaded their native tongue with expressions of Greek or Latin derivation. Cicero, speaking of "old Cato," seems almost to describe More. "His style is rather antiquated; he has some words displeasing to our ears, but which were then in familiar use. Change those terms, which he could not, you will then prefer no speaker to Cato."

But in the combination and arrangement of words, in ordinary phraseology and common habits of composition, he differs more widely from the style that has now been prevalent among us for nearly two centuries. His diction seems a continued experiment to discover the forms into which the language naturally runs. In that attempt he has frequently failed. Fortunate accident, or more varied experiment in aftertimes, led to the adoption of other combinations, which could scarcely have succeeded, if they had not been more consonant to the spirit of the language, and more agreeable to the ear and the feelings of the people. The structure of his sentences is frequently not that which the English language has finally adopted: the language of his countrymen has decided, without appeal, against the composition of the father of English prose.

The speeches contained in his fragment, like many of those in the ancient historians, were probably substantially real, but brightened by ornament, and improved in composition. It could, indeed, scarcely be otherwise: for the history was written in 1513, and the death of Edward IV., with which it opens, occurred in 1483; while Cardinal Morton, who became prime minister two years after that event, appears to have taken young More into his household about the year 1493. There is, therefore, little scope, in so short a time, for much falsification, by tradition, of the arguments and topics really employed. These speeches have the merit of being accommodated to the circumstances, and of being of a tendency to dispose those to whom they were addressed to promote the object of the speaker; and this merit, rare in similar compositions, shows that More had been taught, by the practice of speaking in contests where objects the most important are the prize of the victor, that eloquence is the art of persuasion, and that the end of the orator is not the display of his talents, but dominion over the minds of his hearers. The dying speech, in which Edward exhorts the two parties of his friends to harmony, is a grave appeal to their prudence, as well as an affecting address from a father and a king to their public feelings. The surmises thrown out by Richard against the Widviles are short, dark, and well adapted to awaken suspicion and alarm. The insinuations against the Queen, and the threats of danger to the lords themselves from leaving the person of the Duke of York in the hands of that princess, in Richard's speech to the Privy Council, before the Archbishop of York was sent to Westminster to demand the surrender of the boy, are admirable specimens of the address and art of crafty ambition. Generally speaking, the speeches have little of the vague common-place of rhetoricians and declaimers; and the time is not wasted in parade. In the case, indeed, of the dispute between the Archbishop and the Queen, about taking the Duke of York out of his mother's care, and from the Sanctuary at Westminster, there is more ingenious argument than the scene allows; and the mind rejects logical refinements, of which the use, on such an occasion, is quite irreconcilable to dramatic verisimilitude. The Duke of Buckingham alleged in council, that sanctuary could be claimed only against danger; and that the royal infant had neither wisdom to desire sanctuary, nor the malicious intention in his acts without which he could not require it. To this notable paradox, which amounted to an affirmation that no certainly innocent person could ever claim protection from a sanctuary, when it was carried to the Queen, she answered readily, that if she could be in sanctuary, it followed that her child, who was her ward, was included in her protection, as much as her servants, who were, without contradiction, allowed to be.

The Latin epigrams [*Epigrammata*] of More, a small volume which it required two years to carry through the press at Basle, are mostly translations from the Anthologia, which were rather made known to Europe by the fame of the writer, than calculated to increase it. They contain, however, some decisive proofs that he always entertained the opinions respecting the dependence of all government on the consent of the people, to which he professed his adherence almost in his dying moments. Latin versification was not in that early period successfully attempted in any Transalpine country. The rules of prosody, or at least the laws of metrical composition, were not yet sufficiently studied for such attempts. His Latinity was of the same school with that of his friend Erasmus; which was, indeed, common to the first generation of scholars after the revival of classical study. Finding Latin a sort of general language employed by men of letters in their conversation and correspondence, they continued the use of it in the mixed and corrupted state to which such an application had necessarily reduced it: they began, indeed, to purify it from some grosser corruptions; but they built their style upon the foundation of this colloquial dialect, with no rigorous observation of the good usage of the Roman language. Writings of business, of pleasantry, of familiar intercourse, could never have been composed in pure Latinity; which was still more inconsistent with new manners, institutions, and opinions, and with discoveries and inventions added to those which were transmitted by antiquity. Erasmus, who is the master and model of this system of composition, admirably shows how much had been gained by loosening the fetters of a dead speech, and acquiring in its stead the nature, ease, variety, and vivacity of a spoken and living tongue. The course of circumstances, however, determined that this language should not subsist, or at least flourish, for much more than a century. It was assailed on one side by the purely classical, whom Erasmus, in derision, calls "Ciceronians;" and when it was sufficiently emasculated by dread of their censure, it was finally overwhelmed by the rise of a national literature in every European language.

More exemplified the abundance and flexibility of the Erasmian Latinity in *Utopia*. . . . The idea of the work had been suggested by some of the dialogues of Plato, who speaks of vast territories, formerly cultivated and peopled, but afterwards, by some convulsion of nature, covered by the Atlantic Ocean. These Egyptian traditions, or legends, harmonised admirably with that discovery of a new continent by Columbus, which had roused the admiration of Europe about twenty years before the composition of *Utopia*. This was the name of an island feigned to have been discovered by a supposed companion of Amerigo Vespucci, who is made to tell the wondrous tale of its condition to More, at Antwerp, in 1514: and in it was the seat of the Platonic conception of an imaginary commonwealth. All the names which he invented for men or places were intimations of their being unreal, and were, perhaps, by treating with raillery his own notions, intended to silence gainsayers. The first book, which is preliminary, is naturally and ingeniously opened by a conversation, in which Raphael Hythloday, the Utopian traveller, describes his visit to England; where, as much as in other countries, he found all proposals for improvement encountered by the remark, that,—"Such things pleased our ancestors, and it were well for us if we could but match them; as if it were a great mischief that any should be found wiser than his ancestors." "I met," he goes on to say, "these proud, morose, and absurd judgments, particularly once when dining

with Cardinal Morton at London." "There happened to be at table an English lawyer, who run out into high commendation of the severe execution of justice upon thieves, who were then hanged so fast that there were sometimes twenty hanging upon one gibbet, and added, 'that he could not wonder enough how it came to pass that there were so many thieves left robbing in all places.'" Raphael answered, "that it was because the punishment of death was neither just in itself, nor good for the public; for as the severity was too great, so the remedy was not effectual. You, as well as other nations, like bad schoolmasters, chastise their scholars because they have not the skill to teach them." Raphael afterwards more specially ascribed the gangs of banditti who, after the suppression of Perkin Warbeck's Cornish revolt, infested England, to two causes; of which the first was the frequent disbanding of the idle and armed retainers of the nobles, who, when from necessity let loose from their masters, were too proud for industry, and had no resource but rapine; and the second was the conversion of much corn field into pasture for sheep, because the latter had become more profitable,—by which base motives many landholders were tempted to expel their tenants and destroy the food of man. Raphael suggested the substitution of hard labour for death; for which he quoted the example of the Romans, and of an imaginary community in Persia.

> The lawyer answered, 'that it could never be so settled in England, without endangering the whole nation by it:' he shook his head, and made some grimaces, and then held his peace and all the company seemed to be of his mind. But the cardinal said, 'It is not easy to say whether this plan would succeed or not, since no trial has been made of it; but it might be tried on thieves condemned to death, and adopted if found to answer; and vagabonds might be treated in the same way.' When the cardinal had said this, they all fell to commend the motion, though they had despised it when it came from me. They more particularly commended that concerning the vagabonds, because it had been added by him.

From some parts of the above extracts it is apparent that More, instead of having anticipated the economical doctrines of Adam Smith, as some modern writers have fancied, was thoroughly imbued with the prejudices of his contemporaries against the inclosure of commons, and the extension of pasture. It is, however, observable, that he is perfectly consistent with himself, and follows his principles through all their legitimate consequences, though they may end in doctrines of very startling sound. Considering separate property as always productive of unequal distribution of the fruits of labour, and regarding that inequality of fortune as the source of bodily suffering to those who labour, and of mental depravation to those who are not compelled to toil for subsistence, Hythloday is made to say, that, "as long as there is any property, and while money is the standard of all other things, he cannot expect that a nation can be governed either justly or happily." More himself objects to Hythloday:

> It seems to me that men cannot live conveniently where all things are common. How can there be any plenty where every man will excuse himself from labouring? for as the hope of gain does not excite him, so the confidence that he has in other men's industry may make him slothful. And if people come to be pinched with want, and yet cannot dispose of any thing as their own, what can follow but perpetual sedition and bloodshed;

especially when the reverence and authority due to magistrates fall to the ground; for I cannot imagine how they can be kept among those that are in all things equal to one another.

These remarks do in reality contain the germs of unanswerable objections to all those projects of a community of goods, which suppose the moral character of the majority of mankind to continue, at the moment of their adoption, such as it has been heretofore in the most favourable instances. If, indeed, it be proposed only on the supposition, that by the influence of laws, or by the agency of any other cause, mankind in general are rendered more honest, more benevolent, more disinterested than they have hitherto been, it is evident that they will, in the same proportion, approach to a practice more near the principle of an equality and a community of all advantages. The hints of an answer to Plato, thrown out by More, are so decisive, that it is not easy to see how he left this speck on his romance, unless we may be allowed to suspect that the speculation was in part suggested as a convenient cover for that biting satire on the sordid and rapacious government of Henry VII. which occupies a considerable portion of Hythloday's first discourse. It may also be supposed that More, not anxious to save visionary reformers from a few light blows in an attack aimed at corrupt and tyrannical statesmen, thinks it suitable to his imaginary personage, and conducive to the liveliness of his fiction, to represent the traveller in Utopia as touched by one of the most alluring and delusive of political chimeras.

> *Sir James Mackintosh, "Life of Sir Thomas More," in* The Miscellaneous Works of the Right Honourable Sir James Mackintosh, *edited by R. J. Mackintosh, 1846. Reprint by Carey and Hart, 1848, pp. 43-81.*

JOHN LORD CAMPBELL   (essay date 1861?)

[Campbell was an influential nineteenth-century English political minister and historian. He was extremely active in law reform, holding the offices of solicitor general, attorney general, chief justice of the queen's bench, and lord chancellor, successively. As a historian, he is remembered chiefly for his multivolume Lives of the Lord Chancellors and Keepers of the Great Seal of England *(1845-47) and* The Lives of the Chief Justices of England *(1849-57). G. P. Macdonell has written of the two works: "The merits of [Campbell's]* Lives *are very considerable. They are eminently readable. The style is lively, though rough, careless, and incorrect; every incident is presented effectively; they are full of good stories, and they contain a great deal of information about the history of law and lawyers which is not easily to be found elsewhere." In the following excerpt from his sympathetic biography of More in* Lives of the Lord Chancellors, *Campbell briefly surveys a selection of More's writings, giving highest accolades to* Utopia]

[More's] first literary essay is supposed to have been the fragment which goes under his name as the *History of Edward V. and Richard III,.* though some have ascribed it to Cardinal Morton, who probably furnished the materials for it to his precocious page, having been intimately mixed up with the transactions which it narrates. It has the merit of being the earliest historical composition in the English language; and, with all its defects, several ages elapsed before there was much improvement upon it, this being a department of literature in which England did not excel before the middle of the eighteenth century.

More's *Epigrammata*, though much admired in their day, not only in England, but all over Europe, are now only inspected by the curious, who wish to know how the Latin language was cultivated in the reign of Henry VII. The collection in its present form was printed at Basle from a manuscript supplied by Erasmus, consisting of detached copies made by various friends, without his authority or sanction. His own opinion of their merits is thus given in one of his epistles to Erasmus: "I was never much delighted with my Epigrams, as you are well aware; and if they had not pleased yourself and certain others better than they pleased me, the volume would never have been published." The subjects of these effusions are very multifarious—the ignorance of the clergy—the foibles of the fair sex—the pretensions of sciolists—the tricks of astrologers—the vices and follies of mankind—while they are prompted at times by the warmth of private friendship and the tenderness of domestic affection. (p. 70)

More's controversial writings, on which he bestowed most pains and counted most confidently for future fame, have long fallen into utter oblivion, the very titles of most of them having perished.

But the composition to which he attached no importance, —which, as a *jeu-d'esprit*, occupied a few of his idle hours when he retired from the bar,—and which he was with great difficulty prevailed upon to publish,—would of itself have made his name immortal. Since the time of Plato, there had been no composition given to the world which, for imagination, for philosophical discrimination, for a familiarity with the principles of government, for a knowledge of the springs of human action, for a keen observation of men and manners, and for felicity of expression, could be compared to the *Utopia*. Although the word, invented by More, has been introduced into the language, to describe what is supposed to be impracticable and visionary,—the work (with some extravagance and absurdities, devised perhaps with the covert object of softening the offence which might have been given by his satire upon the abuses of his age and country) abounds with lessons of practical wisdom. (p. 72)

> *John Lord Campbell, "Life of Sir Thomas More from His Resignation of the Great Seal Till His Death," in his* Lives of the Lord Chancellors and Keepers of the Great Seal of England: From the Earliest Times Till the Reign of King George IV, *Vol. II, fifth edition, 1868. Reprint by AMS Press, 1973, pp. 44-77.*

J. S. BREWER   (essay date 1862)

[Brewer was a nineteenth-century English historian and cleric. He achieved high academic distinction late in life, but he is perhaps most admired for his early labors among the London poor and selfless efforts to educate workhouse boys. In the following excerpt from his The Reign of Henry VIII, from His Accession to the Death of Wolsey, *a work originally published as part of the Public Record Office series* Letters and Papers, Foreign and Domestic, of the Reign of Henry VIII *(1862-1932), he relates* Utopia *to social and political conditions in sixteenth-century England and Europe.]*

A modern French author [Jules Michelet], with that sprightliness and lively declamation for which he is justly remarkable, characterizes the *Utopia* of Sir Thomas More as "an insipid romance in which the author has taken great pains to discover truths already realized by the mystic communists of the middle ages in a more original manner. The design of the work is common-place, its matter ordinary; it has little imagination, and less sense of reality." There is not the least reason for supposing that More was ever acquainted with the communistic doctrines of the middle ages, or ever wished to establish them. For common tables and community of goods in the institutions of Utopia, More was indebted to Plato and the laws of Lycurgus; for More was much more familiar with the classical than the middle ages;—and these were introduced for a different purpose than that which M. Michelet surmises. We readily concede that there is not to be found in the *Utopia* the wonderful invention, the inexhaustible wit, the profound learning, the broad farce, the abundant physical coarseness, the sarcasm and unextinguishable laughter, the tenderest and profoundest sentiments masquerading in grotesque and ludicrous shapes, the healthy vigorous humanity, overflowing at one time with clear and beautiful truths, and then anon stranded in pools of mud and filth, that are to be found in Rabelais. But the objects of the two men were as different as their natures. The wit and humour of More is that of the thoughtful observant Englishman, not breaking out into peals of laughter, but so quiet, sedate, and serious as to demand on the part of the reader something of the same habit of quiet thought and observation, to be fully perceived and enjoyed. More hovers so perpetually on the confines of jest and earnest, passes so naturally from one to the other, that the reader is in constant suspense whether his jest be serious, or his seriousness a jest. The book is wonderfully Englishlike; wonderfully like that balancing habit of mind which trembles on the verge of right and wrong, sometimes struggling on in happier times to clearer vision, sometimes, like More, shutting its eyes and relapsing into older impressions unable to endure suspense any longer.

In More's own day the *Utopia* was regarded as a mirror of the political and social evils of the times. "A burgomaster at Antwerp," writes Erasmus, "is so pleased with it, he knows it all by heart." Its popularity is attested by numerous editions and translations. The scene of it is laid in the then scarce-known regions of the West, where Christianity had not yet penetrated. It describes the social and political perfection to which the people of Utopia had arrived by the mere efforts of natural goodness, as compared with the corrupt institutions and manners of Christendom. The Utopians are not entirely free from usages which seem incompatible with a model republic, and this is part of the author's design. They attempt to prevent war by assassination, and bribe the subjects of their enemy to commit treason. But he must be dull indeed, who does not perceive that Utopia when following out these principles, is removed but a few miles from the English Channel, and that a practice which seems the more odious in these upright and wise Utopians was tenfold more unjustifiable in those who, professing the doctrines of Christ never scrupled to employ the same means against their own enemies. Were the intrigues of Henry VIII and his minister Dacre against Scotland more moral than these? Were not their attempts to sow treason and disaffection among the Scotch lords an exact exemplification of this Utopian policy? (pp. 288-89)

But Utopia is nowhere, and was never intended to be, set up as a model to be literally followed. Could More seriously advocate a community of goods, even if as a sound law-

Title page of the first printing of Utopia.

yer he could expect to see the Utopian prohibition verified, that the nations of Europe should have fewer laws and no lawyers? Could he gravely recommend a purely elective monarchy, even if, with his religious views, he might have justified the marriage of priests, to which he has never given any sanction in his writings? But though the *Utopia* was not to be literally followed—was no more than an abstraction at which no one would have laughed more heartily than More himself, if interpreted too strictly—Utopia might serve to show to a corrupt Christendom what good could be effected by the natural instincts of men when following the dictates of natural prudence and justice. If kings could never be elective in Europe, Utopia might show the advantage to a nation where kings were responsible to some other will than their own. If property could never be common, Utopia might teach men how great was the benefit to society when the state regarded itself as created for the well-being of all, and not of a class or a favoured few. Literally property could never be common, except in Utopia; but it might be so in effect in Christian communities when capital and property were more widely diffused,—when the enormous disproportion between the poor and the rich, the noble and the serf, was modified by social improvements,—when laws were simplified, and the statute book disencumbered of obsolete and unintelligible Acts, too often put in force to catch the unwary, and made an instrument of oppression by the crown lawyers.

It might, perhaps, be thought that More attributed too much to nature,—that in the misery and confusion of his times, in the deadlock of all social, political, and religious reforms, in his dissatisfaction at Christianity, as exhibited in the lives of his contemporaries, he gladly turned away to an ideal as little like the reality as possible, and pleased himself, as some did at the French Revolution, with a pure social abstraction removed from all those debasing influences under which men groaned. We might be tempted to think for a moment that he wavered in his allegiance to Christianity, and that the beautiful visions of Platonic republics and ancient patriots, fostered by his classical studies, had for a time overmastered his imagination, as was the case with many others. Christianity, in his days at least, could present no such heroical virtue, no such grace or beauty, as Paganism had done, and was then doing, with an intensity of attraction to the newly-awakened longings of men, of which we can form no conception. Were monks and friars comparable to the ancient philosopher and his supper of herbs? Were Christian kings of the sixteenth century, imperious, headstrong, passionate, and arbitrary, immersed in the games of war and ambition, absorbed by the tournament, or the chase, impatient of contradiction, deaf to good advice—comparable to the Catos, the Reguli, the Spartan or Sabine rulers of the old republics? Had not the advancement of the faith been made a pretext for spoliation and aggrandizement? Had not its teachers taken part rather with the oppressors than the oppressed? Were not half the wars of Christendom traceable to this one cause?—ignoble wars that only fostered the evils under which society laboured, strengthening the oppressor and trampling on the weak? Had More's faith staggered at the trial, it could have occasioned little surprise; but apparently it did not. For Christianity is introduced among the Utopians; it is readily received by them from its secret sympathy with their own opinions and institutions in its purer form.

But a very brief sketch of the Utopian political and social regulations will point out more clearly the prevalent evils of More's days.... [The] endless wars, the faithless leagues, the military expenditure, the money and time wasted upon instruments and means of offence to the neglect of all social improvements, unsettled habits, trains of idle serving-men re-enacting in the streets the interminable brawls of the Montagues and Capulets, broken and disabled soldiers turning to theft, and filling Alsatia for lack of employment, labour disarranged, husbandry broken up, villages and hamlets depopulated to feed sheep, agricultural labourers turned adrift, but forbidden to stray, and driven home from tithing to tithing by the lash, to starve; no poorhouses, no hospitals, though the sweating sickness raged through the land, but the poor left to perish as paupers by the side of the ditches, filling the air with fever and pestilence, houses never swept or ventilated, choked with rotten thatch above and unchanged rushes within, streets reeking with offal and filthy puddles, no adequate supply of water for cleanliness or health, penal laws stringently enforced, more stringently as the evils grew greater, crime and its punishment struggling for the upper hand, justice proud of its executions, and wondering that theft multiplied faster than the gibbet. Then again, and unquestionably the greatest blot upon the reign of Henry VIII. —was the sudden revival of obsolete statutes; as in the punishment of the London apprentices and the *præmunire* in 1530. More's language looks prophetical, as if he

pierced into futurity, and saw beneath the popular and fascinating exterior of Henry VIII. the monarch who should one day use the law, not for the protection, but the oppression of his subjects. "One set of ministers," says the supposed traveller in Utopia,

> will bring forward some old musty laws that have been antiquated by a long disuse, and which, as they have been forgotten by all the king's subjects, so they have also been broken by them; and will urge that the levying of the penalties of these laws, as it will bring in a vast treasure, so also fails not of a very good pretence, *since it would look like the executing of the law and the doing of justice.*

> Another proposes that the judges should be made sure of, that in all causes affecting the king they may always give sentence in his favour, and be sent for to the palace and invited to discuss the matter before the king, that there may be no cause of his, however obviously unjust, in which some among them, either through love of contradiction, or pride of singularity, or desire to win favour, will not find out some pretence or another for giving sentence in the king's behalf.... And there never will be wanting some pretext for declaring in the king's favor;—as, that equity is on his side, or the strict letter of the law, or some forced interpretation of it; or if none of these, that the royal prerogative ought with conscientious judges to outweigh all other considerations. And these notions are fostered by the maxims, that the king can do no wrong, however much he may wish to do it; that not only the property, but the persons of his subjects, are his;—that a man has a right to no more than the king's goodness think fit not to take from him. (pp. 290-93)

Such evils as these could have no place among the Utopians. Their monarchy was elective, their government strictly representative:—"The prince is for life, but he is removable on suspicion of a design to enslave his people." Strange doctrine this in the reign of Henry VIII.! Due provision was made for the health, education, employment, recreation of the people—subjects quite below the consideration of monarchs and ministers in Christian Europe. Every street was twenty feet broad; every house was built of stone, with its garden behind it for health and recreation; a striking contrast to the mean hovels, mud walls, thatched roofs, straggling with overhanging gables, and shutting out both air and light in the metropolis of England. Labour alternated from town to country and from country to town; learning followed work, and work learning. Public lectures were given every morning before daybreak; after supper diversion; summer in their gardens, winter in their public halls, with music and discourse. No games except chess were allowed, or an allegorical tournament between vices and virtues. All, whatever their condition, male or female, noble or ignoble, were set to learn some trade. Six hours for labour, the others for rest; but that rest must be reasonably employed in reading, exercise, or gardening. Labour common, and property common; common halls in every district, "where they all meet and eat;" hospitals without the walls, "so large that they may pass for little towns; by this means, if they had ever such a number of sick, they could lodge them conveniently, and at sufficient distances to prevent contagion." No slaughter-houses permitted within the walls, no offal, no pestilential manufactures. In the country these restrictions were relaxed.

Fathers and grandfathers, sons and daughters-in-law, made one family, and lived under the same roof, like More's own family at Chelsea. In this respect no philosopher ever exemplified his own precepts more perfectly than More. And if we may accept the repeated and uniform assurances of his contemporaries—if the respect and affection of all his household, which accompanied him even to the scaffold, be any test —his own practice must have been the noblest proof of the sound wisdom of his theory. Englishmen and strangers admitted to his acquaintance testify to the peace, purity, love, courtesy, and refinement that reigned supreme in his family; —far more Utopian, when compared with what is known of the private lives of his contemporaries, than any household in Utopia itself.

No wonder, then, that cheerfulness, regard to the welfare and happiness of others, gentleness and good nature, formed a very prominent part in the philosophy of the Utopians, and these not merely as private but public virtues;—that on the same principle gambling, hunting, and field sports were disallowed, as pleasures purchased by the pain of inferior animals, and degenerating into brutality by frequent indulgence. Closely connected with these feelings was the attention paid by the Utopians to the condition of the labouring classes, and their regulations to prevent the workman, skilled or unskilled, from being ground down to that hopeless wretchedness, which at last burst out into open rebellion here and on the continent. (pp. 294-95)

Nor is More less severe against the foreign policy of the governments of Europe; their utter carelessness in breaking treaties however solemnly ratified; their employment of mercenaries; the absence of all controlling power on the part of the popes, who rather imitated than denounced the pernicious practices of the secular rulers. "The Utopians," he says, "make no leagues as other nations do. What is the use of leagues? say they; do you think that a man will care for words whom natural affection fails to reconcile to his fellow-man?" Then adds More, with grave irony:

> In Europe, and especially the parts about us where Christianity is received, the majesty of treaties is everywhere regarded as holy and inviolable, partly from the justice and goodness of kings, partly from the fear and reverence they feel for the sovereign Pontiffs; for as the latter never take engagements upon them which they do not religiously observe, so they enjoin upon all princes to abide by their promises at all hazards, and if they equivocate, subject them to ecclesiastical censures! For they justly consider it a most indecent thing, for them who claim the title of *the faithful* to show *no faith* in their treaties.

Again, in illustration of this topic, More observes: if in their wars against their enemies other means fail, "they sow the seeds of dissension among them, and set up the king's brother or some nobleman to aspire to the crown." "Or," he continues, "if domestic factions languish, they stir up against them the neighbouring nations; and rummaging out some old claims which are never wanting to princes, supply them abundantly with money for the war, but not with their own troops." Then follows a passage aimed so directly against the policy of England that I wonder More had the courage to insert it, only that as France pursued the same methods, unreflecting readers might not

at once perceive how the arrow glanced from one nation to the other:—

> They hire soldiers from all places, but chiefly from the Zapoletæ (the Swiss); a hardy race, patient of heat, cold and labor; strangers to all delights, indifferent to agriculture, careless of their houses and their clothes, studious of nothing but their cattle. They live by hunting and plunder; born only for war, which they watch all opportunities of engaging in, they embrace it eagerly when offered, and are ready to serve any prince that will hire them, in great numbers. They know none of the arts of life, except how to take it away. They serve their employers actively and faithfully; but will bind themselves to no certain terms, and only agree on condition that next day they shall go over to the enemy if he promises larger pay, and veer back again the day after at a higher bidding. As war rarely arises in which a greater part of them is not enlisted on both sides, it often happens that kinsmen and most intimate friends, hired from the same cantons, find themselves opposed, engage and kill one another, regardless of these ties, for no other consideration than that they have been hired to do so for a miserable pay, by princes of opposite interests; and they are so nice in demanding it that they will change sides for the advance of a halfpenny. And yet their wages are of no use to them, for they spend them immediately in low dissipation. They serve the Utopians against all the world, for they are the best paymasters. And as the Utopians look out for good men for their own use at home, they employ the greatest scoundrels abroad; and they think they do a great service to mankind by thus ridding the world of the entire scum of such a foul and nefarious population.

But it is time for me to bring these remarks to a close. If any one wishes to see the real condition of Europe at this period—the arbitrary rule of its monarchs bent on their own aggrandisement, and careless of the improvement of their people—the disputes among their councillors, agreed in one point only, to flatter and mislead their sovereigns—the wide separation between the luxury of the rich and the hopeless misery of the poor—the prevalence of crime—the severe execution of justice, earnest for punishment, but regardless of prevention—the frequency of capital punishment—the depopulation of villages—the engrossing by a few hands of corn and wool—the scarcity of meat—the numbers of idle gentlemen without employment—of idle serving-men and retainers turned adrift on a life of vagabondism:—in short, whoever wishes to see society full of the elements of confusion, requiring only a small spark to fan them into a flame, may read with advantage the *Utopia* of Sir Thomas More. (pp. 295-97)

> *J. S. Brewer, "Two Books of the Period," in his* The Reign of Henry VIII from His Accession to the Death of Wolsey, Vol. I, *edited by James Gairdner, John Murray, 1884, pp. 285-97.*

SIDNEY LEE   (essay date 1907)

[*Lee is best known as an accomplished Shakespearean scholar and as the exacting editor of the* Dictionary of National Biography. *In the latter capacity, he oversaw the writing of most of the* Dictionary's *63 original volumes as well as its first two supplements. In the following excerpt from his* Great Englishmen of the Sixteenth Century, *a work based on research done for the* Dictionary, *he praises the Renaissance spirit of* Utopia *and briefly surveys More's lesser writings.*]

The *Utopia* of Sir Thomas More is the main monument of his genius. It is as admirable in literary form as it is original in thought. (p. 57)

None who read the *Utopia* can deny that its author drank deep of the finest spirit of his age. None can question that he foresaw the main lines along which the political and social ideals of the Renaissance were to develop in the future. There is hardly a scheme of social or political reform that has been enunciated in later epochs of which there is no definite adumbration in More's pages. But he who passes hastily from the speculations of More's *Utopia* to the record of More's subsequent life and writings will experience a strange shock. Nowhere else is he likely to be faced by so sharp a contrast between precept and practice, between enlightened and vivifying theory in the study and adherence in the work-a-day world to the unintelligent routine of bigotry and obscurantism. By the precept and theory of his *Utopia*, More cherished and added power to the new light. By his practical conduct in life he sought to extinguish the illuminating forces to which his writing offered fuel.

The facts of the situation are not open to question. More was long associated in the government of his country on principles which in the *Utopia* he condemned. He acquiesced in a system of rule which rested on inequalities of rank and wealth, and made no endeavour to diminish poverty. In the sphere of religion More's personal conduct most conspicuously conflicted with the aspirations of his Utopians. So far from regarding Pantheism, or any shape of undogmatic religion, as beneficial, he lost no opportunity of denouncing it as sinful; he regarded the toleration in practical life of differences on religious questions as sacrilegious. He actively illustrated more than once his faith in physical coercion or punishment as a means of bringing men to a sense of the only religion which seemed to him to be true. Into his idealistic romance he had introduced a saving clause to the effect that he was not at one with his Utopians at all points. He gave no indication that by the conduct of his personal life he ranked himself with their strenuous foes.

The discrepancy is not satisfactorily accounted for by the theory that his political or religious views suffered change after the *Utopia* was written. No man adhered more rigidly through life to the religious tenets that he had adopted in youth. From youth to age his dominant hope was to fit himself for the rewards in a future life of honest championship of the Catholic Christian faith. No man was more consistently conservative in his attitude to questions of current politics. He believed in the despotic principle of government and the inevitableness of class distinctions. But the breadth of his intellectual temper admitted him also to regions of speculation which were beyond the range of any established religious or political doctrines. He was capable of a detachment of mind which blinded him to the inconsistencies of his double part. The student of More's biography cannot set the *Utopia* in its proper place among More's achievements unless he treat it as proof of his mental sensitiveness to the finest issues of the era, as evidence of his gift of literary imagination, as an impressively fine play of fancy, which was woven by the writer far away from his own work-a-day world in a realm which was not bounded by facts or practical affairs, as they were known to him. Whatever the effects of More's imaginings on readers, whatever their practical bearing in others'

minds on actual conditions of social life, the *Utopia* was for its creator merely a vision, which melted into thin air in his brain as he stood face to face with the realities of life. When the dream ended, the brilliant pageant faded from his consciousness and left not a wrack behind. (pp. 62-4)

As a writer, More's fame mainly depended on his political romance of *Utopia*, which was penned in finished Latin. His Latin style, both in prose and verse, is of rare lucidity, and entitles him to a foremost place among English contributors to the Latin literature of the Renaissance. His *Utopia* is an admirable specimen of fluent and harmonious Latin prose. With the popular English translation of his romance, which was first published sixteen years after his death, he had no concern. Much English verse as well as much Latin verse came from More's active pen. Critics have usually ignored or scorned his English poetry. Its theme is mainly the fickleness of fortune and the voracity of time. But freshness and sincerity characterise his treatment of these well-worn topics, and, though the rhythm is often harsh, and the modern reader may be repelled by archaic vocabulary and constructions, More at times achieves metrical effects which adumbrate the art of Edmund Spenser. Of English prose More made abundant use in treating both secular and religious themes.... [*The History of Richard III.*] is an admirable example of Tudor prose, clear and simple, free from pedantry and singularly modern in construction. Similar characteristics are only a little less conspicuous in More's authentic biography of Pico, the Italian humanist, who, like More himself, yielded to theology abilities that were better adapted to win renown in the pursuit of profane literature.

It is, however, by the voluminous polemical tracts and devotional treatises of his closing career that More's English prose must be finally judged. In controversy More wrote with a rapidity and fluency which put dignity out of the question. Very often the tone is too spasmodic and interjectional to give his work genuine literary value. In the heat of passion he sinks to scurrility which admits of no literary form. But it is only episodically that his anger gets the better of his literary temper. His native humour was never long repressible, and some homely anecdote or proverbial jest usually rushed into his mind to stem the furious torrents of his abuse. When the gust of his anger passed, he said what he meant with the simple directness that comes of conviction, unconstrained by fear. Vigour and freedom are thus the main characteristics of his controversial English prose.

There is smaller trace of individual style in his books of religious exhortation and devotion, but their pious placidity does not exclude bursts both of eloquence and anecdotal reminiscence which prove his wealth of literary energy and of humoursome originality. To one virtue as a writer in English he can make no claim: pointed brevity was out of his range. In Latin he could achieve epigrams, but all his English works in prose are of massive dimensions, and untamable volubility.

For two centuries after his death More was regarded by Catholic Europe as the chief glory of English literature. In the seventeenth century the Latin countries deemed Shakespeare and Bacon his inferiors. It was his Latin writing that was mainly known abroad. But, even in regard to that branch of his literary endeavours, time has long since largely dissipated his early fame. In the lasting literature of the world, More is only remembered as the author of the *Utopia*, wherein he lives for all time, not so much as a man of letters, but in that imaginative rôle, which contrasts so vividly with other parts in his repertory, of social reformer and advocate of reason. In English literary history his voluminous work in English prose deserves grateful, if smaller, remembrance. Despite the many crudities of his utterance, he first indicated that native English prose might serve the purpose of great literature as effectively as Latin prose, which had hitherto held the field among all men of cultivated intelligence. There is an added paradox in the revelation that one who was the apostle in England at once of the cosmopolitan culture of the classical Renaissance and of the medieval dogmatism of the Roman Catholic Church should also be a strenuous champion of the literary usage of his vernacular tongue. But paradox streaks all facets of More's career.

Few careers are more memorable for their pathos than More's. Fewer still are more paradoxical. In that regard he was a true child of an era of ferment and undisciplined enthusiasm, which checked orderliness of conduct or aspiration. Sir Thomas More's variety of aim, of ambition, has indeed few parallels even in the epoch of the Renaissance. Looking at him from one side we detect only a religious enthusiast, cheerfully sacrificing his life for his convictions—a man whose religious creed, in defence of which he faced death, abounded in what seems, in the dry light of reason, to be superstition. Yet surveying More from another side we find ourselves in the presence of one endowed with the finest enlightenment of the Renaissance, a man whose outlook on life was in advance of his generation; possessed too of such quickness of wit, such imaginative activity, such sureness of intellectual insight, that he could lay bare with pen all the defects, all the abuses, which worn-out conventions and lifeless traditions had imposed on the free and beneficent development of human endeavour and human society. That the man, who, by an airy effort of the imagination, devised the new and revolutionary ideal of *Utopia*, should end his days on the scaffold as a martyr to ancient beliefs which shackled man's intellect and denied freedom to man's thought is one of history's perplexing ironies. Sir Thomas More's career propounds a riddle which it is easier to enunciate than to solve. (pp. 90-4)

Sidney Lee, "Sir Thomas More," in his Great Englishmen of the Sixteenth Century, *second edition, 1907. Reprint by Thomas Nelson & Sons, 1910, pp. 44-94.*

G. K. CHESTERTON (essay date 1933)

[*Regarded as one of England's premier men of letters during the first half of the twentieth century, Chesterton is best known today as a colorful bon vivant, a witty essayist, and as the creator of the Father Brown mysteries and the fantasy* The Man Who Was Thursday *(1908). Much of Chesterton's work reveals his childlike enjoyment of life and reflects his pronounced Anglican and, later, Roman Catholic beliefs. His essays are characterized by their humor, frequent use of paradox, and chatty, rambling style. In the following excerpt from an essay written for the anthology* The English Way: Studies in English Sanctity from St. Bede to Newman, *he examines humoristic elements in More's major works.*]

If anyone had looked for the name of Thomas More in the century or so after his death he would probably have found first the isolated mention of a sort of legend: that he was the Man Who Died Laughing. He is mentioned in this manner in more than one of those quaint collections of freaks and monsters and old-world anecdotes such as were common in the whole period from Aubrey to Isaac Disraeli. The story is something of a simplification and an exaggeration; but it is not one which the admirers of Thomas More will in any sense desire to deny. There is no doubt that he died jesting; and that he would have been the first to see the fun of having his death commemorated in a jest-book. In other words, he was not only a humanist, but a humorist; a humorist both in the contemporary and the modern sense. (p. 209)

If, on the other hand, anyone confine his curiosity about Thomas More to an enquiry about the popular notions surrounding the name in quite modern times, he would probably find that More has mostly been remembered as the author of *Utopia*; in some sense as the author of all the Utopias.... (pp. 209-10)

Unfortunately many modern humanists, who know that he even jested in his death, cannot bring themselves to believe that he ever jested in his youth. The fact is that *Utopia* is one mass of the sort of questions which are asked by jesting youth, as by jesting Pilate, even if neither of them waits for an answer. Why should we have all this complicated botheration about private property; how about having property in common, like the monks? Why not assassinate the one foreign statesman who is certainly planning a world-war, instead of massacring millions of harmless people who never wanted any war? Are animals immortal; or why aren't they? Wouldn't it really be a jolly good thing for the country if all lawyers were kicked out of it? Would not divorce be a very comfortable solution of a lot of uncomfortable problems, if only it could be allowed? Might not Nudism be at least a temporary measure; as connected, for instance, with what is now called Companionate Marriage? Is it really possible for a man to think anything except what he does think; and in that case, can it be right to make him responsible even for false doctrine or bad influence? Is it really impossible to have a simpler society, with all the Gordian knots of life cut with this sort of private pocket-knife of common sense? Those are the sort of random rationalistic questions which filled his head, and his period, and his first fantastic book; and if Mr. Bernard Shaw had put them into the mouth of a highly Nonconformist negress, many might now suppose that they were quite novel. But if it be asked how or why a Catholic, let alone a great and holy Catholic, even entertained such ideas, the answer is that a thinking Catholic always does entertain them—if only to reject them. Thomas More did primarily entertain them and did finally reject them. A Catholic is not a man who never thinks of such things. A Catholic is a man who really knows why he does not think they are true. But when people begin to think they are true, to think that far worse things are true, to force the worst things of all upon the world, the situation is entirely different; and cannot be related in any way to the jokes which a young Renaissance humorist put into a book like *Utopia*. (pp. 211-12)

G. K. Chesterton, "Thomas More," in The English Way: Studies in English Sanctity from St. Bede to Newman, *edited by Maisie Ward, 1933. Re-*

print by Books for Libraries Press, 1968, pp. 209-17.

R. W. CHAMBERS   (essay date 1935)

[*Chambers was an English scholar and writer whose interests ranged from early German legends to seventeenth-century English literature. He is especially known for his works on More and his circle, particularly his highly regarded (if sometimes controversial) 1935 biography of More. In the following excerpt from this work, he discusses More's place in the history of English thought and letters.*]

[More] connects Medieval England with Modern England, and he connects England with Europe. Think of him first in connection with the continuity of the English speech, English prose, English literature. To the student of the English language he is a vital link between Middle and Modern English. To the student of English prose his work is the great link which connects modern prose with the medieval prose of Nicholas Love, Walter Hilton, and Richard Rolle, and so with the older English prose of the earlier Middle Ages. To the student of English thought More is equally vital: he points forward to our own times; but he also points back to William Langland, and More and his writings help us to see a continuity running through English literature and history. The late Sir Walter Raleigh said, 'Nothing is more striking than the way English people do not alter'. However that may be, Langland and More deal with somewhat similar problems in a way which does not much alter.

The modern statesman is struck with the modernity of Langland. 'In Piers Plowman is to be found the Englishman of to-day, with the same strength and weakness, the same humour, immutable.' Yet Langland is a Catholic poet of the Middle Ages. So with More. We think of More, and rightly, as our first great modern; as the first great English vernacular historian; or as the first and greatest of an illustrious line of writers of *Utopias*; or as the greatest member of our first group of modern scholars, a man skilled in calling bad names in good Latin; and Dr. Reed has shown us how we have to look to him and his circle for the beginnings of Modern English drama. But More was also the last great man who lived the whole of his life with the England of the Middle Ages yet undestroyed around him; a land of great libraries which had been accumulating since Anglo-Saxon times; of ancient religious houses where the walls were covered with paintings, and the windows shone with the glorious English glass of the Fourteenth and Fifteenth Centuries; a land of schools and hospitals more plentiful than they were to be again for many a day. More is a product of those late Middle Ages of which Dante is the supreme figure; he is the consistent opponent of the new ideas which found literary expression in *The Prince*, and were embodied in the person of Thomas Cromwell. (pp. 359-60)

[The] description of the Utopian state, with its communism, its sacerdotalism, its love of beauty and of symbolic ritual, remains in touch with the Middle Ages. The charges of inconsistency against More arise from our forgetting all this; from our forgetting that his life falls in this last age of English medieval Catholicism, and from our reading back, into his earlier writings, the experience, and even the propaganda, of later generations. Burnet or

Froude feel that *When More wrote the* **Utopia,** *he was in advance of his time. None could see the rogue's face under the cowl clearer than he.* It is just because More *is* medieval that he can 'see the rogue's face under the cowl' without thereby attacking monasticism as an institution. Froude could not; so he calls More a bigot. We might as well think that Fra Angelico was anti-clerical, because, among the group which he depicted as being carried off to Hell from the Last Judgment, we can see the tonsured head, the cardinal's hat, and the bishop's mitre.

In a very similar way the English Reformers misunderstood William Langland. The modern Catholic historian sees in Langland 'the Catholic Englishman *par excellence*, at once the most English of Catholic poets and the most Catholic of English poets', and no one to-day would dispute this judgment. But to John Bale it was clear that William Langland was one of the first disciples of John Wiclif, and that he wrote *Piers Plowman* to reprove the blasphemies of the Papists against God and his Christ. *Piers Plowman* was printed by a Reformer, as good Protestant propaganda.

A little more than a century after More wrote **Utopia,** Francis Bacon wrote his imitation, the *New Atlantis*. A comparison of **Utopia** with the *New Atlantis* may put More's book into its right perspective. It is an odd coincidence, and a helpful one, that our two greatest Lord Chancellors should each have depicted an imaginary commonwealth.

The simplicity of **Utopia,** with its citizens clothed in their Franciscan garb, belongs to an age when voluntary poverty was still an ideal, and an ideal sometimes practised.... [It] was an ideal which More always had before him; we [notice] the spirit of St. Francis in his satisfaction when he finds himself a quite penniless prisoner, dependent for his food upon the charity of that great lady, Mistress Alice: 'Me thinketh God maketh me a wanton, and setteth me on his lap, and dandleth me.' Therefore it is natural that the Prince and the Bishop in Utopia are dressed with the same simplicity as their subjects, distinguished only by a little sheaf, or taper of wax, carried before them. Bacon, on the other hand, combined a carried before them. Bacon, on the other hand, combined a rather childish love of pomp with that very real zeal for the life. When he was married to his 'young wench', a contemporary gossip tells us, 'he was clad from top to toe in purple, and made himself and his wife such store of raiments of cloth of silver and gold that it drew deep into her portion'. It is characteristic of Bacon that when he discusses 'philanthropy' he feels it necessary to utter a warning against unwise self-denial. And so in the *New Atlantis*, a Professor from the College wears gloves set with precious stones, and shoes of peach-coloured velvet; and (what would have shocked More yet further) our Professor has fifty attendants, 'young men all, in white satin loose coats up to the mid-leg, and stockings of white silk, and shoes of blue velvet, and hats of blue velvet, with fine plumes of divers colours set round like hatbands'.

The austerity of the attire of the citizens of Utopia is set off by the ritualistic pomp of the priests' vestments during worship. But we hear nothing of any such Church ritual in the *New Atlantis*.

On the other hand, whilst More does not make his Utopians Christian, and does not give them any sacred book,

Bacon invents an outrageous piece of 'miraculous evangelism', in order to ensure that the *New Atlantis* shall have the canonical books of the Old and New Testament, wrapped in sindons of linen, floated over the ocean in a small ark of cedar wood. It is not that More neglected his Bible; his devotional works contain long passages of translation from the Gospels which should have given him high rank among English Bible-translators. And his interest in Erasmus' *New Testament* is shown, among other things, by his epigrams. Nevertheless, the library which Hythlodaye took with him to Utopia consisted of Greek works of literature and science. Hythlodaye and his companions instructed the Utopians in Greek; and also in the mysteries of the Christian religion; but we hear nothing of any evangelical literature, as yet, in Utopia. Whilst More was writing *Utopia*, the Greek *New Testament* of Erasmus had appeared; here was a chance for More to have brought 'his darling' into his book, as he has brought his other friends. Yet he does not take the opening. The immediate problem of the Utopian converts, as it appears to More, is not how the text of the Gospels can be got out to them, but how a priest is to be appointed to minister the sacraments. Bacon does not bother his head about the apostolic succession among his New Atlanteans. They have got the Word of God.

Surely this difference alone should have been sufficient to show how far More was, at the time of writing *Utopia*, from the Protestantism which has so light-heartedly claimed *Utopia* for its own.

In secular affairs the contrast of Bacon and More is equally marked: Bacon trusts, for the relief of man's estate, to the growth of science; More looks to a more equal distribution of wealth.

Now in England 'Progress' for many centuries moved, not in accordance with the Catholic, medieval, collectivist hopes of More, but along the path indicated by Bacon, the Protestant man of science. And that path *has* led to the 'relief of man's estate', in material things at any rate. Nevertheless, all that had been hoped had not been accomplished, and so the Nineteenth Century saw a revolt, of which the Oxford Movement and *News from Nowhere* were different manifestations. Now it was just because of this return to medievalism that *Utopia* made a strong appeal to the Nineteenth Century, and still makes its appeal. The solemn churches of Utopia move us, while the evangelical miracle of the *New Atlantis* only excites our scepticism. The voluntary poverty of Utopia meets what we feel to be our need. But the wealth lavished upon the Research Professor by the naïve inhabitants of the New Atlantis is bound to cause searchings of heart in the breast of any moderately modest professor; and I speak from thirty years' experience when I say that it always rouses laughter when read to his class. We look back on the *New Atlantis* as a great landmark we have left behind: *Utopia* is still before us.

And so we call *Utopia* 'progressive'. And then we wonder that More resisted 'the progressive movement of his time', forgetting that the charm of *Utopia* lies exactly in the fact that it championed the things, all trace of which 'the progressive movement of his time', in its haste for change and wealth, was sweeping away. Is it not because we are ourselves too inconsistent to appreciate his consistency, that we blame Sir Thomas More? Like those persons wearing

green spectacles of whom Hooker speaks, we think that which we see is green, when indeed that is green whereby we see.

Thomas More ranks with William Langland before him, and Edmund Burke after him, among the greatest of our Reforming Conservatives. Langland, More and Burke are alike in their hatred of oppression and corruption – a hatred which in each case is too fierce to be always just. Yet each, when he finds this hatred leading to revolution, shows marked want of sympathy with the revolutionaries. 'It is no inconsiderable part of wisdom,' said Burke, 'to know how much of an evil ought to be tolerated.' And Burke said this, it is to be noted, not in his Conservative old age, but in the book in which he began his career as a Whig statesman. Burke's sentence might be taken as a motto for much of More's controversial writing against the Reformers; More's constant plea is that the misuse of a good thing does not justify us in abolishing the thing itself.

Langland, More, and Burke place almost first among the order of things which has come down to them, and which they feel it their duty to preserve, such a measure of unity, small or great, as the Christendom of their age has been able to inherit.

The First Book of *Utopia* points back to the medieval ideal of a common Christendom; it is this ideal which makes More hate war among Christian princes, just as it made Langland speak of Edward's French wars as contrary to conscience. This ideal of a united Christendom made Chaucer, who had himself fought in those French wars, pass over as unworthy of record the achievements of his perfect gentle knight in France, whilst he enumerated at length that knight's rather desultory crusades. It is this longing for Unity, Holy Church, and passion against the schism which is destroying it, that inspire the great closing section of *Piers Plowman*:

> Quoth Conscience to all Christians then, my counsel is, we wend
> Hastily into Unity, and hold we us there
> And pray we that a Peace were . . .

It is for 'the common corps of Christendom' that More is always pleading; and for it he died. It might seem that by the death of More and his fellow martyrs, the 'common corps' had been shattered beyond possibility of recovery. Yet by the Eighteenth Century the bitterness of the Wars of Religion had died down. As in the early Sixteenth Century, men might hope for an age of Peace and Reason. Abroad, after the Peace of Utrecht, people were talking, as they had talked in the days of Erasmus two hundred years before, of a League of Peace among Christian Princes. The Eighteenth Century was in a better position to understand More than the later Sixteenth or the Seventeenth, and Addison gloried in More's heroism and in his virtues. From some aspects Swift seems to be More come to life again; in *Gulliver* he gives to *Utopia* the honour, rare with him, of direct and repeated imitation, and he repays his debt by depicting Thomas More as the one modern man worthy to rank with the five noblest men of antiquity. Swift has been described as the soul of Rabelais in a dry place; we might think of him as the mind of Sir Thomas More without More's patience or More's faith, wandering through desert places seeking rest, and finding none. But in nothing is the likeness more strong than in the passion shown by Swift against the futile wars of Christian nations which, when narrated, arouse the disgust alike of the virtuous Houyhnhnms and of the magnanimous giants of Brobdingnag. Few things are more remarkable than the salute passed from Jonathan Swift to Thomas More across the two intervening centuries of futile religious strife; it is a sign that, with the cessation of the Wars of Religion, the standpoint of a common European civilization is again becoming intelligible. At the end of the Eighteenth Century, it is possible for Burke to conceive Western Europe as a unit, before the upheaval of the French Revolution. We cannot but be reminded of More when reading the great passage near the end of the *First Letter on a Regicide Peace*, where Burke eulogizes Europe as 'virtually one great state'. Langland's lament over the Papal schism, More's difference with Henry VIII, Swift's hatred of the Whig war-party, Burke's quarrel with the Jacobins, are all at bottom one: the complaint of the man who longs for unity and peace in Europe against those whom, justly or unjustly, he regards as, in Burke's words, 'making a schism' in the European system.

There is another sentence of Burke which may be a help towards the understanding of Sir Thomas More. When well over sixty, Burke recalled how 'pretty early in his service' he had told the House that 'he had taken his ideas of liberty very low; in order that they should stick to him, and that he might stick to them, to the end of his life'. More had taken his ideas of liberty very low; so low that, one might think, there should have been little difficulty in sticking to them. Yet he stuck to them only at the cost of his life.

More, if we can trust his biographer, spoke freely in Parliament during the reign of Henry VII; his plea for freedom of speech in the parliament of Henry VIII is classic; but, as a Tudor statesman, he necessarily placed the rights of authority very high indeed; if he died for liberty, it was only for that last stronghold of liberty—the right of the free man not to be compelled to say that which he does not believe.

Of course, first and foremost, More gave his life, not for liberty at all, but for Unity, 'in and for the Faith of the Holy Catholic Church'. So he said on the scaffold; at his trial he was able to speak more at length, and it was *then* that he put forward the plea of liberty of conscience. It seems to be agreed that thereby he was claiming for himself a liberty which he denied to others: most of our great historians who have dealt with his trial say so. (pp. 360-66)

More in the *Utopia* depicted the State as laying down what doctrines might be publicly preached and how they might be preached. To disobey is to be guilty of tumult and sedition, and to incur the severest punishment. More held that the heretics *were* so guilty, and deserved severe punishment. More's consistency was put to the extreme test when he found himself faced with the same problem which the heretics had had to face; when the State decided against the view which he held to be true. More allowed himself to be silenced. He maintained this silence both to his fellow-sufferers and to his enemies. His enemies were puzzled. They could not see why a man who submitted so far should not submit farther. More's strictly Utopian attitude comes out at his trial. He is entitled to plead con-

science, he asserts, *just because* he has given no occasion of tumult or sedition.

Not long before his own imprisonment, More had enumerated the cases of the only heretics (seven in all) who, so far as he knew, had suffered death in England in recent times – actually within the preceding eighteen years. He had maintained that, under the law, they had had no wrong. Now, thanks chiefly to Foxe, it is easy to control More's judgment in all seven cases. All these martyrs seem to have been devoted and heroic men, and some of them were assuredly saintly men. But they had all used that 'contentious rebuking and inveighing' which More, when he wrote *Utopia*, thought a penal offence. Further, they had all either recanted, and then deliberately broken their oath, or else they had 'given occasion of tumult and sedition'; most of them had done both these things. His adversaries tried to force More to 'give occasion of tumult and sedition'; by saying that he was afraid of death, they tried to taunt him into uttering treason. If More had publicly and violently denounced the Act declaring the King Supreme Head, after it had been made high treason to do so; if he had then been forgiven, upon making his submission to the King, and swearing to oppose him no more; if he had then quite deliberately broken his oath; it might have been said of him, as he says of the heretics, that he had brought his death upon himself.

I am not saying that these Protestant martyrs were the less heroic because of their momentary weakness. It increases our sympathy, and should not diminish our respect. But More had a strictly legal mind, and could not tolerate such weakness, either in himself or others. In Burke's words, he took his idea of liberty low, and stuck to it. It is just because More kept his claim for freedom of conscience within the narrow limits which he had himself defined twenty years before, in *Utopia*, that we can regard him as a consistent martyr for his ideal of freedom. A low ideal, you may say. Anyway, it was too high for More to hold it and live, in the days of Henry VIII. (pp. 366-68)

> *R. W. Chambers, in his* Thomas More, *Jonathan Cape, 1935, 416 p.*

ROBERT P. ADAMS (essay date 1941)

> [*Adams is an American expert on English Renaissance literature. In the following excerpt, he affirms a satirical unity in* Utopia *based on More's concepts of nature and reason.*]

Although for centuries *Utopia* has been enjoyed as a brilliantly drawn picture of a happy state, it is striking that critics have rarely been able to agree on its significance as satire. Indeed, most aspects of More's *jeu d'esprit* are still controversial. The purpose of this essay is to discover a unified interpretation of *Utopia* in terms of the philosophic ideas underlying the satire as a whole.... (p. 45)

One typical form of criticism has been that which, dismissing the notion that the satire may have unity, asserts that in consequence of psychological conflicts within More's personality the *Utopia* is stuffed with contradictions, which it would be idle to attempt to reconcile, the picture of Utopia being at best only a "renaissance daydream" in which lapses in unity probably represent More's characteristic "humor." Some scholarly editors have been so deeply perplexed by seeming political and religious "paradoxes" in Book II of *Utopia* as to conclude that, if More had a central satiric aim, it must remain lost in doubt. Even Mr. J. H. Lupton, who in most respects is the ablest editor of *Utopia,* admitted bafflement: to him it seemed only paradoxical that More should have represented the Utopians as un-"Chivalrous" in war, although in general they strictly fulfill all social obligations. Thus the Utopian naval strategy, of destroying enemy fleets by "translating" the shore beacons, appeared to him to be only an incomprehensible and "repellent feature of the Utopian character"; while equally unrelated to any unified satiric intention seemed to be the Utopian endeavour to abbreviate wars by purchasing the assassination of enemy leaders. Many are the seeming "inconsistencies" between Utopian practices and More's personal life which have lacked any unified explanation.

Recently, however, Professor R. W. Chambers in particular has presented a wealth of evidence to show that, as far as More's own life is concerned, *Utopia* is highly consistent with More's avowed ideas. Not undertaking a complete analysis of the satire, Mr. Chambers was content, when he had shown the fine integrity of More's character, to remind modern readers again that More was representing, not defending Utopian practices. He did, however, repeat an invaluable critical suggestion, that in the second book of *Utopia* More showed how he thought "enlightened and righteous heathen, . . . heathen philosophers, and, as such, guided solely by the light of reason," ought to behave. An important qualification of this statement must yet be made: the Utopians are guided not merely by "reason" but, most essential of all, strictly by *uncorrupted* "reason" or "nature," which in Utopia is forcibly kept from all possible corruptions to which men are liable. Beginning with this point of departure, it may be possible to reconcile the controversial elements of *Utopia* . . . [and] to reveal a central, highly unified purpose in the famous satire. If this reasoning is just, the notion that Book II of *Utopia* is an illogical, whimsical "renaissance day-dream," artistically inferior to Book I, may be discarded; while the satiric picture of Utopian life itself should appear as a satire, not notable so much for humorous paradoxes, as for the genius of the design and brilliance of its execution into a classic of English romance.

More designed Book I, which he wrote last, as a crafty introduction to the picture of Utopian life itself. Mainly it comprises two realistic dialogues on sore contemporary social problems: first, on the causes of corrupt government and on the duty of princes to rule justly; and, second, on justice, the causes of vagabondage and crime, with the social roots of crime. While the evils attending war are discussed, attention is mainly focussed on the economic and administrative maladies of the whole state. Finally, the first book concludes with Hythlodaye's tantalizing assertion that all the social evils, together with others not yet mentioned, could be eliminated, if property were held in common; moreover, he promised to prove as much in his account of Utopia, which he had seen while in the New World with Amerigo Vespucci. But with Book II More slyly inducts his readers from the European scene into an ingeniously imagined state, whose resemblances to Christian Europe are quite deceiving. Only gradually does it appear that the startling differences between Europe and Utopia exist because in Utopia every free citizen is a philosopher whose life perfectly exemplifies his conceptions that, for uncorrupted men, the good life can be only that led strictly "according to nature" or "reason," even if the aid of divine revelation be lacking. . . . To make clear the unified ideas which govern . . . vital Utopian attitudes and practices, we must analyze the Utopian religious and social philosophy.

The ruling ideas in this philosophy can best be shown by analysis of the essential concepts, concerning "nature" or "reason," from which all important aspects of Utopian life appear to have been developed. Now the sole authority in religion, all citizens agree, is a universal power or "god," which is taken to be apparent to man in the various aspects of the One "nature":

> in this pointe they agree all togethers with the wisest sort, in belevynge that there is one chiefe and pryncipall God, the maker and ruler of the hole worlde. . . . But in this they disagre, that amonge some he is counted one, and amonge some an other. For every one of them, whatsoever that is whiche he taketh for the chiefe God, thynketh it to be the very same nature (*eandem illam prorsus esse naturam*), to whose onlye devyne myght and majestie the som and soveraintie of al thinges, by the consent of all people (*omnium consensu* [sic] *gentium*) is attributed and geven.

All citizens likewise agree that this divine universal power is One, that it is alone entitled to religious veneration; and while men cannot know "god" precisely by their unaided reason, god is evident to man in the orderly universe as everlasting creative power united with and tending to create virtue. . . . (pp. 48-51)

Concerning this deity, or "nature," there are in the Utopian religious philosophy two absolute principles, on which only all freemen *must* strictly agree in order to hold citizenship. These are, first, "that the sowle (of man) ys immortall, and by the bountifull goodnes of God ordeyned to felicitie"; and, second, that from this divine Providence men must expect "that to our vertues and good deades rewardes be apoynted after this lyfe, and to our evell deades punyshementes." Significantly, a freeman who denies or doubts these absolutes (i.e. professes atheism or agnosticism) is promptly classed with brute beasts and madmen, and is at once deprived of all honor, office, and the citizen's privilege of free expression of his thoughts. Since by Utopian definition animals lack "reason," their reasoning here is clearly that a man who makes a declaration can only do so by going contrary to the distinctive best ethical and religious "nature" of (uncorrupted) men. This therefore is *prima facie* evidence of a corrupt "nature": being no longer ruled by "right reason," such individuals meet the Utopian concept of insanity; and clearly in consequence society must isolate from its normal members the one who is no longer aware of social obligations which depend upon uncorrupted "nature" and "reason." (p. 52)

The Utopians generally agree, furthermore, that the virtuous character of the divine ruling "nature" is expressed to man in several mighty gifts, whose potentialities are the foundation of religious and social life. The first "natural" gift, which is regarded as a god-like power distinguishing man as superior in created "nature" to all other living creatures, is the faculty of "reason," together with a capacity for and an inclination toward a life ruled by "reason." The atheist was classed with brute beasts, who by definition lack both (uncorrupted) man's "reason" and distinctive "nature." This faculty is apparent in many ways, for instance in the unique ability of man to appreciate the virtuous purposes of the divine "nature" as expressed in the design and modes of working of the material universe. Thus More wrote that God, "or the very same [i.e. divine] nature," "hathe made (man alone) of wytte and capacytye to consydre and understand the excellencye of so greate a woorke." Since through this faculty of "reason" the divine "nature" and the means to the virtuous, rational life which (it is assumed) "god" intended for man can best be understood, all citizens agree that the criterion of what is good and to be agreed upon, in everyday life as in religion, is "reason," and that man was divinely intended to live "according to nature," being ruled then by "reason" (in the sense of uncorrupted "right reason")…. (pp. 53-4)

After reason the Utopians held the divine "nature's" greatest gift to be man's capacity for and strong inclination toward a close-knit, harmonious family and communal social life, a life distinguished (i.e. as compared with that of brute beasts) by (uncorrupted) man's mutual benevolent solicitude for the common welfare. "Reason" itself, man's most divine faculty, urges men to live joyfully and to help all others, "in respect of the society of nature (*pro naturae societate*)" to live happily. To comfort and aid his fellows, within his species, is distinctively (i.e. "by nature") human,—"…a vertue moste peculiarly belongynge to man (*qua uirtute nulla est homini magis propria*)." (pp. 58-9)

Furthermore, the divine "nature" is a benevolent giver of life and the material necessities of life, not only to man as a superior species, but perhaps even to lower animals as well: "nature" is "…a moste tender and lovynge mother (*parens indulgentissima*)." Since they assume that "…the mercifull clemency of god hath (no) delite in bloud and slaughter," (then clearly reasoning that it would be inconsistent for the benevolent creator of life to enjoy its destruction), the Utopians never make religious sacrifices of living creatures; while by an extension of the same reasoning, as we shall see, they abhor all bloodshed as contrary to "nature" and as gradually destructive of the "clemency" which is the "gentlest affection of our nature." As for the material needs of man, (divine) "nature" has given clear suggestions of the deity's purposes toward man both in the relative amounts and locations of natural resources. That is, "nature [i.e. divine]…hath placed the beste and moste necessarye thynges (e.g. air, earth, water) open a brode"; while providing only small, hidden amounts of such "unnecessary" materials as gold.

Finally, the distinctive Utopian social practices are determined, not only by these two gifts to man from the divine "nature," but also by the peculiar Utopian Epicureanism. While the justification for describing the free, philosopher-citizens as Epicureans is that pleasure is their *summum bonum*, certain significant restrictions in practice are rigidly put upon their concept. For the citizens (as philosophers guided strictly by uncorrupted "reason," with the common welfare always in mind) agree in absolutely dividing "true" (i.e. socially beneficial) from "counterfeit" (i.e. socially injurious) pleasures. The basis of this vital distinction lies in the Utopian religious philosophy. Since it is assumed that divine "nature" planted in (uncorrupted) man a powerful inclination to live in harmonious cooperation with his fellow-men, ruled by "reason," the Utopians infer that only those pleasures which are (i.e. "by nature") "true," "good and honest" and which consequent-

ly enhance the good life should be desired by or permitted to the citizens…. "Reason" itself, as man's most divine gift, prompts man first of course to venerate god, but then above all to lead a joyous Epicurean life, not in selfish privacy, but actively aiding other men to equal felicity, since they are (by inference) equal in the "society of nature." In fact, to help others to live merrily is an almost religious obligation of each citizen…. (pp. 59-61)

[The]—Utopian version of Epicureanism furnishes a concept of psychological motivation according to which every citizen, in his pursuit of pleasure, must subject every form of sensual stimulation to the critical judgment of (uncorrupted) "right reason." The criteria then applied in accepting or rejecting pleasures, as either "true" or "counterfeit," are derived from the Utopian conception of the purposes of the divine "nature," or god, as intending men to create for themselves a good life in which "reason" would be the guide to social cooperation in the interests, not of the individual alone, but most of all of the common welfare. In practice pleasures were in general judged to be "counterfeit" and were forbidden to citizens when, first, they appeared to be contrary to the Utopian concept of "right reason" or man's best "nature" (variously considered as religious, political, ethical, aesthetic, etc.), or, second, when the observed after-effects of a given enjoyment were found to be actually injurious to some one of man's distinctive qualities, upon whose preservation in a healthy state the "society of nature" was believed to depend. The Utopian criteria of "true" pleasure are, on the whole, represented as the wisdom accumulated by painful, extended inductive observation (over 1760 years) on what is vital to as well as most damaging to the good life among uncorrupted men; while these historical conclusions, with the surprising uniformity of opinion as to what comprises "true" or "counterfeit" pleasure, are manifest as "right reason" expressed by the *consensus gentium*. In Utopia coercion of men into agreement with authority was found both undesirable and unnecessary, for when men of "right reason" exercised it in strictly dispassionate discussion, a strong tendency to uniformity of opinion was developed…. [The] outside world provided an inexhaustible supply of examples of the folly and suffering resulting from "counterfeit" pleasures, examples which served as object-lessons in teaching each new Utopian generation to follow only those pleasures which, according to "reason," are *bona atque honesta*. Since much of the keenest "true" pleasure is found in aiding others to live well, it is not surprising that other practical expressions of the *consensus gentium* are found in the Utopian approval of "justice" as "the strongeste and suereste bonde of a common wealthe," and in the cosmopolitan, international extension of this idea into belief in at least the potentiality that all men (if uncorrupted, of course) might be joined in the "strong league" of the "felowshyppe of nature," knit together by mutual "love and benevolence." Finally, the general agreement as to what is "true" pleasure is expressed in a genial assumption that any pleasure which is not known to have injurious social effects may be presumed to be good and honest, excepting evidence of anti-social "nature" which might appear in time. For "no kynde of pleasure (is) forbidden, whereof cummeth no harm."

To be sure the Utopians draw certain conclusions as a result of comparing Utopia with the world outside. For… the Utopians assume that not only they, but all men as a species (if uncorrupted), enjoy the same potentialities for a good life based on the "realization" of the divine "nature's" gifts of capacity for "reason" and loving social co-operation. In contrast with the ostensibly civilized nations outside the happy commonwealth, the Utopians had only made the best of their opportunities. In fact, when the island was first conquered by the original wise prince Utopus (some 1760 years before Hythlodaye's visit), the people were, like renaissance Europeans, "rude, wild" and given to religious strife. To the Utopians therefore, the remarkable advantages of their life, as compared with that suggested in the first book of *Utopia*, were the hard-won rewards of centuries of effort to live "according to nature" or "reason." As for the widespread poverty, disease, greed, mutual hatred of rich and poor, malgovernment, crime and war which seemed characteristic throughout England and Europe in general, such evils indicated (to the Utopians, to Hythlodaye and to More himself) at the very least a disastrous failure of man to benefit greatly from his distinctive potentialities, if indeed existing conditions were not (as was possible) the consequence of wholesale corruption of man's good "nature." In the Utopian view "Nature" endowed men nobly, and then left it largely to man's discretion, whether by corrupting his "high nature" he would become "beastly" or worse, or whether (even without the aid of divine revelation) he would gradually "realize" his gifts in an orderly, peaceful, mutually benevolent "society of nature," "according to reason." The satiric contrast between Utopia and Europe is most stunning and the central purpose most clear when it is seen . . . that the good life in Utopia is represented as achieved by man's wisdom and energy alone, whereas the wretched conditions in Europe were the sorry accomplishment of Christians, who possessed not only the same "natural" gifts as the Utopians but above all the aid of divine revelation. Thus the *Utopia* concludes, while not in despair, yet on a note of judicious pessimism, colored by hopes which had been brightest in 1509, when Henry VIII became king, but which were ebbing while *Utopia* was being written. For even the most corrupt men would never be able to terminate universal "nature's" gifts to man, although their "realization" might be long delayed. If a wise prince (like old Utopus) were disposed to make the right beginning (although improvement at fist might be slow), eventually England, with her matchless resources of men and land, might achieve a rich, stable and peaceful common life even surpassing that of Utopia itself, with the Christian religion added to that of "reason." But "I (must) nedes confesse and graunt," wrote More, as the last words of *Utopia,* "that many thinges be in the Utopian weal publique, which in our cities I may rather wisshe for then hoope after." (pp. 63-5)

> Robert P. Adams, "The Philosophic Unity of More's 'Utopia'," in Studies in Philology, Vol. XXXVIII, No. 1, January, 1941, Pp. 45-65.

WILLIAM J. GRACE (essay date 1947)

[*In the following excerpt, Grace discusses* Utopia *as the serious political vision of a Renaissance statesman.*]

One of the most commonly misunderstood books is the *Utopia* of Sir Thomas More. It is commonly discussed as a mere *jeu d'esprit*, at the expense of ignoring its important and earnest social criticism and the sharp satire of its

presentation. The *Utopia* has been looked upon as a mere aberration in the total work of a man who is otherwise a noteworthy thinker. The common usage of the adjective, "Utopian," indicating an impractical or merely visionary outlook, shows how extensively and how completely the point of one of More's most important works has been missed. (p. 283)

[Sir Thomas More] was not only a saint and an intellectual—he was a realist and a satirist in addition.

The realistic and satiric aspect of More's thought is of particular interest to the consideration of the *Utopia*. This aspect is best illuminated by considering the particular vocation of Sir Thomas More as a councillor to the prince. (p. 284)

The *Utopia* is directly connected with More's work, that of advising the king. This is a work which Machiavelli stresses in *The Prince*. Councillors, according to Machiavelli, must be selected with great care and they must subordinate themselves completely to their master, although they are encouraged to tell him circumspect truths. Francis Bacon of a later day, studying times and occasions and moods so that his own safety is never jeopardized by changes of polity, is a fair example of the Machiavellian model. Yet such councillors ran dangers, as Hamlet put it, of being "first mouthed, to be last swallowed." Nor did Machiavelli advise the prince ever to allow himself to place too much reliance on such men. The prince, as exemplified in the case history of Remiro d'Orco, may sacrifice a faithful minister with impunity if political advantage is to be gained. With typical pessimism, Machiavelli reminds the prince that "men will always prove untrue to you unless they are kept honest by constraint." Ignoring the order of grace, Machiavelli did not suspect that a saint might also be a councillor to the prince.

"Indignatio principis mors est," the disfavor of the prince meant the councillor's death, was a principle for which, as Roper expressly tells us, More had no regard. But both from his character and the nature of his work, More excelled in practical prudence. He did not expect extravagant results from the presentation of the truth and was not disappointed when these results were not forthcoming. But he always *hoped*. He does not have the Machiavellian pessimism that reminds the prince that "men will always prove untrue to you." Raphael Hythlodaye explains at the beginning of the *Utopia* that he does not care, in spite of his knowledge, to be a councillor because of the difficulty of making truth known at court in the midst of conflicting egoisms and jealousies. Yet More, speaking in his own proper person, reproaches Hythlodaye for despairing too easily:

> So the case stondethe in a common wealthe: and so yt ys in the consultatyons of Kynges and prynces. Yf evell opynyons and noughty persuasions can not be utterly and quyte pluckede owte of their hartes; if you can not even as you wold remedye vyces, which use and custome hath confirmed; yet for this cause yow must not leave and forsake the common wealth; you must not forsake the shippe in a tempeste, bycause yowe can not rule and kepe downe the wyndes. No, nor you muste not laboure to dryve into their heades newe and straunge informatyons, whyche yow knowe well shal be nothynge regarded wyth them that be of cleane contrary mindes. But you must with a crafty wile and a subtell

trayne studye and endevoure your selfe, as much as in yow lyethe, to handle the matter wyttelye and hand-somelye for the purpose; and that whyche yowe can not turne to good, so to order it that it be not very badde. For it is not possible for all thynges to be well, onles all men were good: which I thynke will not be yet thys good many yeares.

More's concept of a man's political duty is that the short-comings of rulers and procedures give him no excuse for not exercising his diligence, tact, and influence to bring about as much good and as little ill as possible.

Thomas Cromwell, More's successor duly executed in his own turn, admired Machiavelli's treatise, the tenor of which work is concerned not with what a prince *should* do, but with what a prince *can* do. More, as reported by Roper, particularly warned Cromwell, as the king's new minister, against this very thing: "Master Cromwell," quoth he, "You are now entered into the service of a most noble, wise and liberall prince. If you will followe my poore advice you shall, in your councell gevinge unto his grace, ever tell him what he owght to doe but never tell him what he is able to doe. So that you shewe yourself a true faithfull servant and a right worthy councelour. For if [a] lion knewe his owne strength, harde were it for any man to rule him."

The *Utopia* is an allegory that grows out of More's person-al experience as a councillor, just as the *Pilgrim's Progress* grew out of Bunyan's experience. It is an answer that More is offering to the conflict, always drastic and for high stakes, which he had daily to meet with such patience and discretion. As Chambers remarks, "parts of the *Utopia* read like a commentary on parts of *The Prince*."

For what a prince *can* do and what a prince *ought* to do mark one of the great cleavages of the Renaissance.... The *Utopia* is concerned with indicating what a prince ought to do, and the reasons for doing it. These reasons require an ontological depth, they require a perspective of man and life, that could scarcely be communicated in the intrigue of the court. In the *Utopia* More finds a means of giving counsels on the essentials of government. (pp. 285-88)

More presents a state governed by the light of natural rea-son. To the licentious aspects of the pagan revolt of the Renaissance, a revolt partly connected by way of reaction to the Augustinian denial of the rightful place of natural things, More presents a society not knowing Christ that yet lives with decency and moderation. To a Catholic world, disorganized and morally slothful and yielding spir-itual ideals to Mammon, More reveals a society that by following reason is more praiseworthy than a society that has become indifferent to revelation. To a monarch prac-ticing tyranny More suggests more than once the thought to be found in St. Thomas Aquinas that sovereignty re-sides in the people whose vicar the king is. To the Tudor dynasty More pictures a society whose ruler is selected by a system that is electoral and representative. To a society inaugurating a capitalist destiny More pictures a state whose citizens despise gold, whose purpose it is to use things, not to subordinate things to profits. To contempo-raries who view the stamping out of crime merely as a matter of using the iron hand, More presents a searching sociology which finds in the sins of wealth the basic occa-sions of the lapses of the poor. To a new era soon to ex-

ploit native populations anywhere that they were incapa-ble of defending themselves, More sketches a policy of col-onization for the use of the things of the earth, not for im-perialism. To a Europe bent upon leagues and balances of power, More presents the Utopians as despising leagues as productive of dishonesty and treachery. In contrast to Ma-chiavelli who maintains that a prince ought to have no other aim or thought, nor select anything else for his study, than war and its rules and disciplines, More sketch-es a people to whom there is nothing more inglorious than the glory gained by war.

In presenting a society lived according to the light of rea-son, More follows a medieval tradition, the distinction es-tablished between the virtues taught by reason and those dependent upon Christian revelation. This concept is pres-ent in Dante's poem in which Virgil acts as Dante's guide in secular matters. The virtues of reason—prudence, jus-tice, fortitude and temperance—were considered as attain-able by all men even when the Christian faith had not illu-minated their lives.

It is to be borne in mind, however, that this very restric-tion prevents Utopia from being the best of all possible worlds. The perfect state for More would have been a soci-ety where reason was in conformity with, and illuminated by, divine grace. Several times in his allegory he points out that he does not approve of everything characteristic of *Utopia*. But keeping in mind the emphasis and the re-strictions that More expressly sets down, the points of view and the criticisms of the *Utopia* fall into proper per-spective.

More in sketching his society in the light of reason is a master of irony and satire. *Utopia* is an ironic comment on a Christian world that has forsaken its true traditions. The irony is double-edged, for if the life of reason seems im-practical to men, what must the life of Christian grace with its much more insistent demands seem? The life of More is proof, of course, that it is heroism, impractical or not, that constantly appeals to men, for grace has re-sources that make men stronger and happier even if less comfortable. Nevertheless, for the purpose of his social criticism, More restricts himself to the life of reason, and to such grace as is presupposed for such a life. In contrast to the thought of Luther, More is careful to state that "Reason is servant to Faith, not enemy." He points out in the *Utopia* that some understanding of God is obtainable in the light of reason.... More, believing with St. Thomas Aquinas in the fundamental soundness of human nature, in the rationality and autonomy of man, is not reluctant to emphasize again and again the light of reason.

For this cause he reminds us of the inviolability of the hu-man conscience. He does not anticipate the restoration or the enforcement of truth through external means, a proce-dure that had a fundamental analogy with the Lutheran conception of extrinsic righteousness in the life of grace. The application of force in regard to intellectual or spiritu-al conviction seemed absurd to him. In this outlook he was well ahead of his time. More did not believe that bel-ligerency and bullying were allowable even in the spread-ing of true doctrine. He had no use for "sedition"—any procedure, whatever the motive, that destroys true peace and cooperation. On the subject of religious tolerance. More is not a liberal in the sense of considering all reli-gious experience equally valuable and relevant. But he does take the point of view that no man can be proceeded against by law for what he thinks, for what is locked in his conscience. More himself during the time of his imprisonment and trial maintained that he was under no obligation to reveal what was locked in his mind and conscience to any man living. However, the means of *expressing* and spreading one's views are not merely the concern of the individual person; then the obligations to society enter the picture. More himself was convicted on perjured evidence of having spoken maliciously; in actual fact he kept his views to himself and did not spread "sedition." More himself accepted the principle of contemporary law in regard to sedition. This fact is emphasized in the case of the Christian missionary to the Utopians—who with more "affection than wisdom" denounces the beliefs of the Utopians. He is condemned into exile "not as a despyser of religion, but as a sedicious persone, and a rayser up of dissention amonge the people."

More has an instinct for the historical future when, after the long religious divisions of Europe have had their final effect, common ground must be sought not in faith but in the rule of reason. His conception of religious tolerance has a sense of historical contingency about it that further shows how he anticipated developments. (pp. 288-93)

As we have suggested, More's style in the *Utopia* is often that of a sharp satirist. His humor is, in fact, often comparable to that of Dean Swift. Swift's Gulliver, we recall, is often presented as the unconscious victim of his own intellectual shortcomings, made the more ridiculous by his own unbounded complacency and self-confidence. In informing the king of Brobdingnag of the impressive customs and laws of contemporary England, Gulliver is quite amazed at the king's lack of proper admiration and even comprehension, whereas the reader who can read between the lines is amazed at Gulliver's own lack of self-criticism. Many of the passages of the *Utopia* indicate this technique of the double-edged satire. (pp. 294-95)

The style of the *Utopia* has great variety. Its humor and satiric overtones lighten and contrast direct and hard-hitting criticism. Its surface technique is blunt and direct, with little wasted motion and with emotion tightly suppressed. Contemporaries who think of "reason" or "the rule of reason" as implying dullness, a lack of vivid sensation, can find illustrated in More the more vivid shock that style gives when the author, undeviating from the realities he knows, makes every effort to keep his reaction under intellectual control.

Of course the *Utopia* remains primarily important not for its style and its creative aspects but for the substance of its political and social thought. The *Utopia* is none of the things generally alleged it. It is not "progressive" in the sense of breaking with the past. Machiavelli was "progressive." It is not a young man's dream; it is the point of view of the mature More. Lastly, it certainly is *not* an escapist's or dreamer's world. What the *Utopia* has actually to say refutes this last and most persistent legend. Not only have many of the reforms indicated in the *Utopia* been attempted, but in several instances have become historical realities. But more important and relevant still is the fact that the *Utopia* was written by a prudent man and a prince's councillor as a means, not to escape from reality, but to throw the clear light of reality on perplexing problems and crying social abuses. (p. 296)

William J. Grace, "The Conception of Society in More's 'Utopia'," in THOUGHT, *Vol. XXII, No. 85, June, 1947, pp. 283-96.*

RUSSELL AMES (essay date 1949)

[*In the following excerpt, Ames examines More's views of the peasantry and rebellion as revealed in* Utopia.]

Though More did not believe that professional soldiers could be good citizens—and, indeed, thought them little better than thieves—he knew that citizens could be good soldiers. He has Hythlodaye compare the English favorably with the French soldiery, and then point out that craftsmen and plowmen are not afraid of gentlemen's idle serving men. In short, he had respect for the poor in their contests with the nobility.

The majority of the people in western Europe were semi-independent peasants rather than serfs. By the fifteenth century their conditions had markedly improved. Even the liberal humanist Wimpheling could say: "The peasants in our district and in many parts of Germany have become, through their riches, stiff-necked and ease-loving." In France their position had been worse than in other advanced countries, but under Charles VIII and Louis XII civil war ended, taxes were lightened, and perhaps one-third of the neglected land was returned to cultivation. The peasants had, therefore, some experience, as well as an ideal, of prosperity and freedom.

At the time of *Utopia*, the money economy was radically changing the condition of the peasant. Prices shot far ahead of rents and other income from the land. Landlords, therefore, sought to make good their losses and satisfy their expensive desires by taking land and privileges from the peasants or by driving them back into serfdom.

Another important cause of economic crisis, most serious in England, was the movement of clothmaking to the countryside. The resultant conflict between declining towns and growing villages did not occur in France (or, incidentally, in Utopia); and the comparative economies are well described in John Coke's "Debate between the Heralds of England and France" in which the French Herald says:

> You have more plenty of wolles in Englande to make cloth then we. Yet our clothiers dwell in good townes, who maynteyne th'ynhabitantes and pore people there, so that they get theyr lyvynges by spynnyng and cardyng. . . . It is not so in England, for your clothiers dwel in great fermes abrode in the countrey, havyng howses with commodities lyke unto gentylmen, where aswel they make cloth and kepe husbandry, and also grasse and fede shepe and catell, takyng therby awaye the lyvynges of the pore husbandmen and grasiers. Furthermore in Englande sum one man kepeth in his hands ii or iii fermes, and where hath ben vi or viii persons in every ferme, he kepeth oonly a shepparde or wretched heardman and his wyfe.

The enclosures of which the French Herald speaks were mostly for sheep-farming. Sheep were thought the "mooste profytablest cattell that any man can have," and would double or treble the value of arable land. Peasants were therefore forced to add their numbers to that mass of landless men which had been recently swelled by the breaking up of many bands of feudal retainers. And all these landless men, untrained in handicraft, were generally unemployed and homeless, subject to those ferocious laws against tramps and beggars whose injustice More exposed in *Utopia*.

The government took some rather ineffectual steps to check enclosure. An act of 1515 ordered that all land converted into pasture should be returned to tillage within one year. Wolsey, perhaps influenced by *Utopia*, appointed a commission in 1517 which was to inquire into all enclosures of Tudor times and require offenders to destroy their hedges. When, therefore, Englishmen took matters into their own hands and pulled down hedges, they were, in their way, enforcing the law. More's intense sympathy for the victims of enclosure was thus anti-capitalist and "revolutionary," conservative and radical, at the same time. In what precise circumstances, if any, he might have approved the use of armed violence by the peasantry, it is impossible to say. But certainly the *Utopia* was written with the knowledge that rebellions had recently occurred, were going on at the time, and would doubtless take place in the future. Though More avoids direct comment on the subject, he must have known that his attacks on the nobility and his sympathy for the oppressed people would influence his readers' attitudes toward rebellion.

The peasants resisted the new attacks made on them. Though the great German peasant war did not come till

A woodcut, by Ambrosius Holbein, of the island of Utopia, published in the 1518 Basel edition of Utopia.

1525, there were many uprisings during More's lifetime *before* the writing of *Utopia*, and some of these must have been known to him. Most of the early revolts were German and local; they may not have attracted much attention abroad. Of course More knew of the Cornish rising of 1497, mentioned in *Utopia* itself. Perhaps he had heard, too, of the major revolt of the Ditmarsch peasants which, in 1500, led to the destruction of a Danish army. Certainly with his business, diplomatic, and humanist contacts, he could not have missed news of the rebellions which took place during the years 1513-1516. He would have missed little continental news in those six months, in the latter part of 1515, which he spent in trade centers of the Lowlands talking to merchants and diplomats, and writing the second book of *Utopia*.

In 1513 the *Bund Schuh* underwent one of its frequent suppressions, among the peasants of the upper Rhineland and the Black Forest. In the same year there was a minor Swiss revolt. In 1514 another Swiss uprising was successful; the Poor Konrad succeeded and then failed in Würtemberg; Slovenian peasants had a success; and the *Bund Schuh* failed in Breisgau and Baden. Also in 1514, in Hungary, there was a terrible civil war in which 60,000 peasants died. They had assembled in arms when the papal legate called for a crusade against the Turk and, when their noble masters interfered with the project, rose against them. In the following year revolts broke out in Carinthia and Styria, and were suppressed. In 1516 another failed in Carniola. To whatever degree these foreign conflicts were known to More and his readers, to that same degree his championing of the peasant in *Utopia* was bold, and revolutionary in implication, if only with reference to continental politics.

Kautsky believes that More was wholly opposed to popular revolt. He draws a sharp line between the Utopianism of More and the lower class socialism of the Lollards and of Thomas Münzer; communist leader of the German peasants and proletarians in 1525. The two kinds of socialism should not be entirely divorced. The peasants of 1525 had their middle class theoreticians and leaders like Wendel Hipler; and some of these, like Michael Geismayr and Johan Eberlin, wrote plans of reform which had a distinctly Utopian character. It is very likely, too, that the *Utopia* gave form and direction to the demands and schemes of the German rebels, both rural and urban. The popular election of magistrates and clergy, the restriction or abolition of capitalist organizations, the drastic suppression of luxury and vice, the establishment of social equality, the simplification of law, the economic dispossession of the clergy—all these characteristics of Utopia were proposed by the German revolutionaries and were to some extent put into practice. This fact proves the realistic character of some extreme and seemingly fantastic aspects of Utopia, whether More's book was or was not the direct cause of any action in Germany.

A chief obstacle to the understanding of the Thomas More who wrote *Utopia* is the dependence of so many writers on his later, particularly his polemical, works. Kautsky notes that the *Dialogue Concerning Heresies* (1528) reproaches the Lutherans for making a storm, the peasant war of 1525, which endangered not only the clergy but the nobility and monarchs. This sally against the Lutherans, rather than *Utopia* itself, is used to establish More's views on popular rebellion. More must have known that Luther had become violently anti-peasant. More cared little for most of the German clergy, for the princes and nobles less; but in his bitter controversies with the Lutherans he would pick up almost any club to beat them. Kautsky says that More opposed Lutheranism, not for religious reasons, but because it had stirred popular revolt. It seems more likely that he added a distaste for Lutheran prince-worship to his distaste for Lutheran dogma.

There had been no major uprising of peasants in England since 1497, and there was not to be any till the middle of the sixteenth century. Minor insurrections there were, mainly against enclosures, which were the central target of economic criticism in *Utopia*. Even the London citizens, in 1514, rioted against enclosures of their common land, and succeeded. The common spirit of the time was reported to Wolsey in 1518 when he was told of "grudges and murmurs among the king's subjects; especially in London, where they would think that men went about utterly to destroy them, if, with their other misfortunes, they should also be kept from their fairs and markets. . . ."

Rebelliousness in England—because of its advanced, interwoven, agricultural-commercial economy—probably had a more national character than in any other country. All classes, except for certain sections of the nobility, had grievances against the Crown—the merchants and "lower" commons especially resenting arbitrary police and judicial action, failure to check enclosures, interference with the gilds and companies and, above all, taxation for war. In More's time the most serious threat from the *people*—rather than from the great lords, who were more directly dangerous—came soon after the Spanish revolts and just before the German.

The trouble began with the great subsidy asked in the parliament of 1523, when More was Speaker, for there was "great opposition in the house of commons, opposition which might without much difficulty turn into rebellion; . . . there was a government party in the house of commons, mostly among the knights of the shire, between whom and the burgesses there was a distinct cleavage." Even after a reduced subsidy was finally granted, the commissioners for its collection constantly excused the people to Henry.

Later, in 1525, Wolsey brought the greatest pressure to bear on individual London citizens, but he received no "amicable grants." At this time in many shires there was organized resistance and near rebellion. The clothiers of Suffolk paid the taxes but had to discharge the carders, spinners, weavers, and fullers whom they employed; and a revolt against the Crown was narrowly averted. Rebels were pardoned, however, perhaps because the Crown knew that "in this troublous season the uplandish men of Germany, called bowres, rose in great number, almost a hundred thousand, and rebelled against the princes of Germany."

If More was something of a radical at the time he wrote *Utopia,* there were native English parallels, origins, and precedents for it among townsmen of similar background. The experience of John Rastell in Coventry may exemplify this. Two or three years older than More, he also studied law in London, and he was associated with Thomas and John More in 1499 in furnishing security for a loan from the king. By 1504 he was married to Elizabeth More,

and in that year loaned money to John More, who was fined £100 because of his son Thomas' resistance to a subsidy in parliament. Two years later, Rastell was back in Coventry, succeeding his father as coroner, presiding over the court of statute merchant.

In 1507 Rastell was appointed overseer of the will of a wealthy mercer and ex-mayor, Richard Cooke, who bequeathed two bibles in English to local churches. Here, A. W. Reed believes, "we have an apparent case of Lollardry, and it is interesting to find that Rastell was looked upon as the kind of man who might be expected to see Cooke's directions carried out." During Rastell's youth the craftsmen and other commoners, led by Laurence Saunders, son of a famous mayor, had nearly broken the rule of a conservative recorder and the upper classes. "Rastell," Reed says, "emerged from these and like experiences a radical reformer, and there is little in the social criticism of his brother-in-law's *Utopia* with which he would not find himself in hearty agreement." Besides economic discontent, particularly over the enclosure of public grazing lands, there was a quarrel between the town and clergy over the right of the citizens to control a public school whose master was paid by one of their gilds. "Here again Rastell's subsequent history suggests that he was of the party of the Reformers. . . ."

The implied criticism of peasant rebellion mentioned above—when More reproached the Lutherans for agitation—is only one of many passages in his later works which have been cited to prove his allegiance to some kind of conservatism. It has been noted that the statement on the peasant war needed interpretation in time and context—and so do the others.

It is hard, for instance, to understand More's advising a poor man to starve *with his children* if there is no work and the rich will not provide out of their plenty. Even in 1522, when any kind of rebelliousness was likely to aid the Lutheran cause, this is hard to take from the author of *Utopia*. Yet it is probable that this was only More's way of saying that one should trust in God when all else fails. For a parallel, consider the long *Dialogue of Comfort against Tribulation* which he wrote in the Tower. This tells how a Christian man should submit to the Turkish tyranny, but, as Chambers points out, More was long an advocate of fighting against the Turk and had recently bewailed the failure of Christian princes to aid the emperor in his righteous cause. More seldom advocated a quiescent fatalism. If he had done so more often, his head would have stayed on his shoulders.

Again, we find More defending private property sixteen years after *Utopia* was written, pointing out that if it were all divided up equally, it would shortly return to private hands. It is of some interest to note that this well-worn refutation of communism—perhaps more original and pertinent then than now—attacks a childish theory of communism which Utopia itself did not practice, for Utopia is a communism of ownership, not of equal distribution, and least of all is it a scheme for equal division of money. All this, however, is of incidental interest. To understand the quality of More's thought in this matter, as in others, it is necessary to remember that he was accustomed to observing assaults on the private property of peasants, citizens, and the church. In his time, private property, particularly that of the poor, had to be defended from the rich lords and squires, whereas today, the common people own little property, and we are accustomed to thinking that defense of private property means defending the property of the rich from the socialism of the working class. But wherever his abstract theorizing may have led More, from time to time, we know from *Utopia* what he thought about the dispossession of the poor by a "conspiracy of rich men." He was a strong and passionate man, whose biographers have watered him down. "Sir Thomas More felt, not so much pity for the lot of the poor, as indignation at their wrongs."

It cannot be said with certainty, unless further evidence is forthcoming, that More ever was, or never was, an advocate of popular rebellion. His later works are against it, and the commonwealth of Utopia is not established by it. Of course, if he had been sympathetic to revolt at the time of *Utopia,* it would have been a very dangerous doctrine to promulgate—even under the cover of his "fantasy." (pp. 114-23)

> *Russell Ames, in his* Citizen Thomas More and His Utopia, *Princeton University Press, 1949, 230 p.*

J. K. SOWARDS (essay date 1952)

[*Sowards is an American authority on Renaissance Europe. In the following excerpt, he examines the relationship of More's own political views to his Utopian creation.*]

The two books of the *Utopia* take the form of a dialogue in which Raphael Hythloday appears as the principal speaker and More the secondary figure.... (p. 38)

[A] basic distinction must be made between the views of Hythloday and those of More himself. The opinions of the one are not necessarily those of the other. Sometimes there is agreement; sometimes vigorous disagreement; and sometimes the views of the traveller provide a foil for the arguments of More. The extremity of many of the points made by Hythloday is much beyond the endorsement of More, and he invariably cuts himself off from the speaker by the device of the dialogue. (p. 39)

The tendency to make Hythloday speak for More has caused endless confusion in the interpretation of the *Utopia* and of More's whole career, and has strained the credulity of commentators since the sixteenth century. More remains consistent, in the *Utopia* as in his other works, with his personality, his class, his training, and his faith when the nature and form of the book are properly considered.

The *Utopia* is a very complex work, for it serves as an omnibus to carry many ideas, protests, and programs. It is an unsystematic work, and the themes that run through it are not exhausted in a single place, nor are the arguments ordered according to a particular pattern. Nonetheless, More was definite in his ideas and clear in his convictions. By the year 1516 he had worked out the elements of his personal faith and the structure of his concept of the social order.

One of the most consistently expressed and striking of these convictions to appear in the *Utopia* is More's concern for social justice in a world where materialism was

outrunning its regard for the welfare and the dignity of the simple humanity of man. The theme of social justice was very close to the life of Thomas More. Introspection and a profound religious struggle had finally resolved his own problems of conscience and reason, and with that resolution he had moved out in his thinking to a greater concern for mankind. (p. 40)

More's long experience as lawyer, judge, and man of affairs had brought him time and again to grips with the basic problems of social justice. In the *Utopia* More seeks not a dreamer's escape from the reality of these problems, but a solution which will give solidity to the protest he makes. Book I is a devoted almost entirely to an exhaustive, documented and eloquent statement of this theme of social justice.

After the meeting with Raphael Hythloday both More and Giles are struck with the philosophical excellence of the man. Both wonder why he does not put his great ability at the disposal of some monarch.... (p. 41)

Hythloday, the unbending idealist, sees no place for the philosopher at court and holds that true philosophy will be spurned by the willful kingship as it will be by the thieving economics of the modern state.

In the concluding passages of Book I of the *Utopia* More counters the arguments of the pessimistic Hythloday with the practical wisdom which was always the guiding principle of his life.

> To tell the truth, it seems to me that you should not offer advice which you know will not be considered. What good could it do? How could such a bold discourse influence men whose minds are prepossessed and deeply imbued with contrary aims? Such academic philosophy is not unpleasant among friends in free conversation, but in the King's council, where official business is being carried on, there is no room for it.
>
> "That is what I was saying," Raphael replied. "There is no place for philosophy in the councils of princes."
>
> "Yes there is," I said, "but not for the speculative philosophy which thinks all things suitable for all occasions. There is another philosophy that is more urbane, that takes its proper cue and fits itself to the drama being played, acting its part aptly and well. This is the philosophy you should use. When one of Plautus's comedies is being played and the slaves are joking together, what if you should suddenly appear on the stage in a philosopher's garb and repeat Seneca's speech to Nero from the *Octavia*? Would it not be better to say nothing than to make a silly tragicomedy by mixing opposites? You ruin a play when you add irrelevant and jarring speeches, even if they are better than the play. So go through with the drama in hand as best you can, and do not spoil it because another more pleasing comes into your mind.
>
> "So it is in a commonwealth and in the councils of princes. If evil opinions cannot be quite rooted out, and if you cannot correct habitual attitudes as you wish, you must not therefore abandon the commonwealth. Don't give up the ship in a storm, because you cannot control the winds. And do not force unheard-of advice upon people, when you know that their minds are different from yours. You must strive to guide policy indirectly, so that you make the best of things, and what you cannot turn to good, you can at least make less bad. For it

is impossible to do all things well unless all men are good and this I do not expect to see for a long time."

This, then, is the real spirit of More's position throughout the whole of the *Utopia*. And the reader who enters the fanciful world of Book II must keep it always before him if he is to find there the real opinions of Thomas More. It must stand as a reminder that More does not endorse in his own person, the things which are to come forth. In this foregoing speech is to be found one of the cardinal tenets of the *Utopia*, one of the profound lessons which it intends to teach by indirection, i. e., *that man cannot live in Utopia, that he must live in the world of hard reality, and that he is happier in that world dealing with its perplexities and problems than in Utopia with its decreed happiness and its contentment of compulsion!* Here is the basic counsel of courage and Morian good cheer.

At the conclusion of Book I, the major problem is unequivocally set by Hythloday. To him there is no hope for social justice except in a system of state communism. (pp. 43-5)

Here is portent for the twentieth century, for in these years at the very beginnings of modern times we have stated with clarity and fanatical conviction the essential point of what we consider a peculiarly modern problem. The argument of the philosopher is strong, and it has—as the history of the past four centuries so eloquently attests—an ever fresh appeal to many men of intellect and integrity who seek human happiness and equality and to whom the economic and social brutalities of a competitive society are insufferable. In the answer of Thomas More and in his disagreement lies the way of the moderate marked out as well for our time as for his. Here sharply cut for every age are the inevitable issues of a question which will demand answers of the intelligent as long as men seek security from the gains of their labor.

It is ridiculous and absurd to contend that More could possibly be in agreement with the view set forth by Hythloday! It is not true to the Catholic faith for which he was willing to die, nor to the practical nature of his mind, nor to his position in society as a member of the rising, capitalistic English middle class. Community of goods was something that could not have appealed to More. Much of his public life had already been spent in the service of the economic interests of his class.... In his reply to Hythloday, therefore, the issue of free enterprise and communism is squarely joined:

> "On the contrary," I replied, "it seems to me that men cannot live well where all things are in common. How can there be plenty where every man stops working? The hope of gain will not drive him; he will rely on others and become lazy. If men are stirred by want, and yet no one can legally protect what he has earned, what can follow but continual bloodshed and turmoil, especially when the respect for and the authority of magistrates are lost? I cannot conceive of authority among men that are equal to one another in all things."

In the rejoinder of Hythloday is to be found the kernel of the second book of the *Utopia*. There is a state, he says, in which the precepts he has set forth are honored and form the very basis of government and life, and it is happy and prosperous beyond anything conceived of in contemporary Europe. It is the island kingdon of Utopia.

This state is a dream, a fantasy in which Thomas More cannot and will not share. [According to Henry W. Donner in *Introduction to Utopia (1945)*, *Utopia* is indeed "a protest against the new capitalist system of economics." *But it is not More's protest!* It is not More's purpose that the *Utopia* simply inveigh against the new capitalism but rather that he show in this book one solution—and the most extreme—to the many problems created by that new capitalism. It is his hope that the very absurdity of such a solution make it impractical, but that at the same time, it might work as a catalyst to stir some suitable reaction. The work may be said to have been motivated in part by More's genuine concern for the plight of the poor and his distress at the economic pressures which made them fall from God's image. But to his mind Hythloday's Utopianism is the dreamer's solution which avoids the difficult problems which must be solved in learning to live with capital and in applying the sound principles of reasoned Christian ethics to the conditions of the oppressed.

The whole position of Hythloday that man's happiness can only be secured by the Utopian way of life is again stated and strongly summarized as the conclusion of Book II.

> So when I weigh in my mind all the other states which flourish today, so help me God, I can discover nothing but a conspiracy of the rich, who pursue their own aggrandisement under the name and title of the Commonwealth. They devise ways and means to keep safely what they have unjustly acquired, and to buy up the toil and labor of the poor as cheaply as possible and oppress them. When these schemes of the rich become established by the government, which is meant to protect the poor as well as the rich, then they are law. With insatiable greed these wicked men divide among themselves the goods which would have been enough for all.

> And yet they are far short of the happiness of the Utopians, who have abolished the use of money, and with it greed. What evils they avoid! What a multitude of crimes they prevent! Everyone knows that frauds, thefts, quarrels, contentions, uprisings, murders, betrayals, and poisonings (evils which are commonly punished rather than checked by the severities of the law) would wither away if money were eradicated! Fear, anxiety, worry, care, toil, and sleepless nights would disappear at the same time as money! Even poverty, which seems to need money more than anything else for its relief, would vanish if money were gone....

> If that one monster pride, the first and foremost of all evils, did not forbid it, the whole world would doubtless have adopted the laws of the Utopians long before this, drawn on by a rational perception of what each man's true interest is or else by the authority of Christ our Saviour, who in His great wisdom knows what is best and in His loving kindness bids us do it. Pride measures her prosperity not by her own goods but by others' wants. Pride would not deign to be a goddess, if there were no inferiors she could rule and triumph over. Her happiness shines brightly only in comparison to others' misery, and their poverty binds them and hurts them the more as her wealth is displayed. Pride is the infernal serpent that steals into the hearts of men, thwarting and holding them back from choosing the better way of life.

> Pride is far too deeply rooted in men's hearts to be easily torn out. I am glad, therefore, that the Utopians have achieved their social organization, which I wish all

mankind would imitate. Their institutions give their commonwealth a moral and social foundation for living happy lives, and as far as man can predict, these institutions will last forever. Because they have rooted out ambition and strife along with other vices, they are in no danger of civil wars, which have ruined many states that seemed secure. And as long as they maintain sound institutions and domestic harmony, they can never be overcome by the envious rulers near by, who have often attempted their ruin in vain.

Why should More, as a Christian and a compassionate moralist not agree with this in principle? Surely he does agree with it—in principle. The diagnosis is correct. Pride, he would be happy to admit, is the stumbling block to earthly happiness. But the wisdom which characterizes the man says in the same breath that pride cannot be "legislated out of existence." As long as there are men there will be pride, there will be inequality and want and suffering. Passionate as is the plea of Hythloday and ennobling as it is, he is turning his back upon reality. He is again the speculative philosopher as opposed to the practical philosopher and reformer in Thomas More. More represents the position of Plato when, with longing and deep sadness, he realizes that the philosopher-king is a hybrid creature given to mankind not once in a thousand years. More has seen much of life. He knows that philosophers do not often rule and that when they do the state comes more often to disaster than to happiness. He knows that there is no place for the dreamer in the harsh social, political, and economic world which, in the sixteenth century, is just emerging from the Middle Ages. He makes his summation.

> Thus Raphael finished speaking. I admit that not a few things in the manners and laws of the Utopians seemed very absurd to me: their way of waging war, their religious customs, as well as other matters, but especially [N. B.] the keystone of their entire system, namely, their communal living without the use of money. This one thing takes away all the nobility, magnificence, splendor, and majesty which public opinion commonly regards as the true ornaments of a nation.

Indeed, More might well admit in his own person the absurdity of many of the Utopian customs and laws, for he had created through the figure of Raphael Hythloday an intellectual *tour de force* of pure fantasy. Book II of the *Utopia*, the description of this far away, happy state is a monstrous Cartesian experiment in pure reason. More separates himself from his own background and character in the person of Hythloday and makes the basic assumption that a state can be developed from purely rational principles. In his own person he notes the faults of such a state, for to More reason cannot be the end-all of existence. There is too much Augustinian mysticism in his faith, too much humanity in his philosophy. Utopia is not his ideal. It represents the degree of perfection which a state can achieve from reason and natural law. In this respect the *Utopia* is a brilliant and ingenious fabrication and the sort of thing which so appealed to the Renaissance humanist. Indeed, this book "gained for its author a position among the foremost men of learning in Europe, excelling in wit, erudition, and style." The *Utopia* is at once a plea for reason in More's own age and a warning and exposition of how limiting reason alone can be. (pp. 45-50)

The *Utopia* lays a heavy burden upon the imagination today as in the sixteenth century. It was an intentional fic-

tion to stretch rationality until, for good or ill, it produced a culture the very antithesis of that of More's Europe. The possibilities of such a device were always appealing to Thomas More, for the extremity of the *Utopia* was, as it were, a mirror in which Europe could glimpse herself and perhaps gain some benefit from the distorted image or at least some instructive amusement from the gentle irony of the Utopian way of life. (p. 52)

> *J. K. Sowards, "Some Factors in the Re-Evaluation of Thomas More's 'Utopia'," in* The Northwest Missouri State College Studies, *Vol. XVI, No. 1, June 1, 1952, pp. 31-58.*

J. H. HEXTER (essay date 1952)

[*An American historian, Hexter coedited* Utopia *for* The Yale Edition of the Complete Works of St. Thomas More *and wrote one of the most respected studies of the work,* More's "Utopia": The Biography of an Idea *(1952). In the following excerpt from this study, he discusses More's opinions concerning private property as they are set out in* Utopia.]

The conclusions various scholars have come to about More's attitude toward the institution of property coincide to a remarkable degree with their own predilections on that point, or with their notions of what More should have thought if he was the kind of man they suppose him to be. Thus for Karl Kautsky [in *Thomas More and His Utopia* (1927)] *Utopia* is a socialist vision—and to a considerable extent a Marxian socialist vision—far in advance of its time. In the same way, but in a different sense, several recent Catholic scholars have written of More's social views as if he formed them with the encyclicals *Rerum Novarum* and *Quinquagesimo Anno* in mind. And the most recent Marxist interpretation [Russell Ames, *Citizen Thomas More and His Utopia* (1949)], subtler than Kautsky's, relegates More's views on private property to a secondary place in his social philosophy on the grounds that More was a "middle class man," and that the important part of his thought is that which conforms to the writer's notion of what an "enlightened" sixteenth century bourgeois should think. Many scholars indeed have been so anxious to square More's views on property with their own that they have paid only casual attention either to what More himself said about property in *Utopia* or to how he said it. Yet he had a great deal to say about property there, and it seems to me that an examination of the way he said it can settle as determinatively as such things can be settled what his beliefs on the subject were at the time he wrote *Utopia*.... [Such an examination will enable] us to isolate the views that More expressed in the Netherlands in the work of his first intention from his opinions as he formulated them almost a year later in the additions he made in England. The usefulness of the analysis will be apparent if we apply it to a hypothesis about More's attitude on the institution of property which at present is enjoying a considerable vogue.

In *Utopia* More put the only criticisms of community of property and the only defenses of private property into his own mouth. Because of this coincidence it is argued that these criticisms rather than Hythloday's praise represent the author's own true opinion.... [If my understanding of the structure of *Utopia* is correct], this contention falls flat not once but twice. For there is no defense of private property at all in the *Utopia* of More's first intention, that is, in the Introduction and Discourse written in the Netherlands. The climax and conclusion of that work is Hythloday's magnificent peroration against private property with its theme unmistakably stated at the outset:

> Now I have declared and described unto you, as truly as I could, the form and order of that commonwealth, which verily in my judgment is not only the best, but also that which alone of good right may claim and take upon it the name of a commonwealth or public weal. For in other places they speak still of the commonwealth. But every man procureth his own private wealth. Here where nothing is private, the common affairs be earnestly looked upon.

As he develops his theme he castigates every European realm:

> Therefore when I consider and weigh in my mind all these commonwealths which nowadays anywhere do flourish, so God help me, I can perceive nothing but a certain conspiracy of rich men procuring their own commodities under the name and title of the common wealth.

Finally the Utopian community of property and goods which plucks up by the roots the great occasion for wickedness and mischief is "gladly wished" to all nations. On that note of praise for community of property and goods the original *Utopia—Utopia* as More first intended it—ends.

Still it may be argued that when More got back to England he had a sober second thought. He realized that from *Utopia* as it stood someone might draw the inference which we in fact just drew. To prevent just such a calamity, when he added the new sections to the book he carefully put not one but two defenses of private property into his own mouth.

Perhaps the best way to evaluate this contention is to set down next to each other those two defenses of private property. Here they are:

> *Their common life and community of living without any traffic in money, this alone, which is the ultimate foundation of all their institutions, overthrows all excellence, magnificence, splendor, and majesty—the true proprieties and distinctions of a commonwealth according to the common opinion.*

> Men shall never live there wealthily, where all things be common. For how can there be abundance of goods, or of anything, where every man withdraweth his hand from labor. Whom the regard of his own gain driveth not to work and the hope that he hath of other men's travails maketh him slothful. Then when they be pricked with poverty, and yet no man can by any law or right defend that for his own, which he hath gotten with the labor of his own hands, shall not there of necessity be continual sedition and bloodshed? Specially the authority and reverence of magistrates being taken away, which what place it may have with such men among whom *there are no gradations of rank*, I cannot devise.

Now there is an enormous difference between these two critiques of community of property and goods. The second argument is serious and consequential. It proposes difficulties that any communal scheme must take account of.

The first argument, on the other hand, is simply vapid and frivolous. Frivolous not only from a present-day point of view, but from More's own point of view and that of every contemporary of his who thought seriously about politics. Not one of those contemporaries would have maintained for a moment that what mattered in a commonwealth were splendor, magnificence, and majesty. What mattered to them were order, harmony, justice, peace, and prosperity. In *Utopia* and elsewhere, with a vehemence that does not leave his conviction in doubt, More has set down his own estimate of the role that splendor, magnificence, and majesty play in this world. The rich and royal psalmist, King David, he tells us in the *Dialogue of Comfort*, most highly distinguishes himself not when he displays a glorious pomp, but when "he taketh his wealth for no wealth, nor his riches for no riches, nor in his heart setteth by neither nother, but secretly liveth in a contrite heart and a life penitential."

More's contempt for earthly magnificence and splendor appears not only in his earnest direct denunciations of it in *Utopia*, and in his elimination of all pomp from his ideal commonwealth except in connection with religious worship, but also in his humorous asides, and particularly in his autobiographical aside about the mission of the ambassadors of Anemolia—Land of the Windy Ones—to Utopia. Those splendid and magnificent emissaries, bearers of the majesty of the Anemolians, came to Utopia "determined in the gorgeousness of their apparel to represent very gods." They wore luxurious cloth of gold "with great chains of gold, with gold hanging at their ears, with gold rings upon their fingers, with broaches and *pendants* of gold upon their caps, which glistened full of pearls and precious stones," in order "with the bright shining and glistening of their gay clothing to dazzle the eyes of the silly poor Utopians." Thus splendidly and magnificently got up they paraded through the capital town of Amaurote; but the Utopians had their own ideas about such pompous shows. In Utopia gold chains were for slaves, and precious stones were baubles for children. So the magnificent and splendid Anemolian ambassadors had the joy of hearing young Utopians say to their mothers in wonder: "Look mother how great a lubber doth yet wear pearls and *gems*, as though he were a little child still. But the mother, yea and that also in good earnest: peace, son, sayeth she: I think he be some of the ambassadors' fools."

It is a tale that in 1515 More can tell wryly with a mixture of amusement and ruefulness, since a few months before as ambassador of His splendid and magnificent Majesty, the King of England, he himself had to parade through Bruges bedecked and bedizened as the Anemolian emissaries were. And although it is unlikely that any Flemish child on that occasion called poor More a lubber, there was little need to; no doubt he felt a great enough lubber nevertheless.

Indeed More's revulsion against pomp and display is embedded in levels of his being deeper than his discriminating intellect and rational consciousness. It stems from reasons of his heart and temperament that reason does not know. Not only the most eloquent passages of *Utopia* but his whole life and character are a living and total repudiation on his part of the conspicuous consumption and the false and invidious discriminations implied for him in the terms, "magnificence, splendor, majesty." When he carefully selects that particular group of words to support his "defense" of private property, we may justly suspect the sincerity of his ardor for the cause. Under the circumstances it is really not a defense at all; it is simply treason within the citadel.

Now if anyone honestly wanted to uphold private property, surely he would rest his case with a mature, not with a palpably silly and insincere, argument. More does the opposite. Against Hythloday's magnificent invective hurled at private property at the end of Book II, he sets not the serious but the silly defense of it. This juxtaposition at the very end of the published version of *Utopia* leaves the reader with a feeling of disgust at the evils of private property. This is precisely the effect that anyone in his good senses would expect from such an ending, and More was certainly in his good senses when he wrote it.

Of course More could not put the serious argument against community of property at the end of Book II, because he had already used it near the end of Book I. But why? He wrote both arguments at approximately the same time; why did he make the weak argument the final one? If he was really defending an important position, why did he shoot off all his heavy artillery ammunition before the enemy had brought up the main body of his attacking force? It is a curious tactic for a man committed to the defense of private property, and one that surely calls for explanation. The explanation is not far to seek, but it casts grave doubts on the zeal of the defender—already, as we have seen, not above suspicion.

The argument against community of property at the end of Book I is neither novel nor remarkable, but it is venerable and durable. It raises the two classical problems of egalitarian socialism: the problem of incentives and the problem of order and authority. Where rewards are not proportioned to effective effort, what will induce the worker to give his full share of energy to the common fund of necessary labor? And in a society of equals, whence arises the will to obey the ruling authorities, essential for the maintenance of public order and domestic concord?

We need not seek to evaluate these arguments against egalitarianism and the community of property ourselves; we need only to try to learn how More evaluated them. To this end let us consider them in connection with Hythloday's discourse on the Utopian commonwealth. Now this commonwealth fulfilled precisely the conditions that according to the attack on community of property in Book I must lead to economic and social disaster. In Utopia regard for their own gains did *not* drive men to work, since there were no private gains to regard. All fruits of labor beyond those consumed by their producers went into the common store, and all the necessities of life were freely drawn from that store. Consequently, of course, "no man can ... defend that for his own which he hath gotten with the labor of his own hands." As to gradations of rank in Utopia, they were not utterly destroyed, but they were entirely based on election to office by popular vote, and therefore they fell far below the minimum differentiation of status that respectable people of rank in the sixteenth century deemed essential for the preservation of a properly and decently ordered society. All Utopians have an equal opportunity for education, all do equal labor, and all have an equal voice in the choice of magistrates and priests.

But what of the dire consequences that the argument in Book I against the community of property ascribes to such social arrangements? Is there no "abundance of goods or of anything" in Utopia? On the contrary there is "store and abundance of all things that be requisite either for the necessity or commodity of life." Are the Utopians slothful, "everyman withdrawing his hand from labor"? On the contrary no Utopian has "*victuals* given him until he has ... dispatched so much work as there is wont to be wrought before supper." For the inhabitants of the Fortunate Isle there is indeed "little liberty ... to loiter ... no cloak or pretense to idleness." Does the regime of equality in Utopia take away "the authority and reverence of magistrates"? On the contrary the magistrates are there called fathers and "the citizens willingly exhibit unto them due honor without any compulsion." And far from being prey to "continual sedition and bloodshed," Utopia is a land without "jeopardy of domestical dissension," where "perfect concord remaineth." So the poverty, sloth, and disorder that the argument in Book I supposes to be the consequence of community of property do not exist in Utopia. Instead that land of community of property enjoys the abundance, industriousness, and harmonious order that are supposed to be, but are not, the fruit of the regime of private property.

Indeed it is the rather sour cream of the jest that it is not Utopia but sixteenth century Europe, with its well-rooted institutions of private property, that is running to ruin with scarcity, idleness, and crimes of violence. Such surely is the conclusion that More intends the reader to draw from the social criticism of the Europe of his day so brilliantly and wittily set out in both the *Dialogue* and the Discourse. And this contrast between Europe and Utopia is the consequence of no mere accident. It is the "form and fashion" of Utopian society, its "institutions of life," that have "laid such foundations of their commonwealth, as shall continue and last not only wealthily, but also, as far as man's wit may judge and conjecture, shall endure forever." Among those institutions of life not the least important is community of property. The Utopians live industriously, abundantly, and peacefully not in spite of the community of property practiced there, but in a very considerable measure because of it.

And now we can discern the function in the artistic economy of *Utopia* of the argument against the community of property that More ascribes to himself in Book I. It is revealed by Hythloday's immediate response to it:

> You conceive in your mind either none at all, or else a very false image and similitude of this thing. But if you had been with me in Utopia and had presently seen their fashions and laws, as I did, ... then doubtless you would grant that you never saw people well ordered, but only there.

More's argument serves to set the theme and provide the springboard for Hythloday's description of the Utopian commonwealth, and by the time he has finished describing it, he has not merely defended the community of property in general; he has specifically met all More's objections to it point by point. And this strongly suggests that More made the argument simply that it might be met point by point; that he was setting up a straw man just to have it knocked down. Yet even this does not do full justice to the artfulness of More's procedure when we call to mind that the Discourse which met the objections was written before the **Dialogue** in which they are raised. Thus he did not tailor the answers to fit the objections. In Through-the-Looking-Glass fashion he tailored the objections to fit the answers he already had given. He did not set up a straw man in order to knock it down; he actually set up a straw man that he had already not only knocked down but utterly and completely demolished.

The parts of **Utopia** that More wrote in England represent his second thought only in the very literal sense that they deal in the main with a subject that he had not thought of writing about when he was in the Netherlands. But whenever the course of the added section overlaps that of the original version, the opinions expressed in both coincide exactly one with the other. The only difference in this respect between More's other opinions and his opinions on private property is that in the former case the overlapping is a casual result of the course of the argument he happens at the moment to be pursuing, while in the latter case it is clearly contrived. Only on the subject of property does More obviously go out of his way to use the part of **Utopia** written in England to reinforce a view expressed in the original version of **Utopia** written in the Netherlands. His second thought on the question of property was merely to reiterate and reaffirm his first thought. (pp. 33-43)

J. H. Hexter, in his More's "Utopia": The Biography of an Idea, *Princeton University Press, 1952, 171 p.*

C. S. LEWIS (essay date 1954)

[*Lewis is considered one of the foremost mythopoeic authors of the twentieth century. Indebted principally to George MacDonald, G. K. Chesterton, Charles Williams, and the writers of ancient Norse sagas, he is regarded as a formidable logician and Christian polemicist, a perceptive literary critic, and, perhaps most highly, as a writer of fantasy literature. Also a noted academic and scholar, Lewis held posts at Oxford and Cambridge, where he was an acknowledged authority on medieval and Renaissance literature. A traditionalist in his approach to life and art, he opposed the modern critical movement toward biographical and psychological interpretation, preferring to practice and propound a theory of criticism that stresses the author's intent rather than the reader's presuppositions and prejudices. In the following excerpt from one of his best-known critical works,* English Literature in the Sixteenth Century, Excluding Drama, *he surveys* The History of King Richard III, Utopia, *and More's English controversial and devotional writings, finding much both to praise and to condemn in More's themes and prose style.*]

[Thomas More, who] held his place in our older critical tradition on the precarious tenure of one Latin work, has in recent years been restored to his rightful place as a major English author. (p. 165)

His Latin prose, with the exception of the **Utopia**, may be ignored in a history of English literature, the more so because its chief glory, the **Historia Ricardi Tertii**, can be read in his own unfinished English version. It is an ambitious undertaking modelled on the ancient historians, and in it the long set speeches dear to Thucydides and Livy claim the lion's share. Although their dramatic function is not neglected the author is more interested in them as rhetoric, and Queen Elizabeth pleading for her child's

right to sanctuary is not really much less 'facundious' and forensic than Buckingham addressing the citizens in the Guildhall. More, who had been so purely medieval in his poetry, is here medieval and humanistic at once; he writes for an audience in whom the medieval love of fine talk had been slightly redirected and heavily reinforced by classical example. He expects us to share the enjoyment of the citizens when Buckingham 'rehersed them the same matter again in other order and other wordes, so wel and ornately and natheles so evidently and plaine, with voice, gesture and countenance so cumly and so convenient, that every man much mervailed that herd him'. More is also a lawyer writing for an audience whose education had for the most part a legal twist, and law is the worst influence on his style. He sets out for a whole column the proclamation of Hastings's treasons and probably regards its conveyancing prolixity as an ornament rather than a blemish to his page. The character sketches, pithy and sententious and much indebted to the ancient models, will be more congenial to a modern taste. The portrait of Hastings would not disgrace Tacitus, and that of Jane Shore is a beautiful example of the author's mingled charity and severity. The book now pleases best in those passages which are most intimate—Hastings chatting with his namesake, Richard calling for the mess of strawberries, Richard with his eyes 'whirling' and his hand on his dagger 'like one always ready to strike again', or the lively picture of a queen moving house with 'heavinesse, rumble, haste and businesse ... chestes, coffers, packes, fardelles, trusses ... some lading, some going, some discharging, some coming for more'. It is not an economical style, but it lives. We must not, however, represent a sixteenth-century book as a modern one by over-emphasizing merits which are really subordinate. More is not an early Strachey nor even an early Macaulay. The **Historia** in its entirety will succeed only with readers who can enjoy the classical sort of history—history as a grave and lofty Kind, the prose sister of epic, rhetorical in expression and moral in purpose. If read in the right spirit, More's performance will seem remarkable. He brings to his work a great knowledge of affairs, a sufficient measure of impartiality, a sense of tragedy, and a sense of humour. He makes an attempt, something more than half-hearted, to sift fact from tradition; and to his dramatic moulding of the story Shakespeare's close discipleship is sufficient testimony. He produces a much more interesting example of the new kind of history than Boece.

In 1516 came the **Utopia** which, though it was written in Latin, is so good and has given rise to so many controversies that I should hardly be forgiven if I passed it over in silence. All seem to be agreed that it is a great book, but hardly any two agree as to its real significance: we approach it through a cloud of contradictory eulogies. In such a state of affairs a good, though not a certain, clue is the opinion of those who lived nearer the author's time than we. Our starting-point is that Erasmus speaks of it as if it were primarily a comic book; Tyndale despises it as 'poetry'; for Harpsfield [see excerpt dated 1558] it is a ';vollye invention', 'pleasantly' set forth; More himself in later life classes it and the *Praise of Folly* together as books fitter to be burned than translated in an age prone to misconstruction; Thomas Wilson, fifty years later, mentions it for praise among 'feined narrations and wittie invented matters (as though they were true indeed)'. This is not the language in which friend or enemy or author (when the author is so honest a man as More) refer to a serious philosophical treatise. It all sounds as if we had to do with a book whose real place is not in the history of political thought so much as in that of fiction and satire. It is, of course, possible that More's sixteenth-century readers, and More himself, were mistaken. But it is at least equally possible that the mistake lies with those modern readers who take the book *au grand sérieux*. (pp. 165-67)

The *Utopia* has its serious, even its tragic, elements. It is, as its translator Robinson says, 'fruteful and profitable'. But it is not a consistently serious philosophical treatise, and all attempts to treat it as such break down sooner or later. The interpretation which breaks down soonest is the 'liberal' interpretation. There is nothing in the book on which the later More, the heretic-hunter, need have turned his back. There is no freedom of speech in Utopia. There is nothing liberal in Utopia. From it, as from all other imaginary states, liberty is more successfully banished than the real world, even at its worst, allows. The very charm of these paper citizens is that they cannot in any way resist their author: every man is a dictator in his own book. It is not love of liberty that makes men write Utopias. Nor does the *Utopia* give any colour to Tyndale's view that More 'knew the truth' of Protestantism and forsook it: the religious orders of the Utopians and their very temples are modelled on the old religion. On the other hand, it is not a defence of that old order against current criticisms; it supports those criticisms by choosing an abbot as its specimen of the bad landlord and making a friar its most contemptible character. R. W. Chambers, with whom died so much that was sweetest and strongest in English scholarship, advanced a much more plausible view. According to him the Utopians represent the natural virtues working at their ideal best in isolation from the theological; it will be remembered that they hold their Natural Religion only provisionally 'onles any godlier be inspired into man from heven'. Yet even this leaves some features unaccounted for. It is doubtful whether More would have regarded euthanasia for incurables and the assassination of hostile princes as things contained in the Law of Nature. And it is very strange that he should make Hedonism the philosophy of the Utopians. Epicurus was not regarded by most Christians as the highest example of the natural light. The truth surely is that as long as we take the *Utopia* for a philosophical treatise it will 'give' wherever we lean our weight. It is, to begin with, a dialogue: and we cannot be certain which of the speakers, if any, represents More's considered opinion. When Hythloday explains why his philosophy would be useless in the courts of kings More replies that there is 'another philosophy more civil' and expounds this less intransigent wisdom so sympathetically that we think we have caught the very More at last; but when I have read Hythloday's retort I am all at sea again. It is even very doubtful what More thought of communism as a practical proposal. We have already had to remind ourselves, when considering Colet, that the traditional admission of communism as the law of uncorrupted Nature need carry with it no consequences in the world of practical sociology. It is certain that in the *Confutation* More had come to include communism among the 'horrible heresies' of the Anabaptists and in the *Dialogue of Comfort* he defends private riches. Those who think of More as a 'lost leader' may discount these later utterances. Yet even at the end of the *Utopia* he rejects the Utopian economics as a thing 'founded of no good reason'. The

magnificent rebuke of all existing societies which precedes this may suggest that the rejection is ironical. On the other hand, it may mean that the whole book is only a satiric glass to reveal our own avarice by contrast and is not meant to give us directly practical advice.

These puzzles may give the impression that the *Utopia* is a confused book: and if it were intended as a serious treatise it would be very confused indeed. On my view, however, it appears confused only so long as we are trying to get out of it what it never intended to give. It becomes intelligible and delightful as soon as we take it for what it is—a holiday work, a spontaneous overflow of intellectual high spirits, a revel of debate, paradox, comedy and (above all) of invention, which starts many hares and kills none. It is written by More the translator of Lucian and friend of Erasmus, not More the chancellor or the ascetic. Its place on our shelves is close to *Gulliver* and *Erewhon*, within reasonable distance of Rabelais, a long way from the *Republic* or *New Worlds for Old*. The invention (the 'poetry' of which More was accused) is quite as important as the merits of the polity described, and different parts of that polity are on very different levels of seriousness.

Not to recognize this is to do More grave injustice. Thus the suggestion that the acquisitive impulse should be mortified by using gold for purposes of dishonour is infantile if we take it as a practical proposal. If gold in Utopia were plentiful enough to be so used, gold in Utopia would not

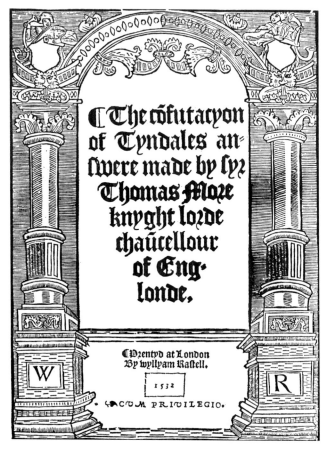

Title page of The confutacyon of Tyndales answere *(1532), More's second denunciation of the English reformer William Tyndale.*

be a precious metal. But if it is taken simply as satiric invention leading up to the story of the child and the ambassadors, it is delicious. The slow beginning of the tale, luring us on from London to Bruges, from Bruges to Antwerp, and thence by reported speech to fabulous lands beyond the line, has no place in the history of political philosophy: in the history of prose fiction it has a very high place indeed. Hythloday himself, as we first see him, has something of the arresting quality of the Ancient Mariner. The dialogue is admirably managed. Mere conversation holds us contented for the first book and includes that analysis of the contemporary English situation which is the most serious and the most truly political part of the *Utopia*. In the second book More gives his imagination free rein. There is a thread of serious thought running through it, an abundance of daring suggestions, several back-handed blows at European institutions, and, finally, the magnificent peroration. But he does not keep our noses to the grindstone. He says many things for the fun of them, surrendering himself to the sheer pleasure of imagined geography, imagined language, and imagined institutions. That is what readers whose interests are rigidly political do not understand: but everyone who has ever made an imaginary map responds at once. (pp. 168-70)

It is idle to expect that More's polemical writings, to which I now turn, should be as good in their own kind as the *Utopia* is in its. In the first place they are commissioned work, undertaken at the instance of the Bishop of London and conscientiously carried out not because More wants to write them but because, on his view, they must be written by someone. There is no evidence that he ever felt a literary and intellectual, as distinct from a religious, vocation to this kind of work. His weariness, until the task has become a habit, is apparent. 'Would God,' he says in the *Confutation*, 'after all my laboure done, so that the remembrance of their pestilent errours were araced out of Englishe mennes heartes and their abominable bookes burned up, myne owne were walked with them, and the name of these matters utterly putte in oblivion.' In the second place More was limited by the very terms of his commission to write for the vulgar.... He was not allowed to fly very high in theology: how high he could have flown if free, I am not qualified to judge. Hooker, writing many years later, gave it as his opinion (*Sermon on Justification*) that More, though a very learned man, had not fully understood the position that his own church was defending against the Lutherans.

One work in this group, the *Dialogue* of 1528, stands apart from the rest. It is the first and the iron has not yet entered into More's soul. The plan of it is good. More feigns a series of visits from a mysterious Messenger who puts forward the Lutheran positions with a disinterested air, disclaiming all belief in them but sometimes betraying it. Considerable dramatic humour results from this device. The discussion is brought to life in true Platonic style by notes of time and place, by interruptions, and by references to Lady More. Passages of hard dialectic are relieved by 'merry tales' and by lengthier speeches which aim at eloquence. As controversy it does not rank very high and perhaps in the circumstances could not: the main questions at issue hardly admit of so popular a treatment. It is easy to put the case for justification by faith as it appears to a text-hunting and ignorant fanatic, and easy to reply in terms of commonplace good sense and morality.

But the real problem, set by the very nature of Christian experience, remains where it was. On saints' miracles More does better, and the marvellous story of the young couple of Walbrook is at once a piece of excellent comedy and an effective argument; but too many pages are wasted on that facile interchange of anecdotal credulity and anecdotal incredulity which you may hear in any casual conversation about spiritualism or flying saucers. A lawyer, we feel, ought to have had something more pertinent to say about the whole nature of evidence. But if this book is not great theology, it is great Platonic dialogue: perhaps the best specimen of that form ever produced in English. Berkeley is urbane and graceful and more profound, but his Hylas and Philonous are mere men of straw beside More and the Messenger. The latter is perhaps too stupidly obstinate and repeats himself too often. No doubt this is so because More wishes to depict the patience of the Papists, but he has not foreseen how severely he would also exercise the patience of his readers. But for the most part the thing is admirably alive. We watch with delight the slow, inevitable progress of the Messenger into snare after snare; and this, together with the richness of its colloquialisms and the wholly excellent humour of its funny stories, will always make the *Dialogue* worth reading.

One more work is worth separate mention before we reach the real slough. The *Supplication of Souls* is a defence of the doctrine of purgatory and More has chosen to put it into the mouth of the souls whom purgatory now contains. The first book, which is almost entirely factual and statistical, contains some of More's best and most muscular prose—for More is happiest when he is not trying to be eloquent. The second book, which has a peculiar literary merit of its own, illustrates a further stage in the degradation of the idea of purgatory. In Fisher the pain has been separated from any spiritual purification, but the torments had at least been inflicted by angels. In More this last link with heaven is severed. The attendants (if that is the right word) are now devils. 'Our keepers', say the imprisoned souls,

> are such as God kepe you from, cruell damned spirites, odious enemies and despitefull tormentours, and theyr companye more horrible and grievous to us than is the payn itself and the intollerable tourmente that they doo us, wherewith from top to toe they cease not to teare us.

The length of the sentence has thus become the sole difference between purgatory and hell. Purgatory is a department of hell. And More's humour, continued even here, somehow increases the horror. Instead of the psalms and litanies which resounded on the sunlit terraces of Dante's mountain from souls 'contented in the flame', out of the black fire which More has imagined, mixed with the howls of unambiguous physical torture, come peals of harsh laughter. All is black, salt, macabre. I make the point not to disgrace a man before whom the best of us must stand uncovered, but because the age we are studying cannot be understood without it. This sort of thing, among others, was what the old religion had come to mean in the popular imagination during the reign of Henry VIII: this was one of the things a man left behind in becoming a Protestant. Nor, I think, is that its only relevance for the history of taste. Has not the wildness of the 'eldritch' poetry in Scotland a secret affinity with it? The thing cannot be proved: but I feel that the burlesque heaven of *Kynd Kit-*

tok springs from the same mood as the serious, yet dreadfully comic, purgatory of the **Supplication**.

Although we have now skimmed more than four hundred columns of the 1557 folio, the greater part of More's controversial writings remains—the **Confutation of Tyndale's Answer**, the **Letter** (against Frith), the **Apology** the **Debellation of Salem and Byzance** and the **Answer to the Poisoned Book**. The earliest criticism ever made on these works is recorded by More himself ('The brethren cannot beare that my writing is so long') and it cannot be seriously questioned. There are indeed differences between them. The **Confutation** is the longest, the harshest, and the dullest. The **Letter** is exceptional not only for its brevity but for its charitable and almost fatherly tone. In the **Apology** we see More being drawn, as all controversialists are drawn, away from the main issue into self-defence. In the **Debellation** what was first undertaken as a duty is only too plainly becoming a habit. More is at pains to excuse himself for answering what in his own judgement needed no answer, and tells us the illuminating fact that this huge treatise was composed in a few days. A not unwelcome air of senility is perceptible in the rambling pages with which it opens and there is charm in the passage where the old lawyer pictures himself once more a young man at a moot. In the **Answer to the Poisoned Book** this loss of grip becomes even more noticeable and we repeatedly escape from the matter in hand into digressions—on gluttony, on the Arian heresy, on the Annunciation, on Free Will, on Judas Iscariot. This twilight is welcome after the heat of such a day.

But in spite of these differences the controversial works, after the **Dialogue**, may well be criticized in the lump. Pure literature they do not aspire to be; and theologically More's commission confines him to stating the 'stock' case for orthodoxy in an entirely popular form. It only remains, therefore, to judge them as specimens of the art of controversy. That this art can produce masterpieces which outlive their occasion, no one who remembers Plato, Hooker, Burke, or Newman will deny. But More's controversies are not on that level. Apart from the deficiencies of his style (a point we must return to) he is hampered by two self-imposed principles which are fatal to the highest kind of success. In the first place he has decided that his case against the heretics should be in his books as the soul is in the body—*tota in toto et tota in qualibet parte*; that the reader, whatever page he lights upon, should find there all that he needs for refutation of the enemy. He is monotonously anxious to conquer and to conquer equally, at every moment: to show in every chapter that every heretical book is wrong about everything—wrong in history, in logic, in rhetoric, and in English grammar as well as in theology. And secondly his method of attacking a book is to go through it page by page like a schoolmaster correcting an exercise, so that the order and emphasis of the discussion are in fact dictated by his opponent. How to throw the grand arguments into bold relief and to condense the lesser, how to decline small points and to answer others while seeming to decline them, where to refresh the reader with some eloquent assault over the ruins of a lately demolished fortification—of all this More has no notion.

Yet even in these books his real talent sometimes appears. Wherever he allows himself to use the weapon of low comedy he is at once excellent. Even the faintest hint of it—as in the last book of the **Confutation** where he transfers the

case against Barnes to two imaginary old women—is sufficient to refresh us; and the fully developed 'merry tales' will bear comparison with anything of the same kind in Chaucer or Shakespeare. It is true that the best of them all, the story of Richard Hunne, comes in the **Dialogue**: but even in the later works we have the goodwife of Culham, *Te igitur clementissime pater*, the lady who stopped her husband's lecture on astronomy, and the woman who talked in church. About these there can be only one opinion; but More has other devices bordering on the comic which do not seem to me so successful. He has the Arnoldian trick of catching up some phrase used by the enemy and ridiculing it by repetition. No instance of this is as good as 'Wragg is in custody', but it can be effective enough when the pilloried phrase has the rhythmic qualities that go to make a good refrain; like 'the great, brode, bottomless ocean sea of evils' in the **Supplication**. But at times it may descend to a kind of nagging or snarling which is unattractive—'I have not contended with Erasmus my derling because I founde no such malicious entente with Erasmus my derling as I fynde with Tyndall. For hadde I founde with Erasmus my derling the shrewde entente and purpose that I fynde in Tyndall, Erasmus my derling should be no more my derling', &c. What is this but the rhetoric of the preparatory school?

The mention of More's humour brings us to the question of his scurrility. From the moral point of view no very serious charge can be made; More is not much more scurrilous, only more amusingly scurrilous, than many of our older controversialists. Even if we judged his scurrility to be a fault it would be hard to wish away a fault so intertwined (or even identical) with what is the chief and often the only merit of these works: that is, the gusto of their hard-hitting, racy, street-corner abuse. It was More's business to appeal to the vulgar, to play to the gallery, and it suited one side of him extremely well. He is our first great cockney humorist, the literary ancestor of Martin Marprelate and Nashe. It would be a loss to his polemical writings if they were purged of their references to heretics who 'have as much shame in their face as a shotten herring hath shrimps in her tail', to 'lowsy Luther' and his disciples' 'long babelary', to 'hammer-heads meete to make horse-shoon in helle'. If he would talk a little less about faggots and Smithfield and about Luther's 'abominable bichery', a theme that almost obsesses him, I for one should have no quarrel with his comic abuse. It is when he is being serious that his abusiveness becomes a literary fault. To rebuke magnificently is one of the duties of a great polemical writer. More often attempts it but he always fails. He loses himself in a wilderness of opprobrious adjectives. He cannot denounce like a prophet; he can only scold and grumble like a father in an old fashioned comedy.

As we read these controversies we become aware that More the author was scarcely less a martyr to his religion than More the man. In obedience to his conscience he spent what might have been the best years of his literary life on work which demanded talents that he lacked and gave very limited scope to those he had. It may well have been no easy sacrifice.

I turn with relief to his devotional works. One of these, the meditation **De IV Novissimis** was early work and might on that account have been treated at the very beginning. I have preferred to place it here, side by side with the **Dia-**

logue of Comfort, in order to bring out the almost laughable, wholly beautiful, contrast between them. The late work written under the shadow of the scaffold, is full of comfort, courage, and humour; the early meditation is a piece of unrelieved gloom. Thus some men's religion fails at the pinch: that of others does not appear to pluck up heart until the pinch comes. The *De IV Novissimis* is, for its darkness, a pendant to the *Supplication*. It may justly be called a religious 'exercise' provided that we do not associate with that word any idea of insincerity. That is to say, it is not an outpouring of individual experience. The theme comes first and is selected for its intrinsic and objective importance; the business of the writer is to find reflections suitable to it. Self-improvement, not self-expression, is the purpose. More's scheme consisted in applying each of the four last things to each of the seven deadly sins in turn, and he gave it up in the middle of applying the first *Novissimum* (death) to the sixth sin (sloth), having thus completed five of the twenty-eight panels or niches intended. Of its value as a devotional work who dares consider himself a judge? If most of it now seems helpless either to encourage or to alarm, the fault may be ours: but not, I think, all ours. Almost everywhere it tries to prove too much. Gross exaggeration of the part played by gluttony in our diseases leaves the conscience undisturbed. The passage in which all life is compared to an illness shows some inability to distinguish between a conceit and an argument. The colours are too dark. In the true late medieval manner More forgets that to paint all black is much the same as not to paint at all. What was intended to be a rebuke of sin degenerates almost into a libel upon life and we are forced into incredulity. It is true that More once assures us that even in the natural order 'virtue bringeth his pleasure and vice is not without pain' but this little taper does not cast its beam very far in the general gloom. The real merits of the book are incidental. The medieval homiletic tradition wisely admitted the grotesque and the comic and where More avails himself of this licence he writes well. The picture of the glutton 'with his belly standing a strote like a taber and his noll totty with drink' is as good as that in the *Ancren Riwle*. We are reminded of Falstaff's death when we read of the dying man 'thy nose sharping, thy legges cooling, thy fingers fimbling'. Few pictures of the deathbed are more vivid than the following:

> Have ye not ere this in a sore sicknes felt it very grievous to have folk babble to you, and namely such thynges as ye sholde make aunswere to, when it was a pain to speake? Thinke ye notnow that it wil be a gentle pleasure when we lye dying, al our body in pain, al our mind in trouble, our soul in sorow, our hearte al in drede, while our life walketh awaiward, while our death draweth toward, while the devil is busy about us, while we lack stomak and strength to beare any one of so manifold heynous troubles, wil it not be as I was about to say, a pleasaunt thing to see before thine eyen and heare at thine eare a rable of fleshly frendes, or rather of flesh flies, skipping about thy bed and thy sicke body (now almost carreyn) crying to thee on every side, What shal I have, what shall I have.... Than shall thyne executours ask for the kayes....

But I have done the author a little more than justice by making one omission and by stopping where I did. More sows from the sack, not from the hand.

The ***Dialogue of Comfort against Tribulation*** is the noblest of all his vernacular writings. It was written in the Tower while More waited for death (for all he knew, death by torture, hanging, cutting down alive, and disembowelling). Its form is an imaginary conversation between two Hungarian gentlemen who foresee the possibility of martyrdom if the Turk comes much nearer. It is thus a fairly close parallel to Boethius' *De Consolatione* and the difference between them is interesting. In Boethius the thought that would be uppermost in any modern mind—that of physical pain—is hardly present at all; in More it is ubiquitous. We feel that we are reading the work of a man with nerves like our own, even of a man sensitive in such matters beyond the norm of his own coarse and courageous century. He discusses at length whether a man should envisage such horrors beforehand. To do so may clearly lead either to false confidence (reckoning with pain's image, not pain) or to despair (reckoning without the grace which will not perhaps be given before the need). His reply is that there is no choice. When once the matter has been raised we cannot refuse to think about it, and to advise us otherwise is 'as much reason as the medicine that I have heard for the toothache, to go thrice about a churchyard and never think on a fox tayle'. He would therefore have everyone, of whatever sex or age, 'often to thinke thereupon'. We must do the best we can, meditating much on the Passion of Christ, never 'full out of feare of fallynge' but 'in good hope and full purpose' to stand. There is no attempt to disguise the situation; 'whan we remember the terrour of shamefull and painefull death, that poynt sodaynly putteth us in oblivion of all that shold be our comfort'. There is here a precision unusual in More. 'Whan we remember'—the mind is numb for hours even in a condemned cell, and then the terror rushes back: and 'sodaynly'. Worse even than this is the haunting fear that the pain itself might force a man 'to forsake our Saviour even in the myddes, and dye there with his synne, and so be damned forever'. Yet when all's said, a man must 'stand to his tackling' and any Christian would be very glad today to have so suffered yesterday.

The theme is almost the gravest that the human mind can entertain, but it must not be supposed that the book is a gloomy one. The ***Dialogue of Comfort*** justifies its title; it overflows with kindliness and humour and the beautiful self-mockery of old age aware of its own garrulity and its own limitations. The 'merry tales' are here in abundance, the old medieval jokes about women, so stale in themselves yet, after all, so amusingly handled, and so touching when we remember the hard road which they are now helping the author to travel. In a slightly different vein the longer story of a false alarm in war is admirably told. But I would not quote much from this book: it is (or was) accessible in a cheap reprint and should be on everyone's shelves.

Of the ***Treatise on the Passion*** in its English form, we have only part from More's own hand; the rest, translated from his Latin by Margaret Roper's daughter. Those who turn to it expecting to find the beauties of the dialogue continued will be disappointed. It is as much exegetical as devotional and takes the form of a commentary on Gerson's *Monatesseron* (a gospel concordance made on a rather clumsy plan). As a Biblical commentator More is wholly medieval. Long ago in the *Supplication* he had used as a proof of the existence of purgatory the fact that Hezekiah wept when told that he must die; here he allegorizes in the old fashion on Our Lord's repetition of the word *Father*, on the name Simon, and on Malchus. From the literary point of view the most unfortunate feature of the book is the indiscretion with which More puts words into the mouth of Christ. It can be done successfully; witness the *Imitation*. But More seems wholly unaware of the dangers involved: it is indeed remarkable how one who had been, as a man, so attentive to the spirit of the Dominical utterances, could have remained, as a critic, so deaf to their style. Already in the ***Answer to the Poisoned Book*** this insensibility had led him to grotesque results ('For I am, as I dyvers times now have told you, the very bread of life'); here it leads to the following:

> Thys is the shorte whyle that is graunted yee and the libertie geven unto darknesse, that now ye maye in the night, which till this howre ye could never be suffered to bring to passe in the daye, like monstruous raveninge fowles, like skriche owles and hegges, like backes, howlettes, nighte crowes and byrdes of the hellye lake, goe aboute with your billes, your tallentes, your teeth and your shyrle shrychinge, outrageouslye, but all in vayne, thus in the darke to flee upon me.

All this (and there is much more than I have quoted) is a gloss on the words 'This is your hour and the power of darkness'; and More cannot see that he is weakening them. It is true that the words quoted are his granddaughter's translation: but those who know More's English best will not say that the style is much inferior to his own, and those who look at the Latin will not find its *bubones striges* and *nycticoraces* much of an improvement on their vernacular equivalents. Yet these errors (of which there are plenty in the ***Treatise***) are balanced by passages of exquisite pathos and insight. The following, also put into the mouth of Our Lord and explaining the final cause of the agony in the garden, is noteworthy—though more, I confess, for the matter than for the style.

> Plucke up thy courage, faint heart, and dispaire never a deale. What though ye be feareful, sory, and weary, and standest in great dread of most painful tormentry that is like to falle upon thee, be of good comfort for all that. For I myself have vanquished the whole worlde, and yet felt I far more feare, sorowe, wearinesse, and much more inward anguish too, whan I considered my most bitter, painful passion to presse so fast uppon me. He that is strong harted may finde a thousand gloryous valiant martyrs whose ensample he may right joyfully follow. But thou, now, o temerous and weke sely shepe, thynke it sufficient for thee onely to walke after me.

Great claims have in modern times been made for More's English prose; I can accept them only with serious reservations. To compare it with that of the *Scale of Perfection* or the *Revelations* of Lady Julian will, in my opinion, only reveal its inferiority to them. The man who sits down and reads fairly through fifty pages of More will find many phrases to admire; but he will also find an invertebrate length of sentence, a fumbling multiplication of epithets, and an almost complete lack of rhythmical vitality. The length of sentence in More is quite different from the fullness of impassioned writers like Cicero or Burke or Ruskin, or from that of close thinkers like Hooker or Coleridge. It is not even the winning garrulity of Montaigne, or not often. Its chief cause is the fact that More never really rose from a legal to a literary conception of clarity and completeness. He multiplies words in a vain endeavour to stop up all possible chinks, where a better artist forces his

conceptions on us by the light and heat of intellect and emotion in which they burn. He thus loses the advantages both of full writing and of concise writing. There are no lightning thrusts: and, on the other hand, no swelling tide of thought and feeling. The style is stodgy and dough-like. As for the good phrases, the reader will already have divined their nature. They come when More is in his homeliest vein: their race and pith and mere Englishry are the great redeeming feature of his prose. They ring in our ears like echoes of the London lanes and Kentish villages; 'whispered in hukermoker', 'damn us all to Dymmingesdale', 'the goose was over the moon', 'every finger shall be a thumb', 'fume, fret, frot, and foam', 'saving for the worshipfull name of wine ichad as leve a drunken water'. They belong to the same world as his merry tales. Nearly all that is best in More is comic or close to comedy.

We think of More, and rightly, as a humanist and a saintly man. On the one hand, he is the writer of the ***Utopia***, the friend of Erasmus, the man whose house became a sort of academy. On the other, he is the man who wanted to be a Carthusian, who used a log of wood for his bolster and wore the hair, the martyr who by high example refused the wine offered him on his way to execution. The literary tragedy is that neither of these sides to his character found nearly such perfect expression in his writings as they deserved. The ***Utopia*** ought to have been only a beginning: his fertility of mind, his humour, and his genius for dialogue ought to have been embodied in some great work, some *colloquies* meatier than those of Erasmus, some satiric invention more gravely droll than Rabelais. As for his sanctity, to live and die like a saint is no doubt a better thing than to write like one, but it is not the same thing; and More does not write like a saint. 'Unction' (in the good sense of that word) is noticeably lacking in his work: the beauty of holiness, the fragrance of the *Imitation* or of St. François de Sales or of Herbert. What is actually expressed in most of his work is a third More, out of whom both the saint and the humanist have been made and with whom (that is both his glory and his limitation) they never lose touch—the Tudor Londoner of the citizen class. However high he rises he remains unmistakably rooted in a world of fat, burgher laughter, contentedly acclaiming well-seasoned jokes about shrewish wives or knavish servants, contemptuous of airs and graces and of what it thinks unnecessary subtleties; a world not lacking in shrewdness, courage, kindness, or honesty, but without fineness. No man even half so wise and good as Thomas More ever showed so little trace of the *cuor gentil*. There is nothing at all in him which, if further developed, could possibly lead on to the graces of Elizabethan and Jacobean literature. It might have led to things which some would prefer, but very different things. (pp. 171-81)

> *C. S. Lewis, "Book II: 'Drab',", in his* English Literature in the Sixteenth Century, Excluding Drama, *Oxford at the Clarendon Press, 1954, pp. 157-317.*

P. ALBERT DUHAMEL   (essay date 1955)

[*Duhamel is an American academic, essayist, and critic. In the following excerpt, he argues that* Utopia *is essentially medieval in methodology.*]

Scholarly concentration almost exclusively on the political content of More's ***Utopia*** as an anticipation of modern liberal thinking has resulted in the unexpected paradox that probably the most medieval of More's works is commonly interpreted as the most Renaissance. Although most of the explicit content of the *Utopia* is concerned with contemporary Renaissance political and economic problems, the implicit heuristic method which determined this content is medieval. Just as some knowledge of the simplified medieval cosmic setting implied by Shakespeare throughout his works is of greater importance to an understanding of his plays than the recognition of any specific historical event which may be alluded to in a particular play, so the explicit content of *Utopia* can be better understood in terms of the Scholastic method which, though only implicit in the work, More employed in the construction of *Utopia* to make his criticism of the world created by an abuse of that method all the more ironical. The failure to recognize how the method controlled the content has been the greatest single obstacle to an understanding of the *Utopia* in its proper context and to its reconciliation with More's life and English works. (p. 99)

The explicit content of More's *Utopia* is the result of the application of that method of investigation employed by the Scholastics.... [St. Anselm of Canterbury's] motto of "Fides quaerens intellectum" roughly summarizes the essence of the method, for it was fundamentally an attempt to reach an understanding of the truths of revelation, or, in other words, to achieve a rational insight into the content of faith. Investigations conducted according to this method started by accepting some statement as true because it was revealed, and then developed by searching for some way in which reason alone might approximate, if not achieve, the same conclusion. For Anselm, faith provided the goal and the impulse to investigate; the revealed truth served as the hypothesis and reason sought to make its content not more certain but merely more intelligible. For More, the Christian community made available to European man by revelation provided the hypothetical ideal, and he sought to demonstrate how closely it might have been approximated through the use of reason alone.

Anselm explains his method with some diffidence at the opening of his *Monologium*. He is writing these meditations, not because he has any conviction about his own ability to reason about these truths, but because he must fulfill the injunction, contained in the first Epistle of Peter (3:15), of first sanctifying the "Lord Christ in your hearts," and then of being "always ready to satisfy everyone that asketh you a reason of that hope which is in you." Anselm, therefore, attempts to show that

> nothing in Scripture should be urged on the authority of Scripture itself but that whatever the conclusion of independent investigation should declare to be true, should, in an unadorned style, with common proofs and with a simple argument, be briefly enforced by the cogency of reason, and plainly expounded in the light of truth. (pp. 103-04)

The world of the early sixteenth century was still dependent in its law, philosophy, theology, ethics, and politics upon the resources of the Scholastic Method, and it was this method that More employed to construct a work which demonstrated the inadequacies of the world the method had produced.

In his *Utopia*, More attempted to define the kind of society which reason alone, but properly directed, might

achieve, and how closely this purely rational society might approximate the ideal of the Christian state in theory, and even surpass contemporary Christian Europe in practice. Although the distinction between reason and revelation had become part of the Christian heritage, More employed the distinction as the Scholastics had, keeping the conclusions of reason separate from those of revelation. Thus the hypothetical Christian state, which would have involved revealed truth in its definition as in the *De Civitate Dei*, is only implied, and the explicit content of *Utopia* is to be understood as the result of demonstration conducted by unaided human reason. The learned reader of More's day understood that More was actually demonstrating the limits of reason in its attempts to define an ideal state, and that he was not actually defining an ideal which, for him certainly, would have required the consideration of the material available through revelation. (p. 105)

The *Utopia* can be read, as it has always been read, by anyone familiar with only "profane" learning. Its full significance, however, cannot be grasped without some knowledge of the implied "divine" knowledge. (pp. 106-07)

If the completely rational state of Utopia surpasses Europe in its integrity and administration of justice, *a fortiori*, how much further would the ideal Christian state surpass this same early sixteenth-century Europe? As Swift employed *le mythe animal*, in the voyage to the Houyhnhnms, to show the irrationality of human conduct, so More used the fiction of the imaginary state to show that Christians without charity are worse than good pagans guided by reason alone. The natural reason of the Utopians, unaided by grace, is superior to the uncharitable Christianity of the Europeans, as the natural reason of the Houyhnhnms is superior to the warped reason of the Europeans. Thus *Utopia* and *Gulliver's Travels* can both be read as meditations upon the foolish pride of European man. (p. 107)

Book II of *Utopia* can be analyzed either logically or descriptively. A descriptive analysis would involve an orderly *explication de texte* which would consider the various details of social, domestic, and political life. More's treatment of the elements of society follows—very roughly, for he was working from memory in Antwerp—the order of chapters 4-12 of Book VII of Aristotle's *Politics*. He begins with a description of the advantages of the location of the island, its cities, and natural resources; proceeds to a discussion of its inhabitants and their occupations, and only then, as in the *Politics* (chapters 13-15), does he analyze the theoretical bases of Utopia. The explicit content of Book II could also be analyzed under the six elements which Aristotle considered necessary for the existence of a state—farmers, artisans, warriors, wealth, priests, judges—and these elements are very heavily stressed in More's probable source, the *Commentary on the Politics* by Aquinas. Such a continuing descriptive analysis would bog down in a multitude of details and is far more appropriate to an edition of the *Utopia*. Finally, it is possible to analyze the second book of *Utopia* in terms of a logical structure which seems to grow out of two principles which are the basis of the entire work. The first principle, the definition of the end of man and consequently of the state, is based on Aristotle's *Politics*. The second principle, the definition of the norm of morality, is derived from the discussion of pleasure in Book IX of Plato's *Republic*.

In their definition of the just state, the Utopians were completely dependent upon a traditional use of reason which they had perfected to the point where in "music, logic, arithmetic, and geometry they have found out in a manner all that our ancient philosophers have taught." Their system of logic had not been refined to such a point that it frustrated the natural movements of the mind in its search for truth, as More thought had happened with logic in the later Scholasticism. Thus the Utopians faced the problem of discovering the just state in the same fashion as the Greeks, whom, More is careful to stress, they most closely resemble. What they lacked of Aristotle and Plato, obviously a hint to the reader, traveller Hythloday was able to supply. Their resources in attacking an intellectual problem would also be similar to those available to the medieval philosopher who set aside the proofs from revelation to answer the gentile who asked the reason "for the hope that was in him." More's method of solving the problem of the just state to be created by reason alone can be described by paraphrasing from chapter 9 of the first book of the *Summa contra Gentiles*. Aquinas says that he will first try to explain the truth which proceeds from faith but which reason can investigate, giving the demonstrative and probable reasons taken from the philosophers and the saints by means of which the truth is confirmed. More cannot, because of the terms of his problem, take Aquinas' second step, which involves the exploration of that truth which surpasses reason and the solution of various objections by supplementing the probable arguments of reason with the certain arguments provided by faith.

Since More limits his arguments to rational ones which, in some matters, can only reach probable conclusions, his Utopians must tolerate certain practices which would be unacceptable to revealed religion. More pictures the Utopians as tolerating mercy killing, divorce, and diversity of religions, practices to which he certainly did not subscribe, and which were outlawed throughout Christian Europe. More thought that, without the Decalogue and its express prohibition "Thou shalt not kill," reason alone would conclude that a man who is suffering from an incurable disease and continuous pain, unable "to do any duty of life, and [who] by overliving his own death is noisome and irksome to others, and grievous to himself" would be wiser to consent to his own death. Although More's Utopians are careful to limit the conditions under which suicide is permitted, they still concede to man an authority over his own life which Christianity would consider an invasion of Divine rights. The Utopians also had a high opinion of the matrimonial bond, but adultery or "intolerable wayward manners" did give either party to the contract the right to seek a license from the council to take another partner. Aquinas argued that the indissolubility of the marriage bond was a natural quality which had not been recognized until after the promulgation of the New Law. There was a right of repudiation under the Old Law which was not finally abandoned until it became obvious that "it was against the nature of the sacrament." So More was squarely within the common teaching of his day in maintaining that reason alone could not have arrived at the idea of the indissolubility of the marriage contract.

The knowledge of God which More attributes to the Utopians is very similar to that which Aquinas maintained in the *Contra Gentiles* was available through reason. Of the Utopians

the most and wisest part believe that there is a certain Godly power (*Contra Gentiles*, I, cap xii-xiii) unknown, incomprehensible, inexplicable, far above the capacity and reach of man's wit (I, cap. xiv), dispersed throughout all the world (I, cap. xliii), not in bigness (I, cap. lxxvi) but in virtue and power (II, cap. xxii). To Him alone they attribute the beginnings, the increasings, the proceedings, the changes, and the ends of all things (II, cap. xv-xxii).

The Utopians had achieved by reason alone a clearer conception of Being and its attributes than the Greeks had. Using the statements of Scripture as hypotheses, the Scholastics constructed proofs of these Divine attributes. The Utopians, without revelation to suggest goals for the flights of reason, have surpassed the Greeks and equalled the Schoolmen. In its 1760 years of continuous development, Utopian philosophy has reached a point which, as a matter of actual recorded history, Western philosophy never achieved without the suggestions of Hebraic and Christian belief. Thus the ideal republic of Utopia is "Nowhere" in two dimensions: Nowhere in space and, more important still, Nowhere in time.

The Utopians consider Christianity an obvious supplement to their own thinking and are thus much readier to accept it than the historical gentile.

> But after they heard us speak of the name of Christ, of His doctrine, laws, miracles, and of the no less wonderful constancy of so many martyrs, whose blood willingly shed brought a great number of nations throughout all parts of the world into their sect, you will not believe with how glad minds they agreed.

More is aware of the theological implications of this acceptance and, in a seemingly off-hand phrase, at once preserves the concept of faith as a gift and also protects it from the charge of being a blind assent. He refuses to decide "whether it were by the secret inspiration of God, or else for that they thought it next unto that opinion which among them is counted the chiefest" that the Utopians accepted Christianity.

Medieval speculation on the problem of the salvation of the heathen also determined the presentation of the alternative explanations of the Utopians' ready acceptance of Christianity. The Schoolmen as well as the earlier Fathers, were preoccupied with the eventual fate of those good pagans who died before the Church could reach them. On the one hand, the Fathers always taught that an act of faith and the remission of original sin through baptism were necessary for salvation. On the other hand, the Fathers also taught that "God wills the salvation of all men, and that no adult is damned but by his own fault." Hugh of St. Victor and Bernard of Clairvaux argued that the minimum of belief necessary for salvation was an explicit belief in God's existence and in His providence, which the Utopians certainly had, and an implicit belief in some mediator between God and man. Aquinas advanced what came to be accepted as the classic solution of the problem in the *De Veritate*. There he argued that, although it is not in our power to know by ourselves alone those things which are proper to faith, yet "if we do as much as in our power lies, that is to say, if we follow the directions of natural reason. God will not permit us to go without what is necessary to us." Further, he thought that it must be held as most certain, "certissime est tenendum," that if anyone followed the dictates of natural reason in seeking good and avoiding evil, God would "either reveal to them by internal inspiration those things which must be believed or send them some preacher of the faith as he sent Peter to Cornelius." Hythloday can thus be called a prophet to the Utopians, and the Rev. Rowland Phillips, Canon of St. Paul's, who was most anxious to go to Utopia to "further and increase" the religion "which is already there begun," may be considered their apostle. More, . . . however, is concerned with the adequacy of the knowledge of the natural law and not with the possible appearance of an apostle. (pp. 107-12)

Throughout his discussion of questions which the Scholastics would have considered proper to natural theology. More is careful to maintain that the Utopians are limited to merely probable conclusions. Without revelation they may only think or believe certain theological propositions are true, but they cannot be certain. Therefore the decree of King Utopus, "that it should be lawful for every man to favor and follow what religion he would, and that he might do the best he could to bring others to his opinion," is a logical consequence of the degree of certitude available in theological matters. Utopus made this decree because he did not dare to

> define and determine . . . unadvisedly [*temere*]; as doubting whether God, desiring manifold and diverse sorts of honour, would inspire sundry men with sundry kinds of religion. And this surely he thought a very unmeet and foolish thing, and a point of arrogant presumption, to compel all other by violence and threatening to agree to the same that thou believest to be true.

Obviously this was neither the attitude of More, who died the "King's good servant but God's first," nor of Catholic Europe, which then professed its faith in the One True Church and silenced the unbeliever at home and abroad.

In religious matters the complete rational man, King Utopus, "gave to every man free liberty and choice to believe what he would" with but two reservations. He charged all men to refrain from entertaining "so vile and base an opinion of the dignity of man's nature, as to think that the souls do die and perish with the body; or that the world runs at all adventures, governed by no divine providence." These principles were considered either immediately apparent or certainly demonstrable, and they could not be denied except through ill will. Further, these two principles are the logical basis of the just state, and to deny them is to deny the very assumptions upon which Utopia was founded.

The Utopians and More reached their conception of the ideal state by following the same order of investigation as Aristotle and Aquinas. They first define the final end of man and from this argue to the purpose of the ideal state. Aquinas, in his commentary on the opening of Book VII of the *Politics,* argues that the rationale of any civil order is determined by the end it is to implement. Since the end of the ideal state is the ensuring of the achievement of the highest end of man, it follows that the final end of man must first be known before the form of the ideal society can be ascertained. For Aquinas, More, and the Utopians, the solution of the ethical problem of what constitutes the good life must therefore precede the solution of the political problem, what constitutes the best form of society. It is precisely in "that part of philosophy which treats of

manners and virtues." ethics, that the reasons and opinions of the Utopians most agree with those of the sixteenth-century Europeans. The Utopians reason of virtue and pleasure, the problems of ethics and morality, "but the chief and principal question is in what thing, be it one or more, the felicity of man consists."

Yet the Utopians do not conduct their investigation of what constitutes the felicity of man entirely within the limits of ethics as a practical science.

> For they never dispute of felicity or blessedness, but they join to the reasons of philosophy certain principles taken out of religion, without the which to the investigation of true felicity, they think reason of itself weak and imperfect.

There are two principles which must be imported from natural theology into the discussions of ethics. They are "that the soul is immortal," and "that to our virtues and good deeds rewards be appointed after this life and to our evil deeds punishments." These are the same two principles which men were required to believe by edict of King Utopus: that the soul lives on after death and that divine providence orders the world morally as well as physically. The Utopians believed that these principles were necessary not only to demonstrate man's end but also to secure order in the state. Remove these fundamental beliefs and "then without any delay they pronounce no man to be so foolish, which would not do all his diligence and endeavor to obtain pleasure by right or wrong."

To define the happiness which is the end of man, More adapts Book IX of Plato's *Republic* as an illustration of the best argumentation available to natural reason on this particular problem. For the Utopians, as for Plato, the end of man and the principle for evaluating whether or not an action is conducive to that end is pleasure.

> In this point they seem almost too much given and enclined to the opinion of them which defend pleasure; wherein they determine either all or the chiefest parts of man's felicity to rest.

More was aware that most of his contemporaries would instinctively recoil from this opinion as proper to Epicureanism as it was then understood. More, therefore, went to to show that pleasure, when properly defined, can be the norm of morality and the end of man.

> But now, sir, they think not felicity to rest in all pleasure, but only in that pleasure that is good and honest; and that, hereto, as to perfect blessedness, our nature is allured and drawn even of virtue.

True pleasure thus depends on a recognition of a hierarchy in the human faculties.

> Pleasure they call every motion and state of the body and mind, wherein man had a natural delectation. Appetite they join to nature, and that not without good cause. For like as not only the senses, but also right reason covets whatever is naturally pleasant, so that it may be gotten without wrong or injury, not letting or debarring a greater pleasure, nor causing painful labor. . . .

True pleasure is, therefore, also natural and prefers the higher good to the lower. Thus the Utopian, like Plato's "man of understanding," will regulate his bodily habit and training, and so far will he be from yielding to brutal and irrational pleasures, that he will regard even health as quite a secondary matter; his first object will be not that he may be fair or strong or well, unless he is likely thereby to gain temperance, but he will always desire so to attemper the body as to preserve the harmony of the soul.

The soul, following the principles established by reason, leads a natural life which is also a virtuous life;

for they define virtue to be a life ordered according to nature; and that we be hereunto ordained by God; and that He doth follow the course of nature, which in desiring and refusing things is ruled by reason." Thus the Utopians can conclude that "even very nature prescribes to us a joyful life, that is to say, pleasure, as the end of all our operations.

The Utopians think the greatest of these pleasures "comes from the exercise of virtue, and conscience of good life." More states, however, that this view of felicity need be accepted only under one condition: "unless any godlier be inspired into man from heaven." More does not discuss whether the Utopians "believe well or not," for he has only undertaken "to show and declare their laws and ordinances, and not to defend them." Yet the illogic of ascetic practices in Utopia is his way of indicating the inadequacies of this view. The only logical attitude for anyone who has accepted natural pleasure as the end of man is to consider any neglect of bodily beauty, fasting, and other customs which "do injury to health, and reject the other pleasant motions of nature" as points of extreme madness, and a "token of man's being cruelly minded towards himself and unkind toward nature." In a long parenthetical clause More indicates that ascetical practices, after the promulgation of Christian revelation, would not be reprehensible but even meritorious. Man might neglect natural pleasures "whiles he doth with a fervent zeal procure the wealth of other benefits, or the common profit, for the which pleasures forborn he is in hope of a greater pleasure of God." The acceptance of fasts and prayers, scourgings and hair shirts as virtuous practices would require a complete revision of the conception of felicity entertained by the Utopians to one wherein the beatitude of spiritual union with God was the goal of life.

In defining the end of man by importing two principles from natural theology, More was imitating Aristotle's procedure in the *Politics*. Where More adapted the ethics of Plato to solve his problem, Aristotle borrowed from his own *Ethics*.

We maintain, and have said in the *Ethics,* if the arguments there adduced are of any value, that happiness is the realization and perfect exercise of virtue, and this not conditional, but absolute.

Aristotle's conclusion is surprisingly similar to that of the Utopians, though their dialectical processes in reaching the conclusion have been different. More now moves ahead with Aristotle.

Since the end of individuals and of states is the same, the end of the best man and of the best constitution must also be the same; it is therefore evident that there ought to exist in both of them the virtues of leisure; for peace, as has been often repeated, is the end of war, and leisure of toil.

More's conception of the purpose of the Utopian society is stated in terms very close to Aristotle's:

In the institution of that weal public this end is only and chiefly pretended and minded that what time may possibly be spared from the necessary occupations and affairs of the commonwealth, all that the citizens should withdraw from the bodily service to the free liberty of the mind and garnishing of the same. For herein they suppose the felicity of this life to consist.

Nothing is so frequently stressed throughout *Utopia* as the obligations of the state to provide the leisure necessary for intellectual development. The chief functions of the Syphograunts are to insure that no one "sit idle and yet that no one work continually like laboring and toiling beasts." Production quotas are determined to provide sufficiency and not superfluity. The resulting freedom of the citizens is to be devoted to some good science. The scheme of values in this ideal state is therefore based on the principle of whether or not a certain practice promotes or curtails the citizens' leisure.

The abolition of private property is not a major point in the logical structure of *Utopia* but an obvious inference from basic principle. The Utopians believe that private ownership is the basis of avarice and the desire for superfluity of goods, which disquiet the mind and destroy private and public peace. Remove the right of private ownership, which is not a natural right according to the Utopians, provide man with a sufficiency, and the entire society is liberated from unnecessary toil and freed to pursue the pleasures of the mind. Again this is not More's real attitude but a logical consequence of the principles to which he has committed his ideal society. It should be pointed out, however, that most of the Church Fathers, and some of the later Scholastics, would have agreed with More that communal ownership of goods was superior to private ownership, and that, in the words of St. Ambrose, "things were made by the creator to be held in common and private ownership is contrary to nature." For St. Chrysostom, the more perfect the nature of the individual the less the need for those "chilling words 'mine' and 'thine.'" Duns Scotus was even of the opinion that one of the consequences of the Fall of Man was the abrogation of the precept of the natural law forbidding the private ownership of goods. Alexander of Hales and St. Bonaventure believed that in a state of innocence all things would have been held in common and nothing would have been restrained within the limits of private ownership. In the *Dialogue of Comfort* More argues very strongly against the common ownership of property because of the present historical state of man, fallen and redeemed but still unable to control his passions through his reason. The Utopian commonwealth must wait, for its realization, upon the perfect rationalist or the perfect Christian, the man without pride. The Utopian attitudes towards war, treaties, the use of mercenaries, and the treatment of natural slaves are also immediate inferences from the Utopian conception of the state as a means of guaranteeing the leisure which is the natural end of man.

Using only reason and the methods of a medieval rationalism, More attempted to demonstrate the failings of contemporary Christian society which was the product of those same forces. More would never have been at home in the Utopian world of universal grays and humorless men vaguely reminiscent of the lands visited by Lemuel Gulliver. More and Swift fought the same enemy, for both believed that

> the respect of every man's private commodity, or else the authority of our saviour Christ . . . would have brought all the world long ago into the laws of this weal public, if it were not that one and only beast, the prince and mother of all mischief, pride, doth withstand it. (pp. 113-19)

The argument for reading *Utopia* in the context of medieval thought can be further strengthened by considering how different More's method was in the composition of some of his other works. While a prisoner in the Tower, More wrote a *Treatise on the Passion* in the construction of which he was guided by the methods of the Renaissance grammarian or humanist. (p. 120)

More's *Treatise on the Passion* was based on the *Monatesseron* of John Gerson, a synthesis of the four Gospel accounts of the passion of Christ. The mood and purpose of the work is to pause "and with entire devotion consider" the events of the passion, searching for the practical significance of the words and actions, so that each man might thereby improve his life. More explores the connotations of words, Jewish antiquities and customs, astronomical calculations, and even some of the stylistic peculiarities of Aramaic. These are the interests of Valla in his examination of the authenticity of the Donation of Constantine and an application of the methods of studying scripture outlined by Erasmus in his *Paraclesis*. More traces the significance of the feast of the Unleavened Bread through the *Dies Azymorum* of the Greeks, and, with the help of St. Jerome, through the *Pascha* of the Hebrews to its ultimate meaning of "immolation." He shows how Eusebius and Chrysostom were correct in their dating of Easter, and how the later Greeks confused their calculations. In a manner which would have delighted William Budé, he discusses the value of the coins Judas received for his betrayal of Christ and concludes that they were worth ten shillings. Words and their fine shades of meaning also occupy him. What is the significance of the two names given to Peter in Mark 14:27, "And he saith to Peter: Simon sleepest thou?" More thinks that "it was a private check given unto him that he called him not by the name of Peter or Cephas," for the name of "Simon" in Christ's day meant "hearing and obedient," and this is the very opposite of what Peter was then doing. More again decides in favor of an ironical interpretation of Christ's words in Mark 4:41, "And he cometh the third time and saith to them: Sleep ye now and take your rest." Only after considering the commentary of St. Augustine on the passage, he concludes that Christ meant the very opposite of what he said, and his decision is based on the vigor of the figurative language. Again, More is puzzled by the precise meaning of "until" (*donec*). Does it mean until Christ's Ascension or is it employed in a completely final sense? He explains the "with desire I have desired" (*desiderio desideravi*) of the Vulgate by reference to the common stylistic practice of the Hebrew of doubling a word to secure emphasis. (pp. 121-22)

Grammar, in the larger sense of the word, thus came to replace the methods of the Scholastic in the solution of theological problems.

All this learned baggage of . . . the *Treatise on the Passion* is only instrumental. It is only a means of acquiring the true Christian philosophy, the philosophy or humanism of Christ as expressed in the Bible. But this Christian wisdom is described, in the *Paraclesis,* as so excellent "that it turns all of the wisdom of the world to folly." This may be the reason why the eminent rationalist, the traveler, Hythloday, is given a name which in Greek means "nonsense." The real Christian must leave behind him the impious curiosities, the incomplete folly, of an excessively rationalistic Scholasticism, and, employing the science of the Christian humanist, seek that knowledge of Christ which results in His imitation. (p. 123)

The *Utopia* is thoroughly Scholastic in its method of construction and largely medieval in its style and content. *Utopia* comes into true focus when it is viewed as the product of the Scholastic Method, revealing the limitations of that method and of the society for which it was largely responsible. The seeming paradoxes which have worried scholars as they tried to reconcile this or that practice in *Utopia* with More's own personal life disappear when it is realized that *Utopia* is only a small part of More's beliefs. It is not necessary to call in More's sense of humor, or a reactionary old age, to account for the Utopian toleration of divorce and religious difference. *Utopia* is all of a piece, marking the end of the Middle Ages and their methods, and the beginning of a Renaissance which was to rely on entirely different methods of investigation and interpretation. (p. 126)

> *P. Albert Duhamel, "Medievalism of More's 'Utopia'," in* Studies in Philology, *Vol. LII, No. 2, April, 1955, pp. 99-126.*

EDWARD SURTZ, S. J. (essay date 1957)

> [*Surtz was an American scholar of English Renaissance literature and a distinguished authority on More's life and writings. In the following excerpt, he analyzes the defense of pleasure in* Utopia.]

The Utopians, Hythloday observes, discuss virtue and pleasure, but the principal point of disputation is "in what thing, be it one or mo, the felicity of man consisteth." The Utopian presupposition is that man's final end is happiness or beatitude. The point at issue is: what is the *object* of this happiness or beatitude? It is worthy of note that the whole controversy is centered about, and is confined to, only two objects: virtue and pleasure. Hence, the protagonists of pleasure are at special pains to refute the defenders of virtue.

In stating that the Utopians hold pleasure to be the object of happiness, Hythloday is careful to introduce a double modification of his statement. To state bluntly that the wisest of pagan peoples were outright hedonists would be too shocking. Hence, he asserts (1) that they "seem almost too much given and inclined" (*propensiores aequo uidentur*) to the defense of pleasure and (2) that they "determine other all or the chiefest part (*potissimam partem*) of man's felicity to rest" in pleasure. These qualifications entail a considerable weakening of the original proposition, and prepare the reader's mind for a more benevolent reception of the Utopian view.

What reasons do the Utopians produce in support of their opinion? First of all, they find in religion "the defense of this so dainty and delicate an opinion." Religion affords them three truths and only three: the immortality of the soul, the special providence of God in ordaining man to happiness, and the reward of virtue and punishment of evil in the next life. But one may read this passage in the *Utopia* several times without seeing how the Utopians discover in religion the "defense" of their theory of pleasure. The basis of their argumentation seems to be the traditional view of the inseparability of religion and morality. The exercise of religion, particularly love and reverence toward God, is the psychological source and foundation of all moral activity, which without religion generally cannot be genuine, complete, constant, and persevering in the face of the difficult temptations and perils of this life. The highest and most weighty motives of moral action—such motives as are found in a God Who is man's final end and object of beatitude and in a God Who is the supreme legislator establishing a sanction in reward or punishment to be encountered in the future life—are absent without religion. Yet at this very time Pietro Pomponazzi (1462-1525) was teaching: "Virtue is independent of the belief in immortality; it is most genuine when practised without reference to reward or punishment." For the Utopians, however, the man who denies the three basic truths mentioned above has no efficacious motive, especially the motive of a future reward, for pursuing good and virtue if the pursuit means the banishment of sweetness from his whole life and even the voluntary toleration of suffering. It is the thought of the sweet pleasures of a future reward which sustains a man when assailed by the powers of evil. The Utopians ask why man forgoes pleasure and suffers pain in the practice of good. The answer expected is that he does so in hope of the joys and delights of the future life of happiness to which God has ordained his immortal soul in reward for his virtue and good works. In a word, "grave, sharp, bitter, and rigorous religion" itself thus affords the "defense" of pleasure as the whole or the greatest part of man's happiness.

But what is the relation between virtue and pleasure for the Utopians? Harsh as the response may seem, one must answer that, in the abstract, virtue is subordinate to pleasure: "all our actions, and in them the virtues themselves, be referred at the last to pleasure as their end and felicity." But this is not subordination in any gross sense. On the contrary, the "chief part" of pleasures of the mind "doth come of the exercise of virtue and conscience of good life." The Utopians practice virtue because they presume that pleasure is inextricably bound up with the performance of virtuous deeds and that a good conscience is a source of gratification. On the relation between the most just life and the most pleasant life, the Utopian thinks much the same as the Athenian in Plato's *Laws*:

> So then the teaching which refuses to separate the pleasant from the just helps, if nothing else, to induce a man to live the holy and just life, so that any doctrine which denies this truth is, in the eyes of the lawgiver, most shameful and most hateful; for no one would voluntarily consent to be induced to commit an act, unless it involves in its consequence more pleasure than pain.

The Utopian subordinates virtue to pleasure, or at least tends to identify the two. To the Stoic, on the other hand, virtue is supreme. The Epicurean says to the Stoic: "Your school dilates on the transcendental beauty of the virtues; but were they not productive of pleasure, who would deem them either praiseworthy or desirable?" Seneca answers that pleasure is but a necessary *concomitant* of virtue, in no way essential to it:

> [I]n the first place, even though virtue is sure to bestow pleasure, it is not for this reason that virtue is sought; for it is not this, but something more than this that she bestows, nor does she labour for this, but her labour, while directed toward something else, achieves this also. . . . [P]leasure is neither the cause nor the reward of virtue, but its by-product, and we do not accept virtue because she delights us, but if we accept her, she also delights us.

The second reason which the Utopians bring forward to sustain their position is that to pleasure, "as to perfect blessedness [*uelut ad summum bonum*], our nature is allured and drawn even of virtue [*ab ipsa uirtute*]." This is a sophistic *tour de force*: to make virtue, in which alone their opponents place man's happiness, serve to prove that pleasure is the highest good! The line of argumentation is the following:

> *Virtue* is life lived according to *nature*. But life lived according to *nature* is the selection and rejection of things according to *reason*. Therefore *virtue* is the selection and rejection of things according to *reason*. But *reason* advises and incites us to lead a life as free from care and full of joy as possible, and to show ourselves helpful, in view of the fellowship arising from nature, in obtaining the same for all other human beings. Therefore *virtue* advises and incites us to lead a life as free from care and full of joy as possible, etc.

With respect to the *first major premise*, when "they define virtue to be a life ordered according to nature" or "according to the prescript of nature," the Utopians would find no objection coming from the Stoics who in general held the same as Zeno. The end of man, the latter says, is a life in agreement with and according to nature; but this life is a life according to virtue, for nature, to be sure, leads us to such a life. Stoic Seneca himself had admitted that Epicurus laid down the same rule for pleasure that the Stoics had laid down for virtue, for "he bids that it obey Nature." The *first minor*, too, would be granted by the Stoics. For, as Cato the Stoic concludes in Cicero's *De Finibus*, "The Chief Good consists in applying to the conduct of life a knowledge of the working of natural causes, choosing what is in accordance with nature and rejecting what is contrary to it." Since the Stoics concede the first major and the first minor, they must concede the *first conclusion*.

The heart of the argument is really the *second minor*, and therefore Hythloday is at some pains to give at length the Utopians' proof for it. The proof is basically a dilemma. A "joyful life, that is to say, a pleasant life" (*uita iucunda, id est, uoluptaria*) is either good or evil. But it is not evil, because nature and humanity bid one to help men as much as possible to a joyful life by relieving their suffering and by restoring their joy. Therefore, a joyful life is good. But if it is good for all other men, it must be good for the individual personally, since nature "equally favoureth all that be comprehended under the communion of one shape, form, and fashion." Therefore, "even very nature (say they) prescribeth to us a joyful life, that is to say, pleasure as the end of all our operations."

It is extremely interesting to observe that at a later period in his life More was to face the problem of joy and tribulation in a far more serious way in his ***Dialogue of Comfort***, Vincent objects that "if it were . . . that perpetual prosperity were to the soul so perilous, and tribulation thereto so fruitful; then were . . . every man bounden of charity, not only to pray God send their neighbour sorrow, but also to help thereto themself." His uncle Antony answers:

> I think in very deed tribulation so good and profitable, that I should haply doubt as you do wherefore a man might labour or pray to be delivered of it, saving that God which teacheth us the one, teacheth us also the other. And as he biddeth us take our pain patiently, and exhort our neighbours to do also the same: so biddeth he us also not let to do our devoir, to remove the pain from us both.

More's final solution is the *natural* answer of the Utopians (insofar as God and nature teach that "thou . . . of duty art bound to procure it [a joyful life] to other . . . [and] to thyself") as supplemented and elevated by the *supernatural* and *Christian* view of faith, prayer, and suffering.

In summary, one may say that the defense of pleasure as the ultimate end of human life is essentially a *declamatio*. Its purpose probably is to incite and provoke to serious thought careless Christians who are behaving as if wealth or glory, not God, were the end of life. More cunningly prejudices the whole question by using the word *pleasure* in its most loose and generic sense. In the best traditions of the *declamatio*, he astonishingly makes religion and virtue serve as two sources of arguments for the supremacy of pleasure. Careful analysis, however, reveals that the final object of Utopian happiness is delight in the presence of God in the next life. (pp. 17-22)

Edward Surtz, S.J., in his The Praise of Pleasure: Philosophy, Education, and Communism in More's Utopia, *Cambridge, Mass.: Harvard University Press, 1957, 246 p.*

RAINER PINEAS (essay date 1968)

[*Pineas is a German-born American academic and critic known for his studies of More and his circle. In the following excerpt from the conclusion of his* Thomas More and Tudor Polemics, *he surveys More's polemical writings, beginning with a brief overview of the principal English controversialists of the age.*]

The main techniques employed by the Reformers in their attack on the Church were the polemical use of secular and ecclesiastical history and the Scriptures.

Their use of history probably played some part in preparing public opinion to accept the assault on clerical wealth and power that Henry embarked on for his own purposes. At least that was the expectation of the government, which attempted to secure the services of Tyndale and which actually recruited Barnes. Henry's favorable reception of Fish and his pamphlet is further evidence of the Crown's appreciation of Protestant historical propaganda. The Reformers' references to ecclesiastical history to demonstrate the nonprimitive origins of Catholic doctrine and practice must be regarded as good strategy, and their citing of actual or imagined incidents of clerical immorality from the chronicles in their criticisms of clerical celibacy and monasticism would have been effective on a popular level.

A chalk drawing by Hans Holbein the Younger of More at about age 49.

Tyndale's translation of the New Testament changed many of the terms the clergy had used to claim scriptural support for their position, while his marginal notes were intended to ensure for the new text an interpretation favorable to the Reformers. Thus on two counts his version was made a vehicle for propaganda. Furthermore, the Reformers' repeated claims that Catholics were afraid of an open Bible—and the reluctance of the clergy to provide such a Bible— implied strongly that neither the behavior nor the doctrine of the Catholic clergy could stand to be measured by the yardstick of the Scriptures.

Looking more broadly at the Reformers' campaign, we find that certain similarities are, of course, apparent between More's technique and that of his opponents. After all, they shared the same educational background so that their use of the disciplines of logic and rhetoric, for instance, is essentially the same. The differences are to be found, I think, in the form of their works, in their use of Scripture, and in their use of history.

Most important to note is that Protestant strategy was a strategy of attack–More's of defense–and that the strategy of attack dictated the form of the works the Reformers wrote. Of this strategy Tyndale was the leading exponent, and his works became prototypes for subsequent Protestant polemics. (Since in all three areas to be discussed– form of work, use of Scripture, and use of history—Tyndale was indebted to Luther, Luther may be regarded as the ultimate source of early Tudor Protestant strategy.)

Tyndale pioneered the two genres on which the Reformers relied: the short treatise of exposition, often of a scriptural passage, such as the *Mammon* and the *Obedience*, descendants of which are Barnes's treatise on the Church, Frith's work on the Eucharist, Joye's exposition of Daniel; and the short, selective analysis of an opponent's work, such as Tyndale's answer to More, in which tradition are Frith's work on purgatory, Barnes's answer to More, and Joye's book against More.

Tyndale's use of Scripture—apart from his translation—again laid the groundwork for subsequent Protestant technique. His insistence on the primacy of Scripture combined with his use of what [I call] a "pliable" Bible provided him with a very convenient document. (His "manipulation" of the Bible was really no different from his "manipulation" of the chronicles; in both instances, in effect, he provided his own source.) And in his "infallible" approach to the Scriptures he was followed by most early and mid-century Protestant polemicists—by Barnes, less by Frith, by Joye, by Turner, by Becon, and, above all, by Bale.

And Tyndale's "new" history, written ultimately . . . by himself, which made the double point that all medieval history had to be "corrected" by Protestant interpretation and that Catholics were historically treasonous, not only had a tremendously damaging effect on the fortunes of the Catholic clergy in England in Tyndale's own day, but was also the "history" adopted by Fish, Barnes, Becon, and especially by Bale, who used Tyndale's historical theories in both his prose works and in *King Johan*, the first Protestant history play.

It is curious that More did not make a greater effort to rebut the Reformers' allegations from history. His attempts in this area were mostly confined to his book against Fish, whose polemical use of history was, however, less extensive and more accurate than that of Tyndale and Barnes. Perhaps More thought it wiser to say as little as possible about the Reformers' historical assertions, which were so favorably received by Henry.

More's most outstanding technique was his use of the dialogue form. Thus in his *Dialogue concernynge heresyes* he was able to present a favorable picture of his own side and an unfavorable one of the Reformers through the creation of a character for himself and for his interlocutor. A similar technique was used against Barnes, for whom an unfavorable character was created and who was defeated by More's spokesmen. The dialogue form also permitted More to return repeatedly to points he wished to treat at some length, without being as obviously repetitious as he was in later works written as straightforward treatises. And More's genius for dialogue and character produced the eloquent souls of his *Supplicacion*, who were in themselves intended as dramatic proof of that work's main thesis.

More's use of humor must also be numbered among his most successful techniques. Enlivening sometimes lengthy doctrinal debate, its earthy quality must have contributed to whatever popular appeal More's polemics enjoyed. That some of More's humor was directed at the foibles of the Catholic clergy, especially in his *Dialogue*, probably enhanced the picture he tried to present of himself as an independent layman who was not a hireling of the clergy. Occasionally, humor served More as a substitute for discussion and, as used against his opponents generally, it implied that there was something ludicrous about both the men and their arguments.

Any attempt to decide who was the victor in the controversy between More and his opponents is a difficult task. The question certainly cannot be answered, as it too often is, according to the particular religious belief of the writer, nor on the basis that in England the cause of Protestantism was ultimately victorious. The triumph of Protestantism was the result of many factors, only one of which was the polemical acumen of its advocates.

However, the fact that almost the entire burden of answering the Reformers in the vernacular was placed on the shoulders of one man—More—hardly helped the Catholic cause, and there can be little doubt that this situation adversely affected the quality of the overlengthy polemics More evidently felt obliged to write after 1529, when he had no leisure for polishing—and pruning—his controversial works. The dearth of English Catholic propaganda in the early and middle Tudor periods is a problem which bears investigation.

More carried out his commission to champion the Church quite brilliantly at first, in his *Dialogue* and in most of his *Supplicacion*. The dramatic devices these works contain make their arguments persuasive and immediate. But More's later defenses, written hastily and under enormous pressure of work, lack force. We know that the prolixity of his *Confutacyon* lost him readers, and the highly technical legal discussions in his works against Saint-German must have had the same effect. In a treatise such as the *Debellacyon*, the "simple and unlearned men" whom More was commissioned to address seem to have been forgotten. Merely on the ground that they failed in their primary function of attracting readers, More's later polemics must be judged poor propaganda.

For on the Protestant side lay all the advantage of attack, in that exposés of abuses usually attract more readers than do defenses of the *status quo*. That Tyndale, Frith, and Fish were widely read—especially Fish—must in a large measure be attributed to the fact that what they had to say was of popular interest. But to the inherent advantage of their position they added the virtue of terseness; they produced "many shorte treatyses"—a deliberate tactic, More thought, and he was probably right.

Thus Protestant propaganda presented a difficult problem, to which More's strategy of exhaustive rebuttal was surely not the correct solution. In this situation, perhaps More should not have attempted a reasoned defense at all, but should have devoted himself instead exclusively to counterattack, possibly in the style of Murner's *Von dem Grossen Lutherischen Narren*.

A few comments should be made about the literary quality of More's polemical works as compared to that of his noncontroversial works.

Since . . . the bulk of More's polemical work was written in great haste under tremendous pressure, and since most of his nonpolemical works were written at greater leisure, one obvious difference is that the latter, as a group, tend to be more polished. Obviously, also, More would make greater efforts to achieve literary polish in the nonpolemical category, since the exhibition of literary elegance would be one of the main objects of the work. Good examples are his *Richard the thirde*, his epigrams, and his *A dialoge of comfort*, written during his imprisonment in the Tower. The one polemical work to which More had time to give some finish in his *Dialogue concernynge heresyes* . . . . It stands in sharp contrast to the piece-meal and formless character of all his other polemics, including the *Supplicacion of soules*, the first book of which contains the central dramatic device of the "souls" but lacks total structure.

More's noncontroversial works also tend to be somewhat less repetitious than the polemical, again chiefly for the reason that when the former were written, More had time to edit what he wrote. *Richard the thirde* and *Utopia* are not at all repetitious, and it should be remembered that the prolix More of the later polemics was at one time master of the concise epigram. The *Dialogue concernynge heresyes* is repetitious, but here the repetition is still controlled and . . . should be regarded as part of More's polemical technique. It is in the *Supplicacion of soules* that he begins to lose control and weary his readers with unnecessary repetition. Evidently the habit carried over later to the noncontroversial *Comfort* which, of course, More wrote under a different kind of pressure.

Understandably, the tone of the polemics is sharp–except the work against Frith—while that of the nonpolemical works is not. Yet in the area of tone the two categories tend to blend, for some of the wonderful satire of *Richard,* the *Utopia,* and the epigrams is essentially the same as the kind of satire More used against his opponents. There is the same masterful characterization and dramatization, as well as the same keen eye for the ridiculous–such as in the Anemolian ambassadors section of the *Utopia* and the picture of Barnes or the David-Bathsheba section in the *Confutacyon,* where More ridicules Tyndale's distinction between sinning and not sinning.

What has been said probably exhausts the points of difference between More's style in the polemical and the nonpolemical works. Essentially, just as the More of the Latin polemics is the More of the English polemics, so the picture of More we get from his works of controversy is not substantially different from the impression of him we get from his other works. For instance, More's flair and penchant for dramatization are evident in everything he wrote. The dramatic structure of the *Dialogue* against Tyndale, of the *Supplicacion,* and of parts of his other polemical works is no less brilliant than that of the *Richard*, the *Utopia*, or the *Comfort*. In fact, as dramatic creation I would put More's "souls" second only to his picture of Richard III—and ahead of any of his Utopian characters, who lack the life of More's "Luther" and "Barnes" as portrayed in the dramatic sketches of the *Responsio* and the *Confutacyon.*

And, of course, More's humor—really inseparable from his dramatizations—runs through all his works. The same keen eye which pierces the pretensions of humanity in the *Utopia* and the epigrams is focused on the self-importance of Luther and Barnes, the specious arguments of Fish, and the claims to impartiality of Saint-German. Essentially,

More's humor consists of the ability to detect the ludicrous and to dramatize it, to make it come alive before our eyes, and then to draw it out to its logical–or rather absurd—conclusions.

Not too surprisingly, again, all of More's methods of argumentation analyzed by Leland Miles in his edition of the *Dialoge of comfort*, such as scriptural barrage, strategically placed anecdote, homey analogy, alliteration, metaphor, wordplay, and merry tales are . . . common to all of More's works. The fact requires no comment; personality does not vary with genre, and style is the man. (pp. 214-20)

Rainer Pineas, in his Thomas More and Tudor Polemics, *Indiana University Press, 1968, 262 p.*

ELIZABETH McCUTCHEON (essay date 1969)

[*McCutcheon is an American scholar and academic who specializes in Neo-Latin literature, the history of rhetoric, and English literature of the sixteenth century. In the following excerpt, she elucidates Raphael Hythloday's function in* Utopia *by reference to the Archangel Raphael.*]

We know how cunningly More named the persons and places in *Utopia*, creating a paradoxical best-place, noplace where the chief city is a phantom, the river waterless, and the ruler without a people. A still more striking proof of what Vives called "his sharpnes of wit" and "his eloquence of phrase" is the name of *Utopia*'s feigned narrator and traveller, Raphael Hythlodaeus. The generic or family name of . . . this truly extraordinary character is generally thought to mean "expert in trifles" or "well-learned in nonsense," but the real paradox depends upon his first name and its associations with the angel Raphael. . . . [The] importance of the name goes beyond More's love of paradox, and is a clue to Raphael's character and crucial in understanding his office and his relationship to the More who hears Raphael's tale of Utopia and the More whose creations Raphael and the *Utopia* are.

As a symbol of man's potential the angels, collectively, fascinated the Renaissance; so the young Thomas More paraphrased Pico della Mirandola's maxim on the dignity of man "that with angel art made to be equal." But the angels and archangels (that is, the last two in the nine orders constituting the angelic hierarchy codified by the pseudo-Dionysius the Areopagite) particularly fascinated Renaissance man, who saw in them a group of rational spiritual beings who were still close to mankind and mediated between the divine world and earth below. Three angels, all archangels, were especially familiar, long loved and known by name: St. Michael, St. Gabriel, and St. Raphael, whose place was assured by his dramatic appearance in the popular apocryphal Book of Tobit.

The fundamental duty of the archangels was well defined by 1500; they served as God's "highest messengers," revealing the "greater mysteries," and to them fell, also, the "governance of a multitude of a city," or "the weal of a multitude," as Bartholomaeus and the *Golden Legend* paraphrase and conflate pseudo-Dionysius and St. Gregory the Great. Two functions which intensify this office were more specifically St. Raphael's. Etymologically his Hebraic name means "the healing of God," and, as the "medicine of God" or the "medicus," the angel physician, he healed the blindness of old Tobit and drove out the demon which troubled Sara, whose marriage to Tobit's son Tobias he also arranged: "And the holy angel of God, Raphael, was sent to heal them both." Equally important for the *Utopia,* he was the traveller-guide to the young Tobias, who set out on his journey to Rages with a man he knew as Azarias (the angel in disguise).

As the implications of these motifs were drawn out, St. Raphael became a symbolic physician who cures souls as well as bodies and illuminates darkened minds. So Pico della Mirandola's *Oration on the Dignity of Man* calls upon Raphael, the "celestial physician, that he may set us free by moral philosophy and by dialectic as though by wholesome drugs." And he became a type of the pilgrim and a guardian who guides men on their journeys both in this life and through it, to their eternal home in heaven: "Also an Angell leadeth us that we wander not out of the way. Tobie 5," as Bartholomaeus writes. Inevitably he became chief of the guardian angels and the patron saint of "peregrinatores," travellers and pilgrims, who set out under his protection: "May God Almighty... order your journey in accordance with His will, and summon His holy angel Raphael as a guardian in this pilgrimage of yours, to accompany you as you go to the place of your desires in peace. And may he bring you back again to us in safety [*cum salute*]."

Two words from "Christe, sanctorum," a hymn attributed to Rabanus Maurus, epitomize the name of Raphael, the most humane of all the archangels. He is the "medicus salutis," the doctor of health—and salvation; the word play the Renaissance loved is part of the phrase. The words were so familiar that William Warham, when Archbishop of Canterbury, can playfully write an Erasmus whose health and pocket are, as usual, ailing: "I have sent you... twenty golden angels, among whom you will find Raphael, the doctor of health [*salutis medicum*], who can easily heal you and restore your former well-being [*sanitatem*]." Even here it is difficult to translate the phrase, for health imperceptibly shades into something non-physical. In the context of the hymn, of course, "salus" comes to stand for salvation. But whether "salus" is "health," "safety," "welfare," or "salvation," the range of concerns is equally true for St. Raphael and Raphael Hythlodaeus, whose overwhelming concern is with what he himself calls "salutem publicam" and the right way to it. It is no easier to translate Hythlodaeus's "salutem," moreover, for though the context calls for welfare, the word carries associations which suggest that for this Raphael, like his prototype, health, welfare, and salvation are inextricably united. (pp. 21-4)

He calls himself a "homuncio," "an insignificant fellow," but More's Raphael dramatically fulfills the general office of his archangelic prototype—or tries to. Like the archangels, his concern is with the commonweal, a point which is acted out for us through much of the first book of the *Utopia.* Though he refuses to attach himself to the service of any king, this is due not to his lack of concern for humanity, but the king and court's, which would lead them to prefer their own blind self-interest to anything which Raphael, who cannot accommodate his teaching to the perverseness of men's morals, might say. For this very reason, he is a teacher or messenger, whose message of health, well-being, and salvation for Western Europe, though thinly disguised as a traveller's tale, is an indict-

ment of sixteenth-century Christian Europe, its avarice and pride.

By the end of the *Utopia* his voice and vision coalesce and he stands before us like a prophet of reform. This too resembles the essentially prophetic role of the archangels, ... whose job it was to carry the highest messages of salvation; compare Bartholomaeus's "Gregorie saith that the office of these Angelles [the Archangels] is to teach good men, and help them of those things that concerne theyr faith, as of the comming of Gods sonne, and of his deedes and lawes." And Raphael himself, conscious of his position, defines it obliquely at least twice. In Book I, for example, he contrasts himself with preachers, "crafty men," who found "that men grievously disliked to have their morals adjusted to the rule of Christ" and "accommodated his teaching to men's morals." At the end of his Utopian revelation he is even more emphatic in an impassioned speech where he argues that "a man's regard for his own interests or the authority of Christ our Savior... would long ago have brought the whole world to adopt the laws of the Utopian commonwealth," were it not for Pride. The Christian overtones of these words are obvious and we see a Raphael who, like other celestial messengers, but ironically unlike most preachers (who, as Colet points out, should be like the angels in their ministry to man), would bring laws which he equates with "salus" to mankind.

And certainly we are made to see Raphael Hythlodaeus as the physician his first name (repeated some twelve times) insists upon, who wishes to heal a state which is sicker than it knows. His technique, like his archangelic prototype's, is a question of illumination. But where St. Raphael opened the eyes of a blind man, this Raphael seeks to open the inner eyes of a nation, to cure this madness which infects so much of the known world. So his own answer to More's initial objections is a matter of vision: "I do not wonder... that it looks this way to you, being a person who has no picture at all, or else a false one, of the situation I mean. But you should have been with me in Utopia and personally seen their manners and customs as I did...."

His name and function are mirrored in an important group of metaphors; again and again, particularly when he is about to introduce the vision which is Utopia, Raphael talks in terms of a cure and uses striking analogies with the physician's art. This sequence, which he initiates, is picked up by More: "If you cannot cure according to your heart's desire vices of long standing, yet you must not on that account desert the commonwealth. You must not abandon the ship in a storm because you cannot control the winds." But Raphael knows his Galen, and he rejects any idea of accommodation by a brilliant medical metaphor (one of several raising the issue of insanity, which simply undercuts More's otherwise persuasive argument and ignores the ship of state metaphor, which is, in its own terms, unanswerable: "By this approach... I should accomplish nothing else than to share the madness of others as I tried to cure their lunacy." A physician who is sick himself cannot cure others, when the illness infects the instrument which effects the cure: the mind which speaks the truth. And, as a final burst of medical metaphors makes abundantly clear, there is, from Raphael's point of view, only one real cure for the evils which have been diagnosed earlier in Book I: the answer Utopia itself provides.

Words of health are strategically placed throughout *Utopia* to reiterate this theme, although the context is partially obscured in translation. Many of these words are underlined even more since they are Raphael's—the healer and physician. But early in Book I More himself comments that he is going to tell us only of "sane ac sapienter institutos ciues," ("well and wisely trained citizens") who "are not everywhere to be found," instead of stale traveller's wonders, and here, at least, we have some idea of his real attitude towards Utopia. His "sane" is echoed at the end of Book I in Raphael's observation that there is only one way to the "salutem publicam" and by his subsequent "sanentur." And Raphael doubles the motif in the last sentence he speaks in the *Utopia*, with words, elegantly accented by parallelism and alliteration, which should drive his message of health-safety-welfare-salvation into even the deafest ears: "salua domi concordia, & salubribus institutis."

For More, medical metaphors and the health motif were always significant, but the image of Raphael as healer, which dominates so much of Book I, is particularly close to the picture More draws of Colet in a letter to him (1504); here (as in *Utopia*) More is preoccupied with the possibility of reform in this world and the nature of the physician-preacher who is to cure a city which is desperately sick. The letter, like *Utopia*, insists upon the integrity and health of the physician; More sees, vividly, that no one will listen to "physicians who are themselves covered with ulcers." But the young More enthusiastically celebrates the alternative, that men will pay attention to a physician like Colet: "Their readiness to allow you to treat their wounds . . . you have yourself proved in the past, and now the universal desire and anticipation of you proclaim it all again."

Twelve years later More is obviously much more sensitive to the difficulties the would-be reformer faces in an imperfect world. And now the optimism inherent in Raphael's name, nature, and healing message is radically qualified by a question which undercuts the earlier and rather naive assumptions of the 1504 letter. Will the man of integrity, he who is best qualified to be a preacher-physician, most able to make a diagnosis, be heard? The final answers (for there are two) are suspended until the end of *Utopia*, but Raphael is quite sure that the answer is "no." Even two members of his present audience, More and Peter Giles, have immediate, if somewhat transparent, objections to the cure this physician, whose integrity is absolute (as Giles's own earlier questions have proven), proposes: More's, economic and psychological, Giles's humanistic: he reverences the claims of antiquity. In the name of Raphael, then, there is throughout the first book an almost unbearable tension between the health he promises and symbolizes and the actual illness of the state, between his enlightenment and man's blindness, his message and man's deafness.

Initially, of course, the Raphael we see is a traveller. This image and the motifs bound up with it dominate the earliest pages of the *Utopia*, and must have been in More's mind from the beginning. Nothing could have been both more natural, and more witty, than to move from St. Raphael, patron saint of travellers, to Raphael, world traveller and explorer, former companion of Amerigo Vespucci. Yet, somewhere below this seemingly realistic and factual (though fictional) surface, the Augustinian image of the just man as a pilgrim, journeying towards a celestial city, is sounded. In the interplay of these two images, held together by Raphael's name and his passionate concern for "peregrinatio," which may mean either travel or a pilgrimage, we have, in fact, More at his most serious and wittiest.

This same interplay explains certain peculiarities in the initial portrait of Raphael, which, if read as an example of realistic fiction, is "somewhat amorphous," in J. H. Hexter's words [in *More's Utopia: The Biography of an Idea* (1952).] When we first meet Raphael, for example, we see, via More, an old, weather-beaten man, indifferent to his appearance, who is a "ship's captain" or "nauclerus." But soon afterwards More plays with this image; as Peter Giles says, "But you are quite mistaken . . . for his sailing has not been like that of Palinurus but that of Ulysses or, rather, of Plato." This is strange indeed if More means simply that Raphael was "wide-awake and observant as a traveller." Why such an emphatic denial? Why this order? More here must be playing upon the word "sailing" [*navigavit*], which becomes a metaphor for Raphael's safe passage through the sea of life, an ancient patristic trope he uses elsewhere. The real contrast is thereby complicated, as Palinurus stands for those who fall asleep at the wheel and plunge into the sea, literally and figuratively, unlike Ulysses, long thought of as a type of the wise man and skillful political expert. But the final contrast is more complete yet, for Plato, whose travels were also understood as a quest for truth, both contemplative and active (moral and political), is certainly not a ship's captain, on the literal level. But on the figurative level his "voyage" is the most appropriate illustration of one who inquires after the true way, and More may well have remembered what St. Augustine says of Plato in his *City of God:* "So he thinking that his invention and Socrates his instructions were all too short of the true ayme of Philosophy, and therefore would needs go travell to any place where Fame told him he might drinke of the fount of noble sapience."

Other details, too, exploit the double image of a traveller in this world and through it, engaged in a search for truth and life. When we read that "He left his patrimony at home—he is a Portuguese—to his brothers . . . ," these two levels actually collide. Even as More is writing this the Portuguese explorers are engaged in plunder on a massive basis; so one account of a Portuguese voyage comments: "Item, on the morning of the twenty-fourth day of this month we went quickly with our whole force, being eight ships all armed, to the town, and did kill all the heathens and plundered the town of great store of gold, silver, pearls, and precious stones, and beautiful garments." The ironic contrast to Raphael's willingness, indeed eagerness, to give up his wealth, his complete lack of concern for material acquisitions, and his joy in discovering a place where gold has no value, is devastating. Does the New Testament command to give up all one has to follow Christ echo, however distantly, here?

The "peregrinatio" motif becomes more and more insistent, as we learn that on the last voyage Raphael "was left behind that he might have his way, being more anxious for travel than about the grave (*peregrinationis magis quam sepulchri curioso*)." The ambiguity which plays about that "peregrinatio" makes it unlikely that this means only that his love of travel was stronger than his fear of death, and the real antithesis becomes the distinction between travel as this symbolizes the way to true life and a merely temporal death. Certainly it is only because he was such an indefatigable "peregrinator" that he has found Utopia and "salus." Finally there is the second of the aphorisms which are constantly on his lips: "From all places it is the same distance to heaven' (*vndique ad superos tantundem esse viae*)." It is very hard to square this aphorism, which resembles one More himself will use when he is imprisoned in the Tower, with any reading of travel as purely geographical, since it effectively negates the anxiety which we have already been told is Raphael's. And of course what this really means is that Raphael's real home is above, his real journey's end is heaven.

Nor is Raphael simply a "peregrinator," a traveller-pilgrim; he is also, like St. Raphael, a guide. This is naturally less specifically developed, being implicit, rather, in his overall function. He has come, if not from heaven, then Utopia, to tell others about this "Happy Land," which Budé calls one of the Fortunate Isles and Hagnopolis, a holy city [see excerpt dated 1517]. And all of Book II witnesses to the effectiveness of Raphael's guidance, as he takes us to a commonwealth where all wealth is common and men love their neighbors, not their purses. At least two "road" metaphors, occurring within a few paragraphs of each other, underline this function and point up both the positive and negative ends of the motif. When he says: "To persons who had made up their minds to go headlong by the opposite road, the man who beckons them back and points out dangers ahead can hardly be welcome," he defines the particular problem which he faces as a would-be guide, incidentally confirming the radical nature of his message. A second metaphor spells out his preoccupation with the true way, and is particularly interesting because it simultaneously plays upon both of Raphael's major offices, linking the way with the end (*salus*): "This wise sage (Plato) to be sure, easily foresaw that the one and only road to the general welfare lies in the maintenance of equality in all respects." We need Raphael's own words, "unam atque unicam illam esse viam ad salutem publicam," for his alliteration and the rimed word-endings insist upon the relationship between the two metaphors. But Plato did not really quite foresee this, as Hexter has demonstrated; this is Raphael's vision, and one which is especially appropriate for a Raphael, a healer and guide, who has sought and found the only commonweal which has the community of interests which means "salus."

Yet a third "road" metaphor occurs at the end of *Utopia*, in the Utopian prayer of thanksgiving and petition which Raphael recites: "He thanks Him for all the benefits received." . . . If he errs in these matters or if there is anything better and more approved by God than that commonwealth or that religion, he prays that He will, of His goodness, bring him to the knowledge of it, for he is ready to follow in whatever path "He may lead him." There is, obviously, an ironic contrast to Raphael's earlier picture of Western Europe blindly following the wrong way, unwilling to listen to any guide, much less to Raphael. The contrast is even more ironic and more complete if More and his readers remembered the often repeated lesson from Tobit, to "Always and in every time bless God and desire of him that he address thy ways. . . ."

The most dramatic moment in all of *Utopia* occurs in the last few paragraphs; only then do we know whether or not

Raphael can effect the cure and be a guide for a commonwealth worthy of the name. We already know that it is unlikely indeed that either king or council would hear his message, and it is no accident that this scene is now recalled. For really, within the *Utopia*, only one simple question remains. Will these good men hear his message, or will they too be deaf? Will Peter Giles, the young, virtuous, open-hearted humanist? Will the More of the narrative, a man devoted to his country, his family, and God? We see one answer; we hear two.

What we see is a Raphael who is . . . "defessum," weary from his long prophetic narrative which attempts the reform of the state. And we see More as he takes the exhausted Raphael by the hand and leads him out of the garden, which suggests their search for an ideal, a paradise, into supper—"as if," Father Surtz has said, "blinded and weakened by the revelation." But this is an extraordinarily ironic reversal, as the guide is guided, the enlightener led into the dark. Surely More is dramatically inverting the gesture which was St. Raphael's, who held the young Tobias by the hand as he guided him safely on his journey. Since there is so little other movement in *Utopia*, the gesture would be significant in any case, but its extraordinary significance is due to its creator, who here, as elsewhere, reveals a love of drama, complicated by his extremely fine sense of the irony of the situation.

This visual irony is amplified, moreover, by verbal irony, for More speaks here as "Moria," that is, the fool. Turning to his readers he tells us, in a cunning speech, that "many things came to my mind which seemed very absurdly established in the customs and laws of the people described." When he has finished his itemized list (which includes their warfare, ceremonies, religion, other institutions, and especially the "common life and subsistence" of the Utopians) there is almost nothing left; we have a "reductio ad absurdum." Yet he cannot tell the "truth" to Raphael; he knew that "he was wearied with his tale," and he also remembered Raphael's comments about men who criticized others to appear wise. And so, still "Moria," he simulates and dissimulates in the best Renaissance tradition with words which should sound familiar, for more than one discussion has been cut off by words like these, spoken on behalf of a *status quo*. His response is very human, but unworthy of Raphael, the truth-seeker: "I therefore praised their way of life and his speech and, taking him by the hand, led him in to supper. I first said, nevertheless, that there would be another chance to think about these matters more deeply and to talk them over with him more fully." The irony of these same words cuts deep indeed, for there will be no other chance to speak, as More knows and says in the very next sentence: "If only this were some day possible!" The wisdom—or folly—of this world proves once again incapable of fully understanding a messenger from another world, unable wholly to see the vision which Raphael has seen with his own eyes. Not the least of the ironies of *Utopia*, then, is that Raphael, healer and guide, will always be Hythlodaeus, a speaker of witty nonsense, to the world as a whole, his vision yet another tall traveller's tale.

But this is not quite the final answer. Raphael has spoken, the vision has been recorded, the cure and the way to health have been proffered, and we have been guided to this Utopia. More, we remember, early alluded to "sane ac sapienter institutos ciues," "well and wisely trained citizens" who "are not everywhere to be found." But they are found in this "No-place," this *Utopia*, which is, like its explorer, Raphael, and the More who created it, no less "salutaris" than "festivus" (1), no less healing and health-giving than witty.

Elizabeth McCutcheon, "Thomas More, Raphael Hythlodaeus, and the Angel Raphael," in Studies in English Literature, 1500-1900, Vol. IX, No. 1, Winter, 1969, pp. 21-38.

GIOVANNI SANTINELLO (essay date 1969)

[*In the following excerpt from an essay originally published in Italian in 1969, Santinello considers the meaning and purpose of* Expositio passionis Christi.]

When Erasmus debated with Colet over the meaning of Christ's sorrow in the Garden, he—although no longer very young—was just at the beginning of his long career as a New Testament "theologian," and the times were less sad than they would be later. Thirty-five years afterwards, we have the *Expositio passionis Christi* of Thomas More....

More wrote his *Expositio passionis* in 1535 while in prison, where he had also written *A Dialogue of Comfort against Tribulation*. He could not finish the work because one fair day his imprisonment was made more severe and he was denied permission to write. The Latin part was translated into English by his grand-daughter Mary Roper Basset. More had composed an earlier part, in English, probably before he was imprisoned. The Latin *Expositio*, based on the texts of the four Gospels, begins with Christ's departure from the Last Supper and his arrival at the Garden of Gethsemane. It breaks off at the moment of his arrest. It thus covers the same Gospel passages that brought about the discussion between Erasmus and Colet, and it has a subtitle analogous to that of the Oxford debate: *De tristitia, taedio, pavore, oratione Christi ante captionem eius*.

More's composition differs in character from Erasmus'. It belongs, like his other Tower works, to what may be called "consolation literature." As in More's other works, beginning with the *Utopia* itself, and as in Erasmus' works, many references to the personal situation of the author, to contemporary events and people, are allowed to appear, sometimes implicitly, sometimes explicitly.

The prayer of Christ occasions a digression on our way of praying: we are distracted, we think of useless things. Our bodily posture itself contrasts with the disposition of a true pray-er (one who prays) placing himself before God. *Insani certe nobis videremur ipsis, si capitalem causam ad hunc tractaremus modum apud mortalem principem*. And yet an earthly king can deprive us only of our bodies, while God has power over our very souls. More's allusion to his own situation is evident, although much veiled. Jesus prays to the Father several times in order that, if it be possible, the cup of his passion may pass from him. He wants, as it were, to show us by his example that it is not wrong to ask God to deliver us from evil, especially in cases where *in magnum (etiam Dei causa) periculum venimus*. Christ needed help and the comforting angel came. Not all martyrs can be alike, comments More. Some are courageous, and know *triumphata morte coelum violenter irrumpere*. Others are afraid, horrified by that which

awaits them, facing death with fear and trembling. God does not prize their sacrifice the less on that account; the wisdom of God, which understands human feeling, knows how to temper the trials in proportion to each one's strength.

Six days had not passed since Christ's triumphal entry into Jerusalem; now he would be condemned to death by the people who had sung hosannas to him. More, who had passed from the Lord Chancellorship to condemnation for treason, emphasizes this passage: *assidue se vertentem humanarum rerum vicissitudinem*. Immediately thereafter, one may read an allusion to Henry VIII: those who condemn Christ are the highest order of Judea, chief priests, Pharisees, scribes, elders of the people: *quodque natura est optimum, ita quum semel coepit in diversum tendere, evadit tandem pessimum*. There is no sin more hateful to God than that *si quis leges ad iniuriam propulsandam natas transferat ad inferendam*.

To some it seems strange that an enlightened man like More could have chosen death for a cause that, in the light of reason, seems to be a superstition. More seems to answer them when he comments on Christ's reproof to Peter after the disciple tried to defend him by striking Malchus, as if to keep him from being obedient to the Father: I have spent my life giving examples of obedience and humility. I have taught that one should obey magistrates, honor one's parents, give to Caesar what is Caesar's and to God what is God's; and now, as I am about to conclude my work, do you wish that I should rend that fabric which I have woven for so long, and that the Son of Man should not be obedient to God?

More is not *animosus;* just as the *Utopia* differs from the moralistic idealism of Erasmus by the realism and pessimism which undergird it, so his martyrdom is a far cry from the fanaticism of the Christian neophyte, inspired by excessive zeal, whom the Utopians condemned for incitement to sedition. At the end of the *Expositio* is a long commentary on the flight of the apostles and on the mysterious figure of the young man who, for a while, followed Christ the prisoner, but who in his turn fled away naked when the soldiers seized him by his shirt (Mk 14.51–52): this final tract is a complex meditation on the legitimacy of flight. If one does not have enough courage to confront the danger, one should flee while there is time. When it is too late, flight becomes a fault, and it would be foolish to save one's present life at the cost of the life to come. One of the articles of faith in the natural religion of *Utopia* is the reward in an after-life. If one flees to avoid being forced to offend God, insofar as one despairs of knowing how to resist by one's own force, even this is foolish and evil, since it is desertion and lack of trust in divine aid. But if, as said at first, it is possible to flee without offending God, then flight is better *quam cunctando captum in horrendi criminis discrimen cadere*. When lawful, hasty fleeing in due time is easy; facing the struggle is difficult and dangerous. The youth fled because his clothes did not hinder him; he could escape naked, leaving his shirt in the hands of the persecutors. But he who is weighed down by clothes that are too heavy, or even by a single poor garment that is too straitly laced, will not be able to get away easily; rather than forfeit the much or the little that he has—to which he is foolishly attached—he will end up falling into the peril. In conclusion, More says, the example of the youth teaches us that, when about to face grave perils from which circumstances do not permit flight, we must be prepared, not weighed down by attachments to our things, but ready to give them up, leaving our garments behind and fleeing naked.

The long meditation on the flight seems to reflect very closely the weighty consideration, the doubts and finally the serenity and decisiveness with which More chose his own road, without fanaticism or ostentation.

He reveals as well the kind of faith and values for which he sacrificed his life. The Son of Man was given into the hands of sinners. The mystical body of Christ, the Church, *christianus videlicet populus*, then as now is threatened by divisiveness: *partes alias truculenti Turcae Christianae ditionis invadunt, alias intestino dissidio multiplices haereticorum sectae dilacerant.* More explicitly thereafter, his profession of faith appears by his quoting in full the Gospel text for the primacy of Peter.

There are frequent hints at the heresies of the reformers and explicit references to the discussions, within the reformers' camp, about the Real Presence: the long quarrel, still alive, of the Bohemian utraquists, the radical position of Zwinglians, *servantes tantum corporis sanguinisque vocabula.* More condemns the reformers, but does not even then forget his former stand in favor of religious toleration. Concerning the utraquists, he writes: *sub utraque specie non solum sumunt ipsi (quae res utcunque posset ferri), sed universos damnant;* that is, they condemn those who do not do as they do; their fault is in being intolerant. Concerning the repression of heresy on the Catholic side, he recalls that, in the episode of Peter's striking Malchus, Christ disapproves not only of the use of the material sword, but also of the spiritual sword, *illum gravem et periculosum excommunicandi gladium,* which is to be used only when *horrenda necessitas* requires it. For the most part, it should be kept back *in clementiae vagina.*

In the **Expositio**, then, More meditates upon his situation and the condition of the times, which appeared to belie the ideals of peace and toleration that had constituted so large a part of his and Erasmus' program for humanistic religious renewal.

To Erasmus he turns in the first pages of his work, which shows the direct influence of the Oxford debate that had unfolded so many years before in a very different climate of hope. The peculiarity of More's text, in comparison with the Erasmus–Colet exchange, is first of all the absence of the controversial tone: some traces of it remain (*miretur aliquis fortasse . . . ; sed hic fortassis obiicias . . .*), but these do not take on a character different from that of the whole work, which . . . is an exposition of Christ's agony as an object of meditation and of comfort. In consequence, the theological and philosophical apparatus used by Erasmus, especially in the second draft of his argument, disappears. All the problems raised by Erasmus and Colet are still present, but they are now fused in a unified treatment that proceeds quickly and that, in the light of good sense, of *pietas* and of a theology—so to speak—of simplicity, dissolves all that remained of the technically theological and philosophical in Erasmus' work. More succeeds, through a single integrating vision, in resolving certain oppositions that had divided Erasmus and Colet. He thus carries out Erasmus's theological program, which was meant not as doctrine for the intellect, but rather food for

the spirit and an exercise of piety in the reading of the sacred text.

What does "Cedron" signify? What does "Gethsemane" signify? Following Erasmus' notes to the *Novum Testamentum,* More relates the significance of these Hebrew words and interprets their sense allegorically. The words of the sacred books, therefore, are not to be read in one sense only, but are fertile with many mysteries. It was this prejudicial question that Colet posed to Erasmus, and that Erasmus refused to debate in depth. More accepts the plurality of scriptural sense, the possibility of diverse interpretations, and makes ample use of this possibility throughout this work. Colet tied his own position to a theological affirmation, which Erasmus did not exclude in his response: the unity of the sense of Scripture depends upon divine inspiration; the multiple sense, upon the weakness of the human interpreter. Concerning the agony in the garden More says expressly: *ab uno pariter ipsius Spiritu universa dictata sunt.* But the unity of divine inspiration does not prohibit human study from struggling with interpretation and does not preclude his exploring diverse senses. On the contrary, what matters to More is the attitude of veneration before the incomprehensibility of God's judgments and his ways. His attitude contrasts with the facile approach of certain *homines novi, subito de terra progerminati theologi,* who maintain their personal interpretations and argue among themselves, conquerors or conquered as the case may be, who thus destroy the *catholicam fidem.* More stands thinking of all the great theological controversies provoked by the reformation, but he attributes the cause of controversy to an attitude that he, with Erasmus, does not share with the reformers: *omnia scire videri volunt.* Evil resides in the pretense to knowledge, in the reduction of theology to science. From that evil the contests and conflicts about interpretations were born. If that attitude is dropped and if, with Colet, one distinguishes between the hidden truth which is one, and the human theological approaches to it, which can be diverse, then the conflicts too cease. Thus one comes to the position of Erasmus and More: the plurality of compatible senses within the unity of revealed and mysterious truth.

Christ in the garden is afraid. Of what? Of death, maintains Erasmus; that his death should not be a cause of the Jews' perdition, maintains Colet in opposition. Now let us read More. An immense heap of suffering crushes *tenerum piumque sanctissimi Servatoris corpus:* the betrayal of Judas, the enemies, the imprisonment, the calumnies, the blasphemies, the blows, the thorns, the nails, the cross and other tortures that will continue for terrible hours. Moreover, he is afflicted by the fear of the disciples, *perditio Judaeorum,* the death of the faithless traitor himself, the unspeakable sorrows of his beloved mother. More has combined the two theses (of Erasmus and Colet); more importantly, he has put them on the same level, binding them together with a single sense of compassion—rich in human and familiar touches: the tender body of Christ at the beginning and the afflicted mother at the end—toward a sorrow and a fear which Christ feels in himself for both his own troubles and all the troubles of others. The contrast between Erasmus and Colet was striking because the sorrows and fear of Christ were placed at levels endowed with different significance: for Erasmus, they were purely human; for Colet, theological and divine. More will go on to say more: all that Christ did or suffered or prayed for in his agony happened to him *ut homine.* Thus for More, even solicitude for the fate of the Jews could be made an integral part of the human sorrows of Christ.

From this question of Christ's human fear came the long justification that Erasmus gave of his thesis. More resolves it by responding to a double interrogative: *potuit? voluit?*

Christ could fear and suffer because, although he was truly God, he was also truly human. He was subject to *humani generis affectus, qui quidem culpa careant,* and these derive *ab inferiore humanitatis suae parte*—that is, his sensible being—in which was seated, as in all men, a natural horror of death. Here are recalled all the concepts that had entered the theological and anthropological fabric of Erasmus, who had leant upon Bonaventure, the Fathers, St. Paul and the stoics. The same thesis is to be found in More, but it is expressed with the intuitive simplicity of good sense, without the over-subtle distinctions that even Erasmus indulged in. More is more truly erasmian than Erasmus. This does not mean, however, that More had no explicit theology; he had that common, clearly defined theology which he accepted without the intricacies of overly scholastic distinctions. Writing in an atmosphere of heresy, he seizes the opportunity to recall the classic heretical oppositions that assert only the human nature or only the divine nature of Christ. For him, the miracles demonstrate his divinity, the agony in the garden, his humanity.

That Christ had been able to suffer is beyond doubt. But why did he choose to? Here again we find, even in More, the objections of Colet that we already know: Christ was required to give an example of strength, for after him there would be a host of strong and courageous martyrs.

More's answer is similar to that of Erasmus, but it is filled and impregnated with the experience he himself is living through. Christ had not willed that his own should in no way *horrerent necem;* his will was that they should not be afraid to the point of fleeing from temporal to eternal death, by denying the faith. He wanted them to be *milites prudentes,* not *stupidos et amentes.* It is better to confront death, when it is impossible to avoid it, than to separate oneself from Christ through fear: *desciscimus autem, si coram mundo fidem eius abnegamus;* but he does not ask us *vim naturae facere,* nor that we should never fear in any case. Thus, when flight does not harm the cause, he agrees that one should eschew torture by fleeing. His providence willed that some martyrs should hide and, when not required to do so, should not reveal themselves as Christians; and that others, on the contrary, should accuse themselves to their persecutors and spontaneously offer themselves to martyrdom. But if anybody found himself in a situation where he must either face torture or deny God, let him not doubt that into *has angustias* he has been led by the will of God himself. He must have every reason to hope that God will either set him free or else assist him in the battle and crown him victor.

Should one believe, perhaps, that martyrs felt no fear? Christ himself has given us an example of it with his fear in the garden and his courage in confronting the cross. More stresses the signs of Christ's human suffering, by noting that he had suffered not only in his body but also, with the terror which caused him to sweat blood, in his soul. Among all the motives for which Christ would not

hide *hos affectus infirmitatis humanae,* pride of place goes to that for which *infirmis infirmus factus, infirmos alios sua infirmitate curaret.* More's insistence on this *infirmitas* is analogous to that of Erasmus on *humanitas: Homo tum hominum causa apud homines loquens humanis verbis reformidationem humanam significavit.* Humanity, which Erasmus at the beginning of the century had loved to see in Christ, is changed in the suffering Christ to the infirm humanity of More awaiting torture. (pp. 456-61)

> *Giovanni Santinello, "Thomas More's 'Expositio Passionis'," translated by Dale B. Billingsley, in* Essential Articles for the Study of Thomas More, *edited by R. S. Sylvester and G. P. Marc'hadour, Archon Books, 1977, pp. 455-61.*

ARTHUR NOEL KINCAID   (essay date 1972)

[*In the following excerpt, Kincaid argues that the structure of* The History of King Richard III *is based on a dramatic conceit by which the moral purpose of the work is expressed.*]

Despite the growing acceptance and appreciation in this century of More's *History of King Richard III* as a literary work, and More as an author of great stylistic brilliance, the dramatic aspect of his writings has been all but ignored and never carefully and systematically studied. In *The History of King Richard III,* More's use of the dramatic approach in his writings reaches its culmination. The structure of this work is essentially founded upon a dramatic conceit, and it is subtly through this dramatic structure that More makes clear the moral intention of the *History.* So closely woven together and so completely interdependent are all the various aspects of the work that without an understanding of its dramatic nature, neither its literary structure nor its moral purpose can be properly comprehended. Failure to view the *History* from this angle has led to centuries of misinterpretation and to insufficient appreciation of its value as a work of art. (pp. 223-24)

For More the theater had the profoundest significance, bound up, as it was to be for Shakespeare, with his whole view of life. Over and over again the image of the theater appears in his works. He employs it in literary criticism when he says of Erasmus's *Encomium Moriae* "that boke of *Moria* dothe in dede but iest vpoon the abuses of such thinges, after the maner of the disours parte in a playe. . . ." In his devotional treatise *The Four Last Things,* he twice employs the theatrical image to illustrate the superficial and transitory nature of life. . . . In *Utopia* More uses the theater image in considering a moral problem which became increasingly urgent to him as he was drawn more and more into government, and which ultimately brought about his death: the extent to which a philosopher should intervene in politics. He wonders whether, by expressing his opinions too boldly, such a man might not risk ruining the "play" by interpolating into it something incongruous.

More's ability to see all sides of a question with equal clarity and his profound sense of the theater have enabled him to create in Richard III a character of many dimensions, a character of such vividness, detail, complexity, and unity that it has remained with us, sharing the stage only with Milton's Satan, as the prime villain of literature.

More, not Shakespeare, was the originator of this portrait, and although Shakespeare heightens it by adding lines and shadings, most of his notable additions to More's portrait are at least inspired by More's implicit suggestions.

The picture emerges as much more than a mere stereotype of evil. It is notable that in writing about an evil character, More prefers the complex process of development and detailed accumulation of evidence to the easier technique of pure vituperation. He gives us first a description of Richard's appearance and personal qualities, and then contrasts Richard in these respects with other characters. This is followed by a narration of his former actions, a continuing analysis of his motives and machinations, and a developing view of the effect he has upon others.

The character is wholly consistent. Every aspect of characterization points him on a determined pursuit of his ambition through the means of dissimulation. This dissimulation, only hinted at in previous "historical" treatments of Richard III, More makes the focal point for his character. Since More was aiming at bringing literary consistency to a character based on historical tradition, this approach was inescapable. It was necessitated by the curious and irreconcilable discrepancies occasionally apparent in the portrait of Richard III—discrepancies resulting from the superimposing of Tudor propaganda on the historical facts of Richard's character and career. To give the character consistency, it was necessary for More to portray him as an actor, a central feature which Shakespeare adopts in his portrayal. (pp. 227-29)

Most writers on the literary nature of More's *History of King Richard III* have alleged that its structure is based upon Richard's determined progress toward the throne, and derives its unity from the central character's manipulation of all the events in the story. To an extent this is true. Richard is introduced very near the opening of the work, and More informs the reader that this character is to be its moving force: "this Dukes demeanoure ministreth in effecte all the whole matter whereof this booke shall entreate."

The *History*'s most recent editor, Richard S. Sylvester, plausibly conjectures [in his 1963 edition of the work] that an earlier draft of More's actually opened with the immediate introduction of Richard rather than with the description of Edward IV. It is in this form that the *History* appears in Grafton's continuation of Hardyng and in Hall. Although the English version continues on to include conjecture concerning the death of the Princes and to introduce Buckingham's rebellion, the Latin version of the *History* concludes with Richard's attainment of his end, his coronation. We may thus perhaps suggest that a structure formed by Richard's manipulation of events as he strives toward the crown, from the inception of his ambition to its fulfillment, represented an earlier plan of More's.

But what we have in the Rastell edition of the English version is somewhat different. Here the work opens with a picture of order and harmony, at the end of Edward IV's reign, which Richard, when he enters, destroys. Toward the conclusion of the history we have a description of Richard's punishment in life through guilt and rebellion, and of his ignominious death. In the final pages before the work breaks off, we are led to see, through the introduction of Morton, the triumph of the rational mind over the

confusions and alienations created by Richard's selfish pursuit of ambition.

Thus throughout the work we have not merely the single driving movement of Richard's progress toward the throne, but another movement as well, which becomes more obvious when we consider the opening and closing of the *History* as they are given in the Rastell edition: the beginning praising Edward IV's peaceful and ideal government, and the ending with the introduction of the rational man's incipient moral victory over the tyrant's minion. This other movement defines the work as an *exemplum,* and those who persist in seeing Richard's progress toward and ultimate achievement of the crown as the sole theme or even the major theme are ignoring the essentially exemplary nature of the work.

This other movement is outlined in the gradual reaction against Richard, which points toward a reestablishment of the state of natural order postulated at the beginning in the ideal reign of Edward IV. Richard's success is only apparent and only temporary. Almost from the beginning, certain characters are able to see through him, and gradually the distrust becomes more and more general. His schemes begin to fail. His greatest crime, the princes' murder, proves to be his greatest failure: he loses his peace of mind, but his victims win the reward of heaven. I think we are justified in calling this movement the primary structure, since it frames the narrative and establishes its moral, then works as an undercurrent, as it pulls against the more obvious but only temporary dominance of Richard in his progression toward the crown, and gradually reemerges toward a reassertion as the *History* breaks off.

The metaphor of the stage is the most important element of this structure, since it defines Richard's position relative to the reader and also to the populace. It is through these relationships that More makes clear his moral purpose. The *History* is similar to a morality play, using an *exemplum* to show how the violation of natural order, particularly on the part of a monarch, whose function should be to uphold and protect order, brings consternation and woe upon the land, and God's punishment on the offender. Like a morality play, it depends for its effect upon the relations between the actor and audience. These take place on two levels. On one level, the reader is the audience, viewing the "history" of the tyrant, observing the tragic struggle for material gain, and, beholding it from the point of view of the *contemptus mundi* tradition, seeing the intrinsic worthlessness of the object of ambition. The irony inherent in this dramatic relationship deflates Richard's apparent success.

On the other level, Richard is an actor watched by an audience *within* the play in which he is leading performer—an audience composed of the other characters and of the general public. He performs for them a series of scenes, to which they react. The subtle shifts of this audience's attitude toward Richard define his gradual downfall. The extent to which the responses of the internal audience (the populace) and the external audience (the reader) combine or diverge adds a further dimension to the work and can be manipulated for mood and emphasis.

More is intentionally placing his readers in the position of a theater audience, for the techniques which he uses to bring the narrative into vivid focus are dramatic in nature: characterization, dialogue, oration, and action. The first few pages introduce *dramatis personae*: Edward IV, the good king at the end of a peaceful and prosperous reign, just, merciful, beloved by his people; Clarence, "a goodly noble Prince"; and Richard, inferior in strength and stature, deformed and ugly, "malicious, wrathfull, enuious."

Direct discourse, which dominates over a third of the work, More skillfully manipulates by leading into it through indirect discourse, from which he shifts unobtrusively. He presents a vivid description of Elizabeth Woodville's receiving, near midnight, news of Rivers and Grey's arrest, and her ensuing consternation and distress as she hastily prepares to enter sanctuary. Then there is a rapid shift to a simultaneously occurring scene at the residence of the Archbishop of York: "Nowe came there one in likewise not longe after myddenighte, fro the Lorde Chaumberlayn vnto the arch bishoppe of Yorke . . . to his place not farre from Westminster."

With the word "nowe," our attention is quickly directed to the new scene, and in that brief passage the set has been altered by the introduction of time, place, and characters. Action ensues: the messenger persuades the servants that this errand is urgent, the servants awaken the Archbishop, who admits the messenger. Then follows a passage in direct discourse, summarizing the effect of the message, and shifting almost imperceptibly into dialogue, bringing the scene into immediate dramatic focus. The Archbishop grants audience to the messenger,

> Of whome hee hard, that these dukes were gone backe with the Kynges grace from Stonye Stratforde vnto Northampton. Notwithstanding sir quod hee, my Lorde sendeth youre Lordeshippe woorde, that there is no feare. For hee assureth you that all shall bee well. I assure him quod the Archebishoppe bee it as well as it will, it will neuer bee so well as wee have seene it.

When the messenger departs, we are returned to the original scene, where the Archbishop now comes to the Queen as she prepares to enter sanctuary.

The dialogues and orations are used for developing character just as much as for expounding messages which the author wishes to convey. At no point is the message permitted to interfere with the characterization. More skillfully manipulates style in dialogue to show both character and change of mood. This is particularly well demonstrated in the scene between Elizabeth Woodville and the Cardinal, who comes to take away the Duke of York. The Queen's obstinacy and anger express themselves first in a series of defiant rhetorical questions, which she answers herself:

> Wherby should I truste that (quod the Quene) In that I am giltlesse? As though they were gilty. In y^t I am with their enemies better beloued than thei? When they hate them for my sake. . . . For I assure you, for that I se some men so gredye withowte any substaunciall cause to haue him, this maketh me much the more farder to deliuer him.

Her rage ultimately rises to sputtering hysteria, as she mocks Richard's words, first with inverted syntax and rapid alterations of subject, then with insistent parallel construction:

But the childe cannot require the priuelege, who tolde hym so? he shal here him aske it and he will. Howbeit this is a gay matter: Suppose he could not aske it, suppose he woulde not aske it, suppose he woulde aske to goe owte, if I say hee shall not, if I aske the priuilege but for my selfe, I say he that agaynst my wyll taketh out him, breaketh the sanctuary.

The humor of the Queen's willful rage and the Cardinal's indignation at her behaving as if "all other . . . saue herselfe, lacked either wit or trouth" serves two purposes in the drama: comic relief for the tension we have had to experience in watching the trap close on its innocent victims, and also an ironic purpose of pointing up through contrast with the humor of the Queen's apparent extravagance of behavior, the genuine terror of the situation in which she and her son stand. Exhausted, chagrined, and reduced to helpless tears at the end of the scene, the Queen parts from her son with words and movements which carry pathos in their simplicity:

> And therewithall she said vnto the child: farewel my own swete sonne, god send you good keping, let me kis you ones yet ere you goe, for God knoweth when we shal kis togither agayne. And therewith she kissed him, & blessed him turned her back and wept and went her way, leauing the childe weping as fast.

The numerous orations are all models of persuasive construction. At the same time they reflect character and situation by use of particular stylistic devices. Edward IV's deathbed oration builds to a desperately emphatic climax in a series of phrases in parallel construction: "I exhort you and require you al, for ye loue that you haue euer borne to me, for the loue y^t I haue euer born to you, for the loue that our lord beareth to vs all, from this time forwarde, all grieues forgotten, eche of you loue other."

Richard's speech to the council in regard to the Duke of York's release from sanctuary is given a pseudo-rational quality through use of long, well-modulated sentences:

> The prosperytye whereof standeth . . . not all in keepynge from enemyes or yll vyande, but partelye also in recreation and moderate pleasure: which he cannot in this tender youthe take in the coumpanye of auncient parsons, but in the famylier conuersacyon of those that bee neyther farre vnder, nor farre aboue his age.

The Cardinal's reply is more rhetorical, deriving emphasis from repetition and alliteration. The build-up of detail which enforces the inviolability of sanctuary leads to a crescendo in the lengthening of the periods. The climax comes in the emphatic repetition and internal rime: "there was neuer so vndeuowte a Kinge, that durst that sacred place violate, or so holye a Bishoppe that durste it presume to consecrate."

Buckingham's reply is scornful and cleverly ironic in contrast. Alliteration falls upon the consonants "w" and "f" throughout: Womannishe feare, naye womannishe frowardenesse. . . ." The word "fear" is brought into utter contempt by a tenfold repetition of it in the course of the speech. Buckingham exhibits a colloquial touch: "yea and ryche menne runne thither with poore mennes goodes . . . and bidde their creditours gooe whistle them." This is reinforced by his shrewd sense of ironical humor: "all the worlde woulde saye that wee wer a wyse sorte of counsaylers about a kynge, that lette his brother bee caste awaye vnder oure noses." He even indulges in playful rime: "sythe the priuileges of that place . . . haue been of long continued, I am not he that woulde bee aboute to breake them. And in good faith if they were nowe to begynne, I woulde not bee he that shoulde bee aboute to make them." A similar style is reproduced for Buckingham later in his oration to the people in favor of Richard's assuming the crown.

More occasionally assumed the customary habit of the morality actor in stepping downstage to the audience to comment on the characters and action, and to state moral messages, in order to be sure that the instructions which the drama conveys are kept constantly in mind. After the death of Hastings, More steps forward to draw our sympathy to him by giving a brief eulogy, and then he presents a moral message for which the episode of Hastings's downfall has served as an *exemplum*: "O good god, the blindnes of our mortall nature, when he most feared, he was in good surety: when he rekened him self surest, he lost his life, & that wᵗ in two howres after."

In the episode of Jane Shore's penance, More, conscious of the difficulty of winning sympathy for a harlot, instead of giving an objective description, addresses the reader directly and makes him share in estimating her beauty: "nothing in her body yᵗ you wold haue changed, but if you would haue wished her somewhat higher." In connection with Mistress Shore, More preaches a lesson in charity, telling us that now she is poor and friendless she is much more worthy of remembrance.

More uses irony to enforce the moral view, often undercutting Richard's pretenses with an ironic comment. This type of irony becomes more frequent and more bitter as the work progresses and Richard's actions become more deeply sinful. More mocks Richard's protestations of piety: he cannot dine until Hastings is executed "for sauing of his othe." He punishes Jane Shore's adultery as if he were "a goodly continent prince clene & fautles of himself, sent oute of heauen into this vicious world for the amendement of mens maners . . ." After the murder of the Princes the irony becomes less playful and more bitter. More points up Richard's desire to have the Princes buried in a better place with the remark: "Loe the honourable corage of a kynge."

These are among the many methods More uses to present a dramatic effect to the reader, putting him in the place of an audience at a play. But if we go into the work itself, we find in effect an actor-audience relationship on another level of reality, as if we are watching a play within a play. Here the audience is the London populace observing the shows staged by Richard, the actor-producer, hypocrite in the original as well as in the modern sense of the word. Ultimately the success or failure of Richard's schemes depends upon the audience's response to them, and we see this response withdrawing from him increasingly as the work progresses, thus outlining the moral structure in theatrical terms.

After Edward IV's death, Richard's feigned regard for the new young king has managed to deceive the public, and the motives for his actions go unquestioned until he stages his first dramatic scene, the arrest of Rivers and Grey. He prepares for this act by first setting a scene: he positions his men along the road and locks the door. Then he stages

a quarrel with Rivers upon false grounds, and answers his denials with arrest. Immediately thereafter he stages another quarrel with Grey, again on grounds which he knows to be false. The distrust into which Richard falls as a result of this action is very short-lived, as if the people could not be sure whether the action were genuine or staged. He recovers his popularity and is named protector.

After this, however, there is nothing Richard does which does not bring suspicion upon him from some quarter. As his movements become more defined in his efforts to obtain possession of the Duke of York, the general fear and distrust become more acute. Elizabeth Woodville clearly sees Richard's "painted processe," and his actions caused "not comen people only that waue with the winde, but wise men also & some lordes, yeke to marke the mater and muse theron." The seeds of distrust have been planted, but have not yet come to the surface.

The Tower council comes at the center of the book and represents the climax of Richard's dissimulation. Richard has carefully planned this culminating scene, and he acts it with perfect timing and aplomb. He enters late and disarms the council by "saluting them curtesly." More then moves the scene into dramatic focus by turning to direct discourse, as Richard asks Morton for strawberries. Richard enters "saieng merely that he had bene a slepe that day. And after a little talking wᵗ them, he sayd vnto yᵉ Bishop of Elye: my lord you haue very good strawberies at your gardayne in Holberne. . . ." From this point on, the scene is played in dialogue. Richard goes out, returning some time later with altered countenance, and after a dramatic silence to heighten the uncertainty of the assembly, he accuses Elizabeth Woodville and Mistress Shore of witchcraft in withering his arm. When Hastings, relying on what he believed was a mutual love between him and the protector, attempts to mitigate his wrath, Richard pretends to take exception at the word "if," accuses Hastings of taking part in the conspiracy, and gives the cue for the elaborate and carefully timed stage machinery, which he had placed in readiness beforehand, to be set in motion: "And therewᵗ as in a great anger, he clapped his fist vpon yᵉ borde a great rappe. At which token giuen, one cried treason without the cambre. Therwith a dore clapped, and in come there rushing men in harneys as many as yᵉ chambre might hold."

Despite Richard's technical skill in executing this scene, those who are present at its performance cease before the end to be taken in. They realize that "this matter was but a quarel," since they know that Elizabeth Woodville would never join in a plot with her late husband's mistress. They are also aware that Richard's accusation of witchcraft is false, since they know that Richard's arm had been deformed from birth. Nor is the populace deceived. As the story of Hastings's death spread over the city, how little it was credited is indicated in the words of the schoolmaster, natural spokesman for the people's reason, who comments on the discrepancy between the length of the proclamation and the brevity of the time between Hastings's execution and its publication. Indeed, says More, "eueri child might wel perceiue, that it was prepared before."

The public reaction becomes more clearly defined during the episode of Jane Shore's penance. Before, it had been a shadowy, secret thing which those who felt it could not verbalize, even to themselves. Then with the schoolmaster's comment one person voiced what all were silently thinking. Now there is outright laughter at Richard's suddenly charging Jane Shore with the adultery which had been common and accepted knowledge for many years past.

Richard takes advantage of the confusion into which the minds of the populace have been thrown to make his decisive move, commissioning a sermon to publicize the illegitimacy of Edward IV's children and his own right to the crown. Again he carefully blocks out a scene, but this time it does not go according to plan. Richard is supposed to enter on the preacher's cue so that he will appear to have been chosen by God. But God refuses to take part in Richards's play. When the protector fails to appear on cue, the preacher, not so expert an actor as Richard himself, bungles the scene and makes a fool of himself by repeating, word for word, a considerable portion of the speech leading up to the cue. This is the worst possible way of covering a delayed entrance, as every actor knows, and as More, the child improviser on Morton's stage, would have been well aware. Instead of merely reporting the preacher's repetition, More actually reproduces it in his text, thus making it possible for the reader to be drawn into the internal play by identifying with the audience within it. He may experience the situation at first hand and share in the embarrassment and levity at the preacher's helplessness. The audience reaction in this case goes completely awry. The scene was calculated to draw audience participation at a certain point, but by the time this point arrives, the audience's willingness to believe in the play has been lost: "the people wer so farre fro crying king Richard, yᵗ thei stode as thei had bene turned into stones, for wonder of this shamefull sermon." Before this, the distrust of Richard's schemes, though invariably present, had been little more than whispered. Now it has become general and overt.

Buckingham's subsequent oration to the people falls under a similar cloud. A brilliant example of persuasive oratory, it fails because the public reaction is not in tune. When his speech arouses no response, Buckingham places himself in a foolish position, like the preacher, by repeating it, and then having the recorder repeat it once again. By means of these repetitions, More depicts the lack of spontaneity and the very careful plotting behind the whole affair. After the second repetition, the only reaction is a general buzzing whisper. Against this background, some "prentices and laddes" and servants of Buckingham "began sodainelye at mennes backes to crye owte as lowde as their throtes would gyue: king Rycharde kinge Rycharde, and threwe vp their cappes in token of ioye." The contrast between the depressed and doubting populace and the sudden noisily enthusiastic shout from a few throats provokes the reader's laughter. But the people are oppressed with sadness. Buckingham thanks them for their unanimous assent. They are caught in a trap. In this instance an effect is achieved in the discrepancy between the reader's and the internal audience's response: the contrast of the reader's laughter with the helplessness of the people's situation makes it seem all the more horrible.

Immediately thereafter, Richard, by prearrangement with Buckingham, stages another show, at Baynard's Castle. He pretends to be surprised by the visit of Buckingham and the city officials, "as though he doubted and partly dystrusted the commyng of suche noumbre vnto him so sodainelye, withoute anye warnyng or knowledge, whyther they came for good or harme." Richard first feigns reluctance to assume the crown, out of loyalty to the young king and fear for his own reputation, but at last he is "forced" to accept it. The people are perfectly well aware that these proceedings represent a previously contrived act, but they excuse it on the grounds of formality.

Before his coronation, Richard plays one more scene in an attempt to disarm the people by pardoning all offenders. In token of this he performs the ritual of taking one of his enemies by the hand, "Whiche thyng the common people reioysed at and praised, but wise men tooke it for a vanitye."

Richard's succession of dramatic scenes succeed or fail for precisely the same reasons as do the plays we see in the theater. The Tower scene is perfect in its technical execution. But the audience, which up to a point have been convinced by it, find a flaw in the argument and at that point realize that it is only fiction. The sermon scene fails because the timing goes wrong. The discomforts of a flustered, inexperienced actor, and the absurd discrepancies produced by the delayed entrance give rise to humor. Buckingham's address fails because, although the acting is good, the audience is not sympathetic with the theme. Like any theater audience of which participation is required, they are reluctant to make fools of themselves by entering into the performance, and coaching makes them balk all the more. When all else fails, men "planted" in the audience attempt to lead the way. The performer then thanks the audience for its helpful participation, but the hypocrisy of the situation makes the majority feel sick and depressed, because, of course, they know that there has been no genuine participation, and the play has proceeded on false grounds. The show whose purpose was ostensibly to entertain them has only exploited them. The final scene, at Baynard's Castle, is smoothly and correctly executed. The audience accept it because it is stylized by nature, but because it is insincere and obviously contrived, they fail to find it appealing.

The *History*'s dramatic images culminate in a passage which overtly expresses the significance inherent in all the scenes leading up to it. In terms of the *History*, the "play within a play," this speech explicitly makes the identification, of which we have been conscious all along, of the populace as audience and the King as leading actor. It stands as a culmination of all the elaborate arrangements of pseudo-theatrical scenes, effects, and posturings which More has had his characters perform throughout the work, and its aptness takes the reader's breath away. But the speech has relevance as well in terms of More's own relations with his audience of readers. He is speaking directly to them here, as the actor in the morality play would address his audience in order to express the play's moral message. He is commenting, on the basis of his own experience and of his premonitions about his own future, on the place of the wise man in government, a dilemma which was troubling his mind at the time of writing the *History*. The speech in even more general terms is a lesson on the frailty, uncertainty, and transience of human life:

> And in a stage play all the people know right wel, that he that playeth the sowdayne is percase a sowter. Yet if one should can so lyttle good, to shewe out of seasonne what acquaintance he hath with him, and calle him by is owne name whyle he standeth in his magestie, one of

his tormentors might hap to breake his head, and worthy for marring of the play. And so they said that these matters bee Kynges games, as it were stage playes, and for the more part plaied vpon scaffoldes. In which pore men be but yᵉ lokers on. And thei yᵗ wise be, wil medle no farther. For they that sometyme step vp and playe wᵗ them, when they cannot play their partes, they disorder the play & do themself no good.

It took a man of considerable experience and insight into all phases of the theater to probe and describe so minutely such a variety of audience reactions. We see in More the talents of the boy page who in his patron's house stepped in among the players and performed parts extempore; the young man who wrote plays and interludes; the lawyer who was so far capable of seeing both sides of the question with sympathy that he was willing to give justice to the devil: and the religious controversialist who created *personae* to represent opposing doctrines and put formidably plausible speeches in the mouth of the opponent.

In *The History of King Richard III,* More's dramatic vision has informed the whole of the work in all of its aspects, creating its structure and, by means of this structure, setting forth its moral message. And in this method lies another facet of More's originality. Instead of overtly moralistic preaching with which the annalists presented their series of *exempla,* More adopts a new approach toward his readers to convey in a method far more subtle and hence more effective his moral view of history. He makes of his readers an audience and presents before them a group of characters playing out a moral tragedy. (pp. 230-42)

> Arthur Noel Kincaid, "The Dramatic Structure of Sir Thomas More's 'History of King Richard III'," in Studies in English Literature, 1500-1900, *Vol. XII, No. 2, Spring, 1972, pp. 223-42.*

ROBERT M. ADAMS (essay date 1975)

[*Adams is a noted American author, editor, and translator. In the following excerpt, he presents his view of More's intent in* Utopia, *offering as well a brief survey of the work's critical history.*]

Utopia is one of those mercurial, jocoserious writings which turn a new profile to every advancing generation, and respond in a different way to every set of questions which is addressed to them. Though small in size and flippant in tone, it is in fact two very heavy books. The first part propounds a set of riddles which every sincere man who enters public life is bound to ask himself, whether he is living in early-capitalist England, late-capitalist America, or any other society dominated by the money-mad and the authority-intoxicated. He must think, What good can I do as an honorable man in a society of power-hungry individuals? What evil will I have to condone as the price of the good I accomplish? And how can I tell when the harm I am doing, by acting as window-dressing for evil, outweighs my potential for good? The second part of *Utopia* offers a set of no less disturbing questions. For example, Can a community be organized for the benefit of all, and not to satisfy the greed, lust, and appetite for domination of a few? How much repression is a good society justified in exercising in order to retain its goodness? And finally, When we give some persons power in our society (as we

must), and appoint others to watch them (as we'd better), who is going to watch the watchers? Can we really stand a society in which everybody watches everybody?

Almost everyone has seen that these are some of the major questions the *Utopia* raises; they include many of the classical questions of political economy and social organization. As for what answers the author of *Utopia* provided, we are still in dispute; he was a complex man who understood very well that it is not always safe or politic to speak one's entire mind—even supposing it is ever possible. [Most authorities] . . . try to calculate the answers More gave to his questions by studying the way in which they are framed or the context in which they occurred to him. Some see him as a man modern far beyond his era, proposing prophetic remedies for the problems of an outworn social system; others see him as a conservative, medieval-minded man whose ideal community was patterned on that of the monastery. Still others deny that he meant anything at all, preferring to describe his book as a joke. Some feel that the book can be understood in terms of its literary form or genre, in terms of its predecessors among the imaginary commonwealths, or in terms of the ideals prevalent among More's literary friends on the Continent. Some find the key to its equivocal patterns of meaning in an equivocal pattern of syntax; some argue that Utopia was a real place located in Peru, and Hythloday a real man who had visited it and talked with More. A gamut of speculation is thus offered to the reader, spreading, if not from the sublime to the ridiculous, at least from the plausible to the improbable.

But, whatever the book "really" meant when it was written, one aspect of it . . . is the enormous influence it had on men's minds. It had this influence not only on socialist Utopians of the nineteenth century like William Morris and Edward Bellamy, but on men of its own time, the sixteenth century. America had been discovered for fewer than twenty-five years when the *Utopia* appeared in print. Europeans knew very little about the new land beyond the ocean, and what information they got from the first explorers was sparse, ill-written, and, worst of all, not very interesting, especially when it was accurate. Just at this moment, More appeared with a finished and elegant literary production, describing some enchanting people who, in addition to all the "natural" virtues like innocence, simplicity, and native honor, had some very sophisticated institutions perfectly suited to comment on the most notorious abuses of contemporary Europe. No wonder the book took European readers by storm. Naive folk of the early sixteenth century swallowed More's account of Utopia as a fair description of the New World; tougher and more practical men still tended, when they came to America, to see the natives as potential Utopians or ex-Utopians. In Mexico and South America the best and most generous of the explorers tried to form the tribes and pueblos they discovered into little Amaurots. These, of course, disintegrated; but throughout the centuries and across most of the American latitudes, there have rarely failed to be found little groups of true believers whose social ideals owed something to the inspiration of More's *Utopia.* The book is thus of special interest to Americans, North and South; it helped to make us what we are today by determining, not our immediate institutions, but the level of our expectations. And in the long run that may be the most important, though the least formal, of our institutions.

If, then, it was a mere joke, More's book was one of the most appealing and influential jokes ever made—consequently, one of the cruelest. And that, I think, takes it outside the limits of More's character. The power of the book's idealism is a real ingredient of its structure; that fact has been demostrated, not in a learned article, but by the testimony of history. We may interpret it as we will, but the way a book like **Utopia** has been read and lived across the centuries is an authentic part of its nature. However we choose to read it, we cannot deprive it of qualities it has proved on the pulses of mankind. On these terms it cannot be other than a compassionate and generous book, as well as a witty one—a book which is interested in living people and the way they live, not just in verbal phantoms and personae. To read it is a test of one's own temper. (pp. vii-ix)

> *Robert M. Adams, in a preface to* "Utopia" by Sir Thomas More: A New Translation, Backgrounds, Criticism, *edited and translated by Robert M. Adams, W. W. Norton & Company, Inc., 1975, pp. vii-ix.*

MERRITT ABRASH (essay date 1977)

[*Abrash is an American academic and author who specializes in Slavonic studies. In the following excerpt, he examines More's "diversions" in* Utopia *to support his thesis that the work is a coherent, consistent whole and that Utopian society is guided solely by a utilitarian principle.*]

Most interpretations of Thomas More's **Utopia** have missed the point of the book. This is not to say that a "correct" interpretation has emerged rendering all others erroneous, but that in the complete absence of consensus on meaning, objective, and significance, the great majority of interpretations are necessarily mistaken in whole or part. The variety is so great that one of the following conclusions must express the real nature of the problem:

A. More expresses himself obscurely through sheer ineptitude.

B. He presents his argument with such subtlety that most readers misunderstand it.

C. The book is deliberately intended to perplex.

D. Readers miss the point because they accept the book too much at face value, thus belaboring the obvious and dismissing the significant.

More was not, of course, an inept writer, nor is anything in **Utopia** obscure in the sense of being difficult to comprehend. Only the point of the work as a whole is obscure, and this only by definition, inasmuch as whatever that point is, a large proportion of readers miss it. To ascribe this to oversubtlety is to deprecate More's skills at argument and exposition—skills which are historically established as very great.

More plausible is the proposition that he introduced perplexities and diversions simply because that was his pleasure. More "starts many hares and kills none," suggests C. S. Lewis, who is committed to the theme that the Discourse on Utopia is a brilliant *jeu d'esprit* and should not be taken as more than that [see excerpt dated 1954]. This interpretation could be valid in the final analysis but is inadmissible as a working hypothesis, since it shades imper-

ceptibly into the assumption that whatever cannot be explained must be a bit of trivia for which no explanation is necessary. By thus foreclosing discussion, the *jeu d'esprit* approach leaves standing all the uncertainties about **Utopia**, to the benefit of neither the reader nor of More himself, who is not known ever to have indicated that his book was merely (in Lewis' words) "a holiday work, a spontaneous overflow of intellectual high spirits."

There is a different set of assumptions which seems more likely to reflect the historical More. Let us assume that he was a careful and subtle writer who had a serious purpose behind every paragraph of this short work. And let us assume that Book I is not only a backdrop of European ills against which Utopia is effectively highlighted, but also may contain parallels with and references to Book II intended to make a point about that same Utopia. In other words, let us assume that More took his book seriously (in the sense that he did not incorporate deliberate false trails or "throwaway lines") and that Book I has something to say about Book II just as Book II obviously does about Book I. These assumptions, which seem appropriate to a man of More's literary skill, intellectual stature and seriousness of purpose, make possible an interpretation of **Utopia** more consistent than any heretofore.

If it is accepted that even the slightest lines in **Utopia** serve a serious purpose, then it is precisely in such lines that the most interesting clues may be found. Otherwise, why did More put in these asides, anecdotes, diversions, or call them what you will? Among interpreters, unfortunately, there has been what might be called a conspiracy of trivialization to avoid serious attention to these odd and inconsequent aspects of **Utopia**. And the occasional scholar who does note them finds himself driven into convoluted and unconvincing reasoning because he does not consider how they might be part of an overall design. H. W. Donner, for instance, makes an effort [in *Introduction to Utopia* (1945)] to explain some of the peculiar and seemingly trivial elements—henceforth collectively labeled "diversions"—but for the most part provides no real enlightenment because he takes them at face value.

Perhaps the best example of the problem is one of the most intriguing of these "diversions": the Utopian custom of premarital observation of prospective mates in the nude. This is hardly one of the mainstays of Utopian society, so it might be assumed that More is merely making a comment on European customs rather than proposing a significant reform. But the explanation Hythlodaeus gives for the procedure raises suspicions about More's purpose:

> We laughed at this custom and condemned it as foolish. They, on the other hand, marvelled at the remarkable folly of all other nations. In buying a colt, where there is question of only a little money, persons are so cautious that though it is almost bare they will not buy until they have taken off the saddle and removed all the trappings for fear some sore lies concealed under these coverings. Yet in the choice of a wife, an action which will cause either pleasure or disgust to follow them the rest of their lives, they are so careless that, while the rest of her body is covered with clothes, they estimate the value of the whole woman from hardly a single handbreath of her, only the face being visible.

Rationally persuasive, beyond a doubt. It is practically impossible to dispute the good sense of the Utopians. A

An imaginary 1518 woodcut by Ambrosius Holbein, showing the bearded Raphael Hythloday, narrator of Utopia, *telling his story to Peter Gillis, John Clement, and More.*

shrewd wit is at work here—but in fact much shrewder than the argument itself suggests.

As an actual social device, this viewing-in-the-nude is not very practical; Donner assumes it is "hardly to be taken literally," and apparently no known society has ever stopped at this peculiar half-way point between traditional Western mores and general premarital sexual experience. Therefore we are back at the point that More is merely making a comment on the Europe of his day. But it cannot be a very significant comment, since the danger of choosing bodily unattractive mates was hardly one of the significant European problems.

In that case, why does More give so much attention to the defense of this Utopian custom? Neither premarital sexual behavior, divorce, adultery nor punishment of criminals is dealt with at such length. The subject matter is intrinsically so slight that it seems out of phase with the surrounding weighty discourse about euthanasia and crime. Yet there it is—two whole paragraphs of it.

What interpreters have overlooked is that the ingenious analogy between choosing a wife and buying a horse neatly obscures the fact that choosing a wife is profoundly different from buying a horse. The actions are meant to serve highly dissimilar purposes and have quite different locations on virtually any scale of values—but it is unneces-

sary to elaborate on this in reference to a humanist of More's sensitivity and discrimination. That what point *is* he making by spelling out a misleading analogy with such persuasive care? To this we shall return when we have uncovered other evidence in *Utopia*.

Another striking bit of description which has escaped consideration in most interpretations of *Utopia* is the compulsory exchange of houses by lot every ten years. This is a truly tyrannical provision, a fitting accompaniment to the absence of locks on doors and the general rule that "nothing is private property anywhere." An extreme application of an extreme rule seems at odds with the Utopian virtues of reason and moderation, but of course this cannot be so unless the author was being inconsistent. Donner again grasps the nettle and finds an explanation based on his study of Vespucci's *Voyages* as a source for *Utopia*: " . . . every ten years they exchange houses, just as the West Indians in Vespucci's *Voyages* moved their habitations every seven or eight years." The odd aspect of the particular point is neutralized by showing that the unattractive custom is merely a bit of contemporary travel lore applied to Utopia with no particular import.

Unfortunately, the travel lore is rather different from Donner's paraphrase, and one does not need to look further than another page of Donner to discover this. There, he *quotes* Vespucci: the natives of the New World "hold their habitations in common, as many as six hundred sharing one building, and every seven or eight years they move the seat of their abodes because they fancy the air to have become infected." This is not at all the same as a rigid periodic exchange of houses by lot; the one case is clearly voluntary, based on fears for physical well-being, while the other is a compulsory manifestation of social policy. In this case, as in the viewing-in-the-nude, "diversions" have always been excluded from interpretations of *Utopia*, either by dismissing them as trivial or ascribing them to More's stock of historical and travel lore. But perhaps they are neither trivial nor even, properly speaking, diversions; perhaps there is an overall interpretive framework of which they are a crucial part and within which they fit with a common purpose.

After the sacred Utopian religious ceremony of First-Feast, "the rest of the day they pass in games and in exercises of military training." These last words may be the briefest "diversion" in *Utopia*, but their significance is not at all commensurate with their length. Engaging in military training on a holy day is not incongruous if, as R. W. Chambers maintains, Utopian religion is based only on the Four Cardinal Virtues and not on the Three Christian Virtues, but it *is* incongruous for a people of whom it is said that "War, as an activity fit only for beasts and yet practiced by no kind of beast so constantly as by man, they regard with utter loathing." Why does More show the Utopians placing an activity they consider spiritually repulsive in close propinquity to their religious festivals?

The fact is that the prevailing Utopian religion is not principally a spiritual matter at all: it is a social institution disguising wholly secular virtues under a religious form. There is no clearer evidence of this than the prayers at the end of the First-Feast, which are conspicuously lacking in spiritual content among the assorted estimable civic sentiments. The prayers say nothing about either moral standards or the state of the individual soul, and, far from reflecting any divine requirements to which a believer must conform, request only that he or she be allowed to live under the best system. Neither heroic nor profound, these prayers brilliantly fulfill the Utopians' intention that "nothing is seen or heard in the temples which does not seem to agree with all in common," and that "the prayers formulated are such as every man may utter without offense to his own belief."

Then what is the function of religion in Utopia? Hythlodaeus never makes a positive statement about this, which is hardly surprising inasmuch as he rules out one possibility after another. Utopian religion is not a means of making people better nor does it provide a bond between man and God (who is described in deistic terms). It does not even purport to provide comfort in distress; the man who dies fearfully is an embarrassment, whereas full attention and ritual are devoted to those who die "cheerfully and full of good hope," i.e., do not need any comfort. All that remains is a form of boosterism—collective self-congratulation about living in a society so well run that it allows unlimited optimism. And, in fact, Utopian life and thought reveal little awareness of doubt, despair or ethical dilemmas.

Even in Utopia, however, there are some situations in which simple optimism is out of place, and one of these—the existence of fools—is described in a way which casts an unexpected light not only upon Utopian religion but upon the whole nature of More's creation:

> They are very fond of fools. It is a great disgrace to treat them with insult, but there is no prohibition against deriving pleasure from their foolery. The latter, they think, is of the greatest benefit to the fools themselves. If anyone is so stern and morose that he is not amused with anything they either do or say, they do not entrust him with the care of a fool. They fear that he may not treat him with sufficient indulgence since he would find in him neither use nor even amusement, which is his sole faculty.

This is a key paragraph in *Utopia*—key in the sense that the flaws in the obvious level of interpretation provide a glimpse of a much different level extending underneath. The immediate effect of the paragraph—similar to the impact of Hythlodaeus' justifications of all other unusual Utopian practices, such as the viewing-in-the-nude—is one of such obvious good sense that the reader is not likely to note that the Utopians have again missed the point. They are "very fond" of fools, and the paragraph dwells on their concern that fools be looked after with kindness. How admirably humane! But why does Hythlodaeus cast this subject in terms of "use" and "amusement, which is his sole faculty?" More, we know, laughed at fools and treated them well. Surely he would not have mistreated them even if he was not amused by them, but the clear implication is that the Utopians might not treat them well if they did not find them worth laughing at. So fools are treated well *because* they are laughed at—not a very inspiring underpinning for the Utopians' renowned humane feelings.

This is not an isolated example. Criminals are put to work and adequately fed instead of being executed; this has always been one of Utopia's most admired features. Yet behind this are no promptings of gentleness or respect for the human individual. The slaves are treated harshly—kept "not only continually at work but also in chains" —and "if they rebel and kick against this treatment, they are thereupon put to death like untameable beasts." A pattern begins to emerge: persons are valued according to their usefulness, and if they have no use they have no value—hence criminals and fools are in equal danger.

It begins to appear, then, that Utopia is a society characterized by a deep preoccupation with functional values—a commitment to what in later times would be known as utilitarianism. "Usefulness" supersedes all other categories, as when the Utopians, who believe that "mercy, the finest feeling of our human nature, is gradually killed off" in those who slaughter food animals, nevertheless require slaves, who share the same human nature, to engage in this spiritually destructive activity. Similarly, these sober and equable people obviously do not go around laughing at each other—but fools should be laughed at because it is their only use. Notably lacking in both these cases is any principle—save usefulness.

Examined with the concept of functional values in mind, Utopia stands revealed as astonishingly consistent—no aspect of the people, their institutions or even their environment fails to contribute to maximum usefulness. The island itself is of a remarkably useful (and unlikely) configuration—a new-moon-like crescent with a narrow entrance into a huge open center, which is protected from the wind by the surrounding land and "lets ships cross in every direction to the great convenience of the inhabitants." This first paragraph of the Discourse is pervaded by an emphasis on usefulness which is never departed from thereafter.

There is no point in methodically reviewing the aspects of Utopia which express the commitment to functional values, since it would mean reviewing the Discourse in its entirety. Identical towns, daily schedules, uniform clothes, population balance, euthanasia, civic religion—it is difficult to find an aspect of Utopian life determined by anything *but* such values. The exclusive reliance on them frequently leads the Utopians to miss the point of human institutions or psychology; this was observed in regard to the viewing-in-the-nude and in fact permeates the whole Utopian attitude toward marriage and sex.

Everything about that attitude makes sense on the basis of marriage as a necessary social institution which must at all costs be made to produce the maximum of stability. The relationship between a man and a woman has no status of its own; it is simply factored into the requirements of the institution. The acceptability of divorce, unexpected though it is from More's pen, follows naturally if divorce is evaluated not as a moral matter but as a variable in the preeminent institution of marriage, which must be protected against excessive strains. It is the evident intention of the Utopians that the society's organization of marital affairs should be just as stable and efficient as its organization of economic affairs—everyone is to marry just as everyone is to work, with deprivation of sex or food the penalty for nonconformity.

The prevalence of functional values makes itself particularly felt in religion. "Who can doubt that he will strive either to evade by craft the public laws of his country or to break them by violence in order to serve his own private desires when he has nothing to fear but laws and no hope beyond the body?"—for this reason, rather than any theological conviction, the Utopians dogmatically insist upon belief in the immortality of the soul and the active role of divine providence in the universe. Similarly, Utopia's renowned religious toleration was instituted by King Utopos purely as a matter of civic convenience, explained by his shrewd observation "that the universal dissensions between the individual sects who were fighting for their country had given him the opportunity of overcoming them all."

Even the "enlightened" Utopian methods of waging war miss the point over and over. Admirers of *Utopia* have never been very happy about the Utopians' attitude toward their Zapoletan mercenaries, whom they unconcernedly send to their deaths because they think "they would be the greatest benefactors to the human race if they could relieve the world of all the dregs of this abominable and impious people." But the underlying utilitarian basis for this is even more revealing: "The Utopians, just as they seek good men to use them, so enlist these villains to abuse them." The Utopians revel in achieving victory "by strength of intellect," but the tactics they boast of are so utterly detached from considerations of morality that More's approval is out of the question.

One of the examples mentioned earlier does not fit so neatly into a framework of functional values, since the changing of houses every ten years does not directly produce any useful result. It serves such a result at one remove, however, since anything that works against the psychology of private property is a valuable social tool in Utopia, which, Hythlodaeus assures us, derives its essential nature from the institution of complete economic communism. Then what about this communism itself—is it any more to More than a functional value subject to whatever strictures *Utopia* implies about that entire philosophy?

More's personal attitude toward communism is obscured by the fact that it is impossible to say with certainty who is speaking for him in the Dialogue of Counsel and the Peroration. The character named More is skeptical in a lukewarm and conventional way, whereas Hythlodaeus is eloquent and impassioned in his denunciations of private property and praises for the effects of communism on Utopia. Since it would be strange indeed for More the author to give all the best lines in the debate over communism to the point of view he opposes, Hythlodaeus' long statements on the subject near the ends of both Books I and II seem intended to make the argument against private property a capstone to everything that has gone before. In view of all this, it is implausible to maintain that More personally opposed communism.

This leads to a further conclusion: if More believed deeply in communism, and Utopia is a society fully based on communism, Utopia must in its general lines represent an expression of More's ideal society. This is a logical conclusion but an unsatisfying one; too many of the "diversions" seem intended to disrupt the unfailingly upbeat portrayal of Utopia's flawless functioning, and what needs to be decided in addition to More's attitude toward communism is his attitude toward Utopia itself and the relationship between these two attitudes.

More's attitude toward the society he created has been variously defined, but all argument has started from a common assumption: that *Utopia* was indeed intended to portray "The Best State of a Commonwealth" (to quote from the title of Book II). It goes without saying that More's creation has much to recommend it to any civilized people at any time, and the delight his fellow humanists took in it is a matter of record. Whatever the deeper implications of the label of functional values, they do not affect the fact that a society run on that principle would deal with many matters in a far more advanced way than the philosophies guiding the European ruling classes of More's day. Yet there are too many Utopian practices which one cannot imagine earning the imprimatur of the humanist of Chelsea.

On the level of daily life, did More really prefer public dining halls for all, run very much like those in nineteenth century boarding schools? It is a mistake to read twentieth century tastes into sixteenth century life, but it is difficult to believe that the vibrant and delightful Chelsea household was run on such regimented lines. It is even harder to accept More as an advocate of using slaves to do the dirty kitchen work.

In the larger field of political and social institutions, Utopia is in some ways an undisguised tyranny. "To take counsel on matters of common interest outside the senate or the popular assembly is considered a capital offense," and "If any person gives himself leave to stray out of his territorial limits and is caught without the governor's certificate, he is treated with contempt, brought back as a runaway, and severely punished. A rash repetition of the offense entails the sentence of slavery"; and "The chief and almost only function of the syphogrants [low-level officials] is to manage and provide that no one sit idle," and, in fact, "being under the eyes of all, people are bound either to be performing the usual labor or to be enjoying their leisure in a fashion not without decency." All this is harsher and more rigid than most large-scale public arrangements familiar to More (except for monasteries, surely the last places in which he wanted to see functional values supreme), so it is likely to be an exaggeration—but for what purpose?

And then there is divorce and euthanasia. Surtz strives manfully to show that More might have been flexible enough about these subjects to approve of Utopian practices, but although the evidence (particularly from Erasmus) carries weight in the case of divorce, there is no getting around the Christian prohibition against euthanasia.

The question of euthanasia provides the clearest specific insight into the conflict between functional values as the guiding philosophy of Utopia and the Christian core of More's thought. The arguments used by Utopian priests and officials when urging suicide on suffering invalids are models of rationality and good sense—a person incurably afflicted is a burden to himself, a trouble to others, and ought no more hesitate to free himself from a tortured existence than from prison and the rack. But elsewhere in *Utopia*—in Book I, it should be noted—Hythlodaeus speaks for himself:

> God has said, "Thou shalt not kill".... But if the divine command against killing be held not to apply where human law justifies killing, what prevents men equally from arranging with one another how far rape, adultery, and perjury are admissable? [If men by mutual consent agree on exemptions from this commandment of God,] will not the law of God then be valid only so far as the law of man permits? The result will be that in the same way men will determine in everything how far it suits them that God's commandments should be obeyed.

These two attitudes are antithetical—which More brings out in even sharper relief through Hythlodaeus' further remark about suicide in Utopia:

> They do believe that death counseled by authority is honorific. But if anyone commits suicide without having obtained the approval of priests and senate, they deem him unworthy of either fire or earth and cast his body ignominiously into a marsh without proper burial.

What clearer illustration could there be of men determining "in everything how far it suits them that God's commandments should be obeyed?"

Since Hythlodaeus' own view in this matter is so opposed to the Utopian view, it needs to be decided which represents More the author rather than any character in the book. About this there can scarcely be any question. But if Utopia embodies a practice unacceptable to More on a profound moral level, it is certainly not his ideal society. In fact, it is *worse* than any society More knew in Europe, which for all its corruption and false gods nowhere sanctioned this particular violation of divine law.

More approves of communism, the backbone of the Utopian social order; he disapproves of the Utopian social order itself. It remains to decide what this approval and disapproval have to do with each other and with Utopia.

The essential nature of Utopia resides in its communism. If it were not communist, it would be an altogether different society. This does not prove the proposition that *because* a society is communist it must become like Utopia, but this, if it could be proved, would resolve the dilemma stated in the previous paragraph. If More felt that communism would in practice surely lead to Utopia, the book's message would be clear. But this conclusion is too important to rest solely on inference; there should be some internal evidence for it.

None of the points made thus far qualify as internal evidence except the contrast between the Utopian justification of euthanasia and Hythlodaeus' warning about the danger in human amendment of divine commandments. But that contrast is not revealed within the Discourse alone; it emerges only when an attractively rational and humane Utopian practice is reconsidered in the light of a statement made in quite another context in Book I. And Book I also contains a "diversion" which seems even more decisively intended to point up the true nature (in More's estimation) of the society described so seductively in Book II. Hythlodaeus is describing a civilized seafaring people south of the equator:

> Their mariners were skilled in adapting themselves to sea and weather. But he reported that he won their extraordinary favor by showing them the use of the magnetic needle of which they had hitherto been quite ignorant so that they had hesitated to trust themselves to the sea and had boldly done so in the summer alone. Now, trusting to the magnet, they do not fear wintry weather, being dangerously confident. Thus, there is a risk that what was thought likely to be a great benefit to them may, through their imprudence, cause them great mischief.

To paraphrase: an intelligent people enhanced their way of life by adopting a particularly useful innovation, but this very success encouraged them to plunge ahead into further enhancements which in actuality were beyond the capabilities of the innovation. As a result, it is likely to "cause them great mischief," or, to use Turner's translation, become "a source of disaster."

This "diversion," which is one of the earliest elements of *Utopia* in presumed order of composition as well as in the finished text, is not likely to be as casual as it seems. It makes no narrative or descriptive contribution whatsoever; in no way does it increase understanding of the Utopian way of life, and it lacks both the color to be an engaging bit of travel lore and the overt lesson to rank with Hythlodaeus' tales of the Polylerites, Achorians, and Macarians. It seems entirely at loose ends, the only item of its type in these introductory pages of Book I. But those few lines provide an abstract of the entire Discourse.

Just as the mariners Hythlodaeus describes would be better off in the long run without the magnetic compass in spite of its evident usefulness, so would the Utopians be better off without communism in spite of its functional advantages. The fault does not lie in communism any more than in the compass; on the contrary, it is the very effectiveness of these innovations that tempts men to apply them beyond their appropriate functions. The mariners extended their new mastery of navigation to winter sailing, which is dangerous for reasons other than those a magnetic compass can overcome; and the Utopians applied their new mastery of economic and social arrangements to aspects of their lives which reflect other values quite outside the criterion of "usefulness." "Overconfidence threatens to convert an apparently useful invention into a source of disaster," and Utopia, to More, *is* a disaster, not in spite of but *because* it is founded on what he freely recognizes to be a useful and, considered purely on its own merits, highly desirable social innovation.

That is why it is not paradoxical for More to approve of communism, the backbone of the Utopian social order, and disapprove of that order itself. Innovation in human affairs, no matter how beneficial, must be kept under tight rein lest the spirit of functional values run rampant. A profoundly conservative statement long before its time.

More has been credited with being ahead of his time in so many respects that perhaps it should not be altogether surprising to find him coming to a conclusion worthy of Burke well in advance of any identifiable school of "conservative" thought. On the other hand, the notion that *Utopia,* which provided the name for the whole genre of ideal societies, was actually conceived as a dystopia smacks of the overingenious. How can there be a family likeness between this puritanical and commonsensical society and, for example, *Brave New World*? Yet only by interpreting *Utopia* as a dystopian vision does it reveal the consistency one would expect from a mind such as More's.

If Utopia is a regimented society which incorporates slavery, divorce and euthanasia, and where professed concern with the finer feelings of humanity does not prevent military training on holy days, laughter at the mentally deficient and subjection of slaves to conditions degrading to human nature, it could not have been More's "Best State of a Commonwealth." Then why did he take the trouble to delineate it with such care? For the same reason as Huxley in *Brave New World* and Zamyatin in *We* —as a warning. For More, as it happens, no technological or ideological trimmings were necessary; with extraordinary skill, he expressed his deepest misgivings about the danger of functional values by depicting their manifestations in the uncomplicated institutions and beliefs of an intelligent and well-meaning people. In essentials, though, the three visions are similar, and *Utopia* should be read with the same mixture of wonderment and distaste as inspired by *Brave New World* and *We*—wonderment at the ingenuity and good intentions behind such a world and distaste for the stunted and regimented human spirit which makes it workable.

There can never be a "final word" on *Utopia*, written as it was by a man of deep complexity in an age which saw the world so differently than ours. But awkward facts must be confronted: the "diversions" have odd implications, there is much in Utopia of which More could not have approved, and the Utopians frequently miss the point about matters important to both Christians and humanists. Interpreters of *Utopia*, in turn, have missed the point that a "utopia" so marred could *not* have been intended at all as "a place or state of ideal perfection". (pp. 27-36)

Merritt Abrash, "Missing the Point in More's 'Utopia','" in Extrapolation, *Vol. 19, No. 1, December, 1977, pp. 27-38.*

LEE CULLEN KHANNA (essay date 1978)

[*In the following excerpt from a paper delivered at a quincentennial More conference held at Thomas More College in 1978, Khanna discusses the portrayal of women in More's English and Latin poetry.*]

Although Thomas More's influence on women's education has been recognized, women in his writings have been too long neglected. The images of women in More's Latin and English poems deserve special attention because they suggest the range of More's literary approaches to women, and because they can serve as a guide to both the seriousness and importance of these differing approaches.

In More's canon women play many parts. Wise queens, utopian priests, innkeepers, vicious wives, teachers, and temptresses are among those to amaze and amuse readers. More's attitude toward these actresses varies from admiring to patronizing, from courtly compliment to empathetic understanding. The sheer number of female characters, and anecdotes about women, testifies to his interest in women; and his modulations of tone suggest a complexity characteristic of the man.

Both the empathetic view of women and satiric attacks on their sex can be seen in the *Epigrammata.* Among the two hundred and fifty epigrams, about twenty mock women. Several of them are translations from the Greek Anthology that was More's primary source and so reflect traditional satire on female vanity, greed, and lust. One epigram, for example, treats the young woman who resisted her rapist until he drew his sword and threatened to leave her. "Terrified by so dire a threat she lay down at once and said, 'Go ahead, but it is an act of violence.'" Another, more typical, satirizes the unfaithful wife:

> My friend Aratus has a fruitful wife—yes, very fruitful wife. No doubt about it, for three times she has conceived children without any assistance from her husband.

In such epigrams More appeals to a stock response, adding only his pointed Latin phrasing to the ancient stereotypes. But these jokes aim only at a quick laugh and never seem to have fully engaged More's imagination. One can measure the difference in both the quality of the poetry and More's relative involvement in his subject by comparing the satiric epigrams to the longer original poems added to the 1520 edition of the *Epigrammata.* The work of More's maturity, two of these poems center on women and are elegant, subtle, and memorable.

The first is an apology to a "certain noble lady" whom More had unwittingly slighted. The fact that the slight was unwitting is an important point in the poem, and More stresses it by setting up polarities between himself and the lady. She had entered his house when he was conversing with a prominent cleric who was so eloquent that More never noticed the lady's arrival. His obtuseness becomes the immediate point of contrast with her. "My eyes," he says, "failed to observe even so brilliant a beauty as hers." The contrast is even more pointed in the Latin where the last word of each line balances the lady's "lumen" against More's "stupor." Looking back at the incident, More is horrified at the failure of his eyes *("O oculos")* which used to be able to spot a radiant girl even at a distance. He wonders whether his eyes are now dimmed through age, the workings of some evil spirit, or the power of the cleric's eloquence. He seems to settle on the latter explanation, for this "mighty prelate" has the power of Orpheus to charm wild beasts. Thus More labels himself a beast by implication, even as he condemned his blindness and stupidity before. The final self-accusation is his own speechlessness, for he failed to acknowledge the lady's presence *("Ut miserum est non posse loqui!")*. Certainly to be dumb at the wrong moment would have been barbarian *(barbaries)* for a humanist, trained in both the moral and aesthetic value of eloquence.

But the lady, although given no opportunity to speak, seems nevertheless to be graced with attributes respected by humanists. She is cultured *("matrona . . . cultu spectanda superbo")*, beautiful, and virtuous. When she enters the drawing room, she proceeds to examine "some choice coins of ancient beauty and, famous herself, enjoyed the famous portraits thereon." Like Budé, like More himself, she values and seems informed about classical coins. Indeed the use of the word *"cultu"* seems to bespeak education as much as elegance. She is cultivated where More is beastly, bright where he is obtuse, graceful and considerate where he is rude or even, he fears, "brutal." She is obviously able to appreciate the eloquence, the learned conversation so valued by humanists because More beseeches the eloquent prelate to apologize in his behalf, assuming of course that she will respond, as More himself did, to his "gift of charming speech."

One of the delights of this charming poem is the exquisite irony of its central opposition. For in the process of opposing his rude, silent, obtuse self to the cultured lady, More reveals his own graciousness, eloquence, and sensitivity. The poem is as elegant as the lady herself, and was perhaps intended for her perusal as well as that of the "mighty prelate." In fact, one of the greatest tributes this poem makes to the lady in question is not finally the courtly elevation of the beautiful woman, but the implicit suggestion that the cleric, the speaker, and the lady are in some sense equals. They may not speak the same language literally ("I have no command of French [my lady speaks only her native French.]") but they share the humanist values of virtue, knowledge of the classics (as the coins suggest), and eloquence. It is the latter, in fact, that is both the "object and the wit" of this deceptively slight poem.

This stylistic grace, or *sprezzatura*, also distinguishes another occasional poem added to the 1520 edition, **"He Expresses Joy at Finding . . . Her Whom He Had Loved as a Mere Boy."** It too is inspired by a woman and is a graceful recollection of youthful infatuation, prompted by a chance meeting many years later. Proust's taste of the madeleine opened a vaster floodgate of memory, but, given the relative brevity of More's poem, its subtlety and delicacy of feeling is hardly less effective. In contrast to the "noble lady" epigram where More did not see the Frenchwoman, the speaker here begins by exclaiming that Elizabeth is "restored to his sight." Indeed the entire poem is about seeing, the various ways of seeing prompted by this woman. "When I was just a boy," the speaker exclaims, "I saw you first: now on the threshold of old age, I see you

again." The two kinds of vision are juxtaposed throughout the poem: the remarkably vivid vision of the beautiful young girl, seen through the eyes of a smitten boy, and the mature vision of a man meditating on the fleeting quality of beauty, the strange twists of destiny.

The mature, realistic vision comes first in the poem. Once, he says, "your face inspired me with innocent devotion." But now, he insists with a startling realism:

> that face is no part of your appearance; where has it gone? When the vision I once loved comes before me, I see, alas, how utterly your actual appearance fails to resemble it. The years, always envious of young beauty, have robbed you of yourself. . . .

The careful courtesy that marked the tribute to the French lady has disappeared. But the very harshness of this confrontation with aging seems to free the speaker for the fullness of memory which follows. Although the lady has been robbed of herself, the speaker has not lost her. "That beauty of countenance," he continues,

> to which my eyes so often clung now occupies my heart. . . . There comes now to my mind that distant day which first revealed you to me as you played amid a group of girls; this was a time when your yellow hair enhanced the pure white of your neck; your lips by contrast with your face were like roses in the snow; your eyes, like stars, held my eyes fast and through them made their way into my heart: I was helpless, as though stunned by a lightningstroke, when I gazed and continued to gaze upon your face.

This romantic scene is unusual in More's canon, as is his use of Petrarchan imagery. Although such imagery becomes all too familiar in later English sonnets, its handling here is startling and effective.

Throughout the poem the emphasis falls on two isolated moments in time—"that distant day" of the Petrarchan vision, and "that notable day" that brings them together after so many years. The joy of the second finally seems to equal the joy of the first, and the two are deliberately confused by the end of the poem. The speaker says, "Our love was blameless; if duty could not keep it so, that day itself *(ipsa dies)* would be enough to keep love blameless still." Does *"ipsa dies"* refer to the original vision or to the meeting that occasioned the poem? The ambiguity is, I believe, deliberate.

The merging of the two days eliminates the unessential to reveal the enduring. Although the speaker confronts the changes wrought by time, his imagination can recreate, and thus perpetuate, the dream of first love. It is ultimately the enduring vision of the heart he celebrates ("That beauty of countenance to which my eyes so often clung now occupies my heart")".

The speaker closes with a hearty good wish for another meeting twenty-five years hence. But in the spirit of the poem it is as much a promise as a fitting farewell, because their innocent love, intensely experienced, has achieved a kind of perpetuity through the power of More's art. The ambiguous *"ipsa dies"* comes close to the emotional triumph over time realized near the end of Shakespeare's sonnets.

The feminine presence in this poem is clearly a positive, even an inspirational one. It is perhaps as romantic as anything in More's work. But we learn little about Elizabeth apart from her Laura-like beauty and its lasting effect.

Another epigram, **"To Candidus: How to Choose A Wife,"** is more informative. Although it has none of the warmth or elusive charm of the recollection of first love, its didacticism affords a clearer view of More's respect for women. In fact, this poem, one of the most popular and, hopefully, most influential of More's epigrams, praises the intellectual and outspoken woman. The heart of the speaker's recommendation to Candidus deals with the value of a learned wife. In fact, forms of the verb to teach *(doceo)* ring through its central lines culminating in the image of Candidus leaving the company of men to return home to his learned wife *("doctaeque coniugis")*. In effect, More applies to a woman his own most dearly held humanist values. Like his friends Colet, Erasmus, and Vives, More believed in the moral and rhetorical value of studying the "oldest and best books" (the best Greek and Latin texts.) But even Colet's school, St. Paul's, did not admit women. In contrast, Thomas More's school at Chelsea did, and, perhaps even more importantly, so did his art.

"Let her be either educated or capable of being educated" *(Instructa literis/Vel talis ut modo/Sit apta literis)*, the speaker exclaims after describing the desirable modesty of the ideal woman's behavior. The value of such education is the sound judgment it confers:

> Happy is the woman whose education permits her to derive from the best of ancient works the principles which confer a blessing on life. Armed with this learning, she would not yield to pride in prosperity, nor to grief in distress—even though misfortune strike her down ... If she is well instructed herself, then some day she will teach your little grandsons, at an early age, to read.... By her comments she would restrain you if ever vain success should exalt you or speechless grief should cast you down. When she speaks, it will be difficult to judge between her extraordinary ability to say what she thinks and her thoughtful understanding of all kinds of affairs.

In this passage one clearly sees More's belief that learning fosters wisdom and eloquence. The "extraordinary ability to say what one thinks and thoughtful understanding of all kinds of affairs" *(summa eloquentia/Iam cum omnium graui/Rerum scientia)* are the goals of humanist education in the Renaissance. But More's application of this new faith in education to a woman is unusual.

It is important to recognize the centrality of humanist values in the poem. Even before the passage on learning, More emphasizes "virtue" as the major attribute of the ideal woman. The speaker urges Candidus to be guided by reason in the selection of a wife, and so dismiss such mundane attractions as beauty and money in favor of "virtutis inclytae" (renowed virtue). The standard translation of "chastity" is misleading here, I think, because it does not include the intellectual, moral, and rhetorical strengths of the woman so important to More's description. Although the speaker goes on to describe the sweetness *("dulcis")*, serenity *("serenitas")*, and modest restraint of her behavior, these traits have less to do with chastity than with the *"modestia"* that is appropriate humility, good, judgment, and moderation in all things. In her speech for example, there should be neither "pointless garrulity" nor "boorish

taciturnity." Surely this golden mean would be desirable for man or woman.

At the end of the poem the speaker returns to the notion of "virtue" once again as the essence of the ideal woman's desirability. The Latin is *"virtutis indole,"* and is repeated twice in the closing lines, again in contrast to beauty and money. [Here Leicester Bradner and Charles Arthur Lynch, in their *Latin Epigrams of Thomas More* (1953),] choose, more accurately I believe, the translation "inborn gift of virtue."

> If nature has denied the gift of beauty to a girl ... if she has this inborn gift of virtue, she would be in my eyes fairer than the swan. If elusive fortune has denied her a dowry ... if she has this inborn gift of virtue, she would be in my eyes richer, Croesus, than you.

Although More's poem is cast in the framework of an appeal to the prospective husband, the virtue he describes goes far beyond chastity. The detailed central passages on education and its effects, and the language chosen *(virtus/scientia/eloquentia)*, demand a broader interpretation of virtue in a woman. Indeed it goes well beyond feminine stereotypes insofar as it incorporates learning and eloquence. Because these attributes apply equally to man or woman this poem clearly demonstrates More's respect for the female mind, a respect unusual for the time.

Although the three Latin poems discussed here are different from one another in style and tone, they are alike in being among the best poems in the *Epigrammata*. They are alike also in presenting positive images of women. There is a similar connection to be noticed when one turns to the English poems.

Among the relatively few English verses, one stands out as exceptionally effective. **"A Ruful Lamentacion,"** an elegy in rhyme royal occasioned by the death of Elizabeth of York (1503), is spoken by Elizabeth herself. She reflects on her untimely death and bids farewell to her family. Such elegies were typically based on a *contemptus mundi* theme, but More's poem is unique, as Frederic Tromly has shown, in its sympathy for the speaker. In fact the elegiac genre is modified, because a sensitive and eloquent woman talks. In this poem a woman is not just the occasion for compliment or meditation, but becomes a model of wisdom.

In the fullness of her character and relationships, however, she goes beyond the ideal but abstract wife of Candidus. We can identify with Elizabeth in her tenderness towards her children as she remembers each in turn. We are moved by her obvious pain at the necessary parting with them, and the many others she still cares for —her husband, her sisters, her subjects. Her solicitude puts her well beyond earlier speakers in the elegiac tradition who were merely sinners bemoaning their own vice and pride. Elizabeth leaves her family reluctantly, but comes to accept the truth of her own mortality, and acquires the wisdom to turn her address to God. She is not a figure to be condemned by the reader for her folly, but to be embraced for her humanity and, finally, her wisdom.

It is especially significant that Thomas More creates a female figure for whom the reader feels such empathy, that he casts his finest English verse in the voice of a female speaker, that through a woman he moves the English elegy from the condemnation of vice to the admiration of virtue.

Modern readers might still ask, however, if Elizabeth is not yet another stereotype. So clearly seen in relation to her husband and children, is she simply the traditional ideal of the chaste good wife? I think not. Although one could hardly doubt Elizabeth of York's chastity, More does not mention it. She is surely the good wife and mother, but her domestic affections do not encompass her. She is a woman of authority and position, and her "wit" as well as her wealth is mentioned in the poem.

The reader sees evidence of wisdom in her ability to properly evaluate the things of this world. She moves quickly from a reliance on her royal blood and enthusiasm over her husband's "castles and towers" to a recognition of other kinds of "edification." In the sixth stanza she exclaims "that costly worke of yours, Myne owne dere lorde, now shall I never see." But the self pity is transformed as she continues to speak to Henry:

> Almighty god vouchsafe to graunt that ye,
> For you and your children well may edefy.
> My palace bylded is, and lo now here I ly.

Her growing insight can almost be traced in these lines as Elizabeth moves beyond worldly claims. Both mundane and spiritual values are included in her witty pun on "edefy." Whereas formerly she had been content with Henry's magnificent buildings, Elizabeth suggests a new kind of edification with the stress on "well" and "edefy" in the second line. Surely she hopes for the intellectual and moral edification of her family here. The fact that her "palace" is now her tomb underscores the need for a new kind of edification. (Modern readers might remember the vanity of building in stone in Shelley's "Ozymandias.")

Finally, there is particular poignancy in her reference to her children. As the embodiment of the ideal wife, Elizabeth was probably moral teacher as well as mother. In hoping that Henry will take up this important task, she demonstrates her continued concern for them, here as elsewhere in the poem. These few lines illustrate the warmth and intelligence of the queen, and the fine play of her mind seen throughout the poem.

Her understanding of the irony of life's unpredictability is visible again in her farewell to her daughter, Margaret. She recalls her dread of Margaret's departure to Scotland after her impending marriage to James IV:

> Now as I gone, and have left you behynde.
> O mortall folke that we be very blynde.
> That we least feare, full oft it is most nye,
> From you depart I fyrst, and lo now here I lye.

Further irony, wisdom, and eloquence are apparent in the final stanza of the poem:

> Adew my lordes, adew my ladies all,
> Adew my faithfull servauntes every chone,
> Adew my commons whom I never shall,
> See in this world, wherefore to the alone,
> Immortal god verely three and one,
> I me commende, thy infinite mercy,
> Shew to thy servant, for lo now here I ly.

In this stanza she turns her attention from members of her court, to her servants, to her people (the commons), and then to God. The movement reflects her painfully acquired wisdom, for she bids farewell to her servants in order to recognize her true role as God's servant. The earlier references to "servants" becomes ironic in terms of the final line, and again reinforces the discrepancy between worldly and spiritual values, the recognition of which constitutes true wisdom. It is not "only a woman's" wisdom here, for it represents Thomas More's interpretation of what wisdom was—for man or woman.

Elizabeth's wisdom and human affection are beautifully expressed throughout the poem. Each stanza gives evidence of her careful choice of words, her sense of irony, her economy of expression. In fact, she embodies the humanist values of eloquence and virtue described abstractly in "Candidus." She is also similar to More's portrayal of her mother, Elizabeth Woodville, in *Richard III*. She joins these other Morean portraits of women in representing the best of Renaissance humanism. As she moves from amazement at her fate, to bitterness, to profound affection for her family, to acceptance of her mortality, she achieves a living voice. She is admirable, yet vulnerable and wonderfully human.

In "**A Ruful Lamentacion**," as in the three Latin poems, More's imaginative energies seem to have been most fully and effectively engaged when he treated women positively. Just as readers of *Richard III* will long remember Shore's wife and the biting wit of Queen Elizabeth Woodville, readers of More's poetry are likely to be most moved by his memory of his lost love, his eloquently witty compliment of the French lady, his strikingly humanistic view of the ideal wife, and his sensitive and eloquent portrait of Elizabeth of York. On the other hand, More's satiric remarks about women, although often amusing, are, like the twenty short epigrams mentioned earlier, nearly always forgettable.

Of course it would be surprising if attitudes towards women in More's art were not as complex, richly varied, occasionally even as contradictory as attitudes towards other important subjects. Evaluating the multiple shifts in tone of this master of jest and earnest is no easy task. But I hope to have shown here that some of More's finest work begins in an appreciation of women as intelligent and sensitive persons, and ends in moving and memorable art. (pp. 78-88)

> *Lee Cullen Khanna, "Images of Women in Thomas More's Poetry," in* Quincentennial Essays on St. Thomas More: Selected Papers from the Thomas More College Conference, *edited by Michael J. Moor, Albion, 1978, pp. 78-88.*

JUDITH P. JONES (essay date 1979)

[*Jones is an American essayist, poet, and critic. In the following excerpt, she discusses the origin and intent of a selection of More's humanist writings.*]

Thomas More's period of greatest literary achievement comes early in his life (ca. 1501-1520) and mirrors his political as well as his humanistic interests. The earliest extant works include a few English poems, a selection of Latin epigrams, many of them translations from the Greek, a Latin translation of some dialogues of the Greek satirist Lucian, and a translation into English of the Latin *Life of*

John Picus, Earl of Mirandula. With the exception of some of the epigrams all were finished before the end of 1506. By 1518, More had published his humanist masterpiece, *Utopia,* and written his *History of Richard III.* Also during this period he wrote to his family and to fellow humanists a series of letters which for both literary and historical reasons are among the most important epistolary documents of the Renaissance. In 1522, he began the *Four Last Things*, a treatise on death which seems strangely out of place during this time of great personal and political success.

The most nearly contemporaneous collection we have of More's earliest writings is the 1557 edition which his nephew, William Rastell, begins with sixteen pages of verse which he says More wrote in his youth for his pastime. They include: **"A meri iest how a sergeant would learne to playe the frere,"** nine verses for some tapestries in the More home, a poem commemorating the death of Henry VII's wife, Queen Elizabeth, and some verses to be used in a preface to the *Book of Fortune.* In the poems we see Thomas More beginning at an early age to write good poetry, and although the English poems are less interesting than the Latin epigrams, they give us insights into More's early literary and philosophical concerns. We see him already a competent poet, writing in the vernacular about the events of his world. The poems reveal his inherent talent for dramatic and humorous narrative as well as his early preoccupation with the transience of life and fortune. The **"Lamentation for the Queen"** has special biographical significance because it describes the royal family which was to play such an important role in the author's life. But it is to the epigrams written over a number of years but not published until 1518 that we must turn for More's first substantial literary effort.

In March of 1518 the third edition of the *Utopia* appeared together with a selection of Latin epigrams by Thomas More, William Lily, and Erasmus. The book was popular enough to be reprinted in December of the same year. In December 1520, More's *Epigrammata* were published separately with significant authorial corrections and revisions. We cannot date all of the epigrams exactly. Although traditionally historians have followed Erasmus, who said that More wrote most of them "when he was still a boy," recent scholarship dates many of the poems between 1509 and 1519, placing them in the period of More's early literary productivity but not exactly in his first youth; he would have been in his thirties at this time. (pp. 32-3)

More's *Epigrammata* begin with the **"Progymnasmata,"** a collection of eighteen epigrams translated by both William Lily and Thomas More from the *Greek Anthology.* Lily, More's friend and fellow scholar, was to become the first High Master of St. Paul's school. The **"Progymnasmata"** give the Greek, followed by More's and Lily's Latin translations. A number of the other epigrams are also from this well-known anthology; still others are translations or adaptations from Diogenes Laertius, Aristotle, Arsenius, and Martial. Two are renditions of English songs. But this account of More's sources still leaves over 150 poems that may be considered original.

The eighteen poems of the **"Progymnasmata"** are our earliest substantial indication of the ideas and problems that were to occupy More for a lifetime. They, like some of the

early English poems, reflect the writer's acute awareness of the unpredictability of fortune and the omnipresent possibility of death: "Now I have reached port; Hope and Luck, farewell. You have nothing to do with me. Now make sport of others"; "Just as surely as I came on earth naked, so surely naked shall I quit it. Why do I struggle in vain, knowing as I do that death is naked?"

Following the **"Progymnasmata"** is a collection of 253 poems by More. It begins with five poems commemorating the marriage and accession of Henry VIII, only three of which may properly be called epigrams. The first of the Henry poems, a long ode on the coronation, is an expression of the humanist's optimistic, perhaps naive, belief that the young king, "whose natural gifts have been enhanced by a liberal education," will bring to Christendom a golden age of learning and peace. From the perspective of the future we are struck by the irony of the lines that describe the wisdom, justice, and moral perfection of the man who was to behead their writer and end the short, scholarly Renaissance in England. Yet More is already aware of the dangers inherent in power and may be warning Henry when he says: "Unlimited power has a tendency to weaken good minds, and that even in the case of very gifted men". But the third poem insists again that Henry's reign ushers in a new Golden Age. The last of the epigrams for Henry VIII is the famous celebration of the union in Henry of the houses of York and Lancaster. Here More develops a conceit in which the two roses, symbolizing the two houses, combine to produce the best qualities of both lines in one flower, the Tudor king.

But it must have been the large number of earthy, dramatic epigrams that caused the immediate popularity of the *Epigrammata.* The poems, which abound with examples of More's genius for making satire, morality, and humor out of everyday events, range from the devotional to the satirical and treat an array of subjects including kingship, government, death, fortune, the clergy, and women. More satirizes drunkards, doctors, spendthrifts, misers, and courtiers.

The emphasis on rulership in the *Epigrammata* points to a concern that pervades More's writing and comes to life in his tragic relationship with Henry VIII. The poems on kingship vividly portray both good rulers and tyrants (no. 14, no. 21, no. 62, no. 91-94, no. 96, no. 97, no. 102, no. 103, no. 182, no. 185, no. 210, no. 211, no. 222). They create an image of the just king who is like a good father to his children or the wise head to the other parts of the body. They define pride and cruelty as the most dangerous qualities in rulers. Epigram 97 is More's most succinct portrayal of the two types of kings:

> What is a good king? He is a watchdog, guardian of the flock. By his barking he keeps the wolves from the sheep. What is the bad king? He is the wolf.

Frequently the ruler is reminded that he, like other men, is governed by the laws of nature: he will suffer sleeplessness from guilt; unless he is just and wise, he will be in great danger; sleep and death render all alike, helpless. Furthermore, a number of the epigrams suggest that the writer had considered the advantages of republican government over monarchy. One says that the king will be safe only so long as he rules in the interest of his subjects (no. 102) and another that he should rule only so long as his subjects wish it (no. 103). Epigram no. 182 is a long consideration of whether a king or a senate governs best. More concludes that bad government is equally bad in both cases but that, if both are good, republican rule is preferable to monarchy because senators can influence one another and because they will be chosen by reason rather than by the chance of royal birth. And senators, unlike kings, are directly responsible to those who elect them.

The attitude toward death expressed in the epigrams is one which remains constant throughout More's life. The poems dealing with death (no. 22, no. 27, no. 28, no. 37, no. 38, no. 52, no. 57, no. 61, no. 62, no. 101, no. 159, no. 243) are dominated be several themes—that death is the great equalizer, coming to kings, slaves, and peasants alike; that it frees all from suffering; that it is foolish to value either good fortune or long life since death wipes everything out in an instant. Furthermore, it is foolish to fear death since it is inevitable but, unlike the misfortunes of life, comes only once and brings lasting peace. Epigram no. 101 suggests the analogy More establishes in the *Dialogue of Comfort* where he compares life to a prison in which we dwell under a death penalty that can be enforced at any moment: "We are all shut up in the prison of this world under sentence of death. In this prison none escapes death."

Another group of poems in the *Epigrammata* requires consideration for historical and biographical as well as literary reasons. These epigrams are the product of a controversy that developed between the French poet Germanus Brixius (or Germain de Brie) and Thomas More. The dispute began with a sea battle which took place on August 10, 1512, between the English ship *Regent* and the French *Cordelèire*. In the midst of the fighting, the *Cordelèire* exploded, causing the destruction of both ships and the drowning of many men, among them the captain of the French vessel, Herve Porzmoguer. The next year, Brixius published an epic poem, *Herveus*, celebrating the battle and romanticizing Porzmoguer's conduct. Thomas More, who resented both the slurs on English honor and the extravagant praise of the French, responded with a collection of epigrams for private circulation. When, a few years later, More published the *Epigrammata*, he considered withholding the controversial epigrams out of respect for the now peaceful relationship between England and France. Although More wrote to Erasmus, who was handling the publication of the poems, and asked him to consider excising the epigrams against Brixius, nine of them appeared in the first edition. The poems attack Brixius's style as well as his biased version of the events. The following year, Brixius replied with the Latin poem *Antimorus*, in which he accuses More of writing fantastic poetry marred by bad Latinity and verse. And, more seriously, he suggests that his opponent had insulted the memory of Henry VII in the poem celebrating the accession of Henry VIII; the poem had of course been written years earlier but was not published until 1518. More perpetuated the debate in his *Epistle to Germanus Brixius* and in the 1520 edition of the *Epigrammata*, which included additional poems against the French writer. Interestingly, however, when More reissued the epigrams, he corrected some of his Latin in accordance with Brixius's criticism. Erasmus's letters indicate that he was finally able to reconcile the two humanists, and that they may even have met.

In the *Epigrammata*, we see foreshadowed many facets of Thomas More's literary future. Already he is a humanist scholar of Greek and Latin, a fiction writer, a satirist, and a polemicist. (pp. 33-6)

As with the *Epigrammata*, it is difficult to give an exact date to More's translation of John Francis's biography of his uncle Giovanni Pico della Mirandula, the renowned Italian Neoplatonist whose broad learning encompassed not only Latin literature and theology but Hebrew and Greek as well—and even included studies in the mysticism of the Jewish Cabala. John Picus, as More calls him, was a devout and scholarly fifteenth-century humanist who, like More, remained a layman despite inclinations toward monastic life. Picus's story would naturally have interested More because it reflected the same conflicts between the religious life, public service, and scholarship that must have dominated this period of his own life. But the influence of Picus on More was intellectual as well as personal; and, no doubt, a great deal of the Platonic influence in More comes through his study of Picus. (p. 40)

The Life of John Picus was a New Year's gift from More to Joyeuce Leigh, a childhood friend who had become a nun in the convent of Poor Clares near London. The dedicatory letter explains that More chose the book because the life and works of Picus teach the Christian virtues of temperance, patience, and humility. In addition to a translation of John Francis's short biography, the book includes selections from the writings of Picus.

The *Life* briefly recounts the career of the wealthy and brilliant Italian humanist, emphasizing his early spirituality and learning. Picus was educated in the laws of the Church but devoted much of his early study to philosophy, science, and theology. By the time he was twenty-three, he had composed a set of 900 theses which constituted something of a compendium of the knowledge of his day, treating subjects in theology, mathematics, astrology, magic, and philosophy. Picus made plans to present his theses at Rome and dispute them with the outstanding scholars of Europe. But Pope Innocent VIII prevented the disputation and appointed a commission to study the controversial theses, some of which were declared heretical or suspect. Picus's defense, the *Apologia*, brought even greater disfavor; papal censures remained until 1493, just one year before his death. (pp. 41-2)

The comments in the dedicatory letter to Joyeuce Leigh considered along with the kinds of changes More makes in translating indicate that he saw in Picus a spiritual example for himself and his reader. The *Life*, as More translates it, derives from several genres of medieval devotional writing. That the book is written in the vernacular for a nun places it in a long tradition of literature composed in English for cloistered women; such instructional and devotional handbooks were very popular throughout the Middle Ages and, according to R. W. Chambers [in *On the Continuity of English Prose from Alfred to More and His School* (1932)], became the means by which English prose style survived the Norman Conquest. The *Life* also shows the influence of the saintly biography, a type which presents the miraculous and holy events in the life of a saint as an inspiring example to the reader. In her [1971 University of Miami dissertation on] the *Life*, Margaret Esmonde says that, though More was, "on the whole, a faithful and literal translator, his omissions and additions have

Title page of More's first substantial literary work, The Lyfe of
Johan Picus *(1510).*

the cumulative effect of trimming Gianfrancesco's adulatory biography down to the concepts he had imbibed in his reading of the vernacular lives of the saints.... More has as his goal not a detailed account of the life and activities of an outstanding individual of the Italian Renaissance but a record of a contemporary example of virtuous living." ... More alters John Francis's account in a way that emphasizes the hero's orthodoxy, spirituality, and virtue. Still, More's choice of a humanist scholar rather than a saint expands the possibilities for Renaissance biography and prefigures the moral and dramatic complexity of his *History of Richard III*, a fragmentary work which is nevertheless one of the first modern historical biographies in English. Finally, and again like *Richard*, the *Life* derives from the literary tradition of the "fall of princes," another genre which functions as an exemplum. The medieval "fall of princes" stresses the fickleness of fortune and the inevitable fall of proud, cruel, and immoral men. The *Life*, however, substantially alters the convention by allowing Picus to transcend the traditionally destructive flaws through spiritual rebirth. Clearly, More is moving toward a kind of biography different from what he found in his models. (p. 43)

The years between 1510 and 1518 were busy ones for Thomas More, both politically and intellectually. Beginning in 1510, he was serving as under-sheriff of London; in 1515 he went to Flanders as royal ambassador; in 1517 he was ambassador to Calais, and by 1518 he had become a member of the King's Council. Nevertheless, he found time between 1513 and 1518 to write two of the masterpieces of English Renaissance humanism, the *Utopia* and the *History of Richard III.* Unlike the *Utopia*, there are many textual and historical problems connected with the *Richard*: it was not published until after More's death; its authorship has been questioned; there are two versions, a Latin and an English one, both unfinished. These facts pose complicated problems for scholars of literature and history.

To begin with the problem of authorship, both internal and external evidence indicate that the book was written between 1514 and 1518 by Thomas More. The earliest authoritative text of the *Richard* in English is Rastell's 1557 edition. The introduction states that this text is from the holograph which More wrote in about 1513 and left unfinished. Rastell also acknowledges More's authorship of the Latin version by incorporating translations of parts of it into his English text. The earliest authoritative text of the Latin *Richard* did not appear until the 1565-66 Louvain edition of More's complete works in Latin. Although the 1557 book is the first authoritative copy in English, manuscript sources were included in Chronicle accounts in 1543, 1548, and 1550; the later two were acknowledged to be from More's text. There seems to be little doubt that his contemporaries attributed the *Richard* to More.

But why More wrote two versions and failed to finish either of them continues to puzzle scholars. The extant Latin and English texts are not exact copies of each other; and the Latin version ends immediately after Richard's coronation, thereby omitting important events of the English account. The Latin *Richard*, which was probably intended for an educated foreign audience, omits some details of the English book, but adds descriptions necessary to the understanding of the non-English reader. Richard S. Sylvester thinks that More wrote the two *Richards*, as he did most of his works, in segments which he later rearranged and refined. He suggests that More may have abandoned his ambitious humanistic project because some of the events of Richard's life were still too politically sensitive for literary consideration.

The problem of the accuracy of More's record and interpretation of King Richard III's life continues to plague historians. More's version became so much a part of the history, legend, and drama of the sixteenth and seventeenth centuries that it is still difficult, if not impossible, to separate what More said from what may or may not have happened. (pp. 46-8)

More's tale projects the Tudor image of Richard III as a deformed monster who usurped the throne by maligning and murdering his own kin. Because it was so early incorporated into the Chronicles of English history and then became the basis for Shakespeare's *Richard III*, More's account has been largely responsible for King Richard's historical reputation. Yet, since the beginning of the seventeenth century, historians have tried to clear Richard of the sixteenth-century charges. And modern historians have brought forth substantial evidence that he was an effective ruler and a loving family man forced to the throne by the instability of the times and by the doubtful legitimacy of his nephews. Furthermore, there is evidence that Edward's sons did not die during Richard's reign and may in fact have been put to death by his successor, Henry VII. (p. 48)

The most important consideration here, however, is the *History of Richard III* as literature, for in it we see clearly for the first time More's genius for telling a story and creating dialogue. R. W. Chambers says that it begins modern historical writing of distinction because it moves away from the dull recording of events toward interpretation and dramatization. Actually, what More creates is indeed more like drama or fiction than history. The book has been seen as a milestone in the development of biography, drama, and history; it may be most accurate to call it our first historical novel. The *Richard* is a series of character studies which More creates by applying his unique dramatic and narrative talents to medieval conventions of biography and history. (pp. 49-50)

By his masterful handling of rhetoric and dramatic circumstance, Thomas More combines the traditions of medieval biography with those of classical tragedy to create a personality that history and literature have been unable to forget. Both Richard S. Sylvester and Robert E. Reiter see in More's *Richard* a reversal of the traditional tendency to eulogize historic heroes. According to Reiter [in his 1970 *Moreana* essay "On the Genre of Thomas More's *Richard III*"], More takes the conventions of the popular saint's life and reverses them in order to depict Richard as the personification of evil. In doing this, he merges form and content to make the book an "inverted panegyric," "a work that expresses in words the eminence of a man's bad qualities." Upon this context, which depicts the protagonist as innately evil, More imposes the complex figure of the tragically powerful man who brings about his own destruction. The effect of the combination of genres is equivocal; Richard, whom More has introduced as courageous and intelligent but born malicious and ugly, changes from a shrewd strategist into a buffoon, and, finally, into a madman capable of killing his brother's children and maligning his own mother. Ultimately, he is destroyed not by his inherently evil nature but by guilt, the strength of which implies that he might have been otherwise. The outcome is ironic as Richard turns his Olympian malice upon himself. By portraying Richard III as a deformed monster and at the same time making him responsible for his fate, More raises the complicated questions of destiny and free will; and in doing so, he places his story in the tradition that links Shakespeare with the classical drama.

But More's talent for dramatic characterization is not limited to his protagonist. There are also brilliant portraits of the Duke of Buckingham, Lord Hastings, Queen Elizabeth, and Jane Shore. Although he is presented as more human than Richard, Buckingham turns out to be almost as ruthless and deceptive. We are told in the beginning that he is honorable and powerful, but he hates the queen and is unremittingly cruel in his opposition to her. He denounces her use of sanctuary in a speech which shows him to be calculating, shrewd, and logical. As Leonard Dean points out [in his 1943 *PMLA* article "Literary Problems in More's *Richard III*"], one of More's most effective techniques of characterization is irony: "This is More's practice; his characters condemn themselves, and we seem to form our own judgment of them. The irony in this method springs, of course, from the disparity between the characters' apparent opinion of themselves and our opinion of them." Thus, Buckingham characterizes himself as

he speaks. In his portrayal of the duke, More is ambivalent as well as ironic. His description of Buckingham's collaboration with Richard elicits sympathy by suggesting that Richard has frightened the duke into cooperating with him. Immediately, however, More dilutes that opinion with a vivid depiction of Buckingham's pragmatic acceptance of his role: "And therefore to thys wicked enterprise, which he beleued coulde not bee voided, hee bent himselfe and went through: and determined, that since the comon mischief could not be amended, he wold tourne it as much as he might to hys owne commodite." Subsequently, the duke enters into the game with such gusto that it becomes increasingly difficult to credit the rumor of his reluctance; he delivers his persuasive speech at the guildhall and participates with complete control in the scene in which he and the lords beg Richard to accept the crown. When Buckingham turns against Richard, More suggests that the betrayal may be explained by Richard's manner of refusing him the reward he requested: "Which so wounded his hert wt hatred & mistrust, that he neuer after could endure to loke a right on king Richard." Here the duke is the loyal supporter, rebuffed and hurt, but immediately we learn that some wise observers doubted this account, knowing that two such evil dissemblers could only survive so long as they remained loyal to one another. Ultimately, More seems to attribute Buckingham's abandonment of Richard to vanity and envy and supposes that the duke pretended loyalty while planning a revolution. The English version of the *History of Richard III* ends with the promise of a conspiracy, "or rather good confederacion," between John Morton and Buckingham and leaves the complexities of the duke's character unresolved. Like Richard, Buckingham is vain, haughty, and dissembling; still we are left with the impression that if this man of great honor, power, and emotion had been better treated, he might have been better behaved.

Like Buckingham, Richard's other follower, Lord Hastings, is powerful and noble, and he despises the queen. But the narrative shows him to be both less powerful and less malicious than Buckingham. Although he hates the queen, Hastings does not realize that his actions will harm her children; this kind of personal and political naïveté is his outstanding characteristic and the cause of his downfall. Richard uses Hastings's reputation for devotion to King Edward to camouflage his own actions and then invents an excuse for executing his ally. The scene in which Richard tricks Hastings into betraying himself accentuates the Lord Chamberlain's profound impercipience; Hastings thinks he can be bold with Richard because of the love between them. More dramatizes Hastings's tragic ignorance of the ways of men and nature in the account of his refusal to heed the ill omens that precede his death. More seems to be speaking for himself when he says: "Thus ended this honorable man, a good knight and a gentle, of gret aucthorite wᵗ his prince, of liuing somewhat dessolate, plaine & open to his enemy, & secret to his frend: eth to begile, as he that of good hart & corage forestudied no perilles. A louing man & passing wel beloued. Very faithful, & trusty ynough, trusting to much."

The *Richard* includes two vivid portraits of women. Queen Elizabeth and Edward IV's former mistress, Jane Shore, are sharply delineated foils to the conniving Richard and his cohorts. With the exception of Richard himself, the queen is the most carefully drawn character in the book. More describes her as the center of political intrigue during her husband's reign, showing both her strength and her vulnerability as she is stripped of all maternal and political privileges. His talent for dramatic setting is nowhere more apparent than in the description of the queen seated "desolate and dismayed" among her possessions, preparing to move herself and her younger son to Church sanctuary because she suspects that she and her children are doomed. Although overcome with grief, the queen is too realistic to be lulled by the Archbishop of York's assurance that everything will be all right. This scene emphasizes the queen's isolation and impotence; the only strength she has left is the strength of her own will, which, although it endures, cannot save her children. We next see the queen energetically arguing with the cardinal, who is using all the tricks of rhetoric and logic, including threats, to pursuade her to surrender her son. Rhetorical skill, intelligence, and emotional control enable the queen to match the cardinal's subtleties, but her efforts are futile. The cardinal makes it clear that he intends to take the boy by force if she refuses to relinquish him. More ends the dialogue with a sympathetic portrait of the queen, standing "a good while in a great study." Knowing that her son may be safer if she surrenders him than if he is forced from her, she turns him over to the cardinal in a moving scene that reveals both her maternal emotions and her political acumen. Still she retains the pride of her position, insisting that she could have kept her son had she seen fit, "whatsoeuer any man say." The irony of More's perspective is obvious as the tableau ends with mother and son weeping and the young duke going to the embraces and kisses of his uncle; the queen's devotion, strength, and sagacity magnify the extent of Richard's chaotic destructiveness.

More uses his usual dramatic techniques of dialogue, rhetoric, and irony to present the queen and the other characters. In contrast, he describes Jane Shore narratively, often distancing himself from his account by reminding the reader that his knowledge of her is based on hearsay. In the description of Richard's motiveless persecution of Jane, More gives a sympathetic account of her life, explaining her sexual immorality and portraying her as generous, intelligent, and kind. In telling how Richard took her possessions and sentenced her to walk through London carrying a candle as a penance for her well-known lustfulness, More shows Jane to be so attractive and modest that the people pity her and despise Richard's malice. Ultimately, his characterization of Jane Shore, like that of the queen, is a comment on Richard. He mitigates Jane's wantonness and praises her generosity with words that mock Richard's "righteousness."

Two literary questions haunt readers of the *History of Richard III:* to what genre does it belong, and why was it never finished? Scholars have answered the questions in various ways. Two writers, R. W. Chambers and A. F. Pollard [see Additional Bibliography], define the issues essential to an assessment of the book. Chambers says that the *Richard* "initiates modern English historical writing" and suggests that More stopped writing it because criticism of "non-moral statecraft" was dangerous under Henry VIII. Like most readers, Chambers notices the inherently dramatic nature of the narrative. In his treatment of the making of *Richard III*, Pollard describes More's sources and concludes that, because of the oral nature of his infor-

mation, the book is "history" only in the loosest sense of the word. According to Pollard, More is not so much writing history as drama; it is "legitimate drama, but illigitimate history." He agrees with Chambers that More probably stopped writing when he became aware of the book's disturbing political relevance. Many critics emphasize the extent to which More uses the techniques of classical rhetoric to develop his story, and C. S. Lewis suggests that the book is more rhetorical than dramatic [see excerpt dated 1954]. Robert E. Reiter sees More's *Richard* as a type of narrative derived from medieval biograpy.

Thus More's *Richard III* has been considered significant in the development of modern history, biography, and drama; it is also important as a precursor of modern narrative fiction. Here at a very early date More experiments with sophisticated novelistic techniques, most notably the manipulation of point of view and the use of the dramatic monologue for characterization. As an aspect of point of view, More distances himself from the story he is telling by continually reminding the reader that his knowledge is secondhand. But he varies this technique in a way that gives more credence to some of his "facts" than to others. Often hearsay must stand on its own, but at times More corrobarates it with such phrases as "some wise mene also weene" "and certayn it is." By thus validating some but not all of what he says, he moves the reader toward an acceptance of his interpretation of historic events and figures. Also, complex narrative passages based on "some says" often begin to sound as if they are being told by an objective third-person narrator. The effect of this mobile perspective coupled with the long, self-revealing monologues is a remarkable combination of credibility and apparent objectivity. In both the *Richard* and the *Utopia*, More experiments with the kind of diffuse point of view not fully realized in English literature until the twentieth century produced the psychological fiction of James Joyce, Virginia Woolf, and D. H. Lawrence. More's methods suggest modern fictional techniques which allow a writer to move freely between the mind of an omniscient third person narrator and the minds of his characters.

But *Richard III* is by no means "art for art's sake"; it is essentially, and again like the *Utopia,* an application of humanist ideals to the moral problems of the sixteenth century. The Latin *Richard* is a humanistic work written for an international audience; both versions are informed by More's knowledge of classical history and rhetoric. It is a kind of history and a good story, but it is also a sermon against tyranny and hypocrisy and a commentary on the tragedy of the human failure to understand the laws of God, man, and nature. (pp. 54-9)

After 1517, Thomas More was increasingly important in the government of Henry VIII. But although his personal fortunes were rising, he must have begun to suspect that Hythlodaeus had been right—for the honest man, a king's court is a trap. England and her European enemies and allies seemed to think war was inevitable and, worse, desirable. The Reformation was adding to the dissension in Europe; and at home, Henry had begun his bloody efforts to secure the succession. In the same year that More became Under-Treasurer, Edward Stafford, Duke of Buckingham, the son of the duke who figures so prominently in the *History of Richard III*, was arrested and executed because Henry thought his royal lineage threatened the throne.

These were the circumstances in 1522 when More and his daughter Margaret each began writing a meditation on Ecclesiasticus 7:40: "In all thy matters remember thy last end, and thou shalt never sin." According to More's biographer Thomas Stapleton, Margaret completed the exercise to the satisfaction of her father who "affirmed most solemnly that that treatise of his daughter was in no way inferior to his own," but More's was never finished. The fragment we have was first published in 1557 in the Rastell edition.

It is tempting to view the unfinished treatise as the fragment of an exercise undertaken by More simply for the edification of his daughter and thus of little consequence to a consideration of his life or writings. In fact, it is important to an understanding of both. The *Four Last Things* shows More to be fully aware not only of the transience of life and success in general, but also of the immediate danger to himself. In his analysis of the relationship between envy and death, he recounts Buckingham's fall in terms that will suggest his own:

> If so were that thou knewest a great Duke, keeping so great estate and princely port in his house that thou, being a right mean man hadst in thine heart a great envy thereat, and specially at some special day in which he keepeth for the marriage of his child a great honourable court above other times; if thou being thereat, and at the sight of the royalty and honour shown him of all the country about resorting to him, while they kneel and crouch to him and at every word barehead begrace him, if thou shouldst suddenly be surely advertised, that for secret treason, lately detected to the King, he should undoubtly be taken the morrow, his court all broken up, his goods seized, his wife put out, his children disinherited, himself cast into prison, brought forth and arraigned, the matter out of question, and he should be condemned, his coat armour reversed, his gilt spurs hewn off his heels, himself hanged, drawn, and quartered, how thinkest thou, by thy faith, amid thine envy shouldst thou not suddenly change into pity?

The treatise is significant for literary as well as biographical reasons; it links the stages in More's intellectual development and demonstrates the integrated quality of his thought. Chronologically, the fragment falls between the periods of humanistic and polemical writings and derives its argument from the Utopian theory of pleasure. But its most specific affinity is with the medieval devotional and mystical writing that so markedly influence the *Life of Picus* and the Tower works.

The *Four Last Things* begins with an introduction to the medicinal value of the verse from Ecclesiasticus, which shows how remembering the four last things (death, doom, pain, and joy) works to prevent the sickness of sin. More sets out to provide a consideration of each of the four things in terms of the seven deadly sins. He begins by explaining the theory of pleasure we first encountered in the letter from John Picus to his nephew and then, fully developed, in the *Utopia*. Here More applies his interpretation of pleasure to the remembrance of the last things in order to prove that the contempation of apparently painful realities is in fact pleasurable. Again, he insists that spiritual pleasure is greater than physical and shows how ignorance and faulty training sometimes cause us to consider unnatural or painful things to be pleasurable. In both *Utopia* and the *Four Last Things,* More compares people who cannot tell pleasure from pain to pregnant women who prefer pitch and tallow to sweets. Here, the cure for our misunderstanding of the pleasure in remembering the last things lies in the practice itself, which inevitably results in the substitution of true for false values.

More begins his meditation with a description of the harsh physical realities of death, the ultimate example of which is Christ's suffering on the cross. The dying man is harassed by the members of his family, who want his goods, and by the devil, who wants his soul. Despite the bleak tone of the book, the author's penchant for drama and comedy enlivens the portrayal of the devil's methods and motivation. In his consideration of death, More uses several metaphors which he will develop years later in the prison *Dialogue of Comfort*. The description of present suffering as a medicine that prevents sin and brings happiness in the future pervades both books, and the *Dialogue* expands to its fullest the image of life as a prison in which we are incarcerated with no hope of escape and under an irrevocable sentence of death.

More sets out to show how the remembrance of each of the four things obviates each of the seven deadly sins. But he breaks off after treating only death and six of the sins: pride, envy, wrath, covetousness, gluttony, and sloth. The treatise begins to grow tedious with the constant emphasis on the senselessness of each sin in the face of impending death.

The argument of the *Four Last Things* resembles the philosophy of pleasure that More developed in the *Utopia*, a theory heavily influenced by classical, especially platonic, thought. But in tone and structure, the work derives from the devotional writing of the middle ages and thereby predicts the direction of More's last works. There are suggestions of the morality play in the parade of the seven deadly sins, the characterization of the devil, and the abandonment of the dying man by the living. The treatise also recalls medieval guides to holy dying, which like the *Four Last Things* depict deathbed temptations and stress the aloneness of the dying man. But the most profound parallels here and in the prison books are with English mystical writing. Undoubtedly, More read and valued books like Walter Hilton's *Scale of Perfection* and *Treatise on the Mixed Life*, Richard Rolle's *Form of Living*, the anonymous *Cloud of Unknowing*, and Nicholas Love's *Meditations on the Life of Christ*—which he would have found in the library of the Carthusians if not in his father's home.

By the Middle Ages, Christian contemplatives had developed a three-stage progression whereby the individual sought communion with God through purgation, illumination, and contemplation. More's meditation on the seven deadly sins suggests the stage of purgation in which the soul strips itself of sin and sensuality. It is [according to Joseph Burnes Collins in *Christian Mysticism in the Elizabethan Age* (1940)] a "period of intense self-discipline, and ceaseless warfare carried on against the vices which beset the soul and tend to deprive it of the virtues." Like his predecessors More insists on the incorporation of active good works into this stage: prayer, alms-deeds, pilgrimages, and fasting as well as discipline and spiritual exercise. The illuminative phase comes with the joyful recognition of the possibility of spiritual perfection. This is the pleasure inherent in the comtemplation of the four last things:

For the pulling out of which weeds by the root, there is not a more meet instrument than the remembrance of the four last things, which as they shall pull out these weeds of fleshly voluptuousness, so shall they not fail to plant in their places not only wholesome virtues, but also marvellous ghostly pleasure and spiritual gladness, which in every good soul riseth of the love of God, and hope of heaven, and inward liking that the godly spirit taketh in the diligent labour of good and virtuous business.

...A penitent beginneth to profit and grow in grace and favour of God when he feeleth a pleasure and quickness in his labour and pain taken in prayer, almsdeeds, pilgrimage, fasting, discipline, tribulation, affliction, and such other spiritual exercise.... Therefore let every man by the labour of his mind and help of prayer, enforce himself in all tribulation and affliction, labour, pain and travail, without spot of pride or ascribing any praise to himself, to conceive a delight and pleasure in such spiritual exercise, and thereby to rise in the love of our Lord, with an hope of heaven, contempt of the world, and longing to be with God.

Illumination is traditionally associated with the contemplation of the humanity of Christ which More suggests here and uses extensively in the Tower works.

In his writings, More left a unique record of an incredibly complex mind—one that seems to have been constantly in the process of combining disparate aspects of experience. The pleasure of spiritual Illumination dominates the *Four Last Things* and indicate a connection between the paradoxical pleasure of meditating on death and the so-called hedonism of *Utopia*. Both depend on the individual's willingness to see present suffering in the light of future spiritual pleasure. And both hold contemplation and the practice of virtue to be the greatest of earthly pleasures. (pp. 77-80)

Judith P. Jones, in her Thomas More, *Twayne Publishers, 1979, 165 p.*

ALISTAIR FOX (essay date 1982)

[*A New Zealander, Fox has written widely on Thomas More and the Henrician Reformation. Reviewing Fox's* Thomas More: History and Providence *(1982) in the* Times Literary Supplement, *Nicolas Barker described the work—from which the following excerpt is taken— as "a portrait, more human than divine but no less heroic for the frailties revealed, wholly sympathetic and wonderfully convincing." Barker added that the biography is "the best book on Thomas More's life and writings to appear since R. W. Chambers's, nearly fifty years ago." Here, Fox offers a close examination of* A Dialogue of Comfort against Tribulation.]

If we suppose that *De Tristitia Christi* was the last work More wrote, and allow sufficient time for him to have written it, then the *Dialogue of Comfort against Tribulation* must have been composed between June 1534 and the early months of 1535. By that time the fifth and sixth sessions of the Reformation Parliament had finally put the seal on the political changes he had been opposing: the clergy had been stripped of their independent right to try heresy by an Act establishing open trials, and the breach with Rome had been confirmed in Acts restraining annates, abolishing Peter's pence, confirming the Submission of the Clergy, and transferring the pope's authority to issue dispensations to the Archbishop of Canterbury.

More's own near escape from inclusion in the Bill of Attainder against the Nun of Kent had also proven how mercilessly his opposition to the king's second marriage would be suppressed should he persist in opposing it as he fully intended. When, in mid-April, More was imprisoned after he had refused to take the oath accompanying the Act of Succession, execution had not yet been prescribed as the punishment for his offence, but it was a future possibility that he might well have envisaged (if he did not, others, such as Chapuys, certainly did). He thus had every incentive for considering what the collapse of his world and his own ominous situation meant in philosophical and religious terms.

Such a consideration was indeed the prime cause and concern of the *Dialogue of Comfort*. Whereas in the *Treatise upon the Passion* More had contemplated universal history in its generalities, he now focused more narrowly upon the calamity he believed had descended upon Europe, and on the predicament of individual men and nations caught up in it. To this end he devised a fictional framework, consisting of the extended metaphor of the Great Turk, and developed a series of analogies within it that allowed him to identify and confront the objects of his perturbations. All of them, he saw, were aspects of the same universal reality of human experience: tribulation. Yet having confronted it, he found in tribulation a cause for hope rather than despair.

Scholarship occasionally shows a tendency to reduce the fictional frame to simple allegory, with the Great Turk representing Henry VIII, or the devil, or the Lutherans, or all three, but to do so is to miss much of the basic point of the *Dialogue*. It is, in effect, far more than a merely partisan piece of anti-Protestant allegory designed to fortify Catholics against future persecution for the old faith. The allegory of the Turk is polysemous rather than simple, in the manner that More thought characterized scripture itself. More's own comments on scriptural exegesis in his *Letter Impugning Frith* provide an appropriate gloss for the way it works. There, he insists on the primacy of the literal sense in all instances where a literal reading can pertain; nevertheless, additional allegorical meanings can reside within the literal sense without replacing it. In the *Treatise upon the Passion* he had demonstrated what he meant by giving elaborate figurative interpretations of literal biblical episodes, such as the bondage of the Israelites under the Pharaoh of Egypt, which 'signifieth the bondage of mankynde vnder the prynce of thys darke world', their delivery and safe passage through the Red Sea, which 'sygnifieth mankynd passyng oute of the dyuels daunger, thorowe the water of baptisme', and their 40 years wandering in the desert, in which 'is there sygnified and fygured, the long payneful wandering of men in the wylde wyldernes of this wreched world ere we can get hence to heauen'. More's own work deliberately reproduced this kind of multilayered structure of meaning in order to achieve universality.

At the literal level, the Turkish threat is presented *per se* in precise and accurate detail. Ever since the fall of Constantinople in 1452 and Athens in 1453, the expansion of the Ottoman Turks had instilled very real fear in the European imagination. They had pillaged as far as Zagreb in 1470, and had repeatedly invaded Hungary in 1473, 1479 and 1493. Several decades later the threat had grown suddenly more menacing when Suleiman the Magnificent captured two of the most important bulwarks of Christendom: Belgrade in 1521 and the island of Rhodes in 1522. After the decisive battle of Mohács in 1526, the Turks seemed poised to invade the very heartland of Christianity.

It is in this context that More places his two Hungarian protagonists, Vincent and Anthony, as they await the final onslaught. Vincent describes the depth of their fear:

> sith the tydynges haue come hether so brymme of the great Turkes interprise into these parties here: we can almost neyther talke nor thynke of any other thyng els, than of his might and our mischefe. There falleth so contynually before the eyen of our hart, a fearefull imaginacion of this terryble thyng / his myghty strength and power, his high malice and hatryd, and his incomparable crueltie, with robbyng, spoylyng, burnyng, and layng wast all the way that his armye commeth / than kyllyng or caryng away, the people far hens fro home.

In a later passage Anthony further details the atrocities of the Turks: the exaction of annual tributes and taxes, the dispossession of Christians from their lands, the levying of children for Janissaries and the seraglio, and forcible conversion to Islam. All these facts, together with accurate references to the internal struggle for the Hungarian crown between Ferdinand, Archduke of Austria, and John Zapolya, Voivode of Transylvania, testify to More's precise knowledge of contemporary developments in the Balkans as reported to Wolsey in numerous official documents.

Significantly, More sets the action in 1527-28 *before* the permanent occupation of Buda by the Turks in the spring of 1529. His use of the literal historical event as a framing fiction thus allowed for the creation of a double perspective: that of the Hungarians, Anthony and Vincent, who are struggling (like More had been from about the same date) to come to terms with the imminent invasion, literal and metaphorical, of their 'country', and that of the European reader who, with the advantage of hindsight, knows that the feared occupation had indeed occurred in the intimated fictional aftermath of the dialogue. Attention focuses, therefore, on the process by which the two protagonists strive to prepare themselves to confront the terrifying experience they fear is about to descend upon them, as the reader knows it will. In depicting that, More was also dramatizing how he himself had evolved out of the state of desperation into which he had been tempted to fall before the field had been won. In this way the *Dialogue* is contrived to provide a spiritual biography of More's response to his own particular circumstances at one level, while at the same time offering a universalized exemplum relevant to all comparable occasions of real or threatened tribulation when and wherever they may occur.

Clearly, the self-sufficient, literal Turkish/Hungarian context contains within it at least two other contexts: one similarly literal, and the other metaphorical. They exist as intermittently obtruded analogies to the main Turkish business, similar, for example, to the political and anagogical strands in the allegory of Spenser's *Faerie Queene*.

The second literal context concerns recent events in European politics. When Vincent expresses fear that 'no small part of our own folke that dwell even here about vs, are (as we here) fallen to hym [the Turk], or all redy confeteryd with hym', one detects a veiled reference to the un-

scrupulous pragmatism of the French. Throughout the 1520s Francis I of France was negotiating with the Turks to form an alliance against Charles V. Vincent's remark could be applied equally to the political alliance between the English administration and anticlericalism that had recently achieved the legislative breach with Rome, so that when Anthony rejoins that the Turk 'hath . . . destroyid our noble yong goodly kyng', his observation, which applies literally to Louis II of Hungary, could bear upon Francis I of France and Henry VIII of England as well. Another remark by Anthony allows for a specific English inference when he claims that 'sinnes the title of the crowne hath comen in question, the good rule of this realme hath very sore decayed / as litle while as it is / And vndowtidly Hungary shall neuer do well, as long as . . . mens myndes harken after newelties, and haue their hartes hangyng vppon a chaunge.' The word 'title' ambiguously raises the question of the 'style' being claimed for Henry as well as the question of the succession. More focuses attention on his own political plight in this context when he makes Vincent observe that good men will be deprived of their goods and bodies 'but yf we turn as they do, and forsake our saviour to / And than (for there ys no born Turke so cruell to christen folke, as is the false christen that falleth fro the fayth) we shall stand in perill yf we percever in the truth, to be more hardely handelyd and dye more cruell deth by our own countremen at home / than yf we were taken hens and caried into Turkey.' Here the allegory could allude to More's sense of his own likely treatment should he persist in refusing to swear to the Oath of Supremacy. Sometimes it is difficult, in fact, to remember as one reads the *Dialogue of Comfort* that Anthony is merely sick and not, like More, in prison fearing the worst.

The political application of the fiction at this level merges with yet another, in which the Turks are likened to the heretics, without precisely being equated with them. When Vincent refers to the growing leniency of his countrymen towards the Turks, his phrasing evokes the countless occasions in the controversies when More uttered the same lament with respect to the attitude of Englishmen to the heretics: 'my thinke I here at myn eare some of our owne here among vs, which with in these few yeres could no more haue born the name of a Turke than the name of the devill, begyn now to fynd litle faute therein'. These lines recall, for instance, the opening of the *Answer to a Poisoned Book*, when More expressed incredulity that Englishmen were now prepared to countenance talk of heresy at their very tables, whereas before a man would have informed upon it 'all thoughe the thing touched hys owne borne brother'. Throughout the controversies More had stressed the analogy between the Lutherans and the Turks, particularly in respect of their infidelity and use of violence. It is not surprising, therefore, that he should have allowed the analogy to surface on several occasions in the *Dialogue of Comfort*. Heresy, along with Henry VIII's political voluntarism and the violence of the Turks, was one of the many manifestations of the larger evil encompassing them all.

That larger evil was the devil himself, and the Great Turk is sometimes described in terms evoking him, as when More refers to 'this terryble thyng' with his 'high malice and hatryd, and his incomparable crueltie'. The depersonalization of the phrase suggests rather more than the historical human figure of Suleiman the Magnificent at that point. The fear instilled by the Turk also makes him like the prophesied Antichrist, at least in the imaginations of the terrified Hungarians. More underlines this by alluding to Christ's reference to the forecast event in Luke 23: 28-30 when he describes their terror: 'These ferefull heps of perill, lye so hevy at oower hartes, whyle we wot not into which we shall fortune to fall, and therefore fere all the worst / that as our sauiour prophesied of the people of Ierusalem, many wysh among vs all redye before the perill come, that the montayns wold ouerwhelm them / or the valeys open and swallow them vpp and keuer them.'

The Turk, together with all that allegorically he represents, is a manifestation of something still larger: the inescapable reality of tribulation in this world and the experience of it. Through the figure of the Turk, More sought to confront the meaning of everything in human experience generally that had the power to perturb the human mind.

The universality of More's concern is indicated in the simplicity of his definition: 'tribulacion semeth generally to signifie nothyng els, but some kynd of grefe, eyther payne of the body or hevynes of the mynd'. The former he was about to suffer, the latter he had already suffered extremely. While book 3 of the *Dialogue of Comfort* progressively narrows its focus to concentrate on painful physical torture and death, it is not to be overlooked that the earlier books are largely concerned with mental and emotional tribulation. The task More had set himself was first to show how hope could be derived from the same experiential realities that can induce despair, and second, to show how he had been able to fortify himself in readiness to 'smyte the devill in the face with a firebrond of charitie'.

Book 1 gives a largely theoretical exposition of how comfort can be achieved. The essential foundation for all hope, More declares, is faith, which is 'in dede the gracious gift of god himself'. The pagan philosophers could never give adequate comfort against tribulation through their natural reasoning because they had no knowledge of the salvation in heaven to which all faith is directed: 'they neuer strech so ferre, but that they leve vntouchid for lak of necessarye knolege, that special poynt, which is not onely the chief comfort of all / but without which also, all other comfortes are nothing / that is to wit the referryng the fynall end of their comfort vnto god'. Once men have attained 'faithfull trust' in God's promise through 'the true beliefe of Goddes woorde', however, they are able to accept that 'by the pacient suffraunce of their tribulacion, they shall attayne his favour / and for their payne receve reward at his hand in heven'.

After the foundation of faith has been laid, one can then understand that tribulation is providentially bestowed. As Anthony explains to Vincent, tribulation is an instrument to drive men *out of* spiritual discomfort and despair: 'And that is one of the causes for the which god sendith it vnto man / for albeit that payne was ordeynyd of god for the punyshment of synne ... yet in this world in which his high mercye giveth men space to be better / the pvnyshment by trybulacion that he sendith, servith ordinarily for a meane of amendment.' The thought here is exactly consistent with that in earlier works such as the *Dialogue Concerning Heresies*; tribulation is both a means of punishment for sin and also an instrument for regeneration. It serves to induce 'the obedient confirmyng of the mans will

vnto god, and ... thankes givyng to god for his visitacion', and thus assists men to recover the obedience, devotion and sole dependence owed to God that they had betrayed at the original Fall. Tribulation cleanses and purges men of their sins as well, so that not only does the patient suffrance of it become 'a mater of merite and reward in heven', but it also serves to remit men's future pain in purgatory.

As far as the particular type of tribulation was concerned, More believed that men could be absolutely certain that God allowed whatever they suffered for the best. This applied both to the pain and the comforting remedy God would always provide: 'let vs nothyng dowt / but that like as his high wisedome better seeth what is best for vs than we can see our selfe / so shall our souerayne goodnes give vs the thyng that shall in dede be best'. All good men, he believed, were afflicted with one general kind of tribulation, consisting of 'the conflyte of the flessh agaynst the sowle / the rebellion of sensualitie agaynst the rule and gouernaunce of reson ... lefte vs by godes ordynaunce to strive agaynst yt and fight with all and by reason and grace to master yt'. Otherwise, men were afflicted variously and severally by diverse kinds of tribulation according to divine wisdom. These included loss of goods, physical sickness, bereavement, disease, mental perturbation, imprisonment, fear of death, and the severest form of all, the fear of damnation.

One of the most grievous forms of tribulation was that of temptation, which More (for obvious personal reasons) held to be as frightening as bodily persecution itself: 'yf we well consider thes two thynges, temptacion and persecution we may fynd that eyther of them is incident to the tother / For both by temptacion the devill persecuteth vs, and by persecucion the devill also temptith vs / and as persecusion is tribulacion to eueryman, so is temptacion tribulacion to euery good man.' More considered the tribulation of temptation to be so important that he organized the whole of book 2 around an exposition of the four kinds of temptation metaphorically figured in the words of Psalm 90:

> *Scuto circumdabit te veritas eius / non temebis a timore nocturno / a sagitta volante in die, a negocio perambulante in tenebris, ab incursu et demonio meridiano*: The trouth of god shall compasse the about with a pavice, thow shalt not be aferd of the nightes feare, nor of the arrow fleyng in the day, nor of the bysynes walkyng about in the darknesses / nor of the incursion or invacion of the devill in the mydde day.

In book 2 these four forms of temptation are treated as four separate demons. *Timor noctu* he identified as 'the tribulacions by which the devyll thorow the suffraunce of god, eyther by hym selfe or other than are his instrumentes, temptith good folke to impacience / as he did Iob'. Generally speaking, this impatience comprised all kinds of imaginary fears, as when 'in the night euery bush to hym that waxeth ones a ferd semeth a thefe'. It also consisted of pusillanimity, excessively scrupulous conscience, and the temptation to suicide. *Sagitta volante in die* he identified as 'the arrow of pride, with which the devill temptith a man / not in the night / that is to wit in tribulacion and aduersite ... but in the day that is to wit in prosperite'. *Negotium perambulans in tenebris* was simply the demon of sensuality – the temptation 'to seke the plea-

sures of the flesh / in eatyng drinkyng and other filthy delite' – and the materialistic greed for wealth.

To the fourth temptation, that arising from the incursion
of the midday devil, or open persecution, More devoted
the entire third book. Even physical torture, he asserted,
was not to be feared, for God would never allow 'the devill with all his faythles tourmentours in this world' to beset any men with more torment than they could endure:

> whan we be of this mynd / and submit our will vnto his,
> and call and pray for his grace: we can tell well inough,
> that he will neuer suffre them to put more vppon vs /
> than his grace will make vs hable to bere / but will also
> with their temptacion prouide for vs a sure waye / For
> / *fidelis est deus* sayth saynt paule / *qui non patitur vos
> temptare / supra id quod potestis sed dat etiam cum ten-
> tatione prouentum vt possitis ferre* / God is (sayth thap-
> postell) faythfull, which suffreth you not to be temptid
> above that you may bere / but giveth also with the
> temptacion a way out.

Either God would ultimately protect men from such persecution, having allowed them in the meantime to experience the dread of it so as 'to drive vs to call for grace', or
else the short pain he would allow to be inflicted on their
bodies would 'tourne vs to eternall profitt'. If men were
surely grounded in faith and confirmed in the hope of
God's assistance, they could receive no harm from persecution: 'that that shall seme harme / shall in dede be to vs
none harm at all / but good / For yf god make vs and kepe
vs good men as he hath promisid to do / yf we pray well
therfor / than saith holy scripture / *Bonis omnia cooperan-
tur in bonum* / vnto good folke, all thinges turne them to
good.' As More said elsewhere, a man might lose his head
and take no harm from it.

For More, the supreme exemplar of this truth was Christ
himself at his passion. Like any ordinary human being,
Christ had experienced 'great horrour and . . . fere . . . in
his own flesh agaynst his paynfull passion'. More believed
that he had suffered in the Garden before the crucifixion
for the express purpose of providing comfort: 'In our fere
let vs remember . . . [it] to thentent that no fere shuld
make vs dispayre.' Meditation of Christ's agony could,
with the assistance of grace, lead a man to 'submit and
conforme' his will to Christ's, just as Christ had submitted
his own will to his father'. As a result, one would be 'com-
fortid with the secret inward inspiracion of his holy sprite'
and hence be able to 'dye for the truth with hym, and therby rayne with hym crownid in eternall glory'.

All the different structural patterns of the ***Dialogue***, in
fact, converge upon the same point: More's demonstration
that Christ's passion archetypally embodies the purpose of
all human experience, individual and common, present,
past and future. One pattern derives from the organization
of the three books around faith, hope and charity respectively. Book 1 declares the necessity for faith as the foundation of all comfort, book 2 shows how men can have
sure hope of God's assistance, and book 3 illuminates the
charity that allows a man to overcome his tribulation. The
progression of the argument through these three Christian
virtues serves to condition Vincent's mind and emotions
to the point where he will be able to strike the devil blind
with 'that fire of charitie throwne in his face' by pitying
and praying for his killers should the worst come to the
worst when the Turks come. Psychologically, the move-

ment through faith, hope and charity reproduces the mental process which, in More's view, can 'quicken' a man's
willingness to imitate Christ even in his passion.

A second pattern organized around the different types of
tribulation leads to the same point. Book 1 deals with tribulation one cannot avoid, and book 2 with tribulation one
willingly suffers, temptation in particular. That in turn is
subdivided into four types, three of which are dealt with
in book 2, and the third of which (that deriving from
physical persecution) is treated at length in book 3. Each
pattern arrives at the vivid visual image of Christ suffering on the Cross:

> the scornefull crowne of sharp thornes beten down vp-
> pon his holy hed, so strayght and so diepe, that on eu-
> ery part his blyssid blode yssued owt and stremyd down
> / his lovely lymmys drawen and strechid out vppon the
> crosse to the Intollerable payne of his forebeten and
> sorebeten vaynes and synewes / new felyng with the cru-
> ell strechyng and straynyng payne far passyng any
> crampe, in euery part of his blyssid body at ones / Than
> the greate long nayles cruelly dryven with hamers tho-
> row his holy handes and fete / and in this horryble
> payne lyft vpp and let hang.

To increase the force of this highly charged climactic image, it is reiterated proleptically in each of the two earlier
books. On the first occasion More sounds the same linguistic chords when he refers to 'all the torment that he
hangyd in / of beatyng / naylyng / and strechyng out all his
lymmes / with the wrestyng of his synews / and brekyng of
his tender vaynes / and the sharpe crown of thorn so
prickyng hym into the hed that his blessid bloude stremyd
down all his face'. On the second occasion More evokes
the image for the sake of parody, in Anthony's tale of the
Carver's wife and her mock crucifixion of her husband, to
illustrate both the suicidal folly and the delusion of seeking to imitate Christ presumptuously. After his wife has
scourged him and driven a crown of thorns on his head,
the Carver 'thought this was inough for that yere, he wold
pray god forbere hym of the remenaunt till good friday
come agayne . . . he longid to folow christ no ferther'. In
this way the structural patterns work through progression,
duplication and convergence to move the reader imaginatively and intellectually into an apprehension of the
book's total meaning.

Through his systematic exploration of the nature and purpose of tribulation, More was able to understand why God
had allowed history to unfold as it had. The assault of the
Turks, the internal dissension within Europe, the threat of
antichristian despotism in England, and the subversion of
the church by heretics were merely macrocosmic exten-
sions of the persecution God had allowed the devil to
wage on mankind since the Fall, and all, he considered,
was for the best, being a manifestation of God's benefi-
cently wise providential disposition.

More's deepened sense of God's way confirmed his growing belief that the Apocalypse was a long way off yet. At
the opening of book 3, when fresh news has arrived of the
Turkish advance, Anthony reassures Vincent that even
should Hungary and much of Christendom be lost to the
Turks, Christ would not allow the enemy completely to
prevail. The historical rhythm of decay followed by renewal would continue until the end of time:

> I nothyng dowt at al, but that in conclucion how bace so euer christendom be brought, it shall spring vp agayne till the tyme be come very nere to the day of dome / wher of some tokens as me thinketh are not comen yet / But som what before that tyme shall christendome be straytid sore, and brought into so narrow a compas, that according to christes wordes / *Filius hominis quum venerit putas inueniet fidem in terra* ... for as apperith in thapocalips and other places of scripture, the fayth shalbe at that tyme so far vaded that he shall for the love of his electes, lest they shuld fall and perish to, abbredge those dayes, and accelerate his comyng.
>
> But as I say me thinketh I mysse yet in my mynde, some of those tokens, that shall by the scripture come a good while before that.

The return of a more balanced historical perspective helped restore More's equilibrium, and once that had happened, he was able to see the escalation of heresy, too, in a new light. At one point in book 1, Vincent questions whether the comforts Anthony has proposed may have been put in doubt by the new doctrines. Many men, he declares, 'affirm for a suer trowth, that ther is no purgatory at all' and 'say ye wot well also, that men merite nothyng at all / but god giveth all for fayth alone'. If these two propositions are true, he continues, they destroy the two main causes for comfort that Anthony has suggested. Anthony's reply reflects a new attitude towards the Lutherans in More himself and as such is worth quoting at length:

> albeit that it is a right hevy thyng to se such variaunce in our beleve rise and grow among our self / to the grete encouragyng of the comen enymies of vs all / wherby they haue our fayth in dirision and cach hope to ouerwhelm vs all / yet do there iij thynges not a litle recomfort my mynd.
>
> The first is, that in some communicacions had of late together, hath aperid good liklyhod of some good agrement to grow in one accord of our fayth /
>
> The second, that in the meane while till this may come to pas, contencions, dispicions, with vncharitable behaviour, is prohibitid and forboden in effect vppon all partes / all such partes I meane as fell before to fight for it.
>
> The Third is, that all germanye for all their diuers opynions / yet as they agre together in profession of christes name / so agre they now together in preparacion of a comen power in defence of christendome ageinst our comen enymye the Turke / And I trust in god that this shall not onely help vs here to strength vs in this warr / but also that as god hath causid them to agre together in the defence of his name / so shall he graciously bryng them to agree together in the truth of his fayth.
>
> Therfor will I let god worke and leve of contention.

Several crucial things are to be noted here. More stresses the common bond uniting all Christians—the profession of Christ's name—rather than the doctrinal differences that divide them into orthodox and heterodox. He also expresses hope that the common Turkish threat might unite them all into one agreement as to the true faith. Finally, he deliberately and decisively repudiates the contention to which he had been accustomed, replacing it with a faith that God is in some way working in events. In spite of the view of a recent editor [Frank Manley, in his and Louis L. Martz's 1976 edition of *A Dialogue of Comfort against*

Tribulation] that Anthony's statements must be taken 'as somewhat satiric' and ironic, there is nothing in tone or content to suggest that More himself did not firmly believe everything that he has Anthony say. The Peace of Nürnberg (1532), which had been reaffirmed in the Peace of Cadan on 29 June 1534—the very time when More was writing the *Dialogue*—had stressed the need for unity and the avoidance of controversy.... More chose to set an example himself by leaving off contention, as both the tone and matter of the *Dialogue of Comfort* attests. As in the *Treatise upon the Passion*, he forgets himself from time to time (as when his treatment of penance and bodily affliction momentarily opens the old wound of Luther's marriage), but his overriding intent is clear – to adopt a more charitable form of behaviour and avoid 'contencions' and 'dispicions'. This is confirmed, for example, in his choice of the word 'christendom' for most of the occasions when formerly he would have written 'church' (which he uses in the *Dialogue* on only two occasions, and then, one feels, inadvertently). 'Christendom' allows conditionally for the inclusion of all those who, as More says, profess the name of Christ regardless of their particular disagreements; 'church', on the other hand, raises the whole divisive spectre which More was trying to lay to rest.

More's new spirit of charitable accommodation is seen even in Anthony's assertion of his own personal belief (and More's) that good works are necessary and meritorious:

> far the more part [of the reformers] are thus farr agreed with vs, that like as we graunt them that no good worke is ought worth to hevyn ward without fayth / and that no good worke of man is rewardable in hevyn of his own nature.... And as we graunt them also that no man may be proude of his workes for his own vnperfit workyng.... As we I say graunt vnto them these thynges / so this one thyng or twayne do they graunt vs agayne / that men are bound to worke good workes yf they haue tyme and power and that who so workith in trew fayth most, shalbe most rewardid.

While More was not prepared to make any further concession in the matter than that, the concession itself testifies to the huge contrast with the inflexible dogmatism of the controversies. The *Dialogue of Comfort* is not a narrowly partisan or bigoted work, which makes it all the more erroneous to identify too precisely the Turk with the reformers.

Once More had been able to step back from events, he seems, without repudiating one jot of his own personal commitment to Latin orthodoxy, to have been almost able to contemplate once again the possibility that he had put into the mind of King Utopus years earlier: that God might desire a varied and manifold worship, and therefore inspire different people with different views.... More knew that if Christendom were to arise again into one accord of faith, as he hoped and expected, it would mean growing into a new consensus rather than returning to the old.

One of the most striking features of the *Dialogue of Comfort* is its proof of the return of More's literary powers. The enforced leisure of imprisonment no doubt gave him time to create an intricately designed, resonant and polished fiction, just as the diplomatic stalemate in Bruges had previously done in 1515, but a far more potent cause was the recovery of his equilibrium and faith.

For the first time since *A Dialogue Concerning Heresies*, More chose the form of the dramatized dialogue – the vehicle of *Utopia*. Within the dialogue, the relation of More's two personae, Vincent and Anthony, to himself is just as complex as that of Morus and Hythlodaeus, and the Messenger and 'More' in the earlier works. It is wrong to make a simple identification of More with Anthony, the old wise man awaiting death, for More dramatizes his experience equally in Vincent, the perturbed and anxious nephew. If anything, Vincent represents the militant self, and Anthony the resolved self, and the depiction of both served to give More himself comfort just as much as he intended it to provide comfort for his family and readers.

The experience Vincent undergoes in the course of the dialogue exemplifies the effect that the book itself is designed to produce. As well, it epitomizes in a 'speaking picture' all that More is trying to say. In effect, he shows as much as he tells, just as he did in *Utopia*, and tried (less successfully) to do in the *Dialogue Concerning Heresies*. In Vincent he also projects the process by which he himself had managed to regain calm and purge himself of the despair with which he had been threatened at the end of his controversial effort.

At the outset, Vincent, too, is so gripped with 'fearefull imaginacion' and 'desperat dreade' that he, along with his family is in 'perill of spirituall drounnyng'. He is so filled with fear that he is tempted to conclude that 'the gretest comfort that a man can haue, ys when he may see that he shall sone be gone'. It is out of this state of spiritual despondency that he arises, by finding within the causes of his fear grounds for faith, hope and charity.

The wise counsel of Anthony provides the instrument by which he is able to confront his tribulation. Anthony himself has 'bene taken prisoner in Turkey ij tymes' earlier in his days; metaphorically speaking, he has suffered the same imprisoning dread in which Vincent is now trapped, and thus, having learnt through experience how to overcome it, can now give and take counsel in the way he later urges all men to do who find themselves in a similar case. His task is to make Vincent realize how he can come to embody the truth mystically signified in his name according to the words of St John (in the person of Christ) in scripture:

> *vincenti dabo edere de ligno vite* / To hym that ouercometh, I shall give hym to eate of the tree of lyfe / And also he that ouercometh shalbe clothid in whyte clothes / and I shall confesse hys name before my father and before his Angelles . . . feare none of those thynges that thow shallt suffre . . . but be faythfull vnto the deth / and I shall give the the crowne of lyfe. He that ouercometh shall not be hurt of the second deth . . . *vincenti dabo manna absconditvm, et dabo illi calculum candidum. Et in calculo nomen nouum scriptum quod nemo scit nisi qui accipit* / To hym that ouercometh will I give manna secret and hid / and I will give hym a white suffrage, and in his suffrage a new name wrytten, which no man knowith but he that receyveth it.

The insistent repetition in these lines draws attention to the action of overcoming, and suggests that More chose the name 'Vincent' deliberately to underline Vincent's function as an exemplar of that process. By the end of the dialogue, Vincent has become fully prepared to fulfil the possibilities inherent in his name, and thus takes his leave

to perform the same task that More himself has just completed: 'I purpose vncle as my pore witt and lernyng will serve me, to put your good counsayle in remembrauns, not in our own langage onely, but in the Almayne tong to.' Without precisely duplicating it, Vincent's intention to translate his projected work evokes the subtitle of the *Dialogue of Comfort* itself: 'made by an hungaryen in laten, and translatyd out of laten into french, and out of french into Englysh'. Through a peculiar telescoping and inversion of the time scale, the past merges in the future as Vincent participates with Anthony, More and Christ himself in a timeless triumph of charity to which experience should serve to draw all good men.

In the course of contriving this drama, More depicted functionally one of the inadequacies he had come to recognize in his old polemical method. After the *Dialogue Concerning Heresies* his literary mode had rapidly disintegrated from representation into assertive diatribe. He must have soon realized that such rambling monstrosities as the *Confutation* were far less help to those in doubt or perplexity than they might otherwise have been had he chosen another method. Something of this realization is dramatized within the *Dialogue of Comfort*.

Book 1, declaring the facts and varieties of tribulation and the need for faith as the foundation for any comfort against it, is closest in manner to the controversies. It is largely theoretical and stark, with most of the talk going to Anthony, who assumes the role of a schoolmaster administering a lecture. Vincent's role is reduced to little more than that of a foil, rather like the Messenger in the last book of *A Dialogue Concerning Heresies*. The effect on Vincent is to make him feel importunate and insignificant, as if his very presence has been a burdensome encumbrance to the wise man: 'you haue evyn shewid me a sample of sufferaunce in beryng my foly so long and so paciently'. He calls an end to the conversation, but nevertheless emboldens himself to request a further meeting.

In the intervening time, Vincent's guilt increases, until, as he charitably declares to Anthony on next seeing him, he had become convinced that any fault was his:

> after my departyng from you, remembring how long we taried together, and that we were all that while in talkyng / And all the labour yours in talkyng so long together without interpawsyng betwene / and that of mater studiouse and displesaunt, all of desease and siknes and other payne and tribulacion: I was in good fayth very sory and not a litell wroth with my selfe for myn own ouer sight, that I had so litell consideried your payne.

Admitting that he had indeed felt '(to sey the trowth) evyn a litell wery', Anthony reciprocates this charitable gesture by confessing that he, too, had felt some remorse after Vincent's departure: '[I wished] the last tyme after you were gone . . . that I had not so told you styll a long tale alone / but that we had more often enterchaungid wordes / and partid the talke betwene vs, with ofter enterparlyng vppon your part.' Anthony, however, will not let Vincent take all the blame: 'in that poynt I sone excusid you, and layd the lak evyn where I found yt / and that was evyn vppon myn own nekke'. It occurred to him that they had been like a nun and her brother: after a long absence abroad, the brother had returned to visit his sister at her convent, but as soon as they met at the locutory grate, she had immediately launched into a sermon on the wretchedness of the world, the frailty of the flesh, and the subtle sleights of the wicked fiend, with plenty of unsolicited counsel besides; eventually, she began to find fault that her brother was not delivering 'some frutfull exortacion', at which he upbraided her: 'By my trouth good sister / quoth her brother I can not for you / for your tong haue neuer ceasid, but said inough for vs bothe.'

In the exchange between Vincent and Anthony, and in this merry tale, More ironically scrutinizes the habit of mind into which he had slipped in his polemical writing. Vincent identifies, in passing, the gloomy oppressiveness of his works once he had lost his sense of humour, perspective and proportion; Anthony, on the other hand, identifies the obsessiveness that can mar the determined expression of a fixed personal viewpoint. More may still have felt that such a hammering method was justified with heretics, as distinct from the non-heretical audience for whom he now wrote, but his professed readiness in word and deed to leave off contention altogether suggests that he had come to accept that it was intrinsically faulty. In any case, the whole episode symbolically figures forth the moment when More steps down from his polemical soapbox, being prepared to re-enter into dialogue, and kissing goodbye at the same time to the hubris that had animated his controversies.

More probes the sigificance of this change of method still further by dramatizing its subsequent effects on the two protagonists.

Vincent is at once drawn out of himself, and reciprocates in kind with another merry tale—about the kinswoman who was content to let her husband have all the words, so long as she spoke them all herself. Just as importantly, he feels that he need no longer forbear boldly to show his folly or be so 'shamfast'. He therefore proceeds to declare more openly and honestly what he really thinks, as when he admits that he finds Anthony's earlier statement that men should in no way seek comfort in any worldly or fleshly thing 'somwhat hard'. Vincent's new honesty in turn induces Anthony to modify the rigidity of his own position. On the matter of mirthful recreation, he admits that he 'dare not be so sore as vtterly to forbyd yet', even though he maintains his prior conviction (and More's) that men should not need it. Even while soberly affirming that he will not be so partial to his own fault ('my selfe am of nature evyn halfe a giglot') as to praise it, he proceeds immediately to tell a very funny story of a holy father's devious strategy to get his sleeping congregation to listen to his sermon. Thereafter, the merry tales flood back with a profusion and inventiveness not seen since the earlier *Dialogue Concerning Heresies*. By book 3 the old literary More had been fully reborn. (pp. 223-42)

A pen-and-ink drawing by Hans Holbein the Younger of Thomas More, his father Sir John More, and the More household.

Alistair Fox, in his Thomas More: History and
Providence, *Basil Blackwell, 1982, 271 p.*

ANTHONY KENNY (essay date 1983)

[*Kenny is a distinguished English philosopher who has written extensively on philosophical thinkers of the past. In the
following excerpt from his full-length study of More, he outlines Raphael Hythloday's description in* Utopia *of the commonwealth of Utopia.*]

Like Plato's *Republic* before it, and the many Utopian
constitutions devised since, More's **Utopia** uses the depiction of an imaginary nation as a vehicle for theories of political philosophy and criticism of contemporary political
institutions. Like Plato, More often leaves his readers to
guess how far the arrangements he describes are serious
political proposals and how far they merely present a
mocking mirror to reveal the distortions of real-life societies. (p. 20)

Utopia is an island, shaped like a crescent moon, five hundred miles long and two hundred across at its broadest
part. It contains fifty-four cities, each surrounded by twenty miles or so of agricultural land. Throughout the country
there are farms, each containing, as well as a pair of serfs,
a household of forty free men and women. These are city-
dwellers who have been sent into the country for a two-
year stint of farming. Twenty are sent each year by rota:
they spend a year learning husbandry from their predecessors and another teaching it to their successors.

All the cities resemble each other in laws, customs and institutions. Each year three elders from each city meet in a
Senate in the capital, Amaurot. In size, shape and situation Amaurot, as described by More, resembles the London of his day. But in one respect Amaurot is startlingly
different: there is no such thing there as privacy or private
property. The terraced houses back on to spacious gardens; the doors to the houses and through them to the gardens swing open easily and are never locked. 'Whoso will,
may go in, for there is nothing within the houses that is
private, or any man's own. And every tenth year they
change their houses by lot.'

In each city, every group of thirty households elects annually a magistrate called a Syphogrant; there are altogether
two hundred of these per city. Each group of ten Syphogrants, with their households, is ruled by a Tranibore, another elected annual magistrate. The Tranibores form the
Council of the supreme magistrate or Prince, who is chosen for life by the Syphogrants from a panel elected by
popular vote. Whenever the Council meets, two Syphogrants must be present, a different pair each day. Nothing
can be decided until it has been debated for three days,
and it is a capital offence to discuss State matters outside
the Council. This is to prevent the princes and Tranibores
from changing the republic into a tyranny. Matters of particular importance are laid before all the assembled
Syphogrants, but nothing is decided until they have had
time to consult their several households. On rare occasions matters may be laid before the Senate of the whole
island.

Every citizen learns agriculture, first in school, and then
during a turn of duty on the farm. In addition every citizen, male or female, is taught a particular craft, such as

cloth-making, masonry, matal-working or carpentry. Utopia is unlike Europe, where differences of class and status
are marked by elaborate distinctions in dress; people all
wear the same clothes, except for a distinction between the
sexes and between the married and the unmarried. All
clothes are home-made in each household.

No one is allowed to be idle, and all must work every day
at their crafts, overseen by a Syphogrant. Citizens can
choose their crafts, but if they wish to specialise in a craft
other than their father's, they must transfer to a household
dedicated to that craft. The working day is brief: Utopians
work for three hours before noon, rest for two hours after
dinner, and then work a further three hours before supper.
They go to bed at eight and sleep for eight hours: the
hours of early morning and evening are thus leisure time
to be spent as each pleases. In the morning there are public lectures, compulsory for those citizens who have been
assigned as scholars, optional for others, male or female.
The evening may be spent in music or in conversation, or
in chess-like games in which numbers devour numbers, or
virtues battle in panoply against vices.

How do the Utopians manage to satisfy all their needs
while working so many fewer hours than Europeans? You
can easily work this out, if you consider how many people
in Europe live idly:

> First, almost all women which be the half of the whole
> number: or else, if the women be somewhere occupied,
> there most commonly in their stead the men be idle.
> Besides this, how great and how idle a company is there
> of priests and religious men, as they call them; put
> thereto all rich men, specially all landed men, which
> commonly be called gentlemen and noblemen – take
> into this number also their servants: I mean all that
> flock of stout bragging swashbucklers. Join to them also
> sturdy and valiant beggars, cloaking their idle life under
> the colour of some disease or sickness.

Even among the few real workers in Europe, many spend
their time producing superfluous luxuries rather than the
things which are necessary for survival, comfort or natural
pleasures. No wonder, then, that in Utopia where no more
than five hundred able-bodied persons in each city-state
are dispensed from manual labour, a six-hour day suffices.

Dispensations are given, by the Syphogrants, on the advice of the priests, only to those who seem specially fitted
for learning and scholarship. From this small class of
scholars are chosen the Utopian priests, Tranibores and
Princes. Syphogrants need not be scholars, but they too
are exempted by law from labour; they take no advantage
of this privilege, however, so as to set others an example
of work.

The work in Utopia is made light, not only by the many
hands, but by the simplicity of the needs they serve. The
buildings, being all communal property, do not suffer
from private neglect, nor are they being continually altered at the whim of new owners. The manufacture of
clothes calls for no great labour, since Utopians prefer
coarse and sturdy wear of undyed cloth.

Occasionally the citizens are summoned from their regular
crafts to perform large-scale public works, such as the
mending of highways. On other occasions, when the economy is thriving, a public proclamation will shorten the
working day. The magistrates do not weary their citizens

with superfluous labour; the keynote of their policy is this: 'What time may possibly be spared from the necessary occupations and affairs of the commonwealth, all that the citizens should withdraw from the bodily service to the free liberty of the mind, and garnishing of the same. For herein they suppose the felicity of this life to consist.'

In More's Utopia, unlike Plato's Republic, the primary social unit is the family or household. Girls, when they grow up, move to the household to which their husbands belong; but sons and grandsons remain in the same household under the rule of the oldest parent until he reaches his dotage and is succeeded by the next oldest. The size of the households is strictly controlled. The number of births is not regulated, nor the number of children under fourteen; but no household may include less than ten or more than sixteen children who have grown up. The excess children in the larger households are moved to households where there are less than the minimum. If the number of households in the whole city grows beyond the statutory limit of six thousand, families are transferred to smaller cities. If every city in the whole island is already fully manned a colony is planted in unoccupied land overseas. If the natives there are unwilling to join them, and resist their settlement, the Utopians will establish the colony by force of arms; 'for they count this the most just cause of war, when any people holdeth a piece of ground void and vacant to no good or profitable use, keeping others from the use and possession of it which, notwithstanding, by the law of nature, ought thereof to be nourished and relieved.' If any of the homeland cities become dangerously undermanned, as has sometimes happened in time of plague, the Utopian colonists are recalled from abroad to make up the lack.

Each household, as explained earlier, will be devoted to a single craft. The products of the household's labour are placed in storehouses in the market-place in the centre of the quarter to which the household belongs. Every householder can carry away from these storehouses, free of charge, anything which he and his family need. In their dealings with each other, the Utopians make no use at all of money.

> For why should anything be denied unto anyone, seeing there is abundance of all things, and that it is not to be feared lest any man will ask more than he needeth? For why should it be thought that a man would ask more than enough, who is sure never to lack? Certainly, in all kinds of living creatures, either fear of lack doth cause covetousness and greed, or, in man only, pride, which counteth it a glorious thing to pass and excel others in the superfluous and vain ostentation of things. The which kind of vice among the Utopians can have no place.

Food, likewise, is distributed freely to every household which needs it: but individual householders have to wait their turn until food has been allotted first of all to the hospitals, on the prescription of doctors, and secondly to the houses of the Syphogrants. These houses contain great halls large enough to contain the whole of the thirty households making up the Syphograncy. Here, at dinner-time and supper-time, a brazen trumpet summons all the households to a communal meal. No one is forbidden to eat at home, but it is frowned on and almost nobody does so. 'It were a folly to take the pain to dress a bad dinner at home, when they may be welcome to good and fine fare so nigh hand at the hall.'

The women of the households take turns to prepare the food and arrange the meals, but they leave the menial and dirty kitchen tasks to the serfs. The tables are set against the walls, as in European monasteries and colleges: the men sit with their backs to the walls, the women on the other side so that they can leave the table easily if they feel unwell or need to attend to a child. The nursing mothers—and Utopian women nurse their own children whenever possible—eat apart with the under-fives in a nursery, which is a 'certain parlour appointed and deputed to the same purpose never without fire and clean water, nor yet without cradles; that when they will, they may down the young infants, and at their pleasure take them out of their swathing clothes, and hold them to the fire, and refresh them with play.' The children over five wait at table, or if they are too young to do so 'they stand by with marvellous silence', having food passed to them from the tables. At every table the diners sit 'four to a mess', as they do to this day in the Inns of Court. The Syphogrant and his wife, and the most senior citizens, sit at a high table on a dais, just like the Benchers of an Inn. They are joined, if there is a church in the Syphograncy, by the priest and his wife.

Both dinner and supper begin with a brief reading from an edifying book; after that, conversation is allowed, and it is specially noted that the elderly are not allowed to monopolise the time with long and tedious talk, but must provoke the young to speak, 'that they may have a proof of every man's wit, and towardness, or disposition to virtue; which commonly in the liberty of feasting, doth shew and utter itself.' Supper lasts longer than dinner, because the working day is over.

> No supper is passed without music. Nor their banquets want no conceits, nor junkets. They burn sweet gums and spices or perfumes, and pleasant smells, and sprinkle about sweet ointments and waters, yea, they have nothing undone that maketh for the cherishing of the company. For they be much inclined to this opinion: to think no kind of pleasure forbidden, whereof cometh no harm.

Travelling in Utopia is carefully regulated. To go from one city-state to another a passport is needed from the Tranibores stating the duration of the absence, and no one is permitted to travel alone. A free ox-cart, with a serf to drive, is provided; but Utopians rarely take advantage of this. For they do not need to carry provisions, since on arriving in another city-state they stay with the members of their profession and work at their crafts just as if they were at home. Travel between city-states without a passport is severely punished, and for a second offence a citizen can be reduced to serfdom. Within the same city-state a man does not need a passport to travel in the country, only 'the good will of his father and the consent of his wife'. But wherever he is, he must do a morning's work before he is given dinner, and an afternoon's work if he is to be given supper. This all ensures that no one is idle, no one goes hungry, and no one needs to beg.

The Utopians travel overseas to trade with other nations: they will export grain, honey, wool, hides, livestock and the like once thay have provided two years' supply of everything for themselves. When their ships arrive abroad, they distribute one-seventh of their cargoes to the poor of the country; the rest they sell at moderate prices. Though the Utopians do not use money among themselves, they need it for a number of international purposes. Iron, gold and silver are their main imports; they use exports principally to build up credit, to be drawn on to make loans to other people or to wage war. As a provision for time of war, they keep a large treasury at home to bribe enemy nationals or to hire mercenaries ('they had rather put strangers in jeopardy than their own countrymen').

Among the most astonishing things about Utopia are the arrangements for preserving the treasury of precious metals. The Utopians see, justly, that iron is of much greater real value than the precious metals. So they are careful not to set any artificial value on gold and silver. They do not lock them away, or work them into fine plate which they would be loath to part with in emergencies. Instead:

> Whereas they eat and drink in earthen and glass vessels – which indeed be curiously and properly made, and yet be of very small value – of gold and silver they make chamber pots and other vessels that serve for most vile uses; not only in their common halls, but in every man's private houses. Furthermore, of the same metals they make great chains, fetters, and gyves, wherein they tie their bondmen. Finally, whosoever for any offence be disgraced, by their ears they hang rings of gold: upon their fingers they wear rings of gold; and around their neck chains of gold: and, in conclusion their heads be tied with gold.

Pearls, diamonds and rubies are cut and polished and given to children to keep with their rattles and dolls.

Hythlodaye recalls that during his visit to Utopia there arrived an embassy from the distant land of Anemolia. The Anemolian ambassadors, ignorant of Utopian customs, sought to impress their hosts by the gorgeousness of their apparel. They wore cloth of gold, and gold necklaces, finger-rings and ear-rings, and caps flashing with pearls and gems. The Utopians took the most simply attired servants to be the leaders of the embassy; the ambassadors they mistook for slaves because of the gold that weighted them down. 'Look, mother,' said one Utopian child, 'there is a great grown fool wearing pearls and jewels as if he were a little boy.' 'Hush, child,' said the mother, 'I think he is one of the ambassador's jesters.' After a few days in Utopia the ambassadors learnt their mistake, and laid aside their fine gear. 'We marvel', the Utopians explained, 'that any men be so foolish as to have delight and pleasure in the doubtful glistering of a little trifling stone, when they may behold any of the stars, and the sun itself.'

Just as the Utopians despise those who take pleasure in jewellery, so too they regard it as madness to take pride in courtly honours. 'What natural or true pleasure', they ask, 'does thou take of another man's bare head, or bowed knees? Will this ease the pain of thy knees, or remedy the frenzy in thine own head?' Likewise, they cannot understand how men can find pleasure in casting dice upon a table, or hearing dogs bark and howl after a hare. What pleasure is there in seeing dogs run?

> But if the hope of slaughter, and the expectation of tearing in pieces the beast, doth please thee, thou shouldest rather be moved with pity to see a silly innocent hare murdered of a dog: the weak of the stronger; the fearful of the fierce; the innocent of the cruel and unmerciful.

So the Utopians regard the cruel sport of hunting as unworthy of free men. Even the slaughter of animals which is necessary for food is not permitted to citizens: only serfs are allowed to become butchers; because through the killing of beasts, they maintain, 'clemency, the gentlest affection of our nature,' decays and perishes little by little.

Though they despise cruel sports, the Utopians enjoy and delight in the pleasures of the body and of the senses, and take pride and joy in their unparalleled health and strength. They are no ascetics, and indeed regard as perverse bodily mortification for its own sake.

> To despise the comeliness of beauty, to waste the bodily strength, to turn nimbleness into slothness, to consume and make feeble the body with fasting, to do injury to health, and to reject the pleasant motions of nature . . . for a vain shadow of virtue, for the wealth and profit of no man, to punish himself, or to the intent he may be able courageously to suffer adversity, which perchance shall never come to him – this to do, they think it a point of extreme madness, and a token of a man cruelly minded towards himself, and unkind towards nature.

But it is the pleasures of the mind, rather than of the body, which most delight the Utopians. Though only a few citizens are dispensed from labour to devote themselves entirely to study, all are taught letters (in their own vernacular) and most men and women devote their leisure throughout life to reading. Before Hythlodaye's visit they were ignorant of Greek and Latin literature, but had made as much progress in music, logic, arithmetic and geometry as any of the classical authors. They were ignorant of modern (that is, medieval) logic, and of astrology; and very much better so. But when they heard a description of Greek literature they were anxious to learn the language; and those who were chosen to do so mastered it within the space of three years. They were delighted to accept from Hythlodaye a fine library of classical texts in Renaissance editions. Indeed, printing and paper-making were the only two European arts which the Utopians envied. Here too they proved quick learners, and acquired both skills in a short time.

In describing the customs of Utopia mention has been made from time to time of serfs. Serfdom is not hereditary slavery: most serfs are Utopians or foreigners reduced to serfdom as punishment for the kind of crime which is elsewhere punishable by death. When Utopians take prisoners in war, they use them as serfs; but they do not buy the prisoners of others as slaves. Labourers from other countries, finding Utopian serfdom preferable to their own drudgery, sometimes become serfs voluntarily; these are given lighter work, and are allowed to return home if ever they please to do so.

The sick are well cared for by the Utopians, who pride themselves on the enlightened and sanitary design of their hospitals. They sit with the incurably diseased and comfort them by every possible means.

> But if the disease be not only uncurable, but also full of continual pain and anguish, the priests and the magistrates exhort the man, seeing he is not able to do any duty of life, and by overliving his own death, is noisome and irksome to others and grievous to himself, that he will determine with himself no longer to cherish that pestilent and painful disease. And seeing his life is to him but a torment, that he will not be unwilling to

die, but rather to take a good hope to him, and either dispatch himself out of that pain, as out of a prison, or a rack of torment, or else suffer himself willingly to be rid out of it by others.

Such a suicide is regarded as a virtuous and noble action; but if a man kills himself without the advice of the priests and the magistrates, he is regarded as unworthy either to be buried or cremated; 'they cast him unburied into some stinking marsh.'

The marriage customs of the Utopians have attracted, or shocked, many of the book's readers. Men marry at twenty-two, and women at eighteen. Those convicted of premarital intercourse are forbidden to marry without a special pardon from the prince, and the heads of their household are disgraced. If promiscuity were allowed, the Utopians say, few would be willing to accept the burdens of monogamous matrimony.

Hythlodaye reports the custom observed by the Utopians in choosing wives and husbands.

> A grave and honest matron sheweth the woman, be she maid or widow, naked to the wooer: and likewise a sage and discreet man exhibiteth the wooer naked to the woman. At this custom we laughed, and disallowed it as foolish. But they on the other part do greatly wonder at the folly of all other nations, which in buying a colt (whereas a little money is in hazard) be so chary and circumspect, that although he be almost all bare, yet they will not buy him, unless the saddle and all the harness be taken off; lest under those coverings be hid some gall or sore. And yet in choosing a wife, which shall be either pleasure or displeasure to them all their life after, they be so reckless that all the residue of the woman's body being covered with clothes, they esteem her scarcely by one hand breadth (for they can see no more but her face), and so do join her to them, not without great jeopardy of evil agreeing together if anything in her body afterward should chance to offend and mislike them.

No doubt, after a marriage is consummated a body may wither or decay; in that case there is no remedy but patience. But before marriage no one should be allowed to conceal deformity beneath deceitful clothes.

Unlike most of their neighbours, the Utopians are monogamous, and marriage is in principle lifelong. However, adultery may break a marriage; the innocent, but not the adulterous, spouse is allowed to remarry. Besides adultery, 'the intolerable wayward manners of either party' provide grounds for divorce and the remarriage of the unoffending spouse. On rare occasions divorce by consent is permitted.

> Now and then it chanceth, whereas the man and woman cannot well agree between themselves, both of them finding other with whom they hope to live more quietly and merrily, that they, by the full consent of them both, be divorced asunder and married again to others. But that not without the authority of the Council: which agreeth to no divorces before they and their wives have diligently tried and examined the matter. Yea, and then also they be loth to consent to it; because they know this to be the next way to break love between man and wife – to be in easy hope of a new marriage!

Adultery is punished with serfdom, and divorce follows automatically unless the guiltless spouse is prepared to share the bondage and drudgery. (Such selfless devotion sometimes wins pardon for the guilty party.) Death is the punishment for repeated adultery: the only crime so punished, other than rebellion by those already condemned to serfdom. Minor matrimonial offences of wives are punished by husbands; the use of cosmetics is regarded as wanton pride, for beauty is less esteemed than probity. 'As love is sometimes won with beauty, so it is not kept, preserved, and continued, but by virtue and obedience.'

Apart from the laws governing marriage, there is little to be told about Utopian municipal law, because of the lack of private property. Altogether, the Utopians have very few laws; they despise the massive tomes of laws and commentaries to be found in other countries. 'They think it against all right and justice, that men should be bound to laws which either be in number more than be able to be read, or else blinder and darker than that any man can well understand them.' Their own laws are simple, and always given the most obvious interpretation. This enables them to dispense altogether with lawyers: they think it better that a man should plead his own case, and tell the same story to the judge that he would tell to his attorney.

The Utopians' virtues have inspired their neighbours to invite Utopian proconsuls to govern them, ruling for a five-year period and then returning home. Such officials are untempted by bribes (for what good is money to them, since they will shortly be returning to a country where it is not used?) and undeflected by malice or partiality (since they are living among strangers). So the two vices which most corrupt commonwealths are absent from the Utopians' allies.

Though the Utopians have allies and friends among other nations, they make no treaties or leagues. If man and man will not league together by nature, the words of treaties will not make them do so, they argue.

> They be brought into this opinion chiefly because, that, in these parts of the world leagues between princes be wont to be kept and observed very slenderly. For here in Europe, and especially in these parts where the faith and religion of Christ reigneth, the majesty of leagues is every where esteemed holy and inviolable: partly through the justice and goodness of princes, and partly at the reverence and motion of the Sovereign Pontiffs. Which, like as they make no promise themselves, but they do very religiously perform the same, so they exhort all princes in any wise to abide by their promises; and them that refuse or deny so to do, by their pontifical power and authority, they compel thereto.

More's irony reveals the degree of contempt into which the pontifical government had been brought, even among loyal Catholics, by the perfidious behaviour of Alexander VI and Julius II. The readiness of rulers to break treaties, he goes on, makes men think that justice is a virtue which is far too plebeian for kings to practise; or at least

> that there be two justices: the one meet for the inferior sort of the people; going a-foot and creeping low by the ground, and bound down on every side with many bands; the other, a princely virtue; which, like as it is of much higher majesty than the other poor justice, so also it is of much more liberty; as to the which, nothing is unlawful that it lusteth after.

Unlike other nations, the Utopians do not regard war as anything glorious; but they are not pacifists either. Both men and women receive regular military training, and they regard war as justified to repel invaders from their own or friendly territory, to liberate peoples oppressed by tyranny, to avenge injustices done to their allies. Pecuniary losses abroad to their own citizens they do not regard as justifying war; but if a Utopian is wrongfully disabled or killed anywhere, they first send an embassy to inquire into the facts, and if the wrongdoers are not surrendered they forthwith declare war. They prefer to win wars by stratagem and cunning than by battle and bloodshed, glorying in victories won by gifts of intellect rather than by the strength and powers that men share with animals.

Their one aim in war is to secure the object which, if it had been granted beforehand, would have prevented the declaration of war; or else, if that is impossible, to punish those at fault so as to deter future wrongdoing. One of their methods of minimising bloodshed is this. When war is declared, they cause posters to be set up secretly throughout enemy territory offering great rewards for the assassination of the enemy king, and smaller but still considerable sums for the deaths of other named individuals, regarded as responsible for the hostilities. This spreads dissension and distrust among the enemy; but it also means that those most likely to be killed in a war are not the general guiltless mass of the enemy nation, but the few wrongdoers among their leaders. For they know that common people do not go to war of their own wills, but are driven to it by the madness of rulers.

When battles do have to be fought abroad, the Utopians employ mercenaries: the fierce, rough Zapoletans, who live in rugged mountains like the Swiss Alps, hardy people who have no trade but fighting and care about nothing but money. Since the Utopians have so much gold, they can outbid rivals in purchasing Zapoletans. Only a small contingent of their own citizens is sent abroad, to accompany the commander and his deputies; and no one is enlisted for foreign service unless he volunteers. If Utopia itself is invaded, however, then all are placed in the front line, on shipboard or on the ramparts, brave men and fainthearts together, men and women alongside each other.

> In set field the wives do stand every one by their own husband's side; also every man is compassed next about with his own children and kinsfolk ... It is a great reproach and dishonesty for the husband to come home without his wife, or the wife without her husband, or the son without his father.

This gives the Utopians unparalleled courage and spirit in battle.

In each battle, as in war generally, the main aim is to destroy the leadership: a band of picked youths is bound by oath to seek out and kill or capture the opposing general. Once the battle is won there is no disordered pursuit or indiscriminate slaughter: the Utopians prefer to take prisoners than to kill the vanquished. They keep truces religiously, and they injure no non-combatants except spies; they never plunder captured cities, but the defeated are obliged to bear the expense of the war once it is over.

The final part of Hythlodaye's account of Utopia concerns religion. Some in Utopia worship heavenly bodies, or departed heroes; but the great majority there believe 'that there is a certain godly power, unknown, everlasting, incomprehensible, inexplicable, far above the capacity and

reach of man's wit,' which they call 'the father of all.' The medley of Utopian superstitions is gradually giving way to the worship of this single supreme being; but the majority do not impose their religious beliefs on others. The founder of Utopia, seeing that religious divisions were a great source of discord,

> made a decree that it should be lawful for every man to favour and follow what religion he would; and that he might do the best he could to bring others to his opinion, so that he did it peaceably, gently, quietly and soberly; without hasty and contentious rebuking and inveighing against others. If he could not by fair and gentle speech induce them unto his opinions, yet he should use no kind of violence and refrain from displeasant and seditious words. To him that would vehemently and fervently in this cause strive and contend, was decreed banishment or bondage.

There was one Utopian who became a convert to Christianity, and proselytised offensively with excessive zeal, consigning all non-Christians to everlasting fire. He was arrested, tried and banished, 'not as a despiser of religion, but as a seditious person and raiser up of dissension among the people.'

The tolerance proclaimed by the founder of Utopia was no mere device for keeping the peace: he thought it might well be true that God inspired different men with different beliefs so that he might be honoured with a varied and manifold worship. Even if only a single religion were true and the rest superstitions, truth is best left to emerge by its own natural strength. But Utopian religious toleration has its limits. It is regarded as base and inhuman to believe that the soul perishes with the body; anyone who professes such an opinion is treated as untrustworthy, excluded from public office and forbidden to defend his belief in public. Those who err on the opposite side, and attribute immortal souls to non-human animals, are left in peace.

Utopians believe not only in immortality, but in a blissful afterlife. For this reason, though they lament illness, they do not regard death, in itself, as an evil. Reluctance to die they take as a sign of a guilty conscience; one who obeys the summons of death with reluctance is viewed with horror and carried out to burial in sorrowful silence. But those who die cheerfully are not buried but cremated amid songs of joy. 'And in the same place they set up a pillar of stone, with the dead man's titles therein graved. When they be come home, they rehearse his virtuous manners and his good deeds. But no part of his life is so oft or gladly talked of, as his merry death.'

The Utopians believe that the dead revisit their friends invisibly and move above the living as witnesses of all their words and deeds. Thus they feel protected as they go about their business, but also deterred from any secret misdoing.

We have seen that the Utopians despise asceticism for its own sake. None the less, there are groups among them who live selfless lives embracing tasks which are rejected as loathsome by others, giving up their leisure to tend the sick, or undertake public works on roads or in field or forest. Some of these people practise celibacy and vegetarianism; others eat flesh, live normal family lives and avoid no pleasure unless it gets in the way of their work. The Utopians regard the former sect as holier but the second sect as wiser.

The Utopians, we are told, have priests of extraordinary holiness 'and therefore very few'. There are thirteen in each city under a bishop, all elected by popular vote in secret ballot. They preside over worship and conduct services, but are also censors of morals: to be rebuked by the priests is a great disgrace. The clergy are not authorised to inflict any punishment other than exclusion from divine service; but this punishment is dreaded more than almost any other.

Women as well as men may become priests, but they are chosen only if they are widows of a certain age. The male priests marry the choicest wives. The priests, male and female, have charge of the education of children and young people. No Utopian court may punish them for any crime. In battle they kneel beside the fighting armies, 'praying first of all for peace, next for victory of their own part, but to neither part a bloody victory'. When victory comes they mingle with their own victorious armies, restraining the fury and cruelty of the soldiers. They have averted such slaughter that their reputation is high among all neighbouring nations. 'There was never any nation so fierce, so cruel and rude, but they had them in such reverence, that they counted their bodies hallowed and sanctified, and therefore not to be violently and unreverently touched.'

Hythlodaye's narrative of the Utopians concludes with a minute description of the feasts with which they keep holy the first and last days of the month and the year, to offer thanks for prosperity past and pray for prosperity future. All family quarrels are reconciled before the feasts; 'if they know themselves to bear any hatred or grudge towards any man, they presume not to come to the sacrifices before they have reconciled themselves and purged their consciences.' 'The priests wear vestments made of birds' feathers, like those of American Indian chiefs. The service ends with a solemn prayer in which the worshippers thank God that they belong to the happiest commonwealth and profess the truest of all religions. The worshipper adds that if he is in error in believing this, 'if there be any other better than either of them is, being more acceptable to God, he desireth him that he will of his goodness let him have knowledge thereof, as one that is ready to follow what way soever he will lead him.' (pp. 20-39)

Anthony Kenny, in his Thomas More, *Oxford University Press, Oxford, 1983, 111 p.*

RICHARD MARIUS (essay date 1984)

[*Marius is a noted American editor, novelist, biographer, and historian. He edited several volumes in* The Yale Edition of the Complete Works of St. Thomas More *and wrote an important, if controversial, biography of More. Of this biography Clarence Miller has written: "Not everyone will agree with all [Marius's] conclusions and speculations about More's feelings, motives, and inner tensions; that would be too much to ask of a writer about such a complex and enigmatic character as More. But everyone should be delighted that such a gifted and knowledgeable writer . . . has finally and brilliantly undertaken the formidable task of seeing More steady and seeing him whole." In the following excerpt from* Thomas More: A Biography, *Marius discusses More's understanding of faith and religion as it is reflected in* Utopia.]

Utopia's religion has often been seen as somehow contrary to the faith for which Thomas More died. But a close study of the religion of the Utopians shows us that More was much less changeable about the things important to him than are most men.

There are some obvious superficial differences between Utopian religion and Catholic faith. Utopians possess a natural religion since it comes from their own perceptions as virtuous human beings and not through some special, historical revelation such as the appearance of God to Moses or of Christ to the world; its dogmas are not found in a sacred book like the Bible. The Utopians are pagans, but pagans of a special sort. Their "natural" theology so resembles the ethical teaching of Christianity that it is no wonder that Raphael could report that many of them were being converted to Christ.

More knew his classical paganism well enough to give some of his Utopians over to the worship of the sun, the moon, and the planets or else to a hero of the past so glorious that a few took him to have been the supreme god. Was More speaking of heroes like Hercules? Or was he implying that the Utopians have some natural intuition of the Christian revelation of the incarnation? The latter supposition is probably the right one: it is in keeping with Christian belief that many ceremonies and literary works from Greek and Roman life were foreshadowings of Christ and doctrines of the church. Virgil's Fourth Eclogue with its promise of a child coming to rule was only one example.

But having nodded toward a restrained and decorous paganism—no bacchic festivals, no orgiastic rites, no human sacrifice, no shedding of blood of any kind—More turned inward to the heart of the best pagan religion and assumed like Plato that behind the multitude of forms lay one grand and eternal reality. He has Raphael say:

> But by far the majority, and those by far the wiser, believe . . . in a certain simple being, unknown, eternal, immense, inexplicable, far above the reach of the human mind, diffused throughout the universe not in mass but in power. Him they call father . . . All the other Utopians too, though varying in their beliefs, agree with them in this respect that they hold there is one supreme being to whom are due both the creation and the providential government of the world.

This variety—hardly variety at all—is beginning to be displaced, so Raphael says, by the steady progress of all toward belief "in that one religion which seems to surpass the rest in reasonableness," the religion Raphael described as that already held by most Utopians.

That religion is harmonious with many of the teachings of Christianity about God and the devotion owed Him by mortals. The view that pagans could know much of God without special revelation was common among Christians. Aquinas is only the best known of a multitude of theologians who thought that any reasonable person of good will could know that God exists and is both infinite and good.

But Christianity is a historical religion and not a religion deduced from first principles. Christians have received revelation. That is, God has intervened in history and told His people things that cannot be known by reason alone. The doctrine of the Trinity, for example, could be neither discovered nor understood by philosophy; it came only through the revelation God made in Christ. Still, although virtuous pagans could not know Christian doctrine, they could win salvation if they lived up to what reason told them of God and the world. Christian theology dealt much more harshly with those who heard the Christian proclamation and turned away; the Utopians were hearing and being converted.

This progressive conversion to Christianity helps us understand the religious toleration in Utopia detailed by Raphael. King Utopus found the Utopians at war with each other over religion when he conquered the island. Indeed his conquest was made possible because the Utopians had been weakened by continual quarrels about religion. He was not himself sure what God wanted in the way of worship. (He could not be sure since he did not know Christianity.) But he did not believe that anyone ought to be compelled to religion by violence. So he laid down three articles of faith that every Utopian had to accept. Everyone had to believe that the human soul was immortal and that after death there is a state of rewards and punishments. Everyone must also believe that the world is guided by divine Providence. People refusing to believe these articles were ostracized by other Utopians, but they were not beaten or put to death. They were forbidden to hold office or share in the civic life, and they were not allowed to argue their beliefs before the common people. Anyone arguing any religious position too vehemently was subject to exile or enslavement.

More could not imagine how anyone could live in civilized society without believing in the immortality of the soul. If we did not believe in punishment after death for sins committed in this life, we would all live like the devil. And if we all lived like the devil, civilization would fall apart. The argument has been common enough in the Western tradition. Voltaire accepted a form of it. So have many others.

The immortality of the soul was being debated in many places as More wrote his ***Utopia.*** The Fifth Lateran Council in 1513 condemned those who denied that the soul was naturally immortal, but the decree did not prevent Pietro Pomponazzi of Bologna from writing in 1516 that no one could prove by reason alone that the soul survived death. Pomponazzi was careful. He claimed that in fact he did believe that the soul was immortal because the church told him to believe and he trusted the church more than reason. It was a "neutral problem," he said, one that could be neither proved nor disproved. But he argued with great and scrupulous care that nothing we observe of human life compels us by reason to suppose that the soul can do without the body any more than the body can endure without the soul. Pomponazzi put reason and faith at odds with each other with the disclaimer that of course he was devoted to the faith. Reason became only a game, although anyone taking the trouble to read his *On the Immortality of the Soul* will see that it was a most important game. Literal-minded modern scholars tend to take Pomponazzi at his word, believing that he did indeed put faith above reason. This modern view seems naïve, and although Pomponazzi did not reveal his innermost feelings, it looks as if his tractate is a cry of naturalism against the prevailing supernaturalism of his day, a supernaturalism that Thomas More upheld all his life and died to vindicate.

To our ears Pomponazzi's argument sounds simple enough. He was being rigorously empirical, commenting not on his authorities but on his experience. In fact, he was much closer to the real teachings of Aristotle on the soul than medieval commentators like Aquinas, who had managed to work their way around Aristotle's dangerous surmises about the indissoluble connection between body and soul. Aquinas held that the natural desire of everyone for immortality proves that the soul is immortal, just as the innate desire of a child to eat proves that there is food. Pomponazzi merely observed that as far as reason could see, people left nothing of themselves behind.

Such a view was not necessarily impious. One could believe that the soul died at the death of the body and that God would resurrect the dead—soul and body—and that the power to live after death was a gift of God's grace, not a quality inherent in the soul. One could argue that the idea of resurrection in the New Testament contradicted the Platonic teaching that the soul was naturally immortal. In some of his more radical early pronouncements, Martin Luther seemed to take this view. William Tyndale, More's great Protestant foe in England, believed in "soul sleep," the unconsciousness of the soul between death and the day of doom. Thomas More, preoccupied with death throughout his life, could not stomach such a reversal of the way Catholics had regarded the soul for centuries.

His Utopians had a social justification for belief in the immortality of the soul. They asked how civilization could survive if people did not believe they would be punished in an afterlife for crimes committed in this world, even if no earthly tribunal convicted them. The Utopians thought society would fall apart without such a belief. They assumed that sin would rush in to overpower anyone left alone, so people had to be watched all the time. Society itself could not do all the watching—although in Utopia privacy was almost as rare as atheism and almost as much suspected. God had to do the watching when, despite the best efforts of the Utopians, citizens managed to be alone.

Pomponazzi held that virtue and vice were their own rewards. The virtuous person was happier than the vicious person, and people would seek happiness naturally if they had the chance. Epicurus and Lucretius in the Greek world had held much the same confidence in human nature; Erasmus seemed to agree. It is an optimism that strikes us as hopelessly romantic, and the minute regulation and implacable openness of Utopian society show that More never shared it.

The Utopians have often seemed optimistic because they favored a philosophy of pleasure called "Epicurean" by modern scholars. More did not mention Epicurus or Epicureanism in ***Utopia,*** and despite the resolute efforts of some recent writers to make More an Epicurean of the spirit, the idea that pleasure was the goal of human life was neither radical nor uncommon in the Middle Ages and the Renaissance. Fortescue in *De laudibus* had taken for granted that human beings desire pleasure. Like More in ***Utopia,*** he held that the highest pleasure always included virtue. Fortescue said that both Stoics and Epicureans were agreed on the point, and it would naturally follow that one should choose the higher pleasures over the lower. More always believed with his Utopians that without strict discipline, the ordinary lot of human beings would be deceived into mistaking lower pleasures for the greatest good. The Utopians have never heard of Adam and Eve; but they recognize original sin.

Raphael tells us that the Utopians support their doctrine of pleasure by reference to their religion. Since religion tells them of a future state of rewards and punishments, they know that the highest pleasure of all is the virtue that, however hard, will be rewarded after death. Without such a belief in immortality, Raphael confesses, the Utopians have no clear standard to tell them the difference between pleasures of the flesh and those of the mind and soul; in fact, they say that people would be foolish to deny themselves some of the pleasures open to the senses in this life if they did not believe in a life to come—a tacit confession of original sin by the Utopians, who have discovered that people have an inclination to do those very things that strict logic and religion forbid.

Utopians must believe in divine Providence; we ... [see this] doctrine in More's story of John Morton's opinions about the rise and fall of kings in *The History of King Richard III*. Christians had to believe in some form of Providence if they were to believe that God had some purpose for creation. Providence would be turned into predestination by Luther and his followers, and More would react vehemently to their teachings. But like most Christians who take God's omnipotence seriously, he was forced to embrace a form of predestination himself in the end. He does not talk about it much in *Utopia*—here Providence seems to mean nothing other than the customary Christian faith that no matter how chaotic the world may seem, God is still in charge. The calamities that seem meaningless—sudden death, illness, or fall from high position—are in fact part of the grand design of God, unfathomable to us but not to Him.

Beyond these three tenets—immortality, an afterlife with punishments and rewards, and Providence—Utopians can hold various religious beliefs without persecution from the authorities. Why did More introduce this element of toleration into his ideal commonwealth? He later became a furious exponent of the traditional Catholic view that heretics should be burned. Did he change his mind? No. (pp. 171-75)

[Some Europeans] believed that the Catholic Church was in great danger even before Luther burst on the scene. They were mostly conservatives. Dorp was one, and old Bishop FitzJames was another. For others the church was so fixed in the life of Europe that they simply had no inkling of the chaos to come. More and Erasmus were different spirits, but in 1515 and 1516 they were united in their confidence that the Catholic Church would always endure, an unbroken vessel holding the culture and the hopes of Christian Europe. More could preach toleration in *Utopia* through Raphael's talkative mouth, and he could thereby call ironic attention to the intolerance of rival theologians, friars, and monastic orders screaming "heresy" at each other over any disagreement.

A certain strain of Neoplatonic romance might also have influenced More. ... [We] do not know much about his early admiration of Pico della Mirandola except that he did translate a short biography of the Italian humanist and mystic. He knew Pico's belief that all religions shared some doctrines—a commonplace of the Neoplatonists in Italy during the later fifteenth century. His friend Marsilio

Ficino suggested that this diversity of religions might have been ordained by God. Pico toiled long, hard, dangerously, and unsuccessfully to reconcile the differences and won for his efforts the hostility of conservative theologians who accused him of heresy and the enmity of a pope who accused him of arrogance. More was never sympathetic to anyone who deviated from the teaching of the church, and in his translation of the biography of Pico, he added a note of his own about Pico's "high mind and proud purpose," which had got him into trouble. Still he must have recognized that many of the accusations lodged against Pico were unfair, and in his *Utopia* he might have resurrected toleration in religion as a rebuke to the intolerance of those who had harassed his ideal man.

But the most plausible reason for religious toleration in *Utopia* is also the simplest: The Utopians were virtuous pagans, living by reason alone and without the revelation that came to Christianity through historical events. They had deduced some general principles, but they did not know Christian doctrine. Had they been intolerant of any religious expression of others, they would have been intolerant of Christianity—and therefore unreasonable. The tour de force that More engineered required religious toleration. Far too much has been made of it.

All the Utopians, by Hythlodaye's account, are steadily advancing toward the high-flown and decorous monotheism most of them already profess. This progress would be more rapid were it not for the superstitious tendency, even among Utopians, to see any misfortune to anyone contemplating a change of religion as a divine punishment, a misinterpretation of coincidence for judgement by God.

But Raphael says that as soon as Christianity was preached to them, the Utopians began to be converted. They were being moved by the name of Christ, his teaching, his character, his miracles, the constancy of the holy martyrs, and the similarity of Christianity to the highest form of their own religion. The conversion was not proceeding without unpleasant incidents: one Utopian convert became so vehement in denouncing other religions that he was sentenced to exile—not because he became a Christian but because he violated the Utopian principle of religious toleration. Here surely we have an ironic reference to the squabbling theologians of Christian Europe.

The Utopian Christians do not yet have a priest to administer the sacraments. Converts could be baptized by members of Raphael's party since, in Catholic doctrine, any Christian (or even non-Christian) can baptize in the absence of a priest. But without a priest, the Utopians are deprived of the other sacraments. When Raphael left them, they were debating whether they might elect one of their number to the priesthood, although such a course would have violated the apostolic succession supposed to be passed on through the sacrament of ordination. New priests had hands laid on their heads by priests who had had hands laid on their heads in a succession going all the way back to the apostles and finally to Christ himself. More would later vehemently defend the apostolic succession, but in *Utopia* Raphael says only that the issue of whether to select a priest or to wait for one had not been resolved by the time he departed.

We may have here a relic of some dinner talk between More and Erasmus. Erasmus would likely have stood for the right of the Utopians to elect their priests and to have them consecrate the eucharist and administer the other sacraments without benefit of ordination. It is hard to imagine More with his reverence for tradition surrendering the orthodox understanding of the sacrament. But at table with friends when he was far from home, in a world where the church seemed secure, such a debate would have been harmless enough. The note that the Utopians had not made up their minds on the subject when Raphael saw them last may have been a witty reference to an argument still unresolved among happily disputatious dinner companions.

It seems clear enough that the Utopians would soon be Christians. In effect, Raphael's story of their conversion is an idealized account of the conversion of the Roman Empire. It is an old maxim of history that those who rule the present command our vision of the past, and the medieval church had a nearly unanimous opinion of how the Romans were converted. Cruel emperors and their cohorts, all inspired by Satan, tried to drown the church in the blood of martyrs. But the martyrs suffered heroically, miracles abounded, the masses were persuaded, and finally God's purpose could be withstood no longer. Not until the eighteenth century was there any general sense among the educated in Europe that the conversion of the Empire had been helped along by greed, violence, chicanery, political intrigue, and wild superstition.

The medieval view of how Rome met Christ could easily be encapsulated in Raphael's story of the conversion of the Utopians. The Romans heard the name of Christ, his teachings, his character, his miracles, and they witnessed the constancy of his many martyrs. The triumph of orthodoxy took a while— three hundred years, in fact. But Christianity won out in the end because it was the perfection of the best in classical civilization, and the wisest and the best Romans were open-minded enough to see the obvious. The mighty works of God done to confirm this faith were such that only the willfully wicked could fail to see that Christ was God's own being in the world.

During those early centuries while Rome was being brought to Christ, the fathers of the church—to More's mind the greatest saints after the apostles—lived and wrote. More could not suppose another incarnation for the benefit of his Utopians, and because they had the wisdom to be open-minded until the true faith came to them, the Utopians would make no martyrs of their first Christians. And More could let himself dream a while of a rebirth of pure Christianity in a new world among people with all the classical virtues and none of the classical vices.

There was one profound difference between how Raphael announced Christianity to the Utopians and how the early fathers had interpreted Christianity to the Roman Empire. To the fathers, the indispensable text was scripture, but Raphael and his band took no Bible with them to Utopia. The omission is startling and not accidental. More knew the Bible well, and Raphael carried with him such a load of Greek books that the Utopians, soon mastering Greek, rapidly began to absorb the best of classical wisdom. But he did not have room in his trunk for a Bible.

Here we have a vision different from that of Erasmus. Erasmus longed for the Bible to become so common, translated into so many vernacular languages, that every-

one could read it—weavers, travelers, plowboys, even Turks and whores. Such a hope was never More's; he thought Christians could have had their faith untarnished and sufficient even if the Bible had never been written. True Christian doctrine was passed along orally from generation to generation in the church, the product of a living community rather than a dead book. That is the spirit we find in *Utopia*.

Like medieval Christians, the Utopians made a distinction between religion and philosophy, but they also held that the two could not be set against one another. A Pietro Pomponazzi would have been greeted with mystification and hostility in Utopia. Raphael tells us that the Utopians never held a discussion about philosophy without using principles taken from religion. Religion could not be revelation in Utopia, but the inseparable joining of religion and reason provides a corollary to More's later argument that reason should always be a handmaid to faith and not faith's master. More never had any use for time-wasting games, and in his mind a Pomponazzi would have made a game of reason and all to no pious purpose.

His was the general opinion of the earlier Middle Ages. Anselm of Canterbury (born an Italian) expressed it when he spoke of the use of reason in religion as "faith seeking understanding." The Christian receives faith from the tradition of the church and through experience with the God revealed through the church. Only then does the believer

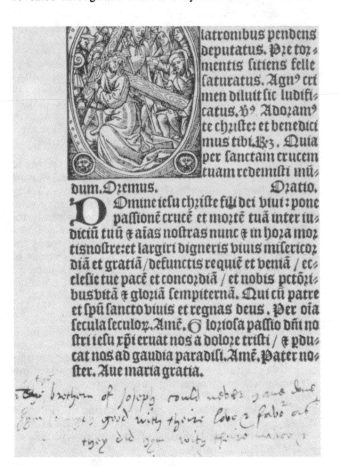

A leaf from More's prayer book, with annotations in More's own hand.

discover that Christian doctrines hold together systematically. They are not absurd. The Christian does not acquire doctrine by reasoning up to it from logic alone. Logical deductions made in a study do not lift us up to the mysteries of God. Nor can reason abstracted from history lead us to the conclusion that Christ was incarnate in Palestine in the early years of the Roman Empire and that he was crucified outside Jerusalem for our sins and that he rose again from the dead so that we, too, can triumph over death.

The Catholic Church always held that deductive reason ("philosophy") was a category different from the revelation of God in history. No logician sitting in a corner without historical knowledge can deduce out of thin air that Caesar crossed the Rubicon or that Columbus discovered America. But one historical reality is known, it can be fitted into a context that allows us some systematic understanding. And once we know what God has done in history, we can see some of the reasons for His act. For example, if we know that Christ died for our sins, we must also see as reasonable the proposition that our depravity must have been far too great for any lesser sacrifice to accomplish our redemption. But such an inference does not begin with abstract reflections on human nature; it begins with the effort to understand a historical event.

More always held this traditional view, that the Christian must accept first what tradition tells about Christ and that only then can reason assemble propositions that make the faith plausible and systematic. And this is his assumption in Raphael's presentation of the relation of philosophy and religion in *Utopia.*

But reason may be defined in many different ways, and sometimes More's use of the word is blurred. He knows the reason that allows us to sort out the various articles of the Christian faith. And he knows also the reason that allows us to make sense of our own experience. That experience includes what we observe of the world, and the Utopians used reason to understand the natural sciences.

When More wrote of "philosophy" in *Utopia,* he seems to have had in mind the basic human faculty for knowing what we observe and for making inferences about it. I may observe a human footprint in the sand, and I may infer that somebody made it by walking there too recently for the print to have been obliterated by wind and rain. I cannot tell much of anything about the person who made the footprint—whether he (or she) was kind and generous or mean and greedy. I cannot tell anything about the person's ancestry or purposes. I can merely observe that a human being has passed by. (pp. 175-79)

Aristotle and his disciples were continually seeking for some way of uniting all that we observe and all our inferences into a great system without contradictions. The Aristotelian is always establishing a truth not self-evident; he does so by means of general principles or observations supposedly clear to everyone, moving upward from discovery to discovery like someone climbing a ladder. Or else he is like a stonemason carefully setting one block of knowledge on top of another. The theory is that in time a perfectly harmonious building of knowledge will encompass all human learning.

Aristotle reasoned up to God—or to a god. But he was like someone studying a footprint on the beach; he could

not deduce much about that god, and Aristotle's deity could just as well be a machine as a loving—and judging—creator. When Aristotle had empirical information, as in observations of natural phenomena, he tried to systematize it, and so he left to us works that tried to reduce physics, poetics, rhetoric, and a host of other subjects to systems that could be easily taught.

Religion in Utopia has a philosophical quality to it. Miracles happen in the commonwealth—though Raphael does not describe any of them. The miracles represent empirical reality; they must be fitted into the general system of knowledge that the Utopians share. What does one infer from miracles? To observe them without inferring the power of God causing them would be an impossible contradiction—at least to the Utopians. So in good Aristotelian fashion, they observe miracles and infer that God is their source. They are reasoning from effect back to cause.

But what kind of God is it? That question apparently gives Utopian "philosophy" the same difficulty that it gives anyone who tries to construct a natural religion by making a chain of inferences from observable phenomena. So More gives us a higher category, a "reason" that is superior to philosophy. We may call it "intuition," though in our day "intuition" has come to mean merely a "hunch" or something equally uncertain. In Plato's thought, intuition is the surest knowledge we can have; it is knowledge we possess directly because we are the beings we are.

All Utopians must believe three things—the immortality of the soul, a future state of rewards and punishments, and a guiding Providence of God. Hythlodaye tells us specifically that these are principles of religion and not of philosophy. That seems to mean that More takes these beliefs to be unmistakable human intuitions.

We may use an illustration that More did not use. If I say that "reason" tells me that the sky is blue and that trees in summer are green, I mean only that the human mind through the mysterious instrument of the eye perceives something that I call "color," which does not seem to be in the perceptions of dogs or cattle. Unless I am color-blind, color is an immediate part of any perception that I have of the physical world. I do not discover color by deductive logic. In fact, when I run into the color-blind person, I find it excruciatingly difficult to explain color at all. I may say that color can be proved because different colors emit different frequencies of light that can be measured. But such a statement is inadequate to demonstrate color to the person who cannot already see it. We can say only that this understanding of frequencies is in harmony with our direct perception, but it cannot replace the perception itself. Without the perception, we cannot give much meaning to statements about frequencies; color remains only a number, something outside ourselves, something fearfully abstract.

In the same way, More seems to be saying that a certain religious consciousness is an immediate perception of human nature and that unless we have it, we are not truly human. From it we can know that the soul is immortal, though we may not be able to explain immortality by "philosophy." It is rather a knowledge that arises from intuition, from our very being. Our natural religious consciousness may be heightened by miracles that provide additional evidence to our spontaneous perception. The God we know by intuition must be assumed to work in His world. But without the intuition that sets them in context, the miracles might be nothing more than frightening and utterly incomprehensible disruptions of the familiar order of nature. We cannot go by logic from miracles to intimate knowledge of God any more than we can pass easily from knowledge of frequencies to proving that colors exist. We must first have the perception; only then can we make sense of the numerical qualities that are a part of color, or the miracles that proceed from God.

"Philosophy" to More is this *outer* thing, a world not immediately open to perception but one we find rather through the block-building of Aristotle that begins with sense experience, then allows us to discover evidence and finally to make connections that assemble the evidence into a system. In moving from the known to the unknown, we use both induction and deduction—processes of the mind that move to conclusions not self-evident. But philosophy of this sort can work only if we trust the sensual perceptions that allow us to assemble the evidence in the first place. The good Aristotelian becomes incredulous, annoyed, even angry when you say to him, "But I don't trust the five senses." In effect, Thomas More—like Cicero—adds a religious sense to the five bodily senses. In his *Utopia*, philosophy based on objective analysis and careful logic can guide us in the quest for moral values only if the religious sense is taken into account. Our five bodily senses can be skewed if we drink too much wine or if we take dope or if we go for days without sleep. In Europe the religious sense was skewed by a grasping and proud society; in Utopia it was allowed full freedom of expression.

The distinction between discursive reasoning and religious intuition in *Utopia* helps us understand the shock that later struck More when he met Protestant heretics with their gloomy insistence on the total depravity of the human soul. The Protestants who denied the natural immortality of the soul seemed to More to be denying one of the fundamental modes by which men and women are able to see themselves as human beings with an eternal worth in the universe.

It was not merely the question of the soul that haunted him; of much profounder significance was the very religious consciousness called into question by the way Protestants approached religion. They claimed to take everything from the Bible, and declared that anything not validated by the express word of scripture could be abandoned. They claimed that the Holy Spirit was necessary to interpret scripture correctly. Still they always held that the book was sufficient to answer all answerable religious questions, and since they disagreed so quickly and so violently with one another, More could denounce them as impossible protagonists of a dead book whereas Catholics espoused a living faith imprinted on the hearts of true Christians. He would ask his foes again and again how they knew the Bible had any value if they rejected the Catholic Church that had given them the Bible in the first place. Turn to the book and reject the church, said he, and you will shortly have no religion at all.

He would write so passionately because to his mind Protestantism threatened not only the Holy Catholic Church but the understanding of human nature that made any religion possible. In his *Utopia* he could hold that we have a natural religious consciousness, and he could assume

that the very presence of the consciousness proved that its object—God Himself—did have an objective existence. This is circular reasoning, to be sure, but it did not seem so to More.

As a Christian he held that the Catholic Church with its centuries of tradition and its hosts of saints was a natural development of the fundamental religious consciousness in all human beings. God had worked with special power in those before Christ whose observance of the natural law purified their lives so that their religious consciousness had the freedom to guide them. He had inspired the great common body of Christendom with proper religious truth, and the existence of the united Catholic Church in time and in space proved that human beings were capable of receiving the special grace of revelation and that they could respond to it with agreement—just as the generality of human beings can recognize colors and agree on the names that should be applied to them although they cannot precisely define them.

Protestantism brought savage and irreconcilable disagreement about religion and called in question humanity's capacity for religious consciousness. To believe that religious consciousness was general and validated by the observable consensus of Catholic history was to believe something about the means God chose to work with the world. God could have worked in other ways; More always admitted that. But in fact human nature and human experience testified to the ways God had chosen, and More thought it evident that God had chosen to work within the religious consciousness implanted in human beings with the image of God Himself at creation. However feeble might be their efforts, humans showed through their innate religious consciousness combined with good will and resolution a capacity to work harmoniously with God. The image of God had been devastated by sin but not destroyed, and all people—Catholics or Utopians—could by their very nature bring themselves into a place where God's grace could meet them and work with them for redemption. However pessimistic the Utopian view of human nature may have been, it fell far short of the total depravity proclaimed by Martin Luther, William Tyndale, Ulrich Zwingli, and the Protestants who came after them.

When Protestants rejected the Catholic Church and its teaching that a united tradition proved the Catholic view of God's working in the world, the worth and very existence of a religious consciousness itself—which, alas, is not as evident to most as light and color—was bound to be questioned. Catholics said, "The truth of the faith is proved by consensus, and consensus arises from the kind of beings we are—religious beings whose religious consciousness is a valid and natural way to God." Protestants said, "Human beings are totally depraved, and any 'natural' consciousness of God is perverted, so that the existence of a religious consciousness in itself tells us nothing at all about how we ought to serve God." Once questions began to be asked about the worth of religious consciousness, any intelligent impartial person could see how hard, how nearly impossible they were to answer in any way that did not mean the collapse of religious belief sustained by rational argument. If this fundamental religious consciousness was only a figment, God might be so different from human beings as to be the "Wholly Other" of modern Protestant conservative theology, a being so different from ourselves that our only attitude must be a patient waiting for Him to speak and a willingness to obey absolutely whatever He tells us. But once the belief in a valid natural religious consciousness in human beings is destroyed, we can just as easily go in the other direction and claim that all religion is merely a figment and that God does not exist.

In *Utopia,* More gave his people a religious consciousness, an intuition that existed above reason but harmonized with it, and without making his Utopians Christians he nevertheless validated the intellectual suppositions about human nature that made belief in Catholic tradition possible. Human beings are like this, no matter where they may be found, he tells us. This kind of human being makes the Catholic Church the most plausible expression of God's incarnation in a single human being, Jesus of Nazareth, and His continued presence in creation through the sacraments of the church and the inspiration of His people. (pp. 179-83)

> *Richard Marius, in his* Thomas More: A Biography, *Alfred A. Knopf, 1984, 562 p.*

ADDITIONAL BIBLIOGRAPHY

Allen, Peter R. "*Utopia* and European Humanism: The Function of the Prefatory Letters and Verses." *Studies in the Renaissance* X (1963): 91-107.
    Discusses the letters and poems written for early editions of *Utopia* by More and his fellow humanists. Allen concludes: "The appended letters and verses . . . share in both the fictional aspect of *Utopia* and its serious intent, and commend it as both a delightful literary game and an important philosophic work."

Anderegg, Michael A. "A Myth for All Seasons: Thomas More." *The Colorado Quarterly* XXIII, No. 3 (Winter 1975): 293-306.
    Cautions against accepting too freely an uncritical view of More as saint and hero non pareil.

Belloc, Hilaire. "The Witness to Abstract Truth." In his *One Thing and Another*, pp. 115-21. London: Hollis & Carter, 1955.
    Examines the nature of More's martyrdom, concluding: "It is our business to give up all for whatever is truth. . . ."

Berger, Harry, Jr. "Utopian Folly: Erasmus and More on the Perils of Misanthropy." *English Literary Renaissance* 12, No. 3 (Autumn 1982): 271-90.
    Maintains that "in their very different ways both *The Praise of Folly* and *Utopia* dramatize the same vitiated attitude toward life, and explore its consequences."

Blake, Mary Elizabeth. "Sir Thomas More." *The Catholic World* LIX, No. 351 (June 1894): 382-84.
    A poem of praise to More's steadfast courage. The poem's speaker is More in the Tower, comforting his daughter Margaret.

Boewe, Charles. "Human Nature in More's *Utopia*." *The Personalist* XLI, No. 3 (Summer 1960): 303-09.
    Investigates More's beliefs concerning the social influence of heredity and environment as they are implied in *Utopia*.

Bolt, Robert. *A Man for All Seasons: A Drama in Two Acts.* New York: Samuel French, Inc., 1962, 134 p.
    An imaginative recreation, based on the earliest eyewitness accounts, of the events leading up to More's execution. The drama was first performed in 1960 and was made into a feature film in 1966.

Bridgett, T. E. *Life and Writings of Sir Thomas More, Lord Chancellor of England and Martyr under Henry VIII.* London: Burns & Oates, Limited, 1891, 458 p.
    An important nineteenth-century biography of More, offering commentary on the author's major and minor works.

Busleyden, Jerome. Letter to Thomas More. In *More's Utopia and Its Critics*, edited by Ligeia Gallagher, pp. 87-9. Chicago: Scott, Foresman and Company, 1964.
    A 1516 letter, originally published in the first edition of *Utopia*, praising Utopia as a model of excellence worthy of imitation in the larger world.

Campbell, W. E. *More's Utopia & His Social Teaching.* London: Eyre & Spottiswoode Publishers Ltd., 1930, 164 p.
    Approaches *Utopia* as the work of "one of those great figures that stand at the parting ways of history."

Chambers, R. W. "The Saga and the Myth of Thomas More." *Proceedings of the British Academy* XII (1926): 179-225.
    A highly favorable overview of More's literary and political careers, documenting changing perceptions of More from the earliest biographies to the first quarter of the twentieth century.

——. *On the Continuity of English Prose from Alfred to More and His School.* Early English Text Society, Original Series, No. 191A. London: Oxford University Press, 1932, clxxiv p.
    Closely examines More's English prose as the culmination of a centuries-old stream of English prose development.

——, ed. *The Fame of Blessed Thomas More: Being Addresses Delivered in His Honour in Chelsea, July 1929.* London: Sheed and Ward, 1929, 132 p.
    Prints eight addresses delivered at the More Memorial Exhibition in 1929. Contributors include Father Ronald Knox, "The Charge of Religious Intolerance"; Henry Browne, S. J., "A Catholic of the Renaissance"; and Bede Jarrett, O. P., "A National Bulwark against Tyranny."

Coogan, Robert. "Petrarch and Thomas More." *Moreana* 21 (February 1969): 19-30.
    Considers the influence of Petrarch's works on More's prose style.

Daly, James J., S. J. "Sir Thomas More, Saint and Humorist." *The Catholic World* CXI, No. 664 (July 1920): 463-70.
    Examines More's "human touch" as it is conveyed in his writings and conversations.

Dean, Leonard F. "Literary Problems in More's Richard III." *PMLA* LVIII, No. 1 (March 1943): 22-41.
    Aesthetic evaluation of the English and Latin versions of *The History of King Richard III*.

Emerson, Ralph Waldo. "Heroism." In his *The Collected Works of Ralph Waldo Emerson*, Volume II: *Essays: First Series*, edited by Alfred R. Ferguson and Jean Ferguson Carr, pp. 145-56. Cambridge: Harvard University Press, Belknap Press, 1979.
    Briefly compares More's "playfulness at the scaffold" with Socrates's condemnation of himself.

Fuller, Thomas. "London: Statesmen." In his *The History of the Worthies of England*, pp. 361-66. 1840. Reprint. New York: AMS Press Inc., 1965.
    A biographical sketch of More, noting that "among his Latin works *Utopia* beareth the bell."

Gibson, R. W. *St. Thomas More: A Preliminary Bibliography of His Works and of Moreana to the Year 1750.* New Haven: Yale University Press, 1961, 499 p.

A descriptive bibliography of early editions of More's works and Moreana, with a bibliography of Utopiana by Gibson and J. Max Patrick.

Grace, Damian, and Byron, Brian. *Thomas More: Essays on the Icon.* Melbourne: Dove Communications, 1980, 129 p.

Collects papers read at a quincentennial More conference held at St. John's College in the University of Sydney. Essayists include Germain Marc'hadour, "Here I Sit: Thomas More's Genius for Dialogue"; A. C. Cousins, "St. Thomas More as English Poet"; and Maureen Purcell, "Dialogue of Comfort for Whom?"

Greenblatt, Stephen. "At the Table of the Great: More's Self-Fashioning and Self-Cancellation." In his *Renaissance Self-Fashioning: From More to Shakespeare,* pp. 11-73. Chicago: The University of Chicago Press, 1980.

Studies More's literary career as it evolved in an age when "there were both selves and a sense that they could be fashioned."

Harbison, E. Harris. "The Intellectual as Social Reformer: Machiavelli and Thomas More." *The Rice Institute Pamphlet* XLIV, No. 3 (October 1957): 1-46.

A comparative study of More's and Machiavelli's approaches to social reform.

Heiserman, A. R. "Satire in the *Utopia.*" *PMLA* LXXVIII, No. 3 (June 1963): 163-74.

Argues that "only an application of the satiric principle . . . explains the apparent discrepancies between More's career and his 'ideal' state, and accounts for the fact that *Utopia* has seemed a *jeu d'esprit,* a philosophical argument, a program for political reform, and an enigmatic document in the history of ideas."

Jones, Emrys. "Commoners and Kings: Book One of More's *Utopia.*" In *Medieval Studies for J. A. W. Bennett, Aetatis Suae LXX,* edited by P. L. Heyworth, pp. 255-72. Oxford: Oxford University Press, Clarendon Press, 1981.

A literary study of *Utopia,* focusing on aesthetic concerns in Book One.

Kaufman, Peter Iver. "Humanist Spirituality and Ecclesial Reaction: Thomas More's Monstra." *Church History* 56, No. 1 (March 1987): 25-38.

A reappraisal of *Utopia*'s place in Renaissance spirituality, arguing that More sought to defend religious formalism in the work.

Kinney, Arthur F. *Rhetoric and Poetic in Thomas More's "Utopia."* Humana Civilitas: Sources and Studies relating to the Middle Ages and the Renaissance, Vol. 5. Malibu, Calif.: Udena Publications, 1979, 36 p.

Studies the rhetorical complexity of *Utopia.*

McConica, James Kelsey. *English Humanists and Reformation Politics under Henry VIII and Edward VI.* Oxford: Oxford University Press, Clarendon Press, 1965, 340 p.

A comprehensive study of English humanism containing scattered references to More and his works.

McCutcheon, Elizabeth. "Denying the Contrary: More's Use of Litotes in the *Utopia.*" *Moreana* 31 (November 1971): 107-21.

Discusses the rhetorical and thematic significance of litotes in *Utopia.*

―――. "Time in More's *Utopia.*" In *Acta Conventus Neo-Latini Turonensis: Troisième Congrès International d'Études Néo-Latins, Tours,* edited by Jean-Claude Margolin, pp. 697-707. Paris: Librairie Philosophique J. Vrin, 1980.

An in-depth analysis of the role of time in *Utopia* and its moral and spiritual implications.

Mason, H. A. *Humanism and Poetry in the Early Tudor Period.* London: Routledge and Kegan Paul, 1959, 296 p.

A full-length study of early Tudor literature, with chapters on More's relation to the humanists, the identity of spirit in the works of More and Erasmus, and *Utopia* as a vindication of Christian humanism.

Metscher, Thomas. "The Irony of Thomas More: Reflections on the Literary and Ideological Status of *Utopia.*" *Shakespeare Jahrbuch* 118 (1982): 120-30.

Discusses the concept of ideal social order in *Utopia,* commenting as well on More and the traditions of radical literature.

Mezciems, Jenny. "Utopia and 'the Thing which is not': More, Swift, and Other Lying Idealists." *University of Toronto Quarterly* 52, No. 1 (Fall 1982): 40-62.

Traces the literary and rhetorical conventions of Utopian fiction from More's *Utopia* to Jonathan Swift's works.

Miles, Leland. "The Literary Artistry of Thomas More: *The Dialogue of Comfort.*" *Studies in English Literature, 1500-1900* VI, No. 1 (Winter 1966): 7-33.

Treats poetic and dramatic devices in *The Dialogue of Comfort,* maintaining that "More exhibits outstanding literary skill in many areas" of the work.

[More, Cresacre]. *The Life and Death of Sir Thomas Moore, Lord High Chancellour of England.* N. p., n. d., 432 p.

A laudatory biography of More by More's great-grandson, published at St. Omer or Douai around 1631, containing scattered remarks on More's writings and a brief appendix treating the works alone.

More, Thomas. "Thomas More to Peter Giles, Sendeth Gretynge." In his *Utopia,* edited by Edward Arber, translated by Ralph Robinson, pp. 21-6. Birmingham, England: n. p., 1869.

A letter from More to Peter Giles, originally published in the first printing of *Utopia,* in which More comments on the purpose and prose style of the work.

Moreana I—(1963—).

A quarterly publication, published by the Amici Thomae Mori, offering articles, book reviews, and abstracts concerning More and his circle.

Morgan, Alice B. "Philosophic Reality and Human Construction in the *Utopia.*" *Moreana* 39 (September 1973): 15-23.

Studies the relationship of the natural and the artificial in *Utopia.*

Perlette, John M. "Irresolution as Solution: Rhetoric and the Unresolved Debate in Book 1 of More's *Utopia.*" *Texas Studies in Literature and Language* 29, No. 1 (Spring 1987): 28-53.

Examines the debate on the question of counsel in Book One of *Utopia.*

Pineas, Rainer. "Thomas More's Use of the Dialogue Form as a Weapon of Religious Controversy." *Studies in the Renaissance* VII (1960): 193-206.

A close survey of More's use of the dialogue form in his controversial works, concluding: "By using the dialogue to discuss the issues rather than just to ridicule his opponents' beliefs, More widened the scope of the Renaissance dialogue of religious controversy."

―――. "Thomas More's Use of Humor as a Weapon of Religious Controversy." *Studies in Philology* LVIII, No. 2 (April 1961): 97-114.

Explores More's controversial works, arguing that "in his bitter struggle to preserve the Catholic faith, More made humor one of his main weapons."

Pollard, A. F. "The Making of Sir Thomas More's *Richard III.*" In *Historical Essays in Honour of James Tait*, edited by J. G. Edwards, V. H. Galbraith, and E. F. Jacob, pp. 223-38. Manchester: Printed for the Subscribers, 1933.
Discusses *The History of King Richard III* in the light of Renaissance historiography.

Raitiere, Martin N. "More's *Utopia* and *The City of God.*" *Studies in the Renaissance* XX (1973): 144-68.
Probes the dichotomy of "natural right and patriarchal authority" in *Utopia*, suggesting that More was influenced by St. Augustine's *City of God.*

Rexroth, Kenneth. "Thomas More: *Utopia.*" In his *Classics Revisited*, pp. 154-59. Chicago: Quadrangle Books, 1968.
A brief review of *Utopia*, describing the work as "a kind of perfected and purified Old Testament."

Reynolds, E. E. *Thomas More and Erasmus.* New York: Fordham University Press, 1965, 260 p.
A comparative study of the lives and literary careers of More and Erasmus by a leading authority on More.

Rowse, A. L. "St. Thomas of Chelsea." *The Spectator* CLIV, No. 5579 (31 May 1935): 924.
Ascribes More's martyrdom to "a deep-rooted spiritual (or intellectual) pride," a "sort of spiritual vanity."

Schoeck, Richard J. *The Achievement of Thomas More: Aspects of his Life and Works.* Victoria: University of Victoria, 1976, 83 p.
Cogent survey of More's life and works.

Smelser, Marshall. "The Political Philosophy of Sir Thomas More as Expressed in His Theological Controversies." *St. Louis University Studies in Honor of St. Thomas Aquinas* 1 (1943): 12-32.
Contends that More's political thought was essentially medieval and that More "was no rationalist in the modern sense."

Sullivan, Frank, and Sullivan, Majie Padberg. *Moreana: Materials for the Study of Saint Thomas More.* 4 vols. Los Angeles: Loyola University of Los Angeles, 1964-68.
An invaluable secondary bibliography of More criticism, citing and evaluating the earliest to the most recent commentary on More. A separate index by Majie Padberg Sullivan alone, *Index to Moreana*, was published in 1971.

Surtz, Edward L., S. J. "Thomas More and Communism." *PMLA* LXIV, No. 3 (June 1949): 549-64.
Attempts to discover More's own attitude toward communism, proceeding from the premise that "there can be no doubt that Raphael Hythloday, like the Utopians, is persuaded that communism is the solution for the social, economic, and political evils of the early sixteenth century."

———. "Logic in Utopia." *Philological Quarterly* XXIX, No. IV (October 1950): 389-401.

Records More's attitude toward contemporary philosophy as it is evidenced in *Utopia.*

———. "Introduction: Utopia Past and Present." In *Utopia,* by St. Thomas More, edited by Edward Surtz, S. J., pp. vii-xxx. New Haven: Yale University Press, 1964.
A short introduction to the major themes and concerns of *Utopia.*

Sylvester, Richard S. "Conscience and Consciousness: Thomas More." In *The Author in His Work: Essays on a Problem in Criticism*, edited by Louis L. Martz and Aubrey Williams, pp. 163-74. New Haven: Yale University Press, 1978.
Explores the role of moral conviction and personal awareness in More's life and works.

———, ed. *St. Thomas More, Action and Contemplation: Proceedings of the Symposium Held at St. John's University, October 9-10, 1970.* New Haven: Yale University Press for St. John's University, 1972, 178 p.
Contains four essays treating More's active and contemplative lives: Richard J. Schoeck, "Common Law and Canon Law in Their Relation to Thomas More"; Louis L. Martz, "Thomas More: The Tower Works"; G. R. Elton, "Thomas More, Councillor (1517 - 1529)"; and Germain Marc'hadour, "Thomas More's Spirituality."

Trapp, J. B., and Herbrüggen, Hubertus Schulte. *"The King's Good Servant": Sir Thomas More, 1477/8-1535.* Ipswich: The Boydell Press, 1977, 147 p.
A generously illustrated catalogue of a More exhibition held at the National Portrait Gallery, London, in 1977. Subjects treated include More's early life in London, his household, his confinement in the Tower, and his posthumous reputation.

Trevor-Roper, Hugh. "The Intellectual World of Sir Thomas More." *The American Scholar* 48, No. 1 (Winter 1978-79): 19-32.
Locates More among his intellectual contemporaries, noting the strong impression made by Platonism on sixteenth-century thought.

Walpole, Horace. "Painters in the Reign of Henry VIII: Hans Holbein (1498-1554)." In his *Anecdotes of Painting in England,* Vol. I, pp. 66-74. London: Henry G. Bohn, 1849.
A biography of the painter Hans Holbein, citing More as "the unblemished magistrate . . . whose humility neither passion nor piety could elate, and whose mirth even martyrdom could not spoil."

Will, George F. "Sir Thomas More: The Limits of Accommodation." In his *The Pursuit of Virtue and Other Tory Notions,* pp. 256-58. New York: Simon and Schuster, 1982.
Thoughts on More's martyrdom, with brief commentary on More's literary works. Will labels *Utopia* "a prescription for gentlemanly totalitarianism."

Willow, Sister Mary Edith. *An Analysis of the English Poems of St. Thomas More.* Bibliotheca Humanistica & Reformatorica, Vol. VIII. Nieuwkoop, Netherlands: B. De Graaf, 1974, 285 p.
A full-length examination of More's English poetry.

William Roper

1496?-1578

English biographer.

Roper is remembered for a single literary work: *The Mirrour of Vertue in Worldly Greatnes; or, The Life of Syr Thomas More Knight*, a biography of the great English humanist and Roman Catholic martyr who lived during the reign of Henry VIII. As a boarder and later as More's son-in-law, Roper was a member of the More household for sixteen years. There he became his father-in-law's confidant and grew to know him intimately—"no one man [livinge] . . . of him and of his doings understood so much as my self," Roper claimed. *The Life* is therefore valued for the light it sheds on More's character and for the glimpses it provides of More's mind during one of the most tumultuous events in Tudor history: More's refusal to accede to Henry VIII's command that he openly acknowledge the king's supremacy in matters of religion in England. Also recognized as a literary work of independent merit, *The Life* is deemed a consummate example of Tudor biography.

Roper was the eldest son of John Roper, a wealthy Kentish landowner, and Jane Fineux Roper, daughter of Sir John Fineux, chief justice of the king's bench. As a member of Lincoln's Inn, John Roper was closely associated with Thomas More and his father, Judge John More, from about 1505 onwards. William was probably born in 1496. Of his youth and early education nothing is known, although one of his first biographers, Anthony à Wood, claimed he was educated "at one of the Universities." Roper entered the More household as a lodger around 1518, the year in which he began to study the law seriously as a member of the Society of Lincoln's Inn. Three years later, in 1521, he married More's eldest daughter, Margaret, who died in 1544. More was extremely fond of Roper but found him argumentative and headstrong. Indeed, at the time of his marriage Roper was, in the words of another of More's early biographers, Nicholas Harpsfield, "a mervailous zealous Protestant"—a characteristic the staunchly Roman Catholic More found wholly repugnant. For promoting the Lutheran doctrine of justification by faith, Roper was charged with open heresy before Cardinal Wolsey; he was spared harsh punishment only "for love borne by the Cardinall to Sir Thomas More." Soon after, Roper renounced Lutheranism under More's influence and embraced the Catholic faith, becoming "the singuler helper and patrone of all Catholikes," according to Harpsfield. In 1529 Roper was elected to parliament as member for Bramber, Sussex. At the time of his father-in-law's execution in 1535 he was active as a prothonotary, a position he had assumed jointly with his father years before and which he held for the remainder of his life. He was also active in public life in Kent, where his most valuable property was located. After More's death Roper apparently suffered little for the king's displeasure against More and his family. He was, however, briefly imprisoned in the Tower of London in 1542 for giving alms to a prominent Catholic. During the reign of Mary, Roper's Catholicism won him favor in government and among the people: he was elected member of parliament for Roches-

William Roper

ter in 1554 and for Canterbury later in the decade. Around this time he wrote *The Life of More*, although the work was not published until 1626. In 1561 Roper became involved in a messy property claim that grew out of an earlier dispute with More's widow, Dame Alice, concerning rights to a parcel in Battersea attained by More in 1529. Under Elizabeth, Roper's religious convictions brought him unwanted attention from the ruling powers. In 1568 he was summoned before the privy council on the charge of having financed the publication of pro-Catholic anti-government tracts. Only his promise to desist saved him from being severely punished. Roper spent the remaining decade of his life discharging the duties of prothonotary and managing his estates. He died in 1578 and was buried in the family vault at St. Dunstan's Church, Canterbury.

In his biography of More, Roper recorded his remembrances and impressions of a man already recognized as a seminal figure in English history. Roper was More's first important biographer; a few brief memorials had been composed shortly after More's death, but they were sketchy at best, unreliable in many details, and failed to convey the essence, the spirit, of the man More. As More's close relative and one of the few living witnesses able or willing to write about More, Roper was motivated by a sense of urgency, devotion to his subject, and the belief that he was especially well suited to the task: "To thentent [very many notable things concerning Sir Thomas Moore] should not all utterley perishe, I have at the desire of divers worshyppfull freinds of mine... declared so much thereof as in my poore judgment seemed worthy to be remembred." Roper is here stating the principal purpose of the biography: to provide a later, "official" biographer with intimate notes on More's life and character, concerning especially the statesman's critical last years. As such, the biography focuses on the circumstances leading up to and surrounding More's crisis of conscience: his winning the king's favor; his elevation to lord chancellor; his misgivings about the king's divorce; his unwillingness to acknowledge publicly the king's claimed supremacy in matters of religion in England; his imprisonment, interrogation, and trial; and his execution. Roper wrote the biography around 1557, twenty-two years after More's death. Immediately the work was taken up by Roper's chosen successor Harpsfield, who based much of his *Life and Death of Sir Thomas Moore, Knight* on it.

Roper's *Life of More* is not a biography in the current sense. Rather, it discloses only "such matters towching [Moore's] life as I could at this present call to remembraunce," according to the author. Roper may have, as he claimed, conceived the biography as notes merely, but many scholars believe he was deeply aware of its purely literary value, too, for the work appears to have been carefully constructed to yield the truest picture of More in the consciest way possible. Each recorded incident is therefore highly revealing of some aspect of More's character, emphasizing what More actually thought about matters high and low, especially domestic and personal ones—a decided departure from the plodding accounts of state careers more typical of the period. "His subject," according to James Mason Cline, "is not More's long career in the world, but the image of his soul." While Donald A. Stauffer has remarked that the biography "rests upon the foundation of traditional hagiology," most critics have found that hagiographical puffing of the sort commonly found in lives of martyrs is minimal. "Roper can tell his tale, and leave it to work its effect, without any attempt to enforce it," wrote R. W. Chambers. Yet readers have noted that *The Life* contains a surprising number of errors. Roper occasionally confused dates, mistook one person for another, or gave inaccurate accounts of political events. Still, two decades or more had elapsed between the events themselves and Roper's recalling them—time enough, most critics agree, for small details to slip from the author's mind. Equally, some of Roper's omissions have proved puzzling, even considering that certain matters ordinarily included in sixteenth-century biographies may not be germane in *The Life*. Roper referred to More's literary works only once and then only in passing—he did not even mention More's celebrated *Utopia* (1516)—and did not explain that More married twice. But if these are faults they are small ones, commentators concur, and in any event Roper made no claim to perfect accuracy or recall: "Very many notable things (not meete to have bine forgotten) throughe neckligens and long contynuans of tyme are slipped out of my mynde."

Roper's biography appears to have gained immediate acceptance as an important account of More's trial and con-

demnation. Writing around 1558 in the dedication of *The Life and Death of Sir Thomas Moore, Knight*, Harpsfield claimed of Roper and his work: "We and our posteritie should knowe to whom to impute and ascribe the welspring of this great benefite, and whom we may accordingly thanke for many thinges nowe come to light of this woorthy man [More], which, perchaunce, otherwise would have bene buried with perpetuall oblivion." Commentators agree that *The Life* helped form early impressions of the More affair, giving as it did a matchless firsthand account of More and his clash with the king's authority. Moreover, as the foundation of Harpsfield's *Life*, its influence was probably strong; for although Harpsfield's biography remained in manuscript even into the present century, it nevertheless enjoyed a fairly wide circulation. Yet early criticism of Roper's *Life* is extremely scarce. Scholars attribute this dearth to two circumstances: (1) the danger connected with harboring, circulating, endorsing, or favorably commenting on "papist" materials in late-sixteenth-century England and (2) the likelihood that the biography was at first considered a historical, ecclesiastical sourcebook of sorts, a mine of information about More, but not a literary composition of independent merit. The exact size of the contemporary audience of Roper's *Life* therefore remains a mystery, but because at least thirteen surviving manuscripts predate the first edition, interest in the work appears to have been considerable. By 1626, when *The Life* first saw print, its publication was justified by its didactic value, historical import, and perceived entitlement to wider circulation. Wrote the anonymous "T. P.," who prepared the manuscript for the press: "Finding, by perusall therof, the same replenished with incomparable Treasures, of no lesse Worthy, and most Christian Factes, then of Wise, & Religious Sentences, Apophthegmes, & Sayings; I deemed it not only an errour to permit so great a light to ly buried, as it were, within the walls of one private Family: but also judged it worthy the Presse, ever of a golden Character (if it were to be had) to the end, the whole World might receave comfort and profit by reading the same." Critical evidence for readership of the biography during the eighteenth and nineteenth centuries is slim. This has suggested to scholars that interest in the More affair may have waned for a time; that Roper's view of More as Catholic martyr was unpopular; that the work was still considered primarily a historical document, not a masterly biography; and that copies of the text were difficult to procure—the latter belief in spite of the appearance of several new editions during the period. With the beatification of More by Leo XIII in 1886, awareness of the man increased appreciably. In time this led to a revival of interest in Roper's *Life* and to the publication of fresh editions.

The elevation of More to sainthood in 1935 coincided with the issuance of a critical text prepared for the Early English Text Society. Although that work's editor, Elsie Vaughan Hitchcock, noted that "the literary value of Roper is... accidental, unpremeditated," there has been a general trend in twentieth-century criticism toward viewing *The Life* as a work of conscious artistry. Increasingly, scholars have observed sophisticated literary techniques in the biography, especially its passages of dramatic dialogue and in the selection and arrangement of material. Writing on the latter issue, Richard S. Sylvester has noted: "Many of [Roper's] scenes appear to be little gems, perfect in their isolation; but the light which they emit is heightened and intensified by similar, yet contrasting, episodes that precede or follow them in the narrative." Another recent critical issue concerns Roper's portrayal of himself in *The Life*. To what extent is the fictional Roper a true representative of the real Roper?

Today Roper's *Life of More* is recognized as a unique portrait of the personality and character of a major English writer, thinker, and politician, a warmly human account of a man who, in the absence of such a portrait, might be perceived as far colder than he actually was, as but a great historical figure. For while More circulated among the intellectual elite of his age, wrote on vexing philosophical issues, and gave up his life for the sake of religious belief, we know from Roper's biography that he had a playful wit, a congenial humor, a deep love for his family, and an abiding faith in the goodness of humankind. This side of More, the human side, complements the abundant testimony concerning More's career as a statesman available elsewhere. Roper's *Life* is therefore the key to a complete understanding of More and, in the words of Chambers, "probably the most perfect little biography in the English language."

PRINCIPAL WORK

The Mirrour of Vertue in Worldly Greatnes; or, The Life of Syr Thomas More Knight, Sometime Lo. Chancellour of England (biography) 1626; also published as *The Lyfe of Sir Thomas Moore, Knighte, Written by William Roper, Esquire, Whiche Maried Margreat, Daughter of the Sayed Thomas Moore*, 1935

*This work was written around 1557.

WILLIAM ROPER (essay date 1557?)

[*In the following preface to* The Life of More, *Roper describes the origin and purpose of his biography, adding his belief that he alone can undertake such a work.*]

Forasmuche as *Sir* Thomas Moore, knighte, sometyme lorde Chauncelor of England, a man of singular vertue *and* of a cleere unspotted consciens, as witnessethe Erasmus, more pure *and* white then the whitest snowe, *and* of such an angelicall witt, as England, he saith, never had the like before, nor never shall againe, unyvarsaly, as well in the Lawes of our owne realme (a study in effecte able to occupy the whole life of a man) as in all other sciences, right well studied, was in his dayes accompted a man worthy perpetuall famous memory: I, William Roper, thoughe most unworthy, his sonne in lawe by mariage of his eldest daughter, knowing [at this daye] no one man [livinge] that of him *and* of his doings understood so much as my self, for that I was contynually resident in his house by the space of xvi yeares and more, thought it therefore my parte to sett forth such matters towching his life as I could at this present call to remembrraunce. Amonge which things, very many notable things (not meete to have bine forgotten) throughe necklingens *and* long contynuans of tyme are slipped out of my mynde. Yeat, to thentent the same should not all utterley perishe, I have at the desire of divers worshyppfull freinds of mine (thoughe very farre

from the grace *and* worthines of them, Nevertheles as farr forthe as my meane wit, memory, *and* [knowledge] wold serve me) declared so much thereof as in my poore judgment seemed worthy to be remembred. (pp. 3-4)

William Roper, in a preface to his The Life of Sir Thomas Moore, Knighte, *edited by Elsie Vaughan Hitchcock, Humphrey Milford, Oxford University Press, 1935, pp. 3-4.*

NICHOLAS HARPSFIELD (essay date 1558?)

[*Harpsfield was an English essayist, theologian, and biographer who is remembered as a staunch champion of Roman Catholicism. For his religious beliefs he was imprisoned in the Fleet in 1559, where he appears to have remained until his death in 1575. Earlier, around 1558, Harpsfield wrote what proved to be one of the major biographies of Thomas More:* The Life and Death of Sir Thomas Moore, Knight. *Although not published until 1932, this work circulated widely in manuscript and was instrumental in promoting More's reputation as a Catholic martyr. Harpsfield's Life of More is avowedly based on Roper's Life; indeed, Roper wrote his work for Harpsfield's benefit, believing Harpsfield to be the man best qualified for the role of "official" biographer of More. In the following excerpt from the dedicatory epistle of his Life of More, Harpsfield expresses his debt to Roper and to Roper's Life.*]

It is, and hath beene, an olde and most auncient custome, not only among the Christians, but longe also before Christes time, at newyeres tyde every man, according to his abilitie, to visite and gratifie with some present his speciall frendes and patrones. Conformable to this custome, I doo at this time (being furnished with no worldly treasure to offer you any riche, pretious gifte) present your woorshipp even with a paper newyeres gifte; but yet suche as I trust, for the devotion of my poore heart toward your woorshipp, shal be no lesse acceptable then was the dishe of water presented once by a poore man to one of the kinges of Persia, where the custome was for every man to welcome and honour the kinges first comming into their quarters with some costly gifte. Which waterish gifte the good king, considering the plaine homely dealing and great and gratefull good will of the saide poore man, not onely tooke in good gree, but made more accompt of then of his riche and pretious giftes. Wherefore I trust, and litle doubt, knowing the goodnes of your gentle nature, and considering the matter comprised in this booke, being the life of the woorthy Sir Thomas More, knight, but that ye will, of your part, in very good part take and accept this my present. Neyther am I so carefull of the acceptation on your behalfe as I am afraide on my owne behalfe, least by my unskilfull handling some part of the woorthines of this man may seeme to some men to be somewhat impaired, blemished, or defaced.... But yet what soever my skill be (which I know well is not correspondent to such an enterprise) I have somewhat the better contentation for that, if I have erred, [you also have erred] in your choyse, in that you appointed no meeter person. (pp. 3-4)

[You] and your familie are by no one thing more adorned, illustred and beautified, then by this woorthy man, Sir Thomas More, in marying his daughter, the excellent, learned and vertuous matrone, mistris Margarete More. He was your woorthy Father in lawe: what say I? your father in lawe? nay, rather your verye father in deede; and though a temporall man, yet your very spirituall father, As one that by his good counsaile and advise, or rather by his instant and devout prayers to God, recovered your lost soule, overwhelmed and full deepe drowned in the deadly, dreadfull depth of horrible heresies.

Ye maye therefore especially at my handes vendicate and challenge to you this my Treatise, And that not onely for causes aforesaid but for other also, forasmuch as ye shall receave, I will not say a pigg of your owne sowe (it were too homely and swinish a terme) but rather a comely and goodly garlande, a pleasaunt, sweete nosegaye of most sweete and odoriferous flowers, picked and gathered even out of your owne garden; ye shall receave a garlande decked and adorned with pretious pearles and stones, The moste orient whereof ye have by your owne travaile procured and gott together, I meane of the good instructions diligently and truely by your industrie gathered, and whereof many ye knowe well by your owne experience, which ye have imparted to me, and furnished me withall. Wherefore as all waters and rivers, according to the saying of holy Scripture, flowe out of the ocean Sea, and thither doo reflowe againe, so it is convenient ye shoulde reape the fruit of your owne labour and industrie, and that it should redounde thither, from whence it originally proceeded; And that we and our posteritie should knowe to whom to impute and ascribe the welspring of this great benefite, and whom we may accordingly thanke for many things nowe come to light of this woorthy man, which, perchaunce, otherwise would have bene buried with perpetuall oblivion. And yet we have also paide some part of the shott, and have not beene altogether [negligent]. We have gleaned, I trust, some good grapes, and have with poore Ruthe leased some good corne, as by the perusing ye shall understand. And thus I committ your Woorshipp to the blessed tuition of the Almightie, who sende you this and many other good and happie newe yeres. (pp. 5-6)

> *Nicholas Harpsfield, "Epistle Dedicatory to Master William Roper," in his* The Life and Death of Sir Thomas Moore, Knight, Sometymes Lord High Chancellor of England, *edited by Elsie Vaughan Hitchcock, 1932. Reprint by Oxford University Press, London, 1963, pp. 3-6.*

THE MIRROUR OF VERTUE IN WORLDLY GREATNES; OR, THE LIFE OF SYR THOMAS MORE KNIGHT (essay date 1626)

[*In the following excerpt from the dedication of the first printing of Roper's* Life of More, *the anonymous critic—the dedication is signed "T. P.," but the author's identity remains unknown—describes the circumstances surrounding the initial publication of the work and suggests its value as an instrument of spiritual comfort and profit.*]

It was my good happe not longe since, in a Friends House, to light upon a briefe History of the Life, Arraignement, and Death of that *Mirrour* of all true Honour, and Vertue *Syr Thomas More*, who by his Wisdome, Learning, & Sanctity, hath eternized his Name, Countrey, & Profession, throughout the Christian World, with immortall Glory, and Renowne.

Finding, by perusall therof, the same replenished with incomparable Treasures, of no lesse Worthy, and most Christian Factes, then of Wise, & Religious Sentences, Apophthegmes, & Sayings; I deemed it not only an errour

to permit so great a light to ly buried, as it were, within the walls of one private Family: but also judged it worthy the Presse, ever of a golden Character (if it were to be had) to the end, the whole World might receave comfort and profit by reading the same. (pp. iii-vi)

> *T. P., "The Epistle Dedicatory," in* The Mirrour of Vertue in Worldly Greatnes; or, The Life of Syr Thomas More Knight, Sometime Lo. Chancellour of England *by William Roper, edited by T. P., n.p., 1626, pp. iii-viii.*

REV. JOHN LEWIS (essay date 1729)

[*Lewis was an English clergyman who wrote extensively on English religious history, local history and topography, and early printing. His historical works evidence a strong Protestant bias but are valued for their original research. In the following excerpt from an essay originally published as the introduction to his 1729 edition of Roper's* Life of More, *he praises Roper's special qualifications as More's biographer but notes his lack of objectivity.*]

Sir Thomas More being a person so very remarkable for his strict virtue, excellent learning, great skill in our municipal laws, his honours and promotions, and lastly for the cause for which he suffer'd a violent death, many have taken in hand to write his history. Of these, that which I now publish [*The Life and Death of Sir Thomas Moore*] as it seems to have been the first written, so all the rest are more or less transcripts of or copies from it. And indeed none of the many other writers of Sir Thomas's Life, can any way pretend to the same advantages and opportunities of knowing him which the author of this little history had, who not only married his beloved daughter, with whom Sir Thomas entrusted his secrets, but who lived sixteen years in the same house with Sir Thomas, and was his attendant and companion almost wherever he went. Accordingly he gives this reason himself for his committing to writing these Memoirs of Sir Thomas's Life, &c. that he knew *his doings and mind no man living so well* [see essay dated 1557?]. (pp. xix-xx)

Mr. Roper seems to have been very well qualified for a writer of Sir Thomas's Life, but his affection for him has had some influence on his pen, so as instead of a history, he has wrote a panegyric. (p. xxiii)

> *Rev. John Lewis, in a preface to* The Life of Sir Thomas More *by William Roper, edited by S. W. Singer, revised edition, Chiswick, 1822, pp. xix-xlii.*

DONALD A. STAUFFER (essay date 1930)

[*Stauffer was a distinguished American novelist, poet, and critic who is best known for his studies of early English biography. In the following excerpt, he emphasizes the vividness of Roper's anecdotal biography, adding that although* The Life of More *is apparently artless, it portrays More's crisis of conscience excellently.*]

[In his *Life of Thomas More,* William Roper] does not mention his idol as the author of *Utopia,* but is careful to inform the reader of the hair shirt Sir Thomas wore, his flagellations, and the hours he spent in devotion; Erasmus and the brilliant circle of humanists who were More's friends are referred to only incidentally, but Roper is meticulous in commending the severe religious discipline which the Lord Chancellor imposed both in his own family and in the nation at large. The life, therefore, rests upon the foundations of traditional hagiology. By accepting at the outset the devout Catholic cast in the biography of a figure soon known as "the blessed Sir Thomas More," the qualities which render Roper's work distinctive and fresh may be more easily ascertained.

Like Cavendish before him, like Walton, like Boswell after him, William Roper does not exclude his own personality from his work. He mentions three wishes of Sir Thomas More's: first, that the Christian world might be at peace; second, that it might be blessed with unity of doctrine; and third, that the question of King Henry's divorce might be amicably settled. Most biographers would have been content with mere enumeration. Roper, however, must make the wishes a vivid part of More's life by giving circumstances. In consequence, he shapes a clear-cut anecdote of an evening walk along the banks of the Thames, whose sweet waters, running softly, at last call forth More's confidences—almost a soliloquy spoken aloud—to his "son Roper." Even the charge of bigotry which forms the sole blot on More's reputation is unconsciously suggested, for they stroll along, in More's phrase, "treading heretics under our feet like ants." The entire biography gives evidence of Roper's retentive and circumstantial memory, since it seems to have been written about 1558, twenty years after the death of the Lord Chancellor. Roper prides himself that no man had equal opportunities to know Sir Thomas, "whom in sixteen years and more, being in his house conversant with him, I could never perceive as much as once in a fume."

The biography abounds in anecdotes to show the dry pungency of More's wit; again and again during his trial, chance remarks, vividly recorded, bring out the vigor and independence of his personality. The King walks with him in the garden, arm around his shoulder, but he is not deceived:

> "Howbeit, son Roper," he says, "I have no cause to be proud thereof, for if my head would win him a castle in France (for there was war between us), it should not fail to go."

The Court requests him to walk in the wedding procession of Ann Boleyn, an action which would tacitly condone Henry's marriage; More replies to the emissaries with the neat parable of the virgin:

> "Now, my Lords," quoth he, "it lieth not in my power but that they may devour me, but God being my good Lord, I will so provide that they shall never deflower me."

He denies the king's conciliatory messengers, and Roper wonders how a man in such desperate condition may be merry:

> "In good faith I rejoiced, son," said he, "that I had given the devil a foul fall, and that with those lords I had gone so far as without great shame I could never go back again."

His integrity cannot be shaken, and when in the tower he is threatened with torture and death, "My lords, quoth he, these terrors be arguments for children, and not for me."

The members of his family are sketched in no less surely—"dearest Meg," who breaks through the crowd to throw her arms around her father's neck as he walks to the Tower, Roper himself with his simple admiration and sharp eye, More's second wife, common and fretful, divided from her husband by a chasm which even imminent death cannot bridge. There are few scenes in literature as tragic as More's final interview with his wife in the Tower, not because an eternal separation is approaching, but because it is already at hand, and has always existed. Her husband's actions are in her mind pure folly, and the story of their entire married life is revealed in the fact that he does not try to explain his motives. . . . (pp. 129-32)

In his living and faithful narrative, with no touch of pretentiousness, Roper has given a summary of More's early life which is well proportioned, and the story of his active years is not passed by without notice. But the larger portion of the biography forms the last act of a drama, the conduct of a great man in adversity, uncompromising and firm in his conviction that neither Parliament nor the King can pass a law that God is not God. In spite of Roper's apparent artlessness, few biographers have equalled him in rendering the last actions of their heroes with the same truth and completeness. (p. 133)

> *Donald A. Stauffer, "Intimate Biography," in his* English Biography before 1700, *1930. Reprint by Russell & Russell, Inc., 1964, pp. 121-74.*

ELSIE VAUGHAN HITCHCOCK   (essay date 1935)

[Hitchcock was an English academic who is best known for her critical editions of Roper's Life of More *and Nicholas Harpsfield's* Life and Death of Sir Thomas Moore, Knight. *In the following excerpt, she considers the literary value of Roper's* Life *and notes factual errors in the work.]*

As far as we know, the **Life of More** is Roper's only contribution to literature. It is not a biography in the modern sense, where the author aims at chronological sequence, careful arrangement of matter, and completeness. Nicholas Harpsfield had been selected by Roper himself as More's official biographer, and Roper, "at the desire of divers worshyppfull freinds" of his, is merely setting forth "such matters towching his life" as he "could at this present call to remembraunce" [see essay dated 1557?]. To Harpsfield the memoir served as Notes, and though he incorporated them word for word, and fully appreciated the literary value of these "good instructions, diligently and truely by . . . industrie gathered," "the moste orient of pretious pearles and stones" [see excerpt dated 1558?], he treated them as Notes, arranging them more logically, weaving them into his other material, and constructing from Roper and his other sources a true biography. We have only to look at what is *not* Roper in Harpsfield, to realise the labour and skill with which Harpsfield "gleaned good grapes and leased good corn."

The literary value of Roper is, as it were, accidental, unpremeditated. His aim is merely to "*sett forth* . . . so much as in his poore judgment seemed worthy to be remembered." There is no verbosity, padding, or preaching, no literary vanity. All is clearly narrated, dignified, effective. "Roper can tell his tale, and leave it to work its effect, without any attempt to enforce it" [see Additional Bibliography citation by R. W. Chambers].

Roper regrets that "very many notable things, not meete to have bine forgotten, throughe necklligens and long contynuans of tyme are slipped out of my mynde." He is writing some twenty years after More's death, certainly not before Mary's reign—it was dangerous to circulate, or even to write, such memoirs earlier—and probably not long before 1557, the date of publication of More's *English Works*.

Some of the omissions interest us. The only reference to More's books is to his writings "in defens of the true Christian religion, against hereseies"—work on which More was actually engaged during Roper's personal contact with him. Roper does not even mention *Utopia*; his attachment to More's household almost certainly dated from the period after 1516. We do not learn from him that More married twice: "the eldest daughter of Master Colte" is not differentiated from "my Lady, his wife," who visits More in the Tower, and tries to scold him into submission to the King's wishes.

Roper's errors are somewhat surprising—of the sort attributable to "necklligens" rather than to "long continuans of tyme":

(1) (*a*) Roper makes More Treasurer instead of Under-Treasurer; Harpsfield corrects. (*b*) And More followed in this office Sir John Cutte, not Weston; Weston followed More. Harpsfield here reproduces Roper's error.

(2) The speech in which More excused himself from the office of Speaker is reported by Roper as "not now extant"; Harpsfield relates the Hannibal-Phormio portion.

(3) Roper errs as to the dates of More's position as Chancellor of the Duchy of Lancaster—actually 1525-9: (*a*) The embassy of More and Wolsey to Charles into Flanders was in August, 1521. Harpsfield incorporates statement from Roper, but omits reference to date. (*b*) Adrian was elected Pope in 1522. Harpsfield does not state that this was during More's Chancellorship of the Duchy, but follows Roper in attributing Wolsey's resentment to the election of Adrian.

(4) "The Frenche kings Sister" is an error for Renée, daughter of Louis XII. Harpsfield follows Roper, adding "the Dutchesse of Alanson."

(5) (*a*) The brief [concerning the legality of the marriage of Henry VIII and Catherine of Aragon] was not found in the Treasury of Spain, but among the papers of the English ambassador of 1494-1509; and (*b*) only a copy was sent to England. Harpsfield adopts Roper's errors.

(6) (*a*) The Court determining the marriage void was held at Dunstable Priory, not at St. Alban's: and (*b*) the marriage to Anne had preceded. Harpsfield, it is surprising, follows Roper.

(7) Five days, not seven, elapsed between More's judgment (1 July) and his execution (6 July). Harpsfield follows Roper.

(8) Elyot's embassy to Charles was in 1531-2. Harpsfield follows Roper.

But these are minor blemishes. For all the More *Lives*, Roper's ranks as the *biographia princeps* ["first biography"], and has always been recognised as one of the masterpieces of English literature. (pp. xliv-xlvii)

Elsie Vaughan Hitchcock, in an introduction to The Lyfe of Sir Thomas Moore, Knighte *by William Roper, edited by Elsie Vaughan Hitchcock, Humphrey Milford, Oxford University Press, 1935, pp. xi-xlvii.*

R. W. CHAMBERS (essay date 1935)

[*Chambers was an English scholar and writer on English language and literature whose interests ranged from early German legends to English authors of the seventeenth century. He is especially known for his works on Thomas More and his circle. In the following excerpt from his biography of More, he praises the artistry of Roper's* Life of More *but cautions readers not to consider the work a consistently reliable historical source.*]

Roper's *Life of More* gives us, in some seventy octavo pages, what is probably the most perfect little biography in the English language.

The historical value of Roper's work has been somewhat overestimated; its value as a work of art has been enormously underrated. People have forgotten that it was written some twenty years after the latest of the events which it records, and that of many of these events Roper was not himself an eyewitness. Roper's dialogues are so cleverly worded that his characters live as do those of Shakespeare. More's wife, Dame Alice, is not less vivid than Mistress Quickly, and indeed uses the same expletives—*Tilly vally, What the good year*. According to Roper, Mistress Alice obtained licence to visit her husband after he had been some time prisoner in the Tower, and 'bluntly saluted him' thus:

'What the good year, Master More,' quoth she, 'I marvel that you, that have been always hitherto taken for so wise a man, will now so play the fool to lie here in this close filthy prison, and be content thus to be shut up amongst mice and rats, when you might be abroad at your liberty, and with the favour and goodwill both of the King and his Council, if you would but do as all the bishops and best learned of this realm have done. And seeing you have at Chelsea a right fair house, your library, your books, your gallery, your garden, your orchard, and all other necessaries so handsome about you, where you might in the company of me your wife, your children, and household, be merry, I muse what a God's name you mean here still thus fondly to tarry.'

After he had a while quietly heard her, with a cheerful countenance he said unto her: 'I pray thee, good Mistress Alice, tell me one thing.'

'What is that?' quoth she.

'Is not this house,' quoth he, 'as nigh heaven as mine own?'

To whom she, after her accustomed homely fashion, not liking such talk, answered, 'Tilly vally, Tilly vally.'

'How say you, Mistress Alice', quoth he, 'is it not so?'

'Bone deus, Bone deus, man, will this gear never be left?' quoth she.

'Well then, Mistress Alice, if it be so,' quoth he, 'it is very well: for I see no great cause why I should much joy, either of my gay house or of anything belonging thereunto, when, if I should but seven years lie buried under the ground, and then arise and come thither again, I should not fail to find some therein that would bid me get me out of doors, and tell me it were none of mine. What cause have I then to like such an house, as would so soon forget his master?'

Now, why do surveys of English literature not think dialogue like this worth notice? Probably because it is dismissed as historical, as something which has nothing to do with the literature of the imagination. Yet surely it is highly imaginative. I do not mean that the interview did not take place; Roper's word proves that it did. But, in the days of Henry VIII, the Tower was not furnished with that 'King's Lugg' within which Sir Walter Scott (in *The Fortunes of Nigel*) represents King James I as hiding, in order to overhear the conversations of prisoners. Whatever James might do, Roper could not, by permission of the Lieutenant, lurk unseen to take notes of the interview between Sir Thomas More and his lady. Roper must presumably have written his account of that interview from memories of the very confused narrative which Mistress Alice brought home with her, more than twenty years before, to the sad house at Chelsea. Now, let anyone try to put down on paper a conversation reported to him, at second hand, twenty years ago, by a woman too worried and too angry to know what she was saying. Further, it would be a grave injustice to Mistress Alice to suppose the conversation to be verbatim. *She* was not the woman, after so brave an opening, to have tamely allowed her batteries to be silenced. But Roper had lived in the same house as his step-mother-in-law 'for sixteen years and more'. The dialogue has its origin, as Wordsworth held that good imaginative writing should have, in emotion recollected in tranquillity.

After More's death there was trouble between Dame Alice and Roper. Dame Alice even accused Roper of having 'gotten away part of her living.' They came at last to an agreement, and we need not suspect malice in Roper's picture of Lady More. More's own writings confirm the picture in every detail. If Roper had learnt how to imitate his mother-in-law, I suspect he learnt it from his father-in-law. Anyway, in More's writings we meet with a certain anonymous lady who is very unmistakably Dame Alice. For example, when More is writing his devotional works in prison, he gives us scraps of the conversation of a certain great lady who, of her charity, visits a certain poor prisoner:

> Whom she found in a chamber (to say the truth) meetly fair, and at the leastwise it was strong enough; but with mats of straw the prisoner had made it so warm, both under the foot and round about the walls, that in these things for the keeping of his health, she was on his behalf glad and very well comforted. But among many other displeasures that for his sake she was sorry for, one she lamented much in her mind, that he should have the chamber door upon him by night made fast by the jailer, that should shut him in. 'For by my troth,' quoth she, 'if the door should be shut upon me, I would ween it would stop up my breath.' At that word of hers the prisoner laughed in his mind (but he durst not laugh aloud, nor say nothing to her, for somewhat indeed he stood in awe of her, and had his finding there, much part, of her charity for alms). But he could not but laugh inwardly. Why, he wist well enough, that she used on the inside to shut every night full surely her own chamber to her, both door and windows too, and used not to open them of all the long night.

The prisoner, we may note, had his maintenance, his 'finding', of her charity. In a letter to Cromwell. Dame Alice tells of the sums she has every week to pay 'for the board-wages of my poor husband and his servant; for the maintaining whereof I have been compelled, of very necessity, to sell part of mine apparel, for lack of other substance to make money off'.

Roper's picture, then, is confirmed by More's own words, in a way which enforces the importance of More's writings both as a check upon his earlier biographers, and as a source for his later ones. This source was scarcely used by Roper, who found sufficient materials for his little book in his own knowledge. Yet, intimate as this knowledge was, Roper depicts himself as holding rather aloof, not quite understanding the man whose memory he later grew to revere. Perhaps this is why, although he draws More as without a fault, he never arouses that dislike which we usually cherish towards the faultless, and those who ask us to revere them. Roper disarms us, by the innocent humility with which he unconsciously shows his own character. Before the trouble over the King's marriage began, Roper congratulated More on England having so Catholic a prince as Henry, and subjects all in one faith agreeing together. All this More admitted, yet he foretold evil to come. Roper protested. More stuck to his prophecy, but would not give his reasons (probably he was not free to give his reasons, even to Roper). Roper, not unnaturally, got flurried and annoyed, and at last turned on his father-in-law:

> I said, 'By my troth, Sir, it is very desperately spoken.' That vile term, I cry God mercy, did I give him. Who, by these words perceiving me in a fume, said merrily unto me, 'Well, well, Son Roper, it shall not be so, it shall not be so.' Whom in sixteen years and more, being in his house conversant with him, I could never perceive as much as once in a fume.

And a certain slowness to follow More's thought persists to the end. In the boat on the way to Lambeth, where (as Roper knew) the oath was to be demanded from More, More sat silent a while, and at last suddenly whispered, 'Son Roper, I thank our Lord the field is won.' 'What he meant thereby,' says Roper, 'I then wist not; yet loath to seem ignorant I answered, "Sir, I am thereof very glad".' These are their last recorded words. For here Roper drops out of the story, and it is Roper's wife who by word and by letter comforted her father during the fifteen months of his imprisonment.

There is something very admirable in the rectitude of memory by which Roper, writing more than ten years after the death of his wife, never claims for himself a share in the peculiar intimacy of More and his daughter Margaret, never forgets the distinction between 'Son Roper' and 'Meg'. This honesty entitles us to believe in the real truth of Roper's dialogues, even where the actual wording must often be his own reconstruction.

We have, then, four main characters – More and his wife, Roper and his wife – acting upon each other. Behind them we have the background of the world, the flesh, and Henry VIII. The world: represented by the Duke of Norfolk, scandalized, when he came to dine with More at Chelsea, to find him in church, singing in the choir, with a surplice on his back. Norfolk protested, as he went arm in arm with his host to the Great House, 'God's body, God's body, my Lord Chancellor, a parish clerk, a parish clerk! You dishonour the King and his office.' More replied, and certainly with truth, that King Henry would not consider the service of God a dishonour to his office. The flesh: Queen Anne Boleyn, More's bitterest enemy, exasperating the king against him by her importunate clamour, yet all the time pitied by her victim, because he realizes 'into what misery, poor soul, she shall shortly come'. King Henry: shown not so much in proper person, as in the reflected light which these anecdotes throw on *him*. Roper refrains from uttering any very direct censure upon his late king, the father of his queen. We have only one glimpse of Henry himself, as he walks after dinner in the garden at Chelsea, holding his arm about More's neck. And the point lies in More's comment afterwards: 'If my head could win him a castle in France, it should not fail to go.'

Amongst the proofs of More's sanctity, his biographers did not forget to place his peculiar gift of prophecy.

We have every reason to believe that Roper preserves truly the atmosphere of the Great House at Chelsea, and this is the important thing for us. But we cannot use Roper's *Life* as a document giving us absolutely reliable evidence of names, places, and dates. Memory plays strange tricks after twenty or thirty years, and Roper was neither a Boswell making systematic notes, nor a historian using documents to check his recollections. We must always keep in mind the apology for lapses of memory with which Roper begins his little book [see essay dated 1557?]; not only has Roper forgotten much which we should have wished him to record, but among the things he records we can trace the confusion, and especially the confusion of chronology, which must ensue if a man trusts entirely to his memory over a space of nearly a generation. Two or three of Roper's mistakes are remarkable. He tells us of More's advancement at Court:

> Then died one Master Weston, Treasurer of the Exchequer whose office, after his death, the king, of his own offer, without any asking, freely gave unto Sir Thomas More.

The office was that of Under-Treasurer, not Treasurer. More was never Treasurer; that post was held at the time by the Duke of Norfolk and was soon to be held by his son. This is a sufficiently careless blunder for an important official, such as Roper, to have committed. But, what is more noteworthy, Sir Richard Weston did not precede More as Under-Treasurer; he followed him (though not immediately), and lived twenty-one years after the date at which he is alleged by Roper to have died, surviving More himself by seven years. Sir Richard Weston lived to stand godfather to another Thomas More, a grandson of Sir Thomas, born three years after his grandfather's execution. For a quarter of a century Weston had been one of the most prominent figures about the Court; there was hardly an official ceremony from which he was absent; and even the violent death of his only son Sir Francis, who was beheaded on the charge of adultery with Queen Anne Boleyn, did not interrupt the even tenor of Sir Richard's attendance upon his King. Roper, one would have thought, must have known Weston well. But Roper is writing more than a dozen years after Weston's death, and time has foreshortened everything. Roper remembers Weston occupying the same office which More occupied, and so he puts his name in place of that of Sir John Cutte,

the Under-Treasurer whom More really succeeded. Roper had probably no clear recollection of Sir John Cutte acting as Under-Treasurer. Other similar inaccuracies of Roper [are found in the *Life*. . . . But there is nothing to shake our confidence in his complete honesty. (pp. 25-31)

R. W. Chambers, "Prologue: The Sources," in his Thomas More, *1935. Reprint by Jonathan Cape, 1962, pp. 15-47.*

JAMES MASON CLINE (essay date 1950)

[In the following excerpt, Cline considers the artistry and spirit of Roper's Life of More.*]*

This intimate and prophetic Memoir *The Lyfe of Sir Thomas Moore, Knighte* has been issued under many titles—but none so inevitably right as this which custom alone has established, without any documentary sanction at all: *Roper's More.* For this was the More Roper remembered; and this was the More he most wanted to be remembered. What title he himself gave his Memoir (if indeed he gave it any) is not known. But his intention is unmistakably clear. Of all the qualities his father-in-law possessed, Roper chose to memorialize only his *goodness*—the essential saintliness of his disposition.

Four hundred years after Sir Thomas' death, the Church confirmed the rightness of Roper's judgment: the figure who was canonized in 1935 was Roper's More.

This was not the More who made the most powerful appeal to the world Roper was addressing. The biographer was writing on the eve of the Elizabethan age—writing, that is, to a world with a rare taste for a life like Thomas More's—for the variety of his interests and actions, for the mere vicissitudes of his public service—even for the sudden splendor of his fall. It was an auspicious attitude—one destined to produce the long pageant of Shakespearean kings, and to find fulfillment in some of the noblest tragedy ever written. But it was not Roper's. He himself had appointed Nicholas Harpsfield to write the official biography, which presumably would tell the world what it wanted to know. There one might read what measure Colet and Erasmus took of More's learning, what figure he cut with Luther and the bishops, what two kings and Wolsey remembered of him as parliamentarian. But the Roper of the Memoir is neither scholar, theologian, nor statesman. He never pretends to judge his father-in-law's greatness —much less to question in any point the veneration the world paid him. All that he simply takes for granted.

What *he* comes forward to attest is the 'cleere unspotted consciens' [see essay dated 1557?] of the man: not what he did, but what he *was*.

The world Sir Thomas lived in would not soon forget the last dramatic image of his imprisonment and death; nor would it fail to pay the honor that men of the Renaissance especially paid to a magnificent gesture of the human spirit. But Roper knew that More's life, and More's death, were not most magnificent in quite this way. *He* knew that the virtue which fulfilled itself on 'St. Thomas' even was born of no sudden or violent determination. To Roper it was the merest revealing of a quiet essence of which he had been aware all his life—had seen so constantly implied in all his father's action, that like his greatness he had taken this for granted, too.

It was a quality as easy for Roper to take for granted as for the world utterly to miss: a modest, quiet, familiar quality, more evident in a chance remark over the supper table in the bosom of the family, than at Westminster or Oxford. Most purely expressed, it was a *manner*—a way of saying and doing things, which more truly communicated itself to Roper in the over-tones of a walk along the quiet river at Chelsea than in the pages of the celebrated *Utopia*. But it was always *there*— essential to the man's character, and indeed, giving the highly individual flavor to his demeanor and wit which others relished as subtly 'characteristic.'

It was not Roper's singular discovery; but now, a generation after More's death, he alone of all living men is best able to illustrate and define it. Unless he speaks, the realest meaning of Sir Thomas More will be lost for ever. And therefore, unequal as are his powers to the duty he must perform, 'yeat to thentent the same should not all utterley perishe,' perform it he will—'knowing at this daye no one man livinge that of him and of his doings understood so much as my self.'

Nothing in Roper's book does him greater credit than his exquisite tact in conveying this insubstantial theme. The world he was addressing—like our own—was only too ready to read into a career like More's an example of the great medieval theme, *Contemptus Mundi*: to find in More's martyrdom a disparagement of merely human values. It is a point of view which generally dominates the Saint's Legend, and exalts the saint to the detriment of the living man. And yet, no perceptive interpretation of Thomas More could minimize his delight in the world; he had a genius for enjoying it. His wit was irrepressible whether in the company of wise men or fools; he had a unique talent for fatherhood; and he loved Chelsea down to the very roots of her trees. To be sure, when forced to choose, he did not choose these: there was one thing better. But the point is, there was *only* one. Therefore he had no cause to lament, as did his great contemporary: 'If I had served God as diligentlie as I have doone the king, he would not have given me over in my greie haires.' More's tragedy was not Wolsey's. But to insist on his asceticism—to ignore his buoyant humanity—would be to deny the nature of *his* tragedy too! Roper chose not to insist at all. He merely implied, and implied in a very special way.

More's was a personality that bred anecdotes as Lincoln's did—possibly because both men liked to speak in parable themselves. And Roper correctly decided to reveal his father-in-law in this homely biographical mode: that is, merely to tell stories about him, and let the man himself emerge. But episodes of the kind which to Roper conveyed the exact flavor of More's reality were neither numerous nor widely known. They were 'family' stories. Their dearth and homeliness, however, were no embarrassment. On the contrary, rarity added a preciousness to the truth they carried. For in their evanescent forms, only shaped to final form after many communal retellings, lived the man they knew better than any one else ever knew him. 'So let them reverently be told once more,' the biography seems to say, 'let them be told with not one little circumstance omitted, just as we are used to tell them.' Later historians, with different aims, have rejected many as insignificant. But their significance for Roper is only

that the family remembered that they happened so; and that the memory of them had the power so inevitably to evoke for them, the man he is commemorating.

For example:

> And albeit outwardly he appeared honorable [i.e. well-dressed] like one of his callinge, yeat inwardly he no such vanityes esteeming, secreatly next his body ware a shirte of heare; which my sister, a yong gentlewoman, in the sommer, as he sate at supper, singly in his doublet and hose, wearing theruppon a plaine shirte, without ruffe or coller, chauncing to spye, began to laughe at it. My wife, not ignorant of his manner, perceyvinge the same, pryvily told him of it; And he, beinge sory that she sawe it, presently amended it...

> The day before he suffred, he sent his shirte of heare (not willing to have it seen) to my wife, his deerely beloved daughter.

Again and again the biography says, 'I remember: it happened just so. Now it all comes back. It was 'a summer evening; we were all together then. . . . Now he is dead.'

Not precisely the episode as it occurred, but the memory of it that survived in the family circle—this was the story Roper had to tell. He himself had lived in More's household for sixteen years, enjoying for that time the prerogative of an eldest son. He now knows that those years—especially the years at Chelsea—were the happiest of his life; and partly for this reason, he cannot as biographer dissociate the memory of his father-in-law from the memory of Chelsea in the time of their prosperity. It is *there* that More is realest to him.

To be sure, twenty years had taken their toll of recollections; still, many remained, and age had made clear a significance in them which youth had not understood. It had given an inkling, at least, of that elusive melancholy, of the gentle wistfulness, that played over his father's spirit even in the flush of his prosperity. As 'Old Mr. Roper' now evokes the image of 'Sonne Roper', he feels a kinship with the older view. He can see all his brothers and sisters—himself like them—all back there at Chelsea again—all young, all sanguine, all assuming in the optimism of youth that the quiet charm of the great estate is the very temper of life itself; and if ever things were to change, they would change as they always had, for the better. He now knows, what Sir Thomas then understood so well—and they never suspected—how utterly mutable was the whole human world that surrounded their pleasant garden. If remoteness of time had blurred the image of some things, it had corrected the memory of others to More's older vision.

Roper's style imparts this mature perspective: this tone of pensive remoteness from the episodes of his story. Of course, it was a fact; he was at great distance from the events he is relating. For one thing, he was no longer 'Sonne Roper.' When he sat down to write, the More and the Chelsea he once knew had been gone more than twenty years. His wife had been dead over ten, and almost every other human tie that bound him to the past had gone the way of time,—not least in importance the youthfulness that experienced it. He was older than the man he remembered as a father. But remembering *that* makes one thing clear: the memory of that man is the most important of his possessions. Nothing he has ever done—nothing he ever will do—can be so great as this simple truth: he knew Sir Thomas More. That alone gives his life what significance it has.

An old man's memory may be allowed to gild the happiest years of his youth with a luminosity which in sober truth they may never have possessed. Roper does not inhibit the tendency. He embraces it—makes it a fact of his art. For he now believes that the very presence of his beloved father on this earth had somehow touched the most commonplace things with its strange beauty. To communicate just *that*: the sense he has of a flow from that spirit of a miraculous energy, striking orchard and river—even the very air of summer with hues of distant and legendary brightness; *this* is his book—so far as we know, the only one he ever wrote.

The essential requirement of such a book is a sustained consistency of tone. And Roper achieves it in the most pervasive of all the materials of his art—in the very rhythm of the prose in which the book is written.

His prose has the truest style a narrator can aim for—the style of a man talking; and in this case, of a man *seeming to remember* as he talks; and yet again, remembering as *he talks about him,* the greatest man he ever knew. In other words, Roper's is an *oral* style, at once familiar and reverential. It constantly sustains the exact attitude of the author to his subject; and its tone, which honestly implies the familiarity and reverence with which he regarded his father-in-law, is imparted to the style of his work generally: to the homely music of its phrases, to the leisurely repose of Chelsea, and to the feeling of solemnity that emanates from the great central figure himself. It is a minute detail, perhaps, the movement of a sentence —as minute as the brush-stroke of a painter. But it is a fact implicit in every aspect of the work. It is important, therefore, that the reader who would truly appreciate Roper's ***'More'*** should savor the exquisite quality of Roper's prose.

Its character is not always most faithfully represented in the purple patches exhibited by the anthologists. The pathetic tableau of Margaret's farewell to her father as he passed from Westminster to the Tower is deservedly classic. So is the staccato dialogue between Dame Alice and her husband in prison—so garrulous as to be almost funny, until the soft lightning of More's irony illumines it with terror. One might add More's epigram for the bishops, and others. Roper is a good dramatist: when his people talk they talk like themselves, and not like him. His *own* style, however, is undramatic, unadorned—not at all like the selections usually chosen to illustrate his book. The example which follows presents no very dramatic substance—one commendable editor omits it; yet in its manner is the essence of Roper's style. "It reads as if he spoke himself," and whoever will read it aloud—slowly—or better, hear it read aloud, will hear in its rhythms an echo of the whole sweet gravity of Roper's book.

> In the tyme somewhat before his trouble
> he wold talke with his wife and children
> of the joyes of heven / and the paynes of hell
>
> of the lyves of holy martires
> of their greivous martirdoms / of their marvelous patiens
> and of their passions and deathes / that they suffred
> rather then they wold offend God

> And what an happie and blessed thinge it was
> for the love of God to suffer losse of goods
> Imprisonement / loss of lands and life also.

> He wold further say unto them / that uppon his faith
> if he might perceyve his wife and children
> wold incourage him to dye in a good cause
> it should so comforte him / that for very joy thereof
> it wold make him merelye / runne to deathe

> He shewed them afore / what trouble might fall unto him

> Wherewith / and the like vertuous talke
> he had so longe before his trouble incouraged them
> that when he after fell into the trouble indeede
> his trouble to them was a great deale the lesse:

> *Quia spicula preuisa / minus laedunt.*

It cannot be claimed for Roper that this style is consistently even. English prose was in its infancy, and there were few approved models to steady his taste. Englishmen still apologized for stooping to write English, and even when they did so, wrote with Latin cadences ringing in their ears. And so, Roper. There are occasions when he purposely inverts 'folk' structure to impart a flavor of Latinity to his rhetoric. His idea of More's petition to the King imitates an early notion of 'high style', a style so inverted and elaborate as to be, in effect, Latin in English. Such prose may be expected in prefatory announcements, or whenever great men or great matters are to be heralded upon his stage. But as mere 'Old Mr. Roper,' recollecting 'Sonne Roper' as he watched Henry VIII, come unexpectedly to dine with Sir Thomas at Chelsea, 'in a fair garden of his' where the King 'walked with him by the space of an houre, holding his arm aboute his necke'—here his utterance is inseparable from the circumstantial memory that prompts it. His world is before you.

From this illusion, then—perhaps from this *fact*—of a man forcing his memory to the utmost, and seeming to speak his recollections just as naturally as they come up to the surface—delivering them often with undue concern for circumstance, and apparent disregard of form—in this complex, the character of the prose is established, and with it the character of Roper's ***More***. His memory is, of course, limited, and it is sometimes faulty; so occasionally is his chronology. But these aberrations do not distort the truth that Roper is telling. He is not writing chronicle history; nor is he writing biography in our sense. His book does not pretend to show us a character shaped by its contact with men and crises. The More Roper portrays was a character quite uninfluenced by the great events in which he played his part. And from beginning to end, this apprehension of More's Being never changes:

> 'It lieth not in my power but that they maye devoure me; but God being my good Lord, I will provide that they shall never deffloure me!'

The character does not develop; it grows in likeness as a painting does—by accretion. The inconsequence of one episode to another, therefore, is no blemish; actually it only contributes to the verisimilitude of the portrait,—an image which enlarges not in size or complexity, but only in clarity and depth.

Now this method—this style—seems to me to achieve the effect of a great dramatic principle—of which Roper very probably had never heard: the unity of time. The work is exactly commensurate with itself. Its author is not endeavoring, as chronicle history used to do, to give the illusion of a whole life in three hours upon the stage. His subject is not More's long career in the world, but the image of his soul. He has told everything he can remember that will mirror it—told it without embellishment, without analysis. There is no more to say; the story achieves its own perfect unity of time—the time it takes to tell it.

Even more insistent is Roper's concern for a unity of *place*. Therefore, the setting of his Memoir is not the wide world of the Renaissance, where Sir Thomas played as conspicuous a part as any Englishman of his time, but Chelsea, More's country-seat on the Thames. This choice of Roper's, at first surprising, becomes, in view of his purpose, intuitively right. For his father-in-law loved Chelsea with a passion that jaundiced all the honors that kept him away from it so much. As a young lawyer he had bought some land near the pleasant village, then about ten miles up the river from London; and as prosperity warranted, he added other lands and buildings to his estate. Roper could remember Chelsea in its flower—when More seems to have kept not merely a country-place, but an academy and a village as well.

Chelsea was known all over the world. Erasmus had heard so much about it he could imagine it from hear-say. Holbein had painted the family portraits there. And they all seem to see it through the eyes of More's affection as a kind of Earthly Paradise of blue and silver mornings. Chelsea is an atmosphere, a state of mind, whose source was the Master of Chelsea himself. For him, especially, it was a place of many voices. Rosemary ran in profusion over the very paths he walked on. He had planted it himself when he first took possession; and he liked to see it spread over his garden walks, 'not onlie because his bees loved it, but because 't is the herb sacred to Remembrance.' Then there was the blossoming orchard where the King had walked with him; and the garden gate that gave on the boat-place, where his liveried bargemen waited while the Lord Chancellor took leave of his family. And all along the walls of his garden were cages and warrens for animals. 'He keeps all sorts of birds,' says Erasmus; 'with apes, foxes, beavers, weazels, and other rareties. The monkey sat to Holbein with the rest of the family.

But More's exuberance was not to be bounded by a mere estate. Like his rosemary it ran over the walls. It was felt in the parish church which he had endowed, and where as Lord Chancellor he was once caught singing in the choir (and not singing very well); it was felt, too, in the home he had founded for the aged of Chelsea and placed under the special charge of his daughter, Margaret Roper. Chelsea was freedom —freedom that released the boundless affection of his nature. And yet the central focus of that affection was none of these. It was the family: a family no doubt impressive in many subtle ways, but obviously impressive for its size.

To make an approximate enumeration, by no means exhaustive, there was to begin with, Sir John More, Judge of the King's Bench, and father of Sir Thomas. His sanguine old age shines in every line that Holbein drew—and is concealed in every one the old man himself ever wrote. 'Matrimony,' he once observed, 'is like a man who puts his hand into a bag containing twenty snakes and one eel. It is twenty to one he catches the eel.' And thus saying, he

married four wives—all excellent women, according to his son.

There was of course, Dame Alice, More's second wife, and Roper's convenient foil to her husband's moderation and unworldliness. *Nec bella nec puella* ["Neither a pearl nor a girl"], More jokingly described her to Erasmus. But if she has come down to us singularly unredeemed by the Graces among whom she lived, let us reflect that during More's long absences from home, she ran Chelsea—a household in which she found herself twice a daughter-in-law, four times a step-mother, and five a mother-in-law. It is questionable whether even Chelsea's wide acres provided range enough to relax the total possibility for tension in such a complex. Besides, the lady herself admits a tendency to sharpness. Returning from confession one day, she smiled upon her husband bidding him 'Be merry; for I purpose now to leave off mine old shrewdness [i.e., shrewishness]—and begin even afresh. (pp. 87-98)

For the busy Lord Chancellor, Chelsea was sanctuary. He had seriously considered retreat when he was a young man—had, in fact, for four years, without vows, observed the strict rule of the Carthusian Brotherhood. And again near the end of his life, his thoughts ran to the cloister. The impulse, Roper knew, was constant and deep; and the increasing press of affairs, despite the honors they brought him, tended to strengthen rather than diminish his desire. Chelsea symbolized retreat—a release for the spirit imprisoned in the King's business, into its own affair—the consideration of itself. Hence the symbolic center of all this throbbing scene, for *Roper's* More, at least, is neither garden, nor orchard, nor rosemary walks—nor even the undeniable pull of the family circle. It is the New Building.

> And because he was desirous for godlye purposes sometyme to be solitary, and sequester himself from worldly company, A good distaunce from his mansion house builded he a place called the newe buildinge, wherein there was a Chappell, a library, and a gallery; In which, as his use was uppon other dayes to occupy himself in prayer and study together, So on the Fridaie, there usually contynewed he from morning till evening, spending his time only in devoute praiers and spirituall exercises.

New Building expressed the whole range of More's humanism, religious and secular. Dame Alice was thinking of it when she called up among the things at Chelsea closest to his heart, 'your library, your bookes, your gallery.' New Building expressed the humanistic passion he so diligently strove to inculcate in the whole family: its ancient coins and medallions, its Roman authors set in a new light the remains of a world that had gone; while its treatises on geography and astronomy, its Holbeins and the new Greek Testament of Erasmus faced the dawning of a new world. Roper's intuition of the meaning of New Building was right; Sir Thomas' own words confirm it. Let one 'choose himself some secret solitary place in his own house, as far from noise and company as he conveniently can, and thither let him some time secretly resort alone. . . There let him open his heart to God . . . and so dwelling in the faithful trust of God's help, he shall well use his prosperity.'

All these impressions lay crowded deep in Roper's mind as he wrote—so deep that they live in his memory not separate and distinct images, but fused into a single sense of place. This is to me best illustrated by an instance he does not record. Sir Thomas had been on a mission to Cambrai for the King. He had returned to England, but was still in conference with the Monarch at Woodstock, when his great barn burned, and with it a neighbor's which had caught fire from the sparks. It was a pretty serious misfortune for all Chelsea. The fall harvest was consumed, and many fields sown to winter grain had been ruined.

Dame Alice was furious, and with some justice blamed the farm-hands. It seemed to her not vengeance but poetic justice that those who had let the barn catch fire should bear the brunt of their carelessness. She therefore prepared to dismiss the laborers; there was no further work to be done that year, and it was their fault there was none. So the poor tenants who knew they faced hunger, now feared they faced unemployment as well. The lamentations in the village rose so high that Giles Heron, husband of More's daughter Cicely, dispatched a letter to Woodstock. Next Sunday it was announced in the parish church that Sir Thomas More had curtailed his conference with the King and got leave to return to Chelsea. In the matter of the fire, no one was to worry. No one would be blamed until he had taken opportunity to investigate for himself. If the ground was indeed ruined, and no labor could be utilized to replant it, let the workers rest assured they would not be turned off until they could find new masters. As for the harvest lost:

> 'Bid them take no thought therefor; for and I should not leave myself a spoon, there shall no poor neighbor of mine, bear any loss happened by any chance in my house.

> 'I pray you, Dame Alice, be with my children and your household merry in God . . . I shall (I think) because of this chance, this next week get leave to come home and see you.'

And so Chelsea relaxed again, though not yet knowing what he could do. Sufficient unto them that he was coming home, and would receive all their troubles into his own large, coarse, capable hands. There was nothing to worry about any more. . . . And *this* was what Roper felt about More. Whether he was apart in his solitary study in New Building, or ambassador in far Cambrai, Chelsea never ceased to shine without a sense of his nearness. That was why, twenty years after, it returned upon his memory, and the memory of many others who had known it in his day, as a kind of Earthly Paradise where it was always summertime—the bright air trembling on the river.

Thus the personality of Roper's More emerges, in part, as an aspect of special time and place. But most important of all, it is realized as *action*. Roper does not 'describe' his father; he tells what he said and did. And his failure to inform us of More's appearance—especially considering the intimacy of their association—cannot fail to disappoint those readers who are unfamiliar with the conventions of the literary form in which Roper was working. For certainly More's figure was striking enough to invite description. We need no more than Holbein's testimony for that; nor the pen of Erasmus which has set the Holbein portrait in motion. He mentions particularly the quick grey eye with flecks in it; the large coarse hands and shambling gait, half scholarly, half rustic—one shoulder higher than the other. But Erasmus was the pioneer of a new school of biography. Roper was old-fashioned.

But fashion—even old-fashion—is as stern a force in art as in behavior. Roper's generation differed more from Boswell's in what it thought worth recording about a man, than Boswell does from Strachey. Biography as an art distinct from history is a comparatively recent phenomenon. When Roper composed his Memoir, even Plutarch was virtually unknown in England, where the familiar forms of 'life-writing' were either Royal Chronicles or Saints' Lives, —biographies, that is, conceived as functions of national or of ecclesiastical history. Human action was important to such chronicles only in proportion as it affected the history of a nation or of the Church. Since the influence of private individuals on these institutions was generally negligible, the lives, even of such extraordinary men as Sir Thomas More, were, in view of his aims, of little interest to the chronicler.

Indeed, even in the record of kings and saints, because little was known either of their outward appearance or individual nature, little could be reported. The chronicle therefore became, perforce, a record of acts—*Acta Sanctorum;* it told what the subject *did*, not what he was. The individualizing mannerism, its relation to the inner world of personality—this was as yet an undiscovered country whose riches were unsuspected: Holinshed had not written and Shakespeare had not been born. Half a dozen stereotypes served for all the kings that ever lived, and the saints required even fewer. So far as the central requirement of a saint's legend was concerned, it was satisfied by a mere record of the acts sufficient to establish his saintliness. Whatever personal attributes the chronicler might wish to add, however interesting, were quite gratuitous.

This was the tradition Roper inherited, and as a saint's legend he conceived his *Life of More.* But he had an eye also to royal chronicle. This too was a record of 'acts'; but the acts of a king are more varied than those of a saint, and they are generally recorded with more brilliance and vigor. Indeed whatever its short-comings as portraiture, for mere narrative energy, royal chronicle in the hands of a master is beyond all praise. And the library at Chelsea must have contained a chronicle by such a master. Its subject was King Richard III, and the master none other than the Master of Chelsea himself! (pp.99-104)

Roper was aware of the virtues of this splendid example of royal chronicle, and also of its single defect. Energy and variety of detail it clearly possessed; but it lacked the cumulative power of total form. The whole was not equal to the sum of its parts. And this need the saint's legend could supply. Deficient by comparison in variety and brightness of episode, it was nevertheless a model of unity; and of unity in the best kind—*action*. However long a saint's legend might be, however numerous its episodes, all were subordinated to one great culminating act—the martyrdom. For the stark vigor of its episodic style, Roper's Memoir is indebted to chronicle; but its greatest obligation is to the legend. . . . Beyond all lesser actions lies the last, the final act which they imply—More's execution. That done, there is no more to say. Less than a hundred and fifty words conclude the story; and they suggest not so much a conclusion as an epilogue: the solemn comment of a tragic chorus enlarging the significance of all that has gone before.

Brief as it is, however, the epilogue offers a very striking confirmation of the structural principle of Roper's book.

From the beginning to this final comment, the episodes of More's life have been viewed obliquely—seen, that is, by the observers at Chelsea—not by one who, like Sir Thomas, occupied the center of a larger stage. In the epilogue such a witness is produced. The distinguished statesman, Sir Thomas Elyot breaks in upon the family circle to tell them what character their father bore, not in England only, but in the great theatre of the world. The man whose actions have for so long seemed of principal concern only to his family, now emerges in a universal light, as they hear that what was happening to their father mattered to every single man and woman in all Christendom.

Yet despite the new emphasis, the final episode does not differ from its predecessors in one essential way: it is still reported *as if* from Chelsea. Where the family actually were—what they were doing through the ghastly last hour of More's life, we are never told. But 'soon after' we hear of the impact of that hour on the court of Charles the Fifth; not literally, as the Emperor received the news, but again, as the account of his receiving it returned to Chelsea. It is the same device Roper has used over and over again to fix our point of view toward More. Indeed, it is so consistently applied that I believe myself justified in regarding these 'returns' upon Chelsea as constituting the natural divisions of the Legend. . . Especially Roper desired that this final episode should, after the manner of a saint's legend, draw up the separate energies of all others within itself, and by its single impact express the whole life of More. And like the others, its setting, also, should be the family circle—the unity of place that colors his memory, and his book. But the *telling* of this total truth he left, not to the limited chorus at home; this time, it is the English Ambassador who is the reporter, and an emperor who speaks for the kings of Christendom:

> 'If we had bine maister of such a servante, of whose doings ourselfe have had these many yeares no small experience, we wold rather have lost the best city of our dominions than have lost such a worthy councellour.' Which matter was by the same Sir Thomas Elliott to my self, to my wife, to maister Clement and his wife, to master John Haywood and his wife, and divers other his Freinds accordingly reported.

In this brief and quiet epitome, time, place and action all converge: Roper's whole book is before you in the instant.

This last episode will serve as well as any to raise one final and fundamental consideration. (pp.106-08)

[This] incident is not related with the scrupulous regard for circumstance which Roper's style so constantly implies. An artist may prefer Roper's version, but historians will point out—as many have—that although Sir Thomas Elyot may have heard the Emperor express the opinion of More which he subsequently reported to the family, the occasion which prompted the Emperor to speak could not have been More's death, for Elyot was not resident in Charles' court when it occurred! Somewhere history has been tampered with to produce a more satisfying and dramatic climax.

The consequences of Roper's distortion, to be sure, are not grave: the character of More is not in the least falsified—nor is the Emperor's opinion, which is only made more telling. Indeed, it might be sympathetically argued that faced with an inconsistency between the facts of his-

tory and the design of his art, the biographer reconciled them brilliantly in the illusion of a higher reality to which both are made contributory. And it might even be more cogently urged that such license in chronology, the extent of which can usually be detected, is as nothing compared with less discernible modifications of motive, of feeling, and the other imponderables of personality which a biographer is constantly required to decide. But it will raise in some minds the question how far this, or indeed any biography which is guilty of such deviation, is to be credited.

The most illuminating opinion I can produce on this whole matter comes not from a biographer but from a novelist. Jean Marie Latour, Willa Cather's archbishop, speaking out of profound emotion, and a newly awakened insight into the character of his life-long friend, says to him, 'I do not see you as you are, Joseph; I see you through my love for you.' Boswell might, with equal candor, have said the same to Johnson—or Roper to More. And they would only have said, in another way, that the attitude of the biographer—the 'love' in which the subject is mirrored—is not only *an* essential creative principle in the art of biography, but perhaps *its most essential one*. For if biography is finally the creation of one personality by another, then it follows that in reading a Memoir like Roper's, we must always be aware of *both* personalities, and aware also, that both have been shaped in some degree by the creative imagination.

But in Roper's Memoir, especially, the attitude of the biographer is insistent in an extraordinary way. Not only is it frequently stated and implied, it is most constantly *dramatized*. 'Sonne Roper' is quite as much a creature of William Roper's art as either Dame Alice or Daughter Margaret; and in the conduct of the legend, the most important figure after Sir Thomas himself! For 'Sonne Roper' is the personification of that 'love' of which the archbishop speaks—the mirror in which the personality of More is imaged. And the reflection none will deny is arrestingly lucid and beautiful. Perhaps the only dissatisfaction a modern would wish to express is that, considering the complexity of the subject, the image is disarmingly simple.

Indeed there is much the mirror fails to reflect—or at least to reflect emphatically. The tracings of that scintillating wit, which even in Elizabethan days was legendary, appear as by accidental necessity in Sonne Roper's memory; and then of a sombre cast. The son could never have understood the opinion that his father was 'born to make jokes' . . . 'better suited to merriment than to gravity.' Into More's genial pessimism toward the constancy of Henry VIII, Sonne Roper reads his own youthful humility. In the very episode alleged to confirm the sweetness of More's temper, he quotes him as mentioning 'some of us, as highe as we seeme to sitt upon the mountaynes, treading heretikes under our feete like antes.' Luther might have doubted the sweetness; he would not like Sonne Roper have been left undazzled by the fire.

But then, neither are we! For time and time again, Roper's honest, circumstantial reporting rises to confute the generous excesses of his adoration. We listen to him as we listen to the story told by a child, delighting in its unworldliness—in its short-sightedness—yet never doubting the essential veracity of the teller. The view is so single, so unaware of other views, that there is, we feel, no temptation to 'reconcile', to misrepresent. And such narrowness has its reward. A memory so intense and fresh, and so naturally meticulous, seems to have conferred upon many episodes, values for our maturer vision which *Sonne* Roper did not consciously create. Reported as they are by the half-comprehending narrator, they color More's speech and action to dream-like lustre, turning him into the semblance of a mysterious visitant not wholly intelligible in the terms of this world. Thus Sonne Roper:

> And whereas he evermore used before, at his departure from his wife and children, whom he tenderly loved, to have them bring him to his boate, and there to kisse them all, and bidd them farewell, Then wold he suffer none of them forthe of the gate to followe him, but pulled the wickatt after him, and shutt them all from him; and with an heavy harte, as by his countenaunce it appeared, with me and our foure servantes there tooke he his boate towards Lambithe. Wherein sitting still sadly awhile, at the last he sodainely rounded me in the yeare, and said: 'Sonne Roper, I thancke our Lord the feild is wonne.' *What he ment thereby I then wist not, yeat loth to seeme ignorant,* I aneswered: 'Sir, I am thereof very glad.'

Thus Sonne Roper: too young, too inexperienced to understand the terrifying implications of More's disclosure. Sonne Roper—but not without an inevitable touch of the inconspicuous biographer to assure us that the teller *remembers* how limited he was! Such is the subtle art of William Roper—*ars celare artem.*

Obviously, then, we must restate our question—must consider not whether William Roper is telling the truth about More, but *what kind of truth* he is telling about him. For he has told a truth no other biographer of More has ever told—or ever will. To do so, he has recreated a youth of naive but incredible memory who recalls his life of sixteen years with Thomas More. The fruit of that experience is an image—an image so simple, so universal as to be all but lost in feeling: the image of the father. Too single for the dramatist, too unrelieved, perhaps, for modern art, it seems to belong in the realm of allegory and saint's legend. Or would, if the character of Sonne Roper were not always there to infuse its ancient form with new life—to personalize its point of view and so inform it with a validity which the anonymous legend of the saint had not possessed.

Yet it is not *solely* the character of Sonne Roper that animates the Memoir, either. The *point of view* itself, though alien to modern art, has its truth, and that truth its power—power to which we still respond when asked to.

But we are not often asked. We sit in the theatre of History having come to see the play, and we can enjoy a tragedy quite as much as a comedy; it is only the power that counts with us. And therefore, if the tragedy is grand enough, grandeur alone redeems the loss that occasioned it. . . . For us. But there is always another audience, though a very small one, for whom this tragedy is but simple sorrow, beyond all power of art to relieve. To that audience Roper belonged. He did not approach the life of More as one who has found a great subject; he wrote to tell us what only a son can know. And however inadequately he may seem to an outsider to have acquitted himself, he has told what no one else could tell. We may know other things, but we can not know better. Nor will experience of the

world, nor the historical point of view equip us to criticize the essential values of his work—values which do not fall within the purviews of such criticism: 'Light that makes things seen, makes some things invisible.' So we must try to see by other lights.

Every one who remembers Woodrow Wilson, friend or foe—and there was little room for others—will recall the peculiar splendor of his battles. Even when he lost a fight, he gained the personal triumph that never deserts a champion; and every one's pulse-beat went up a little when he rode into the lists. But his daughter Eleanor, writing twenty-five years after the event, recalls her feelings on the night of his election with a touch of that awful melancholy with which Sonne Roper watched his father's steps to the chancellorship. Nor is her recollection at all of the triumphant kind which we think we should have felt in her place. Yet who would wish to doubt its validity, its beauty? Indeed, who would dare?

It had been an ominous day for the family, despite every effort to make it otherwise. They had come back to Princeton to await the election returns, and Wilson had whiled away the afternoon revisiting the University grounds. At dinner, according to a rule of long standing, they excluded politics from the conversation; and afterward, while they were still around the table, he read from Browning. . . . Then suddenly, it came. The College bell began to ring wildly, as the distant harmonies of 'Old Nassau' came nearer and louder. The girls ran to an upper window to watch. And all at once nothing was real. Some one dragged a chair out on the porch. Eleanor noticed it was the broken one. But it was too late:

> In all directions, as far as I could see, there were people coming; swarms had already invaded the little garden and were crowded around the porch. . . . And there, sharply silhouetted in the open doorway, a red glare shining full on his face, was father—utterly, utterly unfamiliar.

> The crowd, looking up at him, called on him to speak; but he was silent and those few moments, with the restless throng now utterly still and motionless, are *chrystallized in time for me—sharply separated from all that went before and all that followed.*

> I had a sense of awe—almost of terror. He was no longer the man with whom we had lived in warm, sweet intimacy; he was no longer my father. These people—strangers who had chosen him to be their leader—now claimed him. He belonged to them. . .

> And then I heard his voice. Tears of relief welled into my eyes. It was the same voice that had sung "Peri Meri Dictum Domini," in my childhood.

Four hundred years before, They had chosen Sir Thomas More. He was a splendid champion too—splendid even in catastrophe. Add to their names all the heroes who ever crossed the buskined stage of History to challenge the dramatist with tragic flaws and the mysteries of personality. To their children all this is beside the point. They can not even understand the artist's problem. For they knew these men too, and knew them in a faith so single that their goodness was expressible in the naked simplicity of the act: it needed no explaining. Such a teller, William Roper has created.

The Reader who will thus adumbrate this Memoir will understand the truth that Roper is telling about Sir Thomas More. And he will understand the essential truth about Saint Thomas, too. (pp.108-15)

> *James Mason Cline, "To the Modern Reader: Roper's 'More'," in* The Lyfe of Sir Thomas Moore, Knighte *by William Roper, edited by James Mason Cline, The Swallow Press, 1950, pp. 87-115.*

E. E. REYNOLDS (essay date 1961)

[*In the following excerpt from an essay written in 1961, Reynolds briefly compares Roper's* Life *and Harpsfield's, remarking the unique value of the former.*]

William Roper asked Nicholas Harpsfield to write an account of the life and works of Sir Thomas More, and, to help him, wrote down his own recollections of his father-in-law. Harpsfield incorporated these in his book, but in spite of this, Roper's memoir is a classic in its own right; its freshness is sometimes lost in the larger book. The memoir is not strictly speaking a biography; thus Roper left Harpsfield to deal with such matters as More's writings and controversies while he himself concentrated on recording, in his own vivid fashion, incidents and conversations that remained clear in his memory. Without this small book our knowledge of Sir Thomas More would be much the poorer; it would still be possible, from other sources, to write an account of his public life and of his trial and execution, but we should lack those many intimate details of his family life and of his personality that have made him something more than a great historical figure. (p. v)

> *E. E. Reynolds, in an introduction to* Lives of Saint Thomas More *by William Roper and Nicholas Harpsfield, edited by E. E. Reynolds, Dent, 1963, pp. v-x.*

RICHARD S. SYLVESTER AND DAVIS P. HARDING (essay date 1962)

[*Sylvester was an American scholar of sixteenth-century English literature who wrote extensively on Thomas More and his works. Harding was an American critic of English Renaissance literature. In the following excerpt, they examine aspects of Roper's "calculated art" in* The Life of More, *including characterization, theme, and the essential drama of the biography. An anonymous reviewer in the* Times Literary Supplement *contradicts their conclusions in the excerpt dated 1963.*]

Roper's *Life of More* is, strictly speaking, neither history nor biography. It ... is designed to preserve the image of a great man in terms of his personality and character. For Roper, what More accomplished was not nearly so important as the kind of man he was. Let other men praise his accomplishments and supply the historical details to round out the story of his life. From his privileged position in the More household, a quiet voice from Chelsea, Roper would simply show forth the man as he knew him, both in the time of his prosperity and in the days of his sore tribulation.

For twenty years following More's execution in 1535, Roper remained discreetly silent. There was, on the evidence of the *Life* itself, good reason for his reticence. Henry VIII could hardly be accounted one of the most tolerant men of his age. Not until Catholicism was restored to England with the ascension of Mary to the throne in 1553 did Roper dare to discharge the debt he felt he owed to the memory of Sir Thomas More. When Mary was crowned Queen, Roper was in his mid-fifties and had already well exceeded the life expectancy of the average sixteenth-century Englishman. For a man who loved and reverenced More, who felt that there was "no man living that of him and his doings understood so much" [see essay dated 1557?], the racking thought that he might not live to finish his task must have been almost intolerable. So, during the reign of Mary, he sat down and recorded, honestly and dispassionately, his impressions of the More he knew. "There is nothing," writes R. W. Chambers, More's best biographer, "to shake our confidence in his [Roper's] complete honesty" [see excerpt dated 1935].

Nor can anyone question Roper's proud assertion that he knew Sir Thomas better than any other living man. Roper probably entered More's service sometime during the year 1518 and, as he says in the preamble to his story, he "was continually resident in this house by the space of sixteen years and more." The bond between the two men was strengthened when, in 1521, three years after he had become a member of the household, Roper married Margaret, More's favorite daughter. But the most decisive evidence of More's fondness for Roper comes from the *Life* itself. Time after time More opens his heart to his young companion, and it is during their intimate discourse, man to man, that the reader achieves his clearest insights into the workings of More's mind. More obviously loved Roper. He could therefore indulge the luxury of teasing him, perhaps the most certain sign of his affection. This in itself tells us a good deal about More and something about Roper.

[Like George Cavendish in his *Life and Death of Cardinal Wolsey*] Roper performs a dual function; he is not only the author of the living drama he re-enacts, but also a participant in it. To what extent the real and fictional Ropers are to be identified, we cannot of course ever know. Judging from the historical records. Roper was shrewd, business-like, and efficient, almost grasping. But this side of Roper hardly emerges in the biography. The fictional Roper is simple, direct, unsophisticated—Lemuel Gulliver in sixteenth-century dress. Roper may have had his private reasons for adopting this fictional guise, but that is no great matter. Aesthetically, it avails. The fact of More's greatness, of his indomitable integrity, is imposed upon us by the failure of his closest friend to understand the motives that led him to embrace martyrdom. Roper's fictional guise thus inevitably enhances our growing awareness of More's tragic isolation.

One must not underestimate Roper. His so-called "artlessness" is as fictional as the role in which he casts himself. No one should take seriously his modest disclaimer in the Prologue, he is simply following an old convention and readers who tend to pass off the *Life* as little more than a compilation of notes for some future and more gifted biographer had better take a hard second look. The book from start to finish is finely articulated. It is, as Professor Chambers has said, "one of the most perfect little biographies in the language." This is high praise and from a responsible source.

The key concept—the key word, in fact—is "conscience." The first time the word occurs is in the opening sentence and thereafter it appears again and again until More has reached his personal crisis. The word itself may be said to recapitulate the action of the story. More's conscience first becomes an issue when, as a "beardless boy" in Parliament, he upsets the plans of King Henry VII to exact a "three-fifteenths" subsidy from the people to promote the marriage of his daughter Margaret to James IV of Scotland. From this time on, there is not a single anecdote or episode in the book that does not reflect in some way More's conscience or integrity of character.

The crisis comes, as it had to come, over the King's "great matter"—the vexed question of his divorce from Catherine of Aragon and proposed remarriage, the same crisis which had brought the great Wolsey tumbling down. No mere King, no matter how powerful or wilful, no Parliament, could abrogate the overriding laws of God, as set forth in the Bible and expounded by its holy interpreters. So King Henry, typically and brazenly, tried the last expedient. He appointed More to the post of Lord Chancellor, hoping (as Roper clearly implies) to bribe Sir Thomas into a token acquiescence. The ruse failed, and the long, bitter struggle, which was to end on Tower Hill, began.

What helps to make this story tragic is that More was not essentially of the stuff of which heroes are made. His kind of greatness was thrust upon him. He loved life. He loved his friends and children, and may even have loved his wife, although in the biography his attitude towards her savors more of tolerant good humor than of affection. More, in fact, had a genius for friendship. Even the King and Queen sought him out, and with such zeal that the time came when More, in order to escape from the royal solicitude to the tranquillity of Chelsea, found it convenient to assume the role of court-bore. The strategy worked, and More entered happily into a period of domestic exile. In Roper's pages, this is the only occasion when Sir Thomas could be accused of anything approaching Machiavellian duplicity.

One incident which Roper relates not only reveals More's characteristic warmth and amiability but also provides the reader with an insight into Roper's calculated art. The passage must be quoted in full.

> And for the pleasure he took in his company would his grace [Henry VIII] suddenly sometimes come home to his house at Chelsea, to be merry with him. Whither on a time, unlooked for, he came to dinner to him; and after dinner, in a fair garden of his, walked with him by the space of an hour, holding his arm about his neck. As soon as his grace was gone, I rejoicing thereat told Sir Thomas More how happy he was, whom the King had so familiarly entertained, as I had never seen him to do to any other except Cardinal Wolsey, whom I saw his grace once walk with, arm in arm.
>
> "I thank our Lord, son" quoth he, "I find his grace my very good lord indeed, and I believe he doth as singularly favor me as any subject within this realm. Howbeit, son Roper, I may tell thee I have no cause to be proud thereof, for if my head could win him a castle in France, for then was there war between us, it should not fail to go." (pp. xiv-xviii)

It is wrong to say, as some critics have said, that the book is lacking in drama. There is in fact drama on every page.

In a society dominated by men and women, who, like Wolsey, were devoted to a principle of expediency, More's rectitude is constantly beset by forces from without and within, forces which ultimately he could not cope with. The most dangerous force is that exerted by Henry VIII, whose conscience was not queasy. Indeed, that is one of the reasons why Henry, who genuinely liked More, brought him to the block.

But Sir Thomas himself—and here he stands in direct contrast to Wolsey—does not underestimate the character of Henry VIII, not even from the beginning. The pattern of conflict which begins with Henry VII ends when the son of Henry VII executes him. But this is only part of the pattern. He wins over Henry when the axe falls on Tower Hill, but perhaps his most important victory is the conquest of himself. More was a complicated person. He had always had deep-seated religious impulses; and Roper makes it clear enough that More felt guilty before God because he had not given himself over to a life of sequestration. This sense of guilt is well brought out by Roper. For four years after he qualified himself as a lawyer, "he gave himself to devotion and prayer in the Charterhouse of London." He habitually wore a hair shirt against his skin (Wolsey usually preferred to keep his hair shirts safely tucked away in a bag, conveniently transportable), and, according to Roper, Sir Thomas was given to the practise of mortifying his flesh by periodic self-flagellation. The truth seems to be that More had lost his sense of direction. He did not know where to turn. Imprisoned in the Tower, he makes an important confession to Meg:

> "But I assure thee on my faith, my own good daughter, if it had not been for my wife and you that be my children, whom I accompt the chief part of my charge, I would not have failed long ere this to have closed myself in as strait a room and straiter too."

As a good humanist, More had made his choice, rightly or wrongly. He had chosen the Court and a life of virtuous activity in a world he was already prepared to reject.

"Whom I accompt the chief part of my charge." Torn between the conflicting obligations he felt he owed to his God and those he owed to his prince, More turned to Chelsea and his beloved family. Chelsea was the focal point of his life, his small paradise. . . . In Roper's version, we cannot in fact see the saint for the man. The saint is there but he is implicit in the man, and it is essentially More's humanity which Roper emphasizes.

It is in this light that we must read one of the more poignant passages in the book—More's departure from Chelsea for his trial at Lambeth.

> And whereas he evermore used before, at his departure from his wife and children, whom he tenderly loved, to have them bring him to his boat, and there to kiss them all, and bid them farewell, *then* would he suffer none of them forth of the gate to follow him but pulled the wicket after him, and shut them all from him; and with an heavy heart, as by his countenance it appeared, with me and our four servants there took he his boat towards Lambeth. Wherein sitting still sadly a while, at the last he suddenly rounded me in the ear and said: "Son Roper, I thank our Lord the field is won."

The shutting of the wicket-gate is of course highly suggestive. Having made his decision, More is excluding himself from the world of Chelsea, and all it represents to him, a world to which he will not again return. Roper's observation is characteristic. "I wist not what he meant." Some years later, however, he had second thoughts. "But as I conjectured afterwards, it was for that the love he had to God wrought in him so effectually that it conquered all his carnal affections utterly."

More's tragedy was that he went to the scaffold thinking that no man or woman knew what he meant... (pp. xvii-xx)

A word should be said about the magnificent conclusion of this biography, astonishing as it is in its reticence. Roper does not linger, in the manner of a John Foxe or a professional hagiographer over the details of the execution. He describes it in a few terse paragraphs. Then, instead of the passionate eulogy one might expect at this point, Roper translates the reader abruptly to the court of the Emperor Charles in Europe and records a conversation between the Emperor and Sir Thomas Elyot, alleged to have been England's ambassador to that court. To a shocked ambassador the Emperor relates the news of More's death, and he adds: "And this will we say, that if we had been master of such a servant, of whose doings ourself have had these many years no small experience, we would rather have lost the best city of our dominions than have lost such a worthy counsellor!"

Title page of Roper's sole literary work, The Mirrour of Vertue in Worldly Greatnes; or, The Life of Syr Thomas More Knight *(1626).*

It would be an insensitive reader who did not recall at this point the wistful observation More had made earlier to Roper before he entered the King's service. "If my head could win him a castle in France," he had said, "it should not fail to go." (pp. xx-xxi)

> *Richard S. Sylvester and Davis P. Harding, in an introduction to* Two Early Tudor Lives: The Life and Death of Cardinal Wolsey *by George Cavendish and* The Life of Sir Thomas More *by William Roper, edited by Richard S. Sylvester and Davis P. Harding, Yale University Press, 1962, pp. vii-xxi.*

THE TIMES LITERARY SUPPLEMENT (essay date 1963)

[*The following excerpt is from a review of Richard S. Sylvester and Davis P. Harding's edition of Roper's* Life of More *and George Cavendish's* Life and Death of Cardinal Wolsey. *Here, the anonymous critic rejects Sylvester and Harding's argument that* The Life *is a deliberate, artful experiment in literary form (see excerpt dated 1962).*]

Mr. Sylvester, assisted by Mr. Harding, is concerned with two early Tudor biographies, George Cavendish's *Life and Death of Cardinal Wolsey*, and William Roper's *Life of Sir Thomas More....*

Little need be said about these modernized versions save that they enable the layman to look at Tudor England from the window of a streamlined Pullman car instead of from the back of a mule. The introduction calls for a little more comment, since it raises some disputable matters. The editors have a thesis which can be briefly summarized. While historians, they say, have always recognized the value of both these works as primary sources for the lives of Wolsey and More respectively, they have not accepted them as true biographies. Too much that the historian knows from other sources has been left out of these memoirs. So they accept what these writers have to give, welcoming them as the heralds of a change-over from the Middle Ages to modern times, from the lives of saints and other semi-fictional material which did service as biography in the former period to the more realistic contributions of later times.

Literary critics, on the other hand, have not appreciated the significance of these works. They deserve attention, so the argument runs, as deliberate experiments in literary form, and it is to encourage such a study of them as works of art in themselves that the editors have provided these modernized texts. The argument used to support this theory of Cavendish and Roper as conscious literary artists involves some rather special pleading, and the evidence brought forward is not very convincing. Better far to accept these admirable masterpieces for what they really were meant to be: honest attempts to set down two men's personal impressions of characters they had known, lived with, and admired.

> *"Tudor Worthies," in* The Times Literary Supplement, *No. 3185, March 15, 1963, p. 188.*

HELEN C. WHITE (essay date 1963)

[*White is an American scholar and critic of religious literature. In the following excerpt, she discusses the value of Rop-*

er's Life of More *as personal memoir and hagiographic portrait.*]

That Thomas More was the greatest genius of his country in [his] day, is the claim that his biographers make for him again and again. And even today the lineaments of his personality are better known than those of any of his contemporaries, with the exception of his King. For the picture of More does not have to be reconstructed from his works, as it has to be with so many literary personalities of that time. . . .

[He] is still to be seen through the hagiographic radiance that invests the intimate personal memoir which William Roper, the husband of More's favorite daughter, Margaret, wrote some twenty years after the death of More, but which was published only in 1626 in Paris, *The Mirrour of Vertue in Worldly Greatnes, Or the Life of Syr Thomas More Knight, sometime Lo. Chancellour of England*. . . . [Here] he is seen not only across the transforming tragedy but across the destruction of the whole world to which he belonged. Reading Roper, one thinks, on the lower level, of Castiglione's account of the vanished court of Urbino in *The Courtier*, where the brightness of the past shimmers through the memory of all the disaster that has intervened into a splendor that never was on this earth, nor could be. And, on the higher, one thinks of Plato's account of the death of Socrates. Not only Socrates but the whole world in which Socrates had lived had vanished, and the result was that Plato could present its triumph and its failure alike with that serene and ideal perfection possible only to the heroic scene that will not have to meet the disillusioning test of the morning after the crisis. Only of the dead may the hero-worshiper write with the certainty that is beyond complacency, and the pride which time divests of its arrogance.

There is possible, moreover, a certain impersonality that relieves the hero-worshiper of the onus of his too palpable weakness. There is no suggestion in Plato's *Phaedo* that here is a cause to be vindicated, or an example to be emulated. Nor is there in Roper's *More*. There was an aftermath to that story, grim and pathetic enough, but there is no suggestion of it in Roper's serene pages. It is with the man whose quality is beyond reach of attenuation that Roper is concerned. He does not in any way attempt to exploit it for sympathy for More's relatives, who were to pay their share for the vindication of his principles. He does not even attempt to use the appeal of More's personality for the cause for which he died. Indeed, there is no suggestion in Roper's pages that there was a continuing cause. One might think that the specific issue for which More died had vanished from the world, and only the general remained, latent, like all the basic issues of experience. This is harder to understand than the author's absorption in his subject that made him dismiss the ensuing histories of More's family as irrelevant to the main effect of his theme, as they were, but it is, I think, explicable on one central count, and that is that the world of More had completely vanished, not only the physical but the moral and intellectual and emotional world. That peculiar blend of high Roman simplicity and dignity and English homeliness and humor that characterized this, the main figure of the early English Renaissance, might and probably did recur, but it was not to be found among the martyrs. Whether his son-in-law knew this, with that insight which his humility if not his intelligence gave him, is not easy to prove

by anything he said, but one of the great fascinations of Roper's book is that he writes of these things which he had himself known as if they were quite as vanished for him as they are for us.

That is one of the secrets, too, of [his] Olympian simplicity and serenity. . . . In spite of the fact that his subject had shown from time to time an extraordinary prescience of the future, not, it should be added, of its triumphs, as in the case of most of the prophecies which men like to remember, but of its failures and its disasters, Roper makes no effort to link up More's time with his own. His basic motive was simply to preserve a noble memory and bear his witness to what he had known and loved. For it cannot be stressed too much that this is a personal memoir, and at that a very special type of personal memoir, a memoir from out of the family which meant so much to More. There is nothing of the professional writer, or even of the professional intellectual, about Roper, a fact that stands out most impressively when his account is compared with the accounts of his successors. This is most apparent in the capsule summaries of such relevant transactions in the great world as the disappointment of Wolsey over the papacy and the inception of "the king's business" as a scheme of revenge for the Emperor's responsibility for that disappointment. It is not just that Roper took that whole business more simply than any modern historian would think of doing (more pretentious historians than he ever dreamed of being did, too, at that time), but his account shows that he saw the great world with the same directness and homely simplicity as the domestic world. His eye is for look and word and gesture, not for the diagrams which more intellectual men discern behind the shapes and colors of the sequence of events.

That is one of the reasons why he has been called naïve. Another reason is the role in which he has cast himself in the presentation of his relations with his father-in-law. That is almost always of a rather literal-minded, short-sighted young man whose chief function seems to be to give the wise and far-seeing More a chance to illumine him and us, a sort of hagiographic Dr. Watson, as it were. We must remember, too, that the man who writes this life of More is old Mr. Roper . . . , who is looking back upon the folly and incomprehension of "sonne Roper" from the mature and experienced wisdom of a man now older even than the revered father-in-law of whom he is writing. But it is still true that only a man of a good deal of judgment or of uncommon taste would have been so sparing of his earlier folly, so reticent of his present superior vision. It is customary to say that Roper found help in the pattern of the classic saint's life for the very difficult business of organizing these personal reminiscences, and that is true. From the first sentence of Roper's preface, which finds its kernel in "a man of singular vertue and of a clere unspotted consciens"[see essay dated 1557?], to that wonderfully bare conclusion, "So passed Sir Thomas Moore out of this world to god, uppon the very same daye in which himself had most desired," the basic preoccupation is that of the martyr's life, albeit of a very special martyr, the man who mounted the unsteady scaffold smiling, with a jest: "I pray you, master Lieuetenaunte, see me salf uppe, and for my cominge downe let me shifte for my self." Yet for all the jest, More knew that he was adding his mite to a great tradition. This Roper did not forget, as can be seen in his account of how More dressed himself in his best apparel and the lieutenant protested, "sayenge that he that should have it was but a Javill."

> "What, master Leiuetenaunt," quoth he, "shall I accompte him a Javill that shall doe me his day so singuler a benefitt? Nay, I assure you, were it clothe of gold, I wolde accompt it well bestowed on him, as St Ciprian did, who gave his executioner thirtie peeces of gould." And albeit at length, throughe master Lieuetenauntes importunate persuasion, he altered his apparell, yeat after thexample of that holy martir St Ciprian, did he, of that litle money that was lefte him, send one Angell of gold to his executioner.

One wonders how much Roper, like More, had had that ancient story of Saint Cyprian, one of the purest and the noblest of all time, in his mind throughout.

This general hagiographic approach governs Roper's selection of his material, leading him to say nothing of More's friendship with Erasmus, though he does cite in his preface the praise of Erasmus, more eloquent perhaps, but beside Roper's homespun a little ornate. Nor does he speak of all the throng of visitors from home and abroad, except those who, like King Henry and the Duke of Norfolk, play a part in the tragedy. Nor does he say very much of all that colorful and delightful life of the house and the garden along the river with its view of the city below. But he is quite unpretentiously explicit about More's austerities and his care to conceal them, about his fidelity to religious observance, and his contribution to the intellectual defense of the Church, about his early and late attraction to the contemplative life.

But when it comes to the miraculous, Roper is . . . sober. . . One miraculous cure, that of Margaret, is reported, with careful accounting for the means thereof in the remembrance of the healing "glister" in prayer. And the appropriateness of the day of his death, Saint Thomas of Canterbury's "Even" and the Utas or Octave of Saint Peter is noted, as More had noted it.

But though Roper is . . . sparing of the miraculous . . . , he does admit . . . the gift of prophecy. Clearly, as Roper looked back upon his conversations with More, one of the things that most impressed him was the way in which More had foreseen how things were likely to go when Roper himself had not had the slightest idea, and most even of those older and wiser than he were not much more alert. There is More's early anxiety about the consequences of the "king's matter." Even more impressive is his great care in the midst of professional prosperity and domestic felicity to awaken his family to the possibility of a less comfortable future. But of all these prophetic insights, the most remarkable is that implied in More's prayer that the day might not come when those who now sat on top, "treading heretikes under our feete like antes," would be glad to "let them have their churches quietly to themselfes, so that they wold be contente to let us have ours quietly to our selves." On this occasion Roper permits himself one of his rare rebuttals, "By my troth, sir, it is very desperately spoken!" Perhaps in the light of what had happened since, that protest of his, which almost everyone at that time, heretic and orthodox alike, would have echoed, seemed ironic. But to Roper, who, it may be remembered, tells no stories of divine retribution, that too, now twenty years later, must have seemed prophetic.

It is not easy to tell how far Roper thought this prescience of More's the gift of prophecy of the saints, and how far he deemed it the evidence of his great wisdom. Certainly when More told the young man who had so proudly watched the King put his arm about his neck and walk familiarly with him, that the King would not hesitate to take his head if it would win him one castle in the current war with France, he was merely expressing an estimate of his master's character which was to prove only too correct. And when he warned his friends, the Bishops of Durham, Bath, and Winchester, surely much more experienced men than young Roper, of the hazards of the seemingly nominal compliance of marching in the coronation procession of Queen Anne, he may only have seen that very rapidly moving and complicated situation more steadily and whole than the wisest of his friends. Whatever Roper thought of it all, there is no question of the impressiveness of the cumulative effect. It has been commonly suggested that Roper had a remarkable memory; how remarkable has not been always appreciated. To remember across twenty years not only what his father-in-law said, but how he said it, the very inflection of his voice as revealed in his syntax, is a very remarkable feat. True, he had More's own writing to help him, and no writer was ever more constantly himself than More. Even at the end, in *A Dialoge of Comfort*, when he was most deliberately trying to rise above himself, he cannot, if he would, keep out the homely and breathtakingly apposite story, the flash of dramatic dialogue, the wryly humorous comparison, the ironic turn. All this Roper had to refresh his memory, and up to around some ten years before he presumably wrote his story, he had the help of his wife. With her he must often have talked over these things, doubtless finding in the later consequences much help for understanding what had once seemed so puzzling.

And yet some of Roper's speeches are pretty much the most characteristic utterances of More that we have, and some of them for dramatic incisiveness and grace are so fine that even Shakespeare would not be shamed by them. As A. W. Reed long ago pointed out, More himself not only had a flair for the dramatic, but his house at Chelsea must have been "an academy of dramatic writing and thinking." Roper had remarkable opportunities, but he must also have had remarkable aptitude to profit from them. Only a very unusual sense of the dramatic could keep him from blurring another man's lines, to take it at the lowest.

Roper, also, has a sense of the scene. Take, for instance, the prophecy of the hero's future greatness from the lips of Cardinal Morton, close to the beginning of the life. It is introduced by that unforgettable picture of the brilliant boy stepping into the Christmas play, and without any rehearsal creating a part, on the spur of the moment, more entertaining to the audience than all the carefully prepared witticisms of the players. And, even more important, Roper has a sense of dramatic pattern, of the thrust of action and the revelation of its meaning. When it comes to the final act, how dramatically Roper builds up his climax! How he rises above even the high rafters of Westminster Hall in that speech of More's when he had been condemned and could at last speak out fully. To the Lord Chief Justice, who had marveled that he should stand out against the bishops and the universities and the best learned of the land on the acts of Parliament making the

King the Supreme Head of the Church of England, he answered:

> ...I nothinge doubte but that, thoughe not in this
> realme, yeat in Christendome aboute, of thes well
> lerned Bishoppes and vertuous men that are yeat alive,
> they be not the fewer parte that be of my mind therein.
> But if I should speake of those whiche already be dead,
> of whom many be nowe holy sainctes in heaven, I am
> very sure it is the farre greater parte of them that, all
> the while [they] lived, thoughte in this case that waye
> that I thinck nowe. And therefore am I not bounde, my
> lord, to conforme my consciens to the Councell of one
> Realme against the generall Councell of Christendome.

Higher than that it would not seem that even More could
go, but after the judgment had been given, which, horrible
as it was, Roper did not stop to describe, More went even
above the whole of Christendom with his reminder of
Paul, who had consented to the stoning of Stephen ... :

> More have I not to say, my Lordes, but that like as the
> blessed Apostle St Pawle, as we read in thactes of the
> Apostles, was present, and consented to the death of St
> Stephen, and kepte their clothes that stoned him to
> deathe, and yeat be they [nowe] both twayne holy
> Sainctes in heaven, and shall continue there frendes for
> ever, So I verily [truste], and shall therefore right harte-
> lye pray, that thoughe your lordshippes have now [here]
> in earthe bine Judges to my condemnacion, we may
> yeat hereafter in heaven meerily all meete together, to
> our everlasting salvacion.

After that there is no surprise in that last scene, which
Roper sums up so briefly, knowing as he did from all his
years with More that even at his last minute on earth, he
was thinking of another man's nervousness and how it
might be relieved:

> Then desired he all the people thereaboute to pray for
> him, and to beare witness with him that he should
> [nowe there] suffer death in and for the faith of the holy
> chatholik churche. Whiche done, he kneled downe, and
> after his prayers said, turned to thexecutioner, and with
> a cheerefull countenaunce spake [thus] to him: "Plucke
> upp thy spirites, man, and be not afrayde to do thine
> office; my necke is very shorte; take heede therefore
> thow strike not awrye, for savinge of thine honestye."
> (pp. 116-23)

> *Helen C. White, "The Catholic Martyrs under
> Henry," in her* Tudor Books of Saints and Mar-
> tyrs, *The University of Wisconsin Press, 1963, pp.
> 96-131.*

JOHN MAGUIRE (essay date 1969)

[*In the following excerpt, Maguire contends that Roper's*
Life of More *is a highly artistic work, juxtaposing passages
from the biography and More's letters to prove that Roper
had access to his father-in-law's correspondence.*]

Renaissance biography, though not virgin territory, still
remains largely unplotted ground. Yet even the most cursory surveys have pointed to William Roper's *The Lyfe of
Sir Thomas Moore, knighte,* as one of the most important
landmarks in the field, and More scholars have paid high
tribute to it. For Elsie Vaughn Hitchcock it "has always
been recognized as one of the masterpieces of English literature" [see excerpt dated 1935]. And R. W. Chambers

wrote in glowing terms of Roper's fine "sense of dialogue,
passionate narrative power and dramatic skill", though
adding that Roper lacked "the sense of proportion and
structure which More shows so markedly in *Richard III*"
[see Additional Bibliography]. Even these More scholars,
however, have not recognised that the work has a clearly
indicated controlling theme, is written from a definite
point of view, and manifests a noticeably discernible
structure. But perhaps their most curious oversight is the
failure to recognize Roper's working methods as a biographer, that in composing his supposedly artless memoirs
about his famous father-in-law Roper made astonishingly
sophisticated use of several of More's letters.

Roper's preface to his *Life of More* [see essay dated 1557?]
is too well known to call for more than brief summary and
short quotation here. Very humbly, he begins by setting
forth his reasons for writing the *Life*: More is worthy of
perpetual memory and because Roper knew him better
than had any other living man he has acceded to the request of divers friends to write down "as farr forthe as my
meane wit, memory, and knowledge wold serve me ... so
much thereof as in my poore judgment seemed worthy to
be remembered". This very disarming statement, taken
with Harpsfield's acknowledgment of Roper's help [see excerpt dated 1558?], and his extensive use of the Roper *Life*
in his own biography of More, has contributed to the
widespread myth that Roper had nothing more in mind
than an informal account of somewhat random recollections of More. Chambers obviously believed this, and in
a rather condescending manner has written that More's
own works were ... "scarcely used by Roper, who found
sufficient materials for his little book in his own knowledge.... Roper was neither a Boswell making systematic
notes, nor a historian using documents to check his recollections. We must always keep in mind the apology for
lapses of memory with which Roper begins his little book"
[see excerpt dated 1935]. There is just enough truth in this
statement for it to have been almost universally accepted.
Roper's memory did play tricks on him in many particulars and his errors in the *Life* have been duly noted. But
as far as Roper's use of More's works is a question, the
statement is factually erroneous. Roper expressly refers to
and then quotes almost a hundred words from More's last
letter to his daughter Meg. But there are also several
other passages in the *Life* where Roper makes no reference to
More's letters, although he obviously had them in front of
him as he wrote. Though there are quite a few instances
of parallel wording between events as described by More
in his letters and as reconstructed by Roper in his *Life of
More,* we will look at only a few of the most telling.

It is often asserted by commentators that in the Roper *Life*
and the other early biographies of More Henry's role in
the events leading to More's death is handled with great
reserve. For many and obvious reasons this would apparently have to be true, yet Roper in his *Life* clearly though
indirectly contrasts the dishonorable willfulness and inconsistency of Henry with the honorable and consistent
integrity of his Lord Chancellor. He presents one scene in
which More, on his knees before the king, bemoans the
fact that he cannot be of service in the divorce question
and reminds Henry of

> the most godly wordes that his highnes spake unto him
> at his first coming into his noble service, the most ver-

tuous lesson that ever prince taught his servant, willing him first to looke unto god, and after god to him...

The importance More himself placed on these words of Henry is evident from the fact that he recalled this advice in almost the same words in letters to three rather different correspondents in the time between his retirement from public life and his death. In a letter to Cromwell dated March 5, 1534, More told him of Henry's words

> That I shold fyrst loke unto God and after God unto hym, which moost graciouse wordys was the fyrste lesson also that ever his Grace gave me at my fyrst comyng into his noble servyce.

In a letter written from the Tower in 1534 to Doctor Nicholas Wilson More recalled this same conversation in these words:

> ...his Highenes added therto that I shulde therein loke first unto God and after God unto hym, which word was also the fyrste lesson that his Grace gave me what tyme I came first in to his noble servyce and ...a more gracious lesson coulde there in my mynde never kyng geve his counsaylor or eny his other servaunt.

And finally, describing for his daughter Meg one of his interrogations in the Tower, More wrote:

> Whereto I aunswered...that I had alway from the beginninge truly used myselfe to loking first uppon God and nexte uppon the Kinge according to the lesson that his Highness taught me at my first comminge to his noble service, the most vertuous lesson that ever prynce taught his servaunte...

It is perhaps conceivable that these words were so frequently on More's lips that they were printed indelibly on Roper's memory enabling him to recall them so accurately more than twenty years later; it is likelier that Roper had before him the text of at least one and probably all three of these letters as he wrote. A comparison of the next two passages, however, must remove all reasonable doubt.

When More heard that attempts were being made to link him with "the wykked woman of Canterbery", he wrote Henry, recalling their conversation when the king accepted More's resignation of the chancellorship:

> It pleased your Highnes ferther to say un to me, that for the service which I before had done you (which it than lyked your goodnes far above my deserving to commend) that in eny suit that I should after have un to your Highnes, which either should concerne myn honor (that word it lyked your Highnes to use un to me) or that should perteyne un to my profit, I should fynd your Highnes good and graciouse lord un to me.

Roper describes the same scene in almost identical words:

> ...So pleased it his highnes further to say unto him, that for the service that he had before done hym, in anye sute which he should after have unto him, that either should concerne his honor (for that word it liked his highnes to use unto him) or that should appertaine unto his profitt, he should find his highnes good and gratious Lord unto him.

The mere juxtaposition of these two passages is the single most conclusive evidence for Roper's use of More's letters. The two accounts are so close, and the parenthetic clause about Henry's use of the word "honor" so revealing

as to preclude any other possibility. Yet strangely enough, neither Hitchcock nor Chambers, as familar as they were with both the Roper *Life* and More's letters, ever seemed to see their relationship. Yet as one reads the Roper account of the last years of More's life along with the letters of More to Margaret Roper, Doctor Nicholas Wilson, Cromwell and Henry, and the Margaret Roper-Alice Alington letters, it becomes abundantly clear that the accounts are too similar to be independent. And given that fact, it is no longer possible to believe that Roper's *Life of More* is quite so simple or artless as it is usually believed to be. For Roper did not use More's letters slavishly and he did have his memories and perhaps other sources of information.

But it is perhaps ungenerous for any student/lover of More to carp at the occasional lapses of Chambers and Miss Hitchcock for one simply owes so much to them. And Chambers was righter than he knew when he wrote in glowing terms of Roper's dramatic sense and his ability to write strikingly realistic dialogue. To appreciate fully Roper's artistry in creating scene and dialogue from the stuff of a More letter, we will have to look at two rather lengthy passages.

More's letter of March 5, 1534, to Cromwell touches on an earlier interview he had had with a committee of the Privy Council, including Cromwell, about the matter of the divorce and the Pope's primacy. In it More reminds the Secretary:

> As towching the thyrde point, the prymatie of the Pope, I no thing medle in the mater. Trowth it is, that as I told yow, whan you desyred me to shew yow what I thowght therein, I was myselfe some tyme not of the mynd that the prymatie of that see shold be bygone by thinstitution of God, untill I redd in that mater those thingis that the Kyngis Highnes had written in his moost famouse booke agaynst the heresyes of Marten Luther, at the fyrst reding wherof I moved the Kyngis Highnes either to leve owt that point, or ellys to towche it more slenderly for dowt of such thingis as after myght happe to fall in question bytwene his Highnes and some pope as bytwene pryncis and popis dyverse tymes have done. Wherunto his Highnes answered me that he wold in no wise eny thing minishe of that mater, of which thing his Highnes showed me a secret cause whereof I never had eny thing herd byfore.

Henry's book defending the Pope's primacy against Luther was later a source of acute embarrassment to the King and More had been charged with villainously and traitorously inducing Henry to write it. As Roper reconstructs this appearance of More before some of the Privy Council members, he adds considerable material to it and dramatizes it most effectively:

> When they had thus layd forth all the terrors they coulde ymagine against him: "My lordes", quothe he, "these terrours be arguments for Children, and not for me. But to aunswere that wherewith you doe chifly birden me, I beleave the kinges highnes of his honour will never lay that to my charge; For none is there that can in that pointe say in my excuse more then his highnes himself, who right well knoweth that I never was procurer nor councelour of his majestye thereunto; But after it was finished, by his graces apointment and consent of the makers of the same, only a sorter out and placer of the principall matters therein contayned. Wherein when I founde the Popes aucthority highly de-

fended, I said unto his grace: 'I must put your highnes in remembraunce of one thinge, and that is this. The Pope, as your grace knowethe, is a prince as you are, and in league with all other Christian princes. It may hereafter so fall owte that your grace and he may varye uppon some pointes of the league, whereuppon may growe breach of amitye and warre betweene you bothe. I thincke it best therefore that that place be amended, and his aucthority more sclenderly touched'.

" 'Nay', quoth his grace, 'that shall it not. We are so muche bounded unto the sea of Room that we cannot doe to muche honor unto it'.

"Then did I further put him in remembraunce of the statue of Premunire, whereby a good parte of the Popes pastoral cure here was pared away.

"To that awneswered his highnes: 'Whatsoever impediment to be the contrary, we will set forthe that aucthoritye to the uttermost. For we receaved from that Sea our crowne Imperiall'; which, till his grace with his owne mouthe tould it me, I never heard of before.... "

If one did not already know that Roper in fact had More's letters before him as he wrote, it would perhaps be impossible to argue convincingly from a comparison of only these two passages that Roper was reconstructing his account from the More letter to Cromwell. (Chambers, in fact, quotes both of these passages in his *Thomas More* but sees in the More letter only a confirmation of the essential points of the Roper account. And [in *The Correspondence of Sir Thomas More* (1947)] Elizabeth Rogers speculates rather curiously that More's "secrete cause" was Henry's proof that the Arthur-Katherine marriage had been consummated.) The two accounts are obviously close, though Roper's is longer and more specific in detail. But what are the possible relationships between them? Is it próbable that Roper could recall so accurately conversations held with More more than 20 years earlier, shortly after More's return from this confrontation? It seems far likelier that Roper had before him the text of More's letter to Cromwell (which was printed in Rastell's 1557 edition of More's *English Works,* as were all the letters quoted in this article), called on his memory and perhaps other written sources, and then reconstructed the interview, making the slight changes necessary to increase the dramatic effectiveness of the exchange between More and the Committee as he presents it. If this is so, then the very differences between the two accounts are important in revealing Roper's artistry in transforming More's rather laconic account of this meeting into his own highly dramatic scene.

Renaissance and Classical biographers alike had no scruples about putting fictional speeches into the mouths of their subjects. Nor was the intelligent use of letters as a source and a means of revealing information.... But Roper's use of letters to reconstruct dialogue and dramatic scene is unusually sophisticated for a Renaissance biographer. (pp. 59-64)

> John Maguire, "William Roper's 'Life of More':
> The Working Methods of a Tudor Biographer," in
> Moreana, *Vol. VI, No. 23, August, 1969, pp. 59-*
> *65.*

R[ICHARD] S. SYLVESTER   (essay date 1972)

[In the following excerpt, Sylvester examines the structure and literary technique of Roper's Life of More.*]*

[William Roper's *Life of More* is] the first vernacular biography [of Thomas More] and the basic source for all of the future lives. In assigning this primacy to Roper, I do not mean to neglect Erasmus' sustained character sketch of 1519 (the letter to Hutten) nor to discount the many more or less shrewd comments on More delivered by his contemporaries. These notices are valuable, but, even when taken together, they do not add up to a fully developed view of More's personality. Roper, writing of his father-in-law in the 1550s with intimate affection, claims that "no man living" understood so much of More "and of his doings" as himself [see essay dated 1557?]. It is a proud claim, one which,for many later critics, is scarcely borne out by Roper's spare narrative. Historians have been quick to pounce on Roper's errors of fact. They have often questioned either the basis or the details of several of his anecdotes. At his best, so runs the argument, Roper offers a series of valuable notes; he provides only a *memoir,* and a very limited one at that, telling us nothing about More's international fame and almost completely neglecting More's writings – not even, in fact, mentioning *Utopia* at all.

Whatever justice there may be in views like these, they are singularly unhelpful in that they tend, as negative criticism, to lead readers away from Roper's *Life* instead of attempting to understand his method and to evaluate his very real achievement. We ought rather to ask just what Roper's own "understanding" of More entails, trying then to see how this knowledge can serve to guide us when we come to consider other aspects of More's career which Roper himself does not mention. I am convinced, for my own part, that most of Roper's omissions are quite deliberate. He eschews a full and detailed biography because, for his purposes, it is not necessary. Besides, he had already enlisted the services of, as it were, a top-notch rewrite man, Nicholas Harpsfield, who was to produce, within a year or two, precisely the kind of lengthy narrative that he himself had so scrupulously refrained from writing.

Roper feels, in other words, that a massive agglomeration of facts about More's life will not contribute that much to the essential understanding of his subject. For him, though he preserves a rough chronological progression in his narrative, it is not so much the sequence or the fullness of events that matters, but rather the symbolic value that any given event may have, both in itself and in its relation to other anecdotes which precede or follow it. For the most part, Roper will not analyze, and he will not supply transitions. He tells three little stories to illustrate More's "innocency and clearness" of conscience in refusing to accept bribes; but, instead of continuing in this vein, he asks his readers "by these few . . . with their own judgements wisely to weigh and consider the same." Such a method is essentially dramatic. It asks us to participate in the action as we endeavor to understand—and it indicates, . . . that the influence of Thomas More on William Roper was not merely moral and paternal, but profoundly literary as well.

Roper thus writes out of the fullness of knowledge, but he concentrates his understanding to the utmost, recreating

Thomas More for us in a series of scenes that can easily, as Robert Bolt and others have realized, be transferred directly to the stage. It is not difficult, as my dear friend and teacher, Davis P. Harding, used to remark, to underestimate Roper in this biography. In fact, he almost wilfully compounds our difficulties for us by dramatizing himself, "son Roper", as a naïve misunderstander of many of More's actions. When More, sitting sadly in his boat during his last trip down the Thames from Chelsea to Lambeth, suddenly turns and says, "Son Roper, I thank our Lord the field is won," Roper can only reply "Sir, I am thereof very glad," loath to seem ignorant though "I wist not what he meant thereby."

A scene like this one (and there are many such in the *Life*) enables us to pinpoint one central aspect of Roper's method. By dramatizing his own misunderstanding of More in the past, he provides us with a device through which we can come to comprehend something of the mysterious greatness embodied in a man who seldom failed to understand himself and his surroundings. Roper's seeming lack of control over his story, his hesitancy in analyzing and the insufficiency of his analyses when they are directly offered, are essential to the part which he plays in his narrative. To play a part like this, to cast oneself in such a role, becomes, dramatically, a way of understanding the play itself.

If we are alert to these dramatic values in Roper's biography, then we shall be much less inclined to criticize him for incompleteness. He knows, as author, far more than he understands as character, and this knowledge emerges not only in his creation of his persona but in the structure and placing of his anecdotes. It is true that Roper does not set More's life on an international stage, but the first sentence and the final scene of his *Life* provide a framework which is as universal as sixteenth-century Europe could desire. He starts with a quotation from Erasmus, the most renowned scholar of his day: More was, in Erasmus' words, "more pure and white than the whitest snow, and of such an angelical wit that England never had the like before, nor never shall again." He ends, one hundred pages later, with the judgement of Charles V, delivered, it is said, —and here Roper adjusts history to his purposes—when the emperor received the news of More's death: "We say, that if we had been master of such a servant, of whose doings ourself have had these many years no small experience, we would rather have lost the best city of our dominions than to have lost such a worthy councillor." These two testimonies frame Roper's narrative for us ; sanctioned by the witness of the most learned and the most powerful voices in Europe, he can confidently tell his tale of this "man of singular virtue and of a clear, unspotted conscience." We have been reminded, and the reminder is sufficient, of what "the general council of Christendom" thought of the Thomas More who died for its corporate ideals rather than "conform his conscience to the council of one realm."

Roper's concluding anecdote of the ruler who could value a councillor more than a city is carefully linked to an early episode in the *Life* where More, after patiently suffering through Roper's congratulations on Henry VIII's ardent affection for him, remarks: "Howbeit, son Roper, I may tell thee I have no cause to be proud thereof, for if my head could win him a castle in France, it should not fail to go." More's prophetic words both anticipate and are echoed by Charles' final reflection; the early anecdote lives on in and is enlarged by the later one. Roper's method is brilliantly illustrated by this kind of relationship which he manages to effect between his seemingly self-contained episodes. Many of his scenes appear to be little gems, perfect in their isolation; but the light which they emit is heightened and intensified by similar, yet contrasting, episodes that precede or follow them in the narrative.

Nowhere is this clearer than in the two scenes which Roper employs to show us More at the beginning and at the end of his life. Here is More, aged about fourteen, at the house of Chancellor Morton, where

> though he was young of years, yet would he at Christmas-tide suddenly step in among the players, and never studying for the matter, make a part of his own there presently among them, which made the lookers-on more sport than all the players beside. In whose wit and towardness the Cardinal much delighting, would often say of him unto the nobles that divers times dined with him, "This child here waiting at the table, whosoever shall live to see it, will prove a marvellous man."

More's life, for Roper, begins with its hero on the stage, and it ends with another stage scene:

> And so was he by Master Lieutenant brought out of the Tower, and from thence led towards the place of execution. Where, going up the scaffold, which was so weak that it was ready to fall, he said merrily to master Lieutenant: "I pray you, master Lieutenant, see me safe up, and for my coming down let me shift for my self."

> Then desired he all the people thereabout to pray for him, and to bear witness with him that he should now there suffer death in and for the faith of the holy catholic church. Which done, he kneeled down, and after his prayers said, turned to the executioner, and with a cheerful countenance spake thus to him: "Pluck up thy spirits, man, and be not afraid to do thine office; my neck is very short; take heed therefore thou strike not awry, for saving of thine honesty."

> So passed Sir Thomas More out of this world to God, upon the very same day in which himself had most desired.

Roper tells us, immediately before this final scene, that Henry had requested More to "use few words" at his execution, an ironic request indeed after More had already been convicted for his silence in the king's great matter. But Henry wants no scaffold speeches—he wishes to deny More the opportunity "to make a part of his own," adding words to the prescribed text, as he had done, with Morton's blessing, so many years before at Lambeth Palace. More seems to comply with Henry's request, even though, as he tells Master Pope, he "had purposed at that time somewhat to have spoken." Yet, in his final scene, just as surely as in his first youthful role, More manages to control the action on the stage. This is a shaky, unsound scaffold, quite unlike the festive boards at Lambeth. One's improvisations are limited, but there is no place for bad acting. "Play your part well" ("do thine office"), More instructs his fellow actor. "Your honesty and mine depend upon our acceptance of our roles." Even the exact date of this last performance (July 6, the eve of the feast of Becket and the octave of St. Peter) is arranged in accordance with More's wishes—though not, Roper lets us know, without a bit of providential contrivance.

Thus Roper ties together the opening and the closing scenes of his *Life*, presenting us with his portrait of this man of many parts. The first anecdote is light-hearted, merry, as More performs to the delight of both himself and his audience. Yet even here, for all the twelfth-night gaiety, all the forecast of brilliant accomplishment, the Cardinal's words ("who shall live to see it") cast a momentary shadow of death over the platform. At Tower Hill, on the other hand, the scene is grimly earnest, the audience tearfully sorrowing. But somehow a note of supreme merriment plays about the scaffold. More's wit in the face of death, his confident composure in a performance under pressure, lead us back to the early scene, as we wonder, perhaps, if the truly marvellous side of this man's life is only now about to begin.

More's words to Master Lieutenant ("I pray you, see me safe up, and for my coming down let me shift for myself") can in fact be read as reflecting, in little, the pattern of his whole life. Others—his father, his teachers, friends at court, Wolsey, the king himself—have "seen him safe up," providing roles for him which he did not so much seek as accept when offered. While Roper may overemphasize More's reluctance to become a royal councillor, it remains true that, up to and during the time of his chancellorship, More appears, in the *Life*, as a man who had greatness thrust upon him. As office after office is given to him, he must struggle to preserve a sense of his own identity, even, at one point, deliberately "dissembling his nature," playing the part of the boor, so that the king would not require his attendance at court so frequently. More is not without wit in the first half of the *Life*, but, paradoxically, he is much more serious during his rise than he is after his fall. It is here, fairly early in the *Life*, that Roper tells us of his hair-shirt and of his private flagellation. Most of More's ominous, prophetic statements are uttered while he is in the midst of prosperity and it is then, not later, that he advises his children concerning the wiles of the devil and reminds them that they can't expect to go to heaven on featherbeds.

I spoke above of More's "fall," but the term is not apt. In the matter of his "coming down" More is not the victim of fortune, but rather its master. He now "shifts for himself," resigning the chancellorship of his own accord, and, in Roper's words, "pretending, for certain infirmities of his body," that he was unable any longer to serve. In the second half of the *Life*, his spirits mount as his prosperity wanes. The word "merry" echoes in scene after scene, as More tells his wife and family that, "if they would encourage him [as they will not] to die in a good cause," he would "for very joy thereof, 'merrily run to death.'" He speaks "merrily" to the bishops who come to invite him to Anne Boleyn's coronation, and he puzzles Roper—again—with his "merriness" after his first encounter with the king's commissioners. He plays the fool "merrily" with his wife, Dame Alice, when she visits him in the Tower, and his last words at his trial form a prayer for his judges that "we may yet hereafter in heaven 'merrily' all meet together."

There is one beautifully-situated scene in Roper which seems to sum up the principles through which More exercised his masterly control of his situation. It comes immediately after he has given up the great seal. His family assembles together, all of them worried about their circumstances, for More would now no longer be able to pay all their expenses as he had previously done. More asks for their advice, but no one offers to help. He then assumes the role of speaker himself, "showing his poor mind unto them." "I have been brought up," he says, summarizing his whole career, "at Oxford, at an Inn of Chancery, at Lincoln's Inn, and also in the King's Court . . . from the lowest degree to the highest. Yet I have now little above 100 £ a year left to me. If we are to continue together, all must become contributories; but, by my counsel, it shall not be best for us to fall to the lowest fare first." More then suggests a gradual descent, first to Lincoln's Inn fare, then to New Inn fare, and so forth, remarking as he goes how one can be well content at each level. Finally, if even Oxford fare fails, "then may we yet, with bags and wallets, go a begging together, and hoping that for pity some good folk will give us their charity, at every man's door to sing *Salve Regina,* and so still keep company and be merry together."

This is shifting for oneself with a vengeance! But More's own composure here is never in doubt. Each downward step is as completely foreseen, as carefully rehearsed and as fully controlled, as those last sad steps to the scaffold. Whatever the role, whatever the part assigned, let us play it to the best of our abilities, "merrily" indeed, even if it means becoming the most devotedly happy beggars in Christendom. For the man who has so completely triumphed over himself—and I think this is one thing which Roper means by his constant references to More's "unspotted conscience"—the assumption of such roles is managed with an innocent simplicity. And yet, beneath this calm surface, this easy flexibility, what a sense of struggle and poignant agony! For "conscience," as Roper uses the term to describe More, indicates not only a profound moral integrity; conscience is also, etymologically, and in sixteenth-century usage, a "knowing with," a full and special awareness of both oneself and the world about one. Playing one's part conscientiously entails playing it with full consciousness of the other actors in the drama. The role More felt called upon to play was not, ultimately, one which he could share with his family. In that lay the human tragedy of his death, but in that too lay the grounds of his glory.

If we look back now to consider briefly the genre out of which Roper's biography grows, that of the medieval saint's life, we can, I think, marvel at the transformation he has wrought in it. More's "saintliness" (Roper himself never calls it that) is not of the conventional order. He works no miracles, has no halo around his cradle, never hears voices from heaven, never receives, as did the Nun of Kent, divine revelations of Henry's VIII's wickedness. The trial which Roper describes is not a combat with the devil, but an all-too-human story of a perjured witness and coerced judges. More's virtues are those of the layman, not of the priest, but so too are his trials and sufferings—a fact which he wistfully realizes as, through his window in the Tower, he watches the first band of London Carthusians going "cheerfully to their deaths as bridegrooms to their marriage." The marriages of priests are made in heaven; More's own, as Dame Alice never tired of reminding him, was much more earthly.

More's comments on the execution of the Carthusians take us back, like so many of Roper's later anecdotes, to an earlier scene in the *Life*. We recall how More, while still studying law, had lived for four years in the house of these very same monks, playing the part then of the committed man of religion, testing, trying out the cowl, and finding, in the end, that it did not quite fit. He can sympathize with the painful scene before him now, because he had, in a sense, acted in it earlier; but this recollection scarcely lessens the anguish which he feels at not being able to share their lot. In contrast, he says, to their "strait, hard, penitential and painful life," his own career has been "consumed in pleasure and ease licentiously." But we know, thanks to Roper's telling scenes, that More, even here, is again playing a part, presenting himself as an abject sinner, "a most wicked caitiff," a role that in real life he hardly indulged in, but one which he must assume now as he throws himself on God's mercy.

I do not mean to suggest for a minute that More is being insincere in this moment of self-accusation. He is simply, once again, testing himself, trying out a part, and finding, this time, that it may well suit him perfectly. He is never unaware of the ambiguities posed by the great traditional metaphor of "All the world's a stage," *a topos* which reached back at least to his beloved Lucian and which had recently inspired one the of the most eloquent passages in Pico della Mirandola's *Oration on the Dignity of Man*. The image, as it came down to More, was double-edged: if reality was but a passing show, then human life, in itself, was transitory and had no essential value. One could join, in near despair, the throng of unreflecting fools on the stage; or one could, like the Carthusians, turn away from the theater itself and live only for a transcendent future. But the image, as Pico proclaimed it, could offer a contrary perspective. The playing of different parts by "Protean man" might, if consciously elected, be an educative process. By becoming someone else, man could extend his capacities and perhaps come to understand himself more fully. As Pico had noted, such transformations could be dangerous, for man the actor, if he were not careful, could play parts beneath himself, debasing his capacities instead of enlarging them. Yet the prospect was exciting, dramatically exhilarating, and it did much to shape the aspirations of many a Renaissance man.

More's own employment of the stage *topos,* both in his life and in his art, constantly endeavors to do justice to the several aspects of the image. His supreme ability to play a part is always being checked and balanced, in Roper's biography, by his reluctance to accept a role which he has not chosen for himself. He refuses, again and again, to separate the moral implications of role-playing from the aesthetic satisfactions which it offers. Long before he went to the Tower, he had dwelt, in his meditation on the *Four Last Things* (1522), on the image of life not as a stage, but as a prison, where "the king, by whose high sentence we be condemned to die, would not of this death pardon his own son." But this devout medieval insight did not prevent him, in 1534, from turning his real prison into a stage, telling an uncomprehending Dame Alice that he was quite content in his "gay house" and reminding Master Lieutenant that, if he proved to be an ungrateful guest, he could always be "thrust out of the door."

The comic element in scenes like this, as in the final scene on the scaffold, puzzled many of More's contemporaries, and it has often been slighted or ignored by later critics. The chronicler Edward Hall could not approve of More's jokes in the face of death and he ended his account by remarking that "I cannot tell whether to call him a foolish

wiseman or a wise foolish man." But More knew exactly what he was doing. Since "the field was won" before the battle began, then the battle itself could be treated mockheroically. The king's good servant would never serve (or die) more truly than when he did not serve at all. Nor would More, on the other hand, deliberately seek the alternative role open to him, the martyrdom which he could have chosen by explicitly denying the royal supremacy. He would, perforce, play the martyr's part at the end, but not until he, drawing upon all the resources which his legal training had given him, had used every possible human means "to avoid that indictment."

More's trial at Westminster Hall, as Roper dramatizes it for us, seems almost to take on a kind of sublime absurdity. The conclusion is forgone, the script is rigidly prescribed; the actors, all but one, must play the part which is set down for them. Grim as the farce was, More must have relished the moment when he told the court that he was, as all just men knew, miscast for the role of traitor which had "so wrongfully been imagined" against him. And he must have smiled to himself as he watched Lord Audley, More's successor as Lord Chancellor, try to shrug off the burden of judgement by appealing to Fitz-James, the Lord Chief Justice, for a technical opinion which would validate the proceedings. Fitz-James did himself proud, ignoring every moral issue in the case, ridiculously prefacing his opinion with an oath to St. Julian (the patron saint of hospitality), as he said: "My lords, I must needs confess that if the act of parliament be not unlawful, then is not the indictment in my conscience insufficient." Technically, as Professor Elton has recently shown [in *St. Thomas More: Action and Contemplation* (1972)], Fitz-James was absolutely correct; but the "conscience" upon which he relies here is, like his syntax, a crippling, negative, puny thing, far different from the conscience, and the consciousness, of the man whose story Roper tells.

More could not, one feels, have staged it any better himself. He had, after all, been ever given to the "putting of cases," a habit instilled in him from his years as a law student when, after spending their mornings observing real cases in the courts, the young lawyers would devote their afternoons to moot trials in the mock courts at the Inns. But the hypothetical case, the imagined situation, had now been turned into a matter of life and death. As if to tighten the ironies even further, Roper makes the case for the crown hinge on the "putting of cases," or discussion of hypothetical possibilities, which had occurred during the interview between More and Richard Rich in the Tower. More maintains at his trial that, even if he had spoken the words Rich attributed to him (which he denies), this would not in itself be treasonable, for the conversation "affirmed nothing and was only the putting of cases." But More's crucial distinction between a direct statement, which involves a full personal commitment, and the detached, imaginary entertainment of an idea is lost in a court like this. If one can no longer understand the distinction between the role that a man might elect to play before others and the role which he believed, in his inmost being, to be truly his own, then one must inevitably misunderstand Thomas More. The verdict is "guilty as charged". (pp.47-57)

R[ichard] S. Sylvester, "Roper's 'Life of More'," in Moreana, Vol. IX, No. 36, December, 1972, pp. 47-59.

JUDITH H. ANDERSON (essay date 1984)

[*Anderson is an American scholar of English literature of
the Tudor period. In the following excerpt, she studies the
literary designs of Roper's* Life of More *and compares the
work with Harpsfields* Life.]

In *The Life of Wolsey* Cavendish gives the impression of
coming to terms gradually and for the first time with the
true significance of Wolsey's actions and his own relation
to them. He seems to rejoin his former self as he rediscov-
ers it. Except, perhaps, for the laments about Fortune, we
have little sense in reading Cavendish of how long ago it
was that these things happened, and even the laments, far
from sounding like an older and wiser Cavendish, sound
simply like another, emotional but not very thoughtful,
one.

In contrast to Cavendish's practice, Roper takes care in
The Life of More to remind us of the distance between his
past responses and his present understanding. Roper's
view of More is settled reasonably well even before he
writes: "What he ment thereby I then wist not, yeat loth
to seeme ignorant... But as I conjectured
afterward*es*, it was for [that] the love he had to god
wrought in him so effectually." His judgment of his own
role, if also spontaneously felt, is likewise clear and certain: "I said: 'By my troth, sir, it is very desp*er*ately spoken.' That vyle tearme, I cry god mercy, did I geeve him."
Throughout **The Life of More** Roper's point of view is
more controlled and stabler than is Cavendish's in *The
Life of Wolsey.*

The distance between Roper's present and past responses
has led to descriptions of his "fictional guise" as one that
is "simple, direct, unsophisticated—Lemuel Gulliver in
sixteenth-century dress" [see excerpt by Sylvester and Harding dated 1962]. Gulliver aside (young Roper is not so
fully characterized), the phrase "fictional guise" is useful:
young Roper surely is something of a straight man to
More's wit and wisdom. Still, we must ask in what sense
this guise is "fictional," since presumably it is also true.
The guise appears to be fictional, first, because it is different from *present* truth; second, because it is consistent,
hence controlled or manipulated; and third, because it is
finished, closed or completed.

We might further ask how Roper's self-portrayal differs
from his portrayal of More, how the fictional truth or
truthful fiction of autobiography differs in this admittedly
limited instance from that of biography. Here the chief
difference involves degree rather than kind of awareness.
It lies in the explicitness of the writer's awareness of his
image-making or image-presenting, in his pointed manner
of manipulating his own image to deliberate effect. (pp.
40-1)

Roper's artistry in **The Life of More** lies to a considerable
extent in his genius for the selection and arrangement of
material, for the timing of its presentation, and for the
dramatic analysis of motive. All seem natural and yet
could not be more deliberate: for example, the ironical
counterpointing of More's realistic appraisal of the value
of Henry VIII's affection for him—"if my head [could]
winne him a castle in Fraunce... it should not faile to
goe"—and the words of the Emperor Charles at the end of
The Life when he hears of More's execution—"we wold
rather have lost the best city of our dominions then have

lost such a worthy councellou*r*"; or the pointed nature of
More's leaving his family to answer the summons to Lambeth to take the oaths of succession and supremacy:
"whereas he evermore used before, at his dep*ar*ture from
his wife *and* children... to have them bring him to his
boate.... Then wold he Suffer none of them forthe of the
gate to followe him, but pulled the wickatt after him, *and*
shutt them all from him." Roper, it turns out, accompanies More to London and so looks back, like More, from
the other side of the gate. The closing of that gate is
More's symbolic gesture, but it is also Roper's recollection, selection, and "reading" of the incident.

Another familiar example takes our sense of Roper's artistry further, namely, the parable of the virgin who is the
first to commit a capital offense from the penalty for
which virgins alone are exempted but whose fate is subsequently sealed by a clever counselor: "Let her first be def-
floured, *and* then after may she be devoured." According
to Roper, More tells this parable to several bishops and
then remarks that, although he might well be devoured, he
will take care not to be deflowered by compromising his
views on Henry's divorce and remarriage. Like the closing
of the gate, More's remarks to the bishops illuminate his
motives not only in this incident but in others as well and
do so dramatically. Once again, the dramatization and
analysis of motive are More's own: in More's life, however, it is implausible that the parable stood out—isolated
from daily events or indeed from other moments of
wit—to the degree that it does in Roper's *Life of More.* In
actual life, More's parable might not have served as so
major a commentary on More's actions. Roper does not
tell us that it did; instead, he lets us assume this fact or
find it out for ourselves, as he evidently did. That is, the
image of More we receive through More's own words is,
to the extent that Roper's memory and honesty can be
trusted, More's own, but it is also, perhaps equally, Roper's.

The practice of Harpsfield is illuminating in this connection. Harpsfield knew Roper himself and had Roper's
More open before him as he wrote his own biography of
More. Like Roper's, Harpsfield's reputation for historical
accuracy is fairly good and for truthfulness is excellent.
Yet at times in his biography of More, Harpsfield shifts
into indirect discourse the words More speaks dramatically in Roper's *Life.* At other times Harpsfield omits or alters words and phrases attributed to More by Roper, even
when Roper is the immediate witness of the event. To
take one example: "if my head could winne him a castle
in Fraunce... it should not faile to serve his turne"; as
cited earlier, the final phrase in Roper's *Life* is "faile to
goe." Either Harpsfield did not regard More's speeches in
Roper as verbatim records or else he did not always consider their accuracy important enough to preserve exactly.
The demands of his own way of pre*s*enting More, in fact
of his own image of More, took precedence. In either case,
we are left with the fact and the importance of the biographer's invention.

Although Roper is scrupulously accurate in quoting from
More's last letter from the Tower to his daughter Marga-
ret, he, too, can be shown to have taken liberties with
More's words in the interest of an overall conception in
The Life. In at least one clear instance, Roper skillfully
modifies a letter from More to Henry VIII. The letter re-

fers to Henry's words to More when the latter resigned the chancellorship:

> It pleased your Highnes ferther to say un to me, that for the service which I byfore had done you (*which it than lyked your goodness far above my deserving to commend*) that in eny suit that I should after have un to your Highnes, which either should concerne myn honor (that word it lyked your Highnes to use un to me) or that should perteyne un to my profit, I should fynd your Highnes good and graciouse lord un to me.

Aside from minor alterations in phrasing required by Roper's narrative and an arbitrary preference for *that* or *which*, the italicized parenthesis in the preceding passage indicates his only significant change. Its omission in **The Life** influences tone considerably:

> so pleased it his highnes [further] to say * unto him, that for the * service that he before had done hym, in anye sute which he should after have unto him, that either should concerne his honor (for that word it liked his highnes to use unto him) or that should app*er*taine unto his p*ro*fitt, he should find his highnes good and gratious Lord unto him.

With the omitted parenthesis, More's gratitude for Henry's goodness fades from view; Henry's hypocrisy and Roper's irony become perceptible; More's worth receives greater emphasis. The second parenthesis in the letter, as retained by Roper, intensifies these changes by the addition of that little word "for," which implies that Henry's reference to More's "honor" is amply justified.

Having traced Roper's alterations, however, I should note that he does not assign the passage in question directly to More, as he does the scrupulously quoted words from More's last letter to Margaret. He appears to distinguish sharply between an organizing and even overriding conception of More in **The Life** and untruth or deliberate falsification. His conception coexists persuasively (some might say sophistically) with a lawyer's sense of accuracy.

Terms like *arrangement, design, balance,* or *symmetry* are more fitting to describe Roper's structural practices than is the more rigorous term *pattern*. Roper's "arrangements" are so broad and general or so specific and unextended that they are not properly patterns, although his tendency to make such arrangements might itself be seen as a pattern in the work. Careful arrangement is evident in the long speeches which frame the main body of More's public life. More utters the first speech when he is chosen Speaker of Parliament and the second when he is tried for treason. The first speech is almost the same distance from the opening of Roper's *Life of More*, as is the second speech from its closing, and they share eloquently a concern for the discharge and inviolability of conscience.

Even a casual attempt to outline **The Life** indicates a topical arrangement: youth, public and political involvement, private life, including family life and personal virtues; the problem of King Henry's divorce, withdrawal first from public and then from family life, imprisonment, and death. More's resignation from the chancellorship occurs in the middle of **The Life**, amid pressure from Henry to support his divorce and remarriage. The resignation is immediately preceded by no fewer than five concentrated references to conscience. In the course of them More tells Henry that he would willingly lose a limb to be able to

find some way "with his consciens, safely" whereby he could satisfy Henry's desires and then reminds Henry of the King's own words to him when he first entered into royal service, namely, "to looke unto god, *and* after god to him." To this apology the King replies, "that if he could not [therein] with his consciens serve him, he was content taccept his service otherwise; And using the advice of other [of] his learned councell, whose consciences could well inough agre therewith, wold nevertheles contynewe his gratious favour towards him, *and* never with that matter molest his consciens after." The word "otherwise" could simply mean "in another way" or "differently"; but even with (and even more without) the emendation "therein" from other manuscripts, it could mean "without his conscience" or "unscrupulously." Henry's subsequent reference to the more seviceable consciences of his Council is gratuitous, virtually parenthetical, defensive, and discomforting. The referent of "that matter" in the same sentence is just a little indefinite; it refers to the divorce surely but also suggests the more immediate syntactical possibility, Henry's "gratious favour," a favor with which Henry thought any conscientious subject should reckon as if his life depended on it: *Indignatio principis mors est*," as Norfolk later reminds More.

Henry's uses of the word "conscience," as Roper presents them here, introduce a divorce of another kind in the work, a divorce of moral and political meanings, of private and public roles. The ambiguity—perhaps, literally the duplicity—of Henry's conscience is sinister, rather than merely ironic. Where irony hints at the disunity of truth and, whether bitterly, cynically, or playfully, considers this disunity with some degree of detachment, Henry's ambiguity threatens. It is charged not simply with opposite meanings but, more ominously, with unclearly related ones. His conversation with More and More's decision to resign the chancellorship, which immediately and suggestively follows this conversation, is a carefully designed and controlled turning point at the heart of **The Life of More**.

Despite Roper's interest in design, there are surprisingly few traces of the pattern of a saint's *Life* in **The Life** of this saint. More has his prophetic moments—about Henry's treatment of him, about the coming success of the Reformation, about the future suffering of Anne Boleyn—but Roper treats them as moments of insight or wisdom that are human and, more often than not, shrewd and secular. More's "fervent prayer myraculously" recovers his daughter Margaret from the sweating sickness, but while he is praying, it turns out, he suddenly realizes that a "glister," or enema, is the only way to cure her; the remedy is administered, and she recovers. Miraculous the cure may be, but it is also practical.

Near the end of **The Life,** in reply to the passing of sentence upon him, More suggests an analogy between the condemnation of him and Paul's consenting to the death of St. Stephen and continues, "yeat be they [nowe] both twayne holy Sainctes in heaven, and shall continue there frendes for ever, So I verily [truste], *and* shall therefore right hartelye pray, that thoughe your lordshippes have . . . in earthe bine Judges to my condemnacion, we may yeat hereafter in heaven meerily all meete together." The analogy is aimed essentially at More's judges, instead of at himself, and is notable for its ironical wit and immense generosity. More is not setting himself up as a latter-day

Stephen so much as he is requiring his judges to become truer men, as did Paul.

Perhaps it is finally too neat that Thomas More should die, as is his wish, on "St Thomas even, *and* the utas of St Peeter," on the eve of a day honoring the martyred English saint named Thomas who resisted another King Henry's incursions into ecclesiastical power and in the octave of St Peter, the first head of the Church; but as a matter of historical fact, this is when More was executed, an occasion, I hardly need add, quite beyond his control. In the seemingly providential date of More's execution we find a crucial difference between Cavendish's *Wolsey* and Roper's *More*. In Roper's *Life* such occurrences are not simply staged or put on by the historical actor, and they are not part of a traditional pattern evoked but deliberately unfulfilled by the writer. Instead of suggesting the irony of merely feigned patterns, their presentation suggests patterns beyond our own design.

To an extent unparalleled even in Cavendish, earlier passages foreshadow later ones in Roper's *More* and largely account for our sense of the consistency of More's character. We have already noted relevant parallels: More's first speech on conscience and his last one, his appraisal of his value to Henry and the Emperor Charles's appraisal of More's worth. Many slight echoes subtly but significantly enhance our awareness of design in *The Life*. For example, More's words to Roper after his initial examination before a committee of the Privy Council—"In good Faithe, I rejoyced, sonne ... that I had geven the divell a fowle fall" —recall his teaching to his family much earlier, namely, that "the divell of disposition" is so proud and envious that he fears to assault the persevering man a second time, "least he should therby ... catche a fowle fall himself" and "minister to the man more matter of merite."

Again, the imprisoned More's conversation with Master Rich, who becomes the chief accuser of More, holds memories both of More's earlier reminder to the King of the King's own advice—"first to looke unto god, *and* after god to him"—and of More's earlier response to the Duke of Norfolk's astonishment at finding Lord Chancellor More singing in a church choir with a surplice on his back: to Norfolk's "a p*a*rish clark! you dishonor the king *and* his office," More answers, "the king, yo*u*r master *and* myne, will [*not*] w*i*th me, for serv*i*nge of god, his master, be offended, or therby count his office dishonoured." In the later passage More replies to a sequence of moot cases Master Rich proposes: first, if an act of Parliament were to make Rich king, would More take him for king; second, if by such an act Rich were made Pope, would More take him for Pope. More replies affirmatively to the first proposal and to the second, with a moot case of his own: "Suppose the p*a*rliam*e*nt wold make a lawe that god should not be god"? Should we seek to rationalize Roper's memorial selection and thematic arrangement in all these passages, we might take as our basic text the biblical observation "No man can serve two masters." With this text, other echoes increase in significance: for example, Henry's promising More upon his resignation that More would always "find his highnes good and gratious Lord unto him" and, within a few pages, the conclusion of More's parable of the offending virgin: "they maye devoure me; but god being my good lord, I will p*ro*vide that they shall never deffloure me."

Nearly every detail in the opening of *The Life*—after Roper's prologue and before More's first long speech as Speaker—becomes charged with additional significance as we look back from later stages. Retrospective shading may be a better description of this technique than foreshadowing, although the two types of temporal shading are not entirely separate. Within the first two modern-size pages of Roper's work, we are given a sense of the potential for rich, complex, unified experience in More's life and, as we later realize, a sense of the potential for disunited realities and conflicting demands. Roper's narrative quickly notes More's tutelage in the household of the mighty John Morton, then Archbishop and Lord Chancellor, and his flair for impromptu acting while resident there; his study of Greek, Latin, and then law; his public lectures on St. Augustine, his living for four years, without vow, in a strict community of monks; his first marriage. Within two pages more, Roper relates in some detail and with emphasis how, as a member of Parliament, young More incurred the hostility of Henry VII by blocking his will and how he was then nearly trapped by the dishonest counsel of one of the King's bishops into putting himself into the King's vengeful power. The scenario of willful king, deceptive counselors, and puppet churchmen in More's later life is in retrospect evident already. In yet another two pages, with considerable expansiveness, Roper tells us how More was once appointed to assist the Pope's side in a case involving forfeiture of a ship and argued so effectively that the Pope's side won, at which point, of course, Henry VIII refused to forbear any longer More's entering into his service. Once again the scenario seems prophetic, this time of Henry's insistence that More's conscience should submit to serve royal supremacy in religion.

Seen retrospectively and in outline, the opening of *The Life* begins to look as prearranged as an allegory, and there is still one page to go before More is chosen Speaker. The marginal glosses in Hitchcock's edition suffice for most of the remainder: "His company sought by Henry VIII"; "His liberty thereby much restricted." In order to get some time with his family, More has to feign an attack of dullness, "to dissemble his nature" and gradually from his former "myrthe to [disuse] himself." Early in *The Life*, with favor and preferment still before him, this story is amusing, but later, More's need "to dissemble his nature" in the presence of royal attentions takes a more ominous twist.

Comparison of temporal shading in Roper and Cavendish clarifies the nature of design in each. Shading in Cavendish, the significance beyond the present with which incidents are invested, first suggests a kind of Nemesis and later, as we read on, suggests an order at best ironic and at worst irrational. One incident that stands out at the beginning of Cavendish's *Life* concerns an "officious country gentleman" who clapped Wolsey in the stocks when Wolsey was a schoolmaster and found some years later that Chancellor Wolsey enjoined him to stay in London for about six years. Cavendish worries the moral of this incident at great length, seeing in it a warning to men in authority to remember the impermanence of their power and to be mindful of "god And ffortune." The warning is obviously meant to apply to Wolsey himself and could be said to anticipate a change in his fortunes and even to forecast a reversal of the roles of persecutor and victim. But at the beginning of *The Life*, where Wolsey's power is in the ascendant, this application is incongruous; moreover, so explicit a forecast is forced and in fact too narrow for the life that follows. The difference between this beginning and Roper's is evident: in Roper, the significance of early incidents is richer and better suits what is to come; at the same time it is implied rather than imposed and becomes fully available only later in *The Life*. Again, Cavendish searches, sometimes fumbles, and gradually finds both his art and his meaning, but Roper knows from the outset where he is going.

Roper's temporal shading in the beginning and elsewhere results in a subtler, more pervasive, and more providential effect than is present in Cavendish. By contributing to our impression of the consistency of More's character, Roper's shading greatly influences our sense of stability, even of confidence, in *The Life*, despite flagrant royal injustice. Odd as it may sound, More himself, rather than Roper, seems in charge, or at least aware, of significant designs in his life, which foreshadowing and retrospective shading accentuate: "but god being my good lord, *I* will *p*rovide that they shall never deffloure me"; or again, "to morowe is St Thomas even . . . *therefore* too morowe longe I to goe to god" (emphasis mine, excepting *ro*). In both cases More may be helped by other designers, namely Roper and God, but he, too, is actively helping. With Roper in writing and God in living, More is coauthor of his own integrity.

On the basis of a providential design in *The Life of More* and an ironic one in *The Life of Wolsey*, we cannot generalize absolutely about the world view of their respective authors. Either author's subject, on the one hand a sinner and on the other a saint, obviously influences the overall order effected. But we can see the choice of writing the *Life* of a subject and what is done with the *Life* itself, what is shaped out of its materials, as having in this period at least a direct and necessary relation and even a debt to the writer's own views, values, and experiences. The lawyer Roper's prologue, a detached deposition, comes again to mind, as does Cavendish's ending, where the true point of Wolsey's *Life* is dramatized in his own. In either case the writer is implicated in the work.

As Roper portrays More's character, it is consistent *amid* change, especially amid changing fortunes, and in this respect quite different from the consistency of Cuthbert's life, as from the inconsistencies of Wolsey's. In Roper's *More*, the credibility of rounded character, dramatized motives, real conflict, and developing plot—in short, the credibility of so many of the commonplaces of dramatic art—is reaffirmed, and with it the proximity of Roper's *More* to fiction. More's character is persuasively lifelike in Roper's work, and yet its consistency—its center and focus—suggests fiction. Since, in large part, human centers themselves are fashioned rather than given, it is entirely conceivable that the consistency Roper depicts, illuminates, and heightens so artfully is originally and essentially More's creation.

The coalescence of art and life, of fiction and persuasion, in Roper's *More* will bear momentary analogy with a fiction by Donne, coincidentally a poem that Walton believed directly related to an actual event in Donne's life. The poem "A Valediction: forbidding Mourning," which begins with a deathbed scene and "end[s], where . . . [the poet] begunne," renovates the motto "in my end is my beginning." Both More's and Cuthbert's lives, as presented by Roper and Bede, might be said to reflect a similar cir-

cularity but to do so in significantly distinct ways. From the beginning of written *Life*, Cuthbert's end is settled and known; More's is not. We see More's end in his beginning only in retrospect. Cuthbert's *Life* revitalizes a circular pattern by illustrating it, and More's *Life* refashions a circular pattern to the extent that it becomes nearly indistinguishable from a real life.

Roper's art is elusive because it is artfully hidden. Harpsfield's practices, by contrast with Roper's, again elucidate them. Very near the beginning of his biography, Harpsfield, like Roper, tells of More's trial period in a monastery but expands his report with incidents drawn from much later stages in Roper's *Life of More*: namely, More's remarking that he would never have meddled further with worldly affairs if his daughter Margaret had not been cured and his saying to Margaret when in prison that if it had not been for his wife and children, "he had voluntarily longe ere that time shutt him selfe in as narrowe or narrower a roome then that [*cell*] was." Harpsfield's juxtaposing these remarks with More's early trial of the monastic life makes explicit the consistency of More's character that Roper's temporal shading dramatically implies. At the same time, Harpsfield's rearrangement of incidents in More's life rationalizes and radically limits their meaning. The same remarks in Roper's context are considerably more open-ended and humanly interesting. There they admit the pious meaning Harpsfield finds in them, but they also admit an aura of weariness and at least the temptation to withdraw, merely to retreat, from the arena. Judged by modern standards of completeness and decisiveness, Harpsfield's biography is better than Roper's, as R. W. Chambers judges it in his introduction to Harpsfield [see Additional Bibliography]. But in the passage at hand, which is not atypical, Harpsfield voids the drama of Roper's version, excludes the reader's active involvement in meaning, and remakes More's life in the image of Cuthbert's simplicity—"a life of rigid consistency," as Chambers himself describes Harpsfield's version.

Harpsfield's *Life of More* may be good biography—or at least good "modern" biography—but in comparison with Roper's version, it is less satisfactory art. The passage near the beginning of Harpsfield's biography that has just been described goes on, first to query More's decision not to become a contemplative, since the contemplative life is a higher calling; then to defend More's decision (not every man is bound to become a monk); and finally to justify and to judge More's decision: "God himselfe seemeth to have chosen and appointed this man to another kinde of life, to serve him therein more acceptably . . . and more profitably for the wealth of the Realme and his owne soule also." Harpsfield, for all his virtues as a diligent biographer, would pluck out the heart of More's mystery.

Harpsfield has designs on us. Although his designs stop short of factual dishonesty or distorting omissions, they are explicitly hagiographical and even include, at the end of *The Life*, an extensive comparison of More to St. Thomas of Dover and St. Thomas of Canterbury that ends to More's advantage: "There is therfore in *Sir* Thomas More a deeper cause of martyrdome then in the other twaine." There is nothing remotely comparable in Roper. Yet the designs Harpsfield has on us are not made one with the fabric of More's life. Most often, they alternate with Harpsfield's biographical raw materials, preceding or following them. In doing so, however, they bear mute testimony to another rent in the seams of unified truth in this century, and in this instance the truth rent is biographical.

In Harpsfield's *Life of More*, we meet a ... careful separation of objective and subjective truths, of historical record and authorial interpretation.... From an artistic point of view this separation is regrettable, for as Harpsfield himself believed but perhaps failed fully and imaginatively to grasp, More died at once for the unity of Christendom and for the integrity of the individual conscience: for Harpsfield's More, these two truths, one historical and public and one individual and private, were not in principle at odds and ought not in fact to be so. The presentation, the very form, of Harpsfield's *Life of More*, unlike that of Roper's *Life*, thus seems to work subtly against the unified truth that is, by both these accounts, the deliberately chosen theme of More's being and in this sense is untrue to More's life. Roper's profoundly artful presentation adheres more faithfully to the encompassing idea of unity More himself, by both accounts, embraced. Of the two, it is the more persuasive and, to me, the more truly biographical. It presumes to depict the fundamental principle of More's life—not without a strong sense of conflicting pressures but with an underlying sense of direction still stronger. Roper's *Life* is less nearly complete and more subjective than Harpsfield's, and yet, if it is an idea, an ideal, or a fantasy, it both is artistically and was actually a very real one. If it finally answers to a truth somewhat different from the modern biographer's, the impulse Roper takes to be central to More's life is imagined and reconstructed truly in it.

These comments return us to Roper's role, which is really the role of Roper's art, in *The Life of More*. Roper's sensitivity to the nuances of tone and his dramatic timing of events figure high among the distinctive literary features of his art and among the differences between it and Harpsfield's. The visit of Dame Alice, More's wife, to him in prison, for example, is rightly remembered by readers for its mixture of domestic humor and witty righteousness, for Alice's astringent tongue and More's astringent mind: "(What the good yere, m*aster* Moore,' quoth she, 'I mervaile that you, that have bine alwaies hitherto taken for so wise a man, will nowe so play the foole to lye heare in this close, filthy prison, and be content thus to be shut upp amongst mise *and* rattes, when you might be abroade at y*our* libertye...'" Dame Alice continues for some length in this and in a more appealing vein: when "you might in the company of me your wife, [your] children, *and* howshold be meerye, I muse what a gods name you meane heare still thus fondly to tarye." After More has, Roper points out, "a while quietly heard her," he speaks to her "with a chearefull countenaunce," and effectively shifts the grounds of argument:

> "I pray thee, good m*istris* Alice, tell me one thing."
> "What is that?" quoth shee.
> "Is not this house," quoth he, "as nighe heaven as my owne?"
> To whome shee, after hir accustomed homely fashion, not liking such talke, awneswered, "Tylle valle, Tylle valle!"

Perhaps enough of this scene has been cited to suggest its human credibility, its true-to-life quality, and enough to suggest its dramatic art as well. Roper gives a realistic ti-

rade, natural dialogue, stage directions ("quietly," "chearefull countenaunce"), and tonal analysis to boot ("homely," "not liking"). Without ruining the effect of Dame Alice's initial barrage by overexplaining it, he alerts us to its approach, telling us that she, "at her first cominge, like a simple ignorant woman, *and* somewhat worldly too, with this manner of salutacion bluntlye saluted him." Roper's warning is not intrusive because Dame Alice's speech justifies it and in fact overwhelms its strategic demurrer.

Another reason for the dramatic effect of this scene (and incidentally for Roper's warning) is the context in which it occurs, especially the sharpness of contrast between this scene and the two incidents it follows. The more striking of these begins with More's looking out a window in the Tower and chancing to see the Bridgettine Richard Reynolds and three monks of the Charterhouse, the community in which More once lived, on their way to a brutal execution for their opposition to the King's remarriage and supremacy in religion. The rest of this incident, spoken to More's daughter, concerns his response to what he has seen. The second incident, even briefer than the first, is simply reported to us. The King's Secretary (Thomas Cromwell) comes to More to tell him that the King is "his good and gratious Lorde" and henceforth does not want More to have "any cause of scruple ... to trouble his consciens." Under a pretense of friendship, the Secretary's purpose, like that of the traditional tempter, is to beguile and deceive. Roper observes laconically that More expresses "what comforte he conceaved of ... [*Master Secretary's*] word*es*" by writing a stanza on Fortune's deceptive appearances once the Secretary has departed. Roper's alert to the reader of Dame Alice's approach and her opening salutation follow immediately on the last verses of More's stanza:

> Truste I shall god, to enter in a while
> Hys haven of heaven, sure *and* uniforme;
> Ever after thy [*Fortune's*] calme looke I for [a] storme.

Enter Dame Alice in an attempt to persuade More to settle for another haven in Chelsea. In outline, at least, the unwitting but stormy Dame Alice—though hardly a Miltonic Dalilah—seems the next step in a dramatic series of very human temptations.

A glance at the same incidents in Harpsfield shows Roper's art to be doubly deliberate. Keeping the interview between More and Dame Alice intact as Roper wrote it, Harpsfield moves it into a new context, which could be labeled "collected anecdotes about Dame Alice" and which follows other information about More's household and precedes an extended analysis of More's writings. Some of the anecdotes not to be found in Roper are amusing and valuable pieces of the record of More's life. As we read Roper's interview between More and his wife in Harpsfield, however, we realize that because of its new context, its dramatic impact and memorability are gone. Even Roper's stage directions, though nominally present, have lost much of their force. (pp. 41-51)

Without denying Harpsfield a notable achievement in his *Life of More*, which is worthy in its own comprehensive way, we can perhaps observe of his assembled anecdotes that any good playwright would have known better. Collected anecdotes abstracted from their ongoing, temporal context and then assembled by theme or character are made to *look* forced and lifeless, even if true. Like tales in a joke book, they fail to create a lifelike illusion and, from an artistic viewpoint, are unreal and untrue. Harpsfield's collected anecdotes suggest how much what seems lifelike partakes of art and indeed of illusion and how artistic a form good biography must be.

> *Judith H. Anderson, "Roper: Deliberated Design and Designer," in her* Biographical Truth: The Representation of Historical Persons in Tudor-Stuart Writing, *Yale University Press, 1984, pp. 40-51.*

RICHARD MARIUS   (essay date 1984)

[*Marius is a noted American novelist, biographer, and More scholar. In the following excerpt from his comprehensive biography of More, he considers the merits and limitations of Roper's personal recollections as biography.*]

About 1557 Roper wrote the splendid short biography of More, that has been the heart of every More biography written in English until now.

Roper had an unpleasant side. He was a litigious, grasping man like a great many others of his day. He had some kind of falling-out with his father and was slighted in the elder Roper's will. Son Roper disputed the will until Parliament itself, the supreme court of England, ruled in his favor and gave him a larger share of the estate than his father had intended. After More died, Roper went to court against Dame Alice, More's widow, about some property. At the end of his little biography, he breaks off his moving account of More's life and death to protest with unseemly indignation that the crown and Parliament had robbed him and his wife of property More had tried to transfer to them by putting it in trust. He was for a time, shortly after he married Margaret, a vehement Protestant and wanted to preach the new gospel from Germany. It is not hard to see him as one of the zealots churned up in every tumultuous age, finding in religious conversion a pinnacle from which they may scorn the mob below.

But whatever Roper's character, he loved his father-in-law, and his book is saturated with that devotion.... Roper's More is a saint, although Roper, like Erasmus, is free of the crude miracle-mongering found in conventional saints' legends. He wrote at a time when stories including miracles would not be believed by the educated, and he did not tell them. His aim throughout was to prove that his father-in-law was "a man of singular virtue and of a clear, unspotted conscience" [see essay dated 1557?]. Doubtless he expected More to be canonized by the pope.

Roper's most valuable information came from his personal recollections. More told him many stories, and he witnessed part of More's final ordeal, although he did not attend the trial and execution. The biography takes up fewer than sixty pages in a modern edition; by far the greater part of it considers the last five years of More's life. Roper does not mention *Utopia*.

Roper's More is always calm, always in command of the scene if not of events. Roper claims never to have seen him "in a fume" and gives us a brave, unruffled Christian, doing his duty without wavering and without seeking reward, a Thomas More always doing the right thing merely because it is right, a stoic combining in himself the virtues of devotion, selflessness, sacrifice, and self-control that fifteen hundred years of classical and churchly tradition had held to be supreme among men. Roper's biography is consummate Renaissance art, giving us an ideal man against whom to measure the stature of lesser beings.

But good art is not necessarily good history, and when Roper can be checked, he is often found to be wrong. Sometimes when he cannot be proved in error, we suspect that he has erred because what he tells us is implausible. In his work there is no effort to analyze More, only the desire to prove him above reproach. Roper's is a family history, a literary epitaph designed by one who loved his subject, written for those who also loved him. Such works are devotions, and they seldom show warts and wobblings, but perhaps just because the work shows More in such a mellow and heroic light, it became the most influential thing ever written about him. (pp. xv-xvi)

> *Richard Marius, in an introduction to his* Thomas More: A Biography, *Alfred A. Knopf, 1984, pp. xiii-xxiv.*

ADDITIONAL BIBLIOGRAPHY

Anderegg, Michael A. "Nicholas Harpsfield, Thomas More, and William Roper's Lapse into Heresy." *Notes and Queries* n. s. 23, Nos. 5-6 (May-June 1976): 225-26.

> Comments briefly on Nicholas Harpsfield's use of Roper's *Life of More* in *The Life and Death of Sir Thomas Moore, Knight.*

Beck, Egerton. Review of *The Life of Sir Thomas More, Knighte,* by William Roper. *The Dublin Review* 197, No. 395 (October 1935): 362-63.

> Notices the value of Roper's *Life of More* for "everyone interested in St. Thomas More and his family circle."

Review of *The Life of Sir Thomas More,* by William Roper. *Blackwood's Edinburgh Magazine* XIX, No. 4 (October 1818): 28-34.

> Prints extracts from an 1817 edition of Roper's *Life,* remarking on the work's "exquisite beauty of . . . style."

Chambers, R. W. "The Continuity of English Prose from Alfred to More and His School." In *The Life and Death of Sir Thomas Moore, Knight, Sometymes Lord High Chancellor of England,* by Nicholas Harpsfield, edited by Elsie Vaughan Hitchcock, pp. xlv-clxxiv. Early English Text Society, Original Series, No. 186. London: Oxford University Press for the Early English Text Society, 1932.

> Contains a brief discussion of the value of Roper's *Life of More* as a character sketch and comments on the importance of dramatic dialogue in the work.

Garrett, Constance. "That Mirrour of Vertue, Sir Thomas More." *The Catholic World* CXXXIII, No. 798 (September 1931): 671-77.

> An overview of More's life as it is portrayed in Roper's *Life of More,* maintaining that the work shows Roper to be "a master both at understanding and revealing character."

Harrison, W. E. C. "Pastime with Good Company." *Queen's Quarterly* XLII, No. 4 (Winter 1935): 539-43.

Argues that while the historical value of Roper's *Life of More* may have been overestimated, its literary value is outstanding.

Review of *The Mirrour of Vertue in Worldly Greatnes; or, The Life of Sir Thomas More, Knight,* by William Roper. *The London Quarterly Review* C (October 1903): 394.

Suggests that Roper's *Life of More* "brings us nearer to the great Lord Chancellor than any other memorial of him," adding: "no one can read this touching story without sharing [Roper's] admiration and regard for More."

Reynolds, E. E. *Margaret Roper: Eldest Daughter of St. Thomas More.* New York: P. J. Kenedy & Sons, 1960, 149 p.

A biography of Roper's wife, Margaret More, containing brief commentary on Roper's motive in writing *The Life of More.*

Rowse, A. L. Introduction to *A Man of Singular Virtue; Being a Life of Sir Thomas More by His Son-in-Law William Roper and a Selection of More's Letters,* by William Roper and Thomas More, edited by A. L. Rowse, pp. 9-26. London: The Folio Society, 1980.

A biographical sketch of More containing frequent references to Roper's *Life.*

Singer, S. W. Preface to *The Life of Sir Thomas More,* by William Roper, edited by S. W. Singer, pp. v-xviii. Chiswick: C. Whittingham, 1822.

A general discussion covering the publication history of Roper's *Life* and providing a brief biography of the author. Singer praises *The Life* as a "biographical gem" and recommends it "to the attention of those who are gratified by authentic pictures of ancient manners and ancient virtues."

Acknowledgments

The following is a listing of the copyright holders who have granted us permission to reprint material in this volume of *LC*. Every effort has been made to trace copyright, but if omissions have been made, please let us know.

THE COPYRIGHTED EXCERPTS IN LC, VOLUME 10, WERE REPRINTED FROM THE FOLLOWING PERIODICALS:

Critical Inquiry, v. 14, Spring, 1988 for "Molière and the Sociology of Exchange" by Jean-Marie Apostolides, translated by Alice Musick McLean. Copyright © 1988 by The University of Chicago. Reprinted by permission of the publisher and the translator.

The Explicator, v. 46, Summer, 1988. Copyright © 1988 by Helen Dwight Reid Educational Foundation. Reprinted with permission of the Helen Dwight Reid Educational Foundation, published by Heldref Publications, 4000 Albemarle Street, N.W., Washington, DC 20016.

Extrapolation, v. 19, December, 1977. Copyright 1977 by Thomas D. and Alice S. Clareson. Reprinted by permission of the publisher.

History: The Journal of the Historical Association, n.s. v. 64, October, 1979. © The Historical Association 1979. Reprinted by permission of the publisher.

John Donne Journal, v. 6, 1987. Reprinted by permission of the publisher.

The Listener, v. 101, January 4, 1979 for "Dark Feminist?" by Emrys Jones. © British Broadcasting Corp. 1979. Reprinted by permission of the author.

The Modern Language Review, v. 75, October, 1980 for "Is Tartuffe a Comic Character?" by Brian Nicholas. © Modern Humanities Research Association 1980. Reprinted by permission of the publisher and the author.

Moreana, v. VI, August, 1969; v. IX, December, 1972. Both reprinted by permission of the publisher.

The Polish Review, v. XIV, Winter, 1969. © copyright 1969 by the Polish Institute of Arts and Sciences of America, Inc. Reprinted by permission of the publisher.

Studies in English Literature, 1500-1900, v. IX, Winter, 1969 for "Thomas More, Raphael Hythlodaeus, and the Angel Raphael" by Elizabeth McCutcheon. © 1969 William Marsh Rice University. Reprinted by permission of the publisher and the author./ v. XII, Spring, 1972. © 1972 William Marsh Rice University. Reprinted by permission of the publisher.

Symposium, v. XLI, Summer 1987 for "Religious Parody in Molière's 'George Dandin' " by Dorothy F. Jones. Copyright © the author. Reprinted by permission of the author.

The Times Literary Supplement, n. 3185, March 15, 1963. © Times Newspapers Ltd. (London) 1963. Reproduced from *The Times Literary Supplement* by permission.

THE COPYRIGHTED EXCERPTS IN LC, VOLUME 10, WERE REPRINTED FROM THE FOLLOWING BOOKS:

Adams, Robert M. From a preface to *"Utopia" by Sir Thomas More: A New Translation, Backgrounds, Criticism.* Edited and translated by Robert M. Adams. Norton, l975. Copyright © 1975 by W. W. Norton & Company, Inc. All rights reserved. Reprinted by permission of W. W. Norton & Company, Inc.

Alvarez, A. From *The School of Donne.* Chatto & Windus, 1961. © A. Alvarez 1961. All rights reserved. Reprinted by permission of the author.

Ames, Russell. From *Citizen Thomas More and His Utopia.* Princeton University Press, 1949. Copyright 1949 by Princeton University Press. Renewed 1976 by Russell Ames. Reprinted with permission of the author.

Anderson, Judith H. From *Biographical Truth: The Representation of Historical Persons in Tudor-Stuart Writing.* Yale University Press, 1984. Copyright © 1984 by Yale University. All rights reserved. Reprinted by permission of the publisher.

Andreasen, N. J. C. From *John Donne: Conservative Revolutionary.* Princeton University Press, 1967. Copyright © 1967 by Princeton University Press. All rights reserved. Reprinted with permission of the publisher.

Barnstone, Aliki and Willis Barnstone. From "Emilia Lanier," in *A Book of Women Poets from Antiquity to Now.* Edited by Aliki Barnstone and Willis Barnstone. Schocken Books, 1980. Copyright © 1980 by Schocken Books, Inc. Reprinted by permission of the publisher.

Barnston, Aliki. From "Women and the Garden: Andrew Marvell, Emilia Lanier, and Emily Dickinson," in *Men by Women.* Edited by Janet Todd. Holmes & Meier, 1981. Reprinted by permission of Holmes & Meier Publishers, Inc., 30 Irving Place, New York, NY 10003.

Beilin, Elaine V. From *Redeeming Eve: Women Writers of the English Renaissance.* Princeton University Press, 1987. Copyright © 1987 by Princeton University Press. All rights reserved. Reprinted with permission of the publisher.

Birnbaum, Henrik. From "The Sublimation of Grief: Poems by Two Mourning Fathers," in *For Wiktor Weintraub: Essays in Polish Literature, Language, and History Presented on the Occasion of His 65th Birthday.* Edited by Victor Erlich and others. Mouton, 1975. © copyright 1975 Mouton & Co., Publishers. Reprinted by permission of Mouton de Gruyter, a Division of Walter de Gruyter & Co.

Brodrick, Reverend James, S. J. From a preface to *The Autobiography of Venerable Marie of the Incarnation, O.S.U.: Mystic and Missionary.* Translated by John J. Sullivan, S.J. Loyola University Press, 1964. © 1964 Loyola University Press. Reprinted by permission of the publisher.

Brooks, Cleanth. From "The Language of Paradox," in *The Language of Poetry.* By Philip Wheelwright and others, edited by Allen Tate. Princeton University Press, 1942. Copyright 1942, © 1970 renewed by Princeton University Press. Reprinted with permission of the publisher.

Chapman, Percy Addison. From *The Spirit of Molière: An Interpretation.* Edited by Jean-Albert Bede. Princeton University Press, 1940. Copyright 1940 by Princeton University Press. Renewed 1968 by Mrs. Percy A. Chapman.

Dennis, John. From a letter in *The Critical Works of John Dennis: 1711-1729, Vol. II.* Edited by Edward Niles Hooker. Johns Hopkins Press, 1943. Copyright 1943, The Johns Hopkins Press. Renewed 1970 by Evelyn Hooker. Reprinted by permission of the publisher.

Doolittle, James. From "Human Nature and Institutions in Molière's Plots," in *Studies in Seventeenth-Century French Literature: Presented to Morris Bishop.* Edited by Jean-Jacques Demores. Cornell University Press, 1962. Copyright © 1962 by Cornell University. Used by permission of the publisher, Cornell University Press.

Eliot, Thomas Stearns. From "Donne in Our Time," in *A Garland for John Donne: 1631-1931.* Edited by Theodore Spencer. Cambridge, Mass.: Harvard University Press, 1931. Copyright 1931 by the President and Fellows of Harvard College. Renewed 1959 by Eloise Spencer Wade. Excerpted by permission of the publishers.

Elton, G. R. From *Policy and Police: The Enforcement of the Reformation in the Age of Thomas Cromwell.* Cambridge at the University Press, 1972. © Cambridge University Press 1972. Reprinted with the permission of the publisher.

Erasmus. From an extract from a letter in *The Essential Thomas More.* Edited by James J. Greene and John P. Dolan. New American Library, 1967. Copyright © 1967 by James J. Greene and John P. Dolan. All rights reserved. Reprinted by arrangement with New American Library, a Division of Penguin Books USA Inc., New York, NY.

Erickson, Carolly. From *Great Harry.* Summit Books, 1980. Copyright © 1980 by Carolly Erickson. All rights reserved. Reprinted by permission of Summit Books, a division of Simon & Schuster, Inc.

Fairchild, Hoxie Neale. From *Religious Trends in English Poetry: Protestantism and the Cult of Sentiment, 1700-1740, Vol. I.* Columbia University Press, 1939. Copyright 1939 Columbia University Press, New York. Renewed 1967 by Hoxie Neale Fairchild. Used by permission of the publisher.

Fox, Alistair. From *Thomas More: History and Providence.* Blackwell, 1982. © Alistair Fox 1982. All rights reserved. Reprinted by permission of Basil Blackwell Limited.

Fuller, Edmund. From an introduction to *The Showing Forth of Christ: Sermons of John Donne.* Edited by Edmund Fuller. Harper & Row, 1964. Copyright © 1964 by Edmund Fuller. All rights reserved. Reprinted by permission of Harper & Row, Publishers, Inc.

Gaines, James F. From *Social Structures in Molière's Theater.* Ohio State University Press, 1984. © 1984 by the Ohio State University Press. All rights reserved. Reprinted with permission of the publisher.

Gassner, John. From *Masters of the Drama.* Random House, 1940. Copyright 1940, 1954 by Random House, Inc. Renewed 1968 by Mollie Gassner. Reprinted by permission of the publisher.

Gossman, Lionel. From *Men and Masks: A Study of Molière.* Johns Hopkins Press, 1963. © 1963 by The Johns Hopkins Press. Reprinted by permission of the publisher.

Hampson, Norman. From *Will & Circumstance: Montesquieu, Rousseau and the French Revolution.* University of Oklahoma Press, 1983, Duckworth, 1983. Copyright © 1983 by Norman Hampson. Reprinted by permission of University of Oklahoma Press. In Canada by Gerald Duckworth & Co. Ltd.

Hester, M. Thomas. From *Kinde Pitty and Brave Scorn: John Donne's "Satyres."* Duke University Press, 1982. Copyright © 1982 by Duke University Press, Durham, NC. Reprinted by permission of the publisher.

Hexter, J. H. From *More's "Utopia": The Biography of an Idea.* Princeton University Press, 1952. Copyright 1952 by Princeton University Press. Renewed 1980 by J. H. Hexter. Reprinted by permission of the author.

Hubert, J. D. From *Molière & the Comedy of Intellect.* University of California Press, 1962. Copyright © 1962 by The Regents of the University of California. Reprinted by permission of the publisher.

Jones, Judith P. From *Thomas More.* Twayne, 1979. Copyright 1979 by Twayne Publishers. All rights reserved. Reprinted with the permission of Twayne Publishers, a division of G. K. Hall & Co., Boston.

Kenny, Anthony. From *Thomas More.* Oxford University Press, Oxford, 1983. © Anthony Kenny, 1983. All rights reserved. Reprinted by permission of Oxford University Press.

Khanna, Lee Cullen. From "Images of Women in Thomas More's Poetry," in *Quincentennial Essays on St. Thomas More: Selected Papers from the Thomas More College Conference.* Edited by Michael J. Moore. Albion, 1978. © 1978 Appalachian State University. All rights reserved. Reprinted by permission of the publisher.

Lawrence, Francis L. From *Molière: The Comedy of Unreason.* Tulane Studies in Romance Languages and Literature, 1968. Reprinted by permission of the author.

Lewalski, Barbara K. From "Of God and Good Women: The Poems of Aemilia Lanyer," in *Silent but for the Word: Tudor Women as Patrons, Translators and Writers of Religious Works.* Edited by Margaret Patterson Hannay. Kent State University Press, 1985. Copyright © 1985 by The Kent State University Press. All rights reserved. Reprinted by permission of the publisher.

Mahoney, Mary Denis, O.S.U. From "Venerable Mary of the Incarnation," in *Spirituality through the Centuries: Ascetics and Mystics of the Western Church.* Edited by James Walsh, S.J. Burns & Oates, 1964. Reprinted by permission of the publisher.

Marat, Jean Paul. From "Defense against the Charges," in *The World's Great Speeches.* Edited by Lewis Copeland. Second edition. Dover Publications, Inc., 1958. Copyright © 1958 by Dover Publications, Inc. Renewed 1986 by Copeland and Lamm Inc. All rights reserved. Reprinted by permission of the publisher.

Marie de l'Incarnation. From *The Autobiography of Venerable Marie of the Incarnation, O.S.U.: Mystic and Missionary.* Translated by John J. Sullivan, S.J. Loyola University Press, 1964. © 1964 Loyola University Press. Reprinted by permission of the publisher.

Marie de l'Incarnation. From a letter, translated by Mother Denis Mahoney, in *Marie of the Incarnation: Mystic and Missionary.* By Mother Denis Mahoney, O.S.U. Doubleday & Company, Inc., 1964. Copyright © 1964 by Denis Mahoney. All rights reserved. Reprinted by permission of Mother Denis Mahoney.

Marius, Richard. From *Thomas More: A Biography.* Knopf, 1984. Copyright © 1984 by Richard Marius. All rights reserved. Reprinted by permission of Alfred A. Knopf, Inc.

Martz, Louis L. From *The Poetry of Meditation: A Study in English Religious Literature of the Seventeenth Century.* Yale University Press, 1954. Copyright, 1954, by Yale University Press. Renewed 1982 by Louis L. Martz. All rights reserved. Reprinted by permission of the publisher.

McBride, Robert. From *The Sceptical Vision of Moliere: A Study in Paradox.* Barnes & Noble Books, 1977, Macmillan, London, 1977. © Robert McBride 1977. All rights reserved. Reprinted by permission of Barnes & Noble Books. In Canada by Macmillan, London and Basingstoke.

McKevlin, Dennis J. From *A Lecture in Love's Philosophy: Donne's Vision of the World of Human Love in the "Songs and Sonnets."* University Press of America, 1984. Copyright © 1984 by University Press of America, Inc. All rights reserved. Reprinted by permission of the author.

Mersereau, John, Jr. From "Jan Kochanowski's 'Laments': A Definition of the Emotion of Grief," in *Studies in Russian and Polish Literature: In Honor of Wactaw Lednicki.* Edited by Zbigniew Folejewski and others. Mouton, 1962. © copyright 1962 Mouton & Co., Publishers. Reprinted by permission of Mouton de Gruyter, a Division of Walter de Gruyter & Co.

Miłosz, Czesław. From *The History of Polish Literature.* Second edition. University of California Press, 1983. Copyright © 1969, 1983 by Czesław Miłosz. Reprinted by permission of the publisher.

Molière. From *Eight Plays by Molière.* Translated by Morris Bishop. The Modern Library, 1957. © copyright, 1957, by Morris Bishop. Renewed 1985 by Allison M. K. Bishop. All rights reserved. Reprinted by permission of Random House, Inc.

More, Thomas. From *Selected Letters.* Edited by Elizabeth Frances Rogers. Yale University Press, 1961. Reprinted by permission of the publisher.

Palmer, M. D. From *Henry VIII.* Longman, 1971. © Longman Group Ltd. 1971. All rights reserved. Reprinted by permission of the publisher.

Pineas, Rainer. From *Thomas More and Tudor Polemics.* Indiana University Press, 1968. Copyright © 1968 by Indiana University Press. All rights reserved. Reprinted by permission of the publisher.

Poulet, Georges. From *Studies in Human Time.* Translated by Elliott Coleman. Johns Hopkins Press, 1956. Copyright © 1956 by Johns Hopkins Press. Renewed 1984 by Louis D. Rubin, Jr. Reprinted by permission of the publisher.

Repplier, Agnes. From *Mere Marie of the Ursulines: A Study in Adventure.* Doubleday, Doran & Company, Inc., 1931. Copyright 1931 by Agnes Repplier. Renewed 1958 by the Literary Estate of Agnes Repplier. All rights reserved. Reprinted by permission of the Literary Estate of Agnes Repplier.

Reynolds, E. E. From an introduction to *Lives of Saint Thomas More.* By William Roper and Nicholas Harpsfield, edited by E. E. Reynolds. Dent, 1963. © Text and Introduction, J. M. Dent & Sons Ltd., 1963. All rights reserved. Reprinted by permission of the publisher.

Richards, I. A. From " 'The Exstasie'," in *Master Poems of the English Language.* Edited by Oscar Williams. Trident Press, 1966. Copyright © 1966 by Trident Press. Reprinted by permission of Trident Press, a division of Simon & Schuster, Inc.

Ridley, Jasper. From *Henry VIII.* Constable, 1984, Viking Penguin, 1985. Copyright © 1984, 1985 by Jasper Ridley. All rights reserved. Reprinted by permission of Viking Penguin Inc. In Canada by Constable & Company Limited.

Rowse, A. L. From "Introduction: Shakespeare's Dark Lady," in *The Poems of Shakespeare's Dark Lady: Salve Deus Rex Judaeorum.* By Emilia Lanier. Jonathan Cape, 1978. Introduction © A. L. Rowse 1978. Reprinted by permission of John Johnson Ltd.

Santinello, Giovanni. From "Thomas More's 'Expositio Passionis'," translated by Dale B. Billingsley, in *Essential Articles for the Study of Thomas More.* Edited by R. S. Sylvester and G. P. Marc'hadour. Archon Books, 1977. © 1977 Richard S. Sylvester. All rights reserved. Reprinted by permission of G. P. Marc'hadour.

Scarisbrick, J. J. From *Henry VIII.* University of California Press, 1968. © J. J. Scarisbrick 1968. Reprinted by permission of the publisher.

Sherwood, Terry G. From *Fulfilling the Circle: A Study of John Donne's Thought.* University of Toronto Press, 1984. © University of Toronto Press 1984. Reprinted by permission of the publisher.

Smith, Lacey Baldwin. From *Henry VIII: The Mask of Royalty.* Cape, 1971. © 1971 by Lacey Baldwin Smith. Reprinted by permission of Jonathan Cape Ltd.

Sullivan, John J., S.J. From an introduction to *The Autobiography of Venerable Marie of the Incarnation, O.S.U.: Mystic and Missionary.* Translated by John J. Sullivan, S.J. Loyola University Press, 1964. © 1964 Loyola University Press. Reprinted by permission of the publisher.

Summers, Joseph H. From *The Heirs of Donne and Jonson.* Oxford University Press, 1970, Chatto & Windus, 1970. Copyright © 1970 by Joseph H. Summers. Reprinted by permission of Oxford University Press, Inc. In Canada by the author and Chatto & Windus.

Surtz, Edward, S.J. From *The Praise of Pleasure: Philosophy, Education, and Communism in More's Utopia.* Cambridge, Mass.: Harvard University Press, 1957. Copyright © 1957 by the President and Fellows of Harvard College. Renewed 1985 by Howard J. Gray. Excerpted by permission of the publishers.

Sylvester, Richard S., and Davis P. Harding. From an introduction to *Two Early Tudor Lives: The Life and Death of Cardinal Wolsey* by George Cavendish *and The Life of Sir Thomas More* by William Roper. Edited by Richard S. Sylvester and Davis P. Harding. Yale University Press, 1962. Copyright © 1962 by Yale University. All rights reserved. Reprinted by permission of the publisher.

Tate, Allen. From "The Point of Dying: Donne's 'Virtuous Men'," in *The Forlorn Demon: Didactic and Critical Essays.* Henry Regnery Company, 1953. Copyright 1953, renewed 1981 by Allen Tate. Reprinted by permission of the publisher.

Tjernagel, Neelak Serawlook. From *Henry VIII and the Lutherans: A Study in Anglo-Lutheran Relations from 1521 to 1547*. Concordia, 1965. Copyright © 1965 by Concordia Publishing House. Reprinted by permission of the publisher.

Travitsky, Betty. From "Secular Writings," in *The Paradise of Women: Writings by Englishwomen of the Renaissance*. Edited by Betty Travitsky. Contributions in Women's Studies, No. 22. Greenwood Press, 1981. Copyright © 1981 by Betty Travitsky. All rights reserved. Reprinted by permission of Greenwood Press, Inc., Westport, CT.

Trilling, Lionel. From *Prefaces to The Experience of Literature*. Harcourt Brace Jovanovich, 1979. Copyright © 1967 by Lionel Trilling. Copyright © 1979 by Diana Trilling and James Trilling. Reprinted by permission of Harcourt Brace Jovanovich, Inc.

Walker, Hallam. From *Molière*. Twayne, 1971. Copyright 1971 by Twayne Publishers. All rights reserved. Reprinted with the permission of Twayne Publishers, a division of G. K. Hall & Co., Boston.

Welsh, David. From *Jan Kochanowski*. Twayne, 1974. Copyright 1974 by Twayne Publishers. All rights reserved. Reprinted with the permission of Twayne Publishers, Inc., a division of G. K. Hall & Co., Boston.

White, Helen C. From *Tudor Books of Saints and Martyrs*. The University of Wisconsin Press, 1963. Copyright © 1963 by the Regents of the University of Wisconsin. Reprinted by permission of the publisher.

Woolf, Virginia. From *The Second Common Reader*. Harcourt Brace Jovanovich, 1932. Published in England as *The Common Reader*. Second series. L. & V. Woolf at the Hogarth Press, 1932. Copyright 1932 by Harcourt Brace Jovanovich, Inc. Renewed 1960 by Leonard Woolf. Reprinted by permission of Harcourt Brace Jovanovich, Inc. In Canada by the Literary Estate of Virginia Woolf and The Hogarth Press.

PERMISSION TO REPRINT PHOTOGRAPHS IN LC, VOLUME 10, WAS RECEIVED FROM THE FOLLOWING SOURCES:

Photograph by Publicité Raymond Inc., courtesy of Publicité Raymond Inc. and the Superior of Monastére des Ursulines: p. 248

Courtesy of the Superior of Monastére des Ursulines: p. 254

ISBN 0-8103-6109-4